PENNSYLVANIA GERMAN DICTIONARY

DR. EUGENE S. STINE
PROFESSOR EMERITUS
EAST STROUDSBURG UNIVERSITY

PENNSYLVANIA GERMAN – ENGLISH

ENGLISH - PENNSYLVANIA GERMAN

PENNSYLVANIA GERMAN SOCIETY, INC.
PO BOX 244
KUTZTOWN, PA 19530-0244

PENNSYLVANIA GERMAN DICTIONARY

PENNSYLVANIA GERMAN - ENGLISH
ENGLISH - PENNSYLVANIA GERMAN

Copyright © 2008 Nancy A. Stine

Copyright © 1989, 1990, 1994, 1996 by Eugene S. Stine.
All rights reserved. Printed in the United States of America. Except as permitted under the United States Copyright Act of 1976, no part of this publication may be reproduced or distributed in any form or by any means, or stored in a data base or retrieval system, without the prior written permission of the publisher.

Copyright © 2008
NANCY A. STINE
ASHFIELD, PENNSYLVANIA 18212
ALL RIGHTS RESERVED

Copyright @ 1989, 1990, 1994, 1996
EUGENE S. STINE
LEHIGHTON, PENNSYLVANIA 18235
ALL RIGHTS RESERVED

This Pennsylvania German Society edition, first published in 2008, is an unabridged replication of the first edition of the work published in the Dialect Series of the Pennsylvania German Society in 1996.

Library of Congress Catalog Card Number: 97-066685

ISBN: 0-911122-61-3

Revised 2011

PREFACE

Pennsylvania German Society
and the Eugene R. Stine *Pennsylvania German Dictionary*
known as "the red dictionary"

The Board of the Pennsylvania German Society recognized the immediate need for a dictionary and decided that a re-print of the Eugene R. Stine *Pennsylvania German Dictionary* known as "the red dictionary" was in order. This action is predicated on the need to help preserve the language and to meet the needs of students studying the language, and our constituent members and friends interested in reading and translating the dialect.

The Society is deeply indebted to Nancy and Mark Stine for their generosity and dedication to this project. Mark and Nancy granted permission for the reprint and assisted in developing the final copy. This reprint is an effort to honor, and recognize the contributions to PGS, of their late husband and father Dr. Eugene Stine.

The Society is pleased to present the Stine Dictionary and it is our sincere hope that this will meet the needs of the Pennsylvania German community.

The Pennsylvania German Society

ACKNOWLEDGEMENTS

Whenever a project like this is begun the author has a predetermined idea of what he/she wants to present. It was my idea that I would present a Pennsylvania German to English dictionary which would be an enlargement of the 1990 work. The Board of Directors of the Pennsylvania German Society was enthusiastic about my work but several members thought I should present the dictionary in both German to English and English to German. I wish to thank them for their supportive suggestions since we now have a dictionary never produced before in the Pennsylvania German dialect field of lexicography.

I thank my editor, the Reverend Willard Wetzel, Editor for the Pennsylvania German Society, for his many helpful suggestions concerning the area of publishing. I also thank his wife, Dr. Glenys Waldman, whose education in the Germanic Languages, for her "extra eyes" to proof read the text copy both in German and English.

Last, but not least, I thank my wife Nancy, son Mark and his wife Lori for the patience they have shown during the many hours I spent away from family responsibilities working on the computer to create this dictionary.

Introduction

In the preface of Marcus Bachman Lambert's *Pennsylvania German Dictionary,* originally published by The Pennsylvania German Society in 1924, the author included the observation that no dictionary had ever been published that included both English to Pennsylvania German and Pennsylvania German to English. Now, almost seven decades later, the same Society brings us the dual language dictionary for which Lambert seemed to yearn.

This *Pennsylvania German to English and English to Pennsylvania German Dictionary* has been prepared by Dr. Eugene S. Stine, Pennsylvania German Society Secretary and Professor Emeritus at East Stroudsburg University. In 1990, Dr. Stine published the *Pennsylvania German to English* as a companion to the English to Pennsylvania German one produced by Professor C. Richard Beam. Dr. Stine's interest in this new project was piqued by his discovery of Lambert's comment in the preface to the 1924 dictionary that furthered by the encouragement of some colleagues on The Pennsylvania German Society Board of Directors. The result of this new, first -ever dual language dictionary, containing more than 21,000 Pennsylvania German words and their English counterparts. By way of providing a perspective, note that in his preface, Lambert stated that his 1924 dictionary had 16,438 entries.

Dr. Stine has prepared a descriptive and not a prescriptive dictionary, in which the Lehigh-Northampton County variant of Pennsylvania German is the dominant version or the dialect. The author has taken care, however, to include significant differences from other areas, such as the Lancaster-York County and Schuylkill-Dauphin County regions. Therefore it is important that users study the pronunciation guide included in the front matter. This dictionary documents, as much as possible, and even celebrates regional variations in pronunciation and usage. Therefore it is necessary to understand how these differences are shown by the spellings. The Buffington-Barba system of spelling is used, which The Pennsylvania German Society has been advocating and promoting for years, and has adopted as its official spelling system. It is basely largely on Standard German phonetics (with notable exceptions of the letters **sch, x** and **y,** where German is more likely to use respectively **s, chs, and j).** Nouns are capitalized. Buffington-Barba not only facilitates the standardizing of spelling, but it also makes Pennsylvania German more easily read and understood by speakers of other German dialects and of other European languages.

A word about alphabetization is in order. It will come as no surprise that the text was prepared on a word processor (which Professor Beam has so charmingly baptized with the dialect work ***der Waddefresser***). The alphabetizing mechanism of der Waddefresser reads symbols and numbers before letters. This means that separable-prefix verbs (those written prefix/root, e.g. *Vor/schteh* [to project, be a leader or chairperson] will come before *Vorschteher* [deacon] , of which the prefix is inseparable. Similarly, *nei/schtelle* [place into, put in] will be alphabetized **before** the word nei [new].

Many separable-prefix verbs are shown in this dictionary, but not all. They can be "invented" on the spot, in the same way that prepositions are added at will to verbs in English (e.g., *look in, look out, look over, look through*...). The difference is that in German the separable **pre**fixes are added in **front** of verbs, whereas in English, the prepositions are added as **suf**fixes **after** the verb. Note, moreover, that *overlook* and such **inseparable** verbs cannot usually be thus "invented".

A native of Allentown, Dr. Stine grew up in a bilingual home, speaking English and the Lehigh-Northampton County variant of Pennsylvania German. The author's interest in languages prompted him to the study German and to complete his doctoral dissertation in developmental English skills. In addition to being Secretary of The Pennsylvania German Society, Dr. Stine is a life member of Pennsylvania Dutch Folk Culture Society, a member of the Pennsylvania German Cultural Heritage Center, and The Goschenhoppen Historians, Inc. He has written Pennsylvania German columns for three newspapers and frequently teachers courses in the Pennsylvania German language.

The Rev. Willard W. Wetzel
Editor, The Pennsylvania German Society

and

Dr. Glenys A. Waldman,
Librarian and Curator,
Grand Lodge, F. & A. M. of Pennsylvania

A GUIDE TO PRONUNCIATION

This Guide to Pronunciation is adapted from the Stine PENNSYLVANIA GERMAN TO ENGLISH DICTIONARY published in 1990 (Brookshire Printing Co., Lancaster, PA) pages vi-viii. The spelling and pronunciation follow the Preston A. Barba and Albert F. Buffington "Buffington-Barba System." It is hoped that both students and writers of the dialect will adopt this spelling system, which has been available for over fifty years, as a standard in their work.

Vowels

A vowel is long (1) before a single medial consonant; (2) when doubled; (3) when followed by an h; (4) when final; (5) before a final consonant when Standard German has a long vowel (gut, Not, rot). Almost without exception a vowel is short (1) when followed by two consonants; (2) before a single final consonant unless Standard German has a long vowel (gut, Hut).

Vowel	Pennsylvania German	English Approximation	
a (short)	Sache (things)	a	in what
aa (long)	Aag (eye)	aw	in saw
ae (long)	Baer (bear)	ea	in bear
ae (short)	Paesching (peach)	a	in match
a (r)(long)	darf (may)	a	in father
e (long)	geht (goes) weech (soft)	a	in gate
e (short)	fett (fat)	e	in get
i (long)	ihn (him) Biewel (Bible)	ee	in see
i (short)	bin (am) Biwwel (Bible)	i	in pin
o (long)	rot (red) Boot (boat)	oa	in boat
o (short)	Kopp (head)	u	in cup
u (long)	Blut (blood) Bu (boy)	oo	in moon
u (short)	dumm (stupid)	oo	in cook

Diphthongs

Diphthongs	Pennsylvania German	English Approximation	
au	laut (loud)	ow	in cow
ei	greisch (scream)	i	in pine
oi	Roi (row)	oy	in boy

Consonants

Most of the consonants of Pennsylvania German are pronounced much like they are in American English (b, p, d, t, k, ck, f, h,l, m, n, s, and w). Some of them are associated with letters, which occur in English but with different sounds (v in P.G. = f; sch in P.G. = sh; z in P.G. = ts in English). Some do not occur in American English ch, (ich), ch (ach), and r (in certain positions).

Consonant			Pennsylvania German	English Approximation
b			Bank (bench) Lumbe (rag) robbe (pick,pluck) ab (off,away)	b in bank b in number bb in robber p in bump
ch (following vowel)			ich (I) mache (make)	(Sound not in English) (Sound not in English)
ck			packe (pack) Pack (pack)	ck in picky ck in pack
d			Daal (valley) Dodder (yoke of an egg) Dod (death)	d in dog dd in buddy d in dot
f			finne (find) hoffe (hope) Schof (sheep)	f in find ff in huffy f in hoof
g			Geld (money) Grischt (Christian)	g in gold g in ground
g (between two vowels only)			Aage (eyes)	(Sound not in English)
g (in final position)			Aag (eye)	k in kick
h			Hut (hat)	h in hat
h (silent)			Uhr (clock)	
k			Keenich (king)	k in king
l			Leicht (funeral) Millich (milk) Schlingel (rogue)	l in light ll in silly l in single
m			Mann (man) Besem (broom)	m in man m in broom
n			Not (need) Menner (men) in (in)	n in not nn in banner in in
ng			Ring (ring)	ng in ring
nk			genunk (enough)	nk in sink
p			Parre (pastor) Kopp (head)	p in pastor p in step
r			Trilled in initial and medial position. Vocalic r (after vowel, preceding consonant, or at the end of word) use English *a—father* (Dier; Gaarde) If vocalic *r* is intervocalic, use consonantal *r* sound.	
s			Saddel (saddle) Kissi (cushion) Boss (kiss)	s in sort ss in sissy ss in boss
sch			Schul (school)	sh in shop
t			Tee (tea) Text (text)	t in tea t in next
v			verrickt (crazy)	f in for
w			Wasser (water)	w in water
x			Hex (witch)	x in ax
x (sometimes chs)			waxe, wachse (grow)	x in ax
y			yung (young)	y in yard
z			Zucker (sugar)	ts in hats

Abbreviations	
adj.	Adjective
adv.	Adverb
conj.	Conjunction
dem. adj.	demonstrative adjective
indecl. pronoun	indeclinable pronoun
indef. art.	indefinite article
interj	Interjection
irr.v.	irregular verb
n.	Noun
pl..	plural form
poss. adj.	possessive adjective
poss. pron.	possessive pronoun
pp.	past participle
prep.	Preposition
sg.	Singular
v.	verb

A Word Of Explanation

When the infinitive form of the verb contains a separable prefix, the separable prefix is set off with a line (/). For instance ab/breche (to break off) indicates that ab is separable but the (/) is not written in sentence structure i.e. ab/breche is written abbreche. When this same verb is used in the past participle form the (/) also is not written i.e. ab/breche becomes abgebroche. When more than one past participle is given (for example, pp. verlosse, verlosst), this indicates that more than one form is in use.

When two definite articles (der, die, es) are given, this indicates that both forms are in use.

Any letter or group of letters within parentheses indicates an alternate spelling form of the word which compensates for the local pronunciation of the word. For example, g(e)west is to be read or spelled either gewest or gwest; Kaddu(n) is to be pronounced as either Kaddu or Kaddun.

Verbs which show action to or by oneself are listed alphabetically followed by parentheses with the word sich enclosed, aa/duh (sich --) (dress oneself). The word order in Pennsylvania German is normally sich aa/duh (to dress oneself).

Entries which are noun, verb or adjective phrases have been entered using the major word of the phrase. This word appears in the entry followed by the other phrase words in parentheses e.g. Eck, (es)n. (iwwers --) diagonally.

NOTES

NOTES

NOTES

Aa

Aa-Be-Ze

aa/henke

Aa-Be-Ze (es)n. alphabet

aa/(g)friere, v.; aagfrore, pp. freeze fast to

aa/basse, v.; aagebasst, pp. 1.palm off on; 2.fit 3. (eeni --) tell a lie

aa/baue, v.; aagebaut, pp. 1.build against; 2.build an addition to

aa/bede, v.; aagebet, pp. 1.adore; 2.beseech; 3.worship

aa/befehle, v.; aabefohle, pp. urge

aa/beisse, v.; aagebisse, pp. bite into

aa/belange, v.; aabelangt, pp. belong

aa/biede, v.; aagebodde, pp. 1.make a first bid; 2.offer; 3. (sich--) volunteer

aa/binne, v.; aagebunne, pp. 1.hitch to a post; 2.tie fast; 3. wean (a calf)

aa/blanze, v.; aageblanzt, pp. 1.begin to plant; 2.plant

aa/blaud(e)re, v.; aageblaudert, pp. persuade (someone) to buy or accept (something)

aa/bleiwe, v.; aagebliwwe, pp. remain in place

aa/blicke, v.; aageblickt, pp. 1.behold; 2.look at; 3. observe; 4.view

aa/blinsle, v.; aageblinselt, pp. blink or wink at

aa/blose, v.;aageblose, pp.1.blow up;2.start by blowing

aa/bluge, v.; aageblugt, pp. turn first furrow

aa/bohre, v.; aagebohrt, pp. 1.bore; 2.tap

aa/breche, v.; aagebroche, pp. 1.break open; 2.make a hole in (a case or package)

aa/brenne, v.; aagebrennt, pp. 1.burn down; 2.burn fast to the kettle in cooking; 3.ignite; 4.scorch

aa/briehe, v.; aagebrieht, pp. 1.scald; 2.steep

aa/bringe, v.; aagebrocht, pp. 1.make use of; 2.report; 3.tell

aa/brockle, v.; aagebrockelt, pp. begin to chip

aa/brode, v.; aagebrode, pp. stick to the pan in frying

aa/brumme, v.; aagebrummt, pp. growl at

aa/deide, v.; aagedeit, pp. signify

aa/drede, v.;aagedrede, pp. put in motion with the feet

aa/dreffe,v.;aagedroffe, pp. 1.come across;2.meet with

aa/drehe, v.; aagedreht, pp. turn on (as a light)

aa/dreiwe, v.; aagedriwwe, pp. 1.carry on; 2.start driv-ing; 3.(to play) pranks; 4.urge

aa/duh, v.; aageduh, pp. 1.dress; 2.put on; 3.(sich --) dress oneself;4.(sich viel Mieh --) go to great trouble

aa/faahre, v.; aagfaahre, pp. 1.drive ahead; 2.speak gruffly; 3.turn the first furrow

aa/faarichde, v.; aagfaaricht, pp. 1.draw the first fur-rows through a field in starting to plow; 2.draw in furrows through a plowed field for planting (corn or potatoes)

aa/fackle, v.; aagfackelt, pp. (ebbes --) (to start) something

aa/falle, v.; aagfalle, pp. 1.attack; 2.fall upon

aa/fange,v.;aagfange, pp.1.begin; 2.commence; 3.start

aa/fasse, v.; aagfasst, pp. take hold of

aa/faule, v.; aagfault, pp. begin to rot

aa/fechde, v.; aagfochde, pp. 1.attack; 2.fight; 3.quarrel; 4.tempt (by the devil)

aa/fei(e)re,v.; aagfeirt, pp.1.light; 2.inspire;3.set on fire

aa/feichde, v.; aagfeicht, pp. moisten

aa/feile, v.; aagfeilt, pp. begin to file

aa/feinde, v.; aagfeindt, pp. antagonize

aa/fiedre, v.; aagfiedert, pp. improve by good feeding

aa/fiehle, v.; aagfiehlt, pp. 1.feel at; 2.touch

aa/fiehre, v.; aagfiehrt, pp. 1.deceive; 2.disappoint; 3.fool; 4.cite; 5.quote; 6.lead

aa/fille, v.; aagfillt, pp. fill

aa/fingere, v.; aagfingert, pp. 1.handle; 2.touch

aa/flicke, v.; aagflickt, pp. 1.patch; 2.mend

aa/fransle, v.; aagfranselt, pp. set with a fringe

aa/fratze, v.; aagfratzt, pp. accost in an over bearing manner

aa/fresse, v.; aagfresse, pp. gnaw at

aa/froge, v.; aagfrogt, pp. make inquiry about

aa/gaffe, v.; aagegafft, pp. gape at

aa/geh, v.; aagange, pp. 1.begin; 2.concern; 3.rave; 4.take fire

aa/gewehne, v.; aagewehnt, pp. accustom

aa/gewwe, v.; is aagewwe, pp. 1.lodge information against; 2.make a complaint; 3.report; 4.suggest

aa/gle(e)we, v.; aageglebt, pp. 1.adhere; 2.cleave to; 3. fasten to by sticking on; 4.paste on

aa/gleede, v.; aagegleedt, pp. 1.clothe; 2.dress

aa/globbe, v.; aagegloppt, pp. knock (at)

aa/gnarre, v.; aa(ge)gnatt, pp. 1.growl at; 2.snarl

aa/gnawwere,v.; aagegnawwert, pp.1.gnaw;2.nibble at

aa/gnibbe, v.; aagegnippt, pp. 1.button on; 2.tie on

aa/graunse, v.; aagegraunst, pp. address in a gruff manner

aa/greife, v.; aagegriffe, pp. 1.attack; 2.assail; 3.(to take) hold of; 4.grasp hold on; 5.grip

aa/greische, v.; aagegrische, pp. scream at

aa/griege, v.; aagrickt, pp. 1.get on (an article of cloth-ing); 2.put on

aa/gritzle, v.; aagegritzelt, pp. scribble on

aa/gschteckt, v. (past tense) infected

aa/gschwelle, v.; aagschwolle, pp. (to begin to) swell

aa/gucke, v.; aageguckt, pp. look at

aa/hacke,v.; aaghackt, pp.1.chop into;2.hoe vegetables

aa/hafte, v.; aaghaft, pp. cling to (especially evil conse-quences)

aa/halde, v.; aaghalde, pp. 1.continue; 2.hang on; 3. preserve; 4.stop

aa/harriche, v.; aagharicht, pp. 1.heed; 2.listen to; 3.take advice

aa/hawwe, v.; aaghatt, pp. wear (of clothes)

aa/heele, v.; aagheelt, pp. heal (together, on)

aa/heemle, v.; aagheemelt, pp. 1.have a longing for home; 2.make one feel at home; 3.remind one of home

aa/heere, v.; aagheert, pp. 1.heed; 2.listen to; 3.perceive by listening

aa/helfe, v.; aagholfe, pp. 1.help (a person); 2.put on an article of clothing

aa/henge, v.; aaghonke, pp. cling to

aa/henke, v.; aaghenkt; aaghonke, pp. 1.adhere;2.append; 3.form as fruit on a tree or vine or potatoes on the roots; 4.hang on; 5.put on; 6.sell by persuasion; 7.transmit a disease; 8.(eeni --) tell a lie

Aa

aa/hetze

aa/hetze, v.; aaghetzt, pp. incite

aa/hewe, v.; aaghowe, pp. 1.hold on; 2.lift; 3.start to lift

aa/hitze, v.; aaghitzt, pp. 1.heat; 2.warm up

aa/kedde, v.; aagekett, pp. chain fast

aa/kindiche, v.; aagekindicht, pp. 1.announce; 2.notify

aa/klewe, v.; aageklebt, pp. 1.adhere; 2.cleave to; 3.fasten by sticking on; 4.paste on

aa/knebbe, v.; aagekneppt, pp. button on

aa/kumme, v.; is aakumme, pp. 1.arrive; 2.fare; 3.(druff --) depend upon; 4.(druff -- losse) take a chance; 5.(gut --) prosper

aa/laafe, v.; aageloffe, pp. form a mist on a surface

aa/lache, v.; aagelacht, pp. 1.attract; 2.smile

aa/lande, v.; aagelandt, pp. 1.arrive; 2.land

aa/lange, v.; aagelangt, pp. arrive

aa/lege, v.; aagelekt, pp. 1.commence; 2.go in with a will; 3. invest; 4.put grain in place preparatory to threshing; 5. start a fire

aa/leie, v.; aagelegge, pp. 1.be solicitous; 2.have (something) at heart

aa/liege, v.; aagelogge, pp. belie

aa/locke, v.; aagelockt, pp. 1.allure; 2.entice

aa/losse, v.; aag(e)losst, pp. 1.let on; 2.pretend

aa/mache, v.; aagemacht, pp. 1.light a fire; 2.mix; 3.(sich-- bei ebber) get (into someone's good graces)

aa/mehe, v.; aagemeht, pp. (es Feld --) mow around the field (with the cradle to make way for the reaping machine)

aa/messe, v.; aagemesse, pp. (to take) measurement for clothing

aa/naehe, v.; aagenaeht, pp. sew on

aa/naggle, v.; aagenaggelt, pp. nail on

aa/nemme, v.; aag(e)numme, pp. 1.accept; 2.adopt; 3. engage; 4. join; 5.put up with; 6.receive; 7.support; 8. suppose; 9.take (as paint)

aa/niede, v.; aageniet, pp. rivet

aa/packe, v.; aagepackt, pp. 1.attack; 2.(to take) hold (of); 3.grasp roughly; 4.lay hold of; 5.seize

aa/picke, v.; aagepickt, pp. peck at

aa/raffe, v.; aagerafft, pp. tackle something (with might and main)

aa/ranke, v.; aag(e)rankt, pp.take hold of by means of tendrils

aa/ranse, v.; aageranst, pp. speak gruffly

aa/reeche, v.; aagereecht, pp. touch

aa/rege, v.; aageregt, pp. touch

aa/reisse, v.; aagerisse, pp. 1.take a part of a thing for use; 2.tear into; 3.use part of

aa/reiwe, v.; aageriwwe, pp. 1.grate;2.ignite by rubbing; 3.rub with liniment

aa/richde, v.; aagericht, pp. 1.cause; 2.put dinner on the table; 3.cause trouble; 4.set; 5.stir up

aa/rieche, v.; aageroche, pp. 1.detect by smelling; 2.smell at

aa/riehre, v.; aageriehrt, pp. 1.mix by stirring; 2.touch

aa/robbe, v.; aageroppt, pp. begin to pick

aa/rode, v.; aagerode, pp. suggest

aa/warre

aa/roschde, v.; aageroscht, pp. rust fast

aa/rufe, v.; aagerufe, pp. 1.appeal to; 2.call upon; 3.invoke

aa/saage, v.; aagsaat, pp. 1.announce; 2.bring word 3.notify; 4.say how many (in game of datte)

aa/saufe, v.; aagsoffe, pp. (sich --) 1.begin to feel jolly (from drink); 2.(to start on a) spree

aa/schaele, v.; aagschaelt, pp. (to begin to) peel

aa/schaffe, v.; aagschafft, pp. 1.acquire; 2.procure; 3.provide

aa/schaue, v.; aagschaut, pp. 1.behold; 2.look at; 3.view

aa/scheele, v.; aagscheelt, pp. (to begin to) peel

aa/schicke, v.; aagschickt, pp. (sich --) 1.adapt oneself; 2. behave; 3.make ready

aa/schlagge, v.; aagschlagge, pp. 1.agree with a person (as food); 2.nail; 3.post; 4.produce effect; 5.(zu gering--) underrate

aa/schlibbe, v.; aagschlippt, pp. slip on

aa/schmeechle, v.; aagschmeechelt, pp. 1.coax by soft words; 2.flatter; 3.wheedle; 4.(sich --) curry favor

aa/schmiere, v.; aagschmiert, pp. 1.cheat; 2.grease; 3.trick

aa/schnarre, v.; aagschnatt, pp. 1.scold; 2.speak roughly to

aa/schpanne, v.; aagschpannt, pp. 1.compel; 2.hitch horses to; 3.stretch taut; 4.urge

aa/schpelle, v.; aagschpellt, pp. pin to

aa/schpinne, v.; aagschpunne, pp. 1.hatch an intrigue; 2.(to start) spinning

aa/schplidde, v.; aagschplitt, pp. begin to split

aa/schpritze, v.; aagschpritzt, pp. 1.splash; 2.sprinkle; 3.squirt

aa/schrauwe, v.; aagschraubt, pp. screw fast

aa/schtaahle, v.; aagschtaahlt, pp. 1.put a new steel edge on a tool; 2.sharpen

aa/schtarre,v.; aagschtarrt, pp. 1.mix by stirring; 2.stir up

aa/schtecke, v.; aagschteckt, pp. 1.ignite; 2.infect; 3.(to set) fire (to); 4.(es Licht --) light (the lamp)

aa/schteh, v.; aagschtanne, pp. 1.become; 2.delay; 3.like; 4.please; 5.satisfy

aa/schteibere, v.; aagschteibert, pp. brace or prop

aa/schtelle, v.; aagschtellt, pp. 1.appoint (to ordain); 2.cause; 3.install

aa/schtifde, v.; aagschtift, pp. 1.cause; 2.instigate; 3.suggest

aa/schtosse, v.; aagschtosse, pp. 1.abut; 2.border; 3.join; 4.offend; 5.touch (glasses) in a toast

aa/schtreiche, v.; aagschtriche, pp. paint

aa/schtrenge, v.; aagschtrengt, pp. stretch

aa/schuhe, v.; aagschuht, pp.1.fox (boots); 2.vamp (of a shoe, boot)

aa/schwetze, v.; aagschwetzt, pp. prevail on (someone) to accept (something)

aa/seefe, v.; aagseeft, pp. 1.lather; 2.soap

aa/seh(n)e, v.; aagsehne, pp. 1.look at; 2.regard; 3.respect

aa/setze, v.; aagsetzt, pp. 1.appoint (to ordain); 2.begin; 3.start; 4.set to rise; 5.set up the drinks; 6.take aim

aa/verdraue, v.; aaverdraut, pp. 1.confide a secret; 2.entrust; 3.(to put) trust in

aa/warre, v.; is aawarre, pp. (to become) aware

Aa

aa/waxe

aa/waxe, v.; aagewaxe, pp. 1.become liver grown; 2.join by growing; 3.grow up; 4.grow together

aa/weis(s)e, v.; aagewisse, pp. 1.direct; 2.drill into one; 3.instruct; 4.show

aa/wende, v.; aagewendt, pp. 1.apply; 2.employ; 3.invest; 4.urinate; 5.use

aa/wenne, v.; aagewennt, pp. 1.apply; 2.employ; 3.use

aa/wesche, v.; aagewesche, pp. varnish

aa/wickle, v.; aagewickelt, pp. 1.accomplish by palming off on; 2.start winding on a reel

aa/zaahme, v.; aagezaahmt, pp. 1.attach to oneself; 2.tame (an animal)

aa/zabbe, v.; aagezappt, pp. tap

aa/zeige, v.; aagezeicht, pp. indicate

aa/zettle, v.;aagezettelt, pp.1.put warp on a loom for weaving; 2.start a matter

aa/ziehe, v.; aagezoge, pp. 1.attract; 2.put on; 3.stretch; 4. tighten

aa/ziele, v.; aagezielt, pp. take (good) aim

aa/zinde, v.; aagezindt, pp. ignite

aa/zobbe, v.; aagezoppt, pp. 1.attract fish by little jerks; 2.begin to pull

aa, adv. 1.also; 2.certainly; 3.indeed; 4.to be sure; 5.too; 6.(die Schul is --) school has been called to order; 7.(es feier is --) the fire is made; 8.(ich denk awwer --) well, I am sure; 9.(kummt er --) will he be sure to come; (b) is he coming also; 10.(vun heit --) from today on

aab(e)fehle, v.; aab(e)fohle, pp. 1.enjoin;2.recommend; 3.request; 4.remind emphatically; 5.urge

Aabeginn (der)n. beginning

aabetungswaerdich, adj. adorable

Aabieting (die)n. offer

Aabinngewicht (es)n. hitching weight

Aabinnposchde (der)n.;Aabinnposchde, pl. hitching post

Aabinnrieme (der)n. tie-strap

Aabinnschtee (der)n.; Aabinnschtee, pl. hitching weight

Aablick (der)n. 1.aspect; 2.outlook; 3.sight; 4.view

aabrockle, v.; aagebrockelt, pp. (die Supp --) put crumbs in soup

Aabruch (der)n. break (of day)

Aadacht (die)n. 1.attention; 2.devotion

aadarre, v.; aagedarrt, pp. dry too fast

aadechtich, adj.; adv. 1.attentive; 2.devotional

Aadeel (es)n. 1.part; 2.share

aadeite, v.; aagedeit, pp. 1.hint; 2.signify

Aadenke(s) (es)n. 1.keepsake; 2.memento;3.remembrance

Aader (die)n.; Aadere, pl. 1.artery; 2.vein

Aadler (der)n.; Aadler, pl. 1.eagle; 2.turkey buzzard

aadraage, v.; aagedraage, pp. 1.inform on; 2.give information secretly

aadresche, v.; aagedrosche, pp. begin threshing (generally as to first round with flails)

Aafang (der)n. 1.beginning; 2.origin

aafangs, adv. 1.(at the) present (time); 2.(at the) beginning

aafechding (die)n. 1.contention (usually legal); 2.controversy; 3.quarrel

aagrisse

Aafehles (es)n. 1.feeling for; 2.sympathy

Aafehrung (die)n. 1.citation; 2.deception

Aafenger (der)n. Beginner

Aag (es)n.; Aage, pl. 1.eye; 2.(ebbes im -- hawwe) (a) have some foreign substance in the eye; (b) have something in view; (c) watch something; 3.(ee aagich) one eyed; 4.(weiss vum --) white of the eye

Aageabbel (der)n. pupil (of the eye)

aagebletzlich, adv. immediately

Aageblick (der)n. moment

aageblicklich, adv. momentarily

aagebore, adj. 1.hereditary; 2.inborn; 3.innate; 4.intuitive

Aagebot (der)n. first bid (at public sale)

Aagebraue (die)n., pl. eyebrows

aagebroche, adj. opened

Aagedeckel (der)n.; Aagedeckel, pl. eyelid

Aagedokder (der)n.; Aagedokder, pl. oculist

aageduh, v. (past tense) 1.clothed; 2.dressed

Aageglesser (die)n., pl. 1.eyeglasses; 2.spectacles

aageh, v.; aagange, pp. 1.begin; 2.concern; 3.rave; 4.take fire; 5.(sell geht dich nix --) that is none of your business

Aagehaar (es)n.; Aagehaar, pl. eyelash

aageheere, v.; aageheert, pp. pertain

Aageheidel (es)n. cataract (of the eye)

Aageheidli (es)n. cataract (of the eye)

Aagehoor (die)n. eyelash

Aageld (es)n. 1.earnest money; 2.retainer

Aageleges (es)n. 1.concern; 2.yearning

aagelegge, adj. 1.concerned for; 2.solicitous

Aageluscht (die)n. delight to the eye

Aagemos (es)n. 1.estimate taken by the eye; 2.eyesight

aagenehm, adj. 1.agreeable; 2.comfortable; 3.delightful; 4.pleasurable; 5.welcome

aagenehmlicherweiss, adj. 1.agreeable;2.in an agreeable manner; 3.pleasant

aagescheinlich, adj. evident

Aageschpickel (der)n. 1.act or result of an act held up as a visitation of Providence or warning to evil-doers; 2.any phenomenon; 3.spectacle; 4.tragic sight

Aageschpiegel (der)n. premonition

Aageschpiel (der)n. spectacle

Aageschpiggel (der)n. 1.act or result of an act held up as a visitation of Providence or warning to evil-doers; 2.any phenomenon; 3.spectacle; 4.tragic sight

Aagesicht (es)n. face

Aagewasser (es)n. tears

aagewehne, v.; aagewehnt, pp. 1.(sich ebbes --) form a habit; 2.(sich --) (to become) accustomed

Aagewehnet (die)n. habit

Aagezeeh (der)n. eyetooth

Aagezeige (der)n. eyewitness

aagfault, adj. rotten

aaglaage, v.; aageglaagt, pp. 1.accuse; 2.prosecute

Aagreifer (der)n. attacker

Aagriff (der)n. attack

aagrisse, adj. torn

3

Aa

aagschpellt

aagschpellt, adj. pinned (on)

Aagscht (der)n. August (month)

Aagschtalt (der)n. 1.action; 2.manner of doing anything; 3. move; 4.(so'n -- mache) (a) get ready; (b) prepare

aagschtoche, adj. worm-eaten

aagsehne, adv. respected

Aaguscht (der)n. 1.August (month); 2.Augustus

aagwaxe, adj. liver-grown

Aah!, interj. 1.Ah!; 2.Oh!; 3.also exclamation of satisfaction

aaha!, interj. yes!

aahaltend, adj. continuous (rare use of present participial ending)

aahang (der)n. 1.adherence; 2.appendage

aaheemlich, adj. 1.comfortable; 2.homelike

aahen(k)sich, adj. 1.sticky; 2.tenacious

Aahenger (der)n. 1.adherent; 2.follower

aahengisch, adj. 1.clinging; 2.sticky; 3.tenacious

Aahenker (der)n. adherent

aahenkisch, adj. 1.clinging; 2.sticky; 3.tenacious

aakediere, v.; aakediert, pp. make an arrangement

Aakemmling (der)n. new-comer

aakenne, v.; aakennt, pp. 1.acknowledge; 2.recognize

Aaklach (der)n. complaint

Aalaaf (der)n. starting a run

Aalanges (es)n. 1.longing; 2.yearning

aamarricke, v.; aagemarrickt, pp. 1.mark down; 2.make a note

aamehe, v.; aagemeht, pp. 1.begin mowing; 2.mow around the field with the cradle to make way for the reaping machine

Aamen, interj. amen

Aamet (es)n. 1.aftermath; 2.second crop of hay; 3. (-- mache) secure the second crop of hay

aapalde, v.; aagepalde, pp. keep on (as a coat)

aaranne, v.; aagerannt, pp. 1.growl at; 2.roar at

aardich, adj. decent

aareede, v.; aagereedt, pp. address

aareihe, v.; aagereiht, pp. 1.baste; 2.(sich --) fall in rank

Aarem (der)n.; Erem, pl. arm

aarem, adj.; adv. 1.needy; 2.in need; 3.poor

aaremer Schlucker (der)n. poor wretch

aaremseelich, adj. 1.paltry; 2.pitiful; 3.poor; 4.needy

Aaremvoll (es)n. armful

aarensch, adj. orange

aaretze, v.; aageretzt, pp. 1.accost in a surly manner; 2.goad on; 3.incite

Aarichtdisch (der)n. 1.dresser; 2.kitchen table for dishes

aarm; aarmer; aarmscht, adj. poor; poorer; poorest

Aarmediener (der)n. deacon

Aarmehaus (es)n. poorhouse

Aarmer (en)n. pauper

aarmseelich, adj.; adv. 1.in need; 2.needy; 3.poor; 4.paltry

Aarmut (die)n. poverty

Aaronszwiwwel (die)n. jack-in-the-pulpit

aarote, v.; aagerote, pp. 1.advise; 2.counsel

Aarsch (der)n. 1.arse; 2.buttocks; 3.posterior; 4.butt-end (of an egg)

Aarschdaarem (der)n. the large intestine

Aaverwandti

Aart (die)n. 1.kind; 2.quality; 3.sort; 4.way; 5.(aus der -- schlagge) (a)degenerate; (b)deteriorate; 6.(das es en -- hot) (a)excellently; (b)splendidly; (c)beat the band; (d)well; 7.(noch aller --) like everything; 8.(uff en -- wie) kind o'; sort o'; 9.(uff was fern --) in what way

aasaege, v.; aagseakt, pp. begin cutting with a saw

Aaschein (der)n. 1.appearance; 2.indication

aascheinlich, adj. 1.apparent; 2.evident

aaschiesse, v.; aagschosse, pp. announce or welcome by shooting

Aaschlack (der)n. 1.placard; 2.posted-statement

Aaschlaek (die)n., pl. 1.doings; 2.pranks; 3.(-- fresse) (a) do wonders (ironically); (b) be wool-gathering; (c) gape

aaschliesse, v.; aagschlosse, pp. (sich --) join

aaschmeechle, v.; aagschmeechelt, pp. 1. coax by soft words; 2.(sich --) curry favor

aaschmeechlich, adj. 1.ingratiating; 2.pleasing

aaschmiere, v.; aagschmiert, pp. (sich --) ingratiate oneself

aaschnalle, v.; aagschnallt, pp. buckle on

aaschneide, v.; aagschnidde, pp. cut into

aaschpore, v.; aagschport, pp. incite

Aaschpruch (der)n. 1.application; 2.claim; 3.clamp; 4. demand; 5.request

Aaschprung (der)n. short run before leaping

aaschreiwe, v.; aagschriwwe, pp. charge

aaschtalle, v.; aagschtallt, pp. make preparation for

Aaschtand (der)n. decorum

aaschteckend, adj. 1.contagious; 2.infectious

aaschteesich, adj. scandalous

aaschtehlich, adj. becoming

aaschtelle, v.; aagschtellt, pp. 1.(sich --) (a) act as if; (b) affect an air; (c) cause 2.(sich dumm --) (a) act stupidly; (b) play innocent

aaschtennich, adj. 1.respectable; 2.well-behaved

aaschtick(l)e, v,; aagschtickelt, pp. 1.add a piece to; 2.lengthen

Aaschtifder (der)n. instigator

aaschtimme, v.; aagschtimmt, pp. 1.entune; 2.strike up (a hymn)

Aaschtoss (der)n. 1.offence; 2.scandal

aaschtrecke, v.; aagschtreckt, pp. stretch up

Aaschtreech (die)n., pl. 1.pranks; 2.tricks

Aaschtreicher (der)n. (house) painter

Aaschtreichpensil (der)n. paintbrush

aaschtrenge, v.; aagschtrengt, pp. (sich --) exert oneself

Aaschtrich (der)n. varnish

aaschtricke, v.; aagschtrickt, pp. join by knitting

aaschwatze, v.; aagschwatzt, pp. blacken

aasehnlich, adj. 1.considerable; 2.handsome; 3.reputable; 4.respectable

Aasicht (die)n.1.outlook;2.opinion; 3.sight;4.spectacle; 5.view

aasuche, v.; aagsucht, pp. 1.apply; 2.inquire

aasuckle, v.; aagsuckelt, pp. 1.act the parasite; 2.ingratiate oneself

Aaverwandter (der)n. relative

Aaverwandti (die)n. relative

Aa

aawaerre

aawaerre, v.; aawaerre, pp. 1.dispose of them; 2.get rid of them; 3.sell them

Aawendung (die)n. adaptation

Aawerglaawe (der)n. superstition

aawerglaawisch, adj. superstitious

Aazeeche (der, es)n. 1.omen; 2.sign; 3.token

Aazeiger (der)n. indicator

Aazuck (der)n. 1.attire; 2.suit

aazwinge, v.; aagezwunge, pp. force on (some one)

ab/balsamiere, v.; abgebalsamiert, pp. (to give a) tongue-lashing

ab/balwiere, v.; abgebalwiert, pp. shave off

ab/baschde, v.; abgebascht, pp. brush off

ab/batzle, v.; abgebatzelt, pp. tumble off

ab/beisse, v.; abgebisse, pp. bite off

ab/belze, v.; abgebelzt, pp. skin

ab/bettle, v.; abgebeddelt, pp. 1.obtain by begging or persistency; 2.beg off

ab/bezaale, v.; abbezaalt, pp. pay off

ab/biede, v.; abgebodde, pp. Outbid

ab/binne, v.; abgebunne,pp. 1.furnish or put on the iron-work of a wheel or wagon; 2.hoop; 3.put a hoop on a barrel or cask; 4.remove by tying (a wart); 5.tire

ab/bitte, v.; abgebitt, pp. 1.implore forgiveness or leni-ency; 2. solicit or ask for (something)

ab/blaade, v.; abgeblaadt, pp. 1.pluck leaves from; 2.defoliate; 3.strip off clothing

ab/bleddere, v.; abgebleddert, pp. pluck leaves from

ab/bleeche, v.; abgebleecht, pp. 1.bleach; 2.fade

ab/bleiwe, v.; abgebliwwe, pp. 1.remain at a distance; 2.remain off

ab/bliehe, v.; abgeblieht, pp. cease blooming

ab/bloge, v.; abgeblogt, pp. 1.exhaust by working; 2. (sich --) exhaust oneself by working

ab/blose, v.; abgeblost, pp. 1.blow off; 2.clear up; 3.give vent to one's opinion or feelings; 4.(sich --) (a) boast; (b) brag

ab/breche, v.; abgebroche, pp. 1.break off; 2.stop; 3.(masch --) snap in two

ab/brenne, v.; abgebrennt, pp. burn down

ab/briehe, v.; abgebrieht, pp. scald

ab/briggle, v.; abgebriggelt, pp. drub soundly

ab/brille, v.; abgebrillt, pp. (eens --) cry (a tune)

ab/brockle, v.; abgebrockelt, pp. 1.come off in small particles; 2.crumble

ab/bschtelle, v.; abbschtellt, pp. 1.countermand; 2.postpone

ab/bumbe, v.; abgebumpt, pp. 1.pump off; 2.remove by pumping (to get fresh water)

ab/butze,v.; abgebutzt, pp. 1.clean; 2.clean off; 3. dry (dishes); 4.wipe

ab/dachdle, v.; abgedachdelt, pp. flog

ab/danke, v.; abgedankt, pp. 1.discard; 2.discharge (an official); 3.resign (from an office)

ab/darre, v.; abgedarrt, pp. dry partly (as hay)

ab/decke, v.; abgedeckt, pp. 1.uncover; 2.unroof

ab/deele, v.; abgedeelt, pp. 1.divide; 2.separate; 3.share

ab/deiwle, v.; abgedeiwelt, pp. bedevil

ab/gnabbere

ab/dengle, v.; abgedengelt, pp. cut one short in an argument

ab/detschle, v.; abgedetschelt, pp. touch base (in play-ing hide and seek)

ab/dowe, v.; abgedobt, pp. (sich --) run or rage to exhaustion

ab/draage, v.; abgedraagt, pp. carry off

ab/dradde, v.; abgedratt, pp. trot off

ab/drede, v.; abgedrede, pp. wear off

ab/drehe, v.; abgedreht, pp. 1.turn on a lathe; 2.turn off

ab/dreiwe, v.; abgedriwwe, pp. 1.banish; 2.drive off; 3.expel

ab/drenne, v.; abgedrennt, pp. 1.rip off; 2.un-seem

ab/dresche, v.; abgedrosche, pp. 1.flog soundly; 2.thrash with flail or machine

ab/dricke, v.; abgedrickt, pp. 1.press or pinch off; 2.pull the trigger; 3.fire

ab/drickle, v.; abgedrickelt, pp. dry off

ab/dropse, v.; abgedropst, pp. drop or trickle off

ab/dropsle, v.; abgedropselt, pp. drop or trickle off

ab/duh, v.; abgeduh, pp. 1.postpone; 2.procrastinate; 3.put off; 4.take off

ab/esse, v.; abgesse, pp. eat off

ab/faahre, v.; abgfaahre, pp. 1.start to drive away; 2.haul away

ab/faddiche, v.; abgfaddicht, pp. 1.give the finishing touch; 2.rebuff; 3.send about one's business

ab/falle, v.; abgfalle, pp. 1.apostatize; 2.fall off; 3.lose flesh

ab/fange,v.; abgfange, pp.1.intercept; 2.learn by covert observation

ab/faule, v.; abgfault, pp. rot off

ab/fege, v.; abgfegt, pp. 1.hurry away; 2.scrub off

ab/feile, v.; abgfeilt, pp. file off

ab/fiehre, v.; abgfiehrt, pp. 1.carry off (as water); 2.lead away; 3.purge (for constipation)

ab/fliege, v.; abgflogge, pp. fly off

ab/fliesse, v.; abgflosse, pp. flow off

ab/flitsche, v.; abgflitscht, pp. fly off (as an ax or a stone from the surface of water)

ab/flucke, v.; abgflucht, pp. (eens --)(to utter) profanity

ab/gaerwe, v.; abgegaerbt, pp. 1.flog; 2.tan (skin); 3.thrash

ab/gawwle, v.; abgegawwelt, pp. 1.branch off (as a road); 2.unload grain or hay (with a fork)

ab/geege, v.; abgegeet, pp. 1.cheat;2.drive away hastily; 3.wrest from

ab/geeschle, v.; abgegeeschelt, pp. horsewhip

ab/geh, v.; abgange, pp. 1.begin; 2.come off; 3.pass off; 4.start

ab/gewehne, v.; abgewehnt, pp. wean

ab/giesse,v.;abgschitt;abgegosse(rare usage)pp.pour off

ab/glaare, v.; abgeglaart, pp. 1.clarify; 2.clear off (of weather)

ab/gledde, v.; abgeglett, pp. smooth

ab/glense, v.; abgeglenst, pp. 1.(to be) deflected by some obstruction; 2.glance off; 3.pour off

ab/glitsche, v.; abgeglitscht, pp. 1.slide off; 2.slip off

ab/gloppe, v.; abgegloppt 1.beat off; 2.flog; 3.knock off

ab/gnabbere, v.; abgegnabbert, pp. coitus

Aa

ab/gnawwere

ab/gnawwere, v.; abgegnawwert, pp. gnaw off

ab/gnewwle, v.; abgegnewwelt, pp. tie bundles (of rye straw) with a "Gnewwel"

ab/gnibbe, v.; abgegnippt, pp. 1.tie knots in yarn;2.unbutton

ab/gnicke, v.; abgegnickt, pp. pinch in (of flower buds)

ab/graawe, v.; abgegraawe, pp. 1.dig off; 2.remove by digging

ab/gratze, v.; abgegratzt, pp. scratch or scrape off

ab/greische; abgegrischt, pp. (sich der hals --) scream oneself hoarse

ab/grimmle, v.; abgegrimmelt, pp. crumble (off)

ab/gritzle, v.; abgegritzelt, pp. scribble a copy of

ab/grutze, v.; abgegrutzt, pp. 1.cut poorly; 2.mar by cutting

ab/gscharre, v.; abgschatt, pp. unharness

ab/gucke, v.; abgeguckt, pp. learn by looking on or by stealth

ab/gwaele, v.; abgegwaelt, pp. (sich --) overwork

ab/gwehne, v.; abgwehnt, pp. wean

ab/hacke, v.; abghackt, pp. 1.chop off; 2.decapitate

ab/halte, v.; abghhalt, pp. 1.keep off or away; 2.hold (as court)

ab/handle, v.; abghandelt, pp. 1.discuss; 2.purchase; 3.trade

ab/harriche, v.; abgharricht, pp. 1.ascertain by listening; 2.eavesdrop

ab/haschble, v.; abghaschbelt, pp. unreel (fishing line, yarn, etc.)

ab/hechle, v.; abghechelt, pp. 1.criticize; 2.scold

ab/heele, v.; abgheelt, pp. 1.heal; 2.(to form a) scab

ab/heere, v.; abgheert, pp. 1.grant a hearing; 2.overhear; 3.(sich --) shed the coat

ab/heile, v.; abgheilt, pp. (eens --) cry

ab/helfe, v.; abgholfe, pp. give redress

ab/helle, v.; abghellt, pp. clear off (of weather)

ab/henke, v.; abghonke, pp. 1.detach; 2.slope; 3.take down or off; 4.unhinge; 5.unhook

ab/hewe, v.; abghowe, pp. lift off

ab/hole, v.; abgholt, pp. 1.call for; 2.fetch

ab/howwle, v.; abghowwelt, pp. plane off

ab/hupse, v.; abghupst, pp. hop off or away

ab/kaafe, v.; abkaaft, pp. buy off

ab/kabbe, v.; abgekappt, pp. 1.give a quick retort; 2.reprimand

ab/katze, v.; abgekatzt, pp. 1.abbreviate; 2.shorten

ab/kehre, v.; abgekehrt, pp. sweep off

ab/keime, v.; abgekeimt, pp. remove sprouts (from potatoes)

ab/keldre, v.; abgekeldert, pp. 1.cider or vinegar from the lees; 2.draw off wine

ab/keppe, v.; abgekeppt, pp. decapitate

ab/kiehle, v.; abgekiehlt, pp. 1.cool; 2.refrigerate

ab/koche, v.; abgekocht, pp. 1.boil down; 2.parboil

ab/kumme, v.; is abkumme, pp. 1.escape; 2.get off

ab/laade, v.; abgelaade, pp. unload

ab/laafe, v.; abgeloffe, pp. 1.drain; 2.drop off; 3.run down; 4.run off; 5.start off; 6.turn aside

ab/lauere, v.; abgelauert, pp. 1.eavesdrop; 2.lie in wait; 3.watch for

ab/lause, v.; abgelaust, pp. gain a thing by craft or sharp practice

ab/leddre, v.; abgeleddert, pp. give a good flogging

ab/riwwle

ab/leegele, v.; abgeleegelt, pp. 1.deny; 2.shift blame to another

ab/lege, v.; abgelegt, pp. 1.cast aside; 2.discharge (temporarily)

ab/lehnt, v.; abgelehnt, pp. 1.deny; 2.refuse

ab/leie, v.; abgelegge, pp. be idle temporarily

ab/lese, v.; abgelese, pp. 1.read off; 2.pick off

ab/losse, v.; abgelosst, pp. 1.grant leave; 2.leave off; 3.rebate

ab/maagere, v.; abgemaagert, pp. emaciate

ab/mache, v.; abgemacht, pp. 1.cut (grain); 2.cut down; 3.mow; 4.take off from

ab/madde, v.; abgematt, pp. tire (someone) out

ab/maehe, v.; abgemaeht, pp. (to cut off with a) scythe

ab/maertre, v.; abgemaertert, pp. 1.plague; 2.worry

ab/marricke, v.; abgemarrickt, pp. mark off

ab/meesle, v.; abgemeeselt, pp. 1.chip off; 2.chisel off

ab/mehe, v.; abgemeht, pp. mow down

ab/melke, v.; abgemolke, pp. 1.milk (a cow) dry; 2.milk a cow after calving

ab/messe, v.; abgemesse, pp. 1.measure off; 2.survey land

ab/mole, v.; abgemolt, pp. 1.draw; 2.sketch; 3.copy a picture

ab/moschdere, v.; abgemoschdert, pp. tap off vinegar

ab/munkle, v.; abgemunkelt, pp. prevaricate (in a matter)

ab/nemme (dative)v. (ebber an der Libbe --) read lips

ab/nemme, v.; abgenumme, pp. 1.amputate; 2.become less; 3.lose weight; 4.photograph; 5.subtract; 6.take away from; 7.decrease; 8.take off

ab/newwle, v.; abgenewwelt, pp. 1.clear off; 2.lift (as a fog)

ab/paare, v.; abgepaart, pp. pair off

ab/palde, v.; abgepalde, pp. keep off

ab/petze, v.; abgepetzt, pp. 1.pinch off; 2.(eens --) (a) (take a) nip; (b) (take a) swig

ab/quaele, v.; abgequaelt, pp. (sich --) 1.fret; 2.overwork; 3.worry

ab/raahme, v.; abgeraahmt, pp. 1.separate cream from milk; 2.skim

ab/raame, v.; abgeraamt, pp. clear off (a table)

ab/ranke, v.; abgerankt, pp. clear away superfluous shoots on vines or plants

ab/rapple, v.; abgerappelt, pp. rattle off

ab/reche, v.; abgerecht, pp. rake off

ab/rechle, v.; abgerechelt, pp. 1.deduct; 2.square accounts

ab/reeche, v.; abgereecht, pp. hand over

ab/reese, v.; abgereest, pp. 1.journey; 2.leave on a trip

ab/reisse, v.; abgereest, pp. 1.depart; 2.go on a journey or trip; 3.(sich -- vun) (a) escape; (b) leave

ab/reisse, v.; abgerisse, pp. 1.demolish; 2.part; 3.separate; 4.tear down; 5.tear off

ab/reiwe, v.; abgeriwwe, pp. 1.abrade; 2.rub off

ab/renne, v.; abgerennt, pp. knock off in running

ab/richde, v.; abgericht, pp. 1.arrange; 2.teach animals tricks; 3.train

ab/rinne, v.; abgerunne, pp. 1.drain; 2.drip; 3.run off

ab/ritsche, v.;abgeritscht, pp. 1.glide from; 2.slip; 3.slip from

ab/riwwle, v.; abgeriwwelt, pp. rub off dirt in rivels (rolls)

Aa

ab/robbe

ab/robbe, v.; abgeroppt, pp. 1.pick; 2.pick off; 3.pluck

ab/rolle, v.; abgerollt, pp. 1.roll from or off; 2.unroll

ab/roschde, v.; abgeroscht, pp. rust off

ab/rufe, v.; abgerufe, pp. 1.call off; 2.proclaim

ab/runde, v.; abgerundt, pp. round off

ab/rutsche, v.; abgerutscht, pp. 1.slip off; 2.wear the nap off

ab/saage, v.; abgsaat, pp. 1.decline; 2.refuse; 3.reject 4.revoke; 5.renounce

ab/saddle, v.; abgsaddelt, pp. unsaddle

ab/saege, v.; absaegt, pp. saw off

ab/saufe, v.; abgsoffe, pp. weaken (by suckling)

ab/schaame, v.; abgschaamt, pp. skim off scum (from boiling liquids)

ab/schaawe, v.; abgschaabt, pp. 1.abrade; 2.scrape off

ab/schaere, v.; abgschaerrt, pp. 1.scratch off or away; 2.unharness

ab/schaerfe, v.; abgschaerft, pp. taper

ab/schaffe, v.; abgschafft, pp. 1.discontinue; 2.dispose of; 3. do away with; 4.get rid of; 5.repeal; 6.(sich --) work to excess

ab/schaume, v.; abgschaumt, pp. skim off scum (from boiling liquids)

ab/scheele, v.; abgscheelt, pp. 1.hull; 2.peel off; 3.shell; 4.(sich--) (a) evade; (b) get out of doing something

ab/scheppe, v.; abgscheppt, pp. 1.shovel off; 2.skim off; 3.take away from a liquid

ab/schere, v.; abgschore, pp. shear off

ab/schicke, v.; abgschickt, pp.1.discharge;2.sack (a beau)

ab/schidde, v.; abgschitt, pp. pour off

ab/schiddle, v.; abgschiddelt, pp. 1.shake off; 2.shake out (a rug)

ab/schiesse, v.; abgschosse, pp. 1.discharge (a gun); 2.fire off; 3.reprimand; 4.tell off; 5.(past tense) faded

ab/schiewe, v.; abschowe, pp. 1.push off (the sheaf from a dropper or self-rake reaper); 2.procrastinate; 3.postpone; 4.(sich --) leave hastily

ab/schinne, v.; abgschunne, pp. 1.skin (animals); 2.(sich - -) (a) fag out; (b) flay; (c) overwork

ab/schitte, v.; abgschitt, pp. pour off

ab/schlaamse, v.; abgschlaamst, pp. 1.slope; 2.taper

ab/schlachde, v.; abgschlacht, pp. slaughter

ab/schlagge, v.; abgschlagge, pp. 1.knock off; 2.pronounce an article sold at an auction; 3.(wasser --) urinate

ab/schlecke, v.; abscheckt, pp. lick off

ab/schleiche, v.; abgschliche, pp. sneak away

ab/schleife, v.; abschliffe, pp. 1.grind off; 2.polish

ab/schlenkere, v.; abgschlenkert, pp. shake off

ab/schlibbe, v.; abgschlippt, pp. 1.slip off; 2.steal away

ab/schliesse, v.; abgschlosse, pp. 1.covenant; 2.make an agreement

ab/schlofe, v.; abgschlofe, pp. sleep off (the effects of drink)

ab/schmeisse, v.; abgschmisse, pp. 1.deduct; 2.throw off

ab/schmelze, v.; abgschmolze, pp. 1.drop down in consequence of melting; 2.melt off

ab/schnaebbe, v.; abgschnaeppt, pp. 1.give a curt reply; 2.snap off

ab/schtubbe

ab/schneide, v.; abgschnidde, pp. 1.amputate; 2.cut off; 3.shear

ab/schnelle, v.; abgschnellt, pp. 1.fling off; 2.snap the chalk line (in hewing timber)

ab/schnitzle, v.; abgschnitzelt, pp. whittle off

ab/schpaale, v.; abgschpaalt, pp. 1.break off in spalls; 2.hew logs roughly

ab/schpiele, v.; abgschpielt, pp. 1.play off; 2.pretend; 3.shirk

ab/schpinne, v.; abgschpunne, pp. spin off

ab/schpinne, v.; abgschpunne, pp. (eens --) tell a yarn

ab/schpreche, v.; abschproche, pp. 1.deny; 2.dissuade; 3.refuse

ab/schprenge, v.; abgschprengt, pp. 1.blast off; 2.cause to break or fly off; 3.cause to leave hastily; 4.force off

ab/schpringe, v.; abschprunge, pp. 1.chip off; 2.flee; 3.leap or start suddenly; 4.run away

ab/schraekse, v.; abgschraekst, pp. bevel

ab/schrauwe, v.; abgschraubt, pp. unscrew

ab/schrecke, v.; abgschreckt, pp.1.intimidate;2.scare off

ab/schreiwe, v.; abgschriwwe, pp. 1.copy; 2.transcribe

ab/schridde, v.; abg(e)schritt, pp. pace off

ab/schtaawe, v.; abgschtaapt, pp. remove dust from

ab/schtadde, v.; abgschtatt, pp. (dank --) thank

ab/schtaerme, v.; abgschtaermt, pp. chase away

ab/schtaerwe, v.; abgschtarwe, pp. 1.die; 2.die out

ab/schtambe, v.; abgschtambt, pp. stamp off

ab/schtamme, v.; abgschtammt, pp.(to be) descended from)

ab/schtatte, v.; abgschtatt, pp. thank

ab/schtatze, v.; abgschtatzt, pp. fall off or down

ab/schtecke, v.; abgschteckt, pp. mark off with stakes

ab/schteh, v.; is abgschtanne, pp. 1.abstain; 2.begin to spoil; 3.stand at a distance; 4.turn flat

ab/schtehle, v.; abschtohle, pp. 1.sneak away; 2.steal from

ab/schteige, v.; abschteigt, is abschtigge, pp. 1.alight (from a vehicle); 2.descend; 3.dismount

ab/schtelle, v.; abgschtellt, pp. 1.postpone; 2.unload; 3. (sich --) stand at a distance

ab/schtennich, v. showing signs of decay (as a tree)

ab/schtickle, v.; abgschtickelt, pp. set stakes

ab/schtiege, v.; abgschtigg, pp. dismount

ab/schtimme,v.; abgschtimmt,pp. 1.put to a vote;2.vote down

ab/schtobbe, v.; abgschtoppt, pp. 1.discharge (the baker, milkman, etc.); 2.shut off; 3.stop; 4.stop off

ab/schtolbere, v.; abgschtolbert, pp. stumble away

ab/schtrecke, v.; abgschtreckt, pp. 1.measure; 2.step off

ab/schtreiche, v.; abgschtriche, pp. 1.brush away; 2.level measure of grain

ab/schtriggle, v.; abschtriggelt, pp. curry

ab/schtrippe, v.; abgschtrippt, pp. 1.strip off; 2.(sich --) change one's clothes

ab/schtrofe, v.; abgschtroft, pp. 1.punish; 2.reprimand; 3.reprove

ab/schtubbe, v.; abschtuppt, pp. 1.poke off (with a stick); 2.wear off (by stubbing)

Aa

ab/schwaarde — abgelumpt

ab/schwaarde, v.; abgschwaart, pp. 1.give a beating; 2.saw slabs from a log; 3.take the rind from pork

ab/schweere, v.; abgschwore, pp. 1.swear off; 2.vow to discontinue; 3.renounce

ab/schwenke, v.; abgschwenkt, pp. rinse

ab/schwetze, v.; abgschwetzt, pp. dissuade

ab/sehne, v.; abgsehne, pp. learn by observing

ab/seine, v.; abgseint, pp. sign off

ab/senke, v.; abgsenkt, pp. singe off

ab/senkle, v.; abgsenkelt, pp. plumb

ab/setze, v.; abgsetzt, pp. 1.discharge; 2.dismiss

ab/singe, v.; absunge, pp. (eens --) sing (a tune)

ab/sitze, v.; abgsotze, pp. sit at a distance

ab/suckle, v.; absuckelt, pp. suck off

ab/verdiene, v.; abverdient, pp. earn off a debt by working

ab/waarde, v.; abgewaardt, pp. 1.nurse (a sick person); 2.wait at table

ab/waere, v.; abgwore, pp. 1.urge against doing something; 2.wear off

ab/warne, v.; abgewarnt, pp. 1.keep away; 2.warn

ab/wechsle, v.; abgewechselt, pp. 1.alternate; 2.interchange

ab/weede, v.; abgeweedt, pp. 1.crop the pasturage close; 2.graze on

ab/wehre, v.; abgewehrt, pp. 1.urge against doing something; 2.ward off

ab/weiche, v.; abgeweicht, pp. 1.deviate; 2.depart from; 3.digress; 4.stray

ab/weise, v.; abgewisse, pp. (sich --) 1.turn someone away; 2.make a show of oneself; 3.show off

ab/welke, v.; abgewelkt, pp. wither (and fall off)

ab/wende, v.; abgewendt, pp. avert

ab/wenne, v.; abgewendt, pp. avert

ab/wesche, v.; abgewesche, pp. wash off

ab/wetze, v.; abgewetzt, pp. wear away by whetting

ab/wexle, v.; abgewexelt, pp. vary

ab/wichse, v.; abgewichst, pp. flog

ab/wickle, v.; abgewickelt, pp. 1.uncoil; 2.unfold; 3.unravel; 4.unwind

ab/wiege, v.; abgewoge, pp. weigh (for retail)

ab/wische, v.; abgewischt, pp.1.clean; 2.dust; 3.wipe off

ab/witsche, v.; abgewitscht, pp. 1.glide off or slip; 2.slide; 3.slip away

ab/wohne, v.; abgewohnt, pp. live at a distance

ab/wuhne, v.; abgewuhnt, pp. live at a distance

ab/yoche, v.; abgeyocht, pp. unyoke

ab/zaahme, v.; abgezaahmt, pp. unbridle

ab/zaahne, v.; abgzaahnt, pp. shed the milk teeth

ab/zabbe, v.; abgezappt, pp. 1.bottle; 2.tap

ab/zaerkle, v.; abgezaerkelt, pp. 1.mark off with a pair of compasses; 2.measure very exactly

ab/zanke, v.; abgezankt, pp. 1.scold; 2.upbraid

ab/zebbe, v.; ab(ge)zeppt, pp. skim

ab/zeehle, v.; abgezeehlt, pp. 1.count off; 2.count out; 3.deduct; 4.rattle off; 5.tell; 6.(des kannscht der Finger --) you might know that

ab/zehre, v.; abgezehrt, pp. emaciate

ab/zettle, v.; abgezettelt, pp. 1.dismiss abruptly; 2.finish with

ab/ziehe, v.; abgezoge, pp. 1.abstract; 2.deduct; 3.flay; 4.remove; 5.skin

ab/zobbe, v.; abgezoppt, pp. pull off by light jerks

ab/zwacke, v.; abgezwackt, pp. extort

ab/zwinge, v.; abgezwunge, pp. extort

ab, adj. (gut --) 1.well-fixed; 2.well-off

ab, adv. 1.away; 2.from; 3.off

ab, prep. 1.away; 2.from; 3.off; 4.(er is gans --) (a) he is out of his head; (b) he has severed relations; 5.(-- im Kopp) crazy (off in the head); 6.(er is wennich --) he is a little off his head ; 7.(net iwwel --) not well-off

abaddich, adv., adj. 1.dainty; 2.especial(ly); 3.exclusive (ly); 4.particular(ly); 5.select; 6.special(ly)

abard, adv. 1.particularly; 2.special(ly)

abbardich, adv., adj. 1.dainty; 2.especial(ly); 3.exclusively; 4.particular(ly); 5.select; 6.special(ly)

Abbedeek (die)n.; Abbedeek, pl. 1.drugstore; 2.pharmacy

Abbedeeker (der)n.; Abbedeeker, pl. druggist

Abbedeekerkunscht (die)n. pharmaceutics

Abbeditt (der)n. appetite

abbedittlich, adj. 1.appetizing; 2.beautiful; 3.delicious; 4.nice

Abbel (der)n.; Ebbel, pl. 1.apple; 2.(en laschder Ebbel) many apples

Abbelbaam (der)n. apple tree

Abbelgrutze (der)n. core of an apple

Abbruch (der)n. cessation

Abbutzlumbe (der)n.; Abbutzlumbe, pl. 1.dish towel; 2.tea towel

Abc (der)n. alphabet

Abcbuch (es)n. primer

Abcschitz (der)n. abecedarian

Abdansdaag (der)n. Abdon's Day (July 30)

Abdrack (der)n. 1.duty; 2.excise; 3.tax

Abdrack duh (der)v. 1.damage; 2.undermine (in business)

Abdrickellumbe (der)n. 1.cloth for drying hands or face; 2.towel

Abdritt (der)n. 1.privy; 2.withdrawal

Abdunsdaag (der)n. Abdon's Day (July 30)

Abeer (die)n. strawberry

abeewene, v.; abgeewent, pp. level off

Abendmahl (es)n. 1.Lord's Supper; 2.communion

Abfall (der)n. 1.garbage; 2.leavings; 3.remnant; 4.refuse; 5.off fall; 6.trimmings (around hard soap); 7.waste material

abfeddre, v.; abgfeddert, pp. (sich --) molt

abfeege, v.; abgfeekt, pp. (sich --) become exhausted from over exertion

abfitze, v.; abgfitzt, pp. whip (with a rod)

abfladdre, v.; abgfladdert, pp. fly away slowly

Abgang (der)n. 1.egress; 2.side passage

Abgedderei (die)n. idolatry

abgeddisch, adj. idolatrous

abgehungert, adj. emaciated

abgelbt, adv. worn out

abgelumpt, adv. lean and scurvy (of cats)

Aa

abgemaust

abgemaust, adv. said of an old worn out cat
abgemolke, adv. said of a cow when it is nearly dry
Abgetterei (die)n. idolatry
abgettisch, adj.; adv. idolatrous
abgewinne, v.; abgewinne, pp. win or gain from
abgewore, adj. worn-out
abgezehrt, adj. emaciated
abgezettelt, adv. cut and dried
abglitsche, v.; abgeglitscht, pp. 1.slip off; 2.slide off
Abgott (der)n.; Abgedder, pl. idol
Abgrund (der)n. 1.abyss; 2.precipice
abgschmackt, adj. 1.absurd; 2.tasteless
abgschtanne, adj. stale
abgschtoppt, adj. closed
abgschtumpt, adj. 1.stumpy; 2.worn off
Abhang (der)n. 1.declivity; 2.steep slope
Abharricher (der)n.; Abharricher, pl. listener
abhenki(s)ch, adj. 1.dependent; 2.sloping
abhoore, v.; abgehoort, pp. (sich --) shed the coat
Abkatzing (die)n. abbreviation
Abkatzungszeeche (es)n. 1.dash; 2.apostrophe
Ablaaf (der)n. 1.overflow; 2.sluice
Abloos (der)n. 1.shallow ditch across a road to turn off
  the water; 2.thank-you-ma'am
Abloss (der)n. allowance
ablusche, v.; abgeluchst, pp. get by trickery or cheating
Abnemmede (es)n. marasmus
Abnemmer (der)n.; Abnemmer, pl. photographer
Abnemmes (es)n. 1.marasmus; 2.waning; 3.wasting away
Abraham (der)n. Abraham
Abreissing (die)n. 1.escape; 2.flight
Abrigos (die)n.; Abrigose, pl. apricot
Abrigosebaam (der)n.; Abrigosebeem, pl. apricot tree
Abrill (der)n. 1.April; 2.(in -- schicke) plan an April fool prank
Abrill(e)kalb (es)n. April fool
Abrill(e) Narr (der)n. April fool
Abrille Eesli (es)n. April fool
Abriss (der)n. 1.design; 2.diagram; 3.plan
abrode, v.; abgerode, pp. dissuade
Absalam (der)n. Absalom
Absatz (der)n.; Absetz, pl. 1.heel; 2.ledge; 3.paragraph;
  4.pause; 5.sale of goods; 7.step (from one floor level
  to another); 8.stop
abschaere, v.; abschaert, pp. take the harness from a horse
abscharre, v.; abgschatt, pp. take the harness from a horse
Abschei (der)n. 1.abhorrence; 2.disgust; 3.hatred; 4.horror
abscheilich, adj. 1.abominable; 2.detestable; 3.hateful;
  4.horrible
Abschiddsbreddich (die)n. farewell sermon
Abschied (der)n. departure
abschissich, adj. steep
Abschlaage!, interj. Sold! (said the auctioneer at an auction)
abschleefe, v.; abgschleeft, pp. 1.drag off; 2.wear off by
  dragging
abschliesse, v.; abgschlosse, pp. 1.covenant; 2.make an
  agreement

Adder

Abschnitt (der)n. section
Abschrift (die)n. 1.copy; 2.transcript
abschtumpt, adj. blunt
Abschuss (der)n. declivity
abselut(t), adv. 1.absolutely; 2.(by all) means; 3.insist upon
absenaat, adj. 1.difficult to please; 2.fastidious; 3.finical;
  4.headstrong; 5.obstinate; 6.stubborn
Absetz (der)n. heel
Absicht (die)n. 1.aim; 2.design; 3.purpose
absichtlos, adj. undesigning
abtrinni(s)ch, adj. 1.apostate; 2.disloyal
Abwaarden (die)n. 1.female nurse; 2.waitress
Abwaarder (der)n. 1.male nurse; 2.waiter
Abwarting (die)n. 1.attendance; 2.nursing
Abwartung (die)n. 1.attendance; 2.nursing
Abwechsel (der)n. change
Abwechslung (die)n. 1.change; 2.variety
Abweg (der)n. 1.byroad; 2.byway; 3.wrong road
Abweiser (der)n. shallow ditch across a road
abwennich, adj. 1.alienated; 2.disinclined; 3.opposed
Abwexling (die)n. variety
Abwischer (der)n.; Abwischer, pl. 1.duster; 2.wiper
Abzuck (der)n. 1.deduction; 2.discount
ach!, interj. oh!
achde, v.; geacht, pp. 1.esteem; 2.heed; 3.mind; 4.regard
achding gewwe, adj. be careful
Achel (die)n. awn
acht, achde, adj.; pron. eight
Acht (der, die)n. 1.attention; 2.care; 3.esteem; 4.
  (in -- nemme) (a) bear in mind; (b) take care of; 5.(-- uff
  ebbes hawwe) (a) pay attention to a thing; (b) notice;
  6.(kenn -- hawwe uff ebbes) pay no attention to a thing
acht nemme, v.; genumme, pp. (sich in --) beware
acht/gewwe, v.; achtgewwe, pp. 1.beware; 2.heed; 3.pay
  attention; 4.take care
Achtdaagsuhr (die)n. eight day clock
achteckich, adj. octagonal
Achtel (en)n. eighth (part)
Achter (en)n. eight spot (in cards)
achtgewwe, v. (-- uff ebber, ebbes) care for someone
  (something)
achtich, adj. careful
achting gewwe, adj. be careful
achtlos, adj. 1.careless; 2.indifferent
achtsam, adj. 1.attentive; 2.careful; 3.heedful
Achtung (die)n. esteem
achtzich, adj.; pron. eighty
achzeh, adj.; pron. eighteen
achzichscht, adj. eightieth
Acker (der)n.; Acker, pl. acre
Ackerbau (der)n. agriculture
Adamsabbel (der)n. Adam's apple
Adarn (der)n. horehound
addentlich, adj. decent
Adder (die) n. 1.command; 2.condition; 3.order (in
  business); 4.state

Aa

adder — allemol

adder, conj. or

Adderbreischder (der)n. priest (a member of an order)

addere, v.; geaddert, pp. 1.order; 2.give a business order

Addler (der)n.; Addler, pl. 1.eagle; 2.whole kernel of half a walnut or hickory nut

Addning (die)n. 1.discipline; 2.order

Adem (der)n. Adam

Adem-un-Eva, n. puttyroot

adentlich, adv. orderly

adge, int. goodbye

Adningsgmee (die)n. preparatory service (prior to Holy Communion) Amish

Advent (der)n. Advent

Aebeer (die)n.; Aebeere, pl. strawberry

Aebier (die)n.; Aebiere, pl. strawberry

Aeddick (die)n. attic

aehnlich, adj. 1.alike; 2.similar

Aehnlichkeit (die)n. resemblance

Aehr (die)n. head of grain

Aelkehaal (es)n. alcohol

Aendi (die)n. aunt

Aent(i) (die)n. aunt

Aer(e)bel (die)n.; Aerebel, pl. strawberry

aerblich, adj. 1.contagious; 2.hereditary

aer(ri)yer, adj. worse

Aerbs (die)n.; Aerbse, pl. pea

Aerbsesupp (die)n. pea soup

Aerebe (die)n.; Aerebse, pl. pea

Aerebseschef (die)n.; Aerebseschefe, pl. pea-pod

aerm; aermer; aermscht, adj. poor; poorer; poorest

Aermel (der)n. sleeve

Aermelloch (es)n. sleeve-hole

aermlich, adv. poorly

Aernabbel (der)n. harvest-apple

Aernbreddich (die)n. (harvest)Thanksgiving sermon

aernde, v.; geaernt, pp. harvest

Aernfeld (es)n. harvest field

Aernkichelche (es)n. doughnut

aernschthaft, adj. 1.earnest; 2.serious; 3.sincere

aernschtlich, adv. 1.ardently; 2.earnestly; 3.seriously

Aernsleit (die)n., pl. harvesters

Aernzeit (die)n. harvest time

aerr sei, adj. be confused

aerr warre, adj. become confused

aerr, adj. confused

aerrgeh, v.; aerrgange, pp. go astray

Aerrgraut (es)n. rattlesnake-plantain

aeryere, v.; geaeryert, pp. 1.vex; 2.(sich --) be vexed

aeryerlich, adj. 1.irritable; 2.provoking; 3.vexatious; 4.vexed

Aeryernis (die)n. 1.irritation; 2.vexation

aeryets, adv. somewhere

Aeyer (der)n. 1.fury; 2.vexation

Aff (der)n.; Affe, pl. 1.ape; 2.monkey; 3.silly person

Affegsicht (es)n. 1.mask; 2.ugly face

After (es)n. 1.anus; 2.buttock; 3.posteriors

Aftergschaerr (es)n. quilor harness (the distinctive parts of which were a wide breeching and side or under-belly straps connected with the collar so as to enable horses to hold back a load better in going down hill)

Aggel (die)n. awn

Aggeschpiel (der)n. (any) phenomenon

aha!, interj. aha!

ahne, v.; geahnt, pp. 1.dream of; 2.suspect; 3.think of

Ahning (die)n. inkling

Ahorn (der)n. maple (rare usage)

Ai!, interj. 1.Well!; 2.My goodness!

aich, adv. very

Aiyer (der)n. vexation

aiyerlich, adj. 1.vexatious; 2.vexed

Albrechtsleit (die)n., pl. followers of Jacob Albright later known as the Evangelical Association

Aldaar (der)n.; Aldaare, pl. 1.communion table; 2.altar

Alder (der)n. 1.age; 2.(mei --) (a) boy friend; (b) my beau; (c) my husband; (d) my old man

Aldermann (Schtock) (der)n. southern wood

alders, adv. (ver --) (of) yore

Alderschwech (die)n. infirmity of old age

Alderweiwerglaawe (der)n. 1.a granny's belief; 2.superstition

Aldi (es) n. 1.girl friend; 2.(mei --) (a) girlfriend; (b) my wife

Aldifraa (die)n. common mugwort

Aldimeed (die)n. youth-and-old-age (plant)

all(e)daags(ich), adj. everyday

all, adj. 1.all; 2.every; 3.(-- nix) (a) all in vain; (b) all off

all iwwer, adv. everywhere

Allau (der)n. alum

allbekannt, adj. notorious

Alldaagsgleeder (die)n. 1.everyday clothes; 2.work clothes

alldeweeg, adv. 1.all the way; 2.whole distance

alldiweil, adv. 1.all the time; 2.during this time

alle Aard, pron. miscellaneous

allebeed, pron. both

alle Daag, adv. every day

alle Mol, adv. every time

alle Nacht, adv. nightly

alle Woch, adv. weekly

alle Yaahr, adv. yearly

alle-eens, pron. everyone

Alledaagsblumm (die)n. impatiens sultans

allee, adj.; adv. alone

Alleehandel (der)n. monopoly

alleenich, adv. alone

Alleesei (es)n. state of being alone

allegebott, adv. every now and then

Alleheck (die)n. alder (brush)

Allekur (die)n. Canadian moonseed

Allemengel name applied in colonial times to the north-western part of Lehigh Co. (PA) because of the dire need of the early settlers

allemno, adv. 1.everything considered; 2.it would seem; 3.evidently

allemol, adv.1.every time; 2.(in responses like) amen; 3.most assuredly

Aa

allerarrickscht

allerarrickscht, adj. worst of all
allerbescht, adj. best of all
allerdings, adv. 1.of course; 2.sure enough; 3.to be sure
allererscht, adj. the very first
allerfeinscht, adj. finest of all
allergreescht, adj. largest of all
Allergwalt (die)n. power
allerhand, adj. 1.all sorts of; 2.different; 3.many kinds of; 4.various
Allerheil un (aller) Seel All Saints' and All Souls' Day (Nov. 1 and 2)
Allerheilichi (die)n. All Saints' Day (Nov. 1)
allerhinnerscht, adj. 1.last of all; 2.hindmost
allerlee, adv. 1.all sorts; 2.various kinds
allerlei, adv. 1.all sorts; 2.various kinds
allerlescht, adj. last of all
allerliebscht, adj. 1.dearest; 2.most of all
allernaegscht, adv. 1.most likely; 2.nearest of all; 3.presumably
allerneegscht, adj. nearest of all
allervedderscht, adj. foremost of all
allerwiescht, adj. 1.ugliest of all; 2.worst of all
alles mit nei gnumme, adv.; adj. complete
alles, pron. 1.all; 2.everything
allesmenanner, pron. everything
alleweil, adv. 1.a moment ago; 2.just now; 3.now
allezwee, pron. both
allfatt, adv. 1.always; 2.ever; 3.forever
allfert, adv. 1.always; 2.constantly
allgebott, adj. 1.every now and then; 2.occasionally
allgebreichlich, adj. 1.customary; 2.universal
allgemee, adj. 1.common(ly); 2.universal
allgemee, adv. generally
allgemei, adj. 1.common(ly); 2.universal
allgemein, adj. 1.common(ly); 2.universal
alli Daag, adv. every day
alli Mol, adv. every time
alli Nacht, adv. nightly
alli Woch, adv. weekly
alli Yaahr, adv. yearly
alli-eens, pron. everyone
Allidaagsblumm (die)n. impatiens sultans
alliebber, pron. 1.all; 2.everybody; 3.everyone
alllwwer, adv. 1.everywhere; 2.In all parts
allmechdich, adj. almighty
allmechdich, adv. very
allmenanner, adj. 1.all; 2.altogether
Allowe (die)n. aloe
allrecht, adj. all right
allwissend, adj. omniscient
allzamme, adv. 1.altogether; 2.all at one time
allzeit, adv. 1.always; 2.ever
Almose (die)n., pl. 1.alms; 2.church collection
als, adv. 1.accustomed to; 2.always; 3.as; 4.be; 5.but; 6.continue(d) to; 7.in the habit of; 8.still; 9.used to; 10.while; 11.than

Anndiff(d)i

als, conj.; prep. than
alsdann, adv. then
alsemol, adv. 1.every now and then; 2.occasionally; 3.sometimes
alsfatt, adv. 1.always; 2.constantly
also, adv. that is
Alsodillwatzel (die)n. asphodel
Alt Grischtdaag (der)n. Old Christmas, January 6 (celebrated by the Old Order Amish)
alt Land (es)n. old country (Germany)
alt Leier (die) 1.old ruts; 2.tune the old cow died on; 3. (the same) old (story)
Alt(er)weiwersummer (der)n. Indian Summer
Alt-waare (es)n. state of growing old
alt, adj. 1.old; 2.stale
alt; elder; es elscht, adj. old; older; oldest
altfrankisch, adj. old-fashioned
altfrenkisch, adj. old-fashioned
altgro, adj. hoary
altguckich, adj. 1.aged; 2.having an old look; 3.old-fashioned
Altlicht (es)n. last phase of the moon
altmelkich, adj. nearly dry (of cows)
altmodisch, adj. old-fashioned
Altwarre (es)n. state of growing old
alwer(n), adj. 1.absurd; 2.lacking common sense; 3.unreasonable
Alwerheet (die)n. 1.absurdity; 2.lack of sense
am, prep. at
Amberell (die)n.; Amberelle, pl. umbrella
Ambos (der)n.; Ambose, pl. anvil
Ambosschtand (der)n. anvil mounting
Ambosschtul (der)n. anvil mounting
Ambt (es)n. office
Amerelle (die)n. morello (cherry)
Amerika(a) (es)n. America
amerika(a)nisch, adj. American
Amerikaaner (der)n.; Amerikaaner, pl. American
Amisch (fraa) (die)n. Amish woman
Amisch (mann) (der)n. Amish man
Amisch, adj. Amish
amme = an me at a
ammenent/schicke, v. send to some place
ammenent, adv. somewhere
ammenot/schicke, v. send to some place
ammenot, adv. somewhere
Ammeriele (es)n. Mary Ann
Amschel (die)n.; Amschle, pl. 1.robin; 2.thrush
Amt (es)n. office
Amtsmann (der)n. official
an dem, adv. presumably
an, prep. 1.along; 2.at; 3.by; 4.in; 5.of; 6.to
an, prep.; adv. 1.about; 2.at; 3.on
Andann (der)n. Anthony
andem, adj. 1.(very) likely; 2.presumably
Andiefi (der)n. endive
Andiff(d)i (der)n. endive

Aa

Andiv(v)(d)i

Andiv(v)(d)i (der)n. 1.chicory; 2.endive
andlich, adj. decent
Andreasdaag (der)n. St. Andrew's Day, Nov 30.
Andres (der)n. Andrew
anenanner, adv. 1.fasten together; 2.together
Angel (die)n. 1.awn (of grain); 2.fishhook; 3.hinge of a door; 4.sting of an insect
Angelige (die)n. angelica (plant)
angle, v.; geangelt, pp. fish
Angscht (die)n. fear
Ankel (der)n. uncle
Ankel (die)n. nape (or back of the neck)
Anker (der)n. anchor
ankere, v.; geankert, pp. anchor
annaehre, v.; annaehrt, pp. support
anne = hi compounds of anne are equal to compounds of hi
anne/bschtelle, v.; annebschtellt, pp. announce
anne/hocke, v. (sich --) sit down
anne/kumme, v.; is annekumme, pp. arrive
anne/lege, v.; anneglegt, pp. (sich --) lie down
anne/schicke, v. annegschickt, pp. send to some place
anne/schtelle, v.; annegschtellt, pp. announce
anne/sitze, v.; annegsitzt, pp. (sich --) sit down
Annemar(e)ia (die)n. Ann Mary
annenanner, adv. together
anner, adj.; pron. other
annermol, adj. another time
annerschder, adj.; adv. 1.different; 2.otherwise; 3.various
annerscht, adv. 1.different; 2.otherwise
anneweil, adv. 1.just now; 2.now
ans = an es 1.at the; 2.to the
Anscht (der)n. earnest
anscht, adj. serious
anschtatt(s), prep. instead of
antwadde, v.; geantwatt, pp. 1.answer; 2.reply; 3.respond
Antwatt (die)n.; Antwadde, pl. 1.answer; 2.response; 3.reply
antwatt gewwe, v.; gewwe, pp. answer
antwattlich, adj. 1.amenable; 2.responsible
Aposchdel (der)n. apostle
Apostelg(e)schichte (die)n. Acts of the Apostles
applich, adj. dappled
Araan (die)n. Indian turnip
Araanszwiwwel (die)n. Indian turnip
Arbseschood (die)n. pea-pod
Ardickel (der)n. 1.article; 2.object; 3.product
Ardning (die)n. order
areblich, adj. contagious
Arebse (die)n., pl (-- blicke) shell peas or beans
Arebseschood (die)n.; Arebseschoode, pl. pea-pod
Arem(p)fleger (der)n. poor director
Aremhaus (es)n. poor-house
Arewet(t) (die)n. 1.labor; 2.work; 3.(an -- geh) to go to work; 4.(sich an -- mache) to get to work
Ariyel (die)n.; Arigle, pl. (pipe) organ
Ariyelschpieler (der)n.; Ariyelschpieler, pl. organist
ariyets, adv. somewhere

aus/bauschde

arm(e)slang, adv. (alle --) 1.every little while; 2.every minute
Armedei (die)n. poverty
Armee (die)n. army
Armen (der)n. deacon (Old Order Amish usage)
armle, v.; gearmelt, pp. hug
Armschtuhl (der)n. armchair
Armsleng (die)n. length of an arm
armvollweis, adv. by the armful
Arn (die)n. harvest
arndlich, adj. decent
Arrentschzwiwwel (die)n. 1.jack-in-the-pulpit; 2.Indian turnip
Arrich (die)n. ark
arrick, adj. 1.bad; 2.uncommon; 3.very
arrick, arrickscht, adj. worse, worst
arrig mache, v.; arriggemacht, pp. rage
arrig, adj. 1.bad; 2.uncommon
arrig, adv. very
Arschbacke (der)n. buttock
Arschbaerb (der)n. buttock
Arschloch (es)n. anus
Arwet (die)n. work
Arznei (die)n. medicine
as, adv. 1.as; 2.but
as, conj. since
as, conj.; prep. than
as, pron.; adj.; conj. That
Aschbe (die)n. aspen
Asche (die)n. ash tree
Aschermittwoch (der)n. Ash Wednesday
Ascht (der)n. (rare usage) limb (of a tree)
ass = dass, conj. that
atlich, adj. somewhat
atme, v.; geatmet, pp. breathe
Atschi!, interj. Atchee! (imitation of the sound made in sneezing, sometimes with an added 'Gsundheet')
Attich (der)n. dwarf-elder
au!, interj. oh! ouch!
auf, prep. (rare usage) 1.on; 2.upon
aufaerschteh, v.; aufaerschtanne, pp. rise from the dead
aufaerwecke, v.; aufaerweckt, pp. resuscitate
Aufenthalt (der)n. 1.abode; 2.retreat; 3.whereabouts
Auferschtehing (die)n. resurrection
Aufnahm, (die)n. reception
Aufschlack (der)n. lapel
Aug(u)scht (der)n. August (month)
aus(e)wennich lanne, v.; aus(e)wennich glannt, pp. memorize
aus(e)wennich, adj. 1.(from) memory; 2.outside; 3.on the outside
Aus(en)palt (der)n. reservation for life (in house, room, firewood, etc. in old deeds)
aus/aarde, v.; ausgaart, pp. 1.degenerate; 2.deteriorate
aus/babble, v.; ausgebabbelt, pp. 1.babble; 2.spread tales
aus/baschde, v.; ausgebascht, pp. brush out

Aa

aus/bautsche

aus/bautsche, v.; ausgebautscht, pp. wear out

aus/beisse, v.; ausgebisse, pp. 1.force out by biting; 2.oust; 3.supplant

aus/bezaahle, v.; ausbezaahlt, pp. 1.disburse; 2.pay out

aus/biede, v.; ausgebodde, pp. 1.outwit; 2.serve a quit notice

aus/biggele, v.; ausgebiggelt, pp. iron out

aus/blanze, v.; ausgeblanzt, pp. transplant

aus/blaudre, v.; ausgeblaudert, pp. 1.finish talking; 2. (sich --) talk to one's heart's content

aus/bleeche, v.; ausgebleecht, pp. fade (in color)

aus/bliewe, v.; ausgebliwwe, pp. 1.be long in coming; 2.delay

aus/blose, v.; ausgeblose, pp. blow out (a candle, blast furnace)

aus/bluge, v.; ausgeblugt, pp. 1.plow between the rows of growing plants; 2.plow out potatoes

aus/bohre, v.; ausgebohrt, pp. bore out

aus/breche, v.; ausgebroche, pp. break out (a fire, epidemic disease, eruption)

aus/breede, v.; ausgebreet, pp. spread

aus/brenne, v.; ausgebrennt, pp. 1.burn out; 2.finish burning

aus/briehe, v.; ausgebrieht, pp. 1.incubate; 2.scald (a vessel)

aus/brockle, v.; ausgebrockelt, pp. crumble

aus/brode, v.; ausgebrode, pp. extract fat by frying

aus/bumbe, v.; ausgebumpt, pp. pump dry

aus/butze, v.; ausgebutzt, pp. 1.prune; 2.purge (for constipation); 3.reprimand

aus/daae, v.; ausgedaat, pp. thaw out

aus/daerre, v.; ausgedaerrt, pp. dry out

aus/dauere, v.; ausgedauert, pp. 1.last; 2.preserve

aus/deele, v.; ausgedeelt, pp. 1.deal; 2.distribute; 3.divide among

aus/deiwle, v.;ausgedeiwelt, pp. (sich --) 1.come to the end of a frenzy; 2.give full vent to one's devilishness

aus/denke, v.; ausgedenkt, pp. 1.contrive; 2.think out

aus/diene, v.; ausgedient, pp. serve one's time

aus/dilye, v.; ausgedilgt, pp. extirpate

aus/dowe, v.; ausgedobt, pp. (sich --) 1.give oneself free course in rage; 2.play or other activity

aus/dreele, v.; ausgedreelt, pp. roll out

aus/drehe, v.; ausgedreht, pp. 1.avoid; 2.turn out; 3.wring (out)

aus/dreiwe, v.; ausgedriwwe, pp. 1.drive away; 2.expel; 3.exterminate; 4.oust

aus/drenge, v.; ausgedrengt, pp. 1.force out; 2.supplant

aus/dresche, v.; ausgedrosche, pp. 1.(to finish) threshing; 2.thresh out

aus/dricke, v.; ausgedrickt, pp. (sich --) express oneself

aus/dricke, v.; ausgedrickt, pp. 1.express; 2.press out

aus/drickle, v.; ausgedrickelt, pp. dry out

aus/drinke, v.; ausgedrunke, pp. drink all of

aus/duh, v.; ausgeduh, pp. 1.cancel; 2.cross off the books; 3.undress; 4.(sich --) (a) undress; (b) strip off (clothing)

aus/esse, v.; ausgesse, pp. eat everything in the house

aus/faahre, v.; aus(g)faahre, pp. 1.have one's face covered with pimples; 2.have a rash

aus/hungere

aus/faerrichde, v.; ausgfaerricht, pp. draw furrows for planting

aus/falle, v.; ausgfalle, pp. 1.come out (as hair); 2.drop from the hull (grain); 3.have a disagreement; 4.quarrel; 5.slip the mind

aus/farrichde, v.; ausgfarricht, pp. furrow out

aus/faschle, v.; ausgfaschelt, pp. 1.attempt to gain information; 2.spy out

aus/fasse, v.; ausgfasst, pp. bag grain or feed from bin

aus/fechde, v.; ausgfochde, pp. 1.fight it out; 2.have it out; 3.settle a difference

aus/feile, v.; ausgfeilt, pp. file out

aus/fiehre, v.; ausgfiehrt, pp. 1.carry out; 2.finish; 3.perform

aus/figgere, v.; ausgfiggert, pp. figure out

aus/fille, v.; ausgfillt, pp. fill out or up

aus/finne, v.; ausgfunne, pp. 1.ascertain; 2.discover; 3.find out

aus/fische, v.; ausgfischt, pp. 1.clear (a pond of fish); 2.get information; 3.spy out

aus/fischle, v.; ausgfischelt, pp. spy out

aus/fliege, v.; ausgflogge, pp. leave the nest

aus/fliesse, v.; ausgflosse, pp. 1.flow out; 2.run out

aus/fransle, v.; ausgfranselt, pp. wear to a fringe

aus/fresse, v.; ausgfresse, pp. eat all

aus/(g)friere, v.; ausgfrore, pp. 1.freeze out; 2.perish from freezing

aus/froge, v.; ausgfrogt, pp. 1.interrogate; 2.question minutely

aus/gargle, v.; ausgegargelt, pp. gargle

aus/geh, v.; ausgange, pp. 1.be dismissed; 2.drop out; 3.expire; 4.fade; 5.fall out; 6.go out; 7.result; 8.take a walk

aus/gewwe, v.; ausgewwe, pp. 1.announce; 2.be compelled to stop work from heat or fatigue; 3.expend; 4.yield

aus/gickle, v.; ausgegickelt, pp. finish giggling

aus/glitsche, v.; ausgeglitscht, pp. slip

aus/globbe, v.; ausgeglobbt, pp. 1.beat out; 2.shell (a nut)

aus/graawe, v.; ausgegraawe, pp. excavate

aus/gratze, v.; ausgegratzt, pp. 1.erase; 2.scratch out

aus/greckse, v.; ausgegreckst, pp. finish complaining

aus/greische, v.; ausgegrische, pp. (ebber --) spread evil reports about someone

aus/gritzle, v.; ausgegritzelt, pp. scrawl or scribble over

aus/hacke, v.; ausghackt, pp. (nidder [hoch] --) make the end of the stroke of the scythe (in mowing low [high])

aus/halde, v.; ausghalde, pp. 1.bear; 2.continue; 3. endure; 4.except; 5.exempt; 6.hold out; 7.remain; 8.stipulate

aus/hammere, v.; ausghammert, pp. hammer out

aus/heele, v.; ausgheelt, pp. heal perfectly

aus/heewe, v.; ausghowe, pp. 1.evict; 2.remove

aus/helfe, v.; ausgholfe, pp. 1.aid; 2.assist; 3.help

aus/henke, v.; ausghenkt, pp. 1.detach; 2.unhook

aus/hensle, v.; ausghenselt, pp. 1.chaff; 2.ridicule

aus/hiehle, v.; ausghiehlt, pp. hollow out

aus/hieliche, v.; auskiehlicht, pp. hollow out

aus/hungere, v.; ausghungert, pp. 1.famish; 2.starve

Aa

aus/iewe

aus/iewe, v.; ausgeiebt, pp. 1.go as far as possible; 2.practice; 3.wreak

aus/kaafe, v.; auskaaft, pp. buy out

aus/kehre, v.; ausgekehrt, pp. sweep out

aus/kiehle, v.; ausgekiehlt, pp. cool thoroughly (as a room)

aus/koche, v.; ausgekocht, pp. 1.clean by boiling; 2.extract by boiling

aus/kumme, v.; is auskumme, pp. 1.live on good terms (with); 2.live within one's means; 3.manage on

aus/laade, v.; ausgelaade, pp. unload

aus/laafe, v.;is ausgeloffe, pp. 1.expire;2.drain;3.run out

aus/lache, v.; ausgelacht, pp. 1.laugh at; 2.ridicule

aus/lange, v.; ausgelangt, pp. suffice

aus/laxiere, v.; ausgelaxiert, pp. purge thoroughly

aus/leere, v.; ausgeleert, pp. 1.empty; 2.evacuate; 3.spill

aus/leffle, v.; ausgeleffelt, pp. 1.drop grain in sickling; 2.scoop out

aus/lege, v.; ausgelegt, pp. 1.expend; 2.explain; 3.lay out; 4.plan; 5.prepare a corpse for the coffin

aus/leine, v.; ausgeleint, pp. read lines for repetition in singing

aus/lesche, v.; ausgelescht, pp. extinguish

aus/lese, v.; ausg(e)lese, pp. 1.assort; 2.cull; 3.select; 4.separate into sorts

aus/lewe, v.; ausgelebt, pp. outlive

aus/lifde, v.; ausgelift, pp. ventilate

aus/loche, v.; ausgelocht, pp. (Poschde --) put holes in (a post)

aus/losse, v.; ausg(e)losst, pp. 1.adjourn; 2.let out (a seem); 3.manifest; 4.utter one's mind; 5.wreak upon

aus/mache, v.; ausgemacht, pp. 1.decipher; 2.determine; 3.dig out (potatoes); 4.extinguish (fire); 5.make out;6.matter; 7.plan; 8.settle; 9.shell (corn)

aus/mache, v.; ausgemacht, pp. (gut --) 1.do well; 2.prosper

aus/mauere, v.; ausgemauert, pp. 1.brick up; 2.line with a wall

aus/meesle, v.; ausgemeeselt, pp. chisel out

aus/melke, v.; ausgemolke, pp. drain a cow of all her milk

aus/messe, v.; ausgemesse, pp. 1.gauge; 2.measure out; 3.survey (land)

aus/mischde, v.; ausgemischt, pp. clean a stable

aus/n(a)ehe, v.; ausgen(a)eht, pp. 1.embroider; 2.stitch

aus/nanner, adv. apart

aus/nemme, v.; ausgenumme, pp. 1.draw (fowls); 2.take out in trade

aus/packe, v.; ausgepackt, pp. 1.open a package; 2.unload; 3.unpack (emotionally)

aus/picke, v.; ausgepickt, pp. 1.shell (peas or beans); 2.pick out

aus/raame. v.; ausgeraamt, pp. clear of furniture or rubbish

aus/reeche, v.; ausgereecht, pp. suffice

aus/reisse, v.; ausgerisse, pp. 1.abscond; 2.tear out

aus/reiwe, v.; ausgeriwwe, pp. 1.erase; 2.rub out

aus/richde, v.; ausgericht, pp. 1.attend to; 2.have influence over; 3.perform

aus/ricke, v.; ausgerickt, pp. move out of the way

aus/schreiwe

aus/riege, v.; ausgeriekt, pp. eke out (one's) spite

aus/ritsche, v.; ausgeritscht, pp. 1.lose one's footing; 2.slip

aus/riwwle, v.; ausgeriwwelt, pp. rub out

aus/robbe, v.; ausgeroppt, pp. pull out

aus/rodde, v.; ausgerott, pp.1.exterminate;2.extirpate;3.root out

aus/rolle, v.; ausgerollt, pp. roll out thin

aus/rufe, v.; ausgerufe, pp. 1.call out; 2.proclaim; 3.publish marriage bans

aus/ruh(g)e, v. ; ausgeruugt, pp. (sich --) take a thorough) rest

aus/rutsche, v.; ausgerutscht, pp. slip

aus/saage, v.; ausgsaat, pp. 1.declare; 2.promulgate

aus/saarde, v.; aussaart, pp. sort

aus/saehe, v.; ausgsaeht, pp. sow

aus/saufe, v.; ausgsoffe, pp. 1.drink all; 2.drink to the dregs

aus/schaale, v.; ausgschaalt, pp. 1.peel; 2.shell

aus/schaffe, v.; ausgschafft, pp. 1.carve; 2.pay off a bill with labor; 3.work out

aus/scheele, v.; ausgscheelt, pp. 1.peel; 2.shell

aus/schelde, v.; ausgscholde, pp. scold

aus/schemme, v.; ausgschemmt, pp. 1.cause to feel ashamed; 2.shame

aus/schenke,v.;ausgschenkt,pp. pour out(of a beverage)

aus/schenne, v.; ausgschennt, pp. 1.cause to feel ashamed; 2.reprimand

aus/scheppe, v.; ausgscheppt, pp. bail

aus/schicke, v.; ausgschickt, pp. send out

aus/schidde, v.; ausgschitt, pp. pour out

aus/schiddle, v.; ausgschiddelt, pp. shake out

aus/schiesse, v.; ausgschosse, pp. send out shoots

aus/schlagge, v.; ausgschlagge, pp. 1.send forth shoots or sprouts; 2.spell

aus/schlecke, v.; ausgschleckt, pp. lick out

aus/schliesse, v.; ausgschlosse, pp. 1.exclude; 2.lock out

aus/schlitze, v.; ausgschlitzt, pp. slit

aus/schmelze, v.; ausgschmolze, pp. 1.melt; 2.render (lard)

aus/schnaufe, v.; ausgschnauft, pp. exhale

aus/schnausse, v.; ausgschnausst, pp. snoop through

aus/schneide, v.; ausgschnidde, pp. 1.cut from a pattern; 2.notch; 3.trim

aus/schniere, v.; ausgschniert, pp. unlace

aus/schniffle, v.; ausgschniffelt, pp. pry into

aus/schnitzle, v.; ausgschnitzelt, pp. 1.carve out; 2.whittle

aus/schpanne, v.; ausgschpannt, pp. unhitch (horses from a wagon)

aus/schpauze, v.; ausgschpauzt, pp. spit out

aus/schpiele, v.; ausgschpielt, pp. (sich --) 1.become exhausted; 2.wear out

aus/schpodde, v.; ausgschpott, pp. 1.mock; 2.taunt

aus/schpraehe, v.; ausgschpraet, pp. spread out

aus/schpreche, v.; ausgschproche, pp. 1.pronounce; 2.speak out

aus/schrauwe, v.; ausgschraubt, pp. unscrew

aus/schreiwe, v.; ausgschriwwe, pp. 1.appoint by proclamation; 2.proclaim; 3.write out

Aa

aus/schtambe   **ausgelearnt**

aus/schtambe, v.; ausgschtampt, pp. stamp or beat out

aus/schtarewe, v.; ausgschtarwe, pp.1.become extinct;
   2.die out

aus/schtarre, v.; ausgschtarrt, pp. stir out

aus/schteche, v.; ausgschtoche, pp. dig out with a fork
   (as potatoes)

aus/schtecke, v.; ausgschteckt, pp.1.set out (plants);
   2.transplant; 3.(Kichelcher --) stamp out cookies
   (with a cookie cutter)

aus/schteh, v.; ausgschtanne, pp. 1.bear; 2.endure;
   3.suffer; 4.tolerate

aus/schteiere, v.; ausgschteiert, pp. fit out for housekeeping

aus/schtiege, v.; ausgschtigge, pp. 1.alight from a carriage; 2.dismount

aus/schtiwwere, v.; ausgschtiwwert, pp. drive away

aus/schtobbe, v.; ausgschtoppt, pp. 1.pad; 2.stuff

aus/schtosse, v.; ausgschtosse, pp. 1.exclude; 2.oust

aus/schtrahle, v.; ausgschtrahlt, pp. comb out

aus/schtrecke, v.; ausgschtreckt, pp. 1.stretch out; 2.
   (sich --) (a) stretch oneself; (b) lie at full length

aus/schtreiche, v.; ausgschtriche, pp. 1.cross out; 2.strike out

aus/schtudiere, v.; ausgschtudiert, pp. 1.study out;
   2.study thoroughly

aus/schwenke, v.; ausgschwenkt,pp. (der Hals --) gargle

aus/schwenke, v.; ausgschwenkt, pp. rinse out

aus/schwetze, v.; ausgschwetzt, pp. speak out

aus/schwitze, v.; ausgschwitzt, pp. sweat out

aus/seefe, v.; ausgseeft, pp. scald

aus/sehne, v.; ausgsehne, pp. 1.appear; 2.look; 3.take
   heed (that)

aus/sei, v.; ausgewest, pp. 1.be away from home; 2.be
   extinguished (of a fire); 3.be on bad terms

aus/setze, v.; ausgsetzt, pp. 1.begin; 2.plant out; 3.start
   (out); 4.transplant

aus/sinne, v.; ausgsunne, pp. 1.excogitate; 2.think out

aus/sorde, v.; ausgsort, pp. sort

aus/suche, v.; ausgsucht, pp. 1.search thoroughly;
   2.rummage

aus/suckle, v.; ausgsuckelt, pp. suck out

aus/verkaafe, v.; ausverkaaft,pp. 1.sell by forced
   sale;2.sell out

aus/wandre, v.; ausgewandert, pp. emigrate

aus/waxe. v.; ausgewaxe, pp. 1.attain one's full growth;
   2.send forth shoots or sprouts

aus/weare, v.; ausgwore, pp. wear out

aus/wechsle, v.; ausgewechselt, pp. 1.exchange; 2.trade

aus/weiche, v.; ausgewiche, pp. 1.avoid; 2.elude;
   3.evade; 4.get out of perpendicular; 5.turn out

aus/weisse, v.; ausgeweisst,pp.whitewash (the inside of)

aus/wenne, v.; ausgewennt, pp. 1.evade; 2.turn aside

aus/wexle, v.; ausgewexelt, pp. trade

aus/wickle, v.; ausgewickelt, pp. unwrap

aus/wiege, v.; ausgewoge, pp. weigh out for retail sale

aus/wische, v.; ausgewischt, pp. 1.erase; 2.rub out

aus/witsche, v.; ausgewitscht, pp. 1.slip away; 2.slip out

aus/zaahe, v.; ausgezaaht, pp. (to finish) teething

aus/zaahne, v.; ausgezaahnt, pp. put teeth in a rake

aus/zabbe, v.; ausgezappt, pp. 1.tap; 2.unravel

aus/zacke, v.; ausgezackt, pp. scallop

aus/zeddle, v. ; ausgezeddelt, pp. 1.distribute; 2.peddle out

aus/ziehe, v. 1.trim; 2.(sich --) (a) strip; (b) take off
   (change) one's clothes; 3.doff

aus/zobbe, v.; ausgezoppt, pp. 1.pull out; 2.unravel

aus, prep.; adv. out of

ausbacke, v.; ausgebacke, pp. (do iss ausgebacke) 1.there
   is nothing left; 2.we are at wit's end

ausbacke, v.; ausgebacke, pp. bake sufficiently

Ausbehalt (der)n. reservation for life (of house, room,
   firewood, etc. in old deeds)

Ausbeitzettel (der)n. quit notice

ausbilde, v.; ausgebildt, pp. (sich --) develop physically

ausblose v.; ausgeblose, pp. (eems licht --) (to) kill

ausblude, v.; ausgeblut, pp. bleed

Ausbrechung (die)n. outbreak

ausbreddiche, v.; ausgebreddicht, pp. (sich --) preach to
   the weariness of a congregation

ausbreede, v.; ausgebreet, pp. (sich --) spread oneself

Ausbruch (der)n. 1.breakout; 2.outbreak

Ausdauer (die)n. perseverance

Ausdeeling (die)n. distribution

Ausdreher (der)n. (clothes) wringer

ausdricklich, adv. 1.explicitly; 2.expressly; 3.positively

Ausdruck (der)n. expression

ausenanner/geh, v.; ausenannergange, pp. 1.come
   apart; 2.separate; 3.scatter

ausenanner/lege, v.; ausenannergelegt, pp. lay out separately

ausenanner/mache, v.; ausenannergemacht, pp.
   1.separate; 2.take apart

ausenanner/nemme, v.; ausenannergenumme, pp. take
   apart

ausenanner/setze, v.; ausenannergsetzt, pp. set apart

ausenanner, adj. 1.apart; 2.separate

auserum Moos (die)n. circumference

auserum, adj. around on the outside

ausewendich, adv. outside

ausewennich, adv. outside

Ausfaahres (es)n. skin eruption

Ausfaahring (die)n. skin eruption

ausfaahrisch, adj. 1.eruptive; 2.rash-like

Ausfall (der)n. deficiency

ausfiehrich, adj. 1.eruptive; 2.rash-like

ausfiehrlich, adj. detailed

Ausfiehrung (die)n. achievement

Ausfluss (der)n. emission

Ausgaab (die)n. expenditure

Ausgang (der)n. 1.issue; 2.outlet

ausgange, adj. extinguish

ausgangs, adv. towards the end of

ausgebauert, adj. 1.farmed to death; 2.robbed (of the soil)

ausgebleecht, adj. lost color

ausgedient, adj. 1.useless; 2.worn out

ausgelearnt, adj. having finished one's education

Aa

ausgeloddert

ausgeloddert, adj. 1.dilapidated; 2.rickety
ausgelosse, adj. 1.unruly; 2.wild
ausgemacht, adj. 1.certain; 2.decided upon; 3.downright
ausgenumme, prep. with the exception of
ausgeroscht, adj. rusted
ausgewaxe, adj. 1.full-grown; 2.sprouted
ausgewore, adj. worn-out
Ausgewwer (der)n. distributor
ausgfeekt, adv. exhausted
ausgschpielt, adj. 1.come to an end; 2.exhausted; 3.played out
ausgschtudiert, adj. having finished one's education
ausgucke, v.; ausgeguckt, pp. (sich die aage --) look until one is tired (in expecting some one or in   staring)
ausgwaxe, adj. adult
ausheile, v.; ausgheilt, pp. (sich --) cry oneself to a calm
aushungert, adj. starved
Ausiewung (die)n. exercise
Auskunft (die)n. information
Ausland (es)n. foreign country
Ausleek (der)n. expense
Ausleger (der)n. 1.expositor; 2.interpreter; 3.undertaker
Auslegung (die)n. 1.exposition; 2.interpretation
auslendisch, adj. 1.alien; 2.foreign
auslenn(er)isch, adj. 1.alien; 2.foreign
Auslenner (der)n.; Auslenner, pl. 1.alien; 2.foreigner
Auslifting (die)n. ventilation
ausorte, v.; ausgeort, pp. 1.degenerate; 2.deteriorate; 3.not produce true to breed or variety
ausrechle, v.; ausgrechelt, pp. 1.compute; 2.figure out
Ausrett (die)n.; Ausredde, pl. 1.excuse; 2.pretext
Ausruuf (der)n. proclamation
Ausschlack (der)n. 1.sucker; 2.young shoot (of a plant)
ausschmicke, v.; ausgschmickt, pp. 1.adorn; 2.bedeck
Ausschproch (die)n. pronunciation
Ausscht(e)ier (der)n. 1.bride's clothes and furniture brought to marriage; 2.outfit
ausschtehlich, adj. 1.bearable; 2.tolerable
ausse, adv. 1.outside; 2.on the outside
aussehaer, adv. 1.externally; 2.from without
ausserum, adv. 1.on the outskirts; 2.outside; 3.round about
aussewennich, adv. 1.outside; 2.on the outside
Aussicht (die)n. 1.expectation; 2.prospect; 3.view
Ausverhalt (der)n. reservation for life (of house, room, firewood, etc. in old deeds)
ausverkaaft, adj. sold out
Auswaerfling (der)n. 1.imperfect specimen; 2.out cast
Auswandrer (der)n. emigrant
auswaxe, adj. adult
Auswenger (der)n.; Auswenger, pl. turn in plowing (end of corner of field) (Berks Co., PA)
Auszehring (die)n. 1.consumption; 2.tuberculosis
Autsch!, interj. 1.Oh!; 2.Ouch!
autsche, v.; geautscht, pp. give evidence of pain or soreness
Awendmohl (es)n. 1.Lord's Supper; 2.communion
Awerham (der)n. Abraham
awwer, conj,; adv. but

Azi!

awwerglaawi(s)ch, adj. superstitious
Ax (die)n.; Axe, pl. axle
Ax (die)n.; Ex, pl. ax
Axel (die)n.; Axele, pl. 1.axle; 2.shoulder (human)
Axelgnoche (der)n. shoulder bone
Axeschtiel (der)n. ax-handle
Azi!, interj. Atchee! (imitation of the sound made in sneezing, sometimes with an added 'Gsundheet')

Bb

Ba

Ba (der)n.; Bare, pl. bear (animal)

ba(a)sich, adj. 1.bossy; 2.dictatorial; 3.officious

Baa (der)n. path (through snow)

Baa(h)n mache, v.; Baa(h)n gemacht, pp. open (snow) drifts

Baad (es)n. bath

baade, v.; gebaade; gebaadt, pp. 1.bathe; 2.wade

Baadschtubb (die)n.; Baadschtuwwe, pl. bathroom

Baahn (die)n.; Baahne, pl. bean

baahne, v.; gebaahnt, pp. make a way or path through snow

Baahredraeger (der)n. pallbearer

Baalgaul (der)n. horse with a white forehead

Baalhummel (der)n.   male bumblebee (which has a white forehead)

Baali-oower (der)n. a ball game in which two sides threw the ball over the school-house

baali, adj. bald

baalkeppich, adj. bald-headed

Baalkopp (der)n. bald- headed

Baam (der)n.; Beem, pl. tree

baamblich, adj. 1. awkward; 2. dangling; 3. without energy; 4.wobbly

Baamgaarde (der)n. orchard

Baamgaardegraas (es)n. orchard grass

Baammesser (es)n. pruning hook

Baamolich (der)n. 1.olive oil; 2.sweet-oil

Baamoos (es)n. tree-moss

Baamschul (die)n. nursery (for trees)

Baapscht (der)n.; Baapschde, pl. 1.cactus; 2.hedge-hog cactus; 3.Pope; 4.priest

Baapschtkopp (der)n. 1.cactus; 2.hedge-hog cactus

baar, adj. 1.cash; 2.naked

Baar (der)n. 1.bare; 2.cash; 3.bar

Baardelmae (der)n. 1.Bartholomew; 2.St. Bartholomew's Day August 24

Baare (der)n. 1.haymow; 2.mow

baarfiessich, adj. 1.barefooted; 2.sugarless (of coffee without milk and sugar)

Baargeld (es)n. cash

Baart (der)n.; Baert, pl. 1.beard; 2.chin

Baarzer (der)n. fowl without a tail

Baas (der)n. 1.boss; 2.employer; 3.master; 4.superintendent

baase, v.; gebasst, pp. 1.boss; 2.command; 3.superintend

Baawoll (die)n. cotton

Baawollbam (der)n. cottonwood

baawolle, adj. cotton

Baba (der)n. papa

Babbe (der)n. papa

babbe, v.; gebappt, pp. 1.paste; 2.stick

Babbedeckel (der)n. 1.cardboard; 2.pasteboard

Babbegoi (der)n. parrot

Babbel (der)n. tulip tree

Babbel (die)n. 1.chatterbox; 2.gossip

babbeldeckne, adj. cardboard

Babbelmaul (es)n.; Babbelmeiler, pl. 1.babbler; 2.chatterbox; 3.incessant talker

Babbelwasser (es)n. alcohol

Backoffehaerd

Babbelyacht (die)n. gossiping tour

babbich, adj. sticky

Babble (der)n.; Babble, pl. 1.poplar; 2.tulip tree; 3.white poplar

babble, v.; gebabbelt, pp. 1.babble; 2.chat; 3.chatter; 4.talk fast or incessantly; 5.reveal a secret; 6.tattle

Babbler (der)n. 1.chatterer; 2.gabbler

babblich, adj. 1.chatty; 2.talkative

Babier (der)n.; Babiere, pl. paper

Babierbich(e)li (es)n.; Babierbich(e)lin, pl. pamphlet

Babierche (es)n. 1.little piece of paper; 2.slip of paper

Babierli (es)n. slip of paper

Babiersack (der)n.; Babierseck, pl. paper bag

Babierschitz (der)n. minister who reads sermons from manuscript

Babierschtobber (der)n. paper wad

Babierseckli (der)n.; Babiersecklin, pl. paper bag

Babraa (der)n. 1.garden rhubarb; 2.pie plant

Bach (es)n. brook (rare usage)

Bachbledder (die)n., pl. 1.cow lily; 2.yellow pond-lily

Bachbumbel (die)n. 1.American brooklime; 2.water speedwell

Backabbel (der)n. baking apple

Backdaag (der)n. baking day

Backdroog (der)n. kneading trough

Backe (der)n.; Backe, pl. 1.cheek; 2.hound (of a wagon)

backe, v.; gebacke, pp. 1.bake; 2.harden; 3.(net gans recht gebacke) a little off in the head

Backebaart (der)n. 1.beard; 2.whiskers

Backebuch (es)n.; Backebicher, pl. 1.pocketbook; 2.wallet

Backeffel (es)n. (dem. of Backoffen) summit on the Blue Mountain (west of the Lehigh Gap, PA)

Backerei (die)n. (everlasting) baking

Backes (es)n. baking (a repeated household operation)

Backeschtee (der)n.; Backeschtee, pl. brick

Backeschteeleeger (der)n. bricklayer

backeschteene, adj. (of) brick

backeschteenich, adj. brick

Backeschteeoffe (der)n. brick-kiln

Backeschtick (es)n. brickbat

Backeschtreech (der)n. slap on the cheek

Backett (die)n. baking (enough to last 'til the next baking day)

Backezaah (der)n. molar

Backholz (es)n. oven wood

Backkareb (der)n. basket of braided straw in which rye bread was baked

Backmelassich (der)n. baking molasses

Backmol(t) (die)n.; Backmole, pl. dough-tray

Backmulgratzer (der)n.; Backmulgratzer, pl. scraper (used for scraping out a kneading trough)

Backmult (die)n.; Backmulde, pl. 1.dough-tray; 2.kneading trough

Backoffe (der)n. bake oven

Backoffe reide (der)n. ride the bake oven (said of a young man or woman if, for the second time, a younger brother or sister gets married)

Backoffehaerd (der)n. floor of a bake oven

Bb

Backoffekitsch — bamble

Backoffekitsch (die)n. oven scraper
Backoffeloch (es)n. 1.front of an oven; 2.oven door
Backoffeschiess(er) (der)n.; Backoffeschiesser, pl. baker's peel
Backsach (es)n. pastries
Backschissel (die)n.; Backschissle, pl. wooden baking bowl
Backsoode (der)n. baking soda
Baddalye (die)n. battalion
Badder (der, die)n. 1.bother; 2.trouble; 3.worry
baddere, v.; gebaddert, pp. 1.bother; 2.disturb; 3.(sich--)
  bother oneself
Badderiesle (es)n.; Badderieslin, pl. quail
baddich, adv. 1.dainty; 2.exclusive; 3.particular(ly);
  4.select; 5.special(ly)
Badeau (die)n. boat
Badries(e)li (es)n. 1.partridge; 2.quail
Badriesel (es)n. 1.bobwhite; 2.partridge; 3.quail
Badrieselche (es)n. 1.partridge; 2.quail
bae!, interj. baa!
Baedi (die)n. rowboat
Baeffzes (es)n. piffling talk
baefze, v.; gebaefzt, pp. quarrel
baehe, v.; gebaeht, pp. 1.toast; 2.warm
Baend (die)n. band (of musicians)
Baenk (die)n. 1.bank; 2.credit institution
Baer (der)n.; Baere, pl. 1.bar; 2.bear (animal);
  3. (yunger --) cub
Baerefett (es)n. bear's grease
Baerefuss (der)n. 1.bear's foot; 2.ground pine
Baereglooe (die)n. claw of a bear
Baerehaut (die)n. bearskin
Baergemeeschder (der)n. mayor
baergich, adj. 1.hilly; 2.mountainous
Baerke (die)n. birch
Baerkebaam (der)n. birch tree
Baerlfass (es)n. barrel (by measure)
Baermedickel (der)n. pendulum (of a clock)
Baerrick (der)n. 1.hill; 2.mountain
baerrickab, adj. downhill
Baerrickbalsem (der)n. mountain mint
Baerrickblug (der)n. hillside-plow
Baerrickfeier (es)n. 1.kochia; 2.summer cypress
Baerrickgnabber (der)n. clod-hopper
Baerrickgnippel (der)n. clod-hopper
Baerrickhiwwel (der)n. knoll on a mountain road
baerricknunner, adj. downhill
baerrickruff, adj. uphill (to where the speaker or thinker is)
Baerrickschtee (der)n. stone from the Blue Mountain
Baerrickschtross (die)n. hill-road
Baerricktee (der)n. 1.Blue Mountain tea; 2.sweet scented
  goldenrod
Baerschdebinner (schpringe wie'n --) run like the Old Scratch
baerschdebinner, adj. (wie en -- schaffe [saufe,
  schpringe]) 1.run like the Old Scratch; 2.run like crazy
Baerschdegraas (es)n. poverty-grass
Baerschdelche (es)n. 1.dandy; 2.smartly dressed young fellow
Baerschtubb (die)n.; Baerschtuwwe, pl. 1.barroom; 2.saloon

Baerwelche (es)n. 1.Babby; 2.Barbara
Baerwle (es)n. 1.Babby; 2.Barbara
Baerye (die)n. birch
Baerzel (der)n. 1.backside; 2.posterior
Baerzelschtick (es)n. rump steak
Baesel (die)n. aunty
baetschi!, interj. sound of disgust (uttered by mothers to
  cause a child to desist from taking up or from taking
  some object into the mouth)
baex(i)!, interj. sound of disgust (uttered by mothers to
  cause a child to desist from taking up or from taking
  some object into the mouth)
baf!, interj. bang!
baffze, v.; gebaffzt, pp. 1.bark; 2.quarrel; 3.wrangle
Bahr (die)n. bier
baie, v.; gebait, pp. rock (to sleep)
Bal (der)n. head
balaadsche, v.; gebalaadscht, pp. talk in a long and tiresome manner
Balge (der)n.; Balge, pl. 1.beam (timber); 2.girder; 3.joist
ball, adv. 1.almost; 2.soon
Balle (der)n. 1.bale; 2.ball; 3.ball (of the thumb)
balle, v.; geballt, pp. form in a ball (of snow)
Ballebriggel (der)n. bat (baseball)
Ballebritsch (die)n.; Ballebritsche, pl. bat (baseball)
Ballebudder (der)n. roll-butter
Balledicks (die)n. politics
Ballei, n. pennyroyal
Ballekees (der)n. Dutch cheese
ballemol, adv. soon
Balleschpieler (der)n.; Balleschpieler, pl. ball player
Ballewiesals (es)n. game of ball
Ballfass (es)n.; Ballfesser, pl. 1.barrel; 2.cask; 3.keg;
  4.barrel (by measure)
Balloi, n. pennyroyal
Balluun (der)n. balloon
Balluuner (der)n. balloonist
Balmiermesser (es)n.; Balmiermesser, pl. razor
balsamiere, v.; gebalsamiert, pp. 1.embalm; 2.settle
  one's hash (in an argument)
Balsem (der)n. 1.balsam; 2.mint; 3.peppermint 4.
  (rotschtenglicher --) (a) garden mint; (b) peppermint
Balsem (der)n. (wilder --) spearmint
Balsemabbel (der)n. balsam-apple
Balsembaam (der)n. 1.balsam poplar; 2.balm-of-Gilead
Balsemdemalde (der)n. balsam de Malta
Balsemtee (der)n. 1.peppermint tea; 2.tea from downy mint
Balser (der)n. Balthasar
Balwier(e)messer (es)n.; Balwier(e)messer, pl. razor
Balwiere (der)n. barber
balwiere, v.; gebalwiert, pp. 1. shave; 2.(sich --) shave oneself
Balwierpensil (der)n. shaving-brush
Balwierscheed (die)n. razor-sheath
Balwierseef (die)n. shaving soap
Bambelaerwet (die)n. 1.chores; 2.odd jobs
bamble, v.; gebambelt, pp. 1.dangle; 2.loaf; 3.loiter

Bb

Bammgaarde

Bammgaarde (der)n. orchard

Band (es)n.; Benner, pl. 1.band; 2.bandage; 3.ribbon; 4. certificate of indebtedness; 5.hinge; 6.strap; 7. ligature; 8.certificate of indebtedness

Bandwarem (der)n. tapeworm

Bang (die)n. 1.(-- hawwe) fear; 2.(du brauscht kenn -- hawwe) (a) you need not fear; (b) no danger

bang, adj. 1.afraid; 2.fearful; 3.shy; 4.timid; 5.uneasy

Bangenett (die)n. bayonet

Bangichkeet (die)n. 1.dread; 2.fear; 3.timidity

Bangonett (die)n. bayonet

Bank (die)n.; Benk, pl. 1.bench; 2.pew; 3.workbench

Bankert (der)n. bastard

banne, v.; gebannt, pp. 1.charm; 2.fascinate; 3.subdue by secret power

Banner (der)n. 1.charmer; 2.one who exercises power; 3.magician

Bannet (der)n. bonnet

baple, v.; gebabbelt, pp. prattle

Bapp (die)n. paste

bappe, v.; gebappt, pp. 1.paste; 2.stick

Bar (der)n. 1.bar; 2.bare; 3.cash

Bar(e)hatzichkeit (die)n. mercy

bar(e)mhatzich, adj. merciful

barbaarisch, adv. 1.barbarous; 2.terribly

Barbaraa (der)n. 1.garden rhubarb; 2.pie plant

Bardel (der)n. Bartholomew

baremlich, adj. terrible

Bargamott (der)n. bergamot

barge, v.; gebarkt, pp. 1.borrow; 2.loan; 3.give credit; 4.trust

Bargement (es)n. parchment

Bariye (der)n. 1.agreement; 2.bargain

Bariye (die)n. birch

barmelmaessich, adv. fearfully

barmhaerzich, adj. merciful

barmlich, adj. terrible

Barnd (der)n. Bernhard

Barrasch (der)n. borage

Barretsch (der)n. borage

Barrick (der)n. 1.barrow; 2.gelded boar pig

Barrick (die)n. wig

Barricke (die)n. birch

Barrickebaam (der)n. birch tree

Barrickerinn (die)n. birch bark

Barricks (der)n. (uff -- kaafe) 1.tick; 2.trust

barriere, v.; barriert, pp. 1.obey; 2.physic; 3.purge; (for constipation); 4.(sich schlecht --) misbehave

Barrierung (die)n. purgation

Barrig (der)n.; Barriye, pl. mountain

Barrigbalsem (der)n. mountain mint

Barrigfeier (es)n. 1.kochia; 2.summer cypress

Barrigheisli (es)n. cabin

barrigruff, adv. uphill (toward the speaker)

Barrigtee (der)n. sweet-scented goldenrod

Barschtubb (die)n. barroom

Barzel (der)n. 1.oil gland (of fowl); 2.uropygial gland

Bauchrede

Barzelbaam (der)n. somersault

barzle, v.; gebarzelt, pp. tumble

Baschdard (der)n. bastard

baschde, v.; gebascht, pp. 1.brush; 2.fleece (financially); 3.husk

Baschdert (der)n. 1.illegitimate {child}; 2.cattle of mixed breed; 3.inferior plant or animal; 4.up land grazing area; 5.wet wasteland used for pasture

Baschnaad (die)n.; Baschnaade, pl. parsnip

Bascht (die)n.; Baschde, pl. 1.bristle; 2.brush; 3.husk; 4.inner bark

Baschtholz (es)n.; Baschthelzer, pl. husking pin

Baschtnaad (die)n. parsnip

Bass (der)n. bass (in music)

Bass abschneide (der)v. 1.anticipate; 2.head off; 3.forestall

bass, adj. bass

Bassdrumm (die)n. bass drum

basse, v.; gebasst, pp. 1.amble (of a horses gait); 2.be convenient; 3.suit; 4.fit; 5.pass (in cards)

Basseltang, n. pastime

Bassgeig (die)n.; Bassgeige, pl. 1.bass fiddle; 2.bass violin

Basshann (es)n. 1.bass horn; 2.tuba

bassich, adj. officious

bassiere, v.; bassiert, pp. happen

basslich, adj. 1.convenient; 2.fitting; 3.middling; 4.tolerable

Bassschtimm (die)n. bass voice

Basssinger (der)n. bass singer

Batsch (die)n.; Batschi, pl. 1.child's hand; 2.(die -- (Hand) gewwe) shake hands; 3.('sis alles --) it's all gone to nothing

Batsche, batsche, Kicheli! patty cake, patty cake

batsche, v.; gebatscht, pp. clap (the hands)

Batt (der)n. 1.part; 2.share; 3.(ebber sei -- nemme)(a) side with someone; (b) to take someone's part

batte, v.; gebatt, pp. 1.avail; 2.do good; 3.help; 4.give relief; 5.(es hot nix gebatt) it was unavailing

Batzel (der)n. rump

Batzelbaam (der)n. 1.somersault; 2. (en -- schlagge) (a) tumble; (b) turn a somersault

Batzert (der)n. fowl without a tail

batzich, adj. 1.haughty; 2.impertinent; 3.proud; 4.saucy; 5.spunky

batzle, v.; gebatzelt, pp. tumble

Bau (der)n. 1.plowable land; 2.soil

Baublatz (der)n. building site

Bauch (der)n.; Beich, pl. 1.abdomen; 2.belly; 3.paunch; 4.stomach

Bauchduch (es)n.; Bauchdicher, pl. 1.napkin; 2.serviette

bauche, v.; gebaucht, pp. boil wash

bauchfellich, adj. 1.corpulent; 2.dilapidated

Bauchgart (die)n. 1.belly-band; 2.surcingle

Bauchgatt (die)n. 1.belly-band; 2.surcingle

Bauchgott (der)n. 1.belly-god; 2.gourmand's delight

Bauchgriwwles (es)n. griping in the bowels

bauchlufdich, adj. bloated

Bauchrede (es)n. ventriloquism

Bb

Bauchredner

Bauchredner (der)n. ventriloquist
Bauchreime (der)n. belly strap (harness)
Bauchschwetzer (der)n.; Bauchschwetzer, pl. ventriloquist
Bauchweh (es)n. stomachache
Bauchzuwwer (der)n. 1.bucking tub (for bleaching linen); 2.meat-pickling tub
baue, v.; gebaut, pp. 1.build; 2.till
Bauer (der)n.; Bauere, pl. 1.farmer; 2.jack in a deck of cards (singular form only)
Bauer(e)schtand (der)n. occupation of a farmer
bauere, v.; gebauert, pp. 1.cultivate; 2.farm; 3.raise
Baueregeredschaft (die)n. farming implements
Baueregschar (es)n. farming implements
Bauerehaus (es)n.; Bauersheiser, pl. farmhouse
Bauerei (die)n.; Bauereie, pl. farm
Bauerekoscht (die)n. farmer's fare
Bauersbuh (der)n. boy from the farm
Bauersfraa (die)n. farmer's wife
Bauersleit (der)n. farmer
Bauersmann (der)n. farmer
Bauersmeedel (es)n. girl from the farm
Bauhols (es)n. timber
Baukunscht (die) architecture
Bauland (es)n. cultivatable land
Baumeeschder (der)n. architect
Bauschtee (der)n. building stone
baut, adv. about
Bautz (der)n. 1.bugbear; 2.hobgoblin
bax(i)!, interj. sound of disgust uttered by mothers to cause a little child to desist from taking up or from taking some unfit or improper object into its mouth
beaerdiche, v.; baerdicht, pp. 1.bury; 2.inter
Beaerdichung (die)n. 1.burial; 2.interment
Beamter (der)n. 1.official; 2.one holding office
beantwarte, v.; beantwart, pp. answer a question
Beau (der)n. boy friend
beb(b)ere, v.; gebeb(b)ert, pp. 1.prate; 2.nag
Bech (es)n. 1.pitch; 2.shoemaker's wax
beche, v.; gebecht, pp. 1.pay (fine); 2.wax (threads)
Becher (der)n. goblet
Bechlein (es)n. brook (used only in areas where settlers were largely of Swiss origin)
Bechli (es)n. brook (used only in areas where settlers were largely of Swiss origin)
Beck (der)n. peck
Beckelweh (es)n. backache
Becker (der)n.; Becker, pl. baker
Beckerbrot (es)n. baker's bread
Beckerei (die)n. bakery
Beckerwagge (der)n. baker's wagon
Becki (die)n. Rebecca
bedaerfdich, adj. 1.deserving; 2.in urgent need; 3.needy; 4.poor
bedaerfe, v.; bedaerft, pp. 1.need; 2.want
bedaerflich, adj. 1.in need; 2.needy
Bedaerfnis (es)n. 1.carving of nature; 2.necessity

beed

Bedallye (es) n. 1.battalion; 2.militia drill and the accompanying show
bedanke (sich --)v.; bedankt, pp. thank
bedauere, v.; bedauert, pp. 1.pity; 2.regret
bedauerich, adj. sorrowful
bedauerlich, adj. 1.lamentable; 2.pathetic; 3.pitiful; 4.sad
Beddelfraa (die)n. beggar woman
Beddelmann (der)n. beggar man
beddle, v.; gebeddelt, pp. beg
Beddler (der)n. beggar
Bede(s) (es)n. prayer
bede, v.; gebet, pp. pray
bedecke, v.; bedeckt, pp. 1.bedeck; 2.cover
bedeide, v.; bedeidt, pp. 1.indicate; 2.mean; 3.signify; 4.consider; 5.ponder
bedeierlich, adj. pitiable
bedeitend, adj. considerable
bedeitlich, adj. significant
Bedeitung (die)n. 1.importance; 2.significance
bedenke, v.; bedenkt, pp. 1.consider; 2.ponder
bedenklich, adj. 1.critical; 2.dubious; 3.thought-provoking
bediene, v.; bedient, pp. 1.attend; 2.fill an office; 3.serve
Bediener (der)n. 1.lackey; 2.servant; 3.waiter
Bedienung (die)n. 1.office; 2.service
bedierlich, adj. pitiable
bedinge, v.; bedingt, pp. 1.manure; 2.stipulate
Bedingung (die)n. 1.arrangement; 2.condition; 3.stipulation; 4.terms
bedraage, v.; bedraagt, pp. 1.(a) (sich --) conduct (oneself); (b) behave; 2. (sich schlecht --) misbehave
bedrachde, v.; bedracht, pp. 1.contemplate; 2.observe; 3.view
Bedrachdung (die)n. 1.consideration; 2.mediation
bedrauere, v.; bedrauert, pp. bewail
bedreffe, v.; bedroffe, pp. 1.afflict; 2.concern; 3.happen
bedreibt, adj. 1.depressed; 2.discouraged; 3.sad; 4.sorrowful
Bedriebung (die)n. sadness
bedriege, v.; bedroge, pp. 1.betray; 2.cheat; 3.deceive; 4.defraud; 5.fool; 6.swindle; 7.trick
Bedrieger (der)n. 1.cheat; 2.shark; 3.trickster
Bedriegerei (die)n. 1.cheating; 2.roguery
bedriegerisch, adj. deceptive
bedrieklich, adj. deceptive
bedriewe, v.; bedriebt, pp. sadden
bedrinke, v.; bedrunke, pp. (sich --) (to become) tipsy
bedroddle, v.; bedroddelt, pp. 1.(sich --) (to be) fidgety (over something); 2.(to be) anxious or solicitous
bedroffe, adj. 1.afflict; 2.confound; 3.confuse
Bedruch (der)n. 1.betrayal; 2.deceit; 3.fraud
Bedruck (der)n. deceit
bedrunke, adj. 1.intoxicated; 2.tipsy
Bedruug (der)n. deceit
Bee (es)n.; Bee, pl. leg
beed, adj. both

Bb

Beemche

Beemche (es)n. little tree
Beer (die)n.; Beere, pl. 1.berry; 2.pear
Beerebaam (der)n.; Beerebeem, pl. pear tree
bees, adj. 1.angry; 2.indignant; 3.(genadurt --) of a surly (or bad) disposition; 4. offended; 5.mad; 6.rabid; 7.wicked
Beesding (es)n. 1.felon; 2.whitlow
Beese(m)schtiel (der)n. broomstick
Beesfiewer (es)n. typhoid fever
Beesheet (die)n. 1.iniquity; 2.maliciousness; 3.spite
Beesheit (die)n. 1.iniquity; 2.maliciousness; 3.spite
Beeskatz (die)n. mole (rodent)
befalle, v.; befalle, pp. 1.befall; 2.happen
Befehl (der)n. 1.charge; 2.command; 3.order
befehle, v.; befohle, pp. 1.bid; 2.command; 3.order
befeschdiche, v.; befeschdicht, pp. 1.fasten; 2.strengthen
beffze, v.; gebeffzt, pp. 1.bark; 2.quarrel; 3.wrangle
befiehle, v.; befiehlt, pp. 1.feel of; 2.touch
befinne, v.; befunne, pp. 1. (sich --) to be (as to one's health or condition); 2.(wie befinnter sich?) how is he doing (of a sick person)
beflecke, v.; befleckt, pp. taint
befolge, v.; befolgt, pp. 1.obey; 2.observe
Befolgung (die)n. observance
befreie, v.; befreit, pp. 1.deliver; 2.emancipate; 3.free; 4.rescue
befreinde, v.; befreindt, pp. befriend
Befreiung (die)n. 1.deliverance; 2.discharge; 3.exoneration; 4.release; 5.rescue
befriediche, v.; befreidicht, pp. 1.discharge (a debt); 2.satisfy
Befriedichung (die)n. 1.contentment; 2.satisfaction
befroge, v.; befrogt, pp. question
befze, v.; gebefzt, pp. quarrel
begegne, v.; begegnet, pp. 1.befall; 2.greet; 3.remember to; 4.meet; 5.send regards to
Begehr (der)n. 1.desire; 2.request
begehre, v.; begehrt, pp. 1.demand; 2.desire; 3.wish
begierich, adj. 1.desirous; 2.eager; 3.greedy
Begierichkeet (die)n. 1.eagerness; 2.greediness
Beginn (der)n. 1.beginning; 2.origin
beglaage, v.; beglaagt, pp. 1.bemoan; 2.bewail; 3.(sich --) make a complaint
begleede, v.; begleedt, pp. 1.accompany; 2.clothe; 3.fill an office; 4.invest with
Begleeding (die)n. 1.clothing; 2.moulding
Begleedung (die)n. 1.clothing; 2.vesture
beglicke, v.; beglickt, pp. 1.bless; 2.make happy
begnaadiche, v.; begnaadicht, pp. 1.grant a favor; 2.favor; 3.pardon
Begnaadichung (die)n. pardon
begraawe, v.; begraawe, pp. 1.bury; 2.inter
Begraebnis (es)n. burial (older form of usage)
begraeme, v.; begraemt, pp. (sich --) 1.complain; 2.repine
Begrawwer (der)n. 1.funeral director; 2.undertaker
begreckse, v.; begreckst, pp. (sich --) complain
begreife, v.; begriffe, pp. 1.comprehend; 2.conceive; 3.understand
begreiflich, adj. 1.conceivable; 2.easy; 3.intelligible

bei/schpringe

begrenke, v.; begrenkt, pp. begrudge
Begriff (der)n. 1.comprehension; 2.idea
begriff, v. (im --) be about to
begucke, v.; beguckt, pp. 1.observe; 2.view; 3.scrutinize
begweem, adj. snug
behaapde, v.; behaapt, pp. 1.assert; 2.maintain
behaerze, v.; behaerzt, pp. embrace
behaft, adj. 1.afflicted (with); 2.subject to
behalde, v. 1.keep; 2.preserve
behandle, v.; behandelt, pp. treat
Behandlung (die)n. treatment
behapde, v.; behapt, pp. 1.assert; 2.maintain
behatziche, v.; behatzicht, pp. take to heart
beheefe, v.; beheeft, pp. (sich --) behave (used usually positive)
beheeflich, adj. 1.attentive; 2.complaisant
behelfe, v.; beholfe, pp. (sich --) (to) make shift
behenge, v.; behenkt, pp. (sich --) put on trinkets or jewelry for ornament
behiede, v.; behiet, pp. 1.guard; 2.preserve; 3.protect
behiedes, adv. 1.actually; 2.by thunder; 3.really
behilf(l)ich, adj. 1.helpful; 2.useful
Bei (die)n. cradle
bei greibs! interj. by golly
bei Lewe net! interj. not on your life!
bei/bringe, v.; beigebrocht, pp. 1.administer; 2.allude to; 3.bring; 4.introduce
bei/dabbe, v.; beigedappt, pp. stumble
bei/draage, v.; beigedraage, pp. 1.carry to; 2.contribute
bei/dreiwe, v.; beigedriwwe, pp. drive together
bei/dricke, v.; beigedrickt, pp. press against
bei/faahre, v.; beigfaahre, pp. 1.convey hither by vehicle; 2.haul to a certain place
bei/falle, v.; beigfalle, pp. (dat. of the pronoun) 1.recollect; 2.remember
bei/gage, v.; beigegkt, pp. drive together
bei/griege, v.; beigrickt, pp. 1.acquire; 2.get; 3.fetch; 4.procure
bei/halde, v.; beighalde, pp. keep in place
bei/hole, v.; beigholt, pp. 1.bring near; 2.fetch
bei/kumme, v.; beikumme, pp. 1.come fortuitously; 2.come from; 3.come to a meeting
bei/laafe, v.; beigeloffe, pp. 1.come by chance; 2.come to a gathering
bei/lege, v.; beigelegt, pp. 1.compromise; 2.save; 3.settle a difference
bei/misse, v.; beigemisst, pp. 1.be constrained to appear; 2.must be procured
bei/mixe, v.; beigemixt, pp. admix
bei/ricke, v.; beigerickt, pp. 1.approach; 2.move near; 3.take a seat near
bei/rufe, v.; beigerufe, pp. call near or in
bei/schaffe, v.; beigschafft, pp. 1.procure; 2.provide
bei/schleefe, v.; beigschleeft, pp. drag near or up to
bei/schpringe, v.; beischprunge, pp. 1.assist; 2.come to the aid of; 3.run up to; 4.succor

Bb

bei/schteh · Belskapp

bei/schteh, v.; beischtanne, pp. 1.assist; 2.help; 3.succor
bei/schteht, v.; beigschtanne, pp. endorse
bei/wohne, v.; beigewohnt, pp. 1.attend; 2.be present; 3.(sich --) attend
bei/yaage, v.; beigyaagt, pp. drive together
bei, prep. 1.at; 2.at the house of; 3.amidst; 4.among; 5.by; 6.during; 7.in; 8.near; 9.with
Beiaerwer (der)n. coheir
beichde, v.; gebeicht, pp. 1.acknowledge; 2.confess
Beicht (die)n. confession
Beichtschtuhl (der)n. confessional
Beidel (der)n. 1.bolt (of a flour mill); 2.purse; 3.scrotum
Beidelduch (es)n. bolting-cloth
beidle, v.; gebeidelt, pp. bolt (flour)
Beifall (der)n. 1.applause; 2.approbation; 3.assent
Beifuss (der)n. 1.artemisia; 2.mug-wort
Beig (der)n.; Beiye, pl. mountain
Beigdappter (en)n. person who drops in (with heavy steps)
beigeloffe, v. (pp. of beilaafe) (so en -- Katz) stray
Beigo (die)n. cradle
Beikind (es)n. 1.bastard; 2.illegitimate (child)
Beil (es)n.; Beiler, pl. hatchet
beile, v.; gebeilt, pp. 1.cut; 2.hew
beileiwe net! 1.don't you dare; 2.not as you value your life; 3.on no account
beilo, int. hush-a-by
beilocke, v.; beigelockt, pp. 1.call (fowls, dogs); 2.entice
beim = bei em by him
beim gleene, adv. 1.in small lots; 2.(at) retail
beinaah, adv. 1.almost; 2.nearly
Beinaame (der)n. nickname
beinaegschdem, adv. (very) soon
beinanner, adv. together
beineegscht, adv. almost
beino(och) adv. 1.almost; 2.approximately
Beint (baam) (der)n. pine (tree)
Beint (die)n. pint
Beintblech (es)n. 1.pint-measure; 2.tin cup
Beinthaarz (der)n. 1.pitch; 2.resin
Beis (der)n. bite (of an apple or bread)
beisamme, adv. together
Beischpiel (es)n. 1.example; 2.warning
Beischteier (die)n. contribution
Beiss (der)n. itch
beisse, v.; gebisse, pp. 1.bite; 2.itch; 3.pungent
beissich, adj. 1.acrid; 2.itching; 3.prone to bite; 4. pungent; 5.sharp (to the taste)
Beisszang (die)n. 1.nippers; 2.pincers
beitle, v.; gebeidelt, pp. bolt (flour)
Beitsch (die)n. whip
beitsche, v.; gebeitscht, pp. 1.beat; 2.knock; 3.lash
Beiwatt (es)n.; Beiwadde, pl. 1.adjective; 2.byword
Beiweg (der)n.; Beiwege, pl. 1.byroad; 2.lane
beizeit, adv. in good time
Bekannder (der)n. acquaintance
Bekanndi (die)n. acquaintance

Bekanner (der)n. acquaintance
Bekanni (die)n. acquaintance
bekannt sei, v.; is bekannt gewest, pp. (to be) acquainted
bekannt/mache, v.; bekanntgemacht, pp. 1.announce; 2.introduce; 3.publish; 4.(sich --) introduce (oneself)
bekannt, adj. 1.acquainted; 2.familiar; 3.known; 4. (gut --) well-known
Bekanntmachung (die)n. 1.advertisement; 2.public notice
Bekanntschaft (die)n. acquaintance
Bekehrder (en) n. convert
bekehre, v.; bekehrt, pp. 1.convert; 2.(sich --) convert (one's religious views)
Bekehrung (die)n. conversion
bekenne, v.; bekennt, pp. 1.acknowledge; 2.confess; 3.profess
Bekenntnis (es)n. confession
bekeschdiche, v.; bekeschdicht, pp. 1.board; 2.furnish (food, board)
bekimmere, v.; bekimmert, pp. 1.trouble; 2.(sich --) (a) bother oneself; (b) (to be) concerned about; (c) trouble oneself
bekimmerlich, adj. 1.pitiful; 2.poorly
bekimmerlich, adv. poorly
Bekimmernis (die)n. concern
Beklaachder (der)n. defendant
Beklaager (der)n. accuser
Beklaeger (der)n. accuser
bekreftiche, v.; bekrefticht, pp. confirm
bekumme, v.; is bekumme, pp. 1.agree with (of food); 2.become; 3.fit well (of a garment)
belaage, v. (sich --) make a complaint
belaagre, v.; belaagert, pp. beseige
belaschde, v.; belaschdet, pp. burden
belebt, adj. vivacious
beleege mit, v.; beleekt, pp. cover with
belei(ch)diche, v.; beleidicht, pp. 1.insult; 2.offend
Beleidichung (die)n. 1.insult; 2.offence
belewe, v.; belebt, pp. 1.enliven; 2.vivify
beliddisch, adj. comic
beliebt, adj. 1.beloved; 2.liked; 3.in favor; 4.popular
beliege, v.; beloge, pp. belie
Bell (die); Belle, pl. 1.bell; 2.(-- toole) toll bell (at funerals)
Bella (die)n. king and queen of trumps in datte
belle, v.; gebellt, pp. 1.ring a bell; 2.serenade a newly married couple; 3.tattle
Bellegnippel (der)n. bell-clapper
bellere, v.; gebellert, pp. 1.ask continually; 2.importune; 3.pester; 4.torment
Belleschtrick (der)n. bell-cord
Bellhammel (der)n. 1.bellwether; 2.leader (of a gang)
belohne, v.; belohnt, pp. 1.compensate; 2.recompense; 3.remunerate; 4.reward
Belohning (die)n. 1.compensation; 2.reward
Belohnung (die)n. 1.compensation; 2.reward
belowe, v.; belobt, pp. praise
belse, v.; gebelst, pp. 1.beat; 2.flog; 3.lam
belsich, adj. 1.pithy; 2.spongy (of fruit, radishes)
Belskapp (die)n. 1.fur cap; 2.(letz in der --) off in the head

Bb

Belsnickel

Belsnickel (der)n.; Belsnickel, pl. 1. fur devil; 2. masquerader; 3. Santa Claus; 4.(wieschgaschdich --gfress) a terrible St. Nicholas (Santa Claus) mask

Belsnickler (der)n.; Belsnickler, pl. masquerader

Belsnickelzeit (die)n. Twelvetide, Dec 25 - Jan 6

beluchse, v.; beluchst, pp. cheat

beluhne, v.; beluhnt, pp. 1.compensate; 2.recompense; 3.remunerate; 4.reward

Belz (der)n. 1.fur; 2.pelt; 3.skin; 4.matted growth of hair or grass

Belzibopp (der)n. Beelzebub

Belznickel (der)n.; Belznickel, pl. 1.fur devil; 2.masquerader; 3.Santa Claus

Belznickler (der)n.; Belznickler, pl. masquerader

bemaerricklich, adj. noticeable

Bemaerrickung (die)n. remark

bemarrickbaar, adj. observable

bemarricke, v.; bemarrickt, pp. 1.note; 2.remark; 3.take heed

Bembelaerwet (die)n. 1.chores; 2.odd jobs

Bembeldaag (der)n. 1.day on which no regular work is done; 2.day off

bemble, v.; gebembelt, pp. 1.fool away time; 2.hang loosely

bemiehe, v.; bemieht, pp. 1.trouble; 2.(sich --) (a) exert oneself; (b) (to take the) trouble

benaame, v.; benaamt, pp. 1.dominate; 2.give a name; 3.name

Bendel (der)n. 1.cord; 2.string; 3.tape

Bender (der)n.; Bender, pl. panther

bendere, v.; gebendert, pp. 1.dare; 2.torment

Benediktinwarzel (die)n. avens

benenne, v.; benennt, pp. name

Benennung (die)n. denomination

benewwelt, adj. 1.slightly intoxicated; 2.tipsy

Bengel (der)n. stout lad

Benkel (es)n. little bench

Bennel (der)n. tape

benniche, v.; gebennicht, pp. 1.conquer; 2.subdue

benoochrichde, v.; benoochrichdet, pp. 1.apprise; 2.notify

Bens (der)n.; Bense, pl. 1.cent; 2.penny

Bensegraas (es)n. 1.bog rush; 2.rush

Bensel (es)n. silly child (usually applied playfully)

Bensepetzer (der)n. miser

benutze, v.; benutzt, pp. 1.make profit by; 2.use; 3.utilize

Beobachtung (die)n. observance

bequem, adj. 1.comfortable; 2.convenient; 3.easy; 4.fitting

beraawe, v.; beraabt, pp. 1.bereave; 2.rob; 3.strip of

berausche, v.; berauscht, pp. intoxicate

berechtiche, v.; berechticht, pp. 1.entitle; 2.give a right

berede, v.; beredt, pp. persuade

bereechere, v.; bereechert, pp. treat a horse with vapor (from a rosin, tar, etc. for pneumonia and distemper)

bereie, v.; bereit, pp. repent

bereit, adj. 1.prepared; 2.prompt; 3.ready

Bericht (der)n. report

berichte, v.; bericht, pp. 1.give information of; 2.report

beriehmt, adj. 1.celebrated; 2.famous; 3.renowned

berode, v.; berode, pp. 1.take counsel; 2.deliberate

Betbuch

berotschlagge, v.; berotgschlagge, pp. 1.deliberate; 2.exchange views

Beruf (der)n. calling

beruhiche, v.; beruhicht, pp. 1.pacify; 2.quiet

besarrickt, adj. 1.anxious; 2.solicitous

b(e)schaediche, v.; b(e)schaedicht, pp. injure

b(e)scheediche, v.; b(e)scheedicht, pp. injure

b(e)schenke, v.; b(e)schenkt, pp. 1.make a present; 2.present

beschdle, v.; gebeschdelt, pp. 1.tinker; 2.work at a small job (especially in wood)

bescheide, adj. modest

B(e)schisser (der)n. 1.cheater; 2.crook; 3.dishonest person; 4.fraud

beschitze, v.; beschitzt, pp. protect

Beschitzer (der)n. patron

b(e)schliesse, v.; b(e)schlosse, pp. 1.conclude; 2.finish; 3.resolve

B(e)schluss (der)n. 1.conclusion; 2.resolution

beschreiwe, v.; beschriwwe, pp. describe

Beschreiwung (die)n. description

bescht, adj. best (superlative form of gut)

b(e)schtaetiche, v.; b(e)schtaeticht, pp. 1.confirm; 2.ratify

beschteh, v.; beschtanne, pp. consist

beschtehle, v.; beschtohle, pp. steal from

beschtennich, adv. constantly

b(e)schtimme, v.; b(e)schtimmt, pp. 1.bespeak; 2.fix conditions; 3.set a date for

Beschtli (es)n. small calabash

beschtrofe, v.; beschtroft, pp. 1.avenge; 2.punish

Beschtumbe(die)n.,pl. discarded wax-end threads with bristles

beschuldiche, v.; beschuldicht, pp. 1.accuse; 2.incriminate

beschur, adv. surely

Beschwerde (die)n. 1.mourning; 2.sorrow; 3.woe; 4.trouble

beschwere, v.; beschwert, pp. (sich --) complain (about)

beschwerlich, adj. 1.burdensome; 2.cumbersome; 3.troublesome

Bese(m) (der)n.; Bese(m), pl. broom

Bese(m)schtecke (der)n. broomstick

Besemschtiel (der)n. broomstick

Besemwelschkann (es)n. broom-corn

Besereis (es)n. 1.heath aster; 2.Michaelmas daisy

besetze, v. trim

b(e)sinne, v.; b(e)sunne, pp. (sich --) 1.consider; 2.think over; 3.recall; 4.remember

b(e)sitze, v.; b(e)sesse, pp. 1.own; 2.possess

B(e)sitzer (der)n. 1.owner; 2.possessor; 3.occupant

besonders, adv. particularly

besonner(s), adv. particularly

besser warre, adj. improve (in health)

besser, adj. better (comparative form of gut)

bessere, v.; gebessert, pp. 1.fix; 2.repair; 3.(sich --) (a) (do) better; (b) improve

Bessering (die)n. 1.convalescence; 2.improvement

betaacht, adj. advanced in years

Betbuch (es)n.; Betbicher, pl. prayer book

Bb

Betdaag

Betdaag (der)n. 1.fast day; 2.Thanksgiving
Bethaus (es)n. house of prayer
betschle, v.; gebetschelt, pp. pat (-a-cake)
Betschtund (die)n. prayer meeting
Betschtunn (die)n. 1.hour of prayer; 2.prayer meeting
Bett (es)n.; Bedder, pl. 1.bed; 2.bed (for flowers) 3.layer of grain for threshing by flail; 4. sheaves of grain for threshing by machine; 5.(ins -- geh) go to bed
Bett schtolle (der)n. bed-post
Bettdeck (die)n. 1.bed-quilt; 2.counterpane; 3.coverlet
Bettduch (es)n. bed sheet
bettelgotts!, interj. confound it!
Bettelhem (es)n. Bethlehem
Bettellaus (die)n. tickseed
Bettelmann (der)n. beggar
Bettgleeder (die)n. 1.bedclothes; 2.bedding
bettgrank, adj. sick in bed
Bettlaad (die)n. bedstead
Bettlaaswans (die)n. bedbug
bettlaegerich, adj. bedfast
bettle, v.; gebettelt, pp. beg
Bettleedel (es)n. trundle bed
Bettlehem (es)n. 1.Bethlehem; 2.(noch -- geh) go to bed
Bettler (der)n. beggar
Bettpisser (der)n. piss-a-bed
Bettposchde (der)n. bed-post
Bettsach (es)n. 1.bedclothes; 2.bedding
Bettschisser (der)n. immature contemptible fellow
Bettschprae (die)n. bedspread
Bettschtrick (der)n. bed-cord
Bettschtubb (die)n.; Bettschtuwwe, pl. bedroom
Bettseecher (der)n. 1.dandelion; 2.piss-a-bed
Bettzeit (die)n. bedtime
Bettziech (die)n. feather case (for bed)
Betz (die)n. Elizabeth
bevor, adv., prep. before
bewaare, v.; bewaart, pp. 1.keep; 2.keep safe; 3.guard; 4.preserve
bewege, v.; bewekt, pp. 1.affect; 2.move; 3.stir
Bewegung (die)n. 1.exercise; 2.motion
beweine, v.; beweint, pp. lament
Beweis (der)n. proof
beweise, v.; bewisse, pp. prove
Beweisung (die)n. 1.proof; 2.reference
beweklich, adj. movable
bewilliche, v.; bewillicht, pp. 1.allow; 2.consent to
bewil(l)kumme, v.; bewil(l)kummt, pp. 1.greet; 2.remember to; 3.send regards to
bewohnbaar, adj. inhabitable
bewohne, v.; bewohnt, pp. inhabit
Bewohner (der)n. inhabitant
Bewwi (die)n. 1.Babby; 2.Barbara
beyaae, v.; beyaat, beyatt, pp. 1.affirm; 2.say "yes" to
beyammere, v.; beyammert, pp. 1.bemoan; 2.bewail
beyooe, v.; beyoot, pp. affirm
beyuuse, v.; beyuust, pp. 1.abuse; 2.mistreat; 3.misuse

Biggeleise

Bezaahling (die)n. 1.compensation; 2.fee; 3.pay; 4.payment
Bezaahlsdaag (der)n. pay-day
Bezaahlung (die)n. 1.compensation; 2.fee; 3.pay; 4.payment
bezaale, v.; bezaalt, pp. pay
Bezaerrick (es)n. 1.circuit; 2.district; 3.(im --) in the environs
Bezarrick (es)n. district
bezeige, v.; bezeikt, pp. 1.attest; 2.denote; 3.depose; 4.specify
Bezeigung (die)n. specification
bezwenge, v.; bezwengt, pp. force
bhalde, v.; bhalde, pp. keep
Bibbeli (der)n. penis
Bibs (der)n. penis
Bichelche (es)n. little book
Bicherbinner (der)n. bookbinder
Bicherschank (der)n. bookcase
Bichli (es)n. 1.pamphlet; 2.small thin book
bicke, v.; gebickt, pp. (sich --) 1.bend over; 2.bow; 3.stoop
Bickel (die)n.; Bickels, pl. pickle
Bickelfleesch (es)n. tenderloin
bidde, v.; gebitt, pp. beseech
bidder, adj. bitter
Biddre Selaat (der)n. dandelion
biddri Blaum (die)n.; biddri Blaume, pl. olive
bie! bie! call for chickens
Biebche (es)n. 1.chick; 2.little boy
Biebelche (es)n. chick
Biebli (es)n.; Bieblin, pl. chick
Biebliwelschkaan (es)n. pop-corn
biebse, v.; gebiebst, pp. 1.ail; 2.be sick; 3.mention; 4. peep (of chickens); 5.(er hot kenn watt gebiebst) he did not breathe a word (about it)
Biebser (der)n. 1.cold in the head; 2.gaps (in chicks)
biebsich, adj. 1.ailing (usually of fowls); 2.sickly
biede, v.; gebodde, pp. 1.bid; 2.beat; 3.surpass
Bieder (der)n. bidder
biege, v.; geboge, pp. bend
Biegmaschien (die)n. bending-machine
biegsam, adj. pliable
Bier (die)n.; Biere, pl. 1.berry; 2.pear
Bier (es)n. beer
Bierboddel (die)n. beer-bottle
Bierdrinker (der)n. drinker of beer
Bierebaam (der)n.; Bierebeem, pl. pear tree
Bierfass (es)n. beer-keg
Bierglaas (es)n. beer-glass
Bierheef, (die)n. yeast
Bierwagge, (der)n. brewer's truck
biesse, v.; gebiesst, pp. 1.atone (for); 2.(sei Luschde --) satisfy one's desire (in a good or bad sense)
Biewel (die)n.; Biewele, pl. Bible
Biffel (der)n. 1.blockhead; 2.cow without horns
Biffelochs (der)n. blockhead
Biggelduch (es)n. ironing-cloth
Biggeleise (es)n.; Biggeleise, pl. 1.flatiron; 2.iron (for clothes); 3.sadiron

Bb

biggle — Blatz

biggle, v.; gebiggelt, pp. iron clothes
Bigglerei (die)n. ironing
bigott, adj. 1.by God; 2.by thunder
Bild (es)n.; Bilder, pl. 1.image; 2.likeness; 3.picture
bilde, v.; gebild(e)t, pp. 1. form; 2. shape; 3. (sich --) become educated
Bilderbuch (es)n.; Bilderbicher, pl. picture book
Bilderschtecher (der)n. engraver
Bildnis (es)n. effigy
Bildung (die)n. refinement
billich; billicher; billichscht, adj. cheap, cheaper, cheapest
billiche, v.; gebillicht, pp. 1.approve; 2.grant
Billyoon (die)n. billion
Bimschtee (der)n. pumice
Bindel (der)n. bundle
Bindnis (es)n. alliance
Binn (die)n. bandage
binne, v.; gebunne, pp. 1.bind (together); 2.tie; 3.(fescht --) tie fast
Binner (der)n. binder (in harvest)
Binnschatz (der)n. tying apron
Binnschtriche (der)n. hyphen
Binse (die)n. great bulrush
Birger (der)n. citizen
birgerhaft, adj. naturalized
birgerhaft, v. naturalize
bis uff, prep. up to
bis, prep. 1.as far as; 2.of (in telling time); 3.until; 4.up to
Bischel (es)n. 1.small handful (of grass, weeds); 2.small woods
bischimpe, v.; bschimpt, pp. 1.abuse; 2.defame; 3.disgrace
Bischof (der)n. bishop
Bischop (der)n. bishop
bishaer, adv. hitherto
Bisness (die)n. business
Biss (der)n. 1.bite; 2.sting
Bissel (es)n. 1.bit; 2.a little; 3.short while
bissel, adj. little
bissich, adj. snappish
Bisskatz (die)n.; Bisskatze, pl. 1.polecat; 2.skunk
Bisskatzefett (es)n. skunk oil
Bisskatzegraut (es)n. skunk cabbage
Bisskatzehaut (die)n. skunk's pelt
Bissli (es)n. 1.bit; 2.little; 3.a short while
Bitt (die)n.; Bidde, pl. plea
bitte, v.; gebitt, pp. 1.ask; 2.beseech; 3.pray
bitter, adj. bitter
Bitteraerd (die)n. magnesia
Bitterkasch (die)n. wild cherry
Bitterkneeterich (der)n. smartweed
Bitters (es)n. 1.bitters; 2.drink of spirits
Bitterschtenge(l) (der)n. 1.bitterweed; 2.daisy fleabane; 3.hog weed; 4.Roman wormwood
Bittersiess (es)n. bittersweet
Bitterwaermet (der)n. 1.bitterweed; 2.daisy fleabane; 3.hog weed; 4.Roman wormwood
Bittreschtengel (der)n. great ragweed

Bittreselaat (der)n. dandelion
Bittschrift (die)n. petition
Biwwel (die)n. Bible
Biwwelschpruch (der)n. scripture text
Bix (die)n. 1.female pudendum; 2.rifle
Bixelaaf (der)n. rifle-barrel
Bixemacher (der)n. gunsmith
Bixeschloss (es)n. lock of a rifle
Bixeschtock (der)n. 1.butt-end of a rifle; 2.mandrel
Bixekolwe (der)n. gun stock
Blaan (der)n. 1.design; 2.plan
blaane, v.; geblaant, pp. 1.design; 2.plan
Blaat (es)n.; Bledder, pl. 1.blade; 2.leaf; 3.page
blabbere, v.; geblabbert, pp. 1.blab; 2.chatter; 3.talk fast
blabberich, adj. blabbing
Blabbermaul (es)n.; Blabbermeiler, pl. 1.blabber; 2.chatterbox
Blacke (der)n. 1.spot; 2.patch; 3.small piece of cloth
blackeweis, adv. 1.in limited localities; 2.in spots
blackich, adj. spotted
Blaeckbier (die)n.; Blaeckbiere, pl. blackberry
Blaeckbieregretz (der)n. blackberry itch
Blaeckschmitt (der)n.; Blaeckschmitt, pl. blacksmith
Blaenket (der)n. blanket
blaerre, v.; geblaerrt, pp. 1.bawl; 2.bleat; 3.low
Blaeser (der)n. 1.blowing adder; 2.puff adder
blaffe, v.; geblafft, pp. bark
blaffze, v. (rare usage) bark
Blandaasch(e) (die)n. 1.farm; 2.lot (in derision)
Blaneet (der)n. planet
Blank (die)n.; Blanke, pl. plank
blanke, v.; geblankt, pp. cover with planks
Blanset (die)n. (a) planting
Blansgrumbeer (die)n. seed potato
Blanswelschkaan (es)n. seed corn
Blanz (die)n.; Blanze, pl. 1.herb; 2.plant
blanze, v.; geblanzt, pp. plant
blarre, v.; geblatt, pp. 1.bark; 2.bawl; 3.bellow; 4.low; 5.bleat
Blaschder (es)n. 1.plaster; 2.salve; 3.wearisome talker
blaschdere, v.; geblaschdert, pp. 1.cover with a plaster; 2.treat (oneself) with slave or ointment
blass, adj. 1.dim; 2.indistinct; 3.pale
Blatsche (es)n. smack (on the face or behind)
blatsche, v.; geblatscht, pp. 1.bring the feet down flat; 2.clap; 3.give a report; 4.patter; 5.splash; 6.smack (a child's face or posterior); 7.smack the lips; 8.tattle
Blatscher (der)n. 1.gossip; 2.talebearer; 3.tattler
blatschich, adj. splashing (of a downpour)
Blatt (die)n. plate (of a stove)
Blatt (es)n.; Bledder, pl. 1.blade; 2.leaf; 3.page
blatt, adj. smooth and even
Blattdeitsch (es)n. 1.Low German; 2.Plattdeutsch
blattfiessich, adj. flat footed
Blattzinn (es)n. tin-foil
Blatz (der)n.; Bletz, pl. 1.location; 2.place; 3.room (space); 4.(-- mache) make room

25

Bb

blatze — **Blobarricker**

blatze, v.; geblatzt, pp. burst from internal pressure
Blatzrege (der)n. shower (downpour)
blatzweis, adj. 1.in places; 2.scatteringly
blaudere, v.; geblaudert, pp. 1.chat; 2.talk
blauderich, adj. 1.friendly; 2.talkative; 3.sociable
Blauderyacht (die)n. gossiping tour
Blaum (die)n.; Blaume, pl. plum
Blaume (die)n., pl. (rotbrutziche biddre --) stuffed olives
Blaumebaam (der)n. plum tree
Blaumeschtee (der)n. plum stone
Blech (es)n. 1.tin; 2.tin cup
Blech(e)dach (es)n. tin roof
Bleche (es)n. 1.small patch; 2.small spot
bleche, adj. (of) tin
bleche, v.; geblecht, pp. 1.pay; 2.suffer (for)
Blechegschaerr (es)n. tinware
Blechel (es)n. porringer
blechich, adj. 1.(of) tin; 2.tinny
Blechli (es)n. 1.small patch; 2.small spot
Blechscheer (die)n. tin shears
Blechschmitt (der)n. tinsmith
Blechvoll (es)n. tin-cup-full
Blechwaar (es)n. tinware
Bleckche (es)n. 1.small patch; 2.small spot
blecke, v.; gebleckt, pp. 1.baa; 2.bleat; 3.(die Zeh --) show the teeth (in smiling or anger)
Bleckli (es)n. 1.small patch; 2.srnall spot
Bledder (die)n. foliage
bledle, v.; gebledelt, pp. slice
Bleech(die)n. 1.bleach;2.bleachery;3.greensward for bleaching
bleech, adj. 1.pale; 2.pallid; 3.sallow
bleeche, v.; gebleecht, pp. 1.blanch; 2.bleach; 3.fade; 4.lose color
bleed, adj. 1.diffident; 2.shy; 3.sore; 4.tender (skin); 5.weak (of the eyes)
bleed, adv. bashful
Bleedheet (die)n. 1.bashfulness; 2.diffidence
bleedle, v.; gebleddelt, pp. inoculate (trees)
Bleedsinn (der)n. imbecility
bleen, adj. plain
Bleeser (der)n.; Bleeser, pl. 1.hognose snake; 2.puff adder
blehe, v.; gebleet, pp. starch
Blei (es)n. lead
Bleipensil (der)n. lead pencil
Bleischaffer (der)n. plumber
bleiwe, v. gebliwwe, pp. 1.(-- losse) do without; 2..(iwwer Nacht --) stay for the night; 3.let alone; 4.remain; 5. (sitze --) remain seated; 6. stay
Bleiweiss (es)n. white lead
Bleizucker (der)n. sugar of lead
blendi, adj. plenty
Blenselche (es)n. 1.seedling; 2.small plant
Bleschder (die)n. plaster
bleschdere, v.; gebleschdert, pp. plaster
Bleschderer (der)n.; Blechderer, pl. plasterer
Bleschderkell (die)n. trowel

Bless (die)n. 1.mouth; 2.phiz; 3.white spot on the fore-head of a cow or horse
Blessgsicht (es)n. white face (of a horse)
Blessier (die)n. 1.pleasure; 2.(-- dreiwe) amuse oneself
blessiere, v.; blessiert, pp. (sich --) 1.amuse oneself; 2.have a good time
blessierlich, adj. 1.agreeable; 2.cheerful; 3.pleasant; 4.pleasurable
blet(s)che, v.; gebletscht, pp. 1.paddle; 2.spank; 3.strike with an open hand; 4.applaud
Bletching (die)n. paddling
bletschle, v.; gebletschelt, pp. pat
Blettche (es)n.; Blettcher, pl. saucer
Blettli (es)n.; Blettlin, pl. saucer
blettlich schneide, v. 1.slice; 2.cut into disks (as potatoes)
blettre, v.; geblettert, pp. turn the pages of a book
blettrich, adj. 1.leafy; 2.leaved
Bletzel (es)n. place
bletzlich, adv. 1.abruptly; 2.suddenly
bletzweis, adj. 1.in places; 2.scatteringly
Blick (der)n. 1.cast of the eye; 2.glance; 3.look
Blickaerbs (die)n. pea grown for the pea as distinguished from sugar peas grown for the pod
Blickbohn (die)n. shell bean
blicke, v.; geblickt, pp. 1.peep (of the sun); 2.shell (beans or peas); 3.(die Zeh --) show the teeth
Blicki (es)n. 1.any tin vessel smaller than a pail; 2.blickey; 3.milk pan; 4.small tin kettle
blieh(i)ch, adj. 1.blooming continually; 2.in bloom
Blieh(t) (die)n. 1.blossoms (collective); 2.inflorescence
bliehe, v.; geblieht, pp. 1.bloom; 2.blossom
Bliehknopp (der)n. flower bed
Blimmche (es)n. little flower
blimme, v. flower (Montgomery County, PA)
blind, adj. blind
Blindemeisel (es)n. blindman's buff
blinder Bottboi, n. meatless potpie (Rev. C. Rahn)
Blindhalfder (die)n. 1.blind halter; 2.blinkers
Blindheet (die)n. blindness
blinsle, v.; geblinselt, pp. 1.blink; 2.wink
Blitz (der)n. 1.flash; 2.lightning; 3.menses
blitze, v.; geblitzt, pp. 1.flash; 2.lighten
blitzeblo un dunnergrie formed facetiously (meaningless)
blitzeblo verfrore frozen blue
blitzeblo, adj. dark blue
blitzlich, adv. immediately
Blitzlicht (es)n.; Blitzlichder, pl. flashlight
blo(h), adj. blue
Blobarrgertee (der)n. 1.Blue Mountain tee; 2.sweet scented goldenrod
Blobarrick (der)n. Blue Mountain (named because of the characteristic color when viewed from a distance)
Blobarrick(ger)tee (der)n. 1.Blue Mountain tee; 2.sweet scented goldenrod
Blobarricker (der)n. person living on or near the Blue Mountain

Bb

Blobarriger / bobble

Blobarriger (der)n. person living on or near the Blue Mountain

Blobarrigergraas (es)n. 1.broom grass; 2.broom sedge

Blobier (die)n.; Blobiere, pl. blueberry

Blobottel (die)n. 1.bluebottle; 2.corn flower

Blobottlicher (die)n., pl. grape hyacinth

Block (der)n.; Bleck, pl. 1.block; 2.log; 3.(wie en -- schlofe) sleep like a log

Blockhaus (es)n.; Blockheiser, pl. 1.blockhouse; 2.log cabin

Blockheisel (es)n.; Blockheisli, pl. small blockhouse (log cabin)

Blockheisli (es)n.; Blockheislin, pl. 1.a small blockhouse; 2.log-hut

Blockkett (die)n.; Blockedde,pl. log-chain

Blockscheier (die)n.; Blockscheiere, pl. log-barn

Blockschlidde (der)n. 1.logging sled; 2.sled

Bloder (die)n.; Blodere, pl. blister

blodre, v.; geblodert, pp. blister

Blog (die)n. 1.plague; 2.sickness; 3.trouble; 4.worry

bloge, v.; geblogt, pp. 1.harry; 2.pester; 3.tantalize; 4.tease; 5.torment; 6.trouble; 7.(sich --) worry

Blograas (es)n. 1.Canada bluegrass; 2.wire grass

Blohols (es)n. logwood

Blohuschde (der)n. whooping cough

Blok (die)n. 1.ailment;2.plague;3.sickness;4.toil; 5.trouble

bloos, adj. 1.bare (naked); 2.nude; 3.simply

bloose, v.; gebloose, pp. pant (of humans)

Blos (die)n.; Blose, pl. 1.bladder; 2.blister; 3.bubble

blos, adv. 1.merely; 2.only

Blosballig(s) (der)n. 1.bellows; 2.boastful person; 3.braggart

bloschtengicher Tee (der)n. peppermint tea

blose, v.; geblose, pp. 1.blow; 2.brag; 3.boast; 4.scold

Blosehaus (der)n. 1.bellows; 2.boastful person

Bloshann (es)n. 1.boaster; 2.braggart; 3.dinner-horn

Bloshaus (es)n. 1.boaster; 2.braggart

Blosrohr (es)n. 1.blow-horn; 2.blowhard; 3.boaster; 4.braggart

bloss, adj. naked

blott, adj. 1.bald; 2.bare; 3.uncovered

blottkeppich, adj. 1.baldheaded; 2.bare-headed

Blottkopp (der)n. 1.bald headed; 2.baldheaded person

Blottschaal (die)n. 1.bald headed person; 2.head

Blotz (der)n. 1.jolt; 2.thud

blotze, v.; geblotzt, pp. 1.bruise by falling; 2.jerk; 3.jolt; 4.jounce

Blotzer (der)n.; Blotzer, pl. thank-you-ma'am

Blotzwagge (der)n. 1.farm wagon; 2.wagon without springs

Blovoggel (der)n.; Bloveggel, pl. bluebird

blude, v.; geblut, pp. bleed (also of trees and plants)

bludich, adj. bloody

Blug (der)n.; Blieg, pl. plow

Blug(s)grendel (der)n. plowbeam

Blug(s)hendel (der)n. plow handle

Blug(s)naas (die)n. point of a plowshare

Blug(s)schtrang (der)n. iron plow trace

Blug(s)sech (es)n. coulter

Blug(s)woog (die)n. double-tree used in plowing

bluge, v.; geblugt, pp. plow

Blugschaar (es)n.; Blugschaare, pl. 1.plowshare; 2.share

Blugschleef (es)n. 1.plow shoe; 2.plow drag

Blumm (die)n.; Blumme, pl. flower

Blumme (die)n. menses

Blumme(r)knopp (der)n. flower bud

Blumme(r)krans (der)n. 1.border of flowers; 2.garland; 3.wreath

Blummebaam (der)n. rose of Sharon

Blummebett (es)n. flower bed

Blummeblaat (es)n.; Blummebledder, pp. petal

Blummefraa (die)n. 1.Virgo (6th sign of the zodiac); 2. woman who is very fond of flowers; 3.woman who sells flowers

Blummefreind (der)n. lover of flowers

Blummegraut (es)n. cauliflower

Blummehaffe (der)n.; Blummeheffe, pl. flowerpot

Blummekenner (der)n. botanist

Blummeland (es)n.; Blummelenner, pl. flowerbed

Blummering (der)n. 1.circular flower bed; 2.wreath of flowers

Blummeschtaab (der)n. pollen

Blummeschtiel (der)n.; Blummeschtiel, pl. petiole

Blummeschtock (der)n.; Blummerschteck, pl. 1.flower stalk; 2.flowering plant

Blummeschtrauss (der)n.1.bouquet; 2.posy; 3.stalk with a flower

Blummesome (der)n. flower seed

Blummesume (der)n. flower seed

Blummevoggel (der)n. hummingbird

blummich, adj. 1.flowered; 2.flowery

blump(s)!, interj. 1.bump!; 2.thud!

Blumpsack (der)n. game played with a knotted handkerchief with which blows are dealt

Bluscht (die)n. blossoms (collective)

Blut (es)n. 1.blood; 2.(-- schtille) stop blood; 3.(-- vergiesse) shed blood

Blutaader (die)n.; Blutaadere, pl. 1.artery; 2.vein

Blutfink (der)n. scarlet tanager

Blutgschwaere (der)n. carbuncle

Bluthund (der)n. blood hound

blutich, adv. bloody

Blutoder (die)n.; Blutodere, pl. 1.artery; 2.vein

blutrot, adj. red as blood

Blutschtaerz (der)n. hemorrhage

Blutschtee (der)n. bloodstone

Blutschwamm (der)n. fungus haematodes

Blutsfreind (der)n.; Blutsfreind, pl. relative

Blutsuckler (der)n.; Blutsuckler, pl. 1.bloodsucker; 2.leech

blutt(e)kebbich, adj. 1.bald; 2.bare headed

blutt, adj. bare (bald)

Blutvoggel (der)n. scarlet tanager

Blutwarzel (die)n. 1.bloodroot; 2.turmeric

Blutwascht (die)n. blood pudding

blutwasser, adj. serum

Blutwatzel (die)n. 1.bloodroot; 2.turmeric

Bobb (die)n. 1.baby; 2.doll; 3.puppet

Bobbel(i) (es)n. baby

bobble, v.; bobbelt, pp. pamper

Bb

bobble / Braucherei

bobble, v.; gebobbelt, pp. (to give) birth

Bobbli (es)n.; Bobblin, pl. baby

bobere, v.; gebobert, pp. 1.complain; 2.evince unrest; 3.nag

boberich, adj. 1.loquacious; 2.querulous

boche, v.; gebocht, pp. boast

Bock (der)n.; Beck, pl. 1.buck; 2.ram

Bockbier (es)n. bockbeer

bocke, v.; gebockt, pp. 1.be in heat; 2.rut

Bocksbaart (der)n. stellate sedge

Bockschprung (der)n. 1.buck-jump; 2.caper; 3.gambol; 4.short-jump

bocksecke (en -- aahenge) said of a person in quoits who makes a score of less than 6

Bockseckel (es)n. shepherd's purse

bockseckle, v.; gebockseckelt, pp. 1.defraud; 2.rob

Bockslochgri (wu gehscht hie? En -- buhne roppe) evading an answer to some inquisitive person

Bodde(m) (der)n. 1.bottom; 2.ground; 3.floor; 4.soil

boddegraemisch, adj. 1.foot sore; 2.somewhat helpless; 3.walking with difficulty

boddegrempisch, adj. 1.foot sore; 2.somewhat helpless; 3.walking with difficulty

Boddel (die)n.; Boddle, pl. bottle

Boddelche (es)n. 1.flask; 2.small bottle; 3.vial

boddemlos, adj. 1.quagmire; 2.without sure footing

Boddemriggel (der)n. bottom rail of a worm fence

Boddemscheier (die)n. barn with only one floor as distinguished from a bank barn

Boge (der)n. 1.arc; 2.arch; 3.bow; 4.hair-ribbon; 5.sheet of paper

Boge-flint (die)n. 1.bow; 2.cross-bow

Bogebix (die)n. bow (for shooting)

Bogefenschder (es)n. 1.arched window; 2.bay window

Bogehammer (der)n.; Bogehemmer, pl. pole-pin

Bohn (die)n.; Bohne, pl. bean

Bohnebaam (der)n. 1.catalpa tree; 2.Judas tree

Bohnegraut (es)n. summer savory

Bohnegreidel (es)n. summer savory

Bohnegreitle (es)n. summer savory

Bohneschtecke (der)n. 1.bean pole; 2.tall thin person

Bohrbank (die)n. bench for boring holes in posts

Bohre (der)n.; Bohre, pl. auger

bohre, v.; gebohrt, pp. 1.bore; 2.tap; 3.nag

Bohreise (es)n. bit (carpenter's tool)

Boi (der, es)n. pie

Boibritsch (die)n. pie-paddle

Boigraut (der)n. rhubarb

Boll (die)n. 1.boll (of flax); 2.(chestnut) burr; 3.flax before it is broken

bollere, v.; gebollert, pp. rumble

Bolleryockel (der)n. 1.hog weed; 2.ragweed

Bollhoke (der)n. fuller's teasel

Bollmehl (es)n. middlings

Bollwaerrick (es)n. 1.bolting sieve; 2.tow of first hackling

Bols (die)n. pulse

Bolsoder (die)n. artery

Bolsrohr (es)n. wooden gun for shooting pins and other light projectiles by blowing

Bommerans (die)n. tomato

Bonifazius (der)n. Bonifacius Day (June 5)

Boo (der)n. path (through snow)

Boom (der)n. tree

Boosheet (die)n. 1.iniquity; 2.malice

Boot (es)n.; Boots, pl. boat

boote, v.; geboot, pp. transport commodities in a canal boat

Bootmann (der)n. canal boatman

Bopp (die)n. doll

Borax (der)n. borax

Bord (es)n.; Bord, pl. board (lumber)

Bordkarrich (die)n. gallery (in a church)

Bore (der)n. mow (hay)

Bortsch (die)n. porch

bose, v.; gebost, pp. 1.commit an offence; 2.do something bad

boshaft, adj. spiteful

Bosheet (die)n. 1.iniquity; 2.malice

Bosheit (die)n. 1.iniquity; 2.malice

Boss (der)n.; Bosse, pl. kiss

Bossdaage (die)n., pl. honeymoon

bosse, v.; gebosst, pp. kiss

Bot(t)schaft (die)n. message

Bottboi (der)n. potpie

Bottesch (die)n. potash

bottle, v.; gebottelt, pp. bottle

Bottlerei (die)n. bottling establishment

br!, interj. exclamation of one shivering from cold

braav, adj. 1.brave; 2.good; 3.honest

Braavheit (die)n. bravery

Bracht (die)n. 1.beauty; 2.magnificence; 3.splendor

brachtvoll, adj. 1.magnificent; 2.sumptuous

bradsle, v.; gebradselt, pp. sizzle

Braems (der)n. twitch

braff, adj. well-behaved

bralle, v.; gebrallt, pp. 1.boast; 2.brag

Braller (der)n. 1.boaster; 2.braggart

Brallhans (der)n. 1.boaster; 2.braggart

Brand (der)n. 1.brand; 2.conflagration; 3.ergot; 4.gangrene; 5.mortification; 6.peritonitis

Brandewei (der)n. whiskey

Brandeweifass (es)n. 1.toper; 2.whiskey barrel

Brandschtifder (der)n. incendiary

brau(n), adj. 1.bay (of a horse); 2.brown; 3.russet

brau(n)gehl, adj. dun

Brau(n)watzel (die)n. figwort

brauchba(a)r, adv. 1.necessary; 2.useful

brauchbaar, adj. 1.beneficial; 2.serviceable; 3.useful

Brauchbuch (es)n. 1.manual on powwowing; 2.spell-book

Brauchdokder (der)n. powwow doctor

brauche, v.; gebraucht, pp. 1.need; 2.powwow; 3.stand in need of; 4.use

Braucher (der)n. powwow doctor

Braucherei (die)n. powwowing

Bb

Brauchfraa

Brauchfraa (die)n. powwow doctor
braue, v.; gebraut, pp. brew
Brauer (der)n. brewer
Brauerei (die)n. brewery
braunlich, adj. brownish
Braus (der)n. roar
brause, v.; gebraust, pp. roar
Braut (die)n. bride
Brauticham (der)n. bridegroom
breble, v.; gebrebelt, pp. 1.importune; 2.nag; 3.palaver
Brechaggel (die)n. particle of the outer coating of the flax
    plant separated in the process of breaking
brechdich, adj. 1.beautiful; 2.splendid
breche, v.; gebroche, pp. (sich --) throw up (vomit)
Breche(s) (es)n. vomiting
breche, v.; gebroche, pp. 1.break; 2.check
Brecheise (es)n. crowbar
Brecher (der)n. 1.coal breaker; 2.corn breaker (in a grist mill)
Brechloch (es)n. quarry or hole in which flax was roasted
    and broken
Brechmiddel (es)n. emetic
Brechschtang (die)n. crowbar
breckle, v.; gebreckelt, pp. crumble
Breddich (die)n.; Breddiche, pl. sermon
Breddichamt (es)n. ministry
breddiche, v.; gebreddicht, pp. preach
Breddicher (der)n.; Breddicher, pl. 1.clergyman;
    2.parson; 3.preacher; 4.minister
Breddicherschtul (der)n. pulpit (Montgomery Co. Mennonites)
bredsle, v.; gebredselt, pp. sizzle
breedbeenich, adj. (standing) with one's legs far apart
Breeding (die)n. 1.breadth; 2.width
Breedlatz (der)n. broad front flap of trousers worn by
    Amish men
breedlich, adj. broadly
Breedmaul (es)n. 1.braggart; 2.splay-mouth
breedmeilich, adj. blunt
breednaesich, adj. flat-nosed
breedsichtich, adj. broad-faced
Breem (die)n. horsefly
breese, v.; gebreest, pp. appraise
breet, adj. 1.broad; 2.wide
breetbeenich, adj. standing with one's legs far apart
Breetbeil (es)n.; Breetbeile, pl. broadax
breetgsichtich, adj. broad-faced
Breetlatz (der) n. broad front flap of trousers worn by
    Amish men
breetlich, adj. broadly
Breetmaul (es)n. 1.braggart; 2.splay mouthed
breetmeilich, adj. blunt
breetnaasich, adj. flat nosed
Brei (der)n. pap
breiche, v.; gebreicht, pp. 1.need; 2.use
Breidicham (der)n. bridegroom
Breis (der)n. 1.price; 2.prize
Breis (es)n. wristband

brinselbrau

Breischder (der)n.; Breischder, pl. priest
Brend(e)wei (der)n. brandy
Brendis (der)n.; Brendis, pl. Apprentice
Brengle (der) n.; Brengle, pl. maple-sap-catching-bucket
    (wooden)
brenne, v.; gebrennt, pp. 1.burn; 2.distill; 3.scorch
brennend, adj. 1.burning; 2.lit
Brennerei (die)n., Brennereie, pl. distillery
Brennes(s)el (der)n. (stinging) nettle
Brennglaas (es)n. 1.burning-glass; 2.sun-glass
Brennhaus (es)n.; Brennheiser, pl. distillery
Brennhols (es)n. fire wood
brennsich, adj. burnt (to taste or smell)
Bresibedaat (es)n. (rot --) red precipitate
Bresident (der)n.; Bresidende, pl. president
Bress (die)n. press
Bressen(t) (die)n.; Bressende, pl. 1.jail; 2.prison
Bressent (es)n. present
Brett (es)n. 1.board; 2.bracket
Bretzel (es)n. pretzel
brezis, adj. exactly
Briambel (der)n. long winded talk
Brick (die)n.; Bricke, pl. 1.bridge; 2.(en gwelb --) an
    arched bridge
Brickepeiler (der)n. pier
brie(h)ich, adj. 1.broody (of hens); 2.juicy; 3.liquid
Briederfescht (es)n. annual service for men and boys
    (Moravian)
briederlich, adv. brotherly
Briederlichkeet (die)n. 1.brotherliness; 2.fraternity
Briederschaft (die)n. brotherhood
briee, v.; gebriet, pp. hatch
Brief (der)n. 1.letter; 2.package or paper
Briefbabier (es)n. letter paper
Briefdraager (der)n. letter carrier
Briefdraeger (der)n. letter carrier
Briefelche (es)n. powder (to be taken)
Briefwechsel (der)n. correspondence
Brieh (die)n. 1.broth; 2.gravy; 3.juice; 4.slop
Briehdrog (der)n. scalding trough (in butchering)
briehe, v.; gebrieht, pp. 1.hatch; 2.incubate; 3.parboil; 4.scald
briehe, v.; gebrieht, pp. (oier --) soft-boiled eggs
Briehfass (es)n. scalding vat
Briemaschien (die)n. incubator
Brieschder (der)n. 1.parson (contemptuous); 2.priest
Briggel (der)n. 1.club; 2.cudgel(ing); 3.limb of a tree;
    4.stick; 5.(-- schmeisse) abuse
briggele, v.; gebriggelt, pp. 1.cudgel; 2.club
Briggelhols (es)n. small limbs of trees cut up for firewood
Briggelsupp (die)n. 1.cudgeling; 2.clubbing; 3.flogging
Brill (die)n.; Brille, pl. 1.eyeglasses; 2.spectacles
brille, v.; gebrillt, pp. 1.bawl; 2.cry; 3.roar; 4.weep
Brillescheed (die)n.; Brillescheede, pl. spectacles-case
bringe, v.; gebrocht, pp. 1.bring; 2.fetch
Brinsebedaad (roder)n. larkspur
brinselbrau, adj. brindle

Bb

Britsch

Britsch (die)n. 1.bat; 2.implement used in beating flax from the stem; 3.paddle; 4.(uff der -- sei) be incapacitated for work

britsche, v.; gebritscht, pp. 1.beat with a paddle; 2.flog; 3.paddle something down flat

Briwwe (es)n. 1.privy; 2.toilet; 3.back house

Briwwi (es)n. 1.privy; 2.toilet; 3.back house; 4.out-house

Brocke (der)n. 1.morsel; 2.scrap

Brockel (es)n. 1.bit; 2.crumb

Brockeldings (die)n., pl. trimmings (around hard soap)

Brockelesche (die)n. prickly ash

Brockelsupp (die)n. milk soup (with bread crumbs)

brockle, v.; gebrockelt, pp. 1.break; 2.crumble; 3.break and soak (bread in milk)

Brocklesche (die)n. prickly ash

brocklich, adj. 1.brittle; 2.crisp; 3.crumbly

brode, v.; gebrode, pp. 1.broil; 2.fry; 3.scorch (by the sun); 4.(es is ihm nix rechts --) nothing suits him

Brodpann (die)n.; Brodpanne, pl. frying pan

brodsle, v.; gebrodselt, pp. sizzle

Brofeet (der)n.; Brofeede, pl. prophet

brofesseihe, v.; gebrofesseiht, pp. 1.forecast; 2.predict; 3.prophesy

Brofesser (der)n. professor

Brofit(t) (der)n. 1.gain; 2.profit

brofitlich, adj. profitable

Brombeer (die)n. dewberry

brooche, v.; gebroocht, pp. fallow

Broochland (es)n. fallow land

Brophet (der)n. prophet

Brophezeiung (die)n. 1.prediction; 2.prophecy

Brossan (der)n. crumb (of a loaf of bread)

Brot (es)n. 1.bread; 2.(gebaeht --) toast; 3.(gereescht --) toast

Brotdeeg (der)n. bread dough

Brotfilsel (es)n. stuffing

Brotfresser (der)n. professor (humorous)

Brotgruscht (die)n. bread crust

Brothank (der)n. swinging-shelf

Brotkareb (der)n.; Brotkareb, pl. pannier

Brotpann (die)n. frying pan

Brotschank (der)n. 1.cupboard; 2.pantry

Brotwascht (die)n. 1.(-- in die Pann leere) put (sausage) into the pan; 2.sausage

brotzich, adj. 1.proud; 2.stuck-up

browiere, v.; (ge)browiert, pp. 1.attempt; 2.endeavor; 3.strive; 4.try

Bruch (der)n.; Brich, pl. 1.breach; 2.hernia; 3.rupture; 4.quarry

Bruchband (es)n. truss

Bruchtwaarz (die)n.; Bruschtwaarze, pl. nipple

Brud (die)n. 1.brood (of bees, especially in the comb); 2.litter (of pigs)

Bruder (der)n.; Brieder, pl. brother

Brudermaerder (der)n. fratricide

Brudermard (der)n. fratricide

Bruderskind (es)n. 1.nephew; 2.niece

brumme, v.; gebrummt, pp. 1.buzz; 2.hum; 3.grumble

Brummelochs (der)n. bull

bschteediche

Brummer (der)n.; Brummer, pl. (factory) whistle

brummle,v.; gebrumelt, pp. 1.grumble;2.scold in an undertone

Brummvoggel (der)n. hummingbird

Brunelle (die)n. 1.brunella; 2.self-heal

Brunellegraut (es)n. 1.brunella; 2.self-heal

Brunne (der)n. 1.spring (of water); 2.water well

Brunne(r)wasser (es)n. well-water

Brunnegraawer (der)n. well-digger

Brunnegress (es)n. watercress

Brunnekeller (der)n. deep cellar (usually detached from the house) for cooling butter, etc.

Brunnergraawer (der)n. well digger

Brunnewalz (die)n. windlass (for drawing water)

Brunnewasser (es)n. well water

Bruns (der)n. urine

Brunsbank (die)n. pouter

brunse, v.; gebrunst, pp. urinate

Bruscht (die)n.; Brischt, pl. 1.breast; 2.chest

Bruschtfiewer (es)n. pneumonia

Bruschtgart (die)n. breast strap (of harness)

Bruschtgnoche (der)n. 1.breastbone; 2.wishbone

Bruschtgsims (es)n. wainscoting

Bruschtkaern (es)n. brisket

Bruschtkett (die)n. breast chain (of harness)

Bruschtkummet (es)n. breast collar

Bruschtlappe (der)n. vest

Bruschtschpell (die)n. breastpin

Bruschttee (der)n. 1.checkerberry; 2.wintergreen

Bruschtwaarz (die)n. nipple of the breast

Brut (der)n. litter (of pigs)

brutsich, adj. 1.cross; 2.sulky; 3.sullen

Brutzbank (die)n. 1.pouter; 2.pouting bench

brutze, v.; gebrutzt, pp. 1.fret; 2.pout; 3.sulk; 4.threaten rain

Brutzeck (es)n. pouting corner (corner into which pouting children retire)

brutzich, adj. 1.cross (bees); 2.fretful; 3.peevish; 4.pouty; 5.sulky

Brutzkiwwel (der)n. 1.one given to pouting; 2.one who sulks

brutzle, v.; gebrutzelt, pp. 1.drizzle; 2.simmer

Bruud (die)n. 1.brood of bees (especially in the comb); 2.litter (of pigs)

bsarge, v.; bsarkt, pp. 1.attend to; 2.provide for

bsarkt, adj. 1.careful; 2.provided for; 3.solicitous

bsaufe, v.; bsoffe, pp. (sich --) become intoxicated

Bsch(e)isser (der)n. 1.cheat; 2.fraud; 3.crook

bschaffe, v.; bschaffe, pp. 1.create; 2.form; 3.shape

bscheisse, v.; bschisse, pp. 1.cheat; 2.defraud; 3.swindle

Bscheisserei (die)n. 1.cheating; 2.dishonesty; 3.fraud

bschimpe, v.; bschimpt, pp. 1.abuse; 2.defame; 3.disgrace; 4.taunt

bschinne, v.; bschunne, pp. skin

bschlagge, v.; bschlagge, pp. 1.hew a log; 2.put iron on (a wagon); 3.shoe (a horse); 4.(holz --) hew logs

Bschluss (der)n. conclusion

bschmeisse, v.; bschmisse, pp. 1.pelt; 2.throw at

bschteediche, v.; bschteedicht, pp. 1.confirm; 2.verify

Bb

bschteh — Bumpekiwwel

bschteh, v.; bschtanne, pp. 1.confess; 2.(debei --) (a)be firm in; (b)get along on; (c)manage with

bschtehle, v.; bschtellt; bschtohle, pp. 1.rob; 2.steal from

bschtelle, v.; bschtellt, pp. order

Bschtelling (die)n. appointment

bschtohle, adj. be of a thieving nature

bschtohlnerweis, adv. sneakingly

bschweere, v.; bschwore, pp. swear with an oath

bsetze, v.; bsetzt, pp. 1.lengthen a dress; 2.trim

Bsetzing (die)n. trimming

Bsitzer (der)n.; Bsitzer, pl. possessor

bsoffe, adj. intoxicated

bsonders, adv. particularly

Bsuch (der)n. 1.visit; 2.visitors

bsuche, v.; bsucht, pp. visit

Bsucherei (die)n. (confounded) visiting

bsunders, adv. particularly

bsunne, adj. having presence of mind

Bu (der)n.; Buwe, pl. 1.boy; 2.lad

Bubli (es)n. little boy

Buch (es)n.; Bicher, pl. 1.book; 2.(ins -- schreiwe) (to grant) credit

Buche (die)n. beech tree

buche, adj. (of) beech

Buchebaam (der)n. beech tree

Buchel (die)n. beechnut

Buchhalding (die)n. bookkeeping

Buchhaltung (die)n. bookkeeping

Buchhandlung (die)n. bookstore

Buchs (der)n. 1.boxtree; 2.laurel; 3.wintergreen; 4.(im -- sei) (to be) intoxicated; 5.(nidderer --) (a) checkerberry; (b) wintergreen; 6.(zaahmer --) boxtree

Buchsbaam (der)n. boxtree

Buchsbeer (die)n. 1.checkerberry; 2.teaberry

Buchweeze (der)n. buckwheat

Buchweezekuche (der)n. buckwheat cake

Buchweezemehl (es)n. buckwheat flour

Buchweezenode (die)n., pl. shaped notes

Buchweezeschtroh (es)n. buckwheat straw

Buckel (der) n. 1.back (of human body); 2.hump; 3.slight elevation of ground

Buckel (der)n. (-- weeche) tan

Buckelweh (es)n. 1.backache; 2.lumbago

Bucker (der)n. 1.castrated dog; 2.hardened mucous removed from the nose; 3.heretic; 4.rascal

bucklich, adj. 1.hilly; 2.humpbacked; 3.stoop shouldered; 4.uneven

Budder (der)n. 1.butter; 2.(-- drehe) churn (butter)

Budderbeer (die)n. 1.checker berry; 2.partridge berry

Budderblumm (die)n. 1.buttercup; 2.crowfoot

Budderfass (es)n.; Budderfesse(r), pl. butter churn

Budderhaffe (der)n. butter crock

Budderleffel (der)n. wooden spoon for working butter

Buddermesser (es)n. butter knife

Buddermillich (die)n. buttermilk

Buddermoddel (die)n. 1.butter print; 2.velvet leaf

Buddernuss (die)n. butternut

Budderpress (die)n. butter print

Budderschissel (die)n. wooden dish in which butter is worked

Buddervoggel (der)n. reedbird

Budderwatzel (die)n. wild ginger

Budderzuwwer (der)n.; Budderziwwer, pl. butter tub

Buff (der)n. 1.blow; 2.wack; 3.(alle --) (a) every once in a while; (b) every time

buff!, interj. 1.bang!; 2.slap!

Buhn (die)n.; Buhne, pl. bean

Buhnebaam (der)n. 1.catalpa tree; 2.Judas tree

Buhnegraut (es)n. summer savory

Buhnegreidel (es)n. summer savory

Buhnegreitel (es)n. summer savory

Buhnegreitle (es)n. summer savory

Buhnekeffer (der)n. bean bug

Buhneschtecke (der)n.; Buhneschtecke, pl. 1.bean pole; 2.tall thin person

Buhnesupp (die)n. bean soup

Buk (die)n.; Biek, pl. 1.brace (framework of barn); 2.brace

Bulfer (es)n. powder

Bull (der)n.; Bulle, pl. bull

Bulle (der)n. (so een --) term of contempt for an ignorant bully

bulle, v.; gebullt, pp. long for the bull (of cows)

Bullebeidel (der)n. 1.lady's slipper; 2.moccasin flower

Bullefleesch (es)n. bull beef

Bullekalb (es)n. bull calf

Bullfrack (der)n. bullfrog

Bullhund (der)n. bull dog

Bulli (es)n. a small (immature) bull

Bullirum (der)n. frog

bullirum! onomatopoeic to imitate the croak of a frog

Bullkasch (die)n. oxheart cherry

bullkeppich, adj. obstinate

Bulsoder (die)n. 1.artery; 2.vein

Bulver (es)n. powder

Bulwer (es)n. powder

bumbe, v.; gebumbt, pp. 1.bump; 2.pump

Bumbehandel (der)n. pump-handle

Bumbehaus (es)n.; Bumbeheiser, pl. pump-house

Bumbernickel (der) n. coarse, dark, heavy rye bread of unbolted flour

Bumbeschwengel (der)n. pump-handle

Bumbezott (die)n. pump spout

bumm!, interj. 1.bang!; 2.plump!

Bummelhannes (der)n. 1.Old Peter Tumbledown; 2.slothful and procrastinating person

bummeraalisch, adj. 1.deucedly; 2.fearfully

Bummerans (die)n. tomato

bummere, v.; gebummert, pp. 1.bump; 2.rumble

bummerisch, adj. 1.fearfully; 2.terribly

Bump (der)n. bump

Bump (die)n.; Bumpe, pl. pump

Bumpebett (es). pump floor

Bumpedrog (der)n. pump trough

Bumpekiwwel (der)n. pump piston

Bb

Bumpemacher / buwu!

Bumpemacher (der)n. pump maker
Bumpeschtiel (der)n. pump-handle
Bumpeschtock (der)n. pump
Bumps (der)n. 1.bang; 2.jar; 3.jolt
bumps!, interj. bang!
Bund (der)n. covenant
Bundel (der)n.; Bindel, pl. 1.bundle; 2.sheaf
bundle, v.; gebundelt, pp. bundle (referring to the past custom of bundling)
Bungert (der)n. 1.orchard; 2.(-- aus/butze) prune the orchard
Bungertgraas (es)n. orchard grass
Bunnert (der)n. orchard
Busch (der)n.; Bisch, pl. 1.grove; 2.forest; 3.woods; 4.country
Buschabbel (der)n. 1.May apple; 2.mandrake
Buschbaam (der)n. forest tree
Buschdaab (der)n.; Buschdaawe, pl. letter (in the alphabet)
Buschdaag (der)n.; Buschdaawe, pl. 1.initial; 2.letter of the alphabet
Buscheesel (der)n.; Buscheesel, pl. stick insect
Buschel (der)n.; Buschel, pl. bushel
Buschelkareb (der)n. bushel basket
Buschgnibbel (der)n. 1.clodhopper; 2.rustic
buschich, adj. bushy
Buschknibbel (der)n. clodhopper
Buschland (es)n. woodland
Buschleit (die)n., pl. country people
Buschmick (die)n. 1.forest fly; 2.horse fly
buschtaawiere, v.; buschtaawiert, pp. spell (words)
Buschtee (der)n. dittany
Buschvoggel (der)n. thrush
Buschwaasem (der)n. forest moss
Buschweg (der)n. road through the woods
Buss (die)n. repentance
buss! call for a cat
Buss(e) (die)n. 1.repentance; 2.(busse du) (to) repent
Bussbank (die)n. 1.anxious bench; 2.bench of repentance
Bussdaag (der)n. 1.day of repentance; 2.fast day
Bussem (der)n. bosom
Bussi (die)n. 1.cat; 2.pussy; 3.female pudendum
Bussikatz (die)n. 1.cat; 2.pussy cat
Bussli (die) 1.cat; 2.pussy
Bussli (es)n.; Busslin, pl. kitten
Butscher (der)n.; Butscher, pl. butcher
Butscher-Ax (die)n. cleaver
Butterbeer (die)n. 1.checker berry; 2.partridge berry
Butterbock (der)n. frame on which a churn sets
Butterbohn (die)n. 1.butter bean; 2.lima bean
Butterleffel (der)n. wooden spoon for working butter
Buttermesser (es)n. butter knife
Buttermoddel (die)n. 1.butter print; 2.velvet leaf
Butternuss (die)n. butternut
Butterpress (die)n. butter print
Butterschissel (die)n. wooden dish in which butter is worked
Buttervoggel (der)n. reedbird
Butterwatzel (die)n. wild ginger
Butz(e)li(es)n.; Butz(e)lin, pl. strawberry cleaning

Butze (der)n. 1.afterbirth; 2.placenta (of animals; 3.core of an apple or boil; 4.burnt wick of a candle; 5.long wick end on a burning fat light
Butze (die)n. placenta
butze, v.; gebutzt, pp. 1.clean; 2.dress up; 3.wipe; 4.(beem --) trim trees; 5.(frucht --) winnow grain; 6.(geil --) curry horses; 7.(haus --) clean house; 8.(sich --) deliver the afterbirth
Butzemann (der)n. scarecrow
Butzerei (die)n. (confounded) cleaning
Butzfraa (die)n. charwoman
butzich, adj. 1.short; 2.stunted
Butzing (die)n. placenta
Butzlumbe (der)n. mop
Buweleis (die)n., pl. 1.Spanish needles; 2.tickseed
Buwerutsch (die)n. loose girl
Buweschmaga (der)n.; Buweschmaga, pl. tomboy
Buweschtofft (des) 1.mischievous boys; 2.(these) boys
Buweschtreech (die)n., pl. boyish pranks
Buweschtrofft (des)n. 1.(these) boys; 2.mischievous boys
Buwli (es)n.; Buwlin, pl. little boy
buwu! imitating the bark of a dog

Dd

Daa

Daa (der)n. dew
daa, adv. there
daab, adj. 1.deaf; 2.without kernels (of nuts and grains)
Daadem (der)n.; Daadem(e), pl. date
Daadi (der)n. 1.father; 2.grandfather (Amish usage); 3.papa
daae, v.; gedaat, pp. 1.deposit dew; 2.melt; 3.thaw
Daaf (die)n.; Daafe, pl. baptism
daafe, v.; gedaaft, pp. 1.baptize; 2.christen
Daafel (die)n. (schoolboy's) slate
Daafeldre (die)n.; Daafleit, pl. baptismal sponsors
Daafiewing (die)n. baptismal service (plain)
Daafnaame, (der)n. baptismal name
Daafschei(n) (der)n. baptismal certificate
Daafwasser (es)n. baptismal water
Daafzeige (die)n., pl. sponsors (at baptismal)
Daag (der)n.; Daage, pl. 1.day; 2.daylight; 3.(-- druff) the day
    after; 4.(daags devor) the day before; 5.(daags) during
    the day; 6.(heit iwwer vatzeh --) two weeks from today;
    7.(heit iwwer acht --) this day a week; 8.(hoscht du
    dei -- des lewes!) did you ever!; 9.(im helle --) in bright
    daylight; 10.(sei [mei, dei] -- des lewes net) never;
    11.(seller --e) those days; 12.(varzeh --) two weeks;
    13.(verbeigangne --e) bygone days
Daag des Lewes net!, adv. never (emphatic)
Daag(s)helling (die)n. 1.dawn; 2.daylight
Daagbuch (es)n.; Daagbicher, pl. 1.daybook; 2.diary; 3.journal
Daagdieb (der)n. 1.idler; 2.loafer; 3.scamp; 4.truant
Daage drei, adv. three days or so
Daagebruch (der)n. break of day
daagenacht, adv. (daag un nacht) 1.continually; 2.everlastingly
Daagesaafang (der)n. dawn
Daageslicht (es)n. 1.daylight; 2.light of day
daageweis, adv. 1.by the day; 2.now and then a day;
    3.several days
Daaglehner (der)n.; Daaglehner, pl. day laborer
daaglehnere, v.; gedaaglehnert, pp. work for someone
    on a day by day basis
Daaglehnerhaus (es)n. tenant house
Daagloch (es)n. 1.opening in a wall; 2.small cellar window
Daagluh (der)n. daily wages
Daagsarewett (die)n. day's work
Daagslicht (es)n. dawn
Daagswerk (die)n. day's work
Daaksbruch (der)n. break of day
Daal (es)n.; Daale; Daaler, pl. 1.dale; 2.depression;
    3.hollow; 4.vale; 5.valley; 6.pond
Daaler (der).; Daaler, pl. dollar
Daalernoot (die)n. dollar bill
Daalerros (die)n. aster
daalerweis, adj. dollar by dollar
Daarem (der)n.; Daerem, pl. 1.bowel; 2.(gross --) the
    large intestine
daarnooch, adv. thereafter
daarum, adv. 1.for this; 2.therefore
Daat (die)n.; Daade, pl. 1.act; 2.deed; 3.feat
Daatem (der)n. date

Daerli

Daavid (der)n. David
dabbe, v.; gedappt, pp. 1.grasp for; 2.fumble; 3.step
    (heavily); 4.walk clumsily
dabbele, v.; gedabbelt, pp. 1.step; 2.tramp; 3.fidget (a horse)
dabber, adv. 1.at once; 2.quickly
dabbich, adj. 1.awkward; 2.clumsy
dabei/bleiwe, v. 1.stay with; 2.stick to
dabei/schteh, v. stand by one's guns
dabei/sitze, v. sit by
dabei, adv. among
dabei, prep. 1.among; 2.by that; 3.along with
Dach (es)n.; Decher, pl. roof
dachdle, v.; gedachdelt, pp. 1.beat; 2.flog
Dachdraaf (der)n. eaves
Dachdroff (der)n. eaves-trough or gutter
Dachdrops (der)n. eaves
dache, v.; gedacht, pp. (to put a) roof (on)
Dachfa(e)rscht (der)n. ridgepole
Dachfenschder (es)n.; Dachfenschdere, pl. 1.dormer;
    2.skylight
Dachgiwwel (der)n. point of the roof at the gable-end
Dachkandel (der)n. rainspout
Dachlaade (der)n.; Dachlaade, pl. hatchway (of a roof)
Dachpett (die)n. purlin
Dachrut (die)n. purlin
Dachs (der)n. 1.groundhog; 2.raccoon (a misapprehen-
    sion where used); 3.short-legged dog
dachsbeenich, adj. bandy-legged
Dachschlupper (der)n. (a) drifting snow
Dachschtroh (es)n. thatch
Dachschtul (der)n.; Dachschtiel, pl. 1.ridge-lead;2.roof support
Dachsi (der)n. shorty
dachsich, adj. 1.bent; 2.stooped
Dachwand (die)n. ceiling
Dad (der)n. 1.daddy; 2.father
dadde, adj. there
Daddeldaub (die)n.; Daddeldauwe, pl. turtledove
Daddi (der)n. 1.dad; 2.daddy; 3.grandfather (Amish usage)
daechlich, adj. daily
Daed (der)n. 1.dad; 2.daddy; 3.father; 4.papa;
    5.grandfather (Amish usage)
daedae geh, v. go bye-bye (in speaking to children)
daedlich, adv. deadly
Daefer (der)n.; Daefer, pl. Baptist
Daeger (der)n. dagger
daeglich, adj.; adv. daily
daeklich, adj. daily
Daer (die)n.; Daere, pl. door
daer, dem. adj. this
daer, rel pro. who
Daerbedien (es)n. turpentine
daerbediene, v.; gedaerbedient, pp. apply turpentine
Daerche (es)n. 1.gate; 2.small gate
daereweil, adv. meantime
daerfe, v.; gedaerft, pp. 1.be allowed to; 2.dare; 3.may
Daerli (es)n. 1.gate; 2.small gate

Dd

Daermfett

Daermfett (es)n. intestinal fat (of cattle)
Daermschmals (es)n. intestinal fat (of hogs)
Daermverschtopping (die)n. constipation
Daermwascht (die)n. sausage in casing
Daerr (die)n. place for drying vegetables and fruit
daerr, adj. 1.dry; 2.lean
daerre, v.; gedaerrt, pp. 1.cure; 2.dry
dagege hawwe, v. object
dahaer, adv. for that reason
daheem, adv. home
dahie, adv. thither
dalehafdich, adj. sharing
Dall(e) (die)n. 1.dent; 2.dimple; 3.impression
Dallbopp (die)n.; Dallbobbe, pl. doll
dambe, v.; gedampt, pp. 1.give off vapor; 2.smother;
   3.steam; 4.stew
dambich, adj. 1.steamy; 2.vaporous
damit, adv. therewith
Damm (der)n.; Demm, pl. 1.dam; 2.(do will ich iwwer
   der -- geh) I'll be hanged (damned)
Dammbruscht (die)n. breast of a dam
damme, v.; gedammt, pp. dam
Dammgraas (es)n. pond grass
Dammhig(g)el (der)n. breast of a dam
Damp (der)n. 1.steam; 2.vapor
Dampgnopp (der)n.; Dampgnepp, pl. steamed dumpling
Damploch (es)n. dump hole
Dampnudel (die)n. boiled dumpling
Dangel (der)n. Daniel
Dank (der)n. 1.gratitude; 2.reward; 3.thanks
dank/sage, v.; dankgsaat, pp. offer thanks
dankbaar, adj. 1.grateful; 2.thankful
Dankbaarkeet (die)n. thankfulness
Dankbreddich (die)n. Thanksgiving sermon
danke, v.; gedankt, pp. 1.return a salutation; 2.thank
Dankes (es)n. thanks
dankeswaert worth thanking for
Dankfescht (es)n. Thanksgiving
Danki (der)n. 1.thanks; 2.(-- saage) thank; 3.(-- schee) (a)
   thanks!, (b)thank-you!
Danksaagesdaag (der)n. Thanksgiving
Danksaagung (die)n. Thanksgiving
Dankyaa! 1.thanks!; 2.thank you!
Dankzeige (es)n. reminder
Dann (der)n. 1.spire; 2.steeple
Dann (die)n.; Danne, pl. 1.thorn; 2.(-- im Aag) eyesore;
   3.thorn in the flesh; 4.(grieni --) green-briar;
   5.(hochi --) high blackberry; 6.ton
dann un wann, adv. 1.intermittently; 2.now and then
dann, adv. 1.next; 2.then
dann, conj.; prep. than
Danneros (die)n. sweetbrier
Danneschpell (die)n. 1.red haw; 2.scarlet thorn
Danneschtock (der)n. thornbush
dannich, adj. 1.prickly; 2.thorny
Danz (der)n.; Danze, pl. dance

darrich/falle

danze, v.; gedanzt, pp. dance
Danzer (der)n.; Denzer, pl. dancer
dappe, v.;gedappt, pp. 1.step heavily; 2.walk clumsily
Dappe (der)n. footprint
Dappel (der)n. clumsy fellow
dapper, adv. 1.at once; 2.quickly
Dapperschpring (die)n. diarrhea
Dappes (der)n. clumsy fellow
Dar(re)m (die)n.; Daerm, pl. 1.entrails; 2.intestine
Dardeldaub (die)n. turtle dove
dardle, v.; gedardelt, pp. 1.stagger; 2.sway to and fro
Darebedien (es)n. turpentine
daremlich, adj. 1.dizzy; 2.giddy
Daremseet (die)n. catgut
darigle, v.; gedarigelt, pp. 1.reel; 2.stagger
Dariyel (der)n. vertigo
Darmel (der)n. giddiness
Darn (die)n. thorn
Darneros (die)n. sweet briar
Darneschpell (die)n. 1.red haw; 2.scarlet thorn
Darneschtock (der)n. thorn bush
darnich, adj. thorny
Darr (der)n. 1.tar; 2.(in -- sei) (to be) tipsy
darr, adj. 1.dry; 2.lean; 3.skinny
darrich die Naas, adv. nasal
darrich un darrich, adv. 1.severely; 2.thoroughly
darrich(e)nanner, adj. 1.confusion; 2.helter-skelter
darrich(e)nanner, adv. in confusion
darrich(e)weck, adv. 1.on an average; 2.throughout
darrich/baade, v.; darichgebaadt, pp. wade through
darrich/beisse, v.; darichgebisse, pp. bite through
darrich/blettre, v.; darichgeblettert, pp. turn the leaves
   of a book
darrich/blicke, v.; darichgeblickt, pp. peep through
darrich/blose, v. darichgeblose, pp. 1.blow
   through;2.spend
darrich/bohre, v.; darichgebohrt, pp. 1.bore through;
   2.perforate
darrich/breche, v.; darichgebroche, pp. break through
darrich/brenne. v.; darichgebrennt, pp. 1.burn through;
   2.elope; 3.make a hole by burning; 4.run away
darrich/briggle, v.; darichgebriggelt, pp. beat soundly
darrich/bringe, v. squander
darrich/brode, v.; darichgebrode, pp. fry through
darrich/draage, v.; darichgedraage, pp. bear through
darrich/drede,v.; darichgedrede,pp. wear through by treading
darrich/dreiwe, v.; darichdriwwe, pp. strain (food)
darrich/dresche, v.; darichgedrosche, pp. flog soundly
darrich/dricke, v.; darichgedrickt, pp. press through
darrich/drickle, v.; darichgedrickelt, pp. dry thoroughly
darrich/dringe, v. darichgedrunge, pp. 1.permeate;
   2.penetrate
darrich/dropse, v.; darichgedropst, pp. drop or filter through
darrich/faahre, v.; darichgfaahrt, pp. 1.drive through;
   2.pass through (like a shudder)
darrich/falle, v.; darichgfalle, pp. 1.fall through; 2.fail

34

Dd

darrich/faule

darrich/faule, v.; darichgfault, pp. rot through

darrich/fiehre, v.; darichgfiehrt, pp. 1.carry through; 2.execute

darrich/fresse, v.; darichgfresst, pp. 1.corrode; 2.eat through; 3.(sich --) make one's way under difficulties

darrich/geh, v.; darichgange, pp. 1.abscond (with); 2.escape; 3.run away; 4.go through

darrich/gucke, v.; darichgeguckt, pp. look through

darrich/hacke, v.; darichghockt, pp. 1.chop through with an ax; 2.lash until the skin breaks

darrich/kumme, v.; is darichkumme, pp. 1.come off (well); 2.come through

darrich/laafe, v.; darichgeloffe, pp. 1.run through; 2.walk through

darrich/leddere, v.; darichgeleddert, pp. thrash soundly

darrich/leichde, v.; darichgeleicht, pp. shine through

darrich/lese, v.; darichgelese, pp. 1.peruse; 2.pick over; 3.read

darrich/losse, v.; darichgelosst, pp. allow to pass through

darrich/mache, v.; darichgemacht, pp. 1.bear; 2.endure; 3.experience

darrich/nemme, v.; darichgnumme, pp. take through

darrich/reese, v.; darichgereest, pp. 1.travel through; 2.traverse

darrich/reide, v.; darichgeridde, pp. ride through

darrich/reisse, v.; darichgrisse, pp. tear in two

darrich/reiwe, v.; darichgeriwwe, pp. 1.chafe; 2.rub through

darrich/renne, v.; darichgerennt, pp. 1.pierce; 2.puncture

darrich/rooschde, v.; darichgerooscht, pp.roast (thoroughly)

darrich/rutsche, v.; darichgerutscht, pp. wear through by rubbing

darrich/schaffe, v.; darichgschafft, pp. (si ch --) make one's way under difficulties

darrich/schaudre, v.; darichgschaudert, pp. 1.shudder; 2.thrill

darrich/scheine, v.; darichgscheint, pp. shine through

darrich/schiesse, v.; darichgschosse, pp. 1.get streaked; 2. shoot through; 3.spread (of colors)

darrich/schimmere, v.; darichgschimmert, pp. glimmer through

darrich/schinne, v.; darichschunne, pp. skin through (get through with difficulty)

darrich/schlagge, v.; darichgschlacht, pp. 1.force one's way through; 2.get through as best as one can 3.soak through

darrich/schleefe, v.; darichgschleeft, pp. drag through

darrich/schlibbe, v.; darichgschlippt, pp. 1.escape; 2.slip through

darrich/schlitze, v.; darichgschlitzt, pp. slit through

darrich/schluppe, v.; darichgschluppt, pp. creep through

darrich/schneide, v.; darichgschnidde, pp. 1.cut in two; 2.cut through; 3.intersect

darrich/schnuffle, v.; darichgschnuffelt, pp. 1.rummage; 2.snoop through

darrich/schtecke, v.; darichgschteckt; darichgschtocke, pp. 1.pierce; 2.puncture; 3.stick through

darrich/schteh, v.; darichschtanne, pp. endure to the end

darrich/schtewwere, v.; darichgschtewwert, pp.

Darrlogel

1.rummage; 2.search in every part

darrich/schtreiche, v.; darichgschtriche, pp. 1.cancel; 2.make a mark through

darrich/sehne, v.; darichgsehne, pp. 1.look over (a book); 2.look through; 3.see through

darrich/seihe, v.; darichgseiht, pp. 1.filter; 2.strain liquids; 3.strain through

darrich/setze, v.; darichgsetzt, pp. 1.carry out; 2.enforce

darrich/suche, v.; darichgsucht, pp. 1.ransack; 2.search through

darrich/suddre, v.; darichgsuddert, pp. seep through

darrich/weeche, v.; darichgweecht, pp. 1.flogthoroughly; 2.soak through

darrich/wiehle, v.; darichgewiehlt, pp. turn things topsy- turvy

darrich/witsche, v.; darichgewitscht, pp. 1.escape; 2.slip through

darrich/wolle, v.; darichgewollt, pp. want to go through

darrich/yaage, v.; darichgeyaagt, pp. 1.chase or drive through; 2.squander

darrich/ziehe, v.; darichgezoge, pp. pull or drag through

darrich/zucke, v.; darichgezucht, pp. 1.shudder; 2.twitch

darrich/zwenge, v.; darichzwengt, pp. force (an object) through

darrich/zwinge, v.; darichgezwunge, pp. force a plan through

darrich, adj. tarry (of tar)

darrich, adj. (-- un --) thoroughly

darrich, adv. 1.through; 2.throughout

darrich, prep. during

darrichaus, adv. 1.by all means; 2.on the whole; 3.positively; 4.throughout; 5.(net --) on no account

Darrichbringer (der)n.; Darichbringer, pl. spendthrift

darrichdringlich, adj. penetrable

darrichdriwwe, adj. 1.mischievous; 2.sly

darrichdriwwne Schwammbeere (die)n. strained cranberries

darrichfaahre, adj. 1.streaked; 2.veined

Darrichfall (der)n. diarrhea

Darrichlaaf (der)n. 1.diarrhea; 2.dysentery

darrichnanner/mache, v.; darichnannergemacht, pp.1.jumble up; 2.turn things topsy-turvy

darrichnannergraddle, v.; darichnannergegraddelt, pp.crawl around in great confusion

darrichnannerwiehle, v. turn things topsy-turvy

darrichnass, adj. wet through

darrichschlachdich, adj. variegated

Darrichschnitt (der)n. 1.average; 2.(so im --) on the average

darrichschnittlich, adv. on the average

darrichsichdich, adj. 1.diaphanous; 2.transparent

Darrichwax (der)n. thoroughwort

Darrichwax Tee (der)n. boneset tea

Darrichzuck (der)n. main beam (in a building)

Darradee (die)n. Dorothy

darre, v.; gedarrt, pp. tar

darre, v.; gedatt, pp. 1.cure; 2.dry

Darrlogel (der)n. tar-keg (suspended from the axle of a wagon on long trips)

Dd

Darrlokel — daumesdick

Darrlokel (der)n. tar-keg (suspended from the axle of a wagon on long trips)

Darrschtengel (der)n. sleepy catchfly

Darryockel (der)n. tar-keg (suspended from the axle of a wagon on long trips)

da(r)schdich, adj. thirsty

Da(r)scht (der)n. thirst

dart, adj. there

das, conj. since

das, conj.; prep. than

das, pron.; adj.; conj. that

Dasch (die)n. 1.mouth; 2.pocket (rare usage)

datt drunne, adv. down there

datt(de)mit, adv. with that

datt-driwwer-draus, adv. superior to that

datt, adj. there

datt, adv. yonder

dattanne, adv. 1.into that place (with a verb of motion); 2.thither

dattdarrich, adv. through here

dattdarrichnaus, adv. out through there

dattdarrichnei, adv. 1.in that direction; 2.in through there

dattdarrichniwwer, adv. over through there

dattdarrichnuff, adv. up through there

dattdarrichnunner, adv. down through there

dattdarrichraus, adv. out through there

dattdarrichrei, adv. in through there

dattdarrichriwwer, adv. over through there

dattdarrichrunner, adv. down through there

dattdazu, adv. to that

dattdebei, adv. by that

dattdefor, adv. for that

dattdegege, adv. against that

dattdehinner, adv. 1.back of that; 2.behind that

dattdenewe, adv. there by the side of

dattdevor, adv. in front of that

dattdevun, adv. 1.from that; 2.of that

dattdezu, adv. 1.in addition to that; 2.to that

dattdezwische, adv. in between there

dattdraa, adv. at that

dattdraahi, adv. along there

dattdraanaus, adv. out along there

dattdraaniwwer, adv. out along there

dattdraanuff, adv. up along there

dattdraanunner, adv. down along there

dattdraariwwer, adv. over along there

dattdraus, adv. out there

dattdrinn, adv. in there

dattdriwwer, adv. over that

dattdriwwerdraus, adv. 1.out over that; 2.superior to that

dattdrowwe, adv. up there

dattdruff, adv. 1.on that; 2.on there

dattdruffhie, adv. 1.along that; 2.on the strength of that

dattdruffzus, adv. up that way

dattdrum, adv. about that

dattdrunne, adv. down there

dattdrunner, adv. under that

Datte, 1. name of the Jewish game of cards localized in Allentown, PA; 2. (en --) a run of three cards of the same suit (the seven spot being the lowest card in the deck) in the game of Datte

datte, adj. there

dattebella queen, king and ace, or jack queen and king of trumps in the game of Datte

datthaer, adv. 1.along there; 2.(vun --) from there

datthaerzus, adv. from along there

datthie, adv. there (motion thither)

datthinewe, adv. along the side there

datthinne, adv. back there

datthinnri, adv. back there (with a verb of motion)

datthinnrizus, adv. back in that direction

datthizus, adv. along there

dattmit, adj. with that

dattnaus, adv. out there

dattnauszus, adv. out in that direction

dattnei, adv. 1.in that direction; 2.in there

dattneizus, adv. in that direction

dattnewe, adv. along the side there

dattniwwer, adv. over there

dattniwwerzus, adv. off over in that direction

dattnuff, adv. up there

dattnuffzus, adv. up in that direction

dattnunner, adv. down there

dattnunnerzus, adv. down in that direction

dattraus, adv. out from there

dattrauszus, adv. out from that direction

dattrei, adv. from that direction

dattreizus, adv. in from that direction

dattriwwer, adv. over that way

dattruff, adv. up there

dattrum, adv. thereabout

dattrunner, adv. down that way

dattrunnerzus, adv. down in that direction

dattvaerizus, adv. up front there

dattvaerri, adv. forward there

dattvanne, adv. there in front

dattzerick, adv. back there

dattzerickzus, adv. off back in that direction

Dau (der)n. dew

Daub (die)n.; Dauwe, pl. 1.dove; 2.pigeon; 3.stave of a barrel; 4.(yungi --) squab

Daubert (der)n. male pigeon

dauche, v.; gedaucht, pp. dive

daue, v.; gedaut, pp. 1.melt; 2.thaw

Dauer (die)n. duration

dauere, v.; gedauert, pp. 1.continue; 2.endure; 3.last; 4.pity (to excite pity)

dauerhaft, adj. 1.durable; 2.lasting; 3.strong

dauerunschaad (es is --) it is a great pity

Daume (der)n. thumb

Daumenaggel (der)n. thumbnail

daumesdick, adj. thick as a thumb

Dd

Daumesuckler — Deihenker

Daumesuckler (der)n.; Daumesuckler, pl. thumb-sucking child
Daumling (der)n. 1.thimble; 2.thumb stall
dauschber, adv. 1.dim; 2.twilight
dauschder, adv. 1.dusk; 2.twilight
daused, adj.; pron. thousand
dausellaanisch, adv. awfully (a playfully exaggerating compound)
dausend, adj.; pron. thousand
Dausendfiesser (der)n. 1.millipede; 2.thousand-legger
Dausendgildegraut (es)n. 1.American centaury; 2.bitter-bloom; 3.gentian
dausendmol, adv. thousand times
Dausendreich (es)n. millennium
dausendsapperlott!, interj. gee whiz!
dausendyaehrich Reich (es)n. millennium
dausendyaehrich, adj. millennial
dausich! (ei der --) dear me!
Dauwedieb (der)n. chicken hawk
Dauwegropp (der)n. 1.fumitory; 2.pigeon's crop
Dauwekaschde (der)n. dove-cote
Dauwemillich (die)n. pigeon's milk
Dauwemischt (der)n. pigeon droppings
Dauwenescht (es)n. dove's nest
davun/kumme, v.; davunkumme, pp. recuperate
Dax (der)n. short-legged dog
Daxi (der)n. (glee --) shorty
daxich, adj. stooped
dazu, adv. 1.besides; 2.too
Debbich (der)n. 1.bedspread; 2.quilt
debei, prep. 1.among; 2.by that; 3.along with
debeibliewe, v.; debeigebliwwe, pp. 1.stay with; 2.stick with
debeischteh, v.; debeigschtanne, pp. stand (by one's contentions)
debeisitze, v.; debeigsitzt, pp. sit by
Dechsel (der)n. adze
dechsle, v.; gedechselt, pp. 1.hollow out; 2.thrash; 3.trim down
Deck (die)n. 1.ceiling; 2.cover
Deckbett (es)n. 1.coverlet; 2.featherbed
decke, v.; gedeckt, pp. 1.cover; 2.put roof on; 3.thatch
Deckel (der)n. 1.hat; 2.lid
Deckelglaas (es)n. glass with a lid
Deckelkann (die)n. can with a lid
Decking (die)n. cover
dedarrich, adj. 1.by this means; 2.in this way; 3.through this
deediche, v.; gedeedicht, pp. 1.cause death; 2.kill
deedlich, adj. fatal
Deeg (der)n. dough
Deeg schaffe (der)n. knead dough
deegich, adj. doughy
Deel (es)n., pl. 1.part; 2.share
deel, adj.; pron. some
deel weis, adv. 1.partly; 2.partially
Deele (es)n. some
deele, v.; gedeelt, pp. 1.deal (out); 2.deal (with); 3.divide; 4.part; 5.share
Deeler (die)n. 1.part; 2.share

deelmol, adv. sometimes
deels, adv. partly
deemiedich, adj. humble
Deer (die)n. door
Deer(e)schwell (die)n.; Deer(e)schwelle, pl. 1.doorsill; 2.threshold
Deerche (es)n. small gate
Deereband (es)n. hinge of a door
Deeregnopp (der)n. doorknob
Deerehenk (die)n. door hook
Deereriggel (der)n. bolt of a door
Deereschlissel (der)n. door key
Deereschloss (es)n. door lock
Deerhieter (der)n. porter
deerich(t), adj. foolish
Deerli (es)n. small gate
deete, v.; gedeet, pp. kill
deffendiere, v.; deffendiert, pp. (sich --) 1.defend (oneself); 2.excuse (oneself)
defor 1.for it; 2.in favor of; 3.(-- sei) be in favor of it; 4.(ich kann nix --) I can't help it
Dege (der)n. sword
degege, adv. 1.against it; 2.(ich hab nix --) I have no objections
degleiche, dem. pronoun; the like
degschwische (drin), adv. (in) between
deheem, adv. at home
dehi, adv. 1.along; 2.thither; 3.done for
dehibringe, v.; dehigebrocht, pp. 1.accomplish; 2.bring about
dehinne, adv. back (in, by, at)
dehinner, adv. 1.back of it; 2.behind
dei, adj.(singular); (eier plural) your
deich, adv. 1.I think; 2.I guess; 3.I suppose; 4.no doubt; 5.perhaps
Deich (es)n.; Deicher, pl. 1.dale (depression, hollow); 2.pond; 3.pool; 4.puddle; 5.valley
deich(l)e, v.; gedeich(el)t, pp. lay drain pipes
deich, prep. during
Deichel (es)n.; Deichle, pl. pipe (conduit)
Deichelschneider (der)n.; Deichelschneider, pl. pipe wrench
Deichsel (die)n. 1.human tongue (humorously); 2.pole; 3.wagon tongue
Deichselkett (die)n. pole chain
Deichselnaggel (der)n. pole pin
Deichselscher (die)n. hounds (of a wagon)
Deichselschnall (die)n. buckle on pole strap
deide, v.; gedeidt, pp. point
deier, adj. 1.costly; 2.dear; 3.expensive
Deifel (der)n. 1.Devil; 2.slater's stake
Deifelsabbisswarzel (die)n. 1.devil's bit; 2.flaming star
Deifelszung (die)n. prickly pear
Deifelzeit (die)n. 1.Daylight Saving Time; 2."devil's time"; 3."fast time"
deifle, v.; gedeifelt, pp. 1.bedevil; 2.dare; 3.devil; 4.torment
deiflisch, adj. devilish
Deihenker (die)n. 1.deuce; 2.devil; 3.(der -- is los) there's the devil to pay

Dd

deihenkers / desgleiches

deihenkers, adv. deucedly
deimele, v.; gedeimelt, pp. press with the thumb
Deimling (der)n. 1.thumb bandage; 2.thumb stall
deinesgleiche, indecl. pronoun 1.such as you; 2.your equal
deite, v.; gedeit, pp. 1.explain; 2.point
Deiter (der)n. pointer
deitlich, adj. 1.clear; 2.distinct; 3.explicit; 4.plain
deitsch, adj. German
Deitsch, n.; adj. (Pennsylvania) Dutch
Deitscher (en)n. 1.a German; 2.a Dutchman
Deitscher Kees (der)n. Dutch cheese
Deitschland (es)n. Germany
Deitschlenner (der)n. German (born in Germany)
deitschlennerisch, adj. German
Deiwel (der)n. 1.Devil; 2.slater's stake; 3.(armer --) wretch; 4.(geh zum --) (a) go to the devil; (b).go to hell; 5.(hols der --) sure as fate
deiwelheftich, adj. 1.fearfully; 2.madly
Deiwelsabbis (watzel) (die)n. 1.ague root; 2.colic root; 3.devil's bit; 4.flaming star; 5.golden root; 6.lion's foot; 7.rattlesnake root; 8.unicorn root
Deiwelsdreck (der)n. asafoetida
Deiwelsgewalt (die) (mit --) 1.by all means; 2.with all might
Deiwelskatz (die)n. hell-cat
Deiwelsloch (es)n. cave
deiwle, v.; gedeiwelt, pp. 1.bedevil; 2.devil; 3.torment
deiwlisch, adj. devilish
Deixel (die)n.; Deixle, pl. 1.tongue (human) (humorous usage); 2.wagon-tongue
Deixel!, interj. what the dickens!
Deixelkett (die)n.; Deixelkedde, pl. pole-chain
Deixelnaggel (der)n. pole-pin
Dekterei (die)n. 1.doctoring; 2.dosing (continued); 3. practice of medicine
Delbel (der)n. 1.awkward fellow; 2.yokel
Delbelyaahre (die)n.,pl. 1.awkward years; 2.years of indiscretion
delkich, adj. soggy
Dell (die)n. 1.dell; 2.dent; 3.dimple; 4.impression
Deller (der)n.; Deller, pl. 1.plate; 2.(en erde --) earthen plate
Dellerduch (es)n.; Dellerdicher, pl. 1.napkin; 2.serviette
Dellervoll (der)n. plateful
dem no(och), adv. evidently
Demant (der)n. diamond
demariye, adv. 1.the coming morning (used with a verb in the past, present or future tense); 2.the past morning; 3.this morning
demiedich, adj. humble
demiediche, v.; gedemiedicht, pp. 1.humble; 2.mortify
demit, adv. therewith
demmere, v.; gedemmert, pp. become dusk
Demmerung (die)n. 1.dawn; 2.twilight
demmiddaag, adj. 1.at noon; 2.today noon
demno(och), adv. 1.accordingly; 2.evidently; 3.seemingly
demograadisch, adj. Democratic
Demograat (der)n.; Demograade, pl. Democrat

dempe, v.; gedempt, pp. 1.boil; 2.dampen; 3.stew
Demut (die)n. humility
den Mariye, adv. this morning
den, def. art. the
den, dem. adj. this
denewe/kumme, v.; denewekumme, pp. 1.fail to hit the mark; 2.miss
denewe, adv. 1.at the same time; 2.by the side of
Dengelhammer (der)n.; Dengelhemmer, pl. hammer (for sharpening scythes)
Dengelschtock (der)n.; Dengelschteck, pl. scythe-anvil
dengle, v.; gedengelt, pp. sharpen by hammering out
Dengler (der)n. 1.one who hammers out iron at a forge; 2.(eisi --) one who hammers out iron at a forge
denkbaar, adj. thinkable
denke, v.; gedenkt, pp. 1.imagine; 2.think
Denki (der)n. 1.thanks; 2.(-- saage) thank
Denki! 1.thanks!; 2.thank you!
Denkmol (es)n. 1.memorial; 2.monument
Denkseckli (es)n.; Denksecklin, pl. reminder
Denkzeddel (der)n. reminder
Denkzeeche (es)n. 1.remembrance; 2.reminder
Denkzeige (es)n. remembrance
Denn (die)n. threshing-floor
denn, conj. for (rare usage)
denneweg, adv.1.after this fashion;2.as follows; 3.this way
denno, adv. 1.about it; 2.accordingly; 3.at it
dennoch, adv. accordingly
dennooch, adv. thereafter
dennord, adv. 1.accordingly; 2.after that; 3. subsequently; 4.then
dennort, adv. subsequently
dennot = dennot after that
Dennwand (die)n. threshing-floor wall
denowed, adv. 1.the coming evening (used with a verb in the past, present or future); 2.the past evening; 3.this evening
dense, v.; gedenselt, pp. 1.dance; 2.prance (of a horse)
Denser (der)n. dancer
der, def. art. the
der, pron.; adj.; conj. that
dergleiche, adv. 1.such like; 2.too; 3.(un so --) etc.
derno, adv. 1.after (that); 2.then; 3.afterward(s); 4.subsequently; 5.thereafter; 6.(es is aa --) it is what you would expect
dernooch, adv. thereafter
des(s)emol, adv. this time
des, def. art. the
des, dem. adj. this
des, pron.; adj.; conj. that
Desch (die)n. 1.mouth; 2.vagina
Deschelgraut (es)n. shepherd's purse (also false flax from the similarity of the two plants)
deschperaat, adj. desperate
desde (besser) so much the (better)
desgleiches, adv. 1.the like; 2.too
desgleiches, pron. 1.the like; 2.the same kind

Dd

desmol

desmol, adv. this time
deswege, adv. 1.on that account; 2.for that reason; 3.therefore
Detlausdaag (der)n. Detlaus Day (March 31)
detschle, v.; gedetschelt, pp. pat
devor, adv. before
devun/bleiwe, v.; is devungebliwwe, pp. abstain
devun, adv. 1.away; 2.from it; 3.of it; 4.of that; 5.therefore
devunbringe, v. 1.cause to survive; 2.save
devunfaahre, v. drive away from
devungeh, v. 1.walk off; 2.secede
devungriege, v. 1.get some of; 2.get (someone) away from
devunkumme, v. 1.escape; 2.survive
devunlaafe, v. walk away from
devunnemme, v. 1.partake of; 2.take away from
dewedder, prep. against (it)
deweddermache, v.; deweddergemacht, pp. 1.continue;
    2.fasten to; 3.keep at it
dewege 1.about it; 2.on account of it
deweil, conj. because
dewek, adv. along
Dexel (der)n. adze
dexle, v.; gedexelt, pp. 1.thrash; 2.trim down
Dezember (der)n. December
dezu, adv. 1.also; 2.besides; 3.in addition; 4.to that
dezu, adv. (sie sinn -- nei) they went in pellmell
dezuduh, v.; dezugeduh, pp. 1.add; 2.put in addition
dezukeere, v.; dezugekeert, pp. belong to
dezukumme, v.; is dezukumme, pp. arrive unexpectedly
dezulege, v.; dezugeleegt, pp. lay with
dezumache, v.; dezugemacht, pp. add to
dezurechle, v.; dezugerechelt, pp. reckon in
dezuschticke, v.; dezugschtickt, pp. 1.persevere; 2.persist
dezuschtolpere, v.; dezugschtolpert, pp. come upon
    unexpectedly
dezusetze, v.; dezugsetzt, pp. add to
dezuzehle, v.; dezugegehlt, pp. count in
dezwische, prep. between
dezwischedarrich, adv. through the midst of
dezwischekumme, v. 1.get in between; 2.intervene
dezwischelege, v. lay between
dezwischerede, v. 1.intercede; 2.intermeddle
dezwischeschteh, v. stand between
Dibbel (der)n. dot
dibbeldaanisch, adj. 1.dappled; 2.polka-dotted; 3.spotted
dibbeldunich, adj. 1.dappled; 2.polka-dotted; 3.spotted
dibblich, adj. dappled
dich, (acc.) pron. you
Dichder (der)n.; Dichder, pl. poet
Dichelche (es)n. small cloth
Dicher (der)n. tiger
Dicherlilye (die)n. tiger lily
dichscht, adj. 1.closest; 2.densest
dicht, adv. 1.close; 2.dense; 3.near by
Dichte (die)n., pl. verses
dichter, adj. 1.closer; 2.denser
dichtich, adj. 1.capable; 2.thorough

Dimmelwedder

dichtichlich, adj. thoroughly
dichtsichdich, adj. shortsighted
dick, adj. 1.dense; 2.fat; 3.plump; 4.stout; 5.thick
dickbackich, adj. full-cheeked
Dickbauch (der)n. paunchy person
Dickhals (der)n.; Dickhels, pl. swelling of the neck or throat
Dicking (die)n. thickness
dickkebbich, adj. thickheaded
Dickkopp (der)n. 1.blockhead; 2.self-willed person;
    3.tadpole
dickleiwich, adj. 1.bloated (of animals); 2.constipated;
    3.pot bellied
Dickmillich (die)n. thick-milk
Dicksack (der)n.; Dickseck, pl. potbelly
dickseckisch, adj. paunchy
Dickwazel (die)n.; Dickwazle, pl. mangel-wurzel (root)
    (Waterloo Co. Ontario)
Diddi (der)n. 1.mother's breast; 2.mother's milk; 3.teat; 4.titty
Die Faasnacht kummt hinneno! You old slowpoke!
die wu, pron. those who
die, def. art. the
die, dem. adj. this
Dieb (der)n.; Dieb, pl. 1.burglar; 2.robber; 3.thief
Diebschtaahl (der)n. 1.larceny; 2.theft
diedeldum deido (imitative of jolly music), fiddle-de-dee
Diedre (der)n. Theodoric
dief/denke, v.; diefgedenkt, pp. meditate
dief, adj. 1.deep; 2.profound
Diefing (die)n. depth
diefsinnich, adj. thoughtful
diene, v.; gedient, pp. serve
Diener (der)n.; Diener, pl. 1.clergyman; 2.preacher; 3.servant
Diener der Armen (der)n. deacon (Old Order Amish usage)
Diener zum Watt (Buch) (der)n. minister (Old Order
    Amish Usage)
Dienscht (der)n. (es hot sei --e gedu) it has served its purpose
Dier (die)n.; Diere, pl. door
Dier (es)n.; Diere, pl. (small) animal
Dierche (es)n. 1.gate; 2.small gate; 3.small animal
Diere (die)n., pl. (uffni --) open doors
Dieregaarde (der)n. zoological garden
Dieregschtell (es)n. door frame
Diereschwell (die)n. threshold
Dierknopp (der)n.; Diergnepp, pl. doorknob
Dierli (es)n.; Dierlin, pl. 1.gate; 2.small animal
Dierli-Poschde (der)n.; Dierli-Poschde, pl. gatepost
dies, adj. 1.(so um -- Zeit) so at this time; 2.this (rare usage)
Diesember (der)n. December
Dietli (es)n. dittany
dieweil, conj. while
diewoch, adv. this last week
diezeit, adv. since then
Dill (der)n. dill
Dimmel (es)n. thunder
dimmele, v.; gedimmelt, pp. thunder
Dimmelwedder (es)n. thunderstorm

Dd

Dinde — Dodegraawer

Dinde (der)n. ink
Dindebeer (die)n. 1.poke; 2.pokeweed
Dindeblacke (der)n. ink spot
Dindeboddel (der)n.; Dindeboddle, pl. inkstand
Dindefass (es)n. inkstand
Dindefleck (die)n. ink spot
Dindeglaas (es)n.; Dindeglesser, pl. inkstand
Ding (es)n.; Dinger, pl. 1.thing; 2.(verglinselt --) spoiled
    (or over- indulged) child
dinge, v.; gedingt, gedunge, pp. 1.employ; 2.fertilize;
    3.hire; 4.manure
Dingel(che) (es)n. little thing
Dingrich (der)n. fellow
dings 1.things like that; 2.(kuchedings) used also as end-
    ing of a compound noun, adding the meaning of a
    collection of or variety; 3.(un so --) and so forth
dings mache, v. tell stories
dinke, v.; gedinkt, pp. 1.seem; 2.(sich --) consider one's
    self; 3.(dinkt's dich net) does it not seem to you?; 4.
    (es dinkt mich) it seems to me
dinn, adj. 1.shallow; 2.slender; 3.thin
dinne, v.; gedinnt, pp. thin (out)
dinne Deeg (der)n. batter (for apple fritters)
dinnere, v.; gedinnert, pp. thin out
dinnleiwich, adj. 1.having loose bowels; 2.lanky (person)
dinnschaalich, adj. 1.thin shelled; 2.thin skinned
dinnschwensich, adj. thin-stemmed
Dinschdaag (der)n. Tuesday
dinschdlich, adj. serviceable
Dinscht (der)n. 1.service; 2.(worship) service
Dinschtmeedel (es)n. servant girl
dipplich, adj. spotted
dir, (dative) pron. you
Disch (der)n.; Disch, pl. table
Disch(d)el (die)n.; Dischdle, pl. common thistle
Dischbedaat (der)n. 1.argument; 2.dispute
dischbediere, v.; gedischbediert, pp. 1.argue; 2.dispute
Dischbee (es)n. table leg
Dischblaat (es)n. table leaf
Dischdelfink (die)n. goldfinch
dischder, adj. 1.dim; 2.dusk
dischdere, v.; gedischdert, pp. 1.quiet; 2.pacify; 3.soothe
dischdilliere, v.; gedischdilliert, pp. distill
dischdre, v.; gedischdert, pp. 1.quiet; 2.pacify; 3.sooth
Dischduch (es)n.; Dischdicher, pl. tablecloth
Dischfliggel (der)n. leaf of a table
Dischgawwel (die)n. table fork
Dischgscharr (es)n. dishes
Dischlappe (der)n. dishcloth
Dischligraut (es)n. wild pepper grass
Dischlumbe (der)n. dishcloth
Dischmacher (der)n. cabinetmaker
Dischmesser (es)n. table knife
Dittli (es)n. teat
Ditz (der)n.; Ditze, pl. 1.nipple; 2.teat
Ditzboddel (die)n.; Ditzboddle, pl. 1.milk bottle; 2.nursing
bottle
Ditzli (es)n.; Ditzlin, pl. 1.nipple; 2.teat
diweil, conj. 1.as; 2.while
dizeit, conj. (-- as) since
do degschwische, adv. (in) between
do howwe, adv. up here
do un datt, adv. here and there
do vergange, adv. 1.recently; 2.some time ago
do yetz, adv. recently
do(de)mit, adv. with this
do, adv. here
doanne, adv. 1.here; 2.in this place (with a verb of motion)
dobbel(t), adj. double
dobbel-gsichdich, adj. double (two)-faced
dobbel-laafich, adj. double-barreled
dobbel-schteenich, adj. plaid
dobbel-sinnich, adj. ambiguous
dobble, v.; gedobbelt, pp. double
Dobe (die)n. paw
dobleiwe, v.; dogebliwwe, pp. stay here
doch, adv. 1.anyway; 2.surely; 3.though; 4.to be sure; 5.yet
doch, conj. (er hut's -- gedu) 1.he did it, didn't he?; 2.he
    did it after all
Dochdermann (der)n. son-in-law
Docher (die)n.; Dochdere; Dechder, pl. daughter
Docht (der)n. wick
Dock(e) (die)n. bundle of flax (for spinning)
dock(e), v.; gedockt, pp. put (flax) into bundles for spinning
Dod (der)n. death
Dod(e)sbett (es)n. deathbed
Dod(es)angscht (die)n. paralyzing fear
dod(es)angscht, adv. deathly fear
dod/mache, v.; dodgemacht, pp. kill
dod, adj. 1.dead; 2.(en --es) corpse
dodarrich, adv. 1.through here; 2.through this section
dodarrichnaus, adv. out through here
dodarrichnei, adv. 1.in this direction; 2.in through here
dodarrichniwwer, adv. over in this direction
dodarrichnuff, adv. up through here
dodarrichnunner, adv. down through here
dodarrichraus, adv. out through here
dodarrichrei, adv. over through here
dodarrichriwwer, adv. over through here
dodarrichruff, adv. up through here
dodarrichrunner, adv. down through here
Dodder (der)n. 1.dodder; 2.false flax; 3.shepherd's purse;
    4.yolk of an egg
Dode-ausleger (der)n. undertaker
dodebei, adv. by this
dodedarrich, adv. through this
Dodedraag (die)n. bier
dodefor, adv. for this
dodegege, adv. against this
Dodegleed (es)n. shroud
Dodeglocke (die)n. 1.funeral bell; 2.knell
Dodegraawer (der)n. grave digger

Dd

dodehinner — dorunnerzus

dodehinner, adv. 1.back of this; 2.behind this
Dodekutsch (die)n. hearse
Dodelaad (die)n. coffin
Dodelischt (die)n. 1.list of the dead; 2.obituary
Dodemann (der)n. undertaker
dodenewe, adv. alongside here
dodenno, adv. 1.according to this; 2.after this
Dodesduch (es)n.; Dodesdicher, pl. shroud
Dodesfall (der)n. death
Dodesgleeder (es), pl. shroud
Dodeshunger (der) n. death hunger (if the patient who is mortally ill eats, he will die)
Dodeuhr (die)n. deathwatch
dodevor, adv. before this
dodevun, adv. 1.from this; 2.of this
Dodewaage (der)n.; Dodeweege, pl. hearse
dodewege, adv. 1.from this; 2.of this
Dodezeeche (der)n. death omen
dodgebore, adj. still born
dodgrank, adj. dangerously ill
dodlich, adj. fatal
dodmache, v.; dotgemacht, pp. kill
Dodmacherei (die)n. murder
dodmied, adj. dead tired
dodraa, adv. at this
dodraahie, adv. along here
dodraanaus, adv. out along here
dodrauss, adv. out here
dodrin, adv. in here
dodriwwe, adv. over here
dodriwwer, adv. over this
dodrowwe, adv. up here
dodruff, adv. on here
dodruffhie, adv. 1.along on this side; 2.on the strength of
dodrum, adj. about this
dodrunne, adv. down here
dodrunner, adv. under this
Dodschlack (der)n. manslaughter
Dodschlaeger (der)n. murderer
dodschlagge, v.; dodgschlagge, pp. 1.kill; 2.slay
dohaer, adv. 1.along here; 2.hence; 3.hither
dohaerzus, adv. along here
dohaus, adv. out here
dohie, adv. 1.along this way; 2.here; 3.to this place
dohiefaahre, v. drive along
dohiefalle, v. 1.fall; 2.stumble
dohiezus, adv. along here
dohinne, adv. back here
dohinnrie, adv. back (here) (with a verb of motion)
dohinnriezus, adv. off back in this direction
dohiwwe, adv. 1.on this side; 2.over here
Dohl (es)n. underground conduit for water
dohunne, adv. down here
Dokder (der)n.; Dokder, pl. 1.doctor; 2.physician
Dokder Eisebaart (der)n. (Dr.) Ironbeard = a famous German physician of the 18th century whose cures are

celebrated in a popular P.G. folk song
Dokdersach (es)n. medicine
Dokterbuch (es)n. 1.home doctor; 2.medical work
doktere, v.; gedoktert, pp. 1.adulterate; 2.be attended by a physician; 3.practice medicine; 4.take medicine
Dokterfraa (die) n. woman who dispenses homemade remedies
Dokterschtofft (es)n. medicine
Dolch (der)n. dagger
doll, adj. 1.distracted; 2.frantic; 3.mad; 4.rabid
Dollebaan (die)n. tulip
Dollfuus (der)n. 1.club foot; 2.misshapen foot
dolmetsche, v.; gedolmetscht, pp. 1.explain; 2.gossip; 3.harangue wildly; 4.interpret
Dolmetscher (der)n. interpreter
Dolmetschung (die)n. interpretation
dolmos, adv. at that time
Dominod (der)n.; Dominode, pl. domino (rectangular wooden block with numbers used for playing a game)
domit, adv. with this
Don(i) (der)n. Anthony
donaus, adv. out here
donauszus, adv. out in this direction
donei, adv. in here
doneizus, adv. off in this direction
doniwwer, adv. 1.over here; 2.to the other side
doniwwerzus, adv. off over in that direction
donuff, adv. up here
donuffzus, adv. up in this direction
donunnerzus, adv. down here
Dood (der)n. death
dood/mache, v.; doodgemacht, pp. slay
dood/schlaage, v.; doodgschlaage, pp. slay
Doodebaahr (die)n. bier
Doodes (en)n. a corpse
Doodschlack (der)n. manslaughter
doot, adj. 1.dead; 2.deceased
dootzeidich, adj. old enough to die
Dopp (der)n. top (of a tree)
doppe, v.; gedoppt, pp. (to) top (corn or a tree)
Dor (es)n.; Dore, pl. gate
doraus, adv. out here
dorauszus, adv. out this way
dorei, adv. in here
doreizus, adv. in this way
Doreposchde (der)n.; Doreposchde, pl. gatepost
Dorf (es)n. village (in nursery rhyme only)
Dorheet (die)n. folly
Dorheit (die)n. folly
Dori (der)n. Theodore
Dorn (die)n. thorn
doruff, adv. up here
doruffzus, adv. up this way
dorum, adv. 1.around here; 2.hereabouts
dorunner, adv. down here
dorunnerzus, adv. down this way

Dd

Dos

Dos (die)n. dose
Dottel (der)n. simple person
Dotterblumm (die)n. 1.cowslip; 2.marsh marigold
dottlich, adj. 1.anxious; 2.on tenterhooks
dovaerri, adv. forward here
dovaerrizus, adv. up front here
dovanne, adv. here in front
dowe, v.; gedopt, pp. 1.bluster; 2.rage
Dowwes (der)n. Tobias
dozerick, adv. back in this direction
dozerickzus, adv. back this way
dozumol, adv. 1.at that time; 2.then
draa, adv. at (about, near, of) it
draadenke, v.; draagedenkt, pp. think of it
draaduh, v.; draageduh, pp. 1.add to; 2.put (some one to doing something)
draafehle, v.; draagfehlt, pp. (to be) lacking in something
Draag (die)n. frame on which something is carried
draage, v.; gedraage, pp. 1.bear; 2.carry; 3.drag; 4.wear
draageh, v.; draagange, pp. begin (something)
draagend, adj. with young
Draaget (die)n. as much as one can carry
draagich, adj. with young
draaglaawe, v.; draageglaabt, pp. believe in it
draagriege, v.; draagrickt, pp. get (someone) to do (something)
Draagsack (der)n. uterus of animals
draahalde, v.; draaghalde, pp. (sich --) keep at it
draahenke, v.; draaghenkt, pp. 1.be continually at something; 2.hang (something) at it
draakumme, v.; is draakumme, pp. get to do something
Draam (der)n.; Draame, pl. dream
draamache, v.; draagemacht, pp. (sich --)begin to do something
Draambuch (es)n. dream book
draame, v.; gedraamt, pp. dream
Draamerei, (die)n. (continued) dreaming
draamisse, v.; draagemisst, pp. be compelled to do something
draasei, v.; is draag(e)wesst, pp. 1.be at it; 2.be doing something
draawolle, v.; draagewollt, pp. (to) want to get at doing something
Drach (der) n.; Drache, pl. 1. dragon; 2. kite; 3. meteor; 4.will o' the wisp
drachde, v.; gedracht, pp. 1.pursue; 2.strive after
Dracheloch (es)n. cave
drackdiere, v.; gedrackdiert, pp. 1.abuse cruelly; 2.persecute
dradde, v.; gedratt, pp. 1.gad; 2.trot
Dradder (der)n. trotter
Draeger (der)n.; Draeger, pl. 1.bearer; 2.pallbearer; 3.porter
Draen (die)n.; Draene, pl. tear (drop)
Dramm (der)n. 1.dram; 2.rum; 3.whiskey
Drammratt (die)n. 1.sot; 2.toper
Drammsupp (die)n. soup with rum in it
Drang (der)n. 1.force; 2.forcing; 3.tenesmus
Drangsaal (der)n. 1.misery; 2.torment

Dreckweschp

Drank (der)n. 1.beverage; 2.drink
Drapp (der)n. footmark
Drassem (der)n. unused ends of warp in carpet weaving
Dratsch (die)n. 1.gadabout; 2.gossip
dratsche, v.; gedratscht, pp. 1.gossip; 2.trudge
Dratt (der)n. trot
dratte, v.; gedratt, pp. 1.gad; 2.trot
Dratter (der)n. trotter
drau(e)re, v.; gedrauert, pp. 1.grieve; 2.mourn; 3.wilt (of plants)
Draub (die)n.; Drauwe, pl. grape
draue, v.; gedraut, pp. 1.marry; 2.trust
Drauer (die)n. 1.affliction; 2.grief; 3.mourning; 4.woe
Drauergleed (es)n. mourning garment
Drauerhaus (es)n. house of mourning
drauerich, adj. 1.afflicted; 2.grief-stricken; 3.sad; 4.sorrowful
Drauerichkeet (die)n. sadness
Drauerleit (die)n., pl. mourners
Drauerlied (es)n. dirge
Drauerschtunn (die)n. hour of mourning
Drauerweide (der, die)n. weeping willow
draus(s) prep.; adv. 1.out; 2.outside
draus, adv. (es waerd nix--) nothing will come of it
drausshalde, adv. (to) keep (someone) out
drausssei, adv. (to) be out in the open
Drauwebrieh (die)n. grape juice
Drauwegrischder (es)n. grape arbor
Drauwegrischt (es)n. grape arbor
Drauwehengel (der)n. bunch of grapes
Drauwekaern (die)n. grape seed
Drauwekelter (die)n. grape or wine press
Drauwerank (die)n. grape vine
Drauweschtock (der)n.; Drauweschteck, pl. grapevine
Drauwewei (der)n. grape wine
drebsle, v.; gedrebselt, pp. 1.dribble; 2.fall in small drops
Drechder (der)n. 1.funnel; 2.hopper
Drechderblumm (die)n. 1.bindweed; 2.dogtooth violet; 3.morning glory; 4.petunia; 5.yellow adders tongue
Drechderkuche (der)n.; Drechderkuche, pl. funnel cake
drechdich, adj. with young
Dreck (der)n. 1.dirt; 2.excrement; 3.filth; 4.mud;5.refuse; 6.trifle; 7.(eenicher --) any trifle; 8.(des geht dich kenn -- aa) this is no concern of yours
Dreckhammel (der)n. filthy person
Dreckhund (der)n. 1.rascal; 2.scamp
dreckich mache, v.; dreckich gemacht, pp. make dirty
dreckich, adj. 1.dirty; 2.filthy; 3.lewd; 4.off-color; 5.soiled
Dreckloch (es)n.; Drecklecher, pl. 1.filthy habitation; 2.mud hole; 3.pool; 4.puddle
Dreckriwwel (die)n. roll of dirt (formed on body by rubbing)
Drecksack (der)n. filthy person
Drecksau (die)n. filthy person
Dreckschlibber (der)n. pied-billed grebe
Dreckschwallem (der, die)n. mud swallow
Dreckweschp (die)n. mud wasp

Dd

dredde ... dringe

dredde, v.; gedredde, pp. 1.copulate (of a rooster);
    2.kick; 3.step; 4.tread

Dreed (der)n. kick

Dreeder (der)n. 1.kicker; 2.treadle

Dreegholz (es)n.; Dreeghelzer, pl. rolling pin

Dreelholz (es)n.; Dreelhelzer, pl. rolling pin

dreeschde, v.; gedreescht, pp. 1.comfort; 2.console

dreeschtlich, adj. consoling

dreeschtmiedich, adj. 1.dejected; 2.meditative; 3.meek

dreffe, v.; gedroffe, pp. 1.be lucky in; 2.hit; 3.strike; 4.
    (sich --) (a) chance; (b) happen

Dreffer (der)n. 1.lucky number in a lottery; 2.prize

Dreffloch (es)n. term applied to a person who guesses or
    judges correctly or who boasts of being able to do so

Drefts (die)n. 1.cheat; 2.chess

Dreh (die)n. 1.crank; 2.curve; 3.turn; 4.twist

Drehariyel (die)n. grind-organ

Drehbank (die)n.; Drehbenk, pl. turning lathe

drehe, v.; gedreht, pp. 1.menace; 2.nauseate; 3.threaten;
    4.turn; 5.twist; 6.wring (out); 7.(ebbes --) turn;
    (budder --) churn butter

Drehhendel (der)n. winch

Drehholz (es)n. rolling pin

Drehing (die)n. threat

Drei-Uhr-Schtick, n. mid-afternoon snack

drei, adj.; pron. three

Dreiangel (der)n. triangle (musical instrument)

dreibeenich, adj. three legged

dreiblettrich, adj. three leaved

Dreibraad (es)n. driving wheel

dreibt, v. drive (as the wind the clouds)

dreidoppelt, adj. three ply

dreidraehich, adj. three ply

Dreieck (es)n. triangle

dreieckich, adj. triangular

Dreieehnichkeit (die)n. trinity

dreieenich, adj. triune

dreierlee, adj. of three sorts

dreierlei, adj. of three sorts

dreifach, adj. 1.treble; 2.triple

dreifaechich mache, v. treble

Dreifuus (der)n. 1.tripod; 2.trivet;

Dreigeilswoog (die)n.; Dreigeilswooge, pl. three-horse team

dreigewwe, adj. 1.(to) give in; 2.yield

dreigucke, adj. 1.consider; 2.examine; 3.look (on)

dreihunnert, adj. three hundred

dreimische, v. (sich --) mix up in an affair

dreimol, adv. thrice

dreischlagge, v. pitch in

Dreischpitz (der)n. 1.triangle; 2.trident

dreisehne, v. 1.appear; 2.look; 3.yield a point; 4.(er hut
    arrig --) he was a sight!

dreiseidich, adj. three sided

dreisitzich, adj. three seated

dreissich, adj.; pron. thirty

dreissichscht, adj. thirtieth

dreiwe, v.; gedriwwe, pp. 1.do; 2.drive; 3.engage in; 4. put
    forth leaves; 5.(Hokes Pokes --) (to perform) magic

Dreiwer (der)n.; Dreiwer, pl. 1.coachman; 2.driver; 3.drover

Dreiwoog (die)n. triple-tree

dreiyaehrich, adj. three-year-old

dreizeh, adj.; pron. thirteen

dreizeht, adj. thirteenth

dreizinkich, adj. three-pronged

drenge, v.; gedrengt, pp. urge

Drenk (die)n. watering place

drenke, v.; gedrenkt, pp. 1.water; 2.suckle

Drenkeemer (der)n. watering bucket

Drenkloch (es)n. watering place

drenne, v.; gedrennt, pp. 1.rip; 2.separate; 3.sever

Drennung (die)n. separation

Drepp (die)n.; Drebbe, pl. step (on stairs)

Dreppsche (es)n. little drop

drepsle, v.; gedrepselt, pp. fall in small drops

Dreschbrill (die)n. goggles used by threshers

Dreschdenn (die, es)n.; Dreschdenner, pl. threshing floor

Dreschder (der)n. pomace

dresche, v.; gedrosche, pp. 1.flog; 2.thresh; 3.thrash

Drescher (der)n.; Drescher, pl. thresher

Dreschfleggel (der)n.; Dreschfleggel, pl. flail

Dresching (die)n. beating

Dreschmaschien (die) n.; Dreschmaschiene, pl. threshing
    machine

Dreschzeit (die)n. threshing time

dricke, v.; gedrickt, pp. 1.crush; 2.hug; 3.press; 4.squeeze

Dricker (der)n. trigger

Drickes (es)n. (so'n --) 1.feeling of oppression;2.pressing

drickle, v.; gedrickelt, pp. dry

Drickning (die)n. drought

drickse, v.; gedrickst, pp. 1.threaten or promise without
    fulfilling; 2. (es drickst der ganse Daag) it has been
    threatening (rain) all day

Drickser (der)n. 1.person who hesitates about doing a thing;
    2.person who holds off; 3.shrewd one in pressing a bargain

Driddel (es)n. 1.third; 2.widow's dower

drieb, adj. 1.bleak; 2.cloudy; 3.dejected (of a person);
    4.dim; 5.overcast; 6.muddy

Driebsaal (der)n. 1.distress; 2.sorrow; 3.tribulation

Driebsaal blose, adj. downcast

Dries (die)n. gland

Driese (die)n., pl. 1.(-- brenne dreck) tonsillitis;
    2.(wehe--) tonsillitis

Drill (die)n.; Drille, pl. drill

drille, v.; gedrillt, pp. 1.cause to move; 2.drill; 3.sow with a drill

Driller (der)n. turn button

drillere, v.; gedrillert, pp. trill

Drilling (der)n. 1.triplet; 2.ticking (for feather bed)

Drillseeg (die)n.; Drillseeg, pl. hacksaw

drin, adj. tangled

drin, adv. 1.in; 2.inside; 3.within

dringe, v.; gedrunge, pp. 1.(to be) urgent; 2.urge; 3.
    (druff--) insist upon

Dd

dringend — Drummegnippel

dringend, adj. urgent
Drink (der)n. drink
Drinkblech (es)n. tin cup
Drinke (es)n. 1.drink; 2.drinking; 3.strong drink
drinke, v.; gedrunke, pp. drink
Drinker (der)n. 1.drinker; 2.toper
Drinkes (es)n. beverage
Drinkgeld (es)n. tip, pourboire (on settling a bill)
Drinkschpruch (der)n. toast
Drinkwasser (es)n. drinking water
Drippelarwet (die)n. chores
dripple, v.; gedrippelt, pp. 1.copulate (of a turkey);
    2.move with short steps; 3.trample
Dritt (der)n. 1.kick; 2.tread
dritt, adj. 1.third; 2.(en --er) the figure 3; 3.tray (in cards)
dritte, v.; gedritt, pp. (sich --) (to) happen three times
Drittel (es)n. 1.third; 2.widow's dower
drittelscht, adj. last but two
drittens, adv. thirdly
driwwe, adv. 1.on the other side; 2.over there
driwweliere, v.; gedriwweliert, pp. 1.plague; 2.torment
driwwer/blose, v.; driwwergeblose, pp. blow over
driwwer, adv. 1.across; 2.in the mean while; 3.over it; 4.
    (er is --) he has recovered; 5.(es is nix --) there is
    nothing better
driwwergeh, v.; driwwergange, pp. 1.overhaul; 2.skim
    over; 3.skimp
driwwerkumme, v.; is driwwerkumme, pp. 1.recover; 2.survive
driwwerlaafe, v.; driwwergeloffe, pp. walk over
dro, adv. at (about, near, of) it
Drobbe (der)n.; Drobbe, pl. drop
drobse, v.; gedrobst, pp. drop
drobsle, v.; gedrobselt, pp. drop
droddle, v.; gedroddelt, pp. 1.go; 2.move (slowly); 3.roam
Drog (der)n.; Dreeg, pl. trough
drohde, adj. (of) wire
drohe, v.; gedroht, pp. 1.menace; 2.threaten; 3.threaten rain
Droht (der)n. 1.wax-ends; 2.wire
Drohtgaarn (es)n. shoemaker's thread
Drohtnaggel (der)n. wire nail
Drohtschtumbe, (der)n. 1.shoemaker's ends; 2.wax ends
Drohtzang (die)n.; Drohtzange, pl. (wire) pliers
droie, v.; gedroit, pp. 1.menace; 2.threaten
Droll (der)n. easy trot
Droll (die)n. gadabout
drolle, v.; gedrollt, pp. 1.jog; 2.go along at an easy trot
Drollholz (es)n.; Drollhelzer, pl. rolling pin
drollich, adj. droll
Dron (der)n. 1.fish oil; 2.throne
Dropp (der)n. 1.fellow; 2.(aarmer --) wretch
Droppe (der)n. drop
Droppe (die)n., pl. any liquid medicine
dropse,v.; gedropst,pp. 1.drip;2.fall in drops;3.rain a few drops
dropsle, v.; gedropselt, pp. 1. drip; 2. fall in drops; 3. rain
    a few drops
Droschel (die)n. thrush

Droscht (der)n. 1.consolation; 2.solace 3.(liewer --) (a)
    good Lord!; (b)oh my!
droschtmiedich, adj. 1.dejected; 2.meditative; 3.meek;
    4.satisfied
droschtreich, adj. consoling
Dross (es)n. 1.drill; 2.dross; 3.first line of a nursery rhyme
Drossel (die)n. thrush
drotze, v.; gedrotzt, pp. 1.be defiant; 2.sulk
drowwe, adv. 1.on the top; 2.overhead; 3.up above;
    4.upstairs
drowwedrauss, adv. 1.on the top; 2.up above; 3.upstairs
Druck (der)n. 1.pressure; 2.print
Druckdinde (der)n. printer's ink
drucke, adj. dry
drucke, v.; gedruckt, pp. print
Drucker (der)n.; Drucker, pl. printer
Druckerei (die)n. print shop
Drucksache (die)n., pl. printed matter
druff/blose, v.; druffgeblose, pp. blow on
druff/drehe, v.; druffgedreht, pp. turn on
druff/duh, v.; druffgeduh, pp. apply (a liquid to a surface)
druff/falle, v.; is druffgfalle, pp. fall upon
druff/verlosse, v.; verlosse, pp. (sich --) 1.depend (on
    something/someone); 2.rely upon
druff/zehle, v.; druffgezehlt, pp. count on
druff, adv. 1.(-- aus schticke) (to) insist; 2.(-- aus sei) aim at;
    3.bend one's energies towards; 4.(-- zu) directly towards
    the point or object; 5.(katz --) shortly after; 6.upon
druff, prep. on
druffanne, adv. 1.there at; 2.there on
druffbeitsche, v.; druffgebeitscht, pp. 1.beat; 2.give
    blows; 3.knock on
druffbelse, v.; druffgebelst, pp. strike or hammer on
druffbuffe, v.; druffgebuffe, pp. give a whack
druffgriege, v.; druffgrickt, pp. get blows
druffgucke, v.; druffgeguckt, pp. 1.consider; 2.look on
druffhalde, v.; druffghalde, pp. 1.beat; 2.lay on; 3. (net
    viel --) not to have much regard for
druffhie, adj. 1.on account; 2.on the strength of it
drufflos/schpringe, v.; drufflossgschprunge, pp. run wildly
drufflos/schwetze, v.; drufflossgschwetzt, pp. talk at random
drufflos, adv. vigorously
druffloss/geh, v.; drufflossgange, pp. make a dash for
druffloss/schiese, v.; drufflossgschosse, pp. shoot away
druffschnappe, v.; druffgschnappt, pp. 1.(to) die; 2.kick
    the bucket
druffundewedder, adv. 1.actively; 2.busily; 3.incessantly
Drumbel (die)n. Jew's Harp
Drumbet (die)n. 1.clarion; 2.trumpet
Drumm (die)n. 1.drum; 2.hollow cylinder for heating a room
drumm, adv. 1.about it; 2.for that reason; 3.(ich geb
    nix --) I don't care; 4.(ich bekimmer mich nix --) I
    don't concern myself about it
drummble, v.; gedrummbelt, pp. play on the Jew's harp
drumme, v.; gedrummt, pp. drum
Drummegnippel (der)n. drumstick

Dd

Drummer

Drummer (der)n. drummer
drummle, v.; gedrummelt, pp. drum with the fingers
Drummsaeg (die)n. crosscut saw
Drump (der)n. trump
drumpe, v.; gedrumpt, pp. trump
drumrum, adv. around it
Drun (der)n. fishoil
Drunk (der)n. drink
drunne, adv. 1.below (there); 2.down (there); 3.underneath
drunne, prep. under
drunner un driwwer topsy-turvy
drunner, adv. 1.among; 2.underneath
drunner, prep. under
Drupp (die)n. 1.bevy; 2.drove; 3.herd; 4.flock; 5.group
druppweis, adv. in flocks, herds or bevies
Drutsch (die)n. disreputable woman
Druwwel (der)n. 1.anxiety; 2.exertion; 3.trouble; 4.worry; 5.vexation; 6.(en --) (a) annoyance; (b) nuisance
druwwle, v.; gedruwwelt, pp. 1.trouble; 2.(sich --) worry
du ens 1.doings; 2.goings-on
du liewer Zuschtand!, interj. my goodness!
du, pron. you
Dubbe (der)n. dot
dubbich, adj. dappled
dubblich, adj. flecked
Duch (es)n.; Dicher, pl. 1.cloth; 2.handkerchief
duche, adj. cloth
Duchschtofft (es)n. cloth goods
ducke, v.; geduckt, pp. (sich --) duck
duckmeisich, adj. sneaking
Dudel (der)n. (nau geht der -- aa) now the business (work, trouble) begins
Dudelsack (der)n.; Dudelseck, pl. bagpipe
dudle, v.; gedudelt, pp. 1. hum (a melody); 2. play an instrument badly
Dudler (der)n. bad (instrument) player
dufdich, adj. 1.frosty (applied to still mornings in winter);2.having the appearance of hoar frost in winter or of moisture on polished surface; 3.hazy; 4.misty
Duft (der)n. 1.hoar frost as seen in winter; 2.mist; 3.vapor forming on a polished surface
dufte, v.; geduft, pp. 1.form hoar frost on objects in winter; 2.yield fragrance
duh, v.; geduh, pp. 1.do; 2.perform; 3.(schaade --) damage
dulde, v.; geduldet, pp. 1.bear; 2.tolerate
Dullebaan (die)n.; Dullebaane, pl. tulip
Dulleblumm (die)n. tulip
dumbich, adj. 1.close (of air); 2.hot
dumer 1.do we; 2.we do
dumm aa/schtelle, v.; aagschtelle, pp. (sich --) play innocent
dumm, adj. 1.dumb; 2.ignorant; 3.stupid
dummel, adj. subdued noise
Dummheet (die)n. 1.ignorance; 2.stupidity; 3. (dummheete mache) play a prank; 4.(to) commit an act of poor judgment or folly
Dummheit (die)n.; Dummheide, pl. 1.nonsense; 2.stupidity

Duwacksschtengel

Dummkopp (der)n.; Dummkepp, pl. 1.blockhead; 2.bonehead; 3.dunce; 4.numbskull
Dummlack (der)n. 1.blockhead; 2.bonehead
dummle, v.; gedummelt, pp. (sich --) 1.bustle; 2.hasten; 3.hurry
Dumor (es)n. noise (as in a factory or at a large gathering)
Dumploch (es)n. dump hole
Dun (die)n. down (feathers)
dunke, v.; gedunkt, pp. 1.dip; 2.immerse
dunkel, adj. 1.dark; 2.(dunkle nacht) (the) dark of the moon
dunkelblo, adj. dark blue
dunkelbrau, adj. dark brown
dunkelfarwich, adj. dark colored
dunkelrot, adj. dark red
Dunker (der)n. Dunkard
Dunkes (es)n. 1.gravy; 2.sauce
Dunn (die)n. ton
Dunner (der)n. 1.thunder; 2.(-- uns gewidder) (a) confound it!; (b) damn it!
dunnere, v.; gedunnert, pp. thunder
dunnergrie formed facetiously and added to blitzeblo
dunnerhaagels, adj. 1.awfully; 2.deucedly
dunnerkei(de)l, interj. gee whiz!
dunnerlotters, adj. 1.awfully, 2.confoundedly
Dunnerschdaag (der)n. Thursday
Dunnerschlack (der)n. thunderbolt
dunnerschtinkich, adj. malodorous
Dunnerwetter (es)n. 1.an exclamation and curse; 2.a vituperative term applied to a person; 3.thunderstorm (rare usage)
dunnerwetters (-er) (-i), adj. devil of a
dunschdich, adj. 1.moist; 2.vaporish
Dunscht (der)n. 1.exhalation; 2.vapor
Duppe (der)n. 1.dot; 2.period; 3.spot
dupplich, adj. 1.dotted; 2.spotted; 3.variegated
Duppmeiser (der)n. sneak
duppmeisich, adj. sneaking
dus(e)le, v.; geduselt, pp. 1.be sleepy; 2.nap
dus, adj. soft and low
Duschber (die)n. 1.dusk; 2.twilight
duschber, adv. 1.dim; 2.dusk; 3.twilight
duschde do you?
Duschder (die)n. twilight
duschder, adv. 1.dusk; 2.twilight
dusslich, adj. uneasy
Dutt (die)n.; Dudde, pl. bag
Dutze(n)d (es)n. dozen
dutzenderweis, adj. 1.by dozens; 2.dozens at a time
Duwack (der)n. 1.tobacco; 2.(-- taape) top tobacco
Duwackduch (es)n.; Duwackdicher, pl. tobacco cloth
Duwacksblumm (die)n.; Duwacksblumme, pl. tobacco flower
Duwacksbrieh (die)n. tobacco juice
Duwackschtrick (der)n.; Duwackschtrick, pl. tobacco Rope
Duwacksieb (die)n. tobacco sieve
Duwacksschtengel (der)n. tobacco plant

Ee

eb

eb, conj.; prep. 1.before; 2.sooner than; 3.whether
ebaermlich, adv. 1.awful; 2.miserable; 3.pitiful
Ebbel (der)n. (-- breche) pick (apples)
Ebbelbei (der)n.; Ebbelbei, pl. apple pie
Ebbelboi (der)n.; Ebbelboi, pl. apple pie
Ebbeldritsch (es)n.; Ebbeldritsche, pl. "appletritch"
Ebbelkuche (der)n. apple tart
Ebbelsaes (der)n. apple sauce
ebber, pron. 1. somebody; 2. someone; 3. (yeder --)
　　(a) everybody; (b) everyone
ebbes, adj.; pron. 1. some; 2. something; 3. (-- gleich) (a)
　　something like; (b) something worthwhile;
ebmol(s), adv. occasionally
ebwohl, conj. although
Eck (es) n.; Ecke, pl. 1. angle; 2. corner; 3. out of the way
　　section; 4.nook; 5.(in alle --e) (a) everywhere; (b) high
　　and low; 6.(iwwers --) diagonally
Eckballe (es)n. corner ball (game)
Eckhaus (es)n. corner house
eckich, adj. cornered
Eckschank (der)n.; Eckschenk, pl. corner cupboard
Eckscheit (es)n. carpenter's square
Eckschtee (der)n.; Eckschtee, pl. cornerstone
Eckschtee (die)n. diamonds (in cards)
eckschteenich, adj. checkered
ecksentrisch, adv., adj. eccentric
Edann (der)n. horehound
Edarn (der)n. horehound
edel, adj. noble
Edelmut (der)n. generosity
Edelschtee (der)n. gem
Edorn (der)n. horehound
ee-aermich, adj. one armed
ee, adj. adv. 1.(eem bang warre) (to be) afraid; 2.(eem
　　[dative singular] leed duh) (to be) sorry 3.(eem der
　　Brotkareb heecher henge) put one on shortrations
ee, pron.; adj. one
Eeche (der, die)n. oak
Eeche (die)n. (roti --) red oak
eeche, adj. oaken
Eechebaam (der)n.; Eechebeem, pl. oak tree
eecheblaat (es)n. oak leaf
Eecheholz (es)n. oak wood
Eechel (die)n.; Eechle, pl. acorn
Eecherli (es)n. squirrel
Eechhaas (der)n.; Eechhaase, pl. 1.squirrel 2.(groher --)
　　gray squirrel; 3.(roder --) red squirrel
Eechhaernche (es)n. squirrel
Eechhaesel (es)n. squirrel
Eed (der)n. 1.oath; 2.(en -- nemme) take an oath
eedere, v.; geeidert, pp. ooze lymph from a wound
eefach, adj. simple
eefacht(ich), adj. single (not double)
Eefachtsbensel (es)n. simpleton
Eefachtspensil (es)n. Simpleton
eefeldich, adj. 1.foolish; 2.half-witted; 3.queer; 4.shallow;

eenichariyets

　　5.silly; 6.simple
Eeg (die)n.; Eege, pl. harrow
eege, adj. own
eege, v.; geegt, pp. harrow
Eegedum (es)n. 1.possession; 2.property
Eegeilsbett (es)n. bed for one person only
Eegeilswagge (der)n. one horse wagon
Eegelieb (die)n. egotism
Eegelob (der)n. self praise
eegemechtich, adj. self willed
eegentlich, adv. really
eeges, adj. own
Eegesinn (der)n. willfulness
eegesinni(s)ch, adj. 1.selfish; 2.stubborn; 3.willful
eegne, adj. own
eegne, v.; ge-eegent, pp. 1.own; 2.possess
Eegner (der)n.; Eegner, pl. 1.owner; 2.proprietor
Eehr (es)n. eye (of a needle)
Eek (die)n.; Eege, pl. harrow
Eel (es)n. oil
eelaafich, adj. single barreled
Eelbaam (der)n.; Eelbeem, pl. olive tree
Eelbabble (der)n. Balm of Gilead (salve prepared from
　　the buds of this tree)
Eelbeer (die)n. olive
Eelbier (die)n. olive
Eelblaat (es)n. olive leaf
Eelduch (es)n.; Eeldicher, pl. oilcloth
eele, v.; ge-eelt, pp. 1.lubricate; 2.oil
eeletzich, adj.; adv. singly
Eelfrucht (die)n. olive
eelich, adj. oily
Eeling (die)n. (letschdi --) extreme unction
Eelkann (die)n. oilcan
Eelkennli (es)n. 1.oil gland (of fowl); 2.uropygial gland
Eelkessli (es)n. 1.oil gland (of fowl); 2.uropygial gland
Eelkewwich (es)n. 1.oil gland (of fowl); 2.uropygial gland
Eelschtee (der)n.; Eelschtee, pl. oilstone
Eelwalnuss (die)n. butternut
Eelzeppli (es)n. 1.oil gland (of fowl); 2.uropygial gland
Eemer (der)n. 1.bucket; 2.pail
Eemerhenk (die)n. bail of a bucket
Eemerreef (der)n. bucket hoops
Eemervoll (der)n. pailful
eemervoll, adj. bucketful
eemerweis, adv. by buckets
eemol, adv. 1.once; 2.(uff --) (a) all at once; (b) suddenly
eener, adj. one
eener, adv. (so --) such a one
eener, pron.; adj. 1.a person; 2.one; 3.somebody
eenes Gangs, adv. straightway**eenes,** adj. one
eeni, adj. one
eenich sei, v.; eenich gewest, pp. agree
eenich, adj. 1.agreed; 2.any; 3.harmonious
eenichariyets, adv. anywhere
eenichatiyets, adv. anywhere

Ee

eenichebber

eenichebber, pron. 1.anybody; 2.anyone
eenichebbes, pron. 1.anything; 2.miscellaneous
eenichi Zeit, adv. anytime
Eenichkeit (die)n. 1.peace; 2.unity
eenichmol, adv. Anytime
eens, adj. 1.single (unmarried); 2.(-- ums anner) one after
    the other
eens, pron.; adj. one
eensel, adj. 1.single; 2.singly
eensichebbes, pron. miscellaneous
eensicher, adj. not one
eensicherweis, adj. singly
eensichscht, adv. only
Eensler (der)n. hermit
Eent (der, die, es)n. the one (of several)
eenzel, adj. 1.single; 2.singly
eenzich, adj. 1.single (unmarried); 2.unique
eenzich, adv. only
Eepies (die)n. 1.Christmas cooky (frequently cut in the
    shape of animals); 2.cooky
eeschtimmich, adj. unanimous
eeschtlich, adj. easterly
eeseidich, adj. 1.biased; 2.incomplete; 3.one sided
eeseidich, adj. (-- koppweh) migraine
eesitzich, adj. one seated
eezechtich, adj. singly
Effengeelisch, adj. Evangelical
Effengeelische (die)n. Evangelicals
effentlich, adv. 1.openly; 2.publicly
effne, v.; ge-effnet, pp. open
Effning (die)n. 1.gap; 2.opening
efters, adv. 1.frequently; 2.often
Egel (der)n. 1.disgust; 2.distaste
Eh(e)schtand (der)n. matrimony
Ehe (die)n. matrimony
Ehebreche (es)n. adultery
Ehebrecher (der)n. adulterer
Ehebruch (der)n. adultery
Ehefraa (die)n. wife
Ehemann (der)n. husband
eher, adv. 1.rather; 2.sooner
ehnder, adj. 1.either; 2.rather
ehnder, adv. 1.rather; 2.sooner
Ehr (die)n. 1.head (of grain); 2.honor
ehrbaar, adj. honorable
ehre, v.; ge-ehrt, pp. honor
Ehrenpreis (der)n. common speedwell (Culver's root)
Ehrenpreis (der)n. (hocher --) tall speedwell (Culver's root)
Ehrewatt (es)n. word of honor
Ehrgeiz (der)n. ambition
ehrgeizich, adj. 1.ambitious; 2.eager for pre-eminence
ehrlich, adj. honest
ehrlicherweis, adv. honestly
Ehrlichkeet (die)n. honesty
ehrwaerdich, adj. 1.honorable; 2.venerable
ehrwaerdiche, v.; geehrwaerdicht, pp. reverence

ei/schpanne

ehrze, v.; geehrzt, pp. address one with "ehr"
ei der Dausich!, interj. the dickens!
ei!, interj. 1.oh!; 2.well!; 3.why?
ei/balsamiere, v.; eigebalsamiert, pp. 1.embalm;
    2.perfume; 3.wrap up thickly in clothes
ei/bendle, v.; eigebendelt, pp. 1.hem; 2.lace
ei/bicke, v.; eigebickt, pp. turn in the edge in hemming
ei/bilde, v.; eigebildt, pp. (sich --) 1.imagine; 2.fancy;
    3.be conceited; 4.recollect
ei/binne, v.; eigebunne, pp. 1.bind; 2.wrap up
ei/blose, v.; eigeblose, pp. 1.start the fire in a blast fur-
    nace; 2.whisper into one's ear
ei/dricke, v.; eigedrickt, pp. 1.indent; 2.press together hard
ei/falde, v.; eigfaldt, pp. lay in folds
ei/falle, v.; eigfalle, pp. 1.cave in; 2.occur to; 3.remember
ei/feedle, v.; eigfeedelt, pp. thread
ei/feichde, v.; eigfeicht, pp. moisten
ei/fense, v.; eigfenst, pp. 1.enclose; 2.fence in
ei/geh, v.; eigange, pp. 1.consent; 2.enter; 3.shrink
ei/gewwe, v.; eigewwe, pp. 1.administer medicine;
    2.accede; 3.give in; 4.hand in a bid; 5.yield to
ei/graawe, v.; eigegraawe, pp. 1.bury; 2.inter
ei/hacke, v.; eighackt, pp. 1.chop into; 2.cover with a hoe
    in planting; 3.slander
ei/halde, v.; eighalde, pp. 1.repress; 2.restrict; 3.slacken;
    4.stop
ei/henke, v.; eighanke; eighenkt, pp. hook in
ei/hole, v.; eigholt, pp. overtake
ei/kaafe, v.; eikaaft, pp. buy in
ei/kehre, v.; eigekehrt, pp. 1.begin housekeeping; 2.put up
    at (an inn); 3.stop at
ei/koche, v.; eigekocht, pp. boil down
ei/laade, v.; eigelaade, pp. invite
ei/lege, v.; eiglegt, pp. 1.drop seeds in planting;
    2.enclose; 3.salt down; 4.store up
ei/mache, v.; eigemacht, pp. preserve (fruit)
ei/mummle, v.; eigemummelt, pp. wrap up well
ei/nemme, v.; eigenumme, pp. 1.absorb; 2.adopt; 3.draw
    in; 4.include; 5.move into; 6.take in
ei/richde, v.; eigericht, pp. (sich --) adapt oneself to
    circumstances
ei/richde, v.; eigericht, pp. 1.furnish; 2.fix; 3.prepare;
    4.put in order
ei/salwe, v.; eigsalbt, pp. anoint
ei/scharefe, v.; eigschareft, pp. 1.drill into; 2.instruct
ei/schlagge, v.; eigschlagge, pp. strike (of lightning)
ei/schliesse, v.; eigschlosse, pp. 1.enclose; 2.imprison;
    3.include; 4.lock up
ei/schlofe, v.; eigschlofe, pp. fall asleep
ei/schlummere, v.; eigschlummert, pp. fall (into slumber)
ei/schluppe, v.; eigschlupt, pp. 1.crawl in; 2.slip in
ei/schmiere, v.; eigschmiert, pp. 1.get dirty; 2.lubricate;
    3.rub in grease; 4.sow in wet weather
ei/schneide, v.; eigschnidde, pp. 1.cut (onions or cucum-
    bers) in salt and vinegar; 2.nick
ei/schpanne, v.; eigschpannt, pp. hitch (horses)

Ee

ei/schparre — eihaerte

ei/schparre, v.; eigschpatt, pp. 1.confine; 2.lock up; 3.imprison

ei/schreiwe, v.; eigschriwwe, pp. 1.enroll; 2.inscribe; 3.enter in a book; 4.register

ei/schtimme, v.; eigschtimmt, pp. 1.accord; 2.agree; 3.chime in

ei/seefe, v.; eigseeft, pp. lather

ei/segne, v.; eigsegent, pp. 1.confirm (a person in church); 2.consecrate

ei/setze, v.; eigsetzt, pp. 1.install; 2.ordain; 3.put in

ei/weeche, v.; eigweecht, pp. soak

ei/weide, v.; eigweidt, pp. dedicate

ei/weihe, v.; eigweiht, pp. dedicate

ei/wickle, v.; eigewickelt, pp. 1.implicate; 2.wrap; 3.wrap into

ei/williche, v.; eigewillicht, pp. consent

ei/yaage, v.; eigyaagt, pp. drive in

ei/ziege, v.; eigezoge, pp. 1.absorb; 2.draw in; 3.move into

ei/ziehe, v.; eigezogge, pp. pull in

eiaernde, v.; eigeaernt, pp. harvest

eiballe, v.; eigeballt, pp. roll into balls (butter)

Eibalsamierer (der)n. 1.funeral director; 2.undertaker

eibeisse, v.; eigebisse, pp. bite into

eibiesse, v.; eigebiesst, pp. 1.lose; 2.suffer bodily harm (in an accident)

Eibildichkeet (die)n. conceit

eibildisch, adj. 1.conceited; 2.imaginative; 3.vain

Eibildung (die)n. 1.fancy; 2.imagination

eibilliche, v.; eigebillicht, pp. consent

eibindle, v.; eigebindelt, pp. 1.bundle up; 2.(sich --) dress warmly

eiblaudre, v.; eigeblaudert, pp. 1.get (one) to believe (something); 2.talk (something) into (one)

Eiblick (der)n. 1.hint; 2.mental grasp

eiblicke, v.; eigeblickt, pp. 1.examine; 2.scrutinize

eibluge, v.; eigeblugt, pp. plow in (seed)

eibreche, v.; eigebroche, pp. 1.break (a colt); 2.break in (shoes); 3.enter forcibly

Eibrecher (der)n. burglar

eibrenne, v.; eigebrennt, pp. 1.burn; 2.(eeni --) lie (to someone); 3.(eens --) (a) cheat; (b) give (someone) a blow

eibringe, v.; eigebrocht, pp. 1.bring in income; 2.introduce in a conversation; 3.yield

eibrockle, v.; eigebrockelt, pp. break bread (or crackers) into soup

Eibruch (der)n. burglary

eich, pron. 1.you; 2.to you

eicks wo, adv. somewhere

eidaerre, v.; eigedaerrt, pp. shrink in drying

Eidechs (der)n. lizard

eideele, v.; eigedeelt, pp. divide into parts

Eider (es)n. udder

eidere, v.; geeidert, pp. 1.ooze lymph from a wound; 2.swell the utter before calving

Eideschpiggel (Till) (der)n. Owlglass: a mythical person full of wisdom and pranks frequently lamenting the opposite of what is to happen

Eidie (die)n. idea

eidraage, v.; eigedraage, pp. 1.carry in; 2.yield

eidrehe, v.; eigedreht, pp. 1.turn in; 2.turn in a seem

eidreiwe, v.; eigedriwwe, pp. 1.bring home the cows; 2.collect money

eidrenge, v.; eigedrengt, pp. (sich --) intrude

Eidruck (der)n. 1.emphasis; 2.impression; 3.sensation

eieege, v.; eige-eekt, pp. harrow in (seed)

eier, adj. your (plural)

Eierniss (die)n. offence

eifaahre, v.; eigfaahre, pp. haul into the barn (grain, etc.)

Eifaahrt (die)n. 1.entrance; 2.entrance ramp (to the barn floor); 3.gateway

eifach, adj. 1.not double; 2.plain; 3.simple

eifaedle, v.; eigfaedelt, pp. thread a needle

Eifall (der)n.; Eifalle, pl. 1.fancy; 2.idea; 3.raid; 4.whim

eifalte, v.; eigfalt, pp. lay in small folds

eifange, v.; eigfange, pp. 1.imprison; 2.pen up

eifeddle, v.; eigfeddelt, pp. thread a needle

Eifer (der)n. 1.eagerness; 2.zeal

Eiferer (der)n. zealot

eiferich, adj. 1.eager; 2.excited; 3.zealous

eifersichtich, adj. jealous

Eifersucht (die)n. jealousy

eifiehre, v.; eigfiehrt, pp. 1.induct; 2.introduce; 3.usher in

Eifiehrer (der)n. usher

eifille, v.; eigfillt, pp. 1.bottle; 2.fill up

eifinne, v.; eigfunne, pp. (sich --) (to be) present

Eifluss (der)n. influence

eifrich, adj. 1.busy; 2.eager; 3.earnest; 4.excited; 5.zealous

eifriere, v.; eigfrore, pp. freeze up (for the winter)

Eigang (der)n. 1.entrance; 2.entry

eigawwle, v.; eigegawwelt, pp. 1.eat voraciously; 2.pitch hay or straw in

eigebore, adj. 1.born; 2.native

eigediemlich, adj. peculiar

eigei, interj. 1.exclamation of surprise or deprecation, or (with a different intonation) of endearment in caressingly pressing one's cheek against that of a child; 2.used as noun (geb mir Eigei)

eigelschdere, v.; eigegelschdert, pp. scare (someone)

Eigemachdes (es)n. preserves

Eigendum (es)n. property

Eigeweid(e) (es)n. viscera

eigezogge, adj. 1.backward; 2.diffident; 3.timid

eigfriere, v.; eigfrore, pp. freeze up (for the winter)

eigleppre, v.; eigegleppert, pp. beat (eggs)

eigloppe, v.; eigegloppt, pp. hammer in

eigreife, v.; eigegreifen, pp. 1.make inroads; 2.take part

eigriege, v.; eigrickt, pp. 1.receive; 2.take in

eihacke, v.; eighackt, pp. (nidder (hoch) --) begin the stroke in mowing by cutting low (high)

eihaekle, v.; eighaekelt, pp. hook in

eihaerte, v.; eighaert, pp. 1.harden; 2.inure

Ee

eihafte

eihafte, v.; eighaft, pp. fasten up a dress (with hooks and eyes)

eihalde, v.; eighalde, pp. (eens --) give (someone) a whack

eihandle, v.; eighandelt, pp. 1.procure by trading; 2.purchase

eihauche, v.; eighaucht, pp. 1.breath in; 2.inhale; 3.inspire

eihille, v.; eighillt, pp. wrap up

eihocke, v.; eighockt, pp. 1.keep in its lair (of an animal); 2.stick to the house

eihowwle, v.; eighowwelt, pp. cut cabbage (for sauerkraut)

eikaafe, v.; eikaaft, pp. 1.lay in stock; 2.purchase

Eikumme(s) (es)n. income

eikumme, v.; eikumme, pp. 1.freshen (of a cow); 2.recall; 3.occur to

Eil (die)n.; Eile, pl. 1.haste; 2.owl

Eil (es)n. oil

Eilaading (die)n. invitation

Eiland (es)n.; Eilender, pl. island

eile, v.; ge-eilt, pp. 1.bustle; 2.hasten; 3.hurry

eileichde, v.; eigeleicht, pp. 1.get an idea; 2.(eens --) give a blow or hit

Eileiding, (die)n. introduction

Eileschpiggel (Till) (der)n. Owlglass: a mythical person full of wisdom and pranks frequently lamenting the opposite of what is to happen

eilich, adj. hasty

eimache, v.; eigemacht, pp. (eigemacht Sach) preserves

eimaure, v.; eigemauert, pp. immure

eimische, v.; eigemischt, pp. (sich --) intrude

einaehe, v.; eigenaeht, pp. sew up in

einemme, v.; eigenumme, pp. 1.absorb; 2.cheat; 3.make (a garment) narrower or smaller; 4.take (medicine); 5.take in (also money)

einerlei, adj. all the same

einischde, v.; eigenischt, pp. (sich --) cuddle

einsam, adj. solitary

eirechle, v.; eigerechelt, pp. 1.count in; 2.include

eireggne, v.; eigereggent, pp. (to be) held indoors by rain

eireisse, v.; eigerisse, pp. 1.become a bad custom; 2. make inroads on

eireiwe, v.; eigeriwwe, pp. rub in

Eireschpiggel (Till) (der)n. Owlglass: a mythical person full of wisdom and pranks frequently lamenting the opposite of what is to happen

Eirichding (die)n. 1.arrangement; 2.preparation

eiricke, v.; eigerickt, pp. 1.enter; 2.move in

eiriehre, v.; eigeriehrt, pp. 1.mix; 2.stir in

eiriwwle, v.; eigeriwwelt, pp. 1.crumble something into soup; 2.hint; 3.insinuate

eirutsche, v.; eigerutscht, pp. 1.fall in; 2.slip in

Eis (es)n. 1.ice; 2.(uffs -- schreiwe) (to grant) credit

eis(n), adj. iron

eisaee, v.; eigsaet, pp. sow (a field)

eisaege, v.; eigsaekt, pp. saw into

eisalse, v.; eigsalse, pp. salt down

eisam, adj. solitary

Eisegraas

Eisamkeet (die)n. solitude

eisammle, v.; eigsammelt, pp. 1.collect; 2.gather in; 3.pick

Eisbaerrick (der)n. iceberg

eischaerre, v.; eigschaerrt, pp. 1.bury; 2.scratch in

eischarefe, v.; eigschareft, pp. enjoin

Eischder (die)n.; Eischder, pl. oyster

eischenke, v.; eigschenkt, pp. 1.pour in; 2.pour out

eischeppe, v.; eigscheppt, pp. shovel in

eischicke, v.; eigschickt, pp. send in

eischiewe, v.; eigschowe, pp. 1.force in; 2.push in

eischiffe, v.; eigschifft, pp. embark

eischitte, v.; eigschitt, pp. pour medicine down (an animals throat)

Eischlack (der)n. woof

eischleefe, v.; eigschleeft, pp. creep in

eischleiche, v.; eigschliche, pp. creep in

eischlippe, v.; eigschlippt, pp. slip in

eischlitze, v.; eigschlitzt, pp. 1.slit; 2.tear

eischmeechle, v.; eigschmeechelt, pp. (sich --) ingratiate oneself

eischmiere, v.; eigschmiert, pp. (sich --) ingratiate oneself

eischmuggle, v.; eigschmuggelt, pp. smuggle in

eischnaerre, v.; eigschnaerrt, pp. shrink

eischnalle, v.; eigschnallt, pp. 1.buckle; 2.tighten

eischnee-e, v.; eigschneet, pp. (to) become snowbound

Eischnitt (der)n. 1.groove; 2.incision

eischprenge, v.; eigschprengt, pp. chase in

eischpritze, v.; eigschpritzt, pp. sprinkle (wash) before ironing

eischrecke, v.; eigschreckt, pp. 1.intimidate; 2.scare

eischrenke, v.; eigschrenkt, pp. 1.restrain; 2.shrink

eischt, adj. 1.at the sign of; 2.possibly

eischtaawe, v.; eigschtaabt, pp. 1. covered with dust; 2. sow in dust

eischtaerze, v.; eigschtaertzt, pp. 1.collapse; 2.fall in

eischtecke, v.; eigschteckt, pp. 1.lock up; 2.put into one's pocket

eischteh, v.; eigschtanne, pp. 1.answer; 2.be responsible for; 3.enter service

eischteige, v.; eigschtigge, pp. 1.get into; 2.step into

eischtelle, v.; eigschtellt, pp. 1.forbid; 2.put an end to; 3.put up (cattle) for fattening

eischtewwre, v.; eigschtewwert, pp. 1.chase in; 2.enter abruptly

eischtoppe, v.; eigschtoppt, pp. 1.gorge; 2.stuff in

eischtricke, v.; eigschtrickt, pp. (to) narrow in the toe of a stocking when knitting

eischweere, v.; eigschwore, pp. 1.inaugurate; 2.swear in

eischwetze, v.; eigschwetzt, pp. 1.make one believe; 2.persuade

Eise (es)n. iron

Eise-erz (es)n. iron ore

eise, adj. iron

Eisefresser (der)n. bully

Eisegiesserei (die)n.; Eisegiessereie, pl. foundry

Eisegraas (es)n. 1.Canada bluegrass; 2.wire grass

Ee

Eisegrautwatzel   End

Eisegrautwatzel (die)n. vervain root
Eisehaffe (der)n.; Eisehaffe, pl. iron cook-pot
Eisehammer (der)n. forge
Eisehannes (Till) (der)n. Owlglass: a mythical person full
    of wisdom and pranks frequently lamenting the oppo-
    site of what is to happen
eisehne, v.; eigsehne, pp. 1.comprehend; 2.see the point;
    3.understand
Eisehnes (es)n. 1.consideration; 2.insight
Eiseholz (es)n. 1.blue bush; 2.hop horn-beam
Eisekeidel (der)n. iron wedge
Eisekessel (der)n. iron kettle
Eiseschtor (der)n.; Eiseschtore, pl. hardware store
Eisetzing (die)n. ordination
Eisetzung (die)n. ordination
Eisewarrick (es)n. iron-works
Eisglumpe (der)n. lump of ice
Eisgraut (es)n. clear-grass
Eishaus (es)n.; Eisheiser, pl. icehouse
Eishoke (der)n. ice hook
eisi-gro(h), adj. dappled-gray
Eisibohre (der)n. steel bit
eisich, adj. icy
Eisicht (die)n. insight
eisinke, v.; eigsanke, pp. 1.cave in; 2.sink in
eiskalt, adj. ice cold
Eisop (der)n. hyssop
Eispick (die)n. ice pick
Eissaek (die)n. ice saw
eissaerscht, adv. 1.outer; 2.utmost
Eisschiwwel (der)n. lump of ice
eisserlich, adv. external(ly)
eisuckle, v.; eigsuckelt, pp. suck in
Eiswasser (es)n. ice water
Eiszabbe (der)n.; Eiszabbe, pl. icicle
Eiszang (die)n. ice tongs
Eiwandrer (der)n. immigrant
Eiweiding (die)n. dedication
eiweihe, v.; eigeweiht, pp. dedicate
Eiweihing (die)n. dedication
Eiweiss (es)n. albumen (the white of an egg)
Eiwendung (die)n. 1.excuse; 2.objection; 3.pretex
Eiwenning (die)n. 1.excuse; 2.objection; 3.pretext
eiwetze, v.; eigewetzt, pp. (sich --) bedraggle one's trou-
    sers or dress with mud
eiwilliche, v.; eigewillicht, pp. consent
eiwindle, v.; eigewindelt, pp. swathe
eiwintre, v.; eigewintert, pp. (to) have winter set in
eiwitsche, v.; eigewitscht, pp. slip in
Eiwohner (der)n.; Eiwohner, pl. inhabitant
Eiwuhner (der)n.; Eiwuhner, pl. resident
eiyaage, v.; eigeyaakt, pp. 1.drive or chase in; 2.hole
eiyets (wo), adv. somewhere
eizwinge, v.; eigezwunge, pp. force (one) to swallow
Ekel (der)n. 1.disgust; 2.distaste
ekelhaft, adj. 1.disgusting; 2.distasteful

Ekelhaftichkeit (die)n. loathsomeness
Ekelheftichkeet (die)n. loathsomeness
ekle, v.; ge-ekelt, pp. 1.have a disgust for; 2.be nauseated by
eklich, adj. 1.disagreeable; 2.squeamish
Elbedritsch (es)n.; Elbegritsche, pl.; 2.**Elbedritschel** (es)n.;
    Elbedritschelcher, pl.; 3.**Elbedritschelche** (es)n.;
    Elbedritschelcher, pl.; 4.**Elbedritschli** (es)
    n.;Elbedritschlin, pl.; 5.**Elbegrixel** (es)n.; Elbegrixel-
    cher, pl.; 6.**Elderbritsch** (es)n.; Elderbritsche, pl.;
    7. **Elderdritsch** (es)n.;   Elderdritsche, pl.;
    8. **Eldertwitsch** (es)n.; Eldertwitsche, pl.; 9. **Elefant-
    dritsch** (es)n.; Elefantdritsche, pl.; 10.**Elefantgrixel**
    (es)n.; Elefantgrixelcher, pl.; 11.**Elfedritsch** (es)n.;
    Elfedritsche, pl.; 12. **Elfedritschel** (es)n.; Elfedritschel-
    cher, pl.; 13. **Elfedritschelche** (es)n.; Elfedritschelcher,
    pl.; 14.**Elfedritschli** (es)n.; Elfedritschlin, pl.;
    15.**Elfegrixel** (es)n.; Elfegrixelcher, pl. snipe (mystical
    animal hunted with a sack on cold winter's night)
Eldeschder (der)n. deacon (Old Order Mennonite)
Eldeschtee (der)n. elder in a church
Eldre (die)n., pl. parents
Elefandeschtock (der)n. elephant's (plant)
Element (es)n. element
Elend (es)n. 1.misery; 2. trouble; 3.woe; 4. (en --) (a)
    annoyance; (b) nuisance; (c) vexation
elendich, adj. 1.miserable; 2.pitiful; 3.poor; 4.woeful
Elendsgeglaag (es)n. constant recounting of one's misery
Elendsgweckel (es)n. miserable (little) thing
elf, elfe, adj.; pron. eleven
elfmol, adv. eleven times
elft, adj. eleventh
Eli (der)n. Elias
Eliasdaag (der)n. July 20
Ellboge (der)n.; Ellboge, pl. elbow
El(l)efant (der)n. elephant
Elt (die)n. 1.age; 2.(unnich --) under age
eltlich, adj. elderly
Eltre (die)n., pl. parents
em, prep. to
emol, adv 1.and that ends it; 2.even; 3.formerly; 4.just;
    5.once; 6.sooner or later
emsich, adj. 1.diligent; 2.industrious
en (die) Howwel wu sie die False (tucks) ziege mit tucker
    (for goods)
en annres, pron. another
en mannichmol, adv. many times
en paar, adj. 1.(a) couple; 2.a few; 3.some
**en silwerich (G)Waardeweil un en goldich (G)Nixli mit
    heembringe** nothing (an idiomatic expression to
    children) = to return home empty handed with noth-
    ing for the children
en(t)schuldiche, v.; entschuldicht, pp. 1.excuse; 2.(sich --)
    apologize
En(t)schuldichung (die)n. 1.apology; 2.excuse
en, indef. art. 1.a; 2.an
End (es)n.; Ender, Enner, pl. 1.end; 2.limit

Ee

End(e)rich

End(e)rich (der)n.; Endriche, pl. drake
ende, v.; geendt, pp. 1.end; 2.result
endecke, v.; endeckt, pp. 1.disclose; 2.discover
ender, adj. 1.either; 2.rather
Endiffi (der)n. endive
Endivvi (der)n. chicory
Endivviselaat (der)n. endive (salad)
Endkeitel (der)n. 1.cecum; 2.intestine; 3.the same (of a beef) cleaned and stuffed with sausage meat
endlich, adv. finally
endlos, adj. unending
endweegs, adv. endways
eng, adj. 1. (a) narrow; (b) tight; 2. (-- uff der Bruscht sei) (to) have difficulty in breathing
engbrischdich, adj. asthmatic
engege, prep. toward
engegegeh, adj. (to) go to meet
engegekumme, adj. (to) come to meet
engegelaafe, adj. (to) walk to meet
Engel (der)n.; Engel, pl. angel
Engelblimmli (es)n. 1.corpse plant; 2.Indian pipe
Engelblumm (die)n. 1.corpse plant; 2.Indian pipe
Engelwarzel (die)n. Angelica (plant)
enger, adj. narrower
enghaerzich, adj. narrow minded
Engkeitel (der)n. 1.caecum; 2.intestine; 3.the same (of a beef) cleaned and stuffed with sausage meat
England (es)n. England
Englenner (der)n.; Englenner, pl. Englishman
englisch, adj. 1.English; 2.non-Amish
Englischmann (der)n. Englishman
Engschde (die)n.; Engschde, pl. 1.fear; 2.fright; 3.terror
engschderich, adj. trembly
engschderich, adv. 1.anxious; 2.fearful
en(g)schderlich, adj. 1.anxious; 2.fearful; 3.trembly
en(g)schderlich, adv. 1.anxious; 2.fearful
engschtlich, adv. 1.anxious; 2.fearful
Enkel (der)n. 1.ankle; 2.grandson
Enkelin (die)n. granddaughter (not common usage)
en(n)anner, pron. another
ennere, v.; ge-ennert, pp. 1.alter; 2.change
Ennering (die)n. change
Ennerung (die)n. change
ennlch, adj. 1.any; 2.(-- sei) to agree
ennichareiyets, adv. anywhere
ennichau, adv. 1.anyhow; 2.anyway
ennichebber, pron. 1.anybody; 2.anyone
ennichebbes, pron. anything
ennicheids, adj. anywhere
ennicheiyets, adv. anywhere
ennicher, adj. any
ennicher, adv. 1.anyhow; 2.anyway
ennichhau, adv. anyhow
ennichi Zeit, adv. anytime
ennichi, adj. any
ennihau, adv. 1.anyhow; 2.anyway

Erdschoss

Ent (die)n.; Ende, pl. duck
Entche (es)n. duckling
Enteoi (es)n. duck's egg
entfaernt, adv. distant
Entli (es)n.; Entlin, pl. duckling
entschteh, v.; entschtanne, pp. originate
entsetzlich, adj. 1.awful; 2.terrible
entwedder(s), pron; conj. either
entwedder(s)...odder, pron; conj. either...or
entzickt, adj. 1.enraptured; 2.in a trance
Ephridaa (es)n. Ephrata
Eppelbaam (der)n. apple tree
Eppeldaag (der)n. March 25
Eppelkaern (die)n. apple seed
Eppelkuche (der)n. apple tart
Eppellaab (es)n. apple leaves
Eppelwei (der)n. cider
Er kann so gut schpiele, as die Hinkel doot gehne. play enchantingly well (He plays so enchantingly that the chickens would die because of it.)
Er schwetzt mir kenn Loch hie wu ich eens hab! He won't talk me into it!
er(n)naehre, v.; ernaehert, pp. (sich --) 1.live; 2.make a living; 3.subsist
er(n)naehre, v.; ernaehert, pp. support
er, pron. he
erbaerme, v.; erbaermt, pp. 1.have pity; 2.have mercy
erbaermlich, adj. miserable
erbarme, v.; erbarmt, pp. 1.have pity; 2.have mercy
Erbeer (die)n. strawberry
Erbel (die)n. strawberry
Erbfeind (der)n. arch-enemy
erblicke, v.; erblickt, pp. catch (sight of)
erblos, adj. childless
Erblosser (der)n. testator
Erbschaft (die)n. inheritance
Erd (die)n. 1.earth; 2.world
Erdabbel (der)n. Jerusalem artichoke
Erdballe (der)n. globe
Erdbebung (die)n. earthquake
Erdbeewing (die)n. earthquake
Erdbewung (die)n. earthquake
Erddeel (es)n. part of the earth
erde, adj. earthen
Erdekloss (der)n. earthly
Erdfleh (der) flea-beetle
Erdfloh (der)n.; Erdfleh, pl. plant louse
Erdgeischt (der)n. gnome
Erdglumbe (der)n. clod
erdich, adj. 1.earthen; 2.earthy; 3.earthly
Erdlichdel (es)n. 1.ignis fatuus; 2.will-o'-the- wisp
Erdlicht (es)n.; Erdlichter, pl. 1.jack o' lantern; 2.ignis fatuus
erdne, adj. earthen
Erdreich (es)n. globe
Erdscholle (der)n. 1.clod; 2.lump of earth
Erdschoss (der)n. (lap of) the earth

51

Ee

Erdschpigge

Esch(e)puddel

Erdschpigge (der)n. semaphore
Erdschtreiss (die)n., pl. trailing arbutus
Erdschwamm (der)n. mushroom
Erdziddering (die)n. earthquake
Erebdeel (es)n. inheritance
Erebschaft (die)n. inheritance
erewe, v.; ge-erbt, pp. inherit
Erewer (der)n.; Erewer, pl. heir
erfaahre, v.; erfaahre, pp. 1.experience; 2.learn;3.adept;
    4.versed
Erfaahring (die)n. experience
erfille, v.; erfillt, pp. fulfill
Erfilling (die)n. fulfillment
Erfinder (der)n. inventor
Erfindung (die)n. invention
erfinne, v.; erfunne, pp. invent
erfoddre, v.; erfoddert, pp. require
Erfolk (der)n. 1.event; 2.result
erfreie, v.; erfreit, pp. make glad
erfrische, v.; erfrischt, pp. refresh
Erfrischung (die)n. 1.recreation; 2.refreshment
ergewwe, v.; ergewwe, pp. (sich --) 1.devote oneself;
    2.be resigned; 3.surrender
Ergraut (es)n. rattlesnake plantain
ergreife, v.; ergriffe, pp. 1.comprehend; 2.grab; 3.seize
ergreifich, adj. comprehensible
Ergreifing (die)n. comprehension
ergreiflich adj. comprehensible
ergrinde, v.; ergrindt, pp. 1.fathom; 2.find out
erhalde, v.; erhalde, pp. 1.maintain; 2.preserve; 3.support
Erhaltung (die)n. 1.maintenance; 2.preservation
Erheewer (der)n. elevator belt of a flouring mill
erhehe, v.; erheet, pp. exalt
erhiere, v.; erhiert, pp. (to obtain by) marrying
erhole, v.; erholt, pp. (sich --) 1.recover; 2.regain
Erholung (die)n. recovery
erinnere, v.; erinnert, pp. (sich --) 1.recollect; 2.remember
Erinnerung (die)n. 1.memento; 2.recollection; 3.reminiscence
erkenne, v.; erkennt, pp. recognize
erkindiche, v.; erkindicht, pp. (sich --) inquire
erklaere, v.; erklaert, pp. 1.avow; 2.explain
Erklaerung (die)n. 1.avowal; 2.explanation
erlaawe, v.; erla(a)bt, pp. 1.allow; 2.permit
Erlaawing (die)n. permission
Erlabnis (die)n. permission
erlange, v.; erlangt, pp. 1.acquire; 2.attain; 3.obtain; 4.reach
Erleebnis (die)n. experience
erleese, v.; erleest, pp. 1.redeem; 2.save
Erleeser (der)n. 1.Redeemer; 2.Savior
Erleesung (die)n. redemption
erleewe, v.; erleebt, pp. 1. experience; 2. go through with
Erleheck (die)n. box elder
erleichte, v.; erleicht, pp. illuminate
erleichtere, v.; erleichtert, pp. 1.lessen; 2.lighten
erleide, v.; erlidde, pp. 1.suffer; 2.undergo
erliege, v.; erlogge, pp. trump up lies

erlosse, v.; erlosst, pp. remit
ermaahne, v.; ermaahnt, pp. 1.exhort; 2.remind
Ermaahnung (die)n. 1.exhortation; 2.remonstrance
ermuntere, v.; ermuntert, pp. encourage
Ern (die)n. harvest
Ern(d)karrich (die)n. Harvest Home service
Ern-Versammling (die)n. Harvest Home (plain churches)
ernaehre, v.; ernaehrt, pp. support
Ernbreddich (die)n. Harvest Home
erneire, v.; erneiert, pp. renew
erniedriche, v.; erniedricht, pp. humble
Ernscht (der)n. 1.earnest; 2.seriousness
Erntfescht (es)n. Harvest Home
erquicke, v.; erquickt, pp. 1.quicken; 2.refresh
Erquickung (die)n. 1.recreation; 2.refreshment
Errebbel (die)n. strawberry
erredde, v.; errett, pp. 1.rescue; 2.save
erreeche, v.; erreecht, pp. attain
errichte, v.; erricht, pp. 1.dispose; 2.establish
erschaffe, v.; erschaft, pp. create
Erschaffing (die)n. creation
erschdens, adv. firstly
erschder, adv. 1.rather; 2.sooner
erscheine, v.; erscheint, pp. appear
Erscheinung (die)n. appearance
erschleiche, v.; erschliche, pp. obtain by slow movements
    or delay
erschpare, v.; erschpart, pp. save
erschrecke, v.; erschreckt, pp. terrify
erschrecklich, adj. 1.horrible; 2.terrible
erscht, adj.; adv. first
erscht, adv. 1.first; 2.just; 3.now; 4.only; 5.'til
erschtaune, v.; erschtaunt, pp. 1.astonish; 2.amaze;
    3. wonder; 4.(sich --) be surprised
erschtaunlich, adj.; adv. 1.astonishing; 2.surprising
erschteige, v.; erschteigge, pp. scale
erschticke, v.; erschtickt, pp. suffocate
Erschtling (der)n. heifer that calves for the first time
ersetzlich, adv. 1.awfully; 2.terribly
ersuche, v.; ersucht, pp. beseech
erwaarte, v.; erwaart, pp. 1.await; 2.expect; 3.wait for
erwache, v.; erwacht, pp. waken
erwaehle, v.; erwaehlt, pp. elect
erwecke, v.; erweckt, pp. rouse
erweitre, v.; erweitert, pp. widen
Erz (der)n. ore
erzehle, v.; erzehlt, pp. tell (rare usage)
Erzehler (der)n. narrator
Erzehlung (die)n. narration
erziege, v.; erzogge, pp. breed
Erzphilischder (der)n. consummate pedant
es, def. art. the
es, pron. it
Esch (die)n.; Esche, pl. ashes
Esch(e)puddel (die)n. the last one to rise on Shrove Tues-
    day (day before Ash Wednesday)

Ee

eschdimiere

eschdimiere, v.; ge-eschdimiert, pp. 1.esteem; 2.regard; 3.respect

Esche (die)n. ash tree

Eschelaag (die)n. the brine of leached wood ashes utilized in boiling soft soap

Eschemittwoch (der)n. Ash Wednesday

Eschmann (der)n. ash man

eschtimere, v.; geschtimiert, pp. appreciate

eschtimiere, v.; ge-eschtimiert, pp. 1.esteem; 2.regard

Esel (der)n.; Esel, pl. 1.ass; 2.mule

Eseldreiwer (der)n. mule driver

Eselhutsch (es)n. mule colt

Eselkopp (der)n. blockhead

Eselschtreech (die)n., pl. 1.horseplay; 2.rough pranks

Ess (die)n. raised platform in a blacksmith's shop where the fire and tools are found

Ess-sach(e) (die)n.; pl. 1.eatables; 2.victuals

Ess-schtick (es)n. lunch

Esschank (der)n. 1.larder; 2.pantry

Esse (es)n. 1.(a) eating; (b).food; (c)meal; 2.(en gross --) a big meal

esse, v.; gesse, pp. 1.(a) dine; (b) eat (of humans); 2.(sich gut --) be good eating

Essebell (die)n. large bell erected on a pole and rung to call the men from the field to dinner

Esser (der)n. eater

Esserei (die)n. (much or continued) eating

Essich (der)n. vinegar

Essichbunsch (der)n. vinegar punch (vinegar, sugar, water mixed as a drink for field workers)

Essichfass (es)n. vinegar barrel

Essichgruck (der)n. vinegar jug

Essichhols (es)n. scarlet sumac

Essichmutter (die)n. mother of vinegar

Essichschling (die)n. vinegar punch (vinegar, sugar, water mixed as a drink for field workers)

Esskessel (der)n. dinner pail

Essleffel (der)n. tablespoon

Essschtubb (die)n.; Essschtuwwe, pl. dining room

Esszeddel (der)n. menu

Esszeit (die)n. mealtime

etliche, adj.; pron. some

ettlich, adj. 1.different; 2.various; 3.several

ettzetteraa, adj. et cetera

Evaa (die)n. Eve

Evvengelisch Evangelical

Evvengelium (es)n. gospel

ewe, adj. 1.equal; 2.level; 3.smooth

eweck, adv. 1.absent; 2.away

eweil, adv. 1.a while; 2.meanwhile

Ewekummes (es)n. revenge

ewene, v.; ge-ewent, pp. level

Ewening (die)n. level space

ewich, adj.; adv. 1.eternal; 2.forever; 3.(gaar -- viel) (a) a whole lot; (b) very much; 4.(-- Unruh) perpetual motion

Ewichkeit (die)n. eternity

Exli

ewichlich, adj. forever

Ewichrotzer (der)n.; Ewichrotzer, pl. glanders

Ewichyaeger (der)n. spirit hunter

ewwe, adj. 1.just; 2.simply; 3.you know

Ewwer (der)n.; Ewwer, pl. 1.boar; 2.male pig; 3.hoggish man

ewwer, adv. Upper

Ewwerdeel (es)n. upper part

Ewwergraut (es)n. 1.lady's slipper; 2.moccasin flower

ewwerschich, adv. Upwards

ewwerscht Schpeicher (der)n. attic

ewwerscht Wand (die)n. ceiling

ewwerscht, adj. 1.upper; 2.uppermost

ewwersich, adv. Upwards

ewweviel(ich), adv. 1.immaterial; 2.indifferent

exdraa, adv. Extra

exdroi, adv. Extra

Exel (es)n. 1.hatchet; 2.small ax

Exembel (der)n. example

exeziere, v.; geexeziert, pp. drill

Exli (es)n.; Exlin, pl. little ox

Ff

Faabel

Faabel (die)n. fable

faable, v.; gfaabelt, pp. sleep unsoundly (of ill people)

Faade(m) (der)n. 1.fibre; 2.string; 3.thread

Faahne (die)n.; Faahne, pl. 1.flag; 2.tassel (of corn)

Faahneschtock (der)n. flagstaff

Faahrbrick (die)n. bridge for vehicular traffic

faahre, v.; is gfaahre, pp. 1.drive (a vehicle); 2.haul; 3.ride (on a vehicle); 4.(in die hee --) (a) fly up; (b) resent; (c) start up; 5.(iwwers Maul --) snap a person off

Faahrgeeschel (die)n. (heavy) teamster's whip

Faahrgeld (es)n. fare

faahrlessich, adj. 1.inattentive; 2.negligent

Faahrlessichkeit (die)n. 1.carelessness; 2.negligence

Faahrt (die)n. 1.bars; 2.drive; 3.ford

Faahrweg (der)n.; Faahrwege, pl. 1.carriage road; 2.driveway; 3.road

Faahrzeddel (der)n. railroad ticket

Faamilye (die)n. family

Faaraan (der)n. 1.brake; 2.fern; 3.sweet fern

Faare (der)n. sweet fern

Faas(e)nacht (die)n. Shrove Tuesday

Faasnachtikichelche (es)n. doughnut

Faasnachtkuche (der)n. doughnut

faawle, v.; gfaawelt, pp. 1.talk incoherently (in delirium of severe illness); 2.twaddle

Fabier (es)n.; Fabiere, pl. paper

fache, v.; gfacht, pp. fan

Fackel (die)n. 1.bundle of straw for thatching; 2.torch

Fadderros (die)n. poppy

faddich/mache, v.; faddichgemacht, pp. 1.bring to an end; 2.complete; 3.conclude; 4.finish

faddich, adj. 1.completed; 2.done; 3.finished; 4.ready; 5.(ebbes odder ebber -- sei mit) (to be) finished with (something or someone)

faedmich, adj. 1.fibrous; 2.stringy

faehich, adj. 1.capable; 2.fit

Faehichkeet (die)n. 1.ability; 2.faculty; 3.qualifications

faerdich, adj. 1.done; 2.finished; 3.ready

Faerdinand (der)n. Ferdinand

faerichbutzich, adj. 1.cowardly; 2.shy; 3.timid; 4.timorous

faerichde, v.; gfaericht, pp. 1.dread; 2.fear

faern, adv. 1.distant; 2.remote

faerrich, adj. (was --) 1.what kind of; 2.what sort of

faerrichderlich, adj. 1.dreadful; 2.fearful; 3.frightful

faerriwell, adj. 1.farewell; 2.goodbye

Faerschde (der)n. heel

Faerscht (der)n. 1.ridgepole; 2.space in a building imme-diately under the ridge pole; 3.top of a tree

faerwe, v.; gfaerbt, pp. 1.color; 2.dye

Faerwer (der)n. dyer

Falbel (die)n. 1.flounce; 2.furbelow

Falder (es)n.; Faldere, pl. 1.bars (removable, at entrance to a field or lane); 2.gate

Fall (der)n. 1.case; 2.drop; 3.fall

Fall (die)n.; Falle, pl. trap

Fallbrick (die)n. drawbridge

farze

Falldeer (die)n. trapdoor

Falldier (die)n. trapdoor

falle, v.; gfalle, pp. 1.be contributed; 2.fall

Falletgranke(e)t (die)n. epilepsy

Falliwalder (der)n. pound-apple.

Fallschtrick (der)n. snare

falsch, adj. 1.cross (of a horse); 2.false; 3.untrue; 4. treacherous; 5.(des macht mich --) that provokes me; 6.(-- bliehe) bloom without bearing; 7.(-- mache) provoke; 8.(-- schweere) (to) perjure oneself; 9.(-- warre) (to) acquire a grudge

Falschgsicht (es)n. mask

falschgsichtich, adj. hypocritical

Falschheet (die)n. 1.crossness; 2.latent grudge; 3.resentment; 4.untruth

falschi Zeh (der)n.; falschi Zeh, pl. false teeth

False (die)n., pl. 1.folds; 2.tucks; 3.wrinkles

Falt (die)n.; Falde, pl. 1.crease; 2.fold; 3.pleat; 4.wrinkle

Falter (die)n. bars (at entrance to field or lane)

Familye (die)n. 1.family; 2.(im e -- weg) pregnant

Familyenaame (der)n. surname

Familyeumschtende (die)n. family way

Fang (der)n. catch

fange, v.; gfange, pp. 1.capture; 2.catch; 3.seize; 4.(sich selwer --) contradict oneself; 5.(-- losse) (to)have someone arrested

Fangzaah (der)n.; Fangzeh, pl. 1.fang; 2.tusk

Fanness (die)n.; Fannesse, pl. furnace

fannich, adj. laughable

Far(r)eb (die)n.; Farewe, Farwe, pl. 1.color; 2.paint

far, prep. 1.for; 2.for the benefit of; 3.in exchange for 4.(was --) (a) what kind of; (b) what sort of

Farb (die)n.; Farwe; Farewe, pl. 1.color; 2.paint

Farbkessel (der)n. paint bucket

Farbmiehl (die)n. paint mill

Farbpensil (der)n. paintbrush

farewe, v.; gfarebt, pp. 1.color; 2.dye

Farewell!, interj. 1.adieu!; 2.farewell!

Farewer (der)n.; Farewer, pl. dyer

farewich, adj. colored

farich(t)los, adj. brave

Farichbutz (der)n. coward

farichbutzich, adv. cowardly

farichde, v.; gfaricht, pp. fear

farichderlich, adj. 1.dreadful; 2.terrible

fariche, v.; gfaricht, pp. 1.dread; 2.(sich --) (to be) afraid

farme, v.; gfaamt, pp. confirm

Farness (die)n. furnace

Farrich(t) (die)n.; Farrichde, pl. furrow

Farricht (die)n. 1.fear; 2.fright

Farschde (der)n. heel

Farscht (der)n. ridgepole

fart, adv. 1.away; 2.gone

farwich, adj. colored

Farz (der)n. fart

farze, v.; gfarzt, pp. fart

Ff

Fasandehinkel — Fedderschtiel

Fasandehinkel (es)n. Rhode Island Red (chicken)

Faschde (die)n., pl. Lent

faschde, v.; gfascht, pp. fast (at Lent)

Fascht (die)n. fast (at Lent)

fascht/mache, v.; faschtgemacht, pp. 1.fix; 2.repair

fascht, adj. 1.almost; 2.fast; 3.caught on something; 4.solid; 5.tight

Faschtdaag (der)n. fast day (Amish usage)

faschthalde, v.; faschtghalde, pp. keep hold of

Faschtnacht (die)n. Shrove Tuesday

faschtnemme, v.; faschtgenumme, pp. 1.arrest; 2.take hold of

faschtschtecke, v.; faschtgschtocke, pp. stick fast

faschtwarre, v.; faschtwarre, pp. 1. become stuck; 2. be puzzled

Faschtzeit (die)n. Lent

Fass (es)n.; Fesser, pl. 1.barrel; 2.cask; 3.keg

Fassant (die)n.; Fassande, pl. pheasant

Fassbinner (der)n. cooper

Fassdaub (die)n.; Fassdauwe, pl. stave (of a barrel, cask)

fasse, v.; gfasst, pp. 1.grasp; 2.measure into bags; 3.put into hives (bees); 4.take hold of

Fassenacht (die)n. Shrove Tuesday

Fassere (die)n., pl. 1.fibers; 2.threads

fatt/blaudre, v.; fattgeblaudert, pp. talk on

fatt/bleiwe, v.; fattgebliwwe, pp. 1.remain away; 2.stay away

fatt/bliehe, v.; fattgebieht, pp. continue to bloom

fatt/brauche, v.; fattgebraucht, pp. (to keep on) using

fatt/brenne, v.; fattgebrennt, pp. continue to burn

fatt/daerfe, v.; fattgedaerft, pp. be allowed to go

fatt/dauere, v.; fattgedauert, pp. last

fatt/draage, v.; fattgedraage, pp. carry away

fatt/dreiwe, v.; fattgedriwwe, pp. 1.chase off; 2.drive away

fatt/faahre, v.; fattgfaahre, pp. 1.drive away; 2.haul away

fatt/fiehre, v.; fattgfiehrt, pp. lead away

fatt/fliege, v.; fattgflogge, pp. fly away

fatt/geh, v.; fattgange, pp. 1.depart; 2.leave (on a trip); 3.go away

fatt/halde, v.; fattghalde, pp. continue as an institution

fatt/helfe, v.; fattgholfe, pp. 1.help away; 2.help along

fatt/kenne, v.; fattgekennt, pp. 1.be able to get about; 2.be able to get away

fatt/kumme, v.; is fattkumme, pp. succeed

fatt/laafe, v.; fattgeloffe, pp. walk away

fatt/lewe, v.; fattglebt, pp. continue to live

fatt/loddle, v.; fattgeloddelt, pp. jog along

fatt/mache, v.; fattgemacht, pp. 1.continue; 2.(mach fatt) be gone

fatt/maschiere, v.; fattmaschiert, pp. be off

fatt/misse, v.; fattgemisst, pp. be obliged to go

fatt/nemme, v.; fattgenumme take away

fatt/packe, v.; fattgepackt, pp. (sich --) to be gone

fatt/reggere, v.; fattgreggert, pp. rain on and on

fatt/reide, v.; fattgridde, pp. ride away

fatt/rolle, v.; fattgerollt, pp. roll away

fatt/schaffe, v.; fattgschafft, pp. 1.get rid of; 2.rid

fatt/schicke, v.; fattgschickt, pp. send away

fatt/schiewe, v.; fattgschowe, pp. push away

fatt/schleiche, v.; fattgschliche, pp. sneak away

fatt/schlofe, v.; fattgschlofe, pp. sleep on

fatt/schpringe, v.; fattgschprunge, pp. 1.flee; 2.run away

fatt/schreiwe, v.; fattgschriwwe, pp. 1.continue to write; 2.write to someone at a distance

fatt/schtiwwere, v.; fattgschtiwwert, pp. chase off or away

fatt/setze, v.; fattgsetzt, pp. continue

fatt/wachse, v.; fattgewachst, pp. continue to grow

fatt/wolle, v.; fattgewollt, pp. want to go away

fatt/yaage, v.; fattgeyaagt, pp. chase away

fatt/zackere, v.; fattgezackert, pp. keep on working

fatt/ziehe, v.; fattgezogge, pp. pull away

fatt, adv. 1.absent; 2.away; 3.off

Fattdauer (die)n. 1.continuation; 2.permanence

Fattschritt (der)n. progress

Fatzebrieh (die)n. wet fart

faul, adv. (ebbes --) something wrong

faul, adj. 1.lazy; 2.putrid; 3.rotten

faule, v.; gfault, pp. 1.decay; 2.rot

faulense, v.; gfaulenst, pp. 1.be lazy; 2.loaf; 3.lounge

Faulenzer (der)n.; Faulenzer, pl. 1.idler; 2.lazy person; 3.loafer; 4.sluggard

Faulerkees (der)n. pot cheese

Faulhals (der)n. diphtheria

Faulheet (die)n. laziness

Faulheit (die)n. 1.indolence; 2.laziness

Fauscht (die)n.; 1.fist; 2.(sich die -- voll lache) laugh in one's sleeve; 3.(en -- mache) threaten (with clenched fist)

Fauschthensching (der)n. mitten (with a separate thumb)

Faxe (die)n., pl. 1.nonsense; 2.tomfoolery

faxe, v.; gfaxt, pp. fool

Faxemacher (der)n. 1.buffoon; 2.funny fellow

Febrewaar (der)n. February

fechde, v.; gfochde, pp. fight

Fechder (der)n. fighter

Fechderei (die)n. quarrels

Fecht (der)n. fight

Fechthaahne (der)n. 1.game cock; 2.quarrelsome person

feckle, v.; gfeckelt, pp. coitus

fedd(e)rich, adj. 1.covered with feathers; 2.feathered

Fedder (die)n.; Feddre, pl. 1.feather; 2.pen; 3.spring

Fedderbett (es)n. feather bed

Fedderdeck (die)n. featherbed (cover)

feddere, v.; gfeddert, pl.; 1. feather; 2. (sich --) molt (of chickens)

Fedderfassing (die)n. bed ticking

Fedderhowel (die)n.; Fedderhowwle, pl. tongue and groove plane

Fedderkeidel (der)n. quill

Fedderkissi (es)n. pillow stuffed with feathers

Feddermesser (es)n. penknife

Fedderrohr (es)n. penholder

Fedderschtiel (der)n. penholder

Ff

Feddervieh

Feddervieh (es)n. poultry
Fedderwisch (der)n. feather duster
feddich, adj. 1.fatty; 2.greasy
Feddre schtraube (die)n. resist
feede, v.; gfeedt, pp. remove strings (of beans)
feel, adv. (for) sale
fege, v.; gfegt, pp. 1.clean; 2.run about; 3.sweep; 4.(sich --
)(a) clean up; (b) wash up
Feger (der)n. 1.cleaner; 2.harum-scarum woman;
3.scavenger
Fegerei (die)n. drudgery of cleaning
fehich, adj. 1.able; 2.capable; 3.fit
Fehichkeet (die)n.; Fehichkeit, pl. capability
fehl, adj. (unne --) fail(ing)
fehl, adv. for sale
Fehldritt (der)n. misstep
fehle, v.; g(e)fehlt, pp. 1.ail; 2.fail; 3.lack; 4.miss
fehle, v.; gfehlt, pp. (+dative case) (to be the) matter with
Fehler (der)n.; Fehler, pl. 1.blemish; 2.defect; 3.error;
4. fault; 5.infirmity; 6.mistake; 7.(-- am Hatz hawwe)
(to)have heart trouble
fehlerfrei, adj. perfect
fehlerhaft, adj. 1.faulty; 2.imperfect
Fehlgebort (die)n. miscarriage
fehlgeh, v.; fehlgange, pp. 1.abort; 2.miscarry; 3.miss one's way
fehlgreife, v.; fehlgegriffe, pp. (make a) mistake
Fehlgriff (der)n. blunder
fehl(g)schlagge, v.; fehlgschlagge, pp. 1.abort; 2. miscarry;
3.miss one's blow; 4.fail; 5.turn out unsuccessful
fehlschiesse, v.; fehlgschosse, pp. 1.fail to hit the mark;
2.miss; 3.(to be) mistaken
Fehlschlack (der)n. unsuccessful attempt
Fehlschuss (der)n. miss (in shooting)
Fehlyaa(h)r (es)n. year of poor crops
fei(n), adj. 1.artful; 2.excellent; 3.fine; 4.nice; 5.(en feiner
Kall) opposite of the literal meaning
fei/kaue, v.; feigekaut, pp. chew fine
fei/reisse, v.; feigerisse, pp. tear into pieces
fei, adj. 1.beautiful; 2.nice; 3."stuck up"; 4.(en feiner Kall)
opposite of the literal meaning - a rotten egg guy
Feichdichkeit (die)n. 1.dampness; 2.moistness
feicht, adj. 1.damp; 2.moist
Feichtichkeet (die)n. 1.dampness; 2.moisture
Feichtichkeit (die)n. moisture
Feier (es)n. fire
Feierblotzgrone (der)n. fireplace crane
Feierblumm (die)n. cardinal flower
Feierbohn (die)n.; Feierbohne, pl. 1.(tree) kidney bean;
2.scarlet runner
Feierbrand (der)n. 1.brand; 2.burning stick
Feierbuhn (die)n.; Feierbuhne, pl. 1.(tree) kidney bean;
2.scarlet runner
Feierdaag (der)n.; Feierdaage, pl. holiday
feiere, v.; gfeiert, pp. 1.celebrate; 2.(to start a) fire;
3.keep a fire going
Feiereck (es)n.; Feierecke, pl. fireplace

Feldwelschkann

Feiereifer (der)n. energetic spell
Feierflamm (die)n. red-hot poker plant
Feierfliek (die)n. fire fly
Feierfresser (der)n. 1.bully; 2.fire eater
Feierfunke (der)n. spark
Feierhard (der)n.; Feierhard, pl. 1.hearth; 2.fireplace
Feierhohl (der)n. trammel
Feierholz (es)n. 1.firewood; 2.kindling
feierich, adj. fiery
Feierkeffer (der)n.; Feierkeffer, pl. lightning bug
Feierkolwe (der)n. red nose
feierlich, adj. solemn
Feierlichkeet (die)n. 1.celebration; 2.solemnity
Feiermann (der)n. fireman
Feierowed (der)n. cessation from work
Feierplatz (der)n.; Feierbletz, pl. fireplace
Feierrodeblatt (die)n. cardinal flower
feierrot, adj. fire red
Feierschipp (die)n. fire shovel
Feierschtee (der)n.; Feierschtee, pl. flint
Feiervoggel (der)n.; Feierveggel, pl. 1.firefly; 2.lightning bug
Feierwaerrick (es)n. fireworks
Feierzang (die)n.; Feierzange, pl. fire tongs
Feigebaam (der)n. fig tree
feigloppe, v.; feigegloppt, pp. 1.beat fine; 2.beat to a powder
feignochich, adj. small-boned
feihacke, v.; feikackt, pp. chop fine
feihaerich, adj. snobbish
Feik (die)n. fig
Feil (die)n.; Feile, pl. file
feile, v.; gfeilt, pp. file
feimache, v.; feigemacht, pp. 1.break into small pieces;
2.chop wood (for the stove)
Feind (der)n.; Feind, pl. 1.adversary; 2.enemy; 3.foe
feind, adj. hostile
feindlich, adj. hostile
Feindschaft (die)n. 1.dislike; 2.enmity
feindselich, adj. hostile
feireisse, v.; feigrisse, pp. tear into small pieces
feirich, adj. fiery
feischdle, v.; gfeischdelt, pp. flourish one's fists
feischtenglich, adj. fine (literally and figuratively)
feischtielich, adj. 1.fine; 2.soft
fek, adj. (en alti --) gadabout
Fekfeier (es)n. purgatory
Feld (es)n.; Felder, pl. field
Feldbau (der)n. agriculture
Feldbohn (die)n.; Feldbohne, pl. navy bean
Feldbreddicher (der)n. army chaplain
Feldflasch (die)n. canteen
Feldhaerr (der)n. general
Feldhinkel (es)n. 1.plover; 2.prairie chicken; 3.quail
Feldi (der)n. Valentine
Feldlilye (die)n. 1.Canada lily; 2.meadow lily
Feldmaus (die)n.; Feldmeis, pl. field mouse
Feldwelschkann (es)n. Indian corn

Ff

Feldzuch

fimfmol

Feldzuch (der)n. campaign

Felg (die)n.; Felge, pl. felloe (of a wagon wheel)

Fell (es)n. 1.membrane; 2.pelt; 3.skin

Fellgnopp (der)n. magic bag for curing a membrane over the pupil of the eye

fellich, adv. fully

felsche, v.; gfelscht, pp. forge (records)

Felsching (die)n. 1.changing records; 2.forgery

Felse (der)n.; Felse, pl. 1.boulder; 2.rock

Felsebulwer (es)n. powder used for blasting

Felsekopp (der)n. 1.nigger head; 2.rocky summit; 3. solitary rock (from glacial period)

Felsemoos (es)n. rock-moss

Felsepulfer (es)n. powder used for blasting

felsich, adj. rocky

Fend(y)u (die)n. public sale

fendere, v.; gfendert, pp.; 1.risk; 2.(sich --) (a) risk; (b) venture

Fennichel (der)n. fennel

Fens (die)n.; Fense, pl. fence

Fenschder (es)n.; Fenschdere, pl. window

Fenschderglaas (es)n. windowpane

Fenschdergschtell (es)n. 1.window frame; 2.window seat; 3.window sill

Fenschderkitt (der)n. putty

Fenschderlaade (der)n. shutter

Fenschderraam (der)n. window sash

Fenschderscheib (die)n.; Fenschderscheiwe, pl. pane (of glass)

Fenschdersitz (der)n. 1.window seat; 2.window sill

Fensemaus (die)n.; Fensemeis, pl. chipmunk

Fenseriggel (der)n.; Fenseriggel, pl. fence rail

fer, adv. 1.(-- Parebes) purposely; 2.(-- schur) surely

fer, prep. 1.for; 2.for the benefit of; 3.in exchange; 4.(-- Zeit) ahead of time; 5.(was --) (a) what kind of; (b) what sort of

fer was, conj. why

Ferien (die)n., pl. vacation

Ferri (die)n. ferry

Ferriboot (die)n. ferryboat

Fersandebeer (die)n. 1.checkerberry; 2.partridge berry (Mitchella repens)

Fersant (die)n. pheasant

Fersantehinkel (es)n. breed of fowls somewhat resembling Rhode Island Reds

ferwas, adv. why

Fescht (es)n.; Feschder, pl. 1.banquet; 2.feast; 3. celebration; 4.festival

fescht mache, v.; fescht gemacht, pp. fasten

fescht/babbe, v.; feschtgebabbt, pp. adhere

fescht/hewwe, v.; feschtghowe, pp. hold fast

fescht/kedde, v.; feschtgekett, pp. chain fast

fescht, adj. 1.caught on something; 2.fast; 3.tight

fescht, adv. 1.fast; 2.firm; 3.tight; 4.(--er Leib) constipation

Feschtdaag (der)n. holiday

feschtleiwich, adj. constipated

Feschtred (es)n. speech (at a meeting, banquet)

Fesse(l) (es)n. small keg

Fessli (es)n.; Fesslin, pl. 1.barrel; 2.cask; 3.keg

festlich, adj. festal

Fett (es)n. 1.fat; 2.grease; 3.lard; 4.suet

fett, adj. 1.fat; 2.plump; 3.stout; 4.rich (soil)

Fettamschel (die)n. lard-burning lamp

Fettblacke (der)n. grease spot

Fettbress (die)n. lard press

Fettheffli (es)n. 1.oil gland (of fowl); 2.uropygial gland

fettich, adj. 1.fatty; 2.greasy

Fettkechliche(r) (es)n. cruller

Fettkichelche(r) (es)n. cruller

Fettkuche (der)n. doughnut

Fettlicht (es)n. lamp in which a wick dipped in fat was used

Fettpann (die)n.; Fettpanne, pl. 1.oil gland (of fowl); 2.uropygial gland

Fettschnebbel (der)n. 1.oil gland (of fowl); 2.uropygial gland

Fetze (der)n. shred

Fetzel (die)n. female pudendum

ficke, v.; gfickt, pp. coitus

Fickmiehl (die)n. tit-tat-toe

Fiddelboge (der)n.; Fiddelboge, pl. 1.fiddlestick; 2.violin bow; 3.hieroglyphic; 4.any crooked implement

Fiedel (die)n. fiddle

fiedere, v.; gfiedert, pp. feed

fiederes, v. chores at the barn

fiege, v.; gfiekt, pp.; 1.join; 2.(sich ebbes --) yield

fiehlba(a)r, adj. tangible

fiehle, v.; gfiehlt, pp. 1.feel; 2.(schlecht --) (a) ail; (b) be ill

fiehre, v.; gfiehrt, pp. lead

Fiehrer (der)n. guide

Fiehseiche (es)n. shoat butchered in fall

fiessle, v.; gfiesselt, pp. 1.take short steps; 2.walk rapidly

Fiewer (es)n. fever

Fiewergraut (es)n. feverwort

fiewerisch, adj. feverish

figgere, v.; gfiggert, pp. 1.figure out; 2.reckon

Figur (die)n. figure

Fil(l)sel (es) n. 1. forcemeat; 2. meat scraps left from butchering; 3.sausage; 4.stuffing

Fill (es)n.; Filler, pl. 1.filly; 2.silly person

fille, v.; gfillt, pp. 1.farce; 2.fill; 3.foal

Fill(i) (die)n. 1.abundance; 2.fill

Filli (es)n.; Filler, pl. filly

Filling (die)n. 1.filling; 2.stuffing (of roast fowl)

Filsglaech (der)n. fetlock joint of a horse

Filsing (der)n. stuffing

Filslaus (die)n.; Filsleis, pl. crab louse

fimf Bicher Mosis (die)n. Pentateuch

fimf-feldich, adj. 1.five fold; 2.quintuple

Fimfblettrich, adj. five-leaved

Fimfdaalernot (die)n. five dollar bill

fimfe; fimf, adj. five

fimfeckich, adj. five cornered

Fimffingergraut (es)n. cinquefoil

fimfmol, adj. five times

57

Ff

fimfschteckich

fimfschteckich, adj. five storied
fimfseidich, adj. pentagonal
Fimftel (es)n. fifth (part)
Fimftraad (es)n.; Fimftredder, pl. turntable for front
    wagon wheels
fimfyaahrich, adj. quinquennial
Finfsentschtick (es)n.; Finfsentschticker, pl. nickel (coin)
Finger (der)n.; Finger, pl. 1.finger; 2.tendril;
    3. (lange -- hawwe) be inclined to pilfer
fingere, v.; gfingert, pp. finger
Fingerhensching (der)n. glove
Fingerhut (der)n.; Fingerhiet, pl. thimble
fingeriere, v.; gfingeriert, pp. finger
Fingerling (der) n.; Fingerling, pl. 1. finger-stall; 2. finger
    bandage
Fingernaggel (der).; Fingerneggel, pl. fingernail
Fingerring (der)n. ring (jewelry)
fingersdick, adj. thick as a finger
fingerslang, adj. of the length of a finger
finiere, v.; finiert, pp. veneer
Fink (der)n. finch
finkle, v.; gfinkelt, pp. sparkle
Finne (die)n., pl. garget (a hog disease)
finne, v.; gfunne, pp. 1.find; 2.locate
Finner (der)n.; Finner, pl. finder
Finschder (es)n.; Finschdere, pl. window
finschder, adj. dark
Finschderlaade (der)n. shutter
Finschderniss (die)n.; Finschdernisse, pl. eclipse
fiole, v.; gfiolt, pp. 1.abuse; 2.torment
Fipp (der)n.; Fippe, pl. fipenny bit
Fisch (der) n.; Fisch, pl. 1. fish; 2. Pisces (12th sign of the
    zodiac); 3.tenderloin
Fischangel (die)n. fishhook
Fischbee (der)n. whalebone
fischbele, v.; gfischbelt, pp. feel one's way about (in the dark)
Fischbrud (die)n. spawn
fische, v.; gfischt, pp. 1.angle; 2.fish
Fischeel (es)n. fish oil
Fischel (es)n. little fish
Fischer (der)n. fisherman
Fischerei (die)n. fishery
Fischgaarn (es)n.; Fischgaarne, pl. fishnet
Fischgatt (die)n.; Fischgadde, pl. 1.fish pole; 2.fish rod
Fischgraan (die)n.; Fischgranne, pl. fish bone
Fischhammer (der)n. hand net
Fischhoge (der)n.; Fischhoge, pl. fishhook
Fischkunscht (die)n. ichthyology
Fischli (es)n. tenderloin
Fischlin (die)n., pl. tenderloin
Fischohr (es)n. gill
Fischoier (die)n., pl. 1.fish eggs; 2.roe
Fischreiher (der)n. crane
Fischroiger (der)n. 1.crane; 2.heron
Fischsals (es)n. course salt
Fischschippe (die)n., pl. fish scales

Flaxsume

Fischschlupp (der)n. 1.fishing loop of wire; 2.weel
Fischschtecher (der)n. gig
Fischschubbe (die)n.; Fischschibbe, pl. fishscale
Fischwarem (der)n. earthworm
Fischwieher (der)n. fish pond
Fishroier (der)n. crane
Fitz (die)n. 1.lash; 2.rod; 3.whip
fitze, v.; gfitzt, pp. 1.lash; 2.whip
Fitzeel (es)n. (mit -- schmiere) 1.flog; 2.whip
fitzle, v.; gfitzelt, pp. 1.lash; 2.whip
fix un faddich, adj. completely done
fix un faerdich, adj. all ready
fix, adj. 1.quick; 2.nimble; 3.ready; 4.(aus --) (a) (out of)
    order; (b) (out of) wack; (c) ruined
fix, adv. nimble
flabbe,v.; gflabbt, pp. spank
flach, adj. 1.flat; 2.plain; 3.shallow
flachse, adj. (of) flax
flachse, v.; gflachst, pp. 1.beat; 2.cheat; 3.flog
flachsiere, v.; gflachsiert, pp. 1.handle roughly; 2.lambast
flack(e)re, v.; gflackert, pp. 1.flare; 2.flicker
flack(e)rich, adj. 1.flaring; 2.flickering; 3.inconsistent
Fladderwisch (der)n. 1.fickle girl; 2.wing of turkey or
    goose used for dusting
fladdre, v.; gfladdert, pp. 1.flap; 2.flutter
Flaehm (die)n. 1.flank; 2.(en gfilldi --) stuffed flank
Flaeschlicht (es)n.; Flaeschlichder, pl. flashlight
Flamm (die)n.; Flamme, pl. flame
flamme, v.; gflammt, pp. 1.blaze; 2.flame
Flammkuche (der)n. pancake
Flank (die)n. flank
flankiere, v.; gflankiert, pp. 1.arrange; 2.rove
Flannel (der)n. flannel
flannelle, adj. (of) flannel
Flapp (der)n. 1.flap; 2.flop
flappe, v.; gflappt, pp. 1.flap; 2.flop; 3.spank
flappich, adj. 1.flapping; 2.pendent
Flasch (die)n. 1.flask; 2.small bottle
flatsch!, interj. 1.crash!; 2.smash!
flatsche, v.; gflatscht, pp. 1.gossip; 2.splash in water
Flatterros (die)n. poppy
Flaum (der)n. down
Flaumgraas (es)n. witch grass
Flause (die)n., pl. 1.humbug; 2.tricks
Flax (der)n. flax
Flaxbaue (es)n. flax culture
Flaxbrech (die)n. flax break
Flaxdaerr (die)n. arrangement on which flax is dried
Flaxdotter (der)n. dodder
Flaxhatchel (die)n. hatchel
flaxkebbich, adj. towheaded
Flaxkopp (der)n. towhead
Flaxschwing (die)n. scutch
Flaxseide (der)n. dodder
Flaxsome (der)n. linseed
Flaxsume (der)n. linseed

Ff

flechde

flechde, v.; g(e)flochde, pp. 1.braid; 2.plait

flechich, adj. variegated

Flecht (die)n.; Flechde, pl. braid

Fleck(e) (der)n.; Flecke, pl. 1.patch; 2.spot; 3.small piece of cloth; 4.stain

flecke, v.; gfleckt, pp. 1.spot; 2.stain

fleckich, adj. 1.dappled; 2.soiled; 3.spotted

Fleddermaus (der)n.; Fleddermeis, pl. 1.butterfly; 2.moth

Fledderraad (es)n.; Fledderredder, pl. paddle wheel

Fledderwisch (der)n. feather duster

Fleehgraut (es)n. 1.common smart weed; 2.daisy flea-bane; 3.princes' feather

Fleesch (es)n. meat

Fleeschbank (die)n. meat-bench (on which meat is worked up)

Fleeschbrieh (die)n. broth

Fleeschgawwel (die)n. meat-fork

Fleeschhaffe (der)n. meat-pot (for preserving meat)

Fleeschhoke (der)n. meat-hook

fleeschich, adj. 1.fleshy; 2.meaty

Fleeschmiehl (die)n. meat grinder

Fleeschseeg (die)n.; Fleeschseege, pl. meat-saw

Fleet (die)n. flute

fleeze, v.; gfleezt, pp. (to deposit) silt

Fleggel (der)n.; Fleggel, pl. 1.flail; 2.unmannerly fellow

fleggele, v.; gfleggelt, pp. drub

fleggelhaft, adj. unmannerly

fleggelhaft, adv. 1.impertinent; 2.unmannerly

fleggelhefdich, adv. terribly

Fleggelkilb (die)n. swingle (of a flail)

Fleggelkopp (der)n. U-shaped piece connecting handle and swingle of a flail

Fleggelruut (die)n. handle of a flail

flehe, v.; gfleht, pp. implore

Flehgraut (es)n. 1.daisy fleabane; 2.princes' feather; 3.ragweed; 4.(common) smartweed

Fleiss (der)n. industry

fleissend, adj. flowing

fleissich, adj. 1.busy (diligent); 2.industrious

flenne, v.; gflennt, pp. weep

Flex (die)n. 1.sinew; 2.tendon

flexe, adj. linen

flexich, adj. sinewy

Flick (es)n.; Flick, pl. patch (repair)

flick, adj. 1.full fledged; 2.pubescent; 3.pluck able (of goose feathers at certain seasons)

Flickaerwet(t) (die)n. 1.mending; 2.patching; 3.patchwork

flicke, v.; gflickt, pp. 1.mend; 2.patch; 3.(to do) patchwork

Flicker (es)n.; Flicker, pl. scarlet tanager

Flickeri (die)n. confounded mending

flickrich, adj. 1.flaring; 2.flickering

Flickwese (es)n. 1.act of mending; 2.mending material

Flieg (die)n.; Fliege, pl. fly

fliege, v.; gfloge, pp. fly

fliegend, adj. flying

Fliegzeit (die)n. 1.time when birds of passage take their flight; 2.time when young birds can fly

Frack

Flies (es)n. fuzz

fliesse, v.; gflosse, pp. flow

fliessend, adj. 1.flowing; 2.fluent; 3.running

Fliggel (der)n.; Fliggel, pl. wing

Fliggeldisch (der)n. table with extensions (drop-leaf table)

fliggele, v.; gfliggelt, pp. cut the wing feathers of chickens

Fliggelmauer (die)n. wing wall of a bridge

Fliggelrock (der)n. swallowtail coat

Flindegscheft (es)n. gun stock

Flindekolwe (der)n. gun stock

Flindelaaf (der)n.; Flindeleef, pl. gun barrel

Flindeloch (es)n.; Flindelecher, pl. muzzle

flink, adj. 1.agile; 2.lively; 3.nimble

flink, adv. quick

flinke, v.; gflinkt, pp. 1.shine; 2.sparkle

flinsche, v.; gflinscht, pp. 1.falter; 2.flinch

Flint (die)n.; Flinde, pl. 1.gun; 2.(gezogni --) rifled gun

flischbere, v.; gflischbert, pp. whisper

flissich, adj. 1.liquid; 2.said of discharging matter (from a sore)

flitsche, v.; gflitscht, pp. 1.blaze trees in surveying; 2. glance off; 3. skip stones over water surface; 4.slip off

Flitscher (der)n. 1.milk-pie; 2.slight crack of whip

Flitterwoch (die)n., pl. honeymoon

flitze, v.; gflitzt, pp. 1.flash; 2.flit; 3.move rapidly

Flocke (der)n.; Flocke, pl. flake

flockich, adj. flaky

Floh (der)n.; Fleh, pl. flea

Floor (der)n. crepe

floribus, adv. (in) plenty

Fluch (der)n. 1.curse; 2.(kenn -- waert) not worth a damn

fluche, v.; gflucht, pp. 1.curse; 2.swear

Flucher (der)n. 1.blasphemous person; 2.swearer

Flucherei (die)n. 1.profanity; 2.swearing

Flucht (die)n. 1.escape; 2.flight; 3.stampede

Fluck (der)n. 1.flight; 2.flock; 3.(im --) on the wing

flunke, v.; gflunkelt, pp. sparkle

Fluss (der)n. 1.flood; 2.flux; 3.inflammation; 4.rheumatism

Flussfedder (die)n. fin (of a fish)

flussich, adj. 1.rheumy; 2.scrofulous

Flusskarrell (die)n. amber bead

Flut (die)n. 1.flood; 2.high water

Flutter (die)n. diarrhea

fodd(e)re, v.; gfoddert, pp. 1.ask; 2.claim; 3.demand

Fodderes (es)n. 1.application; 2.claim; 3.demand; 4.request

Foddrung (die)n. requirement

Folge (die)n., pl. consequences

Folger (der)n. follower

folye, v.; gfol(i)gt, pp. 1.follow; 2.listen; 3.obey

foppe, v.; gfoppt, pp. 1.banter; 2.deceive; 3.fool

Forell (die)n., Forelle, pl. trout

Form (die)n. 1.form; 2.mold

Fortsch (der)n. forge

Fotz (die)n. female pudendum

Fraa (die)n.; Weibsleit; Weiwer, pl. 1.wife; 2.(en iw-werausi scheni --) a very pretty woman

Frack (der)n.; Fracke, pl. dress

Ff

Frackmachern / friescht

Frackmachern (die)n. 1.dressmaker; 2.seamstress
Fraktura (die)n., pl. Gothic letters or figures
frakture, v.; gfrakturt, pp. (to) write in Gothic letters
Frankreich (es)n. France
franseesich, adj. French
Fransel (die)n.; Fransle, pl. 1.fringe; 2.tassel
franslich, adj. fringed
Frant (die)n. front
franzeesisch, adj. French
Franzose (die)n.,pl. venereal disease
Fratzel (es)n. 1.heretic; 2.rascal; 3.son-of-a-gun
Fratzhans (der)n. 1.dude; 2.fop
fratzich, adj. foppish
Fratznaesel (es)n. (impudent little) snip
frech, adj. 1.impudent; 2.saucy
Freede (die)n. 1.delight; 2.joy
freedich, adj. 1.gladly; 2.joyfully
frefelhaft, adj. vulgar
frehe, v.; gfreht, pp. (sich --) rejoice
frehlich, adj. 1.cheerful; 2.happy; 3.joyful; 4.merry
Frehlichkeet (die)n. merriment
Frehlichkeit (die)n. 1.joy; 2.pleasure
frei/geh, v.; freigange, pp. (to be) released
frei/gewwe, v.; freigewwe, pp. 1.release; 2.set free
frei/laafe, v.; freigloffe, pp. roam at large (of cattle)
frei/losse, v.; freiglosst, pp. 1.absolve; 2.release
frei/mache, v.; freigemacht, pp. set free
frei/reisse, v.; freigrisse, pp. (sich --) escape
frei/schpreche, v.; freischproche, pp. 1.absolve; 2.set free
frei/setze, v.; freigsetzt, pp. liberate
frei, adj. 1.clear; 2.exempt; 3.free
Freidaag (der)n. Friday
Freide (die)n. 1.delight; 2.joy
Freidefeier (es)n. bonfire
Freidenker (der)n. free thinker
freie, v.; gfreit, pp. 1.court; 2.woo
Freierei (die)n. 1.courtship; 2.wooing
freigew(w)ich, adj. 1. charitable; 2.generous; 3.liberal (in giving)
Freigleeder (die)n.,pl. suit of clothes given an apprentice, servant, hired boy at the end of service
freihaerich, adj. sophisticated
freihalte, v.; 1.defray (someone's) expenses; 2.(sich --) guard against
Freiheit (die)n. 1.freedom; 2.liberty
Freiheitsbaam (der)n. Lombardy popular
Freihlich Neiyaahr!, interj. Happy New Year!
freihzeidich, adv. prematurely
freilich, adj. 1.certainly; 2.to be sure
freilich, adv. 1.certainly; 2.surely; 3.of course
Freimaurer (der)n. Free Mason
Freind (der)n.; Freind, pl. 1.friend; 2.relative
Freind (die)n., pl. 1.relations; 2.relatives
freindlich, adj. 1.amicable; 2.friendly; 3.kind; 4.pleasant
Freindschaft (die)n. 1.friendship; 2.kin; 3.relatives
freindschaftlich, adj. amicable

Freinschaft (der)n. (in -- sei) (to be) related to
Freischul (die)n. public school
freiwillich, adj. voluntarily
freiwillich, adv. 1.freely; 2.voluntarily
Frelichkeet (die)n. mirth
fremd, adj. unfamiliar
Fremder (en)n. stranger
fremm, adj. 1.strange; 2.unacquainted; 3.unfamiliar
Fremmer (der)n. 1.alien; 2.stranger
Fremmi (die)n. alien
Fresch (die)n., pl. spring peepers
Freschmeiler (die)n., pl. snapdragons
Fressdier (es)n. glutton
Fresse (es)n. 1.eating (of animals); 2.food (of dogs); 3.feed (of horses and poultry); 4.rich pickings; 5.(am -- draa sei) gnaw at; 6.(en Fress) (a) a great feed; (b) grand feast
fresse, v.; gfresse, pp. 1.eat (of animals); 2.eat too much or gluttonously (of a person); 3.(sich --) (a) recover; (b) regain
Fresser (der)n.; Fresser, pl. glutton
Fresserei (die)n. gluttony
Fressgranket (die)n. gluttony
Fresshals (der)n. glutton
Fresshunger (der)n. 1.bulimia; 2.voracious appetite
Frewel (der)n. 1.blasphemy; 2.wickedness
frewelhaft, adj. 1.blasphemous; 2.outrageous
Fridder (der)n. Frederick
Fridderich (der)n. Frederick
Fridricke (die)n. Frederica
Friede (der)n. (weiss der --) 1.goodness knows!; 2.sure as you're alive!
Friede (der)n. 1.peace; 2.unity; 3.quiet; 4.(du liewer --) great goodness!; 5.(-- schtifde) restore peace
Friedensgriek (der)n. war for independence
Friedensrichter (der)n. justice of the peace
friedlich, adj. 1.amicable; 2.peaceable; 3.peaceful
Frieh (die)n. (in aller --) early in the morning
frieh, adv. early
Friehabbel (der)n.; Friehebbel, pl. harvest apple
Friehbeer (die)n. early pear
frieher, adv. 1.earlier; 2.formerly
Friehgraut (es)n. early cabbage
Friehgrumbeer (die)n. early potato
Friehling (der)n. spring (season)
Friehling (die)n., pl. spring peepers
Friehseiche (es)n. shoat butchered in fall
Friehschtick (es)n. breakfast
Friehwelschkann (es)n. early corn
Friehyaahr (es)n. spring (season)
Friehyaahrsdaag (der)n. spring day
Friehyaahrswedder (es)n. spring weather
friehzeitich, adj. 1.early; 2.prematurely
Friere(s) (es)n. chill
friere, v.; gfrore, pp. 1.freeze; 2.(es friert mich) I'm shivering
friescht, adv. earliest

Ff

frisch | fuxich

frisch, adj. 1.bold; 2.cool; 3.fresh; 4.new

Frischsalz (es)n. (course) salt

Frissel (es)n. rash

Fritz (der)n. Frederick

Frog(et) (die)n. 1.inquiry; 2.question

froge, v.; gfrogt, pp. 1.ask; 2.demand

froh, adj. 1.happy; 2.glad

fromm, adj. 1.devout; 2.pious; 3.traceable (of animals)

Frommichkeet (die)n. piety

Frommichkeit (die)n. piety

Front (die)n. front

Frosch (der)n.; Fresch, pl. 1.frog; 2.midge (spring peeper); 3.tree frog

Froscht (der)n. frost

frotsich, adj. dudish

Frucht (die)n. 1.fruit of a tree (rare usage); 2.grain (maturing on the field or after it is threshed)

fruchtbaar, adj. 1.fertile; 2.fruitful

Fruchtblans (die)n. cereal

Fruchtfeld (es)n. grain field

Fruchtgawwel (die)n.; Fruchtgawwle, pl. wheat fork

Fruchtgraan (die)n. beard (of grain)

Fruchthaus (es)n. grain elevator

Fruchtkaern (die)n. 1.grain; 2.kernel

Fruchtkammer (die)n. 1.bin; 2.box; 3.case; 4.chest; 5.granary (in the barn)

Fruchtland (es)n. land adapted for grains

Fruchtmaschien (die)n. reaper

Fruchtreff (es)n. grain cradle

frumm, adj. 1.devout; 2.gentle or tractable (of animals); 3.pious

fuchse, v.; gfuchst, pp. coitus

fuchsschwans, adj. a common weed

fuddre, v.; gfuddert, pp. 1.find fault; 2.grumble; 3.remonstrate

Fuder (es)n. 1.feed (for animals); 2.lining (of a garment)

Fuderbank (die)n. feed cutter

Fuderdrog (der)n.; Fuderdreeg, pl. 1.food trough;2.manger; 3.mixing trough (for feed)

fudere, v.; gfudert, pp. line a garment

Fudergang (der)n. 1.entry in a barn along the stalls; 2.feed entry

Fuderzeddel (der)n. menu

fuffzeh, adj.; pron. fifteen

fuffzich, adj.; pron. 1.fifty; 2.a run of four of the same suit (above the seven spot) in the game of datte

fuffzichyaehrich, adj. semi-centennial

Fuggadivus (der)n. 1.rogue; 2.scamp

Fuhr (die)n.; Fuhre, pl. team (of horses, or horses and wagon)

Fuhreleit (die)n. Team Mennonites

Fuhrloh (der)n. 1.(cost of) cartage; 2.haulage

Fuhrmann (der)n.; Fuhrmenner, pl. 1.coachman; 2.driver; 3.drover; 4.teamster

Fuhrmannsgeeschel (die)n. horse whip

Fuhrwaerick (es)n. vehicle

Fuhrwese (es)n. vehicle (usually applied to a carriage or buggy)

Fui!, interj. 1.don't touch! 2.ugh!

Fundament (es)n.; Fundamender, pl. foundation

Fundementmauer (die)n. foundation wall

Fundementschtee (der)n. foundation stone

funggiere, v.; gfunggiert, pp. 1.act; 2.function

Funke (der)n.; Funke, pl. spark

funkel (naagel) nei, adj. (brand) new

Funkezabbe (der)n. spark plug

funkle, v.; gfunkelt, pp. 1.glisten; 2.sparkle

Furcht (die)n. terror

fus(e)rich, adj. fuzzy

Fusser (es)n. fuzz

fussle, v.; gfusselt, pp. finger or hunt in the dark

Fussre (die)n., pl. fuzz

futsch, adv. 1.all into; 2.done for; 3.come to nothing

Fuug (die)n. rabbet

Fuuge (die)n. (aus -- sei) be out of joint

Fuus (der)n.; Fiess, pl. 1.foot; 2.stove-block (placed under stove legs); 3.(zu --) on foot

Fuusbrick (die)n.; Fussbricke, pl. footbridge

Fuusgenger (der)n. pedestrian

Fuusohl (die)n. sole of foot

Fuusweg (der)n.; Fusswege, pl. pathway

Fuusbaad (es)n. foot bath

Fuusdappe (der)n. foot print

Fuusend (es)n. foot end

Fuushald (die)n. foot hold

Fuuspaad (der)n. footpath

Fuusschtoss (der)n. kick

Fux (der)n.; Fix, pl. fox

Fuxgaul (der)n. sorrel horse

fuxich, adj. 1.astute; 2.sly

Gg

Gaab / Garrick

Gaab (die)n.; Gaawa, pl. 1.ability; 2.talent
gaar kenner; kenni; adj., pron. none at all
gaar nix, pron. nothing at all
gaar, adj. 1.cooked thoroughly; 2.well-done
gaar, adv. 1.quite; 2.very
Gaarde (der)n.; Gerde, pl. 1.garden; 2.(-- graawe) (to dig) garden
Gaardebau (der)n. horticulture
Gaardehack (die)n. garden hoe
Gaardelilye (die)n. common white lily
Gaardenaggli (es)n. carnation
Gaardepeffer (der)n.; Gaardepeffer, pl. sweet peppers
Gaardesach (es)n. vegetables
Gaardeselaat (der)n. (cultivated) lettuce
Gaardeweg (der)n. garden path
Gaardezau (der)n. garden fence
Gaarn (es)n. 1.net; 2.twine; 3.yarn
Gaarnschlupp (der)n. mesh
Gaawrel (der)n. Gabriel
Gachnauf (es)n. chattering
Gacke (die)n. 1.chatterer; 2.tiresome talker
Gackel (die)n. chattering silly woman
Gackel (es)n. egg (in child talk)
gackere, v.; gegackert, pp. 1.cackle; 2.chatter
Gackerli (es)n. egg (in child talk)
Gacki (es)n. egg (in child talk)
gackrich, adj. 1.cackling; 2.talkative
gackse, v.; gegackst, pp. 1.cackle; 2.chatter
gadde, v.; gegaddt, pp. 1.switch; 2.whip
gadollisch, adj. catholic
Gadu(n) (der)n. calico
gaebbe, v.; gegaeppt, pp. yawn
gaeh(e), adj. steep
gaehre, v.; gegaehrt; gegohre, pp. ferment
Gaellesse (die)n. suspenders
gaerde, v.; gegaerdt, pp. 1.switch; 2.whip
Gaerdel (der)n. 1.belt; 2.girth; 3.zone; 4.girdle
gaerdle, v.; gegaerdelt, pp. 1.garden; 2.girdle (a tree)
Gaerdler (der)n. gardener
Gaerdli (es)n. little garden
Gaerdner (der)n. gardener
gaern, adv. 1.be likely to; 2.gladly; 3.willingly; 4.(-- esse) (a) be fond of; (b) (to) like (to eat); 5.(-- hawwe) (a) like; (b) (to) be fond of; 6.(mer wolle -- sehne) we will await with interest
Gaerschde (der)n. barley
Gaerscht (der)n. barley
gaerwe, v.; gegaerbt, pp. 1.give a beating; 2.tan
Gaerwerei (die)n. tannery
Gaerwergrub (die)n. tanner's vat
Gaerwerloh (die)n. tanbark
Gaerwersgaul (der)n. (uff em --) afoot
Gaeti (die)n. Katie
Gaewer (der)n.; Gaewer, pl. tanner
gaffe, v.; gegafft, pp. 1.gape; 2.stare; 3.tell tales
gafflich, adj. 1.fidgety; 2.inattentive

Gaffmaul (es)n. telltale
Galge (der)n. gallows
Galgedieb (der)n. scoundrel
Galgeholz (es)n. gallows wood
Galgeschtrick (der)n. scamp
Galgevoggel (der)n. 1.heretic; 2.rascal
Gall (die)n. 1.bile; 2.gall; 3.gallbladder; 4.gallon
Gall(e)blos (der)n. gallbladder
Gall(e)schtee (der)n.; Gall(e)schtee, pl. gallstone
Gall(uun) (die)n.; Gall(uun)e, pl. gallon
Gallebbel (die)n., pl. gall nuts
Galleblech (es)n. gallon measure
Gallefiewer (es)n. bilious fever
gallegrie, adj. green as gall
Galleri(ch) (es)n. 1.pig's feet jelly; 2.souse
Gallesse (die)n. suspenders
Gallewoch (die)n. week of October 16
Gallrich (der)n. 1.pig's feet jelly; 2.souse
Gallrieb (die)n.; Gallriewe, pl. rutabaga
Gallun (die)n. gallon
Galopp (der)n. gallop (nursery rhyme)
Galye (der)n.; Galye, pl. 1.gallows; 2.scaffold
G(a)mander (der)n. germander
Gamber (der)n. camphor
Gamfer (der)n. camphor
Gamm (der)n. rubber
Gammballe (der)n. rubber ball
Gammdeichel (der, es)n. rubber hose
Gammditz (der)n. 1.baby pacifier; 2.rubber nipple
gammel, v.; gegammelt, pp. gamble
Gammler (der)n.; Gammler, pl. gambler
Gammschtiwwel (der)n. rubber boots
Gammschuh (der)n. rubber overshoe
Gang (der)n.; Geng, pl. 1.aisle; 2.corridor; 3.entry hall; 4.hallway; 5.passageway; 6.(eenes --s) (a) directly; (b) straightway; 7.(im --) going
gangbaar, adv. passable
Gangnerkuche (der)n.; 1.doughnut; 2. raised potato cake
Gank (der)n.; Geng, pl. 1.hall; 2.hallway
Gans (die)n.; Gens, pl. 1.goose; 2.silly person
Gansert (der)n.; Gansert, pl. 1.drake; 2.gander
ganz Bedallye (es)n. (the whole) shebang
ganz, adj. whole
ganz, adv. quite
ganz, adv.; adj. entire(ly)
Garb (die)n.; Garwe, pl. sheaf
garbse, v.; gegarbst, pp. belch
Gardien (der)n.; Gardiens, pl. guardian
garewe, v.; gegarebt, pp. tan
Garewer (der)n.; Garewer, pl. tanner
Garewerei (die)n. tannery
Gargelreisser (der)n. tool used by coopers
garigle, v.; gegarigelt, pp. gargle
garn, adv. 1.gladly; 2.willingly
Garret (der)n. 1.attic; 2.garret
Garrick (der)n. 1.cork; 2.stopper

Gg

garricke / Gedruckes

garricke, v.; gegarrickt, pp. cork
Garrickzieger (der)n.; Garrickzieger, pl. cork puller
ga(r)schdich, adj. 1.disagreeable; 2.nasty
garsche, adj. handful
Gart (die)n. 1.belly band; 2.girth
Garyel (die)n. 1. cordial; 2. gargle; 3. throat;
    4. (-- abschneide) cut one's throat
Garyelbloser (der)n. braggart
Garyelreisser (der)n. tool used by coopers
Gascht (der)n. guest
Gass (die)n. occurs (except in the contemptuous meaning of a
    gossip) only in compounds (Wassergass, etc.) in which
    the original meaning of narrow (street) has been lost
Gatt (die)n.; Gadde, pl. 1.belly band; 2.fishing pole;
    3.gad; 4.girth; 5.switch; 6.whip
Gaul (der)n.; Geil, pl. horse
Gaulesel (der)n. male mule
Gaund (der)n.; Geinder, pl. 1.dress; 2.frock; 3.gown
Gaunsch (die)n.; Gaunsche, pl. swing
gaunsche, v.; gegaunscht, pp. 1.spring up and down; 2.swing
gauze, v.; gegauzt, pp. bark
Gauzer (der)n. obstinate cough
Gawwel (die)n.; Gawwle, pl. fork
gawwele, v.; gegawwelt, pp. 1.fork (hay); 2.pitch (hay)
Gawwelgraas (es)n. finger grass
Gawwelschtiel (der)n. fork handle
Gawwelweeg (der)n. fork in a road
Gawwelzinke (die)n. prong (of a fork)
Gax (die)n. tiresome talker
gaxe, v.; gegaxt, pp. cackle
Geardel (es)n. little garden
Geart (die)n. 1.fishing pole; 2.gad; 3.switch; 4.whip
Gebabbel (es)n. (incessant) chatter or babbling
Geback (es)n. (continual) baking
gebaere, v.; gebore, pp. 1.bear (a child); 2.give birth
Gebaerricks (es)n. 1.mountains; 2.mountainous region
Gebaf(f)z (es)n. 1.barking; 2.(violent) quarreling; 3.wrangling
Gebambel (es)n. 1.dangling; 2.dilly-dallying; 3.loitering;
    4.killing time
Gebeck (es)n. baked things
Gebef(f)z (es)n. 1.barking; 2.(violent) quarreling; 3.wrangling
Gebei (es)n.; Gebeier, pl. 1.building; 2.structure
Gebeiss (es)n. incessant biting or itching
Gebelk (es)n. the framing (of a structure)
Gebeller (es)n. (continued) nagging
Gebembel (es)n. 1.dilly-dallying; 2.loitering; 3.killing time
Gebet (es)n.; Gebeder, pl. prayer
Gebetbuch (es)n.; Gebetbicher, pl. prayer book
Gebettel (es)n. incessant begging
Gebisch (es)n. bush(es)
Gebiss (es)n.; Gebisser, pl. 1.bit (of a bridle); 2.set of
    artificial teeth
Geblabber (es)n. 1.chatter; 2.idle talk
Geblaerr (es)n. (continual) bawling or lowing
Geblaff(z) (es)n. 1.barking; 2.quarreling; 3.wrangling
Geblaschder (es)n. (continued) applying of salve

Geblauder (es)n. 1.chatter; 2.(continual) talking; 3.gossip
Gebliet (es)n. 1.blood or family relationship; 2.bloom(s)
Geblos (es)n. 1.blowing; 2.boasting
geblumm, adj. flowered
Geboch (es)n. boasting
geboge, adj. bent
Geboller (es)n. rumbling noise
gebore, v.(no infinitive form); gebore, pp. born
geborni, adj. 1.formerly; 2.nee
Gebort (die)n. birth
Gebortsblatz (der)n. birthplace
Gebortsdaag (der); Gebortsdaage, pl. birthday
Gebott (es)n. 1.bid; 2.command; 3.commandment;
    4.offer; 5.(die zehe --er) the Ten Commandments
Gebrall (es)n. (continual) boasting
Gebrauch (der)n.; Gebreich, pl. 1.custom; 2.fashion;
    3.usage; 4.use
Gebraus (es)n. 1.roaring; 2.rustling
Gebrebel (es)n. 1.(continued) nagging; 2.palaver
Gebreddich (es)n. 1.long-winded talk; 2.preaching
gebreichlich, adv. 1.customary; 2.generally
Gebrill (es)n. (continual) bawling or crying
gebritscht, adv. 1.done up; 2.exhausted; 3.knocked out
Gebrumm (es)n. buzzing (continued)
Gebrummel (es)n. 1.low murmuring; 2.rumor
Gebrutz (es)n. 1.pouting; 2.sulking
Gebun(d) (es)n. bundle (of straw)
Geburt (die)n. birth
Geburtsdaag (der)n.; Geburtsdaage, pl. birthday
geck, adj. (rare usage) 1.nosey; 2.prying
Gedanke (der)n.; Gedanke, pl. 1.idea; 2.thought
gedankelos, adj. 1.scatter-brained; 2.unthinking
gedankevoll, adj. 1.contemplative; 2.thoughtful
Gedans (es)n. (continual) dancing
gedatt, adj. dried
gedaucht, adj. stooped (bent from age)
Gedechtnis (es)n. 1.memory; 2.remembrance
Gedechtnisdaag (der)n. Memorial Day
gedeihe, v.; gediehe, pp. 1.prosper; 2.succeed
gedichdich, adv. 1.severely; 2.thoroughly
Gedicht (es)n.; Gedichde, pl. poem
gedicht, adj. 1.severely; 2.thoroughly
Gedier (es)n.; Gediere, pl. animal
Gediereausschtopper (der)n. taxidermist
Gedimmel (es)n. din
Gedob (es)n. 1.disturbance; 2.(continued) roaring;
    3.raging
Gedratsch (es)n. (continual) gadding
gedrei, adj. 1.faithful; 2.good-hearted; 3.true
gedreilich, adj. 1.faithful; 2.true
Gedrenk (es)n. 1.beverage; 2.drink; 3.liquor
Gedribbel (es)n. pit-a-pat (of feet)
Gedrink (es)n. 1.(act of) drinking; 2.carousing
Gedrops (es)n. (continual) dropping or dripping
gedroscht, adj. 1.confidently; 2.down-cast; 3.meek
Gedruckes (es)n. 1.print; 2.printing

Gg

Gedu

Gedu (der)n. calico
Gedu (es) n. 1.affair; 2.goings on
Gedudel (es)n. monotonous musical performance
Geduld (die)n. patience
geduldich, adj. 1.gentle (of animals); 2.meek; 3.patient
Geduldichkeet (die)n. patience
Gedummel (es)n. subdued noise
Gedumor (es)n. 1.confusion; 2.noise (as in a factory or at a large gathering)
Gedun (der)n. calico
gedunich, adj. (of) calico
Gedunner (es)n. 1.noise; 2.racket; 3.thundering
Geduns (es)n. 1.affair; 2.goings on
Geedel (die)n. god-mother
geeich, prep. toward
Gees (der)n.; Gees, pl. 1.goat; 2.(yunger --) kid
Geesbaart (der)n. goatee
Geesblaat (es)n. climbing honeysuckle
Geesbock (der)n.; Geesbeck, pl. billy goat
Geeschel (die)n.; Geeschle, pl. 1.lash; 2.whip
Geeschelschnur (die) cracker of a horse whip
Geeschelschtock (der)n. whip stock
geeschle, v.; gegeeschelt, pp. 1.lash; 2.scourge; 3.whip
Geescht (der)n. 1.apparition; 2.mind; 3.spirit
Geeshaut (die)n.; Geesheit, pl. goatskin
Geesledder (es)n. 1.goat skin; 2.morocco
gefelkt, adj. fallowed
Gefluch (es)n. 1.profanity; 2.swearing
g(e)fressich, adj. voracious
Gefucker (es)n. to-do
Gefunnenes (en) 1.a foundling; 2.waif
geg(g)e, adv. 1.against; 2.toward
Gegacks (es)n. incessant cackling or chattering
gege Mariye, adv. 1.toward the east; 2.toward morning
gege Naade, adv. 1.towards north; 2.northward
gege(n)waertich, adj. present
gege, adj. steep (of hills)
gege, prep. 1.to; 2.toward
Gegedeel (es)n. 1.contrary; 2.opposite; 3.(er is immer's --) he is always contrary
Gegegift (es)n. antidote
gegehalde, adj. 1.oppose; 2.remind
Gegehaldung (die)n. objection
Gegeik (es)n. (constant) fiddling or fidgeting
gegekalde, adj. 1.oppose; 2.remind
Gegemiddel (es)n. antidote
Gegemittel (es)n. antidote
gegenanner, adv. 1.opposed; 2.opposite or towards each other or one another; 3. (sie sinn immer --) they are always at odds
Gegend (die)n. 1.neighborhood; 2.region; 3.vicinity
gegeniwwer, adv. opposite
Gegeschtand (der)n. 1.object; 2.subject
Gegewart (die)n. 1.presence; 2.present time; 3.vicinity
Gegicker (es)n. giggling
gegisch, adj. silly

Gehorsamkeit

Geglaag (es)n. constant complaining
Geglebber (es)n. 1.clatter; 2.noise; 3.rattling
gegliche, adj. (gut --) well-liked
Geglopp (es)n. (constant) hammering
Geglucks (es)n. (constant) clucking
Gegnarr (es)n. (constant) growling or grumbling
Gegnawwer (es)n. (continual) nibbling
Gegner (der)n. 1.adversary; 2.opponent
Gegnix (es)n. miserliness
Gegnuff (es)n. 1.pommeling; 2.quarreling
Gegnuschder (es)n. being occupied with trifles
Gegnuschel (es)n. pile of junk or trash
Gegramansel (es)n. flummery
Gegratz (es)n. (constant) scratching
Gegrauns (es)n. groaning
Gegrawwel (es)n. 1.crawling; 2.sensation of crawling insects
Gegreider (die)n., pl. herbs
Gegreisch (es)n. 1.shout; 2.yelling
Gegrex (es)n. 1.groaning; 2.grunting
Gegrisch (es)n. 1.howling; 2.report; 3.rumor; 4.yelling
Gegritzel (es)n. scribbling
Geguck (es)n. (continued) gazing or gaping
Gegwacker (es)n. 1.chattering; 2.quacking
gegwehnt (sei)v. (to be) accustomed
gegwolle, v. swell from moisture
geh, v.; gange, pp. 1.endure; 2.go; 3.stand; 4.(aus un ei --) go in and out; 5.(beet --) go in the hole (in Datte)
geh/losse, v.; gehlosst, pp. 1.abrogate; 2.let go
geharriche, v.; karricht, pp. obey
geheem, adj. 1.mysterious; 2.underhanded
Geheemnis (es)n. secret
geheere, v.; gegheert, pp. pertain
geheerich, adv. 1.severely; 2.thoroughly
Gehees (es)n. command
Geheil (es)n. weeping
geheim, adj. 1.mysterious; 2.underhanded
Geheimnis (es)n. secret
gehersam, adj. obedient
gehl, adj. 1.sallow; 2.yellow
gehlbrau(n), adj. tawny
gehlich, adj. 1.jaundiced; 2.yellowish
Gehliem (die)n.; Gehlieme, pl. yellow jacket
Gehlkopp (der)n. copperhead (snake)
Gehlrieb(die)n.; Gehlriewe, pl. 1.carrot; 2.(wildi --) wild carrot
Gehlschpeecht (der)n. flicker (bird)
Gehlsucht (die)n. jaundice
Gehlwarzel (die)n. wild yam
Gehlwasser (es)n. edema
Gehlwassergraut (es)n. pipsissema
Gehlweide (der, die)n. golden willow
Gehlweschp (die)n. yellow jacket
Gehlwoch (die)n. yellow week
Gehorsam (der)n. 1.dutiful; 2.obedience; 3.submissive
gehorsam, adj. 1.obedient; 2.submissive
Gehorsamkeit (die)n. obedience

Gg

gehre — Gemeeschaft

gehre, v.; gegehrt, pp. ferment
Geier (der)n. vulture
Geig (die)n.; Geige, pl. 1.fiddle; 2.violin
geige, v.; gegeigt, pp. 1.fiddle; 2.fidget; 3.teeter on chair balanced on two legs; 4.(uff un ab --) seesaw
Geigeboge (der)n. violin bow
Geigehals (der)n. neck (of violin)
Geigel (die)n.; Geigel, pl. throat
Geigemacher (der)n.; Geigemacher, pl. violin maker
Geiger (der)n. 1.fiddler; 2.violinist
Geigesaddel (der)n. violin bridge
Geigesaet (die)n. violin string
Geigle (die)n. throat
Geilche (es)n. 1.horsey; 2.nag
Geili (es)n. 1.horsey; 2.nag
Geilsbalsem (der)n. horse mint
Geilsbschlagger (der)n. farrier
Geilschar (es)n. 1.gear; 2.harness
Geilscher (es)n. nag
Geilsdeck (die)n. light cover for horses in flying time
Geilsdieb (der)n. horse thief
Geilsdokder (der)n. 1.horse doctor; 2.veterinarian
Geilsdokter (der)n. veterinarian
Geilsdreck (der)n. horse dung
Geilsfleesch (es)n. 1.horse meat; 2.horses
Geilsfuder (es)n. horse feed
Geilsgeeschel (die)n. horsewhip
Geilsgranket (die)n. 1.distemper; 2.epizootic
Geilsgscharrschtang (die)n. gear pole
Geilsgsicht (es)n. kind of mask
Geilshoor (die)n. horse hair
Geilskescht (die)n.; Geilskeschde, pl. horse chestnut
Geilskimmel (der)n. 1.jimsonweed; 2.stramonium; 3. thorn apple
Geilskopp (der)n. horse's head
Geilsmann (der)n. 1.dealer in or handler of horses; 2. lover of horses
Geilsmischt (der)n. horse manure
Geilsschtall (der)n.; Geilschtell, pl. horse stable
Geilsschwanz (der)n.; Geilsschwenz, pl. horsetail
Geilstee (der)n. sweet fern
Geilswatzel (die)n. horse balm
Geilszwiwwel (die)n. Jack-in-the-pulpit
Geischt (der)n.; Gelschder, pl. 1.apparition; 2.ghost; 3. mind; 4.spirit
geischtlich, adj. 1.priestly; 2.spiritual
Geiz (der)n. avarice
geize, v.; gegeizt, pp. 1.stingy; 2.scrimp
Geizhals (der)n. miser
geizich, adj. 1.avaricious; 2.greedy; 3.niggardly; 4.stingy; 5.tight
geizich, adv. miserly
Gekau (es)n. chewing (also the rag)
Gekreider (die)n., pl. herbs
Gekreidersupp (die)n. vegetable soup
Gelaaf (es)n. (constant) walking or gadding

Gelach (es)n. 1.(continued) laughing; 2.laughter
Gelaerm (es)n. 1.ado; 2.noise
gelaernt, adj. learned
Gelammedier (es)n. 1.(continued) lamenting; 2.outcry
Gelander(es)n. 1.banisters; 2.railing
Geld (die) n.; Gelde, pl. 1. (-- verschpritze) spend money lavishly; 2.(-- leie hawwe) (to have) ready money ; 3.(--verbamble) squander money; 4.(lumbich --) unsound (paper) money; 5.money; 6.spayed sow
gelde, v.; gegolde, pp. 1.be accepted; 2.pass (for) amount
Geldgraut (es)n. moneywort
Geldmacherei (die)n. swindle
Geldmaschien (die)n. money making proposition or scheme
Gelds (die)n.; Geldse, pl. spayed sow
Geldsache (die)n., pl. money matters
Geldsack (der)n.; Geldseck, pl. purse
Geldsuckler (der)n.; Geldsuckler, pl. miser
Geldsumm (die)n. 1.fund; 2.sum of money
Gelek (es)n. layer
Gelechter (es)n. laughter
Geleck (es)n. importune coaxing
G(e)leeg (es)n. layer (of hay)
gelege, adj. opportune
Gelegeheit (die)n. 1.chance; 2.opportunity
Gelehrsamkeit (die)n. 1.learnedness; 2.learning
gelehrt, adj. learned
Gelehrter (der)n. scholar
Geleier (es)n. (repeating) the same old story or complaint
geleitert, adj. 1.rectified; 2.refined
G(e)lender (es)n. 1.banister; 2.railing
Geles (es)n. 1.act of reading; 2.much reading
Geleyeheit (die)n. 1.occasion; 2.opportunity
Gelichwicht (es)n. equilibrium
geliebt, adj. beloved
gelind, adj. 1.gentle; 2.mild; 3.smooth
Geling (es)n. 1.heart;2.haslet; 3.liver and lights (of an animal)
Gell(e)?, interj. not so?
gelschderich, adj. 1.(easily) frightened; 2.scared; 3.terror stricken
Gelsd (die)n.; Gelsde, pl. spayed sow
gelse, v.; gegelst, pp. castrate
Gelser (der)n. 1.gelder; 2.unskillful surgeon
Gelte?, interj. not so?
gelte, v.; gegolte, pp. 1.be accepted; 2.pass (for) amount
Gemaad (die)n. swath
gemaahne, v.; gemaahnt, pp. remind
Gemasser (es)n. 1.gnarl or knot (in wood); 2.mixture
Gemech (es)n. male sexual organs
gemechlich, adj. 1.easy; 2.comfortable
G(e)mee (die)n. 1.congregation; 2.(die -- aanemme) (to) join the congregation
gemeenerhand, adj. 1.as a rule; 2.mostly; 3.usually
gemeenichlich, adj. 1.as a rule; 2.usually
Gemeensglied (es) n. 1.church member; 2.member of a congregation
Gemeeschaft (die)n. 1.community; 2.union

Gg

gemeescheflich

gemeescheflich, adj. 1.in common; 2.united

gemein, adj. in common

gemeindlich, adj. 1.congregational; 2.in common

Gemeinheet (die)n. vulgarity

Gemeinschaft (die)n. fellowship

Gemelk (es)n. 1.act of milking; 2.(everlasting) milking; 3.udder

Gemetzel (es)n. carnage

G(e)miess (es)n. meat and vegetables (cooked together)

Gemiet (es)n. 1.mind; 2.mood

gemietlich, adj. 1.comfortable; 2.cozy; 3.down hearted; 4.easy going; 5.soul satisfying

Gemietsort (die)n. 1.character; 2.disposition

Gemisch (es)n. 1.medley; 2.mixture

Gemummel (es)n. (constant) mumbling

Gemunkel (es)n. subdued or unintelligible grumbling

genaa, adj. 1.accurate; 2.exact; 3.precise

Genaeh (es)n. 1.sewing; 2.sewed articles

genau, adj. 1.accurate; 2.exact

geneicht, adj. 1.apt to; 2.inclined

Genetz (es)n. omentum

Genischt (es)n. tangle of weeds or brush

Gensblumm (die)n.; Gensblumme, pl. daisy

Gensdreck (der)n. 1.goose dung; 2.(alle --) every trifle

Genserich (der)n. gander

Gensfedder (die)n. quill

Gensfett (es)n. goose fat

Gensfuss (der)n. 1.girl's game; 2.goose's foot; 3.pentagram

Genshals (der)n. 1.goose's neck; 2.long necked person

Genshaut (die)n. gooseflesh (from cold or fear)

Gensli (es)n.; Genslin, pl. gosling

genslich, adj. enough

Genswei (der)n. 1.Adam's ale; 2.water

Gensyoch (es)n. yoke put on geese to prevent them from creeping through fences

genunk, adj. 1.enough; 2.sufficient

genunk, adv. 1.adequate; 2.ample; 3.enough

genzlich, adv. wholly

Gepeif (es)n. (continued) whistling

Gepischber (es)n. (continued) whispering

Gepulschder (es)n. 1.pad; 2.puffery; 3.stuffing

gepuschdurt, adj. 1.of a certain build and stature; 2.(gut --) (a) shapely; (b) well built

Gequael (es)n. (continual) tormenting or worrying

geraascht, adj. 1.courageous; 2.healthy

Geraebbel (es)n. racket

Geraetschaft (die)n. 1.articles; 2.implements

Gerassel (es)n. rattling

Gerausch (es)n. roaring or rustling

gerdle, v.; gegerdelt, pp. (to dig) garden

Gerdler (der)n. gardener

Gerdner (der)n. gardener

Gerebbelfress (es)n. 1.miscellaneous articles; 2.trash

gerechdich, adj. righteous

Gerechdichkeit (die)n. 1.justice; 2.righteousness

gerecht, adj. 1.equitable; 2.just; 3.righteous

gewaerrt

gerechterweis, adv. 1.in justice; 2.rightly

gereie, v.; gereit, pp. 1.regret; 2.rue

gereinicht, adj. 1.clean; 2.pure

Gereisch (es)n. slight noise

Geretsch (es)n. slanderous gossip

gerhersam, adj. submissive

Gericht (es)n. 1.court (obsolete usage); 2.mess; 3.viands

geriddelt (voll) adv. completely covering the ground (as of apples or potatoes)

gering, adj. slight

geringelt, adv. curled

gerinne, v.; gerunne, pp. 1.clot (of blood); 2.coagulate; 3.curdle (of milk)

Gerischt (der)n. 1.scaffold; 2.walking frame of a sawmill

gerischt, adj. ready

Gerischtholz (es) n. putlog (one of the short timbers that support the flooring of a scaffold)

gern, adv. 1.gladly; 2.willingly

gerode, v.; gerode, pp. 1.turn out; 2.(gut --) (a) thrive; (b) turn out well; (c) yield well; 3.(en guter gerodner Soh) a son who turned out well; 4. (es is ihm net --) he did not succeed

Geros (es)n. frolicking

geroscht, adj. rusted

Gerranne (die)n. geranium

Gerschde (der)n. barley

Gerscht (der)n. barley

Gerschtarn (die)n. barley harvest

Gertrudsdaag (der)n. Gertrude's Day (March 17)

Geruch (der)n. 1.aroma; 2.odor; 3.scent; 4.smell

geruddelt (voll) adv. completely covering the ground (as of apples or potatoes)

Gerumpel (es)n. 1.noise; 2.rumbling

Gerussel (es)n. drizzle

G(e)sang (der)n. singing

geschder, adv. yesterday

G(e)scheft (der)n. business

geschderowed, adv. last evening

gescheftich, adj. busy

Geschenk (es)n. present (gift)

Geschpraech (es)n. conversation

Geschrei (es)n. shout

Geschwetz (es)n. hearsay

Gesell (der)n. companion

Gesellschaft (die)n. society

Gesetz (es)n. 1.commandment; 2.law

Gess (es)n. (act of) eating

gettlich, adj. 1.divine; 2.godly

gewaahr warre, v.; is gewaahrwarre, pp. (to become) aware

gewachsner (en) adult

Gewackel (es)n. (continual) wabbling or shaking

gewaehre losse, v. 1.allow to continue; 2.give free scope; 3.let alone

G(e)waerb (es)n. 1.joint; 2.node (of a plant)

gewaerrt, adv. 1.mixed; 2.tangled; 3.(-- schtroh) straw as it comes from the thresher

Gg

Gewaerz — Gflacker

Gewaerz (es)n.; Gewaerzer, pl. spice
Gewalt (die)n. 1.power; 2.violence
gewaltich, adj. 1.powerful; 2.very
gewaltichlich, adj. mightily
gewaltsam, adj. violent
gewandt, adj. handy
Gewareb (es)n.; Gewarewe, pl. joint (in the human body)
Geweb(b) (es)n. 1.activity; 2.web
Gewefz (es)n. continual barking (of a small dog)
gewehne, v.; gewehnt, pp. accustom
Gewehnet (die)n. habit
gewehnichlich, adv. 1.commonly; 2.ordinarily
gewehnlich, adv. 1.commonly; 2.customary; 3.ordinarily
Gewehr (es)n. 1.gun; 2.weapon
Gewelb (es)n. 1.arc; 2.arch; 3.vault
Gewelbkeller (es)n. arched cellar
gewelbt, adj. arched
Gewelk (es)n. clouds
Gewelsch (es)n. jabbering
Gewesch (es)n. (continual) washing
Gewesser (es)n. 1.flood; 2.(dunner uns --) confound it!
gewessers (gaar), adv. deucedly
Gewewwer (es)n. 1.activity; 2.bustling
Gewex (es)n. 1.goiter; 2.growth; 3.tumor
gewichst, adj. 1.bright; 2.clever; 3.waxed
Gewicht (es)n. weight
gewichtich, adj. weighty
Gewichtschtee (der)n. weight
G(e)widder (es)n. thunder storm
Gewidderregge (der)n. thunder shower
Gewidderrut (die)n. lightning rod
Gewidderschtarm (der)n. thunder storm
Gewidderschtee (der)n. small round glacial stone believed to have been hurled in a bolt of lightning
Gewidderschtreech (der)n. thunderbolt
Gewidderwolk (die)n. thunder cloud
gewiddre, v.; gewiddert, pp. 1.threaten thunder storms; 2.thunder
g(e)widdrich, adj. threatening thunderstorms
Gewiehl (es)n. (continued) rooting or rummaging
Gewilbert (es)n. game (animal)
Gewimmer (es)n. swarming
Gewinn (der)n. gain
G(e)winn (die)n. screw thread
Gewinn (es)n. 1.advantage; 2.gain
gewinne, v.; gewunne, pp. 1.gain; 2.win
Gewinner (der)n. 1.gainer; 2.winner
Gewinsel (es)n. (continued) whining
gewiss, adj., adv. 1.(so -- as alles) (a) really; (b) sure as I'm alive; (c) truly ; 2.certain; 3.certainly; 4.decidedly; 5.indeed; 6.indeed; 7.sure
G(e)wisse (es)n. conscience
gewisse(n)haft, adj. conscientious
gewisselos, adj. conscienceless
gewisslich, adv. decidedly
gewixt, adj. 1.astute; 2.sly

Gewohnheit (die)n. Custom
gewwe, v.; gewwe, pp. 1.(do gebt's nix draus) (a) it will come to nothing; (b) I won't allow it; 2.(er hot mer sei schuld --) he laid the blame on me; 3.(feng --) (a) strike; (b) punish; 4.(was gebt's neies) what's the news; 5.(was hot's --) what has happened; 6.give
Gewwel (der)n. gable
geyaag, adj. 1.fast driving; 2.hunting
Geyacker (es)n. (continual) jogging or driving about
Geyammer (es)n. 1.lamenting; 2.(constant) moaning
Geyeemer (es)n. 1.lamenting; 2.(constant) moaning
geyich, adv. towards
Geyohl (es)n. continued yelling
Geyuck (es)n. 1.fidgeting; 2.jerking
Geyux (es)n. 1.shouting; 2.skylarking
Gezaak (es)n. hesitation
Gezacker (es)n. 1.(constant) driving about; 2.gadding; 3.tiresome driving about
gezackt, adj. 1.indented; 2.toothed
Gezaerr (es)n. (continual) teasing
Gezaerrick(s) (es)n. 1.district; 2.section
Gezank (es)n. (constant) scolding
Gezawwel (es)n. (continual) struggling or wriggling about
gezeppt, adj. braided
Gezewwel (es)n. 1.(yung --) (a) children; (b) young people; 2.commotion
Geziffer (es)n. 1.calculations; 2.insects; 3.markings made with a pencil or pen; 4.vermin
gezogge, adj. 1.drawn; 2.rifled (of a gun); 3.(well) trained (of a child)
Gezwacker (es)n. 1.qualm; 2.twinge
gezwillicht, adj. twilled
Gfaahr (die)n. 1.danger; 2.peril; 3.continual driving; 4.driving; 5.hauling; 6.(in -- bringe) imperil
Gfach (es)n. 1.fence panel; 2.rail section
gfaehrlich, adj. dangerous
Gfaehrlichkeet (die)n. danger
Gfalle (der)n. favor
gfalle, v.; gfalle, pp. 1.like; 2.suit; 3.be satisfied with; 4.please
Gfangner (der)n.; Gfangne, pl. 1.captive; 2.prisoner
gfarlich, adj. dangerous
Gfarz (es)n. farting
Gfecht (es)n. continuous fighting
Gfehler (der)n.; Gfehler, pl. fault
gfehrlich, adj. 1.dangerous; 2.perilous
gfelkt, adj. fallowed
gfellich, adj. 1.agreeable; 2.obliging
Gfellichkeet (die)n. favor
gfelscht, adj. 1.alloyed; 2.counterfeited
Gfengnis (es)n. prison
Gfess (es)n. 1.receptacle; 2.vessel
Gfiehl (es) n. 1.feeling (sense of touch); 2.repeated act of feeling or touching
gfiehllos, adj. 1.torpid; 2.without feeling
Gflacker (es)n. (continual) flickering

Gg

Gfleeztersand / Glavier

Gfleeztersand (der)n. quicksand
Gflicht (die)n. duty
Gflick (es)n. (continual) mending
Gfluch (es)n. cursing (continual)
gformt, adj. 1.formed; 2.shaped
Gfress (es)n. 1.excellent food; 2.face; 3.immoderate eating; 4.miscellaneous articles; 5.mask; 6.mouth; 7.trash 8.ugly
gfressich, adj. voracious
gfriere, v.; gfrore, pp. 1. freeze; 2. (es gfriert mich) I am shivering; 3.(es gfriert) it is freezing
Gfrog (es)n. constant questioning
Gfrornes (es)n. frozen delicacies
gfunne, adj. found
Gfusser (es)n. 1.fuzz; 2.lint
Ghaschbel (es)n. 1.precipitate; 2.thoughtless movement (continued)
gheem, adv. secretly
gheere, v.; gheert, pp. belong
gheert, v.; gheert, pp. pertain
ghuddelt, adj. tangled
Ghuuscht (es)n. incessant coughing
Gibbel (der)n.; Gibbel, pl. 1.peak; 2.pinnacle; 3.summit; 4.top
Gibbelend (es)n. (-- vum Haus) gable-end of the house
Gichder (die)n.; Gichdere, pl. convulsion(s)
Gicht (die)n. gout
Gichtre (die)n., pl. convulsions
Gichtros (die)n.; Gichtrosse, pl. peony
Gichtroschtock (der)n. peony plant
Gick (die)n.; Gicke, pl. sulky (vehicle)
Gickelche (es)n. chicory
gickere, v.; gegickert, pp. 1.giggle; 2.snicker
Gickerigi (der)n. 1.cock-a-doodle-do; 2.rooster
Gickerigu (der)n. 1.cock-a-doodle-do; 2.rooster
gickle, v.; gegickelt, pp. giggle
Gicklifiess (die)n., pl. wild honey suckle
gickse, v.; gegickst, pp. 1.dig (around); 2.nudge in the ribs; 3.poke at; 4.stick; 5.sting
Gickser (der)n. 1.hiccough; 2.sting (of an insect)
giekse, v.; gegiekst, pp. 1.dig (around); 2.nudge in the ribs; 3.poke at; 4.stick; 5.sting
gierich, adj. 1.avaricious; 2.voracious
giesse, v.; gegosse, pp. 1.cast; 2.pour; 3.sprinkle
Giesser (der)n. molder
Giesskann (die)n. sprinkling can
Giesskannekopp (der)n. sprinkler of a sprinkling can
gifdich, adj. 1.poisonous; 2.venomous
Gift (der)n. (ranklich --) poison ivy
Gift (es)n. 1.ivy poisoning; 2.poison; 3.poison ivy; 4.venom
Giftbaschnaad (der)n. wild parsnip
Giftbeer (die)n. poison berry
giftich, adj. poisonous
Giftichkeet (die)n. virulence
Giftschwamm (der)n. toadstool
gilbse, v.; gegilbst, pp. 1.shout; 2.yell
Gilderi (der)n. plover
Gilleri (der)n.; Gilleri, pl. 1.killdeer; 2.plover

Gimpel (der)n. dunce
Ginnihinkel (es)n.; Ginnihinkel, pl. guinea hen
Ginniseiche (es)n. guinea pig
Gippel (der)n. 1.top; 2.summit
Gips (der)n. gypsum
gipse, v.; gegipst, pp. 1.sow (a field) with gypsum; 2.term applied to the sickling of grain by small children
Gipser (der) n. term applied to a tow-headed child who accompanies his parents to the harvest field and cuts grain with the sickle as he is able
Gitar (die)n. guitar
Giwwel (der)n. gable
Giwwelend (es)n. (-- vum Haus) gable-end of the house
Glaabensbekanntnis (es)n. confession of faith
glaablich, adj. 1.credible; 2.plausible
glaage, v.; geglaagt, pp. 1.be indisposed; 2.complain; 3.lament
Glaak (die)n. complaint
glaar, adj. 1.clear; 2.distinct
glaare, v.; geglaart, pp. clear
Glaas (es)n.; Glesser, pl. 1.glass; 2.tumbler
Glaasaag (es)n. glass eye
glaase, adj. (made) of glass
Glaasgraut (es)n. 1.pale touch-me-not; 2.richweed
Glaaskarrell (die)n. glass bead
Glaasschank (der)n. china cupboard
Glaasvoll (es)n. glass full
Glaawe (der)n.; Glaawe, pl. 1.belief; 2.creed; 3.faith
Glaawewexle (der)n. change denominational affiliation
glaawe, v.; geglaabt, pp. 1.believe; 2.think; 3.suppose
Glabberbax (die)n.; Glabberbaxe, pl. piano
Glabbord (es)n.; Glabbaerd, pl. 1.pale; 2.picket; 3.weatherboard
Glabbordfens (die)n.; Glabbordfense, pl. picket fence
Glaech (der)n. link
Glaeger (der)n.; Glaeger, pl. plaintiff
Glaff (die)n.; Glaffe, pl. piano-key
Glaffier (es)n.; Glaffiere, pl. piano
Glamm (die)n.; Glamme, pl. clamp
Glammhoke (der)n. 1.crane hook; 2.dog (in lumbering)
Glansing (die)n. glazing
Glanz (der)n. 1.glitter; 2.luster; 3.shine; 4.splendor
glappe, v.; geglappt, pp. 1.agree; 2.clap (hands); 3.tally
Glarick (der)n.; Glaricke, pl. clerk
Glass (die)n. class
Glassoi (es)n.; Glassoier, pl. nest-egg (of glass)
Glatsch (die)n. gossiping woman
glatt mache, v. smooth
glatt, adj. 1.insinuating; 2.sleek; 3.slippery; 4.(net ar-rig -- haergeh) (a) act rudely or boorishly; (b) (to) keep house in a slovenly manner
Glattbix (die)n. smooth bore rifle
Glatteis (es)n. glazed ice on the ground and on trees
glattschprauich, adj. smooth chaffed (of wheat)
glattschprei-ich, adj. smooth chaffed (of wheat)
Glavier (es)n. piano

Gg

glebbere

glebbere, v.; geglebbert, pp. 1.clatter; 2.rattle

Glebberraad (es)n.; Glebberredder, pl. 1.ratchet; 2.rattle wheel

glebbre, v.; geglebbert, pp. jar

glebich, adj. sticky

Glee (der)n. 1.clover; 2.(weisser --) white clover

glee, adj. 1.(beim gleene) at retail; 2.(en gleenes) (a) baby; (b) small child; 3.(iwwer en gleenes) "yet a little while"; 4.little; 5.petty; 6.small; 7.wee

Gleeblaat (es)n. clover leaf

Gleeblumm (die)n. 1.clover flower; 2.globe amaranth

Gleebutzer (der)n. clover huller

Gleech (es)n.; Gleeche(r), pl. link (in a chain)

Gleed (es)n.; Gleeder, pl. clothes (garment[s])

gleede, v.; gegleedt, pp. clothe

Gleeder (die)n., pl. 1.clothes; 2.garments

Gleederbascht (die)n. clothes brush

Gleederhoke (der)n. clothes hook

Gleederkammer (die)n. 1.clothes closet; 2.wardrobe

Gleederkemmerli (es)n. clothes closet

Gleederschank (der)n.; Gleederschenk, pl. wardrobe

Gleederschtubb (die)n. room for hanging clothes

Gleedrumm (die)n. snare drum

Gleefeld (es)n. clover field

gleeglidderich, adj. small limbed

Gleehoi (es)n. clover hay

Gleekopp (der)n. clover flower

Gleenichkeet (die)n. trifle

Gleenischlangewatzell (die)n. Seneca snake root

Glees (es)n.; Gleeser, pl. 1.rut; 2.track (of a wagon)

Gleeschprau (die)n. clover chaff

Gleeschtengel (der)n. clover stalk

Gleesome (der)n. clover seed

Gleesume (der)n. clover seed

Gleewaasem (der)n. clover sod

gleewich, adj. sticky

glei, adv. 1.at once; 2.soon; 3.without delay

gleich, adj. 1.alike; 2.equal; 3.like; 4.similar

gleich, adv. 1.alike; 2.equally; 3.likely; 4.same

gleichdeitend, adj. synonymous

gleiche, v.; gegliche, pp. 1.enjoy; 2.like; 3.love

gleicherweis, adv. likewise

Gleichewaert (es)n. par value

gleichfellich, adj. equally

gleichfermich, adj. uniform

Gleichgewicht (es)n.; Gleichgewichder, pl. 1.balance; 2.equilibrium; 3.scale

gleichgiltich, adj, unconcerned

gleichgiltichkeit, adj. indifference

gleichgsinnt, adj. like-minded

Gleichheet (die)n. 1.equality; 2.parity

Gleichheit (die)n. 1.equality; 2.parity

gleichlaafend, adj. parallel

Gleichnis (es)n. 1.parable; 2.picture

gleichzeitich, adj. simultaneous

Gleie (die)n. 1.bran; 2.shorts

globbe

Glemm (die)n. 1.dilemma; 2.quandary; 3.pinch; 4.scrape

glemme, v.; geglemmt, pp. 1.pinch; 2.(sich der Finger --) pinch one's finger

glense, v.; geglenst, pp. 1.glitter; 2.shine

glensend, adj. 1.resplendent; 2.shining

glensich, adj. brilliant

gleppre, v.; gegleppert, pp. rattle

glepprich, adj. rattling

Glessaag (es)n. wall eye

Glessel (es)n. little glass full

Glesser (die)n., pl. (eye) glasses

glessern, adj. vitreous

Glessli (es)n. little glass full

Glessur (die)n. glazing

glessure, v.; geglessurt, pp. glaze

Glett (die)n.; Gledde, pl. 1.burdock; 2.burdock burr

Gletteise (es)n. sadiron (rare usage)

glettere, v.; geglettert, pp. climb

Glettewatzel (die)n. burdock root

glewe, v.; geglebt, pp. 1.adhere; 2.stick

glewerich, adj. 1.clotted; 2.gelatinous

Glick (es)n. 1.fortune; 2.good luck; 3.luck; 4.success; 5.(es -- winsche) (a) congratulate; (b) wish success

glicke, v.; geglickt, pp. 1.have good luck; 2.succeed in

Glicker (der)n.; Glicker, pl. 1.marble(s); 2.testicles

glicklich, adj. 1.fortunate; 2.lucky; 3.successful

glicklichweis, adv. 1.as luck would have it; 2.fortunately; 3.luckily

Glickschuss (der)n. unexpected success

glickselich, adj. happy

Glicksfall (der)n. 1.godsend; 2.windfall

Glied (es)n.; Glieder; Glidder, pl. 1.limb; 2.member

Gliederband (es)n. ligament

Gliederschmaerze (die)n., pl. 1.pain in the limbs; 2.rheumatic pains

gliedich, adj. red hot

Gliedwasser (es)n. 1.lymph; 2.synovial fluid

Gliftse (die)n., pl. 1.rocks; 2.wilds

Glimbel (es)n. 1.nodule; 2.nugget; 3.small lump; 4.small roll (of butter)

glimblich, adj. 1.gentle; 2.mild

glimple, v.; geglimpelt, pp. form a lump (of butter in a churn)

Gling (die)n. blade (of a knife)

Glingel (der)n. 1.ball (of yarn); 2.crewel

glingich, adj. prolonged

glingle, v.; geglingelt, pp. 1.jingle; 2.ring; 3.tinkle

Glingschtee (der)n. clingstone

glinsle, v.; geglinselt, pp. 1.flatter; 2.pet

glitsche, v.; geglitscht, pp. 1.slide; 2.slip

glitschich, adj. slippery

glitschiwippi imitating the sound of scissors in cutting

glitzere, v.; geglitzert, pp. 1.gleam; 2.glitter; 3.twinkle

glitzerich, adj. 1.glistening; 2.glittering

globbe, v.; geglobbt, pp. 1.beat; 2.hammer; 3.knock; 4.pound; 5.rap; 6.strike

Gg

Glock — gnetschich

Glock (die)n.; Glocke, pl. 1.bell; 2.(-- toole) toll (at funerals)

Glockeblumm (die)n. 1.blue bell; 2.Canterbury bell; 3.columbine

glodsich, adj. soggy (of ground too wet to plow)

Glofder (es)n. cord (of wood)

Glofderhols (es)n. cord wood

Glooe (der)n. pintle (of a hinge)

Glooe (die)n.; Glooe, pl. 1.claw; 2.cloven foot; 3.paw; 4. talon; 5.clutches

Glooe-Hammer (der)n. claw hammer

glooe, v.; gegloot, pp. (sich fascht --) lay hold of

Glooefett (es)n. neat's foot oil

Glooefuss (der)n. cloven foot

Glooschderfraa (die)n. nun

Glopphaahne (der)n. worn out roue

Glopphengscht (der)n. stallion with retained testicles

gloppiches (ebbes --) something to hammer with

glor, adj. clear

glorensich, adj. 1.clear; 2.simple; 3.whole

Glotz (der)n.; Gletz, pp. block

glotzkebbich, adj. 1.block headed; 2.obstinate; 3.stubborn

Glotzkopp (der)n.; Glotzkepp, pl. 1.blockhead; 2.bonehead; 3.numbskull; 4.obstinate person

Glowe (der)n. (wire) staple

gluch, adj. 1.sage (wise); 2.smart

Gluck (die)n.; Glucke, pp. hen (when with chicks)

Gluckezwiwwel (die)n. multiplier onion

gluckse, v.; gegluckst, pp. 1.cluck; 2.gurgle

glucksich, adj. clucking

Glumbe (der)n. 1.heap; 2.lump; 3.roll of butter

glumbich, adj. 1.cloddy; 2.lumpy

glumpe, v.; geglumpt, pp. 1.form (as butter in the churn); 2.lump

glumsich, adj. clumsy

Glund (die)n. 1.loose woman; 2.slattern

Gluppe (die)n. 1.clutches; 2.hands

Glutzkopp (der)n. blockhead

gluuch, adj. intelligent

Gluut (die)n. 1.glow; 2.heat

gluxe, v.; gegluxt, pp. 1.cluck; 2.gurgle

gluxich, adj. clucking

gmaahne, v.; gmaahnt, pp. remind

Gmee (die)n. 1.church; 2.congregation (in Old Order Amish and Mennonite usage)

Gmeesposchde (der)n. pillar of the church

Gmiesgaarde (der)n. vegetable garden

gna(r)schle, v.; gegnarschelt, pp. gnash

Gnaad(e) (die)n. grace (prayer)

Gnaadebank (die)n.; Gnaadebenk, pp. mercy-seat (in church)

gnaadezeit (die)n. time of grace

gnabbere, v.; gegnabbert, pp. stump about

Gnack (der)n. 1.knot; 2.skein

gnacke, v.; gegnackt, pp. 1.break partially; 2.crack; 3.tick

gnackere, v.; gegnackert, pp. 1.be unsteady (as a table); 2.creak

gnackrich, adj. 1.rickety; 2.tottering; 3.unsteady

gnackse, v.; gegnackst, pp. crack

Gnackwascht (die)n. hard smoked sausage

gnaedich, adj. gracious

Gnaerwel (der)n. 1.cartilage; 2.gristle

gnaerwlich, adj. 1.gnarly (of a tree, apple, or a roughly healed wound); 2.gristly

gnafze, v.; gegnafzt, pp. quarrel

Gnall (der)n. 1.clap; 2.loud report; 3.crack

gnalle, v.; gegnellt, pp. 1.crack; 2.make a loud report

Gnalleise (es)n. 1.(dunner uns --) 1.great guns!; 2.holy smoke; 3.(facetious for a) worthless gun

Gnaller (der)n. cracker (of a whip)

Gnallhitt (die)n. 1.bawdy house; 2.dilapidated building; 3.hovel

gnappe, v.; gegnappt, pp. snap at someone (as a vicious dog)

gnappere, v.; gegnappert, pp. coitus

gnapps, adv. 1.close; 2.near; 3.scanty; 4.scantily; 5.scarcely

gnappse, v.; gegnappst, pp. 1.be sparing with; 2.stint

Gnarre (der)n.; Gnarre, pl. 1.gnarl; 2.knot (in lumber)

gnarre, v.; gegnarrt, pp. 1.croak; 2.grunt; 3.quack

Gnarreloch (es)n.; Gnarrelecher, pl. knothole

gnarrich, adj. 1.gnarly; 2.knotty

Gnarwel (der)n.; Gnarwel, pl. 1.cartilage; 2.gristle

gnarwlich, adj. 1.gnarly (of a tree, apple, or a roughly healed wound); 2.gristly

Gnarze (der)n. 1.blemish in fruit caused by the sting of an insect; 2.core of an apple; 3.nubbin; 4.stumpy old tree

gnarzich, adj. 1.deformed and imperfect (as trees and fruit); 2.knotty

gnatzich, adj. 1.deformed and imperfect (of trees and fruit); 2.knotty

gnaunse, v.; gegnaunst, pp. grumble

gnawwere, v.; gegnawwert, pp. 1.gnaw; 2.nibble

Gnazze (der)n. 1.blemish in fruit caused by the sting of an insect; 2.core of an apple; 3.nubbin; 4.stumpy old tree

Gnechel (der)n.; Gnechel, pl. 1.ankle; 2.knuckle

Gnecht (der)n.; Gnecht, pl. 1.farmhand; 2.hired man; 3.man-servant; 4.(glee --) the boy hired to help on the farm; 5.(gross --) adult hired man

Gneckel (der)n. 1.ankle; 2.knuckle

gnedst, adj. right (sane)

gneedich, adj. gracious

Gneeterich (der)n. 1.knot grass; 2.knotweed

gneffere, v.; gneffert, pp. quarrel

gnefze, v.; gegnefzt, pp. quarrel

Gnefzer (der)n. 1.quarrelsome person; 2.small barking cur

Gnelle (der)n. 1.crack (of a whip); 2.report

gnelle, v.; gegnellt, pp. 1.crack; 2.make a loud report

Gnepp (die)n. dumplings

gneppe, v.; gegneppt, pp. button

gneppich, adj. covered with lumps

Gneppschuh (der)n. button shoe

gnetschich, adj. 1.immature; 2.soggy; 3.soft (especially of bread)

Gg

Gnewwel — Gottheit

Gnewwel (der)n. 1.gag; 2.stick used for twisting a rope or strawband; 3.bolt at the end of a chain; 4.skein; 5.hank

gnewwle, v.; gegnewwelt, pp. 1.gag; 2.twist tight

gnibbe, v.; gegnippt, pp. knot

Gnibbel (der)n..; Gnibbel, pl. 1.club; 2.cudgel; 3.coarse fellow; 4.short stout person

gniblich, adj. sickly

Gnick (es)n. nape (or back of the neck)

gnick gnock tick-tock

gnicke, v.; gegnickt, pp. bend and crack without breaking entirely

Gnicker (der)n. knock

Gnickerli (es)n.; Gnickerlin, pl. stunted fruit

gnickse, v.; gegnickst, pp. (to be) stingy

Gnickser (der)n. miser

Gnie (es)n.; Gnie, pl. 1.elbow of a stove pipe; 2.knee

Gnie biege (die)n. genuflect (Old Order Amish term)

gnie-e, v.; gegniet, pp. kneel

gniedief, adv. up to the knees

gniehoch, adv. knee high

Gniekapp (die)n. kneecap

Gniekehl (die)n. 1.hock; 2.posterior part of the knee joint

Gnieriem(e) (der)n.; Genierieme, pl. (shoemaker's) stirrup or strap

Gniescheib (die)n. 1.kneecap; 2.kneepan

gnieschprunge, adj. kneesprung

Gnieswatzel (die)n. hellebores viridis

Gniewand (die)n. part of the wall between the roof and the floor of a garret

Gnipp (der)n. knot (in a cord)

gnitz, adj. 1.mischievous; 2.tricky

Gnoche (der)n.; Gnoche, pl. bone (human, animal)

Gnochefleesch (es)n. soup bone

Gnochefraas (es)n. caries

Gnochegaul (der)n. skeleton (bony) horse

Gnochelehr (die)n. osteology

Gnochemann (der)n. skeleton

Gnochemehl (es)n. bonemeal

Gnochemiehl (die)n. bone mill

Gnocheseeg (die)n.; Gnocheseege, pl. meat-saw

Gnocheweh (es)n. bone ache

Gnocheyarrigel (der)n. skeleton

Gnocheyockel (der)n. 1.rag and bone collector; 2.skeleton

gnochich, adj. bony

Gnoddel (der)n. 1.chunk; 2.chunky person 3.compact hard droppings of many animals; 4.small lump; 5.turd; 6. (gleener griener --) peas

Gnoddelaerwet (die)n. 1.small chores; 2.tedious job

Gnoddelsupp (die)n. riwwelsoup

Gnoddelwoll (die)n. wool from the rear quarters of a sheep where it is mixed with manure

gnoddelwolle, adj. made of gnoddelwoll

Gnoddelwolleduch (es)n. cloth made from gnoddelwoll

gnoddere, v.; gegnoddert, pp. 1.grumble; 2.scold

gnodderich, adj. 1.grumbly; 2.sulky

gnoddle, v.; gegnoddelt, pp. work in a slow and poky manner

gnoddlich, adj. lumpy

Gnolle (der)n. 1.lump (of sugar); 2.tuber

gnollich, adj. lumpy

Gnootsch-Dokder (der)n. chiropractor

gnootsche, v.; gegnootscht, pp. 1.caress; 2.fondle; 3.handle over much; 4.hug

Gnopp (der)n.; Gnepp, pl. 1.button; 2.knob; 3.lump 4.(schnitz un gnepp); dumplings cooked with dried apples; 5.(gnepp hinnich die ohre hawwe) be tricky; 6.(gnepp im kopp) tricks

Gnopphols (es)n. 1.buttonwood; 2.sycamore

Gnopploch (es)n.; Gnopplecher, pl. buttonhole

Gnoww(el)loch (der)n. garlic

Gnowwlich (der)n. garlic

gnuddere, v.; gegnuddert, pp. scold

gnuffe, v.; gegnufft, pp.1.beat with the fist; 2.hammer lightly; 3.quarrel; 4.pummel

Gnupse (der)n. 1.gag; 2.stick used for twisting a rope of strawband; 3.bolt at the end of a chain; 4.hank; 5.skein

gnuschdre, v.; gegnuschdert, pp. be occupied with trifles

God (die)n. godmother

Goddesdi(e)nscht (der)n. 1.church service; 2.worship

Godelskaern (die)n. cocculus Indicus

Gogelskaern (die)n. cocculus Indicus

Gold (es)n. gold

Goldamschel (die)n.; Goldamschle, pl. Baltimore oriole

golde, adj. golden

goldegehl, adj. golden yellow

Goldendur (die)n. golden tincture

goldni(ch), adj. golden

Goldschaum (der)n. beaten gold (film)

Goldschmitt (der)n. goldsmith

Goldschtick (es)n. gold piece

Goldwarzel (die)n. gold thread

Golopp (der)n. gallop (nursery rhyme)

Golraabi (der)n. kohlrabi

Golraawe (der)n. kohlrabi

Golrieb (die)n. rutabaga

Gorn (es)n. 1.net; 2.worsted; 3.yarn

Gosch (die)n. 1.mouth; 2.mug

Gossduch (es)n. gusset

Gott (der)n.; Gedder, pl. 1.God; 2.(mei -- nochemol!) my goodness!

gottebaermlich, adj. awful

Gottesacker (der)n. cemetery

Gottesblut (es)n. St. John's wort

Gottesdinscht (der)n. divine service

Gottesgaabe (die)n. 1.a child; 2.alms; 3.gift of God

Gotteshaus (es)n. church

Gotteskrefte (die)n., pl. (mit --) with all possible means

Gotteslieb (die)n. 1.charity; 2.divine love

Gottesreich (es)n. kingdom of God

Gotteswatt (es)n. Scripture

Gottfri (der)n. Gottfried

Gottheit (die)n. divinity

Gg

Gottlieb

Gottlieb (der)n. Theophilus
gottlos, adj. 1.ungodly; 2.wicked
Gottlosichkeet (die)n. 1.impiety; 2.godlessness;
   3.wickedness
gottschtraeflich, adj. awfully
gottsdausich, interj. (half playful exclamation) well! well!
gottslebbdaag, interj. well! well!
gottsyemmerlich, adj. terribly
Gottszeit (die)n. Standard Time, "slow time"
gottverdamm, interj. damn it!
gottverdammt, adv. 1.damned; 2.infernal
gottverflucht, adv. 1.damned; 2.accursed
gotzich, adj. 1.single; 2.(aller -- eener) every single one;
   3.(kenn --er Mensch warr datt) not a single person
   was there
Gowe(r)nier (der)n. governor
goweniere, v.; goweniert, pp. govern
Graab (es)n.; Greewer, pl. 1.grave; 2.tomb; 3.trench
Graabblatz (der)n.; Graabbletz, pl. cemetery
Graabhof (der)n.; Graabhef, pl. 1.cemetery; 2.graveyard
Graabmacher (der)n.; Greewermacher, pl. grave digger
   (and formerly also pallbearer)
Graabschtee (der)n.; Graabschtee, pl. 1.gravestone;
   2.headstone; 3.tombstone
Graabschteehacker (der)n. tombstone cutter
graad (dative) **saage,** v. tell straight
graad recht, adj. 1.accurate; 2.exact
graad zu, adv. directly
Graad(e)wohl (es)n. (uff --) haphazard
graad, adj. 1.at once 2.degree; 3.erect; 4.exactly;
   5.measure; 6.slender; 7.straight; 8.(-- im alde) as usual
graad, adv. 1.exactly; 2.right away
graadaus, adj. 1.bluntly; 2.in plain terms; 3.right out
graadement, adj. exactly
graadeweck, adj. 1.bluntly; 2.presently; 3.right out
graadeweck, adv. immediately
Graage (der)n.; Greege, pl. collar
Graahne (der)n. spigot
graahne, v.; gegraahnt, pp. 1.creak; 2.groan
Graam (der)n. 1.grief; 2.heart ache; 3.sadness
Graan (der)n. 1.crane (machine); 2.stopcock; 3.spigot
Graan (die)n.; Graane, pl. 1.awn (of grain) 2.bone (fish)
Graas (es)n. grass
graas(e)grie, adv. green as grass
Graas-schlang (die)n.; Graas-schlange, pl. grass-snake
graasam, adj. cruel
Graasblatz (der)n. lawn
graase, v.; gegraast, pp. 1.graze; 2.weed (a lawn)
Graasfeld (es)n. field in grass
graasfressend, adj. herbivorous
Graashalm (der)n. blade of grass
graasich, adj. 1.grassy; 2.weedy
Graasland (es)n.; Grasslenner, pl. grassland
Graasschier (die)n. grass-shears
Graassens (die)n. scythe
Graassome (der)n. grass seed

gratliere

Graassume (der)n. grass seed
Graawe (der)n.; Greewer, pl. 1.ditch; 2.gutter; 3.trench
graawe, v.; gegraawe, pp. dig
Graawer (der)n. digger
Grabb (die)n.; Grabbe, pl. 1.crow; 2.raven
Grabbefuss (der)n. 1.spotted geranium; 2.spotted cranes bill
Grabbenescht (es)n. crow's nest
Grabbeschnawwel (der)n. 1.spotted geranium; 2.spotted
   cranes bill
grabsche, v.; gegrabscht, pp. 1.be avaricious; 2.grasp;
   3.snatch
grabschich, adj. 1.avaricious; 2.greedy
Grach (der)n. 1.clap; 2.crack; 3.crash; 4.loud report
grache, v.; gegracht, pp. 1.crack; 2.crash; 3.creak; 4.make
   a report
Graddelbohn (die)n.; Graddelbohne, pl. pole bean
Graddelbuhn (die)n.; Graddelbuhne, pl. pole bean
graddle, v.; gegraddelt, pp. 1.climb; 2.crawl; 3.creep
graddlich, adj. 1.astraddle; 2.crawling
Graehaag (es)n. corn (on the foot)
graehe, v.; gegraeht, pp. crow
Graehnaag (es)n. corn (on the foot)
Graemer (der)n. peddler
graemere, v.; gegraemert, pp. peddle
Graenpaep (der)n. grandfather
Graft (die)n.; Grefde, pl. 1.might; 2.power; 3.strength;
   4.vigor
Graftbrieh (die)n. jelly
Grageel (der)n. violent quarrel
grageele, v.; grageelt, pp. 1.quarrel; 2.torment (verbally)
Grageeler (der)n. 1.insistently troublesome person;
   2.quarrelsome person
Grakeel (der)n. violent quarrel
Gramansel (es)n. flummery
Grammenot (die)n. (was dei --) what the deuce!
Gramp (der)n. 1.convulsion; 2.cramp; 3.spasm
Grampet (die)n. 1,(des soll dei -- hole) confound it!;
   2.(gotts --) confound it!; 3.(was dei --) what the deuce!
Granaadabbel (der)n. pomegranate
Granaatabbel (der)n. Queen Anne's pocket melon
   (grown for its fragrance)
Grandel (der)n. plow beam
grank, adj. 1.ill; 2.sick; 3.(en --es) sick person
Grankebett (es)n. sick bed
Granker (der)n.; Granke, pl. patient
Granket (die)n. 1.disease; 2.illness; 3.sickness;
   4.(woman's) courses
Grankheet (die)n. 1.disease; 2.menses; 3.sickness;
   4.(english --) (a) king's evil; (b) scrofula
Grankheit (die)n.; Grankheide, pl. 1.disease; 2.illness;
   3.sickness
Grans (der)n. 1.border; 2.garland; 3.wreath
Grapp (der)n. madder
grappschich, adj. niggardly
Grasschneider (der)n. lawn mower
gratliere, v.; gratliert, pp. congratulate

Gg

Gratz — grense

Gratz (der)n. 1.itch; 2.scratch

gratze, v.; gegratzt, pp.1.scratch;2.(en --s) a tickling sensation

Gratzfiessel (es)n. 1.bow; 2.curtsey

gratzich, adj. 1.crabbed; 2.itching; 3.itchy; 4.partly fermented (of cider); 5.not cordial; 6.pungent; 7.tickling

Grauns (die)n. 1.groaner; 2.grumbler

graunse, v.; gegraunst, pp. 1. grumble; 2. mew; 3. talk indistinctly

graunsich, adj. 1.crabbed; 2.cross; 3.ill- tempered

grausam, adj. cruel

grause, v.; gegraust, pp. 1.nauseate; 2.(to make one) shudder

Graut (es)n.; Greider, pl. 1.cabbage; 2.herb; 3.top of a plant; 4.vegetation; 5.weed

Grautda(r)sch (die)n. heart of cabbage

Grauthammel (der)n. 1.dolt; 2.raw fellow

Grauthowwel (die)n. cabbage cutter

Grautkopp (der)n.; Grautkepp, pl. cabbage-head

Grautkutsch (die)n. frame on posts in which plants, especially cabbage, were raised from seed for transplanting

Grautrieb (die)n. kohlrabi

Grautschtamper (der)n. stamper used in making sauerkraut

Grautschtick (es)n. cabbage patch

Grautschtock (der)n. growing cabbage

Grautselaat (der)n. cabbage slaw

Grautsome (der)n. cabbage seed

Grautsume (der)n. cabbage seed

Grautwarm (der)n. (green) cabbage worm

Grawweles (es)n. crawling sensation

grawwle, v.; gegrawwelt, pp. crawl

grawwlich, adj. crawling

Greadur (die)n. creature

Grebagang (der)n. 1.the act of moving backward; 2.decline

grebbscht, adj. 1.coarsest; 2.roughest; 3.rudest

grebiere, v.; grebiert, pp. 1.die; 2.go to ruin; 3.kick the bucket; 4.(sich --) become ruined

Grebs (der)n. 1.cancer; 2.crab; 3.Cancer (4th sign of zodiac)

Grebsgang (der)n. 1.decline; 2.going backward; 3 .retrogression; 4.(-- geh) go backward; 5.(-- hawwe) (a) (to go) backward(s); (b) fail in health

grebsordich, adj. cancerous

Grecks (die)n. 1.complaint; 2.disease

greckse, v.; gegreckst, pp. 1.ail; 2.grunt

grecksich, adj. 1.ailing; 2.grunting

Grecksmiehl (die)n. person addicted to complaining

Greditt (der)n. 1.credit; 2.(-- gewwe) grant credit

greel, adj. pepper and salt (colored)

Greemer (der)n.; Greemer, pl. peddler

greemere, v.; gegreemert, pp. peddle

Grees (der)n. circle

Grees (die)n. 1.extent; 2.height; 3.magnitude; 4.size

greeschtdeels, adj. mostly

greeser mache, v.; greeser gemacht, pp. enlarge

gref(f)dich, adj. 1.mighty; 2.robust; 3.stout; 4.strong; 5.vigorous

Greh(n)aag (es)n.; Greh(n)aage, pl. corn (on the foot)

grehe, v.; gegreht, pp. crow

Greid (es)n. 1.account; 2.bill; 3.chalk; 4.(in der -- sei) (a) be in a fix; (b) be in for it; (c) owe

Greider (die)n., pl. herbs

greideweiss, adj. white as chalk

greidich, adj. covered with chalk

Greidliwidderbring (der)n. 1.brunella; 2.self-heal

greife, v.; gegriffe, pp. 1.grab; 2.grasp; 3.grip; 4.seize

greine, v.; gegreint, pp. 1.cry; 2.weep

greische, v.; gegrische, pp. 1.bawl; 2.neigh (of horses); 3.scream; 4.shout; 5.shriek; 6.yell; 7.spread tales

greisle, v.; gegreiselt, pp. 1.cause great aversion or nausea; 2.have a horror of

greislich, adj. 1.dreadful; 2.hideous; 3.horrible; 4.terrible; 5.thrilling

Greitliwidderbring (der)n. 1.brunella; 2.self heal

Greitz (es)n.; Greitzer, pl. 1.cross; 2.crucifix;3.misfortune; 4.small of the back; 5.(en --) (a) annoyance; (b) nuisance; (c) vexation

Greitzschpiggel (der)n. mattock

Greitzweg (der)n.; Greitzwege, pl. crossroad

Greiz (es)n. 1.burden; 2.(es is mer en --); 3.(gotts -- nochemol) confound it!; 4.I hate to do it!; 5.(im --hawwe) (to) have lumbago; 6.(iwwers --) crosswise

Greizhols (es)n. scantling

Greizhur (die)n. queen of clubs

greiziche, v.; gegreizicht, pp. crucify

greizlaahm, adj. hip shot

Greizmiehl (die)n. fox and geese

Greizpaad (der)n. cross path

Greizschtroos (die)n. crossroad

Greizweh (es)n. 1.backache; 2.lumbago

greizweis, adv. crosswise

Greizwoch (die)n. week of the Elevation of the Holy Cross (Sept. 14)

Grememm (die)n. grandmother

gremisch, adj. cramped (afflicted with cramp)

grempe, v.; gegrempt, pp. 1.catch in turning; 2.cramp

grempisch, adv. 1.(foot) sore; 2.(walking) with stooping gait

Grenaadeppli (es)n. Queen Anne's pocket melon (grown for its fragrance)

Grendel (der)n. (blug[s] --) plow beam

grenk deuce take you!; (dich soll dei -- hole); (do will ich dei -- griege) I'll be hanged; (gotts --) confound it!; (hols dei --) by golly!; (was dei --) what the deuce!

grenk(er)lich, adj. 1.infirm; 2.invalid; 3.sickly

grenke, v.; gegrenkt, pp. 1.grieve; 2.hurt; 3.regret; 4.vex

Grenkel (es)n. argument

grenket 1.(dich soll dei -- hole) deuce take you!; 2.(wie die --) how the deuce?

grenkle, v.; gegrenk(h)elt, pp. 1.ail; 2.irk; 3.be sickly 4.complain of sickness; 5.take sick

grenklich sei, v.; gewest, pp. 1.ail; 2.be sickly

grenklich, adj. sickly

Grens (die)n. 1.border; 2.limit

grense, v.; gegrenst, pp. 1.be contiguous to; 2.border upon

Gg

grenselos

grenselos, adj. unbounded

Grepp (der)n. (en --) a grudge

greppe, v.; gegreppt, pp. 1.pain; 2.regret; 3.regret the loss of; 4.vex

greppisch, adj. 1.bearing a grudge; 2.miffed

Gresse (die)n. 1.Indian cress; 2.nasturtium

Gret (die)n. Margaret

Gretschel (es)n. (in Hansel un --) in a nursery rhyme, Margaret

Gretz (der)n. (en --) 1.annoyance; 2.crank; 3.grouchy person; 4.itch; 5.nuisance; 6.vexation

Gretz (die)n. (die aldi --) the old crank (of a woman)

gretzich, adj. 1.crabbed; 2.itchy; 3.scabious

grewwelich, adj. gravel

grewwer, adv. coarser

grexe, v.; gegrext, pp. 1.croak; 2.groan; 3.grunt; 4.quack; 5.ail

Gribb (die)n. 1.crib; 2.small bed

gribbe, v.; gegribbt, pp. crib (of horses)

Gribbebeisser (der)n. 1.cribber; 2.cribbing horse

Gribbel (der)n.; Gribbel, pl. cripple

Gribber (der)n. 1.cribber; 2.cribbing horse

gribblich, adj. 1.crippled; 2.poor (in health)

Grick (die); Gricke, pl. crutch

Grick (die)n.; Grecke; Gricke, pl. 1.creek; 2.run; 3.small stream

Grickche (es)n. little pitcher

Grickelche (es)n. little pitcher

Grickselfixel (es)n. 1.fine tracery work; 2.scribbling; 3.vulgar adornment

griddlich, adj. 1.crabbed; 2.cross; 3.fretful; 4.testy; 5.ticklish; 6.trying

grie(n), adj. 1.green; 2.unripe

Grie(n)haus (es)n.; Grienheiser, pl. greenhouse

grie, adj. verdant

Grieg (der)n. war

griege, v.; grickt, pp. 1.acquire; 2.get; 3.obtain; 4.receive; 5.(eens ins Gsicht --) get a blow (slap) in the face

griegehl, adj. yellowish green

Griegel (es)n. 1.mug in which coffee is served (Moravian); 2.small jug

Grieger (der)n. warrior

Griegschiff (es)n. man-of-war (warship)

Griegsmann (der)n. warrior

Griegzeit (die)n. wartime

Griekopp (der)n.; Griekepp, pl. mallard duck (male)

Grieksschiff (es)n. 1.man-of-war; 2.war vessel

grielich, adj. greenish

grien, adj. verdant

griene Schoofgnoodle (die)n. peas

Grie(ner)dunnerschdaag (der)n. Maundy Thursday

Grieschpaa (der)n. verdigris

grieschtenglich Balsem (der)n. spearmint

Griess (der)n. ground corn (for young chickens)

griesse, v.; gegriesst, pl. 1.greet; 2.remember to; 3.salute; 4.send regards

Griewe (die)n., pl. 1.cracklings; 2.greaves

Gritz

Grieweide (der, die)n. white willow

Griff (der)n. 1.clip (of a horseshoe); 2.grip

Griggel (es)n. mug in which coffee is served (Moravian)

Griggelche (es)n. little pitcher

Grille (die)n., pl. 1.whims; 2.(-- im Kopp) (der Wei hot --) the wine is strong

Grimm (die)n. 1.bend; 2.curve; 3.turn

Grimmdar(e)m (der)n. 1.colon; 2.large intestine

grimme, v.; gegrimmt, pp.; (sich --) 1.bend; 2.move

Grimmel (die)n.; Grimmle, pl. crumb

Grimmelboi (der)n. pie covered with crumbs of flour, lard and sugar

grimmich, adj. horrible

Grimming (die)n. 1.bend; 2.curvature

grimmle, v.; gegrimmelt, pp. crumble

Grind (der)n. scab

grinde, v.; gegrindt, pp. 1.establish; 2.found

Grinder (der)n. founder

grindich, adj. scabby

grindkopp, v. (sich en -- aaschwetze) 1.get a battered head; 2.get into trouble

grindlich, adv. 1.severely; 2.thoroughly

Gringel (der)n. circle

grinse, v.; gegrinst, pp. 1.grin; 2.look daggers

Grips (der)n. scruff of the neck

Grips(er) (der)n. 1.chap; 2.little fellow

Grisch (der)n. 1.cry; 2.scream; 3.shout; 4.yell

Grischbel (der)n. proper name

Grischdaag (der)n. Christmas

Grischdaagnacht (die)n. Christmas night

Grischdel (der)n. Christian

Grischdendum (der)n. Christianity

Grischdier (die)n. (enema) syringe

grischdiere, v.; grischdiert, pp. 1.clyster; 2.give an enema

Grischdus (der)n. Christ

Grischkindel (es),n.; Grischkindli(n), pl. Christmas present

Grischt (der)n.; Grischde, pl. Christian

Grischtbaam (der)n. Christmas tree

Grischtblumm (die)n. Christmas flower

Grischtdaag (der)n.; Grischtdaage, pl. 1.Christmas; 2.yule

Grischtdaag(s)baam (der)n.; Grischtdaag(s)beem, pl.Christmas tree

Grischtkindli (es)n. 1.Christmas present; 2.Santa Claus

grischtlich, adj. 1.Christian; 2.devout

Grischtmonet (der)n. December

Grischtnacht (die)n. Christmas eve

Grischtoffel (der)n. Christopher

Grischtowed (der)n. Christmas eve

Grischtwatzel (die)n. hellebores viridis

Grischtyan (der)n. Christian

grislich, adj. 1.horrible; 2.terrible; 3.horrible

Grissel (die)n., pl. 1.cold shivers; 2.thrill; 3.(die -- sinn mer ausgange) I shuddered (at the sight)

grissle, v.; gegrisselt, pp. 1.be distasteful; 2.make one shudder

Gritz (der)n. scratch

Gg

Gritzelfixel — Grummel

Gritzelfixel (es)n. 1.fine tracery work; 2.scribbling; 3.vulgar adornment

gritzle, v.; gegritzelt, pp. scribble

Gritzler (der)n. scribbler

gritzlich, adj. 1.scrawly; 2.scribblingly

griwwle, v.; gegriwwelt, pp. 1.feel a sensation as of a crawling insect; 2.find fault; 3.worry

Griwwles (es)n. 1.creeping sensation; 2.gripes

Grix (der)n. cricket

Grixel (es)n. cricket

Grixer (der)n. cricket

Grixli (es)n.; Grixlin, pl. cricket

gro(h), adj. gray

grob(b), adj.; adv. 1.brusque; 2.coarse; 3.rude; 4.rough; 5.violent

Grobaart (der)n. 1.graybeard; 2.old man

Grobbheet (die)n. 1.coarseness; 2.rudeness

Grobbnickel (der)n. ruffian

grobbscht, adj. 1.coarsest; 2.roughest; 3.rudest

Grod (der)n. two first furrows thrown against each other in plowing to the right

Grod(d)ebalsem (der)n. 1.pennyroyal; 2.sage (tea)

Groddehupse (es)n. leapfrog

Groddetee (der)n. sage (tea)

groeckschteenich, adj. gray plaided

Grohaag (der)n.; Gorhaage, pl. corn (on the foot)

grohoorich, adj. gray haired

Groier (der)n.; Groiere, pl. auctioneer

grokeppich, adj. gray headed

Grokopp (der)n. gray headed

grolich, adj. grayish

Groll (die)n.; Grolle, pl. 1.anger; 2.curl; 3.ringlet; 4.spite

grolle, v.; gegrollt, pp. curl

Grolleise (es)n.; Grolleise, pl. curling iron

grollich, adj. curly

Gron (die)n. crown

Grone (der)n. spigot

Groot (die)n.; Grodde, pl. toad

Grooz (der)n. mold

grooze, v.; gegroozt, pp. 1.become moldy; 2.mold

groozich, adj. moldy

Gropp (der)n. 1.craw (of a fowl); 2.goiter

gross feihlich, adj. 1.big-feeling; 2.haughty; 3.uppish

Gross-soh(n) (der)n. grandson

gross/schwetze, v.; grossgschwetzt, pp. bluster

gross, adj. 1.great; 2.large; 3.tall

gross; greeser; greescht, adj. big; bigger; biggest

grossaagich, adj. large eyed

Grossdaadi (der)n. 1.daddy-longlegs; 2.grandfather

Grossdarem (der)n. large intestine

Grossdochder (die)n. granddaughter

Grossdrumm (die)n. bass drum

Grosseldre (die)n., pl. grandparents

Grossendi (die)n. great aunt

grossfiehlich, adj. conceited

grossfiessich, adj. large footed

grossglidderich, adj. of large build

grossgnochich, adj. large boned

Grosshandel (der)n. wholesale business

grosshatzich, adj. 1.generous; 2.magnanimous

Grosskinskind (es)n.; Grosskinskinner, pl. great grandchild

grosslecherich, adj. full of big holes

Grossmammi (die)n. grandmother

Grossmaul (es)n. 1.blusterer; 2.boaster; 3.braggart

grossmechtich, adj. 1.very large; 2.very tall

grossmeenich, adj. proud

grossmeilich, adj. 1.blustering; 2.boastful; 3.bragging

grossmiedich, adj. 1.proud; 2.self important

Grossmudder (die)n. grandmother

Grossmut (der)n. 1.generosity; 2.magnanimity

Grossonkel (der)n. great uncle

grossordich, adj. 1.grand; 2.great

grossschteh, adv. stand superior

Grossvadder (der)n. grandfather

Grott (die)n. 1.toad; 2.(gleeni --) young girl

Grottebalsem (der)n. American pennyroyal

Grottefuss (der)n. 1.toad's foot; 2.toadstool

Grottegelser (der)n. unskilled surgeon

Grottegickser (der)n. poor pocket knife

Grottehupse (es)n. leapfrog

Grotteschtuhl (der)n. toadstool

growwer, adv. coarser

Grub (die)n.; Gruwe, pl. 1.pit; 2.underground container; 3.vat

grubbe, v.; gegrubbt, pp. 1.dig; 2.grub

Grubbes (es)n. stunted human being or animal

Grubbhack (die)n. 1.grubbing-hoe; 2.mattock

Grubbhackehelm (der)n. mattock helve

grubbich, adj. 1.small; 2.stunted

Grubbs (der)n. 1.brush; 2.scrub

Grubbsefeld (es)n. field grown up in brush

Gruck (der)n.; Griek, pl. 1.pitcher; 2.mug

Grudelrewe (die)n., pl. groundsel

Gruft (die)n. 1.brat; 2.chasm; 3.depth; 4.yawning

Grug (der)n.; Grieg, pl. jug

Grumbeereglicker (der)n. seed ball of the potato

Grumbeereleser (der)n. potato picker

Grumbeereschtengle (der)n. 1.potato stalk; 2.potato top

Grumbeereschtick (es)n. potato patch

Grumbeeresupp (die)n. potato soup

grumm, adj. crooked

grummbeenich, adj. bowlegged

Grummbeer (die)n.; Grummbeere, pl. potato

Grummbeereboi (der)n. potato pie

Grummbeereschaufel (die) n.; Grummbeereschaufle, pl. potato shovel

Grummbier (die)n.; Grummbiere, pl. 1.potato; 2.(gemaeschde --e) mashed potatoes

Grummbiere Saess (es)n. mashed potatoes

Grummbierekeffer (der)n.; Grummbierekeffer, pl. potato bug

Grummbuckel (der)n. humpback

grummbucklich, adj. 1.bent; 2.hilly; 3.humpbacked

Grummel (es)n. 1.low murmuring; 2.rumor

Gg

Grummelwasser

Grummelwasser (es)n. 1.mopish reluctance; 2.sullenness (with suppressed crying)

grummle, v.; gegrummelt, pp. 1.growl; 2.grumble; 3.mutter

grummlich, adj. 1.crabbed; 2.cross; 3.ill-tempered; 4.prone to grumble

Grund (der)n. 1.foundation; 2.ground; 3.reason; 4.soil; 5.(ei du --) my goodness!; 6.(meiner --) by gracious!; 7.(zu -- geh) (a) go to ruin; (b) perish

Grund(d)ax (der)n.; Grund(d)axe, pl. 1.groundhog; 2.woodchuck

Grunddachskitz (die)n. female woodchuck

Grundeeche (die)n. scrub oak

Grundeechel (die)n. acorn of the scrub oak

Grundeis (es)n. 1.flake ice (forming on wet ground); 2. half frozen water in streams

Grundelraawer (die)n. 1.gill; 2.ground ivy

Grundelrewe (die)n. 1.gill; 2.ground ivy

Grundfarb (die)n. 1.color scheme; 2.tone

Grundgretz (der)n. ground itch

Grundkeller (der)n. deep cellar apart from house for cooling milk and other eatables

Grundloch (es)n. pit

Grundmeesel (der)n. iron bar with broad bit for digging post holes

Grundniss (die)n. peanut

Grundsatz (der)n. 1.maxim; 2.principle

Grundsau (die)n.; Grundsei, pl. 1.groundhog; 2.woodchuck

Grundsau Lodsch (der)n. Groundhog Lodge

grundsboddem (vum) from the foundation

Grundschaufel (die)n.; Grundschaufel, pl. shovel

Grundscholle (der)n. clod

Grundschtick (es)n. messuage

Grundschtock (der)n. basement

Grundschtrauss (der)n. 1.gravel plant; 2.trailing arbutus

Grupp (die)n. group

gruschdich, adj. 1.crusty; 2.earthy; 3.out of sorts

Gruscht (die)n. 1.crust; 2.cranky person; 3.country dance; 4.frolic

Gruss (der)n. 1.compliments; 2.salutation

Grusselbier (die)n.; Grusselbiere, pl. gooseberry

Grusselkopp (der)n. curly head

grussle, v.; gegrusselt, pp. curl

grusslich, adj. 1.curled; 2.gristly

Grutze (der); Grutze, pl. 1.applejack; 2.bad whiskey; 3.(corn cob; 4.core (of fruit) ; 5.nubbin; 6.(weeche --)

Grutzepeif (die)n. corncob pipe

Grutzer (der)n. 1.poor sickler; 2.runt; 3.snip

Grutzeschaufel (die)n. pan used in putting corncobs into a stove

grutzich, adj. 1.damaged by the sting of an insect; 2.deformed; 3.stunted

gruuscht, adj. spoiled (of canned fruits)

Gsang (der)n. 1.ditty; 2.singing; 3.song

Gsangbuch (es)n. hymn book

Gsauf (es)n. 1.carousing; 2.hard drinking

Gscha(rr) (es)n.; Gscharre, pl. 1.dishes; 2.harness;

gschosse

3.implements; 4.tools

Gschaerr (es)n. 1.(continued) scratching; 2.scraping

Gschaff (es)n. 1.working; 2.manner of working

Gscharrschank (der)n. 1.cupboard; 2.pantry

Gscharrwescher (der)n. dishwasher

Gscharrweschwasser (es)n. dishwater

Gscharweschlumbe (der)n. dishcloth

Gscharweschschissel (die)n.; Gscharweschschissle, pl. dish pan

gscheffdich, adj. busy

Gscheft (es)n. 1.business; 2.wooden part of an old time gun or rifle; 3.work

gschehe, v.; is gschehe, gschehne, pp. 1.come; 2.happen; 3.occur

gscheid, adj. sage (wise)

Gscheidheet (die)n. 1.cleverness; 2.wisdom

gscheit, adj. 1.clever; 2.intelligent; 3.wise; 4.(net gans recht --) not having all one's senses

Gschelt (es)n. (continual) scolding

Gschenk (es)n.; Gschenker, pl. 1.present; 2.gift

Gschgwall (der)n.; Gschgwalle, pl. squirrel

Gschicht (die)n. 1.affair; 2.history; 3.story; 4.tale

Gschick (der)n. 1.knack; 2.(er kann sich kenn rechder -- gewwe) he hasn't quite got the knack

gschickt, adj. 1.expert; 2.handy; 3.skillful

Gschiess (es)n. (continual) shooting

Gschitt (es)n. (repeated) pouring

Gschittel (es)n. (continual) shaking

Gschlaaf (der)n. slave

Gschlaaferei (die)n. slavery

Gschlauder (es)n. same old story

Gschlawwer (es)n. (continual) slobbering

Gschlecht (es)n. 1.generation; 2.sex

Gschleck (es)n. 1.dainties; 2.delicacies; 3.licking of chops (of a dog); 4.tasting or eating dainties

Gschleckerwese (es)n. delicacies

Gschleff (es)n. 1.any long drawn out work or undertaking; 2.dragging

Gschleich (es)n. (habitual) sneaking or slow movement

Gschlenker (es)n. (continued) jerking or fidgeting

Gschlof (es)n. continued or unusual sleeping

Gschlummer (es)n. (continued) slumbering

Gschmack (der)n. 1.aroma; 2.taste (in some areas)

Gschmatz (es)n. smacking (of the lips in eating or kissing)

Gschmees (es)n. 1.rabble; 2.undesirable person

gschmeidich, adj. 1.slender; 2.svelte

Gschmeiss (es)n. throwing

Gschmier (es)n. 1.mess; 2.smearing; 3.smeary work

Gschmunsel (es)n. 1.grinning; 2.(continual) smiling

Gschnacker (es)n. (incessant) chattering

Gschnarricks (es)n. snoring

Gschnatter (es)n. chattering

Gschnepper (es)n. whittling

Gschnuffel (es)n. 1.secret rummaging; 2.snuffling

Gschockel (es)n. rocking

gschosse, adj. gone to seed (of plants)

Gg

Gschpass

Gschpass (der)n. 1.fun; 2.pleasure
gschpassich, adj. funny
Gschpassvoggel (der)n. 1.droll person; 2.funny chap
Gschpautz (es)n. (constant) spitting
Gschpettel (es)n. 1.derision; 2.sneering
Gschpichte (die)n., pl. 1.tales; 2.(-- mache) play pranks
Gschpiel (es)n. (continual) playing
gschpiere, v.; gschpiert, pp. 1.be sensible of; 2.feel; 3.follow the tracks (of game)
gschpierich, adj. (gut --) comfortable
Gschpott (es)n. (constant) mocking
Gschpraech (es)n. 1.chat; 2.confab; 3.talk
Gschpritz (es)n. 1.(continual) splashing; 2.spirting
gschpruuze, v.; gschpruuzt, pp. ruffle the feathers (of a turkey)
Gschpuck (der)n.; Gschpucker, pl. 1.ghost; 2.spook
Gschpuck(s) (es)n. 1.ghost; 2.hobgoblin; 3.spook
Gschpur (die)n.; Gschpure, pp. 1.track; 2.trace
Gschraub (es) n. 1. (continual) screwing; 2.hesitation or evasion; 3.squirming
Gschrei (es)n. 1.screaming; 2.squealing; 3.yelling
Gschreib (es)n. (continual) writing
Gschriwwenes (es)n. writing
gschrode, adj. chopped
gschtaerickdi Wesch (die)n. starched wash
gschtalle, v.; gschtallt, pp. 1.agree; 2.get along with
Gschtalt (die)n. 1.form; 2.frame
Gschtamp (es)n. (continual) stamping
Gschtank (der)n. stench
gschtarewe, adj. deceased
gschteh, v.; gschtanne, pp. 1.admit to; 2.confess; 3.own up
Gschtell (es) n. 1. frame; 2. (marrickwardiches --) immense person
Gschtichel (es)n. (repeated) innuendos
Gschtick (es)n. cannon
Gschtink (es)n. 1.evil report; 2.stink
gschtiwwelt, adj. fitted out
Gschtiwwer (der)n. 1.caprice; 2.flurry; 3.spell; 4.squall (of snow)
Gschtolper (es)n. 1.hobbling along; 2.(repeated) stumbling
gschtopptevoll, adv. filled to the utmost capacity
Gschtotter (es)n. (constant) stuttering
Gschtreit (es)n. (continual) quarreling
gschtriche, adj. 1.cancelled; 2.(-- mos) stricken measure
Gschtrick (es)n. (constant) knitting
Gschtubb (es)n. 1.nudging; 2.stubbing
gschult, adj. educated
Gschussel (es) n. (continual or repeated) fast or abrupt movements
Gschwaare (der)n. 1.abscess; 2.boil
Gschwaere (der)n. 1.abscess; 2.boil; 3.ulcer
Gschwaerewatzel (die)n. horse balm
Gschwar(e) (der)n.; Gschware, pl. 1.abscess; 2.boil
Gschwarr(e) (der)n. boil
Gschwei (die)n. sister-in-law
gschweige, conj. 1.not to mention; 2.much less

Guckkaschde

gschwelle, v.; gschwolle, pp. swell
Gschwetz (es)n. 1.conversation; 2.gossip; 3.talk; 4.(-- hie un haer) constant bickering; 5.(narrisch --) obscenities
gschwewwelt, adj. 1.three sheets in the wind; 2.tipsy
Gschwier (es)n. 1.boil; 2.ulcer
gschwind, adv. 1.fast; 2.quick; 3.rapid; 4.soon
Gschwindichkeet (die)n. 1.celerity; 2.quickness
Gschwindichkeet (die)n. (inre --) in less than no time
Gschwischder (die)n., pl. brothers and sisters
Gschwischderkind (es)n. 1.cousin; 2.nephew
Gschwischdersoh (der)n. nephew
gschwische, prep. between
gschwischich, prep. between
Gschwitz (es)n. (continued) sweating
gschwolle, adj. swollen
Gschwulscht (die)n. 1.abscess; 2.swelling; 3.tumor
Gseedes (es)n. sod
gsegend, adj. blessed
gselle, v.; gsellt, pp. (sich --) (to) associate
gsellich, adj. 1.companionable; 2.sociable
Gsellschaft (die)n. company
Gsetz (es)n. 1.law; 2.statute
gsetzt, adj. 1.fixed; 2.settled; 3.(gut --) (a) sturdy; (b) well built
Gsicht (es)n.; Gsichder, pl. 1.face; 2.dial; 3.watch or clock face; 4.(en lang, sauer, verdreht, wiescht --mache) make a long, sour, distorted, terrible face; 5. (ins -- saage) tell to one's face
Gsicht(s)fareb (die)n. complexion
gsichtich, adj. double faced
Gsims (es)n. chair-rail (around room to prevent damage to wall)
Gsindel (es)n. rabble
Gsing (es)n. (continual) singing, buzzing
gsoffe, adj. 1.drunk; 2.intoxicated
gsoffe, v. get tipsy
Gsoffner (en)n. drunkard
Gsuch (es)n. (continual) searching or rummaging
Gsuddel (es)n. 1.drizzle; 2.playing in the water puddles (of children)
Gsuddelwese (es)n. dirty work
gsuddle, v.; gsuddelt, pp. play in the water puddles
gsund, adj. healthy
gsund, adv. 1.healthy; 2.hale; 3.well
Gsundheet (die)n. 1.health; 2.(--!), interj. God bless you! (call to another after sneezing)
Gsundheit (die)n. 1.health; 2.(--!), interj. bless you! (call to another after sneezing)
Guck (der)n. 1.appearance; 2.look; 3.looks
gucke, v.; geguckt, pp. 1.appear; 2.look; 3.stare 4.(sich nix meh gleich --) (a) lose all semblance (of corpses); (b) not to look like the same person
Gucker (der)n. 1.eye; 2.onlooker
Guckgummer (die)n. cucumber
guckich, adj. (gut --) good-looking
Guckkaschde (der)n. show

Gg

Guchu(ck)

Gucku(ck) (der)n. cuckoo
Gude(r) Mariye! Good Morning!
guder Naame (der)n. reputation
Guder Owed! Good evening!
gullere, v.; gegullert, pp. 1.coo; 2.gobble (of a turkey)
gulli, gulli call for geese
Gumme (der)n. 1.gum tree; 2.palate; 3.roof of the mouth
    4.(der -- schtecke) pierce the roof of a horse's mouth
    (to relieve blind staggers); 5.(der -- schaawe) recom-
    mended ironically to a person who is finicky in eating
Gummebaam (der)n.; Gummebeem, pl. gum tree
Gummebeer (die)n. gum berry
Gummebrecher (der)n. jawbreaker
Gummer (die)n.; Gummere, pl. 1.cucumber; 2.pickle
Gummerans (die)n. tomato
Gummerche (es)n.; Gummercher, pl. pickle
Gummerebaam (der)n. cucumber tree
Gummrerank (die)n. cucumber patch
Gummreselaat (der)n. pickle salad (cucumber)
Gump (der)n. whet-horn (filled with water or vinegar for
    whetting stone to sharpen scythes)
Gungelrieb (die)n.; Gungelriewe, pl. orchid
Gunn (die)n. 1.favor; 2.honor; 3.good wishes
gunne, v.; gegunnt, pp. 1.begrudge; 2.wish one ill;
    3.(gaern --) (a) gladly wish another's good luck;
    (b) wish well
Gunscht (die)n. favor
Guss (es)n. cast iron
Gusseise (es)n. cast iron
Gut Nacht! Good night!
Gut-n-Owed! Good evening!
gut/mache, v.; gutgemacht, pp. 1.(make) good; 2.restore
gut, adj. 1.good; 2.kind; 3.well; 4.(-- mache) (a) prove a
    statement; (b) make reparations; (c) repair; 5.(-- mann)
    God; 6.(-- heese) approve;7.(-- ab sei) be well-to-do
gut, adv. 1.healthy; 2.well
gutgelannt, adj. well-educated
Guthaerzichkeet (die)n. kind heartedness
Gutmeenichkeet (die)n. kindness
gutmiedich, adj. 1.easy going; 2.good natured; 3.kind
gutriechend, adj. fragrant
gutriechich, adj. fragrant
gutschteh, adj. 1.be responsible; 2.stand well; 3.vouch for
gutwillich, adj. 1.gladly; 2.voluntarily
gutwillicherweis, adj. 1.gladly; 2.voluntarily
Gwaal (die)n. 1.mourning; 2.sorrow; 3.suffering; 4.woe
Gwaart (die)n.; Gwaart, pl. 1.quart; 2.(en katzi --) (a)
    small quart (b) not quite a quart
Gwaartmos (es)n. quart measure
Gwack! sound made to imitate ducks
Gwaddi (der)n. short fat person
Gwadember (der)n. Ember Day
Gwael (die)n. torment
Gwaelaarsch (der)n. 1.trying child; 2.torment
gwaele, v.; gegwaelt, pp. torment
Gwaeleise (es)n. tormenting nagging child

gwunnerich

Gwaelholz (es)n. trying child
gwaelich, adj. tormenting
gwaldich, adv. very
Gwalle (der) n. 1.dried-beef; 2.thick fleshy part of a hind
    quarter of beef
Gwallefleesch (der)n. dried-beef
Gwalt (die)n. strength
gwaltsam, adj. violent
Gwarz (der)n. quartz
gwatsche, v.; (ge)gwatscht, pp. 1.quash; 2."squish" (in mud)
gwaxe, adj. adult
gwaxe, v.; gegwaxt, pp. 1.croak; 2.quack; 3.grunt
Gwecke (die)n. quick-grass
Gweckewasem (der)n. sod filled with couch-grass
Gwecksilwer (es)n. quicksilver
gweele, v.; gegweelt, pp. 1.harass; 2.pester; 3.torment;
    4.tantalize
gweelich, adv. 1.harassing; 2.tormenting
gwehnlich, adj., adv. 1.commonly; 2.generally;
    3.ordinarily; 4.usually
gwehnt, adj. 1.customary; 2.usual
Gwell (die)n. 1.spring (of water); 2.well
gwelle, v.; gegwellt; gegwolle, pp. 1.bubble; 2.ooze out;
    3.parboil; 4.swell from moisture
Gwendeltee (der)n. (creeping) thyme (tea)
Gwetsch (die)n.; Gwetsche, pl. 1.plum; 2.prune
gwetsche, v.; gegwetscht, pp. 1.bruise; 2.pinch; 3.squeeze
Gwetschebaam (der)n.; Gwetschebeem, pl. plum tree
gwetzt, v.; gegwetzt, pp. rub together with a swishing
    sound (of corduroy trousers)
Gwicht (es)n.; Gwichder, pl. weight
Gwiddebaam (der)n.; Gwiddebeem, pl. 1.quince tree;
    2.quinsy
Gwiddekaern (die)n.; Gwiddekaerne, pl quince seed
Gwidder (es)n. 1.thunder; 2.thunderstorm
gwiddere, v.; (ge)widdert, pp. thunder
Gwiddergeil (die)n., pl. thundering horses
Gwidderregge (der)n. thundershower
Gwidderrut (die)n.; Gwidderrude, pl. lightning rod
Gwidderschtang (der)n.; Gwidderschtange, pl. lightning rod
Gwidderschtarem (der)n. thunderstorm
Gwidderschtreech (der)n. thunderbolt
gwieke, v.; gegwiekt, pp. squeak (of mice)
gwilde, v.; gegwillt, pp. quilt
Gwilt (die)n. quilt
Gwinsch (der)n.; Gwinsche, pl. wish
Gwinsi (die)n. 1.quinsy; 2.sore throat
gwisselos, adj. unconscionable
Gwitt (die)n.; Gwidde, pl. quince
Gwunnerfitz (der)n. curiosity
gwunnerich, adj. 1.curious (Old Order Amish usage);
    2.inquisitive

Hh

haabere

haabere, v.; ghaabert, pp. 1.(to raise a) racket; 2.rumble
haabsichdich, adj. 1.avaricious; 2.greedy
Haabsucht (der)n. avarice
Haader (der)n. 1.strife; 2.wrangling
Haagel (der)n. hail
haagele, v.; gehaagelt, pp. hail
haagels, adv. confoundedly
Haagelwetter (es)n. 1.confound it!; 2.hang it all!
Haahne (der)n. 1.hammer or cock of a gun; 2.rooster
Haahnefuuss (der)n. small-flowered crowfoot
Haahnegegrisch (es)n. derogatory gossip
Haahnekamm (der) n. 1.cockscomb; 2.pigweed; 3.red amaranth
Haahnewackel (der)n. playful nickname
Haaland (es)n. field or part of a field when plowed by making all turns to the left
haapere, v.; ghaapert, pp. 1.make a racket; 2.rumble
Haapt (es)n. principal thing
Haaptblatz (der)n. principal place
Haaptgebei (es)n. main building
Haaptkall (der)n. leader
Haaptmann (der)n.; Hauptmenner, pl. 1.captain; 2.leader
Haaptsach (die)n. principal thing
Haaptschtadt (die)n. 1.capital; 2.metropolis
Haaptschtick (es)n. principal part
haaptsechlich, adv. 1.mainly; 2.principally
Haaptsumm (die)n. principal (drawing interest)
Haaptwese (es)n. main point or matter
Haar (es)n. 1.hair; 2.(distant) relationship; 3.(in eem --) (a) (in the) nick of time; (b) by the skin of the teeth
Haarbascht (die)n.; Haarbaschde, pl. hairbrush
Haargnibbel (es)n. knot (woman's hair knot)
haarich, adj. hairy
Haarpusch (der)n. wisp (of hair)
haarscharf, adj. 1.very exact; 2.very sharp
Haarschpell (die)n.; Haarschpelle, pl. hairpin
Haarschwanz (der)n. 1.braid of hair; 2.queue
Haarum! call to horses at the end of a furrow to make a hard turn to the left
Haarz (der)n. resin
haarzich, adj. resinous
Haas (der)n.; Haase, pl. 1.rabbit; 2.(en -- im peffer) there's a difficulty somewhere
Haaschemel (der)n. plowed field (all turns made to the left)
Haasefall (die)n. rabbit trap
Haasefett (es)n. rabbit grease
Haasefleesch (es)n. rabbit meat
Haaseglee (der)n. 1.French clover; 2.oxalis; 3.yellow wood-sorrel
Haasehund (der)n. rabbit-hound
Haasemaul (es)n. 1.harelip; 2.puckered lips
Haasenpeffer (der)n. name of a game of cards
Haaseschlupp (der)n. rabbit snare
Haasetee (der)n. rabbit tea
Haaseyacht (die)n. rabbit hunting
Haasimpeffer (der)n. name of a game of cards

haer/rufe

Haasli (es)n.; Hasslin, pl. bunny (rabbit)
Habbichgraut (es)n. hawkweed
Hack (der)n. 1.blow; 2.lash; 3.sharp rejoinder
Hack (die)n.; Hacke, pl. hoe
Hackbank (die)n. chopping block
hacke, v.; ghackt, pp. 1.chop; 2.hoe; 3.lash; 4.paw (of a horse); 5.(iwwer die Schtrang --) (to kick over the) traces
Hackel (die)n. 1.hackle; 2.hatchel
Hacker (der)n. 1.chopper; 2.hoer
Hackglotz (der)n. chopping block
hackle, v.; ghackelt, pp. hatchel
Hackmarrick (en)n. mark by an ax on a tree
Hackmesser (es)n. cleaver
hadde, v. temper
Hadding (die)n. 1.hardness; 2.temper (of a tool)
Hadyee!, interj. 1.adieu! 2.farewell!
Haefel (es)n. small pot
Haehnche (es)n. 1.cockerel; 2.fop
Haekel (es)n. 1.difficulty; 2.little hook
Haekelche (es)n. crochet needle
haekle, v.; ghaekelt, pp. 1.crochet; 2.hook; 3.limp
Haepter (die)n., pl. 1.bundles (of stalks); 2.heads (of cabbage or lettuce)
Haepterselaat (der)n. head lettuce
haer/bringe, v.; haergebrocht, pp. bring here
haer/bschtelle, v.; haerbschtellt, pp. order to come here
haer/dappe, v.; haergedappt, pp. approach with heavy steps
haer/draage, v.; haergedraage, pp. carry hither
haer/drehe, v.; haergedreht, pp. turn this way
haer/dreiwe, v.; haergedriwwe, pp. drive hither
haer/drolle, v.; haergedrollt, pp. jog along
haer/duh, v.; haergeduh, pp. put or place here
haer/faahre, v.; haergfaahre, pp. drive here (in a vehicle)
haer/fliege, v.; haergflogge, pp. fly hither
haer/geh, v.; haergange, pp. 1.pass off; 2.walk hither; 3.(iwwer ihn --) pitch into him (verbally); 4.(do is es awwer haergange) there were some high doings
haer/gewwe, v.; haergewwe, pp. give here (to some one)
haer/griege, v.; haergrickt, pp. 1.get from; 2.get to this place
haer/halde, v.; haerghalde, pp. bear the brunt
haer/hole, v.; haergholt, pp. fetch here
haer/keere, v.; haergekeert, pp. belong in this place
haer/kumme, v.; haerkumme, pp. 1.come from; 2.come hither
haer/lange, v.; haergelangt, pp. hand over
haer/lege, v.; haergelegt, pp. lay down here
haer/lese, v.; haergelese, pp. read off
haer/locke, v.; haergelockt, pp. 1.coax to a place; 2.entice
haer/losse, v.; haergelosst, pp. allow to come here
haer/nemme, v.; haergenumme, pp. (en fraa --) have intercourse with a woman
haer/reide, v.; haergeridde, pp. ride here (a horse)
haer/richde, v.; haergericht, pp. 1.ruin; 2.spoil
haer/rolle, v.; haergerollt, pp. roll this way
haer/rufe, v.; haergerufe, pp. call here

Hh

haer/rutsche | Halsband

haer/rutsche, v.; haergerutscht, pp. slide toward or near (one)

haer/saage, v.; haergsaagt, pp. 1.relate; 2.repeat

haer/schaffe, v.; haergschafft, pp. 1.convey hither; 2.provide

haer/schleefe, v.; haergschleeft, pp. drag hither

haer/schleiche, v.; haergschliche, pp. sneak hither

haer/schlippe, v.; haergschlippt, pp. slip near

haer/schluppe, v.; haergschluppt, pp. creep or crawl near

haer/schpringe, v.; haergschprunge, pp. run hither

haer/schtamme, v.; haerschtammt, pp. be descended from

haer/schtelle, v.; haergschtelle, pp. 1.set or place here; 2.(sich --) (a) pretend; (b) represent oneself; 3.standhere

haer/shicke, v.; haergschickt, pp. send hither

haer/welse, v. roll (something) to a place

haer/wolle, v. want to come to this place

haer/yaage, v.; haergyaagt, pp. chase this way

haer/ziege, v. 1.move here; 2.pull this way

haer, prep. 1.here; 2.hither

Haerbscht (der)n. 1.autumn; 2 fall

haerchle, v.; ghaerchelt, pp. 1.rattle in the throat; 2.wheeze

Haerd (der)n. 1.hearth; 2.oven floor

Haerd (die)n. 1.flock; 2.herd

haerde, v.; ghaert, pp. 1.harden; 2.temper

Haerdgraas (es)n. herd grass

Haerding (die)n. 1.hardness; 2.temper (of a tool)

haere, v.; ghaert, pp. (sich --) shed the coat or hair

haerli, adv. hardly

haerlich, adj. 1.cheerful; 2.happy; 3.jolly

Haermann (der)n. Herman

haermeniere, v.; haermeniert, pp. 1.carry on (in both senses); 2.get along well together; 3.raise a disturbance

Haern (es)n. brain

Haernenzinding (die)n. brain fever

haernervieh (es)n. cattle

Haernfiewer (es)n. brain fever

Haernschaal (die)n. skull

Haernschaedel (der)n. skull

Haernschaedelhaut (die)n. pericranium

Haernweh (es)n. brain trouble

haernwiedich, adj. mad

Haernzaah (der)n. eyetooth

Haernzoh (der)n. eyetooth

haeroisch, adj. 1.headstrong; 2.resolute; 3.vigorous

haerr(i)yesses! interj. 1.dear me!; 2.good gracious!; 3.good Lord!

haerrevoggel (der)n. jay

haerrge!, interj. 1.dear me!; 2.good gracious!; 3.good Lord!

Haerrgott (der)n. 1.God; 2.the Lord

Haerrin (die)n. mistress

Haerrschaft (die)n. 1.lordship (also used as an expletive)

haerrsche, v.; ghaerrscht, pp. rule

haerryaer(ru)m! interj. good Lord!

haerryammer!, interj. good Lord!

Haerschharngeischt (der)n. 1.hartshorn; 2.liquid ammonia

Haert (der)n. shepherd

haerum, adv. 1.about; 2.round; 3.round about

Haerweeg (der)n. 1.way coming; 2.way hither

haerze, v.; ghaerzt, pp. 1.embrace; 2.love

Haerzel (es)n. darling

Haerzeleed (es)n. 1.mourning; 2.sorrow; 3.woe

haerzus, adj. (on the way) coming

Haesche (es)n. young rabbit

Haffe (der)n.; Heffe, pl. 1.chamber; 2.crock; 3.pot

Haffedeckel (der)n. pot-cover

Haffekees (der)n. cup cheese

Haffeschaerb (die)n. potsherd

Hafte (die)n., pl. (-- un hoke) hooks and eyes

hafte, adj. (to) happen

halb gebacke, adj. half-baked

halb un halb, adv. half and half

halb, adv. half

Halbbruder (der)n.; Halbbrieder, pl. half brother

Halbdaaler (der)n. half-dollar

halbdunkel, adj. shady

Halbdutzend (es)n. half dozen

halbgscheit, adj. 1.cracked; 2.rattlebrained; 3.silly

Halbinsel (die)n. peninsula

Halbkreis (der)n. semi-circle

Halbkuggel (die)n. hemisphere

halbleine, adj. linsey-woolsey

halbleinich, adj. linsey-woolsey

Halbmos (es)n. half measure

Halbnacht (die)n. midnight

halbnarrisch, adj. crack brained

Halbpund (es)n. half a pound

halbscheit, adj. silly

Halbschtiwwel (der)n. 1.bootee; 2.laced shoe

Halbschtreng (die)n., pl. trace-chains

Halbschtunn(d) (die)n. half hour

Halbschweschder (die)n.; Halbschweschdere, pl. half sister

halbverreckt, adj. half dead (of beasts)

halbwechsich, adj. half grown

halbwegs, adv. halfway

halbyaehrich, adj. 1.six months old; 2.semi- annual

halde, v.; ghalde, pp. 1.bridle; 2.conduct; 3.hold; 4.keep; 5.last; 6.observe; 7.restrain; 8.stop; 9.(katz --) keep (a person) short in money; 10.(-- bleiwe) (to be) stuck; 11.(sich in esse --) diet

Halfder (die)n.; Halfdere, pl. halter

Halfderrieme (der)n. halter-strap (on a harness)

Halfterkett (die)n. halter chain

Halleluya (es)n. hallelujah

Hallem (der)n. 1.blade; 2.stalk

Hallich Neiyaahr!, interj. Happy New Year!

hallich, adj. 1.cheerful; 2.happy; 3.splendid

Hallunk (der)n. 1.heretic; 2.rascal; 3.thief

Halm (der)n.; Halme, pl. 1.blade; 2.stalk

Hals (der)n.; Helser, pl. 1.neck; 2.throat

Halsangel (die)n. back of the neck

Halsankel (die)n. back of the neck

Halsauszehring (die)n. 1.bronchitis; 2.laryngitis

Halsband (es)n. 1.collar; 2.necklace

Hh

Halsduck

Halsduch (es)n.; Halsdicher, pl. 1.napkin; 2.neckerchief; 3.necklace; 4.scarf; 5.serviette; 6.small shawl

Halsgnick (es)n. nape (or back of the neck)

Halsgraage (der)n. 1.collar; 2.cravat

Halsreehr (es)n. 1.larynx; 2.windpipe

Halsreime (der)n. leading rope or strap

halsschtarrich, adj. 1.obstinate; 2.stubborn

Halsschtick (es)n. neck (of beef)

Halsweh (es)n. 1.quinsy; 2.sore throat

Halt (die)n. 1.hold; 2.grip

halte, v.; kalte, pp. 1.conduct; 2.hold; 3.keep; 4.last; 5.observe; 6.stop

halt/griege (an ebbes)v.; haltgrickt, pp. catch

halt/nemme, v.; haltgnumme, pp. 1.(to take) a hold (of) 2.grip; 3.grasp roughly; 4.seize

haltbaar, adj. tenable

Halwe (der)n. half-dollar

halwer ausgwaxe, adj. half-grown

halwer gebacke, adj. half-baked

halwer uffgewaxe, adj. half-grown

halwer, adv. half

Halwerdaaler (der)n. half-dollar

Halwergaul (der)n. 1.dock; 2.(breedblettricher --) bitter dock

Hambariyer (die)n. tattletale

Hamm(e)li (es)n. calf

Hammel (der)n. wether

Hammelche (es)n. calf

Hammelfleesch (es)n. mutton

Hammer (der)n. Hemmer, pl. 1. hammer; 2. (en hilsner --) mallet

hammere, v.; ghammert, pp. hammer

Hammergaarn (es)n. dip net

Hammerschlack (der)n. 1.dross; 2.scales of iron

Hammerschtiel (der)n. handle of a hammer

Hammli (es)n.; Hammlin, pl. calf

Hand (die)n.; Hend, pl. 1.hand; 2.handwriting; 3. (ebber -- gewwe) (to shake) hands

Hand aa/schlagge, v.; Hand aagschlagge, pp. pitch in

Hand un Kuss hand and kiss (the kiss of peace in the plain churches of the Pennsylvania Germans)

Handarewett (die)n. handwork

Handballe (der)n. handball

Handbascht (die)n. hand brush

Handbeck (es)n. basin

Handbreeding (die)n. hand's breadth

Handbuch (es)n. manual

Handduch (der)n.; Handdicher, pl. towel

Handel (der)n. 1.barter; 2.business; 3.commerce; 4.craft; 5.trade

Handelschaft (die)n. commerce

Handelsmann (der)n.; Handelsleit, pl. tradesman

Handelwese (es)n. 1.bartering; 2.commerce; 3.trading

Handgelender (es)n. handrail

handgemacht, adj. 1.hand-made; 2.homemade

handgreiflich, adj. plain (comprehensible)

Harnischledder

Handgriff (der)n. 1.grip (of hand); 2. handle

handgross, adj. big as a hand

handhawwe, v.; handghat; handghadde, pp. manage

handiere, v.; handiert, pp. 1.do; 2.work

Handkees (der)n. 1.cheese in balls and ripened; 2.Dutch cheese

handlange, adj. assist masons or bricklayers

Handlanger (der)n.; Handlanger, pl. 1.helper 2.hod-carrier

handle losse, v. (sich --) 1.knock down the price; 2.barter

handle, v.; g(e)handelt, pp. 1.barter; 2.deal; 3.handle; 4.trade

Handlumbe (der)n. 1.handy rag (in the kitchen); 2.towel

Handlung (die)n. 1.business; 2.doings; 3.treatment

Handriggel (der)n. handrail

Handschleefreche (der)n. large rake dragged by hand

Handschreiwes (es)n. handwriting

Handschrift (die)n. handwriting

Handseeg (die)n. handsaw

Handvoll (die)n. handful

Handwarrick (es)n. 1.craft; 2.trade

Handwarricksgschaer (es)n. tools

Handwarricksgscheft (es)n. 1.calling; 2.craft; 3.trade

Handwarricksmann (der)n.; Handswaricksleit, pl. mechanic

Hanf(t) (der)n. hemp

Hang (der)n. 1.declivity; 2.inclination; 3.steep slope

Hank (der)n. 1.slope; 2.suspended shelf for eatables

Hann (es)n.; Hanner, pl. 1.brain; 2.horn

Hannef (der)n. hemp

Hannefsume (der)n. hemp seed

Hannes (der)n. Jack

Hannesel (der)n.; Hannesel, pl. hornet

Hannickel (der)n. John Nicholas

Hanning (der)n. February

Hannschaal (die)n. 1.cranium; 2.skull

Hannschaedel (der)n. skull

Hannscheedel (der)n. 1.cranium; 2.skull

Hannschlack (der)n. stroke

Hannschtreech (der)n. stroke

Hannselnescht (es)n. hornet's nest

Hans (der)n. Jack

Hanskaschber (der)n. jack pudding

hanswarschtle, v.; gehanswarschtelt, pp. 1.act silly; 2.play the clown

Hanswascht (der)n. 1.clown; 2.fool; 3.silly person

Hanswaschtschtreech (die)n., pl. tomfoolery

Hansyarrick (der)n. John George

Hard (die)n. 1.board with low sides for drying fruits and vegetables; 2.group; 3.herd

harde, v.; ghardt, pp. harden

hardich, adj.; adv. 1.quick(ly); 2.swift(ly)

Harebscht (der)n. 1.autumn; 2.fall

Harf(e) (die)n.; Harfe, pl. harp

hariche, v.; gharicht, pp. 1.hear; 2.hearken; 3.listen; 4.obey

harlich, adj. 1.cheerful; 2.happy; 3.glorious; 4.jolly; 5.splendid

Harnischledder (es)n. harness leather

Hh

Harnschlang

Harnschlang (die)n. horned snake
Harnvieh (es)n. cattle
Harr (der)n. Lord
harre, v.; gharrt, pp. wait
Harrevoggel (der)n.; Harreveggel, pl. (blue)jay
harrich, adj. 1.old (of a joke); 2.stale (of a joke)
Harrlichkeit (die)n. glory
hart, adj. 1.firm; 2.hard; 3.severe
Hartgeld (es)n. 1.money in coin; 2.specie
Hasch (der)n.; Hasch, pl. deer
Haschbarig (der)n. deer mountains
Haschbel (der)n. 1.gawk; 2.reel; 3.windlass; 4.silly person
Haschbidaal (der)n. hospital
haschble, v.; ghaschbelt, pp. 1.move precipitately (of persons and horses); 2.reel
haschblich, adj. 1.fidgety; 2.precipitate; 3.unsteady
haschblich, adv. precipitate(ly)
Haschfleesch (es)n. venison
Haschgraas (es)n. 1.green or yellow foxtail
Haschharn (es)n. antler
Haschhaut (die)n. buckskin
Haschkopp (der)n. stag's head
Haschkuh (die)n. 1.female deer; 2.hind; 3.roe
Haschledder (es)n. buckskin
Haschmick (die)n. deer fly
Haschzung (die)n. 1.hart's tongue; 2.rattlesnake weed; 3.walking leaf
Haspittel (der)n. hospital
Hass (der)n. 1.hate; 2.spite
hasse, v.; g(e)hasst, pp. 1.despise; 2.hate
Hasselheck (die)n. hazel bush
Hasselnuss (die)n. hazelnut
Hasselwatzel (die)n. 1.colts-foot; 2.wild ginger
Hatge!, interj. goodbye
hatt, adj. 1.difficult; 2.firm; 3.hard; 4.severe
hattglaawich, adj. skeptical
hatthatzich, adj. hardhearted
hattheerich, adj. deaf
hattlaernich, adj. 1.dull; 2.stupid
hattlannich, adj. 1.dull; 2.stupid
hattleiwich, adj. constipated
hattmeilich, adj. hard mouthed (of horses)
hattneckich, adj. stubborn
Hattriggel (der)n. hop hornbeam
hattschaffich, adj. hard working
Hatyee!, interj. So long!
Hatz (es)n.; Hatzer, pl. heart
Hatz(g)schpaerr 1.common motherwort; 2.digestive disorder in pigs
hatz(h)aftich, adj. 1.bold; 2.courageous; 3.hearty; 4.vigorous
Hatzfehler (der)n. organic disease of the heart
Hatzglobbe(s) (es)n. palpitation (of the heart)
hatzgrank, adj. 1.heartsick; 2.suffering from the heart
hatzhafdich, adj. vigorous
hatzhafdich, adv. hearty
Hatzhols (es)n. heart wood

Hautfareb

hatzich, adj. 1.beloved; 2.dear; 3.good-hearted; 4.(gut --) (a) benevolent; (b) generous;
Hatzkammer (die)n. ventricle
Hatzkauer (der)n. coward
Hatzklemmes (es)n. angina pectoris
Hatzli (es)n. sweetheart
hatzlich, adj. 1.affectionate; 2.cordial; 3.hearty
Hatzlieb (der, die)n. dearest
Hatzschlack (der)n. 1.heart attack; 2.paralysis of the heart
Hatzwatzel (die)n. taproot
Hatzweh (es)n. heart ache
Hauch (der)n. breath
hauche, v.; ghaucht, pp. 1.breathe; 2.expel the breath through the open mouth
Haufe (der)n.; Heife, pl. 1.heap; 2.pile; 3.(en -- mache) cack
Hauns (der)n. hound
Haus (es)n.; Heiser, pl. house
haus/bhalde, v.; hausgebhalde, pp. exclude
haus/losse, v.; hausgelosst, pp. 1.leave out; 2.leave outside; 3.omit
haus, adv. 1.out of doors; 2.out of it; 3.outside
Hausarewett (die)n. housework
Hausbabble (die)n. Lombardy poplar
Hausbutze(s) (es)n. housecleaning
Hausdach (es)n.; Hausdecher, pl. roof of a house
Hausdeer (die)n. outside door (of a house)
Hausdier (die)n. outside door (of a house)
hause, v.; ghaust, pp. 1.be economical; 2.keep house; 3.rage; 4.(-- menanner) live together (man and wife)
Hauseldern (die)n. housekeeper
Hausfiehrer (der)n. housekeeper (of a family where the mother is dead)
Hausfraa (die)n. 1.housewife; 2.lady of the house; 3.mistress
Hausgleed (es)n. negligee
Haushalling (die)n. family
haushalte, adj. 1.be frugal; 2.keep house
Haushaltung (die)n. 1.family; 2.housekeeping
Hausheltern (die)n. housekeeper
Hauslumbe (der)n. shoe-mat
Hausmittel (es)n. home remedy
Hausrod (es)n. furniture
Hausrotschreiner (der)n. cabinetmaker
hauss, adv. 1.out of doors; 2.out of it; 3.outside
Haussache (die)n., pl. house furnishings
Hausschlang (die)n. garter snake
Hausschreiner (der)n. carpenter
Hausscht(e)ier (der)n. 1.clothes and furniture which a bride brings to the marriage; 2.outfit
Hausschteire (der)n. 1.bride's clothes and furniture brought to marriage; 2.outfit
Hausuhr (die)n. clock
Hauswachs (der)n. 1.garden orpine; 2.house leek; 3.live- for-ever
Haut (der)n.; Heit, pl. 1.cuticle; 2.film; 3.hide; 4.membrane; 5.pelt; 6.skin
Hautfareb (die)n. complexion

Hh

Hautgranket

Hautgranket (die)n. skin disease
hawwe, v.; ghat, ghadde, pp. have
Hawwer (der)n. 1. oats; 2.(-- schteckt 'n) he is getting saucy
Hawwer uff/nemme, v. rake and bind oats
Hawwerern (die)n. oat-harvest
Hawwerfeld (es)n.; Hawwerfelder, pl. oat field
Hawwergees (der)n. katydid
Hawwerkaern (die)n. oat grain
Hawwerkeffer (der)n.; Hawwerkeffer, pl. oats-bug
Hawwerkischt (die)n. oat bin
Hawwerlaus (die)n.; Hawwerleis, pl. oat midge
Hawwermehl (es)n. oatmeal
Hawwersack (der)n. 1.oats-bag; 2.(-- heecher henke) reduce the rations
Hawwerschprau (die)n. oat-chaff
Hawwerschtecher (es)n. thumb (in nursery rhyme)
Hawwerschtroh (es)n. oat straw
hawweswaert, adj. valuable
Haydee!, interj. 1.Adieu; 2.Farewell!
Heb (die)n. handle (of a basket)
Hebgarn (es)n. dip net
Heblaad contrivance for loading logs
Hebschtang (die)n. lever
Hechel (die)n. hatchel
hechle, v.; ghechelt, pp. 1.(to give a) tongue-lashing; 2.(iwwer die -- ziehe) take over the coals
Hecht (der)n. 1.pickerel; 2.pike
Hechtgraut (es)n. pickerel-weed
hechze, v.; g(e)hechzt, pp. pant
Heck (die)n.; Hecke, pl. 1.brush (plant); 2.hedge; 3.thicket; 4.(dry) sprig; 5.underbrush; 6.(an (bei) die –e sei) be Johnny on the spot; 7.(sich an die --e mache) get busy
Heckbacke (der)n.; Heckbacke, pl. pouch cheek
Hecke (die)(= pl. of die Heck) 1.hedge; 2.thicket
Heckebascht (die)n. brush made of twigs
Heckedroschel (die)n.; Heckedroschle, pl. thrush
Heckefens (die)n. 1.brush fence; 2.hedge
Heckehoke (der)n.; Heckehoke, pl. trimmer used in cutting bushes
Heckepusch (der)n. clump of bushes
Heckes (die, es)n. thicket
Heckesens (die)n. scythe for cutting briers
heckich, adj. covered with brush
Hecksel (es)n. straw cut fine for feed
Heckselfuder (es)n. feed from cut straw
Heckselkammer (die)n. compartment in a barn for storing cut straw
Heech (die)n. height
Heegel (der)n.; Heegel, pl. scratcher (for gardening)
Heeh (die)n. height
Heekel (es)n. little hook
Heekelche (es)n. crochet needle
Heekelnaadel (es)n. crochet needle
heekle, v.; gheekelt, pp. 1.crochet; 2.hook; 3.limp
heele, v.; gheelt, pp. 1.cure; 2.heal
Heelgraut (es)n. self-heal

Hefdichlich

heem(e)le, v.; gheemelt, pp. 1.be like home; 2.feel at home
heem, adv. 1.home; 2.(gehschde --) home with you (call to a dog)
heembringe, v.; heemgebrocht, pp. 1.bring home; 2.return (things borrowed)
heemdickisch, adj. 1.malicious; 2.underhanded
heemdraage, v. carry home
heemere, v.; gheemert, pp. (sich --) be homesick
Heemet (die)n.; Heemede, pl. home
heemetlos, adj. homeless
heemfaahre, v. 1.drive home; 2.haul home
Heemgebacknes (es)n. home baked
heemgeh, v. go home
heemgemacht, adj. 1.domestic; 2.homemade
heemgewwe, v.; heemgewwe, pp. 1.give back; 2.take revenge
Heemgfiehl (es)n. home feeling
heemgrank, adj. homesick
heemhole, v. fetch home
heemisch, adj. domestic
heemkumme, v. come home
heemlich, adj. 1.homelike; 2.secret; 3.underhanded
heemlich, adv. secretly
heemlicherweis, adv. secretly
Heemlichkeet (die)n. stealth
heemnemme, v.; heemgnumme, pp. take home
heemschicke, v.; heemgschickt, pp. send home
heemschleiche, v.; heemgschliche, pp. steal home
heemschtehle, v.; heemgschtohle, pp. (sich --) return home stealthily
Heemweg (der)n. way home
Heemweh (es)n. homesickness
heemwolle, adj. (to) want to go home
heemziege, v.; heemgezogge, pp. move home
heemzus, adv. 1.homeward; 2.on the way home
heerbaar, adj. audible
heere, v.; gheert, pp. 1.hear; 2.hearken; 3.listen;4.obey; 5.(du muscht mer --) you must obey; 6.(sich--) shed the coat
heereswatt, adj. worth listening to
Heersaage (es)n. hearsay
hees, adj. 1.ardent; 2.hot
heescher, adj. hoarse
Heese (der)n. 1.gambrel; 2.heel; 3.hock; 4.lower part of the hind leg
heese, v.; gheese, pp. 1.be called; 2.bid; 3.call; 4.command; 5.name; 6.request; 7.(gut --) approve
Heesehols (es)n. gambrel (stick used in hanging up hogs in slaughtering)
Heeseholz (es)n. gambrel (stick used to hang up a butchered hog)
heeser, adj. hoarse
Heesli (es)n.; Heeslin, pl. bunny (rabbit)
hefdich, adj. 1.awfully; 2.strongly; 3.vehemently; 4.violently
Hefdichkeet (die)n. 1.vehemence; 2.violence
hefdichlich, adj. violent

Hh

Heffel

Heffel (es)n. little pot
Heffemacher (der)n.; Heffemacher, pl. potter
Heffli (es)n. little pot
Heffner (der)n.; Heffner, pl. potter
Heffnerei (die)n. pottery
Hefli (es)n. lawn
Heflimeher (der)n. lawn mower
Heft (es)n. hilt
Heh (der)n. (in --) up in the air (excited)
Hehl (die)n. 1.cavern; 2.cavity; 3.hollow
hehl halde, v. (to keep) secret
Hehler (der)n.; Hehler, pl. 1.concealer; 2.receiver of sto-
    len goods
Hehling (die)n. 1.cave; 2.cavity; 3.hollow
hehling(s), adv. 1.clandestinely; 2.secretly
hehling, adj. (on the) sly
hehlingerweis, adj. 1.clandestinely; 2.secretly
hehlingerweis, adv. secretly
Hehnli (es)n. male (of birds)
Hei (es)n. hay (rare usage)
hei(e)re, v.; gheiert, pp. marry
Heichelei (die)n. hypocrisy
heichle, v.; gheichelt, pp. act the hypocrite
Heichler (der)n. hypocrite
Heichlerei (die)n. hypocrisy
heichlerisch, adj. hypocritical
Heid(e) (der)n.; Heide, pl. 1.heathen; 2.pagan
Heideland (es)n. heathendom
heider, adj. cheerful
heidesdaags, adv. nowadays
heidich(e)daags, adv. nowadays
heidich, adj. (of) today
heidich, adv. nowadays
heidisch, adj. heathenish
heidzedaags, adv. nowadays
Heifel (es)n. 1.little heap; 2.little pile
heifich, adj. 1.considerably; 2.freely; 3.frequently
heifle, v.; gheifelt, pp. heap up (earth around plants)
Heifli (es)n. 1.little heap; 2.little pile
Heifts (die)n. hives
heil, v.; gheilt, pp. wail
Heiland (der)n. 1.redeemer; 2.the Savior
heile, v.; gheilt, pp. 1.cry; 2.howl; 3.sob; 4.weep
heilenglich, adv. 1.adequate; 2.sufficient
heilich, adj. 1.holy; 2.sacred
heilichdaags, adv. nowadays
heiliche, v.; gheilicht, pp. sanctify
Heilicher (en)n. saint
Heilichi (en)n. saint
heilichsdaags, adj. nowadays
Heilichtum (es)n. sanctuary
Heiling (die)n. 1.cavity; 2.hollow
Heilkunscht (die)n. therapeutics
heillos, adj. wicked
Heilmiddel (es)n. 1.cure; 2.remedy
Heilmittel (es)n. remedy

Hemmergnebbli

heilsam, adj. wholesome
Heinrich (der)n. 1.Henry; 2.(guter --) Good King Henry
    (plant)
Heiraat (die)n. marriage
Heiraats(ge)danke (der)n. thought of marriage
Heiraschbelsgedanke (der)n.thought of marriage
heirich, adj. desirous to marry
Heisel(i) (es)n.; Heiselin, pp. 1.little house; 2.shanty; 3.
    (aus em --) out of one's head
Heisle (es)n. hut
Heisli (es)n.; Heislin, pl. 1.cabin; 2.out house; 3.shanty;
    4.small house; 5.toilet
heislich, adj. 1.domestic; 2.homely
heit, adv. today
Heitche (es)n. 1.film (on milk); 2.membrane
Heitel(i) (es)n. 1.film (on milk); 2.membrane
heitesdaags, adj. nowadays
heitich(e)sdaags, adj. nowadays
heitich, adj. 1.nowadays; 2.of today
heitzedaag, adj. nowadays
heitzedaagich, adv. 1.contemporary; 2.modern
heiyo(bei) hush-a-bye
Held (der)n. hero
helfe, v.; gholfe, pp. 1.assist; 2.avail; 3.do good;4.help;
    5.succor
Helfer (der)n. 1.assistant; 2.helper
helflos, adj. shiftless
Helft (die)n. half
Hell (die)n. hell
hell, adj. 1.bright; 2.clear; 3.distinct; 4.light (of day);
    5.loud; 6.fair (weather); 7.(im --e Daag) in bright
    daylight
hellblo, adj. light blue
hellgro, adj. light gray
Helling (die)n. 1.daylight; 2.dawn; 3.light
hellisch, adj. hellish
Helllicht (es)n. broad daylight
hellrot, adj. light red
Hellsackerment (der)n. term of vituperation
Helm (der)n. 1.handle (of a tool); 2.helve
Hels (der)n.; Helser, pl. neck
helse, adj. wooden
Helsel (es)n. little piece of wood
Helzich (es)n. small wooden dish or goblet
Hembeer (die)n.; Hembeere, pl. raspberry
Hembier (die)n.; Hembiere, pl. raspberry
hemdickisch, adj. treacherous
Hemm (es)n.; Hemmer, pl. shirt
Hemmaermel (der)n. shirt-sleeve
Hemmbierekeffer (der)n. raspberry bug
Hemmche (es)n. 1.little shirt; 2.shirty
Hemmerbreis (es)n. wristband
Hemmerbussem (der)n. shirt bosom
hemmere, v.; ghemmert, pp. hammer
Hemmergnebbli (es)n.; Hemmergnebblin, pl. mallow
    seed pod (in immature state often eaten by children)

Hh

Hemmergneppli   hie un her

Hemmergneppli (es)n.; Hemmergnepplin, pl. mallow seed pod (in immature state, often eaten by children)

Hemmergraage (der)n. shirt collar

Hemmerhendel (der)n. 1.bail; 2.handle

Hemmerknepp (die)n., pl. 1.cheeses; 2.low mallow

Hemmerschwanz (der)n.; Hemmerschwenz, pl. shirttail

Hemmli (es)n. 1.little shirt; 2.shirty

Hen (die)n. height

hendich, adj. 1.convenient; 2.handy; 3.skillful

hendich, adv. handy

hendle, v.; ghendelt, pp. handle

Hendler (der)n. 1.dealer; 2.trader

Hengel (der)n. 1.bunch (grapes); 2.string (fish)

Hengscht (der)n. 1.lecherous man; 2.stallion

Hengschtgraas (es)n. canary grass

henk (bei) by golly

Henk (die)n.; Henke, pl. 1.handle; 2.hinge

Henkbauch (der)n. paunch

henke, v.; ghenkt, g(e)honke, pp. 1.hang; 2.stick to; 3.(der Kopp --) (a) be ashamed; (b) be downcast; 4. (es Maul --) (a) pout; (b) sulk

Henkeglaas (es)n.; Henkeglesser, pl. 1.goblet; 2.mug; 3.tankard

Henkekarb (der)n. basket with a loop handle over the top

Henker (der)n. 1.deuce; 2.hangman

Henkeschloss (es)n. padlock

Henklaade (der)n.; Henklaade, pl. shelf (hanging type)

Henkmaul (es)n.1.drooping mouth; 2.pouter; 3.pouting person

Henkweide (der, die)n. weeping willow

Henner(i) (der)n. Henry

Henni (der)n. Henry

hennicher, adv. 1.anyhow; 2.anyway

hennyer, adv. 1.anyhow; 2.anyway

Hensching (der)n.; Hensching, pl. 1.glove; 2.mitten

hensle, v.; g(e)henselt, pp. 1.be sarcastic; 2.make a laughing stock of; 3.tease

Hepp! giddap (call to horses)

Her(r)ing (der)n. herring

her/beschtelle, v.; herbschtellt, pp. order to come here

her/lange, v.; heregelangt, pp. 1.attain; 2.reach

her/lese, v.; hergelese, pp. 1.read off; 2.tally

her/richde, v.; hergericht, pp. 1.botch; 2.ruin; 3.spoil

her/saage, v.; hergsaat, pp. repeat

her/schaffe, v.; hergschafft, pp. provide

her/schicke, v.; hergschickt, pp. send hither

her/schleiche, v.; hergschliche, pp. sneak hither

her/schtamme, v.; hergschtammt, pp. 1.stem from; 2.(to be) descended

her/schtelle, v.; hergschtellt, pp. (sich --) pretend

her/ziege, v.; hergezogge, pp. move here

her, adv. hither

Herbscht (der)n. 1.autumn; 2.fall

Herbschtros (die)n. (autumn) chrysanthemum

herchle, v.; geherschelt, pp. wheeze

hergeh, v.; hergange, pp. (iwwer ebber --) pitch into (a person)

Herkummes (es)n. origin

Herr (der)n. Lord

herraus! 1.out! 2.get out!

Herreleit (die)n., pl. New Mennonites (followers of John Herr)

herrlich, adj. 1.cheerful; 2.glorious; 3.jolly; 4.lovely; 5.splendid

Herrlichkeit (die)n. glory

Herrnhuder (der)n.; Herrnhuder, pl. Moravian

herrnhuderisch, adj. Moravian

herrsche, v.; gherrscht, pp. rule

Hess (der)n. Hessian

hesselborich, adv. 1.awfully; 2.terribly

Hesselcher (die)n., pl. little boy's trousers

hesseldannisch, adv. terribly

hesseldonisch, adv. 1.awfully; 2.terribly

hesselronisch, adv. 1.awfully; 2.terribly

hesslich, adv.; adj. 1.hateful; 2.terrible; 3.ugly

hetze, v.; ghetzt, pp. 1.hiss; 2.set (dogs) on; 3.set (persons) at variance

hewe, v.; ghowe, pp. 1.hold; 2.lift

Hewer (der)n. lifter (on the stove)

Hewweise (es)n. crowbar

Hewwel (der)n. club

Hex (die)n.; Hexe, pl. 1.sorceress; 2.witch

hexe, v.; ghext, pp. 1.perform magic; 2.witchcraft

Hexebuch (es)n. conjuring book

Hexedans (der) n. fairy ring or circle (where vegetation is lacking owing to fungus growth)

Hexedokder (der)n. witch doctor

Hexeglaawe (der)n. 1.belief in witches; 2.superstition

Hexegraut (es)n. St. John's wort

Hexehols (es)n. witch hazel

Hexekimmel (der)n. 1.jimsonweed; 2.stramonium; 3.thorn apple

Hexel (es)n. straw cut fine for feed

Hexelkammer (die)n. straw (cut fine) storage room (in a barn)

Hexemeeschder (der)n. 1.magician; 2.sorcerer

Hexemehl (es)n. spores (of the ground pine)

Hexerei (die)n. 1.magic; 2.sorcery; 3.something "queer"; 4.witchcraft

Hexeschuss (der)n. 1.(sudden) pain in the hip; 2.powwow word (used in formula for rheumatism); 3.shot fired to kill or drive out a witch

hi! hi!, interj. giggling laugh

hibberdiglibb, adv. slapdash

hibsch, adj. 1.handsome; 2.pretty

Hickeri (es)n. hickory

Hickerinis (der)n. hickory nut

Hickernis-Schtarm (der)n. hickory storm (a brisk wind which causes the hickory nuts to fall)

Hickerniss (die)n., pl. shell barks

hickle, v.; ghickelt, pp. 1.hop on one leg; 2.limp

hie un her, adv. back and forth

Hh

hie un widder

hie un widder, adv. now and then
hie/babble, v.; hiegebabbelt, pp. prate
hie/basse, v. hiegebasst, pp. 1.fit in; 2.(to be) suitable;
   3.(eens --) (a) (to give a) rap; (b) (to give a) slap
hie/batzle, v.; hiegebatzelt, pp. fall over one's feet
hie/bezaahle, v.; hiebezaahlt, pp. 1.pay at a certain
   place; 2.pay down
hie/blanse, v.; hiegeblanst, pp. (sich --) settle down in a
   certain place
hie/blanze, v.; hiegeblanzt, pp. plant in a certain place
hie/blatsche, v.; hiegeblatscht, pp. sprawl
hie/bringe, v.; hiegebrocht, pp. take to a place
hie/bschtelle, v.; hiebeschtellt, pp. order to a certain
   place
hie/daerfe, v.; hiegedaerft, pp. be allowed to go to a
   certain place
hie/dappe, v.; hiegedappt, pp. 1.go to a place by chance
   2.walk clumsily
hie/dargele, v.; hiegedaregelt, pp. reel along
hie/draage, v.; hiegedraage, pp. carry thither
hie/drede, v.; hiegedrede, pp. step in a certain place
hie/drehe, v.; hiegedreht, pp. turn towards
hie/dreiwe, v.; hiegedriwwe, pp. drive to a certain place
hie/drolle, v.; hiegedrollt, pp. trot along
hie/duh, v.; hiegeduh, pp. put into place
hie/faahre, v.; hiegfaahre, pp. drive to a place
hie/falle, v.; hiegfalle, pp. fall down
hie/fiehre, v.; hiegfiehre, pp. lead to a place
hie/fliege, v.; hiegflogge, pp. fly to a place
hie/gackse, v.; hiegegackst, pp. keep on prattling
hie/geh, v.; hiegange, pp. 1.go to a place; 2. lead to
hie/gewwe, v.; hiegewwe, pp. 1.give; 2.hand to
hie/graddle, v.; hiegegraddelt, pp. crawl to a place
hie/gritzle, v.; hiegegritzelt, pp. scribble down
hie/gucke, v.; hiegeguckt, pp. look there
hie/halde, v.; hieghalde, pp. 1.aim; 2.sustain one's part;
   3.(eens --) give a slap
hie/helfe, v.; hiegholfe, pp. assist (a person) to a place
hie/henke, v.; hieghenkt, pp. hang in a place
hie/hewe, v.; hieghowe, pp. reach (to a place)
hie/hocke, v.; hieghockt, pp. 1.seat (in a place); 2.(sich --
) sit down
hie/keere, v.; hiekeert, pp. belong to or in a place
hie/kenne, v.; hiegekennt, pp. be able to get to a place
hie/kumme, v.; is hiekumme 1.become of; 2.get to a place
hie/laafe, v.; hiegeloffe, pp. 1.amount to; 2.run to (of
   liquids); 3.walk to a place
hie/lange, v.; hieglangt, pp. suffice
hie/leie, v.; hiegelegge, pp.1.lay down; 2.(sich --) lie down
hie/losse, v.; hieglosst, pp. allow (a person) to get to a place
hie/mache, v.; hiegemacht, pp. 1.place; 2.put
hie/misse, v.; hiegmisst, pp. be obliged to go to a place
hie/nemme, v.; hiegnumme, pp. take to a place
hie/nischdle, v.; hiegenischdelt, pp. cuddle
hie/rechle, v.; hiegrechelt, pp. 1.calculate; 2.reckon; 3.score
hie/reeche, v.; hiegereecht, pp. suffice

hifdelaahm

hie/reide, v.; hiegridde, pp. jerk near to
hie/richde, v.; hiegericht, pp. 1.botch; 2.ruin; 3.spoil
hie/ricke, v.; hiegerickt, pp. move near
hie/rolle, v.; hiegerollt, pp. roll to
hie/rudre, v.; hiegerudert, pp. row to a place
hie/rufe, v.; hiegerufe, pp. call to a place
hie/rutsche, v.; hiegerutscht, pp. slide to a place
hie/schaffe, v.; hiegschafft, pp. 1.convey to a place;
   2.(sich --) get to a place
hie/schicke, v.; hiegschickt, pp. send to a place
hie/schidde, v.; hiegschidt, pp. pour down
hie/schiewe, v.; hiegschowe, pp. push towards
hie/schlagge, v.; hiegschlagge, pp. 1. strike at something;
   2.(eens --) give a blow
hie/schleefe, v.; hiegschleeft, pp. drag to a place
hie/schleiche, v.; hiegschliche, pp. sneak along
hie/schmeisse, v.; hiegschmisse, pp. throw down
hie/schnelle, v.; hiegschnellt, pp. toss to
hie/schpringe, v.; hiegschprunge, pp. run there
hie/schreiwe, v.; hiegschriwwe, pp. write down
hie/schtatze, v.; hiegschtatzt, pp. fall (headlong)
hie/schtecke, v.; hiegschteckt, pp. 1.stick in place;2.stow
   away
hie/schteh, v.; hiegschtanne, pp. stand idle
hie/schtelle, v.; hiegschtellt, pp. (sich --) take one's place
   or stand
hie/schtelle, v.; hieschtellt, pp. 1.set or put down; 2.(take
   one's) stand
hie/schtrecke, v.; hiegschtreckt, pp. (sich --) lie at full length
hie/schtrecke, v.; hiegschtreckt, pp. stretch out
hie/schwimme, v.; hiegschwumme, pp. swim to a place
hie/sehne, v.; hiegsehne, pp. see as far as
hie/setze, v.; hiegsetzt, pp. 1.set down; 2.(sich --) sit down
hie/weise, v.; hiegewisse, pp. point to
hie/wenne, v.; hiegewennt, pp. (sich --) turn to
hie/winsche, v.; hiegewinscht, pp. (sich --) wish oneself
   there
hie/wolle, v.; hiegewollt, pp. want to go to a place
hie/yaage, v.; hiegyaagt, pp. chase or drive to a place
hie/zackere, v.; hiegezackert, pp. 1.walk heavily; 2.work
   slowly
hie/zehle, v.; hiegezehlt, pp. count down
hie/ziege, v.; hiegezogge, pp. move to a place
hie, adv. there (motion thither)
hiede, v.; ghiedt, pp. 1.mind; 2.watch
hiedichdaagich, adj. (of) today
Hiehling (die)n. 1.cave; 2.cavity; 3.hollow
hielenglich, adj. 1.adequate; 2.sufficient
hielenglich, adv. adequate
hieschdle, v.; ghieschdelt, pp. cough slightly
Hiesicht (die)n. 1.regard; 2.respect; 3.view
Hietche (es)n. little hat
hiete, v.; ghiet, pp. 1.guard; 2.watch; 3.(sich --) be aware
Hietmachern (die)n. milliner
Hieweg (der)n. the way going
hifdelaahm, adj. hip shot

Hh

Hift — hinnernunner

Hift (die)n.; Hifde, pl. hip
Hiftgnoche (der)n.; Hiftgnoche, pl. hipbone
Hifts (die)n.; Hiftse, pl. hip
Hilf (die)n. 1.aid; 2.help
Hilfer (der)n.; Hilfer, pl. helper
hilflos, adj. 1.helpless; 2.shiftless
Hilli (die)n. 1.clothing; 2.(die -- un filli) in abundance
hilsich, adj. wooden
hilze, adj. wooden
Himmel (der)n. 1.heaven; 2.sky
himmelblo, adj. sky blue
Himmelfaahrt(s)daag (der)n. Ascension Day
Himmelferdaag (der)n. Ascension Day
Himmelreich (es)n. kingdom of heaven
Himmelros (die)n. rose of heaven
Himmelsbaam (der)n. ailanthus
Himmelsbrief (der)n. alleged letter of Jesus Christ
himmelswelt (was in der --) what under the sun
himmelwaerts, adv., adj. heavenward
himmlisch, adj. 1.celestial; 2.heavenly
hin, adv. hither
Hingelfresse (es)n. chicken feed
Hinkel (es)n.; Hinkel, pl. 1.chicken; 2.hen
Hinkelche (es)n. 1.chick; 2.little chicken
Hinkeldarm (der)n. 1.chickweed; 2.starwort; 3.(roder --)
    (a) red chickweed; (b) red pimpernel
Hinkeldieb (der)n. chicken thief
Hinkeldreck (der)n. 1.chicken manure; 2.trifling matter
Hinkelfedder (die)n. chicken feather
Hinkelfleesch (es)n. chicken meat
Hinkelfuder (es)n. chicken feed
Hinkelfuss(graas) (es)n. finger grass
Hinkelgnoche (der)n. 1.chicken bone; 2.wishbone
Hinkelhaus (es)n. hen house
Hinkelkaschde (der)n.; Hinkelkaschde, pl. chicken coop
Hinkelkewwich (der)n. chicken coop
Hinkellaus (die)n. chicken louse
Hinkelmischt (der)n. chicken manure
Hinkelnescht (es)n. hen's nest
Hinkeloi (es)n. hen's egg
Hinkelsaddel (der)n. hen roost
Hinkelschtall (der)n. chicken house (coop)
Hinkelschtang (die)n. chicken roost
Hinkelselaat (der)n. red-seeded dandelion
Hinkelwoi (der)n. 1.chicken hawk; 2.(rotschwensicher --)
    red-tailed hawk
Hinkli (es)n.; Hinklin, pl. chick
hinlenglich, adj. sufficient
hinn, prep. 1.in; 2.inside
hinne(r)draa, adv. on behind
hinne(r)her, adv. on behind
hinne(r)no, adv. on behind
hinne(s), prep. 1.behind; 2.in the rear
hinne, adv. (in the) rear
hinnebei, adv. (approaching from the) rear
hinnedraus(s), adv. 1.out back; 2.out in the back country;

3.out in the rear
hinnedrin, adv. in the rear part of
hinnedriwwer, adv. over the back or rump
hinnedrowwe, adv. way up back
hinnedruff, adv. 1.as an after clap; 2.on the rear part of
hinnedrunne, adv. 1.down back; 2.down in the rear
hinnenanner, adv. 1.behind each other; 2.tandem
hinnenannerno adv. 1.in Indian file; 2.in succession
hinnenaus, adv. 1.out behind; 2.out the back way; 3.out
    in the back country
hinnenei, adv. (in by way of the) rear
hinnenewe, adj. off rear (referring to a horse)
hinneniwwer, adv. over in the rear
hinneno, adv. 1.in arrears; 2.(in the) rear; 3.following
    after; 4.on behind
hinnenooch, adv. in the rear
hinnenuff, adv. up by the back way
hinner, adj. 1.after; 2.back; 3.behind; 4.(sei --s) his posterior
hinneraus, adv. out from behind
Hinnerax (die)n. rear axle
Hinnerbacke (der)n.; Hinnerbacke, pl. 1.backside; 2.rear end
Hinnerbarriger (der)n. one living in the back hills
Hinnerbart (der)n. 1.answering back; 2.defense;
    3.standing firm in an altercation
Hinnerbee (es)n. hind leg
Hinnerdeel (es)n. 1.back part (one's rear end); 2.hind
    part; 3.rear; 4.stern
Hinnerdier (die)n. back door
hinnerdrei, adv. 1.after; 2.behind; 3.in pursuit
hinnerdreigeh, adv. follow closely
hinnerdreikumme, adv. follow closely
hinnerdreischlagge, adv. 1.beat up the rear; 2.follow up
hinnerdreischtolbere, v. 1.stumble after; 2.trip
hinnere, v.; ghinnert, pp. 1.clog; 2.prevent; 3.hinder
hinnerfellich, adj. failing
Hinnerfuss (der)n. hind foot
Hinnergang (der)n. 1.deception; 2.decline
hinnergeh, adv. deceive
Hinnerglotz (der)n. back log
Hinnergrund (der)n. background
hinnerhaer, adv. 1.following; 2.in the rear; 3.on behind
Hinnerhalt (die)n. backing
hinnerhand, adj. tardy
Hinnerleib (der)n. venter (of insects)
hinnerlich, adj. (es geh ihm --) 1.he is in poor circum-
    stances; 2.he is doing poorly; 3.he is working under
    some physical disability; 4. troublesome; 5.thwarting
hinnerlich, adv. poorly
hinnerlischdich, adj. 1.cunning; 2.deceitful; 3.treacherous
hinnerlosse, v.; hinnerlosse, pp. leave behind
Hinnerlosseschaft (die)n. estate of a deceased person
hinnernanner, adv. 1.after each other; 2.at odds
hinnernannerno, adv. in succession
hinnerenner, adv. (at) odds
Hinnernis (es)n. 1.hindrance; 2.obstacle
hinnernunner, adv. down the back way

Hh

Hinnerraad

Hinnerraad (es)n. hind wheel
hinnerricksich, adj. backwards
Hinners (der)n. posterior
Hinnerschemel (der)n.; Hinnerschemel, pl. rear bolster
    (of a wagon)
hinnerschich geh, v.; hinnerschichgange, pp. go backward
hinnerschich un varschich, adv. backwards and forwards
hinnerschich, adj. reversed
hinnerschich, adv. backward(s)
hinnerscht-vedderscht, adv. hind-foremost
hinnerscht, adj. 1.hindmost; 2.last; 3.('s -- 's vedderscht)
    hind foremost
Hinnerschtdier (die)n. back door
Hinnerschunke (der)n. ham
hinnersich, adv. backward(s)
hinnerum, adv. 1.around back; 2.secretly
Hinnervaddel (es)n. hind quarter (of beef)
hinnerwaerts, adv. backwards
Hinnerweg (der)n. byroad
hinnewedder, adv. 1.up against in the rear; 2.up against it
hinnich, prep. 1.after; 2.behind; 3.follow up a matter
hinnri, adv. back to a certain place
hinnrizus, adv. 1.back country; 2.out back
Hiob (der)n. Job
Hiobsdroppe (der)n. Job's comfort
Hitt (die)n. 1.cabin; 2.hut
Hitz (die)n. 1.fever; 2.heat spell; 3.turn
hitze, v.; ghitzt, pp. heat
hitzich, adj. 1.fervent; 2.heating; 3.hot headed; 4.passionate
Hitzkopp (der)n. hot head
Hitzoffe (der)n. stove for heating
Hitzpocke (die)n.,pl. prickly heat
Hitzschtreech (der)n. heatstroke
hiwwe un driwwe, adv. 1.(on either) side; 2.(on both) sides
hiwwe, adv. 1.(on this) side; 2.over here
Hiwwel (der)n.; Hiwwle, pl. 1.hill; 2.(-- nuff) uphill;
    3.(-- nunner) downhill
Hiwwelblumm (die)n.; Hiwwelblumme, pl. moss pink
hiwwich, adv. (on this) side
hiwwlich, adj. 1.hilly; 2.undulating
hizus, adv. (on the way) going
hobbere, v.; ghobbert, pp. jolt in passing over a rough
    surface
Hobbertibobb(erti) (der)n. 1.headlong;
    2.Humpty- Dumpty; 3.with a bang
hob(b)rich, adj. rough (of a road, field)
hoch achde, v. 1.esteem; 2.honor; 3.respect
hoch, adj. 1.high; 2.non-Amish; 3.tall; 4.(-- kumme) (to
    be) expensive
hoch; heecher; heechest, adj. high; higher; highest
Hochamt (es)n. (high) mass
hochbeenich, adj. 1.fashionable; 2.grand
hocheibildich, adj. self important
Hocheschisser (der)n. precocious youngster
hochgepreist, adj. 1.costly; 2.expensive
hochhalde, adj. esteem highly

Hoileedere

hochmiedich, adj. 1.haughty; 2.proud; 3.supercilious
Hochmut (der)n. 1.haughtiness; 2.pride
Hochmutsnarr (der)n. vain person (in dress)
Hochmutszibbel (der)n. vain person (in dress)
hochnaasich, adj. 1.haughty; 2."stuck up"; 3.uppish
hochneesich, adj. "stuck up"
hochordich, adj. big-feeling
Hochschtand (der)n. eminence
hochschtendich, adj. eminent
Hochschtuhl (der)n. (baby's) high chair
Hochschul (die)n.; Hochschule, pl. high school
Hochwasser (es)n. 1.flood; 2.high water; 3.inundation
Hochzich (die)n.; Hochziche, pl. 1.nuptial; 2.wedding
Hochzichblumm (die)n. name of a flower
Hochzichdaag (der)n. wedding day
Hochzichgleeder (die)n.,pl. wedding clothes
Hochzichring (der)n. wedding ring
Hochzichschmaus (der)n. wedding dinner
hocke, v.; ghockt, pp. 1.seat; 2.set; 3.sit; 4.squat; 5.(sich -
    -) seat (oneself)
hocke bleiwe, v.; hockegebliwwe, pp. remain seated
Hockschpae (die)n., pl. chips made by a broad ax
Hode (der)n.; Hode, pl. testicle
Hof (der)n.; Hef, pl. 1.farm-place; 2.lawn; 3.yard
Hofdeerle (es)n. gate of a yard fence
Hoffart (der)n. marigold
hoffe, v.; ghofft, pp. hope
Hoffning (die)n. 1.expectation; 2.hope; 3.(uff die -- lewe)
    hope for the best
hoffningsvoll, adj. 1.hopeful; 2.sanguine
Hoffnung (die)n. 1.expectation; 2.hope
hoffnungslos, adj. hopeless
Hohelied (es)n. Song of Solomon
Hohl (es)n. ravine
hohl, adj. 1.concave; 2.hollow
hohlaagich, adj. hollow eyed
Hohle Buhne! nothing to it!
Hohlwarzel (die)n. birthwort
Hohlweg (der)n. sunken road
Hohn (der)n. derision
Hoi (es)n. hay
hoi gawwle, v.; gegawwelt, pp. pitch hay
Hoi mache, v.; gemacht, pp. (to make) hay
Hoi wende, v.; gewennt, pp. turn hay
Hoi wenne, v.; gewennt, pp. turn hay
hoi(i)! call used in driving cattle
Hoibaare (der)n. haymow
Hoibohre (der)n.; Hoibohre, pl. 1.hayloft; 2.haymow
Hoibohrer (der)n. mow (hay)
Hoidenn (es)n.; Hoidenner, pl. 1.hayloft; 2.haymow
Hoiet (die)n. 1.hay-making; 2.hay harvest
Hoifeld (es)n. Hoifelder, pl. hayfield
Hoifisch (der)n. shark
Hoigawwel (die)n.; Hoigawwle, pl. 1.hayfork; 2.pitchfork
Hoihaufe (der)n. haycock
Hoileedere (die)n. 1.hayflats; 2.ladders

Hh

Hoiloch   Hossesackwedder

Hoiloch (es)n.; Hoilecher, pl. hayhole
Hoimesser (es)n. knife for cutting hay in the stack
Hoirechder (es)n. hayhole
Hoireche (der)n. hayrake
Hoireff (es)n.; Hoireff, pl. hayrack
Hoirobber (der)n. hayhook
Hoischreck (die)n.; Hoischrecke, pl. grasshopper
Hoischrecker (der)n.; Hoischrecke, pl. grasshopper
Hoischtall (der)n. hay shed
Hoischtock (der)n.; Hoischteck, pl. haystack
Hoiwagge (der)n. haywagon
Hoiwisch (der)n. wisp of hay
Hoke (der)n.; Hoke, pl. 1.awkward person or horse; 2. hook; 3.scribbling
Hokeblug (der)n. shovel plow
Hokespokes (der)n. 1."funny business"; 2.hocus-pocus
hokle, v.; ghokelt, pp. catch with hooks
hol(l)e, v.; gholt, pp. 1.bring; 2.fetch
Holand(s)watzel (die)n. elecampane
holbrich, adj. rough
hole, v.; gholt. pp. (hol's der Deiwel) (hol's der Schinner) 1.actually; 2.by thunder; 3.sure as fate
Hollenner (der)n. (er is gschprunge wie en --) he ran like the devil
Holler (der)n. 1.elder; 2.(roter --) red-berried elder; 3.(schwatzer --) American elder; 4.(zaahmer --) European elder
Hollerbier (die)n.; Hollerbiere, pl. elderberry
Hollerbix (die)n. popgun (made of hollowed out elder stem)
Hollerblieh (die)n. elder bloom
hollerboller, adv. helter-skelter
Hollerflint (die)n. popgun (made of hollowed out elder stem)
Hollox (der)n. 1.bogie man; 2.Old Nick
Holsabbel (der)n. crab apple
Holsblatz (der)n. place for chopping wood
Holschpaa (der)n. 1.chip; 2.wood shaving
Holsebbli (es)n. wild (ungrafted) apple
Holskaerbs (die)n. winter crookneck squash
Holskohlebrenner (der)n. charcoal burner
Holskopp (der)n. blockhead
Holswagge (der)n. wagon with side-ladders (for hauling wood)
Holz (es)n. wood
Holzbock (der)n.; Holzbeck, pl. 1.sawbuck; 2.stick insect
Holzbohre (der)n. wood bit
Holzesch (die)n. wood ashes
Holzeppeli (es)n. wild (ungrafted) apple
Holzfaaran (der)n. sweet fern
Holzfaare (der)n. sweet fern
Holzfeier (es)n. wood-fire
Holzfeil (die)n. rasp
Holzgnoppbaam (der)n. sycamore
Holzhacker (der)n. woodchopper
Holzhaufe (der)n.; Holzheife, pl. woodpile
Holzheisel (es)n. woodshed
Holzheisli (es)n. woodshed

holzich, adj. 1.wooden; 2.woody
Holzkischt (die)n.; Holzkischde, pl. woodchest
Holzkohl (die)n.; Holzkohle, pl. charcoal
Holzland (es)n.; Holzlenner, pl. woodland
Holzoffe (der)n.; Holzeffe, pl. woodstove
Holzros (die)n. rose of Sharon
Holzsaeg (die)n. woodsaw
Holzschlack (der)n. patch in woods (where timber has been cut and new timber is growing)
Holzschleggel (der)n. maul
Holzschneider (der)n. wood-carver
Holzschopp (der)n. woodshed
Holzschraub (die)n. wooden screw
Holzweg (der)n. (-- naus/geh) 1.disappear; 2.go up the flue; 3. road through a forest (for hauling wood); 4.vanish
Holzzabbe (der)n. 1.wooden peg; 2.wooden stake
hommobaadisch, adj. homeopathic
Hoor (die)n. 1.hair; 2.(es hot em kenn -- geduh) he suffered not the slightest harm
Hoorband (es)n. hair ribbon
Hoorbascht (die)n. hair brush
Hoorbreeding (die)n. hair's breadth
Hoordicking (die)n. hair's breadth
hoorgnapps, adj. 1.close; 2.to a hair
hoorich, adj. 1.hairy; 2.hoary; 3.old (of a joke)
Hoornetz (es)n. hair net
hoorscharf, adj. 1.very exact; 2.very prompt
Hoorschmier (die)n. pomade
Hoorschpell (die)n. hairpin
Hoorschwanz (der)n. 1.braid of hair; 2.pigtail
Hoorwaerwel (der)n. cow-lick
Hopihaufe (der)n.; Hopihaufe, pl. haycock
Hopp (die)n. (wilde --e) clematis
Hoppe (die)n. hops
Hoppeglee (der)n. 1.yellow hop clover; 2.yellow trefoil
Hoppehols (es)n. hop hornbeam
Hoppel (die)n. hopple
Hoppeschtang (die)n. hop pole
hopple, v.; ghoppelt, pp. hopple
hopplich, adj. 1.hobbly; 2.jerkily
hoschde (hoscht du es) have you got it?
Hoseschisser (der)n. 1.precocious youngster; 2.shit-breech
Hoss! giddap (nursery rhyme)
Hosse (die),pl. 1.pants; 2.pantaloons; 3.trousers; 4.(in -- scheisse) besmirch (oneself); 5.(sie hot die -- aa) she wears the breeches
Hosseaarsch (der)n. seat of pants or trousers
Hossebee (es)n. pants leg
Hossebeh (es)n. trousers leg
Hosseblumm (die)n. Dutchman's breeches
Hossedraeger (die)n., pl. suspenders
Hossegnopp (der)n. trousers button
Hosselatz (der)n. fly (on trousers)
Hossesack (der)n.; Hosseseck, pl. pants pocket
Hossesackwedder (es)n. cool weather in which you go about with the hands in the pockets of your pants

Hh

Hosseschittler

Hunsfotz

Hosseschittler (der)n. hoe down
Hosseschlitz (der)n. fly (on trousers)
Hosseschnall (die)n. trousers buckle
Hossesitz (der)n. seat of pants or trousers
hossle, v.; ghosselt, pp. raffle
Host (die)n. host
Hott! gee! (call to horses)
Hottrum! call to horses to turn about to the right
hotzele, v.; ghotzelt, pp. 1.handle; 2.grapple with
howwe, adv. 1.up; 2.upstairs; 3.(do --) up here
Howwel (die)n.; Howwle, pl. plane
Howwelbank (die)n.; Howwelbenk, pl. 1.carpenter's
    bench; 2.workbench
Howweleise (es)n. plane bit (iron)
Howwelschpaa (der)n.; Howwelschpae, pl. shaving
howwle, v.; ghowwelt, pp. plane
Hu hu!, interj. yes
hu!, interj. exclamation of disgust or shivering
hubbere, v.; ghubbert, pp. jolt in passing over a rough
    surface
huberich, adj. uneven (field, road)
Huddel (der)n. 1.fragment; 2.hurry; 3.mixed-up affair;
    4.person or horse that works in a rapid and unsatis-
    factory manner; 5.rag; 6.tangle (in hair); 7.tatter
    8.(was is dei --) what's your hurry?
Huddellumbe (der)n. 1.oven swab; 2.wet rag used in
    cleaning an oven
Huddelschtroh (es)n. tangled straw (out of the thresher)
Huddelwese (es)n. tangled affair
Huddelwisch (der)n. 1.oven swab; 2.wet rag used in
    cleaning an oven
huddle, v.; ghuddelt, pp. 1.sweep up ashes (in an oven);
    2. walk too fast (of horses); 3. work in a hasty and
    unsatisfactory manner; 4.(driwwer naus --) do
    (something) hastily and carelessly
Huddlerei (die)n. 1.confusion; 2.working in an over-hasty
    manner
huddlich, adv. 1.overhasty; 2.careless; 3.confused
huder, adj. 1.rap; 2.snap; 3.(ich gebb kenn -- drum) I
    don't care a rap about it
Huf (der)n.; Hufe, pl. hoof
huf! back up!
Huf(f)eise (es)n. (en -- verliere) have a child out of wedlock
Huf(f)schmitt (der)n. horse shoer
hufe, v.; ghuft, pp. 1.back up (of horses); 2.cause to back
Hufeise (es)n.; Hufeise, pl. horseshoe
Hufhaar (die)n., pl. fetlock
Hufnaggel (der)n.; Hufneggel, pl. hobnail
hui! call used in driving cattle (although this form is
    mostly used in driving a single head)
hui, adj. (vanne -- un hinne fui) appearances are deceptive
hulbrich, adj. 1.rough; 2.uneven
Hullox (der)n. 1.bogieman; 2.Old Nick; 3.(der -- grickt
    dich) the bogieman will get you
Hullu(x) (der)n. 1.bogieman; 2.Old Nick
Hullu! sick 'em! (to a dog)

hulpre, v.; ghulpert, pp. move in a jolting or uneven manner
Hummel (der)n.; Hummle, pl. bumblebee
Hummelnescht (es)n. bumblebee's nest
Hummler (der)n.; Hummler, pl. bumblebee
Hun(d)sblumm (die)n. 1.butter and eggs; 2.toadflax
Hun(d)sbohne (die)n., pl. nonsense
Hun(d)sbuhne (die)n., pl. nonsense
Hun(d)sdreck (der)n. 1.dog excrement; 2.trifle
Hun(d)sgraas (es)n. quitch grass
Hun(d)sgraft (die)n. dog-power (to churn butter, turn
    washing machine)
Hun(d)sgraut (es)n. spreading dogbane
Hun(d)sholz (es)n. dogwood
Hun(d)skachde (der)n.; Hun(d)skachde, pl. 1.doghouse;
    2.kennel
Hun(d)skarrich (der)n. dogcart
Hun(d)skopp (der)n.; Hun(d)skepp, pl. dog's head (skull)
Hun(d)slewe (es)n. 1.dog's life; 2.miserable life
Hun(d)srick (der)n. 1.back; 2.foothill; 3.ridge
Hun(d)sschtall (der)n. 1.dog box; 2.doghouse; 3.kennel
Hun(d)sschtern (die)n. 1.Dog Star; 2.Sirius
Hun(d)strumpel (die)n. 1.mere nothing; 2.rap; 3.trifle
Hun(d)szung (die)n. 1.hounds tongue; 2.rattlesnake weed
Hund (der)n.; Hund, pl. 1.dog; 2.(en beeser --) a mad dog;
    3.(en doller --) a mad dog; 4.(kummt mer iwwer der --,
    so kummt mer iwwer der schwans) (a) the rest is but a
    trifle; (b) we have overcome the main difficulty; 5.(uff
    der -- kumme) (a) be put on the bum; (b) go to the dogs
hunde, v.; gehundt, pp. hunt (game)
Hundel (es)n. pup
hundisch, adj. dogish
Hundli (es)n.; Hindlin, pl. whelp
Hundli (es)n.; Hundlin, pl. 1.pup; 2.puppy
hundsich, adj. 1.debilitated; 2.miserable
hundsiwwel, adj. very miserable
hundsiwwel, adv. miserably
Hunger (der)n. hunger
hungere, v.; ghungert, pp. 1.famish; 2.hunger
hungerich, adj. hungry
Hungersnot (die)n. famine
hunne, adv. 1.down (here); 2.downstairs
hunnemol, adv. surely
hunnert, adj. hundred
Hunnich (der)n. honey
Hunnichabbel (der)n. species of apple
Hunnichbrot (es)n. ginger bread
Hunnichkuche (der)n. ginger bread
Hunnichros (die)n. honeycomb
hunnichsiess, adj. sweet as honey
Hunnichsuckel (es)n. honeysuckle
Hunnichvoggel (der)n. humming bird
Hunnichwasser (es)n. hydromel
Hunsdratt (der)n. dog-trot
Hunsfett (es)n. dog's fat
Hunsfotz (die)n. 1.rap; 2.(ich geb kenn -- drumm) I don't
    care a rap about it

Hh

Hunsfotzegraut   huuschde

Hunsfotzegraut (es)n. hyoscyamus

Hunsglett (die)n. 1.cocklebur; 2.(gleeni --) common
    hounds tongue

Hunsgranket (die)n. distemper

Hunshols (es)n. dogwood

hunsiwwel, adj. very miserably

Hunskopp (der)n. dog's head

Hunsleis (die)n., pl. enchanter's nightshade

Hunsrick (der)n. 1.foothill; 2.ridge

Hunsschtaern (die)n. Dogstar

Hunsschtall (der)n. (dog) kennel

Hunswedder (es)n. very bad weather

Hunswese (es)n. detestable affair

Hunszung (die)n. 1.houndstongue; 2.rattle snake weed

Hup-die-duden-du! up-se-daisy! (used in riding infant on
    knee)

hupse, v.; ghupst, pp. 1.hop; 2.skip

Hupsgrott (die)n. toad

Hur (die)n.; Hure, pl. 1.harlot; 2.prostitute; 3.queen (in
    cards); 4.whore

hure, v.; ghurt, pp. fornicate

Hurebull (der)n. whoremonger

Hurehaus (es)n. brothel

Hurehengscht (der)n. whoremonger

Hurekind (es)n. bastard

Hurenescht (es)n. 1.brothel; 2.dive

Hurerei (die)n. whoring

Hurraah!, interj. hurrah!

hurraahe, v.; ghurraaht, pp. hurrah

Huss, Sau! pig call

Hut (der)n.; Hiet, pl. 1.hat; 2.(in -- bede) pray silently into
    one's hat before taking seat in church

Hutband (es)n. hatband

Hutmacher (der)n.; Hietmacher, pl. hatter

Hutmachern (die)n. female hatmaker

Hutranft (der)n. brim of a hat

Hutsch (der)n.; Hutsche, pl. 1.mess; 2.mistake

Hutsch (es)n. 1.colt; 2.foal

Hutschefuss (der)n. colt's foot

Hutschel(che) (es)n. 1.colt; 2.foal

hutschle, v.; ghutschelt, pp. neigh (of horses)

Hutschli (es)n. 1.colt; 2.foal

Hutzel (die)n. 1.dried peach; 2.(en aldi --) a (wrinkled)
    old woman

Hutzer (der)n. 1.heretic; 2.rascal; 3.son-of-a-gun

hutzlich, adj. 1. shriveled; 2. (es guckt -- aus) things look
    desperate

Hutzucker (der)n. loaf sugar

Huuschde (der)n. cough

huuschde, v.; ghuuscht, pp. cough

Ii

Ich denk awwer aa!

Ich denk awwer aa! Well, I'm sure!
Ich saag Dank(i)! 1.thanks; 2.thank you!
Ich saag Denki! 1.thanks; 2.thank you!
ich, pron. I
Iebing (die)n. practice
Iedrich (der)n. 1.cud (of ruminants); 2.first stomach (of cattle)
Iedrich (der)n. (der -- verliere) unable to chew the cud
iedriche, v.; geiedricht, pp. chew the cud
Iegel (der)n. porcupine
Iem (die)n.; Ieme, pl. honeybee
Iem(s)zeit (die)n. mealtime
Iemebrot (es)n. beebread
Iemebrud (die)n. brood of bees just hatching
Iemefresser (der)n.; Iemefresser, pl. 1.kingbird; 2.bee-eater
Iemekareb (der)n. beehive
Iemekaschde (der)n. beehive
Iemens (die)n.; Iemense, pl. 1.ant; 2.pismire
Iemensehaufe (der)n. anthill
Iemensenescht (es)n. anthill
Iemensepaad (der)n. track of ants in grass
Iemeros (die)n. honeycomb
Iemeschtand (der)n. stand for beehives
Iemeschwarm (der)n. swarm of bees
Iemewachs (der)n. beeswax
Iems (der)n. meal
iewe, v.; geiebt, pp. 1.exercise; 2.try especially; 3.(sich --) retch
Iewing (die)n. practice
Igel (der)n. porcupine
ihm, pron. him
ihr, possessive adj. her
ihresgleiche, adj. 1.like her; 2.of her kind
ihrze, v.; geihrzt, pp. address a person with the pronoun ihr
Ildechs (der)n. lizard
im, prep. in
Imber (der)n. ginger
Imbiss (der)n. light lunch
im Blatz vun, prep. instead of
Imens (die)n.; Imense, pl. 1.ant; 2.pismire
immer in ewich net!, interj. never (emphatic)
immer mehr, adj. more and more
immer, adv. 1.always; 2.ever; 3.forever; 4.(-- un ewich) for ever and ever
immerfart, adj. 1.always; 2.everlastingly
immermeh, adj. more and more
immerwaehrend, adj. 1.everlasting; 2.perpetual
Ims (der)n. meal
imschtand, adj. 1.able to; 2.reckless enough to
Imszeit (die)n. mealtime
in acht nemme, v. 1.take care of; 2.pay attention to
in Add(e)ning, adj. all right
in die Heh faahre, v. 1.resent; 2.start up (in anger)
in eens, zwee, drei, adv. 1.promptly; 2.soon
in schtatz, prep. instead of
in, prep. 1.at; 2.in; 3.into
Indigo (der)n. indigo

iwwer/blose

indressant, adj. interesting
Indresse (die)n., pl. interest (charge for the use of money)
indressiert, adv. interested
inenanner, adj. 1.in(to) one another; 2.tangled
inennanner/mache, v.; inenannergmacht, pp. 1.fit together; 2.put together
infaam(t), adj. 1.confounded(ly); 2.low down
Ingeweid (es)n. 1.entrails; 2.viscera
Inhalt (der)n. content(s)
inne, adv. 1.inside; 2.within
inner, adv. inner
inner, prep. within
inneraus, adv. from within
innerlich, adv. 1.interior; 2.internal
innerscht, adv. inner most
innewaerre, v.; innewaerre, pp. 1.find out; 2.learn
innewennich, adv. inside
ins, prep. into
Insch (der)n.; Insche, pl. Indian
Inschdrument (es)n. instrument
Inschein (der)n.; Inscheine, pl. 1.engine; 2.locomotive
Insching (der)n.; Insching, pl. Indian
Inschingsummer (der)n. Indian summer
Inschlich (es)n. tallow
Inschlichlicht (es)n.; Inschlichlichder, pl. tallow candle
inschtand(l)ich, adj. instantly
Insekt (es)n. insect
Insel (die)n. island
insichtbaar, adj. invisible
inwendich ausse, adv. inside out
inwendich, adv. 1.inside; 2.interior; 3.inward
inwennich, adv. 1.inside; 2.inward
inzweebreche, adv. break in two
inzweefalle, adv. fall apart
inzweeschlagge, adv. break to pieces
inzwische, prep. in between
Irrehaus (es)n. insane asylum
Israael kinner (der)n. children of Israel
Isrel (der)n. Israel (given name)
Iwwel zu Weg, adv. 1.(in a) serious (condition); 2.sicken unto death
iwwel/nemme, v.; iwwelgnumme, pp. resent
iwwel, adj. 1.bad; 2.calamitous; 3.evil; 4.nauseated; 5.(es is mer --) I am sick at the stomach; 6.(-- nemme) take offence; 7.(-- odder wohl) willy-nilly
Iwweldeeder (der)n. evildoer
iwwele, v.; geiwwelt, pp. 1.nauseate; 2.sicken
Iwwelgeruch (der)n. bad odor
iwwelguckich, adj. 1.evil looking; 2.of a bad color
iwwelich, adj. 1.nauseated; 2.nauseating
Iwwelwolle (es)n. malevolence
iwwer Nacht, adv. over night
iwwer un iwwer, adv. repeatedly
iwwer(e)nanner, prep. one above (over, on top of) another
iwwer/baue, v.; iwwergebaut, pp. rebuild
iwwer/blose, v.; iwwergeblost, pp. blow over

92

Ii

iwwer/decke

iwwer/decke, v.; iwwergedeckt, pp. spread (something) over

iwwer/denke, v.; iwwergedenkt, pp. 1.ponder; 2.think over

iwwer/draage, v; iwwergedraage, pp. transfer

iwwer/dreede, v.; iwwerdrede, pp. 1.infringe; 2.transgress; 3.trespass

iwwer/duh, v.; iwwergeduh, pp. 1.do over; 2.put on the stove to boil; 3.(sich --) to over-exert oneself

iwwer/hole, v.; iwwerholt, pp. repeat

iwwer/koche, v.; iwwergekocht, pp. boil over

iwwer/laafe, v.; is iwwergeloffe, pp. 1.flood; 2.inundate; 3.overflow

iwwer/laafe, v.; iwwergelofe, pp. transgress

iwwer/mache, v.; iwwergemacht, pp. 1.make over; 2.repeat; 3.transfer

iwwer/naehe, v.; iwweregenaeht, pp. sew over again

iwwer/nemme, v.; iwwergenumme, pp. take over

iwwer/schinne, v.; iwwergschunne, pp. 1.skim over (do something perfunctorily); 2.skimp

iwwer/schlagge, v.; iwwerschlagge, pp. tumble

iwwer/schlucke, v.; iwwergschluckt, pp. strangle

iwwer/schmeisse, v.; iwwergschmisse, pp. 1.jilt; 2.throw over

iwwer/schmelze, v.; iwwergschmolze, pp. melt again

iwwer/schridde, v.; iwwergschritt, pp. pace over or off

iwwer/schtilbe, v.; iwwergschtilpt, pp. overturn

iwwer/schwetze, v.; iwwergschwetzt, pp. discuss

iwwer/setze, v.; iwwergsetzt, pp. set over

iwwer/welse, v.; iwwergewelst, pp. 1.roll over; 2.overturn

iwwer, adv. 1.past; 2.past (in telling time)

iwwer, prep. 1.across; 2.over; 3.upon; 4.(ee mol --sanner) again and again; 5.(-- un --) repeatedly; 6.(-- kopp un ohre) head over heals; 7.(er is bees -- mich) he is angry with me

iwwerall(ich), adv. everywhere

iwwerall, adj. everywhere

iwweraus, adv. 1.exceedingly; 2.very

Iwwerbarryer (der)n. person living on the other (north) side of the Blue Mountain

iwwerbeenich, adj. cris cross

iwwerbiede, v.; iwwerbodde, pp. 1.outbid; 2.overbid

iwwerbinne, v.; iwwerbunne, pp. hold (under bond or bail)

iwwerbinne, v.; iwwergebunne, pp. tie over

Iwwerbleibsel (es)n. 1.remainder; 2.remnant

iwwerbrenne, v.; iwwergebrennt, pp. burn underbrush or weeds from a tract

Iwwerdeck (die)n. 1.bed-quilt; 2.counterpane; 3.coverlet

iwwerdem(m), adv. 1.momentarily; 2.presently; 3.soon

Iwwerdenn (es)n. loft (above the barn floor)

iwwerdopple, v. reduplicate

iwwerdrachde, v.; iwwerdracht, pp. 1.consider; 2.examine

Iwwerdreder (der)n. 1.offender; 2.transgressor

iwwerdreffe, v.; iwwerdroffe, pp. 1.excel; 2.surpass

iwwerdreiwe, v.; iwwerdriwwe, pp. 1.exaggerate; 2.overdo

iwwerdrissich, adj. 1.disgusted; 2.weary

iwwerduh, v.; iwwer(ge)duh, pp. 1.overdo; 2.(sich --)

iwwerlaade

over exert oneself

iwwerecks, adj. 1.oblique; 2.silly; 3.foolish; 4.awkward

iwwerecksich, adj. contrary

iwwereens rauskumme, v.; iwwereens rauskumme, pp. 1.agree; 2.be in agreement; 3.tally

iwwereens schtimme, v.; gschtimmt, pp. 1.agree; 2.concur

Iwwereiling (die)n. over haste (causing mistakes)

iwwereilt, adj. hasty

iwwereischtimme, v.; iwwereigschtimmt, pp. 1.coincide; 2.concur; 3.harmonize

iwwereischtimmich, adj. consistent

iwwerenannerfalle, v.; iwwerenannergfalle, pp. fall over each other

iwwerfalle, v.; iwwerfalle, pp. 1.astonish (physically); 2.surprise

iwwerfiehre, v.; iwwerfiehrt, pp. convict

iwwerflissich, adj. 1.abundant; 2.superfluous

iwwerflissich, adv. overflowing

Iwwerfluss (der)n. 1.abundance; 2.overflow; 3.plenty; 4.superabundance; 5.surplus

iwwerfresse, v.; iwwerfresse, pp. (sich --) overeat

iwwergelaernt, adj. crack brained

iwwergenunk, adj. 1.abundant; 2.more than enough

Iwwergewicht (es)n. overweight

iwwergewwe, v.; iwwergewwe, pp. (sich --) surrender

iwwergiesse, v.; iwwer(ge)gosse, pp. 1.cast over; 2.suffuse

iwwergrabsche, v.; iwwergrabscht, pp. (sich --) retain an undue proportion

iwwergratze, v.; iwwergegratzt, pp. scratch over

iwwergreife, v.; iwwergriffe, pp. (sich --) overreach oneself

iwwergscheit, adj. 1.conceited; 2.over-smart

iwwergucke, v.; iwwerguckt; iwwergeguckt, pp. look over

iwwerhaapt, adv. 1.by the lot; 2.in general; 3.in lump quantity

Iwwerhand (die)n. 1.upper hand; 2. (-- hawwe) have the upper hand; 3.(-- gewinne) (to gain the) upper hand; 4.(-- nemme) (a) become preponderant; (b) overrun

iwwerhand/nemme, v.; iwwerhandgnumme, pp. overrun

iwwerheere, v.; iwwerheert, pp. overhear

iwwerheifle, v.; iwwerheifelt, pp. overwhelm with

iwwerhewe, v.; iwwerhowe, pp. (sich --) 1.injure oneself by lifting too much; 2.presume; 3.(to become) overheated

iwwerhitze, v.; iwwerhitzt, pp. 1.heat over; 2.overheat

iwwerhole, v.; iwwerholt, pp. 1.catch up with; 2.repeat

Iwwerhosse (die)n., pl. overalls

iwwerhubbe, v.; iwwerhuppt, pp. skip

iwwerhuppe, v.; iwwerhuppt, pp. 1.omit; 2.pass by; 3.skip

Iwwerich (es)n. leftovers

iwwerich, adj. 1.leftover; 2.remaining

Iwweriches (es)n. residue

Iwwerkiddel (der)n. overall jacket (of blue denim)

iwwerkumme, v.; iwwerkumme, pp. 1.conquer; 2.overcome; 3.prevail

iwwerlaade, v.; iwwergelaade, pp. load over

iwwerlaade, v.; iwwerlaade, pp. 1.overload; 2.surfeit

Ii

iwwerlaafe

iwwerlaafe, v.; iwwerloffe, pp. 1.chill; 2.give a feeling of
iwwerlege, v.; iwwergelekt, pp. postpone
iwwerlege, v.; iwwerlekt, pp. 1.consider; 2.ponder
iwwerleschdich, adj. troublesome
iwwerletzich, adv. here and there
iwwerletzich, adv. (-- schtofft) remnants
iwwerlewe, v.; iwwergelebt, pp. live over
iwwerlewe, v.; iwwerlebt, pp. outlive
iwwerlief(f)ere, v.; iwwerlieft, pp. 1.deliver; 2.hand over
iwwerliwwere, v.; iwwerliefert, pp. 1.deliver; 2.hand over
iwwerlosse, v.; iwwerlosse, pp. 1.entrust; 2.relinquish
iwwermaessich, adj. extravagant
iwwermariye, adv. day after tomorrow
iwwermeesich, adj. 1.extravagant; 2.immoderate; 3.superabundant
iwwermeesich, adv. extravagant
iwwermenschlich, adj. superhuman
iwwernacht, adj. overnight
iwwernannernei, adj. 1.in confusion; 2.pell-mell
iwwernannernei, adv. pell-mell
iwwernemme, v.; iwwergenumme, pp. 1.take over; 2.take upon one's self
iwwernemme, v.; iwwernumme, pp. 1.overtake; 2.take advantage of; 3.take charge of; 4.take upon one's self; 5.undertake
iwwerpacke, v.; iwwergepackt, pp. pack over
iwwerrasche, v.; iwwerrascht, pp. 1.astonish; 2.come upon suddenly; 3.surprise
iwwerrechle, v.; iwwerrechelt, pp. (sich --) make one's computation too high
iwwerrechle, v.; iwwerrechelt, pp. overfatigue
Iwwerrescht (der)n. 1.remainder; 2.remnant
Iwwerrock (der)n. overcoat
iwwerrumple, v.; iwwerrumpelt, pp. take by surprise
Iwwersatzer (der)n.; Iwwersatzer, pl. translator
iwwersaufe, v.; iwwersoffe, pp. (sich --) drink too much
iwwerschaffe, v.; iwwergschafft, pp. do over
iwwerschaudre, v.; iwwerschaudert, pp. have a chilly sensation
iwwerschich, adj., adv. upwards
iwwerschiesse, v.; iwwergschosse, pp. 1.flush; 2.pass rapidly over; 3.over reckon
iwwerschlagge, v.; iwwerschlagge, pp. 1.astonish; 2.cover with a thin coat of paint; 3.surprise; 4.temper (air in a room)
iwwerschlechtich, adj. overshot (mill wheel)
iwwerschleefe, v.; iwwergschleeft, pp. drag (a field)
iwwerschmiere, v.; iwwergschmiert, pp. 1.daub; 2.do work hastily
iwwerschnappe, v.; iwwergschnappt, pp. (sich --) 1.betray a secret; 2.talk indiscreetly
iwwerschneppe, v.; iwwergschneppt, pp. fall over from top heaviness
iwwerschpinne, v.; iwwerschpunne, pp. 1.cover with webs; 2.enmesh
iwwerschreiwe, v.; iwwergschriwwe, pp. rewrite

iwwrich

Iwwerschrift (die)n. superscription
iwwerschritte, v.; iwwergschritt, pp. pace over or off
iwwerschritte, v.; iwwerschritt, pp. (to) go too far
iwwerschteh, v.; iwwerschtanne, pp. 1.survive; 2.surmount
iwwerschtende (im) when the horns of the moon point up
iwwerschtock (der)n. skirt (of a dress)
iwwerschtolpere, v.; iwwerschtolpert, pp. stumble over
iwwerschtudiere, v.; iwwerschtudiert, pp. over study (and injure the health)
Iwwerschuh (der)n.; Iwwerschuh, pl. 1.overshoe; 2.rubber
Iwwerschuss (der)n. 1.overshoot; 2.surplus
Iwwerschussraad (es)n. 1.overshot wheel (mill wheel)
iwwerschwemme, v.; iwwerschwemmt, pp. 1.flood; 2.inundate; 3.overflow
Iwwerschwemming (die)n. 1.flood; 2.inundation
iwwersehe, v.; iwwersehne, pp. (sich --) overlook (a matter)
iwwersehe, v.; iwwersehne, pp. 1.oversee; 2.survey
iwwersehne, v.; iwwersehne, pp. (sich --) overlook (a matter)
iwwersehne, v.; iwwersehne, pp. 1.oversee; 2.survey
Iwwersehner (der)n. overseer
iwwersetze, v.; iwwersetzt, pp. translate
Iwwersetzer (der)n. translator
iwwersich, adv. upwards
iwwersichdich, adj. cross-eyed
iwwerwachse, v.; iwwerwachse, pp. overgrow
iwwerwaxe, v.; iwwerwaxe, pp. overgrow
iwwerweil, adv. soon
iwwerweise, v.; iwwerwisse, pp. 1.convince;2.prove (a matter)
iwwerweldich, adj. immense
iwwerweldich, v.; iwwerweldicht, pp. conquer
iwwerweldiche, v.; iwwerweldicht, pp. 1.conquer; 2.overcome; 3.over-power; 4.subdue
iwwerwickle, v.; iwwergewickelt, pp. 1.cover; 2.wind over
iwwerwinde, v.; iwwerwunne, pp. 1.conquer; 2.prevail
iwwerwinne, v.; iwwerwunne, pp. 1.conquer; 2.prevail; 3.subdue
iwwerzeige, v.; iwwerzeicht, pp. convince
Iwwerzeigung (die)n. persuasion
iwwerziege, v.; iwwergezogge, pp. 1.cover; 2.draw over
iwwerziege, v.; iwwerzeicht, pp. convince
iwwerziege, v.; iwwerzogge, pp. upholster
iwwerziehe, v.; iwwerzogge, pp. upholster
iwwerzoge, adj. overcast
Iwwerzuck (der)n. case for a feather bed
iwwerzwaerrich, adv. 1.against the grain; 2.contrary; 3.crossways
iyaiwwerzwarrich, adj. 1.contrary; 2.cross-grained; 3.twisted up
iwwreweil, adv. 1.after a while; 2.soon
iwwrich, adj. 1.left; 2.not wanted; 3.over; 4.remaining; 5.superfluous
iya, 1.yes; 2. why yes (pleasant assent)

Kk

Kaader   Kamilletee

Kaader (der)n.; Kaader, pl. tomcat
Kaaf (der)n. purchase
kaafe, v.; kaaft, pp. 1.buy; 2.purchase
Kaafer (der)n. 1.buyer; 2.purchaser
Kaafgeld (es)n. purchase money
kaafich, adj. eager to purchase
Kaafleit (die)n., pl. 1.buyers; 2.customers
Kaafman (der)n.; Kaafleit, pl. 1.buyer; 2.merchant
kaahl, adj. bare
kaahlkebbich, adj bareheaded
Kaart (die)n.; Kaarde, pl. card
Kabbe, n. lady's handbag
kabbidelfescht, adj. orthodox
kabbiddelfescht, adv. (net gans --) off in the head
Kabesch (die)n. 1.head; 2.mouth
Kabiddel (es)n. chapter
kabutt, adj. 1.dead; 2.done for; 3.ruined
kacke, v.; gekackt, pp. void the bowels
Kaddel (die)n. slovenly woman
Kaddu(n) (der)n. calico
kaddunich, adj. (made of) calico
Kadoffel (die)n. potato (rare usage)
kadollisch, adj. Catholic
Kaefer (der)n.; Kaefer, pl. purchaser
Kaer (die)n.; Kaere, pl. 1.automobile; 2.trowel
Kaer(r)bs (die)n.; Kaer(r)bse, pl. 1.pumpkin; 2.squash
Kaerbsebrei (der)n. pumpkin porridge
Kaerbsekann (die)n. pumpkin seed
Kaerbsekeffer (der)n.; Kaerbsekeffer, pl. squash beetle
Kaerbsekuche, (der)n. pumpkin pie
Kaerbseschtick (es)n. pumpkin patch
Kaerbseschtock (der)n. pumpkin vine
Kaern (die)n.; Kaerne, pl. 1.seed; 2.stone (of fruit)
kaernich, adj. 1.full of seeds; 2.granulated
Kaerper (der)n. body
kaerperlich, adj. bodily
kaerzegraad, adj. 1.perpendicular; 2.perfectly straight; 3.vertical
Kaerzing (die)n. shortness
kaerzlich, adv. 1.not long ago; 2.recently
Kaes (der)n. cheese
Kaesbabbel (die)n. common mallow
kaese, v.; gekaest, pp. 1.curd; 2.turn to cheese
kaesich, adj. 1.lovesick; 2.silly; 3.sour (of milk)
Kaeskopp (der)n. stupid fellow
Kaesmolke (die)n., pl. whey
Kaesseih (die)n. colander
Kaet(i) (die)n. Katie
kafdich, adj. scalloped
Kaffi (der)n. coffee
Kaffibohn (die)n. coffee bean
Kaffieklatsch (der)n. gossiping (coffee party)
Kaffigraut (es)n. 1.chicory; 2.moth mullein; 3.succory
Kaffikann (die)n.; Kaffikanne, pl. coffee pot
Kaffikessel (der)n. coffee pot
Kaffikuche (der)n. coffee cake

Kaffimiehl (die)n. coffee mill
Kaffireeschder (der)n. coffee roaster
Kaffisatz (der)n. coffee grounds
Kaffisupp (die)n. bread broken into coffee
kaflich, adj. 1.ragged; 2.untidy
Kaft (die)n.; Kafde, pl. 1.nick; 2.notch; 3.scallop
kafte, v.; gekaft, pp. notch
kaftich, adj. notched
Kaiser (der)n. emperor
Kaiserdum (es)n. empire
Kaiserkron (die)n. imperial crown
Kaiserreich (es)n. empire
Kaiserskron (die)n. species of lily
Kaktus (der)n. cactus
Kalb (es)n,; Kelwer, pl. 1.calf; 2.foolish person
Kalbascht (die)n. 1.calabash; 2.head
Kalbfell (es)n. calf hide
Kalbfleesch (es)n. veal
Kalbledder (es)n. calfskin
Kalbsgeling (es)n. haslet of a calf
Kalbshaut (die)n. calf's skin
Kalbskopp (der)n. calf's head
Kalbslewwer (die)n. calf's liver
Kalenner (der)n.; Kalenner, pl. 1.almanac; 2.calendar
Kalennerglaawe (der)n. superstition
kalfaktre, v.; gekalfaktert, pp. 1.frolic; 2.romp
kalkich, adj. limy
Kalkmeesel (der)n. coldchisel
Kall (der)n.; Kalls, pl. fellow
Kallianner (der)n. coriander
Kallich (der)n. lime
Kallichbrenner (der)n. lime burner
Kallichoffe (der)n.; Kallicheffe, pl. limekiln
Kallichschtee (der)n. limestone
Kallichschteebodde (der)n. limestone soil
Kallichschteebruch (der)n. limestone quarry
Kallichwasser (es)n. lime water
Kallick (der)n. lime
kallicke, v.; gekallickt, pp. 1.lime; 2.dress with lime
Kalmus (es)n. 1.calamus; 2.sweet flag
Kalmusschwanz (der)n. spadix of calamus
Kalt (der, es)n. cold (illness)
kalt; kelder; keltscht, adj. cold; colder; coldest
Kaltfiewer (es)n. 1.malaria; 2.fever and ague
Kaltmeesel (der)n. coldchisel
kalware, v.; gekalwart, pp. stumble
kalwe, v.; gekalbt, pp. calve
kalwere, v.; gekalwert, pp. (to act) silly
kalwerich, adj. silly
Kambliment (es)n. compliment
Kameel (es)n.; Kameele, pl. camel
Kameelgaarn (es)n. Mohair yarn
Kamf (der)n. combat
Kamille (der)n. 1.camomile; 2.(wilder --) Mayweed
Kamilletee (der)n. camomile tea

Kk

Kamm

Kamm (der)n.; Kamme; Kemm, pl. 1.cog; 2.comb (of a rooster); 3.crest (of a ridge)

Kammer (die)n.; Kemmer, pl. 1..chamber; 2.clothes closet; 3.downstairs sleeping room occupied by the parents (old custom still preserved by the Old Order Amish and Mennonites) 4.room not regularly used

Kammer (es)n. continual hammering

Kammfugler (der)n. bummer

Kammraad (die)n. Kammredder, pl. cogwheel

Kammunikant (der)n. communicant

kampes mentis (net gans --) a little off in the head

Kanaal (der)n.; Kanaale, pl. canal

Kanaalboot (es)n. canal boat

Kanada (es)n. Canada

Kanadaadischdel (die)n. Canada thistle

Kanallye (es)n. 1.rascal; 2.heretic; 3.scamp

Kandel (der)n.; Kandle, pl. 1.rainspout; 2.spout

Kandelzucker (der)n. rock candy

Kandidaat (der)n.; Kandidaade, pl. candidate

Kann (die)n.; Kanne, pl. 1.can; 2.kernel; 3.stone (of fruit)

Kann (es)n. rye

Kannaehr (die)n. head of rye

Kannbliet (die)n. rye blossom

Kannbrot (es)n. rye bread

Kanndramm (der)n. rye whiskey

Kannedeckel (der)n. cover for a can

Kannegiesser (der)n. worthless fellow

Kannfeld (es)n.; Kannfelder, pl. rye-field

Kannmehl (es)n. rye flour

Kannros (die)n. corn poppy

Kannschtock (der)n. 1.rye stalk; 2.stack of rye

Kannschtroh (es)n. rye-straw

Kannsdraub (die)n.; Kannsdrauwe, pl. currants

Kanoon (die)n.; Kanoon, pl. cannon

Kansdrauweschtock (der)n. currant bush

Kansdrauwewei (der)n. currant wine

Kansel (die)n. pulpit

Kanselglopper (der)n. parson

Kanselredner (der)n. pulpit orator

Kansgraut (es)n. St. John's wort

Kanuun (die)n.; Kanuun, pl. cannon

Kapitaal (es)n. capital

Kapp (die) n.; Kappe, pl. 1. beret; 2.cap; 3.hood; 4.sheaf covering of a shock of grain; 5.toe cap (of a shoe); 6.U-shaped piece at the end of the handle of a flail; 7.(die Kappe nemme) take the bonnet (join church)

kappe, v.; gekappt, pp. cap (to provide with a cap)

Kappegraut (es)n. 1.hood-wort; 2.mad-dog; 3.skull-cap

Kappevoggel (der)n. cedar waxwing

kaputt, adj. (out of) wack

kaputt, adv. 1.all in; 2.done for

Karackder (der)n. character

Kard (die)n. 1.card; 2.chart; 3.(--e mixe) shuffle the cards

karde, v.; gekardt, pp. card

Kardedisch (der)n. card table

Kardedischdel (die)n. fuller's teasel

Karrichlaus

Kardmaschien (die)n. carding machine

Kardmiehl (die)n. carding mill

Kareber (der)n.; Kareber, pl. body

Karebet (der)n. carpet

Karebmacher (der)n. basket maker

Karebs (die)n.; Karebse, pl. pumpkin

Karebsegrummbeer (die)n. sweet potato

Karebsegrummbier (die)n. sweet potato

Karebsekuche (der)n. pumpkin pie

Karebseroller (der)n. rustic

Karebseschtick (es)n. pumpkin patch

karebvoll, adj. basketful

Karebweide (die)n. osier (willow)

karessiere, v.; gekaressiert, pp. 1.caress; 2.court

Karfreidaag (der)n. Good Friday

Karfunkel (der)n. carbuncle

Karreb (der)n.; Karreb, pl. basket

Karrebche (es)n. little basket

Karrell (die)n.; Karrelle, pl. 1.baby beads; 2.bead(s)

Karrelle, (die)n. Job's tears, the seed of Coix lacaryma-jobi (an Asiatic grass)

Karrich (der)n. cart (In Old Order Amish usage a two wheeled cart used to train driving horses)

Karrich (die)n.; Karriche, pl. church

Karrich(e)hof (der)n.; Karrich(e)hef, pl. churchyard

Karricharyel (die)n. pipe organ

Karrichbell (die)n. church bell

Karrichbuch (es)n. church record

Karrichdaag (der)n. church day

Karrichdier (die)n. church door

Karrichebenk (die)n., pl. pews

Karrichedi(e)nscht (der)n. church service

Karrichegeld (es)n. 1.alms; 2.church collection

Karricheglaawe (der)n. orthodox belief

Karricheglock (die)n. church bell

Karricheiweihing (die)n. church dedication

Karrichelied (es)n.; Karrichelieder, pl. hymn

Karricheraat (der)n. church council

Karricheschtick (es)n.; Karricheschticker, pl. hymn

Karricheschtul (der)n.; Karricheschtiel, pl. 1.pew; 2.bench

Karrichesitz (der)n. 1.pew; 2.bench

Karrichfenschder (es)n. church window

Karrichfescht (es)n. church festival

Karrichgang (der)n. 1.aisle in a church; 2.attendance at church; 3.going to church

Karrichgaul (der)n. cart horse

Karrichgenger (der)n. churchgoer

Karrichgrischt (der)n. church going Christian

Karrichgschicht (die)n. ecclesiastical history

Karrichhof (der)n.; Karrichhef, pl. 1.cemetery;2.graveyard

Karrichhofflecke (die)n. spots on the skin (liver spots)

Karrichhofkandidaat (der)n. one careless of his health

Karrichhofmauer (die)n. wall surrounding a cemetery

Karrichkalenner (der)n. church almanac

Karrichlaus (die)n. church louse

Kk

Karrichleit

Karrichleit (die)n., pl. 1.church attendants; 2.people going to or from church

Karrichmann (der)n. churchman

Karrichmaus (die)n. church mouse

Karrichposchde (der)n. pillar of the church

Karrichschand (die)n. church scandal

Karrichschul (die)n. 1.church school; 2.parochial school

Karrichtarn (der)n. church steeple

Karrichwese (es)n. 1.church affairs; 2.church disagreement

Karrichzeiding (die)n. church paper or journal

kariyos, adj. 1.odd; 2.strange

Karnligraut (es)n. sweet cicerly

Karrick (der)n. cork

karricke, v.; gekarrickt, pp. cork

Karrickzieger (der)n. corkscrew

Karwel (es)n. 1.collection basket in church; 2.little basket

Karwli (es)n. 1.collection basket in church; 2.little basket

Karwligraut (es)n. sweet cicerly

Karwoch (die)n. Holy Week

Karyanner (der)n. coriander

Karyenner (der)n. coriander

karyos, adj. queer

Kasch (die)n.; Kasche, pl. 1.cherry; 2.virginity; 3.(--breche) take virginity; 4.(-- nemme) take virginity

Kaschber (der)n. 1.funny person; 2.oddly acting person

Kaschde (der)n.; Kaschde, pl. 1.bin; 2.box; 3.chest; 4.coop; 5.head; 6.noodle; 7.runt; 8.snip (of a boy)

Kaschebaam (der)n.; Kaschebeem, pl. cherry tree

Kaschebrieh (die)n. cherry juice

Kaschehatz (der)n. cherry gum

Kaschehoke (der)n. hooked stick used in pulling in limbs of cherry trees in picking cherries

Kaschehols (es)n. cherry wood

Kaschekuche (der)n. cherry tart

Kascheschtee (der)n.; Kascheschtee, pl. cherry pit

Kascheschteener (der)n. cherry pitter

Kasdreelbuhn (die)n. castor oil bean

Kass (die)n. 1.money-box; 2.treasury

Kasset (die)n. corset

Kassinet (es)n. cassinette

Kathrine (die)n. Catherine

Katirsch (die)n. carriage

Kattekism (der)n. catechism

Katz (die)n.; Katze, pl. 1.cat; 2.(des is ver die --) this is no good; 3.(en -- im Sack kaafe) buy a pig in a poke

Katz! scat!

katz, adj. short

katzab, adv. plainly

katzbeenich, adj. short-legged

katze, v.; gekatzt, pp. shorten

Katzedreck (der)n. cat dirt

Katzefisch (der)n. catfish

Katzegegrisch (es)n. caterwauling

Katzegichtre (die)n., pl. conniption fits

Katzegraut (Tee) (es)n. catnip (tea)

Katzekopp (der)n. girls' game

Kehlband

Katzeschwans (der)n. cat tail

Katzevoggel (der)n. catbird

Katzeyammer (der)n. 1.caterwauling; 2.gadding; 3.gossiping

Katzgebet (es)n. short sudden prayer

katzhaarich, adj. short-haired

katzlich, adv. 1.lately; 2.recently; 3.shortly

katzo(o)chd(e)mich, adj. 1.asthmatic; 2.short-winded

katzo(o)demich, adj. short of breath

katzodem, adj. short of breath

katzschtielich, adj. short-handled

katzschwenzich, adj. short-tailed

katzsichdich, adj., adv. 1.myopic; 2.near-sighted

Katzsichdichkeet (die)n.; Katzsichdichkeit, pl. myopia

katzum, adv. (in) short

Kau (der)n. 1.chew; 2.quid

Kauderwelsch (es)n. jargon

Kauduwack (der)n. chewing tobacco

kaue, v.; gekaut, pp. 1.chew; 2."chew over something"; 3."chew the rag"; 4.masticate

kaufdevoll, adv. 1.heaping full; 2.heaping measure

kauftich, adj. heaped

kaum, adv. 1.hardly; 2.scanty; 3.scantily; 4.scarcely

kauscher, adj. (usually used with net) 1.exact; 2.nice; 3.proper; 4.right; 5.(do is aa ebbes net gans recht --) there is something suspicious (queer) about this

Kauz (der)n. 1."queer duck"; 2.strange person

kebbe, v.; gekeppt, pp. top (plants)

Kecherle (es)n. lentil

Kecherli (es)n. soybean

keck, adj. 1.bold; 2.bright; 3.pert

Keddeschtrang (der)n. trace (part of harness) (iron)

kee, adj. 1.no; 2.not any

kee eener, pron. not one

Keefer (der)n. buyer

keemol(s), adv. 1.never; 2.not once

Keenich (der)n.; Keeniche, pl. 1.king; 2.queen bee

Keenichen (die)n. queen

keenichlich, adj. 1.regal; 2.royal

Keenichreich (es)n.; Keenichreicher, pl. kingdom

Keenzeeche (es)n. distinctive mark

Keer (es)n. (sense of) hearing

keere, v.; gekeert, pp. 1.belong; 2.(sich --) (a) behoove; (b) be suitable or proper

Kees (der)n. cheese

Keesbabbel (die)n. mallow

keese, v.; gekeest, pp. 1.curd; 2.turn to cheese

keesich, adj. silly

Keesmolke (die)n. whey

Keesseih (die)n. colander

kefd(l)ich, adj. notched

Keffer (der)n.; Keffer, pl. 1.bug; 2.elegant young fellow; 3.mischievous child(ren)

Keffich (der)n.; Keffiche, pl. coop

keft(l)ich, adj. notched

Kehl (die)n. throat

Kehlband (es)n. 1.brace; 2.throat band

Kk

kehle / Kichedribbel

kehle, v.; gekehlt, pp. choke
Kehlgraut (es)n. jewel weed
Kehlkopp (der)n. larynx
Kehr (die)n. turn (in road)
Kehrdreck (der)n. sweepings
kehre, v.; gekehrt, pp. sweep
Kehrich (der)n. sweepings
Kehrichblech (es)n. dusting pan
keich(l)e, v.; gekeiche(l)t, pp. 1.pant; 2.puff; 3.wheeze
keich(l)ich, adj. 1.asthmatic; 2.panting; 3.short of breath
keiche, v.; gekeicht, pp. 1.puff; 2.wheeze
Keidel (der)n. 1.large piece of bread; 2.wedge
keidle, v.; gekeidelt, pp. 1.wedge; 2.(sich --) become wedged
Keil (der)n. bolt (in dunnerkeil)
Keil (es)n. (continual) crying
Keim (die)n.; Keime, pl. 1.germ; 2.sprout
keime, v.; gekeimt, pp. 1.germinate; 2.remove sprouts
Kelch (der)n.; Kelche, pl. chalice
Kelder (die)n. 1.place where pumice was piled up in old cider mills; 2.winepress
Kelderhaus (es)n. cider press
Kell (die)n.; Kelle, pl. 1.ladle; 2.trowel
Kellebasch (die)n. 1.calabash; 2.head
Keller (der)n.; Kellere, pl. 1.basement; 2.cellar
Kellerdeer (die)n. cellar door
Kellereck (es)n. 1.cellar way; 2.pantry
Kelleresel (der)n. sow bug
kellerfeicht, adj. damp
Kellerhaasli (es)n.; Kellerhasslin, pl. sow bug
Kellerhals (der)n.; Kellerhels, pl. 1.cellar way; 2.outside cellar door
Kellerkeffer (der)n.; Kellerkeffer, pl. sow bug
Kellerkich (die)n. basement (cellar) kitchen
Kellerlaus (die)n.; Kellerleis, pl. sow bug
Kellerluft (die)n. damp air in a cellar
Kellermaus (die)n.; Kellermeis, pl. sow bug
Kellermeisli (es)n.; Kellermeislin, pl. sow bug
Kellerox (der)n.; Kelleroxe, pl. sow bug
Kellerschteek (die)n. cellar steps
Kellich (der)n.; Kelliche, pl. 1.chalice; 2.cup
Kelsche (es)n. blue checkered cotton cloth
kelschich, adj. of checkered cloth
Kelt (die)n. cold(ness)
keltere, v.; gekeltert, pp. crush fruit (especially grapes) for wine (the pressing may be done several days after)
Kelwel (es)n. calf
Kelwerschtreech (die)n., pl. awkward pranks
kem (to) neither one
Kemmerli (es)n. 1.lumber room; 2.small clothes room
ken eener, pron. not one
Kenk (es)n. continued hanging or clinging (to)
kenmol, adv. not once
kenn, adj. no
kenne, v.; gekennt, pp. 1. (to be) able; 2. can; 3.know or understand something; 4.recognize; 5.(-- laerne) become acquainted with

kenner, adj.; pron. 1.none; 2.not any
kenni, adj.; pron. 1.none; 2.not any
Kennzeeche (es)n. distinctive mark
kenns, adj.; pron. 1.none; 2.not any
keppe, v.; gekeppt, pp. 1.behead; 2.decapitated; 3.top (plants)
Keppsche (es)n. 1.little cap; 2.small head (as of a baby)
Kerze (die)n. candle
kerzegraad, adj. 1.perpendicular; 2.perfectly straight; 3.vertical
Keschd(an)eeche (der)n. 1.chestnut oak; 2.rock chestnut oak
Keschdebaam (der)n.; Keschdebeem, pl. chestnut tree
keschdebrau, adj. 1.auburn; 2.chestnut brown
Keschdefareb (die)n. chestnut color
Keschdeholz (es)n. chestnut wood
Keschdepeif (die)n. whistle made of chestnut bark
Keschdeschot (die)n. chestnut burr
Keschdetutt (die) n. holder for berries improvised from chestnut bark
Keschdigel (der)n. chestnut burr
Kescht (die)n.; Keschde, pl. chestnut
keschtlich, adj. costly
Kessel (der) n.; Kessele, pl. 1.hollow enclosed by hills or mountains; 2.kettle; 3.pot
Kesselche (es)n. blickery
Kesselflicker (der)n. tinker
Kesselhenk (die)n. bail of a kettle
Kesselloch (es)n. place for an iron kettle under covered front of old style bakeoven
Kesselschtang (die)n. handlebar
Kett (die)n.; Kedde, pl. 1.chain; 2.(mit Kedde binne) shackle (to tie with chains)
kette, v.; gekett, pp. chain
Kettebrick (die)n. chain bridge
Kettebump (die)n. chain pump
Kettedamm (der)n. dam held by a chain
Kettehoke (der)n. chain hook
Kettehund (der)n. watch dog
Kettekuggel (die)n. chain shot
Ketteschtich (der)n. chain stitch
Ketteschtrang (der)n. iron trace
Ketzel (es)n. kitten
Ketzer (der)n.; Ketzer, pl. 1.heretic; 2.rascal; 3.rogue; 4.scoundrel
Ketzerei (die)n. 1.heresy; 2.tangled affairs
Kewwich (der)n.; Kewwich(e), pl. 1.cage; 2.common evening primrose
kibbe, v.; gekippt, pp. 1.begrudge; 2.(to be) envious; 3.quarrel; 4.topple over
kibbisch, adj. 1.envious; 2.offended
Kich (die)n.; Kiche, pl. kitchen
Kichedeer (die)n. kitchen door
Kichedier (die)n. kitchen door
Kichedisch (der)n. kitchen table
Kichedribbel (der)n. 1.male assistant in kitchen; 2.waiter at table at funerals

Kk

Kichegeraetschaft / Kittel

Kichegeraetschaft (die)n. kitchen utensils
Kichegschar (es)n. kitchen crockery
Kichelche (es)n. 1.little cake; 2.lozenge
Kicheschank (der)n. kitchen cupboard
Kichli (es)n.; Kichlin, pl. 1.cookie; 2.lozenge
kickere, v.; gekickert, pp. 1.giggle; 2.snicker
kidde, v.; gekitt, pp. putty
Kiefer (der)n. cooper
Kiehbacke (der)n. smoked jowl
Kiehband (die, es)n.; Kiehbenner, pl. throat latch (on bridle)
Kiehbauerei (die)n. dairy farm
Kiehbell (die)n.; Kiehbelle, pl. cowbell
Kiehbidders (es)n. tansy
Kiehblaschder (es)n. cow droppings
Kiehblumm (die)n. dandelion
Kiehbohn (die)n.; Kiehbohne, pl. soybean
Kiehdokder (der)n. veterinarian
Kiehdreck (der)n. cow dung
Kiehdreckroller (der)n. 1.applied to a person as a term of opprobrium; 2.tumblebug
Kiehdreiwer (der)n. drover
Kiehfleesch (es)n. beef
Kiehfuder (es)n. fodder for cattle
Kiehkalb (es)n. cow-calf
Kiehkett (die)n. cow chain
kiehl, adj. 1.chilly; 2.cool
kiehle, v.; gekiehlt, pp. 1.cool; 2.refrigerate
Kiehler (der)n. cooler
Kiehlkeller (der)n. cold (storage) cellar
Kiehlwasser (es)n. water used by a blacksmith for cooling his iron
Kiehmischt (der)n. cow dung
Kiehpulwer (es)n. cattle powder
Kiehschleck (die)n. cowlick
Kiehschoop (der)n. cow shelter
Kiehschtaar (der)n. Cowbird
Kiehschtall (der)n.; Kiehschtell, pl. cow stable
Kiehschwans (der)n. 1.cow's tail; 2.(siwwe Kiehschwens ee hoor) distant relationship
Kiehwegli (es)n.; Kiehweglin, pl. cattle path
Kiehzung (die)n. spice cookie
Kieruus (der)n. lampblack
Kilb (der)n. swingle (of a flail)
Kimmel (der)n. caraway
Kimmelbrot (es)n. bread containing caraway seeds
kimmere, v.; gekimmert, pp. (sich --) 1.grieve; 2.meddle in; 3.take an interest in
kimmerlich, adj. 1.distressed; 2.in need; 3.needy
Kimmernis (die)n. 1.anxiety; 2.concern
Kind (es)n.; Kinner, pl. child
Kindbettern (die)n. woman in child-bed
Kinddaaf (die)n. christening
Kindel (es)n. pupil (of the eye)
Kindheet (die) n. 1.childhood; 2.infancy; 3.(die zwett --) dotage
Kindheit (die)n. 1.childhood; 2.infancy

kindisch, adj. childish
kindlich, adv. 1.severely; 2.thoroughly
kindlisch, adj. childish
Kindsbu (der)n. grandson
Kindssuh (der)n. grandson
Kinn (es)n. chin
Kinnbacke (der)n. 1.jaw (bone); 2.smoked jowl
Kinnerdieb (der)n. kidnapper
Kinnerfescht (es)n. service for children
Kinnerfreind (der)n. lover of children
Kinnergleeder (die)n., pl. children's clothing
Kinnergschpiel (es)n. child's play
Kinnerlehr (die)n. catechetical instruction
kinnerlich, adj. childish
Kinnermard (der)n. 1.abortion; 2.infanticide
Kinnerschpass (der)n. childish amusement
Kinnerschpielsach (die)n.; Kinnerschpielsache, pl. toy
Kinnerschtreech (die)n., pl. childish pranks
Kinnersege (der)n. numerous offspring
Kinnerzucht (die)n. noise (made by children)
kinnisch, adj. 1.childish; 2.dotardly
Kinsbett (es) n. 1. confinement; 2. (ins -- kumme) (to be) confined for childbirth
Kinschdler (der)n.; Kinschdler, pl. trick performer
Kinschdlerei (die)n. 1.ability to perform mysteries; 2.powwowing; 3.spiritualistic performances
kinschdlich, adj. 1.artificial; 2.ingenious
Kinskind (es)n.; Kinskinner, pl. grandchild
Kinsmaad (die)n. nursemaid
Kinsnoot (die)n. labor (in childbirth)
Kipp grudge
kippe, v.; gekippt, pp. 1.tip over; 2.topple over
kipprich, adj. speckled
Kirz (die)n. shortness
Kischbel (der)n. giggler
kischblich, adj. 1.giggling; 2.silly
Kischder (der)n. sexton
Kischt (die)n.; Kischde, pl. 1.box; 2.chest; 3.jag
Kiss (der)n. gravel
Kissboddem (der)n. gravelly soil
Kisse (es)n.; Kissin, pl. 1.cushion; 2.pillow
kisse, v.; gekisst, pp. kiss
Kissel (der)n. 1.pebble; 2.sleet
Kisselwedder (es)n. 1.sleet-storm; 2.sleety weather
kisselwetters, adv. confoundedly
Kisses (es)n. kissing
Kissi (es)n.; Kissin, pl. 1.cushion; 2.pillow
kissle, v.; gekisselt, pp. sleet
kisslich, adj. sleety
Kitchegeraetschaft (die)n. kitchen utensils
Kitsch (die)n.; Kitsche, pl. 1.rake; 2.scraper (for removing ashes)
kitsche, v.; gekitscht, pp. scrape with a "Kitsch"
Kitt (der)n. putty
kitte, v.; gekitt, pp. putty
Kittel (es)n. 1.blouse; 2.light coat

Kk

Kittmesser   knicke

Kittmesser (es)n. putty-knife

Kitz (die)n. 1.female cat; 2.female rabbit

Kitzelgraas (es)n. witch grass

Kitzelweide (die)n. pussy willow

kitzle, v.; gekitzelt, pp. 1.fill with secret joy; 2.tickle

Kitzles (es)n. tickling sensation

kitzlich, adj. 1.ticklish; 2.touchy

Kitzn (die)n. female cat

Kiwwel (der)n.; Kiwwel, pl. 1.bucket; 2.bucket of a water wheel; 3.bucket of an elevator; 4.small wooden pail with one long stave for a handle; 5.pump-piston

Kiwwelvoll (der)n. 1.bucketful; 2.pailful

kiwwelvoll, adj. bucketful

Kiyoon (der)n. 1."queer duck;" 2.strange person

klaage, v.; geklaakt, pp. 1.be indisposed; 2.complain; 3.lament

Klaak (die)n. complaint

Klabberdasch (die)n. 1.jabbering person; 2.rickety vehicle

Klaech (der)n. link

Klaeger (der)n. plaintiff

Klaerinett (die)n. clarinet

Klaff (die)n. key (of a piano or organ)

Klamm (die)n. 1.clamp; 2.clothes pin

Klammhoke (der)n. 1.crane hook; 2.dog (in lumbering)

Klang (der)n. 1.echo; 2.ring; 3.sound

klange, v.; geklangt, pp. 1.reverberate; 2.ring; 3.sound

klappe, v.; geklappt, pp. 1.agree; 2.clap (hands); 3.tally

Klapper (der)n. clapper

Klapperschlangewatzel (die) n. 1. lion's-foot; 2.Seneca snakeroot

Klass (die)n. class

Klassis (die)n. classis

Klecks (der)n. blot

Klee (der)n. clover

klee, adj. small

kleede, v.; gekleedt, pp. clothe

Kleie (die)n. 1.bran; 2.shorts

Kleinod (es)n. jewel

Klemm (die)n. 1.dilemma; 2.quandary; 3.pinch; 4.scrape

kleppre, v.; gekleppert, pp. rattle

klepprich, adj. rattling

Klett (die)n. 1.burdock; 2.burdock burr

Kliftse, (die)n., pl. 1.rocks; 2.wilds

Klimpel (es)n. 1.small lump; 2.small roll (of butter)

klimple, v.; geklimpelt, pp. form a lump (of butter in a churn)

Kling (die)n. blade (of a knife)

kling klang! onomatopoeic for the clangor of bells

klinge, v.; geklingt, pp. 1.reverberate; 2.ring; 3.sound

Klingel (der)n. 1.ball (of yarn); 2.crewel

Klingel (die)n. 1.bell; 2.sleigh bell

Klingelsack (der)n. small bag with a long handle used in taking up the collection in church

Klingelseckel (es)n. small bag with a long handle used in taking up the collection in church

Klingelseckli (es)n. small bag with a long handle used in taking up the collection in church

klingle, v.; geklingelt, pp. 1.jingle; 2.ring; 3.tinkle

Klingschtee (der)n. clingstone

Klipp klapp! 1.click clack!; 2.flip flap!

klitsche, v.; gegklitscht, pp. 1.slide; 2.slip

klitschich, adj. slippery

Klooe (die)n. 1.claw; 2.cloven foot; 3.clutches; 4.paw

kloppe, v.; gekloppt, pp. 1.beat; 2.hammer; 3.knock; 4.pound; 5.rap

klor, adj. clear

klore, v.; geklort, pp. 1.clear; 2.clear up

Kloschder (es)n. convent

Kloschderfraa (die)n. nun

Kloster (es)n. convent

Klotz (der)n. 1.block; 2.segment of a tree trunk

Klowe (der)n. (wire) staple

klu(u)ch, adj. 1.clever; 2.prudent; 3.wise

Kluck (die)n. hen (when with chicks)

kluck, adj. 1.cluck; 2.cluck of a liquid running out of a bottle

kluckse, v.; gekluckst, pp. 1.cluck; 2.gurgle

Klumpe (der)n. 1.heap; 2.lump; 3.roll (of butter)

klumpich, adj. lumpy

Kluppe (die)n. 1.clutches; 2.hands

Kluuchheet (die)n. prudence

Kluuchheit (die)n. prudence

Knack (der)n. 1.knot; 2.skein

knacke, v.; geknackt, pp. 1.break partially; 2.crack; 3.tick

Knackwa(r)scht (die)n. 1.hard smoked sausage; 2.saveloy

Knaerps (der)n. 1.chap; 2.little fellow

knaersche, v.; geknaerscht, pp. 1.gnash; 2.grate; 3.grind

Knall (der)n. 1.clap; 2.crack; 3.loud report; 4.(uff -- und fall) in a hurry

knalle, v.; geknallt, pp. 1.crack; 2.make a loud report

Knallhitt (die)n. 1.bawdy house; 2.dilapidated building; 3.hovel

knapps, adj. 1.close; 2.scarcely; 3.stingy

Knarre (der)n. knot (in lumber)

knarre, v.; geknarrt, pp. 1.growl; 2.grumble; 3.scold; 4.snarl

knarrich, adj. 1.gnarly; 2.knotty; 3.prone to grumble

Knarwel (der)n. 1.cartilage; 2.gristle

knarwlich, adj. 1.gnarly (of a tree, apple, or a roughly healed wound); 2.gristly

Knarze (der)n. 1.blemish in fruit caused by the sting of an insect; 2.core of an apple; 3.nubbin; 4.stumpy old tree

knarzich, adj. 1.deformed and imperfect (as trees and fruit); 2.knotty

knawwere, v.; geknawwert, pp. 1.gnaw; 2.nibble

Knecht (der)n.. 1.hired man; 2.male servant

knecke, v.; gekneckt, pp. tick

Kneip (der)n. 1.kitchen paring knife; 2.razor (used jokingly); 3.shoemaker's paring knife

Kneip (die)n. drinking place

Knew(w)el (der)n. 1.bolt at the end of a chain; 2.gag; 3.hank; 4.stick used for twisting a rope or straw band

knewwle, v.; geknewwelt, pp. 1.nag; 2.scold

knicke, v.; geknickt, pp. bend and crack without breaking entirely

Kk

Knie — Kord

Knie (es)n. 1.elbow of a stove pipe; 2.knee
kniee, v.; gekniet, pp. kneel
Knierem (der)n. shoemaker's strap or stirrup
Knierieme (der)n. shoemaker's strap or stirrup
kniffisch, adj. tricky
kniffzich, adj. tricky
Knippel (der)n. 1.club; 2.coarse fellow; 3.cudgel
Knittel (der)n. club
knitz, adj. 1.mischievous; 2.tricky
Knoche (der)n. bone
Knochegaul (der)n. skeleton (bony) horse
Knochelehr (die)n. osteology
Knochemehl (es)n. bonemeal
Knochemiehl (die)n. bone mill
Knocheweh (es)n. bone ache
Knocheyarrigel (der)n. skeleton
knochich, adj. bony
Knoddel (der)n. 1.chunk; 2.chunky person 3.compact hard
  droppings of many animals; 4.small lump; 5.turd
Knoffe (der)n. pommel
knollich, adj. lumpy
knootsche, v.; gegknootscht, pp. 1.fondle; 2.handle over-
  much; 3.hug
Knopp (der)n. 1.button; 2.lump
Knoww(e)lich (der)n. garlic
Knowwelloch (der)n. garlic
Knowwlichgraut (es)n. garlic mustard
knuffe, v.; geknufft, pp. 1.beat with the fist; 2.hammer
  lightly; 3.pummel; 4.quarrel
Kobbekisse (es)n.; Kobbekissi, pl. 1.cushion; 2.pillow
Kobbekissi (es)n. 1.cushion; 2.pillow
Kobbeziech (die)n. pillowcase
Koch (der, die)n.; Kech, pl. cook
Kochabbel (der)n. codling
Kochaerbs (die)n. sweet pumpkin
Kochbohn (die)n. string bean
koche, v.; gekocht, pp. 1.boil; 2.cook; 3.simmer; 4.seethe
Kochegscharr (es)n. utensils
Koches (es)n. cooking
Kochet (die)n. 1.mess (of food); 2.sufficient for one meal
Kochfeier (es)n. coal fire
Kochfleesch (es)n. meat for boiling
Kochgscharr (es)n. utensils
Kochhatte (der)n. iron cook pot
Kochhaus (es)n. summer kitchen (detached)
kochich, adv. 1.boiling; 2.seething
Kochka(e)rbs (die)n. sweet pumpkin
Kochkessel (der)n. 1.boiler; 2.large kettle
Kochleffel (der)n. ladle
Kochoffe (der)n.; Kocheffe, pl. range (stove)
Kochpann (die)n. saucepan
Kochwese(s) (es)n. everlasting cooking
Kod(d)er (der)n. snot (especially when drawn into the
  throat)
Kohl (die)n.; Kohle, pl. coal
Kohle-Eemer (der)n.; Kohle-Eemer, pl. coal scuttle

Kohlebrenner (der)n. charcoal burner
Kohleel (es)n. 1.coal oil; 2.kerosene
Kohleelfass (es)n. petroleum barrel
Kohleelkann (die)n. kerosene can
Kohleellicht (es)n. kerosene lamp
Kohleesch (die)n. ashes of coal
Kohlegrub (die)n. colliery
Kohlekessel (der)n.; Kohlekessel, pl. coal scuttle
Kohlekiwwel (der)n.; Kohlekiwwel, pl. coal scuttle
Kohlhaus (es)n. coal shed
Kohlleeder (die)n. ladder used in mounting the smolder-
  ing charcoal pile
Kohlschtaab (der)n. coal dust
Kohlschtofft (es)n. carbon
kohlschwatz, adv. coal-black
Kokonuss (die)n. coconut
Kollekt (es)n. 1.collect; 2.collection
kollere, v.; gekollert, pp. 1.make a gurgling sound in the
  throat; 2.make the bubbling sound of boiling water
Kollic (der)n. colic
Kolraabi (der)n. kohlrabi
Kolwe (der)n.; Kolwe, pl. 1.ear (human); 2.ear of corn;
  3.nose (of animal); 4.spike of timothy
Kolweblaat (es)n.; Kolwebledder, pl. narrow-leafed plantain
Kolwegraas (es)n. 1.green foxtail; 2.yellow foxtail
Kolwemelde (der)n. purple amaranth
Komma (es)n. comma
Kommood (die)n. 1.bureau; 2.night-stool
kop(u)liere, v.; kop(u)liert, pp. 1. perform the marriage
  ceremony; 2.marry
Kopp (der)n.; Kepp, pl. 1.head; 2.(aus dem --) demented; 3.
  (en -- hawwe) be tipsy; 4. (ich schteck dir
  der -- gschwische dei ohre) a bantering threat to a child;
  5.(sei -- setze) be headstrong; 6.(sie is --s sei) be obstinate
Kopp vedderscht, adv. head first
Kopp-verreisses (es)n. mental exertion
koppschtatze, v.; koppgschtatzt, pp. somersault
Koppaerwet (die)n. brain work
Koppax (die)n. ax used in decapitating fowls
Koppche (es)n.; Koppcher, pl. cup (of cup and saucer)
Koppchekees (der)n. cup cheese
Koppduch (es)n.; Koppdicher, pl. 1.kerchief; 2.shawl
Koppeziech (die)n. pillow case
Koppgraut (es)n. cabbage
Koppi (es)n.; Kopplin, pl. cup
kopple, v.; gekoppelt, pp. join in marriage
Kopp(li)kees (der)n. cup cheese
Kopp-putz (der)n. headdress
Koppschtell (die)n. headstall
koppsleng, adj. a head (taller)
koppsvedderscht, adv. 1.head first; 2.headlong
Koppweh (es)n. headache
Koppwesching (die)n. shampoo
Kor (der)n. 1.body of musicians; 2.choir
Koraal (der)n. choral hymn
Kord (die)n. 1.card; 2.chart; 3.(--e mixe) shuffle the cards

Kk

Kordbendel / krissle

Kordbendel (der)n. cord string
korde, v.; gekordt, pp. card
Kordedisch (der)n. card table
Kordedischdel (die)n. fuller's teasel
Kordmaschien (die)n. carding machine
Kordmiehl (die)n. carding mill
Korgesang (der)n. anthem
Korhemm (es)n. surplice
Koriander (der)n. coriander
Korinne June berry
Kork (der)n. cork
Korkzieger (der)n. corkscrew
Korlied (es)n. anthem
Kornelkasch (die)n. dogwood
Kornett (die)n. cornet
Koschde (die)n.; pl. expense(s)
koschde, v.; gekoscht, pp. cost
koschdefrei, adj., adv. free of cost
Koscht (die)n. 1.board; 2.fare; 3.victuals
koschtbaar, adj. 1.costly; 2.expensive
Koschtgenger (der)n.; Kochetgenger, pl. boarder
koschtlich, adj. expensive
koschtschpielich, adj. 1.costly; 2.expensive
koslich, adj. untidy
Kot (der)n."Owedrot is mariyeschee un Mariyerot bis Owed, Dreck un Kot" mud (as used in Red sky in the evening means fair weather the next day and red in the morning means mud by evening)
Kotz (der)n. vomit
Kotzbohn (die)n. castor oil bean
kotzdunner!, interj. damn it!
kotze, v.; gekotzt, pp. 1.puke; 2.regurgitate; 3.retch; 4.vomit
kotzerich, adj. 1.nauseated; 2.squeamish
kotzgricksel!, interj. 1.by golly!; 2.deuce take it!
kotzmardsapperlott nochermol!, interj. confound it!
kotzsapperment!, interj. the devil!
Kowwel (die)n. top-curl (mostly on the heads of children)
Kraan (der)n. 1.crane; 2.spigot; 3.stopcock
Krabb (die)n. 1.crow; 2.raven
Krach (der)n. 1.crack; 2.crash; 3.report
krache, v.; gekracht, pp. 1.crack; 2.crash; 3.creak; 4.make a report
kraddle, v.; gegkraddelt, pp. 1.climb; 2.crawl; 3.creep
kraddlich, adj. 1.astraddle; 2.crawling
kraehe, v.; gekraeht, pp. crow
Kraemer (der)n. peddler
kraemere, v.; gekraemert, pp. peddle
Kraft (die)n. 1.power; 2.strength; 3.vigor
Kraftbrieh (die)n. jelly
kraftlos, adj. invalid
Krageel (der)n. violent quarrel
krageele, v.; grakeelt, pp. 1.quarrel; 2.torment (verbally)
Krageeler (der)n. 1.insistently troublesome person; 2.quarrelsome person
Kramm (der)n. 1.commodities; 2.wares
Kramp (der)n. 1.convulsion; 2.cramp

krank, adj. 1.sick; 2.(en --es) sick person
Krankebett (es)n. sick bed
krankhaft, adj. morbid
Krankheet (die)n. 1.disease; 2.sickness; 3.mensus
Krans (der)n. 1.border; 2.garland; 3.wreath
Krapp (der)n. madder
kratze, v.; gekratzt, pp. 1.claw; 2.scratch
kratzich, adj. 1. crabbed; 2.itching; 3.not cordial; 4.partly fermented (of cider); 5.pungent; 6.tickling
Kraut (es)n. 1.cabbage; 2.herb; 3.top of a plant; 4.vegetation
krawwle, v.; gekrawwelt, pp. crawl
krawwlich, adj. crawling
Krebs (der) n. 1.cancer; 2.crab; 3.Cancer (4th sign of the zodiac)
Krees (der)n. circle
kreftich, adj. 1.strong; 2.vigorous
Kreid (es)n. 1.account; 2.bill; 3.chalk; 4.(in der -- sei) (a) be in a fix; (b) be in for it; (c) owe
Kreider (die)n., pl. herbs
Kreiderbuch (es)n. treatise on botany
Kreidertee (der)n. herb tea
Kreidliwidderbring (der)n. 1.brunella; 2.self heal
Kreis (der)n. circle
kreische, v.; gekrische, pp. 1.cry; 2.halloo; 3.scream; 4.squeal
kreislich, adj. 1.terrible; 2.thrilling
Kreiz (es)n. 1. cross; 2. crucifix; 3. misfortune; 4. small of the back; 5. (es is mer en --) I hate to do it; 6.(gotts -- nochemol) confound it!; 7. (im -- hawwe) (to) have lumbago; 8. (iwwers --) crosswise
kreiziche, v.; gekreizicht, pp. crucify
krenke, v.; gekrenkt, pp. 1.grieve; 2.hurt; 3.regret; 4.vex
krenkle, v.; gekrenkelt, pp. 1.be sickly; 2.complain of sickness; 3.irk; 4.take sick
Kretz (der)n. 1.crank; 2.grouchy person; 3.itch; 4.(die alt --) (the) old crank
kretzich, adj. 1.crabbed; 2.itchy; 3.scabious
Kricks (der)n. cricket
Kricksel (es)n. cricket
Kriek (der)n. war
Kriksel dei krix! scritch-scratch (imitating the sound of a pen in rapid writing)
Kriksel fixel! scritch-scratch (imitating the sound of a pen in rapid writing)
Krill (die)n. cricket
krimme, v.; gekrimmt, pp. (sich --) 1.bend; 2.move
Krimmel (die)n. crumb
krimmle, v.; gekrimmelt, pp. (sich --) separate into crumbs
krimmle, v.; gekrimmelt, pp. crumble
Krippel (der)n. cripple
kripplich, adj. crippled
Krisch (der)n. 1.cry; 2.scream; 3.shout
Krischkindel (es)n. 1.Christmas present; 2.Santa Claus
Krissel (die)n., pl. 1.cold shivers; 2.thrill; 3.(die -- sinn mer ausgange) I shuddered (at the sight)

Kk

Kritzelfixel — Kuyoon

krissle, v.; gekrisselt, pp. 1.be distasteful; 2.make oneshudder
Kritzelfixel (es)n. 1.fine tracery work; 2.scribbling;
   3.vulgar adornment
kritzle, v.; gekritzelt, pp. scribble
Kritzler (der)n. scribbler
Kroll (die)n. 1.curl; 2.ringlet
krolle, v.; gekrollt, pp. curl
Kroller (der)n. cruller
krollich, adj. curly
Kron (die)n. crown
Krott (die)n. 1.toad; 2.(gleeni --) young girl
Kruck (der)n. 1.jug; 2.mug; 3.pitcher
krumm, adj. crooked
Kruscht (die)n. 1.country dance; 2.cranky person;
   3.crusty; 4.frolic
Krutze (der)n. 1.cob; 2.core (of fruit); 3.nubbin;
   4.(weeche --) (a) applejack; (b) bad whiskey
Kschlaav (es)n. slave
kschlaave, v.; kschlaavt, pp. slave
Kschlaaverei (die)n. slavery
Kss! 1.scat!; 2.sick 'em! (to a dog)
Kubber (es)n. copper
Kubberkessel (der)n. copper kettle
kubbern, adj. copper
Kubberschlang (die)n.; Kubberschlange, pl. Copperhead
   snake
Kubberschmitt (der)n. coppersmith
Kuchbuch (es)n.; Kuchbicher, pl. cookbook
Kuche (der)n.; Kuche, pl. 1.cake; 2.cookie; 3.(en -- setze)
   put a cake in the oven; 4. (gangner --) doughnut
Kucheblatt (die)n. griddle
Kuchedeeg (der)n. cake dough (batter)
Kuchemoddel (die)n. cake cutter
Kucheraedel (es)n. jagging iron
Kucherellche (es)n. dough cutter
Kucheschipp (die)n. cake lifter
Kuchet Aerbse (en)n. mess of peas
Kuckkaschde (der)n. show
Kuddel (der)n.; Kiddel, pl. overall jacket
Kuddelfleck (der)n. tripe
Kuddelwese (es)n. 1.tangled affairs; 2.tangled threads
Kudderments (die)n., pl. (so --) such things
Kuddle (die)n., pl. 1.bowels; 2.guts
Kug(g)el (die)n.; Kug(g)le, pl. bullet
Kuggelbix (die)n. rifle
kuggelfescht, adj. invulnerable
Kuggelform (die)n. bullet mold
Kuggleflint (die)n. rifle
Kuh (die)n.; Kieh, pl. cow
Kuhrinter (die)n., pl. Corinthians
Kuhschtall (der)n.; Kuhschtelle, pl. cow stable
Kumbass (die)n. compass
Kumbliment (es)n. compliment
Kumet (der)n. comet
Kumfermierung (die)n. confirmation
Kumm mit! Come along!

kummbaawel, adj. 1.fit; 2.proper
kumme, v.; is kumme, pp. 1.come; 2.be put in; 3.(ins
   bett --) (to be) confined; 4.(uff die welt--) (to be)
   born; 5.(wie kummt's, dass ...) how is it that ...;
   6.(zu sich --) revive; 7.(zu Hilf --) 1.aid; 2.help
Kummer (der)n. grief
Kummeraad (der)n.; Kummeraade, pl. 1.comrade; 2.pal
Kummet (es)n.; Kummede, pl. (horse) collar
Kummetbloder (die)n. horse collar
Kummetdeck (die)n. 1.housing; 2.hame-cover
Kummetschpaa (der)n.; Kummetschpee, pl. hame (of a
   horse-collar)
Kummetschpaarieme (der)n. hame strap
Kummt er aa? Will he be sure to come?
Kump (der)n. whet-horn (filled with water or vinegar for
   whetting stone to sharpen scythes)
Kumpani (die)n. 1.companion; 2.company
Kumschdaagler (der)n. constable
Kundewidde (die)n. 1.consideration; 2.ingenuity;
   3.thought
kunfermiere, v.; kunfermiert, pp. confirm
Kunfermiering (die)n. confirmation
Kuni (der)n. Conrad
Kunne (der)n. customer
Kunnemiehl (die)n. gristmill doing grinding for toll
Kunnschaft (die)n., pl. 1.craft; 2.customers; 3.custom;
   4.trade
Kunraad (der)n. Conrad
Kunschdaaler (der)n. constable
Kunscht (die)n. 1.ability; 2.art; 3.knowledge; 4.science;
   5.skill; 6.(kenn --) there is no difficulty about this
kupfer (en) a penny
Kupperkopp (der)n. copperhead snake
kupperrot, adv. copper colored
Kupperschtich (der)n. engraving
kupple, v.; gekuppelt, pp. find a partner for another in
   matrimony
Kuppruss (es)n. copperas
Kur(r)asche (die)n. courage
kurraaschich, adj. courageous
kusche, v.; gekuscht, pp. (sich --) 1.lie down; 2.submit;
   3.subside
Kuscht (es)n. incessant coughing
Kusel (die)n. untidy woman
Kuss (der)n. 1.(Holy) Kiss; 2.Kiss of Peace
Kutsch (die)n.; Kutsche, pl. 1.carriage; 2.coach; 3.raised
   platform for raising plants
Kutschel (es)n. (continual) whinnying
kutslich, adj. sloppy
Kutt (die)n. 1.blouse; 2.gown
Kutterments (die)n., pl. 1.so; 2.such things
Kutzel (die)n. untidy woman
kutzlich, adj. untidy
Kuw(w)el (die)n.; Kuw(w)le, pl. bullet
Kuyoon (der)n. 1."queer duck"; 2.strange person

Ll

Laab

Laab (es)n. 1.foliage; 2.leaf
laabe, v.; gelaabt, pp. refresh
Laabfrosch (der)n. 1.tree frog; 2.tree toad
Laabgrott (die)n. 1.tree frog; 2.tree toad
Laabknopp (der)n. leaf bud
Laableis (die)n., pl. aphides
Laad (die)n.; Laade, pl. 1.casket; 2.coffin; 3.load
Laade (der)n.; Laade, pl. 1.cornice; 2.shelf
Laade (der)n.; Leede, pl. shutter
laade, v.; glaade, pp. 1.charge (a gun); 2.load
Laademacher (der)n.; Laademacher, pl. 1.cabinetmaker;
    2.coffin maker; 3.funeral director; 4.undertaker
Laademecher (der)n. 1.coffin maker; 2.undertaker
Laademesser (der)n. 1.funeral director; 2.undertaker
Laadmoos (es)n. measure for powder (in loading a gun)
Laadschtecke (der)n. ramrod
Laaf (der)n.; Leef, pl. 1.current; 2.course; 3.gun barrel;
    4.race; 5.run (off); 6.walk; 7.way
laafe, v.; g(e)loffe, pp. 1. flow (as water); 2. go; 3. run
    (for office); 4.run (of contracts); 5.walk
Laafer (der)n.; Laafer, pl. 1.pedestrian; 2.walker
Laafzeit (die)n. rutting season
Laag (die)n. lye
Laager (der)n.; Laager, pl. camp
Laagseef (die)n. (hard) soap
laahm, adj. lame
laamaesich, adv. lawful
Laarenzius (der)n. St. Lawrence Day, August 10
laawe, v.; gelaabt, pp. 1.refresh; 2.(sich --) shed leaves
Labbe (der)n. rag
Labberhosse (die)n., pl. sailor pants
labbich, adj. 1.careless; 2.negligent; 3.silly
Labbwisch (der)n. spray of leaves
lablos, adj. inanimate
Lach (der)n. laugh
lachdich, adj. 1.soaked; 2.tinted
lache, v.; gelacht, pp. 1.laugh; 2.neigh (of horses); 3.whinny
lachlich, adj. laughable
Lack (die)n. brine in which meat is pickled
Ladann (die)n.; Ladanne, pl. lantern
ladeinisch, adj. Latin
Laeb (der)n. loaf of bread
Laefer (der)n. 1.runner of a sleigh; 2.shoat
Laefersau (die)n. shoat
laerbse, v.; gelaerbst, pp. 1.lisp; 2.speak indistinctly
Laerm(e) (der)n. 1.alarm; 2.noise; 3.tumult
laerme, v.; gelaermt, pp. make a noise
laermend, adj. 1.noisy; 2.obstreperous
laermich, adj. noisy
laerne, v.; gelaernt, pp. 1.educate; 2.learn; 3.teach
Laerrich (die)n. lark
Lafendel (der)n. lavender
Lamm (es)n.; Lemmer, pl. lamb
Lammel (der)n. burly fellow (mostly young boys)
Lampehelling (die)n. lamplight
Lan(d)smann (der)n. 1.countryman; 2.native; 3.neighbor

langschtielich

Land (es)n.; Lenner, pl. 1.country; 2.garden bed; 3.land;
    4.piece of land plowed by making either all right or
    all left turns; 5.soil
Land nufzus, adj. up-country
Landeegner (der)n.; Landeegner, pl. 1.landowner;
    2.yeoman
landfiessich, adj. long footed
Landfuhr (die)n. farmer's conveyance
Landgemee (die)n. country congregation
landhaer, adv. of old
Landkarrich (die)n. country church
Landkord (die)n. 1.chart; 2.map
Landlaafer (der)n. tramp
Landleit (die)n., pl. country people
Landlewe (es)n. country life
Landmesser (der)n.; Landmesser, pl. 1.daddy long legs;
    2.surveyor
landnunnerzus, adj. down-country
Landregge (der)n. steady rain
Landschaft (die)n. 1.district; 2.landscape; 3.section
Landschillgrott (die)n. tortoise
Landschtross (die)n.; Landschtrosse, pl. 1.country road;
    2.highway
Landschul (die)n. country school
Landseit (die)n. land plate (of a plow)
Landvoggel (der)n. land bird
Landvolk (es)n. country people
Landwohning (die)n. country home
lang her, adv. of old
lang zerick, adv. long ago
Lang-gwitt (die, es)n.; Lang-gwidde, pl. coupling pole (of
    the farm wagon)
lang, adj. 1.diluted; 2.long; 3.tall; 4.thin
lang; lenger; lengscht, adj. long; longer; longest
Langaarsch (der)n. deformed fowl or person
langaarschich, adj. 1.deformed; 2.weak
langbeenich, adj. long legged
lange, v.; gelangt, pp. 1.attain; 2.hand to someone;
    3.pass (at the table); 4.reach; 5.suffice; 6.(--[e] fer
    ebbes) (to) aspire (to)
langhi, adv. 1.far off; 2.long
langhoorich, adj. long haired
langkeppich, adj. 1.clever; 2.cunning
Langkwid (die)n. connecting pole of a wagon
langlich, adj. longish
Langmann (der)n. middle finger
langmiedich, adj. 1.forbearing; 2.patient
Langmut (der)n. 1.forbearance; 2.patience
langnaesich, adj. long nosed
Langohr (es)n. 1.ass; 2.mule
langohrich, adj. long eared
langrund, adv. elliptical
langs, adv. at full length
langsam, adj. 1.dull; 2.slow
langschichtich, adj. long drawn out
langschtielich, adj. long handled

Ll

Langschtroh

Langschtroh (es)n. rye-straw

langschwensich, adj. long tailed

langsichtich, adj. 1.hypocritical; 2.long faced

Langversammling (die)n. protracted meeting

langwa(e)rich, adj. tedious

langweile, v.; gelangweilt, pp. 1.(to be) bored; 2.(sich --) (a) be bored; (b) (to be) ennuyed

langweilich, adj. 1.tedious; 2.tiresome; 3.wearisome

langweilich, adv. humdrum

langweis, adv. lengthwise

langwindich, adj. long-winded

Lann (die)n.; Lanne, pl. shaft (of a horse-drawn carriage)

lanne, v.; glannt, pp. 1.instruct; 2.learn; 3.teach

Lanning (die)n. 1.education; 2.learning; 3.schooling

Lans (die)n. lance

Lappaarsch (der)n. 1.negligent person; 2.shiftless person

Lappe (der)n. 1.patch; 2.small piece of cloth; 3.spot

Lapperei (die)n. 1.nonsense; 2.twaddle

Lappes (der)n. negligent person

Lapphund (der)n. 1.negligent person; 2.shiftless person

Lappi (der)n. negligent person

lappich, adj. 1.careless; 2.negligent; 3.silly

Lappichkeet (die)n. 1.carelessness; 2.indifference

larbse, v.; gelarbst, pp. 1.drawl; 2.speak indistinctly

Laschder (es)n. 1.iniquity; 2.vice

laschderhaft, adj. 1.outrageous; 2.vicious

Laschdermaul (es)n. 1.back biter; 2.slanderer

Laschderwese (es)n. iniquitous doings

Lascht (die)n. 1.burden; 2.load

laschtbaar, adj. onerous

lass, adj. 1.careless; 2.indifferent; 3.lax; 4.negligent

Lassichkeit (die)n. 1.lassitude; 2.negligence

Latt (die)n.; Ladde, pl. roofing lath

Lattenaggel (der)n.; Latteneggel, pl. lath nail

Lattwaerrickkessel (der)n. large copper kettle in which apple butter is boiled

Lattwarrick (der)n. apple butter

Lattwarrickriehrer (der)n. stirrer fastened on to the copper kettle (in which apple butter is made)

Latz (der)n. 1.bib; 2.flap; 3.fly (of a man's pants)

lau, adj. indifferent

Lauch (der)n. leek

laude, v.; gelaut, pp. 1.ring (a bell); 2.sound

lauder, adj. 1.all; 2.altogether; 3.nothing but; 4.sheer

lauder, adv. 1.nothing but; 2.merely; 3.only

Lauer (die)n. watch (look)

lauere, v.; gelauert, pp. 1.eavesdrop; 2.lurk; 3.lie in wait; 4.watch

Lauerer (der)n. eavesdropper

Laus (die)n.; Leis, pl. louse

lauschdere, v.; gelauschdert, pp. 1.eavesdrop; 2.listen

lausche, v.; gelauscht, pp. 1.harken; 2.listen

lause, v.; gelaust, pp. 1.delouse; 2.drub; 3.thrash

Laushund (der)n. scamp

Lausknecker (der)n. index finger (in nursery rhyme)

Lauspaad (der)n. part (of hair) (humorous)

Leebli

Laut (der)n. 1.sound; 2.(kenn -- vun sich gewwe) utter no sound

laut, adj. 1.loud; 2.strong (of an odor)

laute, v.; gelaut, pp. 1.be worded; 2.read; 3.ring; 4.sound

lauter, adj. 1.all; 2.altogether; 3.nothing but; 4.sheer

lauwaarm, adj. 1.lukewarm; 2.tepid

Lavendal (der)n. (v=f Lafendal) lavender

Laxier Salz (es)n. Epsom salt

laxiere, v.; gelaxiert, pp. purge (for constipation)

Laxiering (die)n. 1.cathartic; 2.laxative; 3.physic; 4.purgative

Leb(e)wohl (es)n. 1.adieu; 2.farewell

Lebbdaag (der)n. 1.(Gotts --!) well! well!; 2.(mei --) (in) all my life; 3.(sei -- net) never

lebbere, v.; gelebbert, pp. sip

Lebberschulde (die)n.,pl. small debts

lebbi(s)ch, adj. 1.smutty; 2.tasteless; 3.unseasoned

lebhaft, adj. 1.gay; 2.lively; 3.sprightly; 4.vivacious

Lebhaftichkeet (die)n. vivacity

Lebkuche (der)n.; Lebkuche, pl. 1.ginger cake; 2.honey cake

lech(er)lich, adj. laughable

Lechaa (die)n. 1.Lehigh; 2.(die -- Kaft) Lehigh Gap; 3.(die --) the Lehigh River

Lechel (es)n. little hole

lecher(l)ich, adj. 1.funny; 2.laughable; 3.ridiculous

lechere, v.; gelechert, pp. 1.put holes in slate, tin, etc.; 2.(es lechert mich) it makes me laugh

lecherich, adj. 1.full of holes; 2.ludicrous; 3.laughable; 4.ridiculous; 5.(-- mache) ridicule

lechle, v.; gelechelt, pp. smile

Lechli (es)n.; Lechlin, pl. little hole

Leckaarsch (der)n. lickspittle

Leckdrick (die, es)n. electric

Leckdrickuhr (die)n. electric clock

lecke, v.; g(e)leckt, pp. 1.lap; 2.lick

Leckschen (die)n. election

Leddche (es)n. slat

Ledde (der)n. clay (blue)

Leddebodde(m) (der)n. clay soil (blue)

Leddel (es)n. 1.lath; 2.slat

Leddelche (es)n. lath

Ledder (es)n. leather

leddere, v.; geleddert, pp. 1.flog; 2.leather; 3.worst (in a fight)

ledderich, adj. leathery

ledderichweis, adv. 1.out of matrimony 2.(en Kind --) bastard

leddern, adj. leathern

Ledderzang (die)n.; Ledderzange, pl. shoemaker's pliers

leddich, adj. 1.clayey (blue); 2.single (unmarried)

leddicherweis, adj. 1.illegitimate; 2.born out of wedlock

leddicherweis, adv. out of wedlock

lee, adv. alone

Leeb (der)n.; Leewe, pl. 1.Leo (5th sign of the zodiac); 2.lion; 3.loaf (of bread)

Leebli (es)n. lion cub

Ll

Leed

Leed (der)n. (der -- hawwe draa) (to be) tired (of it)

Leed(e) (der)n. 1.grief; 2.mourning; 3.sorrow; 4.woe; 5.(-- hawwe) (to be) tired of it

leede, v.; gleede, gleed, pp. solder

Leeder (die)n.; Leedere, pl. ladder

Leederbaam (der)n.; Leederbeem, pl. ladder-beam

Leederschpross(e) (der)n.; Leederschprosse, pl. rung of a ladder

Leederwaage (der)n.; Leederwegge, pl. ladder-wagon

leedich, adj. tired of

Leedkolwe (der)n. soldering iron

leedmiedich, adj. 1.lonesome; 2.sad; 3.sorrowful

Leefer (der)n.; Leefer, pl. runner (of a sleigh)

Leefersei (die)n. hogs above the size of suckling piglets and smaller than butcher hogs

Leegoi (es)n.; Leegoier, pl. nest-egg

leenich, adv. alone

leer, adj. 1.empty; 2.vacant; 3.void

leere, v.; gleert, pp. 1.pour; 2.(sich --) (to be) suitable

leerkeppich, adj. addle-brained

leer/schteh, v.; leergschtanne, pp. (to be) vacant

Leescht (der)n. shoemaker's last

Leescht (die)n. 1.molding; 2.strip; 3.slat

Leeschthoke (der)n. last hook

Leffel (der)n.; Leffle, pl. 1.spoon; 2.(grosser --) ladle

Leffelgraut (es)n. winter cress

Leffelvoll (der)n. spoonful

Leffermaul (es)n. hang lip

Leffidde (die)n., pl. 1.tale of being henpecked; 2.tale of woe

Leffli (es)n.; Lefflin, pl. (little) spoon

Lefidde (die) n., pl. (ebber die -- ablese) give someone a lecture

Lefts (die)n.; Leftse, pl. lip

lege, v.; g(e)legt, pp. 1. lay; 2. place; 3. put; 4. (sich --) (a) offend; (b) subside; (c) take to one's bed; 5. (sich uff ebbes --) (to make) specialty (of)

Leghinkel (es)n. laying hen

Legschtock (der)n. ovary (in fowls)

Lehme (der)n. clay (red)

Lehmeboddem (der)n. clay soil

lehmich, adj. clayey (red)

lehne, v.; g(e)lehnt, pp. 1.borrow; 2.lean; 3.lend; 4.loan; 5.recline

Lehnebodde(m) (der)n. clay soil (red)

Lehner (der)n. lender

Lehnsbauer (der)n. tenant farmer

Lehnsblatz (der)n. rented place

Lehnshaus (es)n. tenant house

Lehnsmann (der)n.; Lehnsleit, pl. tenant

Lehr (die)n. 1.doctrine; 2.education; 3.learning; 4.lesson

lehre, v.; gelehrt, pp. instruct

Lehrer (der)n. 1.preceptor; 2.teacher

Lei(n)olich (der)n. linseed oil

Leib (der)n. 1.abdomen; 2.belly; 3.paunch; 4.stomach; 5.bodice; 6.body lice

Leibche (es)n. 1.bodice; 2.corset

Leitkolwe

Leibgriwwle(s) (es)n. belly ache

leibhafdich, adv. 1.bodily; 2.identical

Leibschmatze (die)n.,pl. stomachache

Leibschtick (es)n.; Leibschticker, pl. favorite air

Leibweh (es)n. diarrhea

Leich (die)n. corpse

Leichde(n)berichder (der)n. 1.funeral director; 2.undertaker

Leichder (der)n.; Leichder, pl. (paper) taper

Leichehaus (es)n. house of mourning

Leichenbefaahrer (der)n. 1.funeral director; 2.undertaker

leichsinnich, adj. frivolous

Leicht (die)n.; Leichde, pl. 1.body (rare usage); 2.corpse (rare usage); 3.funeral; 4.funeral cortege

leicht, adj. 1.convenient; 2.easy; 3.light; 4.simple

Leichtbreddich (die)n. funeral sermon

leichte, v.; geleicht, pp. 1.give light; 2.lighten; 3.light one's way

Leichter (der)n. 1.lighter; 2.paper taper

leichter, adv. 1.easier; 2.lighter

leichtfiessich, adj. 1.light-footed; 2.swift

leichtfiessich, adj.; adv. swift(ly)

Leichthaus (es)n. house of mourning

Leichtichkeet (die)n. 1.easiness; 2.lightness

Leichtkoschde (die)n., pl. funeral expenses

Leichtmann (der)n. 1.funeral director; 2.undertaker

Leichtsinn (der)n. 1.frivolity; 2.levity

leichtsinnich, adj. thoughtless

Leichtsinnichkeit (die)n. 1.frivolity; 2.thoughtlessness

Leichtversaryer (der)n. 1.funeral director; 2.undertaker

Leid (es)n. 1.affliction; 2.suffering

leid(l)ich, adj. 1.agreeable; 2.indifferent; 3.likeable

leide, v.; gelidde, pp. 1.allow; 2.endure; 3.suffer; 4.tolerate; 5.(gut --) rather like

leidich, adj. comfortable

leie, v.; gelegge; geleye, pp. 1.(to be) sick abed; 2.doze; 3.nap; 4.rest; 5.slumber; 6.(geld -- hawwe) have ready money

Leier (die)n. (die aldi --) 1.old ruts; 2.same old story; 3.tune the cow died on

leiere, v.; geleiert, pp. 1. thrum or drone an air; 2. do something slowly; 3.poke along; 4.work slowly

leilich, adj. short of breath

Leim (der)n. glue

leime, v.; gleimt, pp. glue

Leimkessel (die)n. glue pot

Leimledder (es)n. scraps of leather

Lein (die)n. 1.rein; 2.(thin) rope

Leinduch (es)n.; Leindicher, pl. bed sheet

leine, adj. linen

leinich, adj. linen

leis, adj. 1.faint; 2.low; 3.soft

Leischhowwel (die)n.; Leischhowwle, pl. 1.head-plane; 2.ogee-plane

Leischt (die)n. 1.molding; 2.slat

Leit (die)n. 1.people; 2.(fremmi --) strangers (pl. form)

Leitkolwe (der)n.; Leitkolwe, pl. soldering iron

Ll

leitschei

leitschei, adj. 1.afraid of folks; 2.bashful; 3.shy
Leiwelche (es)n. 1.bodice; 2.corset
Lekeise (es)n. axle plate
Lekhinkel (es)n. laying hen
Lelack (der)n. lilac
lelle, v.; glellt, pp. pant
Lemmel (der)n. burly fellow (mostly of young boys)
lendlich, adj. rural
Leng (die)n. 1.length; 2.(uff die --) in the long run
lenglich, adj. 1.oblong; 2.some what long
lengre, v.; gelengert, pp. 1.extend; 2.lengthen
lengs, adv. at full length
Lennerd (der)n. Leonard
leppere, v.; geleppert, pp. 1.be a steady drinker; 2.sip
Lepperschulde (die)n., pl. 1.debts incurred for drink; 2.small debts
leppisch, adj. 1.insipid; 2.smutty; 3.tasteless; 4.unseasoned
Lerm(e) (der)n. racket
leschdere, v.; geleschdert, pp. 1.blaspheme; 2.slander
leschderhaft, adj. blasphemous
leschderlich, adv. very
Leschdermaul (es)n. shrew
Leschderung (die)n. blasphemy
leschdich, adj. 1.burdensome; 2.wearisome
lesche, v.; gelescht, pp. 1.extinguish; 2.put out (a fire); 3.quench; 4.slake
lese, v.; glese, pp. 1.pick up; 2.read; 3.(des Buch lest vun so sache) this book gives an account of such things
Leser (der)n. 1.picker; 2.reader
Leses (es)n. reading
Leseschtick (es)n. reading selection
Lessichkeit (die)n. negligence
letscht, adj. 1.last; 2.(-- zu guter) (a) finally; (b) wind up with
letscht, adv. (es -- her) 1.here of late; 2.toward the end
letschtyaehrich, adv. last year's
Lettche (es)n. 1.lath; 2.slat
Lette (der)n. clay
Lettel (es)n. 1.lath; 2.slat
lettich, adj. clayey
lettle, v.; gelettelt, pp. lath
Lettli (es)n.; Lettlin, pl. lath
letz mache, v. (sich --) turn inside out
letz rechle, v.; gerechelt, pp. miscalculate
letz sei, v.; is letz gewest, pp. 1.(to be) amiss; 2.wrong
letz, adv. 1.inside out; 2.(-- in der Belskapp) off in the head
Lewe (es)n.; Lewe, pl. 1.bustle; 2.life; 3.living; 4.livelihood; 5.quick (of a nail or horse's hoof); 6.(am (bei) -- sei) (to be) alive; 7.(sei -- net) never; 8. (sei -- uff ebber schweere) enter complaint of assault with intent to kill
Lewe(n)sbeschreiwer (der)n. biographer
Lewe(n)sbeschreiwing (die)n. biography
Lewe(n)sgfaahr (die)n. danger of life
Lewe(n)sgraut (es)n. live-for-ever
Lewe(n)skraft (die)n. 1.strength; 2.vitality
Lewe(n)sschtand (der)n. position in life

lieblich

Lewe(n)sschtrof (die)n. capital punishment
Lewe(n)sunerhalt (der)n. 1.livelihood; 2.sustenance
Lewe(n)sversicherung (die)n. life insurance
Lewe(n)swandel (der)n. biography
Lewe(n)szeeche (es)n. 1.conduct; 2.course of life
Lewe(n)szeit (die)n. lifetime
Lewe(n)sziel (es)n. goal of life
lewe(ns)lang, adv. lifelong
lewe, v.; glebt, pp. (to be) alive
Lewemaul (es)n. snapdragon
lewendich, adj. 1.live; 2.lively; 3.living; 4.maggoty
Lewensbild (es)n. picture of life
Lewensweis (die)n. manner of living
Lewesbalsam (der)n. restorative balsam
Leweslaaf (der)n. biography
leweslang, adv. lifelong
Lewesmiddel (es)n. 1.eatables; 2.foodstuff; 3.provisions
Leweszeit (die)n. lifetime
Lewewohl (es)n. 1.adieu; 2.farewell
Lewewohl!, interj. Farewell!
lewich, adj. 1.alive; 2.lively
Lewwer (die)n.; Lewwere, pl. liver
Lewwerfillsell (es)n. liverwurst
Lewwerflecke (die)n., pl. liver spots
Lewwergraut (es)n. 1.hepatica; 2.liverwort
Lewwerwascht (die)n. liver-pudding
Lewwerwaschtfillsel (es)n. 1.pudding; 2.meat scraps left over from a butchering
liberaal, adj. liberal
Licht (es)n.; Lichder, pl. 1.candle; 2.lamp; 3.light; 4. (eem's -- ausblose) kill a person
Lichtbutzer (der)n. snuffer(s)
Lichtbutzsche(e)r (die)n. snuffer(s)
Lichteil (die)n. miller (moth)
Lichterform (die)n. candle mold
Lichtermacher (der)n. chandler
Lichterschtock (der)n. candlestick
Lichthelling (die)n. early dawn
Lichtmess (die)n. Candlemas, February 2 (All spinning was to be completed.)
Lichtschtraahl (der)n. streak of light
Lick (die)n. 1.gap; 2.(unoccupied) space; 3.spell; 4.while; 5.(en -- dresche) thrash a spell
Lickerisch (der)n. licorice
lickich, adj. 1.(having unoccupied) spaces; 2.small holes; 3.vacant
lidderlich, adj. 1.bawdy; 2.lewd; 3.despicable; 4.foolish; 5.licentious
Lidderlichkeet (die)n. dissoluteness
Lieb (die)n. love
lieb, adj. 1.beloved; 2.dear
lieb, adv.; adj. soon
Liebgreitel (es)n. lovage
Liebhawwer (der)n. lover
lieblich, adj. 1.adorable; 2.lovely; 3.pleasant; 4.savory
lieblich, adv. lovely

Ll

Liebling | los/schiesse

Liebling (der)n. pet
liebreich, adj. kind
liebschde (am --) most of all
Liebschdi (die)n. 1.darling; 2.dear; 3.love; 4.sweetheart
liebscht, adj. dearest
Liebschteckel (es)n. lovage
Lied (es)n.; Lieder, pl. 1.hymn; 2.song
liede, v.; gelied, pp. solder
Liedel (es)n. song
Liederbuch (es)n.; Liederbicher, pl. 1.hymnbook; 2.songbook
Liedli (es)n. song
Lieg (die)n.; Liege, pl. 1.falsehood; 2.lie; 3.untruth
liege, v.; geloge, pp. 1.fib; 2.lie; 3.tell a lie
Liegerei (die)n. 1.repeated or continued lying; 2.slandering
Liegeschtreit (der)n. quarrel due to slander
Liegner (der)n. liar
Liesch(t) (es)n. cattail flag
Lieschkolwe (der)n. cattail spike
liete, v.; geliet, pp. solder
Lietkolwe (der)n. soldering iron
liewe, adj. 1.beloved; 2.dear
liewe, v.; geliebt, pp. 1.caress; 2.like; 3.love
liewenswaert, adj. worthy of love
Liewer (der)n. 1.darling; 2.dear
liewer, adv. 1.dearer; 2.more readily; 3.rather
Liewesbrief (der)n. love letter
lieweshalwer 1.for love's sake; 2.for the sake of
Liewesmahl (es)n. Holy Communion (Dunker usage)
Liewespulwer (es)n. love powder
lieweswaert, adj. worthy of love
Liewi (die)n. 1.darling; 2.dear
liewich, adj. (du --i Zeit!) dear me!
lifde, v.; gelift, pp. ventilate
Lifdel (es)n. (diminutive of die Luft = air) 1.air; 2.breeze
lifdich, adj. 1.airy; 2.breezy
liffere, v.; geliffert, pp. 1.deliver; 2.furnish
Lilye (die)n. lily
Limbaeryer kees (der)n. Limburger cheese
Limmel (der)n. 1.boor; 2.lummox
Lingner (der)n.; Lingner, pl. liar
link, prep. 1.left; 2.(dei --) the left hand
linkerhand, adv. to the left
links-hendich, adj. left-handed
links, adj. 1.left; 2.left handed; 3.to the left
Linne (die)n. linden tree
Linnebaam (der)n. linden tree
Lipp (die)n. lip
lippe, v.; gelippt, pp. lift slightly
Lisbett (die)n. 1.Betsy; 2.Betty; 3.Elizabeth
lischble, v.; gelischbelt, pp. lisp
lischde, v. enlist
lischdich, adj. 1.cunning; 2.mischievous; 3.sly
Lischt (die)n. 1.cunning; 2.list; 3.shrewdness
Liss(i) (die)n. Lizzie
Litanei (die)n. litany
liwwere, v.; geliwwert, pp. deliver

lo, adj. lukewarm
Lob (es)n. 1.character; 2.praise; 3.reputation
Lobgesang (der)n. hymn
Lobreed (die)n. panegyric
Lobschpruch (der)n. doxology
Loch (es)n.; Lecher, pl. 1.burrow; 2.hole; 3.rent; 4.tear
Lochballe (der)n. game of ball
loche, v.; gelocht, pp. 1.bore; 2.hole
Lochposchde (der)n.; Lochposchde, pl. post with holes (for making rail fence)
Lochseeg (die)n. compass saw
Lock (der)n. 1.call; 2.signal
Locke (der)n. lock of wool
locke, v.; gelockt, pp. 1.call; 2.decoy; 3.entice
lockere, v.; gelockert, pp. loosen by shaking or tapping
lockich, adj. having locks
lodd(e)rich, adj. 1.loose; 2.dilapidated; 3.rickety; 4.shaky
loddele, v.; geloddelt, pp. 1.shake (loose); 2.walk slowly
lodder, adj. 1.loose; 2.dilapidated; 3.rickety; 4.shaky
Lodderie (die)n. lottery
lodderlo, adv. 1.all in; 2.fagged out
loddle, v.; geloddelt, pp. 1.bum; 2.shake loose
Lodel (der)n. shiftless person
Logeige (die)n. 1.gillyflower; 2.stock; 3.wall-flower
Loh (der)n. 1.pay; 2.remuneration; 3.wages
Loh (die)n. tanbark
Lohgrub (die)n. tan-pit
Lohmiehl (die)n. mill for grinding bark
lohrot, adj. 1.tanbark color; 2.tawny
Lone (der)n. linchpin
Loone (der)n. support
Loos (die)n.; Loose, pl. sow (female pig)
Lorbeer (die)n. laurel
Los (es)n. 1.destiny; 2.lot
los/binne, v.; losgebunne, pp. untie
los/breche, v.; is losgebroche, pp. 1.break loose; 2.burst out
los/bringe, v.; losgebrocht, pp. accomplish
los/drehe, v.; losgedreht, pp. untwist
los/dricke, v. losgedrickt, pp. pull the trigger
los/faahre, v.; losgfaahre, pp. 1.drive pell-mell; 2.make a rush; 3.make straight for
los/geh, v.; losgange, pp. 1.break loose; 2.go off; 3.(druff --) make a dash for
los/hacke, v.; losghackt, pp. 1.chop away at; 2.lash at
los/helfe, v.; losgholfe, pp. help a person to get loose
los/hoke, v. unhook
los/kaafe, v.; loskaaft, pp. ransom
los/kumme, v.; loskumme, pp. 1.be discharged; 2.get free; 3.(to become) untied
los/losse, v.; losgelosst, pp. 1.release; 2.set free
los/mache, v.; losgemacht, pp. 1.loosen; 2.undo; 3.unfasten; 4.untie
los/reisse, v.; losgerisse, pp. 1.break loose; 2.tear loose
los/schaffe, v.; losgschafft, pp. (sich --) disengage oneself
los/schiesse, v.; losgschosse, pp. discharge (a gun)

los/schlagge — Luwies

los/schlagge, v.; losgschlagge, pp. 1.knock loose; 2.(druff --) strike at wildly
los/schnalle, v.; losgschnallt, pp. unbuckle
los/schneide, v.; losgschnidde, pp. cut loose
los/schpreche, v.; losgschproche, pp. absolve
los/schprenge, v.; losgschprengt, pp. loosen by blasting
los/schpringe, v.; losgschprunge, pp. 1.crack loose; 2.(druff --) run wildly
los/schrauwe, v.; losgschraubt, pp. unscrew
los/schwetze, v.; losgschwetzt, pp. (druff --) talk at random
los/warre, v.; loswarre, pp. 1.dispose of; 2.get loose; 3.throw away
los/weeche, v.; losgeweecht, pp. loosen by softening
los/wickle, v.; losgewickelt, pp. unravel
los/ziege, v.; losgezoge, pp. (iwwer ebber --) haul someone over the coals
los, adj. loose
loschiere, v.; loschiert, pp. 1.abide for a season; 2.lodge; 3.stay for the night
losse, v.; g(e)losst, pp. 1.allow; 2.leave in possession; 3.leave undone; 4.let; 5.let have; 6.(ebber ebbes --) (a) bequeath; (b) will
Lossement (es)n. 1.affair; 2.concern; 3.estate; 4.caboodle; 5.lot
Lovgeige (die)n. (v=f Lofgeige) 1.gillyflower; 2.stock; 3.wall-flower
lowaarm, adv. lukewarm
lowe, v.; gelobt, pp. praise
Lucha (der)n. lynx
luchse, v.; geluchst, pp. 1.cheat; 2.deceive
luck, adj. 1.light (of cake); 2.porous
ludderisch, adj. Lutheran
Luder (es)n. 1.carrion; 2.term of vituperation
Luderblumm (die)n. carrion flower
Luderfuhr (die)n. scavenger's team and wagon
Ludergrabb (die)n. turkey buzzard
Ludergrapp (die)n. turkey buzzard
luderich, adj. foul
luderisch, adj. Lutheran
Luderlewe (es)n. desolate life
Ludermann (der)n. scavenger
luders, adj. 1.awfully; 2.confoundedly
Ludervoggel (der)n. turkey buzzard
Luderwese (es)n. immoral doings
ludre, v.; gludert, pp. stink
lufde, v.; geluft, pp. ventilate
lufdich, adj. 1.airy; 2.breezy
Luft (die)n. 1.air; 2.sky; 3.(heesi --) hot air 4.(in -- geh) explode
luftich, adj. airy
Luftloch (es)n. air hole
Luftrehe (die)n. windpipe
Luftrohr (es)n. windpipe
Luftschiff (es)n.; Luftschiffer, pl. 1.airplane; 2.balloon
Luh (der)n. 1.pay; 2.remuneration; 3.wages
Lumbe (der)n.; Lumbe, pl. rag

Lumbebopp (die)n. rag doll
Lumbegschicht (die)n. rotten affair
Lumbegsindel (es)n. rabble
Lumbehund (der)n. dirty fellow
Lumbekall (der)n. blackguard
Lumbekarrebet (der)n. rag-carpet
Lumbemann (der)n.; Lumbemenner, pl. 1.ragman; 2.scarecrow
Lumberei (die)n. 1.bad business; 2.mixed-up affair; 3.trash; 4.trouble
Lumbesack (der)n.; Lumbeseck, pl. ragbag
Lumbesammler (der)n. rag picker
lumbich, adj. 1.ragged; 2.tattered; 3.wretched
lummerich, adj. 1.limber; 2.limp; 3.supple
Lump (der)n. 1.heretic; 2.n'er-do-well; 3.rascal; 4.scoundrel; 5.villain
Lune (der)n. linchpin
Lung (die)n.; Lunge, pl. lung
Lungefiewer (es)n. pneumonia
Lungefliggel (der)n. lobe of the lung
Lungegraut (es)n. lungwort
Luschde (der)n. 1.appetite; 2.delight; 3.desire; 4.desire for certain things in eating during pregnancy; 5.(sei --biesse) satisfy one's desire (both in a good and a bad sense)
luschdere, v.; geluschdert, pp. 1.enjoy; 2.have a desire
luschderich, adj. 1.having desire; 2.luscious
luschdich, adj. 1.cheerful; 2.gay; 3.jolly; 4.joyful; 5.merry
Luschdichkeet (die)n. glee
luschdiere, v.; geluschdiert, pp. (sich --) enjoy oneself perfectly
Luscht (die)n. 1.merriment; 2.mirth; 3.pleasure; 4.treat
Luschtbaarkeet (die)n. 1.fun; 2.merriment; 3.pleasure
Luschtlewe (es)n. 1.riotous living; 2.sensual living
luschtunfreehlich, adj. 1.happy; 2.jolly
lutsche, v.; gelutscht, pp. suck
Lutteraaner (der)n. Lutheran
luttrisch, adj. Lutheran
Lutzer (die)n.; Lutzer, pl. lantern
Luwies (die)n. Louisa

Mm

Maach | Manierlichkeet

Maach (der)n. poppy
Maad (die)n.; Maade, pl. 1.maid; 2.servant girl
Maag (der)n. poppy
Maage (der)n. stomach
Maagebalsem (der)n. peppermint tea
Maagebidders (es)n. stomach bitters
Maagefiewer (es)n. stomach fever
Maagegramp (der)n. stomach cramps
Maagegrebs (der)n. cancer of the stomach
maager, adj. 1.poor; 2.skinny; 3.slender; 4.unproductive
Maagetee (der)n. peppermint tea
Maagezaah (der)n. stomach tooth (lower canine)
Maahl (es)n. meal
maahle, v.; g(e)maahle, pp. 1.grind (grain); 2.mill
Maahler (der)n.; Maahler, pl. grinder
Maahlerei (die)n. grinding (usually depreciatory)
Maahlmiel (die)n. grist mill
Maahlzeit (die)n. mealtime
Maahne (die)n. mane
Maan(n)i (der)n. Emanuel
Maaran (der)n. (sweet) marjoram
Maa(r)der (der)n. mortar
Maa(r)derbett (es)n. mortar (mixing) box
Maardi (der)n. Martin
Maa(r)tervoggel (der)n. hod
Maarwel (die)n. marble (toy)
Maas (es)n. 1.measure; 2.(iwwer --) without measure
Maasblumm (die)n.; Maasblumme, pl. 1.moss rose; 2.portulaca
mache, v.; gemacht, pp. 1.make; 2.(aaschtalt --) (a) begin; (b) make preparation; 3.(sich --) (a) recover; (b) regain; (c) succeed; 4.(sei Wille --) make one's will; 5.(siess --) sweeten; 6.(zu nix --) undo; 7.(zurecht --) trim
Macht (die)n. 1.might; 2.power
machtlos, adj. helpless
Madaerich (es)n. 1.matter; 2.pus
Madaering (es)n. pus
madde, v.; gematt, pp. murder
Madering (der)n.; 1.matter; 2.pus
Maddedis (der)n. Methodist
Madder (der)n.; Madder, pl. murderer
madderlich, adv. murderous
madderonisch, adj. 1.awfully; 2.frightfully
Madeering (der)n. 1.matter; 2.pus
Madlenewasser (es)n. (contemptuous for) weak coffee
Maed(s)che (es)n.; Maed(s)cher, pl. girl
Maeddedist (der)n. Methodist
Maed(el) (die)n. (en aldi --) an old maid
Maedleis (die)n., pl. 1.all spicies of Bidens whose seeds are broad in proportion to length; 2.tickseed; 3. Spanish needle
Maedschtofft (es)n. 1.mischievous girls; 2.(des --) these girls
Maehd (die)n. (place where) mowing (is done)
maehe, v.; gemaeht, pp. mow
Maeher (der)n. mower
Maehmaschien (die)n. 1.mower; 2.reaper

Maehmesser (es)n. cutter blade (of a mowing machine)
maer(e)b, adj. 1.mellow; ripe; 3.tender
maer(r)b, adj. 1.ripe; 2.cooked thoroughly; 3.tender; 4.well-done
maerde, v.; gemaerdt, pp. 1.assassinate; 2.murder
Maerder (der)n.; Maerder, pl. murderer
maerdere, v.; gemaerdert, pp. 1.torture; 2.torture
Maerderei (die)n. murder
Maerdergschicht (die)n. 1.murder case; 2.murder story
maerderlich, adj. 1.frightfully; 2.murderous
maerderlich, adj. (-- greische) yell to split one's ears
maereb, adj. tender
Maerick (es)n. 1.mark; 2.sign
maericke, v.; gemaerickt, pp. 1.mark; 2.note; 3.take notice
maerickunswaerdich, adj. remarkable
Maer(r) (die)n. 1.mare; 2.nag
Maerrebletter (die)n., pl. lily pads
Maerreoi (es)n. coconut
Maerricker (der)n. marker
maerrickwaerdich, adj. remarkable
Maerrickzeeche (es)n. 1.blaze (on trees); 2.mark
maersche, v.; gemaerscht, pp. crush (in a mortar)
Maerscher (der)n. mortar (apothecaries')
Maert (der)n. Martin
Maerten (der)n. Martin
Maerzeblumm (die)n. violet
maessich, adj. 1.frugal; 2.mighty; 3.moderate; 4.temperate
Maessichkeet (die)n. moderation
Maessichkeit (die)n. moderation
Magneet (es)n. magnet
Mallifitz (die)n. (die gans --) 1.the whole blamed business; 2.the whole thing
Mamm(a) (die)n. 1.mamma; 2.mom; 3.mother
Mammi (die)n. 1.grandmother; 2.mamma; 3.mother
Mammischof (es)n. ewe
manch, adj. many a
mancher, adj. many a
mancherlee, adj. various
Manchfalt (die)n. third stomach of ruminants
manchfalt, adj. manifold
Manchfaltichkeet (die)n. variety
manchi, adj. many a
manchmol, adv. many times
Mandelkaern (die)n. almond
Mandelrock (der)n. (cape) overcoat
Mangel (der)n. 1.lack; 2.necessity; 3.need; 4.want
mangelhaft, adj. 1.imperfect; 2.unsatisfactory
Mangelwazel (die)n. mangel-wurzel (root)
mangle, v.; gemangelt, pp. 1.be lacking; 2.lack
Mangold (der)n. mangel-wurzel (root)
manichmol, adv. 1.many times; 2.many a time;3.sometimes
Manier (die)n. 1.habit; 2.manners; 3.(uff die verderscht --) in first class style
manierlich, adj. 1.genteel; 2.polite
Manierlichkeet (die)n. Politeness

110

Mm

Mann — Maueraerwett

Mann (der) n. (wie en -- unne Koop schwetze) talk nonsense
Mann (der)n.; Menner; Mansleit, pl. 1.husband; 2.man
Mannewell (der)n. Emanuel
mannhaft, adj. manly
Mannheit (die)n. manhood
mannich, adj. many a
Mannier (die)n. manners
mannierlich, adv. mannerly
Mannischt (der)n. Mennonite
mannsaerwet (die)n. 1.heavy work; 2.work for a man
Mannschaft (die)n. team (of men)
mannshoch, adv. of man's stature
Mannskall (der)n.; Mannsleit, pl. 1.male being; 2.man
mannsleitnarrisch, adj. man-crazy
Mannsrock (der)n. gentleman's coat
Mannsvieh (es)n. rough fellow
Mannweib (es)n. 1.amazon; 2.virago
Mantel (der)n. 1.cape; 2.cloak; 3.mantel
marb, adj. ripe
Marbel (die)n. marble (toy)
March (der)n. (rare usage) market
Marchwaagen (der)n. (rare) market wagon
Ma(r)d (der)n. 1.manslaughter; 2.murder
Mardbrenner (der)n. incendiary
Mardbrennerei (die)n. 1.arson; 2.incendiarism
Marddaat (die)n. 1.murder; 2.murderous deed
marde, v.; gemardt, pp. murder
Mardgrisch (der)n. 1.scream; 2.shriek; 3.yell
Mardgschicht (die)n. tale of murder
Mardi (der)n. Martin
mardunisch, adj. 1.awfully; 2.frightfully
mareb, adj. 1.ripe; 2.soft
Mareia (die)n. 1.Maria; 2.Mary; 3.Virgin Mary
Maretyrer Schpiggel (der)n. Martyrs Mirror
Maria (die)n. 1.Maria; 2.Mary; 3.Virgin Mary
Mariche (die)n. 1.Mary; 2.Virgin Mary
Maricheli (es)n. Mary (nursery rhyme)
Marick (es)n.; Marick, pl. mark
maricke, v.; gemarickt, pp. 1.mark; 2.(to take notice)
aware; 3.market produce; 4.note
Maricker (der)n. marker
Marickschtee (der)n. 1.marker; 2.milestone
marickwaddich, adj. remarkable
marickwaddich, adv. notable
Marickzeeche (es)n. mark
Marieheim (es)n. Ascension of the Virgin Mary (Aug. 15)
Marien(s)dischdel (die)n. 1.lady's thistle; 2.Virgin Mary's
thistle
Marien(s)watzel (die)n. 1.valerian; 2.wild marjoram
Marix (es)n. 1.marrow; 2.pith
Mariye (der)n. 1.morning; 2.(aller --) every morning
Mariye-arewett (die)n. morning chores
Mariye-esse (es)n. Breakfast
mariye, adv. 1.tomorrow; 2.(dienders --) (a) are you minded
to do it tomorrow?; (b) will it be convenient tomorrow?

mariyefrieh, adv. tomorrow morning
Mariyegebet (es)n. morning prayer
Mariyeland (es)n. orient
Mariyelendisch (es)n. oriental
Mariyelicht (es)n. dawn
Mariyeschtann (die)n. morning star
Mariyeschtun(d) (die)n. 1.morn; 2.morning (hour)
Mariyesunn (die)n. morning sun
Mariyetender (der)n. huckster (at vendues)
mariyets, adv. in the morning
Markes (der)n. Marcus
Ma(rr) (die)n.; Marre, pl. mare
Ma(rr)esel (der, die)n.; Ma(rr)esel, pl. mare-mule
Ma(rr)land (es)n. Maryland
Marrasch(t)(der)n. 1.mess; 2.mire; 3.mud; 4.slush; 5.swamp
Marrichel (die)n. 1.morel; 2.mushroom
Marrick (der)n. 1.market; 2.market place
Marrickbreis (der)n. market price
Marrickdaag (der)n. market day
Marrickhaus (es)n.; Marrickheiser, pl. market house
Marrickkar(e)b (der)n. market basket
Marrickwagge (der)n. market wagon
marsch, adj. brittle
Maru(n) (der)n. sweet marjoram
Maryerot (es)n. red morning sky
masch, adj. 1.entirely; 2.short off
Maschien (die)n.; Maschiene, pl.
1.automobile;2.contraption; 3.engine; 4.machine
Maschienerie (die)n. machinery
maschiere, v.; maschiert, pp. (sich --) (to be) gone
Mascht (der)n. mast
mascht, adj. 1.fattening (of animals); 2.luxurious (of
plants); 3.pampered
Maschtdarem (der)n. rectum
Maschtochsegraut (es)n. daisy fleabane
Maschtox (der)n. steer (fat or fattening)
Maschtsau (die)n. fat or fattening hog
Maschtvieh (es)n. fat or fattening cattle
mass(e)rich, adj. gnarly
Matratz (die)n.; Matratze, pl. mattress
matt, adj. 1.weak; 2.weary
Mattichkeet (die)n. faintness
mattlich, adj. weakly
Mattsait (es)n.; Mattsaide, pl. supper
Matz (der)n. March
Matzdaag (der)n. March day
Matzfill(i) (es)n. March-foal (person subjected to pranks
on March 1)
Matzhaas (der)n. 1.March hare; 2.(fett wie en --) fat as a
March hare
Matzwedder (es)n. March weather
maudere, v.; gemaudert, pp. 1.brood; 2.droop; 3.hang
the feathers; 4.sulk
maudrich, adj. 1.ailing; 2.drooping
Mauer (die)n. wall
Maueraerwett (die)n. 1.masonry; 2.mason's work

Mm

mauere — Meisli

mauere, v.; gemauert, pp. 1.do mason's work; 2.lay up a wall
Mauerer (der)n.; Mauerere, pl. mason
Mauerhammer (der)n. mason's hammer
Mauerkell (die)n. trowel
Mauerschtee (der)n. building stone
Mauersenkel (der)n. plumb line
Mauerwand (die)n. face of a wall
Maul (es)n.; Meiler, pl. 1.mouth; 2.(eens uffs -- schlagge) give a smack in the face; 3.(en schibbe -- mache) pout; 4.(es -- druffhie schpitze) (to be) eagerly expectant; 5.(es -- halde) shut up; 6.(es -- henke) mope; 7.(es -- zu/binne) gag; 8.(es -- neihenke) interfere; 9.(es -- uff/schparre; uffgschpatt, pp.) (a) gape; (b) yawn; 10.(es -- uffreisse) (a) blab in (b) censure; (c) interfere; 11.(es -- vum Drachloch) the mouth of the cave; 12.(es -- vun der Hehling) the mouth of the cave; 13.(iwwer's -- faahre) snap a person off
Maularigel (die)n. harmonica
Maulbeer (die)n.; Maulbeere, pl. mulberry
Maulbeerebaam (der)n.; Maulbeerebeem, pl. mulberry tree
maule, v.; gemault, pp. 1.grumble; 2.scold
Maulesel (der)n. mule
Maulgrischt (der)n. 1.hypocrite; 2.pretending Christian
maulich, adj. 1.insolent; 2.saucy
Maulkar(e)b (der)n. muzzle
Maulros (die)n. hollyhock
Maulvoll (es)n. mouthful
Maulwar(re)f (der)n. mole (rodent)
Maulwarfgraut (es)n. cypress spurge
Maulzieger (der)n. choke cherry
maunse, v.; gemaunst, pp. 1.complain; 2.meow
Maus (die)n.; Meis, pl. mouse
mausdoot, adv. dead as a doornail
Mausekeenich (der)n.; Mausekeenich, pl. wren
mauseschtill, adj. quiet as a mouse
Mausevoggel (der)n.; Mauseveggel, pl. wren
Mausfall (die)n. mousetrap
Mauskatz (die)n. mouser
Mausloch (es)n.; Mauslecher, pl. mouse-hole
Mausohr (es)n. saxifrage
mausrackedoot, adv. dead as a doornail
Mauszeit (die)n. molting season
Me(e)schder (der)n.; Me(e)schder, pl. master
mechdich, adj. 1.mighty; 2.powerful; 3.strong
mechdich, adv. 1.mighty; 2.very
Meddedischt (der)n. Methodist
Medizin (die)n. medicine
Meebel (der)n. maple
Meechdern (die)n. mistress
meechlich, adv. 1.possible; 2.probably
Meedche (es)n. maiden
Meedel (es)n.; Meed, pl. 1.girl; 2.girl friend; 3.maiden
Meederle (es)n. 1.feather few; 2.fever few
Meedleis (die)n. 1.tick; 2.tickseed (pl. form)
Meedli (es)n.; Meedlin, pl. lass
meege, v.; gemeecht, pp. 1.care (to like); 2.may

meeglich, adv. 1.possible; 2.probably
meeglicherweis, adj. possibly
Meel (die)n. mail
Meelmann (der)n.; Meelmenner, pl. letter carrier
meene, v.; gemeent, pp. 1.express an opinion; 2.intend; 3.mean; 5.think
meenich, adj (gut --) good-hearted
Meening (die)n. 1.intention; 2.meaning; 3.opinion; 4.(die -- saage) give one a piece of one's mind
Meerreddich (die)n. horseradish
Meerreddichbrie (der)n. pap with horseradish and egg
meeschdere, v.; gemeeschdert, pp. 1.master; 2.prevail
Meeschdern (die)n. mistress
Meeschderwatzel (die)n. masterwort
Meesel (der)n.; Meesle, pl. chisel
meesele, v.; gemeeselt, pp. chisel
meeylicherweis, adv. possibly
meh, adj. 1.any longer; 2.more; 3.any more
mehe, v.; gemeht, pp. 1.mow; 2.reap
Meher (der)n.; Meher, pl. mower (person)
Mehl (es)n. 1.flour; 2.meal
Mehlbrei (der)n. pap
Mehlgraut (es)n. meadow-sweet
mehlich, adj. 1.dusty; 2.floury; 3.mealy
Mehlkammer (die)n.; Mehlkammer, pl. pantry
Mehlkischt (die)n. flour chest
Mehlsack (der)n.; Mehlseck, pl. flour bag
Mehlschtaab (der)n. sweepings (of a gristmill)
Mehlsupp (die)n. porridge
Mehmaschien (die)n. 1.mower (machine); 2.reaper
mehner, adj. more
Mehrheet (die)n. 1.majority; 2.plurality
Mehrheit (die)n. majority
mehrschdens, adv. mostly
mehrscht, adj. most
Mehrzaahl (die)n. majority
mei(n); meiner; meini, poss. pron. mine
Meichelmaerder (der)n. assassin
meide, v.; gemeidt, pp. 1.avoid; 2.quit; 3.shun
meiglich, adv. probably
Meil (die)n.; Meile, pl. mile
meileweis, adv. (for) miles
meileweit, adv. miles away
Meilschtee (der)n..; Meilschtee, pl. milestone
mein(e)twege, adv. 1.for all I care; 2.for my sake; 3.on my account
Meind (der, die)n. mind
meinde, v.; gemeindt, pp. 1.mind; 2.remember; 3.obey
Meinding (die)n. shunning
Meinding halde (die)v.; Meinding ghalde, pp. shun
meiner Seel!, interj. my goodness
meiner Siwwe (noch eemol), interj. my goodness!
Meische (es)n. mousey
Meisel (es)n. mouse
meiseschtill, adv. 1.profoundly still; 2.still as a mouse
Meisli (es)n. mousey

112

Mm

Meislinescht / Mick

Meislinescht (es)n.; Meislineschder, pl. tangled hair
Meiy(er)un (der)n. sweet marjoram
Melaasich (der)n. 1.juice extracted by grasshoppers; 2.molasses
Melaasich Brot (es)n. molasses bread
Melasses (der)n. 1.juice exuded by grasshoppers;2.molasses
Melassich (der)n. molasses
Melassichkuche (der)n. molasses cake
Melassichriwwelboi (der)n. shoofly pie
Melassichriwwelkuche (der)n. shoofly cake
Melde (der)n 1.(wilder --) goosefoot; 2.(zaahmer --) (a) lamb's quarters; (b) orach
melde, v.; gemeldt, pp. 1.announce; 2.make known; 3.tell
Meldung (die)n. notification
Meliesegraut (es)n. balm
Melisse (die)n. 1.balm; 2.garden balm
melke, v.; gemolke, pp. milk
Melkeemer (der)n. milkpail
Melkerei (die)n. milking (in all its details)
Melkern (die)n. milkmaid
Melkkuh (die)n.; Melkkieh, pl. milch-cow
Melkschtul (der)n.; Melkschtiel, pl. milking stool
mellenkollisch, adj. 1.hypochondriac; 2.melancholic
Melloon (die)n. melon
Melluun (die)n. melon
Melodei (die)n. melody
Melodie (die)n. melody
Memm (die)n. 1.mom; 2.mother
Memmli (es)n. small metal can provided with a spout which had a perforated button on the end of it, used in feeding infants (the precursor of the nursing bottle)
menanner, adv. 1.in company; 2.jointly; 3.together; 4.(sie hen's --) (a) they are having an altercation; (b) they have an understanding; 5.(sie kenne's --) they get along well together
Meng(e) (die)n. 1.crowd; 2.herd; 3.number
menge, v.; gemengt, pp. mix
Mennche (es)n. 1.little man; 2.male (of birds); 3.also used for Memmli
Menner (der)n. man
Mennischt (der)n.; Mennischde, pl. Mennonite
Mennli (es)n.; Mennlin, pl. little man
mennlich, adj. 1.male; 2.manly; 3.masculine
Mensch (der)n.; Mensche, pl. 1.human being; 2.hussy; 3.mankind; 4.(en lebbischer --) silly person
menschde, adj (am --) 1.most; 2.most of all
menschdens, adv. mostly
Mensche (die)n., pl. people
Mensche(g)pflicht (die)n. moral duty
Menschealter (es)n. generation
Menschebruder (der)n.; Menscherbrieder, pl. fellow man
menschedenke seit, adv. as far back as memory goes
Menschefeind (der)n. misanthrope
Menschefreind (der)n. philanthropist
Menschefresser (der)n.; Menschefrresser, pl. cannibal

Menschegfiehl (es)n. sympathy
Menscheglick (es)n. human happiness
Menschehass (der)n. misanthropy
Menschehatz (es)n. human heart
Menschehilf (die)n. human aid
Menschekind (es)n. human being
Menschekunscht (die)n. human ability
Menschelewe (es)n. human life
Menschepflicht (die)n. moral duty
menscheschei, adj. 1.shy; 2.solitary
Menscheschinner (der)n. 1.grinder; 2.tyrant
Menscheschproch (die)n. human speech
Menscheverschtand (der)n. (human) understanding
Menschewaerrick (es)n. work of man
Menschheet (die)n. human kind
menschlich, adj. human
menscht, adj. most
menschtdeel, adv. mostly
mer, pron. (unaccented form) 1.one; 2.to me; 3.we
mern = mer e (geb -- boss) give me a kiss
meschde, v.; gmescht, pp. fatten (animals)
meschdere, v.; gemeschdert, pp. master
Mesgraut (es)n. white helebore (Veratruum virdi)
Mess (die)n. 1.mass; 2.unbloody sacrifice of the cross; 3.(en schtilli --) low mass
Mess (es)n. brass
Messband (es)n. tape measure
messe, adj. (of) brass
messe, v.; gemesse, pp. 1.contain; 2.gage; 3.hold; 4.measure; 5.survey
Messer (es)n.; Messere, pl. knife
Messergling (die)n. knife blade
Messerkling (die)n. knife blade
Messerkolwe (der)n. haft of a knife
Messerli (es)n. penknife
Messerschaed (die)n. knife sheath
Messerschneid (die)n. knife-edge
Messerschpitze (der)n. 1.pinch (in cooking); 2.point of a knife
Messerschtang (die)n.; Messerschtange, pl. Pitman rod (on a mower)
Messerschtiel (der)n. knife-handle
Messgewand (es)n. vestments
messich, adj. (of) brass
messing, adj. (of) brass
Messraad (es)n.; Messredder, pl. perambulator
Messraahm (der)n. foot measure
Messung (die)n. measurement
Metaal (es)n. metal
Metilde (die)n. Matilda
Metzelsupp (die)n. gift of liver pudding, sausage, etc. made at butchering time
metzle, v.; gemetzelt, pp. 1.butcher; 2.massacre
Miau! meow!
mich (accusative), pron. 1.me; 2.myself
Michel (der)n. Michael
Mick (die)n.; Micke, pl. 1.fly; 2.(en -- nei/duh) stick a drink

Mm

Mickebabier

Mickebabier (es)n. fly paper
Mickeblaschder (es)n. plaster of Spanish fly
Mickedeer (e) (die)n. screen door
Mickedier(e) (die)n. screen door
Mickefall (die)n. fly trap
Mickefenschder (es)n. screen (for window)
Mickegaarn (es)n. fly net
Mickegraut (es)n. wild indigo
Mickegschar (es)n. fly net
Mickeschiss (der)n. flyspeck
Mickevieh (es)n. pest of flies
Mickeweddel (der)n. fly chaser
Mickewehrer (der)n. fly chaser
Mickewoch (die)n. Fly Week
Middaag (der)n. 1.dinner; 2.midday; 3.noon
Middaagarewett (die)n. noon chores
Middaagesse (es)n. dinner (noon meal)
Middaagseit (die)n. south side
Middaagszeit (die)n. noon-time
midde darrich, adv. 1.across; 2.right through
midde unner, adv. amidst
Midde(r)nacht (die)n. midnight
midde(s), adv. 1.amid; 2.in the middle of
Middel (es)n. 1.remedy; 2.run-around; 3.whitlow
Middelalder (es)n. 1.medieval times; 2.middle age of life
middelbaar, adj. 1.indirect; 2.mediate
middeleldich, adj. middle aged
Middelelt (die)n. middle age
Middelheech (die)n. medium height
middelmaessich, adj. 1.medium; 2.moderate; 3.so-so; 4.tolerable
middelmaessich, adv. 1.medium; 2.so-so
Middelmann (der)n. middle-man
Middelmehl (es) n. 1.chop; 2.middlings; 3.shot; 4.second quality flour
Middelmo(o)s (es)n. 1.average; 2.mean; 3.moderation
Middelnaame (der)n. middle name
Middelpunkt (der)n. center (point)
Middelring (der)n. 1.(split) ring (joining the single-tree to the double-tree); 2.middle-ring
middelscht, adj. middle
Middelwand (die)n. partition wall
middle, v.; gemiddelt, pp. (sich --) meddle
mied, adj. 1.fatigued; 2.tired; 3.weary; 4.(-- warre) tire; 5.(sich -- laafe) tire oneself walking
Miedichkeet (die)n. 1.fatigue; 2.tiredness; 3.weariness
Miedichkeit (die)n. 1.fatigue; 2.tiredness; 3.weariness
mieglich, adv. 1.possible; 2.probable
Mieh (die)n. 1.pains; 2.trouble; 3.(-- wert dei) (to be) worth the trouble
Miehl (die)n.; Miehle, pl. mill
Miehldamm (der)n.; Miehldemmer, pl. milldam
Miehldeich (der)n. millpond
Miehlmacher (der)n.; Miehlmacher, pl. millwright
Miehlraad (es)n.; Miehlredder, pl. millwheel
Miehlsaal (die)n. difficulty

Minuddezoiyer

Miehlschtaab (der)n. mill sweepings
Miehlschtee (der)n.; Miehlschtee, pl. millstone
Miehlschteehacker (der)n. millstone cutter
Miehlseelichkeit (die)n. 1.weariness; 2.wretchedness
miehseelich, adj. 1.tiresome; 2.wearisome; 3.wretched
Mielikeffer (der)n. parasitic animal
mieseelich, adj. toilsome
miessich, adj. idle
Miessichgang (der)n. idleness
Miessichkeet (die)n. idleness
mild, adj. 1.gentle; 2.meek; 3.placid
Mildaagraut (es)n. mildewy weeds
Milichschlebbes (es)n. milk-pie
Militz (der)n. militia
Mill(i)yoon (die)n. million
mill(i)yooneweis, adv. (by the) millions
Mill(i)yuun (die)n. million
mill(i)yuuneweis, adv. (by the) millions
Milldaa (der)n. mildew
milldaaich, adj. mildewed
Miller (der)n.; Miller, pl. 1.miller; 2.(der schtaawich --) dusty miller (plant)
Millich (die)n. 1.milk; 2.(maageri --) skim(med) milk
Millichboi (der)n. milk-pie
Millichbrei (der)n. pap
Millicherei (die)n. dairy
Millichfewer (es)n. 1.garget; 2.milk-fever
Millichflitscher (der)n. milk-pie (Hamburg Versammling)
Millichgraawe (der)n. water channel of a spring house
Millichgraut (es)n. 1.milkweed; 2.pleurisy root; 3.wild lettuce
Millichhaar (die)n. down (on the cheek)
Millichhaffe (der)n. milk crock
Millichhaus (es)n.; Millichheiser, pl. 1.dairy; 2.milkhouse
Millichkann (die)n. milk-can
Millichkeller (der)n. cellar for cooling and keeping milk
Millichkuh (die)n.; Mellichkieh, pl. milk-cow
Millichmann (der)n. milkman
Millichmolge (die)n., pl. milk whey
Millichoder (die)n. lacteal vein
Millichsaft (die)n. chyle
Millichseiche (es)n. little pig
Millichseih (die)n. milk-strainer
Millichwagge (der)n. milk wagon
Millichzaah (der)n.; Millichzeh, pl. milk-tooth
Millichzoh (der)n.; Millichzeh, pl. milk-tooth
Mils (die)n. spleen
Milsgranket (die)n. melancholia
Milsgrankheet (die)n. melancholia
milsich, adj. 1.melancholic; 2.splenetic
Milz (die)n. spleen
milzich, adj. splenetic
Minderheet (die)n. minority
Minderheit (die)n. minority
mindlich, adv. orally
Minsfleesch (es)n. mincemeat
Minuddezoiyer (der)n. minute hand

Mm

Minutt / mitnichdem

Minutt (die)n.; Minudde, pl. minute
mir (dative), pron. me
mir, pron. we (accented form)
Mischbel (die)n. persimmon
Mischblebaam (der)n.; Mischblebeem, pl. persimmon tree
Mischbleholz (es)n. persimmon wood
mischde, v.; g(e)mischt, pp. 1.fertilize; 2.manure
mischdich, adj. covered with manure
Mischt (der)n. 1.dung; 2.manure
Mischtbrieh (die)n. 1.manure-juice; 2.manure-liquor
Mischtgawwel (die)n.; Mischtgawwele, pl. manure fork
Mischthaufe (der)n.; Mischtheife, pl. 1.dunghill;
        2.manure pile
Mischthinkel (es)n. common barnyard fowl
Mischthof (der)n.; Mischthe(e)f, pl. 1.barnyard;
        2.manure pile in the barnyard
Mischthoke (der)n. manure hook (for unloading manure)
Mischtschlidde (der)n. 1.manure sled; 2.sledge (on runners)
Mischtschpraehe (der)n. one who spreads manure
Mischtschpreeder (der) n. manure spreader (machine or
        person)
Mischtschpreher (der) n. manure spreader (machine or
        person)
Mischtwagge (der)n. manure wagon
miseraawel, adj. 1.poor; 2.miserable
Miss (die)n. premature birth
Miss(g)falle (es)n. displeasure
Miss(gebort) (die)n. miscarriage
missbrauche, v.; (ge)missbraucht, pp. 1.abuse; 2.mistreat;
        3.misuse
Missdeitung (die)n. misconstruction
missdraue, v.; (ge)missdraut, pp. 1.distrust; 2.mistrust
missdrauisch, adj. 1.distrustful; 2.jealous; 3.suspicious
misse, v.; gemisst, pp. 1.have to; 2.must
Missfalle (es)n. displeasure
missfellich, adj. unacceptable
missfolye, v.; miss(g)folkt, pp. disobey
missgunnisch, adj. 1.begrudging; 2.envious
Missgunscht (die)n. envy
misshandle, v.; misshandelt, pp. mistreat
Misshandlung (die)n. mistreatment
Mission (die)n. mission
Missionsbreddich (die)n. missionary sermon
Missionsbreddicher (der)n. missionary preacher
Missionsgeld (es)n. money for foreign missions
misslich, adj. 1.critical; 2.doubtful; 3.uncertain
missvergunne, v.; missvergunnt, pp. 1.begrudge; 2.envy
missvergunnisch, adj. 1.begrudging; 2.envious; 3.jealous
missvergunnt, adj. envied
Missvergunscht (die)n. envy
Missverschtand (der)n. misunderstanding
missverschteh, v.; missverschtanne, pp. misunderstand
Missverschtendnis (es)n. misunderstanding
mit naegschdem, adv. (very) soon
mit(e)nanner, adv. 1.in company; 2.jointly; 3.together;
        4.(sie hen's --) (a) they are having an altercation;

(b) they have an understanding; 5.(sie kenne's --)
they get along well together
mit(e)nenner, adv. together
mit/bede, v.; mitgebet, pp. join in prayer
mit/bringe, v.; mitgebrocht, pp. bring along
mit/daerfe, v.; mitgedaerft, pp. be allowed to come or go
        along
mit/danse, v.; mitgedanst join in a dance
mit/deele, v.; mitgedeelt, pp. 1.impart; 2.share
mit/draage, v.; mitgedraage, pp. carry along
mit/eischtimme, v.; miteigschtimmt, pp. 1.agree to;
        2.chime in with
mit/esse, v.; mitgesse, pp. join in eating
mit/faahre, v.; mitgfaahre, pp. ride (drive) along with
mit/fridde, v (-- losse) let alone
mit/geh, v.; mitgange, pp. 1.accompany; 2.go with
mit/gewwe, v.; is mitgewwe, pp. give to take along with
mit/helfe, v.; mitgholfe, pp. 1.assist; 2.help along;
        3.extend a hand
mit/hole, v.; mitgholt, pp. bring along
mit/kenne, v.; mitgekennt, pp. be able to go along
mit/koche, v.; mitgekocht, pp. cook several things together
mit/kumme, v.; is mitkumme, pp. come along with
mit/laafe, v.; geloffe, pp. walk along with
mit/lache, v.; mitgelacht, pp. join in the laugh
mit/leide, v.; mitgelidde, pp. 1.suffer with others;
        2.sympathize
mit/leidich, adj. compassionate
mit/locke, v.; mitgelockt, pp. entice
mit/mache, v.; mitgemacht, pp. 1.get along with others;
        2.join in; 3.participate; 4.take part
mit/nemme, v.; mitgenumme, pp. take along with
mit/reide, v.; mitgeridde, pp. ride along with
mit/schaffe, v.; mitgschafft, pp. work along with
mit/schicke, v.; mitgschickt, pp. send along with
mit/schleefe, v.; mitgschleeft, pp. drag along with
mit/schpiele, v.; mitgschpielt, pp. play along with
mit/singe, v.; mitgsunge, pp. sing along
mit/wolle, v.; mitgewollt, pp. want to go along
mit/yuwele, v.; mitgeyuwelt, pp. rejoice along with
mit/ziege, v.; mitgezogge, pp. move along with
mit/ziehe, v.; mitgezogge, pp. pull along with
mit, adv. along
mit, prep. with
mitaus/duh, v.; mituasgeduh, pp. do without
mitaus, conj. 1.except; 2.unless
Mitbruder (der)n. fellow man
Mitgfiehl (es)n. 1.compassion; 2.fellow-feeling; 3.sympathy
Mitgift (die)n. present
Mitglied (es)n.; Mitglieder, pl. member
Mithilf (die)n. 1.aid; 2.assistance
Mitleid(es) (es)n. 1.compassion; 2.sympathy
Mitmensch (der)n. fellow man
Mitnacht (die)n. midnight
mitnachts, adv. (at) midnight
mitnichdem, adv. (by no) means

115

Mm

mitnichtem / munder

mitnichtem, adv. 1.by no means; 2.emphatically not

mitsamde, prep. together with

mitschtimmich, adj. harmonious

Mitschtreiter (der)n. rival

Mitt (die)n. middle

mitt/schtimme, v.; mitgschtimmt, pp. agree

Mitte(r)nacht (die)n. midnight

mittle, v.; gemittelt, pp. (sich --) meddle

Mittler (der)n. mediator

Mittwoch (der)n. Wednesday

mitweegs, adv. 1.halfway; 2.midway

mitzamde(n), prep. together with

mitzamte(n), prep. 1.and all; 2.together with

Mobskopp (der)n.; Mobskepp, pl. 1.dullard; 2.dunce

Moddel (die)n.; Moddle, pl. 1.model; 2.mould (for tallow candles); 3.pattern

Mode (die)n. 1.custom; 2.fashion

Mohlzeit (die)n. wedding

Moi (der)n. May

Moiabbel (der)n.; Moiebbel, pl. 1.May apple; 2.mandrake

Moiblumm (die)n.; Moiblumme, pl. 1.lily of the valley; 2.May apple

moiye, v.; gemoit, pp. picnic on May 1

Mol (die)n. 1.mark; 2.mole (rodent); 3.scar

Mol (es)n. time

mol, adv. 1. once (upon a time); 2. (-- gschwiege) not to mention

mole, v.; gemolt, pp. 1.draw; 2.sketch; 3.paint with oils

Moler (der)n.; Moler, pl. 1.painter; 2.scar

moli, adv. once (upon a time)

Molke (die)n., pl. whey

Molkebeer (die)n. cloudy berry

Molkesupp (die)n. contemptuous for a thin watery soup

Mollekopp (der)n. tadpole

Molligropp (der)n.; Molligrobbe, pl. tadpole

mondgrank, adj. lunatic

Mondhof (der)n. halo (of the moon)

Monet (der)n. month

monetlich, adv. monthly

monetweis, adv. 1.by the month; 2.now and then a month

moobsich, adj. sulky

Moon(d) (der)n.; Moon(d)e, pl. moon

Moon(d)uffgang (der)n. rising of the moon

Moon(d)unnergang (der)n. setting of the moon

Moondaag (der)n. Monday

Moondkalb (es)n. 1.lunatic; 2.man in the moon; 3.mole (rodent)

Moondraude (die)n. honesty (plant)

Moondschei (der)n. moonshine

moondsichdich, adj. somnambular

Moondwechsel (der)n. change of the moon

Moongringel (der)n. halo (of the moon)

moopse, v.; gmoopst, pp. sulk

Moos (es)n. 1.measure; 2.moss

Mooschi (der)n. taffy

Mops (der)n. 1.dull person; 2.dwarf; 3.mope

mopse, v.; gemopst, pp. sulk

mopsich, adv. 1.dwarflike; 2.mopish

Mopskopp (der)n. 1.mope; 2.stupid fellow

Moraal (die)n. morality

moraalisch, adj. having good morals

morallisch, adj. moral

Mord (der)n. 1.murder; 2.(zum -- sackerment), interj.; 3.damn it!; 4.hell and damnation!

Mores (die)n., pl. manners

Mos (es)n. measure

Moschdert (der)n. 1.charlock; 2.mustard

Moschgieder (der)n.; Moschgieders, pl. mosquito

Moschk (der)n. musk

Moschkopp (der)n. 1.mope; 2.stupid fellow

Moschmehl (es)n. 1.cornmeal; 2.mush-meal

Moscht (der)n. must

Mostert (der)n. 1.charlock; 2.mustard

Motto (es)n. motto

Muck (die)n.; Mucke, pl. 1.fly; 2.(en -- nei/duh) stick a drink

mucke, v.; gemuckt, pp. (sich --) 1.budge; 2.move; 3.stir

Muckeblaschder (es)n. plaster of Spanish fly

Muckedeer (die)n. screen door

Muckedier (die)n. screen door

Muckefenschder (es)n. screen (for window)

Muckewoch (die)n. Fly Week

Mudder (die)n. 1.nut (of a bolt); 2.mother (of vinegar); 3.uterus; 4.womb

Mudder (die)n.; Midder; Middere, pl. mother

Mudder ihre Schwescher (der)n. mother's sister (aunt)

muddere, v.; gemuddert, pp. (sich --) resemble (act like) one's mother

Muddergichdre (die) n., pl. 1. hysterics; 2. puerperal convulsions

Muddergraut (es)n. 1.motherwort; 2.Oswego tea

Mudderkaern (die)n. kernel of large size

Mudderleib (der)n. mother's womb

mudderlich, adj. maternal

Muddermaerrick (es)n. mole (on skin)

Muddermard (der)n. matricide

Mudderschof (die)n.; Mudderscheef, pl. ewe

Mudderschprooch (die)n. 1.mother tongue; 2.vernacular

mudderseelichallee, adv. absolutely alone

Mudderwaerm (die)n., pl. supposed cause of rabies in dogs (located under the tongue)

Mudderweh (es)n. hysterics

mudich, adj 1.bold; 2.courageous; 3.daring; 4.spirited

muffle, v.; gmuffelt, pp. speak indistinctly

Muh! moo!

Muhlikuh (die)n; Muhlekieh, pl. "mooley" cow

Mulder, (der)n. 1.miller's toll; 2.multure

muldere, v.; gemuldert, pp. (take the) miller's toll

Mullikopp (der)n. tadpole

mummle, v.; gemummelt, pp. mumble

Mumps (der)n. mumps

Mund (der)n.(rare) mouth

munder, adj. 1.active; 2.hale; 3.lively; 4.well

Mm

munder

munder, adv. 1.healthy; 2.well

Mundschtick (es) n. 1. mouth; 2. mouthpiece (of an instrument); 3.voice

munet, adv (alli --) monthly

Munet (der)n. 1.month; 2.(hinne im --) at the end of the month

munetlich, adj., adv. monthly

munetweis, adj.; adv. by the month

Munfinschderniss (die)n. eclipse of the moon

Munkler (der)n. 1.intriguer; 2.sneak

Munterkeet (die)n. 1.liveliness; 2.vivacity

mupse, v.; gemupst, pp. sulk

mupsich, adj. 1.stupid; 2.sulky; 3.ugly

Mupskoop (der)n. sulky person

murre, v.; gemurrt, pp. croak

Mus(s)fress (es)n. tear-thumb

Muschder (es)n. pattern

Muschderbuch (es)n. pattern book

muschdere, v.; gemuschdert, pp. (sich --) dress up

Muschel (der)n. 1.clam; 2.mussel; 3.shell

Muschgaadnuss (die)n. nutmeg

Muschgratt (die)n. muskrat

Muschgrott (die)n. muskrat

Muschkaadbliet (die)n. mace

Muschkaadnuss (die)n. nutmeg

Muschkeet (die)n. musket

Muschkratt (die)n. muskrat

Muschmelon (die)n.; Muschmelone, pl. muskmelon

Musik (die)n. music

musikaalisch, adj. musical

Musikant (der)n. musician

Musslien (der)n. muslin

Mut (der)n 1.courage; 2.humor; 3.valor; 4.(schlecht zu -- sei) (to be) crabby

mutlos, adv. 1.dejected; 2.discouraged

mutmaase, v.; gemutmaast, pp. 1.presume; 2.surmise

Mutmaasing (die)n. 1.conjecture; 2.presumption; 3.supposition; 4.surmise

mutmaase, v.; gemutmaast, pp. conjecture

mutmoos(s)e, v.; gemutmoost, pp. 1.conjecture;2.presume; 3.surmise

Mutmoosing (die)n. 1.presumption; 2.supposition; 3.surmise

Mutse (die)n., pl. Sunday-go-to-meeting coat (Mennonite)

mutsich, adj. 1.fretful; 2.sulky; 3.touchy

Mutwille (der)n. mischief

mutwillich, adj. 1.malicious; 2.mischievous; 3.playful

mutwillicherweis, adv. 1.intentionally; 2.maliciously

Mutze (der)n.; Mutze, pl. 1.swallowtail; 2.tailcoat

mutzich, adj. 1.fretful; 2.sulky; 3.touchy

Muun(d) (der)n.; Muun(d)e, pl. moon

Muundaag (der)n. Monday

muunhell, adj. moonlit

Muunhelling (die)n. moonlight

Muunlicht (es)n. moonlight

Myusick

Muusfress (es)n. tear-thumb

Myusick (die)n. music

Nn

'n

naggel

'n, pron. 1.a; 2.him; 3.it

Na!, interj. exclamation of impatience (as on failing to thread a needle, or in dropping something, or in knocking against something)

Naab (die)n. 1.hub; 2.nave

naage, v.; genaagt, pp. 1.gnaw; 2.wear

naah/kumme, v.; naahkumme, pp. approach

Naahe (die)n. neighborhood

naahrhafdich, adj. nutritious

naahrhaft, adj. nutritious

Naahring (die)n. nourishment

Naahrung (die)n. nourishment

Naahrungssaft (die)n. chyle

Naahrungsschtofft (es)n. nourishment

Naame (der)n.; Neeme, pl. 1.name; 2.(ledderlich --) maiden name; 3.(schlechder --) (bad) reputation

Naamebuch (es)n. dictionary

Naamegrischt (der)n. 1.pseudo-Christian; 2.pretending Christian

naamens, adv. by the name of

Naamewatt (es)n. noun

Naas (die)n.; Nees, pl. 1.nose; 2.(-- hoch draage) (to be) proud; 3.(-- in alles schtecke) poke one's nose in every-body's business; 4.(-- nuff/runsle) turn up one's nose; 5.(-- ringle) turn up one's nose; 6.(-- runsle) act super-ciliously; 7.(eem ebbes unnich -- reiwe) cast something in a person's teeth; 8.(zu viel in -- hawwe) (to be) tipsy

Naasbee (es)n. nasal bone

Naasegschwetz (es)n. nasal speech

Naasepetzer (der)n. 1.pince-nez; 2.eyeglasses clipped to the nose by a spring

Naaseweis (die)n. smarty

Naasharn (es)n. rhinoceros

naasich, adj. nosey

Naaskaerwerli (es)n.; Naaskaerwerlin, pl. nose-cover (of screen cloth for horse's nose, to protect against flies)

Naasloch (es)n.; Naaslecher, pl. nostril

Naawering (der)n. hub ring

Naazrett (es)n. Nazareth

nach = noch (rare usage)

Nache (der)n. nape (or back of the neck)

nachlessich, adj. negligent

Nacht (die)n.; Nachde; Necht, pl. night

Nachtaerwett (die)n. night work

Nachtblumm (die)n.; Nachtblumme, pl. night-blooming cereus

Nachteil (die)n.; Nachteile, pl. 1.night-hawk; 2.screech owl

Nachtesse (es)n. supper

Nachtgleed (es)n. night-dress

Nachtgschaerr (es)n. (chamber) pot

Nachthaffe (der)n.; Nachthaffe, pl. chamber pot

Nachthemm (es)n.; Nachthemmer, pl. 1.nightgown; 2.nightshirt

Nachtigaal (die)n. nightingale

Nachtkapp (die)n. night cap

Nachtkutt (die)n.; Nachtkudde, pl. nightgown

nachtlich, adv. nocturnal

Nachtlicht (es)n.; Nachtlichder, pl. night-light

Nachtluft (die)n. night air

Nachtmol (es)n. Holy Communion

nachts, adv. (at) night

Nachtschadde (der) n. 1. black nightshade; 2. deadly nightshade; 3.four o'clock

Nachtschtuhl (der)n. chamber stool

Nachtschwitze (es)n. night-sweat

Nachtwandler (der)n. sleepwalker

Nachtwechder (der)n. night watchman

Nacke (der)n. 1.back of the neck; 2.shoulders

nacke, v.; genackt, pp. rest heavily (upon)

nackich, adj. 1.bare; 2.naked; 3.nude

nadd(e), adv. 1.north; 2.toward the north

Nadde (die)n. 1.north; 2.(gege --) toward the north

naddewescht, adv. northwest(erly)

naddlich, adv. northward

Naddlicht (es)n. aurora borealis (northern lights)

Naddschein (der)n. aurora borealis

Naddschtann (die)n. North Star

Naddseit (die)n. north side

Naddweschtwind (der)n. northwest wind

Naddwind (der)n. north wind

nadierlich, adj. 1.naive; 2.natural; 3.physical

nadierlich, adv. naturally

Nadierlichkeet (die)n. naturalness

Nadierlichkeit (die)n. naturalness

Nadurbeschaffenheet (die)n. natural quality

Nadurfarscher (der)n. naturalist

Nadurgaab (die)n. natural gift

Nadurtrieb (der)n. urging of the bowels

Naduur (die)n. nature

Nae(h)disch (der)n. sewing table

Naegli (es)n. clove

Naeh (die)n. neighborhood

naehe, v.; genaeht, pp. sew

Naehern (die)n. 1.dressmaker; 2.seamstress

Naehes (es)n. sewing

Naehkaerwel (es)n. sewing basket

Naehmaschien (die)n.; Naehmaschiene, pl. sewing machine

naehre, v.; genaehrt, pp. 1.nourish; 2.sustain

Naehseide (der)n. sewing silk

naekscht, adv. 1.close; 2.near; 3.nearest; 4.next; 5.(mit [bei] naekschtem) (very) soon

naekschtbescht, adv. next best

naemlich, adj. 1.namely; 2.same

Naer(re)v (die)n. nerve

naerdlich, adv. 1.northerly; 2.toward the north

Naerf (die)n.; Naerfe, pl. nerve

Naerfefiewer (es)n. 1.neurosis; 2.nervous fever

naerfich, adj. 1.nervous; 2.sinewy

Naerveweh (es)n. neuralgia

naeryets, adv. nowhere

Naggel (der)n. Neggel, pl. 1.nail; 2. (en gschnittner--) a forged nail

naggel, v.; genaggelt, pp. nail

Nn

Naggelbohre

Naggelbohre (der)n.; Naggelbohre, pl. gimlet
Naggeleeche (die)n. pin-oak
naggelfascht, adj. immovable
naggelfescht, adj. immovable
Naggelfluss (der)n. 1.felon; 2.whitlow
Naggelgraut (es)n. burnet
naggelnei, adj. brand new
Nammidaag (der)n. afternoon
nanner, pron. 1.each other; 2.one another
nannerno, adv. 1. in rapid succession; 2.one in pursuit of
    another
Narb (die)n. scar
nard, interj. then, lo!
Nard(e) (die)n. north
nard, adv. north
nardlich, adv. northerly
Nardlicht (es)n. aurora borealis
Nardschein (der)n. aurora borealis
Nardschtaern (die)n. northern polestar
nardwescht, adv. northwest(erly)
Nardweschtwind (der)n. northwest wind
Nardwind (der)n. north wind
Naref (die)n.; Narefe, pl. nerve
narefich, adj. nervous
Narr (der)n.; Narre, pl. 1.clown; 2.fool; 3.idiot; 4.lunatic;
    5.(fer en -- halde) (a) fool; (b) make a fool of
narre, adv. only
narre, v.; genatt; gnaart, pp. 1.act foolishly; 2.(to play) pranks
Narreboss (die)n. foolish prank
Narrehaus (es)n. insane asylum
Narreschtick (es)n. nonsense
Narreschtreech (die)n., pl. 1.folly; 2.tomfoolery
Narreschwetz (es)n. foolish talk
Narrheet (die)n. 1.folly; 2.fooler
narrisch, adj. 1.crazy; 2.foolish; 3.insane; 4.mad; 5.
    (-- gschwetz) (a) foolish talk; (b) obscenities
Narrischkeet (die)n. craziness
naryets, adv. nowhere
Nascht (der)n.; Nescht, pl. 1.branch; 2.bough; 3.limb (tree)
naschtich, adj. branchy
nass, adj. 1.wet; 2.(-- mache) (a) rain; (b) wet
Nasseweis (die)n. smarty
nasslich, adj. 1.damp; 2.moist; 3.wetness
nau, adv. 1.now; 2.(vun -- aa) henceforth
Naube (die)n., pl. 1.cunning; 2.difficulty of
    accomplishment; 3.tricks
naus/barge, v.; nausgebarkt, pp. lend
naus/baue, v.; nausgebaut, pp. built out
naus/biege, v.; nausgeboge, pp. bend out
naus/binne, v.; nausgebunne, pp. tie outside
naus/blabbere, v.; nausgeblabbert, pp. blab
naus/blaere, v.; nausgeblaert, pp. 1.blare out; 2.spread
    reports
naus/blaffe, v.; nausgeblafft, pp. spread reports
naus/bluge, v.; nausgeblugt, pp. plow in a
    counter-clockwise direction

naus/schicke

naus/breche, v.; nausgebroche, pp. break out
naus/briggle, v.; nausgebriggelt, pp. drive out with a club
naus/bringe, v.; nausbegrocht, pp. bring out
naus/dinge, v.; nausgedingt, pp. hire out
naus/draage, v.; nausgedraage, pp. carry out
naus/dredde, v.; nausgedredde, pp. kick out
naus/dreiwe, v.; nausgedriwwe, pp. drive out
naus/dresche, v.; nausgedrosche, pp. flog out (of a place)
naus/duh, v.; nausgeduh, pp. 1.eject; 2.oust; 3.put out
naus/faahre, v.; nausgfaahre, pp. haul or drive out
naus/falle, v.; nausgfalle, pp. fall out
naus/fege, v.; nausgfegt, pp. 1.clean; 2.scrub out
naus/fiehre, v.; nausgfiehrt, pp. lead out
naus/foddere, v.; nausgfoddert, pp. challenge
naus/gaerwe, v.; nausgegaerbt, pp. flog out (of a place)
naus/geeschle, v.; nausgegeeschelt, pp. drive out with a
    whip
naus/geh, v.; nausgange, pp. go out
naus/gewwe, v.; nausgewwe, pp. give out
naus/greische, v.; nausgegrische, pp. call out
naus/gucke, v.; nausgeguckt, pp. look out
naus/helfe, v.; nausgholfe, pp. help out (of a place)
naus/hickle, v.; nausghickelt, pp. hobble out
naus/hupse, v.; nausghupst, pp. hop out
naus/keere, v.; nausgekeert, pp. belong outside
naus/kenne, v.; nausgekennt, pp. be able to get out
naus/kumme, v.; nauskumme, pp. come out (to a place)
naus/laafe, v.; nausgeloffe, pp. 1.run out (of liquids);
    2.walk out
naus/lache, v.; nausgelacht, pp. burst out laughing
naus/lange, v.; nausgelangt, pp. 1.hand out; 2.reach out
naus/leichte, v.; nausgeleicht, pp. light the way out
naus/locke, v.; nausgelockt, pp. entice out
naus/mache, v.; nausgemacht, pp. 1.(iwwer ebber --) (a)
    backbite; (b) pick flaws in a person; (c) speak ill of
    someone; 2. (sich --) (a) get out; (b) go out; 4. (soot --)
    (to do) seeding (of wheat and rye) sow a field
naus/misse, v.; nausgemisst, pp. be obliged to go out
naus/packe, v.; nausgepackt, pp. (sich --) 1.be gone;
    2.get out
naus/reeche, v.; nausgereecht, pp. reach out
naus/reide, v.; nausgridde, pp. ride out
naus/renne, v.; nausgerennt, pp. 1.bolt out of a house;
    2.thrust out
naus/ricke, v.; nausgerickt, pp. move out
naus/rolle, v.; nausgerollt, pp. roll out
naus/rufe, v.; nausgerufe, pp. call out
naus/rutsche, v.; gerutscht, pp. slide out
naus/saee, v.; nausgsaet, pp. 1.seed; 2.sow
naus/saehe, v.; nausgsaeht, pp. 1.seed; 2.sow
naus/schaere, v.; nausgschaert, pp. 1.scratch out; 2.sow
    poorly
naus/schaffe, v.; nausgschaft, pp. cause to get out
naus/schenke, v.; nausgschenkt, pp. give away
naus/scheppe, v.; nausgschebbt, pp. shovel out
naus/schicke, v.; nausgschickt, pp. send out

Nn

naus/schidde

naus/schidde, v.; nausgschitt, pp. pour out
naus/schiddle, v.; nausgschiddelt, pp. shake out
naus/schiesse, v.; nausgschosse, pp. shoot or gush out
naus/schiewe, v.; nausgschowe, pp. 1.postpone; 2.push out
naus/schlagge, v.; nausgschlagge, pp. 1.drive a person out by blows; 2.knock out
naus/schleefe, v.; nausgschleeft, pp. drag out
naus/schleese, v.; nausgschlosse, pp. lock out
naus/schlenkere, v.; nausgschlenkert, pp. fling out
naus/schlippe, v.; nausgschlippt, pp. slip out
naus/schluppe, v.; nausgschluppt, pp. crawl out
naus/schmeisse, v.; nausgschmisse, pp. 1.eject; 2.throw out
naus/schnaufe, v.; nausgschnauft, pp. exhale
naus/schnelle, v.; nausgschnellt, pp. fling out
naus/schpaerre, v.; nausgschpaert, pp. 1.bar out; 2.pen out
naus/schpanne, v.; nausgschpannt, pp. stretch or put up (a rope)
naus/schpaue, v.; nausgschpaut, pp. spit out
naus/schpringe, v.; nausschprunge, pp. run out
naus/schtaerze, v.; nausgschtaerzt, pp. tumble out
naus/schtecke, v.; nausgschteckt, pp. 1.protrude; 2.stick out
naus/schtehle, v.; nausgschtole, pp. (sich --) sneak out
naus/schteige, v.; nausgschtigge, pp. 1.alight; 2.climb out
naus/schtelle, v.; nausgschtellt, pp. set out
naus/schtocke, v.; nausgschtockt, pp. plod somewhere with a cane
naus/schtolbere, v.; nausgschtolbert, pp. stumble out
naus/schtosse, v.; nausgschtosse, pp. thrust out
naus/sehne, v.; nausgsehne, pp. look out
naus/setze, v.; nausgsetzt, pp. 1.dispossess; 2.set out
naus/solle, v.; nausgsollt, pp. ought to go out
naus/vendere, v.; nausgvendert, pp. (sich --) venture out
naus/weise, v.; nausgwisse, pp. 1.order out; 2.show out
naus/wickle, v.; nausgewickelt, pp. 1.eject; 2.hustle out
naus/winsche, v.; nausgwinscht, pp. wish someone would leave
naus/yaage, v.; nausgyaagt, pp. chase out
naus/zackere, v.; nausgezackert, pp. jog out
naus, adv. out of
nauszus, prep. (on the way) going (out)
Nawwel (der)n.; Nawwel; Newwel, pl. 1.navel; 2.umbilicus
Nawwelbinn (die)n. navel band
Nawwelbruch (der)n. umbilical hernia
Nawwelschnur (die)n. umbilical cord
ne = ihne, dat. pl. 1.from; 2.of; 3.to them
nechtlich, adv. nightly
neck(s)e, v.; geneckt, pp. 1.tantalize; 2.tease
neck(s)ich, adj. tantalizing
nee, adv. 1.nay; 2.no
neecher, adv. 1.rather; 2.sooner
needich, adj. 1.in need; 2.needy
needich, adv. necessary
neediche, v.; geneedicht, pp. 1.beseech; 2.invite; 3.urge (to accept)
needlich, adj. 1.cross; 2.touchy; 3.in heat (of horses)

nei/drede

neegscht am Dapeet, adv. (in the) nick of time
neegscht, adv. close
neegscht; neecher; neegscht, adv. near; nearer; nearest
neegschtsichdich, adj. near-sighted
neemlich, adj.; adv. namely
Neez (der)n. thread
Neezfaadem (der)n. thread
Neezfadde (der)n. thread
Neger (der)n.; Neger, pl. Negro
negere, v.; gnegert, pp. slave
Negg(e)li (es)n. 1.carnation; 2.clove; 3.small nail
Negg(e)li (es)n.; Negg(e)lin, pl. clove
Neggel (der)n.; Neggel, pl. nail
Neggelche (es)n.; Neggelcher, pl. 1.carnation; 2.clove; 3.small nail
Neggelrobber (der)n. claw-hammer
negscht, adj. next
negschtbescht, adj. next best
Nehern (die)n. dressmaker
nehre, v.; genehrt, pp. nourish
Nei Teschdement (es)n. New Testament
Nei Yaahr (es)n. New Year
Nei Yarick (der)n. New York
Nei-ichkeit (die)n.; Neiichkeide, pl. novelty
Nei-Yaahr-Schitzli (es)n. the last one to get up on New Year's Day
Nei-Yaahr-Schlegel (der)n. the last one to get up on New Year's Day
nei/basse, v.; neigebasst, pp. fit in
nei/baue, v.; neigebaut, pp. build in
nei/beisse, v.; neigebisse, pp. bite into
nei/belse, v.; neigebelst, pp. pound in
nei/biege, v.; neigeboge, pp. bend in
nei/binne, v.; neigebunne, pp. tie in
nei/blabbere, v.; neigeblabbert, pp. blab in
nei/blaerre, v.; neigeblaerrt, pp. interrupt
nei/blaffe, v.; neigeblafft, pp. interrupt
nei/blanze, v.; neigeblanzt, pp. plant in or into
nei/blatsche, v.; neigeblatscht, pp. splash into
nei/blaudre, v.; neigeblaudert, pp. persuade
nei/blicke, v.; neigeblickt, pp. glance in or into
nei/blose, v.; neigeblose, p. blow in
nei/bluge, v.; neigeblugt, pp. plow in a clockwise direction
nei/breche, v.; neigebroche, pp. break into
nei/brenne, v.; neigebrennt, pp.; 1.burn into; 2.(eens --) (a) defraud; (b) give a blow
nei/bringe, v.; neigebrocht, pp. 1.bring in; 2.introduce (in a conversation)
nei/brockle, v.; neigebrockelt, pp. crumble into (as bread in milk)
nei/brunse, v.; neigebrunst, pp. urinate into
nei/dabbe, v.; neigedappt, pp. 1.step into unexpectedly; 2.walk in
nei/dargele, v.; neigedargelt, pp. reel in
nei/draage, v.; neigedraage, pp. carry in
nei/drede, v.; neigedrede, pp. step into

Nn

nei/drehe

nei/drehe, v.; neigedreht, pp. 1.tighten (a screw); 2.turn in
nei/dreiwe, v.; neigedriwwe, pp. drive in
nei/dricke, v.; neigedrickt, pp. indent
nei/drickle, v.; neigedrickelt, pp. dry in
nei/dringe, v. (sich --) 1.intrude; 2.pry
nei/drolle, v.; niegedrollt, pp. trot in
nei/dropse, v.; neigedropst, pp. drop in
nei/duh, v.; neigeduh, pp. put in
nei/dunke, v.; neigedunkt, pp. dip into
nei/dunnere, v.; neigedunnert, pp. enter noisily
nei/faahre, v.; neifaahre, pp. 1.drive in or into; 2.haul in
nei/falle, v.; is neigfalle, pp. fall in
nei/faschle, v. 1.investigate; 2.spy
nei/fiedere, v.; neigfiedert, pp. feed (a threshing machine)
nei/fiehre, v.; neigfiehrt, pp. lead in or into
nei/fille, v.; neigfillt, pp. fill in
nei/fladdere, v.; neigfladdert, pp. flutter in
nei/flechde, v.; neigflochde, pp. twine in
nei/fliege, v.; neigfloge, pp. fly in
nei/fresse, v.; neigfresse, pp. eat into
nei/gaerwe, v.; neigegaerbt, pp. flog in
nei/gaffe, v.; neigegafft, pp. gape in
nei/gauze, v.; neigegauzt, pp. blab in
nei/geh, v.; neigange, pp. 1.enter; 2.go into
nei/gewwe, v.; neigewwe, pp. give in
nei/glaawe, v.; neigeglaabt, pp. believe in
nei/glebbere, v.; neigeglebbert, pp. 1.beat in; 2.enter noisily
nei/glemme, v.; neigeglemmt, pp. pinch in
nei/globbe, v.; neigeglobbt, pp. hammer in
nei/graawe, v.; neigegraawe, pp. dig into
nei/graddle, v.; neigegraddelt, pp. crawl in
nei/gratze, v.; neigegratzt, pp. 1.harrow; 2.scrape into
nei/greische, v.; neigegrische, pp. yell in
nei/griege, v.; neigrickt, pp. get or cause to enter
nei/gritzle, v.; neigegritzelt, pp. scribble in
nei/grubbe, v.; neigegrubbt, pp. grub into
nei/gucke, v.; neigeguckt, pp. look in or into
nei/hacke, v.; neighackt, pp. chop into
nei/halde, v.; neighalde, pp (eens --) give a blow
nei/haschble, v.; neighaschbelt, pp. enter unexpectedly
nei/helfe, v.; neigholfe, pp. help in or into
nei/henke, v.; neighenkt, pp (es Maul --) 1.butt in; 2.interfere; 3.interrupt
nei/hetze, v.; neighetzt, pp. drive in (with dogs)
nei/hokle, v.; neighokelt, pp. hook in
nei/hole, v.; neigholt, pp. fetch in
nei/holpere, v.; neigholpert, pp. hobble in
nei/kenne, v.; neigekennt, pp. be able to get in
nei/kuschle, v. (sich --) snuggle
nei/laafe, v.; neigeloffe, pp. 1.run in (of liquids); 2.walk in
nei/lange, v.; neigelangt, pp. reach in
nei/leere, v.; neigleert, pp. pour into (of grain)
nei/lege, v.; neigelegt, pp. lay in
nei/leichte, v.; neigeleicht, pp (eens --) give (one a blow)
nei/liege, v.; neigeloge, pp. (sich --) obtain a position by lying

nei/schpaerre

nei/locke, v.; neigelockt, pp. entice in
nei/losse, v.; neiglosst, pp. admit
nei/mache, v.; neigemacht, pp. 1.insert; 2.put in place
nei/maricke, v.; neigmarickt, pp. mark in
nei/maule, v.; neigmault, pp. blab in
nei/meesele, v.; neigemeeselt, pp. chisel in
nei/middle, v.; neigemiddelt, pp. (sich --) 1.interfere; 2.meddle
nei/mische, v.; neigemischt, pp. (sich --) 1.interfere; 2.meddle
nei/mixe, v.; neigemixt, pp. admix
nei/packe, v; neigepackt, pp. 1.pack in; 2.(sich --) get in the house
nei/raase, v.; neigeraast, pp. enter tumultuously
nei/raffe, v.; neigerafft, pp. gather in hurriedly
nei/rechle, v.; neigerechelt, pp. 1.include in reckoning; 2.reckon in
nei/regge, v.; neigeregert, pp. spoil by raining
nei/reide, v.; neigeridde, pp. ride in
nei/reisse, v.; neigerisse, pp. tear a slit or hole in
nei/reiwe, v.; neigeriwwe, pp. rub in
nei/renne, v.; neigerennt, pp. 1.stumble in; 2.thrust in
nei/richde, v.; neigericht, pp. (sich --) adapt oneself
nei/ricke, v.; neigerickt, pp. move into
nei/rinne, v.; neigerunnt, pp. leak into
nei/riwwle, v.; neigeriwwelt, pp. rub into as crumbs
nei/rolle, v.; neigerollt, pp. roll in
nei/rudere, v.; neigerudert, pp. row into
nei/rufe, v.; neigerufe, pp. call into (a place)
nei/rutsche, v.; neigerutscht, pp. slide into
nei/saege, v.; neigsaekt, pp. saw into
nei/schaere, v.; neigschaert, pp. sow poorly
nei/schaffe, v.; neigschaft, pp. (sich --) work one's way into a place
nei/schalle, v.; neigschallt, pp. sound into (a place)
nei/scheisse, v.; neigschisse, pp. shit into
nei/schenke, v.; neigschenkt, pp. pour into (of beverages at table)
nei/scheppe, v.; neigschebbt, pp. shovel into
nei/schicke, v.; neigschickt, pp. send in
nei/schidde, v.; neigschitt, pp. pour into
nei/schiesse, v.; neigschosse, pp. shoot into
nei/schiewe, v.; neigschowe, pp. push into
nei/schinne, v.; neigschunne, pp. skimp in seed
nei/schlagge, v.; neigschlagge, pp. 1.go in with a will; 2.knock in
nei/schleefe, v.; neigschleeft, pp. drag in
nei/schleiche, v.; neigschliche, pp. sneak in
nei/schlibbe, v.; neigschlippt, pp. slip in
nei/schluppe, v.; neigschluppt, pp. crawl in
nei/schmeisse, v.; neigschmisse, pp. throw in
nei/schmiere, v.; neigschmiert, pp. (sich --) mix up with
nei/schnubbere, v.; neigschnubbert, pp. pry
nei/schnuffle, v.; neigschnuffelt, pp. poke one's nose into a matter
nei/schpaerre, v.; neigschpaert, pp. 1.lock in; 2.pen up

Nn

nei/schpanne — nettemol

nei/schpanne, v.; neigschpannt, pp. hitch horses to a wagon
nei/schparre, v.; neigschpatt, pp. 1.lock in; 2.pen in
nei/schpaue, v.; neigschpaut, pp. spit in
nei/schpiesse, v.; neigschpiesst, pp. spear with a fork
nei/schpinne, v.; neigschpunne, pp. enmesh
nei/schprenge, v.; neigschprengt, pp. 1.burst in; 2.cause to run in
nei/schpritze, v.; neigschpritzt, pp. 1.inject; 2.splash in
nei/schtaerze, v.; neigschtaerzt, pp. fall into
nei/schtambe, v.; neigschtumpt, pp. stamp into
nei/schteche, v.; neigschtoche, pp. 1.prick; 2.pierce
nei/schtecke, v.; neigschteckt; neigschtocke, pp. 1.invest; 2.pierce; 3.stick or put in a place; 4.tuck in
nei/schteige, v.; neischtigge, pp. enter (a carriage)
nei/schtelle, v.; neigschtellt, pp. set or put in a place
nei/schtewwere, v.; neigschtewwert, pp. chase in
nei/schtimme, v.; neigschtimmt, pp. 1.elect; 2.vote in
nei/schtobbe, v.; neigschtoppt, pp. stuff into
nei/schtocke, v.; neigschtockt, pp. enter stiffly with a cane
nei/schtolpere, v.; neigschtolpert, pp. stumble in
nei/schtosse, v.; neigschtosse, pp. 1.break in; 2.thrust in
nei/schwetze, v.; neigschwetzt, pp. 1.persuade; 2.talk (someone) into (something)
nei/sehne, v.; neigsehne, pp. 1.see into; 2.understand
nei/setze, v.; neigsetzt, pp. set in
nei/sinke, v.; neigsunke, pp. sink in
nei/wachse, v.; neigewachst, pp. grow into
nei/welze, v.; neigewelzt, pp. roll in
nei/wickle, v.; neigewickelt, pp. 1.implicate; 2.wrap into
nei/winsche, v.; neigewinscht, pp. wish (some one) in a place
nei/wolle, v.; neigewollt, pp. want to go in
nei/yaage, v.; neigyaagt, pp. chase in
nei/yoche, v.; neigeyicht, pp. yoke in
nei/yohle, v.; neigeyohlt, pp. shout in
nei/ziehe, v.; neigzoge, pp. 1.move in; 2.pull in
nei, adj. new
nei, adv. anew
nei, prep. 1.in; 2.into
Neibekehrter (der, die)n. new convert
Neid (der)n. envy
neide, v.; geneidt, pp. envy
neidi(s)ch, adj. envious
Neienglenner (der)n. Yankee
neigierich, adj. 1.curious; 2.inquisitive
Neiheit (die)n.; Neiheide, pl. novelty
Neiichkeede (die)n., pl. news
Neiichkeetgreemer (der)n. busybody
Neiichkeidedraeger (der)n. 1.busybody; 2.tattler
Neiland (es)n. newly cleared land
neilich, adv. 1.newly; 2.recently
Neilicht (es)n. new moon
neimodisch, adj. newfangled
Neimoond (der)n. new moon
Neimuund (der)n. new moon
nein(e), adj. nine
Neinder (es)n. nine-spot (of cards)

neineegich, adj. nine-eyed
Neinheidichholz (es)n. nine-bark
Neinmonetros (die)n. garden hydrangea
neint, adj. ninth
Neintel (es)n. ninth
Neinuhrschtick (es)n. nine o'clock snack (served in the field to haying and harvesting hands)
neinzeh, adj. nineteen
neinzeht, adj. nineteenth
neinzich, adj. ninety
Neinzichyaehricher (der)n. nonagenarian
neinzischt, adj. ninetieth
neirunslich, adj. newfangled
neist, adj. decent
Neiyaahrnacht (die)n. New Year's night
Neiyaahrs-gruus (der)n. New Year's greeting
Neiyaahrschitz (der)n.; Neiyaahrschitz, pl. person who shoots in the New Year
Neiyaahrsdaag (es)n. New Year's Day
Neiyaahrswetting (die)n. New Year's banter
Neiyaahrswinsch (der)n. New Year's greeting
Neiyaahrswunsch (der)n.; Neiyaahrswinsche, pl. New Year's greeting
neiyets, adv. nowhere
neizus, adv. on the way (going) in
nemme, v.; gnumme, pp. 1.appropriate; 2.receive; 3.take; 4.(sei Batt --) (a) side with him; (b) take his part; 5.(sei Hinnerbatt --) stand firm (in an altercation)
Nemmer (der)n.; Nemmer, pl. 1.receiver; 2.taker
nengere, v.; genengert, pp. 1.complain constantly; 2.express a longing for; 3.hanker after continually
nenne, v.; genennt, pp. 1.call; 2.mention; 3.name
nenneswaert, adj. worth mentioning
nerscht = erscht 1.just; 2.only
Neschatgweckerli (es)n. terms of endearment (applied to an infant in its cradle)
neschde, v.; genescht, pp. make a nest
Nescht (es)n.; Neschder, pl. 1.bed; 2.nest
Neschtelche (es)n. slip (of plants)
Neschtgwackerli (es)n. terms of endearment (applied to an infant in its cradle)
Neschtli (es)n.; Neschtlin, pl. twig
Neschtoi (es)n.; Neschtoier, pl. nest-egg
Nessi (es)n. outhouse
nesslich, adj. 1.damp; 2.moist; 3.wetness
net aanehmlich, adj. 1.unacceptable; 2.(-- datt) adv. absent
net dief adj. shallow
net draue, v.; net gedraut, pp. mistrust
net emol, adv. not even
net gans kampes off in the head
Net waahr? not so?
net, adv. not
net...un aa net neither...nor
netdesdewennicher, adv. nevertheless
nett, adj. 1.beautiful; 2.nice; 3.neat; 4.pretty; 5.tidy
nettemol, adv. not even

Nn

Netz

Netz (es)n. 1.net; 2.peritoneum; 3.reticulum; 4.yarn

netze, v.; genetzt, pp. 1.sprinkle; 2.wet

Netzhaut (die)n. retina (of the eye)

Netzwaerick (es)n. netting

newe, adv. & prep. 1.alongside; 2.beside; 3.by the side of

newebei, adv. 1.by the by; 2.(coming) from the side; 3.incidentally; 4.(vun --) from the side

newedraa, adv. 1.alongside; 2.beside; 3.by the side of

newedrauss, adv. 1.apart; 2.aside; 3.on a back road; 4.out by; 5.out of the way

Newegaul (der)n. horse harnessed to the right (of the saddle horse)

Newegebei (es)n.; Newegebeier, pl. outbuilding

newehaer, adv. alongside of (in motion)

newehie, adv. 1.alongside of; 2.on the right side (in hitching horses)

Newekoschde (die)n.,pl. extra costs

newem = newe em next to it; him

neweme = newe me next to it; him

Newemensch (der)n. neighbor

newenanner/hocke, v.; newenannerghockt, pp. sit alongside of each other

newenanner/schlofe, v.; newenannergschloft, pp. sleep beside each other

newenanner/setze, v.; newenannergsetzt, pp. set beside each other

newenanner, adv. 1.abreast; 2.beside each other

newenannergeh, adv. walk or go alongside of each other

newenannerhaer, adv. (moving) alongside of each other

newenannerlaafe, adv. walk alongside of each other

newenannerlege, adv. lay alongside of each other

newenannerleie, adv. lie beside each other

newenannerschtelle, adv. set beside each other

newenaus, adv. 1.aside; 2.off to one side

newenei, adv. in at the side (of something in motion)

newes = newe es next to it

Newesach (die)n.; Newesache, pl. non-essential

Neweschtick (es)n. 1.encore; 2.lunch

Neweschtroos (die)n. byway

Newewart (es)n. 1.adverb; 2.curse word

newewedder, adv. against the side

newich, prep. 1.alongside; 2.beside; 3.by the side of

newichenanner, adv. abreast

Newwel (der)n. 1.fog; 2.mist

newwelich, adj. 1.foggy; 2.misty

newwle, v.; genewwelt, pp. 1.drizzle; 2.jestingly of dust as thick as fog; 3.rise like a spray (from the ground in a heavy rain); 4.said of an angry outburst; 5.to be foggy

newwlich, adj. misty

nexe, v.; genext, pp. tease

nichdern, adj. 1.sober; 2.temperate

Nickel (der)n. Nicholas

Nickles (der)n. Nicholas

Nicknaame (der)n. nickname

nidder/bicke, v.; niddergebickt, pp. (sich --) bend down

nidder/brenne, v.; niddergebrennt, pp. burn down

nimmi

nidder/drede, v. niddergedrede, pp. tread down

nidder/ducke, v.; niddergeduckt, pp. 1.dodge; 2.duck

nidder/falle, v.; niddergfalle, pp. fall down

nidder/gaerwe, v.; niddergegaerbt, pp. beat down

nidder/gschlagge, v.; niddergschlagge, pp. 1.beaten down; 2.dejected; 3.in low spirits

nidder/hacke, v.; niddergehackt, pp. chop down

nidder/halde, v.; nidderghalde, pp. 1.aim low; 2.hold low

nidder/lege, v.; niddergelegt, pp. lay down

nidder/losse, v.; nidderglosst, pp. lower

nidder/mache, v.; niddergemacht, pp. chop down

nidder/mehe, v.; niddergemeht, pp. mow down

nidder/reisse, v.; niddergerisse, pp. 1.raze; 2.tear down

nidder/schiesse, v.; niddergschosse, pp. shoot down

nidder/schlagge, v.; niddergschlagge, pp. knock down

nidder/schtelle, v.; niddergschtellt, pp. set (machines) so as to mow lower

nidder/sinke, v.; niddergsunke, pp. sink down

nidder, adj. 1.base; 2.low; 3.vulgar

nidderbeenich, adj. vile

nidderdrechdich, adj. 1.base; 2.despicable; 3.vile

nidderdrechdich, adv. rascally

Nidderdrechdichkeit (die)n. 1.baseness; 2.rascality

niddri Schlange (die)n. Virginia snakeroot

niddrich, adv. lowly

Niddrichkeit (die)n. lowliness

nie, adv. 1.never; 2.(-- kenn) never any; 3.(er dutt -- nix) never

nie net, adv. never

Niedichkeet (die)n. 1.neatness; 2.tidiness

niedlich, adj. 1.beautiful; 2.neat; 3.nice; 4.pretty

Niedlichkeet (die)n. tidiness

niedrich, adj. humble

Nieger (der)n. Negro

niegere, v.; gniegert, pp. slave

niemand, pron. 1. nobody; 2. no one; 3. (net gross mit --) unimportant (meaning little to anyone)

niemols, adv. never

Nier (die)n.; Niere, pl. kidney

Nierefett (es)n. suet

Nieregranket (die)n. 1.Bright's disease; 2.disease of the kidneys

Nieregraut (es)n. sneezewort

Niereinschlich (es)n. suet

Niereschmals (es)n. leaf-lard

Niereschtick (es)n. 1.loin (roast); 2.rump

Niesgraut (es)n. 1.green hellebore (hellebores viridis); 2.white hellebore (Veratrum virde)

niesse, v.; geniesst, pp. sneeze

Niet (der)n. 1.clinch; 2.rivet

niete, v.; geniet, pp. rivet

Nietnaggel (der)n. rivet

nigre, v.; gnigert, pp. neigh (of horses)

nimmand, pron. no one

nimme, adv. 1.never; 2.no more; 3.no longer

nimmermeh, adv. 1.never again; nevermore

nimmi, adv. 1.never; 2.no longer; 3.no more

Nn

nimmimeh / Nixnutzichkeit

nimmimeh, adv. 1.never again; 2.nevermore

ninkere, v.; geninkert, pp. obey the call of nature (in speaking to children)

Nipp (es)n. 1.nip; 2.sip

nischble, v.; gnischbelt, pp. (to be) over-nice (in eating)

nischde, v.; genischt, pp. (sich --) make a nest (as a dog)

nischdle, v.; genischdelt, pp. 1.nestle; 2.snuggle

Niss (die)n. 1.nit; 2.maggots (pl. form)

Nisschisser (der)n.; Nisschisser, pl. gadfly

Nisseel (es)n. oil of butternuts

nissich, adj. nitty

Nitz (die)n.; Nitze, pl. nit

nitzlich, adj. 1.beneficial; 2.profitable; 3.serviceable; 4.useful

nitzlich, adv. necessary

Nitzlichkeet (die)n. utility

niwwer/bezaahle, v.; niwwerbezaahlt, pp. pay over

niwwer/breche, v.; niwwergebroche, pp. break across

niwwer/bringe, v.; niwwergebrocht, pp. bring (get) across

niwwer/draage, v.; niwwergedraage, pp. carry over

niwwer/drehe, v.; niwwergedreht, pp. turn over

niwwer/dreiwe, v.; niwwergedriwwe, pp. drive over

niwwer/duh, v.; niwwergeduh, pp. put across

niwwer/faahre, v.; niwwergfaahre, pp. drive over (in a vehicle)

niwwer/falle, v.; niwwergfalle, pp. fall on the other side

niwwer/fiehre, v.; niwwergfiehrt, pp. lead over

niwwer/fliege, v.; niwwergflogge, pp. fly over

niwwer/gackse, v.; niwwergegackst, pp. gossip across (the fence)

niwwer/gaffe, v.; niwwergegafft, pp. gape across

niwwer/geh, v.; niwwergange, pp. go over

niwwer/gewwe, v.; niwwergewwe, pp. give over

niwwer/graddle, v.; niwwergegraddelt, pp. clamber across

niwwer/greische, v.; niwwergegrische, pp. scream across

niwwer/gucke, v.; niwwergeguckt, pp. look across

niwwer/hacke, v.; niwwerghackt, pp. paw across (of horses)

niwwer/halde, v.; niwwerghalde, pp. hold to the other side

niwwer/harriche, v.; niwwergharricht, pp. listen to what is going on upon the other side

niwwer/helfe, v.; niwwergholfe, pp. help (someone) across

niwwer/hocke, v.; niwwerghockt, pp. (sich --) sit on the other side

niwwer/hupse, v.; niwwerghupst, pp. hop across

niwwer/keere, v.; niwwergekeert, pp. belong on the other side

niwwer/kehre, v.; niwwergekehrt, pp. sweep over

niwwer/kenne, v.; niwwergekennt, pp. be able to get across

niwwer/kessle, v.; niwwergekesselt, pp. make a laborious journey over

niwwer/kumme, v.; is niwwerkumme, pp. come over

niwwer/laafe, v.; niwwergeloffe, pp. 1.run over (of liquids); 2.walk over

niwwer/lege, v.; niwwergelegt, pp. lay over

niwwer/leichte, v.; niwwergeleicht, pp. light the way across

niwwer/lodle, v.; niwwergeloddelt, pp. trudge lazily over

niwwer/misse, v.; niwwergemisst, pp. be obliged to cross

over or pass over

niwwer/nemme, v.; niwwergenumme, pp. take over

niwwer/reeche, v.; niwwergereecht, pp. reach over

niwwer/reisse, v.; niwwergerisse, pp. pull over

niwwer/renne, v.; niwwergerennt, pp. rush over

niwwer/schaffe, v.; niwwergschafft, pp. put or transport over

niwwer/schalle, v.; niwwergschallt, pp. sound across

niwwer/scheppe, v.; niwwergscheppt, pp. shovel over

niwwer/schicke, v.; niwwergschickt, pp. send over

niwwer/schidde, v.; niwwergschitt, pp. pour over

niwwer/schiese, v.; niwwergschosse, pp. shoot over

niwwer/schluppe, v.; niwwergschluppt, pp. creep over

niwwer/schmeise, v.; niwwergschmisse, pp. throw over

niwwer/schnalle, v.; niwwergschnallt, pp. buckle over

niwwer/schnappe, v.; niwwergschnappt. pp. limp over

niwwer/schnelle, v.; niwwergschnellt, pp. jerk over

niwwer/schneppe, v.; niwwergscheppt, pp. tilt over

niwwer/schpringe, v.; niwwerschprunge, pp. run over

niwwer/schridde, v.; niwwergschritt, pp. step across

niwwer/schtecke, v.; niwwergschtocke, pp. fasten over

niwwer/schtelle, v.; niwwergschtellt, pp. set over

niwwer/schtimme, v.; niwwergschtimmt, pp. 1.sound across; 2.vote on the other side

niwwer/schwimme, v.; niwwergschwumme, pp. swim across

niwwer/setze, v.; niwwergsetzt, pp. set over

niwwer/wolle, v.; niwwergewollt, pp. want to get across

niwwer/yaage, v.; niwwergeyaagt, pp. chase to the other side

niwwer/yackere, v.; niwwergeyackert, pp. jog across to

niwwer/yohle, v.; niwwergeyohlt, pp. shout across

niwwer/ziege, v.; niwwergezoge, pp. 1.move over; 2.pull over

niwwer/ziehe, v.; niwwergezoge, pp. 1.move over; 2.pull over

niwwer, adv. 1.across; 2.over

niwwerzus, adv. 1.on the way (going) across; 2.over yonder

nix drin, adj. empty

Nix fer Ungut un gaar nix ver schpeit no harm meant

Nix fer Ungut wann's reggert no harm meant

Nix kumm raus!, interj. nothing doing!

nix meh waert, adj. 1.ruined; 2.out of order; 3.out of wack

nix wa(e)rt, adj. useless

nix Weiders nothing special

nix, adj. zero

nix, pron. 1.naught; 2.nothing; 3. (-- do) (a) nothing of the sort; (b) no you won't; (c) I won't allow it

nixdewennicher, adv. nevertheless

Nixeso!, interj. nothing of the kind!

Nixli mit heembringe return home empty handed with nothing for the children of the house (no candy, etc.)

Nixnutz (der)n. 1.mischief; 2.mischievous child; 3.good for nothing; 4.worthless fellow

nixnutz(ich), adj. 1.mischievous; 2.naughty; 3.worthless

Nixnutzichkeit (die)n. 1.naughtiness; 2.worthlessness

Nn

Nixwisser

Nixwisser (der)n. 1.ignoramus; 2.know-nothing

no, adv. 1.according to; 2.after; 3.by (usually after a noun); 4.then; 5.towards

no, prep. towards

noch nor (rare usage)

noch eens, pron. another

noch Middaag zu, adv. 1.southward; 2.towards the south

noch, adv. 1.still; 2.yet

noch, prep. 1.after; 2.to; 3.towards

Nochber (der)n.; Nochbere, pl. neighbor

Nochberin (die)n. neighbor lady

nochberlich, adj. neighborly

Nochberschaft (die)n. 1.neighborhood; 2.vicinity

Nochberschtick (es)n. neighborly act

Nochbershaus (es)n. neighbor's house

Nochbrebeitscher (der)n. one who slanders his neighbors

nochdem, adv. 1.after that; 2.afterward(s); 3.hereafter

nochdem, conj., pron.; 1.according (to that); 2.after;3.when

nochderhand, adv. afterwards

nochem = noch em after him or it

nochemol, adv. 1.again; 2.once more

nochenanner, adv. 1.consecutively; 2.in succession; 3.one after the other

nochme = noch me after one

Nochmid(d)aag (der)n. afternoon

nochmols, adv. again

nochre = noch re after her

noddlich, adj. 1.dilapidated; 2.rickety

Nodel (die)n.; Nodle, pl. needle

Nodeleehr (die)n. eye of a needle

Nodelloch (es)n. eye of a needle

nodle, v.; genodelt, pp. 1.ply the needle; 2.sew fast

Nofember (der)n. November

Noht (die)n.; Neht, pl. 1.hem; 2.seam

Nome (der)n.; Neeme, pl. name

Nomebuch (es)n. dictionary

Nomegrischt (der) n. 1.pseudo-Christian; 2.pretending Christian

Nomewatt (es)n. noun

nooch, adv. 1.according to; 2.after; 3.by (usually after a noun); 4.past (in telling time); 5.towards

nooch, prep. 1.after; 2.towards

no(och)aarde, v.; no(och)geaart, pp. 1.resemble; 2.take after

no(och)aerwe, v.; no(och)geaerbt, pp. (sich --) be hereditary

no(och)affe, v.; no(och)geafft, pp. 1.ape; 2.imitate

no(och)basse, v.; no(och)gebasst, pp. trudge after

no(och)bede, v.; no(och)gebet, pp. repeat the words of another in prayer

no(och)bezaahle, v.; no(och)bezaahlt, pp. 1. make an additional payment; 2.pay later

no(och)binne, v.; no(och)gebunne, pp. tie sheaves after a cradler

no(och)blaerre, v.; no(och)geblaerrt, pp. bawl or low after

no(och)blaffe, v.; no(och)geblafft, pp. bark after

no(och)graddle

no(och)blanze, v.; no(och)geblanzt, pp. replant

no(och)blaudre, v.; no(och)geblaudert, pp. gossip about

no(och)blicke, v.; no(och)geblickt, pp. look after

no(och)bluge, v.; no(och)geblugt, pp. plow after

no(och)brille, v.; no(och)gebrillt, pp. cry after

no(och)bringe, v.; no(och)gebrocht, pp. bring after

no(och)daerfe, v.; no(och)gedaerft, pp. be allowed to follow

no(och)danse, v.; no(och)gedanst, pp. 1.dance after; 2.imitate in dancing

no(och)dappe, v.; no(och)gedappt, pp. follow

no(och)dapple, v.; no(och)gedappelt, pp. follow in a stiff manner

no(och)darigle, v.; no(och)gedarigelt, pp. stagger after

nooch dem, adv. 1.after this; 2.hereafter

no(och)denke, v.; no(och)gedenkt, pp. 1.consider;2.meditate; 3.reflect

noochdenklich, adj. pensive

noochderhand, adv. afterward(s)

no(och)draage, v.; no(och)gedraage, pp. carry after

no(och)drachde, v.; no(och)gedracht, pp. 1.follow up; 2.lie in wait

no(och)dradde, v.; no(och)gedratt, pp. 1.toddle after; 2.trot after

no(och)draschte, v.; no(och)gedrascht, pp. follow

no(och)dreiwe, v.; no(och)gedriwwe, pp. drive after

no(och)eile, v.; no(och)geeilt, pp. hurry after

no(och)esse, v.; no(och)gesse, pp. 1.eat after the rest; 2.eat at the second table

no(och)faahre, v.; no(och)gfaahre, pp. drive (in a vehicle) after

no(och)fange, v.; no(och)gfange, pp. catch up with

noo(och)faschdle, v.; no(och)gfaschdelt, pp. 1.investigate; 2.pry

no(och)fege, v. follow (someone)

no(och)fiehre, v.; no(och)gfiehrt, pp. lead on behind

no(och)fille, v.; no(och)gfillt, pp. fill up

no(och)flankiere, v.; no(och)gflankiert, pp. roam after

no(och)fliege, v.; no(och)gflogge, pp. fly after

no(och)folge, v.; no(och)gfolgt, pp. 1.follow; 2.imitate; 3.succeed

noochfolger (der)n. successor

no(och)folye, v.; no(och)gfoligt, pp. 1.follow; 2.obey

Noochfolyer (der)n. follower

Noochgebort (die)n. placenta

Noochgeburt (die)n. 1.afterbirth; 2.placenta (of animals)

noochhaer, adv. afterwards

noochhaerich, adj. subsequently

no(och)froge, v.; gfrokt, pp. inquire about

no(och)gaffe, v.; no(och)gegafft, pp. gape after

no(och)geh, v.; no(och)gange, pp. 1.follow; 2.pursue

no(och)gewwe, v.; no(och)gewwe, pp. 1.cave in; 2.give in; 3.give way; 4.recede; 5.sink; 6.yield

no(och)graawe, v.; no(och)gegraawe, pp. dig after

no(och)graddle, v.; no(och)gegraddelt, pp. 1.crawl after; 2.follow with difficulty

Nn

no(och)greische — Notschtall

no(och)greische, v.; no(och)gegrische, pp. shout after

no(och)griege, v.; no(och)grickt, pp. obtain

no(och)gucke, v.; no(och)geguckt, pp. 1.look after; 2.see to

no(och)halde, v.; no(och)ghaldt, pp. 1.keep up with;2.shout at

no(och)haschble, v.; no(och)ghaschbelt, pp. rush after

no(och)heile, v.; no(och)gheilt, pp. cry after

no(och)helfe, v.; no(och)gholfe, pp. 1.help along; 2.improve the occasion

no(och)hetze, v.; no(och)ghetzt, pp. set (dogs) on

no(och)hickle, v.; no(och)ghickelt, pp. limp after

Noochkemmling (der)n. 1.descendent; 2.offspring

no(och)kenne, v.; no(och)gekennt, pp. be able to follow

no(och)kessle, v.; no(och)gekesselt, pp. jog after

no(och)kumme, v.; no(och)kumme, pp. 1.follow; 2.obey

Noochkumme(r) (der)n.; Noochkumme(r), pl. 1.descendent; 2.offspring

Noochkummenschaft (die)n. posterity

Noochkummes (es)n. descendants

Noochkunft (die)n. 1.posterity; 2.the future

no(och)laafe; v.; no(och)gloffe, pp. 1.follow; 2.obey

no(och)lache, v.; no(och)gelacht, pp. laugh after

no(och)lauschdere, v.; no(och)gelauschdert, pp. listen surreptitiously

no(och)leichte, v.; no(och)geleicht, pp. light the way after (someone)

no(och)lese, v.; no(och)glese, pp. pick or read after (someone)

noochlessich, adj. 1.negligent; 2.untidy

Noochlessichkeit (die)n. 1.negligence; 2.remissness

no(och)lewe, v.; no(och)gelebt, pp. conform to

no(och)liege, v.; no(och)geloge, pp. slander

no(och)locke, v.; no(och)gelockt, pp. entice to follow

no(och)losse, v.; no(och)g(e)losst, pp. 1.abate; 2.leave off; 3.relent; 4.slacken

no(och)mache, v.; no(och)g(e)macht, pp. 1.imitate; 2.mimic

Noochmacher (der)n. follower

no(och)maehe, v.; no(och)gemaeht, pp. follow in mowing

no(och)maule, v.; no(och)gemault, pp. scold after (someone)

no(och)misse, v.; no(och)gemisst, pp. be obliged to follow

no(och)naame, v.; no(och)genaamt, pp. name after

no(och)nemme, v.; no(och)gnumme, pp. Takeafter

no(och)packe, v.; no(och)gepackt, pp. hustle after

no(och)peife, v.; no(och)gepiffe, pp. whistle after

no(och)reche, v.; no(och)gerecht, pp. 1.rake after; 2.rake and bind

no(och)rechle, v.; no(och)gerechelt, pp. 1. find out by reckoning; 2.reckon again

no(och)reide, v.; no(och)geridde, pp. ride after

no(och)renne, v.; no(och)gerennt, pp. rush after

no(och)retsche, v.; no(och)geretscht, pp. tell lies behind one's back

Noochricht (die)n. 1.news; 2.notice

no(och)ricke, v.; no(och)gerickt, pp. move after

no(och)rufe, v.; no(och)gerufe, pp. call after

no(och)saage, v.; no(och)gsaat, pp. 1.repeat another's words; 2.speak ill of one (behind his back)

no(och)schaerfe, v.; no(och)gschaerft, pp. give a reminder

no(och)schaffe, v.; no(och)gschafft, pp. 1.convey after a person; 2.make up by working; 3.(sich --) exert oneself to keep up with another

no(och)schalle, v.; no(och)gschallt, pp. sound after

no(och)schicke, v.; no(och)gschickt, pp. send after

no(och)schiesse, v.; no(och)gschosse, pp. 1.follow swiftly; 2.shoot after

no(och)schiewe, v.; no(och)gschowe, pp. push after

no(och)schleefe, v.; no(och)gschleeft, pp. drag after

no(och)schleiche, v.; no(och)schleiche, pp. sneak after

no(och)schluppe, v.; no(och)gschluppt, pp. creep after

no(och)schmeisse, v.; no(och)gschmisse, pp. throw after

no(och)schreiwe, v.; no(och)gschriwwe, pp. follow a model in writing

Noochschrift (die)n. postscript

no(och)schtaerme, v.; no(och)gschtaermt, pp. follow in a rage

no(och)schteh, v.; no(och)gschtanne, pp. serve subsequently

no(och)schtolbere, v.; no(och)schtolbert, pp. stumble after

no(och)schwimme, v.; no(och)schwumme, pp. swim after

no(och)sehne, v.; no(och)gsehnt, pp. look after

nooch sellem, adv. 1. after that; 2.then

nooch sem, adv. 1.after that; 2.then

no(och)singe, v.; no(och)gsunge, pp. follow in singing

no(och)suche, v.; no(och)gsucht, pp. investigate

Noochsummer (der)n. Indian summer

no(och)wachse, v.; no(och)gewachst, pp. 1.come into bearing (of an orchard); 2.grow again

Noochweis (der)n. 1.explanation; 2.proof

no(och)weise, v.; no(och)gewisse, pp. point out in reading

Noochweiser (der)n. index

no(och)wiege, v.; no(och)gwoge, pp. verify the weight

Noochwinter (der)n. latter part of winter

no(och)wolle, v.; no(och)gewollt, pp. want to follow

no(och)yaage, v.; no(och)g(e)yaagt, pp. race after

no(och)zackere, v.; no(och)gezackert, pp. jog after

no(och)zaehle, v.; no(och)gezaehlt, pp. 1.check; 2.count over

no(och)ziege, v.; no(och)gzogge, pp. pull or move after

no(och)ziehe, v.; no(och)zoge, pp. pull or move after

Noodelschpitze (die)n. point of a needle

noodle, v.; genoodelt, pp. ply the needle

Nooi (der)n. Noah

Nooschi (der)n. taffy

nord, adv. then

nore = nooch re after her

nort = dennort after that

Not (die)n. 1.bill; 2.distress; 3.lack; 4.need; 5.note; 6.want

Not (die)n 1.(in --) (a) needy; (b) in need; 2.(-- leide) suffer

Notabbel (der)n. pippin

Notgleech (der)n. open link (for repairing chain)

Notschtall (der)n. trave

Nn

Notschtunn

Notschtunn (die)n. hour of distress
notwendich, adv. necessary
Notwendichkeet (die)n. necessity
notwennich, adv. necessary
Notzeeche (es)n. sign of distress
Nowember (der)n. November
Nubbe (die)n. tricks
nucke, v.; genuckt, pp. 1.doze; 2.give assent by nodding; 3.nod
nuddle, v.; genuddelt, pp. nurse or suck complacently (of an infant)
Nudel (die)n.; Nudle, pl. noodle
Nudelsupp (die)n. noodle soup
nuff/baue, v.; nuffgebaut, pp. build up (somewhere)
nuff/biege, v.; nuffgeboge, pp. bend up
nuff/binne, v.; nuffgebunne, pp. tie up
nuff/blanze, v.; nuffgeblanzt, pp. plant up
nuff/blicke, v.; nuffgeblickt, pp. glance up
nuff/blose, v.; nuffgeblose, pp. blow up
nuff/bringe, v.; nuffgebrocht, pp. bring up
nuff/dappe, v.; nuffgedappt, pp. trudge up
nuff/draage, v.; nuffgedraage, pp. carry up
nuff/drehe, v.; nuffgedreht, pp. put up (the hair)
nuff/dreiwe, v.; nuffgedriwwe, pp. drive up
nuff/drolle, v.; nuffgedrollt, pp. trot up
nuff/duh, v.; nuffgeduh, pp. 1.beat one who plays a lone hand in haasenpeffer; 2.put up
nuff/dunnere, v.; nuffgedunnert, pp. mount stairs noisily
nuff/faahre, v.; nuffgfaahre, pp. drive or haul up
nuff/falle, v.; nuffgfalle, pp. fall up
nuff/fiehre, v.; nuffgfiehrt, pp. lead up
nuff/fladdere, v.; nuffgfladdert, pp. flutter up
nuff/flappe, v.; nuffgflappt, pp. flap up
nuff/fliege, v.; nuffgflogge, pp. fly up
nuff/gawwele, v.; nuffgegawwelt, pp. pitch up (with a fork)
nuff/geh, v.; nuffgange, pp. 1.ascend; 2.rise in price
nuff/glettere,v .; nuffgeglettert, pp. climb up
nuff/graddle, v.; nuffgegraddelt, pp. climb up
nuff/greische, v.; nuffgegrische, pp. call up
nuff/griege, v.; nuffgrickt, pp. (manage to) get up (to a place)
nuff/gucke, v.; nuffgeguckt, pp. look up
nuff/halde, v.; nuffghalde, pp. aim high (with a gun)
nuff/handle, v.; nuffg(e)handelt, pp. raise the price of
nuff/haschble, v.; nuffghaschbelt, pp. rush up
nuff/helfe, v.; nuffgholfe, pp. help up
nuff/henke, v.; nuffghenkt, pp. hang up
nuff/hewe, v.; nuffghowe, pp. lift up
nuff/hole, v.; nuffgholt, pp. fetch or take up
nuff/klempe, v.; nuffgeklempt, pp. turn up edges of tin or zinc
nuff/kumme, v.; nuffkumme, pp. get up (to a place)
nuff/lange, v.; nuffgelangt, pp. reach up
nuff/lege, v.; nuffgelegt, pp. lay up somewhere
nuff/leichte, v.; nuffggeleicht, pp. light (a person) up stairs
nuff/losse, v.; nuffgelosst, pp. allow to go up
nuff/mache, v.; nuffgemacht, pp. 1.hang up; 2.raise
nuff/maerricke, v.; nuffgemaerrickt, pp. mark up
nuff/maschiere, v.; nuffmaschiert, pp. march up

Nummer

nuff/naggle, v.; nuffgenaggelt, pp. nail up
nuff/packe, v.; nuffgepackt, pp. (sich --) go on up
nuff/ranke, v.; nuffgerankt, pp. spread upwards (of vines)
nuff/reeche, v.; nuffgereecht, pp. reach or hand up
nuff/reide, v.; nuffgeridde, pp. ride up
nuff/reisse, v.; nuffgerisse, pp. yank up
nuff/renne, v.; nuffgerennt, pp. 1.bolt upstairs; 2.jerk up
nuff/ricke, v.; nuffgerickt, pp. move up
nuff/rolle, v.; nuffgerollt, pp. roll up
nuff/rufe, v.; nuffgerufe, pp. call upstairs
nuff/runsle, v.; nuffgerunselt, pp (die Naas --) turn up one's nose
nuff/schaffe, v.; nuffgschafft, pp. 1.convey (carry) up; 2.(sich --) work one's way up
nuff/schalle, v.; nuffgschnallt, pp. sound up (to a place)
nuff/scheppe, v.; nuffgscheppt, pp. shovel up somewhere
nuff/schiesse, v.; nuffgschosse, pp. 1.rush up; 2.shoot up
nuff/schlagge, v.; nuffgschlagge, pp. turn up (collar)
nuff/schleefe, v.; nuffgschleeft, pp. drag up
nuff/schleiche, v.; nuffgschliche, pp. sneak up
nuff/schluppe, v.; nuffgschluppt, pp. sneak up
nuff/schmeisse, v.; nuffgschmisse, pp. throw up
nuff/schnalle, v.; nuffgschnallt, pp. buckle up
nuff/schnelle, v.; nuffgschnellt, pp. fling up
nuff/schpelle, v.; nuffschpellt, pp. pin up
nuff/schprenge, v.; nuffgschprengt, pp. chase uphill or upstairs
nuff/schpringe, v.; nuffgschprunge, pp. run up
nuff/schpritze, v.; nuffgschpritzt, pp. splash up
nuff/schrauwe, v.; nuffgschraubt, pp. screw up
nuff/schtarre, v.; nuffgschtatt, pp. 1.poke; 2.stir
nuff/schtecke, v.; nuffgschtocke, pp. put up or stick up
nuff/schteige, v.; nuffgschteigge, pp. climb up
nuff/schtelle, v.; nuffgschtellt, pp. place or set up somewhere
nuff/schtewwre, v.; nuffgschtewwert, pp. chase upstairs
nuff/schtrecke, v.; nuffgschtreckt, pp. stretch up
nuff/schwimme, v.; nuffgschwumme, pp. swim up
nuff/wachse, v.; nuffgwachst, pp. grow up to a certain point
nuff/weise, v.; nuffgewisse, pp. show the way up
nuff/welse, v.; nuffgewelst, pp. roll up
nuff/wenne, v.; nuffgewennt, pp. turn up (sleeves)
nuff/wickle, v.; nuffgewickelt, pp. roll up
nuff/woge, v.; nuffgewogt, pp. (sich --) venture up
nuff/wolle, v.; nuffgewollt, pp. want to go up
nuff/yaage, v.; nuffgeyaakt, pp. chase up
nuff/yohle, v.; nuffgeyolt, pp. shout up
nuff/ziege, v.; nuffgezogge, pp. 1.move up; 2.pull up
nuff/ziehe, v.; nuffgezogge, pp. pull up
nuff/zoppe, v.; nuffgezoppt, pp. jerk up
nuff, adv. 1.up (thither); 2.up to a place
nuffzus, adj. 1.up-country; 2.upward
nuffzus, adv. on the way up
Null (die)n. 1.cipher; 2.naught; 3.zero
null, adj. zero
numme, adv. 1.just; 2.only
Nummer (die)n.; Nummere, pl. 1.figure; 2.number

Nn

nummere

nummere, v.; nummeret, pp. number
Nummereens (der)n. 1.himself; 2.myself; 3.number one
nummereens, adj. 1.first class; 2.first rate
nummero sicher, adv. place of safety
nummeyo by all means
Nummidaag (der)n. afternoon
nummidaags, adv. in the afternoon
nunner/batzle, v.; nunnergebatzelt, pp. tumble down
nunner/betschle, v.; gebetschelt, pp. pat down
nunner/bicke, v.; nunnergebickt, pp. (sich --) bend over
nunner/biege, v.; nunnergeboge, pp. (sich --) bend over
nunner/binne, v.; nunnergebunne; pp. tie down
nunner/bleche, v.; nunnergeblecht, pp. pay down
nunner/blicke, v.; nunnergeblickt, pp. glance down
nunner/breche, v.; nunnergebroche, pp. break down
nunner/brenne, v.; nunnergebrennt, pp. burn down
nunner/draage, v.; nunnergedraage, pp. carry down
nunner/drede, v.; nunnergedrede, pp. 1.trample; 2.tread down
nunner/drehe, v.; nunnergedreht, pp. turn down
nunner/dreiwe, v.; nunnergedriwwe, pp. drive down
nunner/dricke, v.; nunnergedrickt, pp. press down
nunner/ducke, v.; nunnergeduckt, pp. duck
nunner/duh, v.; nunnergeduh, pp. 1.put down; 2.subdue; 3.write down
nunner/esse, v.; nunnergesse, pp. eat (with an effort)
nunner/faahre, v.; nunnergfaahre, pp. drive down
nunner/falle, v.; nunnergfalle, pp. fall down
nunner/faule, v.; nunnergfault, pp. rot down
nunner/flappe, v.; nunnergflappt, pp. flap down
nunner/fliege, v.; nunnergfloge, pp. fly down
nunner/fresse, v.; nunnergfresse, pp. gulp down
nunner/gawwele, v.; nunnergegawwelt, pp. pitch down
nunner/geh, v.; nunnergange, pp. 1.go down; 2.deteriorate; 3.recede; 4.sink
nunner/gewwe, v.; nunnergewwe, pp. hand down
nunner/gloppe, v.; nunnergegloppt, pp. hammer down
nunner/gnalle, v.; nunnergegnellt, pp. shoot down
nunner/gniee, v.; nunnergegniet, pp. kneel down
nunner/graddle, v.; nunnergegraddelt, pp. crawl down
nunner/greische, v.; nunnergegrische, pp. call down
nunner/gucke, v.; nunnergeguckt, pp. look down
nunner/hacke, v.; nunnerghackt, pp. chop down
nunner/heese, v.; nunnergheese, pp. order (one) down
nunner/helfe, v.; nunnergholfe, pp. help down
nunner/hupse, v.; nunnerghupst, pp. hop down
nunner/keere, v.; nunnergekeert, pp. belong down
nunner/kehre, v.; nunnergekehrt, pp. sweep down
nunner/kiehle, v.; nunnergekiehlt, pp. cool down
nunner/klempe, v.; nunnergeklempt, pp. turn down (edges)
nunner/knalle, v.; nunnerknallt, pp. shoot down
nunner/koche, v.; nunnergekocht, pp. boil down
nunner/lege, v.; nunnergelegt, pp. lay down
nunner/losse, v.; nunnergelosst, pp. let down
nunner/mache, v.; nunnergemacht, pp. abase
nunner/maerricke, v.; nunnergemaerrickt, pp. mark down
nunner/misse, v.; nunnergemisst, pp. be obliged to go down

nutzlich

nunner/naggle, v.; nunnergenaggelt, pp. nail down
nunner/nemme, v.; nunnergenumme, pp. take down
nunner/packe, v.; nunnergepackt, pp. (sich --) go down stairs
nunner/reeche, v.; nunnergereecht, pp. reach or hand down
nunner/reisse, v.; nunnergerisse, pp. tear down
nunner/reiwe, v.; nunnergeriwwe, pp. rub down
nunner/renne, v.; nunnergerennt, pp. poke down
nunner/rolle, v.; nunnergerollt, pp. roll down
nunner/rutsche, v.; nunnergerutscht, pp. slide down
nunner/salze, v.; nunnergsalze, pp. salt down
nunner/schleefe, v.; nunnergschleeft, pp. drag down
nunner/schleife, v.; nunnergschliffe, pp. slide down
nunner/schlucke, v.; nunnergschluckt, pp. swallow down
nunner/schnaerre, v.; nunnergschnaerrt, pp. jerk down
nunner/schnalle, v.; nunnergschnallt, pp. buckle down
nunner/schnappe, v.; nunnergschnappt, pp. tilt down
nunner/schprenge, v.; nunnergschprengt, pp. force to rundown
nunner/schpringe, v.; nunnergschprunge, pp. run down
nunner/schreiwe, v.; nunnergschriwwe, pp. record
nunner/schrode, v.; nunnergschrot, pp. eat ravenously
nunner/schtatze, v.; nunnergschtatzt, pp. topple
nunner/schteige, v.; nunnergschtigge, pp. step down
nunner/schtimme, v.; nunnergschtimmt, pp. vote down
nunner/schtosse, v.; nunnergschtosse, pp. push down
nunner/schtrecke, v.; nunnergschtreckt, pp. stretch down
nunner/schwenke, v.; nunnergschwenkt, pp. use as a chaser
nunner/sehne, v.; nunnergsehne, pp. see down
nunner/setze, v.; nunnergsetzt, pp. set down
nunner/weise, v.; nunnergewisse, pp. show the way down
nunner/yaage, v.; nunnergeyaagt, pp. chase down
nunner/ziege, v.; nunnergezogge, pp. move down
nunner/ziehe, v.; nunnergezogge, pp. pull down
nunner, adv. down
nunner, prep (es Land --) down country
Nunnerschrift (die)n. minutes (of a meeting)
nunnerzus, adv. 1.downwards; 2.on the way down
Nuppe (die)n., pl. 1.cunning; 2.tricks
nur, adv. only
nusch(d)le, v.;genusch(d)elt, pp. nurse or suck complacently (of an infant)
Nuss (die)n.; Niss, pl. nut
nutsche, v.; genutscht, pp. suckle
Nutz (der)n. 1.use; 2.worth
nutz, adv. 1.of use; 2.worth
Nutze (der)n. 1.benefit; 2.profit; 3.use
nutze, v.; genutzt, pp. 1.avail; 2.benefit; 3.use
Nutzhols (es)n. in standing timber that part which is available for lumber
nutzlich, adj. beneficial

Oo

O!

Ordning

O!, interj. oh!

ob, conj. 1.if; 2.whether

Obacht (die)n. 1.attention; 2.care

Obdach (es)n. 1.covering; 2.shelter

Obs (es)n. fruit(s)

obschon(n), conj. although

Obscht (es)n. fruit(s)

Obschtbaam (der)n. fruit tree

Obschtyaahr (es)n. year rich in fruit

obsenaat, adj. stubborn

Obst (es)n. fruit(s)

obwohl, conj. although

Ochdem (der)n. 1.breath; 2.(aus --) out of breath

Ochsedrenk (die)n. watering place for cattle

Ochsefuhr (die)n. yoke of oxen

Ochsegraas (es)n. 1.slender cyperus; 2.slender galingale

Ochseyoch (es)n. ox yoke

Ochsezung (die)n. 1.alkanet; 2.bugloss; 3.oxtongue; 4.viper's bugloss

ochsich, adj. 1.brutal; 2.senseless

odder, conj. or

odders = odder es or it

Odem (der)n. 1.breath; 2.(aus --) out of breath

Oder (die)n.; Odere, pl. 1.artery; 2.vein

odere, v.; geodert, pp. ooze from a wound or abraded skin

Odergraut (es)n. rattlesnake weed

oderich, adj. veined

oderlosse, v.; oddergelosst, pp. open a vein

Odermennche (es)n. agrimony

Odermennich (es)n. agrimony

Odermennli (es)n. agrimony

Offe (der)n.; Effe, pl. 1.oven; 2.stove

Offe-elboge (der)n.; Offe-elboge, pl. stovepipe elbow

Offebascht (die)n. stove brush

Offebee (es)n. stove leg

Offeblatt (die)n. plate at front of cook-stove

Offedeckel (der)n. stove lid

Offedeer (die)n. stove door

Offeeise (es)n. lifter (for stove plates)

Offeglaas (es)n. 1.isin-glass; 2.mica

Offelaade (der)n.; Offelaade, pl. shelf on kitchen stove

offenbaar, adj. manifest

offenbaare, v.; (ge)offenbaart, pp. reveal

Offenbaaring (die)n. (Book of) Revelation

offentlich, adv. 1.openly; 2.publicly

Offerohr (es)n. stovepipe

Offeschtupp (die)n. 1.formal room; 2.stove room

Offeschwaerz (die)n. stove polish

oft, adv. often

oftmols, adv. 1.often; 2.ofttimes

oftzeide, adv. ofttimes

Oh!, interj. oh!

Ohmet (es)n. 1.aftermath; 2.second crop; 3.(-- mache) secure the second crop of hay

Ohr (es)n.; Ohre, pl. ear

Ohrbambel (die)n. ear ring

Ohre (die)n., pl (-- schpitze) prick the ears

Ohrebleeser (der)n. 1.talebearer; 2.tattler; 3.telltale

Ohrebloser (der)n. telltale

Ohredroppe (die)n., pl. fuchsia

Ohreglocke (die)n. fuchsia

Ohrelappe (der)n. ear lap

Ohrering (der)n. 1.ear ring; 2.fuchsia

Ohreschmals (es)n. ear wax

Ohreschuh (der)n. shoe provided with a strap for pulling on it

Ohreweh (es)n. ear ache

Ohrfei(k) (die)n. box on the ear

Oi (es)n.; Oier, pl. 1. egg; 2.(es weiss vum --) (a) albumen; (b) the white of an egg

Oidodder (der)n. yolk (of an egg)

Oierdotsch (es)n. omelet

Oierkuche (der)n. 1.omelet; 2.sponge cake

Oiermehl (es)n. omelet

Oierschtock (der)n. ovary (in fowls)

Oii!, interj. exclamation of astonishment

Oischder (die)n. oyster

Oiyerglepperer (der)n. egg beater

Oiyerschaal (die)n. eggshell

Oktober (der)n. October

Oktower (der)n. October

Olanswatzel (die)n. elecampane

Olich (der)n. 1.linseed oil; 2.(-- schlagge) manufacture oil from flaxseed or butternuts

Olichkuche (der)n. mass left after pressing the oil from flaxseed

Olichmehl (es)n. pressings from flaxseed ground for cattle feed

Olichsack (der)n. bag in which the crushed mass was put for pressing flaxseed

Olichschtembel (der)n. stone used in crushing flaxseed (or butternuts) in making oil

Olichschtenner (der)n.; Olichschtenner, pl. vat for holding flaxseed oil

Omet (es)n. 1.aftermath; 2.second crop of hay

Onkel (der)n. uncle

oob, conj. 1.if; 2.whether

Ool (die)n. eel

Oolehaut (die)n. eel skin

Oolehols (es)n. moosewood

Oolekarb (der)n. eel trap

Oos (es)n. 1.carrion; 2.vituperative term

Ooshaahne (der)n.; Ooshaahne, pl. turkey buzzard

Ooshinkel (es)n.; Ooshinkel, pl. turkey buzzard

Oosvog(g)el (der)n. turkey buzzard

Opedildack (es)n. opodeldoc

Opfer (es)n. 1.offering; 2.sacrifice; 3.victim

Opfergeld (es)n. 1.collection; 2.offering

ordentlich, adv. orderly

ordlich neegseht, adv. almost

ordlich, adj. local

ordlich, adv. 1.considerable; 2.queer; 3.quite; 4.rather

Ordning (die)n. 1.discipline; 2.order

Oo

Ordnung

Ordnung (die)n. 1.discipline; 2.order
Orschbackekarreb (der)n. basket (so named because of the shape of the bottom)
Orschdarem (der)n. rectum
Ort (der)n. 1.kind; 2.place; 3.quality; 4.sort; 5.way; 6.(aus der -- schlagge) (a) degenerate; (b) deteriorate; 7.(dass es en -- hott) (a) excellently; (b) splendidly; (c) to beat the band; (d) well ; 8.(noch aller --) like everything; 9.(uff en -- wie) (a) kind o'; (b) sort o'; 10.(uff was fern --) in what way
Oschderblumm (die)n. 1.daffodil; 2.narcissus
Oschderfescht (es)n. Passover
Oschderhaas (der)n. 1.Easter present; 2.Easter rabbit
Oschderlusi (die)n. birthwort
Oschdermariye (der)n. Easter morn
Oschdermondaag (der)n. Easter Monday
Oschderoi (es)n. Easter egg
Oschdersundaag (der)n. Easter Sunday
Oschderwoch (die)n. Easter week
Oschdre (die)n., pl. Easter
Oscht (der)n. east
Osswoi (der)n. turkey buzzard
ouschich, adj. growing in clumps or bunches
Owed (der)n. evening
Owedesse (es)n. supper
Owedrot (es)n. evening glow
oweds, adv. 1.in the evening; 2.(-- denno) the evening after
Owedschtaern (die)n. evening star
Owet (der)n. evening
owwe, adv. above
owwebei, adv. from above
owwedraa, adv. 1.at the top of it; 2.above it
owwedraus, adj. up-country (somewhere)
owwedraus, adv. out up above
owwedrin, adv. up in above
owwedriwwer, adj. superficially
owwedriwwer, adv. over the top
owwedrowwe, adv. 1.up above; 2.upstairs
owwedruff, adv. 1.on the surface; 2.on top; 3.in addition
owwehaer, adv. along the top
owwehie, adv. 1.along the top; 2.along up above
Owweledder (es)n. upper part of a shoe
owwenaus, adj. up-country
owwenaus, adv. out up above
owwenei, adv. up in above
owwenuff, adv. upstairs
owwer = ob er whether he
owwer, adj. upper
Owwerdenn (es)n. loft over the threshing floor
owwerei, adv. 1.from above; 2.from up country
owwerflechlich, adj. superficially
Owwerhand (die)n. 1.superiority; 2.upper hand
Owwerichkeit (die)n. government
Owwerledder (es)n. vamp (of a shoe, boot)
owwerunner, adv. 1.from above; 2.from upstairs
owwewedder, adv. against the top

Oxekarich

owwich, adj. over
owwich, prep. 1.above; 2.over
Ox (der)n. 1.block head; 2.ox; 3.steer; 4.Taurus (2nd sign of the zodiac)
Ox (die)n.; Oxe, pl. ox
Oxekarich (der)n.; Oxekarich, pl. ox-cart

Pp

Paabscht

Paabscht (der)n. Pope
Paad (der)n. path
Paar (es)n. 1.couple; 2.pair
paar, pron., adj. 1.a few; 2.pair; 3.some
paare, v.; gepaart, pp. 1.match; 2.pair; 3.(sich --) mate
paarmol, adv. few times
paarweis, adv. 1.by pairs; 2.by twos
Pack (der)n.; Peck, pl. 1.bundle (of a peddler); 2.pack; 3. package
packe, v.; gepackt, pp. 1.arrest; 2.seize; 3.wrestle
Pae(r)sching (der)n. peach
Paedche (es)n. path
Paedel (es)n. path
Paep (der)n. 1.dad; 2.father
Paerschingbaam (der)n.; Paerschingbeem, pl. peach tree
Paerschingbungert (der)n. peach orchard
Paerschingschtee (der)n.; Paerschingschtee, pl. peach stone
paerseenlich, adj. 1.in person; 2.personal
Paerson (die)n. 1.individual; 2.person
Paert (die)n. 1.part; 2.share
Paertner (der)n. partner
Paertschli (es)n. little porch
Paff (der)n. negative term for minister or priest
Paffekaffe (die)n., pl. nasturtiums
Paffekapp (die)n. skullcap
Paffesack (der)n. priest's (minister's) pocket
Paffeschtofft (es)n. (crowd of) ministers
Pafflekaffle (die)n., pl. nasturtiums
palde, v.; gepalde, pp. keep
Palledix (die)n. politics
Pallem (der)n. palm
Pallemsunndaag (der)n. Palm Sunday
Palm (der)n. palm
Palmblaatt (es)n. palm leaf
Palmsundaag (der)n. Palm Sunday
Pals (die)n. Palatinate
Palscht (der)n. palace
Palz (die)n. Palatinate
Pann (die)n.; Panne, pl. pan
Pannedeckel (der)n. pan-cover
Pannekuche (der)n.; Pannekuche, pl. 1.fritter; 2.pancake
Pannekuchedaag (der)n. Shrove Tuesday
Panneschtiel (der)n. panhandle
Panneschtielche (es)n. jesting name for an infant before it has been baptized
Pannhaas (der)n. scrapple
Pantoffel (der)n. slipper (rare usage)
Pap (der)n. Dad
paplaer, adj. popular
Pappi (der)n. 1.daddy; 2.father
Paradies (es)n. paradise
Parble (die)n. smallpox
Parble (die)n. (-- blanze) vaccinate
Parbleblanz (die)n. vaccine
Parblegrind (der)n. scab of small pox or vaccination
parebes, adv. purposely

Peif

parebislich, adv. purposely
Paredies (es)n. paradise
Paresiesbaam (der)n. ailanthus
Park (der)n. park
Parre (der) n.; Parre, pl. minister or preacher (used by members of the Lutheran and Reformed churches)
Parre(s)fraa (die)n. minister's wife
Parrefresse (es)n. sumptuous feast
Parregeld (es)n. money contributed to the support of the minister (Lutheran and Reformed churches)
parremaessich, adj. clerical
parrenaerrisch, adj. 1. infatuated with parsons; 2. over attentive to parsons
Parreschtell (die)n. parish
Parreskind (es)n. catechumen
Parreskinner (die)n., pl. catechumens
Partei (die)n. party
Paschdor (der)n. pastor
Pasching (der)n. peach
Pasching Ledder (es)n. dried peaches
Paschingsaame (der)n.; Paschingsaame, pl. peach stone
Passionsblumm (die)n. passion flower
patrioodisch, adj. patriotic
Patrioot (der)n. patriot
Pattwaschtfillsel (es) n. 1. meat scraps left over from a butchering; 2.pudding
Paul (der)n. Paul
Pauschbacke (der)n. 1.chubby cheek; 2.swelled-out cheek
pauschbackich, adj. chubby-cheeked
Pauschdier (es)n. marsupial
Pazient (der)n. patient
Peckche (es)n. 1.pimple; 2.small parcel
Pedder (der) n. 1.godfather; 2.(-- un god) sponsors (at baptismal)
Peedche (es)n. path
Peedel (es)n. path
Peeder (der)n. Peter
Peeder un Paul (der)n. Peter and Paul Day, June 29
Peederkett (der)n. Peter in Chains Day, August 1
Pe(e)derli (der)n. parsley
Peedli (es)n.; Peedlin, pl. narrow path
peeke, v.; gepeekt, pp. perform intercourse
Peffer (der)n.; Peffer, pl. 1.pepper; 2.(siesser --) sweet pepper
peffere, v.; gepeffert, pp. 1.pepper; 2.put a high price of something
Peffergraas (es)n. wild pepper grass
Peffergraut (es)n. wild pepper grass
Pefferholz (es)n. spice-wood
Peffermins (der)n. peppermint
Pefferniss (die)n., pl. type of Christmas cookie
pehz, adj. 1.epidemic; 2.long illness
Pei (es)n. pie
Peibritsch (die)n. pie-paddle
Peif (die)n.; Peife, pl. 1.drain pipe; 2.fife; 3.pipe (tobacco); 4.whistle

Pp

Peifarigel

Peifarigel (die)n.; Peifarigele, pl. pipe organ
peife, v.; gepiffe, pp. whistle
Peifel (es)n. pipe
Peifer (der)n.; Peifer, pl. 1.piper; 2.whistler
Peifreehr (die)n. pipe stem
Peifrehe (die)n. pipe-stem
Peil (der)n. arrow
Peiler (der)n.; Peiler, pl. 1.jamb; 2.pier; 3.pillar
Peilesack (der)n. quiver (of arrows)
Peilschpitz (der)n. arrow head
Pein (die)n. 1.affliction; 2.pain; 3.torment
peine, v.; gepeint, pp. long
Peinich (die)n. 1.punishment; 2.plague
peiniche, v.; gepeinicht, pp. 1.plague; 2.torment
Peinis (die)n., pl. peony
peinlich, adj. 1.painful; 2.tormenting
pelsich, adj. Palatine
Pelzer (der)n.; Pelzer, pl. Palatine
penede = wassersupp a soup made of bread, water, salt
    and pepper, (contemptuous for any thin soup)
Pennsilfaani, n. Pennsylvania
Pennsilfaanisch Deitsch, adj. Pennsylvania Dutch (German)
pennsilfaanisch, adj. Pennsylvania
Pennsilweeni Deitsch, adj. Pennsylvania Dutch (German)
Pennsilweeni, n. Pennsylvania
Pennsylvaani, n. Pennsylvania
Pennsylvaanier (der)n. Pennsylvanian
Pensil (der)n. painter's brush
Pescht (die)n.; Peschde, pl. 1.blight; 2.pest; 3.pestilence;
    4.plague; 5.torment
Peschtbloder (die).; Peschtblodere, pl. carbuncle
peschthaft, adj. pestiferous
Pett (die)n. 1.purline; 2.template
Petz (die)n. 1.pinch; 2.tight place
petze, v.; gepetzt, pp. 1.anger; 2.pinch; 3.pinch a top
    crust on pie before baking; 4.vex
Petzer (der)n.; Petzer, pl. 1.pinch; 2.pliers; 3.punch
Pfleech (die)n. fostering care
pflege, v.; gepflegt, pp. 1.foster; 2.tend
pflichdich, adj. 1.bound; 2.responsible
Pflicht (die)n. 1.duty; 2.obligation
Pharisaer (der)n.; Pharisaer, pl. Pharisee
Philepiene (es)n. philippina
Philibbine (die)n. Philippine
Philippine (die)n. Philippine
Philischder (der)n. pedant
Phillipp (der)n. Philip
Philosoph (der)n. philosopher
Philp (der)n. Philip
Pick (die)n. pick ax
Pickder (es)n.; Pickder, pl. 1.photograph; 2.picture
picke, v.; gepickt, pp. 1.pick; 2.use a pick
Pickelfleesch (es)n. pickled meat
pickle, v.; gepickelt, pp. 1.pickle; 2.salt
Pickling (der)n. dried herring
Picknick (die)n. picnic

plaud(e)rich

Pidder (der)n. Peter
piddle, v.; gepiddelt, pp. piddle
Piens (die)n. 1.ailing person; 2.sickly
piense, v.; gepienst, pp. (to be) sickly or ailing
piensich, adj. 1.ailing; 2.complaining; 3.delicate
piepse, v.; gepiepst, pp. 1.ail; 2.be sick; 3.mention;
    4.peep (of chickens)
piesse, v.; gepiesst, pp. sizz (sound made when wetting
    hot iron)
Piewie (der, es)n.; Piewie, pl. peewee (small bird)
Piff (der)n. 1.rap; 2.shrill whistle; 3.straw
Pill (die)n.; Pille, pl. pill
Pilleroller (der)n. facetious for a doctor
Pilverlin (es)n. powder
Pilwe (die)n. pillow
Pilweziech (die)n. pillow case
Pilyer (der)n.; Pilyer, pl. pilgrim
Pilyerrees (die)n. Pilgrim's Progress
Pimpernell (der)n. pimpernel
Pinbohre (der)n.; Pinbohre, pl. pegging awl
Pingschde (die)n., pl. 1.Pentecost; 2.Whitsuntide
Pingschdeblumm (die)n. pinxter flower
Pingschtblumm (die)n.; Pinschtblumme, pl. 1.lilac;
    2.pink; 3.pinxter flower; 4.swamp pink
Pingschtblummeschtock (der)n.; Pingschtblum-
    meschteck, pl. lilac bush
Pingschtmundaag (der)n. Whitmonday
Pingschtnaggel (der)n. 1.lilac; 2.pink; 3.swamp pink
Pingschtsunndaag (der)n. Whitsunday
pink(t)lich, adv. 1.exact; 2.punctual
Pinnaggel (der)n. shoe-peg
Pinnbohre (der)n. pegging awl
Pinschtblumm (die)n.; Pinschtblumme, pl. 1.lilac;
    2.swamp-pink
pinsich, adj. puny
Pipser (der)n. pip
Piro (der)n. bureau
pischbere, v.; gepischbert, pp. whisper
Pischdol (die)n.; Pischdole, pl. pistol
pisse, v.; gepisst, pp. 1.piss; 2.urinate
Pissebett (der)n. dandelion
Pisseeche (der, die)n. piss-oak (hisses when it burns)
pisserich, adj. inclined to urinate
Pitt(er) (der)n. Peter
Piusdaag (der)n. Pius' Day, July 11
Plandaasch (die)n. 1.farm; 2.lot (in derision)
Planet (der)n. planet
Plank (die)n. plank
planke, v.; geplankt, pp. cover with planks
planse, v.; geplanst, pp. plant
Plappermaul (es)n. 1.blabber; 2.chatterbox
Plaschder (die)n. 1.plaster; 2.salve; 3.wearisome talker
Platt (die)n. plate (of a stove)
Platz (der)n.; Pletz, pl. 1.farmstead; 2.place
Platzregge (der)n. downpour
plaud(e)rich, adj. 1.friendly; 2.sociable; 3.talkative

Pp

plaudre

plaudre, v.; geplaudert, pp. 1.chat; 2.talk
Pletzel (es)n. place
plindere, v.; geplindert, pp. plunder
plitsch platsch, adv. slapdash
Plok (die)n. 1.ailment; 2.plague; 3.sickness; 4.toil; 5.trouble
Plug (der)n.; Plieg, Pliek, pl. plow
pluge, v.; geplu(g)kt, pp. plow
Plugschaar (es)n. plowshare
Plugschleef (es)n. 1.plow shoe; 2.plow drag
Plugschtrang (der)n. iron plow trace
Plug(s)grendel (der)n. plow beam
Plug(s)hendel (der)n. plow handle
Plug(s)naas (die)n. point of a plowshare
Plug(s)schleef (die)n. 1.plow drag; 2.plow shoe
Plug(s)schtrang (der)n. iron plow trace
Plug(s)sech (es)n. coulter
Plug(s)woog (die)n. double-tree
plump, adj. plump
plumpe, v.; geplumpt, pp. 1.flop down; 2.plump
plumps!, interj. 1.flop!; 2.thud!
Pock (die)n.; Pocke, pl. pimple
pockich, adj. 1.pimpled; 2.pimply
Poddre (die)n., pl. 1.beads; 2.baby beads
Pohaahne (der)n.; Pohinkel, pl. peacock
Pohaahnefedder (die)n. peacock's feather
Pohinkel (es)n.; Pohinkel, pl. peahen
Pokbeer (die)n.; Pokbeere, pl. pokeberry
poke, v.; gepokt, pp. 1.poke; 2.stir
Poker (der)n. 1.delirium tremens; 2.poker
pokich, adv. poking
Politik(s) (die)n. politics
polschdre, v.; gepolschdert, pp. 1.pad; 2.stuff
Portschgelender (es)n. porch railing
Posaunerkor (der)n. combined trombone players in Moravian ceremonies
Poschde (der)n.; Poschde, pl. 1.pillar; 2.post
Poschde-ax (die)n.; Poschde-ex, pl. post-ax
Poschdebohre (der)n. post-auger
Poschdefens (die)n. post fence
Poschdehund (der)n. post dog (of iron)
Poschdeloch(es)n.; Poschdelecher, pl. post hole
Poschdeschtamber (der)n. tamping tool
Poschtaffis (die)n. post office
Poschtgeld (es)n. postage
Poschtmeeschder (der)n.; Poschtmeeschder, pl. postmaster
Poschtreider (der)n. mounted mail carrier
positiv, adj. positively
Pott (die)n. 1.bud; 2.chamber (vessel)
Pracht (die)n. 1.beauty; 2.magnificence; 3.splendor
prachtvoll, adj. 1.magnificent; 2.sumptuous
pralle, v.; geprallt, pp. 1.boast; 2.brag
Praller (der)n. braggart
Prallhans (der)n. 1.boaster; 2.braggart
Preddich (die)n. sermon
Preddichamt (es)n. ministry
preddiche, v.; gepreddicht, pp. preach

Puttere

Preddicher (der)n. 1.minister; 2.preacher
Preifing (die)n. trial
Preis (der)n. 1.cost; 2.price
Preischder (der)n. 1.parson (contemptuous); 2.priest
Press (die)n. press
presse, v.; gepresst, pp. 1.press; 2.squeeze
Pressent (es)n. present
Pretzel (es)n. pretzel
prezis, adj. exactly
priefe, v.; geprieft, pp. (sich --) examine oneself
Priefing (die)n. 1.trail; 2.warning
Prieschder (der)n. 1.parson (contemptuous); 2.priest
Priggel (der)n. 1.club; 2.clubbing; 3.cudgel; 4.cudgeling; 5.limb of a tree
priggel schmeisse, v. abuse
Prinsipidaat (es)n (rot --) red precipitate
Priwwi (es)n. 1.back house; 2.outhouse
probaat, adj. 1.approved; 2.tried
Produkte (die)n., pl. produce
Professer (der)n. professor
prolaatsche = ballaadsche talk in a long and tiresome manner
Proteschdant (der)n. Protestant
Prunellegraut (es)n. 1.heal-all; 2.self-heal
Psallem (der)n. psalm
Psalm (der)n. psalm
Psalter (der)n. psalter
Psaref (es)n. preserves
psch!, interj. still!
Pserfs (es)n. preserves
pubbe, v.; gepuppt, pp. void the bowels
Puddel (der)n. puddle
puddelnass, adj. soaking wet
puddle, v.; gepuddelt, pp. puddle
puddre, v.; gepuddert, pp. take a dust bath (of fowls)
Pudelhund (der)n.; Pudelhund, pl. poodle
pudre, v.; gepudert, pp. powder
puff!, interj. bang! puff!
puh!, interj. 1.pooh!; 2.whew!
Pulfer (es)n. powder
Puls (der)n. pulse
pulschderich, adj. irregularly ball shaped
Pulver (es)n. powder
Pulwer (es)n. powder
Pulwerhann (es)n. powder horn
Pulwermiehl (die)n. powder-mill
Pund (es)n.; Pund, pl. pound
Pundabbel (der)n. pound-apple
punkich, adj. 1. pithy (of radishes); 2. spongy (of fruit, radishes)
Punkt (der)n.; Punkde, pl. 1.dot; 2.peak; 3.period; 4.point; 5.tip
Puppnacker (der)n. oil gland (of fowl) uropygial gland
Pusch (der)n. 1.clump of grass or shrubbery; 2.tuft
Puschduur (die)n. 1.form; 2.posture; 3.shape
Puscherei (die)n. 1.blunder; 2.botch
Puttere (schtengel) (der)n. moth mullein

133

Pp

Putz

Putz (der)n. miniature landscape (and other scenery used as a setting for the base of a Christmas tree)

putze, v.; geputzt, pp. wet hot pressing iron (with finger to see if it is hot)

puuze, v.; gepuuzt, pp. wet hot pressing iron (with finger to see if it is hot)

puuze

Rr

Raab

Raab (die)n. 1.booty; 2.prey
Raabdier (es)n. beast of prey
Raabe (der)n. raven
Raabnescht (es)n. robber's den
Raabvoggel (der)n. bird of prey
Raache (die)n. revenge
Raachgier (die)n. 1.greediness; 2.revengefulness;
    3. vindictiveness
raachgier(s)ch, adj. 1.avaricious; 2.greedy
raachgierisch, adj. revengeful
Raad (die)n.; Raade, pl. cockle
Raad (es)n.; Redder, pl. wheel
raadich, adj. 1.mangy; 2.scabby
Raadschtul (der)n.; Raadschtiel, pl. wheelchair
Raahm (der)n. cream
Raahmdaader (der)n. milk-pie
Raahmgraut (es)n. wild lettuce
Raahmgriegel (es)n. cream pitcher
Raahmleffel (der)n. 1.skimmer; 2.skimming ladle
Raan (die)n.; Raane, pl. welt
raar, adj. 1.infrequently; 2.rare; 3.scarce
Rarichkeet (die)n. 1.rarity; 2.scarcity
raase, v.; g(e)raast, pp. 1.rage; 2.rave; 3.rush about
raasend, adj. 1.furious; 2.rabid; 3.raging; 4.raving
Raaserei (die)n. 1.fury; 2.madness
raasich, adj. furious
raawe, v.; geraabt, pp. 1.ravish; 2.rob
Raawer (der)n.; Raawer, pl. 1.bandit; 2.robber
Raawerband (die)n. band of robbers
Raawerei (die)n. robbery
Raawes (es)n. the act of robbing someone
Rabbel (es)n.; Rabble, pl. rattle
Rabbelkaschde (der)n. 1.rattletrap; 2.roustabout
rabbelkebbi(s)ch, adj. 1.obstinate; 2.rebellious; 3.stubborn
Rabbelzott (die)n. slattern
rabble, v.; gerabbelt, pp. 1.murmur; 2.rustle
rabblich, adj. 1.dilapidated; 2.rattling
rabsche, v.; gerabscht, pp. (to be) greedy or avaricious
rabschich, adj. 1.greedy; 2.avaricious
Rache (der)n. 1.abyss; 2.mouth
Rachebrecher (der)n. bridle bit for fractious horses
Rachebutzer (der)n.; Rachebutzer, pl. 1.jaw breaker;
    2.napkin; 3.serviette; 4.(a) tough one
Radefall (die)n,.; Raddefalle, pl. rattrap
Raddegift (es)n. rat gut (poison)
Raddenescht (es)n. rat nest
Raddeschwanz (der)n. rattail
raeche, v.; geraecht, pp. avenge
raede, v.; geraedt, pp. 1.sieve; 2.stir (fire)
Raedel (der)n. boom pole (used in binding together a load
    of logs or lumber, or in keeping a load of hay compact)
raerrich, adj. rainy
raessle, v.; graesselt, pp. wrestle
Raetsel (es)n. 1.conundrum; 2.riddle
raetze, v.; geraetzt, pp. moisten and dry alternately (as in
    curing flax)

Raus mit der Fareb!

raffe, v.; gerafft, pp. 1.gather up hastily; 2.snatch
Raffel (die)n. mouth
Raffelgsicht (es)n. mask
Rageet (die)n. rocket
Rahmleffel (der)n. skimmer
rammlich, adj. 1.lascivious; 2.lecherous
Ran (die)n. welt
Ran(e)ft (der)n. 1.edge; 2.rim (of a hat)
Rank (die)n.; Ranke, pl. 1.tendril; 2.vine
ranke, v.; gerankt, pp. put forth vines
Rankegift (es)n. poison ivy
Rankelbohn (die)n. running bean
Rankeldanne (die)n.,pl. 1.dewberry; 2.running brier
rank(l)ich, adj. 1.cirrose; 2.climbing; 3.tangled
Rannli (es)n. 1.run; 2.small stream
Ranse (der)n. 1.belly; 2.large piece; 3.mouth
ranse, v.; geranst, pp. 1.range around; 2.strut
ransich, adj. 1.rancid; 2.rank
Rappelkopp (der)n. dull person
rapple, v.; gerabbelt, pp. rattle
Rappli (es)n.; Rapplin, pl. (baby's) rattle
rapplich, adj. 1.dilapidated; 2.rattling
Raridaet (die)n. a curiosity
rasch(t), adj. 1.hasty; 2.headlong; 3.quick; 4.nimble
rasch, adv. precipitate(ly)
Raschbe(l) (der)n.; Raschbe(l), pl. rasp
raschble, v.; geraschbelt, pp. rasp
raschdich, adj. 1.hearty; 2.vigorous
Rascht (die)n. rest
Rasem (der)n. rosin
rasiere, v.; gerasiert, pp. (sich --) shave (oneself)
Rassel (die)n. rattle
Rasselschlang (die)n. rattlesnake
Rasselschlangebledder (die), pl. rattlesnake weed
Rasselschlangwatzel (die)n. lion's foot
rassle, v.; gerasselt, pp. 1.jar; 2.rattle; 3.rumble; 4.rustle
Ratt (die)n.; Ratte, pl. 1.rat; 2.(en -- schmacke) smell a rat
rau, adj.; adv. 1.rude; 2.rudely; 3.vulgar
Raub (die)n.; Rauwe, pl. caterpillar
raubaschdich, adj.; adv. 1.robust; 2.rough; 3.rude;4.rudely
raubauzich, adj.; adv. 1.rude; 2.rudely
raubeenich, adj. 1.rowdyish; 2.unmannerly
Raubelz (der)n. 1.rowdy; 2.ruffian; 3.unmannerly fellow
raubelzich, adj. 1.rowdyish; 2.unmannerly
Raubengel (der)n. 1.rowdy; 2.ruffian
Raubiggel (der)n. unmannerly fellow
Rauch (der)n. smoke
Raude (die)n. rue
rauh, adj. 1.coarse; 2.inclement; 3.raucous; 4.raw; 5.rough
Rauhbauz (der)n. boor
rauhelsich, adj. hoarse
rauhschaalich, adj. rough-shelled (pear)
Raumaurer (der)n. stonemason
Raup (die)n. caterpillar
Raupenescht (es)n. caterpillars' nest
Raus mit der Fareb! Speak out!

Rr

raus mit!   raus/schaele

raus mit!, interj. out with it!

raus/addere, v.; rausgeaddert, pp. order out

raus/baschde, v.; rausgebascht, pp. brush out

raus/batzle, v.; rausgebatzelt, pp. tumble out

raus/beisse, v.; rausgebisse, pp. 1.bite out; 2.supplant

raus/belse, v.; rausgebelst, pp. pound out

raus/biege, v.; rausgeboge, pp. bend out

raus/biete, v.; rausgebotte, pp. challenge

raus/biggele, v.; rausgebiggelt, pp. iron out

raus/binne, v.; rausgebunne, pp. tie outside

raus/blaerre, v.; rausgeblaerrt, pp. blurt out

raus/blanze, v.; rausgeblanzt, pp. transplant

raus/blatsche, v.; rausgeblatscht, pp. 1.blurt out; 2.utter incautiously

raus/blaudre, v.; rausgeblaudert, pp. cause to change one's mind

raus/bleche, v.; rausgeblecht, pp. pay up (reluctantly)

raus/blicke, v.; rausgeblickt, pp. glance out

raus/blose, v.; rausgeblose, pp. blow out

raus/bluge, v.; rausgeblugt, pp. plow out (as potatoes)

raus/bohre, v.; rausgebohrt, pp. bore out

raus/breche, v.; rausgebroche, pp. break out (of confinement)

raus/brenne, v.; rausgebrennt, pp. burn out

raus/briee, v.; rausgebriet, pp. hatch out

raus/bringe, v.; rausgebrocht, pp. 1.bring out; 2.utter

raus/bumpe, v.; rausgebumpt, pp. pump out

raus/butze, v.; rausgebutzt, pp. clean out

raus/daerfe, v.; rausgedaerft, pp. be allowed out

raus/dappe, v.; rausgedappt, pp. walk out heavily

raus/draage, v.; rausgedraage, pp. carry out

raus/drede, v.; rausgedrede, pp. 1.kick out; 2.tramp out

raus/drehe, v.; rausgedreht, pp. turn out

raus/dreiwe, v.; rausgedriwwe, pp. drive out

raus/dresche, v.; rausgedroscht, pp. thresh out

raus/dricke, v.; rausgedrickt, pp. squeeze out

raus/dropse, v.; rausgedropst, pp. come out in drops

raus/drumme, v.; rausgedrummt, pp. drum out

raus/duh, v.; rausgeduh, pp. 1.evict; 2.put out

raus/dunnere, v.; rausgedunnert, pp. come out tumultuously

raus/faahre, v.; rausgfaahre, pp. 1.be gruff; 2.drive out; 3.fly into a passion

raus/falle, v.; rausgfalle, pp. fall out

raus/fange, v.; rausgfange, pp. catch from a number

raus/fasse, v.; rausg(e)fasst, pp. measure some out

raus/faule, v.; rausgfault, pp. rot out

raus/fitze, v.; rausgfitzt, pp. drive out with a whip

raus/fliege, v.; rausgflogge, pp. fly out

raus/foddre, v.; rausgfoddert, pp. 1.challenge; 2.defy

raus/fresse, v.; rausgfresse, pp. 1.eat out of; 2.(sich --) (a) recoup; (b) recover

raus/gaerwe, v.; rausgegaerbt, pp. drive out by whipping

raus/geh, v.; rausgange, pp. leave

raus/gewwe, v.; rausgewwe, pp. 1.make public; 2.publish

raus/gloppe, v.; rausgegloppt, pp. hammer out

raus/graawe, v.; rausgegraawe, pp. dig out or up

raus/graddle, v.; rausgegraddelt, pp. 1.crawl out; 2.get out of bed

raus/gratze, v.; rausgegratzt, pp. scratch out

raus/griege, v.; rausgrickt, pp. get out

raus/gucke, v.; rausgeguckt, pp. look out

raus/hacke, v.; rausghackt, pp. 1.chop out; 2.hoe out

raus/haschble, v.; rausghaschbelt, pp. come out fortuitously

raus/helfe, v.; rausgholfe, pp. 1.assist; 2.help out; 3.lend a hand

raus/henke, v.; rausghenkt, pp. hang out

raus/hetze, v.; rausghetzt, pp. drive out by dogs

raus/hewe, v.; raughowe, pp. lift out

raus/hole, v.; rausgholt, pp. fetch out

raus/huschde, v.; rausghuscht, pp. cough up

raus/kehre, v.; rausgekehrt, pp. sweep out

raus/kenne, v.; rausgekennt, pp. be able to get out

raus/kotze, v.; rausgekotzt, pp. vomit (it) out

raus/kumme, v.; is rauskumme, pp. 1.become known; 2. be issued 3.come out; 4.emerge; 5.hatch out; 6.result; 7.([iwwer] eens --) tally

raus/laafe, v.; rausgeloffe, pp. 1.run out (of liquids); 2.walk out

raus/laahne, v.; rausglaahnt, pp. lean out

raus/lange, v.; rausgelangt, pp. reach out

raus/lege, v.; raugelekt, pp. lay out

raus/leichte, v.; rausgeleicht, pp. light someone's way out

raus/lese, v.; rausglese, pp. 1.pick out; 2.select

raus/liege, v.; rausgelogge, pp. (sich --) get off by lying

raus/locke, v.; rausgelockt, pp. entice out

raus/loddle, v.; rausgeloddelt, pp. loosen

raus/mache, v.; rausgemacht, pp. 1. dig or remove (as potatoes or stones); 2.(sich --) (a) recover; (b) succeed

raus/maerricke, v.; rausgemaerrickt, pp. mark out

raus/maschiere, v.; rausmaschiert, pp. march out

raus/mehe, v.; rausgemeht, pp. mow around (some obstruction in a field)

raus/misse, v.; rausgemisst, pp. be obliged to get out

raus/nemme, v.; rausgenumme, pp. take out

raus/packe, v.; rausgepackt, pp. (sich --) leave

raus/picke, v.; rausgepickt, pp. pick out

raus/poke, v.; rausgepokt, pp. poke out

raus/reche, v.; rausgerecht, pp. rake out of

raus/reeche, v.; rausgereecht, pp. 1.hand out; 2.reach out

raus/reisse, v.; rausgerisse, pp. tear out

raus/renne, v.; rausgerennt, pp. rush out

raus/ricke, v.; rausgerickt, pp. move out

raus/rinne, v.; rausgerunne, pp. leak out

raus/robbe, v.; rausgeroppt, pp. pull out

raus/rolle, v.; rausgerollt, pp. roll out

raus/roschde, v.; rausgeroscht, pp. rust out

raus/rufe, v.; rausgerufe, pp. call out

raus/rutsche, v.; rausgerutscht, pp. slide out

raus/saage, v.; rausgsaat, pp. speak freely

raus/saege, v.; rausgsaegt, pp. saw out

raus/schaele, v.; rausgschaelt, pp. (sich --) evade

136

Rr

raus/schaffe

raus/schaffe, v.; rausgschafft, pp. (sich --) 1.evade; 2.get
out of; 3.make one's way out

raus/schalle, v.; rausgschallt, pp. sound out from

raus/scharre, v.; rausgschatt, pp. scratch out

raus/scheele, v.; rausgscheelt, pp. (sich --) evade
(responsibility)

raus/scheine, v.; rausgscheint, pp. shine out

raus/schenke, v.; rausgschenkt, pp. pour out (coffee,
milk, etc.)

raus/scheppe, v.; rausgscheppt, pp. dip out

raus/schidde, v.; rausgschitt, pp. pour out

raus/schittle, v.; rausgschittelt, pp. shake out

raus/schlagge, v.; rausgschlagge, pp. 1.beat out; 2.burst
out; 3.(sich --) (a) make good; (b) succeed

raus/schlecke, v.; rausgschlekt, pp. lick out of

raus/schleefe, v.; rausgschleeft, pp. drag out

raus/schleife, v.; rausgschliffe, pp. slide out

raus/schliddle, v.; rausgschiddelt, pp. shake out

raus/schlippe, v.; rausgschlippt, pp. slip out

raus/schmeisse, v.; rausgschmisse, pp. 1.eject; 2.throw out

raus/schmelse, v.; rausgschmolse, pp. melt out

raus/schnaare, v.; rausgschnarrt, pp. utter with a growl

raus/schnabbe, v.; rausgschnappt, pp. utter unguardedly

raus/schnaere, v.; rausgschnaert, pp. jerk out

raus/schneide, v.; rausgschnidde, pp. cut out

raus/schnelle, v; rausgschnellt, pp. jerk out

raus/schneppe, v.; rausgschneppt, pp. tilt out

raus/schpaerre, v.; rausgschpaerrt, pp. lock out

raus/schpanne, v.; rausgschpannt, pp. 1.unharness;
2.unhitch (horses from a wagon)

raus/schprenge, v.; rasugschprengt, pp. 1.blast out;
2.drive out

raus/schpringe, v.; rausgschprunge, pp. run out

raus/schpritze, v.; rausgschpritzt, pp. splash out

raus/schrauwe, v.; rausgschraubt, pp. screw out

raus/schtaerme, v.; rausgschtaermt, pp. storm out

raus/schtampe, v.; rausgschtampt, pp.(come) stamping out

raus/schtarre, v.; rausgschtarrt, pp. stir out

raus/schtatze, v.; rausgschtatzt, pp. tumble out

raus/schteche, v.; rausgschtoche, pp. 1.dig out with a
fork (potatoes); 2.remove from a kettle with a fork

raus/schtecke, v.; rausgschteckt, pp. stick out

raus/schteeniche, v.; rausgschteenicht, pp. chase by
throwing stones

raus/schteh, v.; rausgschtanne, pp. 1.jut out; 2.project

raus/schtelle, v.; rausgschtellt, pp. set out (plants)

raus/schtewwere, v.;rausgschtewwert, pp. chase out

raus/schtimme, v.; rausgschtimmt, pp. defeat by voting
(an official)

raus/schtolpere, v.; rausgschtolpert, pp. stumble out

raus/schtoose, v.; rausgschtoose, pp. project

raus/schtraehle, v.; rausgschtraehlt, pp. comb out

raus/schtrecke, v.; rausgschtreckt, pp. stretch out

raus/schtreiche, v.; rausgschtriche, pp. (sich --) 1.plead
excuses; 2.sound one's own praises

raus/schtreiche, v.; rausgschtriche, pp. 1.exonerate;

rechere

2.shield

raus/schtritze, v.; rausgschtritzt, pp. 1.squirt; 2.sprinkle;
3.splash

raus/schtuppe, v.; rausgschtuppt, pp. prod out of

raus/schwaerme, v.; rausgschwaermt, pp. swarm out

raus/schweere, v.; rausgschwore, pp. swear out (a warrant)

raus/schweese, v.; rausgschweest, pp. 1.leak; 2.ooze

raus/schwemme, v.; rausgschwemmt, pp. flood out

raus/schwenke, v.; rausgschwenkt, pp. rinse out

raus/schwere, v.; rausgschwert, pp. swear out (a warrant)

raus/schwetze, v.; rausgschwetzt, pp. 1.blab out; 2.speak
freely

raus/schwimme, v.; rausgschwumme, pp. swim out

raus/schwinge, v.; rausgschwunge, pp. swing out

raus/sehne, v.; rausgsehne, pp. look out

raus/seihe, v.; rausgseiht, pp. strain out

raus/setze, v.; rausgsetzt, pp. set out (plants)

raus/suche, v.; rausgsucht, pp. 1.pick out; 2.select

raus/suckle, v.; rausgsuckelt, pp. suck out

raus/suddre, v.; rausgsuddert, pp. ooze out

raus/wachse, v.; rausgewachst, pp. grow out

raus/wesche, v.; rausgewesche, pp. wash out

raus/wiehle, v.; rausgewiehlt, pp. root out

raus/witsche, v.; rausgewitscht, pp. slip out

raus/woge, v.; rausgewoge, pp. (sich --) venture out

raus/wolle, v.; rausgewollt, pp. want to come (get) out

raus/yaage, v.; rausgeyaagt, pp. chase out

raus/yutte, v.; rausgeyutt, pp. defraud

raus/zabbe, v.; rausgezappt, pp. tap

raus/zaehle, v.; rausgezaehlt, pp. count out

raus/ziege, v.; rausgezogge, pp. 1.move out; 2.pull (draw)
out

raus/ziehe, v.; rausgezieht, pp. draw out

raus/zoppe, v.; rausgezoppt, pp. jerk out

raus, adv.; prep. out of

Rausch (der)n. 1.intoxication; 2.jag

rauschberich, adj. raucous

rausche, v.; gerauscht, pp. 1.murmur; 2.plash; 3.rustle;
4.splash; 5.swash

Rauschebeidel (der)n. 1.rough fellow; 2.uncouth fellow

rauschend, adj. rousing

Rauscher (der)n. rouser

rauschperich, adj. 1.hoarse; 2.raucous

rauszus, adv. (on the way) coming out

Rauwenescht (es)n. caterpillars' nest

Rawunselgraut (es)n. common evening primrose

Rawwert (der)n. Robert

Reb(e) (die)n.; Rebe, pl. vine

Rebekka (die)n. 1.Becky; 2.Rebecca

Reche (der)n. rake

reche, v.; gerecht, pp. rake

Rechelbuch (es)n. arithmetic (book)

Rechelkunscht (die)n. mathematics

Rechenschaft (die)n. 1.account; 2.reckoning

Recher (der)n.; Recher, pl. 1.one who rakes; 2.rake

rechere, v. rake (Waterloo Co., Ont. usage)

Rr

Recheschtiel — reggnich

Recheschtiel (der)n. rake-handle
rechfaertiche, v.; rechgfaerticht, pp. 1.clear; 2.justify
rechle, v.; gerechelt, pp. 1.calculate; 2.cipher; 3.compute
Rechler (der)n. mathematician
Rechling (die)n. 1.account; 2.bill; 3.calculation; 4.change; 5.charge
Rechmaessichkeet (die)n. legality
rechne, v.; gerechent, pp. 1.cipher; 2.reckon
Rechning (die)n. 1.account; 2.bill; 3.calculation; 4.change
rechschaffich, adj. reliable
Rechschtreit (der)n. law suit
Recht (es)n. 1.law; 2.right; 3.(ebber -- gewwe) agree (with someone); 4.(-- dazu) entitle;
Recht (Hand) (die)n. right-handed
recht mache, v.; gemacht, pp. 1.correct; 2.rectify
recht schtelle, v.; gschtellt, pp. 1.correct; 2.vindicate
recht sei (dative) suit
recht, adj. 1.correct; 2.right; 3.true
recht, adv. very
rechtglaawich, adj. orthodox (in belief)
rechtgleibich, adj. orthodox (in belief)
rechtle, v.; gerechtelt, pp. 1.dispute; 2.wrangle
rechtmeesich, adv. 1.just; 2.lawfully
rechts, adj. 1.right; 2.right-handed; 3.to the right
rechtschaffe, adj. 1.a great deal; 2.honest; 3.reliable; 4.very much; 5.virtuous
rechtschaffich, adj. virtuous
rechtschtelle, v.; rechtgschtellt, pp. vindicate
rechtshandich, adj. right-handed
rechzeitich, adj. 1.at the proper moment; 2.in time
Reckelche (es)n. 1.baby's petticoat; 2.coat
Reder (der)n.; Reder, pl. 1.sifter (for flour); 2.speaker
redde, v.; gerett, pp. 1.rescue; 2.save
Reddel (es)n. 1.little wheel for cutting out cake dough; 2.red chalk
reddi, adj. 1.finished; 2.ready
Reddich (die)n.; Reddiche, pl. radish
Reddichmostert (der)n. wild radish
Reddichsaame (der)n. radish-seed
Reddichsome (der)n. radish-seed
Reddichsume (der)n. radish-seed
redlich, adj. honestly
redour, adv. 1.back; 2.returned
reeche, v.; gereecht, pp. 1.attain; 2.extend; 3.hand; 4.hand out; 5.hold out; 6.reach; 7.suffice
Reed (die)n. speech
reede, v.; gereedt, pp. 1.orate; 2.speak
Reedekunscht (die)n. oratory
Reedel (es)n. 1.red chalk; 2.reddle
Reedle (die)n., pl. measles
Reedner (der)n. 1.orator; 2.preacher
Reef (der)n.; Reef, pl. 1.hoop; 2.rim (of wheel)
Reefaa(re) (der)n. tansy
Reefaa(rt)tee (der)n. tansy tea
Reefaabidders (es)n. tansy bitters
Reefaar(t)bidders (es)n. tansy bitters

Reefaare (der)n. tansy
Reefart (der)n. tansy
Reefeise (es)n. hoop iron
Reefrock (der)n. hoopskirt
Reefschlang (die)n. hoop snake
Reefschneider (der)n. hoop maker
Reefschtecke (der)n. hoop pole
Reefweide (der)n. rose willow
Reehr (die)n. 1.pipe; 2.tube
reel, adj. real
Reemer (der)n.; Reemer, pl. Roman
reemisch, adj. Roman
Rees (die)n.; Reese, pl. 1.journey; 2.progress; 3.voyage; 4.trip
reeschde, v.; gereescht, pp. roast
reese, v.; gereest, pp. 1.journey; 2.travel
Reesel (es)n. Rosie
Reff (es)n.; Reffer, pl. 1.grain cradle; 2.mouth; 3.rack; 4.set of artificial teeth
Reffemiert (der)n. Reformed
Reffschprosse (der)n. round of a rack
Reffzaah(n) (der)n.;Reffzeh, pl. prong of (wooden) grain cradle
Reformiert Karrich (die)n. The Reformed Church (now The United Church of Christ)
Reformiert, adj. Reformed
Reggevoggel (der)n. plover
reggne, v.; gereggnet, pp. rain
rege, v.; geregt, pp. 1.stir; 2.(sich --) (a) move; (b) stir
Regel (die)n. rule
regelmaessich, adj. 1.according to rule; 2.regular
Regelmaessichkeet (die)n. regularity
regere, v.; geregert, pp. rain
Regeschauer (der)n. shower
Regge(r) (der)n. 1.rain; 2.(der -- geht unnerdarrich) the rain is passing to the south
regge(r), v.; gereggert, pp. rain
Reggeboge (der)n. rainbow
Reggebowe (der)n. rainbow
Reggedaag (der)n.;Reggedaage, pl. rainy day
Reggedrobbe (der)n. raindrop
Reggedropp(se) (der)n. raindrop
Reggefass (es)n.;Reggefesser, pl. rain barrel
reggeliere, v.; reggeliert, pp. regulate
Reggemesser (der)n. rain gauge
reggerich, adj. rainy
Reggeschaerm (der)n. umbrella
Reggeschauer (der)n. shower
Reggeschtarem (der)n. rainstorm
Reggewarem (der)n. earthworm
Reggewasser (es)n. rainwater
Reggewetter (es)n. rainy weather
Reggewolk (die)n.; Reggewolke, pl. nimbus
Reggiment (es)n. regiment
reggle, v.; gereggelt, pp. regulate
reggnich, adj. rainy

Rr

regiere

regiere, v.; regiert, pp. 1.govern; 2.reign; 3.rule
Regiering (die)n. government
Regine (die)n. Regina
Regischder (der)n. 1.index; 2.record
regne, v.; geregnet, pp. rain
Rehgraas (es)n. ryegrass
Rehichkeet (es)n. founder
Rehr (die)n. pipe
Rei (die)n. 1.regret; 2.repentance
rei/biege, v.; reigeboge, pp. bend in
rei/binne, v.; reigebunne, pp. tie inside
rei/blose, v.; reigeblose, pp. blow in
rei/breche, v.; reigebroche, pp. break in
rei/bringe, v.; reigebrocht, pp. bring in (toward the speaker)
rei/dappe, v.; reigedappt, pp. enter with heavy steps
rei/draage, v.; reigedraagt, pp. carry in
rei/dreiwe, v.; reigedriwwe, pp. drive in
rei/duh, v.; reigeduh 1.haul into the barn; 2.put in
rei/faahre, v.; reigfaahre, pp. drive in
rei/falle, v.; reigfalle, pp. fall in
rei/fiehre, v.; reigfiehrt, pp. lead in
rei/fliege, v.; reigflogge, pp. fly in
rei/gaffe, v.; reigegafft, pp. gape in
rei/geh, v.; reigange, pp. enter
rei/gewwe, v.; reigewwe, pp. hand in
rei/graddle, v.; reigegraddelt, pp. crawl in
rei/gucke, v.; reigeguckt, pp. look in
rei/helfe, v.; reigholfe, pp. help in
rei/henke, v.; reighenkt, pp. hang (something) inside
rei/hewe, v.; reighowe, pp. lift in
rei/hole, v.; reigholt, pp. fetch in
rei/kenne, v.; reigekennt, pp. be able to come in
rei/kumme, v.; reikumme, pp. come in
rei/laafe, v.; reigloffe, pp. walk in
rei/lange, v.; reigelangt, pp. reach in
rei/lege, v.; reigelekt, pp. lay in
rei/leichte, v.; reigeleicht, pp. light one's way in
rei/locke, v.; reigelockt, pp. 1.call in; 2.entice to enter
rei/losse, v.; reiglosst, pp. reiglesst = Amish usage
    1.entice to enter; 2.let in; 3.permit to enter
rei/maerricke, v.; reigemaerrickt, pp. mark in
rei/misse, v.; reigemisst, pp. be obliged to come in
rei/neediche, v.; reigeneedicht, pp. urge to come in
rei/nemme, v.; reigenumme, pp. take in
rei/packe, v.; reigepackt, pp. 1.pack in; 2.(sich --) come in
rei/reeche, v.; reigereecht, pp. reach in
rei/reggere, v.; reigereggert, pp. rain in
rei/reide, v.; reigeridde, pp. ride in
rei/reisse, v.; reigerisse, pp. tear in
rei/renne, v.; 1.bolt in; 2.enter hurriedly; 3.thrust in
rei/ricke, v.; reigerickt, pp. move in
rei/rinne, v.; reigerunne, pp. leak in
rei/rolle, v.; reigerollt, pp. roll in
rei/rudre, v.; reigerudert, pp. row in
rei/rufe, v.; reigerufe, pp. call in
rei/rutsche, v.; reigerutscht, pp. slide in

reime

rei/schaffe, v.; reigschafft, pp. (sich --) 1.force one's way in; 2.manage to get in
rei/schaffe, v.; reigschafft, pp. get in
rei/schalle, v.; reigschallt, pp. sound in
rei/scheine, v.; reigscheint, pp. shine in
rei/scheppe, v.; reigscheppt, pp. shovel or dip in
rei/schiewe, v.; reigschowe, pp. push in
rei/schlagge, v.; reigschlagge, pp. knock in
rei/schleiche, v.; reigschliche, pp. sneak in
rei/schluppe, v.; reigschluppt, pp. creep in
rei/schmuggle, v.; reigschmuggmelt, pp. smuggle in
rei/schnee-e, v.; reigschneet, pp. snow in
rei/schparre, v.; reigschpatt, pp. pen in
rei/schprenge, v.; reischprengt, pp. 1.burst in; 2.chase in
rei/schpringe, v.; reigschprunge, pp. run in
rei/schtaerme, v.; reigschtaermt, pp. rush in
rei/schtaerze, v.; reigschtaerzt, pp. fall in
rei/schtelle, v.; reigschtellt, pp. set in
rei/schtewwre, v.; reigschtewwert, pp. 1.chase in; 2.enter hastily
rei/schtoose, v.; reigschtoose, pp. push in
rei/wolle, v.; reigewollt, pp. want to come in
rei/zackere, v.; reigezackert, pp. enter with a heavy gait
rei/zehe, v.; reigezoge, pp. pull in
rei/zobbe, v.; reigezoppt, pp. pull in by jerks
rei, adj. 1.clean; 2.pure
rei, adv. in (here)
Reibbascht (die)n. scrubbing brush
Reiblumm (die)n. sweet everlasting (flower)
Reich (es)n. kingdom
reich, adj. 1.opulent; 2.rich; 3.wealthy
Reichdrobbe (die)n., pl. perfume
Reichdum (der)n. 1.riches; 2.wealth
Reicher (der)n. nose
reichfeldich, adj. 1.abundantly; 2.bountifully
reichl(e)ich, adj. 1.abundantly; 2.bountifully
reichlich, adv. plentiful
reide, v.; geridde, pp. ride (a horse)
Reider (der)n.; Reider, pl. 1.jockey; 2.next to the top rail (in a worm fence); 3.rider; 4.trooper
Reie (der)n. instep
reie, v.; gereit, pp. 1.regret; 2.spite
reif, adj. 1.mature; 2.ripe
Reifaare (der)n. tansy
Reifdraub (die)n.; Reifdrauwe, pp. 1.chicken grape; 2.frost grape
Reife (der)n. 1.frost; 2.hoarfrost
reifich, adj. frosty
Reih (die)n. = Roi (die) 1.row; 2.succession; 3.turn
reihe, v.; gereiht, pp. 1.baste; 2.stitch
Reihfaadem (der)n. basting thread
Reihrer (der)n. stirrer
Reim (der)n.; Reime, pl. 1.ballad; 2.rhyme
Reime (der)n. 1.strap; 2.thong (of a flail)
reime, v.; gereimt, pp. 1.rhyme; 2.tally; 3.(sich --) (a) tally; (b) agree

Rr

reimiedich — Riehrleffel

reimiedich, adj. repentant
rein, adj. 1.clean; 2.pure
Reinblumm (die)n. sweet everlasting (flower)
Reinfart (der)n. tansy
Reinheet (die)n. 1.chastity; 2.virtue
reiniche, v.; gereinicht, pp. 1.cleanse; 2.purify
Reiniching (die)n. 1.cleansing; 2.purgation
Reis (der)n. rice
Reis (die)n.; Reise, pl. 1.journey; 2.trip; 3.voyage
Reisbrei (der)n. rice boiled in milk
Reischder (der)n. patch on a boot or shoe
Reischeit (es)n. sway-bar
Reischemel (der)n. (front) body bolster (of a wagon)
Reisel (der)n. 1.nose; 2.proboscis
reisse, v.; gerisse, pp. 1.draw; 2.jerk; 3.move;
    4.pull;5.struggle; 6.tear;7.(sich --) (a) be eager to; (b)
    scramble; (c) struggle
reissend, adv. 1.rapidly; 2.savagely
Reisses (es)n. sharp pains
Reissupp (die)n. rice soup
Reitersalb (die)n. blue ointment
Reitgaul (der)n. 1.mount; 2.riding horse
reiwe, v.; g(e)riwwe, pp. 1.grate; 2.rub; 3.tease
Reiweise (es)n. grater
Reiwerei (die)n. 1.contention; 2.friction
Reiwing (die)n. 1.rubbing; 2.scrubbing
reizus, adv. (on the way) coming in
relange, v.; relangt, pp. attain
Relichion (die)n. religion
renkle, v.; gerenkelt, pp. 1.argue; 2.dispute; 3.quarrel;
    4.wrangle
Renn (der)n. 1.jolt; 2.push; 3.thrust
Renndier (es)n. 1.person or horse that rushes like mad;
    2.reindeer
renne, v.; gerennt, pp. 1.run; 2.rush; 3.thrust
Republikaaner (der)n.; Republikanner, pl. Republican
republikannisch, adj. republican
reschaffe, adj. 1.a great deal; 2.honest; 3.reliable; 4.very
    much; 5.virtuous
Reschdel (es)n. remnant
reschpeckdaawel, adj. respectable
reschpekdiere, v.; reschpekdiert, pp. respect
Reschpekt (der)n. respect
Rescht (es)n. remnant
Reseet (es)n.; Reseede, pl. 1.recipe; 2.receipt
Resein (die)n.; Reseine, pl. raisin
resolutt, adj. 1.determined; 2.resolute
Retch (die)n. 1.busybody; 2.gossip; 3.tattler
Retcher (der)n. tattler
Retour (es)n. sheriff's return
Retschbeddi (die)n. tattletale
Retschbelli (die)n. tattletale
retsche, v.; geretscht, pp. 1.bear tales; 2.gossip; 3.tattle
Retscher (der)n. talebearer
Retscherei (die)n. gossiping
Retschmaul (es)n. tattletale

Retschrett (die)n. speech
Rett (die)n. 1.expression; 2.speech
rette, v.; gerett, pp. save
retze, v.; geretzt, pp. tease
Revier (die)n. Delaware River
Rewollwer (der)n.; Rewollwer, pl. pistol
Rewwer (der)n.; Rewwer, pl. river
Rezept (die)n. 1.prescription; 2.recipe
Rhabarbraa (der)n. rhubarb
Rhummedis (die)n. rheumatism
Rhummedisgraut (es)n. 1.pleurisy root; 2.spotted winter-
    green
Rhummediswarzel (die)n. wild yam
Ribbebuffer (der)n. thump in the ribs
Ribbefell (es)n. pleura
Ribbefleesch (es)n. 1.ribs with meat on them; 2.(spare) ribs
Ribbeschtick (es)n. rib roast
Ribbeschtoos (der)n. jab (in the ribs)
ribbich, adj. 1.ribbed; 2.showing the ribs of a lean horse);
    3.skinny (of horses)
ribbich, adv. ribbed
richde, v.; gericht, pp. 1.direct; 2.judge; 3.put into alignment
Richder (der)n.; Richder, pl. 1.judge; 2.umpire
richdich, adj. correct
Richschtrang (der)n.; Richschtreng, pl. spine
Richtichkeet (die)n. 1.correctness; 2.settlement
Richtscheit (es)n. ten-foot pole
Richtschnur (die)n. 1.rule of action; 2.straight line
Richtung (die)n. direction
Rick (der)n.; Ricke, pl. 1.back (of human); 2.spine
ricke, v.; gerickt, pp. move
rickfellich, adj. 1.in arrears; 2.failing
Rickgrankheit (die)n. rickets
Rickmeesel (der)n. 1.backbone; 2.chine; 3.loin
Rickmeesel (es)n. pork chops
Rickrieme (der)n.; Rickrieme, pl. back strap
Rickschtand (der)n. arrears
Rickschtick (es)n. top sirloin
Rickschtrang (der)n.; Rickschtreng, pl. backbone
Ricksicht (die)n. regard (to) consideration (of)
rickwaerts, adv. backward(s)
Rickweh (es)n. 1.backache; 2.lumbago
Ridderschpor (der)n.; Ridderschpore, pl. larkspur
riddle, v.; geriddelt, pp. 1.accuse; 2.cast up to; 3.shake;
    4.sieve
Rieb (die)n.; Riewe, pl. turnip
Riebsaame (der)n. turnip seed
Riebsaehdaag (der)n. turnip-sowing day, July 25
Riechdroppe (die)n., pl. perfume
rieche, v.; geroche, pp. smell
Riecher (der)n. nose
riehme, v.; geriehmt, pp. praise
riehre, v.; geriehrt, pp. 1.affect; 2.stir
riehrend, adj. 1.affecting; 2.touching
Riehrer (der)n. stirrer
Riehrleffel (der)n.; Riehrleffel, pl. mixing ladle (kitchen)

Rr

Rieme

Rieme (der)n. 1.(leather) strap; 2.rein; 3.thong (of a flail)

Ries (der)n. giant

Rieschder (der)n. patch on a boot or shoe

Riesel (der)n. 1.mouth; 2.nose; 3.proboscis; 4.snout (hog)

Rieselvieh (es)n. swine

riesich, adj. 1.enormous; 2.great

Riewegsicht (es)n. ugly face

Riewekeller (der)n.; Riewekeller, pl. root cellar

Riewenaas (die)n. bottle-nose

Rieweschtick (es)n. turnip patch

Rieweselaat (der)n. turnip salad

Riewesupp (die)n. turnip soup

Riffel (die)n. 1.riffle; 2.ripple

Riggel (der)n. 1.bolt; 2.cross timber; 3.rail

Riggelfens (die)n.;Riggelfense, pp. 1.post fence; 2.rail fence

riggelreide, v.; riggelgeridde, pp. 1.play see-saw; 2.ride (one) on a rail

Riggelschloss (es)n. 1.lock with bolt; 2.stocklock

Riggelweg (der)n. 1.railroad; 2.train

Riggelwegkaers (die)n. train

riggle, v.; geriggelt, pp. bolt

rilpisch, adj.; adv. 1.rude; 2.rudely

Rilps (der)n. rough fellow

rilpse, v.; gerilpst, pp. belch

rilpsich, adj. unmannerly

Rind (es)n.; Rinner, pl. heifer

Rindledder (es)n. 1.neat's leather; 2.upper leather

Rindswambe(r) (der)n. tripe

Ring (der)n. 1.circle; 2.clique; 3.ring (finger ring); 4. (-- schpiele) play ring tag

Ringausschlagge (es)n. ring-tag

Ringbon (der)n. ringbone

ringe, v.; geringt, pp. put a ring through the snout (of a pig or bull)

ringe, v.; grunge, pp. ring

Ringel (es)n. 1.circle; 2.ringlet

Ringelblumm (die)n. marigold

Ringelros (die)n. calendula

ringle, v.; geringelt, pp (die Naas --) turn up one's nose

Ringler (der)n. ringer (at quoits)

Ringmiehl (die)n. girl's game

Ringschlack (der)n. copenhagen game

Ringschtock (der)n. mandrel

ringsrum, adv. all around

Ringwarem (der)n.; Ringwaerm, pl. ringworm

Rinn (die)n. 1.bark (of a tree); 2.rind (of bacon or ham)

Rinn (es)n.; Rind; Rinner, pl. heifer

rinne, v.; gerunne, pp. 1.leak; 2.ooze

Rinneschaeler (der)n. barking spud

Rinssvieh (es)n. 1.cattle; 2.steer; 3.vituperative term

Rinschtickvieh (es)n. head (of cattle)

Rinsfett (es)n. suet

Rinsfleesch (es)n. beef (heifer meat)

Rinskopp (der)n. stubborn person

Rinsledder (es)n. 1.neat's leather; 2.upper leather

Rinszung (die)n. beef tongue

riwwer

Ripp (die)n.; Ribbe, pl. rib

Rippebuffer (der)n. thump in the ribs

Rippefell (es)n. pleura

Rippefleesch (es)n. the ribs with the meat on them

Rippeschtick (es)n. rib (roast)

Rippeschtoos (der)n. dig in the ribs

Rirarridaed (die)n. rarity

Rischbel (die)n. 1.panicle; 2.spike (of yellow or green foxtail)

rischble, v.; gerischbelt, pp. 1.rattle; 2.rustle

rischde, v.; g(e)rischt, pp. 1.make ready; 2.set the table; 3.(sich --) (a) make ready; (b) prepare

Rischderei (die)n. preparation

rischdich, adj. 1.in good health; 2.robust; 3.vigorous

Rischding (die)n. preparation

Rischthaus (es)n. arsenal

Riss (der)n. 1.crack; 2.fissure; 3.rent; 4.tear

rissich, adj. full of cracks

Ritsch (die)n. 1.gadabout; 2.loose woman

Ritscher (der)n.; Ritscher, pl. slip out of the ground (by the plow in plowing)

ritscherd corn salad

ritscherli corn salad

Ritter (der)n. 1.knight; 2.rider

Ritterschpor (der)n. larkspur

Riwwel (die)n.; Riwwle, pl. 1.flour and lard (and sometimes sugar) mixed and rubbed to the consistency of small lumps used as a covering for riwwelkuche; 2.roll of dirt (formed on body by rubbing)

Riwwelkaes (der)n. cheese from scalded skim-milk ripened in a crock

Riwwelkuche (der)n. cake covered with riwwle

Riwwelsupp (die)n. soup made with "Riwwle"

riwwer/breche, v.; riwwergebroche, pp. break over

riwwer/bringe, v.; riwwergebrocht, pp. bring over

riwwer/drehe, v.; riwwergedreht, pp. turn over

riwwer/duh, v.; riwwergeduh, pp. put over

riwwer/falle, v.; riwwergfalle, pp. fall over

riwwer/geh, v.; riwwergange, pp. go over or across

riwwer/gewwe, v.; riwwergewwe, pp. give or hand over

riwwer/graddle, v. riwwergegraddelt, pp. crawl over

riwwer/gucke, v.; riwwergeguckt, pp. look over

riwwer/helfe, v.; riwwergholfe, pp. help across

riwwer/hole, v.; riwwergholt, pp. fetch over

riwwer/hupse, v.; riwwerghupst, pp. hop over

riwwer/kumme, v.; riwwerkumme, pp. come over

riwwer/locke, v.; riwwergelockt, pp. entice over

riwwer/losse, v.; riwwergelosst, pp. allow to come over

riwwer/rufe, v.; riwwergerufe, pp. call over

riwwer/schicke, v.; riwwergschickt, pp. send over

riwwer/schluppe, v.; riwwergschluppt, pp. creep over

riwwer/schmeisse, v.; riwwergschmisse, pp. throw over

riwwer/schtelle, v.; riwwergschtellt, pp. set over

riwwer/setze, v.; riwwergsetzt, pp. set over

riwwer/yaage, v.; riwwergeyaagt, pp. chase over

riwwer, adv. 1.across; 2.over (on this side); 3.over (here); 4.to this side

Rr

riwwerzus

riwwerzus, adv. on the way (coming) across
Riwwle (die)n.; Riwwle, pl. dough crumb
Rock (der)n.; Reck, pl. 1.coat
Rockaermel (der)n.; Rockaermel, pl. coat sleeve
Rocke (der)n. 1.distaff; 2.rye
Rockebrot (es)n. rye bread
Rockegraas (es)n. ryegrass
Rockemehl (es)n. rye flour
Rockfliggel (der)n. coat-tail
Rockgraage (der)n. coat collar
Rocksack (der)n. coat pocket
rode, v.; gerode, pp. 1.advise; 2.guess; 3.suggest
roh, adj. 1.raw; 2.rough; 3.sore
Rohr (es)n. 1.reed; 2.(stove) pipe; 3.spout
Rohrblech (es)n. sheet iron
Rohrloch (es)n. pipe-hole
Rohrschtock (der)n. rattan (cane)
Roi (die)n.; Roie, pl. 1.row; 2.succession; 3.turn; 4.(du
      kummscht aa in die --) your turn will come;
      5. (in -- schtelle) admonish
Roiet (die)n. 1.row; 2.turn
roigeweis, adv. in rows
Roiyet (die)n. 1.round; 2.turn
Rolitsch (die)n. small pieces of beef (stuffed in bags of
      tripe, pickled in dilute vinegar, sliced, fried and
      served with gravy)
Roll (die)n. roll
Roll(e)duwack (der)n. twist tobacco
rolle, v.; gerollt, pp. 1.be served (of sows); 2.roll; 3. (sich -
      -) roll (of horses)
Roller (der)n.; Roller, pl. 1.caster; 2.roller; 3.rolling pin
Rollhols (es)n. rolling pin
rollich, adj. 1.inclined to roll; 2.in heat (of sows); 3.round
Rolliche (die)n. small pieces of beef (stuffed in bags of
      tripe, pickled in dilute vinegar, sliced, fried and
      served with gravy)
Rollmiehl (die)n. rolling mill
Rollschtee (der)n. rubble
Roon (die)n.; Raane, pl. 1.rone; 2.rune; 3.welt
Rooschtnier (der)n.; Rooschtniers, pl. roasting ear
roppe, v.; geroppt, pp. 1.draw; 2.pick; 3.pluck; 4.pull;
      5.move; 6.(ungraut --) weed
Ros (die)n.; Rose, pl. 1.rose; 2.(die feirich --) erysipelas;
      3.(wildi --) wild rose
roschde, v.; geroscht, pp. rust
roschdich, adj. rusty
Roscht (der)n. rust
rose, v.; gerost, pp. 1.frolic; 2.play
Rosegranz (der)n. rosary
Rosein (die)n. raisin
Roserei (die)n. frolicking
Roseschtock (der)n. rosebush
rosich, adj. 1.porous; 2.rosy
Rosmarei (die)n. 1.rosemary; 2.(wilder --) (a) butter and
      eggs (plant); (b) toadflax
rossich, adj. ready for the stallion

ruff/bumbe

Rot (der)n. 1.advice; 2.counsel; 3.(do is guter -- deier) we
      are in a dilemma; 4.(net -- du kenne) not to be able
      to do sufficient 5.(-- gewwe) (a) advise; (b) guess
rot scheckich, adj. speckled red
rot warre, v.; rot warre, pp. Blush
rot, adj. 1.red; 2.ruddy; 3.(kenn --er) (a) nary a red;
      (b) not a cent; 4.(--er hinkeldarm) red pimpernel;
      5.(--er Peffer) Cayenne pepper
rotachdich, adj. reddish
rotbrau(n), adj. auburn
Rotesche (die)n. red ash
Rotfisch (der)n. redfin
Rotgewwer (der)n. 1.advisor; 2.counselor
rotgliedich, adj. red-hot
rothaarich, adj. redheaded
Rothols (es)n. redwood
rotkebbich, adj. redheaded
Rotkopp (der)n.; Rotkepp, pl. 1.redheaded person;
      2.redheaded woodpecker
Rotlaafe (es)n. inflammation
rotlich, adj. reddish
Rotrieb (die)n.; Rotriewe, pl. red beet
rotsa(u)m, adj. advisable
rotschtenglich, adj. red-stemmed
rotseide, adj. (of) red silk
Rotsiesskasche (die)n. variety of un-grafted sweet red cherry
Rott (die)n. gang
rott, v. 1.decayed; 2.dry-rotted
Rotvoggel (der)n.; Rotveggel, pl. redbird
Rotwatzel (die)n. blood root
Rotweide (der, die)n. rose willow
Rotz (der)n. 1.phlegm; 2.snot
rotze, v.; grotzt, pp. snot
Rotzedre (der)n. red cedar
Rotzer (der)n. 1.glanders (in horses); 2.impudent child;
      3.pert child
Rotzfresser (der)n.; Rotzfresser, pl. snot-eater (child)
Rotzhoge (der)n.; Rotzhoge, pl. pert young fellow
Rotzholz (es)n. slippery elm
rotzich, adj. 1.immature; 2.snotty
Rotzkeffer (der)n. impudent person
Rotzleffel (der)n. term of contempt (usually for a callow
      youth)
Rotznaas (die)n.; Rotznaas, pl. 1.fresh young person;
      2.impudent child; 3.pert child
rub(b)lich, adj. 1.uneven (field, road); 2.rough (of a road,
      field)
rubbich, adj. 1.rough (of a road, field); 2.uneven
Ruder (der)n.; Ruder, pl. 1.oar; 2.paddle; 3.rudder
rudere, v.; gerudert, pp. row
Rudi (der)n. Rudolph
Ruf (der)n. call(ing)
rufe, v.; gerufe, pp. call
ruff/binne, v.; ruffgebunne, pp. tie up
ruff/bringe, v.; ruffgebrocht, pp. bring up
ruff/bumbe, v.; ruffgebumpt, pp. pump up

Rr

ruff/bumpe

ruff/bumpe, v.; ruffgebumpt, pp. pump up
ruff/daerfe, v.; ruffgedaerft, pp. be allowed up
ruff/draage, v.; ruffgedraage, pp. carry up
ruff/drehe, v.; ruffgedreht, pp. turn up
ruff/dreiwe, v.; ruffgedriwwe, pp. drive up
ruff/duh, v.; ruffgeduh, pp. put up
ruff/faahre, v.; ruffgfaahre, pp. drive up (in a vehicle)
ruff/fiehre, v.; ruffgfiehrt, pp. lead up
ruff/gawwle, v.; ruffgegawwelt, pp. pitch up
ruff/geh, v.; ruffgange, pp. go up
ruff/gewwe, v.; ruffgewwe, pp. hand up
ruff/graddle, v.; ruffgegraddelt, pp. climb up
ruff/gucke, v.; ruffgeguckt, pp. look up
ruff/hewe, v.; ruffghowe, pp. lift up
ruff/hole, v.; ruffgholt, pp. fetch up
ruff/keere, v.; ruffgekeert, pp. belong up
ruff/kenne, v.; ruffgekennt, pp. be able to get up
ruff/kumme, v.; ruffgekumme, pp come up
ruff/laafe, v.; ruffgelofe, pp. walk up
ruff/lange, v.; ruffgelangt, pp. hand up
ruff/lege, v.; ruffgelegt, pp. lay up
ruff/losse, v.; ruffgelosst, pp. allow to come up
ruff/reide, v.; ruffgeridde, pp. ride up
ruff/renne, v.; ruffgerennt, pp. rush up
ruff/ricke, v.; ruffgerickt, pp. move up
ruff/rufe, v.; ruffgerufe, pp. call up
ruff/schaffe, v.; ruffgschafft, pp. convey up
ruff/schalle, v.; ruffgschallt, pp. sound up
ruff/scheppe, v.; ruffgscheppt, pp. shovel or dip up
ruff/schicke, v.; ruffgschickt, pp. send up
ruff/schiewe, v.; ruffgschowe, pp. push up
ruff/schleefe, v.; ruffgschleeft, pp. drag up
ruff/schmeisse, v.; ruffgschmisse, pp. throw up
ruff/schtelle, v.; ruffgschtellt, pp. set up
ruff/wolle, v.; ruffgewollt, pp. want to get or come up
ruff/yaage, v.; ruffgeyaagt, pp. chase up
ruff/ziege, v.; ruffgezoge, pp. 1.move up; 2.pull up
ruff/ziehe, v.; ruffgezoge, pp. pull up
ruff, adv. 1.up; 2.up to a place; 3.upwards
ruff, adv (es land --) from down country
ruffzus, adv. on the way (coming) up
Rugerei (die)n. (confounded) resting
Ruh (die)n. 1.ease; 2.rest; 3.repose; 4.peace; 5.silence; 6.unity; 7.(sich im -- setze) retire
ruh(g)e, v.; geru(h)gt, pp. 1.recline; 2.rest; 3.sleep
Ruhblatz (der)n. resting place
ruhich, adj. 1.calm; 2.cool and collected; 3.quiet; 4.still; 5.tranquil
Ruhm (der)n. fame
Ruhr (die)n. 1.diarrhea; 2.dysentery
Ruhrgraut (es)n. 1.cudweed; 2.everlasting
Ruhzeit (die)n. 1.holiday(s); 2.time of rest
Rukdaag (der)n. 1.day off; 2.day of rest
Rukschtee (der)n. roundish stone placed on fence posts
Rukschtunn (die)n. (midday) hour of rest
rum/addere, v.; rumgeaddert, pp. order around

rum/froge

rum/bamble, v.; rumgebambelt, pp. loiter
rum/batzle, v.; rumgebatzelt, pp. roll or tumble over and over
rum/biege, v.; rumgeboge, pp. bend around
rum/binne, v.; rumgebunne, pp. tie in another place
rum/blanze, v.; rumgeblanzt, pp. 1.plant in another place; 2.transplant
rum/blarre, v.; rumgeblatt, pp. talk boisterously
rum/blaschdere, v.; rumgeblaschdert, pp. be doctoring or applying plasters continually
rum/blaudre, v.; rumgeblaudert, pp. spread reports
rum/blettre, v.; rumgeblettert, pp. turn the leaves of a book
rum/blicke, v.; rumgeblickt, pp. glance around
rum/blose, v.; rumgeblose, pp. 1.blow around; 2.go about boasting
rum/bluge, v.; rumgeblugt, pp. 1.plow; 2.plow poorly
rum/bringe, v.; rumgebrocht, pp. 1.bring around; 2.bring (another) to one's way of thinking; 3.spend (time)
rum/daafe, v.; rumgedaaft, pp. join another church which requires rebaptism
rum/danse, v.; rumgedanst, pp. 1.cavort; 2.dance around
rum/dappe, v.; rumgedappt, pp. wander around
rum/dargele, v.; rumgedargelt, pp. stagger around
rum/deiwle, v.; rumgedeiwelt, pp. go around raising the devil
rum/demmere, v.; rumgedemmert, pp. run around (all over)
rum/dokdere, v.; rumgedokdert, pp. try all sorts of doctors and medicines
rum/dowe, v.; rumgedopt, pp. rage around
rum/draage, v.; rumgedraage, pp. carry around
rum/drehe, v.; rumgedreht, pp. 1.make a square turn in plowing; 2.reverse; 3.turn around; 4.turn inside out; 5.twist
rum/dreiwe, v.; rumgedriwwe, pp. drive around
rum/dricke, v.; rumgedrickt, pp. squeeze
rum/drinke, v.; rumgedrunke, pp. drink around
rum/dunnere, v.; rumgedunnert, pp. go around noisily
rum/eesle, v.; rumge-eeselt, pp. roam around (especially evenings, Sunday afternoon)
rum/ennere, v.; rumgeennert, pp. change
rum/faahre, v.; rumgfaahre, pp. drive around
rum/faawle, v.; rumgfaawelt, pp. make motions
rum/falle, v.; rumgfalle, pp. tumble about
rum/faschle, v.; rumgfaschelt, pp. pry
rum/fechde, v.; rumgefochde, pp. go around fighting
rum/feischdle, v.; rumgfeischdelt, pp. go around flourishing one's fists
rum/fiehle, v.; rumgfiehlt, pp. feel about
rum/fiehre, v.; rumgfirht, pp. lead about
rum/fiessle, v.; rumgfiesselt, pp. walk around with mincing gate
rum/flankiere, v.; rumgflankiert, pp. 1.gad about; 2.roam about
rum/fliege, v.; rumgfloge, pp. fly around
rum/froge, v.; rumgfrogt, pp. ask one after another

143

Rr

rum/gackse

rum/gackse, v.; rumgegackst, pp. go about gossiping
rum/gaffe, v.; rumgegafft, pp. gape around
rum/geh, v.; rumgange, pp. 1.make the rounds; 2.walk around
rum/gewwe, v.; rumgewwe, pp. hand around
rum/glebbere, v.; rumgeglebbert, pp. make a noise in going around
rum/gleede, v.; rumgegleedt, pp. (sich --) change clothes
rum/gnarre, v.; rumgegnarrt, pp. go about growling
rum/gnaunse, v.; rumgegnaunst, pp. go about complaining
rum/gnickse, v.; rumgegnickst, pp. 1.complain; 2.find fault
rum/gnoddle, v.; rumgegnoddelt, pp. 1.do odd jobs; 2.work leisurely without accomplishing much
rum/gnuschdre, v.; rumgegnuschdert, pp. be occupied with trifles
rum/graawe, v.; rumgegraawe, pp. 1.dig around; 2.dig up and turn over; 3.spade
rum/graddle, v.; rumgegraddelt, pp. crawl around
rum/greckse, v.; rumgegreckst, pp. ail
rum/gucke, v.; rumgeguckt, pp. look around
rum/hacke, v.; rumghackt, pp. hoe up
rum/hammle, v.; rumghammelt, pp. 1.gad about; 2.go around in wet weather or in wet grass
rum/haschble, v.; rumghaschbelt, pp. go around without any fixed purpose
rum/hause, v.; rumghaust, pp. rage around
rum/helfe, v.; rumgholfe, pp. help (one) around
rum/henke, v.; rumghenkt, pp. 1.hang around; 2.hitch (a team of horses) to another wagon; 3.linger; 4.loaf
rum/hewe, v.; rumgghowe, pp. lift around
rum/hickle, v.; rumghickelt, pp. hobble around
rum/hocke, v.; rumghockt, pp. 1.loaf; 2.sit around
rum/hole, v.; rumgholt, pp. 1.fetch; 2.induce (one) to change
rum/hupse, v.; rumghupst, pp. hop about
rum/kessle, v.; rumgekesselt, pp. jaunt around
rum/kumme, v.; is rumkumme, pp. 1.come around; 2.recover; 3.regain
rum/laade, v.; rumglaade, pp. transfer a load
rum/laafe, v.; rumg(e)loffe, pp. 1.gad; 2.tramp; 3.walk around; 4.wander
rum/laerme, v.; rumgelaermt, pp. make a noise
rum/lange, v.; rumglangt, pp. 1.hand about; 2.suffice
rum/lause, v.; rumgelaust, pp. 1.prowl; 2.sneak around
rum/lege, v.; rumgelekt, pp. change the position of
rum/leie, v.; rumgelegge, pp. 1.lie around; 2.loaf
rum/lese, v.; rumgelese, pp. sort over
rum/lodle, v.; rumgelodelt, pp. loaf around
rum/mache, v.; rumgemacht, pp. 1.plow; 2.spade
rum/maerricke, v.; rumgemaerrickt, pp. change the marks of
rum/maschiere, v.; rumgemaschiert, pp. march around
rum/maule, v.; rumgemault, pp. 1.growl; 2.grumble
rum/moddle, v.; rumgemoddelt, pp. remodel
rum/nemme, v.; rurngenumme, pp 1.show around; 2.(un ebber --) embrace
rum/noddle, v.; rumgenodelt, pp. lounge around
rum/packe, v.; rumgpackt, pp. repack

rum/schpringe

rum/pehze, v.; rumgepehzt, pp. be sickly
rum/piddle, v.; rumgepiddelt, pp. 1.dawdle; 2.do odd jobs
rum/piense, v.; rumgepienst, pp. be sickly
rum/poke, v.; rumgepokt, pp. poke around
rum/puddle, v.; rumgepuddelt, pp. splash around
rum/raase, v.; rumgeraast, pp. go about raging
rum/ranke, v.; rumgerankt, pp. twine around
rum/reeche, v.; rumgereecht, pp. 1.hand around; 2.suffice
rum/reese, v.; rumgereest, pp. go wandering about
rum/reide, v.; rumgeridde, pp. ride around
rum/reisse, v.; rumgerisse, pp. jerk around
rum/renne, v.; rumgerennt, pp. rush about aimlessly
rum/ricke, v.; rumgerickt, pp. move around
rum/rieche, v.; rumgeroche, pp. 1.smell; 2.spy out
rum/riehre, v.; rumgeriehrt, pp. 1.stir; 2.stir up
rum/ries(e)le, v.; rumgerieselt, pp. nose around
rum/rolle, v.; rumgerollt, pp. roll around
rum/rutsche, v.; rumgerutscht, pp. 1.move frequently; 2.slide or fidget around
rum/saage, v.; rumgsaat, pp. spread by telling
rum/schaere, v.; rumgschaert, pp. 1.scratch around; 2.seed (a field)
rum/schaffe, v.; rumgschafft, pp. 1.bring about a change in time or position; 2.plow
rum/scharre, v.; rumgschatt, pp. scratch around
rum/schelte, v.; rumgscholte, pp. go around scolding
rum/scheppe, v.; rumgscheppt, pp. shovel or dip from one place to another
rum/schicke, v.; rumgschickt, pp. send around
rum/schiddle, v.; rumgschiddelt, pp. shake around
rum/schiewe, v.; rumgschowe, pp. push about
rum/schinne, v.; rumgschunne, pp. plow poorly
rum/schlagge, v.; rumgschlagge, pp. knock around
rum/schlappe, v.; rumgschlappt, pp. 1.go around in shabby attire; 2.walk around in the wet
rum/schlaudere, v.; rumgschlaudert, pp. loiter
rum/schleefe, v.; rumgschleeft, pp. drag around
rum/schleiche, v.; rumgschliche, pp. sneak around
rum/schlenkere, v.; rumgschlenkert, pp. swing around
rum/schleppe, v.; rumgschleppt, pp. drag around
rum/schluppe, v.; rumgschluppt, pp. creep around
rum/schmeisse, v.; rumgschmisse, pp. 1.throw about; 2.throw around
rum/schnaerre, v.; rumgschnaerrt, pp. jerk around
rum/schnappe, v.; rumgschnappt, pp. limp about
rum/schnuffle, v.; rumgschnuffelt, pp. 1.be inquisitive; 2.snuffle around
rum/schpaade, v.; rumgschpaade, pp. spade
rum/schpanne, v.; rumgschpannt, pp. 1.change the place of a horse from the near to the off side; 2.hitch fresh horses to a vehicle
rum/schpiele, v.; rumgschpielt, pp. play around
rum/schprenge, v.; rumgschprengt, pp. force or gallop or run around
rum/schpringe, v.; rumgschprunge, pp. 1.be wild; 2.gad; 3.run about; 4.run around

Rr

rum/schpucke — Rummel

rum/schpucke, v.; rumgschpuckt, pp. go about at uncanny times or places

rum/schtaerze, v.; rumgschtaerzt, pp. fall around

rum/schtalle, v.; rumgschtallt, pp. make other arrangements

rum/schtarre, v.; rumgschtarrt, pp. 1.move about; 2.stir up

rum/schteh, v.; rumgschtanne, pp. 1.loiter; 2.stand around

rum/schteige, v.; rumgschtigge, pp. change vehicles

rum/schtelle, v.; rumgschtellt, pp. change position of

rum/schtiere, v.; rumgschtiert, pp. scatter about

rum/schtiwwre, v.; rumgschtiwwert, pp. bustle about

rum/schtolbere, v.; rumgschtolbert, pp. stumble about

rum/schtoose, v.; rumgschtoose, pp. jostle about

rum/schtraee, v.; rumgschtraet, pp. scatter about

rum/schtribbe, v.; rumgschtrippt, pp. change clothes

rum/schwenke, v.; rumgschwenkt, pp. swing about

rum/schwewe, v.; rumgschwebt, pp. 1.float about; 2.swing about

rum/schwimme, v.; rumgschwumme, pp. swim about

rum/sehne, v.; rumgschne, pp. have a good view

rum/sei, v. 1.be about; 2.be near

rum/suche, v.; rumgsucht, pp. search around

rum/waerwle, v.; rumgewaerwelt, pp. whirl around

rum/wandre, v.; rumgewandert, pp. 1.range; 2.wander

rum/weise, v.; rumgewisse, pp. show about

rum/wenne, v.; rumgewennt, pp. turn the furrow

rum/wexle, v.; rumgewexelt, pp. 1.change; 2.exchange

rum/wiehle, v.; rumgewiehlt, pp. 1.rummage; 2.turn over by rooting

rum/yaage, v.; rumgeyaagt, pp. 1.chase around; 2.gallop about

rum/yackere, v.; rumgeyackert, pp. jog or drive around the country

rum/yohle, v.; rumgeyohlt, pp. shout around

rum/zackere, v.; rumgezackert, pp. drive about

rum/zaere, v.; rumgezaert, pp. 1.tantalize; 2.tease

rum/zappe, v.; rumgezappt, pp. draw off and put back in a cask

rum/ziehe, v.; rumgezoge, pp.1.change residence; 2.pull around

rum/zoddle, v.; rumgezoddelt, pp. 1.gad about; 2.scatter about

rum, adv. 1.around; 2.round

Rumbel (der)n. 1.affair; 2.business; 3.fun; 4.trick

rumble, v.; gerumbelt, pp. rumble

rumdarigle, v.; rumgedarigelt, pp. stagger around

rumeniere, v.; rumgeniert, pp. 1.break down; 2.ruin

Rumf (der)n. 1.edge (of a bog or dam); 2.hull

rumhaer/addere, v.; rumhaergeaddert, pp. order from one place to another

rumhaer/blose, v.; rumhaergeblose, pp. brag in different places

rumhaer/bralle, v.; rumhaergebrallt, pp. brag in different places

rumhaer/fliege, v.; rumhaergfloge, pp. fly about

rumhaer/gaffe, v.; rumhaergegafft, pp. gape around

rumhaer/geh, v.; rumhaergange, pp. go about

rumhaer/gucke, v.; rumhaergeguckt, pp. look around

rumhaer/kessle, v.; rumhaergekesselt, pp. jog around the country

rumhaer/laafe, v.; rumhaergeloffe, pp. walk around

rumhaer/lege, v.; rumhaergelekt, pp. lay in different places

rumhaer/leie, v.; rumhaergelegge, pp. loaf or bum around

rumhaer/nemme, v.; rumhaergenumme, pp. take from place to place

rumhaer/reese, v.; rumhaergereest, pp. travel from place to place

rumhaer/reide, v.; rumhaergeridde, pp. ride from place to place

rumhaer/renne, v.; rumhaergerennt, pp. rush from place to place

rumhaer/rutsche, v.; rumhaergerutscht, pp. move from place to place

rumhaer/schaffe, v.; rumhaergschafft, pp. work in different places

rumhaer/schmeisse, v.; rumhaergschmisse, pp. throw about

rumhaer/schtolpere, v.; rumhaergschtolpert, pp. stumble around

rumhaer/uffschtelle, v.; rumhaeruffgschtellt, pp. put up at different inns

rumhaer/wachse, v.; rumhaergewachst, pp. grow in different places

rumhaer/wohne, v.; rumhaergewohnt, pp. live in different places

rumhaer/ziege, v.; rumhaergzogge, pp. move from place to place

rumher/blanze, v.; rumhergeblanzt, pp. plant in different places

rumher/blaudre, v.; rumhergeblaudert, pp. spread reports

rumher/bluge, v.; rumhergeblugt, pp. plow for different persons

rumher/greische, v.; rumhergegrische, pp. spread reports

rumher/lause, v.; rumhergelaust, pp. sneak around

rumher/schleiche, v.; rumhergschliche, pp. 1.loiter; 2.prowl; 3.sneak around

rumher/schpringe, v.; rumhergschprunge, pp. 1.run about; 2.run from place to place

rumher/schteh, v.; rumhergschtanne, pp. 1.loiter about; 2.stand around

rumher/schtelle, v.; rumherschtellt, pp. place at different points

rumher/sitze, v.; rumhergsitzt, pp. lounge; 2.sit about

rumher, adv. 1.round; 2.round about

ruminere, v.; geruminiert, pp. ruin

Rumleefer (der)n.; Rumleefer, pl. 1.bum; 2.loafer; 3.tramp; 4.vagabond

Rummedis (die)n. rheumatism

Rummedissgraut (es)n. 1.pleurisy root; 2.spotted wintergreen

Rummel (die)n. variety of large beet

145

Rr

rumore

rumore, v.; gerumort, pp. 1.kick up a row; 2.make a noise
Rump (der)n.; Rumpe, pl. hull (of a vessel)
rumpere, v.; gerumpert, pp. make a big ado
rumps un schtumps, adv. 1.root and branch; 2.totally
Rund (die)n. round
rund, adj. 1.rotund; 2.round
Runding (die)n. 1.curve; 2.roundness
rundleiwich, adj. 1.chunky; 2.paunchy
rundlich, adj. roundish
Rundmeesel (der)n.; Rundmeesle, pl. gouge
Rundzaerkel (der)n. calipers
Rune (die)n., pl. 1.stripes; 2.welts
Runge (der)n. standard (of a wagon)
rungeniere, v.; rungeniert, pp. 1.break down; 2.ruin
Runn (die)n. 1.brook; 2.run
Runne (der)n. standard (of a wagon)
runner/addere, v.; runnergeaddert, pp. order down from a place
runner/batzle, v.; runnergebatzelt, pp. tumble down
runner/biede, v.; runnergebodde, pp. underbid
runner/biege, v.; runnergeboge, pp. bend down
runner/bringe, v.; runnergebrocht, pp. bring down
runner/daerfe, v.; runnergedaerft, pp. be allowed to come down
runner/dreiwe, v.; runnergedriwwe, pp. drive down
runner/falle, v.; is runnergfalle, pp. fall down
runner/geh, v.; runnergange, pp. get down from
runner/griege, v.; runnergrickt, pp. get (something) down
runner/hacke, v.; runnerghackt, pp. chop down
runner/handle, v.; runnerghandelt, pp. beat down the price
runner/helfe, v.; runnergholfe, pp. help down from
runner/henke, v.; runnerghenkt, pp. hang down
runner/hole, v.; runnergholt, pp. fetch down
runner/kumme, v.; runnerkummer, pp. 1.be reduced in circumstances; 2.come down
runner/laafe, v.; runnergeloffe, pp. walk down
runner/leege, v.; runnergeleegt, pp. lay down
runner/leese, v.; runnergeleest, pp. 1.give a person a calling down; 2.read off
runner/losse, v.; runnergelosst, pp. 1.allow to come down; 2.let down
runner/mache, v.; rummergemacht, pp. rain or snow slightly
runner/reeche, v.; runnergereecht, pp. reach down
runner/reisse, v.; runnergerisse, pp. tear down
runner/rufe, v.; runnergerufe, pp. call down
runner/rutsche, v.; runnergerutscht, pp. slide down
runner/schaffe, v.; runnergschafft, pp. (sich --) manage to get down
runner/schaffe, v.; runnergschafft, pp. manage to get (something) down
runner/schidde, v.; runnergschitt, pp. pour down
runner/schiddle, v. runnergschiddle, pp. shake down
runner/schiesse, v.; runnergschosse, pp. shoot down
runner/schlagge, v,; runnergschlagge, pp. knock down
runner/schmeisse, v.; runnergschmisse, pp. throw down
runner/schtatze, v.; runnergschtatzt, pp. topple

Ruukschtunn

runner/schtelle, v.; runnergschtellt, pp. set down
runner/schtosse, v.; runnergschtosse, pp. thrust down
runner/yaage, v.; runnergeyaagt, pp. chase down from
runner/ziehe, v.; runnergezoge, pp. pull down
runner, adv. down (to where the speaker or thinker is)
runner, adv. (vun owwe --) from above
runnerzus, adv. on the way down
ruppich, adj. 1.rough (of a road or the cross terrain of a potato or corn field); 2.uneven
Rusch(d)e (die)n. 1.American elm; 2.(roti --) slippery elm
Ruschebaam (der)n. elm tree
Runsel (die)n. wrinkle
runsle, v.; gerunselt, pp. 1.crease; 2.wrinkle
runslich, adj. wrinkled
Russ (der)n. soot
Russchwallem (der)n. chimney swift
russich, adj. sooty
russle, v.; gerusselt, pp. drizzle
Rut (die)n. rod of a flail
Rutsch (die)n. 1.child who wriggles on its mother's lap; 2.coasting course; 3.gadabout; 4.loose woman; 5.slide; 6.woman who changes residence frequently
rutsche, v.; gerutscht, pp. 1.slide; 2.slip; 3.squirm
rutschich, adj. 1.slippery; 2.squirming (child)
Ruukschtunn (die)n. the midday hour of rest

Ss

Saadan

Saadan (der)n. Satan
saadanisch, adj. satanical
saadonisch, adj. diabolical
Saag (die)n. 1.legend; 2.saying
saage, v.; gsaat, pp. 1.say; 2.tell; 3.(ebber die Meening --) (give someone a) piece of mind
Saam (der)n.; Saame, pl. 1.hem; 2.seam
Saame (der)n. seed
saame, v.; gsaamt, pp. 1.edge; 2.hem
Saametros (die)n. marigold
Saamewelschkann (es)n. seed corn
Saatan (der)n. satan
saatanisch, adj. satanical
Sabbaat (der)n (der grosser --) Saturday before Easter (Moravian)
sabbaatvoll, adj. sacred
Sach (die)n.; Sache, pl. 1.business; 2.concern; 3.matter; 4.thing; 5.(gekennt --) preserves
sachde, adv. 1.quiet; 2.slowly; 3.softly
sachdich, adv. softly
sachdiche, adv. slowly
Sache (die)n. wraps
Sachwascht (die)n. bologna (any kind in a bag)
Sack (der)n.; Seck, pl. 1.bag; 2.paunch; 3.pocket; 4.sack; 5. (en Katz im -- kaafe) buy a pig in a poke; 6.(in --schtecke) (to) pocket; 7.(-- un Pack) (a) luggage; (b) bag and baggage
Sackbendel (der)n. string used in tying a bag
Sackduch (es)n. sackcloth
sacke, v.; gsackt, pp. 1.sag; 2.sink
sackerment!, interj. the deuce!
sackerments, adv. deucedly
Sackmesser (es)n.;Sackmessere,pl. 1.jackknife; 2.penknife; 3.pocketknife
Sackpeif (die)n. bagpipe
Sackrament (es)n. sacrament
Sackuhr (die)n. watch (clock)
sackweis, adv. by bags full
sadde, adv. 1.rather; 2.sort of
Saddel (der)n.; Saddel, pl. saddle
Saddelbank (die)n. saddle-tree
Saddeldeck (die)n. saddlecloth
Saddelgatt (die)n.; Saddelgadde, pl. saddle girth
Saddelgaul (der)n. 1.near horse (of a two-horse team); 2.rear near horse (of a four horse team)
Saddelgnopp (der)n. pommel
Saddelkisse (es)n. pillion
saddle, v.; gsaddelt, pp. saddle
Saddler (der)n.; Saddler, pl. saddler
saeddi! Thank you! (usually used by elders in reminding a small child to say Thank you!)
sae-e, v.; gsaegt, pp. sow
Saees (der)n. 1.Esaias; 2.Isaiah
Saeg (die)n.; Saege, pl. 1.saw; 2.(so dumm as --holz) as stupid as can be
Saegblock (der)n. log to be sawed up

Salzschleck

Saegbock (der)n.; Saegbeck, pl. 1.sawbuck; 2.sawhorse; 3.wood jack
saege, v.; gsaegt, pp. saw
Saegeglamm (die)n.; Saegeglamme, pl. saw clamp
Saeger (der)n. sawyer
Saegezaah (der)n. sawtooth
Saegezoh (der)n. sawtooth
Saegfeil (die)n. saw file
Saegmachter (der)n. saw-rest
Saegmehl (es)n. sawdust
Saegmiehl (die)n. sawmill
Saegrichder (der)n. saw-truer
saehe, v.; gsaeht, pp. sow
Saehmann (der)n. sower
Saesack (der)n. bag slung over the shoulder of a sower
Saet (die)n. 1.cord; 2.string
Saezwiwwel (die)n. squill
safdich, adj. 1.energetically; 2.juicy; 3.piquant (of persons) 4.sappy; 5.smutty; 6.unreliable
safdich, adv. 1.slowly; 2.softly
Saff(e)rich (der)n. 1.safflower; 2.saffron
Saffran (der)n. 1.safflower; 2.saffron
Saft (die)n. 1.juice; 2.sap
saftich, adj. 1.softly; 2.slowly
Sakremant (es)n. sacrament
Sakrischdei (es)n. sacristy
Sal(l)we(i) (der)n. sage (tea)
Salb (die)n. 1.ointment; 2.salve; 3.smear
Salbtee (der)n. sage (tea)
Saldaadeschtreiss (die)n., pl. scarlet sage
Saldaat (der)n. soldier
Saldaatekapp (die)n. soldier's cap
Saldaaterock (der)n. soldier's coat
Sallemann (der)n. Solomon
Salop (der)n. dirty fellow
Salma(n)gundi (es) n. salmagundi (salad plate of meats, anchovies, eggs and vegetables arranged in rows with salad dressing)
Salpederfier (es)n. nitric acid
Salpeeder (der)n. saltpeter
salwe, v.; gsalbt, pp. anoint
Salwen (die)n. selvedge
salwiere, v.; gsalwiert, pp. serve or handle roughly
salwiers, adv. 1.severely; 2.thoroughly
Salz (es)n. 1.salt; 2.(englisch --)Epsom salt
Salz Rewwer (der)n. Salt River
Salzbix (die)n. saltcellar
Salzdroog (der)n.; Salzdreeg, pl. salting trough (for salting meat in preparation for curing) or for cattle
salze, v.; gsalze, pp. salt
Salzfluss (der)n. salt rheum
salzich, adj. 1.high in price; 2.saline; 3.salty
Salzing (die)n. 1.drubbing; 2.salting
Salzlaag (die)n. 1.brine; 2.pickle
Salzlack (die)n. 1.brine; 2.pickle
Salzschleck (die)n. salt lick

Ss

Salzwasser

Salzwasser (es)n. saltwater
samde, prep. together with
Sammetros (die)n. marigold
sammle, v.; gsammelt, pp. 1.collect; 2.gather
Sammlung (die)n. 1.convention; 2.gathering
Samschdaag (der)n. Saturday
Samschdaagskind (es) n. Saturday child (child born on Saturday)
Samt (der)n. velvet
samt(e), prep. together with
samt, adv. together
Sand (der)n. 1.sand; 2.(gfleetzter --) (a) diluvial sand; (b) quicksand
Sanda Klaas (der)n. Santa Claus
Sandbabier (es)n. sandpaper
Sandboddem (der)n. sandy soil
Sandedorn (der)n. bugleweed
sandfarwich, adj. sandy
Sandhaufe (der)n. sandpile
sandich, adj. sandy
Sandkaern (die)n. grain of sand
Sandloch (es)n. sandpit
Sandmann (der)n. sandman
Sandschtee (der)n. sandstone
Sandsibb (die)n. 1.sand screen; 2.sand-sieve
Sandsieb (die)n. 1.sand screen; 2.sand-sieve
sanft, adj. 1.gentle; 2.mild; 3.soft
sanftmiedich, adj. 1.gentle; 2.meek
Sanftmut (der)n. gentleness
Sanickel (die)n. sanicle
Sanickelwatzel (die)n. sanicle
Sankel (der)n. plummet
Sankelschnur (die)n. plumb line
sapperlott!, interj. 1. the deuce!; 2.zounds!
sapperment!, interj. the deuce!
sapperments, adj. deucedly
sarde, v.; gsart, pp. sort
Sarge (die)n. 1.care; 2.trouble
sarge, v.; gsarrickt, pp. 1.care (for); 2.provide
sargefrei, adj. carefree
sargelos, adj. 1.carefree; 2.careless
Sarges (es)n. 1.care; 2.trouble
sarickfeldich, adj. solicitous
Sarig (die)n. sorrow
Sarrich (der)n. 1.bier; 2.coffin
Sarrick (die)n. 1.care; 2.trouble
sarricksam, adj. careful
sarrickvoll, adj. 1.anxious; 2.full of care
Sart (die)n. 1.kind; 2.sort
sarte, v.; gsart, pp. sort
Sarye (die, es)n. 1.sorrow; 2.trouble
sarye, v.; gsarrickt, pp (-- fer ebber) take care of (someone)
Sassafrill (die)n. sarsaparilla
Sassefra(a)s (es)n. sassafras
Sassefrill (die)n (zaahmi --) spikenard (herb of ginseng family)

schaalich

Satt (die)n.; Sadde, pl. 1.kind; 2.sort
satt, adj. 1.satisfied; 2.(ich bin --) I have had enough (to eat); 3.(ich hab's --) I have had enough of it
Satz (der)n. 1.grounds of coffee; 2.leaven; 3.yeast
Satzbloom (die)n. 1.everlasting; 2.cudweed
Satzbritsch (die)n. yeast ladle
satze, v.; gsatzt, pp. mix dough (with wooden paddle)
Satzhaffe (der)n. yeast pot
satzich, adj. yeasty
Satzkuche (der)n. yeast cake
Sau (die)n.; Sei, pl. 1.ace (in cards); 2.hog; 3.swine; 4.sow (female pig); 5. (en gemachti --) a perfect hog (of a person)
Sauballe (der)n. game of ball
saue, v.; gsaut, pp. 1.daub; 2.smear
sauer, adj. sour
Sauerabbel (der)n. sour (tart) apple
Sauerdeeg (der)n. scrapings of the kneading trough
Sauerei (die)n. 1.drunkenness; 2.debauch; 3.hoggishness
Sauereraahmkuche (der)n.; Sauereraahmkuche, pl. sour cream cake
Sauerglee (der)n. wood sorrel
Sauergraas (es)n. sedge
Sauergraut (es)n. sauerkraut
Sauergrautschtembel (der)n. sauerkraut stamper
Sauergrautschtember (der)n. sauerkraut stamper
Sauerka(e)sch (die)n.; Sauerka(e)sche, pl. sour cherry
Sauerrambel (der)n. sorrel
saufe, v.; gsoffe, pp. 1.drink (to excess); 2.suck
Sauferei (der)n. 1.debauch; 2.drunkenness
Saufgichdere (die)n. delirium tremens
Sauflodel (der)n. confirmed drunkard
Sauhund (der)n. dirty scamp
Saukopp (der)n. 1.hog's head; 2.jowl
saumselich, adj. 1.dilatory; 2.listless
saut, adv. south
sauwer, adj. 1.beautiful; 2.clean; 3.clear of weeds; 4.nice; 5.tidy
sauwer mache, v.; sauwer gemacht, pp. clean
Sauwerkeet (die)n. 1.cleanliness; 2.virtue
Sauwerkeit (die)n. virtue
Sawereraahmkuche (der)n.; Sawereraahmkuche, pl. sour cream cake
sch!, interj. 1.hush! 2.sh!
sch(i)ere, v.; gschiert, pp. 1.stir; 2.urge
Schaab (die)n. moth
schaad, adj (es is --) it is a pity
Schaade (der)n. 1.damage; 2.harm; 3.injury
schaadefroh, adj. malicious
Schaademaul (es)n. harelip
schaadlich, adv. harmful
schaadlos, adv. harmless
Schaal (die)n.; Schaale, pl. 1.head; 2.rind; 3.paring; 4.peal; 5.shell (on single-tree); 6.skull
Schaal(e)woog (die)n. 1.balance; 2.scale
schaalich, adj. 1.in layers; 2.scaly; 3.shelly

Ss

Schaam

Schaam (der)n. 1.foam; 2.froth; 3.scum
Schaam (die)n. 1.disgrace; 2.shame
schaame, v.; gschaamt, pp. 1.foam; 2.froth
Schaamgraut (es)n. wild sensitive plant
Schaar (die)n. 1.crowd; 2.multitude
Schaar (es)n. (plow) share
Schaartmaul (es)n. harelip
schaawe, v.; gschaabt, pp. scrape
Schaawer (der)n.; Schaawer, pl. scraper (used for removing pig bristles when butchering)
Schabernack (der)n. 1.prank; 2.trick
Schachdel (en aldi --) 1.an old woman; 2.an old worn out cow
Schack (der)n. shock of grain
schacke, v.; gschackt, pp. set up in shocks (grain)
Schadde (der)n. 1.shade; 2.shadow
Schaddebaam (der)n.; Schaddebeem, pl. shade tree
Schaddebank (die)n. a bench standing under a shade tree
Schaddebild (es)n. shadow-picture
Schaddeseit (die)n. shady side
schaddich, adj. shady
Schaedel (der)n. skull
Schaedelhaut (die)n. pericranium
schaediche, v.; gschaedicht, pp. 1.damage; 2.harm; 3.injure
schaedlich, adj. 1.harmful; 2.injurious; 3.noxious
Schaefel (es)n. lamb
Schaefer (der)n.; Schaefer, pl. shepherd
Schaefli (es)n. lamb
Schaelche (es)n.; Schaelcher, pl. saucer
schaele, v.; gschaelt, pp. 1.pare; 2.peel
Schaeli (es)n. saucer
Schaelmesser (es)n. paring knife
Schaelmiehlche (es)n. apple parer
Schaelschtee (der)n. hulling millstone
Schaep (der)n. sheaf
Schaerb (die) n.; Schaerwe, pl. 1.fragments of crockery or pottery; 2.table crockery; 3.sherd
schaere, v.; gschaert, pp. 1.scrape; 2.scratch
schaerf, adj. sharp
schaerfe, v.; gschaerft, pp. sharpen
Schaerm (der)n. umbrella
schaerre, v.; gschaerrt, pp. 1.hasten; 2.do one's best; 3.scrape; 4.scratch
Schaerwel (die)n. old woman
Schaerz (der)n. 1.jest; 2.joke
schaewisch, adj. Suabian
Schaff-ox (der)n. ox broken to work
Schaffbank (die)n.; Schaffbenk, pl. workbench
Schaffdaag (der)n.; Schaffdaage, pl. 1.weekday; 2.workday
schaffe, v.; gschafft, pp. 1.answer; 2.cultivate; 3.do; 4.ferment; 5.knead; 6.labor; 7.operate; 8.work; 9.(aus em weg --)(a) get rid of; (b) put out of the way; 10.(des schafft net) this won't do; 11.(ich wees was dich schafft) I know what irks you
Schaffgleeder (die)n., pl. working clothes
schaffich, adj. 1.busy; 2.industrious; 3.thrifty

Schatte

Schaffleit (die)n. workfolk
Schaffmann (der)n.; Schaffleit, pl. 1.laborer; 2.worker; 3.workman
Schaft (der)n.; Schafde, pl. 1.shaft; 2.stock (of a gun); 3.wooden part of an old time rifle; 4.(wooden shelf (for storing canned goods in cellar)
Schalk (der)n. 1.rogue; 2.wag
Schalkheet (die)n. 1.cunning; 2.roguery
Schalkyaahr (es)n. leap year
Schall (der)n.; Schalle, pl. 1.echo; 2.sound
Schallach (es)n. scarlet fever
Schallachfiewer (es)n. scarlet fever
Schallachfrissel (es)n. scarlet rash
Schallack (der)n. 1.rogue; 2.wag
Schallbrett (es)n. sounding board
schalle, v.; gschallt, pp. 1.sound; 2.reverberate
Schallhann (es)n. speaking trumpet
Schallicks (der)n. 1.rogue; 2.wag
schalu, adj. 1.clever; 2.cunning
Schamm (die)n. modesty
Schampanyer (der)n. champagne
Schan(d) (die)n. 1.disgrace; 2.dishonor; 3.shame
schandbaar, adj. 1.disgraceful; 2.shameful
schandbaarlich, adj. shamefully
schandeshalwer, adv. 1.to avoid disgrace; 2.for appearances' sake
Schandfleck (die)n. 1.blemish; 2.disgrace; 3.slander
schandlich, adj. 1.disgraceful; 2.shameful
schandlos(ich), adj. shameless
Schandwese (es)n. scandalous affair
Schank (der)n.; Schenk, pl. cupboard
Schankmacher (der)n. cabinetmaker
Schannschde (der)n. chimney
Schannschte(e) (der)n. chimney
Scharbock (der)n. scurvy
schare, v.; gschart, pp. shear
scharef, adj. 1.acrid; 2.keen; 3.sharp; 4.shrewd
scharefe, v.; gschareft, pp. sharpen
scharefsichdich, adj. 1.sagacious; 2.sharp-eyed
Scharefsinn (der)n. sagacity
scharf, adj. 1.sharp; 2.shrewd
scharfaagich, adj. hawk eyed
Scharfseit (die)n. (cutting) edge
scharfsichdich, adj. sagacious
scharfsinnich, adj. shrewd
scharmand, adj. 1.beautiful; 2.elegant; 3.fine; 4.very good
scharmant, adj. 1.beautiful; 2.elegant; 3.fine; 4.very good
Scharnschde (der)n. chimney
Scharnschderuss (die)n. flower-of-tan (plant)
Scharnschtee (der)n. chimney
Scharnschteefeger (der)n. chimney sweep
Scharnschteeloch (es)n. pipe hole into a chimney
scharre, v.; gschatt, pp. scratch
Scharz (der)n. apron
Scharzbendel (der)n. apron string
Schatte (der)n. 1.shade; 2.shadow

Ss

schatte

schatte, v.; gschatt, pp 1.(batt's nix, so schatt's nix) no harm in trying; 2.(es schatt ihm nix) it serves him right; 3.(nix --) (a) no matter; (b) (to do) no harm

Schattebaam (der)n. shade tree

Schattebild (es)n. shadow picture

Schatteseit (die)n. shady side

schattich, adj. shady

Schatz (der)n.; Schatz, pl. 1.apron; 2.sweetheart; 3.treasure

Schatzbendel (die)n., pl. string (apron)

Schatzfell (es)n. leather apron

Schatzkammer (die)n. treasury

Schatzmeeschder (der)n. treasurer

Schauder (der)n. 1.horror; 2.shiver

schaudere, v.; gschaudeert, pp. 1.shiver; 2.shudder

schauderhafdich, adj. 1.frightful; 2.shocking; 3.terrible

schauderhaft, adj. 1.frightful; 2.shocking; 3.terrible

schauderlich, adj. 1.dreadful; 2.shuddering

Schauer (der)n. shower

schauer(l)ich, adj. 1.dreadful; 2.shuddering

schauere, v.; gschauert, pp. shower

schauerich, adj. shuddering

Schaufel (die)n. 1.scoop-shovel; 2.spade

Schaufelblug (der)n.; Schaufelblieg, pl. shovel plow

Schaufeleek (die)n. cultivator

Schaufelhaendel (der)n.; Schaufelhaendle, pl. shovel-handle

schaufle, v.; gschaufelt, pp. 1.cultivate; 2.eat rapidly; 3.shovel

Schaum (der)n. 1.foam; 2.froth; 3.lather; 4.scum

schaume, v.; gschaumt, pp. 1.foam; 2.froth

schaumich, adj. 1.foamy; 2.frothy; 3.lathery

Schaumkel (die)n.; Schaumkele, pl. 1.skimmer; 2. skimming ladle

Schaumkuche (der)n. pastry dough with meringue covering baked in shape of a pie

Schaumleffel (der)n.; Schaumleffele 1.skimmer; 2.skimming ladle

Schebber (der)n. 1.dipper; 2.ladle

Scheck (die)n. spotted cow

scheckich, adj. 1.dappled; 2.piebald; 3.spotted; 4.variegated

Scheckikuh (die)n. spotted cow

Schee(d)wasser (es)n. 1.aqua fortes; 2.nitric acid

schee, adj. 1.beautiful; 2.handsome; 3.nice; 4.pretty

scheech, adj. 1.pale; 2.terrified

scheeche, v.; gscheecht, pp. 1.chase away; 2.drive away

Scheed (die)n. 1.case; 2.scabbard; 3.sheath

Scheedbrief (der)n.; Scheedbriefe, pl. divorce

scheede, v.; gscheede, pp. 1.divorce; 2.separate; 3.(en gscheedni fraa) a grass-widow

Scheedel (der)n. part in the hair

scheediche, v.; gscheedicht, pp. 1.divorce; 2.injure

scheedle, v.; gscheedelt, pp. part (the hair)

scheedlich, adj. 1.harmful; 2.injurious

scheedlich, adv. harmful

Schee(d)wasser (es)n. 1.aqua fortes; 2.nitric acid

Scheeheet (die)n. beauty

scheel, adj. 1.blind in one eye; 2.one-eyed; 3.spotted

scheisslich

scheele, v.; gscheelt, pp. shell

Scheelgraut (es)n. celandine

Scheer (die)n. shears

Schef (die)n.; Schefe, pl. 1.pod; 2.shell

Scheffer (der)n.; Scheffer, pl. 1.industrious person; 2.laborer; 3.workman

scheffich, adj. 1.busy; 2.industrious

Scheft (der)n. stock of a gun

schei, adj. shy

Scheib (die)n. 1.pane of glass; 2.target

scheide, adj. 1.part; 2.separate

scheide, v.; gscheide, pp. 1.part; 2.separate

Scheideckel (der)n. 1.blinker; 2.eyelid

scheidoot, adj. seemingly dead

scheie, v.; gscheit, pp. 1.be frightened; 2.shy; 3.(sich --) (a) be afraid; (b) fear; (c) shrink from

Scheier (die)n.; Scheiere, pl. barn

Scheierbesem (der)n. barn broom

Scheierbrick (die)n. entrance ramp (approach to the threshing floor of the bank barn)

Scheierbruder (der)n. Knight of the Golden Circle (of Civil War times)

Scheierdach (es)n.; Scheierdecher, pl. barn roof

Scheierdor (es)n.; Scheierdore, pl. barn door (at the rear of the barn)

scheiere, v.; gscheiert, pp. scour

Scheiereil (die)n.; Scheiereile, pl. barn owl

Scheiereili (es)n.; Scheiereilin, pl. (infant) barn owl

Scheiergang (der)n. passageway in barn

Scheierhiwwel (der)n. entrance ramp (to the barn floor)

Scheierhof (der)n.; Scheierhef, pl. 1.barnyard; 2.farmyard

Scheierschwalm (der)n.; Scheierschwalme, pl. barn swallow

scheiheilich, adj. hypocritical

Scheiheilichkeet (die)n. hypocrisy

Scheiledder (es)n.; Scheileddere, pl. 1.blind halter; 2.blinkers

Scheilheilicher (der)n.; Scheiheilicher, pl. hypocrite

Schein (der)n. 1.appearance; 2.glare; 3.glitter

scheinbaar, adj. 1.apparently; 2.ostensibly; 3.plausible; 4.seemingly; 5.spacious

scheinbaar, adv. seemingly

scheinbarlich, adj. evidently

scheine, v.; gscheint, pp. 1.appear; 2.glitter; 3.seem; 4.shine

scheinlich, adv. evidently

scheins, adv. 1.apparently; 2.evidently; 3.it would seem

Scheiss (die)n. 1.diarrhea; 2.dysentery

Scheissdreck (der)n. 1.turd; 2.(des geht dich kenn -- aa) that is none of your business

scheisse, v.; gschisse, pp. 1.shit; 2.void the bowels; 3.(ich -- der druff) I don't give a hang for what you say

Scheisshaffe (der)n.; Scheisshaffe, pl. (chamber) pot

Scheisshaus (es)n.; Scheissheiser, pl. outhouse

Scheisshoke (der)n. hock (of animals)

scheissich, adj. 1.failing to meet expectations; 2.insignificant

Scheisskammer (die)n. outhouse

scheisslich, adj. 1.abhorrent; 2.terrible

Ss

Scheissloch

Scheissloch (es)n.; Scheisslecher, pl. toilet hole
Scheisspog (der)n. scamp
schelde, v.; gscholde, pp. 1.rebuke; 2.reprimand; 3.scold
Schelf (es)n.; Schelfer, pl. 1.cornice; 2.shelf
schelle, v.; gschellt, pp. 1.sound; 2.reverberate; 3.ring;
    4.(des hot awwer gschellt) there was some row
Schellem (der)n. 1.knave; 2.rogue; 3.wretch
Schellgraut (es)n. celandine
Schellix (der)n. rogue
Schelm (der)n. 1.knave; 2.rogue; 3.wretch; 4.(grick's
    der --) the deuce take it
Schelmerei (die)n. 1.roguery; 2.villainy
Schelmlied (es)n.; Schelmlieder, pl. roguish song
Schemel (der) n. 1.bolster; 2.frame on which a log lies in
    sawing; 3.sawhorse; 4.trestle
Schemelnaggel (der)n. bolster pin
schemme, v.; gschemmt, pp. 1.(schemm dich) shame on
    you; 2.(sich --) (a) blush; (b) (to be) ashamed
schende, v.; gschendt, pp. 1.ravish; 2.violate
Schender (der)n. ravisher
schendlich, adj. 1.disgraceful; 2.pitiful; 3.scandalous;
    4.shameful
Schenkaasche (die)n. present (gift)
schenke, v.; gschenkt, pp. 1.make a present; 2.to present
Schenkel (der)n. 1.leg; 2.thigh
Schenkelgnoche (der)n. thighbone
Schenker (der)n. donor
Schenkung (die)n. donation
Schepfer (der)n. creator
Schepfung (die)n. creation
schepp, adj. 1.crooked; 2.lopsided; 3.not straight; 4. oblique;
    5.wry; 6.(en -- watt gewwe) never to utter a cross word
Scheppbool (die)n. dipper
scheppe, v.; gscheppt, pp. 1.dip; 2.shovel
Schepper (der)n. dipper
Schepphund (der)n. collie
Scheppkiwwel (der)n. pail
Scheppleffel (der)n. ladle
Scheppmaul (es)n. wry mouth
scheppmeilich, adj. 1.sarcastic; 2.wry-mouthed
scheppseidich, adj. lopsided
Scher (die)n.; Schere, pl. scissors
schere, v.; gschore, pp. 1.clip; 2.shear
schetzbaar, adj. valuable
schetze, v.; gschetzt, pp. 1.appraise; 2.consider; 3. esti-
    mate; 4.prize; 5.value
Schetzel (es)n. sweetheart
Schetzung (der)n. 1.estimate; 2.valuation
Schewing (der)n. chewing (Towhee)
schewwetzich, adj. 1.awry; 2.bungled; 3.crooked;
    4.imperfect; 5.scabrous
Schgidders (der)n. 1.diarrhea; 2.dysentery
schgoffle, v. heap up (earth around plants)
Schgweier (der)n. 1.Justice of the Peace; 2.District Justice
Schibb (die)n.; Schibbe, pl. dandruff
Schibbe (die)n., pl. scales of fish

Schiffsboot

Schibbesau (die)n. ace of spades
schibbich gucke, v. (to look) sheepish
schibbich, adj. scaly
schichder, adj. 1.shy; 2.timid
schichderich, adj. 1.shy; 2.timid
schicke, v.; gschickt, pp. (sich net --) misbehave
schicke, v.; gschickt, pp. 1.send; 2.(sich --) (a) adapt
    (oneself); (b) conduct (oneself)
schicke mache, v.; gemacht, pp. make it convenient
Schickelche (es)n. small shoe
schicklich, adj. 1.convenient; 2.decent; 3.suitable
Schicklichkeit (die)n. tact
Schicksaal (es)n. 1.doom; 2.fate
Schiddelgawwel (die)n.; Schiddelgawwle, pl. wooden fork
schiddle, v.; gschiddelt, pp. 1.jar; 2.shake; 3.shiver;
    4.vibrate; 5.wag; 6.(die Hend --)(to) shake hands
Schiddler (der)n. shaker of a threshing machine
Schiebbettlaedche (es)n. trundle bed
Schiebdor (es)n.; Schiebdore, pl. sliding door (on barn)
Schiebfenschder (es)n. sash-window
Schiebschtoff(t) (es)n. 1.middling; 2.chop; 3.shot
schiele, v.; gschielt, pp. squint
Schien(e)kar(e)b (der)n. splint basket
Schiene (die)n. 1.splint (used in making baskets, brooms
    and chair-seats); 2.rails (of a railroad) pl. form
Schienebese(m) (der)n. hickory splint broom
Schieneschtul (der)n. chair with splint seat
Schier (es)n. share
schier gaar, adv. 1.almost; 2. very nearly; 3.(-- gaarli) very
    nearly; 4.(net --) adv. hardly
Schiessbaawoll (die)n. gun cotton
Schiessbriggel (der)n. 1.fowling piece; 2.gun
schiesse, v.; gschosse, pp. 1.blast; 2.move fast; 3.run to seed;
    4.seed; 5.shoot; 6.(der bock --) do wonders (sarcastically)
Schiessgewehr (es)n. 1.gun; 2.shooting iron
Schiesskolwe (der)n. blunderbuss
Schiesspulwer (es)n. gunpowder
schiewe, v.; gschowe, pp. 1.push; 2.shove
Schiewer (der)n.; Schiewer, pl. 1.drawer; 2.slide; 3.sliding
    bolt (of a door)
Schiewerli (es)n. 1.bolt for a door-latch; 2.trundle bed
Schiff (die)n.; Schiffe, pl. dandruff
Schiff (es)n.; Schiffer, pl. 1.ship; 2.vessel
Schiffaahrt (die)n. navigation
Schiffbruch (der)n. shipwreck
Schiffel (der)n. weaver's shuttle
Schiffer (der)n. skipper
schifferich, adj. 1.dapple-gray; 2.shaly; 3.slaty; 4.slate
    colored; 5.speckled
Schifferschtee (der)n. 1.shale; 2.slate
schifferschteenich, adj. 1.barred; 2.shaley; 3.slaty;
    4.speckled
Schiffleit (die)n., pl. crew (of a vessel)
Schiffmann (der)n. sailor
schiffrich, adj. speckled
Schiffsboot (es)n. launch

Ss

Schild — Schlamp

Schild (es)n. 1.shield; 2.sign
Schildgraut (es)n. skullcap
Schildposchde (der)n. signpost
schilkse, v.; gschilkst, pp. cast stolen glances
Schillgrott (die)n.; Schillgrodde, pl. 1.tortoise; 2.turtle
Schillgrottebletter (die)n., pl. yellow pond lily
Schilling (der)n. shilling
S(ch)illscheit (es)n.; S(ch)illscheider, pl. 1.single-tree;
    2.whiffle-tree
schimb(er)lich, adj. shameful
schimbe, v.; gschimbt, pp. revile
schimfe, v.; gschimft, pp. 1.abuse; 2.defame; 3.disgrace;
    4.rebuke
schimm(e)lich, adj. moldy
Schimmel (der)n.;Schimmel,pl. 1.mold; 2.white
    horsewith small black spots
schimmere, v.; gschimmert, pp. 1.glimmer; 2.shine
schimmerich, adj. shimmering
Schimp (der)n. 1.blemish; 2.disgrace; 3.dishonor
schimp(er)lich, adj. 1.ignominious; 2.shameful
schimpe, v.; gschimpt, pp. 1.abuse; 2.defame; 3.disgrace
Schimpnaame (der)n. 1.nickname; 2.opprobrious epithet
Schindel (die)n.; Schindle, pl. 1.shingle; 2.splint for set-
    ting bones; 3.(mit Schindle decke) shingle
schindel, v.; gschindelt, pp. 1.(to apply) splints (to a bro-
    ken bone); 2.shingle
Schindeldach (es)n.; Schindeldecher, pl. shingle-roof
Schindeldecker (der)n.; Schindeldecker, pl. 1.petty
    fault-finder; 2.shingler
Schindelmacher (der)n.; Schindelmacher, pl. Shingle-maker
Schindelnaggel (der)n.; Schindelneggel, pl. Shingle-nail
schindle, v.; gschindelt, pp. 1.apply splints to broken
    bones; 2.shingle
Schindluder (der)n. scamp
Schindmaerr (die)n. jade
Schinke (der)n. ham
Schinnbee (es)n. shinbone
Schinnbloder (die)n. contusion
schinne, v.; gschunne, pp. 1.overwork; 2.skin; 3.skimp
Schinner (der)n. 1.deuce; 2.oppressor; 3.scavenger
Schinnerei (die)n. drudgery
Schinnerhannes (der)n. 1.man who hauls away dead
    animals; 2.scavenger
schinners, adv. deucedly
Schinnluder (der)n. scamp
Schinnoos (es)n. carrion
Schipp (die)n. 1.scoop; 2.shovel; 3.spade; 4.spade (in
    cards); 5.(-- an schtiel) the whole business
Schippelche (es)n. lamb
Schippeli (es)n. lamb
Schippesiwweter (der)n. fore-flusher
Schippli (es)n.; Schipplin, pl. lamb
S(ch)ippschaft (die)n. 1.concern; 2.gang; 3.set
Schippsche (es)n (en -- mache) 1.hang the lip; 2.pout
Schirm (der)n. protection
Schiss (der)n. 1.excrement; 2.speck (of flies); 3.trivial matter

Schissel (die)n.; Schissle, pl. 1.bowl; 2.dish; 3.vessel
Schisselblumm (die)n. daffodil
Schisser (der)n.; Schisser, pl. 1.shaver; 2.youngster
schitte, v.; gschitt, pp. pour
Schitz (der)n. 1.gunner; 2.hunter; 3.marksman;
    4.Sagittarius (9th sign of the zodiac); 5.shot
schitze, v.; gschitzt, pp. protect
Schiwwel (der)n. 1.chunk; 2.lump
Schiwwel (die)n. spade
Schiwwer (der)n.; Schiwwere, pl. 1.shale (formation);
    2.piece of slate
schiwwer-schteenich, adj. 1.barred (like barred Ply-
    mouth Rock fowls); 2.shaly; 3.slaty; 4.speckled
schiwwerich, adj. 1.dapple-gray; 2.shaley; 3.gravelly;
    4.slate-colored; 5.slaty; 6.speckled
Schiwwerschtee (der)n. 1.shale; 2.slate
schiwwerschteenich, adj. 1.barred; 2.shaly; 3.slaty;
    4.speckled
schiwwitzich, adj. 1.awry; 2.bungled; 3.crooked;
    4.imperfect; 5.scabrous
Schklaaf (der)n. slave
schklaafe, v.; gschlaaft, pp. slave
Schklaaferei (die)n. slavery
Schlaag (der)n. 1.apoplexy; 2.stroke (paralysis)
Schlaam (der)n. 1.slime; 2.mire; 3.mud
schlaams, adj. 1.slanting; 2.sloping
schlaamse, v.; gschlaamst, pp. 1.slant; 2.slope
schlabbe, v.; gschlappt, pp. slop
Schlabbes (der)n. slovenly person
schlabbich, adj. 1.careless; 2.disheveled; 3.sloppy;
    4.unkempt; 5.untidy
schlachde, v.; gschlacht, pp. 1.butcher; 2.kill
Schlacht (die)n.; Schlachde, pl. battle
Schlachtdaag (der)n. butchering day
Schlachthaus (es)n.; Schlachtheiser, pl. slaughterhouse
schlachtich, adj. 1.streaked; 2.streaky
Schlachtmann (der)n. butcher (rare usage)
Schlachtvieh (es)n. cattle fattened for slaughtering
Schlachtzeit (die)n. butchering season (December)
Schlack (der)n. 1.apoplexy; 2.slap; 3.slight blow;
    4.stroke; 5.whack; 6.tribe; 7.variety
Schlackhammer (der)n.; Schlackhemmer, pl. rock hammer
schlade, v.; gschlacht, pp. 1.butcher; 2.slaughter
Schlaefer (der)n. sleeper
schlaeferich, adj. 1.drowsy; 2.dull; 3.sleepy
Schlaeger (die)n. 1.fighter; 2.striker
Schlaegerei (die)n. fight
Schlaek (die)n., pl. 1.flogging; 2.whipping
schlaerbse, v.; gschlaerbst, pp. eat with a smacking sound
schlaff, adj. slack
schlagge, v.; gschlaage, pp. 1.beat; 2.break (an egg in a
    dish); 3.hit; 4.kick (of a horse); 5.strike; 6.(en
    Droot --) pace off (in plowing); 7.(sich --) succeed
schlambich, adj. slovenly
Schlamm (der)n. 1.mire; 2.mud; 3.slime; 4.ooze
Schlamp (die)n. sloven

Ss

Schlang / schliesslich

Schlang (die)n.; Schlange, pl. 1.reptile; 2.snake; 3.worm (in distilling apparatus); 4.(gleeni --) Virginia snakeroot

Schlangebiss (der)n. Snakebite

Schlangedokter, (der)n. 1.dragon-fly; 2.devil's darning needle

Schlangegiesser (der)n. dragonfly

Schlangegraas (es)n. stinking eryngo

Schlangehaut (die)n. snake skin

Schlangehieder (der)n. dragonfly

Schlangewatzel (die)n. snakeroot

Schlangwatzel (die) n 1. (grossi, hochi, schwatzi --) black cohosh; 2.(gleeni, niddri --) Virginia snakeroot

schlank, adj. 1.slender; 2.svelte

Schlapp (die)n. 1.swill; 2.untidy woman

schlappe, v.; gschlappt, pp. 1.slop; 2.(es Maul --) drop or lower the lip

Schlappeemer (der)n. slop bucket

Schlappes (der)n. slovenly person

Schlappfass (es)n.; Schlappfesser, pl. 1.slop barrel; 2.swill barrel

schlappfiessich, adj. walking in a slovenly manner

Schlappfuus (der)n. slovenly walker

Schlapphut (der)n.; Schlapphiet, pl. 1.soft felt man's hat; 2.sun-bonnet

schlappich, adj. untidy

Schlappmaul (es)n. 1.fly trap (facetious); 2.hang-lip

Schlaraffegsicht (der)n. mask

schlarbse, v.; gschlarebst, pp. lisp

schlarre (adj. 1.big morsel; 2.large piece

schlau, adj. 1.astute; 2.cunning; 3.mischievous; 4.of a pleasing sensation (mostly in a vulgar manner); 5.sly; 6.tricky

Schlauch (der)n. sheath of a horse

Schlauder (es)n. same old story

Schlaufeleeg (die)n. cultivator

Schlawwer (es)n. saliva

Schlawwerduch (es)n.; Schlawwerdicher, pl. (baby) bib

schlawwere, v.; gschlawwert, pp. 1.drool; 2.slobber

schlawwerich, adj. slobbering

Schlawwermaul (es)n. person who slobbers

schlebbe, v.; gschleppt, pp. snare game

Schlechdes (es)n. evil

Schlechdichkeit (die)n. 1.badness; 2.evil; 3.meanness; 4.wickedness

schlecht fiehle, v.; gfiehlt, pp. 1.ail; 2.be sickly

schlecht uff/fiehre, v.; schlecht (sich --) uffgfiehrt, pp. misbehave

schlecht, adj. 1.bad; 2.evil; 3.vile; 4.wicked

schlechtguckich, adj. bad looking

Schlechtichkeet (die)n. 1.badness; 2.meanness; 3.wickedness

Schleck (der)n. 1.a taste; 2.lick; 3.little bit

schlecke, v.; gschleckt, pp. 1.lap; 2.lick

Schlecker (der)n.; Schlecker, pl. tongue (of shoe) (humorous)

Schleckerei (die)n. 1.dainties; 2.sweets

Schleckerwese (es)n. sweets

Schleckes (es)n. 1.dainties; 2.sweets

Schleef (die)n. 1.manure sled; 2.sledge (on runners)

schleeferich, adj. drowsy

Schleefgaarn (es)n. 1.drag-net; 2.seine

Schleefreche (der)n. drag rake

schleffe, v.; gschleeft, pp. drag

Schleffelwedder (es)n. thawing weather

schleffle, v.; gschleffelt, pp. 1.melt; 2.thaw

Schleggel (der)n. 1.maul; 2.sledgehammer; 3.mallet

schleggele, v.; gschleggelt, pp. struggle

Schleggelhammer (der) n.; Schleggelhemmer, pl. sledgehammer

schleggle, v.; gschleggelt, pp. use a sledge

Schleich (die)n. 1.slowpoke; 2.sneaking person

schleiche, v.; gschliche, pp. 1.slink; 2.sneak; 3.steal; 4.walk slowly; 5.walk stealthy

Schleicher (der)n. silent fart

Schleier (der)n. mourning veil

schleife, v.; gschleift, pp. drag

schleife, v.; gschliffe, pp. 1.grind; 2.sharpen; 3.skate; 4.slide

Schleifschtee (der)n.; Schleifschtee, pl. grindstone

Schleim (der)n. 1.mucilage; 2.mucus; 3.slime

schleimich, adj. 1.mucilaginous; 2.slimy

Schlem (der)n. 1.rogue; 2.wretch

schlendere, v.; gschlendert, pp. 1.gawk about; 2.idle

Schlenk (die)n. 1.sling; 2.thumb-latch

schlenkere, v.; gschlenkert, pp. 1.fling; 2.shake vigorously; 3.swing

schlenkerich, adj. 1.loose-jointed; 2.swinging

Schleppche (es)n. small load

schleppe, v.; gschleppt, pp. 1.carry a heavy load; 2.drag; 3.snare game

Schleppschlecker (der)n. sycophant

schlibbe, v.; gschlippt, pp. 1.slip; 2.snare game; 3.steal

schlibberich, adj. 1.mischievous; 2.slippery; 3.sly

schlibbich, adj. slippery

schlichde, v.; gschlicht, pp. settle

Schlicht (der)n. sizing (put on wagon covers to weatherproof them)

schlicht, adj. simple

schlichte, v.; gschlicht, pp. 1.adjust a quarrel; 2.settle

Schlichthols (es)n. shoemaker's sleeking stick

Schlichthowwel (die)n. smoothing plane

schlick, adj. crafty

Schlickser (der)n. hiccough

schlicksere, v.; gschlicksert, pp. hiccough

Schlicksergramp (der)n. hysteria

Schlidde (der)n. 1.sled; 2.sleigh

Schliddebaah (die)n. sleighing

Schliddebell (die)n. sleigh bell

Schliddefaahre (es)n. sleigh-riding

Schliddeleefer (der)n. runner (of a sleigh)

Schlier (der)n. 1.abscess; 2.carbuncle

Schliess (die)n. 1.counterpin; 2.lock (of a canal); 3.lockgate (of a dam); 4.key

schliesse, v.; gschlosse, pp. lock

schliesslich, adj. in conclusion

153

Ss

Schliffel

Schliffel (der)n. 1.big stout fellow; 2.rowdy
Schliffelmiehl (die)n. merry-go-round
Schliffer (der)n.; Schliffere, pl. splinter
schlifferich, adj. splintery
schlifferschteenich, adj. slaty
schlimm, adj. 1.bad; 2.sad; 3.serious
schlimm grank, adj, very ill
Schlimmscht (es)n. worst
Schling (die)n. 1.hot punch; 2.sling
Schlingel (der)n. 1.awkward fellow; 2.rogue
Schlipp (der)n. slip
schlipp schlapp imitative of the splashing sound of a
    waterwheel
Schlissel (der)n.; Schlissle, pl. key
Schlisselblettche (es)n. keyhole guard
Schlisselblumm (die)n.; Schlisselblumme, pl. 1.cowslip;
    2.hyacinth; 3.primrose
Schlisselloch (es)n.; Schlissellecher, pl. keyhole
Schlissellochblettche (es)n. keyhole guard
Schlisselring (der)n. key-ring
Schlitz (der)n. 1.hole; 2.placket; 3.slit; 4.tear
schlitze, v.; gschlitzt, pp. slash
Schlitzholz (es)n. shoemaker's sleeking stick
schlitzohrich, adj. 1.artful; 2.crafty; 3.cunning;
    4.mischievous; 5.sly
Schliwwer (der)n.; Schliwwere, pl. 1.jag; 2.splinter
schliwwere, v.; gschliwwert, pp. 1.splinter; 2.(es -- losse)
    (a) break loose; (b) let 'er go
schliwwerich, adj. splintery
schliwwerich, adv. rascally
Schlixer (der)n. hiccough
Schlixergramp (der)n. hysteria
Schlodderfuus (der)n. person walking with a shambling gate
schlodere, v.; gschlodert, pp. 1.dawdle; 2.shamble
schlodle, v.; gschlodert, pp. 1.dawdle; 2.shamble
Schlof (der)n. 1.sleep; 2.temple (side of the head);
    3.(im -- sei), (am --e sei) (to be) asleep
Schlofbank (die)n.; Schlofbenk, pl. bunk
Schlofdrobbe (die)n., pl. 1.opiate; 2.soporific
schlofe, v.; gschlofe, pp. sleep
Schlofkammer (die)n.; Schloffkemmer, pl. bedroom
Schlofkapp (die)n. nightcap
Schlofkopp (der)n. (to be) sleepy headed
Schlofkummeraad (der)n. bed fellow
Schlofleis (die)n., pl. 1.sandman; 2.sleepiness
schlofschtermich, adv. nightmarish
Schlofschtubb (die)n.; Schlofschtuwwe, pl. bedroom
schloidere, v.; gschlodert, pp. shamble
Schloofdrobbe (die)n., pl. opiate
Schloofmiddel (es)n. opiate
Schloss (die)n. hailstone
Schloss (es)n.; Schlesser, pl. 1.lock; 2.snap (fastener)
schlosse, v.; gschlosse, pp. hail
Schlosser (der)n.; Schlosser, pl. locksmith
Schlosseschtarm (der)n. hail-storm
Schlossewedder (es)n. hail-storm

Schmatz

Schlott (die)n. onion top
Schlotterfuss (der)n. person walking with a shambling gait
schlotze, v.; gschlotzt, pp. suck
Schlotzer (der)n.; Schlotzer, pl. 1.nipple; 2.pacifier
schluchze, v.; gschluchzt, pp. 1.sigh; 2.sob; 3.weep
Schluck (der)n. 1.mouthful; 2.swallow (food or liquid)
schlucke, v.; gschluckt, pp. 1.gulp; 2.swallow
Schlucker (der)n. 1.esophagus; 2.throat; 3.(aarmer --)
    (a) poor devil; (b) wretch
Schluckerli (es)n. throat
Schluckse (es)n. hiccough
Schluckser (der)n. hiccough
schlumbich, adj. slatternly
schlumblich, adj. soggy
Schlummer (der)n. 1.doze; 2.slumber
schlummere, v.; gschlurnmert, pp. 1.doze; 2.slumber
schlummerich, adj. drowsy
schlummre, v.; gschlummert, pp. 1.doze; 2.nap; 3.slumber
Schlump (die)n. slattern
schlumpich, adj. slatternly
schlumsich, adj. slatternly
Schlund (der)n. 1.gullet; 2.throat
Schlupp (der)n.; Schlipp, pl. 1.bow (tied like a necktie);
    2.loop; 3.noose; 4.ribbon
schluppe, v.; gschluppt, pp. 1.crawl; 2.creep
Schlupploch (es)n. 1.hole; 2.hole to crawl out through;
    3.loophole
Schlur(r)i (der)n. good-for-nothing fellow
Schluss (der)n. 1.conclusion; 2.end
Schlusslied (es)n. closing hymn
Schlutzer (der)n. sugar-teat (baby's pacifier of bread and
    sugar)
schmaal, adj. narrow
Schmaaler (der)n. drink of whiskey
schmachde, v.; gschmacht, pp. languish
Schmack (der)n. scent
schmacke, v.; gschmackt, pp. 1.smell (in certain areas);
    2. taste; 3.(der Schmittschapp schmackt) the black-
    smith shop smells (of burning hoof); 4.(en Ratt --)
    smell a rat
schmackhaft, adj. 1.delicious; 2.palatable; 3.toothsome
Schmackwaerscht (der)n. person who tasted the sausage
    meat for condiments
schmaehe, v.; gschmaeht, pp. 1.revile; 2.taunt
schmaert, adj. 1.intelligent; 2.smart
Schmaerze (die)n., pl. pain
schmaerze, v.; gschmaerzt, pp. 1.cause pain; 2.pain
schmaerzhaft, adj. 1.painful; 2.sore
schmaerzlich, adj. painful
Schmalsbress (die)n. lard press
Schmalz (es)n. lard
Schmalzschtenner (der)n. lard can
Schmarotzerei (die)n. parasitism
Schmarre (der)n. 1.cut; 2.slash
Schmatz (der)n.; Schmatze, pl. 1.ache; 2.hearty kiss;
    3.smack; 4.pain

Ss

schmatze

schmatze, v.; gschmatzt, pp. 1.ache; 2.make a smacking sound; 3.be in pain; 4.smack; 5.smart; 6.taste or eat with a smacking sound; 7.hurt (oneself)

Schmaus (der)n. feast

schmause, v.; gschmaust, pp. 1.feast; 2.revel

Schmauserei (die)n. debauch

schmecke, v.; gschmeckt, pp. 1.smell (in certain areas); 2.taste

Schmeechle, v.; gschmeechelt, pp. 1.fawn; 2.flatter; 3.soothe

Schmeechler (der)n. flatterer

schmeelich, adj. 1.flattering; 2.insinuating

Schmeesmick (die)n. bluebottle (fly)

Schmeichelei (die)n. flattery

Schmeicherei (die)n. flattery

schmeisse, v.; gschmisse, pp. 1.cast; 2.throw; 3.toss

Schmeissgaarn (es)n. casting net

Schmelme applied to several varities of grass

schmelse, v.; gschmolse, pp. 1.melt; 2.smelt

Schmelzoffe (der)n. 1.furnace; 2.ore smelter

Schmelzpann (die)n. 1.oil gland (of fowl); 2.uropygial gland

Schmetterling (der)n. butterfly (rare usage)

schmicke, v.; gschmickt, pp. adorn

Schmier (die)n. 1.grease; 2.ointment; 3.salve

schmiere, v.; gschmiert, pp. 1.bribe; 2.blarney; 3.daub; 4. lubricate; 5. rub with ointment; 6. smear; 7.spread something on bread

Schmiererei (die)n. 1.any (long continued) smeary or greasy work; 2.doctoring; 3.mixed-up affair

schmierich, adj. 1.muddy; 2.miry; 3.smeary; 4.sticky

Schmierkann (die)n. oilcan

Schmierkees (der)n. cottage cheese

Schmierseef (die)n. soft soap

Schmierwese (es)n. smeary or greasy work

Schmitt (der)n.; Schmitt, pl. blacksmith

schmitte, v.; gschmitt, pp. carry on the blacksmith's trade

Schmitthammer (der)n. blacksmith's hammer

Schmittschapp (der)n.; Schmittschepp, pl. smithy

Schmittzaerkel (der)n. calipers

Schmittzang (die)n. blacksmith's tongs

schmoddere, v.; gschmoddert, pp. smother

schmodderich, adj. 1.close (of air); 2.sultry

schmodich, adj. sultry

Schmok (der)n. smoke

schmoke, v.; gschmokt, pp. smoke

Schmokhaus (es)n.; Schmokheiser, pl. smokehouse

schmokich, adj. smoky

Schmokpeif (die)n. 1.smoke pipe; 2.(en erdne --) an earthen pipe

Schmokwedder (es)n. Indian summer

Schmookdaage (die)n. Indian summer

schmore, v. 1.fry; 2.stew

schmudich, adj. sultry

schmuggle, v.; gschmuggelt, pp. cheat

schmunsle, v.; gschmunselt, pp. 1.grin; 2.smile

schmunslich, adj. smiling

schnause

Schmutz (der)n. 1.dirt; 2.filth; 3.grease; 4.hearty kiss; 5.lard; 6.smack

Schmutzblacke (der)n. grease spot

schmutze, v.; gschmutzt, pp. 1.kiss; 2.lubricate

Schmutzheffli (es)n. 1.oil gland (of fowl); 2.uropygial gland

schmutzich, adj. 1.dirty; 2.greasy; 3.lewd; 4.off-color; 5.muddy; 6.smutty; 7.sordid

Schmutzkeidel (es)n. 1.oil gland (of fowl); 2.uropygial gland

Schmutzkennli (es)n. 1.oil gland (of fowl); 2.uropygial gland

Schmutzlicht (es)n. fat light

schnabbe, v.; gschnappt, pp. snap

schnabble, v.; gschnappt, pp. 1.nod; 2.give assent by nodding; 3.doze

schnack, adj. 1.well-fitting (of clothes); 2.well-shaped (of girls)

schnackerich, adj. 1.slender; 2.slim

schnackich, adj. 1.dainty in eating; 2.sneaky

schnaddre, v.; gschnaddert, pp. 1.shake from cold; 2.tremble

Schnaerkel (der)n. 1.funny saying; 2.joke

Schnaerr (der)n. jerk

Schnaerr (die)n. jerky young woman

schnaerre, v.; gschnaerrt, pp. 1.convey in a rig; 2.jerk

schnaerrfiessich, adj. spring-halted

Schnaerrvoggel (der)n.; Schnaerrveggel, pl. Humming bird

Schnaffler (der)n.; Schnaffler, pl. nosey fellow

schnaflich, adj. nosey

schnaixe, v.; gschnaixt, pp. snore

Schnall (die)n.; Schnalle, pl. buckle

schnalle, v.; gschnallt, pp. buckle

Schnapp (die)n. snap

schnappe, v.; gschnappt, pp. 1.limp; 2.nod; 3.snap; 4.(noch luft --) gasp

Schnappgalye (der)n. lever-pump

Schnapps (der)n. 1.spirits; 2.whiskey; 3.(en -- nemme) take a drink of whiskey

Schnappsack (der)n.; Schnappseck, pl. 1.haversack; 2.knapsack

schnapse, v.; gschnapst, pp. drink spirits

Schnarefeggelgsicht (es)n. 1.false face; 2.mask; 3.used contemptuously of a human face

schnarixe, v.; gschnarixt, pp. snore

Schnarixer (der)n. snorer

Schnarrbaart (der)n. moustache

schnarre, v.; gschnarrt, pp. 1.snarl; 2.speak gruffly

schnarre, v.; gschnatt, pp. 1.jerk; 2.jolt; 3.snarl

schnarrich, adj. gruff

Schnarveggelche (es)n. hummingbird

Schnarvoggel (der)n.; Schnarveggel, pl. hummingbird

schnattre, v.; gschnaddert, pp. 1.gabble; 2.quack (of ducks); 3.tremble; 4.chatter (of teeth)

schnaube, v. snort (of a horse or pig)

schnaufe, v.; gschnauft, pp. 1.breathe; 2.(to be) short of breath

schnause, v.; gschnaust, pp. 1.eat secretly; 2.purloin; 3.secure eatables by stealth

Ss

Schnauser(n)   schnubbere

Schnauser(n) (der, die)n. busybody

schnausich, adj. 1.dainty in eating; 2.overly curious

Schnaut (die)n. wry mouth

Schnauzbaart (der)n. moustache

schnauze, v.; gschnauzt, pp. snort (of animals, especially pigs)

schnauzich, adj. snappish

schnawlich, adj. nosey

Schnawwel (der)n.; Schnawwel, pl. 1.spout (of teapot); 2.visor (of a cap)

Schnawwel (der)n.; Schnawwele, pl. 1.beak; 2.bill

Schnawwelkeppli (es)n. pointed cap

schnebbe, v.; gschneppt, pp. 1.lift with a lever; 2.snare; 3.tilt

Schnebber (der)n. 1.snapping turtle; 2.trigger

schnebberich, adj. talkative

schneberich, adj. unstable (of boards)

Schneck (die)n.; Schnecke, pl. snail

Schneckeharn (es)n. 1.conch; 2.peculiarly shaped instrument used as a dinner horn

Schneckehaus (die)n. snail-shell

schneckerich, adj. 1.slender; 2.slim

Schneckeschteek (die)n. winding stairs

Schnee (der)n. snow

schnee-e, v.; gschneet, pp. snow

Schneeballe (der)n. snowball

Schneeballebaam (der)n. snowball tree

Schneeblug (der)n.; Schneeblieg, pl. snowplow

Schneeblumm (die)n.; Schneeblumme, pl. snowdrop

Schneebrocke (der)n. snowflake

Schneeflocke (der)n. snowflake

Schneegans (die)n. wild goose

Schnee(g)schtiwwer (der)n. 1.snow squall; 2.snowstorm

schneeich, adj. snowy

Schneeschaufel (die)n. snow-shovel

Schneeschtar(e)m (der)n. snow storm

Schneevoggel (der)n. 1.junco; 2.snowbird

Schneewasser (es)n. snow-water

schneeweiss, adj. snow-white

Schneewind (der)n. wind bringing snow

Schneid (die)n. cutting edge of a tool

Schneidbank (die)n. drawing-bench

schneide, v.; gschnidde, pp. 1.cut; 2.castrate; 3.geld; 4.reap grain with a sickle; 5.spay; 6.(Haar --) (to) cut hair

Schneideise (es)n. 1.die; 2.screw tap

Schneider (der)n.; Schneider,pl. 1.daddy-longlegs; 2.tailor

schneidere, v.; gschneidert, pp. tailor

Schneiderkuraaschi, n. corn gromwell

Schneidern (die)n. seamstress

Schneidgschaerr (die)n. edged tool

Schneidmesser (es)n.; Schneidmesser, pl. drawknife

schneize, v.; gschneizt, pp. (sich --) blow the nose by pressing a finger against the side of the nostril

schnell, adj.; adv. 1.quick(ly); 2.rapid(ly); 3.swift(ly)

schnelle, v.; gschnellt, pp. 1.fling; 2.fillip; 3.jerk; 4.let fly

Schneller (der)n. 1.fillip; 2.insect which attacks smoked meat; 3.leaping beetle; 4.marble(s) 5.spring; 6.trigger

Schnellichkeet (die)n. 1.swiftness; 2.velocity

Schnellichkeit (die)n. 1.swiftness; 2.velocity

Schnellkeffer (der)n.; Schnellkeffer, pl. 1.click beetle (which attacks smoked ham); 2.leaping beetle

Schnellposcht (die)n. tattletale

Schnellschreiwer (der)n. 1.stenographer; 2.shorthand writer

Schnellwoog (die)n. steelyard

Schnepp (die)n. 1.catch; 2.simpleton; 3.snap; 4.snipe (game bird); 5.sulky; 6.(er is uff der --) he is undecided

Schneppermaul (es)n. chatterbox

schneppre, v.; gschneppert, pp. chatter

Schnewwel (der)n. 1.beak; 2.bill

Schnewwli (es)n. 1.oil gland (of fowl); 2.uropygial gland

Schnibbelche (es)n. snip

Schnickel (der)n. penis

Schnickelfritz (der)n. mischievous child

Schnidder (der)n.; Schnidder, pl. 1.sickler; 2.reaper

Schnidderlich (der)n. chives

schnieki(s)ch, adj. 1.dainty in eating; 2.fastidious; 3.mischievous; 4.sneaky; 5.sly

schnier, adv. nearly

schniere, v.; gschniert, pp. 1.cheat; 2.lace

Schnierleibche (es)n. corset

Schnierschtiwwel (der)n. laced boot

Schnippche (es)n (en -- mache) pout

Schnippelche, (es)n. snip

schnipple, v.; gschnippelt, pp. snip

Schnippler (der)n. 1.nibbler; 2.one who only nibbles at things (at the table)

schnippse, v.; gschnippst, pp. 1.sob; 2.weep

Schnipsel (es)n. snip

schnipsle, v.; gschnipselt, pp. whittle

Schnitt (der)n. cut

Schnitter (der)n. 1.gelder; 2.reaper; 3.sickler

Schnitt(er)lich (der)n. chives

Schnittling (der)n. slip

Schnittloch (der)n. chives

Schnitz (die)n.; Schnitz, pl. 1.dried fruit; 2.fibs; 3.sections of apple; 4.(-- un Gnepp) apples (sliced and dried) and dumplings

Schnitzboi (der)n.; Schnitzboi, pl. snitz pie

schnitze, v.; gschnitzt, pp. 1.halve or quarter fruit; 2.tell a fib

Schnitzelbank (die)n. 1.drawing bench; 2.name of a popular song

Schnitzkuche (der)n. pie made of schnitz

schnitzle, v.; gschnitzelt, pp. whittle

Schnitzriwwelkuche (der) n. tart (made of dried apples covered with sugared crumbs)

schnobe, v.; gschnobt, pp. snort

Schnok (die)n.; Schnoke, pl. 1.gnat; 2.mosquito

Schnubbe (der)n. 1.rheum; 2.cold in the head

schnubbe, v.; gschnuppt, pp. 1.sniff; 2.sniffle; 3.snuffle; 4.take snuff

schnubbere, v.; gschnubbert, pp. 1.pry; 2.sniffle

Ss

schnubbich

schnubbich, adj. 1.sneaking; 2.snoopy

schnuddle, v.; gschnuddelt, pp. 1.drink in a sloppy manner; 2.take to drink; 3.take strong drink; 4.over drink (booze)

Schnuffelbochs (die)n. busybody

schnuffle, v.; gschnuffelt, pp. 1.pry; 2.rummage; 3.sniffle

Schnuffler (der)n.; Schnuffler, pl. 1.busybody; 2.spy

Schnupf (der)n. snuff

Schnupfharn (es)n. mull (fabric)

Schnupp (die)n. snap

Schnuppduch (es)n.; Schnuppdicher, pl. handkerchief

Schnuppduwack (der)n. Snuff

Schnuppe (der)n. cold (in the head)

schnuppe, v.; gschnuppt, pp. 1.sniff; 2.snuffle; 3.take snuff

schnuppere, v.; gschnuppert, pp. meddle with another's property; 2.pry; 3.sniffle

schnupperich, adj. prying

schnuppich, adj. 1.dainty in eating; 2.fastidious; 3.sneaking; 4.snoopy

Schnur (die)n. 1.cord; 2.lace; 3.lash; 4.string; 5.twine; 6. (iwwer die -- hacke) (a) go wrong; (b) kick over the traces

Schnurbaerdli (es)n. little moustache

Schnurbort (der)n. moustache

schnure, v.; gschnurt, pp. (sich --) lace (as a corset)

schnurschtracks, adj. 1.directly; 2.erect; 3.slender; 4.straight

schnurschtracks, adv. 1.at once; 2.directly; 3.straight

Schnut (die)n. 1.snoot; 2.snout (hog); 3.wry mouth; 4. (en -- mache) (a) make a face; (b) pout

Schnutz (der)n. 1.sections of (dried) fruit; 2.smack; 3.term of endearment (applied to an infant in its cradle) 4.(-- un Gnepp) apples (sliced and dried) and dumplings

Schocheri (der)n. name of a foothill in Lynn Township, Lehigh County

Schockel (die)n.; Schockle, pl. 1.cradle; 2.crib (for an infant)

Schockelleefer (der)n.; Schockelleefer, pl. runner (of a rocking chair)

Schockellied (es)n. lullaby

Schockelschtul (der)n.; Schockelschtiel, pl. rocking chair

Schocklaad (der)n. chocolate

schockle, v.; gschockelt, pp. rock (on a chair)

Schockler (der)n,; Schockler, pl. 1.rocking chair; 2.rocker; 3.one who rocks

Schodde an der Keddeschtreng (der) (leather) sheath on iron traces

schoddere, v.; gschoddert, pp. (to cause to) tremble

schoddre, v.; gschoddert, pp. shake

Schof (es)n.; Schof, pl. sheep

Schofbeer (die)n. sheepberry

Schofbelz (die)n. sheepskin

Schofbock (der)n.; Schofbeck, pl. 1.he-sheep; 2.ram

Schofgnoddel (der)n. 1.black haw; 2.sheep excrement

Schofgnoddelbeer (die)n. sheepberry

Schofgnoddletee (der) n. decoction made from sheep

Schpaerwel

excrement formerly administered to bring out the rash of measles or scarlet fever

Schofhammel (der)n. wether

Schofhaut (die)n. sheepskin

Schofheider (der)n. shepherd

Schofhund (der)n. 1.collie; 2.sheep dog

schofisch, adj. sheepish

Schofkasch (die)n. sheepberry

Schofknoddel (der)n. 1.black haw; 2.sheep excrement

Schofkopp (der)n. 1.blockhead; 2.chump

Schoflaus (die)n. 1.hounds tongue; 2.stickseed; 3.tick

Schofleis (die)n. tick

Schofli (es)n.; Schoflin, pl. lamb

Schofmischt (der)n. sheep manure

Schofnaas (die)n. 1.sheep's nose; 2.variety of apples

Schofrippe (die)n., pl. yarrow

Schofscher (die)n. sheep shears

Schofschtall (der)n. sheepfold

Schofseckel (der)n. shepherd's purse

Schoftee (der)n. horse-tail (plant)

Scholle (der)n. clod

Schollehupser (der)n. 1.clodhopper; 2.rustic

schollich, adj. cloddy

schone, v.; gschont, pp. 1.favor; 2.spare; 3.treat with forbearance

Schooffleesch (es)n. mutton

Schopp (der)n.; Schepp, pl. shed

Schoppe (der)n (am -- nemme) take a good hold of (in nape of neck)

Schoppscheier (die)n. shed-barn

Schoss (der)n. lap

Schossduch (es)n.; Schossdicher, pl. napkin

Schot (die)n. 1.pod; 2.shell

Schotebaam (der)n. catalpa

Schotebohn (die)n. pod bean

schottere, v.; gschottert, pp. 1.cause to tremble; 2.shake

Schottscheier (die)n.; Schottschiere, pl. 1.storage place for grain, hay, straw (outbuilding); 2.shed-barn

Schpaa (der)n. 1.chip; 2.wood shaving

Schpaade (der)n. spavin

schpaade, v.; gschpaade, pp. spade

Schpaal (der)n.; Schpaale; Schpalde, pl. 1.chip (of stone); 2.spall

schpaare, v.; gschpaart, pp. 1.economize; 2.save; 3.spare

schpaarsam, adj. 1.economical; 2.frugal; 3.saving

Schpaarsamkeit (die)n. 1.economy; 2.frugality

Schpaat (die)n. spade

Schpacht (der)n.; Schpachde, pl. spoke (in a wheel)

Schpaech(t) (der)n. 1.flicker; 2.woodpecker

schpaerlich, adj. scarce

Schpaerling (der)n. sparrow

Schpaerrbalke (der)n. break beam

schpaerreweit, adj. wide (open)

Schpaerrglotz (der)n. brake block

Schpaerrit (der)n. spirits

Schpaerwel (die)n. persimmon

Ss

Schpalde

Schpalde (die)n., pl. chips
schpalde, v.; gschpalt, pp. split
Schpaldeise (es)n. iron used in splitting rails
Schpalt (der)n. 1.crack; 2.crevice
Schpaltax (die)n.; Schpaltex, pl. splitting axe
Schpange (die)n. bracelet (rare usage)
schpanisch, adj. Spanish
Schpank (der)n. spunk
schpanki, adj. daring
schpankich, adj. 1.daring; 2.spunky
Schpann (der)n. span
Schpanne (die)n., pl. pin oaks
schpanne, v.; gschpannt, pp. 1.cock (a gun); 2.(to be) tight; 3.stretch
Schpanneeche (die)n. pin-oak
Schpannpett (die)n. cross beam
Schpannsaeg (die)n. wood saw
Schpannseel (es)n.; Schpannseele, pl. tether
Schpanodel (die)n.; Schpanodle, pl. Spanish needle
schparige, v.; gschparigt, pp. 1.court; 2.go courting
Schparkett (die)n.; Schparkedde, pl. log-chain
Schparr (die)n.; Schparre, pl. brake
Schparre (der)n.; Schparre, pl. 1.rafter; 2.(er hut en --los); (er hut en -- zu viel odder eener zu wennich) he is a bit off in the head
schparre, v.; gschpatt, pp. stand open
Schparregra(a)s (es)n. asparagus
Schparreschwengel (der)n. brake handle (on a farm wagon)
Schparrkett (die)n.; Schparrkedde, pl. 1.brake chain; 2.log chain
Schparwel (die)n. persimmon
Schparwelbaam (der)n. persimmon tree
Schpass (der)n. 1.fun; 2.pleasure; 3.(-- mache) be funny; 4.(voll --) (a) funny; (b) humorous
Schpassgedicht (es)n. doggerel
schpassich, adj. 1.funny; 2.laughable; 3.ridiculous; 4.odd
Schpassvoggel (der)n. 1.droll person; 2.joker
Schpatz (der)n. 1.mason's hawk; 2.sparrow
Schpatze (der)n. taffy
Schpatzesupp (die)n. soup of left-overs
schpatziere, v.; gschpatziert, pp. 1.court; 2.go courting; 3.promenade
Schpau (der)n. 1.saliva; 2.spittle
Schpau (es)n. spit
Schpaubax (die)n.; Schpaubaxe, pl. 1.cuspidor; 2.spittoon
schpaue, v.; gschpaut, pp. spit
Schpautz, (der)n. 1.saliva; 2.spittle
Schpautzbax (die)n. cuspidor
schpautze, v.; gschpautzt, pp. spit
Schpauz (der, es)n. 1.saliva; 2.spittle
schpauze, v.; gschpauzt, pp. spit
Schpechthaahne (der)n. 1.flicker; 2.woodpecker
Schpeck (der)n. 1.bacon; 2.profit
Schpeckdaagel (der)n. spectacle
Schpeckdaakel (der)n. spectacle

Schpielkummeraad

Schpeckdief (es)n. 1.spyglass; 2.telescope
Schpeckdraub (die)n.; Schpeckdrauwe, pl. fox grape
schpeckeliere, v.; gschpeckeliert, pp. speculate
Schpeckmaus (es)n.; Schpeckmeis, pl. bat (mammal)
Schpeckmeisli (es)n.; Schpeckmeislin, pl. bat (mammal)
Schpeckschwaart (die)n. rind (of bacon or ham)
Schpeckseit (die)n. flitch of bacon
schpedde, v.; gschpett, pp. taunt
Schpedder (der)n. mocker
schpeddle, v.; gschpeddelt, pp. 1.mock; 2.taunt
Schpeech (der)n.; Schpeeche, pl. spoke (in a wheel)
Schpeecht (der)n.; Schpeechde, pl. woodpecker
Schpeicher (der) n. 1.second floor; 2.second story (in a dwelling)
Schpeicherschteeg (die)n. garret stairs
schpeide, v.; gschpeidt, pp. spite
Schpeidel (der)n. gore
schpeidele, v.; gschpeidelt, pp. set a gore in a garment
Schpeikeeg (die)n. spike-toothed harrow
Schpeis (die)n. 1.food; 2.nourishment
Schpeit (der)n. 1.malice; 2.spite
schpeitvoll, adj. 1.malicious; 2.spiteful
Schpekdaagel (der)n. 1.spectacle; 2.strange sight
Schpekdief (es)n. 1.spy glass; 2.telescope
schpekeliere, v.; gschpekeliert, pp. speculate
Schpektabille (die)n. bleeding heart
Schpektakel (der)n. 1.spectacle; 2.strange sight
Schpell (die)n. pin
schpelle, v.; gschpellt, pp. pin
Schpellebaam (der)n. 1.hawthorn; 2.honey locust tree
Schpellekisse (es)n. pin cushion
Schpels (der)n. spelt
schpende, v.; gschpendt, pp. 1.spend; 2.squander
Schpengler (der)n. 1.tinker; 2.tinsmith
Schpetter (der)n. mocker
schpettle, v.; gschpeddelt, pp. 1.mock; 2.sneer; 3.taunt
schpettlich, adj. 1.mockingly; 2.sneeringly
schpettlich, adv. mockingly
Schpetzel (es)n. sparrow
Schpetzli (es)n. any small bird
Schpichde (die)n.,pl. 1.funny stories; 2.tales
schpidde, v.; gschpitt, pp. spite (Montgomery Co., PA)
Schpiel (es)n. game
Schpielbank (die)n.; Schpielbenk, pl. sink
Schpielblatz (der)n. playground
Schpielche (es)n. small spool
schpiele, v.; gschpielt, pp. 1.play; 2.play cards; 3.rinse; 4.said of cattle in rutting time; 5.(Balle --) (to) play ball
schpiele, v.; gschpielt, pp (Nepsel --) play tip-cat
Schpieler (der)n. 1.gambler; 2.player
Schpieles (es)n. music (as entertainment)
Schpielhaus (es)n. children's playhouse
Schpielich (der)n. distiller's swill
schpielich, adj. 1.amorous; 2.passionate
Schpielkord (die)n. playing card
Schpielkummeraad (der)n. playmate

158

Ss

Schpiellumbe / Schpruch

Schpiellumbe (der)n. dishrag

Schpielmann (der)n. musician

Schpielsach (die)n.; Schpielsache, pl. toy

Schpielschissel (die)n. dish pan

Schpielwasser (es)n. dishwater

schpiere, v.;schpiert, pp. 1.be sensible of; 2.feel; 3.follow the tracks (of games)

Schpiess (der)n. 1.halberd; 2.pike; 3.spear

schpiesse, v.; gschpiesst, pp. spear

Schpiesshoke (der)n. ice hook

Schpiggel (der)n.; Schpiggle, pl. mirror

schpiggle, v.; gschpiggelt, pp. reflect

Schpillumbe (der)n. dishcloth (Amish usage)

Schpillwasser (es)n. dishwater (Amish usage)

Schpinaat (der)n. spinach

Schpindel (der)n. 1.axle; 2.spindle

Schpindelpann (die)n. step-box

schpindlich, adj. 1.slender; 2.spindling

Schpinn (die)n.; Schpinne, pl. spider

schpinne, v.; gschpunne, pp. 1.purr; 2.spin

Schpinnegraut (es)n. spiderwort

Schpinnenescht (es)n.; Schpinneneschder, pl. cobweb

Schpinner (der)n.; Schpinner, pl. tendril

Schpinnerocke (der)n. distaff

Schpinneweb (es)n.; Schpinnewewer, pl. 1.cobweb; 2.spiderweb

Schpinnraad (es)n.; Schpinnredder, pl. spinning wheel

Schpion (der)n. 1.scout; 2.spy

schpione, v.; gschpiont, pp. 1.go on a still hunt; 2.spy out

Schpitz (der)n. penis

Schpitz(e) (der)n. 1.peak; 2.point; 3.tip

Schpitzbu(h) (der)n. 1.heretic; 2.knave; 3.rascal

schpitze, v.; gschpitzt, pp. 1.make sharp; 2.put a point on; 3.sharpen; 4.(die Ohre --) (a) be all attention; (b) prick the ears; 5.(sich uff ebbes --) (a) anticipate; (b) look forward to

Schpitzewettrich (der)n. 1.narrow-leafed plantain; 2.ribgrass

schpitzich, adj. 1.peaked; 2.pointed

schpitzohrich, adj. 1.clever; 2.keen

schplidde, v.; gschplitt, pp. split

Schplitt (der)n. split

schplitte, v.; gschplitt, pp. split

schpodde, v.; gschpott, pp. 1.mock; 2.mimic

schpoddich, adv. mockingly

Schpoo (der)n.; Schpee, pl. 1.chip; 2.wood shaving

Schpore (der)n. 1.fruit spur; 2.spur

schpot; schpeeder; es schpeedscht, adj. late; later; latest

Schpotgraut (es)n. late cabbage

Schpott (der)n. 1.derision; 2.mockery; 3.scorn

schpotte, v.; gschpott, pp. 1.jeer; 2.mimic; 3.mock; 4.rail

schpottich, adj. mockingly

Schpottnaame (der)n. nickname

Schpottvoggel (der)n. mocking bird

schpottwolfel, adj. ridiculously cheap

Schpotyaahr (es)n. 1.autumn; 2.fall

Schpotyaahrsdaag (der)n. autumn day

Schpotyaahrswetter (es)n. autumn weather

Schpotyaahrswind (der)n. autumn wind

schpraddle, v.; gschpraddelt, pp. spread out (like a plant)

schpraddlich, adj. spread out

Schprae (die)n. 1.bedding for animals; 2.spread

schpraehe, v.; gschpraet, pp. spread

schpranze, v.; gschpranzt, pp. strut

schpratzle, v.; gschpratzelt, pp. sputter (of boiling mush)

Schprau (die)n. 1.chaff; 2.(gladdi --e) smooth chaff (wheat)

Schprau(er)sack (der)n.; Schprau(er)seck, pl. chaff bag (used as mattress)

Schpraukisse (es)n. bolster

schprauze, v.; gschprauzt, pp. sprawl out

schpreche, v.; gschproche, pp. 1.speak; 2.talk (of formal speech only)

Schprecher (der)n. 1.orator; 2.speaker

schprechlich, adj. spotted

schpreize, v.; gschpreizt, pp. ruffle the feathers (like a turkey)

schprenge, v.; gschprengt, pp. 1.blast; 2.force to run; 3.pursue; 4.rout

Schprengpulwer (es)n. blasting powder

schprettle, v.; gschpreddelt, pp. 1.scatter; 2.spread

Schprichwart (es)n. 1.adage; 2.proverb

Schpriggel (der)n. 1.body bow (of a wagon); 2.tilt lath

Schpring (die)n. spring (of water)

Schpringarwet duh (die)v. run an errand

Schpringblumm (die)n.; Schpringblumme, pl. touch-me-not

Schpringdapper (die)n. diarrhea

schpringe, v.; gschprunge, pp. 1.jump; 2.run; 3.skip; 4.spring (of lumber)

Schpringegraawe (der)n. 1.runnel; 2.water space in a spring house

Schpringegress (es)n. watercress

Schpringer (der)n.; Schpringer, pl. 1.urchin; 2.(en gleener --) (a) half grown boy; (b) toddler; (c) young cattle

Schpringers (die)n. dysentery

Schpringewasser (es)n. spring water

Schpringfedder (die)n. watch spring

Schpringhaus (es)n. spring house

Schpringschtock (der)n.; Schpringschteck, pl. lancet

Schpringwedder (es)n. 1.spring weather; 2."run" weather

Schpritz (die)n. 1.hand fire pump; 2.syringe

schpritze, v.; gschpritzt, pp. 1.splash; 2.sprinkle; 3.squirt

Schpritzer (der)n. 1.shower; 2.sprinkle (of rain)

Schprochkenner (der)n. linguist

schprock, adj. 1.brittle; 2.crisp; 3.fragile

Schprooch (die)n. 1.speech; 2.language; 3.(power of) speech; 4.voice

Schproochbax (die)n. larynx

schproose, v.; gschproozt, pp. (sich --) ruffle the feathers (like a turkey)

Schprosse (der)n. 1.round; 2.rung

Schpruch (der)n.; Schprich, pl. 1.saying; 2.scripture text

Ss

Schpruchlied

Schpruchlied (es)n. gnomic song
Schprung (der)n. 1.crack; 2.jump; 3.leap
Schprungrieme (der)n. martingale
Schpuchte (die)n., pl. capers
Schpuck(s) (es)n.; Schpucke, pl. 1.ghost; 2.spook 3.wraith
schpucke, v.; gschpuckt, pp. 1.have ghostly manifestations; 2.be haunted; 3.spit
Schpulche (es)n. small spool
Schpule (der)n. 1.bobbin; 2.spool
schpule, v.; gschpult, pp. wind on spools
Schpuli (der)n. trickster
Schpund (der)n. splint
Schpund(e)bohre (der)n.; Schpund(e)bohre, pl. 1.auger for boring bung holes; 2.gouge
Schpunde (der)n. 1.bung; 2.sapwood
Schpundeloch (es)n.; Schpundelecher, pl. bunghole
Schpundholz (es)n. sapwood
Schpundi (der)n. 1.nut (silly person); 2.sap
Schpunk (der)n. 1.ghost; 2.specter
Schpur (die)n.; Schpure, pl. 1.trace; 2.track
schpure, v.; gschpurt, pp. 1.follow instructions; 2.follow the track; 3.trace
schpuuze, v.; gschpuuzt, pp. spit
Schrackack katydid (onomatopoeic)
schraeks, adj. 1.aslant; 2.oblique
schraeksaagich, adj. cross eyed
schraekse, v.; gschraekst, pp. 1.cant; 2.slant off
Schramm (die)n. scar
schrankle, v.; gschrankelt, pp. walk unsteadily (from weakness)
schranklich adj. unsteady (in gait)
Schraub (die)n.; Schrauwe, pl. screw
Schraubschtock (der)n. vise
schrauwe, v.; gschraubt, pp. 1.dicker; 2.evade; 3.screw; 4.squirm
Schrauwedreher (der)n. screwdriver
Schrauwezieher (der)n. screwdriver
schreckballisch, adj. terrible
schreckbollisch, adj. terrible
Schrecke (der)n. 1.fright; 2.horror; 3.scare;4.terror
Schrecke (die)n., pl. grasshoppers
schrecke, v.; gschreckt, pp. 1.frighten; 2.intimidate;3.scare
schrecklich, adj. 1.hideous; 2.horrible; 3.terrible
schreegs, adj. oblique
Schreibbabier (es)n. writing paper
Schreibdisch (der)n. writing table
schreie, v.; gschreit, pp. shout
Schreiner (der)n.; Schreiner, pl. 1.cabinetmaker; 2.carpenter; 3.joiner
schreiwe, v.; gschriwwe, pp. write
Schreiwer (der)n.; Schreiwer, pl. 1.conveyancer; 2.penman; 3.scribe; 4.writer
Schreiwes (es)n. 1.document; 2.writing; 3.written agreement; 4.(-- un es Rechles) reading, writing and arithmetic
schrenke, v.; gschrenkt, pp. shrink (a tire, cloth)
schreppe, v.; gschreppt, pp. cup

Schtachelsau

Schreppkopp (der)n. cupping glass
schridde, v.; gschritt, pp. 1.pace; 2.step
schriddich, adv. 1.gradually; 2.step by step
Schrief (der)n. sheriff
Schrift (die)n. 1.handwriting; 2.scripture
Schriftler (der)n. theologue
schriftlich, adj. 1.(according to) scripture;2.writing
schriftmeesich, adj. scriptural
Schriftschteller (der)n. author
Schritt (der)n.; Schridde, pl. 1.pace; 2.step (walking)
schrittweis(s), adv. 1.gradually; 2.step by step
schrode, v.; gschrot, pp. 1.crush; 2.grind coarsely; 3.grind into chop
Schrot (die)n. 1.chop; 2.middlings; 3.shot
Schrotflint (die)n.; Schrotflinde, pl. shotgun
Schrotfuder (es)n. cut feed mixed with chop
Schrotmeesel (der)n. chisel hammer
Schrotmiehl (die)n.; Schrotmiehle, pl. gristmill
Schrotsack (der)n. 1.chop bag; 2.shot pouch
Schrume (die)n. scar
Schrumm (die)n. scar
Schrunn(e) (die)n. 1.bruise; 2.chap; 3.crack; 4.mark; 5.scar
Schtaab (der)n. dust
Schtaab (der)n.; Schtaawe, pl. staff
Schtaabbascht (die)n. brush
Schtaabduch (es)n. dusting cloth
Schtaabfischel (es)n. larva of carpet moth
Schtaablumbe (der)n. dust cloth
Schtaabwisch (der)n. duster
Schtaagefens (die)n.; Schtaagefense, pl. 1.snake fence; 2.worm fence
schtaagefensich, adj. zigzag
schtaahle, adj. (of) steel
schtaahle, v.; gschtaahlt, pp. 1.harden; 2.temper
Schtaake (der)n. stake
Schtaakefens (der)n.; Schtaagefense, pl. stake fence (zig-zag)
Schtaakeloch (es)n. hole in which the stake of a worm fence is placed
Schtaal (der)n. steel
schtaans, adv. confoundedly
Schtaar (der)n. 1.blackbird; 2.cataract (of the eye)
Schtaat (der)n. 1.commonwealth; 2.pride; 3.state; 4.(en grosser -- draus/mache) (to be) proud
schtaatlich, adj. grand
schtaawe, v.; gschtaabt, pp. 1.give off dust; 2.go pell mell
schtaawich, adj. dusty
Schtachel (der)n.; Schtachle, pl. sting (of a bee)
Schtachel (die)n. 1.round rung; 2.thorn; 3.prickle
Schtachelband (es)n.; Schtachelbenner, pl. muzzle (spiked) for calves (to prevent sucking cow)
schtachele, v.; gschtachelt, pp. (to attempt to) sting (as a bee when it is held fast)
Schtachelgraut (es)n. thorn apple
Schtachelgummer (die)n. gherkin
Schtachelsau (die)n. porcupine

Ss

Schtachelschwein — Schtecke

Schtachelschwein (es)n. porcupine
schtachlich, adj. 1.prickly; 2.thorny
Schtadt (die)n.; Schtedt, pl. 1.city; 2.town
Schtadtleit (die)n., pl. 1.city folk; 2.villagers
Schtadtlewe (es)n. city life
Schtadtraat (der)n. city council
Schtadtwagge (der)n. market wagon
schtaedich, adv. steadily
schtaerblich, adj. 1.dying; 2.mortal
Schtaerblichkeit (die)n. mortality
Schtaerick (die)n. starch
schtaericke, v.; gschtaerickt, pp. starch
Schtaerm (der)n. storm
schtaerme, v.; gschtaermt, pp. 1.rave; 2.(to take by) storm
Schtaermer (der)n. boisterous fellow
Schtaern (die)n.; Schtaerne, pl. 1.block (of a quilt); 2.forehead; 3.star; 4.white mark on the face of a horse or cow
Schtaernband (es)n. forehead strap (of a bridle)
Schtaernblumm (die)n.; Schtaernblumme, pl. 1.aster; 2.hyacinth; 3.narcissus; 4.star of Bethlehem
schtaernehell, adj. starlit
Schtaernehimmel (der)n. firmament
Schtaernekenner (der)n. astronomer
Schtaerneschnuppe, (die)n. falling star
schtaernhaayels, adj. deucedly
schtaernhaaylich, adj. deucedly
schtaernich, adj. starry
Schtaernrieme (der)n. head piece of a bridle
schtaernriesel!, interj. thunderation!
schtaerns, adv. 1.confoundedly; 2.very
Schtaerrick (die)n. 1.starch; 2.strength
schtaerricke, v.; gschtaerrickt, pp. 1.invigorate; 2.starch; 3.strengthen
Schtaerrickungsmittel (es)n. tonic
Schtaerwes (es)n. dying
schtaerwesgrank, adj. dangerously ill
schtaerze, v.; gschtaerzt, pp. 1.cause to fall; 2.dish (a wheel); 3.fall; 4.overthrow; 5.tumble
Schtaerzing (die)n. dish (of a wheel)
schtaetich, adj. 1.constantly; 2.steadily
Schtaffel (die)n. 1.round; 2.rung
Schtaik (die)n. starch
schtaik, adj.; adv. swift(ly)
schtaike, v.; gschtaikt, pp. starch
Schtall (der)n.; Schtell, pl. 1.stable; 2.stall
Schtalldier (die)n. stable-door
schtalle, v.; gschtallt, pp. 1.agree; 2.get along together; 3.stable
Schtallgnecht (der)n. hostler
Schtalling (die)n. stabling
schtambe, v.; gschtampt, pp. 1.stamp; 2.tamp
Schtamber (der)n.; Schtamber, pl. 1.masher; 2.stamper
Schtamm (der)n. 1.race; 2.stem; 3.trunk; 4.tribe
schtamme, v.; gschtammt, pp. 1.be descended (from); 2.come from
Schtamploch (es)n. stamping hole (made by horses in chasing flies)
Schtand (der)n. 1.condition; 2.rank; 3.stand; 4.state
schtandhafdich, adj. 1.steadfast; 2.sturdy
schtandhaft, adj. 1.firm; 2.steadfast; 3.steady; 4.stout
Schtang (die)n.; Schtange, pl. 1.rod; 2.pole
Schtangeglaas (es)n. wineglass
Schtann (der)n.; Schtanne, pp. star
Schtann (die)n.; Schtanne, pl. 1.brow; 2.forehead; 3.white mark on the forehead of a cow or horse; 4.(-- runsle) frown
Schtannblumm (die)n. hyacinth
schtannich, adj. starry
Schtar(e)m (der)n. storm
schtaremich, adj. stormy
schtarewe, v.; is gschtarewe, pp. die
Schtarich (der)n. stork
Schtarichelgaarn (es)n. seine
Schtarick (die)n. 1.starch; 2.strength
schtarick, adj. 1.robust; 2.stout;3.steadfast; 4.strong; 5.sturdy
schtarick, adj.; adv. 1.fast; 2.swift(ly)
schtarme, v.; gschtarmt, pp. (to be) stormy
schtarmich, adj. stormy
Schtarmwind (der)n. 1.gale; 2.storm
schtarnkebbich, adj. stubborn
Schtarr (der)n. cataract
schtarr, adj. 1.fixed; 2.staring; 3.stiff
Schtarre (der)n. 1.dead limb; 2.dead tree; 3.visible part of a decayed tooth
schtarre, v.; gschtarrt, pp. 1.poke; 2.stir
Schtarrich (der)n. stork
schtarrick, adj. 1.fast; 2.robust; 3.stout; 4.strong; 5.(er is -- draa) he is hard at work
schtarrkebbich, adj. 1.obstinate; 2.stubborn
Schtarrkopp (der)n. stubborn person
Schtarze (der)n. 1.root (of a decayed tooth); 2.stub; 3.stump
schtattfinne, v.; schtattgfunne, pp. 1.occur; 2.take place
schtatts, prep (-- vun) instead of
Schtatz (der)n. tumble
schtatze, v.; gschtatzt, pp. 1.topple; 2.tumble
schtauche, v.; gschtaucht, pp. 1.bend in; 2.jolt; 3.strain; 4.wrench
schtebbe, v.; gschteppt, pp. 1.quilt; 2.stitch
Schtechabbel (der)n. 1.belladonna; 2.stramonium; 3.jimsonweed; 4.thorn apple
schteche, v.; gschtoche, pp. 1.pierce; 2.prick; 3.stab; 4.stick; 5.sting
Schtecher (der)n.; Schtecher, pl. 1.stinger (of a bee); 2.sting of an insect
schtechgraut prickly lettuce
Schtechmick (Die)n. forest fly
schtechselaat prickly lettuce
Schtecke (der)n. 1.cane; 2.stick

161

Ss

schtecke

schtecke, v.; gschteckt, pp. 1.be hidden; 2.plant; 3.stay; 4.stick; 5.(-- bleiwe) (a) stalled (with a load); (b) stop short; 6. (die Naas in alles --) poke one's nose in every-body's business; 7.(ebber [ebbes] --) (to give a) tip; 8.(geld in ebbes --) invest money in some-thing; 9.(ich will's ihm --) I'll give him a tip; 10.(wu hoschde gschtocke) where have you been keeping yourself

Schteckebohn (die)n. pole bean

Schteckedier (es)n.; Schteckediere, pl. stick insect

Schteckegaul (der)n. hobby horse

Schteckereide (es)n. riding a hobby-horse

Schteckle (es)n. hide-and-seek

Schteckli (es)n. hide-and-seek

Schteckli (es)n (-- schtecke) stick game ("sticking the stick") (Amish)

Schteddel (es)n.1.hamlet; 2.town; 3.village; 4.(-- nuf/geh) (to go) uptown

Schteddelche (es)n. village

Schteddelleit (die)n. 1.city folk; 2.villagers

Schteddli (es)n. hamlet

Schtedler (der)n.; Schtedler, pl. 1.town resident; 2.villager

Schtedlermeedel (es)n.; Schtedlermeed, pl. town girl

Schtedt(el)che, (es)n. village

Schtedtche (es)n. 1.hamlet; 2.village; 3.town

Schtedtli (es)n. town

Schtee (der)n.; Schtee, pl. 1.grindstone; 2.stone; 3.(-- breche) quarry (stone)

schtee-alt, adj. very old

Schtee-esel (der)n.; Schtee-esel, pl. jackass

Schteeblatt (die)n. large flat stone

Schteebloder (die)n. contusion (of the foot)

Schteebock (der)n. Capricorn (10th sign of the zodiac)

Schteebohrer (der)n. drill

Schteeboot (es)n.; Schteeboot, pl. 1.stone-boat (hauled stones on canal); 2.manure sled; 3.sledge (on run-ners)

Schteebrecher (der)n.; Schteebrecher, pl. stone crusher

Schteebruch (der)n.; Schteebrich, pl. 1.hernia; 2.rupture; 3.stone quarry

Schteeche (es)n. pebble

Schteedrepp (die)n.; Schteedrebbe, pl. stone step

Schteedruck (der)n. lithograph

Schtee-eil (die)n. barn owl

Schtee-eselfill (es)n. jackass-colt

Schteefaare brake (fern)

Schteefens (die)n.; Schteefense, pl. stone fence

Schteeg (die)n.; Schteege, pl. 1.footbridge; 2.stairs; 3.stairway

Schteeglee (der)n. stone clover

Schteeglone (der)n.; Schteeglone, pl. railing (of a stair)

Schteegruck (der)n. stone jug

Schteehacker (der)n.; Schteehacker, pl. stonecutter

Schteehammer (der)n.; Schteehemmer, pl. stone sledge

Schteehaufe (der)n. pile of stones

schtennich

Schteekeizli (es)n. little screech owl

Schteekgelender (es)n. banisters

Schteekohl (die)n. anthracite coal

Schteemauer (die)n. stone wall

schteenalt, adj. very old

schteene, v.; gschteent, pp. remove the stones (from cherries)

schteenich, adj. 1.of stone; 2.stony

schteeniche, v.; gschteenicht, pp. 1.stone; 2.throw stones

schteere, v.; gschteert, pp. 1.disturb; 2.trouble

Schteeroi (die)n. stone row (often as a fence between two fields)

Schteeschleegel (der)n. sledge

Schteeschlidde (der)n.; Schteeschlidde, pl. 1.manure sled; 2.stone boat; 3.sled; 4.sledge (on runners)

Schteewagge (der)n. wagon rigged for hauling stones

schteh, v.; gschtanne, pp. 1.be; 2.stand

schtehle, v.; gschtohle, pp. steal

Schtehler (der)n. thief

Schtehlerei (die)n. burglary

Schteiber (der)n.; Schteiber, pl. 1.brace; 2.prop

schteibere, v.; gschteibert, pp. (sich --) 1.hesitate; 2.(to be) stubborn

schteibere, v.; gschteibert, pp. brace

Schteibiggel (der)n. stirrup

schteibre, v. (sich --) resist

schteiere, v.; gschteiert, pp. steer

Schteiermann (der)n. 1.helmsman; 2.pilot

Schteierraad (es)n. steering wheel

schteif, adj. 1.formal; 2.rigid; 3.stiff;4.thick

schteifhalsich, adj. obstinate

Schteifheit (die)n. stiffness

Schteifing (der)n. buckram

Schteigbiggel (der)n. stirrup

schteige, v.; gschtigge, pp. rise

schteik, adv. 1.fast; 2.swift (Amish pronunciation)

Schteirruder (der)n. rudder

Schtell (die)n. 1.charge; 2.employment; 3.place; 4.position; 5.situation

schtelle, v.; gschtellt, pp. 1.place; 2.put; 3.set up; 4.(sich --) (a) act as if; (b) stand ready for attack

Schtellgaarn (es)n. stalker (kind of fish net)

Schtellung (die)n. 1.attitude; 2.location

Schtels (die)n. stilt

Schtembel (der)n. 1.pounder; 2.stamper

Schtember (der)n. stamper

schtende, v. 1.endure; 2.stand

Schtengel (der)n. 1.stalk; 2.stem; 3.stick (of candy); 4.weed

Schtengelbauer (der)n. poor farmer

Schtengelglaas (es)n. wineglass

Schtengli (es)n. 1.stalk; 2.stem; 3.stick (of candy); 4.weed

Schtenner (der)n.; Schtenner, pl. 1.soap-making vat; 2.tub; 3.stand for salting meat; 4.upright

schtennich, adj. constantly

Ss

schteppe

schteppe, v.; gschteppt, pp. 1.quilt; 2.stitch

schterde, v.; gschter(d)t, pp. start

Schtetzelche (es)n. cuff (in ballad only)

schtewwere, v.; gschtewwert, pp. 1.disperse; 2.scatter

Schtibbche (es)n. small room

Schtich (der)n. 1.steep stretch of road; 2.sting; 3.twinge; 4.twitch

schtichdunkel, adv. pitch dark

schtichele, v. gschtichelt, pp. hint

schtichle, v.; gschtichelt, pp. 1.make insinuating allusions; 2.twit

Schtichler (der)n. person who makes insinuating allusions

Schtichlerei (die)n. making insinuating allusions

Schtick (es)n. 1.patch; 2.part; 3.piece; 4.slice; 5.stretch; 6.(en -- weck) afar; 7.(in eem -- fatt) incessantly; 8.(schticker sex) (a) six or so; (b) half a dozen or so

schtick wegs, adv. part of the way

schticke, v.; gschtickt, pp. 1.persist; 2.stay; 3.stick

Schtickel (der)n. stake

Schtickel (es)n. 1.short way; 2.small piece

Schtickeldebbich (der)n. patchwork quilt

schtickere, v.; gschtickert, pp. quilt

Schtickerei (die)n. quilting

Schtickfluss (der)n. croup

schtickich, adj. 1.close; 2.sticky; 3.stuffy

schtickle, v.; gschtickelt, pp. quilt

Schtickli (es)n. 1.short way; 2.small piece

schtickweis, adv. 1.piecemeal; 2.(at) retail; 3.singly

Schtieber (der)n.; Schtieber, pl. raised cake

Schtiefbruder (der)n.; Schtiefbrieder, pl. step-brother

Schtiefdaadi (der)n. step-father

Schtiefdochder (die)n. step-daughter

Schtiefgrossmammi (die)n. step-grandmother

Schtiefkett (die)n. stay-chain

Schtiefkind (es)n.; Schtiefkinner, pl. step-child

Schtiefmammi (die)n. step-mother

Schtiefmudder (die)n. step-mother

Schtiefschweschder (die)n. step-sister

Schtiefsohn (der)n. step-son

Schtiefvadder (der)n. step-father

schtiege, v.; is gschtigge, pp. 1.ascend; 2.rise; 3.mount

Schtiehlche (es)n. 1.child's chair; 2.(hoch --) child's highchair

Schtiel (der)n.; Schtiel, pl. 1.handle; 2.helve

Schtier (der)n. 1.steer; 2.Taurus (2nd sign of the zodiac)

schtiere, v.; gschtiert, pp. copulate (of cattle)

schtifde, v.; gschtifde, pp. 1.instigate; 2.stir up

Schtiffel (der)n.; Schtiffel, pl. boot

schtiffle, v.; gschtiffelt, pp. to "sport" boots

schtill/schteh, v.; schtillgschtanne, pp. 1.stand still; 2.stop

schtill/schweige, v.; schtillgschweicht, pp. 1.(keep) mum; 2.(to keep) silent

schtill, adj. 1.calm; 2.quiet; 3.silent; 4.still; 5.tranquil

schtill sei, v. 1.shut up; 2.(to keep) silent

schtille, v.; gschtillt, pp. 1.appease; 2.pacify; 3.quiet; 4.silence; 5.soothe

Schtillschtand (der)n. 1.stagnation;

schtocke

2.standstill;3.suspension

Schtillschweige (es)n. silence

Schtimbel (der)n. small remainder

Schtimbelroi (die)n. (short) row (at the end of a field)

Schtimm (die)n.; Schtimme, pl. 1.voice; 2.vote

schtimme, v.; gschtimmt, pp. 1.tune; 2.vote; 3.(net iwwer eens --) not to tally

Schtimmgawwel (die)n. tuning fork

Schtimmgewwer (der)n.; Schtimmgewwer, pl. voter

Schtimmlerei (die)n. 1.botch; 2.bungled work; 3.delayed work

Schtimmrecht (es)n. franchise

Schtimpel (der)n. small remainder

Schtimpelroi (die)n. short row (at one end of a field)

Schtimplerei (die)n. 1.botch; 2.bungled work; 3.delayed work

Schtink (der)n. bad odor

Schtinkblumm (die)n.; Schtinkblumme, pl. marigold

Schtinkbock (der)n.; Schtinkbeck, pl. 1.dirty rascal;2.marigold; 3.sot

schtinke, v.; gschtunke, pp. stink

Schtinker (der)n.; Schtinker, pl. 1.mean person; 2.silent fart; 3.stinker

Schtinker (die)n., pl. marigold

Schtinkert (der)n. vile-smelling animal

schtinkich, adj. 1.foul; 2.rank (odor); 3.smelly; 4.stuffy

Schtinkkees (der)n. hand or Dutch cheese

Schtinkkeffer (der)n.; Schtinkkeffer,pl. stinkbug

Schtinkluder (der)n. 1.carrion; 2.vituperative term

Schtippche (es)n. (small) room

Schtitz (der)n.; Schtitze, pl. 1.small wooden vessel used in carrying water to workmen; 2.sprinkling can; 3.top hat

schtitze, v.; gschtizt, pp. 1.depend on; 2.expect

Schtitzhut (der)n. 1.stovepipe hat; 2.top hat

Schtiwwel (der)n.; Schtiwwel, pl. boot

Schtiwwelgnecht (der)n. bootjack

Schtiwwelhols (es)n. boot-tree

Schtiwwelmann (der)n. man with a penchant for wearing boots

Schtiwwelzieger (der)n. bootjack

Schtiwwer (der)n. 1.caprice; 2.flurry; 3.spell; 4.squall

Schtiwwich (der)n. movable circular wooden vat varying in height from less than a foot to 4 feet

schtiwwich voll, adv. overflowing

schtiwwle, v.; gschtiwwelt, pp. walk

schtobbe, v.; gschtoppt, pp. 1.darn; 2.halt; 3.quit; 4.stop; 5.stop up; 6.stuff

Schtobbelfeld (es)n. stubble-field

Schtobber (der)n. stopper

Schtock (der)n.; Schteck, pl. 1.bush; 2.cane; 3.plant; 4.stack; 5.skirt (of a dress); 6.story (of a building); 7.walking stick

schtock Englisch adj. thoroughly English

schtockblind, adj. stone blind

Schtockbuhn (die)n.; Schtockbuhne, pl. bush bean

schtockdaub, adj. stone-deaf

schtockdunkel, adj. pitch dark

schtocke, v.; gschtockt, pp. 1.make a stack; 2.walk rapidly with a cane

Ss

schtockebbich | Schtriche

schtockebbich, adj. stubborn
Schtockros (die)n. rose plant
Schtockschraub (die)n. screw of a vice
schtoddere, v.; gschtoddert, pp. 1.stammer; 2.stutter
schtodderich, adj. stuttering
Schtoff(t) (es)n. 1.(dress) material; 2.goods; 3.rabble; 4.riff-raff; 5.stuff
Schtoffel (der)n. 1.Christopher, used as a nickname; 2.(es --) blockhead
Schtoffelgluck (die)n. uncouth fellow
Schtol (die)n. stole
schtolbere, v.; gschtolbert, pp. stumble
Schtolle (der)n. 1.ball of snow formed under a horse's hoof; 2.calk; 3.foot (of a chair or bedstead)
Schtollfuss (der)n. club foot
schtolpere, v.; gschtolpert, pp. stumble
schtolperich, adj. prone to stumble
schtols Heinrich (der)n. good King Henry (plant)
Schtolz (der)n. pride
schtolz, adj. haughty
schtolzich, adj. stylish
schtoose, v.; gschtoose, pp. 1.churn (butter); 2.hook (of cattle); 3.jostle; 4.poke; 5.push; 6.shove
schtoppe, v.; gschtoppt, pp. 1.darn; 2.plug; 3.stop up; 4.stuff
Schtoppel (die)n. stubble
Schtoppelfeld (es)n. stubble field
Schtopper (der)n. 1.stopper; 2.wad
schtopple, v.; gschtobbelt, pp. seed a stubble-field in the same crop
schtopplich, adj. stubbly
Schtoppnodel (die)n.; Schtoppnoddle, pl. darning needle
Schtor (der)n.; Schtore, pl. store
Schtori (die)n.; Schtories, pl. 1.story; 2.tale
Schtorkibber (der)n.; Schtorkibber, pl. storekeeper
Schtorkipper (der)n.; Schtorkipper, pl. merchant
Schtorm (der)n. storm
Schtoss (der)n. 1.gust; 2.jar; 3.jog 4.knock; 5.push; 6.thrust
Schtosseise (es)n. tool used in digging graves to secure a straight edge
Schtosswoi (der)n. chicken hawk
schtottere, v.; gschtottert, pp. 1.stammer; 2.stutter
schtotterich, adj. 1.stammering; 2.stuttering
schtowwelich, adj. obstinate
schtowwerich, adj. 1.obstinate; 2.stubborn
Schtraal (der) n.; Schtraale, pl. 1. beam (ray); 2. bolt (of lightning)
schtraale, v.; gschtraalt, pp. radiate
schtraallich, adj. 1.radiant; 2.ray like
schtrack(s), adj. 1.straight; 2.erect; 3.slender; 4.straightaway
schtraee, v.; gschtraet, pp. 1.bed (a stable or cattle); 2.spread; 3.strew
schtraehe, v.; gschtraet, pp. spread (bed a stable or cattle)

schtraehmich, adj. 1.streaked; 2.striped
Schtraeme (der)n. 1.band; 2.strip; 3.welt
schtraff, adj. 1.erect; 2.stiff
schtramble, v.; gschtrambelt, pp. 1.kick; 2.struggle; 3.trample
Schtrang (der)n.; Schtreng, pl. 1.gear; 2.skein (of spun flax); 3.trace (part of harness); 4.(iwwer -- hacke) rebel
Schtrapatze (die)n., pl. 1.hardship; 2.sufferings
Schtratz (der)n. strut
Schtratz (die)n. diarrhea
schtratze, v.; gschtratzt, pp. strut
schtraube, v.; gschtraubt, pp. 1.ruffle; 2.(die Feddre --) ruffle the feathers; 3.(sich --) (a) act rebelliously; (b) resist
Schtrauss (der)n.; Schtreiss, pl. 1.bunch of flowers; 2.posy
Schtraw(w)atz (der)n. 1.disagreement; 2.row
schtrawwatzich, adj. refractory
schtrawwle, v.; gschtrawwelt, pp. 1.kick; 2.struggle
Schtrawwler (der)n.; Schtrawwler, pl. nickname for members of the Evangelical denomination
Schtreck (die)n. 1.stretch; 2.tract
schtrecke, v.; gschtreckt, pp. stretch
Schtreech (der)n.; Schtreech, pl. 1.blow; 2.joke; 3.prank; 4.stroke; 5.(aus --) out of commission
Schtreef(e) (der)n. 1.streak; 2.strip; 3.stripe
schtreefich Grass (es)n. puzzle grass
schtreefich, adj. striped
Schtreel (der)n.; Schtreel, pl. comb
schtreele, v.; gschtreelt, pp. (sich --) comb (oneself)
schtreemich, adj. striped
schtreiche, v.; gschtriche, pp. 1.pat; 2.strike; 3.stroke; 4.(sich --) sound one's own praises
Schtreichholz (es)n.; Schtreichhelzer, pl. 1.match (for lighting a fire); 2.strickle
schtreichle, v.; gschtreichelt, pp. 1.pat; 2.stroke
Schtreichler, n. pretzel
Schtreichrieme (der)n. strop
schtreide, v.; gschtridde, pp. 1.argue; 2.contend; 3.dispute; 4.litigate; 5.quarrel; 6.wrangle
Schtreiderei (die)n. (continued) quarreling or wrangling
schtreidich warre, adj. quarrel
schtreidich, adj. quarreling
schtreidich, adv. (at) odds
Schtreiss (die)n., pl. 1.plumes on a lady's hat; 2.tassels
Schtreissel (es)n. 1.narrow twisted strip of dough (on top of a pie); 2.nosegay; 3.pretzel; 4.small round cakes;5.small tassel; 6.sprig
Schtreit (der)n. 1.quarrel; 2.strife; 3.wrangle
schtreng, adj. 1.rigorous; 2.severe; 3.strict
schtrenge, v.; gschtrengt, pp. 1.exert; 2.strain; 3.wrench
schtribbe, v.; gschtrippt, pp. (sich --) strip off (clothing)
Schtrich (der)n. 1.rope; 2.streak; 3.strip; 4.stripe
Schtriche (der)n.; Schtriche, pl. 1.line; 2.stroke; 3.teat (of a cow)

Ss

schtrichweis

schtrichweis, adv. 1.by narrow sections; 2.in streaks

schtricke, v.; gschtrickt, pp. knit

Schtrickes (es)n. knitting

Schtrickhalfder (die)n.; Schtrickhalfder, pl. rope halter

Schtricknoddel (die)n. knitting needle

Schtrickschtrump (der)n. unfinished stocking

schtriebich, adj. 1.streaked; 2.striped

Schtriehme (der)n. 1.band; 2.strip; 3.welt

Schtrieme (der)n. welt

Schtriggel (der)n. currycomb

schtriggle, v.; gschtriggel, pp. 1.curry; 2.fleece someone

schtrikt, adj. 1.severe; 2.strict; 3.stringent

Schtrimpelche (es)n. baby's sock

Schtrimpmacher (der)n. hosier

Schtripp (der)n. strip

schtrippe, v.; gschtrippt, pp. 1.provide with strips or laths; 2.strip; 3.(Welschkann --) husk corn

Schtripphut (der)n. woman's sun bonnet

Schtritt (der)n.; Schtridde, pl. stride

Schtritz (die)n. syringe

Schtritzbix (die)n. squirt gun

schtritze, v.; gschtritzt, pp. 1.sprinkle; 2.splash; 3.squirt

Schtrof (die)n. 1.fine; 2.punishment

schtrofbaar, adj. punishable

schtrofe, v.; gschtroft, pp. 1.fine; 2.punish

Schtrofing (die)n. reproof

Schtroh (es)n. straw

Schtrohbank (die)n. straw cutter

Schtrohblumm (die)n. straw flower

Schtrohbohre (der)n. straw mow

Schtrohdach (es)n.; Schtrodecher, pl. thatched roof

Schtrohdenn (es)n.; Schtrohdenner, pl. straw mow

Schtrohfackel (die)n. straw bundle (used in burning hornet's nests, etc.)

Schtrohfeier (es)n. passing excitement

Schtrohhalm (der)n. straw haulm

Schtrohhaufe (der)n. straw heap

Schtrohhoke (der)n.; Schtrohhoke, pl. straw-hook (pitchfork with bent tines)

Schtrohhut (der)n.;Schtrohhiet,pl. straw hat

Schtrohkisse (es)n. straw bolster

Schtrohl (der)n. ray

Schtrohmann (der)n. dummy

Schtrohsack (der)n.; Schtrohseck, pl. straw mattress

Schtrohschtock (der)n.; Schtrohschteck, pl. straw stack

Schtrohseel (es)n. straw band (for tying sheaves)

Schtrohwisch (der)n. wisp of straw

schtroie, v.; gschtroit, pp. bed (animals)

Schtrom (der)n. 1.current; 2.stream

Schtross (die)n.; Schtrosse, pl. 1.road; 2.street

schtrubbich, adj. 1.bristly; 2.long-haired; 3.rough; 4.rough-coated; 5.tousled

schtruddle, v.; gschtruddelt, pp. 1.speak indistinctly; 2.sputter

schtrudle, v.; gschtrudelt, pp. spout

Schtrump (der)n.; Schtrimp, pl. 1.sock; 2.stocking

schu!

Schtrumpbendel (der)n.; Schtrumpbendle, pl. garter

Schtrumpsocke (der)n. foot of a stocking

Schtrupp (der)n. hame hook

schtruppe, v.; gschtruppt, pp. strip

Schtrupphaahne (der)n. cock with ruffed plumage

Schtrupphut (der)n.; Schtrupphiet, pl. sun-bonnet

Schtruppnodel (die)n. bodkin

schtrutze, v.; gschtrutzt, pp. 1.parade; 2.strut

Schtruwutz (der)n. 1.disagreement; 2.row

Schtruwwelkopp (der)n. person with disheveled hair

Schtruwwertz (der)n. 1.disagreement; 2.row

schtruwwli(ch), adj. 1.disheveled; 2.unkempt; 3.uncombed

schtruwwlich Nans (die)n. ragged robin

Schtu(h)l (der)n.; Schtiel, pl. chair

Schtubb (die)n.; Schtuwwe, pl. room (in a house)

schtubbe, v.; gschtuppt, pp. 1.root (of hogs); 2.stub one's toe

schtubbich, adj. 1.balky; 2.dumpy; 3.dwarfish; 4.obstinate; 5.stubborn

schtublich, adj. stubbly

Schtudent (der)n.; Schtudende, pl. student

schtudiere, v.; gschudiert, pp. study

Schtuf (die)n. 1.little porch; 2.stair; 3.step (on stair); 4.stoop

Schtuhldaub (die)n. stool pigeon

Schtulgang (der)n. 1.discharge of the bowels; 2.excrement; 3.stool

Schtumbe (der)n. stump (of a tree, tooth, limb)

schtumbe, v.; gschtumpt, pp. 1.challenge; 2.stump

Schtumbefens (die)n. stump-fence

Schtumberobber (der)n. stump puller

Schtumbewasser (es)n. water in the hollow of a stump

schtumbich, adj. 1.stocky; 2.stumpy

schtumbiere, v.; schtumbiert, pp. 1.abuse; 2.chaff; 3.cow; 4.heckle

schtumm, adj. 1.mute; 2.tongue-tied

Schtummer (der)n. mute person

schtump, adj. 1.blunt; 2.dull

schtumpnaasich, adj. pug nosed

Schtumpschwans (der)n. bobtailed horse or dog

schtumpschwensich, adj. bobtailed

Schtund (die)n.; Schtunde, pl. hour

Schtunn (die)n.; Schtunne, pl. 1.hour; 2.(die gut --) goodness itself

Schtunneglaas (es)n. hourglass

Schtunnezioger (der)n. hour hand

schtupid, adj. stupid

Schtupp (die)n. room (in a house)

schtupprich, adj. stubborn

Schtuppvoll (der)n. roomful

Schtutz (der)n (uff der --) 1.on the spur of the moment; 2.suddenly; 3.undecided

schtutze, v.; gschtutzt, pp. 1.butt; 2.hesitate; 3.pause

Schtutzer (der)n. beau

schu!, interj. shoo!

Ss

Schub

Schwaarm

Schub (der)n. shove
Schubbe (die)n. scarf
Schuck (der)n. 1.shoe; 2.short downpour of rain or gust of wind; 3.short time
schucke, v.; gschuckt, pp. toss (a ball)
schuckweis, adv. 1.(by) starts; 2.intervals
Schuer (der)n. shower
schuere, v.; gschuert, pp. shower
schuerich, adj. showery
schuffle, v.; gschuffelt, pp. 1.sniff; 2.sniffle
Schuft (der)n. 1.heretic; 2.rascal
Schuh (der)n.; Schuh, pl. shoe
Schuhbascht (die)n. shoe-brush
Schuhbech (es)n. cobbler's wax
Schuhbendel (der)n. shoelace
Schuhbla(e)cke (der)n. shoe blacking
Schuhbutzer (der)n. 1.doormat; 2.shoe-mat
Schuhdinde (der)n. shoemaker's blacking
schuhflicke, v.; gflickt, pp. repair shoes
Schuhflicker (der)n. cobbler
Schuhgnopp (der)n. shoe-button
Schuhgratzer (der)n. shoe-mat
Schuhhammer (der)n. cobbler's hammer
Schuhkapp (die)n. cap of a shoe
Schuhlumbe (der)n. doormat
Schuhmacher (der)n.; Schuhmacher, pl. shoemaker
Schuhmacherbaam (der)n.; Schuhmacherbeem, pl. sumac tree
Schuhmacherdrott (der)n. shoemaker's thread
Schuhraahme (der)n. welt
Schuhreime (der)n. shoelace
Schuhschnall (die)n. shoe-buckle
Schuhsohl (der)n. shoe-sole
Schul (die)n. school
Schulbaas (der)n. school superintendent
Schulbu (der)n.; Schulbuwe, pl. schoolboy
Schulbuch (es)n.; Schulbicher, pl. schoolbook
Schuld (die)n.; Schulde, pl. 1.crime; 2.debt; 3.fault; 4.guilt
Schuldaag (der)n.; Schuldaage, pl. school-day
Schulde (die)n., pl. 1.bills; 2.debts; 3.indebtedness
Schulde (die)n., pl (-- mache) incur (debts)
Schulder (die)n. shoulder (human)
Schulderblaat (es)n. shoulder blade
schuldere, v.; gschuldert, pp. shoulder
schuldich, adj. 1.due; 2.guilty; 3.indebted; 4.owing; 5.(ebber -- sie) (dative) owe
Schuldichkeet (die)n. duty
Schuldner (der)n. debtor
schule, v.; gschult, pp. (to) school
Schuler (der)n.; Schieler, pl. 1.disciple; 2.pupil; 3.scholar
Schulgeld (es)n. tuition
Schulhalde, v.; Schulghalde, pp. teach school
Schulhaus (es)n.; Schulheiser, pl. schoolhouse
Schulhausbank (die)n.; Schulhausbenk, pl. school bench
Schulhof (der)n.; Schulheef, pl. schoolyard
Schuling (die)n. 1.education; 2.schooling

Schulkorreggder (der)n. school director
Schulkummeraad (der)n.; Schulkummeraade, pl. schoolmate
Schulmaedel (es)n.; Schulmaed, pl. schoolgirl
Schulmann (die)n.; Schulmenner, pl. 1.schoolmaster; 2.teacher
Schulme(e)schder (der)n. teacher (male)
Schulme(e)schdern (die)n. teacher (female)
Schulschtubb (die)n.; Schulschtubbe, pl. schoolroom
Schulschwenser (der)n. truant
Schulsuperintend (der)n. superintendent of schools
Schultax (der)n. school tax
Schulter (die)n. shoulder
schultere, v.; gschultert, pp. 1.assume (responsibility); 2.shoulder
Schulyaahr (es)n.; Schulyaahre, pl. school year
Schum(a)eck (es)n. sumac
Schumacher (der)n. cobbler
Schumack (es)n. sumac
Schumackbaam (der)n. ailanthus
schune, v.; gschont, gschunt, pp. 1.favor; 2.spare; 3.treat with forbearance
Schunke (der)n.; Schinke, pl. ham
Schunkefleesch (es)n. shoulder (ham)
schunn(t), adv. already
schunn, adv. (er waerd -- dezu sehne) he'll be sure to see it
schunnemol, adv. once before
schunscht, adv. otherwise
schunscht, conj. 1.else; 2.or
Schuppe (die)n. 1.fish-scale; 2.scurf
Schuppkaich (der)n.; Shuppkaiche, pl. wheelbarrow
Schuppkarich (der)n.; Schuppkariche, pl. wheelbarrow
Schupplaad (die)n.; Schupplaade, pl. drawer
schur, adj. 1.sure; 2.certain
Schuschder (der)n. 1.cobbler; 2.shoemaker
Schuss (der)n. 1.blast; 2.chute; 3.shoot; 4.sprout; 5.shot; 6.(im -- sei) be in a hurry
Schuss-scheier (die)n. 1.lean-to; 2.shed-barn
Schussbloder (die)n. sty (on the eyelid)
Schussbord (es)n. tailboard
Schussbrett (es)n. tailboard
Schussbulfer (es)n. gunpowder
Schussel (der)n. 1.person or horse given to abrupt or rapid movements; 2.scatterbrain
schussle, v.; gschusselt, pp. 1.bustle; 2.race along
schussweis, adv. 1.by fits and starts; 2.by jerks
Schuster (der)n. 1.cobbler; 2.shoemaker
Schuttscheier (die) n.; Schuttscheire, pl. straw-barn with adjustable roof
Schutz (der)n. 1.refuge; 2.shelter
schutze, v.; schutzt, pp. 1.safeguard; 2.shelter
Schutzscheier (die)n.; Schutzscheire, pl. storage place for grain, hay, straw (out building)
Schwa(e)rzing (die)n. blacking
Schwaad (die)n. swath
Schwaan (der)n. swan
Schwaarm (der)n. swarm

Ss

Schwaart | schwelle

Schwaart (die)n. 1.rind of bacon or ham; 2.rough fellow; 3.slab

schwaarte, v.; gschwaart, pp. flog

Schwaartli (es)n. 1.blue flag; 2.iris; 3.flag

schwach, adj. 1.feeble; 2.infirm; 3.weak

Schwachheet (die)n. weakness

Schwachheit (die)n. weakness

schwachsinnich, adj. weak-minded

Schwaegern (die)n. sister-in-law

Schwaer (der)n. father-in-law

Schwaerdaadi (der)n. father-in-law

Schwaere (der)n. 1.abscess; 2.boil

schwaerme, v.; gschwaermt, pp. swarm

Schwaermudder (die)n. mother-in-law

Schwaerneeter (der)n. 1.scamp; 2.son-of-a-gun

Schwaernoot (die)n. deuce

Schwaert (es)n. sword

Schwaertli (es)n. 1.blue flag; 2.iris

schwaewisch, adj. Suabian

Schwal(le)me (der)n.; Schwalme, pl. swallow (bird)

Schwalmenescht (es)n. swallow's nest

Schwamm (der)n. 1.mushroom; 2.toadstool; 3.meadow; 4.punk; 5.sponge; 6.swamp

Schwammdischdel (die)n. swamp-thistle

Schwammeeche (die)n. swamp white oak

Schwammgraas (es)n. meadow-grass

schwammich, adj. 1.quaggy; 2.soft; 3.swampy; 4.wet

Schwammbeere (die)n.; pl. cranberries

Schwammkaader (der)n. runagate

Schwammriesel (der)n. mole (rodent)

Schwammweide (die)n. pussy willow

Schwang (der)n (im -- sei) be current

schwanger, adj. pregnant

schwanke, v.; gschwankt, pp. sway

schwankich, adj. 1.swaying; 2.unsteady

Schwann (der)n. swan

Schwannaggel (die)n. buckshot

Schwansschtick (es)n. back rump

Schwanz (der)n.; Schwenz, pl. tail

Schwanzfedder (die)n. tail-feather

Schwanzgribs (es)n. 1.oil gland (of fowl); 2.uropygial gland

Schwanzrieme (der)n. crupper

Schwanzsupp (die)n. oxtail soup

Schwardaadi (der)n. father-in-law

Schwardochder (die)n. daughter-in-law

Schwarm (der)n. swarm

schwarme, v.; gschw(a)ermt, pp. swarm

schwarz, adj. 1.black; 2.(en Schwarzer) a Negro; 3.(--e parble) small pox

schwarzbeenich, adj. black legged

schwarzbrau, adj. dark brown

Schwarzdarn (die)n. black thorn

Schwarzeeche (die)n. black oak

Schwarzesch (die)n. black ash

Schwarzkasch (die)n. black (mazard) cherry

Schwarzkopp (der) n. 1. black-headed person; 2. female

bumblebee (so called because its face is black while that of the male is white)

Schwarzmaulbeer (die)n. red mulberry

schwarzrot, adj. dark red

schwarzunblo, adj. 1.black and blue; 2.livid

Schwarzwalniss(baam) (der)n. black walnut

Schwarzwatzel (die)n. comfrey

Schwarzweide (der, die)n. black willow

Schwatsdarn (die)n. black thorn

schwatz, adj. black

schwatzbeenich, adj. black legged

schwatzbrau, adj. dark brown

schwatzdreckich, adj. very dirty

Schwatze (die)n. smallpox

Schwatzeeche (die)n. black oak

Schwatzer (en)n. Negro

Schwatzesch (die)n. black ash

Schwatzing (die)n. blacking

Schwatzkasch (die)n. black (mazard) cherry

Schwatzkopp (der) n. 1. black headed person; 2. female bumblebee (so called because its face is black while that of the male is white)

Schwatzmaulbeer (die)n. red mulberry

schwatzrot, adj. dark red

schwatzunblo, adj. 1.black and blue; 2.livid

Schwatzvoggel (der)n.; Schwatzfeggel, pl. blackbird

Schwatzwalniss(baam) (der)n. black walnut

Schwatzwatzel (die)n. comfrey

Schwatzweide (der, die)n. black willow

Schweb (die)n. swing beam (used in raising a bucket out of a well)

schweche, v.; gschwecht, pp. 1.unnerve; 2.weaken

schwechlich, adv. weakly

Schwechlichkeet (die)n. 1.sickliness; 2.weakness

Schwechlichkeit (die)n. 1.sickliness; 2.weakness

Schweedrieb (die)n. rutabaga (Waterloo Co., Ontario, Canada)

Schweeger (der)n.; Schweeger, pl. brother-in-law

Schweegerdochder (die)n. daughter-in-law

schweere, v.; gschwore, pp. 1.make oath; 2.swear

Schwees (der)n. sweat

schwees(s)e, v.; gschwees(s)t, pp. 1.leak; 2.ooze; 3.weld (solder)

Schweesdrobbe (der)n. sweat drop

Schweesduch (es)n. cloth put on face of a corpse

Schweesfux (der)n. sorrel horse

Schweffel-helzich (es)n.; Schweffel- helzicher, pl. match (for lighting a fire)

Schweffel-schtecke (es)n.; Schweffel-schtecke, pl. match (for lighting a fire)

Schwei (die)n. sister-in-law

schweige, v.; gschweicht, pp. (to be) silent

Schweini(ng) (die),n. 1.atrophy (of a muscle); 2.sweeny

schweiyend, adj. silent

Schwell (die)n. 1.ground plate; 2.sill

schwelle, v.; gschwolle, pp. swell

167

Ss

Schwelme

Schwelme applied to several varieties of grass

Schwemmche (es)n. little meadow

schwemme, v.; gschwemmt, pp. 1.deposit (sand or silt); 2.overflow (of streams)

Schwenckfelder (der)n. member of the religious sect founded by Kaspar Schwenckfeld

schwenke, v.; gschwenkt, pp. 1.rinse; 2.sway; 3.turn; 4.wave

Schwenkfelder (der)n. timber-raiser (in building)

Schwenkzuwwer (der)n.; Schwenkziwwer, pl. rinsing tub (for family washing)

schwenslich, adj. applied to a mare that is given to switching her tail

Schwenz (die)n., pl (rote --) princes' feather

schwenze, v.; gschwenzt, pp. (to dock the) tail (of horses, dogs, sheep)

schwenzle, v.; gschwenzelt, pp. 1.wag; 2.wiggle; 3.walk with a mimicking gate

schwer, adj. 1.difficult; 2.heavy; 3.weighty

Schwerbruder (der)n. brother-in-law

Schwerdaadi (der)n. father-in-law

schwerlich, adj. 1.hardly; 2.scarcely; 3.somewhat heavy

schwerlich, adv. scarcely

schwermiedich, adj. melancholy

Schwermudder (die)n. mother-in-law

Schwerneeder (der)n. 1.scamp; 2.son of a gun

Schwerschweschder (die)n. sister-in-law

Schwertli (es)n. 1.blue flag; 2.iris; 3.flag

Schweschder (die)n.; Schweschdere, pl. 1.nun; 2.sister

Schweschderkind (es)n.; Schweschderkinner, pl. niece or nephew

schweschderlich, adj. sisterly

Schwester(n)fescht (es)n. Sister Service (annual, for women and girls, Moravian)

schwetze, v.; gschwetzt, pp. 1.speak; 2.talk; 3.(ebber en Loch in der Kopp --) (dative) talk one's head off; 4.(feischtenglich --) talk fine; 5.(-- iwwer ebber) talk about (someone)

Schwetzer (der)n.; Schwetzer, pl. 1.orator; 2.speaker; 3.talker

schwewe, v.; gschwebt, pp. 1.float; 2.glide

Schwewwel (der)n. Sulphur

Schwewwel-helzich (es)n.; Schwewwel-helzicher, pl. match (for lighting a fire)

Schwewwel-schtecke (es)n.; Schwewwel-schtecke, pl. match (for lighting a fire)

Schwewwelbliet (die)n. flowers of sulphur

Schwewwelsauer (die)n. sulphuric acid

schwewwle, v.; gschwewwelt, pp. 1.asphyxiate with sulphur fumes; 2.make it hot for someone

Schwiegerdochder (die)n. daughter-in-law

Schwiegermudder (die)n. mother-in-law

Schwiegern (die)n. mother-in-law

Schwiegersoh (der)n. son-in-law

Schwiegersuh (der)n. son-in-law

Schwiegervadder (der)n. father-in-law

sechse

schwiel, adj. sultry

schwiele, v.; gschwole, pp. swell

Schwimmblatz (der)n.; Schwimmbletz, pl. swimming hole

schwimme, v.; gschwumme, pp. 1.float; 2.swim

Schwimmer (der)n.; Schwimmer, pl. swimmer

Schwimmlichdel (es) n. piece of paper floating in a cup or saucer filled with fat and lit to furnish light

Schwimmloch (es)n.; Schwimmlecher, pl. swimming hole

schwind, adj. quick

Schwindel (der)n. 1.giddiness; 2.humbug; 3.swindle; 4.vertigo

schwindle, v.; gschwindelt, pp. 1.(to be) dizzy; 2.swindle

Schwindler (der)n.; Schwindler, pl. swindler

Schwindlerei (die)n. 1.fraud; 2.swindle; 3.swindling

schwindlich, adj. dizzy

Schwing (die)n. 1.pole; 2.rod; 3.swing; 4.whip

schwinge, v.; gschwunge, pp. 1.beat (limbs of a chestnut tree to bring down nuts); 2.flog; 3.scutch; 4.swing; 5.vibrate

Schwingfedder (die)n. large wing feather

Schwingfelderkuche (der)n. Dutch cake

Schwingmesser (es)n. swingle

Schwingmiehl (die)n. scutch

Schwingraad (es)n. scutch

Schwingwaerick (es)n. tow

Schwinne (die)n. 1.atrophy (of a muscle); 2.sweeny

schwinne, v.; gschwinne; gschwunne, pp. vanish

Schwitz (der)n. sweat

schwitze, v.; gschwitzt, pp. 1.be clouded by moisture; 2.suffer; 3.sweat

Schwitzgegreider (die)n., pl. sudorific herbs

schwitzich, adj. 1.sweated; 2.sweaty

Schwitzing (die)n. sweating

Schwob (der)n.; Schwowe, pl. 1.cockroach; 2.Suabian; 3.term of ridicule

Schwoger (der)n.; Schweeger, pl. brother-in-law

Schwort (die)n. 1.rind of bacon or ham; 2.rough fellow; 3.slab

schworte, v.; gschwort, pp. flog

Schwortemaage (der)n. pig's stomach filled and pressed

Schwowefall (die)n. cockroach trap

Schwoweland (es)n. Suabia

Schwoweschtreech (die)n., pl. 1.nonsense; 2.tomfoolery

Schwung (die)n. 1.sweep; 2.swing

Schwungraad (es)n. balance wheel

Schwupp (der)n. swoop

schwuppe, v.; gschwuppt, pp. 1.beat; 2.defeat; 3.strike

Schwur (der)n. 1.oath; 2.vow

se = zu to

Sebb (die)n. sieve

Sech (es)n. 1.coulter (on plow); 2.jointer

Sechbluk (der)n. plow with a jointer

sechs, adj 1.six; 2.(meiner --) by golly

Sechsdel (es)n. 1.sixth of a barrel of beer; 2.sixth part

sechsder, adj six spot of cards

sechse, adj. six

Ss

sechseckich

sechseckich, adj. hexagonal
sechshunnert, adj. six hundred
sechsmol, adj. six times
sechst, adj. sixth
sechsyaehrich, adj. six years old
sechzeh, adj.; pron. sixteen
sechzeht, adj. sixteenth
sechzich, adj.; pron. sixty
sechzichscht, adj. sixtieth
Seckche (es)n. little bag
Seckel (der)n. scrotum
Seckelwetzer (der)n. scamp
seckendiere, v.; seckendiert, pp. (sich --) 1.defend one's self; 2.know what to do; 3.stand up against; 4.take one's own part
Seckli (es)n.; Secklin, pl. little bag
seddich, v.; gseddicht, pp. satisfy
See (der)n. 1.ocean; 2.sea
see! see! kum! call for cows
Seech (der)n. urine
seeche, v.; gseecht, pp. urinate
Seechgrott (die)n. toad
Seef (die)n. soap
Seef(e)wasser (es)n. soapsuds
seefe, v.; gseeft, pp. soap
Seefefett (es)n. soap-fat
Seefeschaum (der)n. lather
seefich, adj. soapy
Seefschissel (die)n. soap-dish
Seegraas (es)n. seaweed
seegrank, adj. seasick
Seegranket (die)n. seasickness
Seehund (der)n. seal
seeisch, adj. maritime
Seel (die)n.; Seele, pl. soul
Seel (es)n. straw for tying sheaves
Seeledokder (der)n. negative term for minister
seelich, adj. 1.blessed; 2.happy; 3.saved (religious sense)
Seelichkeet (die)n. salvation
Seelsaryer (der)n. pastor
seene, v.; gseent, pp. 1.filter; 2.strain (liquids)
Seener (der)n. 1.filter; 2.strainer
Seeraawer (der)n. pirate
Seereis (die)n. voyage
Seeschaal (die)n. 1.seashell; 2.voyage
Seet (die)n. string (violin)
Seevoggel (der)n. gull
Seezwiwwel (die)n. 1.sea onion; 2.squill
seftich, adj. 1.having a bad reputation; 2.indecent
Seftle (es)n. jelly
Sege (der)n. 1.benediction; 2.blessing
Segel (es)n. sail
Segelduch (es)n. sailcloth
segle, v.; gsegelt, pp. 1.be in a hurry; 2.sail
segne, v.; gsegent, pp. bless
Segund (die)n.; Segunde, pl. second (measure of time)

Seigranket

Segundezeeche (es)n. second hand (of a clock)
Segundezoier (es)n. second hand (of a clock)
sehne, v.; gsehnt, pp. 1.have a longing desire; 2.long
sehne, v.; gsehne, pp. 1.look; 2.see
Sehnern (die)n. daughter-in-law
sehneswaert, adj. worth seeing
Sehnsucht (die)n. longing
sehr, adv. very (used rarely)
sei Lebbdaag net!, adv. never (emphatic)
sei Lewe(s) net!, adv. never (emphatic)
sei, poss. adj. his
sei, v.; is g(e)west, pp. (to) be
Seibaerzel (der)n. purslane
Seiballe (der)n. pig-ball (Amish game, "Stay pig"!)
Seibaschde (die)n. bristle (pig)
Seibengel (der)n. 1.boor; 2.brute
Seiblos (die)n. hog's bladder (when dried, used as a purse or tobacco pouch)
Seibohn (die)n. horse bean
Seiche (es)n. suckling pig
seiddem, prep. since
Seide (der)n. silk
Seideblaat (es)n. side trace
Seideblatt (es)n.; Seidebledder, pl. side tree
Seidefleesch (es)n. 1.bacon; 2.flitch
Seidel (der)n. beer tankard
Seidemiehl (die)n. silk mill
Seider (der)n. cider
seider, prep. since
Seiderpress (es)n. cider press
Seideschpeck (der)n. bacon
Seideschteche (es)n. stitch in one's side
Seideschtick (es)n. 1.bacon; 2.flitch
Seidewar(e)m (der)n. silkworm
seidich, adj. silken
seidlings, adj., adv. 1.edgeways; 2.sideways
Seidreck (der)n. 1.hog excrement; 2.matter of no importance
Seidrog (der)n. hog trough
Seidschtross (die)n. side street
seidwaerts, adj., adv. sideways
seidweks, adj., adv. sideways
Seieemer (der)n. swill-bucket
Seierei (die)n. 1.hoggishness; 2.mess; 3.obscene talk
seierlich, adj. tart
Seifass (es)n.; Seifesser, pl. 1.slop barrel; 2.swill-barrel
Seifenger (der)n. contrivance for catching hogs by the leg
seiferich, adv. 1.(with a) sigh; 2.sighing
Seifleesch (es)n. pork
seifze, v.; gseifzt, pp. 1.sigh; 2.sob; 3.weep
Seifzer (der)n.; Seifzer, pl. sigh
seifzerich, adj. 1.sighing; 2.with a sigh
Seigalye (der)n. cross-like structure on which slaughtered hogs are hung
Seigelser (der)n. gelder
Seigieg (die)n. 1.calathumpian violin; 2.horse fiddle
Seigranket (die)n. hog cholera

169

Ss

Seigrumbeere — sexeckich

Seigrumbeere (die)n., pl. culls (of potatoes)
Seih (die)n. 1.filter; 2.strainer
Seihduch (es)n. cloth for straining
seihe, v.; gseiht, pp. 1.filter; 2.strain through; 3.strain (liquids)
seii(s)ch, adj. 1.gluttonous; 2.hoggish; 3.piggish
Seikaerbs (die)n. field pumpkin
Seikamille (der)n. 1.mayweed; 2.stinking camomile
Seikaschde (der)n. slovenly person
Seikiwwel (der)n. swill-bucket
Seil (die)n. awl
seilebbdaag, adv. always
Seiledder (es)n. hog skin
Seilewe (es)n. beastly life
seilewe(s), adv. 1.always; 2.ever; 3.(-- net) never
Seili (es)n. 1.little pig; 2.suckling pig
Seimaage (der)n. hog's stomach, the same cleaned and filled (as an edible)
sein(e)sgleiche(s) 1.of his own kind; 2.such as he
Seinawwel (der)n. sheath of a hog (hung up for the birds in winter)
seine, v.; gseint, pp. sift
Seiner (der)n.; Seiner, pl. sieve
Seinescht (es)n. 1.dirty hole; 2.pig's litter
Seiohr (es)n. pig's ear
Seiohreblaat (es)n. plantain leaf
Seiriesel (der)n. dirty fellow
Seisaufe (es)n. swill
Seischneider (der)n. gelder (of hogs)
Seischtall (der)n. hog pen
Seischwans (der)n. pig's tail
Seit (die)n.; Seide, pl. side
seit, prep. since
seitlings, adv. sideways
Seitloh (der)n. 1.(casual) emoluments; 2.side-wages
Seitschtross (die)n. side street
seitwaerts, adv. sideways
seitwegs, adv. sideways
Seiwelschkann (es)n. nubbins
seiwere, v.; gseiwert, pp. 1.cleanse; 2.(sich --) deliver the afterbirth
Seiwering (die)n. 1.afterbirth; 2.placenta (of animals)
seiwerlich, adj. 1.clean; 2.cleanly; 3.tidy
Seiyoch (es) n. yoke put on hogs to prevent them from creeping through fences
Sekritaer (der)n. secretary
Sekt (die)n. sect
Selaat (der)n. 1.lettuce; 2.salad; 3.(wilder --) wild lettuce
Selaatbrieh (die)n. salad dressing
selbscht, pron. self
Selbschtmard (der)n. suicide
selde, adv. seldom
seldsam, adj. 1.strange; 2.unaccountable
selewe, adv. 1.always; 2.ever; 3.(-- net) never
selich, adj. 1.blessed; 2.happy; 3.saved
Sell (die)n. cell

sell, pron. that one
sell, pron.; adj.; conj. that
sellem, adv. 1.then; 2.dative of *sell*
sellemno according to that
sellemol(s), adv. 1.at that time; 2.in those times; 3.in times past; 4.then
seller, pron. that one
seller, pron.; adj.; conj. that
Selleri (der)n. celery
Sellerich (der)n. celery
selleweg, adv. that way
selli, dem. adj. those
selli, pron. that one
selli, pron.; adj.; conj. that
selliweil, adv. during that time
seltsam, adj. strange
Selwen (die)n. selvedge
selwer(t), pron. self
sem = sellem dative of *sell*
Seminaar (es)n. seminary
Semmli (es)n. legislature
Semmlimann (der)n. legislator
Senaador (der)n. senator
Senaat (der)n. senate
Senger (der)n. singer
Senkblei (es)n. 1.plumb; 2.plumb line
senke, v.; gsenkt, pp. 1.sag; 2.settle; 3.sink; 4.singe
Senkel (der)n. plummet
Senkelschnur (die)n. plumb line
senkle, v.; gsenkelt, pp. plumb
senkrecht, adj. 1.perpendicular; 2.vertical
Sens (die)n.; Sense, pl. 1.scythe; 2.(deitschi --) (German) scythe (broad-blade)
Sensewar(e)f (der)n. 1.handle (of a scythe); 2.snath
Seperdent (der)n. superintendent
Sepp (der)n. Joe
Seppi (die)n. 1.Josephine; 2.Josie
September (der)n. September
sercht = es ercht the first
Serwe (der)n. 1.hired boy; 2.hired man; 3.(indentured) servant
Serwebu (der)n. hired (indentured) boy
Serwemann (der)n. 1.hired (indentured) man;2.manservant
Serwenmaedechen (die)n. servant girl
Sessel (der)n. armchair
settiche, v.; gsetticht, pp. 1.appease; 2.satisfy
Setz, n. clinch iron
setze, v.; gsetzt, pp. 1.start brooding (of a hen); 2.(sich --) seat (oneself); 3.set; 4.sit down
Setzer (der)n. compositor
Setzet (die)n. setting (of eggs)
sex; sexe, pron. six
Sexdel (es)n. 1.sixth part; 2.sixth of a barrel
Sexdelball (en)n. 1/6 barrel
sexeckich, adj. hexagonal

Ss

sexmol — sinne

sexmol, adv. six times
sexyaerich, adj. six years old
Shnadderli (es)n. souse (pig's feet)
Sibb (die)n. sieve
sibbe, v.; gsibbt, pp. 1.screen; 2.sieve; 3.sift
sichde, v.; gsicht, pp. sieve
Sichel (die)n.; Sichle, pp. sickle
sicher, adj. 1.certain; 2.safe; 3.secure; 4.sure
sicher, adj.; adv. safe(ly)
Sicherheet (die)n. certainty
sichle, v.; gsichelt, pp. cut with a sickle
Sichler (der)n.; Sichler, pl. sickler
Sicht (die)n. 1.eyesight; 2.outlook; 3.view
sichtbaar, adj. visible
sichtbarlich, adj. perceptibly
sichte, v.; gsicht, pp. 1.sieve; 2.winnow
sidder, prep. since
siddlich, adj. 1.southerly; 2.southern
siddlich, adv. southerly
sie, pron. 1.her; 2.she; 3.them; 4.they
sie, pron. you (occasionally used as a mark of respect in addressing a person, especially a minister)
sie selwer, pron. herself
Sieb (die)n.; Siewe(r), pl. 1.screen; 2.sieve
Siebdeer (die)n. screen door
sieche, v.; gsiecht, pp. conquer
siechreich, adj. victorious
siede, v. simmer
siedlich, adj. southern
siedlich, adv. southerly
siege, v.; gsiecht, pp. conquer
Siegel (es)n. seal
Siek (der)n. victory
siene, v.; gsient, pp. strain (liquids)
Sienerli (es)n.; Sienerlin, pl. strainer
sies = sie es; sie iss she is
siess, adj. sweet
Siessabbel (der)n.; Siessebbel, pl. sweet apple
Siessbaerke (der, die)n. black birch
Siesseraahmkuche (der)n.; Siessraahmkuche, pl. sweet cream cake
Siesseroomkuche (der)n.; Siessroomkuche, pl. Sweet cream cake
Siesses (es)n. 1.sugar; 2.sweets
Siessfennichel (der)n. sweet cicerly
Siessfleesch (es)n. sweetbread (thymus of a young animal used for food)
Siessgraas (es)n. sweet vernal grass
Siessgrummbeer (die)n.; Siessgrumbeere, pl. sweet potato
Siessholswatzel (die)n. licorice stick
Siessholz (es)n. 1.birch; 2.licorice root
Siesskasch (die)n.; Siesskasche, pl. sweet cherry
Siesskuche (der)n.; Seisskuche, pl. 1.favorite cake; 2.sweet cake
siesslich, adj. sweetish
Siesswatzel (die)n. sweet cicely

Siesswelchkann (es)n. sweet corn
sietsam, adj. softly
siffe, v.; gsifft, pp. sip
Siffer (der)n. drunkard
Sigaer (die)n.; Sigaere, pl. cigar
Siggel (es)n. seal
siggele, v.; gsiggelt, pp. seal
Siggelwachs (der)n. sealing wax
Silfeschder (der)n. last one to get up on New Year's Day
Silli (der)n. last one to get up on New Year's Day
Sillscheidhoke (der)n.; Sillscheidhoke, pl. singletree hook
Sillscheit (es)n.; Sillscheider, pl. 1.single-tree; 2.whiffle tree
Silvaanus (der)n. Silvanus
Silwer (es)n. silver
silwer(n), adj. (of) silver
Silwerbabble (die)n. white poplar
Silwerfisch (der)n.; Silwerfisch, pl. silverfish
Silwerglett (die)n. litharge
Silwergraas (es)n. knotgrass
Silwersand (der)n. pewter sand
Silwerschmitt (der)n. silversmith
Silwerschtick (es)n. silver coin
Silweschder (der)n. last one to get up on New Year's Day
Sim (der)n. 1.Simeon; 2.Simon
Simbel (der)n. 1.silly person; 2.simpleton
Simmbild (es)n. emblem
simmeliere, v.; gsimmeliert, pp. meditate
simmer = sinn mer are we
Simmet (der)n. cinnamon
Simmetrinn (die)n. cinnamon
Simpel (der)n. 1.silly person; 2.simpleton
Sims (der)n. 1.cornice; 2.shelf
Sin(d) (die)n.; Sin(d)e, pl. 1.sin; 2.(ee -- un ee schand) a wicked shame
Sindebock (der)n. scapegoat
Sindefall (der)n. Fall (of man)
Sinder (der)n.; Sinder, pl. sinner
Sindeschuld (die)n.; Sindeschulde, pl. sore (as punishment for sin)
Sindflut (die)n. deluge
Sindfrewel (der)n. iniquity
sindhafdich, adj. sinful
Sindhafdichkeit (die)n. sinfulness
sindhaft, adj. sinful
sindiche, v.; gsindicht, pp. sin
Singbuch (es)n.; Singbicher, pl. hymnbook
singe, v.; gsunge, pp. 1.sing; 2.warble
Singer (der)n.; Singer, pl. singer
Singern (die)n. female singer
Singing (die)n. song service
Singschtick (es)n.; Singschticker, pl. song
Singschul (die)n. singing school
sinke, v.; gsunke, pp. sink
Sinkloch (es)n.; Sinklecher, pl. 1.cesspool; 2.sinkhole
Sinn (der)n. 1.mind; 2.sense; 3.(im -- hawwe) intend
sinne, v.; gsunne, pp. 1.meditate; 2.think

Ss

sinter — Summerheisel

sinter, adv. since
Sirrop (der)n. syrup
Siss alles batsch! It's all gone to nothing!
Siss net der Wart It's not worthwhile
sittsam, adj. 1.demure; 2.modest
Sitz (der)n.; Sitze, pl. seat
sitze, v.; gsitzt, gsotze, pp. 1.sit; 2.(-- losse) jilt
Sitzfleesch (es)n (er hot kenn --) he can't sit still
Sitzloch (es)n. 1.anus; 2.arse
siwwe, adj,; pron. seven
siwwefach, adj. sevenfold
siwwerschteenich, adj. barred
Siwweschleafer (der)n. (long) sleeper
Siwweschleefer (der)n. Seven Sleepers Day, June 27
siwwet, adj. seventh
siwweter (en), adj. seven spot in cards
Siwweyaeger (der)n. spirit hunter
siwwezeh, adj.; pron. seventeen
siwwezeht, adj. seventeenth
siwwezich, adj.; pron. seventy
siwwezichscht, adj. seventieth
Skorpion (der)n. Scorpio (8th sign of the zodiac)
so eens, adj.; adv.; pron. such
So willkumm wie en Sau imme Yuddehaus As welcome as a pig in a synagogue
so yaahreweis, adv. (in) odd or scattering years
so, adj.; adv.; conj. 1.so; 2.such
so, conj. according (to that)
soball, adv. as soon as
Socke (der) n. 1. remains of woven goods; 2.(foot of a) stocking; 3.sock
Sodbrenne(s) (es)n. 1.heartburn; 2.water-brash
soddere, v.; gsoddert, pp. simmer
soddich, adj.; adv.; pron. such
Sode (die)n. soda
sodegleiche, adj. such like
Sofe (es)n. sofa
sogaar, adj.; adv. even
sogaar, adv. truly
Soh (der)n. son
Sohl (die)n. 1.ground plate; 2.sole
sohle, v.; gsohlt, pp. 1.flog; 2.sole; 3.charge an exorbitant price
Sohlledder (es)n. sole-leather
Sohn (der)n. son
Sohnsfraa (die)n.; Sohnsweiwer, pl. daughter-in-law
soich, adj.; adv.; pron. such
solang, adv. as long as
Soldaat (der)n.; Soldaade, pl. soldier
solle, v.; gsollt, pp. 1.are to; 2.be intended to; 3.be said to
sollich, adj.; adv.; pron. such
Some (der)n. 1.growing grain; 2.seed
some = so me
Somefeld (es)n. sowed field in wheat or rye
Someglee (der)n. clover for seed
Somekaern (die)n. grain of seed
Somekeim (die)n. cotyledon

Somekopp (der)n. seedpod
Someschtaab (der)n. pollen
Somewelschkann (es)n. seed corn
Soot (die)n. 1.(growing) grain; 2.seed; 3.season for sowing winter cereals
Sootfeld (es)n. sowed field in wheat or rye
Sootfrucht (die)n. seed grain
Sootgrummbeer (die)n. seed potato
Sootkarn (es)n. seed rye
Sootlaerrich (die)n. field lark
Sootweeze (der)n. seed wheat
Sootwelschkann (es)n. seed corn
sore = so eenr (dative sing fem) so one
soviel, conj. 1.as much (as); 2.for all
soweit, conj. as far (as)
sozesaage, conj. 1.as good as; 2.almost; 3.just about
Subbefleesch (es)n. soup meat
Subbegnoche (der)n. soup bone
Subbekell (die)n.; Subbekelle, pl. soup ladle
Subbeleffel (der)n. tablespoon
Subbeschissel (die)n. 1.soup dish; 2.tureen
suche, v.; gsucht, pp. 1.look for; 2.search for; 3.seek
Sucht (die)n. 1.ailment; 2.complaint; 3.plague
Suckelfill (es)n. suckling filly
Suckelsau (die)n. suckling pig
Suckelsei (die)n. piglets of suckling age
Sucki (es)n. calf
suckle, v.; gsuckelt, pp. 1.play the parasite; 2.sip; 3.suck
Suckler (der)n. 1.parasite; 2.sucker (person)
Sudd(e) (die)n. south
sudde, adv. south
Suddelarewett (die)n. sloppy work
Suddelwedder (es)n. drizzly weather
suddere, v.; gsuddert, pp. simmer
suddle, v.; gsuddelt, pp. 1.be foggy; 2.drizzle; 3.splash in water
suddlich, adj. 1.drizzling; 2.rainy; 3.wet
suddlich, adv. southern
suddre, v.; gsuddert, pp. 1.burn as a smothered fire; 2.simmer
suddwescht, adv. southwest
Suff (der)n. intoxication
Suh (der)n.; Seh, pl. son
Suhnsfraa (die)n.; Suhnsweiwer, pl. daughter-in-law
suk! call for cows
sumbich, adj. swampy
Sume (der)n. seed
Sumeschtaab (der)n. pollen
Summ (die)n. 1.amount; 2.sum
summe, v.; gsummt, pp. 1.drone; 2.hum
Summer (der)n. summer
Summerbeer (die)n. summer pear
Summerblog (die)n. summer complaint
Summerfleck (die)n.; Summerflecke, pl. freckle
summerfleckich, adj. freckled
Summergranket (die)n. summer complaint
Summerheisel (es)n. summer kitchen

172

Ss

Summerheisli

Summerheisli (es)n. 1.summerhouse; 2.summer kitchen

Summerhitz (die)n. summer heat

summerich, adj. summer-like

Summerkich (die)n. summer kitchen

Summerpocke (die)n., pl. rash

summers, adv. (in the) summer

Summerschul (die)n. summer school

Summervoggel (der)n. butterfly

Summerwascht (die)n. bologna (for use in summer)

Summerwedder (es)n. summer weather

Sump (der)n. 1.bog; 2.marsh; 3.swamp

sumpich, adj. marshy

Sumploch (es)n. swampy spot

sumse, v.; gsumst, pp. hum

sunderbaar, adj. 1.peculiar; 2.quaint; 3.queer; 4.strange;
    5.unexpected

Sunn (die)n. sun

Sunndaag (der)n. Sunday

Sunndaagschul (die)n. Sunday school

Sunndaagsgleeder (die)n.,pl. Sunday clothes

Sunndaagshals (der)n 1.windpipe; 2.(ebbes in der -- griege)
    draw something into the windpipe while swallowing

sunndaagsich, adj. Sunday

Sunndaagskind (es)n. Sunday child (child born on Sunday)

sunne, v.; gsunnt, pp. 1.expose to the sun; 2.(sich --) bask in
    the sun

Sunneblumm (die)n.; Sunneblumme, pl. sunflower

Sunnedebbich (der)n. quilt pattern

Sunnefinschdernis(s) (die)n. eclipse of the sun

Sunnefisch (der)n. sunfish

Sunnefleck (die)n. freckle

Sunneglaas (es)n. sunglass

Tt

taadle

taadle, v.; getaadelt, pp. 1.censure; 2.find fault
Taadler (der)n. fault-finder
Taasel (die)n. 1.fringe; 2.tassel
Tabernaakel (der)n. tabernacle
Taermin (der)n. 1.term; 2.limit
Takt (der)n. 1.bar in music; 2.rhythm
Talent (es)n. 1.natural gift; 2.talent
Tamaet(i)s (die)n., pl. tomato
Tamaetsbrieh (die)n. tomato juice
Tand (der)n. toy
Tann (der)n. 1.spire; 2.steeple
Tanne (die)n. fir
Tarm (der)n. 1.spire; 2.steeple
Tarn (der)n. 1.spire; 2.steeple
Tatz (die)n. 1.fingers; 2.paw
tausend, adj., pron. thousand
Tax (der)n.; Taxe, pl. tax
taxbaar, adj. taxable
Taxbezaahler (der)n.; Taxbezaahler, pl. taxpayer
taxe, v.; getaxt, pp. 1.charge; 2.tax
taxfrei, adj. tax-exempt
Taxgeld (es)n. money for taxes
Tee (der)n. 1.tea; 2.(im -- sei) (to be) tipsy
Teeblaat(es)n.; Teebledder, pl. tea leaf
Teeblettche (es)n. saucer
Teebletti (es)n. saucer
Teegraut (es)n. golden-rod
Teekann (die)n.; Teekanne, pl. teapot
Teekessel (der)n.; Teekessele, pl. teakettle
Teeleffel (der)n.; Teeleffele, pl. teaspoon
Teeleffelvoll (der)n. teaspoonful
Teeleffli (es)n.; Teelefflin, pl. teaspoon
Teelefflivoll (der)n. teaspoonful
Tempel (der)n. temple
tempere, v.; getempert, pp. (sich --) 1.be temperate; 2.calm down; 3.use moderation
Teschdament (es)n. Testament
Text (der)n. text
Ticher (der)n. tiger
ticke, v.; getickt, pp. tick
Tiddel (der)n. title
tiddeliere, v.; tiddeliert, pp. coax
Tieschern (die)n. 1.schoolmaster; 2.teacher
Till(i) (der)n. Tilghman
Till(i) (die)n. Tillie
Tinktur (die)n. tincture
Titel (der)n. title
Tock (die) bundle of flax (for spinning)
Tollbeer (die)n. belladonna
Tollkasch (die)n. belladonna
Tomaetskeffer (der)n. tomato bug
Ton (der)n. 1.sound; 2.tone
Tour (die)n. 1.trip; 2.turn (especially a customary act of the kind); 3.walk
trachte, v.; getracht, pp. 1.pursue; 2.strive after
Traen (die)n.; Traene, pl. tear (drop)

Tyrann

trakdiere, v.; trakdiert, pp. abuse cruelly
Trank (der)n. 1.beverage; 2.drink
Trapp (der)n. footmark
trapp, tripp, trapp! imitating the sound of heavy steps
trappe, v.; getrappt, pp. step (heavily)
trau(e)re, v.; getrauert, pp. 1.grieve; 2.mourn; 3.wilt (of plants)
traurich, adj. 1.afflicted; 2.sad
treeschde, v.; getreescht, pp. console
treeschtmiedich, adj. 1.dejected; 2.meditative; 3.meek
trei, adj. 1.faithful; 2.true
Treie (die)n. troth
treihaerzich, adj. 1.faithful; 2.simple-hearted
treilos, adj. faithless
trenne, v.; getrennt, pp. 1.rip; 2.separate; 3.sever
Trennung (die)n. separation
trimme, v.; getrimmt, pp. trim
Trommel (die)n. jew's harp
Troscht (der)n 1.consolation; 2.(liewer --) interj. (a)good Lord!; (b) oh my!
trostmiedich, adj. 1.dejected; 2.meditative; 3.meek; 4.satisfied
trostreich, adj. consoling
Trotz (der)n. defiance
trotz, prep. in spite of
trotze, v.; getrotzt, pp. 1.be defiant; 2.sulk
trotzich, adj. 1.defiant; 2.spiteful
Trotzkopp (der)n. headstrong person
Trunkebold (der)n. drunkard
tschaae, v.; getschaat, pp. 1.chew; 2.masticate
Turm (der)n. 1.spire; 2.steeple
Tutt (die)n.; Tudde, pl. bag
Tyrann (der)n. tyrant

Uu

ubeholfe, adj. helpless

Ufer (es)n. 1.bank; 2.shore

uff barigs, adv. on credit

uff der Schnepp, adj. (to be) undecided

uff un ab, adv. back and forth

Uff-fiehrung (die)n. conduct

Uff-frischung (die)n. refreshment

uff/backe, v.; uffgebackt, pp. use up in baking

uff/baerschde, v.; uffgebaerscht, pp. brush up

uff/balixe, v.; uffgebalixt, pp. mix up

uff/banke, v.; uffgebankt, pp. bank (a fire)

uff/basse, v.; uffgebasst, pp. 1.beware; 2.pay attention; 3.take care; 4.watch out

uff/baue, v.; uffgebaut, pp. 1.build up; 2.construct; 3.erect

uff/beisse, v.; uffgebisse, pp. bite open

uff/bessere, v.; uffgebessert, pp. ameliorate

uff/biege, v.; uffgeboge, pp. bend up or open

uff/bindle, v.; uffgebindelt, pp. get (a woman) in the family way

uff/binne, v.; uffgebunne, pp. 1.rake and bind (in harvest); 2.tie up

uff/blaehe, v.; uffgeblaeht, pp. bloat

uff/blaschdere, v.; uffgeblaschdert, pp. patch up

uff/blaudre, v.; uffgeblaudert, pp. 1.palm off on; 2.persuade

uff/bleiwe, v.; gebliwwe. pp. 1.remain open; 2.stay up

uff/blicke, v.; uffgeblickt, pp. look up

uff/blocke, v.; uffgeblockt, pp. 1.block up; 2.build a log house

uff/blose, v.; uffgeblost, pp. 1.blow open; 2.blow up; 3.inflate

uff/bluge, v.; uffgeblugt, pp. plow up

uff/bome, v. wind up a warp on a cylinder preparatory to weaving rag carpet

uff/brauche, v.; uffgebraucht, pp. use up

uff/breche, v.; uffgebroche, pp. 1.adjourn; 2.break up; 3.go bankrupt

uff/brenne, v.; is uffgebrennt, pp. burn up

uff/bringe, v.; uffgebrocht, pp. 1.adduce (against a person); 2.rear (a child); 3.restore (a sick person)

uff/buckere, v.; uffgebuckert, pp. 1.damage; 2.dent; 3.mar

uff/butze, v.; uffgebutzt, pp. 1.clean up; 2.(sich --) (a) clean up; (b) dress up; (c) winnow grain

uff/daae, v.; uffgedaat, pp. 1.melt; 2.thaw

uff/damme, v.; uffgedammt, pp. dam

uff/darre, v.; uffgedatt, pp. dry up

uff/decke, v.; uffgedeckt, pp. 1.disclose; 2.expose;3.uncover

uff/deele, v.; uffgedeelt, pp. apportion

uff/denke, v.; uffgedenkt, pp think up

uff/dopple, v.; uffgedoppelt, pp. double up

uff/draage, v.; uffgedraage, pp. serve

uff/drede, v.; gedredde, pp. step on

uff/drehe, v.; uffgedreht, pp. 1.screw open; 2.turn up; 3.untwine

uff/drenne, v.; uffgedrennt, pp. rip

uff/dricke, v.; uffgedrickt, pp. squeeze open

uff/drickle, v.; uffgedrickelt, pp. 1.evaporate; 2.dry up; 3.shrivel

uff/driewe, v.; uffgedriebt, pp. become cloudy

uff/drinke, v.; uffgedrunke, pp. drink up

uff/drumme, v.; uffgedrummt, pp. arouse interest

uff/ducke, v.; uffgeduckt, pp. raise the head or body suddenly

uff/duh, v.; uffgeduh, pp. 1.adorn; 2.preserve (fruit); 3.put on (a hat); 4.put up (hay); 5.(ebbes --) repair something; 6.(sich --) (a) adorn; (b) dress up

uff/eege, v.; uffge-eekt, pp. loosen by harrowing

uff/eegne, v.; uffge-eegnet, pp. 1.admit to (something); 2.confess; 3.own up

uff/esse, v.; uffgesse, pp. eat up

uff/faahre, v.; uffgfaahre, pp. 1.fly up in anger; 2.rise abruptly

uff/falle, v. uffgfalle, pp. 1.cause an open wound by falling; 2.fall on; 3.fall open

uff/fange, v.; uffgfange, pp. snatch up

uff/feichde, v.; uffgfeicht, pp. moisten

uff/feiere, v.; uffgfeiert, pp. 1.make a fire better; 2.(to start a) fire

uff/feile, v.; uffgfeilt, pp. file open

uff/fiedre, v.; uffgfiedert, pp. 1.improve by good feeding; 2.use up as fodder

uff/fiehre, v.; uffgfiehrt, pp 1.(sich schlecht --) misbehave; 2.(sich --) behave

uff/flackere, v.; uffgflackert, pp. flame up

uff/flamme, v.; uffgflammt, pp. flame up

uff/flattre, v.; uffgflattert, pp. flutter up

uff/fliege, v.; is uffgfloge, pp. burst open

uff/folge, v.; uffgfolkt, pp. follow up

uff/fresse, v.; uffgfresse, pp. devour

uff/frische, v.; uffgfrischt, pp. refresh

uff/gawwle, v.; uffgegawwelt, pp. pick up (with a fork)

uff/geblose, v. bloated

uff/gedrosse, v. bloated

uff/geduh, v. dressed up

uff/geh, v.; uffgange, pp. 1.become undone; 2.bloom; 3.melt; 4.open; 5.sprout; 6.thaw

uff/geklaert, v. enlightened

uff/gelebt, v. 1.cheerful; 2.jolly

uff/gelese, v.; 1.picked up; 2.(en --nes Kind) an illegitimate child

uff/gepulschdert, v. 1.disarranged; 2.messed

uff/gewe, v.; uffgewwe, pp. 1.abrogate; 2.give up; 3.quit

uff/gfriere, v.; uffgfrore, pp. freeze up

uff/glaare, v.; uffgeglaart, pp. clear up

uff/globbe, v.; uffgegloppt, pp. open by hammering

uff/gnebbe, v.; uffgegneppt, pp. unbutton

uff/gneppe, v. uffgegneppt, pp. unbutton

uff/gnibbe, v.; uffgegnippt, pp. unbutton

uff/graawe, v.; uffgegraawe, pp. 1.dig up; 2.disinter

uff/graddle, v.; uffgegraddelt, pp. get up with difficulty

uff/grapsche, v.; uffgegrapscht, pp. grasp up

uff/gratze, v.; uffgegratzt, pp. 1.scratch open; 2.start off suddenly

Uu

uff/griege

uff/griege, v.; uffgrickt, pp. 1.arrange; 2.cause to rise; 3.originate

uff/grimmle, v.; uffgegrimmelt, pp. crumble up

uff/gritzle, v.; uffgegritzelt, pp. use up in scribbling

uff/grumble, v.; uffgegrumbelt, pp. crumble up

uff/grussle, v.; uffgegrusselt, pp. curl up

uff/gscha(e)rre, v.; uffgscha(e)rrt; uffgschatt, pp. put harness on a horse

uff/gschwelle, v.; uffgschwolle, pp. swell up

uff/gucke, v.; uffgeguckt, pp. look up

uff/gwelle, v.; uffgegwellt, pp. 1.spring up; 2.swell; 3.swell from moisture

uff/hacke, v.; uffghackt, pp. 1.chop up; 2.cut open; 3.cut up (a carcass); 4.hoe

uff/halde, v.; uffghalde, pp. 1.delay; 2.detain; 3.hinder; 4.keep up; 5.retard; 6.stand by one's guns; 7.tarry; 8.(sich iwwer ebbes --) worry about something; 9.(sich --) reside

uff/harriche, v.; uffgharricht, pp. 1.give ear; 2.listen

uff/haufe, v. hoard

uff/hawwe, v.; uffghat, pp. 1.have on; 2.have open; 3.wear

uff/heere, v.; uffgheert, pp. 1.cease; 2.halt; 3.stop

uff/heifle, v.; uffgheifelt, pp. pile up

uff/helfe, v.; uffgholfe, pp. 1.give a lift; 2.help up

uff/helle, v.; uffghellt, pp. clear up

uff/henke, v.; uffghenkt, pp. 1.hang up; 2.suspend

uff/hetze, v.; uffghetzt, pp. stir up

uff/hewe, v.; uffghowe, pp. 1.economize; 2.hold back; 3.keep for future use; 4.lift up; 5.pick up; 6.save; 7.up hold

uff/hitze, v.; uffghitzt, pp. heat up

uff/hocke, v.; uffghockt, pp. sit up (especially with a sick person)

uff/hoke, v.; uffghokt, pp. 1.detach; 2.unclasp; 3.unhook

uff/huddle, v.; uffghuddelt, pp. 1.confuse; 2.(en)tangle

uff/hutzle, v.; uffghutzelt, pp. 1.dry up; 2.shrivel

uff/kaafe, v.; uffkaaft, pp. buy up

uff/kaue, v.; uffgekaut, pp. chew up

uff/kehre, v.; uffgekehrt, pp. sweep up

uff/kenne, v.; uffgekennt, pp. be able to get up

uff/kindiche, v. annul

uff/kinne, v. 1.give notice of leaving; 2.(to serve a) quit notice

uff/klappe, v.; uffgeklabbert, pp. fly open

uff/koche, v.; uffgekocht, pp. boil up

uff/kumme, v.; is uffkumme, pp. 1.recover from an illness; 2.prosper; 3.rise; 4.spring up; 5.sprout

uff/kumme, v.; uffkumme, pp. (-- losse) 1.acknowledge; 2.admit

uff/laade, v.; uffgelaade, pp. load

uff/laafe, v.; uffgelofe, pp. 1.become inflamed; 2.walk up to

uff/laese, v. convalesce

uff/laure, v.; uffgelauert, pp. lie in ambush

uff/lege, v.; uffgelegt, pp. 1.apply; 2.economize; 3.impose; 4.inflict; 5.lay by; 6.lay up (stones); 7.save; 8.(sich --) protest

uff/leichte, v.; uffgeleicht, pp. light up

uff/scheppe

uff/leie, v.; uffgelegge, pp. 1.lie open; 2.rest upon; 3.(sich --) become bedsore

uff/lese, v.; uffglese, pp. 1.catch (contagious disease); 2.pick up (potatoes, stones)

uff/lewe, v.; uffglebt, pp. 1.spend; 2.use up in living

uff/lockere, v.; uffgelockert, pp. loosen

uff/losse, v.; uffgelosst, pp. 1.abate; 2.keep on; 3.leave open; 4.permit to get up; 5..stop

uff/lowe, v.; uffgelobt, pp. praise

uff/maahle, v.; uffgemaahlt, pp. grind up

uff/mache, v.; uffgemacht, pp. 1.open; 2.make up (to become reconciled); 3.raise (money) 4.undo; 5.unfasten; 6.(es Feld --) open the field

uff/maericke, v.; uffgemaerickt, pp. 1.mark down; 2.record

uff/meschde, v.; uffgemescht, pp. fatten

uff/messe, v.; uffgemesse, pp. measure (grain)

uff/misse, v.; uffgemisst, pp. be compelled to get up

uff/muntre, v. encourage

uff/nemme, v.; uffgenumme, pp. 1.arrest; 2.entertain; 3.nominate; 4.resume; 5.take offense; 6.take up

uff/packe, v.; uffgepackt, pp. 1.gather; 2.improve; 3.pack up

uff/palde, v.; uffgepalde, pp. keep on (one's hat)

uff/petze, v.; uffgepetzt, pp. pinch open

uff/picke, v.; uffgepickt, pp. 1.gather; 2.improve; 3.pick up

uff/poke, v.; uffgepokt, pp. stir up

uff/quelle, v.; uffgequellt, pp. 1.spring up; 2.swell

uff/raahme, v.; uffgeraahmt, pp. 1.put in order; 2.redd up; 3.tidy up

uff/raffe, v.; uffgerafft, pp. snatch up

uff/reche, v.; uffgerecht, pp. rake up

uff/rege, v.; uffgeregt, pp. 1.excite; 2.stir up

uff/reisse, v.; uffgerisse, pp. 1.open wide; 2.tear open;3. (es Maul --) (a) accuse; (b) find fault

uff/reiwe, v.; uffgeriwwe, pp. rub open

uff/retze, v.; uffgeretzt, pp. arouse

uff/richde, v.; uffgericht, pp. 1.erect; 2.raise

uff/riddle, v.; uffgeriddelt, pp. 1.cast up (to someone); 2.shake up

uff/riege, v.; uffgeregt, pp. 1.excite; 2.stir up

uff/riehre, v.; uffgriehrt, pp. 1.agitate; 2.excite; 3.rouse; 4.stir up

uff/rischde, v.; uffgerischt, pp. make preparations for meals (at funerals)

uff/robbe, v.; uffgeroppt, pp. 1.pluck; 2.pull up

uff/rolle, v.; uffgerollt, pp. 1.roll up; 2.unroll

uff/roschde, v.; uffgeroscht, pp. rust away

uff/rufe, v.; uffgerufe, pp. call up

uff/saage, v.; uffsaat, pp. recite

uff/saame, v.; uffgsaamt, pp. hem

uff/saddle, v.; uffgsaddelt, pp. 1.put saddle on; 2.saddle (someone) with

uff/saege, v.; uffgsaegt, pp. saw up

uff/sammle, v.; uffgsammelt, pp. collect

uff/saufe, v.; uffgsoffe, pp. 1.drink up; 2.spend in drink

uff/schaerre, v.; uffgschaerrt, pp. scratch open

uff/scheppe, v.; uffgscheppt, pp. shovel up

Uu

uff/schidde

uff/schidde, v (eens --) take a drink
uff/schiddle, v.; uffgschiddelt, pp. shake up
uff/schiesse, v.; uffgschosse, pp. 1.grow up fast; 2.shoot up
uff/schiewe, v.; uffgschowe, pp. 1.postpone; 2.procrastinate
uff/schinne, v.; uffgschunne, pp. abrade
uff/schitte, v.; uffgschitt, pp (eens --) take a drink
uff/schlagge, v.; uffgschlagge, pp. 1.open; 2.post advance in price; 3.raise (the frame of a building); 4.(en Eise --) shoe a horse; 5. (sich der Kopp --) abrade one's head by knocking it against
uff/schliesse, v.; uffgschlosse, pp. unlock
uff/schlitze, v.; uffgschlitzt, pp. slit open
uff/schmeisse, v.; uffschmisse, pp. 1.abrogate; 2.back out; 3.relinquish; 4.resign; 5.vomit
uff/schmelze, v.; uffgschmolze, pp. melt up
uff/schmicke, v.; uffgschmickt, pp. adorn
uff/schmutze, v.; uffgschmutzt, pp. 1.begrease; 2.sleek up
uff/schnabbe, v.; uffgschnappt, pp. tilt
uff/schnalle, v.; uffgschnallt, pp. 1.buckle on; 2.unbuckle
uff/schnebbe, v.; uffgschneppt, pp. pry up
uff/schneide, v.; uffgschnidde, pp. cut open or up
uff/schniere, v.; uffgschniert, pp. unlace
uff/schpaare, v.; uffgschpaart, pp. save
uff/schpaerre, v.; uffgschpaerrt, pp.; 1.open wide; 2.(es Maul --) (a) gape; (b) yawn
uff/schpanne, v.; uffgschpannt, pp. 1.open (an umbrella); 2.put up a line
uff/schparre, v.; uffgschpatt, pp. 1.economize; 2.open wide; 3.save
uff/schpiele, v.; uffgschpielt, pp. play up
uff/schpinne, v.; uffgschpinnt, pp. use up in spinning
uff/schpitze, v.; uffgschpitzt, pp (Duwack --) put tobacco up on the laths
uff/schplidde, v.; uffgschplitt, pp. split up
uff/schpraue, v.; uffgschpraut, pp. (sich --) ruffle the feathers (of a turkey)
uff/schpringe, v.; is uffgschprunge, pp. 1.burst open; 2.chap (of hands); 3.jump up
uff/schreiwe, v.; uffgschriwwe, pp. 1.charge; 2.record; 3.register; 4.write down
uff/schtachle, v. 1.incite; 2.stir up
uff/schtaerme, v.; uffgschtaermt, pp. rise in anger
uff/schtarre, v.; uffgschtarrt, pp. 1.agitate; 2.excite; 3.stir up
uff/schteche, v.; uffgschtoche, pp. open with a pointed instrument
uff/schtecke, v.; uffgschteckt; uffgschtocke, pp. 1.put up; 2.wager
uff/schteh, v.; uffgschtanne, pp. 1.set up; 2.stand open; 3.stand up
uff/schteibere, v.; uffgschteibert, pp. prop open or up
uff/schteige, v.; uffgschtigge, pp. 1.ascend; 2.come on (a thunderstorm); 3.rise
uff/schtelle, v.; uffgschtellt, pp. 1.erect; 2.put up; 3.stop (at an inn)
uff/schtickere, v.; uffgschtickert, pp. piece
uff/schtifde, v.; uffgschtift, pp. 1.egg on; 2.instigate;

uffgebleht

3.provoke
uff/schtiwwre, v.; uffgschtiwwert, pp. 1.flush (a bird); 2.rouse
uff/schtobbe, v.; uffgschtoppt, pp. clog
uff/schtosse, v.; uffgschtosse, pp. belch
uff/schtrecke, v.; uffgschtreckt, pp. stretch up
uff/schwelle, v.; uffgschwolle, pp. 1.bloat; 2.swell up
uff/schwetze, v.; uffgschwetzt, pp. 1.palm off on; 2.talk someone in to taking; 3.talk up (to a person)
uff/setze, v.; uffgsetzt, pp. 1.put on (a hat); 2.set up; 3.treat
uff/sitze, v.; uffgsotze, pp. 1.be convalescent; 2.sit up
uff/suche, v.; uffgsucht, pp. 1.look up; 2.search for
uff/waarde, v.; uffgewaart, pp. wait on
uff/wache, v.; uffgewacht, pp. wake up
uff/waerme, v.; uffgewaermt, pp. warm up
uff/waxe, v.; uffgwaxe, pp. 1.grow up; 2.mature
uff/wecke, v.; uffgeweckt, pp. 1.arise; 2.awaken; 3.rouse; 4.wake
uff/weeche, v.; uffgeweecht, pp. 1.soak; 2.soften by soaking
uff/weise, v.; uffgeweist, pp. show
uff/wenne, v.; uffgewennt, pp. 1.ted hay; 2.turn for drying
uff/wesche, v.; uffgewesche, pp. 1.scrub (a floor); 2.wash up
uff/wickle, v.; uffgewickelt, pp. 1.wrap; 2.untwine; 3.unwrap; 4.wind up
uff/wiehle, v.; uffgewiehlt, pp. root up
uff/wische, v.; uffgewischt, pp. (to make a big) spread for someone
uff/wolle, v.; uffgewollt, pp. want to get up
uff/yaage, v.; uffgeyaagt, pp. 1.chase from a lair; 2.drive out of bed
uff/zaahme, v.; uffgezaahmt, pp. bridle (a horse)
uff/zehle, v.; uffgezehlt,pp. 1.add (up); 2.count up
uff/zehre, v.; uffgezehrt, pp. 1.consume; 2.waste away
uff/ziege, v.; uffgezoge, pp. 1.bring up; 2.raise; 3.rear
uff/ziehe, v.; uffgezoge, pp. 1.raise; 2.train; 3.wind up
uff/ziggele, v.; uffgeziggelt, pp. put harness on a horse
uff/zwacke, v.; uffgewackt, pp. play a sharp trick upon
uff/zwinge, v.; uffgezwunge, pp. force upon
uff, adv. open
uff, prep. 1.at; 2.up; 3.upon
uff, prep., adv.; 1.on; 2.(-- Barigs kaafe) (to buy on) tick (on credit); 3.(-- der Brutzbank sitze) (a) pout; (b) sulk; 4.(-- der Schtell) immediately; 5.(-- der Schtutz) (a) (on the) spur of the moment; (b)suddenly; 6.(-- die Leng) (in the long) run; 7.(-- em Dapeet) on the point (of); 8.(-- em Grebsgang sei) (a) fail in health; (b) (to go) backward(s); 9.(-- em Weg) on the way; 10.(-- emol) (a) abruptly; (b) suddenly; 11.(-- en Aart wie) sort of; 12.(-- graad(e)wohl) haphazard(ly); 13.(-- Parebes) purposely; 14.(-- und ab geige) seesaw; 15. (ebbes -- die Daerr duh) place something for drying
uffe(e)mol, adv. 1.abruptly; 2.all at once; 3.suddenly
uffe, adv. open
Uffen(t)halt (der)n. whereabouts
uffenanner, adv. (on) top of one another
uffenbaar, adv. evident
uffgebindelt, adj. pregnant
uffgebleht, adj. bloated

Uu

uffgeblosse / umduh

uffgeblosse, adj. 1.bloated; 2.pregnant

uffgschafft, adj. excited

Uffgwaxaner (der)n.; Uffgwaxni, pl. adult

uffgwaxe, adj. adult

Uffhalding (die)n. 1.abode; 2.upkeep

Uffhebrieme (der)n. strap to rein up a horse's head

Ufflauerer (der)n. lurker

uffme = uff me on one

Uffmuntering (die)n. encouragement

uffne, adj. open

uffnemme mit Hand und Kuss receive (into the fellow-ship) with a handshake and kiss (the ritual greeting of the plain churches)

Uffnemmer (der)n. person who raked and bound the grain after the man with a grain-cradle

uffnich, adv. openly

Uffning (die)n. opening

uffre = uff re on her

uffrichdich, adj. 1.sincere; 2.upright; 3.true

Uffriehrer (der)n. insurgent

uffriehrisch, adj. 1.fractious (of a horse); 2.rebellious; 3.uneasy

uffriehrisch, adv. agitated

Uffrohr (der)n. 1.commotion; 2.uproar

Uffruhr (der, die)n. 1.uproar; 2.tumult

uffs = uff es on it

Uffsatz (der) n.; Uffsetz, pl. step (from one floor level to another)

Uffschpielbank (die)n. sink

Uffschpiellumbe (der)n. dishcloth

Uffschpielschissel (die)n. dish pan

Uffschpielwasser (es)n. dishwater

uffschtennich, adj. 1.provoked; 2.resentful

Uffschtosses (es)n. belching

uffsetzich, adj. 1.obstinate; 2.vexed

Uffwaarting (die)n. 1.hospitality; 2.waiting on

uffwaerts, adv. upwards

Uffwaxener (der)n.; Uffgwaxeni, pl. adult

Uhmet (es)n. 1.aftermath; 2.second crop of hay; 3.(-- mache) secure the second crop of hay

Uhr (die)n.; Uhre, pl. clock

uhr, adv. o'clock

Uhregsicht (es)n. clock dial

Uhrekaschde (der)n. clock case

Uhremacher (der)n.; Uhremacher, pl. 1.clock maker; 2.watchmaker

Uhreschpring (die)n. clock spring

Uhrewaerrick (es)n. works of a clock

Uhrezeeche (es)n.; Uhrezeeche, pl. hand of clock

Ulla (die)n. dim of Ulrike, celebrated in the "Ulla, Ulla ei" ballad

Ulme (die)n. elm

um/batzle, v.; umgebatzelt, pp. tumble over

um/blose, v.; umgeblose, pp. 1.blow down; 2.blow over

um/bluge, v.; umgeblugt, pp. turn with the plow

um/bringe, v.; umgebrocht, pp. 1.kill; 2.(sich --) commit suicide

um/draue, v.; umgedraut, pp. distrust

um/drehe, v.; umgedreht, pp. 1.revolve; 2.turn away; 3.turn around; 4.turn over; 5.twirl

um/faahre, v.; umgfaahre, pp. 1.drive over; 2.make a detour

um/falle, v.; umgfalle, pp. 1.fall down; 2.fall over; 3.tip

um/fasse, v.; umgfasst, pp. 1.measure into other containers; 2.twine about

um/geh, v.; umgange, pp. 1.go out of one's way; 2.handle; 3.make a detour; 4.manage

um/gnalle, v.; umgegnallt, pp. shoot down

um/hacke, v.; urnghackt, pp. cut down

um/henke, v.; umghonke, pp. enclose with curtains

um/kehre, v.; umgekehrt, pp. 1.invert; 2.reverse; 3.turn back; 4.turn around; 5.turn over

um/kumme, v.; is umkumme, pp. 1.perish; 2.be killed

um/mehe, v.; umgemeht, pp. mow down

um/niede, v.; umgeniet, pp. 1.clinch; 2.rivet

um/reisse, v.; umgerisse, pp. 1.demolish; 2.tear down

um/renne, v.; umgerennt, pp. 1.knock over; 2.upset

um/rolle, v.; umgerollt, pp. roll over

um/saege, v.; umgsaegt, pp. saw down

um/schiesse, v.; umschosse, pp. shoot down

um/schiewe, v.; umgschowe, pp. push over

um/schmeisse, v.; umgschmisse, pp. 1.throw down; 2.upset; 3.void an agreement; 4.vomit

um/schtaerze, v.; umgschtaertzt, pp. 1.fall over; 2.overturn; 3.tilt; 4.tumble; 5.upset

um/schtalle, v.; umgschtallt, pp. 1.change; 2.make other arrangements

um/schtatze, v.; umgschtatzt, pp. upset

um/schtilbe, v.; umgschtilpt, pp. 1.invert; 2.turn over (upside down)

um/schtosse, v.; umgschtosse, pp. 1.knock over; 2.overthrow

um/sehne, v.; umgsehne, pp. (sich --) 1.cast about; 2.look around; 3.seek

um/wandle, v.; umgewandelt, pp. transform

um/welse, v.; umgewelst, pp. 1.revolve; 2.overturn

um/yaage, v.; umgeyaagt, pp. blow down

um, prep.; 1.around; 2.(der Baam is --) the tree is down; 3.(ich geb nix -- die Aerwet) (a) I don't care for work; (b) I don't mind work; 4.(so -- vier Uhr) about four o'clock; 5.(-- ihr Wille) for her sake; 6.(-- sei Geld kumme) lose one's money

umarme, v.; umarmt, pp. 1.embrace; 2.hug

umbedenkt, adj. unexpected

umbehilfich, adj. 1.awkward; 2.helpless

umbeholfe, adj. helpless

umbekannt, adj. unfamiliar

umbekehrt, adj. unconverted

umbennich, adj. unruly

umbiege, v.; umgeboge, pp. bend over or down

umblessierlich, adj. 1.disagreeable; 2.unpleasant

umbreche, v.; umgebroche, pp. break down

umdrauisch, adj. distrustful

Umdrehung (die)n. rotation

umduh, v.; umgeduh, pp. 1.inquire; 2.look about; 3.look after

177

Uu

umenanner

umenanner, adv. around one another
Umens (die)n.; Umense, pl. 1.ant; 2.prismire
Umensepaad (der)n. track of ants in grass
Umfang (der)n. circumference
umfasse, v.; umfasst, pp. 1.embrace; 2.twine about
umfasse, v.; umgfasst, pp. measure into other containers
Umgang (der)n. 1.acquaintance; 2.intercourse
Umgangsschproch (die)n. vernacular
Umgeduld (die)n. impatience
umgeduldich, adj. impatient
Umgegend (die)n. 1.neighborhood; 2.surrounding country; 3.vicinity
umgeh, v.; umgange, pp (-- mit) have dealings with
umgenglich, adj. sociable
umgfarr, adv. about
Umglaawe (der)n. 1.disbelief; 2.unbelief
Umglick (es)n. misfortune
umgnicke, v.; umgegnickt, pp. bend and fall over without
breaking entirely
Umgraut (es)n. 1.undisciplined youth; 2.weed
Umgrees (die)n. 1.surrounding section; 2.periphery
umgsund, adj. 1.unhealthy; 2.unwell
umgwehnlich, adj. unusual
Umhang (der)n. curtain
umhendich, adj. unhandy
Umhenkel (es)n. window curtain
umher/laafe, v.; is umhergeloffe, pp. 1.gad; 2.wander
umher, adv. round
Umlaaf (der)n. 1.circulation; 2.whitlow
umlege, v.; umgelekt, pp. lay over or on the side
umleidich, adj. uncomfortable
umleidlich, adj. 1.disagreeable; 2.unlovable
umleie, v.; umgelegge, pp. lie flat (after having been
blown or knocked down)
umleitlich, adj. 1.disagreeable; 2.uncomfortabl
ummache, v.; umgemacht, pp. cut down (a tree)
Ummacht (die)n. swoon
ummanierlich, adj. unmannerly
um(m)echdich, adj. unconscious
ummechdich warre, v.; is ummechdich warre, pp. 1.faint;
2.swoon
ummenschlich, adj. inhuman
ummieglich, adj. impossible
Umrees (die)n. circuit
umringe, v.; umringt, pp. surround
Umruh (die)n. 1.restlessness; 2.unrest
umruhich, adj. restless
ums = um es around it
ums = um e (eens -- anner) one after the other
Umschlack (der)n. 1.cover; 2.wrapper
umschlagge, v.; umgschlagge, pp. 1.fold over; 2.knock
down
umschreiwe, v.; umschriwwe, pp. paraphrase
Umschtand (der)n.; Umschtende, pl. 1.condition;
2.circumstance
umschuldich, adj. 1.blameless; 2.guileless; 3.innocent

unbeweklich

umsehne, v.; umgsehne, pp. (eb mer sich -- kann) before
one is aware of it
umsunscht, adv. (in) vain
umvergleichlich, adv.; adj. incomparable
umverschtennich, adj. unreasonable
Umweg (der)n. detour
umwische, v.; umgewischt, pp. knock down
un(a)e(r)baermlich, adj. 1.extremely; 2.not to be endured; 3.terribly
un, conj. 1.and; 2.(-- so der gleiche); 3.(a) (-- so fatt);
(b) (-- so weiter); etcetera
unaardich, adj. 1.mischievous; 2.naughty; 3.unmannerly
Unaart (die)n. naughtiness
unabbeditlich, adj. 1.disagreeable to taste or smell; 2.not
appetizing
unabhengich, adj. independent
unachtsam, adj. careless
Unachtsamkeet (die)n. carelessness
unaehnlich, adj. 1.dissimilar; 2.unlike
unaerdraeglich, adj. intolerable
unaerfaahre, adj. inexperienced
Unaerfaahring (die)n. 1.ignorance; 2.verdancy
unaerheert, adj. unheard-of
unaerlaabt, adj. 1.illicit; 2.not permitted
unaerlebt, adv. unheard-of
unaermesslich, adj. immeasurable
unaerschprechlich, adj. inexpressible
unaerwaart, adj. unexpected
Unardning (die)n. disorder
unaschtendich, adj. unbecoming
unausschprechlich, adj. inexpressible
unbardeiisch, adj. 1.impartial; 2.neutral
unbaremhartzich, adj. 1.relentless; 2.unmerciful
unbarmhaerzich, adj. unmerciful
Unbarmhaerzichkeet (die)n. 1.cruelty; 2.unmercifulness
unbedacht, adj. 1.indiscrete; 2.thoughtless(ly); 3.without
thinking
unbedenkt, adj. 1.indiscrete; 2.thoughtless(ly); 3.without
thinking
unbegreiflich, adj. incomprehensible
unbehilf(l)ich, adj. 1.awkward; 2.helpless
unbehofft, adj. unexpected
unbeholfe, adj. 1.awkward; 2.helpless; 3.unhandy;
4.wooden
unbekannt, adj. 1.strange; 2.unfamiliar; 3.unknown
unbekehrt, adj. unconverted
unbekimmert, adj. indifferent
unbennich, adj. 1.uncontrollable; 2.untamable
unbequem, adj. uncomfortable
unbeschraue, adj. unnoticed
unbeschtimmt, adj. 1.doubtful; 2.dubious; 3.indefinite;
4.uncertain
unbeschtritte, adj. undisputed
unbestimmt, adj. uncertain
unbewechlich, adj. immovable
unbeweklich, adj. immovable

Uu

unblessierlich

unblessierlich, adj. 1.disagreeable; 2.unpleasant
unbrowiert, adj. untried
Undaedeli (es)n. 1.blemish; 2.flaw
Undank (der)n. ingratitude
undankbaar, adj. ungrateful
undeitlich, adj. 1.indistinct; 2.obscure; 3.vague
undenklich, adj. 1.immemorial; 2.unthinkable
unedlich, adj. ignoble
uneenich, adj. disagreeing
uneenich sei, v.; uneenich gewest, pp. disagree
Uneenichkeit (die)n. discord
unehrlich, adj. dishonest
Unehrlichkeet (die)n. dishonesty
unendeckt, adj. undiscovered
unendlich, adv. infinite
unerbaermlich, adj. unbearable
unerbaermlich, adv. terribly
unerlaabt, adj. not permitted
unermesslich, adj. 1.immeasurable; 2.immense
unerwaard, adj. unexpected
unewe, adj. uneven
unfaehich, adj. 1.incapable; 2.unable
Unfall (der)n.; Unfelle, pl. 1.accident; 2.mischance;
    3.mishap
unfehlbaar, adj. unfailing
Unflaat (der)n. 1.mischievous child; 2.nuisance
unflaet, adj. 1.mischievous; 2.nasty
unflatt, adj. mischievous
unfrehlich, adj. 1.disgruntled; 2.sour
unfreindlich, adj. 1.uncanny; 2.unfriendly; 3.unkind;
    4.unpleasant (of weather)
Unfruch (der)n. disorder
unfruchtbaar, adj. sterile
ung(e)faehr, adj. about
ungaern, adj. unwillingly
unge-eschdimiert, adj. not respected
ungebacke, adj. lacking common sense
ungebascht, adj. 1.rowdyish; 2.unbrushed
ungebore, adj. unborn
ungebutzt, adj. 1.uncleaned; 2.unmannerly
Ungeduld (die)n. impatience
ungeduldich, adj. impatient
ungeeschdimiert, adj. 1.not appreciated; 2.not respected
Ungeheier (es)n. monster
ungeheier, adj. 1.awfully; 2.huge; 3.immense;
    4.monstrous; 5.vast
ungehorsam, adj. disobedient (Old Order Mennonite
    usage)
Ungehorsamkeit (die)n. disobedience
ungelaernt, adj. illiterate
Ungemach (es)n. 1.burden; 2.discomfort
ungemietlich, adj. 1.uncanny; 2.unpleasant
ungerecht, adj. 1.unjust; 2.unrighteous
ungerechterweis, adv. unjustly
ungern, adv. unwilling
Ungeschtalt (es)n. deformed object

unnedarich

ungeschtiem, adj. 1.boisterous; 2.inclement
ungewehnlich, adj. uncommon
ungewiss, adj. uncertain
ungeziemt, adj. unbecoming
Ungeziffer (es)n. 1.bugs; 2.insects; 3.mob; 4.rabble;
    5.vermin
ungezogge, adj. 1.ill-bred; 2.unruly
ungfaahr, adj. unexpected
ungfarr, adv. about
unggfaehr, adj. about
unglaabich, adj. incredible
Unglaawe (der)n. 1.disbelief; 2.infidelity; 3.unbelief
unglaawich, adj. incredulous
ungleich, adj. 1.dissimilar; 2.unlike
Unglick (es)n. 1.accident; 2.misfortune
unglicklich, adj. 1.accidental; 2.meeting with an accident;
    3.unlucky; 4.wretched
Unglicksdaag (der)n. unlucky day
Unglicksoi (es)n. unusually small egg
unglor, adj. dim
ungraad, adj. 1.crooked; 2.odd; 3.uneven
Ungraut (es)n. 1.undisciplined youth; 2.weed
ungsalze, adj. unsalted
ungscheit, adj. 1.foolish; 2.unwise
ungschickt, adj. 1.awkward; 2.clumsy
ungsund, adj. 1.unhealthy; 2.unwell
ungut, adj (nix fer --) no offence I hope
Unheel (es)n. 1.harm; 2.mischief
unheemlich, adj. 1.creepy; 2.uncanny; 3.uneasy; 4.weird
Unheemlichkeit (die)n. weirdness
Unheil (es)n. mischief
unhendich, adj. unhandy
unkluch, adj. imprudent
Unkoschde (die)n., pl. costs
unleid(l)ich, adj. 1.disagreeable; 2.unbearable; 3.unlovable
unleserlich, adj. illegible
unmaessich, adj. intemperate
unmanierlich, adj. 1.absurd; 2.lacking common sense;
    3.unreasonable; 4.unmannerly
unmanierlich, adv.; adj. 1.impertinent; 2.impolite;
    3.unmannerly
Unmeeglichkeet (die)n. impossibility
unmenschlich, adj. 1.cruel; 2.inhuman
Unmieglichkeet (die)n. impossibility
unmietich, adj. displeased
Unnaame (der)n. nickname
unnadierlich, adj. unnatural
unne End, adv. infinite
unne Gwisse, adj. unconscionable
unne(re)nanner, adv. 1.among themselves; 2.between
    each other; 3.one below the other; 4.mutually
unne, adv. 1.below; 2.in a lower place
unne, prep. without
unnebei, adv. from below
unnedarich, adv. 1.through below; 2.(der Regge geht --)
    the rain is passing to the south

Uu

unnedraa   unrein

unnedraa, adv. 1.at the bottom; 2.beneath
unnedrauss, adv. in the lower part (geographically)
unnedrin, adv. 1.in below; 2.in the bottom
unnedrunner, adv. beneath
unneedich, adj. unnecessary
unnefehl, adj. without fail
unneher, prep. along the bottom
unnenaus, prep. out below
unnenei, prep. in below
unner/aerdisch, adj. underground
unner/bleiwe, v.; unnergebliwwe, pp. stay under (water)
unner/bluge, v.; unnergeblugt, pp. plow under (as a cover crop)
unner/dricke, v.; unnergedrickt, pp. 1.depress; 2.oppress; 3.repress; 4.suppress
unner/geh, v.; unnergange, pp. 1.set (of the sun); 2.sink
unner/hewe, v.; unnerghowe, pp. hold under
unner/lege, v.; unnergelekt, pp. lay (something) under (as a stone under a wheel to hold a wagon on a slope)
unner/nemme, v.; unnergenumme, pp. 1.attempt; 2.undertake
unner/schetze, v.; unnergschetzt, pp. 1.depreciate; 2.underrate
unner/schiewe, v.; unnergschowe, pp. push under
unner/schrecke, v.; unnergschreckt, pp. tuck under (as the end of the band in binding grain)
unner/schreiwe, v.; unnergschriwwe, pp. sign
unner/schteh, v. (sich --) 1.dare; 2.presume
unner/schtelle, v.; unnergschtellt, pp. place or set under
unner/schtitze, v.; unnergschtitzt, pp. 1.patronize; 2.support
unner/schtrecke, v.; unnergschtreckt, pp. tuck under (as the end of the band in binding grain)
unner/setze, v.; unnergsetzt, pp. set under
unner/suche, v.; unnergsucht, pp. 1.investigate; 2.examine
unner/zeichne, v. sign
unner, adj. lower
unner, prep. 1.among; 2.under; 3.underneath
unneraus, adv. out below
Unnerdaahn (der)n. underling
unnerdaenich, adj. subservient
Unnerdeel (es)n. lower part
Unnerdricker (der)n. oppressor
Unnerdrickung (die)n. oppression
unnerei, adj. (approaching) in below
unnererdisch, adj. underground
Unnergang (der)n. 1.downfall; 2.ruination; 3.setting
Unnergleeder (die)n., pl. 1.underclothes; 2.underwear
unnergraawe, v.; unnergegraawe, pp. undermine
Unnerhalt (der)n. maintenance
Unnerhemm (es)n.; Unnerhemmer, pl. undershirt
Unnerholz (es)n. underbrush
Unnerhosse (die)n. 1.drawers; 2.underpants
unneriwwer, adv. across down below
Unnerlehrer (der)n. tutor
Unnerleib (der)n. abdomen
unnerm = unner em under him or them

unnerme = unner me under one
unnern = unner en under him
unnernemme, v.; unnernumme, pp. (sich --) attempt
unnernemme, v.; unnernumme, pp. undertake
Unnernemmung (die)n. 1.enterprise; 2.undertaking
unnerraus, adv. out below
unnerre = unner re under her
Unnerricht (der) n. 1. instruction; 2. (in der -- geh) attend catechetical instruction
Unnerrichtslehr (die)n. catechetical instruction
Unnerrock (der)n.; Unnerreck, pl. 1.petticoat; 2.under jacket; 3.underwear
unners = unner es under it
unners(ch)ich, adj. downwards
unnerschetze, v.; unnergschetzt, pp. underrate
Unnerschitt (der)n. difference
unnerschittlich, adj. 1.different; 2.various
unnerschlechdich, adj. undershot
unnerschreiwe, v.; unnerschriwwe, pp. sign
Unnerschreiwer (der)n. signer
Unnerschrift (die)n. signature
unnerschteh, v. presume
Unnerschtehende (im) when the horns of the moon are turned downward
unnerschtitze, v.; unnerschtitzt, pp. 1.patronize; 2.support
unnerscht's ewwerscht, adv., adj. 1.topsy-turvy; 2.upside down
unnerschuche, v.; unnersucht, pp. research
Unnersuchung (die)n. 1.inquiry; 2.investigation; 3.trial
unneruff, adv. up from below
unnerum, adv. around below
unnerwege losse, v.; unnerwege gelosst, pp. 1.refrain from; 2.stop
unnerwegs, adv. on the way
unnerweils, adv. 1.meantime; 2.meanwhile
Unnerwelt (die)n. hades
unnerzeiche, v. sign
Unnerzuck (der)n. undercurrent
unnes = unne es without it
unnewedder, adv. 1.against below; 2.at the bottom
unni Verseimes, adv. 1.abruptly; 2.suddenly
unni/duh, v.; unnigeduh, pp. do without
unni, prep. without
unnich, prep. 1.among; 2.below; 3.beneath; 4.under; 5.without
unnichem = unnich em under him
unnichme = unnich me under one (but not "without a")
unnichre = unnich re under her (but not "without a" [fem])
unnichs = unnich es 1.under it; 2.without it
unnilengscht, adv. recently
unnitz(ich), adj. 1.good for nothing; 2.mischievous
unnitz, adj. good for nothing
unordich, adj. impolite
Unrecht (es)n. injustice
unrechtmaessich, adj. illegal
unreif, adj. immature
unrein, adj.; 1.unclean; 2.(--i zeit) menstrual period

Uu

unrichdich | **Uumeeglichkeet**

unrichdich, adj. false
Unrichdichkeet (die)n. inaccuracy
Unrot (der)n. 1.dirt; 2.rubbish; 3.undesirable person or animal
Unruh (die)n. 1.escapement (of a watch); 2.restlessness; 3.unrest
unruhich, adj. 1.restless; 2.uneasy
uns, pron. 1.ourself; 2.ourselves; 3.us
unschaedlich, adj. harmless
Unscheeheet (die)n. homeliness
unschicklich, adj. 1.inconvenient; 2.improper
unschtaerblich, adj. immortal
unschtaetich, adj. 1.inconstant; 2.restless
Unschuld (die)n. innocence
Unschuldich Kindelsdaag (der)n. Innocents' Day (Dec. 28)
unschuldich, adj. 1.blameless; 2.guileless; 3.innocent
unsereem, pron. 1.ourself; 2.ourselves
unsereems, pron. such as we
unsereens, pron. 1.ourself; 2.ourselves; 3.such as we
unsicher, adj. 1.precarious; 2.uncertain
Unsinn (der)n. nonsense
unsinnich, adj. 1.nonsensical; 2.senseless
uns(r)er(s), pron. 1.our; 2.ours
unsri, pron. 1.our; 2.ours
Unsumm (die)n. immense amount
unverdeelt, adj. undivided
unverdient, adj. undeserved
unverdrosse, adj. 1.diligent; 2.unawed; 3.undeterred; 4.with alacrity
unvergesslich, adj. unforgettable
unvergleichlich, adj. incomparable
unvergunnisch, adj. uncharitable
unverhofft, adj. unexpected
unverlessich, adj. unreliable
unverletzt, adj. unhurt
unverninfdich, adj. 1.foolish; 2.unreasonable
Unvernunft (die)n. 1.ignorance; 2.lack of reason
unverschaemlich, adj. impudent
unverschaemt, adj. impudent
unverschrocke, adj. undismayed
unverschtaert, adj. undisturbed
Unverschtand (der)n. 1.absurdity; 2.(lack of) sense; 3.senseless person
Unverschtang (der)n. 1.absurdity; 2.lack of sense
unverschtennich, adj. 1.absurd; 2.lacking common sense; 3.unreasonable
Unverschtennichkeit (die)n. 1.absurdity; 2.lack of sense
unversehne, adj. unaware
unversichert, adj. unprotected
unverzaacht, adj. 1.intrepid; 2.undismayed
unverzaagt, adj. courageous
unverzaakt, adj. 1.intrepid; 2.undismayed
unvorsichdich, adj. 1.careless; 2.improvident; 3.thoughtless
unwaahr, adj. untrue
Unwaahret (die)n. untruth
Unwaahrheet (die)n. untruth
Unwaahrheit (die)n. untruth

unwaahrscheinlich, adv. 1.improbable; 2.unlikely
Unwedder (es)n. 1.storm; 2.stormy weather
unwillens, adj. unwilling
unwillich, adj. loath
unwissend, adj. 1.ignorant; 2.unknowingly
unwohl, adj. 1.unhealthy; 2.unwell; 3.sick
unwohl, adv. not well
unwohr, adj. untrue
Unzaahl (die)n. great number
unzaehlich, adj. numberless
unzeidich, adj. 1.immature; 2.unripe
unzichtich, adj. 1.dissolute; 2.immoral
Unzucht (die)n. naughtiness
unzufridde, adj. 1.discontent; 2.dissatisfied
unzugenglich, adj. inapproachable
Urenkel (der)n. great grandchild
Urgrossdaddi (der)n. great grandfather
Urgrossmutter (die)n. great grandmother
Urgrossvadder (der)n. great grandfather
Urhewer (der)n. 1.instigator; 2.originator
Ursach (die)n.; Ursache, pl. 1.cause; 2.incentive; 3.reason
urschpringlich, adv. 1.from the beginning; 2.originally
Urschprung (der)n. 1.origin; 2.source
Urteil (es)n. 1.judgement; 2.sentence
urteile, v.; geurteilt, pp. 1.judge; 2.sentence
Urvatter (der)n. forefather
uscht, adv. 1.just; 2.just now; 3.only
uubaerschdich, adj. uncivil
uubaerschtich, adj. uncivil
uubarmhaerzich, adj. unmerciful
uubedenkt, adj. inadvertently
uubeholfe, adj. helpless
uubekannt, adj. unknown
uubekehrt, adj. unconverted
uubekimmert, adj. careless
uubennich, adj. 1.uncontrollable; 2.untamable
uubeschreiblich, adj. indescribable
uubewusst, adj. in ignorance
uublessierlich, adj. unpleasant
Uudank (der)n. ingratitude
uuehrlich, adj. dishonest
uugerecht, adj. 1.unjust; 2.unrighteous
Uuglaawe (der)n. 1.disbelief; 2.unbelief
uuglablich, adj. incredible
uugscheit, adj. 1.foolish; 2.unwise
uugschickt, adj. 1.awkward; 2.clumsy
uugsund, adj. 1.unhealthy; 2.unwell
uuheemlich, adj. 1.creepy; 2.uncanny; 3.weird
uuhendich, adj. 1.inconvenient; 2.unhandy
uuleidich, adj. 1.disagreeable; 2.uncomfortable
Uumacht (die)n. swoon
uumanieerlich, adj. impolite
uumanierlich, adj. unmannerly
uumechdich, adj. 1.in a faint; 2.swooning
uumeeglich, adj. impossible
Uumeeglichkeet (die)n. impossibility

Uu

Uumensch

Uumensch (der)n. 1.brute; 2.monster
uumieglich, adj. impossible
Uumieglichkeet (die)n. impossibility
Uurecht (es)n. injustice
uuschuldich, adj. 1.blameless; 2.innocent
uuvergenglich, adj. 1.everlasting; 2.immortal
uuvergunnisch, adj. 1.envious; 2.uncharitable
uuvermeidlich, adj. inevitably
Uuwedder (es)n. 1.storm; 2.stormy weather
Uuzaahl (die)n. immense number
Uuzucht (die)n. 1.noise; 2.rumpus; 3.unseemliness
Uwing (die)n. 1.disturbance; 2.noise

Uwing

Vv

Vaddel   verbaerge

Vaddel (der) (-- Daaler)n. quarter ($0.25)

Vaddel (es)n. 1.advantage; 2.gain; 3.quarter (1/4)

Vaddelball (en)n. 1/4 barrel

Vaddelpund (es)n. quarter of a pound

Vaddelschtunn (die)n. quarter of an hour

vaddelyaerich, adv. quarterly

Vadder (der)n. father

vaddere, v.; gvaddert, pp. 1.adopt; 2.(sich --) resemble one's father

vadderhand, adv. 1.(in) advance; 2.previously

Vadderland (es)n. fatherland

vadderlich, adj. fatherly

Vaddermard (der)n. patricide

Vaddernaus (es)n. paternoster

Vadderunser (es)n. 1.Lord's Prayer; 2.paternoster

Vaddle (es)n. 1.advantage; 2.gain

vadem, adv. previously

Vaerdel (der) (-- Daaler)n. quarter ($0.25)

Vaerdel (es)n. quarter (1/4)

vaerri, prep. 1.front (in a vehicle, room or crowd with a verb of motion); 2.forward

vaers(ch)ich, adj. forward

Vaersch(t) (der)n. 1.stanza; 2.verse

Va(e)rtel (der)n. 1.advantage; 2.knack

Vammiddaag (der)n. forenoon

vanne-druff, adv. on the front part

vanne, adv. 1.before; 2.in front

vannebei, adv. (coming) from the front

vannedraa, adv. 1.at the head; 2.ahead

vannedraus, adv. 1.in front; 2.out front

vannedrin, adv. in the front part of

vanneher, adv. 1.ahead; 2.(by way of) preface

vannehie, adv. to the front

vannenaus/bezaa(h)le, v.; vannenausbezaa(h)lt, pp. pay in advance

vannenaus/faahre, v.; vannenausgfaahre, pp. 1.drive ahead; 2.drive at the head

vannenaus/geh, v.; vannenausgange, pp. leave by the front way

vannenaus/reide, v.; vannenausgeridde, pp. ride in advance

vannenaus/saage, v. vannenausgsaat, pp. 1.predict; 2.tell in advance

vannenaus/schicke, v.; vannenausgschickt, pp. send on before

vannenaus/sehne, v.; vannenausgsehne, pp. foresee

vannenaus/wisse, v.; vannenausgewisst, pp. know in advance

vannenaus/yaage, v.; vannenausgyaagt, pp. 1.chase out the front way; 2.chase ahead; 3.drive out at the head of

vannenaus, adv. 1.ahead; 2.in advance; 3.beforehand; 4.out by the front way

vannenei, adv. 1.in by the front way; 2.into the front

Vannenewegaul (der)n. the off horse of the two leaders

vanneniwwer, adv. (crossing) over in front

vannenuff, adv. 1.up by the front; 2.up in front

vannerei, adv. in by the front way

vannerum, adv. 1.round (about) in front; 2.around by the front way

vanneweck, adv. 1. before everything else; 2. (taken or collected) in advance

vannewedder, adv. against in front

vannre = vanne re in front of her

vannrem = vanne em in front of him

var, adv. 1.ago; 2.before

Varscht (der)n. verse

vartelhaft, adj. advantageous

vatzeh, adj.; pron. fourteen

vatzich, adj.; pron. forty

vedder, adj. 1.fore; 2.front

Vedderbeh (es)n.; Vedderbeh, pl. foreleg

Vedderfiess (die)n. forefeet

Veddergschar (es)n. harness of the lead horse

vedderscht, adj. 1.first; 2.foremost; 3.front

Vedderschunke (der)n. ham shoulder

Vedderschunkefleesch (es)n. shoulder (ham)

Veggelche (es)n. little bird

Veggelmischt (der)n. 1.droppings of birds; 2.guano

Veggli (es)n.; Vegglin, pl. little bird

Veilche (es)n. violet

Veiolich (die)n. violet

velleicht, adv. perhaps

Vellich Diener (der)n. Bishop (Old Order Amish usage)

vellich, adj. fully

vendere, v.; gvendert, pp. 1.risk; 2.venture; 3.(sich --) (a) risk; (b) venture

Vendu (die)n. auction

Vendugroier (der)n. auctioneer

ver, adv. ago

verachde, v.; veracht, pp. despise

Verachdung (die)n. contempt

veracht, adj. despised

veraerre; v.; veraerrt, pp. (sich --) go astray

veraerwe, v.; veraerbt, pp. bequeath

veraeryere; v. (sich --) to be vexed

veraeryerlich, adj. 1.provoking; 2.vexatious

Veraeryernis (die)n. vexation

veraeryert, adj. angry (bees)

veraiyerlich, adj. vexatious

veralders, adv. 1.formerly; 2.in olden times; 3.of yore

veralt, adj. timeworn

verantwarte, v.; verantwart, pp. 1.answer for; 2.(sich --) justify oneself

verantwartlich, adj. accountable

Verantwartlichkeet (die)n. accountability

verardne, v.; verardent, pp. 1.enact; 2.order

Verardning (die)n. 1.order; 2.regulation

verarme, v.; verarmt, pp. become poverty stricken

veraryere, v.; veraiyert, pp. vex

verbabble; v.; verbabbelt, pp. (sich --) 1.(to blab out a) secret; 2.talk too long

verbacke, v.; verbacke, pp. use up in baking

verbaerge, v.; verborge, pp. conceal

183

Vv

verbamble

verbamble, v.; verbambelt, pp. 1.fool away; 2.neglect; 3.squander money

verbarge, v.; verbarkt, pp. give on credit

verbasse, v.; verbasst, pp. 1.neglect; 2.overlook; 3.pass in cards

verbatsche, v.; verbatscht, pp. botch

verbaue, v.; verbaut, pp. build up closely

verbei/bringe, v.; verbeigebrocht, pp. bring past

verbei/dreiwe, v.; verbeigedriwwe, pp. drive past

verbei/faahre, v.; verbeigfaahre, pp. drive past (in a vehicle)

verbei/fiehre, v.; verbeigfiehrt, pp. lead past

verbei/fliege, v.; verbeigfloge, pp. fly past

verbei/geh, v.; verbeigange, pp. pass

verbei/kenne, v.; verbeigekennt, pp. be able to get past

verbei/kumme, v.; verbeikumme, pp. pass by

verbei/laafe, v.; verbeigeloffe, pp. walk past

verbei/losse, v.; verbeigelosst, pp. allow to pass

verbei/reide, v.; verbeigeridde, pp. ride past

verbei/renne, v.; verbeigerennt, pp. rush past

verbei/schiesse, v.; verbeigschosse, pp. rush past

verbei/schiewe, v.; verbeigschowe, pp. push past

verbei/schleefe, v.; verbeigschleeft, pp. drag past

verbei/schleiche, v.; verbeigschliche, pp. sneak past

verbei/schtolpere, v.; verbeigschtolpert, pp. stumble past

verbei/sei, v.; verbeigewest, pp. be over

verbei/yaage, v.; verbeigeyaagt, pp. dash past

verbei, adv. 1.bygone; 2.over; 3.past; 4.past (in telling time); 5.finished

verbeigehend, adj. passing

verbeisse, v.; verbisse, pp. 1.chew up; 2.crush with the teeth; 3.gnaw at

verbelze, v.; verbelzt, pp. 1.beat with the fist; 2.crush; 3.pommel

verbemble, v.; verbembelt, pp. 1.fool away; 2.neglect; 3.squander money; 4.waste time; 5.(geld --) squandermoney

verbessre, v.; verbessert, pp. 1.amend; 2.better; 3.improve; 4.reform

Verbessring (die)n. improvement

verbiddert, adj. embittered

verbiede, v.; verbodde, pp. 1.forbid; 2.prohibit

verbiege, v.; verboge, pp. bend out of shape

verbinne, v.; verbunne, pp. 1.bind; 2.combine; 3.engage; 4. join; 5. oblige; 6.tie up; 7.unite; 8.(sich --) obligate oneself

Verbinnerei (die)n. uniting of new and old members of Grundsau lodge

Verbinnung (die)n. 1.compact; 2.junction

verblaschdert schmiere, v.; verblaschdert gschmiert, pp. smear all over

verblatsche, v.; verblatscht, pp. 1.blab out a secret; 2.splash with mud

verblaud(e)re, v.; verblaudert, pp. 1.lead astray; 2.over-persuade; 3.(sich --) (a) (to blab out a) secret; (b) talk too long

verblaudre losse; v. (sich --) permit oneself to be persuaded

verdaue

verblenne, v.; verblennt, pp. 1.blind; 2.dazzle

Verblennerei (die)n. 1.illusion; 2.witchcraft; 3.witchery

verbleschdere, v.; verbleschdert, pp. 1.overdo (in plastering or the use of salve); 2.plaster up

verblicke, v.; verblickt, pp. pluck (to pieces)

verbliehe, v.; verblieht, pp. stop blooming

verblieht, adj. faded

verbliffe, v.; verblifft, pp. 1.disconcert; 2.nonplus

verblosse, v.; verblosse, pp. pass over

verblotze, v.; verblotzt, pp. 1.bruise by falling; 2.crush by falling

verblude; v.; verblut, pp. (sich --) 1.besmear with blood; 2.bleed

verbluffe, v.; verblufft, pp. nonplus

verblummt, adj. covered with flowers or designs

verbobbelt, adj. pampered

verbobble, v.; verbobbelt, pp. 1.baby; 2.coddle; 3.pamper

verboge, adj. bent

Verborge (es)n. 1.concealed; 2.secret

Verbrauch (der)n. 1.consumption; 2.use

verbrauche, v.; verbraucht, pp. use up

Verbreche (es)n. 1.crime; 2.offence

verbreche, v.; verbroche, pp. break (into pieces)

Verbrecher (der)n.; Verbrecher, pl. 1.criminal; 2.felon

verbrechlich, adj. fragile

verbreckle, v.; verbreckelt, pp. break into small pieces

verbreede, v.; verbreet, pp. spread

verbreite, v.; verbreit, pp. spread

verbrenne, v.; verbrennt, pp. 1.be consumed by flames; 2.burn up; 3.suffer from burning

verbriehe, v.; verbrieht, pp. 1.over scald (a hog or fowl); 2.scald

verbriet, adj. spoiled (of an egg that has been set too long; of plants)

verbriggele, v.; verbriggelt, pp. 1.beat; 2.cudgel

verbrillt, adj. given to crying

verbringe, v.; verbrocht, pp. squander

verbrunse, v.; verbrunst, pp. bepiss

verbrutzt, adj. prone to pout

verbuckere, v.; verbuckert, pp. 1.botch; 2.mar; 3.ruin; 4.spoil

verbutzt, adj. stunted

verdaage, v.; verdaagt, pp. adjourn

verdabbe, v.; verdappt, pp. trample

Verdacht (der)n. suspicion

verdaerblich, adj. pernicious

verdamme, v.; verdammt, pp. damn

Verdammnis (die)n. damnation

verdanke, v.; verdankt, pp. 1.(to have to) thank for; 2.owe to

verdappe; v.; verdappt, pp. (sich --) 1.give oneself away; 2.lose one's way

verdarebt, adv. very

verdarewe, adj. spoiled

verdarewe, v.; verdarewe, pp. 1.botch; 2.ruin; 3.spoil

verdarre, v.; verdatt, pp. wither

verdaschde, v.; verdascht, pp. die from thirst

verdatt, adj. 1.dried up; 2.withered

verdaue, v.; verdaut, pp. digest

Vv

Verdauung

Verdauung (die)n. digestion
verdechdich, adj. suspicious
verdeele, v.; verdeelt, pp. 1.distribute; 2.divide up; 3.part; 4.separate from; 5.share
Verdeelung (die)n. division
verdeffendiere; v.; verdeffendiert, pp. (sich --) 1.excuse or defend oneself; 2.insist; 3.justify oneself
verdeihenkert, adv. 1.deucedly; 2.enormously; 3.very
verdeiwelt, adj. 1.devilish(ly); 2.very
verdenke, v.; verdenkt, pp. 1.blame for; 2.take amiss
Verdi(e)nscht (der)n. 1.earnings; 2.pay; 3.reward; 4.wage(s)
verdiene, v.; verdient, pp. earn
verdilye, v.; verdilgt, pp. 1.destroy; 2.exterminate (weeds); 3.obliterate
verdinfdich, adj. sensible
verdinge; v.; verdingt, pp. (sich --) hire out
verdinschtlich, adj. meritorious
verdokdere, v.; verdokdert, pp. spend with doctors
verdollt, adv. 1.confoundedly; 2.deucedly
verdolmetsche, v.; verdolmetscht, pp. interpret
verdopple, v.; verdoppelt, pp. 1.double; 2.reduplicate
verdottle; v.; verdottelt, pp. (sich --) shit in one's pants
verdraage, v.; verdraage, pp. 1.abort; 2.agree with (of food); 3.miscarry; 4.fit well
Verdraue (es)n. 1.have confidence; 2.trust
verdraue, v.; verdraut, pp. 1.have confidence; 2.trust
verdrauensvoll, adj. 1.reliable; 2.trusting
verdraulich, adj. 1.insinuatingly; 2.reliable
verdrecke, v.; verdreckt, pp. 1.soil; 2. (sich --) soil one's person or clothes
verdrede, v.; verdrede, pp. 1.represent; 2.trample on
verdrehe, v.; verdreht, pp. 1.bend; 2.distort; 3.turn away; 4.turn the wrong way; 5.twist; 6.wrench
verdreiwe, v.; verdriwwe, pp. 1.banish; 2.drive away; 3.drive off; 4.exterminate
verdribble, v.; verdribbelt, pp. 1.mark by stepping on; 2.trample down
verdricke, v.; verdrickt, pp. 1.crush; 2.mash; 3.press; 4.squeeze
verdrickle, v.; verdrickelt, pp. 1.be forgotten; 2.die out; 3.dry up; 4.fail to materialize
verdriele, v.; verdrielt, pp. spill water (all over the floor)
verdriesse, v.; verdrosse, pp. 1.displease; 2.offend; 3.vex
verdriesslich, adj. 1.provoking; 2.snappish; 3.troublesome; 4.vexatious; 5.vexed
verdrillt, v.; verdrillt, pp. spill water (all over the floor)
verdrisslich, adj. tedious
verdroddle; v.; verdroddelt, pp. (sich --) be anxious or solicitous
verdrosse, adj. offended
Verdruss (der)n. bad feelings
verduckle, v.; verduckelt, pp. (to keep) secret
verduh, v.; verduh, pp. squander
verdunisch, adj. 1.squandering; 2.wasteful
verdunkle, v.; verdunkelt, pp. darken
verdunnere, v.; verdunnert, pp. waste money or posses-

Vergang

sions riotously
verduppt, adj. 1.dotted; 2.specked
verdutze, v.; verdutzt, pp. ruin
verdutzt, adj. 1.despised; 2.mopish; 3.sheepish; 4.spoiled
vereeniche, v.; vereenicht, pp. 1.combine; 2.unify; 3.unite
vereewiche, v.; vereewicht, pp. perpetuate
verehre, v.; verehrt, pp. 1.adore; 2.honor; 3.revere; 4.venerate
Verehrung (die)n. veneration
Vereinichde Brieder (die)n., pl. United Brethern (church)
verekelt, adj. disgusted
verelende, v.; verelendt, pp. pine away in misery
verennere, v.; verennert, pp. 1.alter; 2.change; 3.vary
Verennering (die)n. 1.alteration; 2.change
verennerlich, adj. 1.changeable; 2.variable
Verennerung (die)n. 1.alteration; 2.change
verewiche, v.; verewicht, pp. perpetuate
verewicht, adj. 1.deceased; 2.late; 3.of blessed memory
verfaahre, v.; verfaahre, pp. 1.act; 2.crush by driving over; 3.handle; 4.proceed
Verfall (der)n. ruin
verfalle, v.; verfalle, pp. 1.be due; 2.fall to pieces; 3.(go to) ruin
verfaule, v.; verfault, pp. 1.decay; 2.rot
verfault, adj. rotten
verfehle, v.; verfehlt, pp. 1.fail; 2.miss
verfelsche, v.; verfelscht, pp. 1.adulterate; 2.falsify
Verfelschung (die)n. adulteration
verfiehre, v.; verfiehrt, pp. 1.lead astray; 2.mislead; 3.seduce
Verfiehrer (der)n. 1.seducer; 2.tempter
verfinschdere, v.; verfinschdert, pp. 1.eclipse; 2.obscure
verfinschdert, adj. eclipsed
verflammt, adj. 1.awful(ly); 2.confounded(ly) Euphemistic for verdammt and verflucht (partaking of the form of each word)
verflecke, v.; verfleckt, pp. 1.blot; 2.soil; 3.spot
verflicke, v.; verflickt, pp. (to put a) patch on
verflickt, adj. 1.confounded(ly); 2.deuced(ly)
verfliege, v.; verflogge, pp. 1.pass away; 2.vanish
verfliesse, v.; verflosse, pp. pass (of time)
verflixt, adj. 1.confounded(ly); 2.deuced(ly)
verfluche, v.; verflucht, pp. 1.curse; 2.swear
verfochde, adj. 1.continually involved in quarrels; 2.quarrelsome
verfolge, v.; verfolgt, pp. persecute
verfranselt, adj. fringed
verfresse, adj. gluttonous
verfresse, v.; verfresse, pp. 1.devour; 2.spend for dainties; 3.squander on food
verfriere, v.; verfrore, pp. freeze
verfuggere, v.; verfuggert, pp. squander
vergaffe; v.; vergafft, pp. (sich --) 1.be mistaken in; 2.captivated by good looks; 3.loiter; 4.stare at
Vergang (der)n (im --) passing away

Vv

Vergange(n)heit   verhext

Vergange(n)heit (die)n. past
vergange, adv. 1.bygone; 2.past
vergaxt, adj. talkative
vergebens, adv. in vain
vergeblich, adj. 1.in vain; 2.unavailing
vergeh, v.; vergange, pp. 1. dissolve; 2.cease to exist;
    3.pass over; 4.elapse; 5.dispel
vergelde, v.; vergolde, pp. 1.reward; 2.give tit for tat
vergelschdere, v.; vergelschdert, pp. 1.confuse;
    2.flbbergast; 3.frighten; 4.terrify
vergelse, v.; vergelst, pp. 1.castrate; 2.geld
vergelte, v.; vergolte, pp. 1.give tit for tat; 2.repay;
    3.reward
vergenglich, adj. 1.soluble; 2.transient
vergesse, v.; vergesse, pp. 1.forget; (sich --) make a
    blunder
vergesslich, adj. forgetful
Vergessmichnet (die)n. forget-me-not
vergewens, adv. in vain
vergewwe, v.; vergewwe, pp. 1.forgive; 2.pardon
Vergewwing (die)n. forgiveness
vergiesse, v.; vergosse, pp (blut --) shed blood
vergifte, v.; vergift, pp. poison
verglaage, v.; verglaagt, pp. 1.accuse; 2.make a com-
    plaint against; 3.sue at court; 4.(sich --) complain
vergleede; v.; vergleedt, pp. (sich --) disguise oneself
Vergleich (der)n. comparison
vergleiche, v.; vergliche, pp. 1.compare; 2.liken
vergleichlich, adj. 1.comparable; 2.similar
Vergleichnis (es)n. picture
verglennere, v.; verglennert, pp. make smaller
vergnawwere, v.; vergnawwert, pp. nibble at
vergnechere, v.; vernechert, pp. ossify
vergnibbe, v.; vergnippt, pp. knot
vergniechlich, adj. 1.contented; 2.ennuied
vergniecht, adj. 1.cheerful; 2.content; 3.joyful; 4.merry
Vergniege (der)n. 1.contentment; 2.pleasure
vergniege; n.; vergniecht, pp. (sich --) amuse oneself
vergnipple, v.; vergnippelt, pp. 1.beat; 2.club
vergnoddelt, adj. knotted
vergnoddle, v.; vergnoddelt, pp. 1.entangle; 2.knot up
vergnootsche, v.; vergnootscht, pp. 1.fondle; 2.soil or
    mess by handling
vergolde, v.; vergoldt, pp. gild
vergraage, v.; vergraage, pp. 1.agree with (of food);
    2.bear; 3.endure
vergraawe, v.; vergraawe, pp. 1.bury; 2.dig a hole in the
    ground with an implement or by burrowing; 3.inter
Vergraawes (es)n. burial
vergrache, v.; vergracht, pp. burst with a loud report
Vergraebnis (es)n. burial
vergratze, v.; vergratzt, pp. 1.mar (by cutting); 2.scratch;
    3.spoil by scratching
vergratzt, adj. scratched
vergraunse; v.; vergraunst, pp. (sich --) complain irritably
vergreckse; v.; vergreckst, pp. (sich --) 1.complain; 2.croak

vergreesere, v.; vergreesert, pp. 1.enlarge; 2.magnify
Vergreeseringsglaas (es)n. 1.magnifying glass; 2.microscope
vergribbelt, adj. deformed
vergribble, v.; vergribbelt, pp. cripple
vergrimmle, v.; vergrimmelt, pp. crumble
vergripple, v.; vergrippelt, pp. 1.cripple; 2.maim
vergrische, adj. (prone to) scream (or cry)
vergritzle, v.; vergritzelt, pp. 1.cover with scribbling;
    2.waste in scribbling
vergrooze, v.; vergroozt, pp. 1.become moldy; 2.mold
vergrumple, v.; vergrumpelt, pp. crumple
vergruschde; v.; vergruscht, pp. (sich --) become crusty
    or encrusted
vergrutze, v.; vergrutzt, pp. mar in cutting
vergucke; v.; verguckt, pp. (sich --) 1.become infatuated;
    2.get a wrong impression from looking
vergunne, v.; vergunnt, pp. 1.begrudge; 2.envy
vergunnisch, adj. 1.begrudging; 2.envious; 3.jealous
vergunnt, adj. envied
vergwetscht, adj. bruised
verhacke, v.; verhackt, pp. chop to pieces
verhaerte, v.; verhaert, pp. harden
verhafdich, adv. 1.indeed; 2.really; 3.truly
verhaffdich, adj. 1.decidedly; 2.really
verhafte, v.; verhaft, pp. arrest
verhaftich, adj. 1.actually; 2.certainly; 3.really; 4.truly;
    5.veracious
verhalde; v.; verhalde, pp. (sich --) refrain
verhammere, v.; verhammert, pp. hammer to pieces
verhammle, v.; verhammelt, pp. 1.bedraggle; 2. (sich --)
    bedraggle one's clothes
verhandelbaar, adv. negotiable
verhandle, v.; verhandelt, pp. 1.sell off; 2.trade off
verharde, v.; verhardt, pp. harden
verhaschble; v. (sich --) 1.get entangled; 2.make awk-
    ward movements
verhasse, v.; verhasst, pp. despise
verhasst, adj. 1.despised; 2.hated
verhaue, v.; verhaut, pp. beat up
verhause, v.; verhaust, pp. 1.botch; 2.destroy; 3.ruin;
    4.soil; 5.soil diapers
verhechle, v.; verhechelt, pp. 1.haul over the coals; 2.heckle
Verheer (es)n. reprimand
verheere, v.; verheert, pp. 1.devastate; 2.give a hearing;
    3.reprimand
verhehle, v.; verhehlt, pp. conceal
verheide, v.; verheit, pp. prevent
verheiere; v.; verheiert, pp. (sich --) marry
verheilt, adj. prone to cry
verheire, v.; verheiert, pp. change (one's name) by marrying
Verheltnis (es)n. relation
verhenke, v.; verhonke, pp. bedeck (with ribbons, etc.)
verhenkert, adj. 1.confoundedly; 2.devilishly
verhensle, v.; verhenselt, pp. 1.haul over the coals; 2.shame
verhexe, v.; verhext, pp. bewitch
verhext, adj. bewitched

Vv

verhiete

verhiete, v.; verhiet, pp. 1.avoid; 2.prevent
verhinnere, v.; verhinnert, pp. 1.hinder; 2.impede; 2.prevent
Verhinnerung (die)n. prevention
verhitze, v.; verhitzt, pp. overheat
verhopbasse, v.; verhopbasst, pp. 1.miss; 2.neglect; 3.overlook
verhopple; v.; verhoppelt, pp. (sich --) get one's feet entangled
verhuddelt, adj. 1.confused; 2.(en)tangled; 3.in confusion; 4.mixed up;
verhuddle, v.; verhuddelt, pp. 1.confuse; 2.(en)tangle
verhungere, v.; verhungert, pp. starve
verhungert, adj. emaciated
verhunse, v.; verhunst, pp. 1.botch; 2.ruin; 3.spoil
verhure, v.; verhurt, pp. waste one's living with harlots
verhutzelt, adj. 1.ragged; 2.wrinkled
veriwwer, adv. 1.ceased; 2.finished; 3.over; 4.past
veriwwergeh, v.; veriwwergange, pp. pass over
verkaafe, v.; verkaaft, pp. sell
Verkaafer (der)n. seller
verkaffle, v.; verkaffelt, pp. soil
verkatze, v.; verkatzt, pp. 1.abbreviate; 2.shorten
verkaue, v.; verkaut, pp. chew
Verkeefer (der)n. seller
verkefdle, v.; verkefdelt, pp. spoil by notching
verkehrt, adj. 1.amiss; 2.crazy; 3.demented; 4.incoherent; 5.mixed-up; 6.perverse; 7.topsy-turvy; 8.wrong
verkelde; v.; verkeldt, pp. (sich --) catch (a cold)
Verkelding (die)n. cold (illness)
verkeschdiche, v.; verkeschdicht, pp. furnish (food, board)
verkiddert, adj. silly
verkindiche, v.; verkindicht, pp. announce publicly
verkinne, v.; verkinnt, pp. announce publicly
verkleckse, v.; verkleckst, pp. blot
verknechert, v. 1.become bony; 2.ossified
verknipp(l)e, v.; verknippelt, pp. knot so it is difficult to undo
verknippe, v.; vergnippt, pp. knot
verkoche, v.; verkocht, pp. fall to pieces in cooking
verkollebiere, v.; verkollebiert, pp. 1.abuse to distraction; 2.confuse; 3.spoil by abuse
verkollebiert, adj. spoiled
verkutzle, v.; verkutzelt, pp. (to make) untidy
verlaafe; v.; verloffe, pp. 1.run off (of liquids); 2.(sich --) (a) lose one's way; (b) stray
verlabbe, v.; verlappt, pp. 1.miss; 2.muff; 3.neglect
verlache, v.; verlacht, pp. 1.deride; 2.ridicule
verlaeret disliked
verlaerne, v.; verlaernt, pp. 1.forget; 2.unlearn
Verlange (es)n. 1.desire; 2.longing
verlange, v.; verlangt, pp. 1.ask; 2.demand; 3.desire; 4.require; 5.want
verlappelt, adj. dilapidated
verlappert, adj. dilapidated
verlause losse, v.; verlause gelosst, pp. (to let go to) ruin
verlause, v.; verlaust, pp. become lousy
verlechere, v.; verlechert, pp. dry out so as to leak
verlechert, adj. given to laughing or giggling

Vermeege

verleed sei (+ dative case)v. despair
verleed, adj. 1.depressed; 2.discouraged; 3.discontented; 4.disgusted; 5.tired
verleede, v.; verleedt, pp. tired of
verleedich, adj. 1.depressed; 2.discouraged
verleedtsam, adj. 1.discouraging; 2.tiresome; 3.wearisome
verleegele, v.; verleegelt, pp. deny
verleegne, v.; verleegnet, pp. deny
verleere, v.; verleert, pp. 1.pour out; 2.spill
verlege, v.; verlegt, pp. 1.mislay; 2.misplace
verlegele, v.; verlegelt, pp. deny
verlegge, adj. troubled
Verleggeheet (die)n. 1.embarrassment; 2.trouble
verlegne, v.; verlegelt, pp. deny
verlehne, v.; verlehnt, pp. 1.let; 2.lease; 3.loan (to others); 4.rent
verleicht, adv. perhaps
verleichtere, v.; verleichtert, pp. lighten
verlengere, v.; verlengert, pp. 1.extend; 2.lengthen; 3.prolong
verleppere, v.; verleppert, pp. waste in drink
verleschdere, v.; verleschdert, pp. 1.blaspheme; 2.defame
Verleschderung (die)n. 1.blasphemy; 2.defamation
verlesche, v.; verlescht, pp. extinguish
verlese, v.; verlese, pp. 1.read off; 2.tally
verlessich, adj. reliable
verletze, v.; verletzt, pp. 1.botch; 2.damage; 3.injure; 4.ruin; 5.spoil
verletzlich, adj. violable
Verletzung (die)n. violation
verlewe, v.; verlebt, pp. 1.spend; 2.use in living
verliebt, adj. in love (with)
verliere, v.; verlore, pp. lose
verliewe; v.; verliebt, pp. (sich --) fall in love
verlocke, v.; verlockt, pp. 1.decoy; 2.entice
verloddert, adj. dilapidated
verloffe, adv. 1.astray; 2.expired; 3.past
verlogge, adj. mendacious
verlosse, v.; verlosse, pp. 1.abandon; 2.depart; 3.desert; 4.forsake; 5.leave (on a trip)
verlossich, adj. dependent
verlumbe, v.; verlumbt, pp. 1.run down; 2.(to go to) ruin
verlumpt, adj. 1.dilapidated; 2.neglected; 3.ragged; 4.run down; 5.worn down
verluschdiere; v.; verluschdiert, pp. (sich --) enjoy oneself (especially clandestinely)
Verluscht (der)n. 1.damage; 2.loss
vermaahle, adj. 1.powdered; 2.pulverized
vermaahne, v.; vermaahnt, pp. 1.admonish; 2.exhort; 3.reprove
Vermaahning (die)n. 1.admonition; 2.short address to the relatives of the deceased at a funeral
vermache, v.; vermacht, pp. 1.bequeath; 2.will
vermaericke, v.; vermaerickt, pp. 1.make marks on; 2.mark up
vermaule, v.; vermault, pp. defame
vermaunst given to irritable complaining
Vermeege (es)n. 1.ability; 2.property

Vv

vermehre — verschinne

vermehre; v.; vermehrt, pp. (sich --) 1.multiply; 2.propagate

Vermehrung (die)n. 1.increase; 2.multiplication

vermetzle, v.; vermetzelt, pp. 1.butcher; 2.castrate; 3.massacre

vermische, v.; vermischt, pp. mix up

vermisse, v.; vermisst, pp. miss

vermucke; v.; vermuckt, pp. (sich --) 1.budge; 2.move; 3.stir (always with a negative)

vermude, v.; vermut, pp. presume

vermummt, adj. masked

vermuschdere; v.; vermuschdert, pp. (sich --) masquerade

vermutlich, adv. 1.presumably; 2.probably

vernaddert = vernarrt 1.crazy over; 2.infatuated with

vernaehe, v.; vernaeht, pp. use up in sewing

vernaggle, v.; vernaggelt, pp. 1.fasten down with nails; 2.lame in shoeing (a horse)

vernarre, v.; vernarrt, pp. fool

vernemme, v.; vernumme, pp. 1.comprehend; 2.understand

vernewwele, v.; vernewwelt, pp. (to become) tipsy

vernichde, v.; vernicht, pp. 1.annul; 2.destroy; 3.undo

verninfdich, adj. reasonable

vernoochlessiche, v.; vernoochlessicht, pp. neglect

vernuddle, v.; vernuddelt, pp. 1.slobber; 2.soil; 3.suck

Vernumft (die)n. common sense

Vernunft (die)n. common sense

verpeffert, adj. spoiled with too much pepper

verpflichde, v.; verpflicht, pp. oblige

Verpflichtung (die)n. obligation

verpisse, v.; verpisst, pp. spoil by urinating on

verpusche, v.; verpuscht, pp. 1.bungle; 2.spoil in making

verquetsche, v.; verquetscht, pp. 1.bruise; 2.contuse; 3.crush

Verraeter (der)n. traitor

verraeze, v.; verraezt, pp. spoil or damage by weathering

verralders, adv. of yore

verrammle; v.; verrammelt, pp. (sich --) bedraggle oneself

verranst worn out

verrechle; v.; verechelt, pp. (sich --) make a mistake in calculating

verrecke, v.; verreckt, pp. 1.die; 2.kick the bucket

verreese, v.; verreest, pp. (to go) traveling

verrege; v.; verregt, pp. (sich --) 1.budge; 2.move; 3.stir

verrege, v.; verregt, pp. 1.move; 2.stir

verreggere, v.; verreggert, pp. spoil by rainy weather

verreisse, v.; verrisse, pp. 1.rend; 2.tear (to pieces)

verreiwe, v.; verriwwe, pp. 1.rub out; 2.rub to powder

Verrengt (es)n. sprain

verrenke, v.; verrenkt, pp. 1.dislocate; 2.sprain; 3.twist

verretsche, v.; verretscht, pp. slander

verretscht, adj. slanderous

verrichde, v.; verricht, pp. accomplish

verricke, v.; verrickt, pp. displace

verrickt, adj. 1.absurd; 2.crazy; 3.deranged; 4.insane; 5.lunatic; 6.mad; 7.out of place; 8.zany

verrieche, v.; verroche, pp. lose odor

verriehre, v.; verriehrt, pp. mix by stirring

verriessle, v.; verriesselt, pp. upset

verrisse, adj. tatter

verriwwle, v.; verriwwelt, pp. rub fine

verrobbe, v.; verroppt, pp. 1.play pranks; 2.pull apart; 3.tear to pieces

verrode, v.; verrode, pp. 1.advise; 2.betray; 3.inform on

verroschde, v.; verroscht, pp. rust

verroscht, adj. rusted

Verrot (der)n. treason

verrumeniere, v.; verrumeniert, pp. ruin

verrumple, v.; verrumpelt, pp. 1.disarrange; 2.dishevel; 3.make full of creases

verrungeniere, v.; verrungeniert, pp. ruin

verrunsle, v.; verrunselt, pp. wrinkle

versaage, v.; versaagt, pp. 1.deny; 2.withhold permission

versaege, v.; versaegt, pp. saw into pieces

versalze, v.; versalzt, pp. spoil with too much salt

versammle; v.; versammelt, pp. (sich --) 1.assemble; 2.get together; 3.meet

Versammling (die)n. 1.assembly; 2.congregation; 3.meeting; 4.(lang --) protracted (prayer) meeting

Versammlinghaus (es)n. meeting house

Versammlung (die)n. 1.assembly; 2.congregation; 3.meeting

versar(i)ye, v.; versarigt, pp. 1.supply; 2.tend

Versatz (der)n. 1.possession; 2.(er hut's im --) he has it in his power

versaue, v.; versaut, pp. 1.make dirty; 2.soil

versaufe, v.; versoffe, pp. 1.drink (to excess); 2.drown; 3.spend in drink

verschaere, v.; verschaert, pp. 1.scatter by scratching; 2.spoil by scratching

verschaffe, v.; verschafft, pp. 1.procure; 2.provide; 3.work up material

verschalle, v.; verschallt, pp. 1.pass into oblivion; 2.vanish

verscheeche, v.; verscheecht, pp. frighten away

verscheie, v.; verscheit, pp. abhor

verscheisse; v.; verschisse, pp. (sich --) besmirch (oneself)

verschelde, v.; verscholde, pp. 1.berate; 2.scold

verschenke, v.; verschenkt, pp. 1.give away; 2.make a present of

verschenne, v.; verschennt, pp. 1.be ironical; 2.deface; 3.disfigure; 4.mar; 5.rail at

verschennere, v.; verschennert, pp. 1.beautify; 2.embellish

Verschennerung (die)n. embellishment

verschidde, v.; verschitt, pp. spill

verschiddlich, adj. 1.different; 2.varied; 3.various

verschieden, adj. various

verschiedlich, adj. 1.different; 2.varied; 3.various

verschiesse, v.; verschosse, pp. 1.(to use up in) shooting; 2.(to riddle by) shooting

verschiewe, v.; verschowe, pp. 1.disarrange; 2.misplace

verschimbiere, v.; verschimbiert, pp. 1.rail at; 2.vilify

verschimfe, v.; verschimft, pp. 1.defame; 2.scold

verschimmelt, adj. moldy

verschimpe, v.; verschimpt, pp. 1.bungle up; 2.disfigure

verschinne, v.; verschunne, pp. 1.abrade; 2.break the bark of a tree; 3.lacerate; 4.(sich --) abrade (the skin)

Vv

verschinnert — verschtewwere

verschinnert, adj. 1.confounded(ly); 2.devilishly

verschitte, v.; verschitt, pp. spill

verschittle, v.; verschiddelt, pp. 1.rack down; 2.scatter

verschlabbe, v.; verschlappt, pp. 1.bespatter; 2.soil; 3.spill

verschlagge, v.; verschlagge, pp. 1.break (to knock to pieces); 2.smash

verschlawwere, v.; verschlawwert, pp. 1.beslobber; 2.(sich --) slobber over oneself

verschlecke, v.; verschleckt, pp. 1.lick all over; 2.taste (in testing)

verschleefe, v.; verschleeft, pp. 1.drag away; 2.mislay; 3.misplace

verschlenkere, v.; verschlenkert, pp. 1.dissipate; 2.waste

verschliesse, v.; verschlosse, pp. lock (up)

verschlimmere, v.; verschlimmert, pp. worsen

verschlinge, v.; verschlunge, pp. 1.gulp down; 2.swallow

verschlitze, v.; verschlitzt, pp. slit up

verschliwwere, v.; verschliwwert, pp. splinter

verschlofe; v.; verschlofe, pp. 1.(sich --) oversleep; 2.(-- sei) (to be) sleepy headed

verschlucke; v.; verschluckt, pp. (sich --) choke

verschluppe; v.; verschluppt, pp. (sich --) hide

verschmacke, v.; verschmackt, pp. take a taste of

verschmaerze, v.; verschmaerzt, pp. 1.forget; 2.put up with; 3.tolerate

verschmeisse, v.; verschmisse, pp. 1.break into pieces by throwing; 2.scatter grass in a swath; 3.smash

verschmelze, v.; verschmolze, pp. 1.dissolve; 2.melt

verschmiere, v.; verschmiert, pp. 1.bedaub; 2.besmear; 3.soil; 4.(sich --) (a) besmear; (b) soil

verschmiert, adj. soiled

verschmitzt, adj. 1.sly; 2.mischievous

verschmoddere, v.; verschmoddert, pp. smother

verschmutze, v.; verschmutzt, pp. 1.soil with grease; 2.(sich --) begrease oneself

verschnabbe; v.; verschnappt, pp. (sich --) slip (in speaking)

verschnaerre, v.; verschnaerrt, pp. jerk apart (or to pieces)

verschnawwelt, adj. talkative

verschnee-e, v.; verschneet, pp. 1.(to be) snowbound; 2.(to spoil by) snowing

verschneide, v.; verschnidde, p. 1.castrate; 2.cut into pieces

verschnitzle, v.; verschnitzelt, pp. whittle away

verschnuddle, v.; verschnuddelt, pp. soil (by slopping)

verschoddere, v.; verschoddert, pp. 1.rend asunder; 2.shiver to pieces

verscholle, v.; verschollt, pp. vanish

verschone, v.; verschont, pp. 1.favor; 2.spare

verschosse, adj. 1.faded; 2.lost color; 3.shot away; 4.shot to pieces

verschottere, v.; verschottert, pp. 1.rend asunder; 2.shiver to pieces

verschowe, adv (-- im haernkaschde) 1.batty in the belfry; 2.out of one's mind

verschpaare, v.; verschpaart, pp. 1.economize; 2.save for the future; 3.spare

verschpaehe, v.; verschpraet, pp. spread

verschpaete; v.; verschpaet, pp. (sich --) 1.be behind in time; 2.be late

verschpalde, v.; verschpalt, pp. split

verschpaue, v.; verschpaut, pp. bespit

verschpiele, v.; verschpielt, pp. gamble away

verschpinne, v.; verschpunne, pp. 1.cover with cobwebs; 2.use up in spinning

verschplidde, v.; verschplitt, pp. split

verschpodde, v.; verschpott, pp. 1.deride; 2.ridicule

verschpraddelt, adj. spread out

verschpraddle; v.; verschpraddelt, pp. (sich --) be astonished

verschpraee, v.; verschpraet, pp. spread

Verschpreche(s) (es)n. 1.pledge; 2.promise

verschpreche, v.; verschproche, pp. 1.pledge; 2.promise

verschprenge, v.; verschprengt, pp. 1.blast; 2.cause to burst

verschpringe, v.; is verschprunge, pp. 1.burst; 2.explode

verschpritze, v.; verschpritzt, pp. bespatter

verschproche, adj. betrothed

verschprunge, adj. sprung (of a window, door)

verschrecke, v.; verschrocke, pp. 1.frighten; 2.horrify; 3.scare; 4.terrify

verschreiwe, v.; verschriwwe, pp. 1.convey (in writing); 2.prescribe

verschrumbelt, adj. shriveled

verschtaawe, v.; verschtaabt, pp. cover with dust

verschtaerricke, v.; verschtaerrickt, pp. strengthen

verschtambe, v.; verschtampt, pp. stamp to pieces

Verschtand (der)n. 1.cause; 2.common sense; 3.intellect; 4.reason; 5.wit

verschtarzelt, adj. cut short

verschtauche, v.; verschtaucht, pp. 1.jolt; 2.sprain

verschtaune, v.; verschtaunt, pp. 1.surprise; 2.(sich --) (a) (to be) amazed; (b) astonished; (c) surprised

verschtaunlich, adv.; adj. 1.astonishing; 2.surprising

verschtaunt, adj. astonished

verschteche, v.; verschtoche, pp. prick or sting full of holes

verschtecke, v.; verschteckt, pp. hide

verschteckelt, adj. hidden

verschteckle, v.; verschteckelt, pp. 1.hide; 2.(sich --) hide oneself

verschteege, v.; verschteekt, pp. sell (at auction)

verschteere, v.; verschteert, pp. 1.bother; 2.destroy; 3.disturb; 4.frighten

Verschteerung (die)n. 1.distraction; 2.disturbance

verschteeye, v.; verschteegt, pp. sell at auction

verschteh, v.; verschtanne, pp. 1.comprehend; 2.understand

verschtelle, v.; verschtellt, pp. 1.change the position of; 2.(sich --) (a) disguise; (b) pretend

Verschtelling (die)n. pretense

verschtendich, adj. 1.sensible; 2.well-behaved

verschtendich, adv. orderly

verschtendlich, adj. understandable

Verschtendnis (es)n. understanding

verschtennich, adj. 1.sensible; 2.well-behaved

verschtewwere, v.; verschtewwert, pp. Scatter

Vv

verschticke

verschticke, v.; verschtickt, pp. 1.asphyxiate; 2.smother; 3.suffocate

verschtickere, v.; verschtickert, pp. 1.cut in pieces; 2.patch; 3.mend

verschtifde, v.; verschtift, pp. 1.entice; 2.lead astray; 3.prejudice against (another)

verschtimmelt, adj. spoiled

verschtimmle, v.; verschtimmelt, pp. 1.botch; 2.mutilate; 3.ruin; 4.spoil

verschtimmt, adj. 1.discordant; 2.displeased

verschtimple, v.; verschtimmelt, pp. 1.botch; 2.mutilate; 3.spoil

verschtiwwert, adj. 1.distraught; 2.driven out; 3.scattered

verschtobbe, v.; verschtoppt, pp. 1.clog; 2.plug; 3.stop a hole or leak

verschtoche, adj. pierced

verschtockt, adj. obdurate

verschtohle, adv. 1.clandestinely; 2.underhandedly

verschtohlenerweis, adv. 1.clandestinely; 2.stealthily

Verschtopping (die)n. constipation

verschtoppt, adj. 1.constipated; 2.stopped

verschtosse, v.; verschtosse, pp. 1.disown; 2.reject

verschtruwwele, v.; verschtruwwelt, pp. dishevel

verschtumbiere, v.; verschtumbiert, pp. abuse

verschtutzt, adj. 1.ruined; 2.spoiled (of plants)

verschune, v.; verschont, pp. 1.favor; 2.spare

verschunne, adj. 1.bruised; 2.scratched

verschwaerze; v.; verschwaerzt, pp. (sich --) get black

verschweche, v.; verschwecht, pp. weaken

verschweere, v.; verschwore, pp. 1.conspire; 2.(sich --) vow

verschweige, v.; verschweicht, pp. 1.keep silent; 2.keep to oneself (as a secret)

verschwelle, v.; verschwolle, pp. swell

verschwende, v.; verschwendt, pp. waste

Verschwendung (die)n. extravagance

verschwenne, v.; verschwendt, pp. waste

verschwetze; v.; verschwetzt, pp. (sich --) 1.blab a secret; 2.gossip

verschwetze losse; v. (sich --) permit oneself to be persuaded

verschwetze, v.; verschwetzt, pp. 1.persuade; 2.talk someone into (something)

verschwiche, adj. 1.reticent; 2.silent

verschwinde, v.; verschwindt, pp. disappear

verschwinne, v.; verschwunne, pp. 1.disappear; 2.vanish

verschwitze, v.; verschwitzt, pp. soil or spoil by sweating

verschwitzt, adj. soiled by sweating

verschwolle, adj. swollen

verseeche, v.; verseecht, pp. spoil by urinating on

verseefe, v.; verseeft, pp. (sich --) (commit) suicide by drowning

verseefe, v.; verseeft, pp. drown

Versehe (es)n. mistake

versehe, v.; versehne, pp. provide for

Versehne (es)n. mistake

verwaxe

versehne, v.; versehne, pp. provide for

verseihe, v.; verseiht, pp. said of a cow when she is in that period of gestation before calving when she gives no milk

verseime, v.; verseimt, pp. 1.neglect; 2.miss

Verseimung (die)n. omission

versenke, v.; versenkt, pp. 1.scorch; 2.singe

versetze, v.; versetzt, pp. 1.carry out; 3.change the place of; 4.displace; 5.give

Versetzung (die)n. transposition

versichere, v.; versichert, pp. 1.assure; 2.secure;3.warrant

Versichering (die)n. 1.insurance; 2.guarantee; 3.warranty

versindiche; v.; versindicht, pp. (sich --) sin

versinke, v.; versunke, pp. 1.sink; 2.sink out of sight

versoddere, v.; versoddert, pp. seep away

versoffe, adj. intoxicated

versoffner (en), adj. a drunken fellow

versohle; v.; versohlt, pp. (sich --) begrime one's trousers

versohle, v.; versohlt, pp. flog thoroughly

verstarwe, adj (--ner, --ni, --nes) 1.deceased; 2.late

Versuch (der)n. 1.effort; 2.taste; 3.trial

versuche, v.; versucht, pp. 1.attempt; 2.experience; 3.taste; 4.tempt; 5.try

Versuchung (die)n. temptation

versuddere, v.; versuddert, pp. seep away

versuddle, v.; versuddelt, pp. 1.mess up; 2.ruin; 3.soil

verummeniere, v.; verummeniert, pp. ruin

verungeniere, v.; verungeniert, pp. ruin

verunglicke, v.; verunglickt, pp. 1.go amiss; 2.meet with an accident

verursache, v.; verursacht, pp. cause

verwa(e)rre, v.; verwa(e)rrt, pp. 1.addle; 2.bewilder; 3.confuse; 4.(sich --) become confused

verwaahre, v.; verwaahrt, pp. keep carefully

Verwaahring (die)n. protection

verwaarde, v.; verwaardt, pp. expect

verwache, v.; verwacht, pp. (to be unable to) sleep

verwaerfe, v.; verworfe, pp. reject

verwaerricke, v.; verwaerrickt, pp. forfeit

verwalte, v.; verwalt, pp. administer

Verwalter (der)n. administrator

verwandle, v.; verwandelt, pp. 1.change; 2.transmute

Verwandlung (die)n. transmission

Verwandschaft (die)n. relatives

Verwandte(r) (der)n. relative

verwarixe, v.; verwarixt, pp. choke

verwarne, v.; verwarnt, pp. (fore)warn

verwarrickse, v.; verwarrickst, pp. choke (intransitive)

verwart, adj. perplexed

verwarzelt, adj. closely rooted

verwatt, adj. 1.perplexed; 2.tangled

verwatzle; v.; verwatzelt, pp. (sich --) 1.be all impatience; 2.lost in amazement

verwaxe, v.; verwaxe, pp. 1.lose with age; 2.outgrow; 3.overgrown (with weeds)

Vv

Verwechsling

Verwechsling (die)n. change
Verwechslung (die)n. change
verweeche, v.; verweecht, pp. become too soft
verweese, v.; verweest, pp. molder
verwehne, v.; verwehnt, pp. 1.coddle; 2.spoil (a child)
verwehre, v.; verwehrt, pp. 1.prevent; 2.prohibit
verweigere, v.; verweigert, pp. refuse
verweile, v.; verweilt, pp. 1.linger; 2.stay; 3.tarry; 4.while away (time); 5.(sich --) pass the time
verwelke, v.; verwelkt, pp. wither
verwenderisch, adj. extravagant
verwenkle, v.; verwenkelt, pp. wither
verwenne, v.; verwennt, pp. 1.apply; 2.spend
verwenniche, v.; verwennicht, pp. make less
Verweser (der)n. guardian
verweslich, adj. liable to decay
verwetze, v.; verwetzt, pp (die Hosse --) cover the inside of the trouser leg with mud and moisture from walking inmud or wet grass
verwexle, v.; verwexelt, pp. 1.change; 2.take for another
verwickle, v.; verwickelt, pp. 1.confuse; 2.entangle; 3.implicate; 4.ravel; 5.tangle
Verwicklung (die)n. 1.maze; 2.tangle
verwiehle, v.; verwiehlt, pp. root over (a field)
verwieschde, v.; verwiescht, pp. devastate
verwildert, adj. grown up in weeds and brush
verwille, v.; verwillt, pp. 1.bequeath; 2.will
verwilliche, v.; verwillicht, pp. 1.accede to; 2.comply with; 3.grant
verwinsche, v.; verwinscht, pp. 1.curse; 2.imprecate
verwische, v.; verwischt, pp. 1.catch hold of; 2.detect; 3.erase; 4.obliterate
verwunde, v.; verwundt, pp. wound
verwunnere; v.; verwunnert, pp. (sich --) 1.amaze; 2.wonder
verwunnere, v.; verwunnert, pp. astound
veryaage, v.; veryaagt, pp. 1.chase away; 2.rout
veryuxe, v.; veryuxt, pp. 1.blow in; 2.gamble
verzaacht, adj. 1.afraid; 2.shy; 3.timid
verzaage, v.; verzaacht; verzaakt, pp. despair
verzabbe, v.; verzappt, pp. tap (out)
verzackere, v.; verzackert, pp. 1.botch up; 2.ornament; 3.squander
verzaerne, v.; verzaernt, pp. 1.anger; 2.(sich --) become angry
verzanne, v.; verzannt, pp. 1.anger; 2.incense; 3.provoke; 4.vex; 5.(sich --) become angry
verzannt, adj. 1.angry; 2.enrage; 3.indignant
verzappe, v.; verzappt, pp. tap (out)
verzehle, v.; verzehlt, pp. 1.narrate; 2.tell
verzehre, v.; verzehrt, pp. 1.consume; 2.devour
verzeichne, v.; verzeicht, pp. record
verzeihe, v.; verzeiht, pp. 1.forgive; 2.pardon; 3.tarry
verzeite, adv. 1.formerly; 2.in olden times
verzickere, v.; verzickert, pp. ornament
verzickt, adj. 1.enraptured; 2.out of one's mind; 3.wild
verziege, v.; verzogge, pp. 1.tarry; 2.warp; 3.wait
verziehe, v.; verzoge, pp. warp

Voggelnescht

verzimmere, v.; verzimmert, pp. 1.fix; 2.repair
verzobbe, v.; verzoppt, pp. pull to pieces
verzottle, v.; verzottelt, pp. 1. drop; 2. lose in hauling or handling
verzucke, v.; verzuckt, pp. 1.budge; 2.move; 3.shrug; 4.twitch; 5.distort
verzwaerwle, v.; verzwaerwelt, pp. blow into whirls or tangles
verzwenge, v.; verzwengt, pp. 1.elbow aside; 2.hold back; 3.restrain
verzwickt, adj. 1.awkward; 2.queer; 3.(-- wese) darn thing
Viech (es)n. 1.confounded rabble; 2.cattle
Vieh (es)n. 1.confounded rabble; 2.cattle
Viehdokder (der)n.; Viehdokder, pl. veterinarian
Viehdreiwer (der)n. drover (of cattle)
viehisch, adj. 1.beastly; 2.brutish
Viehsalz (es)n. rock salt
viel, pron; adj. 1.many; 2.much
Vieleck (es)n. polygon
vielerlee, adj. 1.different; 2.various
vielfeldich, adj. manifold
Vielfrass (der)n. 1.glutton; 2.sloth
vielleicht, adv. 1.maybe; 2.perhaps
Vielweiwerei (die)n. polygamy
vier, adj (so um die --) about 4 o'clock
vier, adj.; pron. four
vierbeenich, adj. quadruped
vierblettrich, adj. four leafed
vierdausend, adj., pron. four thousand
vierdraehdich, adj. four ply
viere, adj.; pron. four
Viereck (es)n. 1.quadrangle; 2.rectangle
viereckich, adj. 1.quadrangular; 2.rectangular; 3.square
vierfiessich, adj. quadruped
vierfeldich, adj. quadruple
Viergeilsfuhr (die)n. four horse team
vierhendich, adj. four handed
vierhunnert, adj., pron. four hundred
Vieruhr-Schtick (es)n. (mid-afternoon) snack
viermol, adv. four times
vierreddich, adj. four wheeled
vierschtechich, adj. four storied
vierschtimmich, adj. (for) four voices or parts
viersitzich, adj. four seated
Viert Yuli (der)n. Fourth of July
viert, adj. fourth
viertens, adj. fourthly
vierter (en) four spot in cards
vieryaehrich, adj. four years old
Violi (es)n. violet
visidiere, v.; visidiert, pp (v = f) 1.examine; 2.inspect
Visier (es)n. sight (of a rifle)
Voggel (der)n.; Veggel, pl. bird
Voggelfuss (der)n. birdfoot violet
Voggelkaschde, (der)n. bird house
Voggelnescht (es)n. bird's nest

Vv

Voggeloi — Vorhang

Voggeloi (es)n. bird's egg
Voggelsbohn (die)n. speckled bean
Volk (es)n. 1.folk; 2.lot; 3.nation; 4.set
volkreich, adj. populous
Volksaage (die)n. folklore
voll Angscht, adv. 1.anxious; 2.fearful
voll/mache, v.; vollgemacht, pp. fill
voll, adj. 1.full; 2.replete
vollbringe, v.; vollbrocht, pp. 1.carry out; 2.complete
vollende, v.; vollendet, pp. finish
vollens, adj. fully
vollfiehre, v.; vollfiehrt, pp. 1.carry out; 2.execute
vollfille, v.; vollfillt, pp. fulfill
Vollicht (es)n. full moon
vollkumme, adj. 1.entirely; 2.perfect
Vollmacht (die)n. authority
vollmechdich, adv. mightily
vollmechtiche, v.; vollmechticht, pp. empower
Vollmoond (der)n. full moon
vollschder, adj. 1.at length; 2.completely; 3.finally; 4.finished
vollschtennich, adv. complete
vollschtoppe, v.; vollgschtoppt, pp. cram full
vollyaarich, adj. of age
vollyeahrich, adj. of age
vor(d)ich, adj. a while ago
vor/bringe, v.; vorgebrocht, pp. 1.produce; 2.propose
vor/draage, v.; vorgedraage, pp. present
vor/drehe, v.; vorgedreht, pp. turn ahead (a clock)
vor/geh, v.; vorgange, pp. 1.precede; 2.take place
vor/gewwe, v.; vorgewwe, pp. 1.have a pretext; 2.pretend
vor/halde, v.; vorghalde, pp. 1.remand; 2.reproach; 3.upbraid
vor/kumme, v.; vorkumme, pp. 1.anticipate; 2.beat; 3.come forward; 4.forestall; 5.happen; 6.seem
vor/laade, v.; vorgelaade, pp. summon
vor/lege, v.; vorgelegt, pp. 1.accuse of; 2.upbraid
vor/lese, v.; vorgelese, pp. 1.read aloud; 2.read before singing
vor/losse, v.; vorgelosst, pp. 1.allow to pass; 2.permit to come to the front
vor/mache, v.; vorgemacht, pp (ebber ebbes --) show (another) how to do something
vor/nemme; v.; vorgenumme, pp. (sich --) purpose
vor/reide, v.; vorgeridde, pp. 1.outstrip in riding; 2.ride past another (in the same direction)
vor/ricke, v.; vorgerickt, pp. place or push forward
vor/rutsche, v.; vorgerutscht, pp. 1.slide ahead; 2.slip ahead
vor/saage, v.; vorgsaat, pp. 1.forecast; 2.line out a hymn; 3.predict; 4.prophesy
vor/schicke, v.; vorgschickt, pp. send up ahead
vor/schiewe, v.; vorschowe, pp. push forward
vor/schlagge, v.; vorgschlagge, pp. propose
vor/schmeisse, v.; vorg(e)schmisse, pp. 1.accuse; 2.cast

up to (one); 3.reproach (with)
vor/schpringe, v.; vorschprunge, pp. 1.run ahead of; 2.run to the head of
vor/schteh, v.; vorgschtanne, pp. project
vor/sehne, v.; vorgsehne, pp. 1.foresee; 2.(sich --) (a) be cautious; (b) provide for oneself
vor/setze, v.; vorgsetzt, pp. prescribe
vor/sitze, v.; vorgsotze, pp. take a seat up front
vor/zehle, v.; vorgezehlt, pp. tell (someone) what is what
vor/ziege, v.; vorgezogge, pp. prefer
vor, prep. 1.ahead; 2.before
voraa/geh, v.; voraagange, pp. 1.precede; 2.proceed; 3.progress
voraa/kumme, v.; voraakumme, pp. 1.progress; 2.thrive
voraa, adv. forward
voraahelfe, v.; voraagholfe, pp. help on the way
voraus/setze, v.; vorausgsetzt, pp. 1.support; 2.suppose
voraus, adv. in advance
Vorb(e)reiding (die) n. preparatory service (prior to Holy Communion [Lutheran and Reformed])
Vorbau (der)n. 1.forebay; 2.overhang (of a P.G. barn)
Vorbauer (der)n. overhang (of the P.G. barn)
Vorbedeidung (die)n. 1.omen; 2.portent
vorbedeite, v.; vorbedeit, pp. portend
vorbei/schleiche, v.; vorbeigschliche, pp. sneak past
vorbereide, v.; vorbereidt, pp. prepare
vorbiege; v.; vorgeboge, pp. (sich --) bend forward
vord, adv. a while ago
Vordeel (es)n. 1.advantage; 2.gain
vordem, adv. 1.before this; 2.formerly; 3.previously
vorderhand, adv. 1.(in) advance; 2.beforehand; 3.previously
vordreffich, adj. excellent
vorduh, v.; vorgeduh, pp. set or put ahead
vore, adv. a while ago
voreege, v.; voreeekt, pp. harrow before sowing
Voreldre (die)n., pl. ancestors
voremyaahr, adv. last year
vorfaahre, v.; vorgfaahre, pp. 1.drive past; 2.outstrip another in driving
Vorfall (der)n. event
vorfalle, v.; vorgfalle, pp. happen
Vorgang (der)n. 1.happening; 2.vestibule
vorgeblich, adj. ostensible
Vorgenger (der)n. 1.ancestor; 2.leader
vorgeschder, adv. day before yesterday
vorgeschdrowed, adv. evening before last
Vorgrund (der)n. foreground
vorgucke, v.; vorgeguckt, pp. 1.anticipate; 2.be on the alert
vorhaer, adv. 1.before; 2.in advance; 3.previously
vorhaergeh, v.; verhaergange, pp. precede
vorhaersaage, v.; vorhaergsaat, pp. 1.predict; 2.tell in advance
vorhaerwisse, v.; vorhaergewisst, pp. know in advance
Vorhang (der)n. curtain

Vv

vorhawwe

vorhawwe, v.; vorghatt, pp. 1.be at; 2.be engaged in; 3.be up to; 4.have in mind

vorher/geh, v.; vorhergange, pp. precede

vorher/saage, v.; vorhersaagt, pl. 1.predict; 2.prognosticate; 3.tell in advance

vorher, adv. 1.before; 2.formerly; 3.previously

vorich, adj. 1.a while ago; 2.former

Vorlaaf (der)n. (in distilling) the first run of spirits

vorlaafe, v.; vorgeloffe, pp. 1.walk ahead; 2.walk to the head

Vorlaafer (der)n.; Vorlaafer, pl. 1.forerunner; 2.harbinger

Vorleses (es)n. reading (of something out loud)

vorm = vor em before him or it

vormaehe, v.; vorgemaeht, pp. lead the mowers

Vormaeher (der)n. leader of the mowers

Vormann (der)n. foreman

vorme = vor me before one or it

Vormiddaag (der)n. forenoon

vormiddaags, adv. in the forenoon

vormyaahr, adv. last year

vorn = vor en before him or it

Vornaame (der)n.; Vorneeme, pl. forename

vornehm, adj. excellent

vornehmscht, adj. very best

vornemlich, adj. 1.chiefly; 2.particularly

Vornemmes (es)n. undertaking

Vornome (der)n. given name

vorraedich, adv. 1.in store; 2.on hand

Vorrang (der)n. 1.advantage; 2.prestige

Vorrecht (es)n. 1.prerogative; 2.privilege

Vorreed (die)n. preface

vorrenne, v.; vorgerennt, pp. dash ahead

vorriddle, v.; vorgeriddelt, pp. cast up (something) to (someone)

Vorrot (der)n. 1.hoard; 2.provision

Vorsarig (die)n. 1.foresight; 2.provision

vorschaffe, v.; vorgschafft, pp. 1. put (something) into a forward position; 2.(sich --) get up ahead

Vorschein (der)n. appearance

Vorschlack (der)n. proposal

vorschneide, v.; vorgschnidde, pp. lead the sicklers

vorschpanne, v.; vorgschpannt, pp. hitch additional horses in front

vorschreiwe, v.; vorgschriwwe, pp. write as a copy

Vorschrift (die)n. fraktur sample given as a gift

Vorscht(eh)er (der)n. deacon

Vorschteher (der)n. deacon

vorschtelle; v.; vorgschtellt, pp. (sich --) imagine

vorschtelle, v.; vorgschtellt, pp. personate

Vorschtelling (die)n. 1.anticipation; 2.imagination

Vorschtellung (die)n. 1.anticipation; 2.imagination

Vorschtimmer (der)n. song leader

vorschtrecke, v.; vorgschtreckt, pp. advance (money)

Vorschtubb (die)n. anteroom

Vorschuss (der)n.; Vorschuss, pl. 1.forebay; 2.overhang (of a P.G. barn); 3.overshoot

vurrand = voraa

Vorsehnes (es)n. foresight

vorsei, v.; vorgewest, pp. 1.be ahead; 2.have a case on at court

Vorsenger (der)n. leader of the choir

vorsichdich, adj. 1.careful; 2.cautious; 3.provident

Vorsicht (die)n. 1.caution; 2.precaution; 3.foresight; 4.warines

vorsinge, v.; vorgsunge, pp. lead the singing

Vorsinger (der)n.; Vorsinger, pl. song leader

Vorsitzer (der)n.; Vorsitzer, pl. 1.chairman; 2.president

Vorurteil (es)n. prejudice

Vorvedder (die)n., pl. 1.ancestors; 2.forefathers

vorwaerts, adv. 1.ahead; 2.forward

Vorwart (es)n. 1.forward; 2.preface

Vorwinter (der)n. early part of the winter

vorwitzich, adj. 1.bold; 2.courageous; 3.forward; 4.indiscrete; 5.snoopy

vorwitzich, adv. precipitate(ly)

Vorzuck (der)n. 1.advantage; 2.preference

vorzus, adv. forward

vum, prep. 1.from; 2. of

vumme = vun me of one

vun Alders her (from) of old

vun dann, adv. thence

vun neiem, adv. anew

vun selwer(t) willichweis, adv. voluntarily

vun, prep. 1.from; 2.of

vunanner/reise, v.; vunannergerisse, pp. tear apart

vunenanner/geh, v.; vunenannergange, pp. 1.part; 2.separate

vunenanner, adv. 1.apart; 2.separate

vunenannerkumme, v.; vunenannerkumme, pp. become separated

vunre = vun re 1.from her; 2.of her

vunwege, conj. 1.because; 2.since

vunwege, prep. 1.about; 2.concerning; 3.since

vurrand = voraa forward

Ww

Waache

Waache (der)n. wagon
Waachen (der)n. wagon
Waade (die)n. calf (of human leg)
waade, v.; gewaade, pp. wade
waage, v.; gewaagt, pp. 1.dare; 2.venture
Waagenaggel (der)n. pin or bolt of a double-tree
Waagereef (der)n.; Waagereef, pl. 1.hoop; 2.tire
Waageschopp (der)n. implement shed
Waahl (die)n. 1.choice; 2.election; 3.option; 4.selection;
   5.(in -- schteh) (to be) undecided
waahle, v.; gewaahlt, pp. 1.be undecided; 2.hesitate
waahr, adj. true
waahretlich, adj. verily
Waahretsaager (der)n. 1.fortune teller; 2.soothsayer
waahrhafdich, adv. 1.actually; 2.certainly; 3.really;
   4.truly; 5.veracious
waahrhaft, adj. truthful
Waahrheit (die)n. truth
waahrlich, adj. verily
waahrsaage, v.; waahrgsaat, pp. 1.divine; 2.tell fortune
Waahrsaager (der)n. 1.fortune teller; 2.soothsayer
waahrscheinlich, adv. 1.apparently; 2.probably
Waahrscheinlichkeet (die)n. 1.likelihood; 2.probability
Waalfisch (der)n. whale
Waar (die)n. 1.goods; 2.ware
waar(e)m, adj. warm
waarde, v. stay
waared, v.; gwaard, pp. wait
waarem, adj. warm
Waarhaus (es)n. warehouse
Waart (die)n. on the watch
waarte, v.; gewaart, pp. wait
Waartfraa (die)n. midwife
Waarting (die)n. 1.attendance; 2.nursing
Waartung (die)n. 1.attendance; 2.nursing
wa(a)rum, adv. why
Waarz (die)n.; Waarze, pl. 1.nipple; 2.teat; 3.wart
waarzich, adj. warty
wabble, v.; gewabbelt, pp. 1.shake; 2.wabble
wabblich, adj. 1.rickety; 2.shaky
Wach(t)nacht (die)n. 1.night vigil (with a corpse); 2.wake;
   3.watch
wach(t)sa(a)m, adj. 1.alert; 2.vigilant
wache, v.; gwacht, pp. 1.keep awake; 2.watch
wachere = wache keep awake
Wacheschtee (der)n. flint
Wachholder (der)n. juniper
Wachholler (der)n. juniper
Wachhollerbeer (die)n. juniper berry
wachse, v.; gewachst, pp. wax
Wachsgnopp (der)n. swollen gland
wachsich, adj. 1.thrifty (of plants); 2.waxen
Wachsschtok (der)n. begonia
Wacht (die)n. 1.wake; 2.watch
Wachthund (der)n. watchdog
Wacke (der)n. 1.boulder; 2.cobble; 3.quartz

Waerrwese

wacker mache, v.; gemacht, pp. 1.awaken; 2.wake
wacker warre, v.; is wacker warre, pp. awaken
wacker, adj. 1.alert; 2.awake; 3.wakeful 4.(-- [wackerich]
   sei) (to be) awake
wack(e)rich, adj. 1.alert; 2.awake; 3.wakeful
wackich, adj. soil covered with small boulders
wackle, v.; gewackelt, pp. totter (to shake, wobble)
wacklich, adj. 1.shaky; 2.wobbly
Wadaag (der)n.; Wadaage, pl. workday
Wadaagsgleeder (die)n., pl. working clothes
wadde, v.; gewaade, pp. 1.bathe; 2.wade
Waddebuch (es)n.; Waddebicher, pl. 1.dictionary;
   2.vocabulary
Waddel (der)n. 1.burly fellow (mostly of young boys);
   2.stout
Waddin (die)n. landlady
waddlich, adj. verbal
waehle, v.; gewaehlt, pp. 1.choose; 2.elect
waehre, v.; gewaehrt, pp. 1.continue; 2.last
waehrend, prep. during
waer, v. (past tense of be) 1.were; 2.would be
Waer(ric)kmesser (es)n. butteris
waerd 1.becomes; 2.will
waerdaags, adv. weekdays
Waerdaagsgleeder (die)n., pl. working clothes
Waerderswese (es)n. confounded thing
waerdich, adj. worthy
waere, v.; gewore, pp. wear
waerecklich, adv. really
waerfe, v. litter (of sows)
Waerfel (der)n.; Waerfle, pl. dice
waerfle, v.; gewaerfelt, pp. shoot crap
waerflich, adj. (cut) in cubes
Waergel (es)n. handful of finished flax
Waerick (es)n. tow
waericklich, adv. 1.really; 2.truly
Waerkelholz (es)n. rolling pin
waerklich, adv. 1.really; 2.truly
Waerklichkeet (die)n. reality
waerksam, adj. 1.effective; 2.efficient
Waerkzeich (es)n. 1.implement; 2.tool
Waermche (es)n. 1.little worm; 2.(en horrich -- puppe)
   fidget with impatience
waerme; v.; gewaermt, pp. 1.warm; 2.(sich --) warm
   oneself
waermich, adj. wormy
Waerming (die)n. 1.heat; 2.flogging; 3.warmth
waerr, adj. confused
waerre, v.; warre; waerre, pp. 1.become; 2.change;
   3.shall; 4.will; 5.(es waerd net) it is not a success
Waerrick (es)n. 1.tow; 2.work(s)
waerricke, adj. of flax
waerricke, v.; gewaerrickt, pp. choke
Waerrickgawwel (die)n. distaff
Waerrickhaus (es)n. workhouse
Waerrwese (es)n. confusion

Ww

waerschde / Warfschaufel

waerschde, v.; gewaerscht, pp. (to make) sausage
waerschtche (es)n. little sausage
Waerschtdrechder (der)n. sausage stuffer
Waerschtfleesch (es)n. sausage meat
Waerschtmaschien (die)n. meat chopper
Waerschtschiesser (der)n. sausage stuffer
Waert (der)n. 1.value; 2.worth
waert, adj. (ebbes --) worthwhile
waert, adv. (er is nix --) 1.he has no property; 2.he is good for nothing; 3.worth
waertlich, adj. 1.literal; 2.verbal
waertschafte, v.; gewaertschaft, pp. 1.be busy at or with; 2.get along
Waertung (die)n. value
waertvoll, adj. valuable
Waerwel (der)n. 1.crown; 2.eddy; 3.middle of the skull; 4.turn button; 5.whirl
waerwle, v.; gewaerwelt, pp. whirl
Waerzeich (es)n. tool
Wa(e)rzelche (es)n. rootlet
Waesevadder (der)n. prothonotary
Waffel (die)n. 1.mouth; 2.waffle
Waffeleise (es)n. waffle iron
Wagge (der)n.; Wegge, pl. wagon
Waggeachs (die)n. axle tree
Waggedeck (die)n. wagon cover
Waggedeixel (die)n. wagon-tongue
Waggeglees (der)n. wheel rut
Waggeleeder (die)n. hay rack (on a wagon)
Waggeraad (es)n.; Waggeredder, pl. wagon wheel
Waggereef (der)n. tire
Waggesaddel (der)n.; Waggesaddel, pl. saddle on the saddle horse
Waggeschmier (die)n. axle grease
Waggeschnepp (die)n. jack
Waggeschopp (der)n.; Waggeschepp, pl. wagon-shed
Waggeschpaerr (die)n. brake
Waggewinn (die)n. screw jack
Wagner (der)n. wheelwright
Wahret (die)n. 1.truth; 2.(die Deitscher --) plain truth; 3. (fer -- saage) really
Waisehaus (es)n. orphan's home
Waisekind (es)n.; Waisekinner, pl. orphan
Wald (der)n. 1.dense growth (figurative); 2.forest (rare usage)
Waldhaehr (der)n. jay
Walfisch (der)n. whale
Wall(i) (der)n. 1.Valentine; 2.Walter
Wallebletter (die)n., pl. yellow pond lily
Wallem (die)n.; Walme, pl. ridge or heaped row (in which sweet potatoes are planted)
wallicke, v.; gewallickt, pp. beat
Walnus (die)n.; Walnis, pl. walnut
Walnusbaam (der)n.; Walnusbeem, pl. walnut tree
Walnusholz (es)n. walnut wood
Walnusrinn (die)n. bark of the walnut tree

Walnusschaal (die)n. walnut shell
walte, v.; gewaltet, pp. 1.govern; 2.leave to the disposition of (God)
Walz (die)n. 1.land roller; 2.roller; 3.windlass
walze, v.; gewalzt, pp. 1.flatten out (with a roller); 2.roll (earth)
Walzer (der)n. waltz
Wambe(r) (der)n. 1.belly; 2.large lump (resembling a cow's stomach); 3.maw; 4.stomach (of cattle)
wammer = wann mer 1.if a person; 2.if one; 3.if we
wammerm = wammer em if one
wammern = wammer en if he
Wammes (der)n.; Wammes, pl. 1.jacket; 2.short coat; 3.vest; 4.waistcoat
wamsche, v.; gewamscht, pp. 1.beat; 2.flog
Wand (die)n.; Wend, pl. 1.(inside) wall; 2.(rocky) cliff
Wandbabier (es)n. wall paper
Wandbegleedung (die)n. wainscoating
Wandbopp (die)n. wallflower (sarcastic)
Wanddeppich (der)n. tapestry
Wandel (der)n. 1.conduct; 2.course of life; 3.mode of life
wandere, v.; gewandert, pp. 1.roam; 2.wander
Wandlaus (die)n. 1.bedbug; 2.(so griddlich as en --) said of a very grouchy person
wandle, v.; gewandelt, pp. 1.act; 2.move; 3.travel; 4.walk
Wange (die)n. cheek (rare usage)
Wangelabbe (der)n. wattle
Wangner (der)n. wagon-builder
wanke, v.; gewankt, pp. 1.(to be) unstable; 2.stagger; 3.waver; 4.wobble
wankelmiedich, adj. 1.fickle; 2.irresolute; 3.vacillating
wankle, v.; gewankelt, pp. 1.totter; 2.waver
wanklich, adj. 1.shaky; 2.unsteady
wann, adv (mach as --) pretend
wann, conj. if
wann, conj.; pron. when
wannd = wann du when you
wannde = wann du when you
wanndem = wann du em when he
wanndeme = wann du me when one
wanndre = wann du re when she
wanne, v.; gewarnt; gwannt, pp. 1.forewarn; 2.warn
Wanning (die)n. warning
wanns = wann es when it
Wans (die)n.; Wanse, pl. bedbug
Wansegeruch (der)n. odor of bedbugs
Wansenescht (es)n. 1.buggy house; 2.shack
wansich, adj. 1.buggy; 2.full of bedbugs
Wardaag (der)n. weekday
wardaags, adv. weekdays
Wardaagsgleeder (die)n. working clothes
Warem (der)n. worm
waremich, adj. wormy
Waremmiddel (es)n. vermifuge
Warf (der)n. 1.handle of a scythe; 2.snathe; 3.wharf
Warfschaufel (die)n. scoop-shovel

Ww

warge

warge, v.; gewarrickt, pp. choke
Warick (es)n. 1.deeds; 2.work
waricklich, adv. 1.actually; 2.really; 3.truly
warixe, v.; gewarixt, pp. 1.gag; 2.hawk; 3.vomit
Warm (der)n.; Waerm, pl. worm
Warmet (der)n (wilder --) ragweed
Warmet (der)n (zaahmer --) wormwood
Warmgraut (es)n. wormseed
warmich, adj. wormy
Warmschtich (der)n. wormhole
warmschtichich, adj. worm-eaten
Warmut (es)n (wilder --) ragweed
warne, v.; gewarnt, pp. 1.forewarn; 2.warn
Warning (die)n. warning
warre, v.; is warre, pp. 1.become; 2.get
Warref (der)n. 1.handle of a scythe; 2.snathe
warricke, v.; gewarrickt, pp. choke
Warscht (die)n. sausage
Wart (der)n. 1.value; 2.worth
Wart (es)n. word
wart, adv. worth
wartreich, adj. wordy
Wartschpiel (es)n. pun
Warzel (die)n. root
warzle, v.; gewarzelt, pp. take root
warzlich, adj. full of roots
Was der Dausich! what the dickens!
was ewwer?, pron. whatever?
was fa(e)rich? 1.what kind of?; 2.what sort of?
was fer ----? (what) sort (of) ----?
was fer? what kind of?
was, pron. what
was, rel. pron. that which
Wascht (die)n. 1.sausage; 2.(frischi --) fresh sausage; 3.
    (gschmokdi --) smoked sausage
Waschtdeeg (der)n. ground sausage meat
Waschtdrechder (der)n. sausage-stuffer
Waschtfleesch (es)n. sausage meat
Waschtmaschien (die)n. meat chopper
Waschtschiesser (der)n. sausage-stuffer
Waschtschtobber (der)n. sausage-stuffer
Wass iss do uff? What's the matter here?
wass(e)rich, adj. watery
Wassem (der)n. sod
Wasser (es)n. 1.water; 2.(-- ab/schlagge) urinate; 3.
    (-- losse) urinate; 4.(darich's -- baade [weaade]) to
    wade through the water
Wasserabbel (der)n. variety of apple
Wasserbabble (der, die)n. buttonwood
Wasserbaerke (die)n. river birch
Wasserbank (die)n.; Wasserbenk, pl. 1.sink; 2.water bench
Wasserblos (die)n. bubble
Wasserboddel (die)n.; Wasserboddle, pl. water bottle
Wasserbool (die)n. dipper
Wasserdroppe (der)n. drop of water
Wassereemer (der)n. bucket

Wax

Wasserfall (der)n. waterfall
Wasserfass (es)n. water barrel
Wassergawwel (die)n.; Wassergawwle, pl. divining rod
Wassergeitz (der)n. diving beetle
Wassergraawe (der)n. ditch
Wassergrog (der)n. water-trough
wasserich, adj. watery
Wasserkaft (die)n. water gap
Wasserkiwwel (der)n. bucket (especially of a well)
Wasserlilye (die)n. 1.pond lily; 2.water lily
Wasserloch (es)n.; Wasserlecher, pl. 1.pond; 2.pool;
    3.puddle; 4.water hole
Wassermaerrick (es)n. watermark
Wassermann (der)n. Aquarius (1st sign of the zodiac)
Wassermelon (die)n. watermelon
Wassermelun (die)n.; Wassermelune, pp. watermelon
Wassermiehl (die)n. water mill
Wassernot (die)n. water famine
Wasserpann (die)n. shallow pool (in woods or in low ground)
Wasserparble (die)n. chicken pox
Wasserpitschbaam (der)n. sycamore
Wasserraad (es)n.; Wasserredder, pl. waterwheel
Wasserrecht (es)n. water right
Wasserschei (die)n. hydrophobia
Wasserschlang (die)n.; Wasserschlange, pl. water snake
Wasserschlibber (der)n.; Wasserschlibber, pl. pied-billed grebe
Wasserschpritz (die)n. 1.squirt; 2.water engine
Wasserschtitz (der)n. bucket (wooden used on the farm)
Wasserschtraehme, n. soggy streak in bread
wasserschtraemich, adj. soggy (of bread)
Wassersenf (der)n. watercress
wassersichdich, adj. poor in quality (of apples)
Wassersimpel (der)n. temperance crank
Wassersucht (die)n. dropsy
Wassersuchtgraut (es)n. wild ginger
Wassersupp (der)n. 1.soup of bread, water, salt, and
    pepper; 2.(contemptuous for) any thin soup
Wasservoggel (der)n. water bird
Wasserwaerrick (es)n. waterworks
Wasserwagge (der)n. water wagon
Wasserzieg (der, die)n. diving rod
Watt (der)n.; Wadde, pl. 1.innkeeper; 2.landlord; 3.taverner
Watt (die)n. wad(ding)
Watt (es)n.; Wadde, pl. 1.promise; 2.word
Wattche (es)n. 1.word; 2.(kenn --) not a word
Watterbuch (es)n. 1.dictionary; 2.vocabulary
Wattin (die)n. landlady
Wattschaft (die)n. 1.bustle; 2.confusion; 3.hotel busi-
    ness; 4.hotel-stand
Wattsfrau (die)n. landlady
Wattshaus (es)n.; Wattsheiser, pl. 1.hotel; 2.tavern
Watzel (die)n.; Watzle, pl. root (of a plant)
Watzelche (es)n.; Watzelcher, pl. rootlet
watzle, v.; gewatzelt, pp. (to take) root
Wautz (der)n. hobgoblin
Wax (der)n. wax

Ww

Waxblumm

Waxblumm (die)n. wax flower
Waxbopp (die)n. wax doll
waxe, v.; gewaxe, pp. 1.thrive; 2.grow
waxich, adj. 1.growing; 2.thrifty (of plants); 3.waxen
Waxlicht (es)n.; Waxlichder, pl. taper
Waxschmier (die)n. 1.ointment; 2.salve; 3.(grafting) wax
wearge, v.; gewaerrickt, pp. choke
Webb (es)n. web
Webschtul (der)n.; Webschtiel, pl. loom
Webzettel (der)n. 1.carpet chain; 2.warp
Wechder (der)n.; Wechder, pl. 1.sentinel; 2.watchman
wechentlich, adj. weekly
wechlich, adj. weekly
wechslich, adj. changeable
Wechsling (die)n. change
Weck (der)n.; Weck, pl. 1.bun; 2.roll; 3.rusk; 4.small light-cake
weck sei, v.; weck g(e)west, pp. be absent
weck/addere, v.; weckgeaddert, pp. order away
weck/balke, v. spend
weck/barge, v.; weckgebarkt, pp. lend out
weck/baschde, v.; weckgebascht, pp. brush away
weck/batzle, v.; weckgebatzelt, pp. tumble away
weck/beile, v.; weckgebeilt, pp. hew away
weck/beisse, v.; weckgebisse, pp. keep away by biting
weck/bemble, v.; weckgebembelt, pp. 1.fritter away; 2.waste
weck/biege, v.; weckgeboge, pp. bend away
weck/binne, v.; weckgebunne, pp. tie in another place
weck/bleiwe, v.; weckgebliwwe, pp. 1.remain away; 2.stay away
weck/blicke, v.; weckgeblickt, pp. glance away
weck/blose, v.; weckgeblose, pp. blow away
weck/brauche, v.; weckgebraucht, pp. cause to disappear by powwowing
weck/breche, v.; weckgebroche, pp. break or crumble away
weck/brenne, v.; is weckgebrennt, pp. burn down
weck/briggle, v.; weckgebriggelt, pp. drive away with a club
weck/bringe, v.; weckgebrocht, pp. 1.bring away; 2.cause to disappear
weck/bumbe, v.; weckgebumpt, pp. pump away
weck/butze, v.; weckgebutzt, pp. 1.clean away; 2.pilfer
weck/dabbe, v.; weckgedappt, pp. trudge away
weck/daerfe, v.; weckgedaerft, pp. be allowed to go away
weck/daerre, v.; weckgedaerrt, pp. dry away
weck/draage, v.; weckgedraage, pp. carry away
weck/dreiwe, v.; weckgedriwwe, pp. drive away
weck/drinke, v.; weckgedrunke, pp. drink all of
weck/duh, v.; weckgeduh, pp. 1.abolish; 2.put away; 3.remove
weck/eile, v.; weckgeeilt, pp. hasten away
weck/esse, v.; weckgesse, pp. 1.eat all of; 2.eat up quickly
weck/faahre, v.; weckgfaahre, pp. drive away (in a vehicle)
weck/falle, v.; weckgfalle, pp. lose flesh (as in illness)
weck/fange, v.; weckgfange, pp. 1.catch; 2.snatch away
weck/faule, v.; weckgfault, pp. rot away
weck/fiehre, v.; weckgfiehrt, pp. lead away
weck/fladdre, v.; weckgfladdert, pp. flutter away
weck/flappe, v.; weckgflappt, pp. flop away

weck/rufe

weck/flause, v.; weckgflaust, pp. filch
weck/fliege, v.; weckgflogge, pp. fly away
weck/fresse, v.; weckgfresse, pp. eat up greedily
weck/gawwle, v.; weckgegawwelt, pp. pitch away (with a fork)
weck/geh, v.; is weckgange, pp. 1.depart; 2.disappear; 3.go away; 4.leave; 5.pass over
weck/gewwe, v.; weckgewwe, pp. 1.betray; 2.give away
weck/grabsche, v.; weckgegrabscht, pp. snatch away
weck/graddle, v.; weckgegradelt, pp. crawl away
weck/gratze, v.; weckgegratzt, pp. scratch away
weck/griege, v.; weckgrickt, pp. 1.get (some one) away; 2.induce to leave
weck/gucke, v.; weckgeguckt, pp. look away
weck/hacke, v.; weckghackt, pp. cut or chop down
weck/halde, v.; weckgehalde, pp. 1.avoid; 2.keep someone away; 3.ward off; 4.(sich --) absent (oneself)
weck/haschble, v.; weckghaschbelt, pp. leave thoughtlessly
weck/helfe, v.; weckgholfe, pp. help (someone) away
weck/henke, v.; weckghenkt, pp. hang away
weck/hewe, v.; weckghowe, pp. lift away
weck/hole, v.; weckgholt, pp. fetch away
weck/hupse, v.; weckghupst, pp. hop away
weck/kehre, v.; weckgekehrt, pp. sweep away
weck/kenne, v.; weckgekennt, pp. be able to get away
weck/kumme, v.; weckkumme, pp. 1.come away; 2.disappear; 3.(schlecht --) fare badly
weck/laafe, v.; weckgeloffe, pp. 1.leave without notice; 2.run away (of liquids); 3.walk away
weck/lause, v.; weckgelaust, pp. 1.filch; 2.steal
weck/lege, v.; weckgelegt, pp. 1.lay away; 2.(sich --) go to bed
weck/lehne, v.; weckglehnt, pp. 1.lend; 2.let; 3.loan; 4.rent
weck/lese, v.; weckglese, pp. pick away
weck/lifte, v. lift away
weck/locke, v.; weckgelockt, pp. 1.call off (a dog); 2.decoy; 3.entice
weck/losse, v.; weckgelosst, pp. leave away
weck/mache, v.; weckgemacht, pp. remove
weck/maehe, v.; weckgemaeht, pp. remove by mowing
weck/misse, v.; weckgemisst, pp. be compelled to get away
weck/narre, v.; weckgenaart, pp. part with foolishly
weck/nemme, v.; weckgenumme, pp. 1.cause to disappear; 2.cure; 3.remove; 4.take away
weck/packe, v.; weckgepackt, pp. 1.pack away; 2.(sich --) get away
weck/raahme, v.; weckgeraahmt, pp. remove
weck/raffe, v.; weckgerafft, pp. grasp away (from someone)
weck/reide, v.; weckgeridde, pp. ride away
weck/reisse, v.; weckgerisse, pp. 1.snatch away; 2.tear down (a building)
weck/renne, v.; weckgerennt, pp. 1.rush away; 2.thrust away
weck/rinne, v.; weckgerunne, pp. leak away
weck/rolle, v.; weckgerollt, pp. roll away
weck/roppe, v.; weckgeroppt, pp. remove by plucking
weck/roschde, v.; weckgeroscht, pp. rust away
weck/rufe, v.; weckgerufe, pp. call away

Ww

weck/rutsche   Wedderleger

weck/rutsche, v.; weckgerutscht, pp. slide away
weck/saege, v.; weckgsaegt, pp. saw off
weck/schaffe, v.; weckgschafft, pp. 1.dispose of; 2.get rid of; 3.remove
weck/schalle, v.; weckgschallt, pp. sound at a distance
weck/scharre, v.; weckgschatt, pp. scratch away
weck/schaufle, v.; weckgschaufelt, pp. shovel away
weck/scheele, v.; weckgscheelt, pp. peel off
weck/schenke, v.; weckgschenkt, pp. give away
weck/scheppe, v.; weckgscheppt, pp. 1.dip away; 2.shovel away
weck/schere, v.; weckgschore, pp. shear off
weck/schicke, v.; weckgschickt, pp. send away
weck/schidde, v.; weckgschitt, pp. 1.pour away; 2.pour out (of liquids)
weck/schiesse, v.; weckgschosse, pp. use up in shooting
weck/schiewe, v.; weckgschowe, pp. shove away
weck/schinne, v.; weckgschunne, pp. 1.abrade; 2.plow poorly
weck/schlagge, v.; weckgschlagge, pp. knock away
weck/schleefe, v.; weckgschleeft, pp. drag away
weck/schleiche, v.; weckgschliche, pp. sneak away
weck/schlenkere, v.; weckgschlenkert, pp. fling away
weck/schlibbe, v.; weckgschlippt, pp. 1.elude; 2.steal away
weck/schluppe, v.; weckgschluppt, pp. creep into a place of concealment
weck/schmeisse, v.; weckgschmisse, pp. 1.dispose of; 2.throw away
weck/schmelze, v.; wechgschmolze, pp. melt away
weck/schnabbe, v.; weckgschnappt, pp. snatch away
weck/schnaerre, v.; weckgschnaerrt, pp. snatch away
weck/schneide, v.; weckgschnidde, pp. cut away
weck/schnelle, v.; weckgschnellt, pp. jerk away
weck/schpaue, v.; weckgschpaut, pp. spit out
weck/schprenge, v.; weckgschprunge, pp. cause to run away
weck/schpringe, v.; weckgschprunge, pp. 1.flee; 2.run away
weck/schridde, v.; weckgschritt, pp. step away
weck/schtecke, v.; weckgschtocke, pp. 1.conceal; 2.put in a safe place
weck/schtehle, v.; weckgschtohle, pp. steal away
weck/schtelle, v.; weckgschtellt, pp. set away
weck/schtolpere, v.; weckgschtolpert, pp. stumble away
weck/schtosse, v.; weckgschtosse, pp. 1.push away; 2.spurn
weck/sehne, v.; weckgsehne, pp. see off (to a distance)
weck/setze, v.; weckgsetzt, pp. set away
weck/vendere; v.; weckvendert, pp. (sich --) venture away
weck/weise, v.; weckgewisse, pp. show away
weck/wesche, v.; weckgewesche, pp. wash away
weck/wische, v.; weckgewischt, pp. wipe away
weck/wolle, v.; weckgewollt, pp. want to go away
weck/yaage, v.; weckgeyaagt, pp. chase away
weck/zackere, v.; weckgezackert, pp. 1.go along haltingly; 2.work slovenly
weck/ziege, v.; weckgezogge, pp. 1.move away; 2.pull away
weck/ziehe, v.; weckgezogge, pp. 1.move away; 2.pull away

weck, adv. 1.absent; 2.away; 3.off
wecke, v.; geweckt, pp. wake
Wecker (der)n. one who wakens
Weckuhr (die)n. alarm clock
weckzus, adv. 1.away from; 2.(on the way) going
wedde, v.; g(e)wett, pp. 1.bet; 2.gamble; 3.wager
Weddel (der)n. 1.paddle; 2.tail
Wedder (der)n. Aries (1st sign of the zodiac)
Wedder (es)n. 1.storm; 2.thunderstorm; 3.weather 4.(beim --!) by thunder!; 5.(er draut dem -- net recht) (a) he is cautious; (b) he is suspicious 6.(es gebt gut --) is said when everything in the dishes on the table at a meal is eaten
wedder/bappe, v.; weddergebappt, pp. paste against
wedder/dappe, v.; weddergedappt, pp. walk up against
wedder/drede, v.; weddergedrede, pp. firm (against something) by treading
wedder/faahre, v.; wedderfaahre, pp. 1.befall; 2.drive against (as against a rock in plowing); 3.happen
wedder/fliege, v.; weddergflogge, pp. fly against
wedder/gloppe, v.; weddergegloppt, pp. hammer against
wedder/halde, v.; wedderghalde, pp. 1.endure; 2.resist; 3.sustain one's part
wedder/halte, v.; wedderghalte, pp. 1.(hart --) (a) be difficult to get done; (b) be long in happening; 2.(die ax --) steady by holding an ax against
wedder/kumme, v.; wedderkumme, pp. get against
wedder/laafe, v.; weddergeloffe, pp. 1.run up against a snag in one's plans; 2.walk up against
wedder/laahne, v.; weddergelaahnt, pp. lean against
wedder/leie, v.; weddergelegge, pp. lie against
wedder/naggle, v.; weddergenaggelt, pp. nail against
wedder/renne, v.; weddergerennt, pp. run up against
wedder/schiewe, v.; weddergschowe, pp. push against
wedder/schlagge, v.; weddergschlagge, pp. knock against
wedder/schmeisse, v.; weddergschmisse, pp. throw against
wedder/schpringe, v.; weddergschprunge, pp. run against
wedder/schtaerze, v.; weddergschtaerzt, pp. fall against
wedder/schteh, v.; weddergschtanne, pp. resist
wedder/schtosse, v.; weddergschtosse, pp. 1.abut; 2.border; 3.bump against; 4.join; 5.knock against
wedder/ziehe, v.; weddergezogge, pp. pull against
wedder, prep. against
Wedderbatt (der)n 1.opposition; 2.(ebber -- halde) oppose in an argument
Wedderbrofeet (der)n. weather prophet
Wedderbrophet (der)n. weather prophet
weddere, v.; geweddert, pp. 1.thunder and lighten; 2.weather
Wedderglaas (es)n.; Wedderglesser, pl. 1.barometer; 2.weatherglass
Wedderhaahne (der)n. weathercock
Wedderhex (die)n. (carpenter's) tool for scribing angles
Wedderleech (der)n. lightning
wedderleeche, v.; gewedderleecht, pp. lighten
wedderlege, v.; wedderlegt, pp. 1.deny; 2.oppose
Wedderleger (der)n. opponent

Ww

wedderleichde

wedderleichde, v.; gewedderleicht, pp. lighten
wedderlich, adj. 1.disgusting; 2.nauseating
Weddermann (der)n. weatherman
weddernanner, adv. one against the other
Wedderrut (die)n. lightning rod
wedders, adv. fearfully
Wedderschtand (der)n. resistance
wedderschteh, v.; wedderschtanne, pp. 1.be disdainful; 2.offer resistance; 3.oppose; 4.withstand
Weddes (es)n. betting
Wedding (die)n. bet
weddle, v.; geweddelt, pp. 1.swing; 2.wave; 3.wag the tail (of a dog)
Wedel (der)n. 1.fly-chaser; 2.paddle; 3.tail; 4.whisk
Weeb (es)n. web
weech/mache, v.; weechgemacht, pp. soften
weech, adj. soft
weeche, v.; geweecht, pp (der Buckel --) 1.flog; 2.tan
weechhatzich, adj. soft-hearted
weechmeilich, adj. soft-mouthed (of horses)
Weed (die)n. pasture
weede, v.; gweedt, pp. 1.browse; 2.graze (of cattle)
Weedfeld (es)n. pasture field
Weedland (es)n. pasture
weeich, prep. 1.about; 2.because of; 3.on account of
Weeze (der)n. wheat
Weeze-aern(t) (die)n. wheat harvest
Weezeaehr (die)n. head of wheat
Weezebodde(m) (der)n. soil adapted for growing wheat
Weezebrot (es)n. wheat bread
Weezefeld (es)n. wheat field
Weezekaern (die)n. grain of wheat
Weezekaschde (der)n.; Weezekaschde, pl. wheat-bin
Weezelaus (die)n. Hessian fly
Weezemehl (es)n. wheat flour
Weezeschprau (die)n. wheat chaff
Weezeschtroh (es)n. wheat straw
Weg (der)n.; Wege, pl. 1.road; 2.direction; 3.way; 4.(aus em --) out of the way; 5.(aus em -- schaffe) put out of the way; 6.(um -- sei) be (somewhere) about; 7.(-- mache) repair roads
Wegdred(d)er (der)n. 1.knotgrass; 2.(breeder --) com-monplantain
Wege (der)n (deitschi --) Dutch ways
wege, prep. 1.about; 2.because of; 3.on account of
wegem = wege em because of him
wegeme = wege me because of one
Wegerich (der)n. narrow leaved plantain
Weggel(i) (es)n. buggy
Weggelche (es)n. buggy
Wegli (es)n. path
Wegmacher (der)n. road repairer
Wegmeeschder (der)n. supervisor (of roads)
Wegner (der)n. wagon-builder
wegre = wege re because of her
wegs, adv (graades --) 1.immediately; 2.right away

Weis

Wegschdeier (der)n (er hot der -- nimmi) he is so weak that he is not able to walk
Wegschisser (der)n. sty (on the eyelid)
Wegweiser (der)n.; Wegweiser, pl. 1.guidepost; 2.signboard; 3.signpost
Weh(er)hals (der)n. diphtheria
weh/duh, v.; wehgeduh, pp. 1.ache; 2.pain; 3.(to be) painful; 4.(sich --) (a) hurt (oneself); (b) injure
weh, adj. 1.painful; 2.sore; 3.(ebbes --es) sore
wehe, v.; geweht, pp. 1.blow (of the wind); 2.wave
Wehhals (der)n.; Wehhels, pl. 1.sore throat; 2.tonsillitis
wehle, v.; gewehlt, pp. 1.choose; 2.elect; 3.select; 4.pick out
wehre, v.; gewehrt, pp. 1.keep off; 2.(sich --) (a) defend; (b) resist
Wei (der)n. wine
wei!, interj. why!
Weib (es)n.; Weiwer, pl. 1.wife; 2.woman (rarely used singular in both meanings)
Weibarig (der)n. vineyard
Weibche (es)n. female (of birds)
Weiblanz (die)n. rhubarb
weiblich, adj. 1.effeminate; feminine); 2.female; 3.feminine; 4.womanly
Weiblumm (die)n. grape hyacinth
Weibottel (die)n. grape hyacinth
Weibress (die)n. winepress
Weibsbild (es) n. 1. female; 2. woman (feminine term corresponding to der Mannskall)
Weibshemm (es)n. chemise
Weibsleit (die)n., pl. womenfolk
weibsleitnarrisch, adj. (crazy over) women
Weibsmensch (es)n.; Weibsleit, pl. 1.female; 2.woman
Weiche (der)n.; Wieche, pl. lamp wick
weiche, v.; gewiche, pp. 1.retreat; 2.yield
weichlich, adj. effeminate
Weide (der, die)n. willow
Weidebaam (der)n.; Weidebeem, pl. willow tree
Weidekareb (der)n. wicker basket
weider, adv. 1.farther; 2.further; 3.onward 4.wider
weiders, adv. 1.farther; 2.special(ly)
Weidraub (die)n. wine grape
Weifass (es)n. wine barrel
Weigaarde (der)n. vineyard
Weigeischt (der)n. alcohol
Weiglaas (es)n. wineglass
Weiglessli (es)n. grape hyacinth
Weiglessliche (es)n. grape hyacinth
weihe, v.; geweiht, pp. bless
Weiher (der)n. 1.fish dam; 2.weir
Weihnachte (die)n., pl. Christmas
Weihwasser (es)n. holy water
Weil (die)n. 1.a while; 2.(space of) time
weil, conj. 1.because; 2.while
weile, v.; geweilt, pp. 1.tarry; 2.while
weine, v.; geweint, pp. 1.weep; 2.whine
Weis (die)n. 1.manner; 2.melody; 3.tune

Ww

weis/mache | wem

weis/mache, v.; weisgemacht, pp. 1.misrepresent; 2.make someone believe something

weis/saage, v. forecast

Weischtee (der)n. cream of tartar

Weischtock (der)n. vine

weise, v.; gewisse, pp. 1.direct; 2.point out; 3.show

Weisheet (die)n. wisdom

Weisheit (die)n. wisdom

Weiss der Friede! Sure as you're alive!

Weiss der Himmel! Sure as I'm alive!

weiss der Zuschtand, adv. really

weiss mache, v.; weiss gemacht, pp. whiten

weiss, adj. white

weissaage, v. prophesy

Weissaaging (die)n. prophecy

Weissaayung (die)n. prophecy

Weissbabble (die)n. white poplar

Weissbeind (die)n. white pine

Weissbrot (es)n. wheat (white) bread

Weisschtee (der)n. tarter

weisschtengicher Tee (der)n. peppermint tea

Weissdarn (der)n. hawthorn

weisse, v.; g(e)wisse, pp. 1.display; 2.indicate; 3.show

weisse, v.; geweisst, pp. whitewash

Weisseeche (der, die)n. white oak

Weissesche (die)n. white ash

weissgliedich, adj. incandescent

Weissgraut (es)n. boiled cabbage

weisskebbich, adj. white-headed

Weisskopp (der)n.; Weisskepp, pl. 1.male bumblebee; 2.person with white hair; 3.tow haired child; 4.(wie en -- schpringt) run helter-skelter

weissle, v.; geweisselt, pp. whitewash

weisslich, adj. whitish

Weissmaulbeer (die)n. white mulberry

Weissmehl (es)n. wheat flour

Weisspensil (der)n. whitewash brush

Weisswacke (der)n. quartz

Weisswalnuss (der)n. butternut

Weisszedre (der)n. white cedar

weit ab, adv. afar

weit weck, adv. afar

weit, adj. 1.far; 2.long; 3.wide

weithaer, adv. from afar

weithie, adv. in the distance

Weiting (die)n. width

weitleftich, adj. 1.distant; 2.elaborate; 3.sporadic

weitrum, adv. far and wide

Weiwasserkessel (der)n. holy water font

Weiwel (es)n. 1.little woman; 2.wifey

Weiwerfeind (der)n. misogynist

weiwisch, adj. effeminate

welbe, v.; gewelbt, pp. arch

Welfling (die)n. cheapness

welk, adj. 1.withered; 2.wilted

Welkche (es)n. small cloud

welke, v.; gewelkt, pp. 1.whither; 2.wilt

Well (die)n.; Welle, pl. wave

well, adv., pron. which

well, interj. well

Wellbaam (der)n. 1.axle (of a wheel); 2.wooden shaft of a mill wheel

welle, v.; gewellt, pp. 1.bubble; 2.desire; 3.intend; 4.want; 5.will; 6.wish wash; 7.(net --) not thrive

Wellebletter (die)n., pl. yellow pond lily

weller, adv.; pron. which

Welleschlack (der)n. breaker

welli, adv.; pron. which

welsch, adj. indistinctly

Welsche (die)n. Welsh

welsche, v.; gewelscht, pp. jabber

Welschhaahne (der)n.; Welschhaahne; Welschhinkel, pl. (turkey) gobbler

Welschhinkel (es)n.; Welschhinkel, pl. turkey

Welschkann (es)n. Indian corn

Welschkannausmacher (der)n. corn sheller

Welschkannblanzer (der)n. corn planter

Welschkannblicker (der)n. corn sheller

Welschkannfeld (es)n.; Welschkannfelder, pl. corn field

Welschkanngareb (der)n.; Welsckanngarewe, pl. corn shock

Welschkanngeik (die)n. cornstalk fiddle

Welschkanngribb (die)n. corncrib

Welschkanngrutze (der)n.; Welschkanngrutze, pl. corncob

Welschkannhaar (die)n. corn silk

Welschkannheisel (es)n.; Welschkannheisli, pl. corncrib

Welschkannkolwe (der)n. ear of corn

Welschkannkuche (der) n.; Welschkannkuche, pl. 1.corn fritter; 2.Johnny cake

Welschkannlaab (es)n. corn fodder

Welschkannmehl (es)n. cornmeal

Welschkannschack (der)n.; Welschkannschack, pl. corn shock

Welschkannscheeler (der)n.; Welschkannscheeler, pl. corn sheller

Welschkannschtengel (der)n. cornstalk

Welschkannschtick (es)n. patch of corn

welse, v.; gewelst, pp. 1.roll; 2.wallow

Welt (die)n. world

Weltbrieschder (der)n. secular priest

Weltdeel (es)n. 1.area; 2.part of the earth; 3.section

Weltgrieg (der)n. world war

Welti (der)n. Walter

Weltkreis (der)n. world

Weltlaerning (die)n. wisdom

weltlich, adj. 1.mundane; 2.secular; 3.temporal; 4.worldly

Weltlichkeet (die)n. worldliness

Weltlieb (die)n. worldliness

Weltluscht (die)n. mundane pleasure

Weltmensch (der)n. worldling

Weltsinn (der)n. worldliness

welze, v.; gewelzt, pp. roll (earth)

wem sei, pron. whose

wem, pron. whom

Ww

wen(n)ichschdens

wen(n)ichschdens, adv. at least

wen, pron. whom

wende, v.; gewennt, pp. 1.ted; 2.turn

Wennbrett (es)n. moldboard

wenne, v.; gewennt, pp. 1.ted hay; 2.turn for drying

Wenneise (es)n. 1.moldboard; 2.wrench

Wenner (der)n. tedder

wennich, adj.; pron. some

wennich; wennicher; es wennichscht, adj. little; less; least

Wennrich (der)n. cant hook (wooden lever used to handle logs)

Wennring (der)n. cant hook (wooden lever used to handle logs)

Wennseit (die)n. moldboard side of a plow

wer, pron. who

werewwer, pron. whoever

Werkgawwel (die)n. distaff

Wesch (die)n. 1.laundry; 2.wash; 3.(-- aaschpritze) sprinkle wash

wesch (puddel) **nass,** adj. drenched

Wesch-schteiber (der)n. clothes prop

Weschb (die)n.; Weschbe, pl. wasp

Weschbenescht (es)n. wasp-nest

Weschbeschtich (der)n. sting of a wasp

Weschblo (die)n. blueing

Weschb(l)ock (der)n. washing stool

Weschbool (die)n. washbasin

Weschdaag (der)n. wash day

wesche; v.; gewescht, pp. 1.wash; 2.(sich --) wash (oneself)

Wescherei (die)n. confounded washing (laundry)

Weschern (die)n. washerwoman

Wesches (es)n. washing

Weschfraa (die)n.; Weschweiwer, pl. 1.laundrywoman; 2.washerwoman

Weschglamm (die)n. clothespin

Weschhaus (es)n. wash house

Wesching (die)n. washing

Weschkareb (der)n. clothes basket

Weschkessel (der)n. wash boiler

Weschkich (es)n. wash house

Weschlein (die)n.; Weschleine, pl. wash line

Weschlumbe (der)n. 1.washcloth; 2.washrag

Weschmachien (die)n. washing machine

weschnass, adj. soaking wet

Weschp (die)n. wasp

Weschpegerranne (die)n. geranium with scented leaves

Weschpenescht (es)n. wasp nest

weschpuddelnass, adj. soaking wet

Weschschdeiber (der)n. clothes prop

Weschschissel (die)n.; Weschschissle, pl. 1.basin; 2.washbasin

Weschschpell (die)n. clothespin

Wescht (der)n. west

Wescht (die)n. vest

wescht, adj.; adv. western

weschtlich, adv. 1.western; 2.westward

Weschwasser (es)n. water in which clothes have been washed

widderhole

Weschwringer (der)n. clothes wringer

Weschzuwwer (der)n.; Weschziwwer, pl. washtub

Wese (es)n. 1.being; 2.thing

Wese(s) (es)n. 1.disagreement; 2.row; 3.(net viel -- mache) settle a matter (offhand)

wessere, v.; gewessert, pp. water

wesserich, adj. 1.liquid; 2.watery

Wett (die)n. bet

wett = wott would

wette, v.; gewett, pp. bet

Wetting (die)n. bet

Wettschtaahl (der)n. butcher's steel

Wettschtee (der)n. whetstone

wettschteenich, adj. 1.course (of cake); 2.sandy

Wetz (der)n. whetting

wetze, v.; gewetzt, pp. 1.rub together with a swishing sound (of corduroy trousers); 2.whet

Wetzer (der)n. penis

Wetzkoom (der)n. whet-horn (filled with water or vinegar for whetting stone to sharpen scythes)

Wetzkump (der)n. whet-horn (filled with water or vinegar for whetting stone to sharpen scythes)

Wetzschtee (der)n. whetstone

wewe, v.; gewewe, pp. 1.wave; 2.weave; 3.wig-wag

Wewer (der)n.; Wewer, pl. weaver

Wewerzeddel (der)n. warp

wewwere, v.; gewewwert, pp. 1.bustle; 2.swarm

Wewwi (es)n. 1.hurt (in speaking to children); 2.sore

Wexel (der)n. 1.change (small coins); 2.(sudden) turn

Wexelfiewer (es)n. intermittent fever

wexich, adj. 1.favorable to growth; 2.flourishing; 3.thrifty

wexle, v.; gewexelt, pp. 1.change; 2.exchange

Wibbe(r)willblumm (die)n. 1.Indian paintbrush; 2.painted cup

Wibberwill (der)n. whippoorwill

Wibberwillschtock (der)n.; Wibberwillschteck, pl. pinxter flower

wibble, v.; gewibbelt, pp. 1.shake; 2.wobble

wichdich, adj. 1.important; 2.weighty

Wichs (die)n. 1.beating; 2.flogging; 3.mess; 4.paste

wichse, v.; gewichst, pp. 1.beat; 2.polish

Wickel (der)n. 1.flax wound round the distaff; 2.half fool; 3.lap of the winding frame; 4.roll; 5.(am -- nemme) take by the hair

Wickelschtock (der)n. horizontal flax reel

wickle, v.; gewickelt, pp. 1.roll; 2.warp; 3.wind; 4.wrap

Widd (die)n. withe

widde = willst du do you want to

Widder (der)n. Aries (1st sign of the zodiac)

Widder(ver)kau (der)n. 1.chewing the cud; 2.quid

widder, adv. 1.again; 2.once more; 3.(-- draa gehne) resume

widderbaerschdich, adj. 1.contrary; 2.stubborn

widdere, v.; gewiddert, pp. 1.feel disgust; 2.go against the grain; 3.scent; 4.smell

Widdergebort (die)n. regeneration

widderher/schtelle, v.; widderhergschtellt, pp. restore

widderhole, v.; widderholt, pp. 1.reiterate; 2.repeat

Ww

Widderholung / Winkeleck

Widderholung (die)n. repetition
widderkaue, v.; widdergekaut, pp. chew the cud
Widderkumm (der)n. loose strife
widderlich, adj. 1.disgusting; 2.nauseating
widderrufe, v.; widderrufe, pp. revoke
Widdersaager (der)n. adversary
widderschpreche, v.; widdergschproche, pp. contradict
Widderschpruch (der)n. contradiction
Widderschtand (der)n. resistance
widderschteh, v.; widderschtanne, pp. 1.nauseate; 2.pall; 3.resist; 4.withstand
Widderwaerdichkeet (die)n. 1.contrariness; 2.unpleasantness
Wie bischt? How do you do!
Wie geht's? Good day! (How are you?)
Wie heescht? What's your name?
Wie viel? How much?
Wie-lenger-wie-lenger, n. ground pine
Wie-lenger-wie-liewer, n. ground pine
wie, adv.; conj. 1.according (to that); 2.as; 3.how
wie, prep. 1.like; 2.than
Wieche (der)n.; Wieche, pl. wick
Wiechgaarn (es)n. wick cord
wiede, v.; gewiet, pp. rave
Wiederkau (die)n. sweet-scented fern
wiedich, adj. 1.furious; 2.mad; 3.rabid; 4.raving
wiedich bees, adj. infuriated
Wieg (die)n.; Wiege, pl. cradle (for an infant)
wiege, v.; gewoge, pp. 1.weigh; 2.(sich --) weigh oneself
Wiegelied (es)n. lullaby
wiehle, v.; gewiehlt, pp. 1.root (of hogs); 2.rummage
Wiek (die)n. cradle
Wies (die)n. meadow
wieschderlich, adj. 1.very bad-tempered; 2.very disagreeable
Wieschderlichkeet (die)n. disagreeableness
wiescht mache; v.; wiescht gemacht, pp. (sich --) soil the diaper (of infants)
wiescht viel, adv. terribly much
wiescht, adj. 1.bad; 2.cruel; 3.disagreeable; 4.malicious; 5.ugly; 6.unruly; 7.(er hut -- gemacht) he raised Cain
wieschtgaschdich, adj. 1.malicious; 2.very disagreeable
wiete, v.; gewiet, pp. rave
wieviel, adv. 1.how many; 2.ow much
wievielt, adv. 1.what number; 2.which
wiffel, adv. 1.how many; 2.how much
wiffelt, adv. 1.what number; 2.which
wild, adj. 1.peculiar; 2.savage; 3.unruly; 4.wild
Wildbret (es)n. venison
Wildernis (die)n. wilderness
Wildfeier (es)n. 1.erysipelas; 2.wildfire
Wildfleesch (es)n. proud flesh
Wildheet (die)n. 1.unruliness; 2.wildness
Wildkasch (die)n.; Wildkasche, pl. 1.choke cherry; 2.June berry; 3.wild cherry
Wildkatz (die)n. wildcat
Wille (der)n. will
Wille mache, v.; gemacht, pp. (sei --) make one's will

wille, adj. made of wool
wille, prep. (um [ihr] --) for (her) sake
willens, adj. willing
willich, adj. willing
Wil(l)kumm (der)n. welcome
Wil(l)kumm!, interj. welcome!
wimmele, v.; gewimmelt, pp. 1.cry feebly (of a sick child); 2.groan; 3.moan
wimmle, v.; gewimmelt, pp. 1.be alive with; 2.swarm
Wind (der)n. 1.wind; 2.twaddle; 3.(-- griege vun ebbes) get wind of something
Windbeidel (der)n. 1.blusterer; 2.undependable person
Windblumm (die)n. anemone
Windel (der)n.; Windle, pl. 1.diaper; 2.swaddling clothes
Windelschpell (die)n. safety pin
Winder (der)n. winter
Winderabbel (der)n. winter apple
Winderbeer (die)n. winter pear
Winderdaag (der)n. winter day
windere, v.; gewindert, pp. winter
Windergleeder (die)n., pl. winter clothes
Windergrie (die)n. 1.partridge berry (Matchella repens); 2.wintergreen
winderisch, adj. wintery
Windermarye (der)n. winter morning
Windermunet (der)n. winter month
Winderobscht (es)n. winter fruit
Winderreddich (der)n. winter radish
winders, adv. (in the) winter
Winderseit (die)n. north side
Winderwedder (es)n. winter weather
Winderweeze (der)n. winter wheat
Winderzwiwwel (die)n.; Winderzwiwwle, pl. multiplier onions
windgebroche, adj. 1.having the heaves; 2.heavy
Windhund (der)n. any long slender dog (also applied to other animals and even to persons)
windich, adj. 1.talkative; 2.windy
Windkaft (die)n. wind gap
Windkolick (der)n. wind colic
Windmiehl (die)n. 1.windmill; 2.winnowing mill
Windraad (es)n. wind-wheel
windrich, adj. wintery
Windroi (die)n. windrow
Windros (die)n. anemone
windschtill, adj. calm
Windschtoss (der)n. gust
Windsuckler (der)n. cribbing horse
Windwaerwel (der)n. whirlwind
Windwolk (die)n. cloud presaging windy weather
Wink (der)n. 1.sign; 2.wink
winke, v.; gewunke, pp. 1.beckon; 2.wink
Winkel (der)n. 1.angle; 2.corner; 3.gusset; 4.square
winkel, adj. square
Winkelbohre (der)n. brace (tool)
Winkeleck (es)n. the right-angled corner

Ww

Winkeleise

Winkeleise (es)n. square (carpenter's tool)

Winn (die)n.; Winne, pl. 1.pulley; 2.screw; 3.screw jack; 4.windlass

Winne (die)n. 1.black bindweed; 2.field bind- weed; 3.hedge bindweed

Winnel (die)n. diaper

winnisch, adj. 1.crooked; 2.out of shape; 3.warped

Winsch (der)n.; Winsche, pl. wish

winsche, v.; gewinscht, pp. wish

Winscher (der)n.; Winscher, pl. member of a New Year's greeting party

Winsches (es)n. wish

Winsching (die)n. New Year's greeting

winsle, v.; gewinselt, pp. 1.whine; 2.whimper

Winterfrucht (die)n. grain sown in fall and the resulting growth

Wintergraut (es)n. cabbage for winter use

Winterhols (es)n. firewood for the winter

winterisch, adj. wintery

wintrich, adj. wintery

Wipphand (die)n. upper hand

Wisch (der)n. 1.wiper; 2.wisp

wisch, adj (en --) (a) a small number; (b) several

Wischbel (der)n. small bunch or wisp (of hay)

wischble, v.; gewischbelt, pp. 1.murmur; 2.move back and forth; 3.rustle

Wischbleholz (es)n. persimmon wood

wische, v.; gewischt, pp. wipe

Wischel (es)n. 1.lock; 2.tuft; 3.wisp

Wischer (der)n. 1.mat; 2.wiper

Wischli (es)n. 1.lock; 2.tuft; 3.wisp

Wischpel (die)n. persimmon

wischpel = mischpel persimmon

wischwasch 1.bosh; 2.claptrap

Wiss (die)n.; Wisse, pl. 1.meadow; 2.pasture

Wissbaam (der)n. boom-pole (used on hay wagon)

wisse losse, v.; wisse gloss (glesst = Amish usage 1.inform; 2.let know

wisse, v.; gwisst, pp. 1. know; 2.(mer kennt net --) there's no telling; 3.(weiss der himmel) sure as I'm alive

Wissel (der)n. weasel

Wisselche (es)n. weasel

Wisselhaut (die)n. weasel skin

Wissemaus (die)n. meadow mouse

Wissenschaft (die)n. 1.knowledge; 2.science

wissentlich, adj. knowingly

wittere, v.; gewittert, pp. 1.scent (of horses); 2.smell

Wittfraa (die)n.; Wittweiwer, pl. 1.widow; 2. (hinnerlossni --) relict

Wittmann (der)n.; Wittmenner, pl. widower

Wittring (die)n. 1.climate; 2.weather

Wittrung (die)n. weather

Witz (der)n. 1.wit; 2.witticism

Witzbold (der)n. 1.funny fellow; 2.jokesmith

Witzel (es)n. little pig

witzich, adj. 1.over smart; 2.witty

Wiwwel (die)n.; Wiwwle, pl. weevil

Woll(e)graut

Wiwwelsucht (die)n. nettle-rash

wiwwle, v.; gewiwwelt, pp. swarm

Wix (der)n. sophisticated fellow

Wix (die)n. paste

wixe, v.; gewixt, pp. polish

wo, pron. where

wo, rel. pron. 1.which; 2.who

Woch (die) n.; Woche, pl. 1. week; 2. (aafangs --) at the beginning of the week; 3.(en --ner sex) six weeks or so; 4.(hinnes --) at the end of the week

wochelang, adv. (for) weeks

Wochend (es)n. weekend

wodarich, adv. whereby

woge, v.; gewogt, pp. 1.dare; 2.risk; 3.venture

Wogenaggel (der)n. pin or bolt of a double tree (usually with the head shaped like a hammer)

woher, adv. whence

wohl, adj., adv. 1.healthy; 2.well

wohlaan!, interj. 1.'tis well!; 2.well!

wohlbekannt, adj. noted

Wohldaat (die)n. benefaction

Wohlfaahrt (die)n. welfare

Wohlgemut (der)n. wild marjoram

Wohlgeruch (der)n. perfume

Wohlgfalle (der)n. favor

wohlhaabend, adj. rich

wohluff, adj. 1.cheerful; 2.joyful; 3.merry

Wohnblatz (der)n.; Wohnbletz, pl. 1.abode; 2.residence

wohne, v.; gwohnt, pp. 1.dwell; 2.live; 3.reside

wohnhaft, adj. 1.domiciled; 2.resident

Wohnhaus (es)n. dwelling

Wohning (die)n. 1.dwelling; 2.place of dwelling

Wohnung (die)n. 1.dwelling; 2.place of dwelling

wohr, adj. true

Wohret (die)n. truth

wohretlich, adj. verily

wohrhafdich, adv. really

wohrhaft, adj. truthful

wohrhaftich, adj. 1.actually; 2.certainly; 3.really; 4.truly; 5.veracious

wohrlich, adj. verily

wohrsaage, v.; wohrsaat, pp. 1.divine; 2.tell fortunes

Wohrsaager (der)n. 1.fortune teller; 2.soothsayer

Woi (der)n.; Woi, pl. hawk

Wolf (der)n.; Welf, pl. wolf

wolfel; welfler; welflescht, adj. cheap; cheaper; cheapest

Wolfhaut (die)n. wolf-robe

wolfich, adj. 1.avaricious; 2.greedy; 3.voracious; 4.wolfish

Wolfsbuhn (die)n. lupine

wolfschtraehmich, adj. brindled

Wolk (die)n.; Wolke, pl. cloud

Wolkebruch (der)n. cloudburst

wolkich, adj. cloudy

wolkschtreemich, adj. brindled

Woll (die)n. wool

Woll(e)graut (es)n. mullein

Ww

woll   Wutzsau

woll; adj. 1.of course; 2.well

wolle, adj. woolen

wolle, v.; gewollt, pp. 1.intend; 2.to want to; 3.will; 4.wish; 5.(net --) not thrive

Wolleblaat (es)n.; Wollebledder, pl. mullein leaf

Wolleflies (der)n. woolen fleece

Wolleschtengel (der)n. mullein

Wollfell (es)n. sheep's skin

Wollgaarn (es)n. worsted

Wollgemut (der)n. 1.mountain sage; 2.wild marjoram

wollich, adj. woolen

Wollraad (es)n. spinning wheel for wool

wollschtraemich, adj. brindled

wollschtreemich, adj. brindled

Wonne (die)n. 1.delight; 2.joy

Woog (die)n.; Wooge, pl. 1.balance; 2.double-tree; 3.Libra (7th sign of the zodiac); 4.scale

wooghelsich, adj. daring

wott, v. 1.wish; 2.would

woxe; v.; gewoxt, pp. (sich --) regurgitate

wu anne? (to) what place?

wu anne, adv. 1.to what place; 2.where to

wu hie, adv. where to

wu mit, adv. wherewith

wu, conj. as

wu, pron. where

wu, rel. pron. 1.which; 2.who

wudarich, adv. whereby

wuher, adv. whence

wuhie, adv. 1.where to; 2.whither

Wuhnblatz (der)n.; Wuhnbletz, pl. 1.abode; 2.residence

wuhne, v.; gewuhnt, pp. 1.dwell; 2.live; 3.reside

wuhnhaft, adj. 1.domiciled; 2.resident

Wuhning (die)n.; Wuhninge, pl. 1.abode; 2.dwelling

wull, adj. 1.I suppose; 2.it is true; 3.of course; 4.well

wull, adv. of course

wulli! call for geese

Wund (die)n. wound

wund, adj. 1.chafed; 2.sore

Wundblascher (es)n. salve

Wunddokder (der)n. surgeon

wunde, v.; gewundt, pp. wound

wunderbaar, adj. 1.marvelous; 2.wonderful

Wundgraut (es)n. goldenrod

Wundnarb (die)n. scar

Wundschmatze (die)n., pl. pain in an old wound

Wunner (die, es)n. 1.miracle; 2.prodigy; 3.wonder

wunnerbaar, adj. 1.marvelous; 2.wonderful

wunnere, v.; gewunnert, pp. 1.wonder; 2.(es wunnert mich) I wonder; 3.(sich --) wonder

Wunnerfitz (der)n.; Wunnerfitz, pl. 1.busybody;2.curiosity; 3.inquisitive person

wunnerfitzich, adj. 1.curious; 2.inquisitive; 3.prying

wunnerlich, adj. 1.demented; 2.inquisitive; 3.melancholy; 4.strange; 5.wonderful

Wunnernaas (der)n. busybody

wunnernaasich, adj. inquisitive

Wunnernaus (die)n. inquisitive person

wunners, adv. 1.great shakes; 2.wonderfully

wunnerschee, adj. very beautiful

wunnerschtolz, adj. very proud

wunnerselde, adv. rarely

wunnerswaert, adj. 1.admirable; 2.worthwhile

wunnervoll, adj. wonderful

wuns(l)ich glee, adj. very small

wuns(l)ich, adj. 1.small; 2.wee

Wunsch (der)n. wish

wunz(l)ich, adj. 1.small; 2.wee

wuppsch, adv. 1.in a jiffy; 2.whiz!

Wurfschaufel (die)n. scoop

wurum, adv. whereabout

Wusch (der)n. clump or bunch (of hair)

wusslich, adj. 1.agile; 2.lively; 3.nimble; 4.sprightly

Wut (die)n. 1.anger; 2.fury; 3.rage; 4.wrath

Wutgraut (es)n. 1.mad-dog skullcap; 2.madweed

Wutschtee (der)n. mad-stone

Wutz (die)n. 1.hog; 2.pig

Wutzelche (es)n. 1.little pig; 2.piggy

Wutzlein (es)n. 1.little pig; 2.piggy

Wutz(l)i (es)n.; Wutzlin, pl. piglet

Wutzsau (die)n. 1.hog; 2.pig

Yy

ya

ya, adv. 1.yes; 2.(-- was ich saage wott) (a) oh, by the way; (b) I was going to say

yaage, v.; geyaagt, pp. 1.chase; 2.drive (as the wind the clouds); 3.drive fast; 4.hunt

Yaaghund (der)n.; Yaaghund, pl. hound

Yaahr (es)n.; Yaahre, pl. year

Yaahrbuch (es)n.; Yaahrbicher, pl. yearbook

Yaahr(e)szeit (die)n. season

yaahreweis, adv. several years

Yaahrgang (der)n. season

yaahrlich, adv. yearly

Yaard (es)n. yard (measure)

Yaardschtecke (der)n. yardstick

yachde, v.; gyacht, pp. make noise

yachdich, adj. noisy

Yacht (die)n. 1.hunt; 2.lark; 3.noise

yachtich, adj. noisy

Yackbautsch (der)n. hunting bag

yackere, v.; geyackert, pp. jog along

yae(h)rich, adj. a year-old

Yaeger (der)n. shirker (man who goes to town and neglects his farm work)

yaegere, v.; geyaegert, pp. hunt

Yaegerei (die)n. hunting

yaehlings, adv. 1.precipitately; 2.sheer down

yaehre, v.; geyaehrt, pp. 1.ferment; 2.(sich --) have a birthday

Yaehrlichfescht (es)n. anniversary

Yaehrling (der)n. yearling

Yaehrsdaag (der)n.; Yaehrsdaage, pl. birthday

yaerich, adv. year old

yaerlich, adv. annual

Yakob (der)n. Jacob

Yakobus (der)n. St. James Day, July 25

Yammer (der)n. 1.misery; 2.trouble

Yammer un Elend! Oh, misery!

Yammerdaal (es)n. vale of tears

yammere, v.; geyammert, pp. 1.groan; 2.lament; 3.moan; 4.(sich --) move one to pity

Yanuaar (der)n. January

Yarick (der)n. George

yauchze, v.; geyauchzt, pp. shout

Yauner (der)n. swindler

yaunse, v.; geyaunst, pp. 1.complain; 2.grumble; 3.yelp

yautze, v.; geyautzt, pp. 1.bark; 2.shout

Yawatt (es)n. 1.assent; 2.yes

ye!, interj (ach [du] --!) dear me

ye, adv. ever (rare usage)

yeder, adj. each

yedermann, adj. 1.everybody; 2.everyone

yeders, adj. 1.each one; 2.everyone

yeders, pron. 1.each; 2.everyone

yederzeit, adv. at all times

yedesmol, adv. 1.each time; 2.every time

yedoch, adv. however

Yeeger (der)n.; Yeeger, pl. hunter

Yuchend

yeemere, v.; geyeemert, pp. groan

Ye(e)sus (der)n. Jesus

Ye(e)sus (der)n (-- Mensche Erleeser) I.H.S.

Ye(e)susbrief (der)n. alleged letter of Jesus

Ye(e)sus Grischdus (der)n. Jesus Christ

yehaer, adv (vun --) from the remotest time

yehre, v.; geyehrt, pp. ferment

yeklich, adj. each

yemmerlich, adj. 1.deplorable; 2.pitiful

yemols, adv. ever

Yenner (der)n. January

Yennerkalb (es)n.; Yennerkelwer, pl. person born inJanuary

Yess (der)n. 1.flurry (of temper); 2.tantrum

yetz nau, adv. now

yetzich, adj. present (time)

Yinger (der)n.; Yinger, pl. disciple

Yingling (der)n. 1.young person; 2.youth

yo, adv. 1.yes; 2.(geh -- net weck) don't leave under any circumstances

Yoch (die)n. 1.oxtongue; 2.viper's bugloss

Yoch (es)n.; Yecher, pl. ox-yoke

yoche, v.; geyocht, pp. yoke

Yochholz (es)n. yoke

Yochschtick (es)n. chuck rib

Yockel (der)n. 1.Jack; 2.Jakey

Yockli (der)n. 1.Jack; 2.Jacob; 3.Jakey

yodle, v.; geyodelt, pp. yodel

Yoel (der)n. Joel

Yohannes (der)n. John

Yohannsgraut (es)n. St. John's wort

yohle, v.; geyohlt, pp. 1.bay (of a hound in hunting); 2.bark; 3.shout

Yohr (es)n. year

Yohr(e)zeit (die)n. season

yohraus, adv. year out

yohre, v. ferment

yohrei, adv. year in

yohrelang, adj. 1.for years; 2.(in) odd or scattered years; 3.several years in succession

Yohrgang (der)n. season

Yohrhunnert (es)n. century

Yohrsdaag (der)n. festival or anniversary day, September 24 (Schwenckfelder)

Yohrzaahl (die)n. 1.date; 2.year

Yokkob (der)n. Jacob

Yoli (der)n. dim. of Joseph or Joel

yomere, v.; geyomert, pp. 1.groan; 2.moan

Yones (der)n. 1.Jonas; 2.Jonathan

Yoni (der)n. 1.Jonas; 2.Jonathan

Yorch (der)n. George

Yordan (der)n. Jordan

Yost (der)n. Yost

Yowatt (es)n. 1.assent; 2.yes

yubele, v.; geyubelt, pp. shout

Yubelfescht (es)n. Jubilee

Yuchend (die)n. youth

Yy

yucke · yuxich

yucke, v.; geyuckt, pp. 1.fidget; 2.jerk
Yuckschnepp (die)n. spotted sandpiper
Yuddekasch (die)n.; Yuddekasche, pl. ground-cherry
Yudderei (die)n. overcharging
Yugend (die)n. youth
Yuli (der)n. July
Yung (der)n.; Yunge, pl. boy
yung, adj. young
Yungfraa (die)n. 1.virgin; 2.Virgo (6th sign of the zodiac)
yungleidisch, adj. 1.snobbish; 2.snooty
Yuni (der)n. June
yuschdament, adv. exactly
Yuschdis (der)n. justice of the peace
yuscht, adv. 1.just; 2.just now; 3.only
Yutt (der)n.; Yudde, pl. 1.atlas bone; 2.Jew; 3.(der
    ewiche --) impatiens (flowering plant)
yutte, v.; geyutt, pp. 1.bargain; 2.cheat; 3.haggle
Yuttenaas (die)n. Jewish (aquiline) nose
yuuse, v.; gyuust, pp. 1.apply; 2.employ; 3.use
Yux (der)n. 1.jerk; 2.Indian whoop; 3.shout
yuxe, v.; geyuxt, pp. 1.have a lark; 2.shout
yuxich, adj. 1.boisterous; 2.sportive

Zz

zaage

zaage, v.; gezaakt, pp. hesitate
Zaah (der)n.; Zeh, pl. tooth
Zaahdokder (der)n. dentist
Zaahfleesch (es)n. gum(s)
Zaahgschwaere (der)n. tooth ulcer
Zaahkeenich (der)n. wren
Zaahl (die)n. number
Zaahlaad (die)n. 1.jawbone; 2.tooth socket
zaahllos, adj. numberless
zaahlreich, adj. numerous
Zaahlwatt (es)n. 1.figure; 2.numeral
Zaahm (der)n.; Zehm, pl. bridle
zaahm, adj. tame
zaahme, v.; gezaahmt, pp. tame
zaahne, v.; gezaahnt, pp. teeth
Zaahreeb (die)n. 1.climbing false buckwheat; 2.Virginia creeper
Zaahrieb (die)n.; Zaahriewe, pl. 1.man-of-the-earth; 2.Virginia creeper
Zaahschlibber (der)n. wren
Zaahweh (es)n. toothache
Zaam (der)n. reins
Zaamziggel (der)n. reins
zaart, adj. 1.crisp; 2.short; 3.tender
Zaaschlipper (der)n. wren
Zabbe (der)n.; Zabbe, pl. 1.peg; 2.pin; 3.tenon; 4.plug; 5.stopper; 6.bung; 7.faucet; 8.spigot
Zabbeloch (es)n.; Zabbelecher, pl. 1.mortise; 2.peg-hole
zachich, adj. pointed
Zacke (der)n. 1.branch; 2.fruit-spur; 3.projection; 4.prong; 5.scallop-edge; 6.tooth
zackere, v.; gezackert, pp. 1.jog along; 2.plant corn in checkerboard fashion; 3.plow
zackich, adj. 1.pointed; 2.toothed
zackle, v.; gezackelt, pp. 1.notch; 2.tooth
zacklich, adj. 1.pointed; 2.toothed
zaeh, adj. 1.tough; 2.viscous
Zaehbascht (die)n. toothbrush
Zaehbutzer (der)n. toothpick
Zaehche (es)n. toothie
Zaehdokder (der)n. dentist
Zaehglepperes (es)n. chattering of the teeth
Zaehichkeet (die)n. toughness
Zaehknaersche (es)n. gnashing of the teeth
zaehlbaar, adj. numerable
zaehle, v.; gezaehlt, pp. 1.calculate; 2.count; 3.depend upon
Zaehler (der)n. teller
Zaehlung (die)n. numeration
Zaehpulwer (es)n. tooth powder
Zaehropper (der)n. tooth extractor
zaere, v.; gezaert, pp. 1.tease; 2.tug
zaerife, v.; gezaerift, pp. 1.quarrel; 2.wrangle
Zaerkel (der)n. compass (circle dividers)
Zaerkelsaeg (die)n. circular saw
zaerkle, v.; gezaerkelt, pp. circle
zamme/babbe, v.; zammegebappt, pp. stick together
zamme/backe, v.; zammegebackt, pp. stick together in baking

zamme/hewe

zamme/baerschde, v.; zammegebaerscht, pp. brush up
zamme/balle, v.; zammegeballt, pp. form in a ball
zamme/basse, v.; zammegebasst, pp. 1.fit together; 2.(to be) suited to each other
zamme/batzle, v.; zammegebatzelt, pp. tumble down
zamme/belse, v.; zammegebelst, pp. slam together
zamme/bicke; v. zammegebickt, pp. (sich --) bend over
zamme/biege, v.; zammegeboge, pp. bend together
zamme/binne, v.; zammegebunne, pp. tie together
zamme/blanze, v.; zammegeblanzt, pp. plant together
zamme/blatsche, v.; zammegeblatscht, pp. pack the ground (as by a heavy rain)
zamme/blaudre, v.; zammegeblaudert, pp. talk together
zamme/bleiwe, v.; zammegebliwwe, pp. remain together
zamme/bluge, v.; zammegeblugt, pp. plow in partnership
zamme/breche, v.; is zummegebroche, pp. break down
zamme/bringe, v.; zammegebrocht, pp. gather
zamme/daerfe, v.; zammegedaerft, pp. be allowed to meet
zamme/daerre, v.; zammegedaerrt, pp. dry up
zamme/dappe, v.; zammegedappt, pp. meet (by chance)
zamme/draage, v.; zammegedraage, pp. 1.carry together; 2.collect
zamme/drehe, v.; zammegedreht, pp. twist together
zamme/dricke, v.; zammegedrickt, pp. 1.compress; 2.indent; 3.press together hard
zamme/drickle, v.; zammegedrickelt, pp. dry up
zamme/dripple, v.; zammegedrippelt, pp. tramp down
zamme/duh, v.; zammegeduh, pp. 1. assembled; 2. put together
zamme/faahre, v.; is zammegfaahre, pp. 1.haul together; 2.shrink; 3.start (from fright)
zamme/falle, v.; zammegfalle, pp. 1.collapse; 2.fall down
zamme/fasse, v.; zarnmegfasst, pp. 1.gather up; 2.grasp
zamme/fidde, v.; zammegfitt, pp. fit together
zamme/fiege, v.; zammegfiegt, pp. 1.fit together; 2.fly together; 3.go to smash
zamme/gaerwe, v.; zammegegaerbt, pp. drive together by beating
zamme/geh, v.; zammegange, pp. 1.come (of butter); 2.congregate; 3.shrink
zamme/gfriere, v.; zammegfrore, pp. freeze together
zamme/gloppe, v.; zammegegloppt, pp. hammer together
zamme/gnicke, v.; zammegegnickt, pp. collapse
zamme/gnippe, v.; zammegegnippt, pp. knot together
zamme/gnootsche, v.; zammegegnootscht, pp. mess by handling
zamme/grache, v.; zammegegracht, pp. crash down
zamme/gratze, v.; zammegegratzt, pp. 1.amass by hoarding; 2.scratch together
zamme/hacke, v.; zammeghackt, pp. chop down
zamme/haerde, v.; zammeghaerdt, pp. herd together
zamme/halte, v.; zammeghalte, pp. hold together
zamme/heele, v.; zammegheelt, pp. heal (together)
zamme/helfe, v.; zammegholfe, pp. help to get together
zamme/henke, v.; zammeghenkt, pp. hang together
zamme/hewe, v.; zammeghowe, pp. hold together

Zz

zamme/hocke

zamme/hocke, v.; zammeghockt, pp. sit together
zamme/hole, v.; zammegholt, pp. assemble
zamme/huddle, v.; zammeghuddelt, pp. gather in a hasty manner
zamme/kaafe, v.; zammekaaft, pp. buy up
zamme/keere, v.; zammegekeert, pp. belong together
zamme/kehre, v.; zammegekehrt, pp. sweep up
zamme/kenne, v.; zammegekennt, pp. be able to get together
zamme/kette, v.; zammegekett, pp. chain together
zamme/kumme, v.; is zammekumme, pp. 1.assemble; 2.get together; 3.meet
zamme/laafe, v.; zummegeloffe, pp. 1.assemble; 2.get together; 3.meet; 4.come together (in a social gathering)
zamme/lause, v.; zammegelaust, pp. hoard
zamme/leere, v.; zammegeleert, pp. pour from one vessel into another
zamme/lege, v.; zammeglegt, pp. 1.contribute jointly; 2.fold
zamme/lese, v.; zammegelese, pp. gather
zamme/lewe, v.; zammegelebt, pp. live together
zamme/locke, v.; zammegelockt, pp. call together
zamme/losse, v.; zammegelosst, pp. permit to come together
zamme/maahle, v.; zammegemaahle, pp. grind
zamme/mache, v.; zammegemacht, pp. 1.collect; 2.gather
zamme/maehe, v.; zammegemaeht, pp. mow down
zamme/mische, v. zammegemischt, pp. mix
zamme/naehe, v.; zammegenaeht, pp. sew together
zamme/naggle, v.; zammegenaggelt, pp. nail together
zamme/nemme, v.; zammegenumme, pp. 1.gather up; 2.take together
zamme/packe, v.; zammegepackt, pp. pack
zamme/palde, v.; zammegepalde, pp. keep together
zamme/petze, v.; zammegepetzt, pp. 1.pinch shut; 2.together
zamme/quetsche, v.; zammequetscht, pp. crush
zamme/raffe, v.; zammegerafft, pp. gather hastily
zamme/reche, v.; zammegerecht, pp. rake up
zamme/reeche, v.; zammegereecht, pp. reach together
zamme/reide, v.; zammegeridde, pp. ride together
zamme/reisse, v.; zammegerisse, pp. tear down
zamme/reiwe, v.; zammegeriwwe, pp. rub together
zamme/renne, v.; zammegerennt, pp. collide
zamme/ricke, v.; zammegerickt, pp. move up to each other
zamme/rolle, v.; zammegerollt, pp. roll up
zamme/rufe, v.; zammegerufe, pp. 1.call together; 2.convene
zamme/rumple, v.; zammegerumpelt, pp. put in disorder
zamme/sammle, v.; zammegsammelt, pp. gather
zamme/schaerre, v.; zammegschaerrt, pp. 1.accumulate; 2.scratch together
zamme/schaffe, v.; zammegschaft, pp. 1.gather; 2.work together
zamme/schiesse, v.; zammegschosse, pp. shoot down
zamme/schiewe, v.; zammegschowe, pp. push together
zamme/schlagge, v.; zammegschlagge, pp. 1.clash; 2.knock down; 3.knock to pieces
zamme/schleefe, v.; zammegschleeft, pp. bring together

zammenei

by dragging
zamme/schleiche, v.; zammegschliche, pp. 1.meet secretly; 2.sneak together
zamme/schluppe, v.; zammegschluppt, pp. creep together
zamme/schmeisse, v.; zammegschmisse, pp. 1.demolish; 2.throw down
zamme/schnaerre, v.; zammegschnaerrt, pp. shrivel up
zamme/schnalle, v.; zammegschnallt, pp. strap or buckle together
zamme/schpaare, v.; zammegschpaart, pp. hoard
zamme/schpaerre, v.; zammegschpaerrt, pp. pen up together
zamme/schpanne, v.; zammegschpannt, pp. 1.each of two men to furnish a horse to be worked together as a team; 2.harness (horses) together
zamme/schpelle, v.; zammegschpellt, pp. pin together
zamme/schpringe, v.; zammegschprunge, pp. run together
zamme/schreiwe, v.; zammegschriwwe, pp. correspond
zamme/schrumble, v.; zammegschrumbelt, pp. shrivel
zamme/schtaerze, v.; zammegschtaerzt, pp. 1.fall down; 2.fall in
zamme/schtecke, v.; zammegschtocke, pp. stick together
zamme/schteh, v.; zammegschtanne, pp. stand together
zamme/schteppe, v.; zammegschteppt, pp. sew together
zamme/schticke, v.; zammegschtickt, pp. stick together
zamme/schtosse, v.; zammegschtosse, pp. 1.adjoin; 2.collide; 3.churn; 4.join together
zamme/schweese, v.; zammegschweest, pp. weld
zamme/schwemme, v.; zammegschwemmt, pp. collect by flooding
zamme/schwetze, v.; zammegschwetzt, pp. talk together
zamme/sei, v.; zammegewest, pp. be together
zamme/setze, v.; zammegsetzt, pp. compose
zamme/wachse, v.; zammegewachst, pp. grow together
zamme/warzle, v.; zammegewarzelt, pp. have roots intertwine
zamme/wickle, v.; zammegewickelt, pp. wrap together
zamme/wohne, v.; zammegewohnt, pp. live together
zamme/wolle, v.; zammegewollt, pp. want to get together
zamme/yaage, v.; zammegeyaagt, pp. chase together
zamme/zehle, v.; zammgzehlt, pp. add (up)
zamme/ziehe, v.; zammegezogge, pp. 1.move into the same house; 2.pull together
zamme/zwenge, v.; zammegezwengt, pp. force together
zamme/zwinge, v.; zammegezwunge, pp. force together
zamme, adv. together
Zammelaaf (der)n. social gathering
zammenanner, adv. together
zammenannerfaahre, v.; zammernannergfaahre, pp. drive together
zammenannergeh, v.; zammenannergange, pp. 1.gather in one place; 2.go together
zammenei, adv. 1.in together; 2.separable prefix of verbs, adding the ideas pell-mell, crowding, precipitately, abruptly, voraciously

208

Zz

zammenunner ... Zell

zammenunner, adv. 1.down together; 2.separable prefix of verbs, adding the idea of pell-mell, crowding, precipitately, abruptly, voraciously

zammer, adv. together

zammernannerkumme, v.; zammernannergkumme, pp. 1.come together by appointment; 2.meet unexpectedly

zamt(e), adv. 1.together with; 2.with; 3.(mit --) pack, bag and baggage, and all

Zange (die)n. tongs

Zank (der)n. 1.altercation; 2.contention; 3.strife

zanke, v.; gezankt, pp. 1.scold; 2.wrangle

Zankerei (die)n. 1.contention; 2.strife

zankich, adj. 1.faultfinding; 2.scolding

Zanking (die)n. scolding

Zann (der)n. 1.anger; 2.indignation; 3.ire; 4.rage; 5.temper; 6.wrath

zannich mache, v.; zannich gemacht, pp. anger

zannich, adj. 1.angry (bees); 2.indignant; 3.peevish; 4.wroth

zappe, v.; gezappt, pp. tap

Zappeeche (die)n. swamp white oak

Zapper (der)n. tapster

zapple, v.; gezappelt, pp. 1.dangle; 2.kick; 3.struggle

zareffe, v.; gezarefft, pp. wrangle

zarfe, v.; gezareft, pp. quarrel

Zarickelseeg (die)n.; Zarickelseege, pl. circular saw

zarre, v.; gezatt, pp. tease

Zau (der)n. paling fence (rare usage)

Zauber (der)n. spell

zaudere, v.; gezaudert, pp. 1.be slow about; 2.hesitate

Zaunkeenich (der)n. wren

zawwle, v.; gezawwelt, pp. 1.kick; 2.struggle; 3.wiggle

zawwlich, adj. 1.restless; 2.wiggling

ze = zu 1.at; 2.closed; 3.to

ze reh foundered

zeah, adj. viscous

Zebbche (es)n. 1.little peg; 2.uvula

zebbe, v.; gezeppt, pp. plait

Zech (die)n. 1.bill; 2.reckoning; 3.score

Zeck (die)n.; Zecke, pl. 1.scolding person; 2.tick

Zeeche (es)n. 1.hand of a clock; 2.omen; 3.sign; 4.sign of the zodiac

zeeche, v.; gezeecht, pp. 1.carouse; 2.drink

Zeedre (der)n. cedar

Zeedre Baum (der)n. cedar tree

zeedre, v.; gezeedert, pp. sing or trill (only of the singing or trilling of hens)

Zeedrehols (es)n. cedar wood

Zeedrekischt (die)n. cedar chest

Zeh blecke (die)v. show the teeth (animal)

zeh, adj. tough

Zehbascht (die)n. toothbrush

Zehblicker (der)n. toothpick

Zehbutzer (der)n. toothpick

Zehche (es)n. toothie

Zehe (der)n.; Zehe, pl. toe

Zehe Gebodde (die)n. Ten Commandments

Zehe(de)deel (es)n. tenth part

Zehe-Cent-Schtick (es)n.; Zehe-Cent-Schticker, pl. dime

zehe, adj.; pron. ten

Zehed(e)l (es)n. tenth

Zeheder (en) ten spot (in cards)

Zehefuusschtecke (der)n. ten-foot pole

zehejaahrich, adj. ten years old

zehemol, adv. ten times

zehet, adv. tenth

Zehichkeet (die)n. toughness

Zehland (die)n. tooth-socket

zehle, v.; gezehlt, pp. 1.add; 2.count on; 3.expect; 4.numerate; 5.presume

Zehler (der)n. teller

zehme, v., gezehmt, pp. tame

Zehpulwer (es)n. tooth powder

zehre, v.; gezehrt, pp. 1.consume; 2.spend

Zehrgeld (es)n. spending money

Zehring (die)n. spending money

Zehrobber (der)n. tooth extractor

Zehschtarer (der)n.; Zehschtarer, pl. toothpick

Zeichnis (es)n. 1.evidence; 2.testimony; 3.(-- gewwe) (a) attest; (b) testify

zeideweis, adv. 1.at times; 2.periodically

zeidich, adj. 1.ripe; 2.seasonable

zeidiche, v.; gezeidicht, pp. 1.mature; 2.ripen

Zeiding (die)n.; Zeidinge, pl. newspaper

Zeidingdrager (der)n. newsboy

Zeidingschreiwer (der)n. newspaper reporter

Zeige (der)n. witness

zeige, v.; gezeikt, pp. generate

Zeigegeld (es)n. witness fee

Zeignis (es)n. 1.testimony; 2.(-- gewwe) testify

Zeiknis (es)n. 1.evidence; 2.testimony

Zeil (die)n. line (rare usage)

Zeit (die)n.; Zeite, pl. 1.menses; 2.time; 3.(-- verdreiwe) pass time (away); 4.(bei -- kumme) come early; 5.(die -- biete) (a) pass the time of day; (b) salute; 6. (fer 'n --) temporarily; 7.(langsami --) Standard Time ("slow time"); 8.(schtaricki --) (a) Daylight Saving Time; (b) "devils time"; (c) "fast time"; 9. (sei -- schteh) serve one's apprenticeship

zeiteweis, adv. 1.at times; 2.for a time

Zeitgeischt (der)n. spirit of the times

Zeithaer (en) for some time now

Zeiting (die)n. newspaper

Zeitlang (es)n. longing

zeitlich, adj. 1.early; 2.in time; 3.punctual; 4.temporal

zeitlich, adv. timely

Zeitpunk (der)n. epoch

Zeitverdreib (der)n. pastime

Zeitwaart (es)n. verb

Zelaat (der)n. 1.lettuce; 2.salad; 3.(wilder --) wild lettuce

Zelaatvoggel (der)n.; Zelaatveggel, pl. gold finch

zeletscht, adv. 1.at last; 2.finally; 3.last

Zell (die)n. cell

Zz

Zellerich

Zellerich (der)n. celery

zellerich = selleri celery

Zelt (es)n.; Zelder, pl. tent

Zeltduch (es)n. tent cloth

Zelthaus (es)n. tent

Zengel (der)n.; Zengel, pl. pendulum (of a clock)

Zenkel (der)n.; Zenkel, pl. plummet

Zenkrin (die)n. 1.scold; 2.termagant; 3.virago

Zeppelche (es)n. 1.helpless babe; 2.uvula

zerechtlege, v.; zerrechtgelegt, pp. lay out in order

zerechtmache, v.; zerechtgemacht, pp. 1.fix; 2.prepare; 3.trim

zerechtschtelle, v. zerechtgschtellt, pp. 1.correct someone; 2.set in order

Zeremonie (die)n. ceremony

zerick un vari, adv. back and forth

zerick/baerschde, v.; zerickgebaerscht, pp. brush back

zerick/bezaahle, v.; zerickbezaahlt, pp. 1.refund; 2.pay back

zerick/biege, v.; zerickgeboge, pp. bend back

zerick/binne, v.; zerickgebunne, pp. tie back (the off horse)

zerick/blaudre, v.; zerickgeblaudert, pp. give back talk

zerick/bleiwe, v.; zerickgebliwwe, pp. 1.be deficient; 2.remain behind

zerick/bringe, v.; zerickgebrocht, pp. 1.bring back; 2.return

zerick/daerfe, v.; zerickgedaerft, pp. be allowed to come back

zerick/dappe, v.; zerickgedappt, pp. trudge back

zerick/demme, v.; zerickgedemmt, pp. dam up

zerick/denke, v.; zerickgedenkt, pp. think back

zerick/draage, v.; zerickgedraage, pp. carry back

zerick/drehe, v.; zerickgedreht, pp. turn back

zerick/dreiwe, v.; zerickgedriwwe, pp. 1.drive back; 2.repulse

zerick/duh, v.; zerickgeduh, pp. put or set back

zerick/dummle; v.; zerickgedummelt, pp. (sich --)hurry back

zerick/faahre, v.; zerickgfaahre, pp. drive back (in a vehicle)

zerick/falle, v.; zerickgfalle, pp. 1.fall back; 2.fall behind; 3.retreat

zerick/falte, v.; zerickgfalte, pp. fold back

zerick/fiehre, v.; zerickgfiehrt, pp. lead back

zerick/fliege, v.; zerickgfloge, pp. fly back

zerick/foddre, v.; zerickgfoddert, pp. demand back

zerick/gaffe, v.; zerickgegafft, pp. gape back

zerick/geeschle, v.; zerickgegeeschelt, pp. drive back with a whip

zerick/geh, v.; zerickgange, pp. 1.go back; 2.go to ruin; 3.recede; 4.retreat; 5.return

zerick/gewwe, v.; zerickgewwe, pp. 1.give back; 2.repay; 3.retaliate

zerick/gloppe, v.; zerickgegloppt, pp. beat back

zerick/gnarre, v.; zerickgegnarrt, pp. give a surly answer

zerick/gneppe, v.; zerickgegneppt, pp. button back

zerick/griege, v.; zerickgrickt, pp. 1.recover; 2.regain

zerick/gucke, v.; zerickgeguckt, pp. look back

zerick/hacke, v.; zerickghackt, pp. 1.give a sharp rejoinder; 2.kick (of a horse)

zerick/halde, v.; zerickghalde, pp. 1.check; 2.hold back; 3.reserve; 4.restrain

zerick/hawwe, v.; zerickghatt, pp. have back

zerick/schprenge

zerick/helfe, v.; zerickgholfe, pp. help in return

zerick/henke, v.; zerickghenkt, pp. 1.rein up; 2.stay on behind

zerick/hewe, v.; zerickghowe, pp. hold back

zerick/hocke, v.; zerickghockt, pp. sit (in) back

zerick/hole, v.; zerickgholt, pp. fetch back

zerick/kaafe, v.; zerickgekaaft, pp. buy back

zerick/kenne, v.; zerickgekennt, pp. be able to get back

zerick/kumme, v.; zerickkumme, pp. 1.come back; 2.fall behind (in obligations); 3.return

zerick/laafe, v.; zerickgeloffe, pp. walk back

zerick/laahne, v.; zerickgelaahnt, pp. lean back

zerick/lache, v.; zerickgelacht, pp. laugh back or in return

zerick/lege, v.; zerickgelegt, pp. 1.lay back; 2.lay by; 3.save; 4.(sich --) recline

zerick/lehne, v.; zerickgelehnt, pp. recline

zerick/leie, v.; zerickgelegge, pp. lie back

zerick/losse, v.; zerickgelosst, pp. 1.leave behind; 2.permit to go back

zerick/mache, v.; zerickgemacht, pp. 1.remove to the rear (as straw in threshing); 2.(sich --) hurry back

zerick/maule, v.; zerickgemault, pp. talk back

zerick/misse, v.; zerickgemisst, pp. be obliged to return

zerick/nemme, v.; zerickgnumme, pp. 1.return; 2.take back

zerick/packe; v.; zerickgepackt, pp. (sich --) be off and get back

zerick/palde, v.; zerickgepalde, pp. keep back

zerick/reeche, v.; zerickgereecht, pp. reach back

zerick/reide, v.; zerickgeridde, pp. ride back

zerick/reisse, v.; zerickgerisse, pp. jerk back

zerick/renne, v.; zerickgerennt, pp. 1.rush back; 2.thrust back

zerick/rolle, v.; zerickgerollt, pp. roll back

zerick/rudere, v.; zerickgerudert, pp. row back

zerick/rufe, v.; zerickgerufe, pp. recall

zerick/rutsche, v.; zerickgerutscht, pp. slide back

zerick/saage, v.; zerickgsaagt, pp. retort

zerick/schaerre, v.; zerickgschaerrt, pp. scratch back

zerick/schaffe, v.; zerickgschafft, pp. convey back

zerick/schalle, v.; zerickgschallt, pp. re-echo

zerick/schelte, v.; zerickgscholte, pp. scold in return

zerick/scheppe, v.; zerickgscheppt, pp. dip or shovel back

zerick/schicke, v.; zerickgschickt, pp. send back

zerick/schiewe, v.; zerickgschowe, pp. shove back

zerick/schitte, v.; zerickgschitt, pp. pour back

zerick/schlagge, v.; zerickgschlagge, pp. 1.revert; 2.strike back

zerick/schleefe, v.; zerickgschleeft, pp. drag back

zerick/schluppe, v.; zerickgschluppt, pp. creep back

zerick/schmeisse, v.; zerickgschmisse, pp. 1.cause to fall behind; 2.throw back

zerick/schnalle, v.; zerickgschnallt, pp. strap or buckle back

zerick/schnappe, v.; zerickgschnappt, pp. limp back

zerick/schneide, v.; zerickgschnidde, pp. 1.cut back; 2.top

zerick/schnelle, v.; zerickgschnellt, pp. jerk back

zerick/schneppe, v.; zerickgschneppt, pp. tilt back

zerick/schprenge, v.; zerickgschprengt, pp. cause to beat a hasty retreat

Zz

zerick/schpringe | Zohlaad

zerick/schpringe, v.; zerickgschprunge, pp. run back
zerick/schritte, v.; zerickgschritt, pp. step back
zerick/schtaerze, v.; zerickgschtaerzt, pp. fall back
zerick/schtamme, v.; zerickgschtammt, pp. be descended from
zerick/schtech, v.; zerickschtanne, pp. abstain
zerick/schteh, v.; zerickgschtanne, pp. 1. abstain; 2. be backward; 3.stand back
zerick/schtelle, v.; zerickschtellt, pp. reject
zerick/schtewwre, v.; zerickgschtewwert, pp. chase back
zerick/schtosse, v.; zerickgschtosse, pp. repel
zerick/schwetze, v.; zerickgschwetzt, pp. talk back
zerick/sehne, v.; zerickgsehnt, pp. 1.look back; 2.see back
zerick/sei, v.; is zerickgewest, pp. 1.be backward; 2.be behind
zerick/setze, v.; zerickgsetzt, pp. (give one) a set back
zerick/weise, v.; zerickgewisse, pp. refer (back)
zerick/winsche, v.; zerickgewinscht, pp. wish back
zerick/wolle, v.; zerickgewollt, pp. want to go back
zerick/yaage, v.; zerickgeyaagt, pp. chase back
zerick/ziehe, v.; zerickgezoge, pp. 1.pull back; 2.retreat; 3.secede; 4.withdraw
zerick/zoppe, v.; zerickgezoppt, pp. jerk back
zerick, adv. 1.ago; 2.back
Zerickbezaahling (die)n. revenge
Zerickfall (der)n. relapse
zerickzus, adv. 1.backwards; 2.in the back country; 3.on the way back
zerickzusfalle, adv. fall backwards
zerickzusgeh, adv. 1.fail; 2.go into a decline
zesaage, adj. barely
Zettel (der)n. 1.label; 2.note; 3.short letter; 4.slip of paper; 5.ticket; 6.warp in weaving
Zettelend (es)n. end of a piece of woven carpet
zewege bringe, adv. accomplish
Zi(g)einer (der)n.; Zi(g)einer, pl. Gypsy
Zibbel (der)n. 1.oil gland (of fowl); 2.uropygial gland
Zibbelkapp (die)n.; Zibbelkabbe; Zibbelkepp, pl. 1.pointed cap; 2.peaked (woolen) cap
zichdiche, v.; gezichdicht, pp. 1.admonish; 2.chastise
Zickel (es)n. 1.little rascal; 2.shaver; 3.urchin
zickzack, adv. zigzag
Zidder (die)n. zither
zidder, prep. since
ziddere, v.; geziddert, pp. 1.quiver; 2.shudder; 3.tremble
zidderich, adj. 1.nervous; 2.trembly
Zidderli (der)n. souse (pig's feet jelly)
Zidderwackel (der)n. nervous wobble
Ziech (die)n. (bed) tick
Ziegblaschder (es)n. plaster for drawing (blistering)
Ziegbrunne (der)n. well with bucket and rope or chain
Ziegdaag (der)n. moving day
ziege, v.; gezoge, pp. 1.draw; 2.move; 3.pull
Ziegenbock (der)n. billy goat (nursery rhyme only)
Zieggaul (der)n. draft horse
Ziegloch (es)n. pipe hole
Ziegmesser (es)n. drawing knife
Ziegochs (der)n. draft ox

ziehe, v.; gezoge, pp. 1.draw; 2.pull; 3.move; 4.train
Ziel (es)n. 1.aim; 2.goal
ziele, v.; gezielt, pp. aim
ziemlich viel, adj. considerable
Zier (die)n. 1.ornament; 2.sweetheart
zier, adj. 1.prettily; 2.smartly
ziere, v.; geziert, pp. adorn
zierlich, adj. nicely
Zierraat (die)n. ornament
Ziffer (der)n.; Ziffere, pl. 1.figure; 2.numeral
Zifferblaat (es)n. dial (of a clock)
ziffere, v.; geziffert, pp. 1.cast up accounts; 2.cipher
Ziggel (der)n. 1.bridle; 2.tile
zimberlich, adj. 1.delicate; 2.weak
Zimmer (es)n. room (rare usage)
zimmere, v.; gezimmert, pp. 1.construct of wood; 2.tinker
Zimmermann (der)n. rough carpenter
zimmlich, adv. 1.nearly; 2.pretty; 3.pretty good; 4.rather; 5.tolerable
zimmlich glei, adv. 1.shortly; 2.very soon
zimmlich naegscht, adj. very near
zinde, v.; gezindt, pp. 1.ignite; 2.kindle
Zindhols (es)n. 1.kindling wood; 2.match (rare usage)
Zindloch (es)n. touch hole
Zindpann (die)n. touch hole
Zindpulwer (die)n. priming
zing charm word repeated in powwowing
zingle, v.; gezingelt, pp. 1.give a tingling sensation; 2.wag the tongue
Zink (es)n. zinc
Zinke (der, die)n. prong (of a fork)
Zinkegraas (es)n. finger grass
Zinkharn (es)n. cornet
zinkich, adj. prolonged
Zinn (es)n. 1.pewter; 2.tin; 3.tin cup
zinne, adj. (of) tin
zinnich, adj. 1.(of) tin; 2.tinny
zinter, adv. since
Zion (es)n. Zion
zipp! 1.cheep!; 2.chirp!
Zippche (es)n. chirping sparrow
Zippel (der)n. 1.foolish person; 2.tip
zische, v.; gezischt, pp. 1.boil; 2.hiss
Zittche (es)n. chirping sparrow
zitter, adv. since
zitterem = zitter em since one
ziwwele, v.; geziwwelt, pp. 1.correct; 2.pull ears
Ziwwerche (es)n. small tub
Zoddelbank (die)n. sink
zoddele, v.; gezoddelt, pp. 1.drop unintentionally; 2.scatter
Zoddelmann (der)n.; Zoddelmenner, pl. 1.rag man; 2.tramp
zoddlich, adj. 1.ragged; 2.shaggy; 3.tattered
Zoh (der)n.; Zeh, pl. tooth
Zohfleesch (es)n. gum(s)
Zohgschwaere (der)n. ulcer on a tooth
Zohlaad (die)n. 1.jawbone; 2.tooth socket

211

Zz

zohne | zufellich

zohne, v.; gezohnt, pp. teeth
Zohreeb (die)n. 1.climbing false buckwheat; 2.Virginia creeper
Zohrieb (die)n. 1.man-of-the-earth; 2.Virginia creeper
Zohweh (es)n. toothache
Zoiger (der)n. hand of a clock
Zoll (der)n.; Zoll, pl. inch
Zollhaus (es)n. (road) toll house
Zollschtaab (der)n. foot rule
Zollschtaag (der)n. foot rule
Zooschlipper (der)n. wren
Zoppe (der)n. 1.nape of the neck; 2.rag; 3.tatter
zoppe, v.; gezoppt, pp. 1.jerk; 2.pick; 3.pull
zoppich, adj. 1.ragged; 2.rough; 3.unkempt
Zopplein (der)n.; Zoppleine, pl. jerk-line
Zoppziegel (der)n.; Zoppziggle, pl. check rein
Zott (die)n. 1.female pudendum; 2.spout (of coffee or tea pot)
Zottel (der, die)n. 1.lewd woman; 2.rag
Zotteleeche (die)n. pin oak
zowwele, v.; gezowwelt, pp. pull (ears)
zu(g)friere, v.; zugfrore, pp. freeze up
zu-schnee-e, v.; zugschneet, pp. snow in
zu/bringe, v.; zugebrocht, pp. 1.pass (time); 2.spend
zu/decke, v.; zugedeckt, pp. cover up
zu/dreffe; v.; zugedroffe, pp. (sich --) 1.come to pass; 2.happen
zu/dreffe, v.; zugedroffe, pp. encounter
zu/gewwe, v.; zugewwe, pp. 1.accede; 2.admit; 3.allow
zu/haue, v.; zugehaut, pp. 1.hit; 2.strike
zu/losse, v.; zuglosst, pp. 1.admit; 2.leave closed
zu/mache, v.; zug(e)macht, pp. 1.close; 2.shut
zu/mude, v.; zugemut, pp. expect (someone) to
zu/nemme, v.; zugnumme, pp. 1.gain (weight); 2.increase
zu/ri(s)chde, v.; zugeri(s)cht, pp. prepare
zu/schiewe, v.; zugschowe, pp. push shut
zu/schlagge, v.; zugschlagge, pp. 1.assist a blacksmith in welding tires; 2.slam
zu/schmiere, v.; zugschmiert, pp. 1. stop up cracks (with plaster, etc.); 2.smear shut
zu/schpelle, v.; zugschpellt, pp. pin together
zu/schpreche, v.; zugschproche, pp. 1.encourage; 2.urge on; 3.urge to eat heartily
zu/schpringe, v.; zugschprunge, pp. 1.clap shut; 2.close; 3.come to the aid of; 4.run up to
zu/schtecke, v.; zugschteckt, pp. 1.give clandestinely; 2.plug; 3.stop a hole or leak; 4.clog
zu/schtobbe, v.; zugschtoppt, pp. stop up
zu/schtrecke, v.; zugschtreckt, pp. 1.add to; 2.(to make a) shortcut
zu/wickle, v.; zugewickelt, pp. wrap up
zu/zabbe, v.; zugezappt, pp. 1.plug; 2.stop a hole or leak; 3.clog
zu/ziehe, v.; zugezoge, pp. pull tight
zu, adj. shut
zu, adv. too
zu, prep. to
zubaue, v.; zugebaut, pp. obstruct by building
zubinne, v.; zugebunne, pp. tie up

zubleiwe, v.; zugebliwwe, pp. remain closed
zubleschdre, v.; zugebleschdert, pp. plaster up
zublocke, v.; zugeblockt, pp. block up
zublose, v.; zugeblose, pp. drift shut (of roads by snow)
Zubreiding (die) n. preparatory service (prior to Holy Communion)(Mennonite)
zuchdich, adj. noisy
zuchrich, adj. saccharine
Zucht (die)n. 1.noise; 2.order; 3.training; 4.(en -- verfiehre) (to raise) a racket
Zuchthaus (es)n. penitentiary
Zuchthengscht (der)n. stallion
Zuchtmaerr (die)n. brood mare
Zuck (der)n. 1.draft; 2.moving (of household belongings); 3.pull
Zuckblaschder (es)n. plaster (for drawing)
zucke, v.; gezucht, pp. 1.jerk; 2.twitch
Zucker (der)n. sugar
Zucker(g)schleck (es)n. candy
Zuckerarebse (die)n.; Zuckerarebse, pl. sugar peas (pod peas)
Zuckerbaam (der)n. sugar maple
Zuckerbool (die)n. sugar bowl
Zuckerbretzel (es)n. pretzel covered with sugar instead of salt
Zuckerbusch (der)n.; Zuckerbisch, pl. sugar maple grove
Zuckerfass (es)n. sugar barrel
Zuckergnolle (der)n. lump of sugar
zuckerich, adj. 1.of sugar; 2.sugary
Zuckerlattwarick (der)n. sugar applebutter (made with sugar, not boiled down)
Zuckermaul (es)n. person with a sweet tooth
zuckern, adv. of sugar
Zuckerrieb (die)n. sugar beet
Zuckersach (es)n. 1.candies; 2.sweets
Zuckerscheifli (es)n.; Zuckerscheiflin, pl. sugar candy (hard, made of maple sugar)
Zuckerschtengel (es)n. stick of candy
Zuckerschtengelche (es)n. stick of candy
Zuckerschtengli (es)n. stick of candy
zuckersiess, adv. sweet as sugar
Zuckerwasser (es)n. maple sap
zuckich, adj. twitchy
Zuckloch (es)n. 1.air hole; 2.flue
zudem, adv. 1.besides; 2.in addition
zudraage; v.; zugedraage, pp. (sich --) happen
Zudraue (es)n. confidence
zudraue, v.; zugedraut, pp. 1.confide in; 2.credit with
zudrauisch, adj. trusting
zudrehe, v.; zugedreht, pp. 1.shut off; 2.turn off
zudricke, v.; zugedrickt, pp. close (by squeezing)
zue, adj. closed
zuerscht, adv. 1.first; 2.in the first place
zufaahre, v.; zugfaahre, pp. 1.drive on; 2.fill (a place) with vehicles parking
zufaerrichde, v.; zugfaerricht, pp. plow under (as potatoes)
Zufall (der)n. 1.accident; 2.case
zufalle, v.; zugfalle, pp. 1.devolve upon; 2.fall in; 3.happen
zufellich, adj. 1.accidentally; 2.by haphazard

212

Zz

zufellicherweis / zwedder

zufellicherweis, adj. accidentally

zufiege, v.; zugfliekt, pp. 1.add to; 2.credit (one) with; 3.inflict

Zuflucht (die)n. refuge

zufridde, adj. 1.contented; 2.satisfied

Zufriddeheet (die)n. 1.contentment; 2.satisfaction

Zugang (der)n. 1.access; 2.admission

zugeh, v.; zugange, pp. 1.close; 2.happen

zugeh, v.; zugange, pp (wie geht's zu bei eich) how are things going with you

Zugeheer (es)n. appurtenances

zugenglich, adj. 1.accessible; 2.approachable

zugerischt, adj. prepared

zuglappe, v.; zugeglappt, pp. slam shut

zugnippe, v.; zugegnippt, pp. button up

zugreife, v.; zugegriffe, pp. 1.begin; 2.take hold of

zugriege, v.; zugrickt, pp. get to close (a door)

zugrund/geh, v.; zugrundgange, pp. perish

zugschoppt, adj. constipated

zugucke, v.; zugeguckt, pp. look on

zuhalte, v.; zughalte, pp. keep closed

zuharriche, v.; zugharricht, pp. listen

zuhawwe, v.; zughatt, pp. have closed

zuheele, v.; zugheelt, pp. heal up

zuheere, v.; zugheert, pp. listen

Zuheerer (der)n. 1.auditor; 2.listener

zuhewe, v.; zughowe, pp. hold shut

zuklemme, v.; zugeklemmt, pp. 1.close by pressing together; 2.grip hard; 3.press together

Zukumft (die)n. future

zukumme, v.; zukumme, pp. 1.accrue; 2.appertain to; 3.regain consciousness

Zukunft, (die)n. future

zulege, v.; zugelekt, pp. cover with (boards)

zuletscht, adv. 1.at last; 2.finally; 3.last

Zulossung (die)n. admittance

zum = zu em to him

zumaure, v.; zugemauert, pp. wall up

zume = zu me to one

Zunaame (der)n. surname

zunaehe, v.; zugenaeht, pp. sew up

zunaggele, v.; zugenaggelt, pp. nail up

Zunahm (der)n. increase

zuner, adj. closed

Zung (die)n.; Zunge, pl. tongue (human)

zuni, adj. closed

zunischde, v.; zugenischt, pp. 1.overrun with weeds or briers; 2.overspin (of the tent caterpillar)

Zunome (der)n. surname

zuranke, v.; zugerankt, pp. become covered with vines

zure = zu re to her

zurechle, v.; zugerechelt, pp. 1.add to; 2.ascribe

zurecht, adj. ready

zurecht, adv. 1.in good order; 2.ready

zureisse, v.; zugerisse, pp. pull shut

zuriggele, v.; zugeriggelt, pp. bolt

Zuritt (der)n. admission

zurufe, v.; zugerufe, pp. hail

zus = zu es to it

Zusatz (der)n. addition

zuschaffe, v.; zugschafft, pp. 1.amass; 2.procure

zuschand/geh, v.; zuschandgange, pp. perish

Zuschlackhammer (der)n. sledgehammer

zuschliesse, v.; zugschlosse, pp. lock

zuschmeisse, v.; zugschmisse, pp. fill up

zuschnalle, v.; zugschnallt, pp. buckle

zuschneee, v.; zugschneet, pp. snow in

zuschniere, v.; zugschniert, pp. 1.strangle; 2.(die Kehl --) strangle (a person)

zuschpinne, v.; zugschpunne, pp. cover with spider webs

zuschreiwe, v.; zugschriwwe, pp. 1.ascribe to; 2.charge

Zuschtand (der)n.; Zuschtende, pl. 1.case; 2.condition; 3.plight; 4.situation; 5.state

zuschtelle, v.; zugschtellt, pp. 1.block up; 2.close down; 3.obstruct

zuschtoppe, v.; zugschtoppt, pp. stop up

zuschtreeme, v.; zugschtreemt, pp. flow towards

zuschwemme, v.; zugschwemmt, pp. cover with silt or sand

zusehne, v.; zugsehne, pp. look on

zusetze, v.; zugsetzt, pp. 1.add to; 2.increase

Zuverdraue (es)n. 1.confidence; 2.reliance

Zuversicht (die)n. confidence

zuversichtlich, adj. confidently

zuvor, adv. 1.before; 2.formerly

Zuwachs (der)n. increase

zuwachse, v.; zugewachse, pp. become grown over

zuwidder, prep. 1.adverse; 2.contrary; 3.disagreeable

Zuwwer (der)n.; Ziwwer, pl. tub

zwaar, adv. truly

zwacke, v.; gezwackt, pp. (to be) grasping or miserly

zwackich, adj. warty

Zwaerichax (die)n. twibill

Zwaerichpeif (die)n.; Zwaerichpeife, pl. 1.fife; 2.piccolo

Zwaerichsack (der)n. 1.saddle-bags; 2.shoulder-bag

Zwaerl (der)n. whirl

zwaerne, v.; gezwaernt, pp. twist (yarn)

Zwaernraad (es)n. twisting wheel (in spinning)

Zwaerrick (der)n (en rechter --) trouble maker

Zwaerwel (der)n. 1.eddy; 2.whirl

zwaerwle, v.; gezwaerwelt, pp. 1.eddy; 2.whirl

Zwang (der)n. 1.coercion; 2.cramp; 3.force; 4.urging of the bowels

zwansich, adj.; pron. twenty

Zwansichschdel (es)n. twentieth (part)

zwansichscht, adj. twentieth

Zwarich (der)n. dwarf

Zwarichsack (es)n. shoulder bag

Zweck (der)n. 1.aim; 2.design; 3.object; 4.purpose

zweckmaessich, adj. appropriate

Zwedde Grischtdaag (der)n. Second Christmas, Dec. 26

zweddens, adv. secondly

zwedder (en)n. deuce in cards

Zz

zwee

zwee, adj.; pron. two

zweeaerlee, adv. (of) two kinds

zweebeenich, adj. two-legged

zweedoddrich, adj. (having) two yolks

zweedoppelt, adv. double

zweefach, adj. two-fold

Zweegeilswagge (der)n.; Zweegeilswegge, pl. two-horse wagon

zweegsichtich, adj. two-faced

zweekeppich, adj. of different mind

zweemol, adv. twice

zweereddrich, adj. two-wheeled

zweeschneidich, adj. double edged

zweeschpennich, adj. double

zweeschteckich, adj. two-storied

zweeseidich, adj. two-faced

zweesitzich, adj. two-seated

Zweewoog (die)n.; Zweewooge, pl. double-tree

zweeyaahrich, adv. two years old

zweeyaehrich, adj. two years old

Zweifel (der)n. doubt

zweifelhaft, adj. doubtful

zweifle, v.; gezweifelt, pp. doubt

Zweig (die)n.; Zweige, pl. 1.graft; 2.scion; 3.twig

zweige, v.; gezweigt, pp. graft (a tree)

Zweikschmier (die)n. grafting wax

Zweiwel (der)n. doubt

zweiwle, v.; gezweiwelt, pp. doubt

zwelf; zwelfe, adj.; pron. twelve

Zwelfde (es)n. twelfth (part)

zwelft, adv. twelfth

zwenge, v.; gezwengt, pp. 1.compel; 2.force

zwett Mol (es)n. second time

zwett, adj. second

zwette; v.; gezwett, pp. (sich --) 1.become two years old; 2.happen twice

zwetteltscht, adj. next to the oldest

zwettglennscht, adj. next to the smallest

zwettgreescht, adj. next to the largest

Zwickel (der)n.; Zwickel, pl. 1.clown; 2.gore; 3.fool

Zwickelzwack (der)n. crazy loon

Zwieschpalt (der)n. 1.misunderstanding; 2.trouble-maker

zwillere, v.; gezwillert, pp. warble

Zwillich (der)n. twill

zwillichde, v.; gezwillicht, pp. twill

Zwilling (der)n.; Zwilling, pl. 1.Gemini (3rd sign of the zodiac); 2.twin

Zwillingbobbli (es)n.; Zwillingbobblin, pl. twin

zwinge, v.; gezwunge, pp. 1.coerce; 2.force; 3.persuade; 4.talk into

zwische, prep. between

zwischedarich, adv. through and between

zwischedrin, adv. in between

zwischem = zwische em between it

zwischeme = zwische me between one

zwischenei, adv. 1.in between (in motion); 2.interlarded

Zwiwwlekuche

zwischere = zwische re between her

zwisches = zwisch es between it

zwischich, prep. between

zwiterich, adj. 1. glistening; 2. rapidly; 3. shimmering tremulously

zwitschere, v.; gezwitschert, pp. 1.sing (of birds); 2.twitter

zwitscherich, adj. shimmering tremulously

Zwitter (der)n. 1.bisexual pig or fowl; 2.human hermaphrodite

zwitzere, v.; gezwitzert, pp. 1.shimmer tremulously; 2.twitter

Zwiwwel (die)n.; Zwiwwle, pl. 1.onion; 2.(gleeni Zwiwwle) onion sets

Zwiwwelschlott (die)n. onion top

Zwiwwelschuss (der)n. onion top

Zwiwwelsupp (die)n. onion soup

zwiwwle, v.; gezwiwwelt, pp. 1.beat; 2.cheat

Zwiwwlekuche (der)n. onion pie

NOTES

NOTES

NOTES

NOTES

NOTES

NOTES

Aa

a   **accident**

a 1.en, indef. art.; 2.n, pron.

abandon verlosse, v.; verlosse, pp.

abase nunner/mache, v.; nunnergemacht, pp.

abate no(och)losse, v.; no(och)g(e)losst, pp.

abbreviate 1.ab/katze, v.; abgekatzt, pp.; 2. verkatze, v.; verkatzt, pp.

abbreviation Abkatzing (die)n.

abdomen 1.Bauch (der)n.; Beich, pl.; 2.Leib (der); 3.Unnerleib (der)n.

Abdon's Day (July 30) 1.Abdansdaag (der)n.; 2.Abdunsdaag (der)n.

abecedarian Abcschitz (der)n.

abhor verscheie, v.; verscheit, pp.

abhorrence Abschei (der)n.

abhorrent scheisslich, adj.

abide for a season loschiere, v.; loschiert, pp.

ability 1.Faehichkeet (die)n.; 2.Gaab (die)n.; Gaawe, pl.; 3. Kunscht (die)n.; 4.Vermeege (es)n.

ability to perform mysteries Kinschdlerei (die)n.

able 1.fehich, adj.; 2.kenne, v.; gekennt, pp.

able to imschtand, adj. 1.**come in** rei/kenne, v.; reigekennt, pp.; 2.**follow** no(och)kenne, v.; no(och)gekennt, pp.

able to get 1. **a place** hie/kenne, v.; hiegekennt, pp.; 2.fatt/kenne, v.; fattgekennt, pp.; 3.**across** niwwer/kenne, v.; niwwergekennt, pp.; 4. **away** (a) fatt/kenne, v.; fattgekennt, pp.; (b) weck/kenne, v.; weckgekennt, pp.; 5.**back** zerick/ kenne, v.;zerickgekennt, pp.; 6.**get up** (a) ruff/kenne, v.;ruffgekennt, pp. (b) uff/kenne,v. uffgekennt, pp.; 7. **in** nei/kenne, v.; neigekennt, pp. 8.**out** (a) naus/kenne, v.;nausgekennt, pp.; (b) raus/kenne,v.; rausgekennt, pp.;9.**past** verbei/kenne, v.; verbeigekennt, pp.; 10.**together** zamme/kenne, v.; zammegekennt, pp.

able to go along mit/kenne, v.; mitgekennt, pp.

abode 1.Aufenthalt (der)n.; 2.Uffhalding (die)n.; 3.Wohnblatz (der)n.; 4.Wuhnblatz (der)n.; Wuhnbletz, pl.; 5.Wuhning (die)n.; Wuhninge, pl.

abolish weck/duh, v.; weckgeduh,pp.

abominable abscheilich, adj.

abort 1.fehl/geh, v.; fehlgange, pp.; 2. fehl/schlagge, v.; fehlgschlagge, pp.; 3. verdraage, v.; verdraage, pp.

abortion Kinnermard (der)n.

about (a) an, prep.; adv.; (b) baut, adv.; (c) haerum, adj.; (d) rum/sei, v.; (e) umgfarr, adv.; (f) ung(e)faehr, adi; (g) ungfarr, adv.; (h) unggfaehr, adv.; (i) vunwege, prep.; (j) weeich, prep.; (k) wege, prep.; 2.**that** dattdrum, adv.; 3.**this** dodrum, adj.; 4.**to** begriff, v. (im --)

about 4 o'clock 1.vier, adj. (so um die --); 2.um, prep. (so -- vier Uhr)

above 1.owwe, adv.; 2.owwich, prep.

above it owwedraa, adv.

abrade 1.ab/reiwe, v.; abgeriwwe, pp.; 2.ab/schaawe, v.;abgschaabt, pp.; 3.uff/schinne, v.; uffgschunne, pp.; 4.verschinne, v.; verschunne, pp.; 5.weck/schinne,v.; weckgschunne, pp.

abrade (the skin) verschinne (sich --), v.; verschunne, pp.

abrade one's head (by knocking it against) uff/schlagge,

v.; uffgschlagge, pp. (sich der Kopp --)

Abraham 1.Abraham (der)n.; 2.Awerham (der)n.

abreast 1.newenanner, adv.; 2.newichenanner, adv.

abrogate 1.geh/losse, v.; gehlosst, pp.; 2.uff/gewe, v.; uffgewwe, pp.; 3.uff/schmeisse, v.; uffschmisse, pp.

abruptly 1.bletzlich, adv.; 2.uff, prep., adv.(-- emol); 3.unni Verseimes, adv.

Absalom Absalam (der)n.

abscess 1.Gschwar(e) (der)n.; Gschware, pl.; 2.Gschwaare (der)n.; 3.Gschwaere (der)n.; 4.Gschwulscht (die n.; 5.Schlier (der)n.; 6.Schwaere (der)n.

abscond aus/reisse, v.; ausgerisse, pp.

absent 1.eweck, adv.; 2.fatt, adv.; 3.net datt, adv.; 4.weck, adv.; 5.weck sei, v.; weck g(e)west, pp.

absent (oneself) weck/halde v. (sich --); weckghalde, pp.

absolutely abselut(t), adv.

absolutely alone mudderseelichallee, adv.

absolve 1.frei/losse, v.; freeglosst, pp.; 2.frei/schpreche, v.; freischproche, pp.; 3.los/schpreche, v.;losgschproche, pp.

absorb 1.ei/nemme, v.; eigenumme, pp.; 2.ei/ziege, v.; eigezoge, pp.

abstain 1. ab/schteh, v.; iss abgschtanne, pp.; 2.devun/bleiwe, v.; is devungebliwwe, pp.; 3. zerick/schtech, v.; zerickschtanne, pp.; 4.zerick/schteh, v.;zerickgschtanne, pp.

abstract ab/ziehe, v.; abgezoge, pp.

absurd 1.abgschmackt, adj.; 2.alwer(n), adj.; 3.unmanierlich, adj.; 4.unverschtennich, adj.; 5.verrickt, adj.

absurdity 1.Alwerheet (die)n.; 2.Unverschtand (der)n.; 3.Unverschtang (der)n.; 4.Unverschtennichkeit (die)n.

abundance 1.Fill(i) (die)n.; 2.Iwwerfluss (der)n.

abundant 1.iwwerflissich, adj.; 2.iwwergenunk, adj.

abundantly 1.reichfeldich, adj.; 2.reichl(e)ich, adj.

abuse 1.beyuuse, v.; beyuust, pp.; 2.Briggel (der)n. (--schmeisse); 4. bschimpe, v.; bschimpt, pp.; 5. fiole, v.; gfiolt, pp.; 6.missbrauche, v.; (ge)missbraucht, pp.; 7. priggel schmeisse, v.; 8. schimfe, v.; gschimft, pp.; 9. schimpe, v.; gschimpt, pp.; 10. schtumbiere, v.; schtumbiert, pp.; 11. verschtumbiere, v.; verschtumbiert, pp.

abuse cruelly trakdiere, v.; trakdiert, pp.

abuse to distraction verkollebiere, v.; verkollebiert, pp.

abut 1. aa/schtosse, v.; aagschtosse, pp.; 2.wedder/schtosse, v.; weddergschtosse, pp.

abyss 1.Abgrund (der)n.; 2.Rache (der)n.

accede 1.ei/gewwe, v.; eigewwe, pp.; 2.zu/gewwe, v.; zugewwe, pp.

accede to verwilliche, v.; verwillicht, pp.

accept aa/nemme, v.; aag(e)numme, pp.

accepted 1. gelde, v.; gegolde, pp.; 2. gelte, v.; gegolte, pp.

access Zugang (der)n.

accessible zugenglich, adj.

accident 1.Unfall (der)n.; Unfelle, pl.; 2.Unglick (es)n.; 3.Zufall (der)n.

221

Aa

accidental

accidental unglicklich, adj.

accidentally 1.zufellich, adj.; 2.zufellicherweis, adj.

accompany 1.begleede, v.; begleedt, pp.; 2.mit/geh, v.; iss mitgange, pp.

accomplish 1.los/bringe, v.; losgebrocht, pp.; 2.verrichde,v.; verricht, pp.; 3.zewege bringe, adv.

accomplish by palming off on aa/wickle, v.; aagewickelt, pp.

accord ei/schtimme, v.; eigschtimmt, pp.

according (to that) 1.nochdem, conj.; 2.sellemno, conj.; 3.so, conj.; 4.wie, adv., conj.

according to 1.no, adv.; 2.nooch, adv.

according to rule regelmaessich, adj.

according to scripture schriftlich, adj.

accordingly 1.denno, adv.; 2.dennoch, adv.

accost in a surly manner aaretze, v.; aageretzt, pp.

accost in an over bearing manner aa/fratze, v.; aagfratzt, pp.

account 1. Greid (es)n.; 2. Kreid (es)n.; 3. Rechenschaft (die)n.; 4. Rechling (die)n.; 5. Rechning (die)n.

accountability Verantwartlichkeet (die)n.

accountable verantwartlich, adj.

accrue zukumme, v.; zukumme, pp.

accumulate zamme/schaerre, v.; zammegschaerrt, pp.

accurate 1.genaa, adj.; 2.genau, adj.; 3.graad recht, adj.

accuse 1.aaglaage, v.; aageglaagt, pp.; 2.beschuldiche, v.; beschuldicht, pp.; 3.riddle, v.; geriddelt, pp.; 4.uff/reisse, v.; uffgerisse, pp. (es Maul --); 5.verglaage, v.;verglaagt, pp.; 6.vor/schmeisse, v.; vorg(e)schmisse, pp.

accuse of vor/lege, v.; vorgelegt, pp.

accuser 1.Beklaager (der)n.; 2.Beklaeger (der)n.

accustom 1.aa/gewehne, v.; aagewehnt, pp.; 2.gewehne, v.; gewehnt, pp.

accustomed 1.aagewehne (sich --) v.; aagewehnt pp.; 2.aagegwehnt (sei)v.

accustomed to als, adv.

ace (in cards) Sau (die)n.; Sei, pl.

ace of spades Schibbesau (die)n.

ache 1.Schmatz (der)n.; Schmatze, pl.; 2.schmatze, v.; gschmatzt, pp.; 3.weh/duh, v.; wehgeduh, pp.

achievement Ausfiehrung (die)n.

acknowledge 1.aakenne, v.; aakennt, pp.; 2.beichde, v.;gebeicht, pp.; 3.bekenne, v.; bekennt, pp.; 4.uff/kumme, v.; uffkumme, pp. (-- losse)

acorn 1. Eechel (die) n.; Eechle, pl.; 2. (of the scrub oak) Grundeechel (die)n.

acquaintance 1.Bekann(d)er (der)n.; 2.Bekann(d)i (die)n.; 3.Bekanntschaft (die)n.; 4.Umgang (der) n.

acquainted 1.bekannt, adj.; 2.bekannt sei, v.; is bekannt gewest, pp.

acquire 1.aa/schaffe, v.; aagschafft, pp.; 2.bei/griege, v.; beigrickt, pp.; 3.erlange, v.; erlangt, pp.; 4.griege, v.; grickt, pp.

acquire a grudge falsch, adj. (-- warre)

acre Acker (der)n.; Acker, pl.

acrid 1.beissich, adj.; 2.scharef, adj.

adherence

across 1.iwwer, prep.; 2.midde darrich, adv.; 3.niwwer, adv.; 4.riwwer, adv.

across down below unneriwwer, adv.

act 1.funggiere, v.; gfunggiert, pp.; 2.verfaahre, v.; verfaahre, pp.; 3.wandle, v.; gewandelt, pp.; **as if** 1.aaschtelle (sich --)v.; aagschtellt, pp.; 2.schtelle (sich --)v.; **foolishly** narre, v.; genatt; gnaart, pp.; **of drinking** Gedrink (es)n.; **of eating** Gess (es)n.; **of going to church** Karichgang (der)n.; **of mending** Flickwese (es)n.; **of milking** Gemelk (es)n.; **of moving backward** Grebagang (der)n.; **of reading** Geles (es)n.; **of robbing someone** Raawes (es)n.; **or result of an act held up as a visitation of Providence or warning to evil-doers** 1.Aageschpickel der)n.; 2.Aageschpiggel (der)n.; **rebelliously** schtraube (sich --), v.; **rudely or boorishly** glatt, adj. (net arrig --haergeh); **silly** (a) hanswarschtle, v.; gehanswarschtelt, pp.; (b) kalwere, v.; gekalwert, pp.; **stupidly** aaschtelle, v.; aagschtellt, pp. (sich dumm --); **superciliously** Naas (die)n. (-- runsle); **the hypocrite** heichle, v.; gheichelt, pp.; **the parasite** aasuckle, v.; aagsuckelt, pp.

action Aagschtalt (der)n.

active munder, adj.

activity 1.Geweb(b) (es)n.; 2.Gewewwer (es)n.

Acts of the Apostles Apostelg(e)schichte (die)n.

actually 1.behiedes, adv.; 2.hole, v.; gholt. pp.; (hol's der Deiwel) (hol's der Schinner); 3.verhaftich, adj.; 4.waahrhafdich, adv.; 5.waricklich, adv. 6.wohrhaftich, adj.

adage Schprichwart (es)n.

Adam Adem (der)n.

Adam's ale Genswei (der)n. ; **apple** Adamsabbel (der)n.

adapt (oneself) 1.schicke (sich --)v.; gschickt, pp.; 2.aa/schicke (sich --)v.; aagschickt, pp.; 3.nei/richde (sich --) v.; neigericht, pp. **oneself to circumstances** ei/richde (sich --)v.; eigericht, pp.

adaptation Aawendung (die)n.

add zehle, v.; gezehlt, pp.; **(up)** 1.uff/zehle, v.; uffgezehlt, pp.; 2.zamme/zehle, v.; zammegzehlt, pp.; **a piece to** aaschtick(l)e, v.; aagschtickelt, pp.; **to** 1. dezumache, v.; dezugemacht, pp.; 2. dezusetze, v.;dezugsetzt, pp.; 3. zu/schtrecke, v.; zugschtreckt, pp.; 4. zufiege, v.; zugfliekt, pp.; 5. zurechle, v.; zugerechelt, pp.; 6.zusetze, v.; zugsetzt, pp.

addition Zusatz (der)n.

addle verwa(e)rre, v.; verwa(e)rrt, pp.; **brained** leerkeppich, adj.

address aareede, v.; aagereedt, pp.; **a person with the pronoun ihr** ihrze, v.; geihrzt, pp.; **in a gruff manner** aa/grdunse, v.; aagegraunst, pp.; **one with ehr** ehrze, v.; geehrzt, pp.

adduce (against a person) uff/bringe, v.; uffgebrocht, pp.

adept erfaahre, v.; erfaahre, pp.

adequate 1.genunk, adv. 2.helenglich, adj., adv.

adhere 1.aa/gle(e)we, v.; aageglebt, pp.; 2.aa/henke, v.; aaghenkt; aaghonke, pp.; 3.aa/klewe, v.; aageklebt, pp.; 4.fescht/babbe, v.; feschtgebabbt, pp.; 5. glewe, v.; geglebt, pp.

adherence Aahang (der)n.

222

Aa

adherent / agree

adherent 1.Aahenger (der)n.; 2.Aahenker (der)n.

Adieu 1.Farewell!, interj.; 2.Hadyee!, interj.; 3.Haydee!, interj.; 4.Leb(e)wohl (es)n.; 5.Lewewohl (es)n.

adjective Beiwatt (es)n.; Beiwadde, pl.

adjoin zamme/schtosse, v.; zammegschtosse, pp.

adjourn 1.aus/losse, v.; ausg(e)losst, pp.; 2.uff/breche, v.; uffgebroche, pp.; 3.verdaage, v.; verdaagt, pp.

adjust a quarrel schlichte, v.; gschlicht, pp.

administer 1.bei/bringe, v.; beigebrocht, pp.; 2.verwalte, v.; verwalt, pp.; **medicine** ei/gewwe, v.; eigewwe, pp.

administrator Verwalter (der)n.

admirable wunnerswaert, adj.

admission 1.Zugang (der)n.; 2.Zuritt (der)n.

admit 1.nei/losse, v.; neiglosst, pp.; 2.uff/kumme, v.; uffkumme, pp. (-- losse); 3.zu/gewwe, v.; zugewwe, pp.; 4.zu/losse, v.; zuglosst, pp.; **to** gschteh, v.; gschtanne, pp.; **something** uff/eegne, v.; uffge-eegnet,pp.

admittance Zulossung (die)n.

admix 1.bei/mixe, v.; beigemixt, pp.; 2.nei/mixe, v.; neigemixt, pp.

admonish 1. Roi (die) n. (in -- schtelle) 2. vermaahne, v.; vermaahnt, pp.; 3.zichdiche, v.; gezichdicht, pp.

admonition Vermaahning (die)n.

ado Gelaerm (es)n.

adopt 1.aa/nemme, v.; aag(e)numme, pp.;2.vaddere, v.; gvaddert, pp.

adorable 1.aabetungswaerdich, adj.; 2.lieblich, adj.

adore 1.aa/bede, v.; aagebet, pp.; 2.verehre, v.; verehrt, pp.

adorn 1.ausschmicke, v.; ausgschmickt, pp.; 2.schmicke, v.; gschmickt, pp.; 3.uff/duh, v.; uffgeduh, pp.; 4.uff/schmicke, v.; uffgschmickt, pp.; 5.ziere, v.; geziert, pp.

adult 1.aus(g)waxe, adj.; 2.gewachsner (en --); 3.gwaxe,adj.; 4.Uffgwaxaner (der)n.; Uffgwaxni, pl.; 5.uffgwaxe,adj.; 6.uff/gewachse, v.(en uffgewachsner); 7.Uffwaxener (der)n.; Uffgwaxeni, pl.; **hired man** 1.Gnecht (der)n. 2.(gross --)

adulterate verfelsche, v.; verfelscht, pp.

adulteration Verfelschung (die)n.

adulterer Ehebrecher (der)n.

adultery 1.Ehebreche (es)n.; 2.Ehebruch (der)n.

advance (money) vorschtrecke, v.; vorgschtreckt, pp.

advanced in years betaacht, adj.

advantage 1.Gewinn (es)n.; 2.Va(e)rtel (der)n.; 3.Vaddel (es)n ; 4.Vordeel (ee)n ; 5.Vorrang (der)n.; 6.Vorzuck (der)n.

advantageous vartelhaft, adj.

Advent Advent (der)n.

adverb Newewart (es)n.

adversary 1.Feind (der)n.; Feind, pl.; 2.Gegner (der)n.; 3. Widdersaager (der)n.

adverse zuwidder, prep.

advertisement Bekanntmachung (die)n.

advice Rot (der)n.

advisable rotsaum, adj.

advise 1.aarote, v.; aagerote, pp.; 2.rode, v.; gerode pp.; 3.Rot (der)n. (-- gewwe); 4.verrode, v.; verrode, pp.

advisor Rotgewwer (der)n.

adze 1.Dechsel (der)n.; 2.Dexel (der)n.

afar 1.Schtick (es)n. (en -- weck); 2.weit ab, adv.; 3. weit weck, adv.

affair 1.Gschicht (die)n.; 2.Lossement (es)n.; 3.Rumbel (der)n.

affairs 1.Gedu(ns) (es)n.

affect 1.bewege, v.; bewekt, pp.; 2.riehre, v.; geriehrt, pp.; **an air** aaschtelle (sich --)v.; aagschtellt, pp.

affecting riehrend, adj.

affectionate hatzlich, adj.

affirm 1.beyaae, v.; beyaat, beyatt, pp.; 2.beyooe, v.; beyoot, pp.

afflict 1.bedreffe, v.; bedroffe, pp.; 2.bedroffe, adj.

afflicted 1.traurich, adj.; 2.behaft, adj.

affliction 1.Leid (es)n.; 2.Pein (die)n.

afoot Gaerwersgaul (der)n. (uff em --)

afraid 1.bang, adj.; 2.eem bang warre, v.; is warre, pp.; 3.fariche (sich --)v.; gfaricht, pp.; 4.scheie (sich --)v.; 5.verzaacht, adj.; **of folks** leitschei, adj.

after 1.hinner, adj.; 2.hinnerdrei, adv.; 3.hinnich, prep.; 4.no,adv.; 5.noch, prep.;6.nochdem, conj.;7.nooch, adv.; 8.nooch,prep.; **a while** iwwreweil, adv.; **clap** (as an --) hinnedruff, adv.;**each other** hinnernanner, adv.; **her** 1.nochre = noch re; 2.nore = nooch re; **one** nochme = noch me; **that** 1.dennord, adv.;2. dennot = dennot; 3.nochdem, adv.; 4.nooch sellemn adv.; 5. nooch sem; 6.nort = dennort; **them** nochem = noch em; **this** 1.dodenno, adv.; 2.nooch dem, adv.

afterbirth 1.Butze (der)n.; 2.Noochgeburt (die)n.; 3.Seiwering (die)n.

aftermath 1.Aamet (es)n.; 2.Ohmet (es)n.; 3.Omet (es)n.; 4.Uhmet (es)n.

afternoon 1.Nammidaag (der)n.; 2.Nochmid(d)aag (der) n.; 3.Nummidaag (der)n.

afterward(s) 1.nochdem, adv.; 2.no(o)chderhand, adv.; 3.noochhaer, adv.

again 1.nochemol, adv.; 2.nochmols, adv.; 3.widder, adv.; **and again** iwwer, prep. (ee mol --s anner)

against 1.eeg(g)e, adv.; 2.degege, adv.; 3.wedder, prep.; **(it)** dewedder, prep.; **below** unnewedder, adv.; **in front** vannewedder, adv.; **that** dattdegege, adv.; **the grain** iwwerzwaerrich, adj.; **the side** newewedder, adv.; **the top** owwewedder, adv.; **this** dodegege, adv.

age 1.Alder (der)n.; 2.Elt (die)n.

aged altguckich, adj.

agile 1.flink, adj.; 2.supel, adj.; 3.wusslich, adj.

agitate 1.uff/riehre, v.; uffgriehrt, pp.; 2.uff/schtarre, v.; uffgschtarrt, pp.

agitated uffriehrisch, adv.

ago 1.var, adv.; 2.ver, adv.; 3.zerick, adv.

agree 1.eenich sei, v.; eenich gewest, pp.; 2.ei/schtimme, v.; eigschtimmt, pp.; 3.ennich, adj.; 4.glappe, v.; geglappt, pp.; 5.gschtalle, v.; gschtallt, pp.;

(Continued on page 224)

Aa

agree (continued)

(Continued from page 223)

6.iwwereens rauskumme, v.; iwwereens rauskumme, pp.; 7.iwwereens schtimme, v.; gschtimmt, pp.; 8.klappe, v.; geklappt, pp.; 9.mitt/schtimme, v.; mitgschtimmt, pp.; 10.reime (sich --)v.; gereimt, pp.; 11.schtalle, v.; gschtallt, pp.; **to** mit/eischtimme, v.; miteigschtimmt, pp.; **with** (of food) 1.aa/schlagge, v.; aagschlagge, pp.; 2.bekumme, v.; is bekumme, pp.; 3.verdraage, v.; verdraage, pp., 4.vergraage, v.; vergraage, pp.; **with someone** Recht (es) n. (ebber -- gewwe);

agreeable 1.aagenehm, adj.; 2.aagenehmlicherweiss, adj.; 3.blessierlich, adj.; 4.gfellich, adj.; 5.leid(l)ich, adj.

agreed eenich, adj.

agreement Bariye (der)n.

agriculture 1.Ackerbau (der)n.; 2.Feldbau (der)n.

agrimony 1.Odermennche (es)n.; 2.Odermennich (es)n.; 3.Odermennli (es)n.

Ah! Aah!, interj.

aha! aha!, interj.

ahead 1.vannedraa, adv.; 2.vanneher, adv.; 3.vannenaus, adv.; 4.vor, prep.; 5.vorwaerts, adv.; 6.vorsei, v.; vorgewest, pp.; **of time** fer Zeit, prep.

aid 1.aus/helfe, v.; ausgholfe, pp.; 2.Hilf (die)n.; 3.kumme, v.; kumme, pp. (zu Hilf --); 4.Mithilf (die)n.

ail 1.biebse, v.; gebiebst, pp.; 2.fehle, v.; g(e)fehlt, pp.;3.fiehle (schlecht --), v.; gfiehlt, pp.; 4.greckse, v.; gegreckst, pp.; 5.grenkle, v.; gegrenk(h)elt, pp.; 6.grenklich sie, v.; grenklichgewest, pp.; 7.grexe, v.; gegrext, pp.; 8.peipse, v.; gepiebst, pp.; 9.rum/greckse, v.; rumgegreckst, pp.

ailanthus 1.Himmelsbaam (der)n.; 2.Paresiesbaam (der) n.; 3.Schumackbaam (der)n.

ailing 1.grecksich, adj.; 2.maudrich, adj.; 3.piensich, adj.; **(usually of fowls)** biebsich, adj.; **person** Piens (die)n.

ailment 1.Blok (die)n.; 2.Plok (die)n.; 3.Sucht (die)n.

aim 1.Absicht (die)n.; 2.hie/halde, v.; hieghalde, pp.; 3.Ziel (es)n.; 4.ziele, v.; gezielt, pp.; 5.Zweck (der)n.

aim (with a gun) **high** nuff/halde, v.; nuffghalde, pp.; **low** nidder/halde, v.; nidderghalde, pp.

air 1.Lifdel (es)n. (diminutive of die Luft = air); 2.Luft (die) n.; **hole** 1.Luftloch (es)n.; 2.Zuckloch (es)n.

airplane Luftschiff (es)n.; Luftschiffer, pl.

airy 1.lifdich, adj.; 2.lufdich, adj.; 3.luftich, adj.

aisle Gang (der)n.; Geng, pl.; **in a church** Karrichgang (der)n.

alarm Laerm(e) (der)n.; **clock** Weckuhr (die)n.

albumen 1.Oi (es)n. (es weiss vum --); 2.Eiweiss (es)n.

alcohol 1.Aelkehaal (es)n.; 2.Babbelwasser (es)n.; 3.Weigeischt (der)n.

alder (brush) Alleheck (die)n.

alert 1.wach(t)sa(a)m, adj.; 2.wacker, adj.; 3.wackerich, adj.

alien 1.auslendisch, adj.; 2.auslenn(er)isch, adj. 3.Auslenner (der)n.; Auslenner, pl.;4.Fremmer (der) n.;5.Fremmi (die)n.

alienated abwennich, adj.

alight naus/schteige, v.; nausgschtigge, pp.; **from a vehi-**

alone

cle ab/schteige, v.; abschteigt, is abschtigge, pp.; **from a carriage** aus/schtiege, v.; ausgschtigge, pp.

alike 1.aehnlich, adj.; 2.gleich, adj.; adv.

alive 1.Lewe (es)n.; Lewe, pl.; (am (bei) -- sei); 2.lewe, v.; glebt, pp.; 3.lewich, adj.; **with** wimmle, v.; gewimmelt, pp.

alkanet Ochsezung (die)n.

all 1.all, adj.; 2.alles, pron.; 3.alliebber, pron.; 4.allmenanner, adj.; 5.lauder, adj.; 6.lauter, adj.; **around** ringsrum, adv.; **at once** 1.eemol, adv. (uff --); 2.uffe(e)mol, adv.; **at one time** allzamme, adv.; **attention** schpitze, v.; gschpitzt, pp. (die Ohre --); **impatience** verwatzle (sich --)v.; verwatzelt, pp.; **in** 1.kaputt, adv.; 2.lodderlo, adv.; **in vain** all, adj. (-- nix); **into** futsch, adv.; **off** all, adj. (-- nix); **ready** fix un faerdich, adj.; **right** 1.allrecht, adj.;2. in Add (e)ning, adj.; **sorts** 1.allerlee, adv.; 2.allerlei, adv.; **sorts of** allerhand, adj.; **the same** einerlei, adj.; **the time** alldiweil, adv.; **the way** alldeweeg, adv.

All Saints' and All Souls' Day (Nov. 1 and 2) 1.Allerheil un (aller) Seel; 2.Allerheilichi (die)n.

alliance Bindnis (es)n.

allow 1.bewilliche, v.; bewillicht, pp.; 2.erlaawe, v.; erla(a)bt, pp.; 3.leide, v.; gelidde, pp.; 4.losse, v.; g(e)losst, pp.; 5. zu/gewwe, v.; zugewwe, pp.; **a person to get to a place** hie/losse, v.; hieglosst, pp.; **over** riwwer/losse, v.; riwwergelosst, pp.; **to come down** runner/losse, v. runnergelosst, pp.; **to come here** haer/losse, v.; haergelosst, pp.; **to continue** gewaehre losse, v.; **to go up** nuff/losse, v.; nuffgelosst, pp.; **to pass** 1.verbei/losse, v.; verbeigelosst, pp.; 2.vor/losse, v.; vorgelosst, pp.; **to pass through** darich/losse, v.; darichgelosst, pp.; **up** ruff/losse, v.; ruffgelosst, pp.

allowance Abloss (der)n.

allowed out raus/daerfe, v.; rausgedaerft, pp.;

allowed to come back zerick/daerfe, v.; zerickgedaerft, pp.; **to come down** runner/daerfe, v.; runnergedaerft, pp.; **to come or go along** mit/daerfe, v.; mitgedaerft, pp.; **to follow** no(och)daerfe, v.; no(och)gedaerft, pp.; **to go** fatt/daerfe, v.; fattgedaerft, pp.; **to go away** weck/daerfe, v.; weckgedaerft, pp.; **to go to a certain place** hie/daerfe, v.; hiegedaerft, pp.; **to meet** zamme/daerfe, v.; zammegedaerft, pp.; **up** ruff/daerfe, v.; ruffgedaerft, pp.

alloyed gfelscht, adj.

allude to bei/bringe, v.; beigebrocht, pp.

allure aa/locke, v.; aagelockt, pp.

almanac Kalenner (der)n.; Kalenner, pl.

almighty allmechdich, adj.

almond Mandelkaern (die)n.

almost 1.ball, adv.; 2.beinaah, adv.; 3.beineegscht, adv.; 4.beino, adv.; 5.beinooch, adv.; 6.fascht, adj.; 7.ordlich neegseht, adv.; 8.schier gaar, adv.; 9.sozesaage, conj.

alms 1.Almose (die)n., pl.; 2.Gottesgaabe (die)n.; 3.Karrichegeld (es)n.

aloe Allowe (die)n.

alone 1.allee, adj.; adv.; 2.alleenich, adv.; 3.lee, adv.; 4.leenich, adv.;.

Aa

along — anthill

along 1.an, prep.; 2.dewek, adv.; 3.mit, adv.; **here** 1.dodraahie, adv.; 2.dohaerzus, adv.; 3.dohiezus, adv.; **the bottom** unneher, prep.; **the side there** 1.datthinewe, adv.; 2.dattnewe, adv.; **the top** owwehaer, adv.; **there** 1.dattdraahi, adv; 2.datthaer, adv.; 3.datthizus, adv.; **up above** owwehie, adv.; **with** 1.dabei, prep.; 2.debei, prep.

alongside 1.newe, adv.; prep.; 2.newedraa, adv.; 3.anewich, prep.; **here** dodenewe, adv.; **of** newehie, adv.; **of** (in motion) newehaer, adv.

alphabet 1.Aa-Be-Ze (es)n.; 2.Abc (der)n.

already schunn(t), adv.

also aa, adv.

altar Aldaar (der)n.; Aldaare, pl.

alter 1.ennere,v.; ge-ennert, pp.;2.verennere,v.; verennert, pp.

alteration 1.Verennering (die)n.; 2.Verennerung (die)n.

altercation Zank (der)n.

alternate ab/wechsle, v.; abgewechselt, pp.

although 1.ebwohl, conj.; 2.obschon(n), conj.; 3.obwohl, conj.

altogether 1.allmenanner, adj.; 2.allzamme, adv.; 3.lauder, adj.; 4.lauter, adj.

alum Allau (der)n.

always 1.allfatt, adv.; 2.allfert, adv.; 3.allzeit, adv.; 4.als, adv.; 5.alsfatt, adv.; 6.immer, adv.; 7.immerfart, adj.; 8.seilebbdaag, adv.; 9.seilewe(s), adv; 10.selewe, adv.

amass zuschaffe, v.; zugschafft, pp. ; **by hoarding** zamme/gratze, v.; zammegegratzt, pp.

amaze 1. erschtaune, v.; erschtaunt, pp.; 2. verwunnere (sich --) v.; verwunnert, pp.

amazed verschtaune (sich --)v.; verschtaunt, pp.

amazon Mannweib (es)n.

amber bead Flusskarrell (die)n.

ambiguous dobbel-sinnich, adj.

ambition Ehrgeiz (der)n.

ambitious ehrgeizich, adj.

amble (of a horses gait) basse, v.; gebasst, pp.

ameliorate uff/bessere, v.; uffgebessert, pp.

amen 1.Aamen, interj.; 2.allemol, adv. (used in responses)

amenable antwattlich, adj.

amend verbessre, v.; verbessert, pp.

America Amerika(a),n.

American 1.amerika(a)nisch, adj.; 2.Amerikaaner (der)n.; Amerikaaner, pl.; **brooklime** Bachbumbel (die)n.; **elder** Holler (der) n. (schwatzer --); **elm** Rusch(d)e (die)n. **pennyroyal** Grottebalsem (der)n.

amicable 1.freindlich, adj.; 2.freindschaftlich, adj.; 3.friedlich, adj.

amid midde(s), adv.

amidst 1.bei, prep.; 2.midde unner, adv.

Amish Amisch, adj.; **man** Amischmann (der)n.; **woman** Amischfraa (die)n.

amiss 1.verkehrt, adj.; 2.letz sei, v.; is letz gewest, pp.

among 1.bei, prep.; 2.dabei, adv.; 3.unner, prep.; 4.unnich, prep.; **themselves** unne(re)nanner, adv.

amorous schpielich, adj.

amount Summ (die)n.; **to** hie/laafe, v.; hiegeloffe, pp.

ample genunk, adv.

amputate 1.ab/nemme, v.; abgenumme, pp.; 2.ab/schneide, v.; abgschnidde, pp.

amuse oneself 1. Blessier (die) n. (-- dreiwe); 2. blessiere (sich --) v.; blessiert, pp.; 3. vergniege (sich --) v.; vergniecht, pp.

an en, indef. art.

ancestor Vorgenger (der)n.

ancestors 1.Voreldre (die)n., pl.; 2.Vorvedder (die)n., pl.

anchor 1.Anker (der)n.; 2.ankere, v.; geankert, pp.

and un, conj.; **all** mitzamte(n), prep.; **so forth** dings (un so --); **that ends it** emol, adv

Andrew Andres (der)n.

anemone 1.Windblumm (die)n.; 2.Windros (die)n.

anew 1.nei, adv.; 2.vun neiem, adv.

angel Engel (der)n.; Engel, pl.

Angelica (plant) 1.Angelige (die)n.; 2.Engelwarzel (die)n.

anger 1.Groll (der)n.; 2.petze, v.; gepetzt, pp.; 3.verzaerne, v.; verzaernt, pp.; 4.verzanne, v.; verzannt, pp.; 5.Wut (die)n.; 6.Zann (der)n.; 7.zannich mache, v.; zannich gemacht, pp.

angina pectoris Hatzklemmes (es)n.

angle 1.Eck (es)n.; Ecke, pl.; 2.Winkel (der)n. **(for fish)** fische, v.; gfischt, pp.

angry 1.bees, adj.; 2.verzannt, adj.; **outburst** newwle, v.; genewwelt, pp.; **(bees)** 1.veraeryert, adj.; 2.zannich, adj.

animal Gedier (es)n.; Gediere, pl.

ankle 1.Enkel (der)n.; 2.Gnechel (der)n.; Gnechel, pl.; 3.Gneckel (der)n.

Ann Mary Annemar(e)ia (die)n.

anniversary Yehrlichfescht (es)n.

announce 1.aa/kindiche, v.; aagekindicht, pp.; 2.aa/saage, v.; aagsaat, pp.; 3.anne/bschtelle, v.; annebschtellt, pp.; 4.anne/schtelle, v.; annegschtellt, pp.; 5.aus/gewwe, v.; ausgewwe, pp.; 6.bekannt/mache, v.; bekanntgemacht, pp.; 7.melde, v.; gemeldt, pp.; **or welcome** (by shooting) aschiesse, v.; aagschosse, pp.; **publicly** 1.verkindiche, v.; verkindicht, pp.; verkinne, v.; verkinnt, pp.

annoyance 1.Elend (es)n. (en --); 2.Greitz (es)n. (en --); 3.Gretz (der)n. (en --)

annual 1.yaerhrich, adv.; 2.yaehrlich, adv.

annul 1.uff/kindiche, v.; 2.vernichde, v.; vernicht, pp.

anoint 1.ei/salwe, v.; eigsalbt, pp.; 2.salwe, v.; gsalbt, pp.

another 1.en annres, pron.; 2.en(n)anner, pron.; 3.noch eens, pron.; **time** 1.annermol, adj.

answer 1.antwadde, v.; geantwatt, pp.; 2.Antwatt (die)n.; Antwadde, pl.; 3.antwatt gewwe, v.; antwatt gewwe, pp.; 4.eischteh, v.; eigschtanne, pp.; 5.schaffe, v.; gschafft, pp.; **a question** beantwarte, v.; beantwart, pp.; **for** 1.verantwarte, v.; verantwart, pp.

answering back Hinnerbart (der)n.

ant 1.lemens (die)n.; lemense, pl.; 2.Imens (die)n.; Imense, pl.; 3.Umens (die)n.; Umense, pl.

antagonize aa/feinde, v.; aagfeindt, pp.

anteroom Vorschtubb (die)n.

anthem 1.Korgesang (der)n.; 2.Korlied (es)n.

anthill 1.Iemensehaufe (der)n.; 2.Iemensenescht (es)n.

225

Aa

Anthony

Anthony 1.Andann (der)n.; 2.Don(i) (der)n.
anthracite coal Schteekohl (die)n.
anticipate 1.Bass abschneide (der)v.; 2..schpitze, v.;
    gschpitzt, pp. (sich uff ebbes --); 3.vor/kumme, v.;
    vorkumme, pp.; 5.vorgucke, v.; vorgeguckt, pp.
anticipation 1.Vorschtelling (die)n.; 2.Vorschtellung (die)n.
antidote 1.Gegegift (es)n.;2.Gegemiddel (es)n.;
    3.Gegemittel (es)n.
antler Haschharn (es)n.
anus 1.After (es)n.; 2.Arschloch (es)n.; 3.Sitzloch (es)n.
anvil Ambos (der)n.; Ambose, pl.; **mounting**
    1.Ambosschtand (der)n.; 2.Ambosschtul (der)n.
anxiety Kimmernis (die)n.
anxious 1.besarickt, adj.; 2.engschderich, adv.; 3.engschderlich,
    adj.; adv.; 5.engschtlich, adv.; 6.enschderlich, adv.;
    7.sarrickvoll, adj.; 8.voll Angscht, adv.; **bench** Bussbank
    (die)n.; **or solicitous** verdroddle (sich --)v.; verdroddelt, pp.
any 1.eenich, adj.; 2.ennich, adj.; 3.ennicher, adj.;
    4.ennichi, adj.; **longer** meh, adj.; **more** meh, adj.
anybody 1.eenichebber, pron.; 2.ennichebber, pron.
anyhow 1.ennichau, adv.; 2.ennicher, adv.; 3.ennichhau,
    adv.; 4.ennihau, adv.; 5.hennicher, adv.; 6.hennyer, adv.
anyone 1.eenichebber, pron.; 2.ennichebber, pron.
anything 1.eenichebbes, pron.; 2.ennichebbes, pron.
anytime 1.eenichi Zeit, adv.; 2.eenichmol, adv.; 3.ennichi
    Zeit, adv.
anyway 1.ennichau, adv.; 2.ennicher, adv.; 3.ennihau,
    adv.; 4.hennicher, adv.; 5.hennyer, adv.
anywhere 1.eenichariyets, adv.; 2.eenichatiyets, adv.;
    3.ennichareiyets, adv.; 4.ennicheids, adj.;
    5.ennicheiyets, adv.
apart 1.aus/nanner, adv.; 2.ausenanner, adj.;
    3.newedrauss, adv.; 4.vunenanner, adv.
ape 1.Aff (der)n.; Affe, pl.; 2.no(och)affe, v.; no(och)geafft, pp.
aphides Laableis (die)n., pl.
apologize 1.en(t)schuldiche (sich --)v.; en(t)schuldicht, pp.
apology En(t)schuldichung (die)n.
apoplexy 1.Schlaag (der)n.; 2.Schlack (der)n.
apostate abtrinni(s)ch, adj.
apostatize ab/falle, v.; abgfalle, pp.
apostle Aposchdel (der)n.
apostrophe Abkatzungszeeche (es)n.
apparent aascheinlich, adj.
apparently 1.scheinbaar, adj.; 2.scheins, adv.;
    3.waahrscheinlich, adv.
apparition 1.Geescht (der)n.; 2.Geischt (der)n.; Geischder, pl.
appeal to aa/rufe, v.; aagerufe, pp.
appear 1.aus/sehne, v.; ausgsehne, pp.; 2.erscheine, v.;
    erscheint, pp.; 3.gucke, v.; geguckt, pp.; 4.scheine, v.;
    gscheint, pp.
appearance 1.Aaschein (der)n.; 2.Erscheinung (die)
    n.;3.Guck (der)n.; 4.Schein (der)n.; 5.Vorschein (der)
    n.; **of hoar frost in winter or of moisture on pol-
    ished surface** dufdich, adj.
appearances are deceptive hui, adj.(vanne -- un hinne fui)
appease 1.schtille, v.; gschtillt, pp.; 2.settiche, v.; gsetticht, pp.

April

append aa/henke, v.; aaghenkt; aaghonke, pp.
appendage Aahang (der)n.
appertain to zukumme, v.; zukumme, pp.
appetite 1.Abbeditt (der)n.; 2.Luschde (der)n.
appetizing abbedittlich, adj.
applaud blet(s)che, v.; gebletscht, pp.
applause Beifall (der)n.
apple Abbel (der)n.; Ebbel, pl.; **butter** Lattwarrick (der)n.;
    leaves Eppellaab (es)n.; **parer** Schaelmiehlche (es)n.;
    pie 1.Ebbelbei (der) n.; Ebbelbei,; pl.; 2.Ebbelboi
    (der)n.; Ebbelboi, pl.; **sauce** Ebbelsaes (der)n.; **seed**
    Eppelkaern (die)n.; **tart** 1.Ebbelkuche (der)n.;
    2.Eppelkuche (der)n.; **tree** 1.Abbelbaam (der)n.;
    2.Eppelbaam (der)n.
applejack 1.Grutze (der)n. (weeche --); 2.Krutze (der)n.
apples (sliced and dried) and dumplings Schnitz (die)n.
    (-- un Gnepp); **apples** (very many) Abbel (der)n.
    (en laschder --)
appletritch 1.Ebbeldritsch (es)n.; 2.Ebbeldritsche, pl.
application 1.Aaschpruch (der)n.; 2.Fodderes (es)n.
apply 1.aa/wende, v.; aagewendt, pp.; 2.aa/wenne, v.;
    aagewennt, pp.; 3.aasuche, v.; aagsucht, pp.;
    4.uff/lege, v.; uffgelegt, pp.; 5.verwenne, v.;
    verwennt, pp.; 6.yuuse, v.; gyuust, pp.; **a liquid to a
    surface** druff/ duh, v.; druffgeduh, pp.; **splints to a
    broken bone** 1.schindel, v.; gschindelt, pp.;
    2.schindle, v.; gschindelt, pp.; **turpentine**
    daerbediene, v.; gedaerbedient, pp.
applying of salve Geblaschder (es)n.
appoint (by proclamation) aus/schreiwe, v.; ausgschri-
    wwe, pp.; **appoint (to ordain)** 1.aa/schtelle, v.;
    aagschtellt, pp.; 2.aa/setze, v.; aagsetzt, pp.
appointment Bschtelling (die)n.
apportion uff/deele, v.; uffgedeelt, pp.
appraise 1.breese, v.; gebreest, pp.; 2.schetze, v.;
    gschetzt, pp.
appreciate eschtimere, v.; geschtimiert, pp.
apprentice Brendis (der)n.; Brendis, pl.
apprise benoochrichde, v.; benoochrichdet, pp.
approach 1.bei/ricke, v.; beigerickt, pp.; 2.naah/kumme,
    v.; naahkumme, pp.; **with heavy steps** haer/dappe,
    v.; haergedappt, pp.
approachable zugenglich, adj.
approaching from the rear hinnebei,adv.;**in below** unne-
    rei, adj.
approbation Beifall (der)n.
appropriate 1.nemme, v.; gnumme, pp.; 2.zweckmaessich, adj.
approve 1. billiche, v.; gebillicht, pp.; 2.heese, v.;
    gheese, pp. (gut --)
approved probaat, adj.
approximately 1.beino, adv.; 2.beinooch, adv.
appurtenances Zugeheer (es)n.
apricot Abrigos (die)n.; Abrigose, pl.; **tree** Abrigosebaam
    (der)n.; Abrigosebeem, pl.
April Abrill (der)n.; **fool** 1.Abril(le)kalb (es)n.; 2.Abrill(e)
    Narr (der)n.; 3.Abrille Eesli (es)n.

Aa

apron — assemble

apron 1. Schatz (der) n.; Schatz, pl.; 2.Schar(t)z (der) n.; Schar(t)z, pl.; **string** 1. Schatzbendel (der) n.; 2.Schar(t)zbendel (der)n.

apt to geneicht, adj.

aquafortis Schee(d)wasser (es)n.

Aquarius (11th sign of the zodiac) Wassermann (der)n.

arc 1.Boge (der)n.; 2.Gewelb (es)n.

arch 1.Boge (der)n.; 2.Gewelb (es)n.;3.welbe, v.; gewelbt, pp.; **enemy** Erbfeind (der) n

arched gewelbt, adj.; **bridge** Brick (die)n. (en gwelb--); **arched cellar** Gewelbkeller (es)n.; **window** Bogefenschder (es)n.

architect Baumeeschder (der)n.

architecture Baukunscht (die)

ardent hees, adj.

ardently aernschtlich, adv.

are to solle, v.; gsollt, pp.

are we simmer = sinn mer

Are you minded to do it tomorrow? mariye, adv. (dienders --)

area Weltdeel (es)n.

argue 1.renkle,v.; gerenkelt, pp.;2.schtreide, v.; gschtridde, pp.

argument Grenkel (es)n.

Aries (1st sign of the zodiac)1.Wedder (der)n.;2.Widder (der)n.

arise uff/wecke, v.; uffgeweckt, pp.

arithmetic (book) Rechelbuch (es)n.

ark Arrich (die)n.

arm Aarem (der)n.; Erem, pl.

armchair 1.Armschtuhl (der)n.; 2.Sessel (der)n.

armful Aaremvoll (es)n.

army Armee (die)n.; **chaplain** Feldbreddicher (der)n.

aroma 1.Geruch (der)n.; 2.Gschmack (der)n.

around 1.rum, adv.; 2.um, prep.; **back** hinnerum, adv.; **below** unnerum, adv.; **by the front way** vannerum, adv.; **it** 1.drumrum, adv.; 2.ums = um es **on the outside** auserum, adj.; **one another** umenanner, adv.

arouse uff/retze, v.; uffgeretzt, pp.; **interest** uff/drumme, v.; uffgedrummt, pp.

arrange 1.ab/richde, v.; abgericht, pp.; 2. flankiere, v.; gflankiert, pp.; 3.uff/griege, v.; uffgrickt, pp.

arrangement 1.Bedingung (die)n.; 2.Eirichding (die) n. **on which flax is dried** Flaxdaerr (die)n.

arrears Rickschtand (der)n.

arrest 1.faschtnemme, v.; faschtgenumme, pp.; 2.packe, v.; gepackt, pp.; 3.uff/nemme, v.; uffgenumme, pp.; 4.verhafte, v.; verhaft, pp.

arrive 1.aa/kumme, v.; is aakumme, pp.; 2.aa/lande, v.; aagelandt, pp.; 3. aa/lange, v.; aagelangt, pp.; 4. anne/kumme, v.; is annekumme, pp.; **unexpectedly** dezukumme, v.; is dezukumme, pp.

arrow Peil (der)n.

arrowhead Peilschpitz (der)n.

arse 1.Aarsch (der)n.; 2.Sitzloch (es)n.

arsenal Rischthaus (es)n.

arson Mardbrennerei (die)n.

art Kunscht (die)n.

artemisia Beifuss (der)n.

artery 1.Aader (die) n.; Aadere, pl.; 2.Blutaader (die) n.; Blutaadere, pl.; 3.Blutoder (die)n.; Blutodere, pl.; 4.Bolsoder (die)n.Bulsoder (die)n.;5.Oder (die)n.; Odere, pl.

artful 1.fei(n), adj.; 2.schlitzohrich, adj.

article Ardickel (der)n.

articles Geraetschaft (die)n.

artificial kinschdlich, adj.

as 1.als, adv.; 2.as, adv.; 3.wie, adv.; conj.; 4.wu, conj.; **a rule** 1.gemeenerhand, adj. ; 2.gemeenichlich, adj. **far as** 1.soweit, conj.; 2.bis, prep.; **far back as memory goes**; menschedenke seit, adv.; **follows** denneweg, adv.; **good as** sozesaage, conj.; **long as** solang, adv.; **luck would have it** glicklichweis, adv.; **much as** soviel, conj.; **much as one can carry** Draaget (die)n.; **soon as** soball, adv.; **stupid as can be** Saeg (die)n. (so dumm as -- holz); **usual** graad, adj. (graad -- im alde); **welcome as a pig in a synagogue** So willkumm wie en Sau imme Yuddehaus

asafoetida Deiwelsdreck (der)n.

ascend 1.nuff/geh, v.; nuffgange, pp.; 2.schtiege, v.; is gschtigge, pp.; 3.uff/schteige, v.; uffgschtigge, pp.

Ascension Day 1.Himmelfaahrt(s)daag (der)n.; 2.Himmelferdaag (der)n.

Ascension of the Virgin Mary (Aug. 15) Marieheim (es)n.

ascertain aus/finne, v.; ausgfunne, pp.; **by listening** ab/hariche, v.; abgharicht, pp.

ascribe zurechle, v.; zugerechelt, pp.; **to** zuschreiwe, v.; zugschriwwe, pp.

ash-tree 1.Asche (die)n.; 2.Esche (die)n.

Ash Wednesday 1.Aschermittwoch (der)n.; 2.Eschemittwoch (der)n.

ashamed 1.henke, v.; ghenkt, pp.; (der Kopp --) 2.schemme (sich --)v.; gschemmt, pp.

ashes Esch (die)n.; Esche, pl.; **of coal** Kohleesch (die)n.

ashman Eschmann (der)n.

aside 1.newedrauss, adv.; 2.newenaus, adv.

ask 1.bitte, v.; gebitt, pp.; 2.fodd(e)re, v.; gfoddert, pp.; 3.froge, v.; gfrogt, pp.; 4. verlange, v.; verlangt, pp. **continually** bellere, v.; gebellert, pp.

ask one after another rum/froge, v.; rumgfrogt, pp.

aslant schraeks, adj.

asleep Schlof (der)n.(am [im]) -- sei);

asparagus Schparregra(a)s (es)n.

aspect Aabllck (der)n.

aspen 1.Aschbe (die)n.; 2.asphodel; 3.Alsodillwatzel (die)n.

asphyxiate verschticke, v.; verschtickt, pp.; **with sulphur fumes** schwewwle, v.; gschwewwelt, pp.

aspire lange, v.; gelangt, pp. (--[e] fer ebbes)

ass (animal) 1.Esel (der)n.; Esel, pl.; 2.Langohr (es)n.

assail aa/greife, v.; aagegriffe, pp.

assassin Meichelmaerder (der)n.

assassinate maerde, v.; gemaerdt, pp.

assemble 1.versammle (sich --)v.; versammelt, pp.; 2.zamme/hole, v.; zammegholt, pp.; 4.zamme/kumme, v.; is zammekumme, pp.; 5.zamme/laafe, v.; 6.zummegeloffe, pp.

Aa

assembled | aurora borealis

assembled 1.zamme/duh, v.; zarnmegeduh, pp.;
2.Versammling (die)n.

assembly Versammlung (die)n.

assent 1.Beifall (der)n.; 2.Yawatt (es)n.; 3.Yowatt (es)n.;
4.behaapde, v.; behaapt, pp.

assert behapde, v.; behapt, pp.

assist 1.aus/helfe, v.; ausgholfe, pp.; 2.bei/schpringe, v.;
beischprunge, pp.; 3.bei/ schteh, v.; beischtanne,
pp.; 4.helfe, v.; gholfe, pp.; 5.mit/helfe, v.; mitgholfe,
pp.; 6.raus/helfe, v.; rausgholfe, pp.; **assist** (a person)
to a place hie/helfe, v.; hiegholfe, pp.; **a blacksmith
in welding tires** zu/schlagge, v.; zugschlagge, pp.;
masons or bricklayers handlange, adj.

assistance Mithilf (die)n.

assistant Helfer (der)n.

associate gselle (sich --)v.; gsellt, pp.

assort aus/lese, v.; ausg(e)lese, pp.

assume (responsibility) schultere, v.; gschultert, pp.

assure versichere, v.; versichert, pp.

aster 1.Daalerros (die) n.; 2. Schtaernblumm (die) n.;
Schtaernblumme, pl.

asthmatic 1. engbrischdich, adj.; 2. keich(l)ich, adj.; 3.
katzo(o)chd(e)mich, adj.

astonish 1.erschtaune, v.; erschtaunt, pp.; 2.iwwerrasche,
v.; iwwerrascht, pp.; 3.iwwerschlagge, v.; iwwerschlagge, pp.; **(physically)** iwwerfalle, v.; iwwerfalle, pp.

astonished 1.verschtaune (sich --)v.; verschtaunt, pp.;
2.verschtaunt, adj.; 3.verschpraddle (sich --)v.;
verschpraddelt, pp.

astonishing 1.erschtaunlich, adj.; adv.; 2.verschtaunlich,
adv.; adj.

astound verwunnere, v.; verwunnert, pp.

astraddle 1.graddlich, adj.; 2.kraddlich, adj.

astray verloffe, adv.

astronomer Schtaernekenner (der)n.

astute 1.fuxich, adj.; 2.gewixt, adj. 3.schlau, adj.

at 1.am, prep.; 2.an, prep.; adv.; 3.bei, prep.; 4.in, prep.;
5.uff, prep.; 6.ze = zu; **at it** (about, near, of) 1.draa,
adv.; 2. denno, adv.; 3.dro, ad; **a amme** = an me; **all
times** yederzeit, adv.; **full length** 1.langs, adv.; 2.lengs,
adv.; **home** deheem, adv.; **last** 1.zeletscht, adv.;
2.zuletscht, adv.; **least** wen(n)ichschdens, adv.; **length**
vollschder, adj.; **midnight** mitnachts, adv.; **night** nachts,
adv.; **odd** 1. hinnernanner, adv.; 2.hinnernenner, adv.
3.schtreidich, adv.; **once** 1.glei, adv.; 2.graad, adj.;
3.schnurschtracks, adv.; **retail** 1.beim gleene, adv.;
2.glee, adj. (beim gleene); **that** dattdraa, adv.; **that
time** 1.dolmos, adv.; 2.sellemols, adv. **at the** ans = an
es; **beginning** aafangs, adv.; **beginning of the week**
Woch (die)n. (aafangs --); **bottom** 1.unnedraa, adv.;
2.unnewedder, adv.; **end of the month** Munet (der)n.
(hinne im --); **end of the week** Woch (die)n.
(hinnes --); **head** vannedraa, adv.; **house of** bei, prep.
present (time) fangs, adv.; **proper moment** rechzeitich,
adj.; **sign of** eischt, adj.; **top of it** owwedraa, adv.

at this dodraa, adv.; **time** 1.zeideweis, adv.; 2.zeiteweis, adv.

Atchee! 1.Atschi!, interj.; 2.Azi!, interj. (imitation of the
sound made in sneezing, some-times with an added
'Gsundheet').

atlas bone Yutt (der)n.

atone (for) biesse, v.; gebiesst, pp.

atrophy (of a muscle)1.Schweini(ng) (die),n.;2.Schwinne
(die)n.

attach to oneself aa/zaahme, v.; aagezaahmt, pp.

attack 1.aa/falle, v.; aagfalle, pp.; 2.aa/fechde, v.; aagfochde, pp.; 3.aa/greife, v. aagegriffe, pp. 4.aa/
packe, v.; aagepackt, pp.; 5.Aagriff (der)n.

attacker Aagreifer (der)n.

attain 1.erlange, v.; erlangt, pp.; 2.erreeche, v.; erreecht, pp.;
3.her/lange, v.; heregelangt,; pp.; 4.lange, v.; gelangt,
pp.; 5.reeche, v.; gereecht, pp.; 6.relange, v.; relangt,
pp.; **one's full growth** aus/waxe, v.; ausgewaxe, pp.

attempt 1.browiere, v.; (ge)browiert, pp.; 2.unner/
nemme, v.; unnergenumme, pp.; 3.unnernemme
(sich --) v.; unnernumme, pp.; 4.versuche, v.; versucht, pp.; **to gain information** aus/faschle, v.;
ausgfaschelt, pp.; **to sting** (as a bee when it is held
fast) schtachele, v.; gschtachelt, pp.

attend 1.bediene, v.; bedient, pp.; 2.bei/wohne, v.;
beigewohnt, pp.; 3.bei/wohne (sich --)v.; beigewohnt, pp.; **catechetical instruction** Unnerricht (der)
n. (in der -- geh); **to** 1.aus/richde, v.; ausgericht,
pp.;2.bsarge, v.; bsarkt, pp.

attendance 1. Abwarting (die) n.; 2. Abwartung (die) n.;
3. Waarting (die) n. 4. Waartung (die) n.; **at church**
Karrichgang (der)n.

attended by a physician doktere, v.; gedoktert, pp.

attention 1.Aadacht (die)n.; 2.Acht (der, die)n.; 3.Obacht (die)n.

attentive 1.aadechtich,adj.;adv.; 2.achtsam,adj.
3.beheeflich,adj.

attest 1.bezeige, v.; bezeikt, pp.; 2.Zeichnis (es)n.
(-- gewwe)

attic 1.Aeddick (die)n.; 2.ewwerscht Schpeicher (der)n.;
3.Garret (der)n.

attire Aazuck (der)n.

attitude Schtellung (die)n.

attract 1.aa/lache, v.; aagelacht, pp.; 2.aa/ziehe, v.; aagezoge,
pp.; **fish by little jerks** aa/zobbe, v.; aagezoppt, pp.

auburn 1.keschdebrau, adj.; 2.rotbrau(n), adj.

auction Vendu (die)n.

auctioneer 1.Groier (der)n.; Groiere, pl.; 2.Vendugroier (der)n.

audible heerbaar, adj.

auditor Zuheerer (der)n.

auger Bohre (der)n.; Bohre, pl.

auger for boring bung holes 1.Schpund(e)bohre (der)n.;
Schpund(e)bohre, pl.

August (month) 1. Aagscht (der) n.; 2. Aaguscht (der) n.;
3.Aug(u)scht (der)n.

Augustus Aaguscht (der)n.

aunt 1.Aendi (die)n.; 2.Aent(i) (die)n.

aunty Baesel (die)n.

aurora borealis 1.Naddschein (der)n.; 2.Nardlicht (es)n.;

Bb

baa

baa blecke, v.; gebleckt, pp.

baa! bae!, interj.

baby 1.Baerwelche (es)n.; 2.Baerwle (es)n.; 3.Bewwi (die) n.; 4.Bobb (die)n.; 5.Bobbel(i)(es)n.; 6.Bobbli (es)n.; Bobblin, pl.; 7.glee, adj.; (en gleenes); 8.verbobble, v.; verbobbelt, pp.; **beads** 1.Karell (die)n.; Karelle, pl.; 2.Poddre (die)n., pl.; **bib** Schlawwerduch (es)n.; Schlawwerdicher, pl.; **high chair** Hochschtuhl (der)n.; **pacifier** Gammditz (der)n.; **petticoat** Reckelche (es) n.; **rattle** Rappli (es)n.; Rapplin, pl.; **sock** Schtrimpelche (es)n.

babble 1.aus/babble, v.; ausgebabbelt, pp.; 2.babble, v.; gebabbelt, pp.

babbler Babbelmaul (es)n.; Babbelmeiler, pl.

back 1.hinner, adj.; 2.Hun(d)srick (der)n.; 3.redour, adv.; 4.zerick, adv.; **and forth** 1.hie un her, adv.; 2.uff un ab, adv.; 3.zerick un vari, adv.; **here** (with a verb of motion) dohinnrie, adv.; **(in, by, at)** dehinne, adv.; **(of human body)** 1.Buckel (der)n.; 2.Rick(der)n.; Ricke, pl.; **biter** Laschdermaul (es)n.; **bone** Rickmeesel (der)n.; Rickschtrang (der)n.; Rickschtreng, pl.; **country** hinnrizus, adv.; **door** 1.Hinnerdier (die) n.; 2.Hinnerschtdier (die)n.; **here** dohinne, adv.; **house** 1.Briwwe (es)n.; 2.Briwwi (es)n.; 3.Priwwi (es) n.; **in that direction** datthinnrizus, adv.; **in this direct** dozerick, adv.; **log** Hinnerglotz (der)n.; **of the neck** 1.Halsangel (die)n.; 2.Halsankel (die)n.; 3.Nacke (der) n.; **out** uff/schmeisse, v.; uffschmisse, pp.; **part** (one's rear end) Hinnerdeel (es)n.; **rump** Schwansschtick (es)n.; **there** (with a verb of motion) datthinnri, adv.; **there** 1.datthinne, adv.; 2.dattzerick, adv.; **this way** dozerickzus, adv.; **to a certain place** hinnri, adv.

backache 1.Beckelweh (es)n.; 2.Buckelweh (es)n.; 3.Greizweh (es)n.; 4.Rickweh (es)n.

backbite naus/mache, v.; nausgemacht, pp.(iwwer ebber --)

background Hinnergrund (der)n.

backing Hinnerhalt (die)n.

backside 1.Baerzel (der)n.; 2.Hinnerbacke (der)n.; 3.Hinnerbacke, pl.

backstrap Rickrieme (der)n.; Rickrieme, pl.

backward 1.eigezogge, adj.; 2.hinnerschich, adv.; 3.hinnersich, adv.; 4. rickwaerts, adv.; 5. hinnerricksich, adj. 6. hinnerwaerts, adv.; 7.zerick/schteh, v.; zerickgschtanne, pp.; 8.zerick/sei, v.; is zerickgewest, pp.; 9.zerickzus, adv.

backwards and forward hinnerschich un varschich, adv.

bacon 1.Schpeck (der)n.; 2.Seidefleesch (es)n.; 3.Seideschpeck (der)n.; 4.Seideschtick (es)n.

bad 1.arig, adj.; 2.arrick, adj.; 3.iwwel, adj.; 4.schlecht, adj.; 5.schlimm, adj.; 6.wiescht, adj.; **business** Lumberei (die)n.; **feelings** Verdruss (der)n.; **instrument player** Dudler (der)n.; **looking** schlechtguckich, adj.; **odor** 1.Iwwelgeruch (der)n.; 2.Schtink (der)n.; **reputation** seftich, adj.; **tempered** wieschderlich, adj.; **weather** Hunswedder (es)n.; **whiskey** 1.Grutze

band

(der)n. (weecher --); 2.Krutze (der)n. (weecher --)

badness 1.Schlechdichkeit (die)n.; 2.Schlechtichkeet (die)n.

bag 1.Dutt (die)n.; Dudde, pl.; 2.Sack (der)n.; Seck, pl.; 3.Tutt (die)n.; Tudde, pl.; **and baggage** Sack (der)n. (--un Pack); **grain or feed from bin** aus/fasse, v.; ausgfasst, pp.; **in which the crushed mass was put for pressing flaxseed** Olichsack (der)n.; **slung over the shoulder of a sower** Saesack (der)n.

bagpipe 1.Dudelsack (der)n; Dudelseck, pl.; 2.Sackpeif (die)n.

bail 1.aus/scheppe, v.; ausgscheppt, pp.; 2.Hemmerhendel(der)n.; **(of a bucket)** Eemerhenk (die)n.; **(of a kettle)** Kesselhenk (die)

bake backe, v.; gebacke, pp.; **oven** Backoffe (der) n.; **sufficiently** ausbacke, v.; ausgebacke, pp.

baked thing Gebeck (es)n.

baker Becker (der)n.; Becker, pl.

baker's bread Beckerbrot (es)n.; **peel** 1.Backoffeschiess (der); 2.Backoffeschiesser (der)n. Backoffeschiesser, pl.; **wagon** Beckerwagge (der)n.

bakery Beckerei (die)n.

baking Geback (es)n.; **(a repeated household operation)** Backes (es)n.; **('til the next baking day)** Backett (die)n.

baking-apple Backabbel (der)n.

baking day Backdaag (der)n.

baking molasses Backmelassich (der)n.

baking soda Backsoode (der)n.

balance 1.Gleichgewicht (es)n.; 2.Schaal(e)woog (die)n.; 3.Woog (die)n.; Wooge, pl.

balance wheel Schwungraad (es)n.

bald 1.baali, adj.; 2.blott, adj.; 3.blutt(e)kebbich, adj.

baldhead 1. baalkeppich, adj.; 2. Baalkopp (der) n.; 3. blottkeppich, adj.; 4.Blottkopp (der)n.; 5.Blottschaal (die)n.

bale Balle (der)n.

balky schtubbich, adj.

balky as hell (of a horse) Galgeholz (es)n. (falsch wie --)

ball Balle (der)n.; **(of the thumb)** Balle (der)n.; **(of yarn)** 1.Glingel (der)n.; 2.Klingel (der)n.

ball game in which two sides threw the ball over the school house Baall-oower (der)n.

ball of snow formed under a horse's hoof Schtolle (der) n.

ball player Balleschpieler (der)n.; Balleschpieler, pl.

ballad Reim (der)n.; Reime, pl.

balloon 1.Balluun (der)n.; 2.Luftschiff (es)n.; Luftschiffer, pl.

balloonist Balluuner (der)n.

Balm of Gilead (salve prepared from the buds of this tree) 1. Eelbabble (der)n.; 2.Balsembaam (der)n.; 3.Balsem (der)n.

balm 1.Meliesegraut (es)n.; 2.Melisse (die)n.

balsam apple Balsemabbel (der)n.

balsam de Malta Balsemdemalde (der)n.

balsam poplar Balsembaam (der)n.

Balthasar Balser (der)n.

Baltimore oriole Goldamschel (die)n.; Goldamschle, pl.

band 1.Band (es)n.; Benner, pl.; 2.Schtraeme (der)n.; 3.Schtriehme (der) n.; **of musicians** Baend (die) n.; **of robbers** Raawerband (die)n.

Bb

bandage / bay

bandage 1.Band (es)n.; Benner, pl.; 2.Binn (die)n.
bandit Raawer (der)n.; Raawer, pl.
bandy-legged dachsbeenich, adj.
bang 1.Bumps (der)n.; 2.baf!, interj.; 3.buff!, interj.;
  4.bumm!, interj.; 5.bumps! interj.; **bang! (puff!)**
  puff!, interj.
banish 1.ab/dreiwe, v.; abgedriwwe, pp.; 2.verdreiwe,
  v.; verdriwwe, pp.
banister 1.G(e)lender (es)n.; 2.Gelander(es) n.; 3.
  Schteekgelender (es) n.
bank 1.Baenk (die)n.; 2.Ufer (es)n.; **a fire** uff/banke, v.;
  uffgebankt, pp.
banquet Fescht (es)n.; Feschder, pl.
banter foppe, v.; gfoppt, pp.
bantering threat to a child Kopp (der)n. (ich schteck dir
  der -- gschwische dei Ohre)
baptism Daaf (die)n.; Daafe, pl.
baptismal certificate Daafschei(n) (der)n.; **name**
  Daafnaame, (der)n.; **service** (plain) Daafiewing (die)n.;
  sponsors 1. Daafeldre (die)n. pl.; Daafleit (die)n. pl.;
  water Daafwasser (es)n.
baptist Daefer (der)n.; Daefer, pl.
bar 1.Baer (der)n.; Baere, pl.; 2.Bar (der)n.; **in music** Takt
  (der)n.; **out** naus/schpaerre, v.; nausgschpaert, pp.
Barbara Bewwi (die)n.
barbarous barbaarisch, adv.
barber Balwiere (der)n.
bare 1.Bar (der)n.; 2.blott, adj.; 3.kaahl, adj.; 4.nackich,
  adj.; (**bald**) blutt, adj.; (**naked**) bloos, adj.
barefooted baarfiessich, adj.
bareheaded 1.blottkeppich, adj ; 2.kaahlkebbich, adv.
barely zesaage, adj.
bargain yutte, v.; geyutt, pp.
bark 1.baffze, v.; gebaffzt, pp.; 2.beffze, v.; gebeffzt, pp.;
  3.blaffe, v.; geblafft, pp.; 4.blaffze, v. (rare useage);
  5.blarre, v.; geblatt, pp.; 6.gauze, v.; gegauzt, pp.;
  7.yautze, v.; geyautzt, pp.; 8.yohle, v.; geyohlt, pp.;
  after no(och)blaffe, v.; no(och)geblafft, pp.; **of a tree**
  Rinn (die)n.; **of the walnut tree**; Walnusrinn (die)n.
barking 1.Gebaf(f)z (es)n.; 2.Gebef(f)z (es)n.; 3.Geblaff(z)
  (es)n.; **spud** Rinneschaeler (der)n.
barley 1.Gaerschde (der)n.; 2.Gaerscht (der)n.; 3.Gerschde (der)
  n.; 4.Gerscht (der)n.; **harvest** Gerschtarn (die)n.
barn Scheier (die)n.; Scheiere, pl.; **broom** Scheierbesem
  (der)n.; **door** (at the rear of thebarn) Scheierdor (es) n.;
  Scheierdore, pl.; **owl** 1.Scheiereil (die) n.; Scheiereile,
  pl.; 2. Schtee-eil (die) n.; **roof** Scheierdach (es) n.;
  Scheierdecher, pl.; **swallow** Scheierschwalm (der)n.;
  Scheierschwalme, pl.; **with only one floor** (as
  distinguished from a bank barn) Boddemscheier (die)n.
barnyard 1.Mischthof (der)n.; Mischthe(e)f, pl.;
  2.Scheierhof (der)n.; Scheierhef, pl.
barometer Wedderglaas (es)n.; Wedderglesser, pl.
barred 1.schifferschteenich, adj.; 2.schiwwerschteenich,
  adj.; 3.siwwerschteenich, adj.; **barred** (like barred
  Plymouth Rock fowl) schiwwer-schteenich, adj.

barrel 1.Ballfass (es)n.; Ballfesser, pl.; 2.Fass (es)n.;
  Fesser, pl.; 3.Fessli (es)n.; Fesslin, pl.; (**by measure**)
  1.Baerlfass (es)n.; 2.Ballfass (es)n.; Ballfesser, pl.
barroom 1.Baerschtubb (die)n.; Baerschtuwwe, pl.;
  2.Barschtubb (die)n.
barrow Barick (der)n.
bars Faahrt (die)n.; (**at entrance to field or lane**) 1.Falder
  (es n.; Faldere, pl.; 2.Falter (die)n.
barter 1.Handel (der)n.; 2.handle losse (sich --)v.;
  3.handle, v.; g(e)handelt, pp.
bartering handelwese (es)n.
Bartholomew 1.Baardelmae (der)n.; 2.Bardel (der)n.
base 1.nidder, adj.; 2.nidderdrechdich, adj.
baseball bat 1.Ballebriggel (der)n.; 2.Ballebritsch (die)n.;
  Ballebritsche, pl.;
basement 1.Grundschtock (der)n.; 2.Keller (der)n.; Kellere, pl.; (**cellar**) **kitchen** Kellerkich (die)n.
baseness Nidderdrechdichkeit (die)n.
bashful 1.bleed, adv.; 2.leitschei, adj.
bashfulness Bleedheet (die)n.
basin 1.Handbeck (es)n.; 2.Weschschissel (die)n.;
  Weschschissle, pl.
bask in the sun sunne (sich --)v.; gsunnt, pp.
basket 1.Karreb (der)n.; Karreb, pl.; 2.Orschbackekarreb
  (der)n.; **maker** Karrebmacher (der)n.; **of braided
  straw in which rye bread was baked** Backkarreb
  (der)n.; **with a loop handle over the top** Henkekarrb
  (der)n.
basketful karrebvoll, adj.
bass bass, adj.; (**in music**) Bass (der)n.; **drum**
  1.Bassdrumm (die)n.; 2.Grossdrumm (die)n.; **fiddle**
  Bassgeig (die)n.; Bassgeige, pl.; **horn** Basshann (es)n.;
  singer Basssinger (der)n.; **voice** Bassschtimm (die)n.
bastard 1.Bankert (der)n.; 2.Baschdard (der)n.; 3.Beikind (es)
  n.; 4.Hurekind (es)n.; 5.ledderichweiss, adv.(en Kind --)
baste 1.aareihe, v.; aagereiht, pp.; 2.reihe, v.; gereiht, pp.
basting thread Reihfaadem (der)n.
bat Britsch (die)n.;(**mammal**) 1. Schpeckmaus (es) n.;
  Schpeckmeis, pl.; 2.Schpeckmeisli (es)n.;
  Schpeckmeislin, pl.
bath Baad (es)n.
bathe 1. baade, v.; gebaade; gebaadt, pp.; 2. wadde,
  v.; gewaade, pp.
bathroom Baadschtubb (die)n.; Baadschtuwwe, pl.
battalion 1.Baddalye (die)n. 2.Bedalye (es)n.
batter (for apple fritters) dinne Deeg (der)n.
battle Schlacht (die)n.; Schlachde, pl.
batty in the belfry verschowe, adv. (-- im Haernkaschde)
bawdy lidderlich, adj.; **house** 1.Gnallhitt (die)n.;
  2.Knallhitt (die)n.
bawl 1.blaerre, v.; geblaerrt, pp.; 2.blarre, v.; geblatt, pp.;
  3.brille, v.; gebrillt, pp.; 4.greische, v.; gegrische, pp.;
  or low after no(och)blaerre, v.; no(och)geblaerrt, pp.
bawling or crying Gebrill (es)n.; **or lowing** Geblaerr (es)n.
bay (of a horse) brau(n), adj.; **of a hound in hunting** yohle, v.;
  geyohlt, pp.; **window** Bogefenschder (es)n.

Bb

bayonet

bayonet 1.Bangonett (die)n.; 2.Bangenett (die)n.

be 1.als, adv.; 2.schteh, v.; gschtanne, pp.; **(somewhere) about** Weg (der)n. (um -- sei); **at** vorhawwe, v.; vorghatt, pp.; **the matter with** fehle, v.; gfehlt, pp.

bead(s) 1.Karell (die)n.; Karelle, pl.; 2.Poddre (die)n., pl.

beak 1.Schnawwel (der)n.; Schnawwele, pl.; 2.Schnewwel (der)n.; Schnewwele, pl.

beam (ray) Schtraal (der)n.; Schtraale, pl.; **(timber)** Balge (der)n.; Balge, pl.

bean 1.Baahn (die)n.; Baahne, pl.; 2.Bohn (die)n.; Bohne, pl.; 3.Buhn (die)n.; Buhne, pl.; **bug** Buhnekeffer (der) n.; **pole** 1.Bohneschtecke (der)n.; 2.Buhneschtecke (der)n.; Buhneschtecke, pl.; **soup** Buhnesupp (die)n.

bear 1.aus/halde, v.; ausghalde, pp.; 2.aus/schteh, v.; ausgschtanne, pp.; 3.Ba (der)n.; Bare, pl.; 4.Baer (der)n.; Baere, pl.; 5.vergraage, v.; vergraage,pp.; **a child** gebaere, v.; gebore, pp.; **in mind**; Acht (der, die)n. (in -- nemme); **tales** retsche, v.; geretscht, pp. **the brunt** haer/halde, v.; haerghalde, pp.; **through (a burden)** darich/draage, v.; darichgedraage, pp.

bear's foot Baerefuss (der)n.; **grease** Baerefett (es)n.

bearable ausschtehlich, adj.

beard 1.Baart (der)n.; Baert, pl.; 2.Backebaart (der)n.; **(on the cheeks only) of grain** Fruchtgraan (die)n.

bearing a grudge greppisch, adj.

bearskin Baerehaut (die)n.

beast of prey Raabdier (es)n.

beastly viehisch, adj.; **life** Seilewe (es)n.

beat 1.beitsche, v.; gebeitscht, pp.; 2.belse, v.; gebelst, pp.; 3.biede, v.; gebodde, pp.; 4.flachse, v.; gflachst, pp.; 5.globbe, v.; geglobbt, pp.; 6.kloppe, v.; gekloppt, pp.; 7.schlagge, v.; gschlaage, pp.; 8.schwuppe, v.; gschwuppt, pp.; 9.verbriggele, v.; verbriggelt, pp.; 10.vergnipple, v.; vergnippelt, pp.; 11.vor/kumme, v.; vorkumme, pp.; 12. wallicke, v.; gewallickt, pp.; 13.wamsche, v.; gewamscht, pp.; 14. wichse, v.; gewichst, pp.; 15. zwiwwle, v.; gezwiwwelt, pp.; **eggs** eigleppre, v.; eigegleppert, pp.; **limbs of a chestnut tree to bring down nuts** schwinge, v.; gschwunge, pp.; **back** zerick/gloppe, v.; zerickgegloppt, pp.; **down** nidder/gaerwe, v.; niddergegaerbt, pp.; **down the price** runner/handle, v.; runnerghandelt, pp.; **fine** feigloppe, v.; feigegloppt, pp.; **in** nei/glebbere, v.; neiglebbert, pp.; **off** ab/gloppe, v.; abgegloppt pp.; **one** (who plays a lone hand in haasenpeffer) nuff/duh, v.; nuffgeduh, pp.; **out** 1.aus/globbe, v.; ausgeglobbt, pp.; 2.raus/schlagge, v.; rausgschlagge, pp.; **soundly** darich/briggle, v.; darichgebriggelt, pp.; **the band** Aart (die)n. (das es en -- hot); **to a powder** feigloppe, v.; feigegloppt, pp.; **up** verhaue, v.; verhaut, pp.; **up the rear** innerdreischlagge, adv.; **with a paddle** britsche, v.; gebritscht, pp.; **with the fist** 1.gnuffe, v.; gegnufft, pp. 2.knuffe, v.; geknufft, pp.; 3.verbelze, v.; verbelzt, pp.

beaten down nidder/gschlagge, v.; niddergschlagge, pp.; **gold** (film) Goldschaum (der)n.

beating 1.Dresching (die)n.; 2.Wichs (die)n.

beau Schtutzer (der)n.

bed-stead

beautiful 1.abbedittlich, adj.; 2.brechdich, adj.; 3.fei, adj.; 4.nett, adj.; 5.niedlich, adj.; 6.sauwer, adj.; 7.scharmand, adj.; 8.scharmant, adj.; 9.schee, adj. 10.(very beautiful) wunnerschee, adj.

beautify verschennere, v.; verschennert, pp.

beauty 1.Bracht (die)n.; 2.Pracht (die)n.; 3.Scheeheet (die)n.

because 1.deweil, conj.; 2.vunwege, conj.; 3.weil, conj.; **of** 1.weeich, prep.; 2.wege, prep.; **of her** wegre = wege re; **of one**; 1.wegem = wege em; 2.wegeme = wege me

beckon winke, v.; gewunke, pp.

become 1.aa/schteh, v.; aagschtanne, pp.; 2.bekumme, v.; is bekumme, pp.; 3.waerre, v.; warre; waerre, pp.; 4.warre, v.; is warre, pp.; **a bad custom** eireisse, v.; eigerisse, pp.; **acquainted with** kenne, v.; gekennt, pp. (-- laerne); **angry** 1.verzaerne (sich --)v.; verzaernt, pp.; 2.verzanne (sich --), v.; verzannt, pp.; **aware** gewaahr warre, v.; is gewaahrwarre, pp.; **bedsore** uff/leie (sich --)v.; uffgelegge, pp.; **bony** verknechert, v.; **cloudy** uff/driewe, v.; uffgedriebt, pp.; **confused** 1.aerr warre, adj.; 2. verwa(e)rre (sich --)v.; verwa(e)rrt, pp.; **covered with vines** zuranke, v.; zugerankt, pp.; **crusty or encrusted** vergruschde (sich --)v.; vergruscht, pp.; **dusk** demmere, v.; gedemmert, pp.; **educated** bilde (sich --) v.; gebild(e)t, pp.; **exhausted** aus/schpiele (sich --) v.; ausgschpielt, pp.; **exhausted from over exertion** abfeege (sich --)v.; abgfeekt, pp.; **extinct** aus/schtarewe, v.; ausgschtarewe, pp.; **grown over** zuwachse, v.; zugewachse, pp.; **infatuated** vergucke (sich --)v.; verguckt, pp.; **inflamed** uff/laafe, v.; uffgelofe, pp.; **intoxicated** bsaufe (sich --)v.; bsoffe, pp.; **known** raus/kumme, v.; is rauskumme, pp.; **less** ab/nemme, v.; abgenumme, pp.; **livergrown** aa/waxe, v.; aagewaxe, pp.; **lousey** verlause, v.; verlaust, pp.; **moldy** 1.grooze, v.; gegroozt, pp.; 2.vergrooze, v.; vergroozt, pp.; **of** hie/kumme, v.; is hiekumme; **overheated** iwwerhitze (sich --)v.; iwwerhitzt, pp.; **poverty stricken** verarme, v.; verarmt, pp.; **preponderant** Iwwerhand (die)n. (-- nemme); **ruined** grebiere (sich --) v.; grebiert, pp.; **separated** vunenannerkumme, v.; vunenannerkumme, pp.; **snowbound** eischnee-e, v.; eigschneet, pp.; **stuck** faschtwarre, v.; faschtwarre, pp.; **tipsy** vernewwele, v.; **become** vernewwelt, pp.; **too soft** verweeche, v.; verweecht, pp.; **two years old** zwette (sich --) v.; gezwett, pp.; **undone** uff/geh, v.; uffgange, pp.; **untied** los/kumme, v.; loskumme, pp.; **wedged** keidle (sich --)v.; gekeidelt, pp.

becoming aaschtehlich, adj.;

bed 1.Bett (es)n.; Bedder, pl.; 2.Nescht (es)n.; Neschder, pl.; **(a stable or cattle)** schtraee, v.; gschtraet, pp.; **(animals)** schtroie, v.; gschtroit, pp.; **(for flowers)** Bett (es)n.; Bedder, pl.; **(for one person only)** Eegeilsbett (es)n.; **fellow** Schlofkummeraad (der)n.; **sheet** 1.Bettduch (es)n.; 2.Leinduch (es)n.; Leindicher, pl.; **tick** Ziech (die)n.; **ticking** Fedderfassing (die)n.

bed-cord Bettschtrick (der)n.;

bed-post 1.Bettposchde (der)n.; 2.Bett schtolle (der)n.;

bed-stead Bettlaad (die)n.

Bb

bed-quilt / belly ache

bed-quilt 1.Bettdeck (die)n.; 2.Iwwerdeck (die)n.
bedaub verschmiere, v.; verschmiert, pp.
bedbug 1.Bettlaaswans (die)n.; 2.Wandlaus (die)n.;
   3.Wans(die)n.; Wanse, **pl.**
bedclothes 1.Bettgleeder (die)n.; 2.Bettsach (es)n.
bedding 1.Bettgleeder (die)n.; 2.Bettsach (es)n.; **(for ani-mals)** Schprae (die)n.
bedeck 1.ausschmicke, v.; ausgschmickt, pp.; 2.bedecke,
   v.; bedeckt, pp.; **(with ribbons, etc.)** verhenke, v.;
   verhonke, pp.
bedevil ab/deiwle, v.; abgedeiwelt, pp.
bedfast bettlaegerich, adj.
bedrag verhammle, v.; verhammelt, pp.
bedraggle **(one's clothes)** verhammle (sich --)v.; verhammelt,
   pp.; **(one's trousers or dress with mud)** eiwetze (sich --)
   v.; eigewetzt, pp.; **oneself** verrammle (sich --)v.;
   verrammelt, pp.
bedroom 1.Bettschtubb (die)n.; Bettschtuwwe, pl.;
   2.Schlofkammer (die)n.; Schloffkemmer, pl.;
   3.Schlofschtubb (die)n.; Schlofschtuwwe, pl.
bedspread Bettschprae (die)n.
bedtime Bettzeit (die)n.
bee-eater lemefresser (der)n.; lemefresser, pl.
beebread lemebrot (es)n.
beech **(tree)** 1.Buche (die)n.; 2.Buchebaam (der)n.
beechnut Buchel (die)n.
beef 1.Kiehfleesch(es); 2.Rinsfleesch (es)n.; **tongue**
   Rinszung (die)n.
beehive 1.lemekareb (der)n.; 2.lemekaschde (der)n.
Beelzebub Belzibopp (der)n.
beer Bier (es)n.; **bottle** Bierboddel (die)n.; **glass** Bierglaas
   (es)n.; **keg** Bierfass (es)n.; **tankar** Seidel (der)n.
beeswax lemewachs (der)n.
befall 1.befalle, v.; befalle, pp.; 2.begegne, v.; begegnet,
   pp.; 3.wedder/faahre, v.; wedderfaahre, pp.
before 1.bevor, adv., prep.; 2.devor, adv.;3.eb, conj.; prep.;
   4.vanne, adv.; 5.var, adv.; 6.vor, prep.;7.vorhaer, adv.;
   8.vorher, adv.; 9.zuvor, adv.; **everything else**
   vanneweck, adv.; **him** 1.vorm = vor em; 2.vorn = vor en;
   one vorme = vor me; **one is aware of it** umsehne (sich -
   -) v.;   umgsehne, pp.(eb mer sich -- kann); **this**
   1.dodevor, adv.; 2.vordem, adv.
beforehand 1.vannenaus, adv.; 2.vorderhand, adv.
befriend befreinde, v.; befreindt, pp.
beg 1.beddle, v.; gebeddelt, pp.; 2.bettle, v.; gebettelt,
   pp. **for mercy** Wedder (es)n. (um gut -- bitte); **off**
   ab/bettle, v.; abgebeddelt, pp.
beggar **(man)** 1. Beddelmann (der) n.; 2. Beddler (der)
   n.;   3. Bettelmann (der) n.; 4. Bettler (der) n.;
   (woman) Beddelfraa (die)n.
begin 1. aa/fange, v.; aagfange, pp.; 2. aa/geh, v.; aagange,
   pp.; 3.aa/setze, v.; aagsetzt, pp.; 4.ab/geh, v.; abgange, pp.;
   5.aus/setze, v.; ausgsetzt, pp.; 6.mache, v.; gemacht, pp.;
   (aaschtalt --) 7.zugreife, v.; zugegriffe, pp.; **cutting with a**
   saw aasaege, v.; aagseakt, pp.; **housekeeping** ei/kehre, v.;
   eigekehrt, pp.; **mowing** aamehe, v.; aagemeht, pp.; **some-**
   thing draageh, v.; draagange, pp.; **the stroke in mowing by**

cutting low (high) eihacke, v.; eighackt, pp. (nidder
   [hoch] --); **threshing (generally as to first round with flails)**
   aadresche, v.; aagedrosche, pp.; **to chip** aa/ brockle, v.;
   aagebrockelt, pp.; **to do something** draamache (sich --)v.;
   draagemacht, pp.; **to feel jolly (from drink)** aa/saufe (sich --
) v.; aagsoffe, pp.; **to file** aa/feile, v.; aagfeilt, pp.; **to peel**
   aaschaele, v.; aagschaelt, pp.; **to pick** aa/robbe, v.;
   aageroppt, pp.; **to plant** aa/blanze, v.; aageblanzt, pp.; **to**
   pull aa/zobbe, v.; aagezoppt, pp.; **to rot** aa/faule, v.;
   aagfault, pp.; **to split** aa/schplidde, v.; aagschplitt, pp.; **to**
   spoil ab/schteh, v.; abgschtanne, pp.
beginner Aafenger (der)n.
beginning 1.Aabeginn (der)n.; 2.Aafang (der)n.; 3.Beginn (der)n.
begonia Wachsschtok (der)n.
begrease uff/schmutze, v.; uffgschmutzt, pp.; **(oneself)**
   verschmutze (sich --)v.; verschmutzt, pp.
begrime **(one's trousers)** versohle (sich --)v.; versohlt, pp.
begrudge 1.begrenke, v.; begrenkt, pp.; 2.gunne, v.; gegunnt,
   pp.; 3.kibbe, v.; gekippt, pp.; 4.missvergunne,v.; missvergunnt, pp.; 5.vergunne, v.; vergunnt, pp.
begrudging 1.missgunnisch, adj.; 2.missvergunnisch, adj.;
   3.vergunnisch, adj.
behave 1.aa/schicke (sich --)v.; aagschickt, pp.;
   2.bedraage (sich --)v.; bedraagt, pp.; 3.uff/fiehre
   (sich --)v.; uffgfiehrt, pp.; **(used usually positive)**
   beheefe (sich --)v.; beheeft, pp.
behead keppe, v.; gekeppt, pp.
behind 1.dehinner, adv.; 2.hinne(s), prep.; 3.hinner, adj.;
   4. hinnerdrei, adv.; 5.hinnich, prep 6.zerick/sei, v.; is
   zerickgewest, pp.; **each other** hinnenanner, adv.; **in**
   time verschpaete (sich --)v.; verschpaet, pp.; **that**
   dattdehinner, adv.; **this** dodehinner, adv.
behold 1.aa/blicke, v.; aageblickt, pp.; 2.aa/schaue, v.;
   aagschaut, pp.
behoove keere (sich--)v.; gekeert, pp.
being Wese (es)n.; **occupied with trifles** Gegnuschder (es)n.
belch 1.garbse, v.; gegarbst, pp.; 2.rilpse, v.; gerilpst, pp.;
   3.uff/schtosse, v.; uffgschtosse, pp.
belching Uffschtosses (es)n.
belie 1.aa/liege, v.; aagelogge, pp.; 2.beliege, v.; beloge, pp.
belief Glaawe (der)n.; Glaawe, pl.; **in witches** Hexeglaawe
   (der)n.
believe glaawe, v.; geglaabt, pp.; **in** nei/glaawe, v.; neigeglaabt,
   pp.; **in it** draaglaawe, v.; draageglaabt, pp.
bell 1.Bell (die); Belle, pl.; 2.Glock (die)n.; Glocke, pl.; 3.Klingel
   (die)n.; **(erected on a pole and rung to call the men**
   from the field to dinner) Essebell (die)n.; **clapper** Bellegnippel (der)n.; **cord** Belleschtrick (der)n.
belladonna 1.Schtechabbel (der)n.; 2.Tollbeer (die)n.;
   3.Tollkasch (die)n.
bellow blarre, v.; geblatt, pp.
bellows 1.Blosballig(s) (der)n.; 2.Blosehaus (der)n.
bellweather Bellhammel (der)n.
belly 1.Bauch (der)n.; Beich, pl.; 2.Leib (der)n.; 3.Ranse
   (der)n.; 4.Wambe(r) (der)n.
belly ache Leibgriwwle(s) (es)n.; **band** 1.Bauchgatt (die)n.;
   2.Bauchgart (die)n.; 3.Gart (die)n.; 4.Gatt (die)n.;
   Gadde, pl.

Bb

belly-god / bier

belly-god Bauchgott (der)n.

bellystrap (harness) Bauchreime (der)n.

belong 1.aa/belange, v.; aabelangt, pp.; 2.gheere, v.; gheert, pp.; 3.keere, v.; gekeert, pp.; **down** nunner/keere, v.; nunnergekeert, pp.; **in this place** haer/keere, v.; haergekeert, pp.; **on the other side** niwwer/keere, v.; niwwergekeert, pp.; **outside** naus/keere, v.; nausgekeert, pp.; **to** dezukeere, v.; dezugekeert, pp.; **to or in a place** hie/keere, v.; hiekeert, pp.; **together** zamme/keere, v.; zammegekeert, pp.; **up** ruff/keere, v.; ruffgekeert, pp.

beloved 1.beliebt, adj.; 2.geliebt, adj.; 3.hatzich, adj.; 4.lieb, adj.; 5.liewe, adj.

below 1.unne, adv.; 2.unnich, prep.

belt Gaerdel (der)n.

bemoan 1.beglaage, v.; beglaagt, pp.; 2.beyammere, v.; beyammert, pp.

bench 1.Bank (die)n.; Benk, pl.; 2.Karricheschtul (der)n.; Karricheschtiel, pl.; 3.Karrichesitz (der)n.; **(for boring holes in posts)** Bohrbank (die)n.; **(standing under a shade tree)** Schaddebank (die)n.; **of repentance** Bussbank (die)n.

bend 1.biege, v.; geboge, pp.; 2.Grimm (die)n.; 3.grimme (sich --)v.; gegrimmt, pp.; 4.Grimming (die)n.; 5. krimme (sich --) v.; gekrimmt, pp.; 6.verdrehe, v.; verdreht, pp.; **and crack** (without breaking entirely) 1.gnicke, v.; gegnickt, pp.; 2.knicke, v.; geknickt, pp. 2.umgnicke, v.; umgegnickt, pp.; **around** rum/biege, v.; rumgeboge, pp.; **away** weck/biege, v.; weckgeboge, pp.; **back** zerick/biege, v.; zerickgeboge, pp.; **down** 1.nidder/bicke (sich --), v.; niddergebickt, pp.; 2.runner/biege, v.; runnergeboge, pp.; **forward** vorbiege (sich --)v.; vorgeboge, pp.; **in** 1.nei/biege, v.; neigeboge, pp.; 2.rei/biege, v.; reigeboge, pp.; 3.schtauche, v.; gschtaucht, pp.; **one's energies towards** druff, adv. (-- aus sei); **out;** 1.naus/biege, v.; nausgeboge, pp.; 2.raus/biege, v.; rausgeboge, pp.; **out of shape** verbiege, v.; verboge, pp.; **over;** 1.bicke (sich--), v.; gebickt, pp.; 2.nunner/bicke (sich --), v.; nunnergebickt, pp.; 3.nunner/biege (sich --), v.; nunnergeboge, pp.; 4.zamme/bicke (sich --)v. zammegebickt, pp.; **over** (or down) umbiege, v.; umgeboge, pp.; **together** zamme/ biege, v.; zammegeboge, pp.; **up** nuff/biege, v.; nuffgeboge, pp.; **up** (or open) uff/biege, v.; uffgeboge, pp.

bending machine Biegmaschien (die)n.

beneath 1.unnedraa, adv.; 2.unnedrunner, adv.; 3.unnich, prep.

benediction Sege (der)n.

benefaction Wohldaat (die)n.

beneficial 1.brauchbaar, adj.; 2.nitzlich, adj.; 3.nutzlich, adj.

benefit 1.Nutze (der)n.; 2.nutze, v.; genutzt, pp.

benevolent hatzich, adj. (gut --)

bent 1.geboge, adj.; 2.grummbucklich, adj; 3.verboge, adj.

bepiss verbrunse, v.; verbrunst, pp.

bequeath 1.losse, v.; gelosst, pp.; (ebber ebbes --); 2.veraerwe, v.; veraerbt, pp.; 3.vermache, v.; vermacht, pp.; 4.verwille, v.; verwillt, pp.

berate verschelde, v.; verscholde, pp.

bereave beraawe, v.; beraabt, pp.

beretta Kapp (die)n.; Kappe, pl.

bergamot Bargamott (der)n.

Bernhard Barnd (der)n.

berry 1.Beer (die)n.; Beere, pl.; 2.Bier (die)n.; Biere, pl.

beseech 1.aa/bede, v.; aagebet, pp.; 2.bidde, v.; gebitt, pp; 3.bitte, v.; gebitt, pp.; 4.ersuche, v.; ersucht, pp.; 5.neediche, v.; geneedicht, pp.

beseige belaagre, v.; belaagert, pp.

beside 1.newe, adv.; prep.; 2.newedraa, adv.; 3.newich, prep.; **each other** newenanner, adv.

besides 1.dezu, adv.; 2.zudem, adv.

beslobber verschlawwere, v.; verschlawwert, pp.

besmear 1.verschmiere (sich --)v.; verschmiert, pp.; 2.verschmiere, v.; verschmiert, pp.; **with blood** verblude (sich --)v.; verblut, pp.

besmirch (oneself) 1.Hosse (die)n. (in -- scheisse); 2.verscheisse (sich --)v.; verschisse, pp.

bespatter 1.verschlabbe, v.; verschlappt, pp.; 2.verschpritze, v.; verschpritzt, pp.

bespeak b(e)schtimme, v.; b(e)schtimmt, pp.

bespit verschpaue, v.; verschpaut, pp.

best (very) vornehmscht, adj.; **of all** allerbescht, adj.

bet 1.wedde, v.; g(e)wett, pp.; 2.Wedding (die)n.; 3.Wett (die)n.; 4.wette, v.; gewett, pp.; 5.Wetting (die)n.

betray 1.bedriege, v.; bedroge, pp.; 2.verrode, v.; verrode, pp.; 3.weck/gewwe, v.; weckgewwe, pp.; **a secret** iwwerschnappe (sich --)v.; iwwergschnappt, pp.

betrayal Bedruch (der)n.

betrothed verschproche, adj.

Betsy Lisbett (die)n.

better verbessre, v.; verbessert, pp.

betting Weddes (es)n.

Betty Lisbett (die)n.

between 1.dezwische, prep.; 2.gschwischich, prep.; 3.zwische, prep.; 4.zwischich, prep.; **each other** unne (re)nanner, adv.; **her** zwischere = zwische re; **it** zwisches = zwisch es; **one** 1.zwischem = zwische em; 2.zwischeme = zwische me

bevel ab/schraekse, v.; abgschraekst, pp.

beverage 1.Drinkes (es)n.; 2.Gedrenk (es)n.; 3.Trank (der) n.

bewail 1.bedrauere, v.; bedrauert, pp.; 2.beglaage, v.; beglaagt, pp.; 3.beyammere, v.; beyammert, pp.; 4.acht nemme, v.; genumme, pp. (sich in --)

beware 1.acht/gewwe, v.; achtgewwe, pp.; 2.uff/basse, v.; uffgebasst, pp.

bewilder verwa(e)rre, v.; verwa(e)rrt, pp.

bewitch verhexe, v.; verhext, pp.

bewitched verhext, adj.

biased eeseidich, adj.

bib Latz (der)n.

Bible 1.Biewel (die)n.; Biewele, pl.; 2.Biwwel (die)n.

bid 1.befehle, v.; befohle, pp.; 2.biede, v.; gebodde, pp.; 3.Gebott (es)n.; 4.heese, v.; gheese, pp.

bidder Bieder (der)n.

bidens (all species of whose seeds are broad in proportion to length) Maedleis (die)n., pl.

bier 1.Bahr (die)n.; 2.Dodedraag (die)n.; 3.Doodebaahr (die)n.; 4.Sarrich (der)n.

Bb

big

big (as a hand) handgross, adj.; **feeling** 1.gross feihlich, adj.; 2.hochordich, adj.; **morsel** schlarre (adj).; **(stout fellow)** Schliffel (der)n.; **bigger; biggest** gross; greeser; greescht, adj.

bile Gall (die)n.

bilious fever Gallefiewer (es)n.

bill 1.Greid (es)n.; 2.Kreid (es)n.; 3.Not (die)n.; 4.Rechling (die)n.; 5.Rechning (die)n.; 6.Schnawwel (der)n.; Schnawwele, pl.; 7.Schnewwel (der)n.; 8.Zech (die)n.

billion Billyoon (die)n.

bills Schulde (die)n., pl.

billy goat Geesbock (der)n.; Geesbeck, pl.; **goat** (nursery rhyme only) Ziegenbock (der)n.

bin 1.Fruchtkammer (die)n.; 2.Kaschde (der)n.; Kaschde, pl.

bind 1.ei/binne, v.; eigebunne, pp.; 2.verbinne, v.; verbunne, pp.; **together** binne, v.; gebunne, pp.

binder (in harvest) Binner (der)n.

bindweed Drechderblumm (die)n.

biographer Lewe(n)sbeschreiwer (der)n.

biography 1.Lewe(n)sbeschreiwing (die)n.; 2.Lewe(n)swandel (der)n.; 3.Leweslaaf (der)n.

birch 1.Baerke (die)n.; 2.Baerye (die)n.; 3.Baricke (die)n.; 4.Bariye (die)n.; 5.Siessholz (es)n.; **bark** Barickerinn (die)n.; **tree** 1.Baerkebaam (der)n.; 2.Barickebaam (der)n.

bird Voggel (der)n.; Veggel, pl.; **(any small)** Schpetzli (es)n.; **egg** Voggeloi (es)n.; **house** Voggelkaschde, (der)n.; **nest** Voggelnescht (es)n.; **of prey** Raabvoggel (der)n.

birdfoot violet Voggelfuss (der)n.

birth 1.Gebort (die)n.; 2.Geburt (die)n.

birthday 1.Gebortsdaag (der); Gebortsdaage, pl.; 2. Geburtsdaag (der)n.; Geburtsdaage, pl.; 3.Yaehrsdaag (der)n.; Yaehrsdaage, pl.

birthplace Gebortsblatz (der)n.

birthwort 1.Hohlwarzel (die)n.; 2.Oschderlusi (die)n.

bisexual (pig or fowl) Zwitter (der)n.

Bishop (Old Order Amish usage) Vellich Diener (der)n.

bishop 1.Bischof (der)n.; 2.Bischop (der)n.

bit 1.Bissel (es)n.; 2.Bissli (es)n.; 3.Brockel (es)n.; **(carpenter's tool)** Bohreise (es)n.; **(of a bridle)** Gebiss (es)n.; Gebisser, pl.

bite 1.beisse, v.; gebisse, pp.; 2.Biss (der)n.; **of an apple or bread** Beis (der)n.; **into** 1.aa/beisse, v.; aagebisse, pp.; 2.eibeisse, v.; eigebisse, pp.; 3.nei/beisse, v.; neigebisse, pp.; **off** ab/beisse, v.; abgebisse, pp.; **open** uff/beisse, v.; uffgebisse, pp.; **out** raus/beisse, v.; rausgebisse, pp.; **through** darich/beisse, v.; darichgebisse, pp.

bitter 1.bidder, adj.; 2.bitter, adj.; **bloom** Dausendgildegraut (es)n.; **dock** Halwergaul (der)n. (breedblettricher --)

bitters Bitters (es)n.

bittersweet Bittersiess (es)n.

bitterweed 1.Bitterschtenge(l) (der)n.; 2.Bitterwaermet (der)n.

blab 1.blabbere, v.; geblabbert, pp.; 2.naus/blabbere, v.; nausgeblabbert, pp.; **a secret** verschwetze (sich --)v.; verschwetzt, pp.; **in** 1.Maul (es)n. (es -- uffreisse); 2.nei/blabbere, v.; neigeblabbert, pp.; 3.nei/gauze,

blast

v.; neigegauzt, pp.; 4.nei/maule, v.; neigmault, pp.; **out** raus/schwetze, v.; rausgschwetzt, pp.; **out a secret** 1.verbabble (sich --)v.; verbabbelt, pp.; 2.verblatsche, v.; verblatscht, pp.; 3.verblaudre (sich --)v.; verblaudert, pp.

blabber 1.Blabbermaul (es)n.; Blabbermeiler, pl.; 2.Plappermaul (es)n.

blabbing blabberich, adj.

black 1.schwarz, adj.; 2.schwatz, adj.; **(mazard) cherry** 1.Schwarzkasch (die)n.; 2.Schwatzkasch (die)n.; **and blue** 1.schwarzunblo, adj.; 2.schwatzunblo, adj.; **ash** 1.Schwarzesch (die)n.; 2.Schwatzesch (die)n.; **bindweed** Winne (die)n.; **birch** Siessbaerke (der, die)n.; **cohosh** Schlangwatzel (die)n. (grossi, hochi, schwatzi --); **haw** 1.Schofgnoddel (der)n.; 2.Schofknoddel (der)n.; **headed person** 1.Schwatzkopp (der)n.;2.Schwarzkopp (der)n.; **legged** 1.schwarzbeenich, adj.; 2.schwatzbeenich, adj.; **nightshade** Nachtschadde (der)n.; **oak** 1.Schwarzeeche (die)n.; 2.Schwatzeeche (die)n.; **thorn** 1.Schwarzdarn (die)n.; 2.Schwatsdarn (die)n. **walnut** 1.Schwarzwalniss (baam) (der)n.; 2.Schwatzwalniss(baam) (der)n.; **willow** 1.Schwarzweide (der, die)n.; 2.Schwatzweide (der, die)n.

blackberry Blaeckbier (die)n.; Blaeckbiere, pl.; **itch** Blaeckbieregretz (der)n.

blackbird 1.Schtaar (der)n.; 2.Schwatzvoggel (der)n.; Schwatzfeggel, pl.

blacken aaschwatze, v.; aagschwatzt, pp.

blackguard Lumbekall (der)n.

blacking 1.Schwa(e)rzing (die)n.; 2.Schwatzing (die)n.

blacksmith 1.Blaeckschmitt (der)n.; Blaeckschmitt, pl.; 2.Schmitt (der)n.; Schmitt, pl.; **shop smells** (of burning hoof) schmacke, v.; gschmackt, pp. (der Schmittschapp schmackt)

blacksmith's hammer Schmitthammer (der)n.; **tongs** Schmittzang (die)n.

bladder Blos (die)n.; Blose, pl.

blade (of a knife) 1.Gling (die)n.; 2.Kling (die)n.; **of a plant** 1.Blaat (es)n.; Bledder, pl.; 2.Blatt (es)n.; Bledder, pl.; 3.Hallem (der)n.; 4.Halm (der)n.; Halme, pl.; **of grass** Graashalm (der)n.

blame for verdenke, v.; verdenkt, pp.

blameless 1.umschuldich, adj.; 2.unschuldich, adj.; 3.uuschuldich, adj.

blanch bleeche, v.; gebleecht, pp.

blanket Blaenket (der)n.

blare out naus/blaere, v.; nausgeblaert, pp.

blarney schmiere, v.; gschmiert, pp.

blaspheme 1.leschdere, v.; geleschdert, pp.; 2.verleschdere, v.; verleschdert, pp.

blasphemous 1.frewelhaft, adj.; 2.leschderhaft, adj.; **person** Flucher (der)n.

blasphemy 1.Frewel (der)n.; 2.Leschderung (die)n.; 3.Verleschderung (die)n.

blast 1.schiesse, v.; gschosse, pp.; 2.schprenge, v.; gschprengt, pp.; 3.Schuss (der)n.; 4.verschprenge, v.; verschprengt, pp.; **off** ab/schprenge, v.; abgschprengt, pp.; **blast out** raus/schprenge, v.; rasugschprengt, pp.

Bb

blasting powder

blustering

blasting powder Schprengpulwer (es)n.

blaze flamme, v.; gflammt, pp.; **on trees** Maerrickzeeche (es)n.; **trees in surveying** flitsche, v.; gflitscht, pp.

bleach 1.ab/bleeche, v.; abgebleecht, pp.; 2.Bleech (die) n.; 3.bleeche, v.; gebleecht

bleacher Bleech (die)n.

bleat 1.blaerre, v.; geblaerrt, pp.; 2.blarre, v.; geblatt, pp.; 3.blecke, v.; gebleckt, pp.

bleed 1.ausblude, v.; ausgeblut, pp.; 2.verblude (sich --)v.; verblut, pp.; **(also of trees and plants)** blude, v.; geblut, pp.

bleeding heart Schpektabille (die)n.

blemish 1.Fehler (der)n.; Fehler, pl.; 2.Schandfleck (die)n.; 3.Schimp (der)n.; 4.Undaedeli (es)n.; **in fruit (caused by the sting of an insect)** 1.Gnarze (der)n.; 2.Gnazze (der)n.; 3.Knarze (der)n.

bless 1.beglicke, v.; beglickt, pp.; 2.segne, v.; gsegent, pp.; **you!** (call to another after sneezing) 1.Gsundheet (die)n. (--!); 2.Gsundheit (die)n. (--!)

blessed 1.gsegend, adj.; 2.se(e)lich, adj.

blessing Sege (der)n.

blickery Kesselche (es)n.

blickey Blicki (es)n.

blight Pescht (die)n.; Peschde, pl.

blind 1.blind, adj.; 2.verblenne, v.; verblennt, pp.; **in one eye** scheel, adj.

blindhalter 1.Blindhalfder (die)n.; 2.Scheiledder (es)n.; Scheileddere, pl.

blindman's buff Blindemeisel (es)n.

blindness Blindheet (die)n.

blink 1.aa/blinsle, v.; aageblinselt, pp.; 2.blinsle, v.; geblinselt, pp.

blinker Scheideckel (der)n.

blinkers 1.Blindhalfder (die)n.; 2.Scheiledder (es)n.; Scheileddere, pl.

blister 1.Bloder (die)n.; Blodere, pl. 2.blodre, v.; geblodert, pp.; 3.Blos (die)n.; Blose, pl.

bloat 1.uff/blaehe, v.; uffgeblaeht, pp.; 2.uff/schwelle, v.; uffgschwolle, pp.

bloated 1.bauchlufdich, adj.; 2.uff/geblose, v.; 3.uff/gedrosse, v.; 4.uffgebleht, adj.; 5.uffgeblosse, adj.

block 1.Block (der)n.; Bleck, pl.; **of a quilt** Schtaern (die) n.; Schtaerne, pl.; **up** 1.uff/blocke, v.; uffgeblockt, pp.; (a) zublocke, v.; zugeblockt, pp.; (b) zuschtelle, v.; zugschtellt, pp.

blockhead 1.Biffel (der)n.; 2.Biffelochs (der)n.; 3.Eselkopp (der)n.; 4. Glotz (der)n.; Gletz, pp.; 5. Glotzkopp (der) n.; Glotzkepp, pl; 6.Glutzkopp (der)n.; 7.Holskopp (der)n.; 8.Klotz (der)n.; 9.Ox (der)n.; 10Schofkopp (der)n.; 9.Schtoffel (der)n. (es --)

blockheaded glotzkebbich, adj.

blockhouse Blockhaus (es)n.; Blockheiser, pl.

blood Blut (es)n.; **hound** Bluthund (der)n.; **or family relationship** Gebliet (es)n.; **pudding** Blutwascht (die)n.; **root** 1.Blutwarzel (die)n.;2.Blutwatzel (die) n.;3.Rotwatzel (die)n.

bloodstone Blutschtee (der)n.

bloodsucker Blutsuckler (der)n.; Blutsuckler, pl.

bloody 1.bludich, adj.; 2.blutich, adv.

bloom 1.bliehe, v.; geblieht, pp.; 2.uff/geh, v.; uffgange, pp.

bloom(s) Gebliet (es)n. **without bearing** (falsch --), adj.

blooming continually blieh(i)ch, adj.

blossom bliehe, v.; geblieht, pp.

blossoms (collective) 1.Blieh(t) (die)n.; 2.Bluscht (die)n.

blot 1.Klecks (der)n.; 2.verflecke, v.; verfleckt, pp.; 3.verkleckse, v.; verkleckst, pp.

blouse 1.Kittel (es)n.; 2.Kutt (die)n.

blow 1.blose, v.; geblose, pp.; 2.Buff (der)n.; 3.Hack (der)n.; 4.Schtreech (der)n.; Schtreech, pl.; **around** rum/blose, v.; rumgeblose, pp.; **away** weck/blose, v.; weckgeblose, pp.; **down** 1.um/blose, v.; umgeblose, pp.; 2.um/yaage, v.; umgeyaagt, pp.; **horn** Blosrohr (es)n.; **in** 1.nei/ blose, v.; neigeblose, pp.; 2.rei/blose, v.; reigeblose, pp.; 3.veryuxe, v.; veryuxt, pp.; **into whirls or tangles** verzwaerwle, v.; verzwaerwelt, pp.; **of the wind** wehe, v.; geweht, pp.; **off** ab/blose, v.; abgeblost, pp.; **on** druff/blose, v.; druffgeblose, pp.; **open** uff/blose, v.; uffgeblost, pp.; **out** raus/blose, v.; rausgeblose, pp.; **out** (a candle, blast furnace) aus/blose, v.; ausgeblose, pp.; **over** 1.driwwer/blose, v.; driwwergeblose, pp.; 2.iwwer/ blose, v.; iwwergeblost, pp.; 3.um/blose, v.; umgeblose, pp.; **the nose by pressing a finger against the side of the nostril** schneize (sich --)v.; gschneizt, pp.; **up** 1.aa/blose, v.; aageblose, pp.; 2.nuff/blose, v.; nuffgeblose, pp.; 3. uff/blose, v.; uffgeblost, pp.

blowhard Blosrohr (es)n.

blowing Geblos (es)n.; **adder** Blaeser (der)n.

Blue Mountain (Eastern Pennsylvania)(named because of characteristic color when viewed from a distance) Blobarrick (der)n.; **tea** 1.Baerricktee (der)n.; 2.Blobarrgertee (der)n.; 3.Blobarrick(ger)tee (der)n.

blue blo(h), adj.; **bell** Glockeblumm (die)n.; **bush** Eiseholz (es)n.; **checkered cotton cloth** Kelsche (es)n.; **ointment** Reitersalb (die)n.

blueberry Blobier (die)n.; Blobiere, pl.

bluebird Blovoggel (der)n.; Bloveggel, pl.

bluebottle Blobottel (die)n.; **fly** Schmeesmick (die)n.

blueflag 1.Schwaartli (es)n.;2.Schwaertli (es)n.;3.Schwertli (es)n.

blueing Weschblo (die)n.

bluejay Harrevoggel (der)n.; Harreveggel, pl.

blunder 1.Fehlgriff (der)n.; 2.Puscherei (die)n.

blunderbuss Schiesskolwe (der)n.

blunt 1.abschtumpt, adj.; 2.breedmeilich, adj.; 3.breetmeilich, adj.; 4.schtump, adj.

bluntly 1.graadaus, adj.; 2.graadeweck, adj.

blurt out 1.raus/blaerre, v.; rausgeblaerrt, pp.; 2.raus/blatsche, v.; rausgeblatscht, pp.

blush 1.rot warre, v.; rot warre, pp.; 2.schemme (sich --) v.; gschemmt, pp.

bluster gross/schwetze, v.; grossgschwetzt, pp.

blusterer 1.Grossmaul (es)n.; 2.Windbeidel (der)n.

blustering grossmeilich, adj.

235

Bb

boar

boar Ewwer (der)n.; Ewwer, pl.

board 1.bekeschdiche, v.; bekeschdicht, pp.; 2.Brett (es)n.; 3.Koscht (die)n.; **(lumber)** Bord (es)n.; Bord, pl.; **with low sides for drying fruits and vegetables** Hard (die)n.

boarder Koschtgenger (der)n.; Kochetgenger, pl.

boast 1.ab/blose (sich --)v.; abgeblose, pp.; 2.blose, v.; geblose, pp.; 3.boche, v.; gebocht, pp.; 4.bralle, v.; gebrallt, pp.; 5.pralle, v.; geprallt, pp.

boaster 1.Bloshann (es)n.; 2.Bloshaus (es)n.; 3.Blosrohr (es)n.; 4.Braller (der)n.; 5.Brallhans (der)n.; 6.Grossmaul (es)n.; 7.Prallhans (der)n.

boastful 1.Blosballig(s) (der)n.; 2.Blosehaus (der)n.; 3.grossmeilich, adj.

boasting 1.Geblos (es)n.; 2.Geboch (es)n.; 3.Gebrall (es)n.

boat 1.Badeau (die)n.; 2.Boot (es)n.; Boots, pl.

bobbin Schpule (der)n.

bobtailed schtumpschwensich, adj.; **horse or dog** Schtumpschwans (der)n.

bobwhite Badriesel (es)n.

bock beer Bockbier (es)n.

bodice 1.Leib (der)n.; 2.Leibche (es)n.; 3.Leiwelche (es)n.

bodily 1.kaerperlich, adj.; 2.leibhafdich, adv.

bodkin Schtruppnodel (die)n.

body 1.Kaerper (der)n.; 2.Kareber (der)n.; Kareber, pl.; 3.Leicht (die)n.; Leichde, pl. (rare usage); **bow** (of a wagon) Schpriggel (der)n.; **lice** Leib (der)n.; **of musicians** Kor (der)n.

bog Sump (der)n.; **rush** Bensegraas (es)n.

bogieman 1.Hollox (der)n.; 2.Hullox (der)n.; 3.Hullu (der) n.; 4.Hullux (der)n.

boil (on the skin)1.Gschwaare (der)n.; 2.Gschwaere (der) n.; 3.Gschwar(e) (der)n.; Gschware, pl.; 4.Gschwarr (e) (der)n.; 5.Gschwier (es)n.; 6.Schwaere (der)n.; 7.zische, v.; gezischt, pp.; **(cooking)** 1.koche, v.; gekocht, pp.; **down** 1.ab/koche, v.; abgekocht, pp.; 2.ei/koche, v.; eigekocht, pp.; 3.nunner/koche, v.; nunnergekocht, pp.; **over** iwwer/koche, v.; iwwergekocht, pp.; **up** uff/koche, v.; uffgekocht, pp.; **wash** bauche, v.; gebaucht, pp.

boiled cabbage Weissgraut (es)n.; **dumpling** Dampnudel (die)n.

boiler Kochkessel (der)n.

boiling kochich, adv.

boisterous 1.ungeschtiem, adj.; 2.yuxich, adj.; **fellow** Schtaermer (der)n.

bold 1.frisch, adj.; 2.hatz(h)aftich, adj.; 3.keck, adj.; 4.mudich, adj.; 5.vorwitzich, adj.

boll (of flax) Boll (die)n.

bologna (any kind in a bag) Sackwascht (die)n.; **for use in summer** Summerwascht (die)n.

bolster 1.Schemel (der)n.; 2.Schpraukisse (es)n.; **pin** Schemelnaggel (der)n.

bolt 1.Riggel (der)n.; 2.riggle, v.; geriggelt, pp.; 3.zuriggele, v.; zugeriggelt, pp.; **at the end of a chain** 1.Gnewwel (der)n.; 2.Knew(w)el (der)n.; **flour** 1.beidle, v.; gebeidelt, pp.; 2.beitle, v.; gebeidelt, pp.;

botanist

for a door latch Schiewerli (es)n.; **in dunnerkeil** Keil (der)n.; **of a door** Deereriggel (der)n.; **of a flour mill** Beidel (der)n.; **of lightning** Schtraal (der)n.; Schtraale, pl.; **in rei/renne**, v.; **out of a house** naus/renne, v.; nausgerennt, pp.; **upstairs** nuff/renne, v.; nuffgerennt, pp.

bolting cloth Beidelduch (es)n.; **sieve** Bollwaerrick (es)n.

bone 1.Gnoche (der)n.; Gnoche, pl.; 2.Knoche (der)n.; **(fish)** Graan (die)n.; Graane, pl.; **ache** 1.Gnocheweh (es)n.; 2.Knocheweh (es)n.; **mill** 1.Gnochemiehl (die) n.; 2.Knochemiehl (die)n.

bonehead 1.Dummkopp (der)n.; Dummkepp, pl.; 2.Dummlack (der)n.; 3.Glotzkopp (der)n.; Glotzkepp, pl.

bonemeal 1.Gnochemehl (es)n.; 2.Knochemehl (es)n.

boneset tea Darichwax Tee (der)n.

bonfire Freidefeier (es)n.

Bonifacius Day (June 5) Bonifazius (der)n.

bonnet 1.Bannet (der)n.; 2.Schtrupphut (der)n.; Schtruppheit, pl.

bony gnochich, adj.; knochich, adj.

Book of Revelation Offenbaaring (die)n.

book Buch (es)n.; Bicher, pl.

bookbinder Bicherbinner (der)n.

bookcase Bicherschank (der)n.

bookkeeping 1.Buchhalding (die)n.; 2.Buchhaltung (die)n.

bookstore Buchhandlung (die)n.

boom pole (used in binding either a load of logs or lumber, or in keeping a load of hay compact) 1.Raedel (der)n.; 2.Wissbaam (der)n.

boor 1.Limmel (der)n.; 2.Rauhbauz (der)n.; 3.Seibengel (der)n.

boot 1.Schtiffel (der)n.; Schtiffel, pl.; 2.Schtiwwel (der)n.; Schtiwwel, pl.; **tree** Schtiwwelhols (es)n.

bootee Halbschtiwwel (der)n.

bootjack 1.Schtiwwelgnecht (der)n.; 2.Schtiwwelzieger (der)n.

booty Raab (die)n.

borage 1.Barrasch (der)n.; 2.Barretsch (der)n.

borax Borax (der)n.

border 1.aa/schtosse, v.; aagschtosse, pp.; 2.Grans (der) n.; 3.Grens (die)n.; 4.Krans (der)n.; **of flowers** Blumme(r)krans (der)n.; **upon** grense, v.; gegrenst, pp.

bore 1.aa/bohre, v.; aagebohrt, pp.; 2.bohre, v.; gebohrt, pp.; 3.loche, v.; gelocht, pp.; **out** 1.aus/bohre, v.; ausgebohrt, pp.; 2.raus/bohre, v.; rausgebohrt, pp.

bored 1.langweile (sich --)v.; gelangweilt, pp.; 2.langweile, v.; gelangweilt, pp.

born 1.eigebore, adj.; 2.kumme, v.; kumme, pp. (uff die welt --) 3.gebore, v.(no infinitive form); gebore, pp.; **out of wedlock** leddicherweis, adj.

borrow 1.barge, v.; gebarkt, pp.; 2.barye, v.; gebarigt, pp.; 3.lehne, v.; g(e)lehnt, pp.

bosh wischwasch

bosom Bussem (der)n.

boss 1.Baas (der)n.; 2.baase, v.; gebasst, pp.

bossy ba(a)sich, adj.

botanist Blummekenner (der)n.

Bb

botch

botch 1.her/richde, v.; hergericht, pp.; 2.hie/richde, v.;
hiegericht, pp.; 3.Puscherei (die)n.; 4.Schtimmlerei (die)n.;
5.Schtimplerei (die)n.; 6.verbatsche, v.; verbatscht, pp.;
7.verbuckere, v.; verbuckert, pp.; 8.verdarewe, v.; verdarewe, pp.; 9.verhunse, v.; verhunst, pp.; 10.verletze, v.;
verletzt, pp.; 11.verschtimmle, v.; verschtimmelt, pp.;
12.verschtimple, v.; verschtimmelt, pp.

botch up verzackere, v.; verzackert, pp.

both 1.allebeed, pron.; 2.allezwee, pron.; 3.beed, adj.

bother 1.Badder (der,die)n.; 2.baddere, v.; gebaddert,
pp.; 3.verschteere, v.; verschteert, pp.; **oneself**
1.baddere (sich --), v.; gebaddert, pp.; 2.bekimmere
(sich --)v.; bekimmert, pp.

botsch verhause, v.; verhaust, pp.

bottle 1.ab/zabbe, v.; abgezappt, pp.; 2.Boddel (die)n.;
Boddle, pl.; 3.bottle, v.; gebottelt, pp.; 4.eifille, v.;
eigfillt, pp.; **nose** Riewenaas (die)n.

bottling establishment Bottlerei (die)n.

bottom Bodde(m) (der)n.; **rail of a worm fence**
Boddemriggel (der)n.

bough Nascht (der)n.; Nescht, pl.

boulder 1.Felse (der)n.; Felse, pl.; 2.Wacke (der)n.

bound pflichdich, adj.

bountifully 1.reichfeldich, adj.; 2.reichl(e)ich, adj.

bouquet Blummeschtrauss (der)n.

bow bicke (sich --), v.; gebickt, pp.;

bow Boge (der)n.; **for shooting** 1.Bogeflint (die)n.;
2.Bogebix (die)n. 3.Gratzfiessel (es)n.; **tied like a
necktie** Schlupp (der)n.; Schlipp, pl.

bowel Daarem (der)n.; Daerem, pl.

bowels Kuddle (die)n., pl.

bowl Schissel (die)n.; Schissle, pl.

bowlegged grummbeenich, adj.

box 1.Fruchtkammer (die)n.; 2.Kaschde (der)n.; Kaschde,
pl.; 3.Kischt (die)n.; Kischde, pl.; **on the ear** Ohrfei(k)
(die)n.

box elder Erleheck (die)n.

boxtree 1.Buchs (der)n.; 2.Buchs (der)n. (zaahmer --);
3.Buchsbaam (der)n.

boy 1.Bu (der)n.; Buwe, pl.; 2.Yung (der)n.; Yunge, pl.;
friend 1.Alder (der)n.; (mei --) 2.Beau (der)n.; **from
the farm** Bauersbuh (der)n.

boyish pranks Buweschtreech (die)n., pl.

brace 1.Buk (der)n.; Diek, pl.; 2.Kehlband (es)n.;
3.Schteiber (der)n.; Schteiber, pl.; 4.schteibere, v.;
gschteibert, pp.; **(framework of barn)** Buk (die)n.;
Biek, pl.; **(tool)** Winkelbohre (der)n. **or prop**
aa/schteibere, v.; aagschteibert, pp.

bracelet (rare usage) Schpange (die)n.

bracket Brett (es)n.

brag 1.ab/blose (sich --)v.; abgeblose, pp.; 2.blose, v.; geblose,
pp.; 3.bralle, v.; gebrallt, pp.; 4.pralle, v.; geprallt, pp.; **in
different places** 1.rumhaer/blose, v.; rumhaergeblose, pp.
2.rumhaer/bralle, v.; rumhaergebrallt, pp.

braggart 1.Blosballig(s) (der)n.; 2.Bloshann (es)n.;
3.Bloshaus (es)n.; 4.Blosrohr (es)n.; 5.Braller (der)
n.;6.Brallhans (der)n.; 7.Breedmaul (es)n.;

break

8.Breetmaul (es)n.; 9.Garyelbloser (der)n.; 10.Praller
(der)n. 11.Prallhans (der)n.

braid 1.flechde, v.; g(e)flochde, pp.; 2.Flecht (die)n.;
Flechde, pl.; **of hair** 1.Haarschwanz (der)n.;
2.Hoorschwanz (der)n.

braided gezeppt, adj.

brain 1.Haern (es)n.; 2.Hann (es)n.; Hanner, pl.; **fever**
1.Haernenzinding (die)n.; 2.Haernfiewer (es)n. **trouble** Haernweh (es)n.; **work** Koppaerwet (die)n.

brake 1.Faaraan (der)n.; 2.Schparr (die)n.; Schparre, pl.;
3.Waggeschpaerr (die) n.; **(fern)** Schteefaare; **block**
Schpaerrglotz (der)n.; **chain** Schparrkett (die)n.;
Schparrkedde, pl.; **handle** (on a farm wagon)
Schparreschwengel (der)n.

bran 1.Gleie (die)n.; 2.Kleie (die)n.

branch 1.Nascht (der)n.; Nescht, pl.; 2.Zacke (der)n.; **off**
(as a road) ab/gawwle, v.; abgegawwelt, pp.

branchy naschtich, adj.

brand 1.Brand (der)n.; 2.Feierbrand (der)n.; **new** 1.funkel
(Naagel) nei, adj.; 2.naggelnei, adj.

brandy Brend(e)wei (der)n.

brass 1.Mess (es)n.; 2.messe, adj.

brat Gruft (die)n.

brave 1.braav, adj.; 2.farich(t)los, adj.

bravery Braavheit (die)n.

breach Bruch (der)n.; Brich, pl.

bread Brot (es)n.; **broken into coffee** Kaffisupp (die)n.;
containing caraway seeds Kimmelbrot (es)n.; **dough**
Brotdeeg (der)n.

breadcrust Brotgruscht (die)n.

breadth Breeding (die)n.

break 1.breche, v.; gebroche, pp.; 2.brockle, v.;
gebrockelt, pp.; **a colt** eibreche, v.; eigebroche, pp.;
an egg in a dish schlagge, v.; gschlaage, pp.; **into
pieces** verbreche, v.; verbroche, pp.; **of day** Aabruch
(der)n.; **(to knock to pieces)** verschlagge, v.;
verschlagge, pp. **across** niwwer/breche, v.;
niwwergebroche, pp.; **and soak** (bread in milk)
brockle, v.; gebrockelt, pp.; **beam** Schpaerrbalke
(der)n.; **bread** (or crackers) **into soup** eibrockle, v.;
eigebrockelt, pp.; **down** 1.nunner/breche, v.;
nunnergebroche, pp.; 2.rumeniere, v.; rumgeniert,
pp.; 3.rungeniere, v.; rungeniert, pp.; 4.umbreche, v.;
umgebroche, pp.; 5.zamme/breche, v.; is zummegebroche, pp.; **in** 1.nei/schtosse, v.; neigschtosse, pp.;
2.rei/breche, v.; reigebroche, pp.; **in** (shoes)
eibreche, v.; eigebroche, pp.; **in two** inzweebreche,
adv.; **into** nei/breche, v.; neigebroche, pp.; **into
pieces by throwing** verschmeisse, v.; verschmisse,
pp.; **into small pieces** 1.feimache, v.; feigemacht,
pp.; 2.verbreckle, v.; verbreckelt, pp.; **loose**
1.los/breche, v.; is losgebroche, pp.; 2.los/geh, v.;
losgange, pp.; 3.los/reisse, v.; losgerisse, pp.;
4.schliwwere, v.; gschliwwert, pp. (es -- losse); **of day**
1.Daagebruch (der)n.; 2.Daaksbruch (der)n.; **off**

(Continued on page 238)

Bb

break (continued)   broom

(Continued from page 237)

ab/breche, v.; abgebroche, pp.; **off in spalls**
ab/schpaale, v.; abgschpaalt, pp.; **open** aa/breche,
v.; aagebroche, pp.; **or crumble away** weck/breche,
v.; weckgebroche, pp.; **out** naus/breche, v.;
nausgebroche, pp.; **out** (a fire, epidemic disease,
eruption) aus/breche, v.; ausgebroche, pp.; **out** (of
confinement) raus/breche, v.; rausgebroche, pp.;
over riwwer/breche, v.; riwwergebroche, pp.; **partially** 1.gnacke, v.; gegnackt, pp.; 2.knacke, v.;
geknackt, pp.; **the bark of a tree** verschinne, v.;
verschunne, pp.; **through** darich/breche, v.;
darichgebroche, pp.; **to pieces** inzweeschlagge, adv.;
up uff/breche, v.; uffgebroche, pp.

breaker Welleschlack (der)n.

breakfast 1.Friehschtick (es)n.; 2.Mariye-Esse (es)n.

breakout Ausbruch (der)n.

breast Bruscht (die)n.; Brischt, pl.; **chain** (of harness)
Bruschtkett (die)n.; **of a dam** 1.Dammbruscht (die)n.;
2.Dammhig(g)el (der)n.; **strap** (of harness)
Bruschtgart (die)n.

breastbone Bruschtgnoche (der)n.

breastcollar Bruschtkummet (es)n.

breastpin Bruschtschpell (die)n.

breath 1.Hauch (der)n.; 2.Ochdem (der)n.; 3.Odem (der)n.

breathe 1.atme, v.; geatmet, pp.; 2.hauche, v.; ghaucht,
pp.; 3.schnaufe, v.; gschnauft, pp.; **in** eihauche, v.;
eighaucht, pp.

breed erziege, v.; erzogge, pp.; **of fowls** (somewhat resembling Rhode Island Reds) Fersantehinkel (es)n.

breeze Lifdel (es)n. (diminutive of die Luft = air)

breezy 1.lifdich, adj.; 2.lufdich, adj.

brew braue, v.; gebraut, pp.

brewer Brauer (der)n.

brewer's truck Bierwagge, (der)n.

brewery Brauerei (die)n.

bribe schmiere, v.; gschmiert, pp.

brick 1.Backeschtee (der)n.; Backeschtee, pl.;
2.backeschteenich, adj.; **kiln** Backeschteeoffe (der)
n.; **up** aus/mauere, v.; ausgemauert, pp.

brickbat Backeschtick (es)n.

bricklayer Backeschteeleeger (der)n.

bride Braut (die)n.

bride's clothes and furniture (brought to marriage)
1.Ausscht(e)ier (der)n.; 2.Hausscht(e)ire (der)n.

bridegroom 1.Brauticham (der)n.; 2.Breidicham (der)n.

bridge Brick (die)n.; Bricke, pl.; **for vehicular traffic**
Faahrbrick (die)n.

bridle 1.halde, v.; ghalde, pp.; 2.Zaahm (der)n.; Zehm, pl.;
a horse uff/zaahme, v.; uffgezaahmt, pp.; **bit** (for
fractious horses) Rachebrecher (der)n.

bright 1.gewichst, adj.; 2.hell, adj.;

Bright's disease Nieregranket (die)n.

brilliant glensich, adj.

brim (of a hat) Hutranft (der)n.

brindle brinselbrau, adj.

brindled 1.wolfschtraehmich, adj.; 2.wolkschtreemich,
adj.; 3.wollschtraemich, adj.; 4.wollschtreemich, adj.

brine 1.Salzlaag (die)n.; 2.Salzlack (die)n.; **in which meat
is pickled** Lack (die)n.; **of leached wood ashes utilized in boiling soft soap** Eschelaag (die)n.

bring 1.bei/bringe, v.; beigebrocht, pp.; 2.bringe, v.;
gebrocht, pp.; 3.hol(l)e, v.; gholt, pp.; **(get) across**
niwwer/bringe, v.; niwwergebrocht, pp.; **about**
dehibringe, v.; dehigebrocht, pp.; **about** (a change in
time or position) rum/schaffe, v.; rumgschafft, pp.;
after no(och)bringe, v.; no(och)gebrocht, pp.; **along**
1.mit/bringe, v.; mitgebrocht, pp.; 2.mit/hole, v.;
mitgholt, pp.; **another to one's way of thinking**
rum/bringe, v.; rumgebrocht, pp.; **around**
rum/bringe, v.; rumgebrocht,pp.; **away** weck/bringe,
v.; weckgebrocht, pp.; **back** zerick/bringe, v.;
zerickgebrocht, pp.; **down** runner/bringe, v.;
runnergebrocht, pp.; **here** haer/bringe, v.;
haergebrocht, pp.; **home** heembringe, v.;
heemgebrocht, pp.; **home the cows** eidreiwe, v.;
eigedriwwe, pp.; **in** nei/bringe, v.; neigebrocht, pp.;
in (toward the speaker) rei/bringe, v.; reigebrocht,
pp.; **in income** eibringe, v.; eigebrocht, pp.; **near**
bei/hole, v.; beigholt, pp.; **out** 1.naus/ bringe, v.;
nausbegrocht, pp.; 2.raus/bringe, v.; rausgebrocht,
pp.; **over** riwwer/bringe, v.; riwwergebrocht, pp.;
past verbei/bringe, v.; verbeigebrocht, pp.; **the feet
down flat** blatsche, v.; geblatscht, pp.; **to an end**
faddich mache, v.; faddichgemacht, pp.; **together** (by
dragging) zamme/schleefe, v.; zammegschleeft, pp.;
up; 1.nuff/bringe, v.; nuffgebrocht, pp.;
2.ruff/bringe, v.; ruffgebrocht, pp.; 3. uff/ziege, v.;
uffgezoge, pp.; **word** aa/saage, v.;aagsaat, pp.

brisket Bruschtkaern (es)n.

bristle Bascht (die)n.; Baschde, pl.; **(pig)** Seibaschde (die)n.

bristly 1.schtrubbich, adj.; 2.schtrubbich, adj.

brittle 1.brocklich, adj.; 2.marsch, adj.; 3.schprock, adj.;
4.schprock, adj.

broad breet, adj.; **daylight** Helllicht (es)n.; **faced**
1.breedsichtich, adj.; 2.breetgsichtich, adj.; **front flap
of trousers** (as worn by Amish men) 1.Breedlatz (der)
n.; 2.Breetlatz (der)n.

broadax Breetbeil (es)n.; Breetbeile, pl.

broadish 1.breedlich, adj.; 2.breetlich, adj.

broil brode, v.; gebrode, pp.

bronchitis Halsauszehring (die)n.

brood maudere, v.; gemaudert, pp.; **of bees (especially in
the comb)** Bru(u)d (die)n.; **mare** Zuchtmaerr (die)n.;
of bees (just hatching) Iemebrud (die)n.

broody (of hens) brie(h)ich, adj.

brook 1.Runn (die)n.; 2.Bach (es)n. (rare usage);
3.Bechlein (es)n.; 4.Bechli (es)n. (used only in areas
where settlers were largely of Swiss origin)

broom Bese(m) (der)n.; Bese(m), pl.; **corn** Besemwelschkann (es)n.; **grass** Blobarrigergraas (es)n.;
sedge Blobarrigergraas (es)n.

Bb

broomstick — bung

broomstick 1.Beese(m)schtiel (der)n.; 2.Bese(m)schtecke (der)n.; 3.Besemschtiel (der)n.

broth 1.Brieh (die)n.; 2.Fleeschbrieh (die)n.;3.Fleeschsupp (die)n.

brothel 1.Hurehaus (es)n.; 2.Hurenescht (es)n.

brother Bruder (der)n.; Brieder, pl.; **in-law** 1.Schweeger (der)n.; Schweeger, pl.; 2.Schwerbruder (der)n.; 3.Schwoger (der)n.; Schweeger, pl.

brotherhood Briederschaft (die)n.

brotherliness Briederlichkeet (die)n.

brotherly briederlich, adv.

brothers and sisters Gschwischder (die)n., pl.

brow 1.Schtann (die)n.; Schtanne, pl.

brown brau(n), adj.

brownish braunlich, adj.

browse weede, v.; gweedt, pp.

bruise 1.gwetsche, v.; gegwetscht, pp.; 2.Schrunn(e) (die)n.; 3.Schrunn(e) (die)n.; 4.verquetsche, v.; verquetscht, pp.; **by falling** 1.blotze, v.; geblotzt, pp.; 2.verblotze, v.; verblotzt, pp.; 3.vergwetscht, adj.

bruised verschunne, adj.

brunella 1.Brunelle (die)n.; 2.Brunellegraut (es)n. 3.Greidliwidderbring (der)n.; 4.Greitliwidderbring (der)n.; 5.Kreidliwidderbring (der)n.

brush 1.baschde, v.; gebascht, pp.; 2.Bascht (die)n.; Baschde, pl.; 3.Grubbs (der)n.; 4.Schtaabbascht (die)n.; **(made of twigs)** Heckebascht (die)n.; **away** 1.ab/schtreiche, v.; abgschtriche, pp.; 2.weck/baschde, v.; weckgebascht, pp.; **back** zerick/baerschde, v.; zerickgebaerscht, pp.; **fence** Heckefens (die)n.; **off** ab/baschde, v.; abgebascht, pp.; **out** 1.aus/baschde, v.; ausgebascht, pp.; 2.raus/baschde, v.; rausgebascht, pp.; **plant** Heck (die)n.; Hecke, pl.; **up** 1.uff/baerschde, v.; uffgebaerscht, pp.; 2.zamme/baerschde, v.; zammegebaerscht, pp.

brusque grobb, adj.

brutal ochsich, adj.

brute 1.Seibengel (der)n.; 2.Uumensch (der)n.

brutish viehisch, adj.

bubble 1.Blos (die)n.; Blose, pl.; 2.gwelle, v.; gegwellt; gegwolle, pp.; 3.Wasserblos (die)n.; 4.welle, v.; gwellt, pp.

buck Bock (der)n.; Beck, pl.; **jump** Bockschprung (der)n.

bucket 1.Eemer (der)n.; 2.Kiwwel (der)n.; Kiwwel, pl.; 3.Wasseremer (der)n.; **(especially of a well)** Wasserkiwwel (der)n.; **(wooden used on the farm)** Wasserschtitz (der)n.; **hoops** Eemerreef (der)n.; **of an elevator** Kiwwel (der)n.; Kiwwel, pl. **bucketful** 1.eemervoll, adj.; 2.Kiwwelvoll (der)n.;3.kiwwelvoll, adj.

bucking tub (for bleaching linen) Bauchzuwwer (der)n.

buckle 1.eischnalle, v.; eigschnallt, pp.; 2.Schnall (die)n.; Schnalle, pl.; 3.schnalle, v.; gschnallt, pp.; 4.zuschnalle, v.; zugschnallt, pp.; **down** nunner/schnalle, v.; nunnergschnallt, pp.; **on** 1.aaschnalle, v.; aagschnallt, pp.; 2.uff/schnalle, v.; uffgschnallt, pp.; **on pole strap** Deichselschnall (die)n.; **over** niwwer/schnalle, v.; niwwergschnallt, pp.; **up** nuff/schnalle, v.; nuffgschnallt, pp.

buckram Schteifing (der)n.

buckshot Schwannaggel (die)n.

buckskin 1.Haschhaut (die)n.; 2.Haschledder (es)n.

buckwheat Buchweeze (der)n.; **cake** Buchweezekuche (der)n.; **flour** Buchweezemehl (es)n.; **straw** Buchweezeschtroh (es)n.

bud Pott (die)n.

budge 1.mucke (sich --)v.; gemuckt, pp.; 2.vermucke (sich --)v.; vermuckt, pp.; 3.verrege (sich --)v.; verregt, pp.; 4.verzucke, v.; verzuckt, pp.

buffoon Faxemacher (der)n.

bug Keffer (der)n.; Keffer, pl.

bugbear Bautz (der)n.

buggy (bug) 1.wansich, adj.; 2.Weggel(i) (es)n.; 3.Weggelche (es)n.; **house** Wansenescht (es)n.

bugleweed Sandedorn (der)n.

bugloss 1.Ochsezung (die)n.; 2.Ochsezung (die)n.

bugs Ungeziffer (es)n.

build baue, v.; gebaut, pp.; **(a log house)** uff/blocke, v.; uffgeblockt, pp.; **against** aa/baue, v.; aagebaut, pp.; **an addition to** aa/baue, v.; aagebaut, pp.; **in** nei/baue, v.; neigebaut, pp.; **up** uff/baue, v.; uffgebaut, pp.; **up** (closely) verbaus, v.; verbaut, pp.; **up** (somewhere) nuff/baue, v.; nuffgebaut, pp.

building Gebei (es)n.; Gebeier, pl.; **site** Baublatz (der)n.; **stone** 1.Bauschtee (der)n.; 2.Mauerschtee (der)n.; **out** naus/baue, v.; nausgebaut, pp.

bulimia Fresshunger (der)n.

bull 1.Brummelochs (der)n.; 2.Bull (der)n.; Bulle, pl.; **beef** Bullefleesch (es)n.; **calf** Bullekalb (es)n.; **dog** Bullhund (der)n.

bullet 1.Kug(g)el (die)n.; Kug(g)le, pl.; 2.Kuw(w)el (die)n.; Kuw(w)le, pl.; **mould** Kuggelform (die)n.

bullfrog Bullfrack (der)n.

bully 1.Eisefresser (der)n.; 2.Feierfresser (der)n.

bum 1.loddle, v.; geloddelt, pp.; 2.Rumleefer (der)n.; Rumleefer, pl.

bumblebee 1.Hummel (der)n.; Hummle, pl.; 2.Hummler (der)n.; Hummler, pl.

bumblebee's nest Hummelnescht (es)n.

bummer Kammfugler (der)n.

bump 1.bumbe, v.; gebumbt, pp.; 2.bummere, v.; gebummert, pp.; 3.Bump (der)n.; 4.bump!; 5.blump(s)!; **against** wedder/schtosse, v.; weddergschtosse, pp.

bun Weck (der)n.; Weck, pl.

bunch of flowers Schtrauss (der)n.; Schtreiss, pl.; **grapes** 1.Drauwehengel (der)n.; 2.Hengel (der)n.

bundle 1.Bindel (der)n.; 2.Bundel (der)n.; Bindel, pl.; **(referring to the past custom of bundling)** bundle, v.; gebundelt, pp.; **of a peddler** Pack (der)n.; Peck, pl.; **of flax** (for spinning) 1.Dock(e) (die)n.; 2.Tock (die); **of straw** (for thatching) 1.Fackel (die)n. 2.Gebun(d) (es)n.;

bundle up eibindle, v.; eigebindelt, pp.

bundles (of stalks) Haepter (die)n., pl.

bung 1.Schpunde (der)n.; 2.Schpunder (der)n.; 3.Zabbe (der)n.; Zabbe, pl.

239

Bb

bunghole — buy

bunghole Schpundeloch (es)n.; Schpundelecher, pl.

bungle verpusche, v.; verpuscht, pp.; **up** verschimpe, v.; verschimpt, pp.

bungled 1.schewwetzich, adj.; 2.schiwwitzich, adj.; **work** 1.Schtimmlerei (die)n.; 2.Schtimplerei (die)n.

bunk Schlofbank (die)n.; Schlofbenk, pl.

bunny (rabbit) 1.Haasli (es)n.; Hasslin, pl.; 2.Heesli (es)n.; Heeslin, pl.

burden 1.belaschde, v.; belaschdet, pp.; 2.Greiz (es)n.; 3.Lascht (die)n.; 4.Ungemach (es)n.

burdensome 1.beschwerlich, adj.; 2.leschdich, adj.

burdock 1.Glett (die)n.; Gledde, pl.; 2.Klett (die)n.; root Glettewatzel (die)n.

bureau 1.Kommood (die)n.; 2.Piro (der)n.

burglar Eibrecher (der)n.

burglary 1.Eibruch (der)n.; 2.Schtehlerei (die)n.

burial 1.Beaerdichung (die)n.; 2.Begraebnis (es)n. (older form of usage;) 3.Vergraawes (es)n.; 4.Vergraebnis (es)n.

burly fellow (mostly of young boys) 1.Lammel (der)n.; 2.Lemmel (der)n.; 3.Waddel (der)n.

burn 1.brenne, v.; gebrennt, pp.; 2.eibrenne, v.; eigebrennt, pp.; (as a smothered fire) suddre, v.; gsuddert, pp.; **underbrush or weeds from a tract** iwwerbrenne, v.; iwwergebrennt, pp.; **down** 1.aa/brenne, v.; aagebrennt, pp.; 2.ab/brenne, v.; abgebrennt, pp.; 3.nidder/brenne, v.; niddergebrennt, pp.; 4.nunner/brenne, v.; nunnergebrennt, pp.; 5.weck/brenne, v.; is weckgebrennt, pp.; **fast to the kettle** aa/brenne, v.; aagebrennt, pp.; **into** nei/brenne, v.; neigebrennt, pp.; **out** 1.aus/brenne, v.; ausgebrennt, pp.; 2.raus/brenne, v.; rausgebrennt, pp.; **up** 1.uff/brenne, v.; is uffgebrennt, pp.; 2.verbrenne, v.; verbrennt, pp.

burnet Naggelgraut (es)n.

burning brennend, adj.; **glass** Brennglaas (es)n.; **stick** Feierbrand (der)n.

burnt (to taste or smell) brennsich, adj.; **wick of a candle** Butze (der)n.

burrow Loch (es)n.; Lecher, pl.

burst verschpringe, v.; is verschprunge, pp.; **from internal pressure** blatze, v.; geblatzt, pp.; **with a loud report** vergrache, v.; vergracht, pp.; **in** 1.nei/schprenge, v.; neigschprengt, pp.; 2.rei/schprenge, v.; reischprengt, pp.; **open** 1.uff/fliege, v.; is uffgfloge, pp.; 2.uff/schpringe, v.; is uffgschprunge, pp.; **out** 1.los/breche, v.; is losgebroche, pp.; 2.raus/schlagge, v.; rausgschlagge, pp.; **out laughing** naus/lache, v.; nausgelacht, pp.

bury 1.beaerdiche, v.; beardicht, pp.; 2.begraawe, v.; begraawe, pp.; 3.ei/graawe, v.; eigegraawe, pp.; 4.eischaerre, v.; eigschaerrt, pp.; 5.vergraawe, v.; vergraawe, pp.

bush Schtock (der)n.; Schteck, pl.

bush(es) Gebisch (es)n.

bushbeans Schtockbuhn (die)n.; Schtockbuhne, pl.

bushel Buschel (der)n.; Buschel, pl.; basket Buschelkareb (der)n.

bushy buschich, adj.

busily druffundewedder, adv.

business 1.Bisness (die)n.; 2.G(e)scheft (der)n.; 3.Gscheft (es)n.; 4.Handel (der)n.; 5.Handlung (die)n.; 6.Rumbel (der)n.; 7.Sach (die)n.; Sache, pl.

bustle 1.eile, v.; ge-eilt, pp.; 2.Lewe (es)n.; 3.schussle, v.; gschussel, pp.; 4.Wattschaft (die)n.; 5.wewwere, v.; gewewwert, pp.; **about** rum/schtiwwre, v.; rumgschtiwwert, pp.

bustling Gewewwer (es)n.

busy 1.eifrich, adj.; 2.gescheftich, adj.; 3.gscheffdich, adj.; 4.schaffich, adj.; 5.scheffich, adj.; (diligent) fleissich, adj.; **at or with** waertschafte, v.; gewaertschaft, pp.

busybody 1.Neiichkeetgreemer (der)n.; 2.Neiichkeidedraeger (der)n.; 3.Retch (die)n.; 4.Schnuffelbochs (die)n.; 5.Schnuffler (der)n.; Schnuffler, pl.; 6.Wunnerfitz (der)n.; Wunnerfitz, pl.; 7.Wunnernaas (der)n.; (**male; female**) Schnauser(n) (der,die)n.

but 1.als, adv.; 2.as, adv.; 3.awwer, conj.; adv.

butcher 1.Butscher (der)n.; Butscher, pl.; 2.metzle, v.; gemetzelt, pp.; 3.schlachde, v.; gschlacht, pp.; 4.schlade, v.; gschlacht, pp.; 5.vermetzle, v.; vermetzelt, pp.; 6.Schlachtmann (der)n. (rare usage)

butcher's steel Wettschtaahl (der)n. **plant** Heck(die)n.; Hecke, pl.; Schlachtdaag (der)n.

butchering season (December) Schlachtzeit (die)n.

butt schtutze, v.; gschtutzt, pp.; **end** 1.(of a rifle) Bixeschtock (der)n.; 2.(of an egg) 3.Aarsch (der)n.; **in** nei/henke, v.; neighenkt, pp. (es Maul --)

butter Budder (der)n.; **and eggs** (flower) 1.Hun(d)sblumm (die)n.; 2.Rosmarei (die)n. (wilder --);**bean** Butterbohn (die)n.;**churn** Budderfass (es)n.; Budderfesse(r), pl.; crock Budderhaffe (der)n.; **print** 1.Buddermoddel (die)n.; 2.Budderpress (die)n.; 3.Buttermoddel (die)n.; 4.Butterpress (die)n.; tub Budderzuwwer (der)n.; Budderziwwer, pl.

buttercup Budderblumm (die)n.

butterfly 1.Fleddermaus (der)n.; Fleddermeis, pl.; 2.Schmetterling (der)n. (rare usage;) 3.Summervoggel (der)n.

butteris Waer(ric)kmesser (es)n.

butterknife 1.Buddermesser (es)n.; 2.Buttermesser (es)n.

buttermilk Buddermillich (die)n.

butternut 1.Buddernuss (die)n.; 2.Butternuss (die)n.; 3.Eelwalnuss (die)n.; 4.Weisswalnuss (der)n.

buttock 1.Aarsch (der)n.; 2.After (es)n.; 3.Arschbacke (der)n.; 4.Arschbaerb (der)n.

button 1.gneppe, v.; gegneppt, pp.; 2.Gnopp (der)n.; Gnepp, pl.; 3.Knopp (der)n.;**back** zerick/gneppe, v.; zerickgegneppt, pp.; **on** 1.aa/gnibbe, v.; aagegnippt, pp.; 2.aa/knebbe, v.; aagekneppt, pp.; **shoe** Gneppschuh (der)n.; **up** zugnippe, v.; zugegnippt, pp.

buttonhole Gnopploch (es)n.; Gnopplecher, pl.

buttonwood 1.Gnopphols (es)n.; 2.Wasserbabble (der, die)n.

buy kaafe, v.; kaaft, pp.; **a pig in a poke** Katz (die)n. (en -- im Sack kaafe); **back** zerick/kaafe, v.; zerickgekaaft, pp.; **in** ei/kaafe, v.; eikaaft, pp.; **off** ab/kaafe, v.; abkaaft, pp.; **on tick** (credit) uff, prep., adv. (-- Barigs kaafe); out aus/kaafe, v.; auskaaft, pp.; **up** 1.uff/kaafe, v.; uffkaaft, pp.; 2.zamme/kaafe, v.; zammekaaft, pp.

Bb

buyer

byword

buyer 1.Kaafer (der)n.; 2.Kaafman (der)n.; Kaafleit, pl.;
    3.Keefer (der)n.

buyers Kaafleit (die)n., pl.

buzz brumme, v.; gebrummt, pp.

buzzing (continued) Gebrumm (es)n.

by 1.an, prep.; 2.bei, prep.; **all means** 1.abselut(t), adv.;
    2.nummeyo; **bagfuls** sackweis, adv.; **buckets**
    eemerweis, adv.; **fits and starts** schussweis, adv.;
    God bigott, adj.; **golly** 1.bei greibs, interj.; 2.henk
    (bei); 3.sechs, adj.; (meiner --); 4.grenk (hol's
    dei --); 5.kotzgricksel!, interj.; **gracious!** Grund (der)
    n. (meiner --); **haphazard** zufellich, adj.; **him** beim =
    bei em; **jerks** schussweis, adv.; **narrow sections**
    schtrichweis, adv.; **no means** 1.mitnichdem, adv.;
    2.mitnichtem, adv.; **pairs** paarweis, adv.; **starts**
    schuckweis, adv.; **that** 1.dabei, prep.; 2.dattdebei,
    adv.; 3.debei, prep.; **the month** 1.monetweis, adv.;
    2.munetweis, adj.; adv.; **the name of** naamens, adv.;
    the armful armvollweis, adv.; **the by** newebei, adv.;
    the lot iwwerhaapt, adv.; **the millions**
    1.mill(i)yooneweis, adv.; 2.mill(i)yuuneweis, adv.; **the
    side of** 1.denewe, adv.; 2.newe, adv. & prep.;
    3.newedraa, adv.; 4.newich, prep.; **this** dodebei,
    adv.; **thunder** 1.behiedes, adv.; 2.bigott, adj.; 3.hole,
    v.; gholt. pp. (hol's der Deiwel); (hol's der Schinner);
    4.Wedder (es)n. (beim --!); **twos** paarweis, adv.

bygone 1.verbei, adv.; 2.vergange, adv.

bygone days Daag (der)n. (verbeigangne --e)

byroad 1.Abweg (der)n.; 2.Beiweg (der)n.; Beiwege, pl.;
    3.Hinnerweg (der)n.

byway 1.Abweg (der)n.; 2.Neweschtroos (die)n.

byword Beiwatt (es)n.; Beiwadde, pl.

Cc

cabbage

cabbage 1.Graut (es)n.; Greider, pl.; 2.Koppgraut (es)n.; 3.Kraut (es)n.

cabbage (for winter use) Wintergraut (es)n.; **cutter** Grauthowwel (die)n. **head** Grautkopp (der)n.; Grautkepp, pl.; **patch** Grautschtick (es)n.; **seed** 1.Grautsome (der)n.; 2.Grautsume (der)n.; **slaw** Grautselaat (der)n.

cabin 1.Barigheisli (es)n.;2.Heisli (es)n.; Heislin, pl.;3.Hitt(die)n.

cabinetmaker 1.Dischmacher (der)n.; 2.Hausrotschreiner (der) n.; 3.Laademacher (der)n.; Laademacher, pl.; 4.Schankmacher (der)n.; 5.Schreiner (der)n.; Schreiner,pl.

cack Haufe (der)n. (en -- mache)

cackle 1.gackere, v.; gegackert, pp.; 2.gackse, v.; gegackst, pp.; 3.gaxe, v.; gegaxt, pp.

cackling gackrich, adj.

cactus 1.Baapscht (der)n.; Baapschde, pl.; 2.Baapschtkopp (der)n.; 3.Kaktus (der)n.

caecum 1.Endkeitel (der)n.; 2.Engkeitel (der)n.

cage Kewwich (der)n.; Kewwich(e), pl.

cake Kuche (der)n.; Kuche, pl.; **covered with riwwles** Riwwelkuche (der)n.; **cutter** Kuchemoddel (die)n.; **dough** (batter) Kuchedeeg (der)n.; **lifter** Kucheschipp (die)n.

calabash 1.Kalbascht (die)n.; 2.Kellebasch (die)n.

calamitous, adj. iwwel

calamus Kalmus (es)n.

calathumpian violin Seigieg (die)n.

calculate 1.hie/rechle, v.; hiegrechelt, pp.; 2.rechle, v.; gerechelt, pp.; 3.zaehle, v.; gezaehlt, pp.

calculation 1.Rechling (die)n.; 2.Rechning (die)n.

calculations Geziffer (es)n.

calendar Kalenner (der)n.; Kalenner, pl.

calendula Ringelros (die)n.

calf 1.Hammelche (es)n.; 2.Hamm(e)li (es)n.; 3.Hammli(es) n.; Hammlin, pl.; 4.Kalb(es)n,; Kelwer, pl.; 5.Kelwel (es) n.; 6.Sucki (es)n.; **of human leg** Waade (die)n.

calf's head Kalbskopp (der)n.; **liver** Kalbslewwer (die)n.; **skin** 1.Kalbfell (es)n.; 2.Kalbledder (es)n.; 3.Kalbshaut (die)n.

calico 1.Gadu(n) (der)n.; 2.Gedu (der)n.; 3.Gedun (der)n.; 4.Kaddu(n) (der)n.

calipers 1.Rundzaerkel (der)n.; 2.Schmittzaerkel (der)n.

calk Schtolle (der)n.

call 1.heese, v.; gheese, pp.; 2.Lock (der)n.; 3.locke, v.; gelockt, pp.; 4.nenne, v.; genennt, pp.; 5.rufe, v.; gerufe, pp.; **after** no(och)rufe, v.; no(och)gerufe, pp.; **away** weck/rufe, v.; weckgerufe, pp.; **down** 1.nunner/greische, v. nunnergegrische, pp.; 2.runner/rufe, v.; runnergerufe, pp.; **for** ab/hole, v.; abgholt, pp.; **for a cat** buss! interj.; **for chickens** bie! bie!; **for cows** 1.see! see! kum!; 2.suk!; **for geese** 1.gulli, gulli; 2.wulli! **(fowls, dogs)** beilocke, v.; beigelockt, pp.; **here** haer/rufe, v.; haergerufe, pp.; **in** 1.rei/locke, v.; reigelockt, pp.; 2.rei/rufe, v.; reigerufe, pp.; **into** (a place) nei/rufe, v.; neigerufe, pp.; **near or in** bei/rufe, v.; beigerufe, pp.; **off** 1.ab/rufe, v.; abgerufe, pp.; 2.(a dog) weck/locke, v.; weckgelockt, pp.; **out** 1.aus/rufe, v.; ausgerufe, pp.; 2.naus/ greische, v.;

cant

nausgegrische, pp.; 3.naus/ rufe, v.; nausgerufe, pp.; 4.raus/rufe, v.; rausgerufe, pp.; **over** riwwer/rufe, v.; riwwergerufe pp.; **to a place** hie/rufe, v.; hiegerufe, pp.; **to horses** 1.(at the end of a furrow to make a hard turn to the left) haarum!; 2.(to turn about to the right) hottrum! **together**; 1.zamme/locke, v.; zammegelockt, pp.; 2.zamme/rufe, v.; zammegerufe, pp.; **up** 1.nuff/greische, v.; nuffgegrische, pp.; 2.ruff/rufe, v.; ruffgerufe, pp.; 3.uff/rufe, v.; uffgerufe, pp.; **upon** aa/rufe, v.; aagerufe, pp.; **upstairs** nuff/rufe, v.; nuffgerufe, pp.; **used in driving cattle** 1.hoi(i)!; **used in driving cattle** 2.(this form is mostly used in driving a single head) hui!

call(ing) Ruf (der)n.

called heese, v.; gheese, pp.

calling 1.Beruf (der)n.; 2.Handwaricksgscheft (es)n.

calm 1.ruhich, adj.; 2.schtill, adj.; 3.windschtill, adj.; **down** tempere (sich --)v.; getempert, pp.

calve kalwe, v.; gekalbt, pp.

camel Kameel (es)n.; Kameele, pl.

camomile Kamille (der)n.; **tea** Kamilletee (der)n.

camp Laager (der)n.; Laager, pl.

campaign Feldzuch (der)n.

camphor 1.Gamber (der)n.; 2.Gamfer (der)n.

can 1.Kann (die)n.; Kanne, pl.; 2.kenne, v.; gekennt, pp.; **(provided with a spout which had a perforated button on the end of it, used in feeding infants, the precursor of the nursing bottle)** Memmli (es)n.; **with a lid** Deckelkann (die)n.

Canada Kanada (es)n.; **bluegrass** 1.Blograas (es)n.; 2.Eisegraas(es)n.; **lily** Feldlilye (die)n.; **thistle** Kanadaadischdel (die)n.

Canadian moonseed Allekur (die)n.

canal Kanaal (der)n.; Kanaale, pl.; **boat** Kanaalboot (es)n.; **boatman** Bootmann (der)n.

canary grass Hengschtgraas (es)n.

cancel aus/duh, v.; ausgeduh, pp.

cancelled gschtriche, adj.

Cancer (4th sign of the zodiac) Krebs (der)n.

cancer 1.Grebs (der)n.; 2.Krebs (der)n.; **of the stomach** Maagegrebs (der)n.

cancerous grebsordich, adj.

candidate Kandidaat (der)n.; Kandidaade, pl.

candies Zuckersach (es)n.

candle 1.Kerze (die)n.; 2.Licht (es)n.; Lichder, pl.; **mould** Lichterform (die)n.

Candlemas, February 2 Lichtmess (die)n.

candlestick Lichterschtock (der)n.

candy Zucker(g)schleck (es)n.

cane Schtecke (der)n.

cannibal Menschefresser (der)n.; Menschefrresser, pl.

cannon 1.Gschtick (es)n.; 2.Kanoon (die)n.; Kanoon, pl.; 3.Kanuun (die)n.; Kanuun, pl.

cant schraekse, v.; gschraekst, pp.; **hook** (wooden lever used to handle logs) 1.Wennrich (der)n.; 2.Wennring (der)n.

Cc

canteen

canteen Feldflasch (die)n.

Canterybury bell Glockeblumm (die)n.

cap Kapp (die)n.; Kappe, pl.; **of a shoe** Schuhkapp (die)n.; **(to provide with a cap)** kappe, v.; gekappt, pp.

capability Fehichkeet (die)n.; Fehichkeit, pl.

capable 1.faehich, adj.; 2.fehich, adj.

cape Mantel (der)n.; **(type of overcoat)** Mandelrock (der)n.

caper Bockschprung (der)n.

capers Schpuchte (die)n., pl.

capital 1.Haaptschtadt (die)n.; 2.Kapitaal (es)n.; **punishment** Lewe(n)sschtrof (die)n.

caprice 1.Gschtiwwer (der)n.; 2.Schtiwwer (der)n.

Capricorn (10th sign of the zodiac) Schteebock (der)n.

captain Haaptmann (der)n.; Haaptmenner, pl.

captivated by good looks vergaffe (sich --)v.; vergafft, pp.

captive Gfangner (der)n.; Gfangne, pl.

capture fange, v.; gfange, pp.

caraway Kimmel (der)n.

carbon Kohlschtofft (es)n.

carbuncle 1.Blutgschwaere (der)n.; 2.Karfunkel (der)n.; 3.Peschtbloder (die). Peschtblodere, pl.; 4.Schlier (der)n.

card 1.Kaart (die)n.; Kaarde, pl.; 2.Kard (die)n.; 3.karde, v.; gekardt, pp.; 4.Kord (die)n.; 5.korde, v.; gekordt, pp.; **table** 1.Kardedisch (der)n.; 2.Kordedisch (der)n.;

cardboard 1.Babbedeckel (der)n.; 2.babbeldeckne, adj.

cardinal flower 1.Feierblumm (die)n.; 2.Feierrodeblatt (die)n.

carding machine 1.Kardmaschien (die)n.; 2.Kordmaschien (die)n.; **mill** 1.Kardmiehl (die)n.; 2.Kordmiehl (die)n.

care 1.Acht (der, die)n.; 2.Obacht (die)n.; 3.Sarrick (die)n.; 4.Sarge (die)n.; 5.Sarges (es)n.; **for** sarge, v.; gsarrickt, pp.; **for someone** (something) achtgewwe, v. (-- uff ebber [ebbes]); **(to like)** meege, v.; gemeecht, pp.;

carefree 1.sargefrei, adj.; 2.sargelos, adj.

careful 1.achding gewwe, adj.; 2.achtich, adj.; 3.achting gewwe, adj.; 4.achtsam, adj.; 5.bsarkt, adj.; 6.sarricksam, adj.; 7.vorsichdich, adj.

careless 1.achtlos, adj.; 2.labbich, adj.; 3.lappich, adj.; 4.lass, adj.; 5.sargelos, adj.; 6.schlabbich, adj.;7.unachtsam, adj.; 8.unvorsichdich, adj.; 9.uubekimmert, adj.

carelessness 1.Faahrlessichkeit (die)n.;2.Lappichkeet (die) n.; 3.Unachtsamkeet (die)n.

caress 1.gnootsche, v.; gegnootscht, pp.; 2.karessiere, v.; gekaressiert, pp.; 3.liewe, v.; geliebt, pp.

caries Gnochefraas (es)n.

carnage Gemetzel (es)n.

carnation 1.Gaardenaggli (es)n. 2.Negg(e)li (es)n.; 3.Neggelche (es)n.; Neggelcher, pl.

carouse zeeche, v.; gezeecht, pp.

carousing Gsauf (es)n.

carpenter 1.Hausschreiner (der)n.; 2.Schreiner (der)n.; Schreiner, pl.

carpenter's bench Howwelbank (die)n.; Howwelbenk, pl.

carpenter's square Eckscheit (es)n.

carpet Karrebet (der)n.

carpet chain Webzettel (der)n.

cast

carriage 1.Katirsch (die)n.; 2.Kutsch (die)n.; Kutsche, pl.; **road** Faahrweg (der)n.; Faahrwege, pl.

carrion 1.Luder (es)n.; 2.Oos (es)n.; 3.Schinnoos (es)n.; 4.Schtinkluder (es)n.; **flower** Luderblumm (die)n.

carrot Gehlrieb (die)n.; Gehlriewe, pl.

carry draage, v.; gedraage, pp.; **after** no(och)draage, v.; no(och)gedraage, pp.; **a heavy load** schleppe, v.; gschleppt, pp.; **along** mit/draage, v.; mitgedraage, pp.; **around** rum/draage, v.; rumgedraage, pp.; **away** 1.fatt/draage, v.; fattgedraage, pp.; 2.weck/draage, v.; weckgedraage, pp.; **back** zerick/draage, v.; zerickgedraage, pp.; **down** nunner/draage, v.; nunnergedraage, pp.; **hither** haer/draage, v.; haergedraage, pp.; **home** heemdraage, v.; **in** 1.eidraage, v.; eigedraage, pp.; 2.nei/draage, v.; neigedraage, pp.; 3.rei/draage, v.; reigedraagt, pp.; **off** ab/draage, v.; abgedraagt, pp.; **off** (as water) ab/fiehre, v.; abgfiehrt, pp.; **on** 1.aa/dreiwe, v.; aagedriwwe, pp.; 2.(in both senses); haermeniere, v.; haermeniert, pp.; 3.(the blacksmith's trade) schmitte, v.; gschmitt, pp.; **out** 1.aus/fiehre, v.; ausgfiehrt, pp.; 2.naus/draage, v.; nausgedraage, pp.; 3.raus/draage, v.; rausgedraage, pp.; 4.versetze, v.; versetzt, pp.; 5.vollbringe, v.; vollbrocht, pp.; 6.vollfiehre, v.; vollfiehrt, pp.; **over** niwwer/draage, v.; niwwergedraage, pp.; **thither** hie/draage, v.; hiegedraage, pp.; **to** bei/draage, v.; beigedraage, pp.; **together** zamme/draage, v. zammegedraage, pp.; **up** 1.nuff/draage, v.; nuffgedraage, pp.; 2.ruff/draage, v.; ruffgedraage, pp.

cart (In Old Order Amish usage a two wheeled cart used to train driving horses) Karrich (der)n.; **horse** Karrichgaul (der)n.

cartilage 1.Gnaerwel (der)n.; 2.Gnarwel (der)n.; Gnarwel, pl.; 3.Knarwel (der)n.

carve aus/schaffe, v.; ausgschafft, pp.; **out** aus/schnitzle, v.; ausgschnitzelt, pp.

carving of nature Bedaerfnis (es)n.

case 1.Fall (der)n.; 2.Fruchtkammer (die)n.; 3.Scheed (die) n.; 4.Zufall (der)n.; 5.Zuschtand (der)n.; Zuschtende, pl.; **for a feather bed** Iwwerzuck (der)n.; **on at court** vorsei, v.; vorgewest, pp.

cash 1.baar, adj.; 2.Baargeld (es)n.; 3.Bar (der)n.

cask 1.Ballfass (es)n.; Ballfesser, pl. 2.Fass (es)n.; Fesser, pl.; 3.Fessli (es)n.; Fesslin, pl.

casket Laad (die)n.; Laade, pl.

cassinette Kassinet (es)n.

cast 1.giesse, v.; gegosse, pp.; 2.schmeisse, v.; gschmisse, pp.; **about** um/sehne (sich --)v.; umsehne, pp.; **aside** ab/lege, v.; abgelegt, pp.; **iron** 1.Guss (es)n.; 2.Gusseise (es)n.; **of the eye** Blick (der)n.; **over** iwwergiesse, v.; iwwer(ge)gosse, pp.; **something** (in a person's teeth) Naas (die)n. (eem ebbes unnich die -- reiwe); **stolen glances** schilkse, v.; gschilkst, pp.; **up** (something to someone) 1.uff/riddle, v.; uffgeriddelt, pp.; 2.vorriddle, v.; vorgeriddelt, pp.; **up accounts** ziffere, v.; geziffert, pp.; **up to** 1.riddle, v.; geriddelt, pp.; 2.(one) vor/ schmeisse, v.; vorg(e)schmisse, pp.

243

Cc

caster | cent

caster Roller (der)n.; Roller, pl.

casting net Schmeissgaarn (es)n.

castor oil bean 1.Kasdreelbuhn (die)n.; 2.Kotzbohn (die)n.

castrate 1.gelse, v.; gegelst, pp.; 2.schneide, v.; gschnidde, pp.; 3.vergelse, v.; vergelst, pp.; 4.vermetzle, v.; vermetzelt, pp.; 5.verschneide, v.; verschnidde, pp.

castrated dog Bucker (der)n.

casual emoluments Seitloh (der)n.

cat 1.Bussi (die)n.; 2.Bussikatz (die)n.; 3.Bussli (die);) 4.Katz (die)n.; Katze, pl.; **dirt** Katzedreck (der)n.; **(old, worn out)** abgemaust, adv.; **tail** Katzeschwans (der)n.

catalpa tree 1.Bohnebaam (der)n.; 2.Buhnebaam (der)n.; 3.Schotebaam (der)n.

cataract 1.Aageheidel (es)n.; 2.Aageheidli (es)n.; 3.Schtaar(der)n.

catbird Katzevoggel (der)n.

catch 1.Fang (der)n.; 2.fange, v.; gfange, pp.; 3.halt/griege (an ebbes)v.; haltgrickt, pp.; 4.Schnepp (die)n.; 5.weck/fange, v.; weckgfange, pp.; **a cold** verkelde v.; verkeldt, pp. ; **contagious disease** uff/lese, v.; uffglese, pp.; **from a number** raus/fange, v.; rausgfange, pp. **hold of** verwische, v.; verwischt, pp.; **in turning** grempe, v.; gegrempt, pp.; **sight of** erblicke, v.; erblickt, pp.; **up with** 1.iwwerhole, v.; iwwerholt, pp.; 2.no(och)fange, v.; no(och)gfange, pp.; **with hooks** hokle, v.; ghokelt, pp.

catechetical instruction 1.Kinnerlehr (die) n.;2.Unnerrichtslehr (die)n.

catechism Kattekism (der)n.

catechumen 1.Parreskind (es)n.; 2.Parreskinner (die)n., pl.

caterpillar 1.Raub (die)n.; Rauwe, pl.; 2.Raup (die)n.; **nest** 1.Raupenescht (es)n.; 2.Rauwenescht (es)n.

caterwauling 1.Katzegegrisch (es)n.; 2.Katzeyammer (der)n.

catfish Katzefisch (der)n.

catgut Daremseet (die)n.

cathartic Laxiering (die)n.

Catherine Kathrine (die)n.

Catholic 1.gadollisch, adj.; 2.kadollisch, adj.

catnip (tea) Katzegraut (Tee) (es)n.

cattail flag Liesch(t) (es)n.; **spike** Lieschkolwe (der)n.

cattle 1.Haernervieh (es)n. 2.Harnvieh (es)n.; 3.Rinsvieh (es)n.; 4.Viech (es)n.; 5.Vieh (es)n.; **fattened for slaughtering** Schlachtvieh (es)n.; **in rutting time** schpiele, v.; gschpielt, pp.; **of mixed breed** Baschdert (der)n.; **path** Kiehwegli (es)n.; Kiehweglin, pl.; **powder** Kiehpulwer (es)n.

caught on something 1.fascht, adj.; 2.fescht, adj.

cauliflower Blummegraut (es)n.

cause 1.aa/richde, v.; aagericht, pp.; 2.aa/schtelle, v.; aagschtellt, pp.; 3.aa/schtifde, v.; aagschtift, pp.; 4.aaschtelle (sich --)v.; aagschtellt, pp.; 5.Ursach (die) n.; Ursache, pl.; 6.Verschtand (der)n.; 7.verursache, v.; verursacht, pp.; **an open wound by falling** uff/falle, v. uffgfalle, pp.; **great aversion or nausea** greisle, v.; gegreiselt, pp.; **pain** schmaerze, v.; gschmaerzt, pp.; **to back** hufe, v.; ghuft, pp.; **to beat a hasty retreat** zerick/schprenge, v.; zerickgschprengt, pp.; **to break or**

fly off ab/schprenge, v.; abgschprengt, pp.; **to burst** verschprenge, v.; verschprengt, pp.; **to change one's mind** raus/blaudre, v.; rausgeblaudert, pp.; **to disappear** 1.weck/bringe, v.; weckgebrocht, pp.; 2.weck/nemme, v.; weckgenumme, pp.; **to disappear (by powwowing)** weck/brauche, v.; weckgebraucht, pp.; **to fall** schtaerze, v.; gschtaerzt, pp.; **to fall behind** zerick/schmeisse, v.; zerickgschmisse, pp.; **to feel ashamed** 1.aus/schemme, v.; ausgeschemmt, pp.; 2.aus/schenne, v.; ausgeschennt, pp.; **to get out** naus/schaffe, v.; nausgschaft, pp.; **to leave hastily** ab/schprenge, v.; abgschprengt, pp.; **to rise** uff/griege, v.; uffgrickt, pp.; **to run away**; weck/schprenge, v.; weckgschprunge, pp.; **to run in** nei/schprenge, v.; neigschprengt, pp.; **to tremble** 1.schoddere, v.; gschoddert, pp.; 2.schottere, v.; gschottert, pp.; **trouble** aa/richde, v.; aagericht, pp.

caution Vorsicht (die)n.

cautious 1.vorsichdich, adj.; 2.vor/sehne (sich --)v.; vorgsehne, pp.

cave 1.Deiwelsloch (es)n.; 2.Dracheloch (es)n.; 3.Hehling (die)n.; 4.Hiehling (die)n.; **in** 1.ei/falle, v.; eigfalle, pp.; 2.eisinke, v.; eigsanke, pp.; 3. (och)gewwe, v.; no(och)gewwe, pp.

cavern Hehl (die)n.

cavity 1.Hehl (die)n.; 2.Hehling (die)n.; 3.Heiling (die)n.; 4.Hiehling (die)n.

cavort rum/danse, v.; rumgedanst, pp.

Cayenne pepper rot, adj. (--er Peffer)

cease uff/heere, v.; uffgheert, pp.; **blooming** ab/bliehe, v.; abgeblieht, pp.; **to exist** vergeh, v.; vergange, pp.

ceased veriwwer, adv.

cedar 1.Zeeder (der)n.; 2.Zeedre (der)n.; **tree** Zeedre (der)n. (-- Baam); **chest** Zeedrekischt (die)n.; **waxwing** Kappevoggel (der)n.; **wood** Zeedrehols (es)n.

ceiling 1.Dachwand (die)n.; 2.ewwerscht Wand (die)n.

celandine 1.Scheelgraut (es)n.; 2.Schellgraut (es)n.

celebrate feiere, v.; gfeiert, pp.

celebrated beriehmt, adj.

celebration 1.Feierlichkeet (die)n.; 2.Fescht (es) n.;Feschder, pl.

celerity Gschwindichkeet (die)n.

celery 1.Selleri (der)n.; 2.Sellerich (der)n.; 3.Zellerich (der) n.; 4.zellerich = selleri

celestial himmlisch, adj.

cell 1.Sell (die)n.; 2.Zell (die)n.

cellar Keller (der)n.; Kellere, pl.; **door** Kellerdeer (die)n.; **for cooling and keeping milk** Millichkeller (der)n.; **steps** Kellerschteek (die)n.

cellarway 1.Kellereck (es)n.; 2.Kellerhals (der)n.; Kellerhels, pl.

cemetery 1.Gottesacker (der)n.; 2.Graabblatz (der)n.; Graabbletz, pl.; 3.Graabhof (der)n.; Graabhef, pl.; 4.Karrichof (der)n.; Karrichhef, pl.

censure 1.Maul (es)n. (es -- uffreisse;); 2.taadle, v.; getaadelt, pp.

cent Bens (der)n.; Bense, pl.

Cc

center

center (point) Middelpunkt (der)n.

century Yohrhunnert (es)n.

cereal Fruchtblans (die)n.

ceremony Zeremonie (die)n.

certain 1.ausgemacht, adj.; 2.gewiss, adj.; 3.schur, adj.; 4.sicher, adj.

certainly 1.freilich, adj., adv.; 2.gewiss, adv.; 3.verhaftich, adj.; 4.waahrhafdich, adv.; 5.wohrhaftich, adj.; 6.Sicherheet (die)n.

certificate of indebtedness Band (es)n.; Benner, pl.

cessation Abbruch (der)n.; **from work** Feierowed (der)n.

cesspool Sinkloch (es)n.; Sinklecher, pl.

chafed wund, adj.

chaff 1.aus/hensle, v.; ausghenselt, pp.; 2.Schprau (die)n.; 3.schtumbiere, v.; schtumbiert, pp.; **bag** (used as a mattress) Schprau(er)sack (der)n.; Schprau(er)seck, pl.

chain 1.Kett (die)n.; Kedde, pl.; 2.kette, v.; gekett, pp.;**bridge** Kettebrick (die)n.; **fast** 1.aa/kedde, v.; aagekett, pp.; 2.fescht/kedde, v.; feschtgekett, pp.; **hook** Kettehoke (der)n.; **pump** Kettebump (die)n.; **shot** Kettekuggel (die)n.; **stitch**Ketteschtich (der)n.; **together** zamme/kette, v.; zammegekett, pp.

chair Schtu(h)l (der)n.; Schtiel, pl.; **rail** (around room to prevent damage to wall) Gsims (es)n.; **with splint seat** Schieneschtul (der)n.

chairman Vorsitzer (der)n.; Vorsitzer, pl.

chalice 1.Kelch (der)n.; Kelche, pl.; 2.Kellich (der)n.; Kelliche, pl.

chalk Kreid (es)n.

challenge 1.naus/foddere, v.; nausgfoddert, pp.; 2.raus/biete, v.; rausgebotte, pp.; 3.raus/foddre, v.; rausgfoddert, pp.; 4.schtumbe, v.; gschtumpt, pp.

chamber pot 1.Haffe (der)n.; Heffe, pl.; 2.Kammer (die) n.; Kemmer, pl.; 3.Pott (die)n.; 4.Nachtgschaerr (es)n.; 5.Nachthaffe (der)n.; Nachthaffe, pl.; 6.Scheisshaffe (der)n.; Scheisshaffe, pl.; **stool** Nachtschtuhl (der)n.

champagne Schampanyer (der)n.

chance Gelegeheit (die)n.

chandler Lichtermacher (der)n.

change (alter) 1.verennere, v.; verennert, pp.; 2.Verennering (die)n.; 3.Verennerung (die)n.; 4.verwandle, v.; verwandelt, pp. ; **(because of a mistake)** 1.Verwechsling (die)n.; 2.Verwechslung (die)n.; 3.verwexle, v.; verwexelt, pp.; **(for variety)** 1.Abwechslung (die)n.; 2.Ennering (die)n.; 3.Ennerung (die)n.; **(make other arrangements)** um/schtalle, v.; umgschtallt, pp.; **(money)** 1.Rechling (die)n.; 2.Rechning (die)n.; 3.Abwechsel (der)n.; 4.Wechsling (die)n.; 5.Wexel (der)n. (small coins); **one's name by marrying** verheire, v.; verheiert, pp.; **(to change)** 1.rum/ennere, v.; rumgeennert, pp.; 2.rum/wexle, v.; rumgewexelt, pp.; 3.wexle, v.; gewexelt, pp.; **clothes** 1.ab/schtrippe v.; abgschtrippt, pp.; 2.rum/gleede (sich --) v.; rumgegleedt, pp.; 3.rum/schtribbe, v.; rumgschtrippt, pp.; **denominational affiliation** Glaawe wexle (der)n.; **of the moon** Moondwechsel

chase

(der)n.; **position of** rum/schtelle, v.; rumgschtellt, pp.; **residence** rum/ziehe, v.; rumgezoge, pp.; **the marks of** rum/maerricke, v.; rumgemaerrickt, pp.; **the place of a horse from the near to the off side** rum/schpanne, v.; rumgschpannt, pp.; **the position of** 1.rum/lege, v.; rumgelekt, pp.; 2.verschtelle, v.; verschtellt, pp.; **to** 1.waerre, v.; warre; waerre, pp.; **vehicles** rum/schteige, v.; rumgschtigge, pp.

changeable 1.verennerlich, adj.; 2.wechslich, adj.

changing records Felsching (die)n.

chap 1.Grips(er) (der)n.; 2.Knaerps (der)n.; **(of hands)** uff/schpringe, v.; is uffgschprunge, pp.

chapter Kabiddel (es)n.

character 1.Gemietsort (die)n.; 2.Karackder (der)n.; 3.Lob (es)n.

charcoal Holzkohl (die)n.; Holzkohle, pl.; **burner** 1.Holskohlebrenner (der)n.; 2.Kohlebrenner (der)n.

charge 1.aaschreiwe, v.; aagschriwwe, pp.; 2.Befehl (der) n.; 3.Rechling (die)n.; 4.Schtell (die)n.; 5.taxe, v.; getaxt, pp.; 6.uff/schreiwe, v.; uffgschriwwe, pp.; 7.zuschreiwe, v.; zugschriwwe, pp.; **a gun** laade, v.; glaade, pp.; **an exorbitant price** sohle, v.; gsohlt, pp.

charitable freigew(w)ich, adj.

charity Gotteslieb (die)n.

charlock 1.Moschdert (der)n.; 2.Mostert (der)n.

charm banne, v.; gebannt, pp.; **word repeated in pow-wowing** zing

charmer Banner (der)n.

chart 1.Kard (die)n.; 2.Kord (die)n.; 3.Landkord (die)n.

charwoman Butzfraa (die)n.

chase yaage, v.; geyaagt, pp.; **ahead** vannenaus/yaage, v.; vannenausgyaagt, pp.; **around** rum/yaage, v.; rumgeyaagt, pp.; **away** 1.ab/schtaerme, v.; abgschtaermt, pp.; 2.fatt/yaage, v.; fattgeyaagt, pp.; 3.scheeche, v.; gscheecht, pp.; 4.veryaage, v.; veryaagt, pp.; 5.weck/yaage, v.; weckgeyaagt, pp.; **back** 1.zerick/schtewwre, v.; zerickgschtewwert, pp.; 2.zerick/yaage, v.; zerickgeyaagt, pp.; **by throwing stones** raus/schteeniche, v.; rausgschteenicht, pp.; **down** 1.nunner/yaage, v.; nunnergeyaagt, pp.; 2.runner/yaage, v.; runnergeyaagt, pp.; **from a lair** uff/yaage, v.; uffgeyaagt, pp.; **in** 1. eischprenge, v.; eigschprengt, pp.; 2.eischtewwre, v.; eigschtewwert, pp.; 3.nei/schtewwere, v.; neigschtewwert, pp.; 4.nei/yaage, v.; neigyaagt, pp.; 5.rei/schprenge, v.; reischprengt, pp.; 6.rei/schtewwre, v.; reigschtewwert, pp.; **off** (or away) 1.fatt/dreiwe, v.; fattgedriwwe, pp.; 2.fatt/schtiwwere, v.; fattgschtiwwert, pp.; **or drive to a place** hie/yaage, v.; hiegyaagt, pp.; **out** 1.naus/yaage, v.; nausgyaagt, pp.; 2.raus/schtewwere, v.; rausgschtewwert, pp.; 3.raus/yaage, v.; rausgeyaagt, pp.; **out the front way** vannenaus/yaage, v.; vannenausgyaagt, pp.; **over** riwwer/yaage, v.; riwwergeyaagt, pp.; **this way** haer/yaage, v.; haergyaagt, pp.; **to the other side** niwwer/yaage, v.; niwwergeyaagt, pp.; **together** zamme/yaage, v.; zammegeyaagt, pp.; **up** 1.nuff/yaage, v.; nuffgeyaakt, pp.; 2.ruff/yaage, v.; ruffgeyaagt, pp.; **uphill or upstairs** 1.nuff/schprenge, v.; nuffgschprengt, pp.; 2.nuff/schtewwre, v.; nuffgschtewwert, pp.

245

Cc

chasm — chilly

chasm Gruft (die)n.

chastise zichdiche, v.; gezichdicht, pp.

chastity Reinheet (die)n.

chat 1.babble, v.; gebabbelt, pp.; 2.blaudere, v.; geblaudert, pp.; 3.Gschpraech (es)n.; 4.plaudre, v.; geplaudert, pp.

chatter 1.babble, v.; gebabbelt, pp.; 2.blabbere, v.; geblabbert, pp.; 3.gackere, v.; gegackert, pp.; 4.gackse, v.; gegackst, pp.; 5.Geblabber (es)n.; 6.Geblauder (es)n.; 7.schneppre, v.; gschneppert, pp.

chatterbox 1.Babbel (die)n.; 2.Babbelmaul (es)n.; Babbelmeiler, pl.; 3.Blabbermaul (es)n.; Blabbermeiler, pl.; 4.Plappermaul (es)n.; 5.Schneppermaul (es)n.

chatterer 1.Babbler (der)n.; 2.Gacke (die)n.

chattering 1.Gachnauf (es)n.; 2.Gegwacker (es)n.; 3.Gschnatter (es)n.; **of the teeth** 1.schnattre, v.; gschnaddert, pp.; 2.Zaehglepperes (es)n.; **silly woman** Gackel (die)n.

chatty babblich, adj.

cheap, cheaper, cheapest 1.billich; billicher; billichscht, adj.; 2.wolfel; welfler; welflescht, adj.

cheapness Welfling (die)n.

cheat 1.aa/schmiere, v.; aagschmiert, pp.; 2.ab/geege, v.; abgegeet, pp.; 3.bedriege, v.; bedroge, pp.; 4.Bedrieger (der)n.; 5.beluchse, v.; beluchst, pp.; 6.Bsch(e)isser (der)n.; 7.bscheisse, v.; bschisse, pp.; 8.eibrenne, v.; eigebrennt, pp. (eens --); 9.einemme, v.; eigenumme, pp.; 10.flachse, v.; gflachst, pp.; 11.luchse, v.; geluchst, pp.; 12. schmuggle, v.; gschmuggelt, pp.; 13.schniere, v.; gschniert, pp.; 14.yutte, v.; geyutt, pp.; 15.zwiwwle, v.; gezwiwwelt, pp.

cheater B(e)schisser (der)n.

cheating 1.Bedriegerei (die)n.; 2.Bscheisserei (die)n.

check 1.breche, v.; gebroche, pp.; 2.no(och)zaehle, v.; no(och)gezaehlt, pp.; 3.zerick/halde, v.; zerickghalde, pp.; **rein** Zoppziegel (der)n.; Zoppziggle, pl.

checkerberry 1.Bruschttee (der)n.; 2.Buchs (der)n. (nidderer --) 3.Buchsbeer (die)n.; 4.Budderbeer (die) n.; 5.Butterbeer (die)n.; 6.Fersandebeer (die)n.

checkered eckschteenich, adj.

cheek 1.Backe (der)n.; Backe, pl.; 2.Wange (die)n. (rare usage)

cheep! zipp!

cheerful 1.blessierlich, adj.; 2.frehlich, adj.; 3.haerlich, adj.; 4.hallich, adj.; 5.harlich, adj.; 6.heider, adj.; 7.herrlich, adj.; 8.luschdich, adj.; 9.uff/gelebt, v.; 10.vergniecht, adj.; 11.wohluff, adj.

cheese 1.Kaes (der)n.; 2.Kees (der)n.; **(from scalded skim milk ripened in a crock)** Riwwelkaes (der)n.; **(in balls and ripened)** Handkees (der)n.

cheeses Hemmerknepp (die)n., pl.

chemise Weibshemm (es)n.

cherry Kasch (die)n.; Kasche, pl.; **gum** Kaschehatz (der)n.; **juice** Kaschebrieh (die)n.; **pit** Kascheschtee (der)n.; Kascheschtee, pl.; **pitter** Kascheschteene (der)n.; **tart** Kaschekuche (der)n.; **tree** Kaschebaam (der)n.;

Kaschebeem, pl.; **wood** Kaschehols (es)n.

chess Drefts (die)n.

chest 1.Bruscht (die)n.; Brischt, pl.; 2.Fruchtkammer (die) n.; 3.Kischt (die)n.; Kischde, pl.

chestnut Kescht (die)n.; Keschde, pl.; **brown** keschdebrau, adj.; **burr** 1.Boll (die)n.; 2.Keschdeschot (die)n.; 3.Keschdigel (der)n.; **color** Keschdefareb (die)n.; **oak** Keschd(an)eeche (der)n.; **tree** Keschdebaam (der)n.; Keschdebeem, pl.; **wood** Keschdeholz (es)n.

chew 1.Kau (der)n.; 2.kaue, v.; gekaut, pp.; 3.tschaae, v.; getschaat, pp.; 4.verkaue, v.; verkaut, pp.; **fine** fei/kaue, v.; feigekaut, pp.; **over something** kaue, v.; gekaut, pp.; **the cud** 1.iedriche, v.; geiedricht, pp.; 2.widderkaue, v.; widdergekaut, pp.; 3.Widder(ver)kau (der)n.; **the rag** kaue, v.; gekaut, pp.; **up** 1.uff/kaue, v.; uffgekaut, pp.; 2.verbeisse, v.; verbisse, pp.

chewing (also the rag) Gekau (es)n.; **tobacco** Kauduwack (der)n.

chewink Schewing (der)n.

chick 1.Bieb(el)che (es)n.; 2.Biebli (es)n.; Bieblin, pl.; 3.Hinkelche (es)n.; 4.Hinkli (es)n.; Hinklin, pl.

chicken Hinkel (es)n.; Hinkel, pl.; **bone** Hinkelgnoche (der) n.; **coop** 1.Hinkelkaschde (der)n.; Hinkelkaschde, pl.; 2.Hinkelkewwich (der)n.; **feather** Hinkelfedder (die) n.; **feed** 1.Hingelfresse (es)n.; 2.Hinkelfuder (es)n.; **grape** Reifdraub (die)n.; Reifdrauwe, pp.; **hawk** 1.Dauwedieb (der)n.; 2.Hinkelwoi (der)n.; 3.Schtosswoi (der)n.; **house** (coop) Hinkelschtall (der)n.; **louse** Hinkellaus (die)n.; **manure** 1.Hinkeldreck (der)n.; 2.Hinkelmischt (der)n.; **meat** Hinkelfleesch (es)n.; **pox** Wasserparble (die)n.; **(roost)** Hinkelschtang (die)n.; **thief** Hinkeldieb (der)n.

chickery Gickelche (es)n.

chickweed Hinkeldarm (der)n.

chicory 1.Andiv(v)(d)i (der)n.; 2.Endivvi (der)n.; 3.Kaffigraut (es)n.

chiefly vornemlich, adj.

child 1.Gottesgaabe (die)n.; 2.Kind (es)n.; Kinner, pl. **(illegitimate)** uff/gelese, v. (en --nes Kind); **who wriggles on its mother's lap** Rutsch (die)n.; **out of wedlock** Huf(f)eise (es)n. (en -- verliere) **child's chair** Schtiehlche (es)n.; **hand** Batsch (die)n.; Batschi, pl.; **highchair** Schtiehlche (es)n. (hoch --); **play** Kinnergschpiel (es)n.

childhood Kindheit (die)n.

childish 1.kindisch, adj.; 2.kindlisch, adj.; 3.kinnerlich, adj.; 4.kinnisch, adj.; **amusement** Kinnerschpass (der)n.; **pranks** Kinnerschtreech (die)n., pl.

childless erblos, adj.

children of Israel Israael kinner (der)n.

children's clothing Kinnergleeder (die)n., pl.; **playhouse** Schpielhaus (es)n.

chill 1.Friere(s) (es)n.; 2.iwwerlaafe, v.; iwwerloffe, pp.

chilly kiehl, adj.; **sensation** iwwerschaudre, v.; iwwerschaudert, pp.

Cc

chime — circle

chime in ei/schtimme, v.; eigschtimmt, pp.; **with** mit/eischtimme, v.; miteigschtimmt, pp.

chimney 1.Schannschde (der)n.; 2.Schannschte(e) (der)n.; 3.Scharnschde (der)n.; 4.Scharnschtee (der)n.; **sweep** Scharnschteefeger (der)n.; **swift** Russchwallem (der)n.

chin 1.Baart (der)n.; Baert, pl.; 2.Kinn (es)n.

china cupboard Glaasschank (der)n.

chine Rickmeesel (der)n.

chip 1.Holschpaa (der)n.; 2.Schpaa (der)n.; 3.Schpoo (der)n.; Schpee, pl.; **of stone** Schpaal (der)n.; Schpaale; Schpalde, pl.; **off** 1.ab/meesle, v.; abgemeeselt, pp.; 2.ab/schpringe, v.; abschprunge, pp.

chipmunk Fensemaus (die)n.; Fensemeis, pl.

chips Schpalde (die)n., pl.; **made by a broad ax** Hockschpae (die)n., pl.

chiropractor Gnootsch-Dokder (der)n.

chirp! zipp!

chirping sparrow 1.Zippche (es)n.; 2.Zittche (es)n.

chisel 1.Meesel (der)n.; Meesle, pl.; 2.meesele, v.; gemeeselt, pp.; **hammer** Schrotmeesel (der)n.; **in** nei/meesele, v.; neigemeeselt, pp.; **off** ab/meesle, v.; abgemeeselt, pp.; **out** aus/meesle, v.; ausgemeeselt, pp.

chives 1.Schnidderlich (der)n.; 2.Schnitt(er)lich (der)n.; 3.Schnittloch (der)n.

chocolate Schocklaad (der)n.

choice Waahl (die)n.

choir Kor (der)n.

choke 1.kehle, v.; gekehlt, pp.; 2.verschlucke (sich --)v.; verschluckt, pp.; 3.verwarixe, v.; verwarixt, pp.; 4.waerricke, v.; gewaerrickt, pp.; 5.warge, v.; gewarrickt, pp.; 6.warricke, v.; gewarrickt, pp.; 7.wearge, v.; gewaerrickt, pp.

choke (intransitive) verwarrickse, v.; verwarrickst, pp.

choke cherry 1.Maulzieger (der)n.; 2.Wildkasch (die)n.; Wildkasche, pl.

choose 1.waehle, v.; gewaehlt, pp.; 2.wehle, v.; gewehlt, pp.

chop 1.hacke, v.; ghackt, pp.; 2.Middelmehl (es)n.; 3.Schiebschtoff(t) (es)n.; 4.Schrot (die)n.; **away at** los/hacke, v.; losghackt, pp.; **bag** Schrotsack (der)n.; **down** 1.nidder/hacke, v.; nidderghackt, pp.; 2.nidder/mache, v.; niddergemacht, pp.; 3.nunner/hacke, v.; nunnerghackt, pp.; 4.runner/hacke, v.; runnerghackt, pp.; 5.zamme/hacke, v.; zammeghackt, pp.; **fine** feihacke, v.; feikackt, pp.; **into** 1.aa/hacke, v.; aaghackt, pp.; 2.ei/hacke, v.; eighackt, pp.; 3.nei/hacke, v.; neighackt, pp.; **off** ab/hacke, v.; abghackt, pp.; **out** raus/hacke, v.; rausghackt, pp.; **to pieces** verhacke, v.; verhackt, pp.; **up** uff/hacke, v. uffghackt, pp.; **wood** (for the stove) feimache, v.; feigemacht, pp.

chopped gschrode, adj.

chopper Hacker (der)n.

chopping block 1.Hackbank (die)n.; 2.Hackglotz (der)n.

choral hymn Koraal (der)n.

chores 1.Bambelaerwet (die)n.; 2.Bembelaerwet (die)n.; 3.Drippelarwet (die)n.; **at the barn** fiederes, v.

Christ Grischdus (der)n.

christen daafe, v.; gedaaft, pp.

christening Kinddaaf (die)n.

Christian 1.Grischdel (der)n.; 2.Grischt (der)n.; Grischde, pl.; 3.grischtlich, adj.; 4.Grischtyan (der)n.

Christianity Grischdendum (der)n.

Christmas 1.Grischdaag (der)n.; 2.Grischtdaag (der)n.; Grischtdaage, pl.; 3.Weihnachte (die)n., pl. **Christmas cookie** 1.Eepies (frequently cut in the shape of animals) 2.Pefferniss (die)n., pl.; **eve** 1.Grischtnacht (die)n.; 2.Grischtowed (der)n.; **flower** Grischtblumm (die)n.; **night** Grischdaagnacht (die)n.; **present** 1.Grischkindel (es),n.; Grischkindli(n), pl.; 2.Grischtkindli (es)n.; 3.Krischkindel (es)n.; **tree** 1.Grischtbaam (der)n.; 2.Grischtdaag(s)baam (der)n.; Grischtdaag(s)beem, pl.

Christopher 1.Grischtoffel (der)n. 2.Schtoffel (der)n. (used as a nick- name)

chubby cheek Pauschbacke (der)n.; **cheeked** pauschbackich, adj.

chuck rib Yochschtick (es)n.

chump Schofkopp (der)n.

chunk 1.Gnoddel (der)n.; 2.Knoddel (der)n.; 3.Schiwwel (der)n.

chunky rundleiwich, adj.; **person** 1.Gnoddel (der)n.; 2.Knoddel (der)n.

church 1.Gmee (die)n.; 2.Gotteshaus (es)n.; 3.Karrich (die) n.; Karriche, pl.; **affairs** Karrichwese (es)n.; **almanac** Karrichkalenner (der)n.; **attendants** Karrichleit (die)n., pl.; **bell** 1.Karrichbell (die)n.; 2.Karricheglock (die)n.; **collection** 1.Almose (die)n., pl.; 2.Karrichegeld (es)n.; **council** Karricheraat (der)n.; **day** Karrichdaag (der)n.; **dedication** Karricheiweihing (die)n.; **disagreement** Karrichwese (es)n.; **door** Karrichdier (die)n.; **festival** Karrichfescht (es)n.; **going Christian** Karrichgrischt (der) n.; **louse** Karrichlaus (die)n.; **member** Gemeensglied (es)n.; **mouse** Karrichmaus (die)n.; **paper or journal** Karrichzeiding (die)n.; **record** Karrichbuch (es)n.; **scandal** Karrichschand (die)n.; **school** Karichschul (die)n.; **service** 1.Goddesdi(e)nscht (der)n.; 2.Karrichedi(e) nscht (der)n.; **steeple** Karrichtarn (der)n.; **window** Karrichfenschder (es)n.

churchgoer Karrichgenger (der)n.

churchman Karrichmann (der)n.

churchyard Karrich(e)hof (der)n.; Karric(e)hef, pl.

churn zamme/schtosse, v.; zammegschtosse, pp.; **butter** 1.Budder (der)n. (-- drehe); 2.schtoose, v.; gschtoose, pp.

chute Schuss (der)n.

chyle 1.Millichsaft (die)n.; 2.Naahrungssaft (die)n.

cider 1.Eppelwei (der)n.; 2.Seider (der)n.; **vinegar from the lees** ab/keldre, v.; abgekeldert, pp.; **press** 1.Kelderhaus (es)n.; 2.Seiderpress (es)n.

cigar Sigaer (die)n.; Sigaere, pl.

cinnamon 1.Simmet (der)n.; 2.Simmetrinn (die)n.

cinquefoil Fimffingergraut (es)n.

cipher 1.Null (die)n.; 2.rechle, v.; gerechelt, pp.; 3.rechne, v.; gerechent, pp.; 4.ziffere, v.; geziffert, pp.

circle 1.Grees (der)n.; 2.Gringel (der)n.; 3.Krees (der)n.; 4.Kreis (der)n.; 5.Ring (der)n.; 6.Ringel (es)n.; 7.zaerkle, v.; gezaerkelt, pp.

Cc

circuit

circuit 1.Bezaerrick (es)n.; 2.Umrees (die)n.
circular flower bed Blummering (der)n.
circular saw 1.Zaerkelsaeg (die)n.; 2.Zarickelseeg (die)n.;
Zarickelseege, pl.
circulation Umlaaf (der)n.
circumference 1.auserum Moos (die)n.; 2.Umfang (der)n.;
3.Umschtand (der)n.; Umschtende, pl.
cirrose ranklich, adj.
citation Aafehrung (die)n.
cite aa/fiehre, v.; aagfiehrt, pp.
citizen Birger (der)n.
city Schtadt (die)n.; Schtedt, pl.; **council** Schadtraat (der)
n.; **folk** 1.Schadtleit (die)n.; Schteddler, pl.;
2.Schtadtleit (die)n., pl.; 3.Schteddelleit (die)n.; **life**
Schadtlewe (es)n.
claim 1.Aaschpruch (der)n.; 2.fodd(e)re, v.; gfoddert, pp.;
3.Fodderes (es)n.
clam Muschel (der)n.
clamber across niwwer/graddle, v.; niwwergegraddelt, pp.
clamp 1.Aaschpruch (der)n.; 2.Glamm (die)n.; Glamme,
pl.; 3.Klamm (die)n.
clandestinely 1.hehling(s), adv.; 2.hehlingerweis, adj.;
3.verschtohle, adv.; 4.verschtohlenerweis, adv.
clap 1.blatsche, v.; geblatscht, pp. 2.Gnall (der)n.; 3.Grach
(der)n.; 4.Knall (der)n.; **hands** 1.batsche, v.; gebatscht,
pp.; 2.glappe, v.; geglappt, pp.; 3.klappe, v.; geklappt,
pp.; **shut** zu/schpringe, v.; zugschprunge, pp.
clapper Klapper (der)n.
claptrap wischwasch
clarify ab/glaare, v.; abgeglaart, pp.
clarinet Klaerinett (die)n.
clash zamme/schlagge, v.; zammegschlagge, pp.
class 1.Glass (die)n.; 2.Klass (die)n.
classis Klassis (die)n.
clatter 1.Geeglebber (es)n.; 2.glebbere, v.; geglebbert, pp.
claw 1.Glooe (die)n.; Glooe, pl.; 2.Klooe (die)n.; 3.kratze,
v.; gekratzt, pp.; **hammer** 1.Glooe-Hammer (der)n.;
2.Neggelrobber (der)n.; **of a bear** Baereglooe (die)n.
clay Lette (der)n.; **(blue)** Ledde (der)n.; **(red)** Lehme (der)n.;
soil 1.Lehmeboddem (der)n.; 2.(blue) Leddebodde(m)
(der)n.; 3.(red) Lehnebodde(m) (der) n.
clayey lettich, adj.; **(blue)** leddich, adj.; (red) lehmich, adj.
clean 1.ab/butzt, v.; abgebutzt, pp.; 2.ab/wische, v.;
abgewischt, pp.; 3.butze, v.; gebutzt, pp.; 4.fege, v.;
gfegt, pp.; 5.gereinicht, adj.; 6.naus/fege, v.; nausgfegt,
pp.; 7.rei, adj.; 8.rein, adj.; 9.sauwer mache, v.; sauwer
gemacht, pp.; 10.seiwerlich, adj.; **a stable** aus/mischde,
v.; ausgemischt, pp.; **away** weck/butze, v.; weckgebutzt
pp.; **by boiling** aus/koche, v.; ausgekocht, pp.; **house**
butze, v.; gebutzt, pp. (Haus --); **off** ab/butzt, v.;
abgebutzt, pp.; **out** raus/butze, v.; rausgebutzt, pp.; **up**
1.fege (sich --)v.; gfekt, pp.; 2.uff/butze (sich --)v.;
uffgebutzt, v.; 3.uff/butze, v.; uffgebutzt, pp.
cleaner Feger (der)n.
cleaning (confounded) Butzerei (die)n.
cleanliness Sauwerkeet (die)n.

clodhopper

cleanly 1.sauwer, adj.; 2.seiwerlich, adj.
cleanse 1.reiniche, v.; gereinicht, pp.; 2.seiwere, v.;
gseiwert, pp.
cleansing Reiniching (die)n.
clear 1.frei, adj.; 2.glaar, adj.; 3.glaare, v.; geglaart, pp.;
4.glor, adj.; 5.glorensich, adj.; 6.hell, adj.; 7.klor, adj.;
8.klore, v.; geklort, pp.; 9.rechfaertiche, v.;
rechgfaerticht, pp.; **a pond of fish** aus/fische, v.;
ausgfischt, pp.; **of furniture or rubbish** aus/raame. v.
ausgeraamt, pp.; **(of weeds)** sauwer, adj.; **away superfluous shoots** (on vines or plants) ab/ranke, v.;
abgerankt, pp.; **off** 1.ab/newwle, v.; abgenewwelt, pp.;
2.(a table) ab/raame, v.; abgeraamt, pp.; 3.(of weather)
a.ab/glaare, v.; abgeglaart, pp.; b.ab/helle, v.; abghellt,
pp.; **up** 1.ab/blose, v.; abgeblost, pp.; 2.klore, v.;
geklort, pp.; 3.uff/glaare, v.; uffgeglaart, pp.;
4.uff/helle, v.; uffghellt, pp.
cleave to 1.aa/gle(e)we, v.; aageglebt, pp.; 2.aa/klewe, v.;
aageklebt, pp.
cleaver 1.Butscher-Ax (die)n.; 2.Hackmesser (es)n.
clematis Hopp (die)n. (wildi --e)
clergyman Breddicher (der)n.; Breddicher, pl.
clerical parremaessich, adj.
clerk Glarick (der)n.; Glaricke, pl.
clever 1.gewichst, adj.; 2.gscheit, adj.; 3.klu(u)ch, adj.;
4.langkeppich, adj.; 5.schalu, adj.; 6.schpitzohrich, adj.
cleverness Gscheidheet (die)n.
click beetle (which attacks smoked ham) Schnellkeffer
(der)n.; Schnellkeffer, pl.
click clack! klipp klapp!
climate Wittring (die)n.
climb 1.glettere, v.; geglettert, pp.; 2.graddle, v.; gegraddelt,
pp.; 3.kraddle, v.; gegkraddelt, pp.; **out** naus/schteige,
v.; nausgschtigge, pp.; **up** 1.nuff/glettere,v .;
nuffgeglettert, pp.; 2.nuff/graddle, v.; nuffgegraddelt,
pp.; 3.nuff/schteige, v.; nuffgschteigge, pp.;
4.ruff/graddle, v.; ruffgegraddelt, pp.
climbing ranklich, adj.; **false buckwheat** 1.Zaahreeb (die)
n.; 2.Zohreeb (die)n.; **honeysuckle** Geesblaat (es)n.
clinch 1.Niet (der)n.; 2.um/niede, v.; umgeniet, pp.; **iron**
Setz, n.; **to** 1.aa/henge, v.; aaghonke, pp.; 2.(especially
evil consequences) aa/hafte, v.; aaghaft, pp.
clinging 1.aahengisch, adj.; 2.aahenkisch, adj.
clingstone 1.Glingschtee (der)n.; 2.Klingschtee (der)n.
clip schere, v.; gschore, pp.; **of a horseshoe** Griff (der)n.
clique Ring (der)n.
cloak Mantel (der)n.
clock 1.Hausuhr (die)n.; 2.Uhr (die)n.; Uhre, pl.; **case**
Uhrekaschde (der)n.; **dial** Uhregsicht (es)n.; **spring**
Uhreschpring (die)n.
clockmaker Uhremacher (der)n.; Uhremacher, pl.
clod 1.Erdglumbe (der)n.; 2.Erdscholle (der)n.;
3.Grundscholle (der)n.; 4.Scholle (der)n.
cloddy 1.glumbich, adj.; 2.schollich, adj.
clodhopper 1.Baerrickgnabber (der)n.; 2.Baerrickgnippel
(der)n.; 3.Buschgnibbel (der)n.; 4.Buschknibbel (der)
n.; 5.Schollehupser (der)n.

Cc

clog | cockscomb

clog 1.hinnere, v.; ghinnert, pp.; 2.uff/schtobbe, v.; uffgschtoppt, pp.; 3.verschtobbe, v.; verschtoppt, pp.; 4.zu/schtecke, v.; zugschteckt, pp.; 5.zu/zabbe, v.; zugezappt, pp.

close 1.gnapps, adv.; 2.hoorgnapps, adj.; 3.knapps, adj.; 4.naekscht, adv.; 5.neegscht, adv.; 6.schtickich, adj.; 7.zu/mache, v.; zug(e)macht, pp.; 8.zugeh, v.; zugange, pp.; **by pressing together** zuklemme, v.; zugeklemmt, pp.; **by squeezing** zudricke, v.; zugedrickt, pp.; **down** zuschtelle, v.; zugschtellt, pp.

close (of air) schmodderich, adj.

closed 1.abgschtoppt, adj.; 2.ze = zu; 3.zue, adj.; 4.zuner, adj.; 5.zuni, adj.

closely rooted verwarzelt, adj.

closing hymn Schlusslied (es)n.

clot (of blood) gerinne, v.; gerunne, pp.

cloth 1.duche, adj.; 2.Abdrickellumbe (der)n.; **for straining** Seihduch (es)n.; **made from gnoddelwoll** Gnoddelwolleduch (es)n.; **put on face of a corpse** Schweesduch (es)n.; **goods** Duchschtofft (es)n.

clothe 1.aa/gleede, v.; aagegleedt, pp.; 2.begleede, v.; begleedt, pp.; 3.gleede, v.; gegleedt, pp.; 4.kleede, v.; gekleedt, pp.

clothed aageduh, v. (past tense)

clothes 1.Gleed (es)n.; Gleeder, pl.; 2.Gleeder (die)n., pl.; **basket** Weschkareb (der)n.; **brush** Gleederbascht (die) n.; **closet** 1.Gleederkammer (die)n.; 2.Gleederkemmerli (es)n.; 3.Kammer (die)n.; Kemmer, pl.; **hook** Gleederhoke (der)n.; **prop** 1.Wesch-schteiber (der)n.; 2.Weschschdeiber (der)n.; **wringer** 1.Ausdreher (der)n.; 2.Weschwringer (der)n.

clothespin 1.Klamm (die)n.; 2.Weschglamm (die)n.; 3.Weschschpell (die)n.

clothing 1.Begleeding (die)n.; 2.Begleedung (die)n.; 3.Hilli (die)n.

clotted glewerich, adj.

cloud 1.Wolk (die)n.; Wolke, pl.; 2.Gewelk (es)n.

cloud (presaging windy weather) Windwolk (die)n.

cloudburst Wolkebruch (der)n.

clouded by moisture schwitze, v.; gschwitzt, pp.

cloudy 1.drieb, adj.; 2.wolkich, adj.

cloudy berry Molkebeer (die)n.

clove 1.Naegli (es)n.; 2.Negg(e)li (es)n.; 3.Negg(e)li (es)n.; Negg(e)lin, pl.; 4.Neggelche (es)n.; Neggelcher, pl.

cloven foot 1.Glooe (die)n.; Glooe, pl.; 2.Glooefuss (der) n.; 3.Klooe (die)n.

clover 1.Glee (der)n.; 2.Klee (der)n.; **(for seed)** Someglee (der)n.; **chaff** Gleeschprau (die)n.; **field** Gleefeld (es) n.; **flower** 1.Gleeblumm (die)n.; 2.Gleekopp (der)n.; **hay** Gleehoi (es)n.; **huller** Gleebutzer (der)n.; **leaf** Gleeblaatt (es)n.; **seed** 1.Gleesome (der)n.; 2.Gleesume (der)n.; **sod** Gleewaasem (der)n.; **stalk** Gleeschtengel (der)n.

clown 1.Hanswascht (der)n.; 2.Narr (der)n.; Narre, pl.; 3.Zwickel (der)n.; Zwickel, pl.

club 1.Briggel (der)n.; 2.briggele, v.; gebriggelt, pp.; 3.Gnibbel (der)n.; 4.Hewwel (der)n.; 5.Knippel (der) n.; 6.Knittel (der)n.; 7.Priggel (der)n.; 8.vergnipple, v.; vergnippelt, pp.; **foot** Schtollfuss (der)n.

clubbing 1.Briggelsupp (die)n.; 2.Priggel (der)n.

cluck 1.gluckse, v.; gegluckst, pp.; 2.gluxe, v.; gegluxt, pp.; 3.kluck, adj.; 4.kluckse, v.; gekluckst, pp.; **of a liquid running out of a bottle** kluck, adj. **clucking** 1.glucksich, adj.; 2.gluxich, adj.

clump (of bushes) Heckepusch (der)n.; **of grass or shrubbery** Pusch (der)n.; **or bunch of hair** Wusch (der)n.

clumsy 1.dabbich, adj.; 2.glumsich, adj.; 3.ungschickt, adj.; 4.uugschickt, adj.; **fellow** 1.Dappel (der)n.; 2.Dappes (der)n.

clutches 1.Glooe (die)n.; Glooe, pl.; 2.Gluppe (die)n.; 3.Klooe (die)n.; 4.Kluppe (die)n.

clyster grischdiere, v.; grischdiert, pp.

co-heir Beiaerwer (der)n.

coach Kutsch (die)n.; Kutsche, pl.

coachman Fuhrmann (der)n.; Fuhrmenner, pl.

coagulate gerinne, v.; gerunne, pp.

coal Kohl (die)n.; Kohle, pl.; **black** kohlschwatz, adv.; **breaker** Brecher (der)n.; **dust** Kohlschtaab (der)n.; **fire** Kochfeier (es)n.; **oil** Kohleel (es)n.; **scuttle** 1.Kohle-Eemer (der)n.; Kohle-Eemer, pl.; 2.Kohlekessel (der)n.; Kohlekessel, pl.; 3.Kohlekiwwel (der)n.; Kohlekiwwel, pl.; **shed** Kohlhaus (es)n.

coarse 1.grobb, adj.; 2.rauh, adj.; **fellow** Knippel (der)n.

coarser 1.grewwer, adv.; 2.growwer, adv.

coarsest 1.grebbscht, adj.; 2.grobbscht, adj.

coasting course Rutsch (die)n.

coat 1.Reckelche (es)n.; 2.Rock (der)n.; Reck, pl.; **collar** Rockgraage (der)n.; **pocket** Rocksack (der)n.; **sleeve** Rockaermel (der)n.; Rockaermel, pl.; **tail** Rockfliggel (der)n.

coax tiddeliere, v.; tiddeliert, pp.; **by soft words** 1.aa/ schmeechle, v.; aagschmeechelt, pp.; 2.aaschmeechle, v.; aagschmeechelt, pp.; **to a place** haer/locke, v.; haergelockt, pp.

cob Krutze (der)n.

cobble Wacke (der)n.

cobbler 1.Schuhflicker (der)n.; 2.Schumacher (der)n.; 3.Schuschder (der)n.; 4.Schuster (der)n.

cobbler's hammer Schuhhammer (der)n.; **wax** Schuhbech (es)n.

cobweb 1.Schpinnenescht (es)n.; Schpinneneschder, pl.; 2. Schpinneweb (es)n.; Schpinnewewer, pl.

cocculus Indicus 1.Godelskaern (die)n.; 2.Gogelskaern (die)n.

cock (a gun) schpanne, v.; gschpannt, pp.

cock-a-doodle-do 1.Gickerigi (der)n.; 2.Gickerigu (der)n.

cock with ruffed plumage Schtrupphaahne (der)n.

cockerel Haehnche (es)n.

cockle Raad (die)n.; Raade, pl.

cocklebur Hunsglett (die)n.

cockroach Schwob (der)n.; Schwowe, pl.; **trap** Schwowefall (die)n.

cockscomb Haahnekamm (der)n.

Cc

coconut

coconut 1.Kokonuss (die)n.; 2.Maerreoi (es)n.

coddle 1.verbobble, v.; verbobbelt, pp.; 2.verwehne, v.;
verwehnt, pp.

codling Kochabbel (der)n.

coerce zwinge, v.; gezwunge, pp.

coercion Zwang (der)n.

coffee Kaffi (der)n.; **bean** Kaffibohn (die)n.; **cake** Kaffikuche
(der)n.; **grounds** Kaffisatz (der)n.; **mill** Kaffimiehl (die)n.;
pot 1.Kaffikann (die)n.; Kaffikanne, pl.; 2.Kaffikessel
(der)n.; **roaster** Kaffireeschder (der)n.

coffin 1.Dodelaad (die)n.; 2.Laad (die)n.; Laade, pl.;
3.Sarrich (der)n.; **maker** 1.Laademacher (der)n.;
Laademacher, pl.; 2.Laademecher (der)n.

cog Kamm (der)n.; Kamme; Kemm, pl.

cogwheel Karnmraad (die)n.; Kammredder, pl.

coincide iwwereischtimme, v.; iwwereigschtimmt, pp.

coire 1.ab/gnabbere, v.; abgegnabbert, pp.; 2.feckle, v.;
gfeckelt, pp.; 3.ficke, v.; gfickt, pp.; 4.fuchse, v.;
gfuchst, pp.; 5.gnappere, v.; gegnappert, pp.

colander 1.Kaesseih (die)n.; 2.Keesseih (die)n.

cold (illness) 1.Biebser (der)n.; 2.Kalt (der, es)n.;
3.Verkelding (die)n.; 4.Schnubbe (der)n.; 5.Schnuppe
(der)n.; **(storage) cellar** Kiehlkeller (der)n.; **shivers**
1.Grissel (die)n., pl.; 2.Krissel (die)n., pl.; **colder;**

coldest kalt; kelder; keltscht, adj.; **cold(ness)** Kelt (die)n.

coldchisel 1.Kalkmeesel (der)n.; 2.Kaltmeesel (der)n.

colic Kollic (der)n.; **root** Deiwelsabbis (watzel) (die)n.

collapse 1.eischtaerze, v.; eigschtaertzt, pp.;
2.zamme/falle, v.; zammegfalle, pp.;
3.zamme/gnicke, v.; zammegegnickt, pp.

collar 1.Graage (der)n.; Greege, pl.; 2.Halsband (es)n.;
3.Halsgraage (der)n.

collect 1.eisammle, v.; eigsammelt, pp.; 2.Kollekt (es)n.;
3.sammle, v.; gsammelt, pp.; 4.uff/sammle, v.;
uffgsammelt, pp.; 5.zamme/draage, v.; zammegedraage,
pp.; 6.zamme/mache, v.; zammegemacht, pp.; **by flooding** zamme/schwemme, v.; zammegschwemmt, pp.;
money eidreiwe, v.; eigedriwwe, pp.

collection 1.Kollekt (es)n.; 2.Opfergeld (es)n.; **basket in
church** 1.Karwel (es)n.; 2.Karwli (es)n.

collide 1.zamme/renne, v.; zammegerennt, pp.;
2.zamme/ schtosse, v.; zammegschtosse, pp.

collie 1.Schepphund (der)n.; 2.Schofhund (der)n.

colliery Kohlegrub (die)n.

colon Grimmdar(e)m (der)n.

color 1.faerwe, v.; gfaerbt, pp.; 2.Farb (die)n.; Farwe;
Farewe, pl.; 3.farewe, v.; gfarebt, pp.; 4.Far(r)eb (die)n.;
Farewe, Farwe, pl.; **scheme** Grundfarb (die)n.

colored far(e)wich, adj.

colt 1.Hutsch (es)n.; 2.Hutschel (es)n.; 3.Hutschelche (es)
n.; 4.Hutschli (es)n.

colts-foot 1.Hasselwatzel (die)n.; 2.Hutschefuss (der)n.

comb Schtreel (der)n.; Schtreel, pl. **(of a rooster)** Kamm (der)
n.; Kamme; Kemm, pl.; **oneself** schtreele (sich --)v.;
gschtreelt, pp.; **out** 1.aus/schtrahle, v.; ausgschtrahlt,
pp.; 2.raus/schtraehle, v.; rausgschtraehlt pp.

combat Kamf (der)n.

commence

combine 1.verbinne, v.; verbunne, pp.; 2.vereeniche, v.;
vereenicht, pp.

Come along! Kumm mit!

come 1.gschehe, v.; is gschehe, gschehne, pp.; 2.kumme, v.; is
kumme, pp.; **(of butter)** zamme/geh, v.; zammegange,
pp.; **across** aa/dreffe, v.; aagedroffe, pp.; **along with**
mit/kumme, v.; is mitkumme, pp.; **apart** ausenanner/geh,
v.; ausenannergange, pp.; **around** rum/kumme, v.; is
rumkumme, pp.; **away** weck/kumme, v.; weckkumme,
pp.; **back** zerick/kumme, v.; zerickkumme, pp.; **by chance**
bei/laafe, v.; beigeloffe, pp.; **down** runner/kumme, v.;
runnerkummer, pp.; **early** Zeit (die)n. (bei -- kumme);
fortuitously bei/kumme, v.; is kumme, pp.; **forward**
vor/kumme, v.; vorkumme, pp.; **from** 1.bei/kumme, v.; is
kumme, pp.; 2.haer/kumme, v.; haerkumme, pp.;
3.schtamme, v.; gschtammt, pp.; **home** heemkumme, v.;
in 1.rei/kumme, v.; reikumme, pp.; 2.rei/packe (sich --)v.;
reigepackt, pp.; **into bearing** (of an orchard)
no(och)wachse, v.; no(och)gewachst, pp.; **off** 1.ab/geh, v.;
abgange, pp.; 2. (in small particles) ab/brockle, v.;
abgebrockelt, pp.; **on** (a thunderstorm) uff/schteige, v.;
uffgschtigge, pp.; **out** 1.raus/kumme, v.; is rauskumme,
pp.; 2.(as hair) aus/falle, v.; ausgfalle, pp.; 3.(fortuitously)
raus/haschble, v.; rausghaschbelt, pp.; 4.(in drops)
raus/ dropse, v.; rausgedropst, pp.; 5.(to a place)
naus/kumme, v.; nauskumme, pp.; 6.(tumultuously)
raus/ dunnere, v.; rausgedunnert, pp.; **over**
1.niwwer/kumme, v.; is niwwerkumme, pp.;
2.riwwer/kumme, v.; riwwerkumme, pp.; **stamping out**
raus/schtampe, v.; rausgschtampt, pp.; **through**
darich/kumme, v.; is darichkumme, pp.; **to a gathering**
bei/laafe, v.; beigeloffe, pp.; **to a meeting** bei/kumme, v.;
is kumme, pp.; **to an end** ausgschpielt, adj.; **to meet**
engegekumme, adj.; **to nothing** futsch, adv.; **to pass**
zu/dreffe (sich --) v.; zugedroffe, pp.; **to the aid of** 1.
bei/schpringe, v.; beischprunge, pp.; 2.zu/schpringe, v.;
zugschprunge, pp.; **to the end of a frenzy** aus/deiwle (sich
--)v.; ausgedeiwelt, pp.; **together** (by appointment)
zammernannerkumme, v.; zammernannergkumme, pp.;
together (in a social gathering) zamme/laafe, v.;
zummegeloffe, pp.; **up** ruff/ kumme, v.; ruffgekumme,
pp.; **upon suddenly** iwwerrasche, v.; iwwerrascht, pp.;
upon unexpectedly dezuschtolpere, v.; dezugschtolpert,
pp.

comet Kumet (der)n.

comfortable 1.aagenehm, adj.; 2.aaheemlich, adj.;
3.bequem, adj.; 4.gemechlich, adj.; 5.gemietlich,
adj.; 6.gschpierich, adj. (gut --); 7.leidich, adj.

comfrey 1.Schwarzwatzel (die)n.; 2.Schwatzwatzel (die)n.

comic beliddisch, adj.

coming from the front vannebei, adv.; **from the side**
newebei, adv.

comma Komma (es)n.

command 1.Adder (die)n.; 2.baase, v.; gebasst, pp.;
3.Befehl (der)n.; 4.befehle, v.; befohle, pp.; 5.Gebott
(es)n.; 6.Gehees (es)n.; 7.heese, v.; gheese, pp.

commandment Gesetz (es)n.

commence 1.aa/fange, v.; aagfange, pp.; 2.aa/lege, v.; aagelekt, pp.; 3.Handel (der)n.; 4.Handelschaft (die)n.;
5.Handelwese (es)n.

250

Cc

commit an offence · condition

commit an offence bose, v.; gebost, pp.

commit suicide um/bringe (sich --)v.; umgebrocht, pp.; **by drowning** verseefe (sich --)v.; verseeft, pp.

commodities Kramm (der)n.

common barnyard fowl Mischthinkel (es)n.; **evening primrose** 1.Kewwich (der)n.; Kewwich(e), pl.; 2.Rawunselgraut (es)n.; **houndstongue** Hunsglett (die)n. (gleeni --); **mallow** Kaesbabbel (die)n.; **motherwort** Hatz(g)schpaerr; **mugwort** Aldifraa (die)n.; **plaintain** Wegdred(d)er (der)n. (breeder --); **sense** 1.Vernumft (die)n.; 2.Vernunft (die)n.; 3.Verschtand (der)n.; **smartweed** Flehgraut (es)n.; **speedwell** (Culver's root) Ehrenpreis (der)n.; **thistle** Disch(d)el (die)n.; Dischdle, pl.; **weed** fuchsschwans, adj.; **white lily** Gaardelilye (die)n.

common(ly) 1.allgemee, adj.; 2.allgemei, adj.; 3.allgemein, adj.

commonly 1.gewehnichlich, adv.; 2.g(e)wehnlich, adv.

commonwealth Schtaat (der)n.

commotion 1.Gezewwel (es)n.; 2.Uffrohr (der)n.

communicant Kammunikant (der)n.

communion 1.Abendmahl (es)n.; 2.Awendmohl (es)n.

communion table Aldaar (der)n.; Aldaare, pl.

community Gemeeschaft (die)n.

compact Verbinnung (die)n.; **hard droppings** (of many animals) Knoddel (der)n.

companion 1.Gesell (der)n.; 2.Kumpani (die)n.

companionable gsellich, adj.

company 1.Gsellschaft (die)n.; 2.Kumpani (die)n.

comparable vergleichlich, adj.

compare vergleiche, v.; vergliche, pp.

comparison Vergleich (der)n.

compartment in a barn (for storing cut straw) Hecksel-kammer (die)n.

compass Kumbass (die)n.

compass (circle dividers) Zaerkel (der)n.; **saw** Lochseeg (die)n.

compassion 1.Mitgfiehl (es)n.; 2.Mitleid(es) (es)n.

compassionate mit/leidich, adj.

compel 1.aa/schpanne, v.; aagschpannt, pp.; 2.zwenge, v.; gezwengt, pp.

compelled to do something draamisse, v.; draagemisst, pp.; **to get away** weck/misse, v.; weckgemisst, pp.; **to get up** uff/misse, v.; uffgemisst, pp.; **to stop work from heat or fatigue** aus/gewwe, v.; ausgewwe, pp.

compensate 1.belohne, v.; belohnt, pp.; 2.beluhne, v.; beluhnt, pp.

compensation 1.Belohning (die)n.; 2.Belohnung (die)n.; 3.Bezaahling (die)n.; 4.Bezaahlung (die)n.

complain 1.begraeme (sich --)v.; begraemt, pp.; 2.begreckse (sich --)v.; begreckst, pp.; 3.bobere, v.; gebobert, pp.; 4.glaage, v.; geglaagt, pp.; 5.klaage, v.; geklaakt, pp.; 6.maunse, v.; gemaunst, pp.; 7.rum/gnickse, v.; rumge-gnickst, pp.; 8.verglaage (sich --)v.; verglaakt, pp.; 9.vergreckse (sich --)v.; vergreckst, pp.; 10.yaunse, v.; geyaunst, pp.; **about** beschwere (sich --)v.; beschwert, pp.; **of sickness** 1.grenkle, v.; gegrenkelt, pp.; 2.krenkle,

v.; gekrenkelt, pp.; **constantly** nengere, v.; genengert, pp.; **irritably** vergraunse (sich --)v.; vergraunst, pp.

complaining piensich, adj.

complaint 1.Aaklach (der)n.; 2.Glaak (die)n.; 3.Grecks (die)n.; 4.Klaak (die)n.; 5.Sucht (die)n.

complaisant beheeflich, adj.

complete 1.alles mit nei gnumme, adv.; adj.; 2.faddich mache, v.; faddichgemacht, pp.; 3.vollbringe, v.; vollbrocht, pp.; 4.vollschtennich, adv.; 5.faddich, adj.

completely vollschder, adj.; **covering the ground** (as of apples or potatoes) 1.geriddelt (voll) adv.; 2.geruddelt (voll) adv.; **done** fix un faddich, adj.

complexion 1.Gsicht(s)fareb (die)n.; 2.Hautfareb (die)n.

compliment 1.Kambliment (es)n.; 2.Kumbliment (es)n.

compliments Gruss (der)n.

comply with verwilliche, v.; verwillicht, pp.

compose zamme/setze, v.; zammegesetzt, pp.

compositor Setzer (der)n.

compounds of anne are equal to compounds of hi anne = hi

comprehend 1.begreife, v.; begriffe, pp.; 2.eisehne, v.; eigsehne, pp.; 3.ergreife, v.; ergriffe, pp.; 4.vernemme, v.; vernumme, pp.; 5.verschteh, v.; verschtanne, pp.

comprehensible ergreifich, adj.

comprehension 1.Begriff (der)n.; 2.Ergreifing (die)n.

compress zamme/dricke, v.; zammegedrickt, pp.

compromise bei/lege, v.; beigelegt, pp.

compute 1.ausrechle, v.; ausgrechelt,pp.; 2.rechle, v.; gerechelt, pp.

computer Komputer (der)n.

comrade Kummeraad (der)n.; Kummeraade, pl.

concave hohl, adj.;

conceal 1.verbaerge, v.; verborge, pp.; 2.verhehle, v.; ver-hehlt, pp.; 3.weck/schtecke, v.; weckgschtocke, pp.

concealed Verborge (es)n.

concealer Hehler (der)n.; Hehler, pl.

conceit Eibildichkeet (die)n.

conceited 1.eibildisch, adj.; 2.grossfiehlich, adj.; 3.ei/bilde (sich --)v.; eigebildt, pp.; 3.iwwergscheit, adj.

conceivable begreiflich, adj.

conceive begreife, v.; begriffe, pp.

concern 1.aa/geh, v.; aagange, pp.; 2.Aageleges (es)n.; 3.Bekimmernis (die)n.; 4.Kimmernis (die)n.; 5.Lossement (es)n.; 6.S(ch)ippschaft (die)n.

concerned about bekimmere (sich --)v.; bekimmert, pp.; **for** aagelegge, adj.

concerning vunwege, prep.

conch Schneckeharn (es)n.

conclude 1.b(e)schliesse, v.; b(e)schlosse, pp.; 2.faddich mache, v.; faddichgemacht, pp.

conclusion 1.B(e)schluss (der)n.; 2.Bschluss (der)n.; 3.Schluss (der)n.

concur iwwereischtimme, v.; iwwereigschtimmt, pp.

condition 1.Adder (die)n.; 2.Bedingung (die)n.; 3.Schtand

(Continued on page 252)

Cc

condition (continued)   construct

(Continued from page 251)

(der)n.; 4.Umschtand (der)n.; Umschtende, pl.;
5.Zuschtand (der)n.; Zuschtende, pl.

conduct 1.halde, v.; ghalde, pp.; 2.Lewe(n)szeeche (es)n.;
3.Uff-fiehrung (die)n.; 4.Wandel (der)n.; **oneself**
1.bedraage (sich --)v.; bedraagt, pp.; 2.schicke (sich --
)v.; gschickt, pp.

confab Gschpraech (es)n.

confess 1.beichde, v.; gebeicht, pp.; 2.bekenne, v.;
bekennt, pp.; 3.bschteh, v.; bschtanne, pp.;
4.gschteh, v.; gschtanne, pp.; 5.uff/eegne, v.;
uffge-eegnet, pp.

confession 1.Beicht (die)n.; 2.Bekenntnis (es)n.; **of faith**
Glaabensbekanntnis (es)n.

confessional Beichtschtuhl (der)n.

confide a secret aa/verdraue, v.; aaverdraut, pp.; **in**
zudraue, v.; zugedraut, pp.

confidence 1.Verdraue (es)n.; 2.verdraue, v.; verdraut,
pp.; 3.Zudraue (es)n.; 4.Zuverdraue (es)n.;
5.Zuversicht (die)n.

confidently 1.gedroscht, adj.; 2.zuversichtlich, adj.

confine ei/schparre, v.; eigschpatt, pp.

confined 1.Kinsbett (es)n. (ins -- kumme); 2.kumme, v.;
kumme, pp.(ins Bett --)

confinement (for childbirth) Kinsbett (es)n.

confirm 1.b(e)schtaetiche, v.; b(e)schtaeticht, pp.;
2.bekreftiche, v.; bekrefticht, pp.; 3.bschteediche, v.;
bschteedicht, pp.; 4.farme, v.; gfaamt, pp.;
5.kunfermiere, v.; kunfermiert, pp.; **a person in**
church ei/segne, v.; eigsegent, pp.

confirmation 1.Kumfermierung (die)n.; 2.Kunfermiering (die)n.

confirmed drunkard Sauflodel (der)n.

conflagration Brand (der)n.

conform to no(och)lewe, v.; no(och)gelebt, pp.

confound bedroffe, adj.

confound it 1.bettelgotts!, interj.; 2.Gewesser (es)n. (dunner
uns --); 3.Grampet (die)n. (des soll dei -- hole);
4.Grampet (die)n.(Gotts --); 5.Grampet (die)n.(Gotts --);
6.Greiz (es)n. (Gotts -- nochemol); 7.grenk (Gotts --);
8.Haagelwetter (es)n.; 9.kotzmardsapperlott nochermol!, interj.; 10.Kreiz (es)n. (Gotts -- nochemol)

confounded thing Waerderswese (es)n.

confounded(ly) 1.dunnerlotters, adj.; 2.haagels, adv.; 3.infaam
(t), adj.; 4.kisselwetters, adv.; 5.luders, adj.; 6.schtaans,
adv.; 7.schtaerns, adv.; 8.verdollt, adv.; 9.verflickt, adj.;
10.verflixt, adj.; 11.verhenkert, adj.; 12.verschinnert, adj.

confuse 1.bedroffe, adj.; 2.uff/huddle, v.; uffghuddelt,
pp.; 3.verhuddle, v. verhuddelt, pp.; 4.verkollebiere,
v.; verkollebiert, pp.; 5.verwa(e)rre, v.; verwa(e)rrt,
pp.; 6.verwickle, v.; verwickelt, pp.

confused 1.aerr, adj.; 2.vergelschdert, adj.3.waerr, adj.

confusion 1.Gedumor (es)n.; 2.Huddlerei (die)
n.;3.Waerrwese (es)n.; 4.Wattschaft (die)n.

congratulate 1.Glick (es)n. (es -- winsche); 2.gratliere, v.;
gratliert, pp.

congregate zamme/geh, v.; zammegange, pp.

congregation 1.G(e)mee (die)n. (in Old Order Amish and
Mennonite usage); 2.Versammling (die)n.;
3.Versammlung (die)n.

congregational gemeindlich, adj.

conjecture 1.Mutmaasing (die)n.; 2.mutmaase, v.;
gemutmaast, pp.; 3.mutmoose, v.; gemutmoost, pp.

conjuring book Hexebuch (es)n.

connecting pole (of a wagon) Langkwid (die)n.

conniption fits Katzegichtre (die)n., pl.

conquer 1.benniche, v.; gebennicht, pp.; 2.iwwerkumme,
iwwerkumme, pp.; 3.iwwerweldich(e), v.;
iwwerweldicht, pp.; 4.iwwerwinde, v.; iwwerwunne,
pp.; 5.iwwerwinne, v.; iwwerwunne, pp.; 6.sieche, v.;
gsiecht, pp.; 7.siege, v.; gsiecht, pp.

Conrad 1.Kuni (der)n.; 2.Kunraad (der)n.

conscience G(e)wisse (es)n.

conscienceless gewisselos, adj.

conscientious gewisse(n)haft, adj.

consecrate ei/segne, v.; eigsegent, pp.

consecutively nochenanner, adv.

consent 1.ei/geh, v.; eigange, pp.; 2.ei/williche, v.;
eigewillicht, pp.; 3.eibilliche, v.; eibillicht, pp.; **to**
bewilliche, v.; bewillicht, pp.

consequences Folge (die)n., pl.

consider 1.b(e)sinne (sich --)v.; b(e)sunne, pp.;
2.bedeide, v.; bedeidt, pp.; 3.bedenke, v.; bedenkt,
pp.; 4.iwwerdrachde, v.; iwwerdracht, pp.;
5.iwwerlege, v.; iwwerlekt, pp.; 6.no(och)denke, v.;
no(och)gedenkt, pp.; 7.schetze, v.; gschetzt, pp.

considerable 1.aasehnlich, adj.; 2.bedeitend, adj.;
3.ordlich, adv. 4.ziemlich viel, adj.

considerably heifich, adj.

consideration 1.Bedrachdung (die)n.; 2.Eisehnes (es)n.;
3.Kundewidde (die)n.

consist beschteh, v.; beschtanne, pp.

consistent iwwereischtimmich, adj.

consolation Troscht (der)n.

console 1.dreeschde, v.; gedreescht, pp.; 2.treeschde, v.;
getreescht, pp.

consoling 1.dreeschtlich, adj.; 2.droschtreich, adj.;
3.trostreich, adj.

conspire verschweere, v.; verschwore, pp.

constable 1.Kumschdaagler (der)n.; 2.Kunschdaaler (der)n.

constant bickering Gschwetz (es)n. (-- hie un haer);

clucking Geglucks (es)n.; **complaining** Geglaag (es)n.;
driving about Gezacker (es)n.; **questioning** Gfrog (es)
n.; **recounting of one's misery** Elendsgeglaag (es)n.

constantly 1.allfert, adv.; 2.alsfatt, adv.; 3.beschtennich,
adv.; 4.schtaetich, adj.; 5.schtennich, adj.

constipated 1.dickleiwich, adj.; 2.feschtleiwich, adj.;
3.hattleiwich, adj.; 4.verschtoppt, adj.; 5.zugschoppt, adj.

constipation 1.Daermverschtopping (die)n.; 2.fescht, adv.
(--er leib); 3.Verschtopping (die)n.

constrained to appear bei/misse, v.; beigemisst, pp.

construct uff/baue, v.; uffgebaut, pp.; **of wood** zimmere,
v.; gezimmert, pp.

Cc

consume

consume 1.uff/zehre, v.; uffgezehrt, pp.; 2.verzehre, v.; verzehrt, pp.; 3.zehre, v.; gezehrt, pp.

consumed by flames verbrenne, v.; verbrennt, pp.

consummate pedant Erzphilischder (der)n.

consumption 1.Auszehring (die)n.; 2.Verbrauch (der)n.

contagious 1.aaschteckend, adj.; 2.aerblich, adj.

contain messe, v.; gemesse, pp.

contemplate bedrachde, v.; bedracht, pp.

contemplative gedankevoll, adj.

contemporary 1.heitzedaagich, adv.; 2.heitzedaagich, adv.

contempt Verachdung (die)n.

contemptuous (for a thin watery soup) 1.Molkesupp (die) n.; 2.Wassersupp (der)n.

contend schtreide, v.; gschtridde, pp.

content(s) 1.vergniecht, adj.; 2.Inhalt (der)n.

contented 1.vergniechlich, adj.; 2.zufridde, adj.

contention 1.Reiwerei (die)n.; 2.Zank (der)n.; 3.Zankerei (die)n.; **(usually legal)** aafechding (die)n.

contentment 1.Befriedichung (die)n.; 2.Vergniege (der)n.; 3. Zufriddeheet (die)n.

contiguous to grense, v.; gegrenst, pp.

continual barking (of a small dog) Gewefz (es)n.; **driving** Gfaahr (es)n.; **hammering** Kammer (es)n.; **or repeated fast or abrupt movements** Gschussel (es)n.;

continually involved in quarrels verfochde, adj.

continuation Fattdauer (die)n.

continue 1.aa/halde, v.; aaghalde, pp.; 2.aus/halde, v.; ausghalde, pp.; 3.fatt/mache, v.; fattgemacht, pp.; 4.fatt/setze, v.; fattgesetzt, pp.; 5.waehre, v.; gewaehrt, pp.; **as an institution** fatt/halde, v.; fattghalde, pp.; **to bloom** fatt/bliehe, v.; fattgebieht, pp.; **to burn** fatt/brenne, v.; fattgebrennt, pp.; **to grow** fatt/wachse, v.; fattgewachst, pp.; **to live** fatt/lewe, v.; fattglebt, pp.; **to write** fatt/schreiwe, v.; fattgschriwwe, pp.

continue(d) to als, adv.; **hanging or clinging (to)** Kenk (es) n.; **or unusual sleeping** Gschlof (es)n.; **quarreling or wrangling** Schtreiderei (die)n.; **yelling** Geyohl (es)n.

continuous aahaltend, adj. (rare use of present participial ending); **fighting** Gfecht (es)n.

contradict widderschpreche, v.; widdergschproche, pp.; **oneself** fange, v.; gfange, pp. (sich selwer --)

contradiction Widderschpruch (der)n.

contraption Maschien (die)n.; Maschiene, pl.

contrariness Widderwaerdichkeet (die)n.

contrary 1.Gegedeel (es)n.; 2.iwwerecksich, adj.; 3.iwwerzwaerrich, adj.; 4.iwwerzwarrich, adj.; 5.widderbaerschdich, adj.; 6.zuwidder, prep.

contribute bei/draage, v.; beigedraage, pp.; **jointly** zamme/lege, v.; zammeglegt, pp.

contributed falle, v.; gfalle, pp.

contribution Beischteier (die)n.

contrivance for catching hogs by the leg Seifenger (der) n.; **for loading logs** Heblaad

contrive aus/denke, v.; ausgedenkt, pp.

controversy aafechding (die)n.

contuse verquetsche, v.; verquetscht, pp.

copperas

contusion Schinnbloder (die)n.; **of the foot** Schteebloder (die)n.

conundrum Raetsel (es)n.

convalesce uff/laese, v.

convalescence Bessering (die)n.

convalescent uff/sitze, v.; uffgsotze, pp.

convene zamme/rufe, v.; zammegerufe, pp.

convenient 1.basse, v.; gebasst, pp.; 2.basslich, adj.;3.bequem, adj.; 4.hendich, adj.; 5.hendich, adj.; 6.leicht, adj.; 7.schicklich, adj.

convent 1.Kloschder (es)n.; 2.Kloster (es)n.

convention Sammlung (die)n.

conversation 1.Geschpraech (es)n.; 2.Gschwetz (es)n.

conversion Bekehrung (die)n.

convert 1.Bekehrder (en)n.; 2.bekehre, v.; bekehrt, pp. **one's religious views** bekehre (sich --)v.; bekehrt, pp.

convey (carry) up nuff/schaffe, v.; nuffgschafft, pp.; **in writing** verschreiwe, v.; verschriwwe, pp.; **after a person** no(och)schaffe, v.; no(och)gschafft, pp.; **back** zerick/schaffe, v.; zerickgschafft, pp.; **hither** haer/schaffe, v.; haergschafft, pp.; **hither by vehicle** bei/faahre, v.; beigfaahre, pp.; **in a rig** schnaerre, v.;gschnaerrt, pp.; **to a place** hie/schaffe, v.; hiegschafft, pp.; **up** ruff/schaffe, v.; ruffgschafft, pp.

conveyancer Schreiwer (der)n.; Schreiwer, pl.

convict iwwerfiehre, v.; iwwerfiehrt, pp.

convince 1.iwwerweise, v.; iwwerwisse, pp.; 2.iwwerzeige, v.; iwwerzeicht, pp.; 3.iwwerziege, v.; iwwerzeicht, pp.

convulsion 1.Gramp (der)n.; 2.Kramp (der)n.

convulsion(s) 1.Gichder (die)n.; Gichdere, pl.; 2.Gichtre (die)n., pl.

coo gullere, v.; gegullert, pp.

cook 1.Koch (der, die)n.; Kech, pl.;2.koche; v.: gekocht, pp. **several things together** mit/koche, v.; mitgekocht, pp.

cookbook Kuchbuch (es)n.; Kuchbicher, pl.

cooked thoroughly 1.gaar, adj.; 2.maer(r)b, adj.

cookie 1.Eepies (die)n. (made at Christmas time); 2.Kichli (es)n.; Kichlin, pl.; 3.Kuche (der)n.; Kuche, pl.

cooking Koches (es)n.

cool 1.ab/kiehle, v.; abgekiehlt, pp.; 2.frisch, adj.; 3.kiehl, **corner** adj.; 4.kiehle, v.; gekiehlt, pp.; **and collected** ruhich, adj.; **down** nunner/kiehle, v.; nunnergekiehlt, pp.; **thoroughly** (as a room) aus/kiehle, v.; ausgekiehlt, pp.; **weather** (in which you go about with the hands in the pocket of your pants) Hossesackwedder (es)n.

cooler Kiehler (der)n.

coop 1.Kaschde (der)n.; Kaschde, pl.; 2.Keffich (der)n.; Keffiche, pl.

cooper 1.Fassbinner (der)n.; 2.Kiefer (der)n.

copenhagen game Ringschlack (der)n.

copper 1.Kubber (es)n.; 2.kubbern, adj.; **colored** kupperrot, adv.; **kettle** 1.Kubberkessel (der)n.; 2.(in which applebutter is boiled) Lattwaerrickkessel (der)n.

copperas Kuppruss (es)n.

253

Cc

copperhead snake — court

copperhead snake 1.Gehlkopp (der)n.; 2.Kubberschlang (die)n.; Kubberschlange, pl.; 3.Kupperkopp (der)n.

coppersmith Kubberschmitt (der)n.

copulate (of cattle) schtiere, v.; gschtiert, pp.

copy 1.ab/schreiwe, v.; abgeschriwwe, pp.; 2.Abschrift (die)n.

copy a picture ab/mole, v.; abgemolt, pp.

cord 1.Bendel (der)n.; 2.Saet (die)n.; 3.Schnur (die)n.; **of wood** 1.Glofder (es)n.; 2.Glofderhols (es)n.; **string** Kordbendel (der)n.

cordial 1.Garyel (die)n.; 2.hatzlich, adj.

core (of an apple or boil) Butze (der)n.

core (of an apple) 1.Abbelgrutze (der)n.; 2.Gnarze (der)n.; 3.Gnazze (der)n.; 4.Knarze (der)n.; **of fruit** 1.Grutze (der); Grutze, pl.; 2.Krutze (der)n.

coriander 1.Kallianner (der)n.; 2.Karyanner (der)n.; 3.Karyenner (der)n.; 4.Koriander (der)n.

Corinthians Kuhrinter (die)n., pl.

cork 1.Garrick (der)n.; 2.garricke, v.; gegarrickt, pp.;3.Karrick (der)n.; 4.karricke, v.; gekarrickt, pp.; 5.Kork (der)n.; **puller** Garrickzieger (der)n.; Garrickzieger, pl.

corkscrew 1.Karrickzieger (der)n.; 2.Korkzieger (der)n.

corn (in a grist mill) Brecher (der)n.; **on the foot** 1.Graehaag (es) n.; 2.Graehnaag (es)n.; 3.Greh(n)aag (es)n.; Greh(n)aage, pl.; 4.Grohaag (der)n.; Gorhaage, pl.; **field** Welschkannfeld (es)n.; Welschkannfelder, pl.; **flower** Blobottel (die)n.; **fodder** Welschkannlaab (es)n.; **gromwell** Schneiderkuraaschi, n.; **planter** Welschkannblanzer (der)n.; **poppy** Kannros (die)n.; **salad** 1.ritscherd; 2.ritscherli; **sheller** 1.Welschkannausmacher (der)n.; 2.Welschkannblicker (der)n.; 3.Welschkannscheeler (der)n.; Welschkannscheeler, pl.; **silk** Welschkannhaar (die)n.

corncob 1.Grutze (der); Grutze, pl.; 2.Welschkanngrutze (der)n.; Welschkanngrutze, pl.

corncob pipe Grutzepeif (die)n.

corncrib 1.Welschkanngribb (die)n.; 2.Welschkannheisel (es)n.; Welschkannheisli, pl.

corner 1.Eck (es)n.; Ecke, pl.; 2.Winkel (der)n.; **ball** (game) Eckballe (es)n.; **cupboard** Eckschank (der)n.; Eckschenk, pl.; **house** Eckhaus (es)n.

cornered eckich, adj.

cornerstone Eckschtee (der)n., Eckschtee, pl.

cornet 1.Kornett (die)n.; 2.Zinkharn (es)n.

cornfritter Welschkannkuche (der)n.; Welschkannkuche, pl.

cornice 1.Laade (der)n.; Laade, pl.; 2.Schelf (es)n.; Schelfer, pl.; 3.Sims (der)n.

cornmeal 1.Moschmehl (es)n.; 2.Welschkannmehl (es)n.

cornshock 1.Welschkanngareb (der)n.; Welschkanngarewe, pl.; 2.Welschkannschack (der)n.; Welschkannschack, pl.

cornstalk Welschkannschtengel (der)n.; **fiddle** Welschkanngeik (die)n.

corpse 1.dod, adj. (en --es); 2.Doodes (en)n.; 3.Leich (die) n.; 4.Leicht (die)n.; Leichde, pl. (rare usage); **plant** 1.Engelblimmli (es)n.; 2.Engelblumm (die)n.

corpulent bauchfellich, adj.

correct 1.recht, adj.; 2.recht mache, v.; gemacht, pp.; 3.recht schtelle, v.; gschtellt, pp.; 4.richdich, adj.; 5.ziwwele, v.; geziwwelt, pp.; **someone** zerechtschtelle, v. zerechtgschtellt, pp.

correctness Richtichkeet (die)n.

correspond zamme/schreiwe, v.; zammegschriwwe, pp.

correspondence Briefwechsel (der)n.

corridor Gang (der)n.; Geng, pl.

corset 1.Kasset (die)n.; 2.Leibche (es)n. 3.Leiwelche (es) n.; 4.Schnierleibche (es)n.

cost 1.koschde, v.; gekoscht, pp.; 2.Preis (der)n.; **of cartage** Furhloh (der)n.

costly 1.hochgepreist, adj.; 2.keschtlich, adj.; 3.koschtbaar, adj.; 4.koschtschpielich, adj.

costs Unkoschde (die)n., pl.

cottage cheese Schmierkees (der)n.

cotton 1.Baawoll (die)n.; 2.baawolle, adj.

cottonwood Baawollbam (der)n.

cotyledon Somekeim (die)n.

cough 1.Huuschde (der)n.; 2.huuschde, v.; ghuuscht, pp.; **slightly** hieschdle, v.; ghieschdelt, pp.; **up** raus/huschde, v.; rausghuscht, pp.

coulter 1.Blug(s)sech (es)n.; 2.Plug(s)sech (es)n.; 4.Sech (es)n.

counsel 1.aarote, v.; aagerote, pp.; 2.Rot (der)n.

counsellor Rotgewwer (der)n.

count zaehle, v.; gezaehlt, pp.; **down** hie/zehle, v.; hiegezehlt, pp.; **in** 1.dezuzehle, v.; dezugegehlt, pp.; 2.eirechle, v.; eigerechelt, pp.; **off** ab/zeehle, v.; abgezeehlt, pp.; **on** 1.druff/zehle, v.; druffgezehlt, pp.; 2.zehle, v.; gezehlt, pp.; **out** 1.ab/zeehle, v.; abgezeehl pp.; 2.raus/zaehle, v.; rausgezaehlt, pp.; **over** no(och)zaehle, v.; no(och)gezaehlt, pp.; **up** uff/zehle, v.; uffgezehlt,pp.

counterfeited gfelscht, adj.

countermand ab/bschtelle, v.; abbschtellt, pp.

counterpane 1.Bettdeck (die)n.; 2.Iwwerdeck (die)n.

counterpin Schliess (die)n.

country 1.Busch (der)n.; Bisch, pl.; 2.Land (es)n.; Lenner, pl.; **church** Landkarrich (die)n.; **congregation** Landgemee (die)n.; **dance** Kruscht (die)n.; **home** Landwohning (die) n.; **life** Landlewe (es)n.; **people** 1.Buschleit (die)n., pl.; 2.Landleit (die)n., pl.; 3.Landvolk (es)n.; **road** Landschtross (die)n.; Landschtrosse, pl.; **school** Landschul (die)n.

countryman Lan(d)smann (der)n.

couple 1.en paar, adj.; 2.Paar (es)n.

coupling pole (of the farm wagon) Lang-gwitt (die, es)n.; Lang-gwidde, pl.

courage 1.Kur(r)asche (die)n.; 2.Mut (der)n.

courageous 1.geraascht, adj.; 2.hatz(h)aftich, adj.; 3.kurraaschich, adj.; 4.mudich, adj; 5.unverzaagt, adj.; 6.vorwitzich, adj.

course Laaf (der)n.; Leef, pl.; **of cake** wettschteenich, adj.; **of life** 1.Lewe(n)szeeche (es)n.; 2.Wandel (der) n.; **salt** F(r)ischsalz (es)n.

courseness Grobbheet (die)n.

court 1.freie, v.; gfreit, pp.; 2.karessiere, v.; gekaressiert, pp.; 3.schparige, v.; gschparigt, pp.; 4.schpatziere, v.; gschpatziert, pp.; 5.Gericht (es)n. (obsolete usage)

Cc

courtship

courtship Freierei (die)n.

cousin Gschwischderkind (es)n.

covenant 1.ab/schliesse, v.; abgschlosse, pp.; 2.Bund (der)n.

cover 1.bedecke, v.; bedeckt, pp.; 2.Deck (die)n.; 3.Decking (die)n.; 4.iwwerwickle, v.; iwwergewickelt, pp.; 5.iwwerziege, v.; iwwergezogge, pp.; 6.Umschlack (der)n.; **for a can** Kannedeckel (der)n.; **the inside of the trouser leg with mud and moisture from walking in mud or wet grass** verwetze, v.; verwetzt, pp. (die hosse --); **up** zu/decke, v.; zugedeckt, pp.; **with** beleege mit, v.; beleekt, pp.; **with a hoe in planting** ei/hacke, v.; eighackt, pp.; **with a plaster** blaschdere, v.; geblaschdert pp.; **with a thin coat of paint** iwwerschlagge, v.; iwwerschlagge, pp.; **with boards** zulege, v.; zugelekt, pp.; **with cobwebs** verschpinne, v.; verschpunne, pp.; **with dust** verschtaawe, v.; verschtaabt, pp. ; **with planks** 1.blanke, v.; geblankt, pp.; 2.planke, v.; geplankt, pp.; **with scribbling** vergritzle, v.; vergritzelt, pp.; **with silt or sand** zuschwemme, v.; zugschwemmt, pp.; **with spider webs** zuschpinne, v.; zugschpunne, pp.; **with webs** iwwerschpinne, v.; iwwerschpunne, pp.; **with brush** heckich, adj.; **with chalk** greidich, adj.; **with dust** eischtaawe, v.; eigschtaabt, pp.; **with feathers** fedd(e)rich, adj.; **with flowers or designs** verblummt adj.; **with lumps** gneppich, adj.; **with manure** mischdich, adj.

covering Obdach (es)n.

coverlet 1.Bettdeck (die)n.; 2.Iwwerdeck (die)n.

cow 1.Kuh (die)n.; Kieh, pl.; 2.schtumbiere, v.; schtumbiert, pp.; **(old worn out)** Schachdel (en aldi --) **calf** Kiehkalb (es)n.; **chain** Kiehkett (die)n.; **droppings** 1.Kiehblaschder (es)n.; 2.Kiehdreck (der)n.; 3.Kiehmischt (der)n.; **lily** Bachbledder (die)n., pl.; **shelter** Kiehschopp (der)n.; **stable** 1.Kiehschtall (der)n.; Kiehschtell, pl.; 2.Kuhschtall (der)n.; Kuhschtelle, pl.; **when it is nearly dry** 1.abgemolke, adv.; 2.verseihe, v.; verseiht, pp.; **without horns** Biffel (der)n.;

cow's tail Kiehschwans (der)n.

coward 1.Farichbutz (der)n.; 2.Hatzkauer (der)n.

cowardly 1.faerichbutzich, adj.; 2.farichbutzich, adv.

cowbell Kiehbell (die)n.; Kiehbelle, pl.

cowbird Kiehschtaar (der)n.

cowlick 1.Hoorwaerwel (der)n. 2.Kiehschleck (die)n.

cowslip Schlisselblumm (die)n.; Schlisselblumme, pl.

cozy gemietlich, adj.

crab 1.Grebs (der)n.; 2.Krebs (der)n.; **apple** Holsabbel (der)n.; **louse** Filslaus (die)n.; Filsleis, pl.

crabbed 1.gratzich, adj.; 2.graunsich, adj.; 3.gretzich, adj.; 4.griddlich, adj.; 5.grummlich, adj.; 6.kratzich, adj.; 7.kretzich, adj.

crabby Mut (der)n. (schlecht zu -- sei)

crack 1.gnacke, v.; gegnackt, pp.; 2.gnackse, v.; gegnackst, pp.; 3.gnalle, v.; gegnellt, pp.; 4.gnelle, v.; gegnellt, pp.; 5.Grach (der)n.; 6.grache, v.; gegracht, pp.; 7.knacke, v.; geknackt, pp.; 8.Knall (der)n.; 9.knalle, v.; geknallt, pp.; 10.Krach (der)n.; 11.krache, v.; gekracht, pp.;12.Riss (der)n.; 13.Schpalt (der)n.; 14.Schprung (der)n.;15.Schrunn(e) (die)n.

crack (of a whip) Gnelle (der)n.; **brained** 1.halbnarrisch adj.; 2.iwwergelaernt, adj.; **loose** los/schpringe, v.; losgschprunge, pp.

creature

cracked 1.halbgscheit, adj.; 2.halbgscheit, adj.

cracker (of a whip) 1.Gnaller (der)n.; 2.Geeschelschnur (die)

cracklings Griewe (die)n., pl.

cradle 1.Bei (die)n.; 2.Beigo (die)n.; 3.Schockel (die)n.; Schockle, pl.; 4.Wiek (die)n.; 5.Wieg (die)n.; Wiege, pl.

craft 1.Handel (der)n.; 2.Handwarrick (es)n.; 3.Handwarricksgscheft (es)n.; 4.Handwarrick (es)n.; 5.Handwarrick (es)n.; 6.Kunnschaft (die)n., pl.

crafty 1.schlick, adj.; 2.schlitzohrich, adj.

cram full vollschtoppe, v.; vollgschtoppt, pp.

cramp 1.Gramp (der)n.; 2.grempe, v.; gegrempt, pp.; 3.Kramp (der)n.; 4.Zwang (der)n.

cramped (afflicted with cramp) gremisch, adj.

cranberries Schwammbeere (die)n.; pl.

crane 1.Fischreiher (der)n.; 2.Fischroiger (der)n.; 3.Fishroier (der)n.; 4.Kraan (der)n.; **(machine)** Graan (der)n.; **hook** 1.Glammhoke (der)n.; 2.Klammhoke (der)n.

cranium 1.Hannschaal (die)n.; 2.Hannscheedel (der)n.; 3.Hannscheedel (der)n.

crank 1.Gretz (der)n.; 2.Kretz (der)n.

cranky person 1.Gruscht (die)n.; 2.Kruscht (die)n.

crash 1.flatsch!, interj.; 2.grache, v.; gegracht, pp.; 3.Krach (der)n.; 4.krache, v.; gekracht, pp.; **down** zamme/grache, v.; zammegegracht, pp.

cravat Halsgraage (der)n.

craw (of a fowl) Gropp (der)n.

crawl 1.graddle, v.; gegraddelt, pp.; 2.grawwle, v.; gegrawwelt, pp.; 3.kraddle, v.; gegkraddelt, pp.; 4.krawwle, v.; gekrawwelt, pp.; 5.schluppe, v.; gschluppt, pp.; **after** no(och)graddle, v.; no(och)gegraddelt, pp.; **around** 1.rum/graddle, v.; rumgegraddelt, pp.; 2.(in great confusion) darichnannergraddle, v.; darichnannergegraddelt, pp.; **away** weck/graddle, v.; weckgegradelt, pp.; **down** nunner/graddle, v.; nunnergegraddelt, pp.; **in** 1. ei/schluppe, v.; eigschlupt, pp.; 2.nei/graddle, v.; neigegraddelt, pp.; 3.nei/schluppe, v.; neigschluppt, pp.; 4.rei/graddle, v.; reigegraddelt, pp.; **out** 1.naus/schluppe, v.; nausgschluppt, pp.; 2.raus/graddle, v.; rausgegraddelt, pp.; **over** riwwer/graddle, v. riwwergegraddelt, pp.; **to a place** hie/graddle, v.; hiegegraddelt, pp.

crawling 1.Gegrawwel (es)n.; 2.graddlich, adj.; 3.grawwlich, adj.; 4.kraddlich, adj.; 5.krawwlich, adj.; **sensation** Grawweles (es)n.

craziness Narrischkeet (die)n.

crazy 1.narrisch, adj.; 2.verkehrt, adj.; 3.verrickt, adj.; **(off in the head)** ab, prep. (-- im Kopp); **loon** Zwickelzwack (der)n.; **over** vernaddert = vernarrt; **over women** weibsleitnarrisch, adj.

creak 1.gnackere, v.; gegnackert, pp.; 2.graahne, v.; ge-graahnt, pp.; 3.krache, v.; gekracht, pp.

cream Raahm (der)n.; **of tartar** Weischtee (der)n.; **pitcher** Raahmgriegel (es)n.

crease 1.Falt (die)n.; Falde, pl.; 2.runsle, v.; gerunselt, pp.

create 1.bschaffe, v.; bschaffe, pp.; 2.erschaffe, v.; er-schaft, pp.; 3.Erschaffing (die)n.; 4.Schepfung (die)n.

creator Schepfer (der)n.

creature Greadur (die)n.

Cc

credible — crush

credible glaablich, adj.

credit Greditt (der)n.; **(one) with** zufiege, v.; zugfliekt, pp.; **institution** Baenk (die)n.; **with** zudraue, v.;zugedraut, pp.

creed Glaawe (der)n.; Glaawe, pl.

creek Grick (die)n.; Grecke; Gricke, pl.

creep 1.kraddle, v.; gegkraddelt, pp.; 2.schluppe, v.; gschluppt, pp.; **after** no(och)schluppe, v.; no(och)gschluppt, pp.; **around** rum/schluppe, v.; rumgschluppt, pp.; **back** zerick/schluppe, v.; zerickgschluppt, pp.; **in** 1.eischleefe, v.; eigschleeft, pp.; 2.eischleiche, v.; eigschliche, pp.; 3.rei/schluppe, v.; reigschluppt, pp.; **into a place of concealment** weck/schluppe, v.; weckgschluppt, pp.; **or crawl near** haer/schluppe, v.; haergschluppt, pp.; **over** 1.niwwer/schluppe, v.; niwwergschluppt, pp.; 2.riwwer/schluppe, v.; riwwergschluppt, pp.; **through** darich/schluppe, v.; darichgschluppt, pp.; **together** zamme/schluppe, v.; zammegschluppt, pp.

creeping sensation Griwwles (es)n.; **thyme** (tea) Gwendeltee (der)n.

creepy 1.unheemlich, adj.; 2.uuheemlich, adj.

crepe Floor (der)n.

crest of a ridge Kamm (der)n.; Kamme; Kemm, pl.

crevice Schpalt (der)n.

crew (of a vessel) Schiffleit (die)n., pl.

crewel 1.Glingel (der)n.; 2.Klingel (der)n.

crib Gribb (die)n.; **(for an infant)** Schockel (die)n.; Schockle, pl.; (of horses) gribbe, v.; gegribbt, pp.

cribber 1.Gribbebeisser (der)n.; 2.Gribber (der)n.

cribbing horse 1.Gribbebeisser (der)n.; 2.Gribber (der)n.; 3.Windsuckler (der)n.

cricket 1.Grix (der)n.; 2.Grixel (es)n.; 3.Grixer (der)n.; 4.Grixli (es)n.; Grixlin, pl.; 5.Kricks (der)n.; 6.Kricksel (es)n.; 7.Krill (die)n.

crime 1.Schuld (die)n.; Schulde, pl.;2.Verbreche (es)n.

criminal Verbrecher (der)n.; Verbrecher, pl.

cripple 1.Gribbel (der)n.; Gribbel, pl.;2.Krippel (der)n.; 3.vergribble, v.; vergribbelt, pp.; 4.vergripple, v.; vergrippelt, pp.

crippled 1.gribblich, adj.; 2.kripplich, adj.

crisp 1.brocklich, adj.; 2.zaart, adj.

criss cross iwwerbeenich, adj.

critical 1.bedenklich, adj.; 2.misslich, adj.

criticise ab/hechle, v.; abghechelt, pp.

croak 1.gnarre, v.; gegnarrt, pp.; 2.grexe, v.; gegrext, pp.; 3.gwaxe, v.; gegwaxt, pp.; 4.murre, v.; gemurrt, pp.; 5.vergreckse (sich --)v.; vergreckst, pp.

crochet 1.haekle, v.; kaeghelt, pp.; 2.haekle, v.; kaeghelt, pp.; 3.heekle, v.; gheekelt, pp.; **needle** 1.Haekelche (es)n.; 2.Heekelche (es)n.; 3.Heekelnaadel (es)n.

crock Haffe (der)n.; Heffe, pl.

crook 1.B(e)schisser (der)n.; 2.Bsch(e)isser (der)n.

crooked 1.grumm, adj.; 2.krumm, adj.; 3.schepp, adj.; 4.schewwetzich, adj.; 5.schiwwitzich, adj.; 6.ungraad, adj.; 7.winnisch, adj.; **implement** Fiddelboge (der)n.; Fiddelboge, pl.

crop the pasturage close ab/weede, v.; abgeweedt, pp.

cross 1.brutsich, adj.; 2.graunsich, adj.; 3.Greitz (es)n.; Greitzer, pl.; 4.griddlich, adj.; 5.grummlich, adj.; 6.Kreiz (es)n.; 7.needlich, adj.; **beam** Schpannpett (die)n.; **bees** brutzich, adj.; **bow** Boge-flint (die)n.; **eyed** 1.iwwersichdich, adj.; 2.schreaksaagich, adj.; **grained** iwwerzwarich, adj.; **-like structure** (on which slaughtered hogs are hung) Seigalye (der)n.; **of a horse** falsch, adj.; **off the books** aus/duh, v.; ausgeduh, pp.; **out** aus/schtreiche, v.; ausgschtriche, pp.; **path** Greizpaad der)n.; **timber** Riggel (der)n.

crosscut saw Drummsaeg (die)n.

crossing over in front vanneniwwer, adv.

crossness Falschheet (die)n.

crossroad 1.Greitzweg (der)n.; Greitzwege, pl.; 2.Greizschtroos (die)n.

crossways iwwerzwaerrich, adj.

crosswise 1.Greiz (es)n. (iwwers--); 2.greizweis, adv.; 3.Kreiz (es)n. (iwwers --)

croup Schtickfluss (der)n.

crow 1.Grabb (die)n.; Grabbe, pl.; 2.graehe, v.; gegraeht, pp.; 3.grehe, v.; gegreht, pp.; 4.Krabb (die)n.; 5.kraehe, v.; gekraeht, pp.

crow's nest Grabbenescht (es)n.

crowbar 1.Brecheise (es)n.; 2.Brechschtang (die)n.; 3.Hewweise (es)n.

crowd 1.Meng(e) (die)n.; 2.Schaar (die)n.; **of ministers** Paffeschtofft (es)n.

crowfoot Budderblumm (die)n.

crown 1.Gron (die)n.; 2.Kron (die)n.; 3.Waerwel (der)n.

crucifix 1.Greitz (es)n.; Greitzer, pl.; 2.Kreiz (es)n.

crucify 1.greiziche, v.; gegreizicht, pp.; 2.kreiziche, v.; gekreizicht, pp.

cruel 1.graasam, adj.; 2.grausam, adj.; 3.unmenschlich, adj.; 4.wiescht, adj.

cruelty Unbarmhaerzichkeet (die)n.

cruller 1.Fettkechliche(r) (es)n.; 2.Fettkichelche(r) (es)n.; 3.Kroller (der)n.

crumb 1.Brockel (es)n.; 2.Grimmel (die)n.; Grimmle, pl.; 3.Krimmel (die)n.

crumb (of a loaf of bread) Brossan (der)n.

crumble 1.ab/brockle, v.; abgebrockelt, pp.; 2. aus/brockle, v.; ausgebrockelt, pp.; 3.breckle, v.; gebreckelt, pp.; 4.brockle, v.; gebrockelt, pp.; 5.grimmle, v.; gegrimmelt, pp.; 6.krimmle, v.; gekrimmelt, pp.; 7.vergrimmle, v.; vergrimmelt, pp.; **into** (as bread in milk) nei/brockle, v.; neigebrockelt, pp.; **off** ab/grimmle, v.; abgegrimmelt, pp.; **something into soup** eiriwwle, v.; eigeriwwelt, pp.; **up** 1.uff/grimmle, v.; uffgegrimmelt, pp.; 2.uff/grumble, v.; uffgegrumbelt, pp.

crumbly brocklich, adj.

crumple vergrumple, v.; vergrumpelt, pp.

crupper Schwanzrieme (der)n.

crush 1.schrode, v.; gschrot, pp.; 2.verbelze, v.; verbelzt, pp.; 3.verdricke, v.; verdrickt, pp.; 4.verquetsche, v.; verquetscht, pp.; 5.zamme/quetsche, v.; zammequetscht, pp.;

(Continued on page 257)

Cc

Crush (continued)

(Continued from page 256)

by driving over verfaahre, v.; verfaahre, pp.; **by falling** verblotze, v.; verblotzt, pp.; **fruit (especially grapes) for wine (especially grapes) (the pressing may be several days later)** keltere, v.; gekeltert, pp.; **in a mortar** maersche, v.; gemaerscht, pp.; **with the teeth** verbeisse, v.; verbisse, pp.

crust Gruscht (die)n.

crusty 1.gruschdich, adj.; 2.Kruscht (die)n.

crutch Grick (die); Gricke, pl.

cry 1.ab/heile, v.; abgheilt, pp. (eens --); 2.brille, v.; gebrillt, pp.; 3.greine, v.; gegreint, pp.; 4.Grisch (der) n.; 5.heile, v.; gheilt, pp.; 6.kreische, v.; gekrische, pp.; 8.Krisch (der)n.; **a tune** ab/brille, v.; abgebrillt, pp. (eens --) **after** 1.no(och)brille, v.; no(och)gebrillt, pp.; 2.no(och)heile, v.; no(och)gheilt, pp.; **feebly (of a sick child)** wimmele, v.; gewimmelt, pp.; **oneself to a calm** ausheile (sich --) v.; ausgheilt, pp.

crying Keil (es)n.

cub Baer (der)n. (yunger --)

cuckoo Gucku(ck) (der)n.

cucumber 1.Guckgummer (die)n.; 2.Gummer (die)n.; Gummere, pl.; **patch** Gummrerank (die)n.; **tree** Gummerebaam (der)n.

cud (of ruminants) Iedrich (der)n.

cuddle 1.einischde (sich --)v.; eigenischt, pp.; 2.hie/nischdle, v.; hiegenischdelt, pp.

cudgel 1.briggele, v.; gebriggelt, pp.; 2.Gnibbel (der)n.; 3.Knippel (der)n.; 4.Priggel (der)n.; 5.verbriggele, v.; verbriggelt, pp.

cudgel(ing) 1.Briggel (der)n.; 2.Priggel (der)n.; 3.Briggelsupp (die)n.

cudweed 1.Ruhrgraut (es)n.; 2.Satzbloom (die)n.

cuff (in ballad only) Schtetzelche (es)n.

cull aus/lese, v.; ausg(e)lese, pp.

culls (of potatoes) Seigrumbeere (die)n., pl.

cultivable land Bauland (es)n.

cultivate 1.bauere, v.; gebauert, pp.; 2.schaffe, v.; gschafft, pp.; 3.schaufle, v.; gschaufelt, pp.

cultivated lettuce Gaaredselaat (der)n.

cultivator 1.Schaufeleek (die)n.; 2.Schlaufeleeg (die)n.

cumbersome beschwerlich, adj.

cunning 1.hinnerlischdich, adj.; 2.langkeppich, adj.; 3.lischdich, adj.; 4.Lischt (die)n.; 5.Naube (die)n., pl.; 6.Nuppe (die)n., pl.;7.Schalkheet (die)n.; 8.schalu, adj.; 9.schlau, adj.; 10.schlitzohrich, adj.

cup 1.Kellich (der)n., Kelliche, pl.; 2.Koppi (es)n.; Kopplin, pl.; 3.schreppe, v.; gschreppt, pp.; **(of cup and saucer)** Koppche (es)n.; Koppcher, pl.

cupboard 1.Brotschank (der)n.; 2.Gscharrschank (der)n.; 3. Schank (der)n.; Schenk, pl.

cupcheese 1.Haffekees (der)n.; 2.Koppchekees (der)n.; 3. Koppkees (der)n.; 4.Kopplikees (der)n.

cupping glass Schreppkopp (der)n.

curd 1.kaese, v.; gekaest, pp.; 2.keese, v.; gekeest, pp.

cure 1.heele, v.; gheelt, pp.; 2.Heilmiddel (es)n.; 3.Heilmiddel (es)n.; 4.weck/nemme, v.; weckgenumme, pp.

---

curiosity 1.Gwunnerfitz (der)n.; 2.Raridaet (die)n.; 3.Wunnerfitz (der)n.; Wunnerfitz, pl.

curious 1.neigierich, adj.; 2.wunnerfitzich, adj.; 3.gwunnerich, adj. (Old Order Amish usage)

curl 1.Groll (die)n.; Grolle, pl.; 2.grolle, v.; gegrollt, pp.; 3.grussle, v.; gegrusselt, pp.; 4.Kroll (die)n.; 5.krolle, v.; gekrollt, pp.; **up** uff/grussle, v.; uffgegrusselt, pp.

curled 1.geringelt, adv.; 2.grusslich, adj.

curling iron Grolleise (es)n.; Grolleise, pl.

curly 1.grollich, adj.; 2.krollich, adj.; **head** Grusselkopp (der)n.

currant bush Kansdrauweschtock (der)n.; **wine** Kansdrauwewei (der)n.

currants Kannsdraub (die)n.; Kannsdrauwe, pl.

current 1.Laaf (der)n.; Leef, pl.; 2.Schtrom (der)n. 3.Schwang (der)n. (-- sei)

curry 1.ab/schtriggle, v.; abschtriggelt, pp.; 2.schtriggle, v.; gschtriggel, pp.; **a favor** aa/schmeechle (sich --)v.; aagschmeechelt, pp.; **horses** butze, v.; gebutzt, pp. (geil --)

currycomb Schtriggel (der)n.

curse 1.Fluch (der)n.; 2.fluche, v.; gflucht, pp.; 3.verfluche, v.; verflucht, pp.; 4.verwinsche, v.; verwinscht, pp.; **word** Newewart (es)n.

cursing (continual) Gfluch (es)n.

curtain 1.Umhang (der)n.; 2.Vorhang (der)n.

curtsey Gratzfiessel (es)n.

curvature Grimming (die)n.

curve 1.Dreh (die)n.; 2.Grimm (die)n.; 3.Runding (die)n.

cushion 1.Kisse (es)n.; Kissin, pl.; 2.Kissi (es)n.; Kissin, pl.; 3.Kobbekisse (es)n.; Kobbekissi, pl.; 4.Kobbekissi (es)n.

cuspidor Schpaubax (die)n.; Schpaubaxe, pl.

custom 1.Gebrauch (der)n.; Gebreich, pl.; 2.Gewohnheit (die)n.; 3.Kunnschaft (die)n., pl.; 4.Mode (die)n.

customary 1.allgebreichlich, adj.; 2.gebreichlich, adv.; 3.gewehnlich, adv.; 4.gwehnt, adj.

customer Kunne (der)n.

customers 1.Kaafleit (die)n., pl.; 2.Kunnschaft (die)n., pl.

cut 1.beile, v.; gebeilt, pp.; 2.Schmarre (der)n.; 3.schneide, v.; gschnidde, pp.; 4.Schnitt (der)n.; **and dried** abgezettelt, adv.; **away** weck/schneide, v.; weckgschnidde, pp.; **back** zerick/schneide, v.; zerickgschnidde, pp.; **cabbage (for sauerkraut)** eihowwle, v.; eighowwelt, pp.; **down** 1.ab/mache, v.; abgemacht, pp.; 2.um/hacke, v.; umghackt, pp.; 3.(a tree) ummache, v.; umgemacht, pp.; **feed (mixed with chop)** Schrotfuder (es)n.; **from a pattern** aus/schneide, v.; ausgschnidde, pp.; **grain** ab/mache, v.; abgemacht, pp.; **hair** schneide, v.; gschnidde, pp. (Haar --); **in cubes** waerflich, adv.; **into** aaschneide, v.; aagschnidde, pp.; **into disks (as potatoes)** blettlich schneide, v.; **into pieces** 1.verschneide, v.; verschnidde, pp.; 2.verschtickere, v.; verschtickert, pp.; **loose** los/schneide, v.; losgschnidde, pp.; **off** 1.ab/schneide, v.; abgschnidde, pp.; 2.(with a scythe) ab/maehe, v.; abgemaeht, pp.; **one short in an argument** ab/dengle, v.; abgedengelt, pp.; **one's throat** Garyel (die)n. (-- abschneide); **onions or cucumbers in salt and vinegar** ei/schneide, v.; eigschnidde, pp.; **open or up** 1.uff/hacke, v.; uffghackt pp.; 2.uff/schneide, v.; uffgschnidde, pp.; **or chop down** weck/hacke, v.;

(Continued on page 258)

cut (continued)

(Continued from page 257)

weckghackt, pp.; **out** raus/ schneide, v.; rausgschnidde, pp.; **poorly** ab/grutze, v.; abgegrutzt, pp.; **short** verschtarzelt, adj.; **the wing feathers of chickens** fliggele, v.; gfliggelt, pp.; **through** darich/schneide, v.; darichgschnidde, pp.; **up** (a carcass) uff/hacke, v.; uffghackt, pp.; **with a sickle** sichle, v.; gsichelt, pp.

cuticle Haut (der)n.; Heit, pl.

cutter blade (of a mowing machine) Maehmesser (es)n.

cutting edge Scharfseit (die)n.; **of a tool** Schneid (die)n.

cypress spurge Maulwarfgraut (es)n.

Dd

dad — deadly

dad 1.Paep (der)n.; 2.Pap (der)n.
daddy 1.Daddi (der)n.; 2.Daed (der)n.; 3.Pappi (der)n. **long legs** 1.Landmesser (der)n.; Landmesser, pl.; 2.Grossdaadi (der)n.; 3.Schneider (der)n.; Schneider,pl.
daffodil 1.(die)n.; 2.Schisselblumm (die)n.
dagger 1.Daeger (der)n.; 2.Dolch (der)n.
daily 1.daechlich, adj.; 2.daeglich, adj., adv.; 3.daeklich, adj.
daily wages Daagluh (der)n.
dainties 1.Gschleck (es)n.; 2.Schleckerei (die)n.; 3.Schleckes (es)n.
dainty 1.abaddich, adv., adj.; 2.abbardich, adv., adj.; 3.baddich, adv.; **in eating** 1.schnackich, adj.; 2.schnausich, adj.; 3.schnieki(s)ch, adj.; 4..schnuppich, adj.
dairy 1.Millicherei (die)n.; 2.Millichhaus (es)n. Millichheiser, pl.
dairy farm Kiehbauerei (die)n.
daisy fleabane 1.Bitterschtenge(l) (der)n.; 2.Bitterwaermet (der)n.; 3.Fle(e)hgraut (es)n.; 4.Gensblumm (die)n.; Gensblumme, pl.; 5.Maschtochsegraut (es)n.
dam 1.Damm (der)n.; Demm, pl.; 2.damme, v.; gedammt, pp.; 3.uff/damme, v.; uffgedammt, pp.; **(held by a chain)** Kettedamm (der)n.; **up** zerick/demme, v.; zerickgedemmt,pp.
damage 1.Abdrack duh (der)v.; 2.duh, v.; geduh, pp.; (schaade --); 3.Schaade (der)n.; 4.schaediche, v.; gschaedicht, pp.; 5.uff/buckere, v.; uffgebuckert, pp.; 6.erletze, v.; verletzt, pp.; 7.Verluscht (der)n.
damaged (by the sting of an insect) grutzich, adj.
damn verdamme, v.; verdammt, pp.; **it!** 1.Dunner (der)n. (-- uns gewidder); 2.gottverdamm, interj.; 3.kotzdunner!, interj.; 4.Mord (der)n. (zum -- sackerment)
damnation Verdammnis (die)n.
damned 1.gottverdammt, adv.; 2.gottverflucht, adv.
damp 1.feicht, adj. 2.kellerfeicht, adj.; 3.nasslich, adj.; 4.nesslich, adj.; **air in a cellar** Kellerluft (die)n.
dampen dempe, v.; gedempt, pp.
dampness 1.Feichtichkeet (die)n.; 2.Feichdichkeit (die)n.
dance 1.Danz (der)n.; Danze, pl.; 2.danze, v.; gedanzt, pp.; **after** no(och)danse, v.; no(och)gedanst, pp.; **around** rum/danse, v.; rumgedanst, pp.
dancer 1.Danzer (der)n.; Denzer, pl.; 2.Denser (der)n.
dancing Gedans (es)n.
dandelion 1.Bettseecher (der)n.; 2.Biddre Selaat (der)n.; 3.Bittreselaat (der)n.; 4.Kiehblumm (die)n.; 5.Pissebell(der)n.
dandruff 1.Schibb (die)n.; Schibbe, pl.; 2.Schiff (die)n.; Schiffe, pl.
dandy Baerschdelche (es)n.
danger 1.Gfaahr (die)n.; 2.Gfaehrlichkeet (die)n.; **of life** Lewe(n)sgfaahr (die)n.
dangerous 1.gfaehrlich, adj.; 2.gfarlich, adj.; 3.gfehrlich, adj.
dangerously ill 1.dodgrank, adj.; 2.schtaerwesgrank, adj.
dangle 1.bamble, v.; gebambelt, pp.; 2.zapple, v.; gezappelt, pp.
dangling 1.baamblich, adj.; 2.Gebambel (es)n.
Daniel Dangel (der)n.
dappled 1.applich, adj.; 2.dibblich, adj.; 3.dubbich, adj.;

4.fleckich, adj.; 5.scheckich, adj.; **gray** 1.eisi-gro(h), adj.; 2.schifferich, adj.; 3.schiwwerich, adj.
dare 1.bendere, v.; gebendert, pp.; 2.daerfe, v.; gedaerft, pp.; 3.deifle, v.; gedeifelt, pp.; 4.unner/schteh (sich --) v.; 5.waage, v.; gewaagt, pp.; 6.woge, v.; gewogt, pp.
daring 1.mudich, adj.; 2.schpanki, adj.; 3.schpankich, adj.; 4.wooghelsich, adj.
dark 1.dunkel, adj.; 2.finschder, adj.; **blue** 1.blitzeblo, adj.; 2.dunkelblo, adj.; **brown** 1.dunkelbrau, adj.; 2.schwarzbrau, adj.; 3.schwatzbrau, adj.; **colored** dunkelfarwich, adj.; **red** 1.dunkelrot, adj.; 2.schwarzrot, adj.; 3.schwatzrot, adj.
darken verdunkle, v.; verdunkelt, pp.
darling 1.Haerzel (es)n.; 2.Liebschdi (die)n.; 3.Liewer (der) n.; 4.Liewi (die)n.
darn 1.schtobbe, v.; gschtoppt, pp.; 2.schtoppe, v.; gschtoppt, pp.; **thing** verzwickt, adj. (-- wese)
darning needle Schtoppnodel(die)n.; Schtoppnoddle, pl.
dash Abkatzungszeeche (es)n.; **ahead** vorrenne, v.; vorgerennt, pp.; **past** verbei/yaage, v.; verbeigeyaagt, pp.
date 1.Daadem (der)n.; Daadem(e), pl.; 2.Daatem (der)n.; 3.Yohrzaahl (die)n.
daub 1.iwwerschmiere, v.; iwwergschmiert, pp.; 2.saue, v.; gsaut, pp.; 3.schmiere, v.; gschmiert, pp.
daughter Dochder (die)n.; Dochdere; Dechder, pl.; **in-law** 1.Schwardochder (die)n.; 2.Schweegerdochder (die) n.; 3.Schwiegerdochder (die)n.; 4.Sehnern (die)n.; 5.Sohnsfraa (die)n.; Sohnsweiwer, pl.; 6.Suhnsfraa (die)n.; Suhnsweiwer, pl.
David Daavid (der)n.
dawdle 1.rum/piddle, v.; rumgepiddelt, pp.; 2.schlodere, v.; gschlodert, pp.; 3.schlodle, v.; gschlodert, pp.
dawn 1.Daagesaafang (der)n.; 2.Daagslicht (es)n.; 3.Mariyelicht (es)n.
day Daag (der)n.; Daage, pl.; **after** Daag (der)n.; Daage, pl. (-- druff); **after tomorrow** iwwermariye, adv.; **day before yesterday** 1.Daag (der)n.; Daage, pl. (Daags devor); 2.vorgeschder, adv.; **laborer** Daaglehner (der)n.; Daaglehner, pl.; **of repentance** Bussdaag (der)n.; **of rest** Rukdaag (der)n.; **off** 1.Bembeldaag (der)n.; 2.Rukdaag (der)n.; **on which no regular work is done** Bembeldaag (der)n.
day's work 1.Daagsarewett (die)n.; 2.Daagswerk (die)n.
Daylight Saving Time Zeit (die)n. (schtaricki --)
daylight 1.Daag (der)n.; Daage, pl.; 2.Daag(s)helling (die) n.; 3.Helling (die)n.
dazzle verblenne, v.; verblennt, pp.
deacon 1.Aarmediener (der)n.; 2.Armen (der)n. (Old Order Amish usage); 3.Diener der Armen (der)n. (Old Order Amish usage); 4.Eldeschde (der)n.; 5.Eldeschder (der)n. (Old Order Mennonite); 6.Vorscht(eh)er (der)n.
dead 1.dod, adj.; 2.kabutt, adj.; **as a doornail** 1.mausdoot, adv.; 2.mausrackedoot, adv.; **limb or tree** Schtarre (der)n.; **tired** dodmied, adj.
deadly daedlich, adv.; **nightshade** Nachtschadde (der)n.

Dd

deaf — delicate

deaf hattheerich, adj.

deal 1.aus/deele, v.; ausgedeelt, pp.; 2.handle, v.; g(e)handelt, pp.; **with** deele, v.; gedeelt, pp.

dealer Hendler (der)n.; **in or handler of horses** Geilsmann (der)n.

dear 1.deier, adj.; 2.hatzich, adj.; 3.lieb, adj.; 4.Liebschdi (die)n.; 5.liewe, adj.; 6.Liewer (der)n.; 7.Liewi (die)n.; **me** 1.ye!, interj. (ach [du] --!); 2.dausich! interj. (ei der --); 3.haerr(i)yesses, interj.; 4.haerrge!, interj.; 5.liewich, adj. (du --i zeit!)

dearer liewer, adv.

dearest 1.allerliebscht, adj.; 2.Hatzlieb (der, die)n.; 3.liebscht, adj.

death 1.Dod (der)n.; 2.Dodesfall (der)n.; 3.Dood (der)n.; **hunger** (If the patient who is mortally ill eats, he will die)Dodeshunger (der)n.; **omen** Dodezeeche (der)n.

deathbed Dod(e)sbett (es)n.

deathly fear dod(es)angscht, adv.

deathwatch Dodeuhr (die)n.

debauch 1.Sauerei (die)n.; 2.Sauferei (der)n.; 3.Schmauserei (die)n.

debilitated hundsich, adj.

debt Schuld (die)n.; Schulde, pl.

debtor Schuldner (der)n.

debts incurred for drink Lepperschulde (die)n., pl.

decapitate 1.ab/hacke, v.; abghackt, pp.; 2.ab/keppe, v.; abgekeppt, pp.; 3.keppe, v.; gekeppt, pp.

decay 1.faule, v.; gfault, pp.; 2.verfaule, v.; verfault, pp.

decayed rott, v.

deceased 1.doot, adj.; 2.gschtarewe, adj.; 3.verewicht, adj.; 4.verstarwe, adj. (--ner, --ni, --nes)

deceit 1.Bedruch (der)n.; 2.Bedruck (der)n.; 3.Bedruug (der)n.

deceive 1.aa/fiehre, v.; aagfiehrt, pp.; 2.bedriege, v.; bedroge, pp.; 3.foppe, v.; gfoppt, pp.; 4.hinnergeh,adv.; 5.luchse, v.; geluchst, pp.

December 1.Dezember (der)n.; 2.Diesember (der)n.; 3.Grischtmonet (der)n.

decent 1.aardich, adj.; 2.addentlich, adj.; 3.andlich, adj.; 4.arndlich, adj.; 5.neist, adj.; 6.schlicklich, adj.

deception 1.Aafehrung (die)n.; 2.Hinnergang (der)n.

deceptive 1.bedriegerisch, adj.; 2.bedrieklich, adj.

decided upon ausgemacht, adj.

decidedly 1.gewiss, adv.; 2.gewisslich, adv.; 3.verhaffdich, adj.

decipher aus/mache, v.; ausgemacht, pp.

declare aus/saage, v.; ausgsaat, pp.

decline 1.ab/saage, v.; abgsaat, pp.; 2.Grebagang (der)n.; 3.Grebsgang (der)n.

declivity 1.Abhang (der)n.; 2.Abschuss (der)n.; 3.Hang (der)n.

decoction made from sheep excrement (formerly administered to bring out the rash of measles or scarlet fever) Schofgnoddletee (der)n.

decorum Aaschtand (der)n.

decoy 1.locke, v.; gelockt, pp.; 2.verlocke, v.; verlockt, pp.; 3.weck/locke, v.; weckgelockt, pp.

decrease ab/nemme, v.; abgenumme, pp.

dedicate 1.ei/weide, v.; eigweidt, pp.; 2.ei/weihe, v.; eig-weiht, pp.

dedication 1.Eiweiding (die)n.; 2.Eiweihing (die)n.

deduct 1.ab/rechle, v.; abgerechelt, pp.; 2.ab/schmeisse, v.; abgchmisse, pp.; 3.ab/zeehle, v.; abgezeehlt, pp.; 4.ab/ziehe, v.; abgezoge, pp.

deduction Abzuck (der)n.

deed Daat (die)n.; Daade, pl.

deeds Warick (es)n.

deep cellar (usually detached from the house) for cooling butter, etc. 1.Brunnekeller (der)n.; 2.Grundkeller (der)n.

deer Hasch (der)n.; Hasch, pl.; **fly** Haschmick (die)n.; **mountains** Haschbarig (der)n.

deface verschenne, v.; verschennt, pp.

defamation Verleschderung (die)n.

defame 1.bischimpe, v.; bschimpt, pp.; 2.bschimpe, v.; bschimpt, pp.; 3.schimfe, v.; gschimft, pp.; 4.schimpe, v.; gschimpt, pp.; 5.verleschdere, v.; verleschdert, pp.; 6.vermaule, v.; vermault, pp.; 7.verschimfe, v.; verschimft, pp.

defeat schwuppe, v.; gschwuppt, pp.; **by voting** (an official) raus/schtimme, v.; rausgschtimmt, pp.

defect Fehler (der)n.; Fehler, pl.

defend wehre (sich --)v.; g(e)wehrt, pp.; **one's self** seckendiere (sich --)v.; seckendiert, pp.

defendant Beklaachder (der)n.

defense Hinnerbart (der)n.

defiance Trotz (der)n.

defiant 1.trotze, v.; getrotzt, pp.; 2.trotzich, adj.

deficiency Ausfall (der)n.

deficient zerick/bleiwe, v.; zerickgebliwwe, pp.

deflected (by some obstruction) ab/glense, v.; abgeglenst, pp.

defoliate ab/blaade, v.; abgeblaadt, pp.

deformed 1.Grutzich, adj.; 2.langaarschich, adj.; 3.vergribbelt, adj.; **fowl or person** Langaarsch (der)n.; **and imperfect** (as trees and fruit) 1.gnarzich, adj.; 2.knarzich, adj.; 3.gnatzich, adj.; **object** Ungeschtalt (es)n.

defraud 1.bedriege, v.; bedroge, pp.; 2.bockseckle, v.; gebockseckelt, pp.; 3.bscheisse, v.; bschisse, pp.; 4.nei/brenne, v.; neigebrennt, pp. (eens --); 5.raus/yutte, v.; rausgeyutt, pp.

defray (some one's expenses) freihalte, v.

defy raus/foddre, v.; rausgfoddert, pp.

degenerate 1.Aart (die)n. (aus der -- schlagge); 2.aus/aarde, v.; ausgaart, pp.; 3.ausorte, v.; ausgeort, pp.; 4.Ort (die)n. (aus der -- schlagge)

degree graad, adj.

dejected 1.drieb, adj.; 2.mutlos, adv.; 3.nidder/gschlagge, v.; niddergschlagge, pp.; 4.treeschtmiedich, adj.; 5.trostmiedich, adj.; **Delaware River** Revier (die)n.

delay 1.aa/schteh, v.; aagschtanne, pp.; 2.aus/bliewe, v.; ausgebliwwe, pp.; 3.uff/halde, v.; uffghalde, pp.

delayed work 1.Schtimmlerei (die)n.; 2.Schtimplerei (die)n.

deliberate 1.berode, v.; berode, pp.; 2.berotschlagge, v.; berotgschlagge, pp.

delicacies 1.Gschleck (es)n.; 2.Gschleckerwese (es)n.

delicate 1.piensich, adj.; 2.zimberlich, adj.

Dd

delicious

delicious 1.abbedittlich, adj.; 2.schmackhaft, adj.
delight 1.Freede (die)n.; 2.Freide (die)n.; 3.Luschde (der) n.; 4.Wonne (die)n.; **to the eye** Aageluscht (die)n.
delightful aagenehm, adj.
delirium tremens 1.Poker (der)n.; 2.Saufgichdere (die)n.
deliver 1.befreie, v.; befreit, pp.; 2.iwwerlief(f)ere, v.; iwwerlieft, pp.; 3.iwwerliwwere, v.; iwwerliefert, pp.; 4.liffere, v.; geliffert, pp.; 5.liwwere, v.; geliwwert, pp.; **the afterbirth** 1.butze (sich --)v.; gebutzt, pp.; 2.seiwere (sich --)v.; gseiweert, pp.
deliverance Befreiung (die)n.
dell Dell (die)n.
delouse lause, v.; gelaust, pp.
deluge Sindflut (die)n.
demand 1.Aaschpruch (der)n.; 2.begehre, v.; begehrt, pp.; 3.fodd(e)re, v.; gfoddert, pp.; 4.Fodderes (es)n.; 5.froge, v.; gfrogt, pp.; 6.verlange, v.; verlangt, pp.; **back** zerick/foddre, v.; zerickgfoddert, pp.
demented 1.Kopp (der)n. (aus dem --); 2.verkehrt, adj.; 3.wunnerlich, adj.
Democrat Demograat (der)n.; Demograade, pl.
Democratic demograadisch, adj.
demolish 1.ab/reisse, v.; abgerisse, pp.; 2.um/reisse, v.; umgerisse, pp.; 3.zamme/schmeisse, v.; zammegschmisse, pp.
demure sittsam, adj.
denomination Benennung (die)n.
denote bezeige, v.; bezeikt, pp.
dense dicht, adj., adv.; **growth** (figurative) Wald (der)n.
dent 1.Dell (die)n.; 2.uff/buckere, v.; uffgebuckert, pp.
dentist 1.Zaahdokder (der)n.; 2.Zaehdokder (der)n.
deny 1.ab/leegele, v.; abgeleegelt, pp.; 2.ab/lehnt, v.; abgelehnt, pp.; 3.ab/schpreche, v.; abschproche, pp.; 4.verleegele, v.; verleegelt, pp.;5.verleegne, v.; verleegnet, pp.; 6.verlegele, v.; verlegelt, pp.; 7.verlegne, v.; verlegelt, pp.; 8.versaage, v.; versaagt, pp.; 9.wedderlege, v.; wedderlegt, pp.
depart 1.ab/reisse, v.; abgereest, pp.; 2.fatt/geh, v.; fattgange, pp.; 3.verlosse, v.; verlosse, pp.; 4.weck/geh v.; is weckgange, pp.; **from** ab/weiche, v.; abgeweicht, pp.
departure Abschied (der)n.
depend (on something/someone) druff/verlosse (sich --) v.; verlosse, pp.; **upon** 1.aa/kumme, v.; is aakumme, pp. (druff --); 2.schtitze, v.; gschtizt, pp.; 3.zaehle, v.; gczochlt, pp.
dependent 1.abhenki(s)ch, adj.; 2.verlossich, adj.
deplorable yemmerlich, adj.
depose bezeige, v.; bezeikt, pp.
deposit (sand or silt) 1.schwemme, v.; gschwemmt, pp.; 2.fleeze, v.; gfleezt, pp.
depreciate unner/schetze, v.; unnergschetzt, pp.
depress unner/dricke, v.; unnergedrickt, pp.
depressed 1.bedreibt, adj.; 2.verleed, adj.; 3.verleedich, adj.
depression Daal (es)n.; Daale; Daaler, pl.
depth Diefing (die)n.
deranged verrickt, adj.

deuce

deride 1.verlache, v.; verlacht, pp.; 2.verschpodde, v.; verschpott, pp.
derision 1.Gschpettel (es)n.; 2.Hohn (der)n.; 3.Schpott (der)n.
derogatory gossip Haahnegegrisch (es)n.
descend ab/schteige,v.; abschteigt, is abschtigge, pp.
descended (from) 1.ab/schtamme, v.; abgschtammt, pp.; 2.schtamme, v.; gschtammt, pp.; 3.haer/schtamme, v.; haerschtammt, pp.; 4.zerick/schtamme, v.; zerickgschtammt, pp.
descendent 1.Noochkemmling (der)n.; 2.Noochkumme(r) (der)n.; Noochkumme(r), pl.
describe beschreiwe, v.; beschriwwe, pp.
description Beschreiwung (die)n.
desert verlosse, v.; verlosse, pp.
deserving bedaerfdich, adj.
deshevel verschtruwwele, v.; verschtruwwelt, pp.
design 1.Abriss (der)n.; 2.Absicht (die)n.; 3.Blaan (der)n.; 4.blaane, v.; geblaant, pp.; 5.Zweck (der)n.
desire 1.Begehr (der)n.; 2.begehre, v.; begehrt, pp.; 3.Luschde (der)n.; 4.luschdere, v.; geluschdert, pp.; 5.luschderich, adj.; 6.Verlange (es)n.; 7.verlange, v.; verlangt, pp.; 8.welle, v.; gewellt, pp.; **for certain things in eating during pregnancy** Luschde (der)n.
desirous begierich, adj.; **to marry** heirich, adj.
desolate life Luderlewe (es)n.
despair 1.verleed sei (+ dative case)v.; 2.verzaage, v.; verzaacht; verzaakt, pp.
desperate deschperaat, adj.
despicable 1.lidderlich, adj.; 2.nidderdrechdich, adj.
despise 1.hasse, v.; g(e)hasst, pp.; 2.verachde, v.; veracht, pp.; 3.veracht, v.; 4.verhasse, v.; verhasst, pp.
despised 1.verdutzt, adj.; 2.verhasst, adj.
destiny Los (es)n.
destroy 1.verdilye, v.; verdilgt, pp.; 2.verhause, v.; ver-haust, pp.; 3.vernichde, v.; vernicht, pp.; 4.verschteere, v.; verschteert, pp.
detach 1.ab/henke, v.; abghonke, pp.; 2.aus/henke, v.; ausghenkt, pp.; 3.uff/hoke, v.; uffghokt, pp.
detailed ausfiehrlich, adj.
detain uff/halde, v.; uffghalde, pp.
detect verwische, v.; verwischt, pp.; **by smelling** aa/rieche, v.; aageroche,pp.
deteriorate 1.Aart (die)n. (aus der -- schlagge); 2.aus/aarde, v.; ausgaart, pp.; 3.ausorte, v.; ausgeort, pp.; 4.nunner/geh, v.; nunnergange, pp.; 5.Ort (die)n. (aus der -- schlagge)
determine aus/mache, v.; ausgemacht, pp.
determined resolutt, adj.
detestable abscheilich, adj.; **affair** Hunswese (es)n.
Detlaus Day (March 31) Detlausdaag (der)n.
detour Umweg (der)n.
deuce 1.Henker (der)n.; 2.Schinner (der)n.; 3.Schwaernot (die)n.; **(in cards)** zwedder (en)n.; **the deuce!** 1.sackerment!, interj.; 2.sapperlott!, interj.; 3.sapperment!, interj.; **take it!** kotzgricksel!, interj.; **take you!** grenk(et) (dich soll dei -- hole)

Dd

deucedly — direct

deucedly 1.bummeraalisch, adj.; 2.deihenkers, adv.; 3.dunnerhaagels, adj.; 4.gewessers (gaar), adv. 5.sackerments, adv.; 6.sapperments, adj.; 7.schinners, adv.; 8.schtaernhaayels, adj.; 9.schtaernhaaylich, adj.; 10.verdeihenkert, adv.; 11.verdollt, adv.; 12.verflickt adj.; 13.verflixt, adj.

develop physically ausbilde (sich --)v.; ausgebildt, pp.

devestate 1.verheere, v.; verheert, pp.; 2.verwieschde, v.; verwiescht, pp.

deviate ab/weiche, v.; abgeweicht, pp.

devil 1.deifle, v.; gedeifelt, pp.; 2.Deihenker (die)n.; 3.deiwle, v.; gedeiwelt, pp.; **of a** dunnerwetters (-er) (-i), adj.

devil's bit Deiwelsabbis (watzel) (die)n.; **time** (daylight savings time) Deifelzeit (die)n.

devilish(ly) 1.verdeiwelt, adj.; 2.verhenkert, adj.; 3.verschinnert, adj.

devlish 1.deiflisch, adj.; 2.deiwlisch, adj.

devolve upon zufalle, v.; zugfalle, pp.

devote oneself ergewwe (sich --)v.; ergewwe, pp.

devotion Aadacht (die)n.

devotional aadechtich, adj.; adv.

devour 1.uff/fresse, v.; uffgfresse, pp.; 2.verfresse, v.; verfresse, pp.; 3.verzehre, v.; verzehrt, pp.

devout 1.fromm, adj.; 2.frumm, adj.; 3.grischtlich, adj.

dew 1.Daa (der)n.; 2.Dau (der)n.

dewberry 1.Brombeer (die)n.; 2.Rankeldanne (die)n.,pl.

diabolical saadonisch, adj.

diagnoally Eck (es)n. (iwwers --)

diagram Abriss (der)n.

dial Gsicht (es)n.; Gsichder, pl.; **of a clock** Zifferblaatt (es)n.

diamond Demant (der)n.

diamonds (in cards) Eckschtee (die)n.

diaper 1.Windel (der)n.; Windle, pl.; 2.Winnel (die)n.

diarrhea 1.Dapperschpring (die)n.; 2.Darichfall (der)n.; 3.Flutter (die)n.; 4.Leibweh (es)n.; 5.Ruhr (die)n.; 6.Scheiss (die)n.; 7.Schgidders (der)n.; 8.Schpringdapper(die)n.; 9.Schtratz (die)n.

diary Daagbuch (es)n.; Daagbicher, pl.

dice Waerfel (der)n.; Waerfle, pl.

dicker schrauwe, v.; gschraubt, pp.

dictatorial ba(a)sich, adj.

dictionary 1.Naamebuch (es)n.; 2.Nomebuch (es)n.; 3.Waddebuch (es)n.; Waddebicher, pl.; 4.Watterbuch (es)n.

did you ever! Daag (der)n. (hoscht du dei -- des lewes!)

die 1.ab/schtaerwe, v.; abgschtarwe, pp.; 2.grebiere, v.; grebiert, pp.; 3.Schneideise (es)n.; 4.schtarewe, v.; is gschtarewe, pp.; 5.verrecke, v.; verreckt, pp.; **from thirst** verdaschde, v.; verdascht, pp.; **out** 1.ab/schtaerwe, v.; abgschtarwe, pp.; 2.aus/schtarewe, v.; ausgschtarwe, pp.; 3.verdrickle, v.; verdrickelt, pp.

diet halde, v.; ghalde, pp. (sich in esse --)

difference Unnerschitt (der)n.

different 1.allerhand, adj.; 2.annerschder, adj.; adv.; 3.annerscht, adv.; 4.ettlich, adj.; 5.unnerschittlich, adj.; 6.verschiddlich, adj.; 7.verschiedlich, adj.; 8.vielerlee, adj.

difficult 1.hatt, adj.; 2.schwer, adj.; **to get done** wedder/halte, v. wedderghalte, pp. (hart --); **to please** absenaat, adj.

difficulty 1.Haekel (es)n.; 2.Miehlsaal (die)n.; in breathing eng, adj. (-- uff der bruscht sei); **of accomplishment** Naube (die)n., pl.

diffidence Bleedheet (die)n.

diffident 1.bleed, adj.; 2.eigezogge, adj.

dig 1.graawe, v.; gegraawe, pp.; 2.grubbe, v.; gegrubbt, pp.; **a hole** (in the ground with an implement or by burrowing) vergraawe,v.; vergraawe,pp.; **after** no(och)graawe, v.; no(och)gegraawe, pp.; **around** 1.gickse, v.; gegickst, pp.; 2.giekse, v.; gegiekst, pp.; 3.rum/graawe, v.; rumgegraawe, pp.; **garden** 1.Gaarde (der)n. (-- graawe); 2.gerdle, v.; gegerdelt, pp.; **in the ribs** Rippeschtoos (der)n.; **into** nei/graawe, v.; neigegraawe, pp.; **off** ab/graawe, v.; abgegraawe, pp.; **or remove** (as potatoes or stones) raus/mache, v.; rausgemacht, pp.; **out** (potatoes) aus/mache, v.; ausgemacht, pp.; **out or up** raus/graawe, v.; rausgegraawe, pp.; **out with a fork** (as potatoes) 1.aus/ schteche, v.; ausgschtoche, pp.; 2.raus/schteche, v.; rausgschtoche, pp.; **up uff/graawe,** v.; uffgegraawe, pp.; **up and turn over** rum/graawe, v.; rumgegraawe, pp.

digest verdaue, v.; verdaut, pp.

digestion Verdauung (die)n.

digger Graawer (der)n.

digress ab/weiche, v.; abgeweicht, pp.

dilapidated 1.ausgeloddert, adj.; 2.bauchfellich, adj.; 3.lodd(e)rich, adj.; 4.lodder, adj.; 5.noddlich, adj.; 6.rabblich, adj.; 7.rapplich, adj.; 8.verlappelt, adj.; 9.verlappert, adj.; 10.verloddert, adj.; 11.verlumpt, adj.; **building** 1.Gnallhitt (die)n.; 2.Knallhitt (die)n.

dilatory saumselich, adj.

dilemma 1.Klemm (die)n.; 2.Glemm (die)n.

diligent 1.emsich, adj.; 2.unverdrosse, adj.

dill Dill (der)n.

dilly-dallying 1.Gebambel (es)n.; 2.Gebembel (es)n.

diluted lang, adj.

diluvial sand Sand (der)n. (gfleetzter --)

dim 1.blass, adj.; 2.drieb, adj.; 3.unglor, adj.

dime Zehe-Cent-Schtick (es)n.; Zehe-Cent-Schticker, pl.

dimple 1.Dall(e) (die)n.; 2.Dell (die)n.

din Gedimmel (es)n.

dine esse, v.; gesse, pp.

dining room Essschtubb (die)n.; Essschtuwwe, pl.

dinner (noon meal) 1.Middaag (der)n.; 2.Middaagesse (es)n.; **horn** Bloshann (es)n.; **pail** Esskessel (der)n.

dip scheppe, v.; gscheppt, pp.; **away** weck/scheppe, v weckgscheppt, pp.; **into** nei/dunke, v.; neigedunkt, pp.; **net** 1.Hammergaarn (es)n.; 2.Hebgarn (es)n.; **or shovel back** zerick/scheppe, v.; zerickgscheppt, pp.; **out** raus/scheppe, v.; rausgscheppt, pp.

diphtheria 1.Faulhals (der)n.; 2.Weh(er)hals (der)n.

dipper 1.Schebber (der)n.; 2.Scheppbool (die)n.; 3.Schepper (der)n.; 4.Wasserbool (die)n.

direct 1.aa/weis(s)e, v.; aagewisse, pp.; 2.richde, v.; gericht, pp.; 3.weise, v.; gewisse, pp.

262

Dd

direction   disliked

direction 1.Richtung (die)n.; 2.Weg (der)n.; Wege, pl.

directly 1.Gang (der)n. (eenes --s); 2.graad zu, adv.; 3.schnurschtracks, adj.; 4.schnurschtracks, adv.; **towards** the point or object druff, adv. (-- zu)

dirge Drauerlied (es)n.

dirt 1.Schmutz (der)n.; 2.Unrot (der)n.

dirty schmutzich, adj.; **(very)** schwatzdreckich, adj.;

fellow 1.Lumbehund (der)n.; 2.Sallop (der)n.; 3.Seiriesel (der)n.; **hole** Seinescht (es)n.; **rascal** Schtinkbock (der)n.; Schtinkbeck, pl.; **scamp** Sauhund (der)n.; **work** Gsuddelwese (es)n.

disagree uneenich sie, v.; uneenich gewest, pp.

disagreeable 1.eklich, adj.; 2.ga(r)schdich, adj.; 3.umblessierlich, adj.; 4.umleidlich, adj.; 5.umleitlich, adj.; 6.unabbeditlich, adj.; 7.unblessierlich, adj.; 8.unleid(l)ich, adj.; 9.uuleidich, adj.; 10.wiescht, adj.; 11.zuwidder, prep.; **(very)** 1.wieschderlich, adj.; 2.wieschtgaschdich, adj.

disagreeableness Wieschderlichkeet (die)n.

disagreeing uneenich, adj.

disagreement 1.Schtraw(w)atz (der)n.; 2.Schtruwutz (der)n.; 3.Schtruwwertz (der)n.; 4.Wese(s) (es)n.

disappear 1.Holzweg (der)n. (-- naus/geh); 2.verschwinde, v.; verschwindt, pp.; 3.verschwinne, v.; verschwunne, pp.; 4.weck/geh, v.; is weckgange, pp.; 5.weck/kumme, v.; weckkumme, pp.

disappoint aa/fiehre, v.; aagfiehrt, pp.

disarrange 1.verrumple, v.; verrumpelt, pp.; 2.verschiewe, v.; verschowe, pp.; 3.uff/gepulschdert, v.

disbelief 1.Umglaawe (der)n.; 2.Unglaawe (der)n.; 3.Uuglaawe (der)n.

disburse aus/bezaahle, v.; ausbezaahlt, pp.

discard ab/danke, v.; abgedankt, pp.

discarded waxend threads with bristles Beschtumbe (die)n., pl.

discharge 1.ab/schicke, v.; abgschickt, pp.; 2.ab/setze, v.; abgsetzt, pp.; 3.Befreiung (die)n.; **a debt** befriediche, v.; befreidicht, pp.; **a gun** 1.ab/schiesse, v.; abgschosse, pp.; 2.los/schiesse, v.; losgschosse, pp.; **an official** ab/ danke, v.; abgedankt, pp.; **of the bowels** Schtulgang (der)n.; **temporarily** ab/lege, v.; abgelegt, pp.; **the baker, milkman, etc.** ab/schtobbe, v.; abgschtoppt, pp.

discharged los/kumme, v.; loskumme, pp.

discharging matter (from a sore) flissich, adj.

disciple 1.Schuler (der)n.; Schieler, pl.; 2.Yinger (der)n.; Yinger, pl.

discipline 1.Addning (die)n.; 2.Ordnung (die)n.; 3.Ordnung (die)n.

disclose 1.endecke, v.; endeckt, pp.; 2.uff/decke, v.; uffgedeckt, pp.

discomfort Ungemach (es)n.

disconcert verbliffe, v.; verblifft, pp.

discontent unzufridde, adj.

discontented verleed, adj.

discord Uneenichkeit (die)n.

discordant verschtimmt, adj.

discount Abzuck (der)n.

discountinue ab/schaffe, v.; abgschafft, pp.

discouraged 1.bedreibt, adj.; 2.mutlos, adv.; 3.verleed, adj.; 4.verleedich, adj.

discouraging verleedtsam, adj.

discover 1.aus/finne, v.; ausgfunne, pp.; 2.endecke, v.; endeckt, pp.

discuss 1.ab/handle, v.; abghandelt, pp.; 2.iwwer/schwetze, v.; iwwergschwetzt, pp.

disease 1.Granket (die)n.; 2.Grankheet (die)n.; 3.Grankheit (die)n.; Grankheide, pl.; 4.Grecks (die)n.; 5.Krankheet (die)n.; **of the kidneys** Nieregranket (die)n.

disengage oneself los/schaffe (sich --)v.; losgschafft, pp.

disfigure 1.verschenne, v.; verschennt, pp.; 2.verschimpe, v.; verschimpt, pp.

disgrace 1.bischimpe, v.; bschimpt, pp.; 2.bschimpe, v.; bschimpt, pp.; 3.Schaam (die)n.; 4.Schan(d) (die)n.; 5.Schandfleck (die)n.; 6.schimfe, v.; gschimft, pp.; 7.Schimp (der)n.; 8.schimpe, v.; gschimpt, pp.

disgraceful 1.schandbaar, adj.; 2.schandlich, adj.; 3.schendlich, adj.

disgruntled unfrehlich, adj.

disguise verschtelle (sich --)v.; verschtellt, pp.; **oneself** vergleede (sich --)v.; vergleedt, pp.

disgust 1.Egel (der)n.; 2.Ekel (der)n.; 3.Abschei (der)n. **for** ekle, v.; ge-ekelt, pp.

disgusted 1.iwwerdrissich, adj.; 2.verekelt, adj.; 3.verleed, adj.

disgusting 1.ekelhaft, adj.; 2.wedderlich, adj.; 3.widderlich, adj.

dish Schissel (die)n.; Schissle, pl.; **of a wheel** 1.schtaerze, v.; gschtaerzt, pp.; 2.Schtaerzing (die)n.

dishes 1.Dischgscharr (es)n.; 2.Gscha(rr) (es)n.; Gscharre, pl.

dishevel verrumple, v.; verrumpelt, pp.

disheveled 1.schlabbich, adj.; 2.schtruwwli(ch), adj.

dishonest 1.unehrlich, adj.; 2.uuehrlich, adj.; 3.B(e) schisser (der)n.

dishonesty 1.Bscheisserei (die)n.; 2.Unehrlichkeet (die)n.

dishonor 1.Schan(d) (die)n.; 2.Schimp (der)n.

dishpan 1.Gscharweschschissel (die)n. Gscharweschschissle, pl.; 2.Schpielschissel (die)n.; 3.Uffschpielschissel (die)n.

dishrag Schpiellumbe (der)n.

dishtowel 1.Abbutzlumbe (der)n.; Abbutzlumbe, pl.; 2.Dischlappe (der)n.; 3.Dischlumbe (der)n.; 4.Gscharweschlumbe (der)n.; 5.Uffschpiellumbe (der)n.; 6.Schpillumbe (der)n. (Amish usage)

dishwasher Gscharrwescher (der)n.

dishwater 1.Gscharrweschwasser (es)n.; 2.Schpielwasser (es)n.; 3.Uffschpielwasser (es)n.; 4.Schpillwasser (es) n. (Amish usage)

disinclined abwennich, adj.

disinter uff/graawe, v.; uffgegraawe, pp.

dislike Feindschaft (die)n.

disliked verlaeret

Dd

dislocate

dislocate verrenke, v.; verrenkt, pp.

disloyal abtrinni(s)ch, adj.

dismiss ab/setze, v.; abgsetzt, pp.; **abruptly** ab/zettle, v.; abgezettelt, pp.

dismissed aus/geh, v.; ausgange, pp.

dismount 1.ab/schteige,v.; abschteigt, is abschtigge, pp.; 2.ab/schtiege, v.; abgschtigge, pp.; 3.aus/schtiege, v.; ausgschtigge, pp.

disobedience Ungehorsamkeit (die)n.

disobedient ungehorsam, adj. (Old Order Mennonite usage)

disobey missfolye, v.; miss(g)folkt, pp.

disorder 1.Unardning (die)n.; 2.Unfruch (der)n.

disown verschtosse, v.; verschtosse, pp.

dispel vergeh, v.; vergange, pp.

disperse schtewwere, v.; gschtewwert, pp.

displace verricke, v.; verrickt, pp.

display weisse, v.; g(e)wisse, pp.

displease 1.verdriesse, v.; verdrosse, pp.; 2.unmietich, adj.; 3.verschtimmt, adj.

displeasure Miss(g)falle (es)n.

dispose errichte, v.; erricht, pp.; **of** 1.ab/schaffe, v.; abgschafft, pp.; 2.los/warre, v.; loswarre, pp.; 3.weck/schaffe, v.; weckgschafft, pp.;4.weck/schmeisse, v.; weckgschmisse, pp.; **of them** aawaerre, v.; aawaerre, pp.

disposition Gemietsort (die)n.

dispossess naus/setze, v.; nausgsetzt, pp.

dispute 1.Dischbedaat (der)n.; 2.dischbediere, v.; gedischbediert, pp.; 3.rechtle, v.; gerechtelt, pp.; 4.renkle, v.; gerenkelt, pp.; 5.schtreide, v.; gschtridde, pp.

disreputable woman Drutsch (die)n.

dissatisfied unzufridde, adj.

dissimilar 1.unaehnlich, adj.; 2.ungleich, adj.

dissipate verschlenkere, v.; verschlenkert, pp.

dissolute unzichtich, adj.

dissoluteness Lidderlichkeet (die)n.

dissolve 1.vergeh, v.; vergange, pp.; 2.verschmelze, v.; verschmolze, pp.

dissuade 1.ab/schpreche, v.; abschproche, pp.; 2.ab/schwetze, v.; abgschwetzt, pp.; 3.abrode, v.; abgerode, pp.

distaff 1.Rocke (der)n.; 2.Schpinnerocke (der)n.; 3.Waerrickgawwel (die)n.; 4.Werkgawwel (die)n.

distainful wedderschteh, v.; wedderschtanne, pp.

distant 1.entfaernt, adv.; 2.faern, adv.; 3.weitleftich, adj.; **relationship** 1.Kiehschwenz (der)n. (siwwe --); 2.Kiehschwans (der)n. (siwwe Kiehschwens ee Hoor)

distaste 1.Egel (der)n.; 2.Ekel (der)n.

distasteful 1.grissle, v.; gegrisselt, pp.; 2.ekelhaft, adj.; 3..krissle, v.; gekrisselt, pp.

distemper 1.Geilsgranket (die)n.; 2.Hunsgranket (die)n.

distill 1.brenne, v.; gebrennt, pp.; 2.dischdilliere, v.; gedischdilliert, pp.

distiller's swill 1.Schpielich (der)n.; 2.Brennerei (die)n., Brennereie, pl.

distillery Brennhaus (es)n.; Brennheiser, pl.

distinct 1.deitlich, adj.; 2.glaar, adj.; 3.hell, adj.

do

distinctive mark 1.Keenzeeche (es)n.; 2.Kennzeeche (es)n.

distort 1.verdrehe, v.; verdreht, pp.; 2.verzucke, v.; verzuckt, pp.

distraction Verschteerung (die)n.

distraut verschtiwwert, adj.

distress Not (die)n.

distressed kimmerlich, adj.

distribute 1.aus/deele, v.; ausgedeelt, pp.; 2.aus/zeddle, v.; ausgezeddelt, pp.; 3.verdeele, v.; verdeelt, pp.

distribution Ausdeeling (die)n.

distributor Ausgewwer (der)n.

District Justice Schgweier (der)n.

district 1.Bezaerrick (es)n.; 2.Bezarick (es)n.; 3.Gezaerrick (s) (es)n.; 4.Landschaft (die)n.

distrust 1.missdraue, v.; (ge)missdraut, pp.; 2.um/draue, v.; umgedraut, pp.

distrustful 1.missdrauisch, adj.; 2.umdrauisch, adj.

disturb 1.baddere, v.; gebaddert, pp.; 2.schteere, v.; gschteert, pp.; 3.verschteere, v.; verschteert, pp.

disturbance 1.Gedob (es)n.; 2.Uwing (die)n.; 3.Verschteerung (die)n.

ditch 1.Graawe (der)n.; Greewer, pl.; 2.Wassergraawe (der)n.

dittany 1.Buschtee (der)n.; 2.Dietli (es)n.

ditty Gsang (der)n.

dive 1.dauche, v.; gedaucht, pp.; 2.Hurenescht (es)n.

divide 1.ab/deele, v.; abgedeelt, pp.; 2.deele, v.; gedeelt, pp.; **among** aus/deele, v.; ausgedeelt, pp.; **into parts** eideele, v.; eigedeelt, pp.; **up** verdeele, v.; verdeelt, pp.

divine 1.gettlich, adj.; 2.waahrsaage, v.; waahrgsaat, pp.; 3.wohrsaage, v.; wohrsaat, pp.; **love** Gotteslieb (die)n. **service** Gottesdinscht (der)n.

diving beetle Wassergeitz (der)n.

divining rod 1.Wassergawwel (die)n.; Wassergawwle, pl.; 2.Wasserzieg (der, die)n.

divinity Gottheit (die)n.

division Verdeeling (die)n.

divorce 1.Scheedbrief (der)n.; Scheedbriefe, pl.; 2.scheede, v.; gscheede, pp.; 3.scheediche, v.; gscheedicht, pp.

dizzy 1.schwindle, v.; gschwindelt, pp.; 2.schwindlich, adj.

do 1.handiere, v.; handiert, pp.; 2.schaffe, v.; gschafft, pp.; **away with** ab/schaffe, v.; abgschafft, pp.; **better** bessere (sich --) v.; gebessert, pp.; **good** 1.batte, v.; gebatt, pp.; 2.helfe, v.; gholfe, pp.; **mason's work** mauere, v.; gemauert, pp.; **no harm** schatte, v.; gschatt, pp. (nix --); **odd jobs** ghuddelt, pp. (driwwer naus --) 1.rum/gnoddle, v.; rumgegnoddelt, pp.; 2.rum/piddle, v.; rumgepiddelt, pp.; **one's best** schaerre, v.; gschaerrt,pp.; **over** 1.iwwer/duh, v.; iwwergeduh, pp. 2.iwwerschaffe, v.; iwwergschafft, pp.; **patchwork** flicke, v.; gflickt, pp.; **something bad** bose, v.; gebost, pp.; **something hastily and carelessly** huddle, v.; **something slowly** leiere, v.; geleiert, pp.; **well** aus/mache, v.; ausgemacht, pp. (gut --); **without** 1.bleiwe, v.; gebliwwe, pp. (-- losse); 2.mitaus/duh, v.; mituasgeduh, pp.; 3.unni/duh, v.; unnigeduh, pp.; **wonders** (ironically) Aaschlaek (die)n., pl. (-- fresse); **wonders** (sarcastically) schiesse, v.; gschosse, pp. (der bock --); **work hastily** iwwerschmiere, v.; iwwergschmiert, pp.; **you want to** widde = willst do; **you?** duschde

264

Dd

dock — downwards

dock Halwergaul (der)n.; **the tail** (of horses, dogs, sheep) schwenze, v.; gschwenzt, pp.

doctor (facetious) Pilleroller (der)n.; Dokder (der)n.; Dokder, pl.

doctoring Schmiererei (die)n.; **or applying plasters continually** rum/blaschdere, v.; rumgeblaschdert, pp.

doctrine Lehr (die)n.

document Schreiwes (es)n.

dodder 1.Flaxdotter (der)n.; 2.Flaxseide (der)n.

dodge nidder/ducke, v.; niddergeduckt, pp.

does it not seem to you? dinke, v.; gedinkt, pp. (dinkt's dich net)

doff aus/ziehe (sich --)v.; ausgezoge, pp.

Dog Star Hun(d)sschtern (die)n.

dog Hund (der)n.; Hund, pl. **(any long slender, also applied to other animals and even to persons)** Windhund (der)n.; **(in lumbering)** 1.Glammhoke (der)n.; 2.Klammhoke (der)n.; **box** Hun(d)sschtall (der)n.; **excrement** 1.Hun(d)sdreck (der)n.; 2.Hun(d)sdreck (der)n.; **kennel** Hunsschtall (der)n.; **power** (to churn butter, turn washing machine) Hun(d)sgraft (die)n.; **trot** Hunsdratt (der)n.

dog's fat Hunsfett (es)n.; **head** 1.Hunskopp (der)n.; 2.Hun(d)skopp (der)n.; Hun(d)skepp, pl.; **life** Hun(d)slewe (es)n.

dogcart Hun(d)skarrich (der)n.

doggerel Schpassgedicht (es)n.

doggish hundisch, adj.

doghouse 1.Hun(d)skachde (der)n.; Hun(d)skachde, pl.; 2.Hun(d)skachde (der)n.; Hun(d)skachde, pl.

dogtooth violet Drechderblumm (die)n.

dogwood 1.Hun(d)sholz (es)n.; 2.Hunshols (es)n.; 3.Kornelkasch (die)n.

doing something draasei, v.; is draag(e)wesst, pp.

doings 1.Aaschlaek (die)n., pl.; 2.Handlung (die)n.

doll 1.Bobb (die)n.; 2.Dallbopp (die)n.; Dallbobbe, pl.

dollar Daaler (der)n; Daaler, pl.; **bill** Daalernoot (die)n.; **by dollar** daalerweis, adj.

dolt Grauthammel (der)n.

domestic 1.heemgemacht, adj.; 2.heemisch, adj.; 3.heislich, adj.

domiciled 1.wohnhaft, adj.; 2.wuhnhaft, adj.

dominate benaame, v.; benaamt, pp.

don't leave under any circumstances yo, adv. (geh -- net weck); **touch!** Fui!, interj.; **you dare** beileiwe net!, interj.

donation Schenkung (die)n.

done 1.faddich, adj.; 2.faerdich, adj.; **for** 1.dehi, adv.; 2.futsch, adv.; 3.kabutt, adj.; 4.kaputt, adv.; **up** gebritscht, adv.

donor Schenker (der)n.

doom Schicksaal (es)n.

door 1.Daer (die)n.; Daere, pl.; 2.Deer (die)n.; 3.Dier (die)n.; Diere, pl.; **frame** Dieregschtell (es)n.; **hook** Deerehenk (die)n.

doorkey Deereschlissel (der)n.

doorknob 1.Deeregnopp (der)n.; 2.Dierknopp (der)n.; Diergnepp, pl.;

doorlock Deereschloss (es)n.

doormat 1.Schuhbutzer (der)n.; 2.Schuhlumbe (der)n.

Dorothy Darradee (die)n.

dose Dos (die)n.

dosing (continued) Dekterei (die)n.

dot 1.Dibbel (der)n.; 2.Dubbe (der)n.; 3.Punkt (der)n.; Punkde, pl.

dotage Kindheet (die)n. (die zwett --)

dotardly kinnisch, adj.

dotted verduppt, adj.

double 1.dobbel(t), adj.; 2.dobble, v.; gedobbelt, pp.; 3.verdopple, v.; verdoppelt, pp.; 4.zweedoppelt, adv.; 5.zweeschpennich, adj.; **(two)-faced** 1.dobbel-gsichdich, adj.; 2.gsichtich, adj.; **barreled** dobbel-laafich, adj.; **edged** zweeschneidich, adj.; **tree** (scale) 1.Woog (die)n.; Wooge, pl.; 2.Zweewoog (die)n.; Zweewooge, pl.; **tree** (used in plowing) 1.Blug(s)woog (die)n.; 2.Plugswoog (die)n.; **up** uff/dopple, v.; uffgedoppelt, pp.

doubt 1.Zweifel (der)n.; 2.zweifle, v.; gezweifelt pp.; 3.Zweiwel (der)n.; 4.zweiwle, v.; gezweiwelt, pp.

doubtful 1.misslich, adj.; 2.unbeschtimmt, adj.; 3.zweifelhaft, adj.

dough Deeg (der)n.; **crumb** Riwwle (die)n.; Riwwle, pl.; **cutter** Kucherellche (es)n.; **tray** 1.Backmol(t) (die)n.; Backmole, pl.; 2.Backmult (die)n.; Backmulde, pl.

doughnut 1.Aernkichelche (es)n.; 2.Faasnachtikichelche (es)n.; 3.Faasnachtkuche (der)n.; 4.Fettkuche (der)n.; 5.Gangnerkuche (der)n.

doughy deegich, adj.

dove-cote Dauwekaschde (der)n.; **nest** Dauwenescht (es)n.

down 1.Flaum (der)n.; 2.nunner, adv.; **along there** dattdraanunner, adv.; **back** hinnedrunne, adv.; **cast** 1.Driebsaal blose, adj.; 2.gedroscht, adj.; 3.henke, v.; ghenkt, pp. (der Kopp --); **country** nunner, prep. (es Land --); **country** landnunnerzus, adj.; **feathers** Dun (die)n.; **here** 1.dodrunne, adv.; 2.dohunne, 3.hunne, adv.; adv.; 3.donunnerzus, adv.; 4.dorunner, adv.; **in that direction** 1.dattnunnerzus, adv.; 2.dattrunnerzus, adv.; **on the cheek** Millichhaar (die)n.; **that way** dattrunner, adv.; **the back way** hinnernunner, adv.; **there** 1.dattdrunne, adv.; 2.dattnunner, adv.; **there** drunne, adv.; **this way** dorunnerzus, adv.; **through here** 1.dodarrichnunner, adv.; 2.dodarrichrunner, adv.; **through there** 1.dattdarichnunner, adv.; 2.dattdarichrunner, adv.; **together** zammenunner, adv. **to where the speaker or thinker is** runner, adv.;

downfall Unnergang (der)n.

downhill 1.baerrickab, adj.; 2.baerricknunner, adj.; 3.Hiwwel (der)n. (-- nunner)

downpour Platzregge (der)n.

downright ausgemacht, adj.

downstairs sleeping room (occupied by the parents) [old custom still preserved by the Old Order Amish and Mennonites] Kammer (die)n.; Kemmer, pl.

downwards 1.nunnerzus, adv.; 2.unners(ch)ich, adj.

Dd

doxology ··· drive

doxology Lobschpruch (der)n.

doze 1.leie, v.; gelege; geleye, pp.; 2.nucke, v.; genuckt, pp.; 3.Schlummer (der)n.; 4.schlumm(e)re, v.; gschlummert, pp.; 5.schnabble, v.; gschnappt, pp.

dozen Dutze(n)d (es)n.

dozens at a time dutzenderweis, adj.

draft Zuck (der)n.

drag 1.draage, v.; gedraage, pp.; 2.schleffe, v.; gschleeft, pp.; 3.schleife, v.; gschleift, pp.; 4.schleppe, v.; gschleppt, pp.; **a field** iwwerschleefe, v.; iwwergschleeft, pp.; **after** no(och)schleefe, v.; no(och)gschleeft, pp.; **along with** mit/schleefe, v.; mitgschleeft, pp.; **around** 1.rum/schleefe, v.; rumgschleeft, pp.; 2.rum/schleppe, v.; rumgschleppt, pp.; **away** 1.verschleefe, v.; verschleeft, pp.;2.weck/schleefe, v.; weckgschleeft, pp.; **back** zerick/schleefe, v.; zerickgschleeft, pp.; **down** nunner/schleefe, v.; nunnergschleeft, pp.; **hither** haer/schleefe, v. haergschleeft, pp.; **in** nei/schleefe, v.; neigschleeft, pp.; **near or up to** bei/schleefe, v.; beigschleeft, pp. **net** Schleefgaarn (es)n.; **off** abschleefe, v.; abgschleeft, pp.; **out** 1.naus/schleefe, v.; nausgschleeft, pp.; 2.raus/ schleefe, v.; rausgschleeft, pp.; **past** verbei/schleefe, v.; verbeigschleeft, pp.; **rake** Schleefreche (der)n.; **through** darich/schleefe, v.; darichgschleeft, pp.; **to a place** hie/schleefe, v.; hiegschleeft, pp.; **up** 1.nuff/schleefe, v.; nuffgschleeft, pp.; 2.ruff/schleefe, v.; ruffgschleeft, pp.

dragging Gschleff (es)n.

dragonfly 1.Schlangegiesser (der)n.; 2.Schlangehieder (der)n.

drain 1.ab/laafe, v.; abgeloffe, pp.; 2.ab/rinne, v.; abgerunne, pp.; 3.aus/laafe, v.; is ausgeloffe, pp.; **a cow** (of all her milk) aus/melke, v.; ausgemolke, pp.

drainpipe Peif (die)n.; Peife, pl.

drake 1.End(e)rich (der)n.; Endriche, pl.; 2.Gansert (der) n.; Gansert, pl.

draught horse Zieggaul (der)n.; **ox** Ziegochs (der)n.

draw 1.ab/mole, v.; abgemolt, pp.; 2.mole, v.; gemolt, pp.; 3.reisse, v.; gerisse, pp.; 4.robbe, v.; geroppt, pp.; 5.ziege, v.; gezoge, pp.; 6.ziehe, v.; gezoge, pp.; **fowls** aus/nemme, v.; ausgenumme, pp.; **furrows for planting** aus/faerrichde, v.; ausgfaerricht, pp.; **in** 1.ei/nemme, v.; eigenumme, pp.; 2.ei/ziege, v.; eigezoge, pp.; **in furrows through a plowed field for planting** (corn or potatoes) aa/faarichde, v.; aagfaaricht, pp.; **off and put back in a cask** rum/zappe, v.; rumgezappt, pp.; **off wine** ab/keldre, v.; abgekeldert, pp.; **out** raus/ziehe, v.; rausgezieht, pp.; **over** iwwerziege, v.; iwwergezogge, pp.; **something into the windpipe while swallowing** Sunndaagshals (der)n. (ebbes in der -- griege); **the first furrows through a field in starting to plow** aa/faarichde, v.; aagfaaricht, pp.

drawbridge Fallbrick (die)n.

drawer 1.Schiewer (der)n.; Schiewer, pl.; 2.Schupplaad (die)n.; Schupplaade, pl.

drawers (underwear) Unnerhosse (die)n.

drawing bench 1.Schneidbank (die)n.; 2.Schnitzelbank (die)n.; **knife** 1.Ziegmesser (es)n.; 2.Schneidmesser (es)n.; Schneidmesser, pl.

drawl larbse, v.; gelarbst, pp.

drawn gezogge, adj.; **out work or undertaking** Gschleff (es)n.

dread 1.Bangichkeet (die)n.; 2.faerichde, v.; gfaericht, pp.; 3.fariche, v.; gfaricht, pp.

dreadful 1.faerrichderlich, adj.; 2.farichderlich, adj.; 3.greislich, adj.; 4.schauderlich, adj.; 5.schauer(l)ich, adj.

dream 1.Draam (der)n.; Draame, pl.; 2.draame, v.; gedraamt, pp.; **of** ahne, v.; geahnt, pp.

dreambook Draambuch (es)n.

drenched wesch (puddel) nass, adj.

dress 1.aa/duh, v.; aageduh, pp.; 2.aa/gleede, v.; aagegleedt, pp.; 3.Frack (der)n.; Fracke, pl.; 4.Gaund (der)n.; Geinder, pl.; **material** Schtoff(t) (es)n.; **oneself** aa/duh (sich --)v.; aageduh, pp.; **up** 1.butze, v.; gebutzt, pp.; 2.muschdere (sich --)v.; gemuschdert, pp.; 3.uff/butze (sich --)v.; uffgebutzt, pp.; 4.uff/duh (sich --)v.; uffgeduh, pp.; **warmly** eibindle (sich --)v.; eigebindelt, pp.

dressed aageduh, v. (past tense)

dressed up uff/geduh, v.

dresser Aarichtdisch (der)n.

dressmaker 1.Frackmachern (die)n.; 2.Naehern (die)n.; 3.Nehern (die)n.

dried gedatt, adj.; **beef** 1.Gwalle (der)n.; 2.Gwallefleesch (der)n.; **fruit** Schnitz (die)n.; Schnitz, pl.; **herring** Pickling (der)n.; **peach(es)** 1.Hutzel (die)n.; 2.Pasching Ledder (es)n.; **up** verdatt, adj.

drift shut (of roads by snow) zublose, v.; zugeblose, pp.

drill 1.Drill (die)n.; Drille, pl.; 2.drille, v.; gedrillt, pp.; 3.Dross (es) n.; 4.exeziere, v.; geexeziert, pp.; 5.Schteebohrer (der)n.; **into** ei/scharefe, v.; eigschareft, pp.; **into one** aa/weis(s)e, v.; aagewisse, pp.

drink 1.Drank (der)n.; 2.Drink (der)n.; 3.drinke, v.; gedrunke, pp.; 4.Drunk (der)n.; 5.Gedrenk (es)n.; 6.Trank (der)n.; 7.zeeche, v.; gezeecht, pp.; **all** 1.aus/drinke, v.; ausgedrunke, pp.; 2.aus/saufe, v.; ausgsoffe, pp.; 3.weck/drinke, v.; weckgedrunke, pp.; **around** rum/drinke, v.; rumgedrunke, pp.; **in a sloppy manner** schnuddle, v.; gschnuddelt, pp.; **of whiskey** Schmaaler (der)n.; **spirits** 1.Bitters (es)n.; 2.schnapse, v.; gschnapst, pp.; **to excess** 1.saufe, v.; gsoffe, pp.; 2.versaufe, v.; versoffe, pp.; **to the dregs** aus/saufe, v.; ausgsoffe, pp.; **too much** iwwersaufe (sich --)v.; iwwersoffe, pp.; **up** 1.uff/drinke, v.; uffgedrunke, pp.; 2.uff/saufe, v.; uffgsoffe, pp.

drinker of beer Bierdrinker (der)n.

drinking Drinke (es)n.; **place** Kneip (die)n.; **water** Drinkwasser (es)n.

drip ab/rinne, v.; abgerunne, pp.

drive 1.Faahrt (die)n.; 2.faahre, v.; is gfaahre, pp.; **(as the wind the clouds)** 1.dreibt, v.; 2.yaage, v.; geyaagt, pp.; **a person out by blows** naus/schlagge, v.; nausgschlagge, pp.; **about** rum/zackere, v.; rumgezackert, pp.; **after** no(och)dreiwe, v.; no(och)gedriwwe, pp.; **after** (in a vehicle) no(och)faahre, v.; no(och)gfaahre, pp.; **against** (a rock in plowing) wedder/faahre, v.; wedderfaahre, pp.; **ahead** 1.aa/faahre, v.; aagfaahre, pp.; 2.vannenaus/faahre, v.; vannenausgfaahre, pp.; **along** dohiefaahre, v.; **around** 1.rum/dreiwe, v.; rumgedriwwe, pp.; 2.rum/faahre, v.; rumgfaahre, pp.; **at the head** vannenaus/faahre, v.; vannenausgfaahre, pp.; **away** 1.aus/dreiwe, v.; ausgedriwwe, pp.; 2.aus/schtiwwere, v.; ausgschtiwwert,

(Continued on page 267)

Dd

drive (continued)

(Continued from page 266)

pp.; 3.fatt/dreiwe, v.; fattgedriwwe, pp.; 4.scheeche, v.; gscheecht, pp.; 5.verdreiwe, v.; verdriwwe, pp.; 6.weck/dreiwe, v.; weckgedriwwe, pp.; 7.weck/faahre, v.; weckgfaahre, pp.; **away from** devunfaahre, v.; **away hastily** ab/geege, v.; abgegeet, pp.; **away with a club** weck/briggle, v.; weckgebriggelt, pp.; **back** 1.zerick/dreiwe, v.; zerickgedriwwe, pp.; 2.zerick/faahre, v.; zerickgfaahre, pp.; **back with a whip** zerick/geeschle, v.; zerickgegeeschelt, pp.; **down** 1.nunner/dreiwe, v.; nunnergedriwwe, pp.; 2.nunner/faahre, v.; nunnergfaahre, pp.; 3.runner/dreiwe, v.; runnergedriwwe, pp.; **fast** yaage, v.; geyaagt, pp.; **here** (in a vehicle) haer/faahre, v.; haergfaahre, pp.; **hither** haer/dreiwe, v.; haergedriwwe, pp.; **home** heemfaahre, v.; **in** 1.ei/yaage, v.; eigyaagt, pp.; 2.nei/dreiwe, v.; neigedriwwe, pp.; 3.rei/dreiwe, v.; reigedriwwe, pp.; 4.rei/faahre, v.; reigfaahre, pp.; **(with dogs)** nei/hetze, v.; neighetzt, pp.; **in or into** (with a vehicle) nei/faahre, v.; neifaahre, pp.; **off** 1.ab/dreiwe, v.; abgedriwwe, pp.; 2.verdreiwe, v.; verdriwwe, pp.; **on** zufaahre, v.; zugfaahre, pp.; **or chase in** eiyaage, v.; eigeyaakt, pp.; **or haul up** nuff/faahre, v.; nuffgfaahre, pp.; **out** 1.naus/dreiwe, v.; nausgedriwwe, pp.; 2.raus/dreiwe, v.; rausgedriwwe, pp.; 3.raus/faahre, v.; rausgfaahre, pp.; 4.raus/schprenge, v.; rasugschprengt, pp.; **out at the head of** vannenaus/yaage, v.; vannenausgyaagt, pp.; **out by dogs** raus/hetze, v.; rausghetzt, pp.; **out by whipping** raus/gaerwe, v.; rausgegaerbt, pp.; **out of bed** uff/yaage, v.; uffgeyaagt, pp.; **out with a club** naus/briggle, v.; nausgebriggelt, pp.; **out with a whip** 1.naus/geeschle, v.; nausgegeeschelt, pp.; 2.raus/fitze, v.; rausgfitzt, pp.; **over** 1.niwwer/dreiwe, v.; niwwergedriwwe, pp.; 2.niwwer/faahre, v.; niwwergfaahre, pp.; 3.um/faahre, v.; umgfaahre, pp.; **past** 1.verbei/dreiwe, v.; verbeigedriwwe, pp.; 2.verbei/faahre, v.; verbeigfaahre, pp.; 3.vorfaahre, v.; vorgfaahre, pp.; **pell mell** los/faahre, v.; losgfaahre, pp.; **to a place** 1.hie/dreiwe, v.; hiegedriwwe, pp.; 2.hie/faahre, v.; hiegfaahre, pp.; **together** 1.bei/dreiwe, v.; beigedriwwe, pp.; 2.bei/gage, v.; beigegkt, pp.; 3.bei/yaage, v.; beigyaagt, pp.; 4.zammenannerfaahre, v.; zammernannergfaahre, pp.; **together** (by beating) zamme/gaerwe, v.; zammegegaerbt, pp.; **up** 1.nuff/ dreiwe, v.; nuffgedriwwe, pp.; 2.ruff/dreiwe, v.; ruffgedriwwe, pp.; 3.ruff/faahre, v.; ruffgfaahre, pp.

driven out verschtiwwert, adj.

driver 1.Dreiwer (der)n.; Dreiwer, pl.; 2.Fuhrmann (der)n.; Fuhrmenner, pl.

driveway Faahrweg (der)n.; Faahrwege, pl.

driving Gfaahr (es)n ; **wheel** Dreihraad (es)n.

drizzle 1.brutzle, v.; gebrutzelt, pp.; 2.Gerussel (es)n.; 3.Gsuddel (es)n.; 4.newwle, v.; genewwelt, pp.; 5.russle, v.; gerusselt, pp.; 6.suddle, v.; gsuddelt, pp.

drizzling suddlich, adj.

drizzly weather Suddelwedder (es)n.

droll drollich, adj.; **person** 1.Gschpassvoggel (der)n.; 2.Schpassvoggel (der)n.

drone summe, v.; gsummt, pp.

drool schlawwere, v.; gschlawwert, pp.

droop maudere, v.; gemaudert, pp.

drooping maudrich, adj.; **mouth** Henkmaul (es)n.

drop 1.Drobbe (der)n.; Drobbe, pl.; 2.drobse, v.; gedrobst, pp.; 3.drobsle, v.; gedrobselt, pp.; 4.Droppe (der)n.;

5.Fall (der)n.; 6.verzottle, v.; verzottelt, pp. **down** (in consequence of melting) ab/schmelze, v.; abgschmolze, pp.; **from the hull** (grain) aus/falle, v.; ausgfalle, pp.; **grain in sickling** aus/leffle, v.; ausgeleffelt, pp.; **in** nei/dropse, v.; neigedropst, pp.; **of water** Wasserdroppe (der)n.; **off** ab/laafe, v.; abgeloffe, pp.; **or filter through** darich/dropse, v.; darichgedropst, pp.; **or lower the lip** schlappe, v.; gschlappt, pp. (es Maul --); **or trickle off** ab/drops(l)e, v.; abgedropselt, pp.; **out** aus/geh, v.; ausgange, pp. **seeds in planting** ei/lege, v.; eiglegt, pp.; **unintentionally** zoddele, v.; gezoddelt, pp.

dropping or dripping Gedrops (es)n.

droppings of birds Veggelmischt (der)n.

dropsy Wassersucht (die)n.

dross 1.Dross (es)n.; 2.Hammerschlack (der)n.

drought Drickning (die)n.

drove Drupp (die)n.

drover 1.Dreiwer (der)n.; Dreiwer, pl.; 2.Fuhrmann (der) n.; Fuhrmenner, pl.; 3.Kiehdreiwer (der)n. 4.Viehdreiwer (der)n. (of cattle)

drown 1.versaufe, v.; versoffe, pp.; 2.verseefe, v.; verseeft, pp.

drowsy 1.schlaeferich, adj.; 2.schleeferich, adj.; 3.schlummerich, adj.

drub 1.fleggele, v.; gfleggelt, pp.; 2.lause, v.; gelaust, pp.; **soundly** ab/briggle, v.; abgebriggelt, pp.

drubbing Salzing (die)n.

drudgery Schinnerei (die)n.; **of cleaning** Fegerei (die)n.

druggist Abbedeeker (der)n.; Abbedeeker, pl.

drugstore Abbedeek (die)n.; Abbedeek, pl.

drum drumme, v.; gedrummt, pp.; **out** raus/drumme, v.; rausgedrummt, pp.; **with the fingers** drummle, v.; gedrummelt, pp.

drummer Drummer (der)n.

drumstick Drummegnippel (der)n.

drunk gsoffe, adj.

drunkard 1.Gsoffner (en)n.; 2.Siffer (der)n.; 3.Trunkebold (der)n.

drunken fellow versoffner (en), adj.

drunkenness 1.Sauerei (die)n.; 2.Sauferei (der)n.

dry 1.daerre, v.; gedaerrt, pp.; 2.darre, v.; gedatt, pp.; 3.drickle, v.; gedrickelt, pp.; 4.drucke, adj.; **away** weck/daerre, v.; weckgedaerrt, pp.; **dishes** ab/butzt, v.; abgebutzt, pp.; **in** nei/drickle, v.; neigedrickelt, pp.; **off** adrickle, v ; abgedrickelt, pp.; **dry too fast** aadarre, v.; aagedarrt, pp.; **out** 1.aus/daerre, v.; ausgedaerrt, pp.; 2.aus/drickle, v.; ausgedrickelt, pp.; **out so as to leak** verlechere, v.; verlechert, pp.; **partly** (as hay) ab/darre, v.; abgedarrt, pp.; **rotted** rott, v.; **sprig** Heck (die)n.; Hecke, pl.; **thoroughly** darich/drickle, v.; darich-gedrickelt, pp.; **up** 1.uff/darre, v.; uffgedatt, pp.; 2.uff/drickle, v.; uffgedrickelt, pp.; 3.uff/hutzle, v.; uffghutzelt, pp.; 4.verdrickle, v.; verdrickelt, pp.; 5.zamme/daerre, v.; zammegedaerrt, pp.; 6.zamme/drickle, v.; zammegedrickelt, pp.

dubious 1.bedenklich, adj.; 2.unbeschtimmt, adj.

duck 1.ducke (sich --)v.; geduckt, pp.; 2.Ent (die)n.; Ende,

(Continued on page 268)

Dd

duck (continued)   **dysentary**

(Continued from page 267)

pl.; 3.nidder/ducke, v.; niddergeduckt, pp.;
4.nunner/ducke, v.; nunnergeduckt, pp.; **egg** Enteoi
(es)n.

duckling 1.Entche (es)n.; 2.Entli (es)n.; Entlin, pl.

dude Fratzhans (der)n.

dudish frotsich, adj.

due 1.schuldich, adj.; 2.verfalle, v.; verfalle, pp.

dull 1.hattlaernich, adj.; 2.hattlannich, adj.; 3.langsam,
adj.; 4.schlaeferich, adj.; 5.schtump, adj.; **person**
1.Mops (der)n.; 2.Rappelkopp (der)n.

dullard Mobskopp (der)n.; Mobskepp, pl.

dummy Schtrohmann (der)n.

dump hole Damploch (es)n.

dumplings Gnepp (die)n.; **cooked with dried apples**
Gnopp (der)n.; Gnepp, pl. (schnitz un gnepp)

dumpy schtubbich, adj.

dun brau(n)gehl, adj.

dunce 1.Dummkopp (der)n.; Dummkepp, pl.; 2.Gimpel
(der)n.; 3.Mobskopp (der)n.; Mobskepp, pl.

dung Mischt (der)n.

dunghill Mischthaufe (der)n.; Mischtheife, pl.

Dunkard Dunker (der)n.

duration Dauer (die)n.

during 1.bei, prep.; 2.darich, prep.; 3.deich, prep.;
4.waehrend, prep.; **that time** selliweil, adv.; **the day**
Daag (der)n.; Daage, pl. (daags); **this time** alldiweil,
adv.

dusk 1.dischder, adj.; 2.duschber, adv.

dust 1.ab/wische, v.; abgewischt, pp.; 2.Schtaab (der)n.

dustcloth Schtaablumbe (der)n.

duster 1.Abwischer (der)n.; Abwischer, pl.;
2.Schtaabwisch (der)n.

dusting cloth Schtaabduch (es)n.; **pan** Kehrichblech (es)n.

dusty 1.mehlich, adj.; 2.schtaawich, adj.; **miller** (plant)
Miller (der)n. (der schtaawich --)

Dutch cake Schwingfelderkuche (der)n.; **cheese**
1.Ballekees (der)n.; 2.Deitscher Kees (der)n.;
3.Handkees (der)n.; **ways** Wege (der)n. (Deitscher --)

Dutchman Deitscher (en)n.

Dutchman's breeches Hosseblumm (die)n.

dutiful Gehorsam (der)n.

duty 1.Abdrack (der)n.; 2.Gflicht (die)n.; 3.Pflicht (die)n.;
4.Schuldichkeet (die)n.

dwarf 1.Mops (der)n.; 2.Zwarich (der)n.; **elder** Attich (der)
n.

dwarfish schtubbich, adj.

dwarflike mopsich, adv.

dwell 1.wohne, v.; gwohnt, pp.;2.wuhne, v.; gewuhnt, pp.

dwelling 1.Wohnhaus (es)n.; 2.Wohning (die)n.
3.Wohnung (die)n. 4.Wuhning (die)n.; Wuhninge, pl.

dye faerwe, v.; gfaerbt, pp.

dyer Faerwer (der)n.; Farewer, pl.

dying 1.schtaerblich, adj.; 2.Schtaerwes (es)n.

dysentery 1.Darichlaaf (der)n.; 2.Ruhr (die)n.; 3.Scheiss
(die)n.; 4.Schgidders (der)n.; 5.Schpringers (die)n.

268

Ee

each

each 1.yeder, adj.; 2.yeders, pron.; 3.yeklich, adj.; **of two men** (to furnish a horse to be worked together as a team)zamme/schpanne, v.; zammegschpannt, pp.; **one** yeders, adj.; **other** nanner, pron.; **time** yedesmol, adv.

eager 1.begierich, adj.; 2.eif(e)rich, adj.; **for preeminence** ehrgeizich, adj.; **to be** reisse (sich --)v.; gerisse, pp.; **to purchase** kaafich, adj.

eagerly expectant Maul (es)n. (es -- druffhie schpitze)

eagerness 1.Begierichkeet (die)n.; 2.Eifer (der)n.

eagle 1.Aadler (der)n.; Aadler, pl.; 2.Addler (der)n.; Addler, pl.

ear Ohr (es)n.; Ohre, pl.; **(human)** Kolwe (der)n.; Kolwe, pl.; **ache** Ohreweh (es)n.; **lap** Ohrelappe (der)n.; **of corn** Kolwe (der)n.; Kolwe, pl.; 2.Welschkannkolwe (der)n.; **ring** 1.Ohrbambel (die)n.; 2.Ohrering (der)n.; **wax** Ohreschmals (es)n.

earlier frieher, adv.

earliest friescht, adv.

early 1.frieh, adv.; 2.friehzeitich, adj.; 3.zeitlich, adj.; **cabbage** Friehgraut (es)n.; **corn** Friehwelschkann (es)n. **dawn** Lichthelling (die)n.; **in the morning** Frieh (die)n. (in aller --); **part of the winter** Vorwinter (der)n.; **pear** Friehbeer (die)n.; **potato** Friehgrumbeer (die)n.

earn verdiene, v.; verdient, pp.; **off a debt by working** ab/verdiene, v.; abverdient, pp.

earnest 1.aernschthaft, adj.; 2.Anscht (der)n.; 3.eifrich, adj.; 4.Ernscht (der)n.

earnestly aernschtlich, adv.

earnings Verdi(e)nscht (der)n.

earth Erd (die)n.

earthen 1.erde, adj.; 2.erdich, adj.; 3.erdne, adj.; **pipe** Schmokpeif (die)n. (en erdne --); **plate** Deller (der)n. (en erdne --)

earthly 1.Erdekloss (der)n.; 2.erdich, adj.

earthquake 1.Erdbebung (die)n.; 2.Erdbeewing (die)n.; 3.Erdbewung (die)n.; 4.Erdziddering (die)n.

earthworm 1.Fischwarem (der)n.; 2.Reggewarem (der)n.

earthy 1.erdich, adj.; 2.gruschdich, adj.

ease Ruh (die)n.

easier leichter, adv.

easily frightened gelschderich, adj.

easiness Leichtichkeet (die)n.

east Oscht (der)n.

Easter Oschdre (die)n., pl.; **egg** Oschderoi (es)n.; **Monday** Oschdermondaag (der)n.; **morn** Oschdermariye (der)n.; **present** Oschderhaas (der)n.; **rabbit** Oschderhaas (der) n.; **Sunday** Oschdersundaag (der)n.; **week** Oschderwoch (die)n.

easterly eeschtlich, adj.

easy 1.begreiflich, adj.; 2.bequem, adj.; 3.gemechlich, adj.; 4.leicht, adj.; **going** 1.gemietlich, adj.; 2.gutmiedich, adj.; **trot** Droll (der)n.

eat (of animals) fresse, v.; gfresse, pp.; **(of humans)** esse, v.; gesse, pp.; nunnergesse, pp.; **after the rest** no(och)esse, v.; no(och)gesse, pp.; **all aus/fresse,** v.; ausgfresse, pp.; **all of** weck/esse, v.; weckgesse, pp.; **at the second table**

eight

no(och)esse, v.; no(och)gesse, pp.; **everything in the house** aus/ esse, v.; ausgesse, pp.; **into** nei/fresse, v.; neigfresse, pp.; **off** ab/esse, v.; abgesse, pp.; **out of** raus/fresse, v.; rausgfresse, pp.; **rapidly** schaufle, v.; gschaufelt, pp.; **ravenously** nunner/schrode, v.; nunnergschrot, pp.; **secretly** schnause, v.; gschnaust, pp.; **through** darich/fresse, v.; darichgfresst, pp.; **too much or gluttonously** (of a person) fresse, v.; gfresse, pp.; **up** uff/esse, v.; uffgesse, pp.; **up greedily** weck/fresse, v.; weckgfresse, pp.; **up quickly** weck/esse, v.; weckgesse, pp.; **voraciously** eigawwle, v.; eigegawwelt, pp.; **with an effort** nunner/esse, v.; **with a smacking sound** schlaerbse, v.; gschlaerbst, pp.

eatables 1.Ess-sach(e) (die)n.; pl.; 2.Lewesmiddel (es)n.

eater Esser (der)n.

eating Esse (es)n.; **(of animals)** Fresse (es)n.

eaves 1.Dachdraaf (der)n.; 2.Dachdrops (der)n.; **trough or gutter** Dachdroff (der)n.

eavesdrop 1.ab/hariche, v.; abgharicht, pp.; 2.ab/lauere, v.; abgelauert, pp.; 3.lauere, v.; gelauert, pp.; 4.lauschdere, v.; gelauschdert, pp.

eavesdropper Lauerer (der)n.

eccentric ecksentrisch, adv., adj.

ecclesiastical history Karichgschicht (die)n.

echo 1.Klang (der)n.; 2.Schall (der)n.; Schalle, pl.

eclipse 1.Finschderniss (die)n.; Finschdernisse, pl.; 2.verfinschdere, v.; verfinschdert, pp.; **of the moon** Munfinschderniss (die)n.; **of the sun** Sunnefinschdernis(s) (die)n.

eclipsed verfinschdert, adj.

economical 1.hause, v.; ghaust, pp.; 2.schpaarsam, adj.

economize 1.schpaare, v.; gschpaart, pp. 2.uff/hewe, v.; uffghowe, pp.; 3.uff/lege, v.; uffgelegt, pp.; 4.uff/ schparre, v.; uffgschpatt, pp.; 5.verschpaare, v.; verschpaart, pp.

economy Schpaarsamkeit (die)n.

eddy 1.Waerwel (der)n.; 2.Zwaerwel (der)n.; 3.zwaerwle, v.; gezwaerwelt, pp.

edema Gehlwasser (es)n.

edge 1.Ran(e)ft (der)n.; 2.saame, v.; gsaamt, pp.; **of a bog or dam** Rumf (der)n.

edged tool Schneidgschaerr (die)n.

edgeways seidlings, adj., adv.

educate laerne, v.; gelaernt, pp.

educated gschult, adj.

education 1.Lanning (die)n.; 2.Lehr (die)n.; 3.Schuling (die)n.

eel Ool (die)n.; **skin** Oolehaut (die)n.; **trap** Oolekarb (der)n.

effective waerksam, adj.

effeminate 1.weiblich, adj.; 2.weichlich, adj.; 3.weiwisch, adj.

efficient waerksam, adj.

effigy Bildnis (es)n.

effort Versuch (der)n.

egg Oi (es)n.; Oier, pl.; **(in child talk)** 1.Gackel (es)n.; 2.Gackerli (es)n.; 3.Gacki (es)n.; **beater** Oiyerglepperer (der)n.; **on** uff/schtifde, v.; uffgschtift, pp.

eggshell Oiyerschaal (die)n.

egotism Eegelieb (die)n.

egress Abgang (der)n.

eight achde, acht, adj.; pron.; **day clock** Achtdaagsuhr (die)n.; **spot** (in cards) Achter (en)n.

269

Ee

eighteen achzeh, adj.; pron.
eighth (part) Achtel (en)n.
eightieth achzichscht, adj.
eighty achtzich, adj.; pron.
either 1.ehnder, adj.; 2.ender, adj.; 3.entwedder(s), pron; conj.
either...or entwedder(s)...odder, pron; conj.
eject 1.naus/duh, v.; nausgeduh, pp.; 2.naus/schmeisse, v.; nausgschmisse, pp.; 3.naus/wickle, v.; nausgewickelt, pp.; 4.raus/schmeisse, v.; rausgschmisse, pp.
eke out (one's) spite aus/riege, v.; ausgeriekt, pp.
elaborate weitleftich, adj.
elapse vergeh, v.; vergange, pp.
elbow Ellboge (der)n.; Ellboge, pl.; **aside** verzwenge, v.; verzwengt, pp.; **of a stove pipe** 1.Gnie (es)n.; Gnie, pl.; 2.Knie (es)n.
elder Holler (der)n.; **(in church)** 1.Eldeschde (der)n.; 2.Eldeschtee (der)n.
elderberry Hollerbier (die)n.; Hollerbiere, pl.
elderbloom Hollerblieh (die)n.
elderly eltlich, adj.
elecampane 1.Holand(s)watzel (die)n.; 2.Olanswatzel (die) n.
elect 1.erwaehle, v.; erwaehlt, pp.; 2.nei/schtimme, v.; neigschtimmt, pp.; 3.waehle, v.; gewaehlt, pp.; 4.wehle, v.; gewehlt, pp.
election 1.Leckschen (die)n.; 2.Waahl (die)n.
electric Leckdrick (die, es)n.; **clock** Leckdrickuhr (die)n.
elegant 1.scharmand, adj.; 2.scharmant, adj.; **young fellow** Keffer (der)n.; Keffer, pl.
element Element (es)n.
elephant 1.Elefant (der)n.; 2.El(l)efant (der)n.
elephant's ear Elefandeschtock (der)n.
elevator belt (of a flouring mill) Erheewer (der)n.
eleven 1.elf, adj.; pron.; 2.elfe, adj.; pron.; **times** elfmol, adv.
eleventh elft, adj.
Elias Eli (der)n.
Elizabeth 1.Betz (die)n.; 2.Lisbett (die)n.
elliptical langrund, adv.
elm Ulme (die)n.; **tree** Ruschebaam (der)n.
elope darich/brenne. v.; darichgebrennt, pp.
else schunscht, conj.
elude 1.aus/weiche, v.; ausgewiche, pp.; 2.weck/schlibbe, v.; weckgschlippt, pp.
emaciate 1.ab/maagere, v.; abgemaagert, pp.; 2.ab/zehre, v.; abgezehrt, pp.
emaciated 1.abgehungert, adj.; 2.abgezehrt, adj.; 3.verhungert, adj.
emancipate befreie, v.; befreit, pp.
Emanuel 1.Maan(n)i (der)n.; 2.Mannewell (der)n.
embalm 1.balsamiere, v.; gebalsamiert, pp.; 2.ei/balsamiere, v.; eigebalsamiert, pp.
embark eischiffe, v.; eigschifft, pp.
embarrassment Verleggeheet (die)n.
embellish verschennere, v.; verschennert, pp.
embellishment Verschennerung (die)n.
Ember Day Gwadember (der)n.
embittered verbiddert, adj.

emblem Simmbild (es)n.
embrace 1.behaerze, v.; behaerzt, pp.; 2.haerze, v.; ghaerzt, pp.; 3.haerze, v.; ghaerzt, pp.; 4.rum/nemme, v.; rumgenumme, pp.(un ebber --); 5.umarme, v.; umarmt, pp.; 6.umfasse, v.; umfasst, pp.
embroider aus/n(a)ehe, v.; ausgen(a)eht, pp.
emerge raus/kumme, v.; is rauskumme, pp.
emetic Brechmiddel (es)n.
emigrant 1.Auswandrer (der)n.; 2.aus/wandre, v.; ausgewandert, pp.
eminance Hochschtand (der)n.
eminent hochschtendich, adj.
emission Ausfluss (der)n.
emperor Kaiser (der)n.
emphasis Eidruck (der)n.
emphatically not mitnichtem, adv.
empire 1.Kaiserdum (es)n.; 2.Kaiserreich (es)n.
employ 1.aa/wende, v.; aagewendt, pp.; 2.aa/wenne, v.; aagewennt, pp.; 3.yuuse, v.; gyuust, pp.
employer Baas (der)n.
employment Schtell (die)n.
empower vollmechtiche, v.; vollmechtict, pp.
empty 1.aus/leere, v.; ausgeleert, pp.; 2.leer, adj.; 3.nix drin, adj.
enact verardne, v.; verardent, pp.
enchanter's nightshade Hunsleis (die)n., pl.
enclose 1.ei/fense, v.; eigfenst, pp.; 2.ei/schliesse, v.; eigschlosse, pp.; **with curtains** um/henke, v.; umghonke, pp.
encore Neweschtick (es)n.
encounter zu/dreffe, v.; zugedroffe, pp.
encourage 1.ermuntere, v.; ermuntert, pp.; 2.uff/muntre, v.; 3.zu/schpreche, v.; zugschproche, pp.
encouragement Uffmuntering (die)n.
end 1.End (es)n.; Ender, Enner, pl.; 2.ende, v.; geendt, pp.; 3.Schluss (der)n.; **of a piece of woven carpet** Zettelend (es)n.
endeavor browiere, v.; (ge)browiert, pp.
endive 1.Andiefi (der)n.; 2.Andiff(d)i (der)n.;3.Andiv(v)(d)i (der)n.; 4.Endiffi (der)n.; **salad** Endivviselaat (der)n.
endorse bei/schteht, v.; beigschtanne, pp.
endure 1.aus/halde, v.; ausghalde, pp.; 2.aus/schteh, v.; ausgschtanne, pp.; 3.darich/mache, v.; darichgemacht, pp.; 4.dauere, v.; gedauert, pp.; 5.geh, v.; gange, pp.; 6.leide, v.; gelidde, pp.; 7.schtende, v.; 8.vergraage, v.; vergraage,pp.; 9.wedder/halde, v.; wedderghalde, pp.; **to the end** darich/schteh, v.; darichschtanne, pp.
endways endweegs, adv.
enema syringe Grischdier (die)n.
enemy Feind (der)n.; Feind, pl.
energetic spell Feiereifer (der)n.
energetically safdich, adj.
enforce darich/setze, v.; darichgsetzt, pp.
engage 1.aa/nemme, v.; aag(e)numme, pp.; 2.verbinne, v.; verbunne, pp.; **in** 1.dreiwe, v.; gedriwwe, pp.; 2.vorhawwe, v.; vorghatt, pp.

Ee

engine | especial(ly)

engine 1.Inschein (der)n.; Inscheine, pl.; 2.Maschien (die) n.; Maschiene, pl.

England England (es)n.

English englisch, adj.

Englishman 1.Englenner (der)n.; Englenner, pl.; 2.Englischmann (der)n.

engraver Bilderschtecher (der)n.

engraving Kupperschtich (der)n.

enjoin 1.aab(e)fehle, v.; aab(e)fohle, pp.; 2.eischarefe, v.; eigschareft, pp.

enjoy 1.gleiche, v.; gegliche, pp.; 2.luschdere, v.; geluschdert, pp.; **oneself** (especially clandestinely) verluschdiere (sich --)v.; verluschdiert, pp.; **onself perfectly** luschdiere (sich --)v.; geluschdiert, pp.

enlarge 1.greeser mache, v.; gresser gemacht, pp.; 2.vergreesere, v.; vergreesert, pp.

enlightened uff/geklaert, v.

enlist lischde, v.

enliven belewe, v.; belebt, pp.

enmesh 1.iwwerschpinne, v.; iwwerschpunne, pp.; 2.nei/ schpinne, v.; neigschpunne, pp.

enmity Feindschaft (die)n.

ennuied 1.langweile (sich --)v.; gelangweilt, pp. 2.vergniechlich, adj.

enormous riesich, adj.

enormously verdeihenkert, adv.

enough 1.genslich, adj.; 2.genunk, adj.

enrage verzannt, adj.

enraptured 1.entzickt, adj.; 2.verzickt, adj.

enroll ei/schreiwe, v.; eigschriwwe, pp.

enscribe ei/schreiwe, v.; eigschriwwe, pp.

entangle 1.uff/huddle, v.; uffghuddelt, pp.; 2.vergnoddle, v.; vergnoddelt, pp.; 3.verhuddle, v.; verhuddelt, pp.; 4.verwickle, v.; verwickelt, pp.

entangled verhuddelt, adj.

enter 1.ei/geh, v.; eigange, pp.; 2.eiricke, v.; eigerickt, pp.; 3.nei/geh, v.; neigange,pp.; 4.rei/geh, v.; reigange, pp.; **abruptly** eischtewwre, v.; eigschtewwert, pp.; **a carriage** nei/schteige, v.; neischtigge, pp.; **complaint of assault** (with intent to kill) Lewe (es)n. (sei -- uff ebber schweere); **forcibly** eibreche, v.; eigebroche, pp.; **hastily** rei/schtewwre, v.; reigschtewwert, pp.; **hurriedly** rei/renne, v.; **in a book** ei/schreiwe, v.; eigschriwwe, pp.; **noisily** 1.nei/dunnere, v.; neigedunnert, pp.; 2.nei/glebbere, v.; neiglebbert, pp.; **service** eischteh, v.; eigschtanne, pp.; **stiffly with a cane** nei/schtocke, v.; neigschtockt, pp.; **tumultuously** nei/raase, v.; neigeraast, pp.; **unexpectedly** nei/haschble, v.; neighaschbelt, pp.; **with a heavy gait** rei/zackere, v.; reigezackert, pp.; **with heavy steps** rei/dappe, v.; reigedappt, pp.

enterprise Unnernemmung (die)n.

entertain uff/nemme, v.; uffgenumme, pp.

entice 1.aa/locke, v.; aagelockt, pp.; 2.beilocke, v.; beigelockt, pp.; 3.haer/locke, v.; haergelockt, pp.; 4.locke, v.; gelockt, pp.; 5.mit/locke, v.; mitgelockt, pp.; 6.verlocke, v.; verlockt, pp.; 7.verschtifde, v.; verschtift, pp.;

8.weck/locke, v.; weckgelockt, pp.; **in** nei/locke, v.; neigelockt, pp.; **out** 1.naus/locke, v.; nausgelockt, pp.; 2.raus/locke, v.; rausgelockt, pp.; **over** riwwer/locke, v.; riwwergelockt, pp.; **to enter** 1.rei/locke, v.; reigelockt, pp.; 2.rei/losse,v.; reiglosst, pp. reiglesst = Amish usage; **to follow** no(och)locke, v.; no(och)gelockt, pp.

entirely 1.ganz, adv.; adj.; 2.masch, adj.; 3.vollkumme, adj.

entitle berechtiche, v.; berechticht, pp.

entrails Ingeweid (es)n.

entrance 1.Eifaahrt (die)n.; 2.Eigang (der)n.; **ramp** 1. (approach to the threshing floor of the bank barn) Scheierbrick (die)n.; 2.(to the barn floor) 1.Eifaahrt (die)n.; 3.Scheierhiwwel (der)n.

entrust 1.aa/verdraue, v.; aaverdraut, pp.; 2.iwwerlosse, v.; iwwerlosse, pp.

entry Eigang (der)n.; **in a barn along the stalls** Fudergang (der)n.

entune aaschtimme, v.; aagschtimmt, pp.

envied 1.missvergunnt, adj.; 2.vergunnt, adj.

envious 1.kibbe, v.; gekippt, pp.; 2.kibbisch, adj.; 3.missgunnisch, adj.; 4.missvergunnisch, adj.; 5.neidi (s)ch, adj.; 6.uuvergunnisch, adj.; 7.vergunnisch, adj.

envy 1.Missgunscht (die)n.; 2.missvergunne, v.; missvergunnt, pp.; 3.Missvergunscht (die)n.; 4.Neid (der)n.; 5.neide, v.; geneidt, pp.; 6.vergunne, v.; vergunnt, pp.

Ephrata Ephridaa (es)n.

epidemic pehz, adj.

epilepsy Falletgranke(e)t (die)n.

epizootic Geilsgranket (die)n.

epoch Zeitpunk (der)n.

epsom salt 1.Laxier Salz (es)n.; 2.Salz (es)n. (englisch --)

equal 1.ewe, adj.; 2.gleich, adj.

equality 1.Gleichheet (die)n.; 2.Gleichheit (die)n.

equally 1.gleich, adv.; 2.gleichfellich, adj.

equilibrium 1.Gelichwicht (es)n.; 2.Gleichgewicht (es)n.; Gleichgewichder, pl.

equitable gerecht, adj.

erase 1.aus/gratze, v.; ausgegratzt, pp.; 2.aus/reiwe, v.; ausgeriwwe, pp.; 3.aus/wische, v.; ausgewischt, pp.; 4.verwische, v.; verwischt, pp.

erect 1.schnurschtracks, adj.; 2.schtrack(s), adj.; 3.schtraff, adj.; 4.uff/baue, v.; uffgebaut, pp.; 5.uff/richde, v.; uffgericht, pp.; 6.uff/schtelle, v.; uffgschtellt, pp.

ergot Brand (der)n.

ernest money Aageld (es)n.

error Fehler (der)n.; Fehler, pl.

eruptive 1.ausfaahrisch, adj.; 2.ausfiehrich, adj.

erysipelas 1.Ros (die)n. (die feirich --); 2.Wildfeier (es)n.

Esaias Saees (der)n.

escape 1.ab/kumme, v.; is abkumme, pp.; 2.ab/reisse, v. (sich -- vun); 3.Abreissing (die)n.; 4.darich/geh, v.; darichgange, pp.; 5.Flucht (die)n.; 6.frei/reisse (sich --), v.; freigrisse, pp.

escapement (of a watch) Unruh (die)n.

esophagus Schlucker (der)n.

especial(ly) 1.abaddich, adv., adj.; 2.abbardich, adv., adj.

Ee

establish

establish 1.errichte, v.; erricht, pp.; 2.grinde, v.; gegrindt, pp.

estate Lossement (es)n.; **of a deceased person** Hinnerlosseschaft (die)n.

esteem 1.achde, v.; geacht, pp.; 2.Acht (der, die)n.; 3.Achtung (die)n.; 4.eschdimiere, v. ge-eschdimiert, pp.; 5.eschtimiere, v.; ge-eschtimiert, pp.; 6.hoch achde, v.; **highly** hochhalde, adj.

estimate 1.schetze, v.; gschetzt, pp.; 2.Schetzung (der)n. **taken by the eye** Aagemos (es)n.

et cetera 1.dergleiche, adv. (un so --); 2.ettzetteraa, adj.; 3.un, conj. (-- so der gleiche); (-- so fatt); (-- so weiter)

eternal ewich, adj.; adv.

eternity Ewichkeit (die)n.

European elder Holler (der)n. (zaahmer --)

evacuate aus/leere, v.; ausgeleert, pp.

evade 1.ab/scheele (sich --)v.; abgscheelt, pp.; 2.aus/weiche, v.; ausgewiche, pp.; 3.aus/wenne, v.; ausgewennt, pp.; 4.raus/schaele (sich --)v.; rausgschaelt, pp.; 5.raus/schaffe (sich --)v.; rausgschafft, pp.; 6.schrauwe, v.; gschraubt, pp.; **responsibility** raus/scheele (sich --)v.; rausgscheelt, pp.

evading an answer to some inquisitive person Bockslochgrie (wu gehscht hie? En -- buhneroppe)

Evangelical 1.Effengeelisch, adj.; 2.Evvengelisch

Evangelicals Effengeelische (die)n.

evaporate uff/drickle, v.; uffgedrickelt, pp.

Eve Evaa (die)n.

even 1.emol, ad. v. 2.sogaar, adj.; adv.

evening 1.Owed (der)n.; 2.Owet (der)n.; **after** oweds, adv. (-- denno); **before last** vorgeschdrowed, adv.; **glow** Owedrot (es)n.; **star** Owedschtaern (die)n.

event 1.Erfolk (der)n.; 2.Vorfall (der)n.

ever 1.allfatt, adv.; 2.allzeit, adv.; 3.immer, adv.; 4.seilewe(s), adv.; 5.selewe, adv.; 6.yemols, adv.; 7.ye, adv. (rare usage)

everlasting 1.immerwaehrend, adj.; 2.Ruhrgraut (es)n.; 3.Satzbloom (die)n.; 4.uuvergenglich, adj.

everlastingly 1.daagenacht, adv. (daag un nacht); 2.immerfart, adj.

every all, adj.; **day** alli Daag, adv.; **little while** arm(e)slang (alle), adv.; **minute** arm(e)slang (alle), adv.; **morning** Mariye (der) n. (aller --); **now and then** 1.all(e)gebott, adj.; 2.alsemol, adv.; **once in a while** Buff (der)n. (alle --); **single one** gotzich, adj. (aller -- eener); **time** 1.alli Mol, adv.; 2.Buff (der)n. (alle --); 3.yedesmol, adv. **trifle** Gensdreck (der)n. (alle --)

everybody 1.alliebber, pron.; 2.ebber, pron. (yeder --); 3.yedermann, adj.

everyday all(e)daags(ich), adj.; **clothes** Alldaagsgleeder (die)n.

everyone 1.alli-eens, pron.; 2.alliebber, pron.; 3.ebber, pron. (-- yeder); 4.yedermann, adj.; 5.yeders, adj., prn.

everything 1.alles, pron.; 2.allesmenanner, pron.; **considered** allemno, adv.

everytime allemol, adv.

everywhere 1.alliwwer, adv.; 2.Eck (es)n. (in alle --e); 3.iwwerall(ich), adv.; 4.iwwerall, adj.

exclusive(ly)

evict 1.aus/heewe, v.; ausghowe, pp.; 2.raus/duh, v.; rausgeduh, pp.

evidence 1.Zeichnis (es)n.; 2.Zeiknis (es)n.

evident 1.aagescheinlich, adj.; 2.aascheinlich, adj.; 3.uffenbaar, adv.

evidently 1.allemno, adv.; 2.demno, adv.; 4.demnooch, adv.; 5.scheinbarlich, adj.; 6.scheinlich, adv.; 7.scheins, adv.

evil 1.iwwel, adj.; 2.Schlechdes (es)n.; 3.Schlechdichkeit (die)n.; 4.schlecht, adj.; **looking** iwwelguckich, adj.; **report** Gschtink (es)n.

evildoer Iwweldeeder (der)n.

evince unrest bobere, v.; gebobert, pp.

ewe 1.Mammischof (es)n.; 2.Mudderschof (die)n.; Mudderscheef, pl.

exact 1.genaa, adj.; 2.genau, adj.; 3.graad recht, adj.; 4.pink(t)lich, adv.; **(usually used with net)** kauscher, adj.; **(very)** 1.haarscharf, adj.; 2.hoorscharf, adj.

exactly 1.brezis, adj.; 2.graad, adv., adj.; 3.graadement, adj.; 4.prezis, adj.; 5.yuschdament, adv.

exaggerate iwwerdreiwe, v.; iwwerdriwwe, pp.

exalt erhehe, v.; erheet, pp.

examine 1.dreigucke, adj.; 2.eiblicke, v.; eigeblickt, pp.; 3.iwwerdrachde, v.; iwwerdracht, pp.; 4.unner/suche, v.; unnergsucht, pp.; 5.visidiere, v.; visidiert, pp. (v = f)

examine oneself priefe (sich --)v.; geprieft, pp.

example 1.Beischpiel (es)n.; 2.Exembel (der)n.

excavate aus/graawe, v.; ausgegraawe, pp.

exceedingly iwweraus, adv.

excel iwwerdreffe, v.; iwwerdroffe, pp.

excellent 1.fei(n), adj.; 2.vordreffich, adj.; 3.vornehm, adj.; **food** Gfress (es)n.

excellently 1.Aart (die)n. (das es en -- hot); 2.Ort (die)n. (das es en -- hott)

except mitaus, conj.

exchange 1.aus/wechsle, v.; ausgewechselt, pp.; 2.rum/wexle, v.; rumgewexelt, pp.; 3.wexle, v.; gewexelt, pp.; **views** berotschlagge, v.; berotgschlagge, pp.

excise Abdrack (der)n.

excite 1.uff/rege, v.; uffgeregt, pp.; 2.uff/riege, v.; uffgeregt, pp.; 3.uff/riehre, v.; uffgriehrt, pp.;4.uff/schtarre, v.; uffgschtarrt, pp.; 5.eiferich, adj.; 6.eifrich, adj.

excited uffgschafft, adj.

exclamation of astonishment oii!, interj.; **of disgust or shivering** hu!, interj.; **of impatience** (as on failing to thread a needle, or in dropping something, or in knocking against something) Na!, interj.; **of one shivering from cold** br!, interj.; **of satisfaction** Aah!, interj.; **of surprise or deprecation** (or with a different intonation of endearment in cressingly pressing one's cheek against that of a child) eigei, interj.

exclude 1.aus/schliesse, v.; ausgschlosse, pp.; 2.aus/schtosse, v.; ausgschtosse, pp.; 3.haus/bhalde, v.; hausgebhalde, pp.

exclusive baddich, adv.

exclusive(ly) 1.abaddich, adv., adj.; 2.abbardich, adv., adj.

Ee

excogitate

extreme unction

excogitate aus/sinne, v.; ausgsunne, pp.

excrement Schtulgang (der)n.

excrementum 1.Dreck (der)n.; 2.Schiss (der)n.

excuse 1.Ausrett (die)n.; Ausredde, pl.; 2.Eiwendung (die) n.; 3.Eiwenning (die)n.; **oneself** 1.deffendiere (sich --)v.; deffendiert, pp.; 2.en(t)schuldiche, v.; entschuldicht, pp.; 3.En(t)schuldichung (die)n.; **or defend oneself** verdeffendiere (sich --)v.; verdeffendiert, pp.

execute 1.darich/fiehre, v.; darichgfiehrt, pp.; 2.vollfiehre, v.; vollfiehrt, pp.

exempt 1.aus/halde, v.; ausghalde, pp.; 2.frei, adj.

exercise 1.Ausiewung (die)n.; 2.Bewegung (die)n.; 3.iewe, v.; geiebt, pp.

exert schtrenge, v.; gschtrengt, pp.; **oneself** 1.aaschtrenge (sich --)v.; aagschtrengt, pp.; 2. bemiehe (sich --) v.; bemieht, pp.; **oneself** (to keep up with another) no(och)schaffe (sich --)v.; no(och)gschafft, pp.

exertion Druwwel (der)n.

exhale 1.aus/schnaufe, v.; ausgschnauft, pp.; 2.naus/schnaufe, v.; nausgschnauft, pp.

exhaust oneself by working ab/bloge (sich --)v.; abgeblogt, pp.

exhausted 1.ausgfeekt, adv.; 2.ausgschpielt, adj.; 3.gebritscht, adv.

exhort 1.ermaahne, v.; ermaahnt, pp.; 2.vermaahne, v.; vermaahnt, pp.

exhortation Ermaahnung (die)n.

exonerate raus/schtreiche, v.; rausgschtriche, pp.

exoneration Befreiung (die)n.

expect 1.erwaarte, v.; erwaart, pp.; 2.schtitze, v.; gschtizt, pp.; 3.verwaarde, v.; verwaardt, pp.; 4.zehle, v.; gezehlt, pp.; **someone to** zu/mude, v.; zugemut, pp.

expectation 1.Aussicht (die)n.; 2.Hoffning (die)n.; 3.Hoffning (die)n.; 4.Hoffnung (die)n.

expel ab/dreiwe, v.; abgedriwwe, pp. aus/dreiwe, v.; ausgedriwwe, pp.; **the breath** (through the open mouth) hauche, v.; ghaucht, pp.

expend 1.aus/gewwe, v.; ausgewwe, pp.; 2.aus/lege, v.; ausgelegt, pp.

expenditure Ausgaab (die)n.

expense Ausleek (der)n.

expense(s) Koschde (die)n.; pl.

expensive 1.deier, adj. 2.hoch, adj. (-- kumme) 3.koschtlich, adj.; 4.koschtschpielich, adj.

experience 1.darich/mache, v.; darichgemacht, pp.; 2. erfaahre, v.; erfaahre, pp.; 3.Erfaahring (die)n.; 4.Erleebnis (die)n.; 5.erleewe, v.; erleebt, pp.; 6.versuche, v.; versucht, pp.

expert gschickt, adj.

expire 1.aus/geh, v.; ausgange, pp.; 2.aus/laafe, v.; is ausgeloffe, pp.

expired verloffe, adv.

explain 1.aus/lege, v.; ausgelegt, pp.; 2.erklaere, v.; erklaert, pp.

explanation 1.Erklaerung (die)n.; 2.Noochweis (der)n.

explicit deitlich, adj.

explicitly ausdricklich, adv.

explode 1.Luft (die)n. (in -- geh); 2.verschpringe, v.; is verschprunge, pp.

expose uff/decke, v.; uffgedeckt, pp.; **to the sun** sunne, v.; gsunnt, pp.

exposition Auslegung (die)n.

expositor Ausleger (der)n.

express aus/dricke, v.; ausgedrickt, pp.; **a longing for** nengere, v.; genengert, pp.; **an opinion** meene, v.; gemeent, pp.; **oneself** aus/dricke (sich --)v.; ausgedrickt, pp.

expression 1.Ausdruck (der)n.; 2.Rett (die)n.

expressly ausdricklich, adv.

extend 1.lengre, v.; gelengert, pp.; 2.reeche, v.; gereecht, pp.; 3.verlengere, v.; verlengert, pp.; **a hand** mit/helfe, v.; mitgholfe, pp.

extent Grees (die)n.

exterminate 1.aus/dreiwe, v.; ausgedriwwe, pp.; 2.aus/rodde, v.; ausgerott, pp.; 3.verdreiwe, v.; verdriwwe, pp.; 4.verdreiwe, v.; verdriwwe, pp.

exterminate (weeds) verdilye, v.; verdilgt, pp.

externally 1.aussehaer, adv.; 2.eisserlich, adv.

extinguish 1.aus/lesche, v.; ausgelescht, pp.; 2.ausgange, adj.; 3.lesche, v.; gelescht, pp.; 4.verlesche, v.; verlescht, pp.; **(fire)** aus/mache, v.; ausgemacht, pp.

extinguished (of a fire) aus/sei, v.; ausgewest, pp.

extirpate 1.aus/dilye, v.; ausgedilgt, pp.; 2.aus/rodde, v.; ausgerott, pp.

extort 1.ab/zwacke, v.; abgezwackt, pp.; 2.ab/zwinge, v.; abgezwunge, pp.

extra 1.exdraa, adv.; 2.exdroi, adv.; **costs** Newekoschde (die)n.,pl.

extract by boiling aus/koche, v.; ausgekocht, pp.; **fat by frying** aus/brode, v.; ausgebrode, pp.

extravagance Verschwendung (die)n.

extravagant 1.iwwermaessich, adj.; 2.iwwermeesich, adj.; adv.; 3.verwenderisch, adj.

extreme unction Eeling (die)n. (letschdi --)

273

Ff

fable — farmyard

fable Faabel (die)n.

face 1.Aagesicht (es)n.; 2.Gfress (es)n.; 3.Gsicht (es)n.; Gsichder, pl.; **of a wall** Mauerwand (die)n.

factory whistle Brummer (der)n.; Brummer, pl.

faculty Faehichkeet (die)n.

fade 1.ab/bleeche, v.; abgebleecht; pp.; 2.aus/geh, v.; ausgange, pp.; 3.bleeche, v.; gebleecht, pp.; **in color** aus/bleeche, v.; ausgebleecht, pp.

faded 1.verblieht, adj.; 2.verschosse, adj.; **(past tense usage)** ab/schiesse, v.; abgschosse, pp.

fag out ab/schinne (sich --)v.; abgschunne, pp.

fagged out lodderlo, adv.

fail 1.darich/falle, v.; darichgfalle, pp.; 2.fehl/gschlagge, v.; fehlgschlagge, pp.; 3.fehle, v.; g(e)fehlt, pp.; 4.verfehle, v.; verfehlt, pp.; 5.zerickzusgeh, adv.; **in health** uff, prep., adv. (-- em Grebsgang sei); **to hit the mark** fehl/schiesse, v.; fehlgschosse, pp.; **to materialize** verdrickle, v.; verdrickelt, pp.

fail(ing) fehl, adj. (unne --)

failing 1.hinnerfellich, adj.; 2.rickfellich, adj.; **to meet expectations** scheissich, adj.

faint 1.leis, adj.; 2.ummechdich warre, v.; is ummechdich warre, pp.

faintness Mattichkeet (die)n.

fair (weather) hell, adj.

fairy ring or circle (where vegetation is lacking owing to fungus growth) Hexedans (der)n.

faithful 1.gedrei, adj.; 2.gedreilich, adj.; 3.trei, adj.; 4.treihaerzich, adj.

faithless treilos, adj.

Fall (of man) Sindefall (der)n.

fall 1.dropsle, v.; gedropselt, pp.; 2.Fall (der)n.; 3.falle, v.; gfalle, pp.; 4.Harebscht (der)n.; 5.Herbscht (der)n.; 6.Schpotyaahr (es)n.; 7.schtaerze, v.; gschtaerzt, pp.; **against** wedder/schtaerze, v.; weddergschtaerzt, pp.; **apart** inzweefalle, adv.; **around** rum/schtaerze, v.; rumgschtaerzt, pp.; **asleep** ei/schlofe, v.; eigschlofe, pp.; **back** 1.zerick/falle, v.; zerickgfalle, pp.; 2.zerick/schtaerze, v.; zerickgschtaerzt, pp.; **backwards** zerickzusfalle, adv.; **behind** zerick/falle, v.; zerickgfalle, pp.; **behind (in obligations)** zerick/kumme, v.; zerickkumme, pp.; **down** 1.hie/falle, v.; hiegfalle, pp.; 2.nidder/falle, v.; niddergfalle, pp.; 3.nunner/falle, v.; nunnergfalle, pp.; 4.runner/falle, v.; is runnergfalle, pp.; 5.um/falle, v.; umgfalle, pp.; 6.zamme/falle, v.; zammegfalle, pp.; 7.zamme/schtaerze, v.; zammegschtaerzt, pp.; **headlong** hie/schtatze, v.; hiegschtatzt, pp.; **in** 1.eirutsche, v.; eigerutscht, pp.; 2.eischtaerze, v.; eigschtaertzt, pp.; 3.nei/falle, v.; is neigfalle, pp.; 4.rei/falle, v.; reigfalle, pp.; 5.rei/schtaerze, v.; reigschtaerzt, pp.; 6.zamme/schtaerze, v.; zammegschtaerzt, pp.; 7.zufalle, v.; zugfalle, pp.; **in drops** 1.drebsle, v.; gedrebselt, pp.; 2.drepsle, v.; gedrepselt, pp.; 3.dropse, v.; gedropst, pp.; **in love** verliewe (sich --) v.; verliebt, pp.; **in rank** aareihe (sich --) v.; aagereiht, pp.; **into** nei/schtaerze, v.; neigschtaerzt, pp.; **into slumber** ei/schlummere, v.; eigschlummert, pp.; **off** ab/falle,

v.; abgfalle, pp.; **off or down** ab/schtatze, v.; abgschtatzt, pp.; **on** uff/falle, v. uffgfalle, pp.; **on the other side** niwwer/falle, v.; niwwergfalle, pp; **open** uff/falle, v. uffgfalle, pp.; **out** 1.aus/geh, v.; ausgange, pp.; 2.naus/falle, v.; nausgfalle, pp.; 3.raus/falle, v.; rausgfalle, pp.; **over** 1.riwwer/falle, v.; riwwergfalle, pp.; 2.um/falle, v.; umgfalle, pp.; 3.um/schtaerze, v.; umgschtaertzt, pp.; **over each other** iwwerenannerfalle, v.; iwwerenannergfalle, pp.; **over from top heaviness** iwwerschneppe, v.; iwwergschneppt, pp.; **over one's feet** hie/batzle, v.; hiegebatzelt, pp.; **to pieces** verfalle, v.; verfalle, pp.; **to pieces in cooking** verkoche, v.; verkocht, pp.; **up** nuff/falle, v.; nuffgfalle, pp.; **upon** 1.aa/falle, v.; aagfalle, pp.; 2.druff/falle, v.; is druffgfalle, pp.

falling star Schtaerneschnuppe, (die)n.

fallow brooche, v.; gebroocht, pp.; **land** Broochland (es)n.

fallowed g(e)felkt, adj.

false 1.falsch, adj.; 2.unrichdich, adj.; **face** Schnarefeggelgsicht (es)n.; **flax** Dodder (der)n.; **teeth** falscher Zeh (der)n.; falschi Zeh, pl.

falsehood Lieg (die)n.; Liege, pl.

falsify verfelsche, v.; verfelscht, pp.

falter flinsche, v.; gflinscht, pp.

fame Ruhm (der)n.

familiar bekannt, adj.

family 1.Fa(a)milye (die)n.; 3.Haushalling (die)n.; 4.Haushaltung (die)n.; **way** Familyeumschtende (die)n.

famine Hungersnot (die)n.

famish 1.aus/hungere, v.; ausghungert, pp.; 2.hungere, v.; ghungert, pp.; 3.hungere, v.; ghungert, pp.

famous beriehmt, adj.

fan fache, v.; gfacht, pp.

fancy 1.ei/bilde (sich --)v.; eigebildt, pp.; 2.Eibildung (die) n.; 3.Eifall (der)n.; Eifalle, pl.

fang Fangzaah (der)n.; Fangzeh, pl.

far weit, adj.,adv.; **and wide** weitrum, adv.; **off** langhi, adv.

farce fille, v.; gfillt, pp.

fare 1.aa/kumme, v.; is aakumme, pp.; 2.Faahrgeld (es)n.; 3.Koscht (die)n.; **badly** weck/kumme, v.; weckkumme, pp. (schlecht --)

farewell 1.faerriwell, adj.; 2.farewell!, inter.; 3.hadyee!, interj.; 4.Leb(e)wohl (es)n.; 5.Lewewohl!, inter.; **sermon** Abschiddsbreddich (die)n.

farm 1.bauere, v.; gebauert, pp.; 2.Bauerei (die)n.; Bauereie, pl.; 3.Blandaasch(e) (die)n.; 4.Plandaasch (die)n.; **place** Hof (der)n.; Hef, pl.; **wagon** Blotzwagge (der)n.

farmed to death ausgebauert, adj.

farmer 1.Bauer (der)n.; Bauere, pl.; 2.Bauersleit (der)n.; 3.Bauersmann (der)n.

farmer's conveyance Landfuhr (die)n.; **fare** Bauerekoscht (die)n.; **wife** Bauersfraa (die)n.

farmhand Gnecht (der)n.; Gnecht, pl.

farmhouse Bauerehaus (es)n.; Bauersheiser, pl.

farming implements 1.Baueregeredschaft (die)n.; 2.Baueregschar (es)n.

farmstead Platz (der)n.; Pletz, pl.

farmyard Scheierhof (der)n.; Scheierhef, pl.

Ff

farrier — female

farrier Geilsbschlagger (der)n.

fart 1.Farz (der)n.; 2.farze, v.; gfarzt, pp.; 3.Fatz (der)n.; Fatze, pl.

farther weider(s), adv.

farting Gfarz (es)n.

fascinate banne, v.; gebannt, pp.

fashion 1.Gebrauch (der)n.; Gebreich, pl.; 2.Mode (die)n.

fashionable hochbeenich, adj.

fast 1.fascht, adj.; 2.fescht, adv., adj.; 3.gschwind, adv.; 4.schtar(r)ick, adj.; adv.; 5.schteik, adv.; **(at Lent)** 1.faschde, v.; gfascht, pp.; 2.Fascht (die)n.; **day** 1.Betdaag (der)n.; 2.Bussdaag (der)n.; 3.Faschtdaag (der)n. (Amish usage); **driving** geyaag, adj.; **time** Deifelzeit (die)n.

fasten 1.befeschdiche, v.; befeschdicht, pp.; 2.fescht mache, v.; fescht gemacht, pp.; **by sticking on** aa/klewe, v.; aageklebt, pp.; **down with nails** vernaggle, v.; vernaggelt, pp.; **over** niwwer/schtecke, v.; niwwergschtocke, pp.; **to** deweddermache, v.; deweddergemacht, pp.; **to by sticking on** aa/gle(e)we v.; aageglebt, pp. **together** anenanner, adv.; **up a dress** (with hooks and eyes) eihafte, v.; eighaft, pp.

fastidious 1.absenaat, adj.; 2.schniekich, adj. 3.schnuppich, adj.

fat 1.dick, adj.; 2.Fett (es)n.; 3.fett, adj.; **as a March hare** Matzhaas (der)n. (fett wie en --); **light** Schmutzlicht (es)n.; **or fattening** 1.**cattle** Maschtvieh (es)n.; **2.hog** Maschtsau (die)n.

fatal 1.deedlich, adj.; 2.dodlich, adj.

fate Schicksaal (es)n.

father 1.Dad (der)n.; 2.Daed (der)n.; 3.Paep (der)n.; 4.Pappi (der)n.; 5.Vadder (der)n.; **in-law** 1.Schwaer (der)n.; 2.Schw(a)erdaadi (der)n.; 3.Schwardaadi (der)n.; 4.Schwiegervadder (der)n.

fatherland Vadderland (es)n.

fatherly vadderlich, adj.

fathom ergrinde, v.; ergrindt, pp.

fatigue 1.Miedichkeet (die)n.; 2.Miedichkeit (die)n.

fatigued mied, adj.

fatten uff/meschde, v.; uffgemescht, pp.; **(animals)** 1.mascht, adj.; 2.meschde, v.; gmescht, pp.

fatty 1.feddich, adj.; 2.fettich, adj.

faucet Zabbe (der)n.; Zabbe, pl.

fault 1.Fehler (der)n.; Fehler, pl.; 2.Gfehler (der)n., Gfehler, pl.; 3.Schuld (die)n.; Schulde, pl.; **finder** Taadler (der)n.; **finding** zankich, adj.

faulty fehlerhaft, adj.

favor 1.begnaadiche, v.; begnaadicht, pp.; 2.Gfalle (der) n.; 3.Gfellichkeet (die)n.; 4.Gunn (die)n.; 5.Gunscht (die)n.; 6.schone, v.; gschont, pp.; 7.schune, v.; gschont, pp.; 8.verschone, v.; verschont, pp.; 9.verschune, v.; verschont, pp.; 10.Wohlgfalle (der)n.

favorable to growth wexich, adj.

favorite air Leibschtick (es)n.; Leibschticker, pl.; **cake** Siesskuche (der)n.; Seisskuche, pl.

fawn schmeechle, v.; gschmeechelt, pp.

fear 1.Angscht (die)n.; 2.Bang (die)n. (-- hawwe;) 3.Bangichkeet (die)n.; 4.Engschde (die)n.; Engschde, pl.; 5.faerichde, v.; gfaericht, pp.; 6.farichde, v.; gfaricht, pp.; 7.Farricht (die)n.; 8.scheie (sich --)v.

fearful 1.bang, adj.; 2.engschderich, adv.; 3.engschderlich, adj., adv.; 4.engschtlich, adv.; 5.enschderlich, adv.; 6.faerrichderlich, adj.; 7.voll Angscht, adv.; 8.barmelmaessich, adv.

fearfully 1.bummeraalisch, adj.; 2.bummerisch, adj.; 3.wedders, adv.

feast 1.Fescht (es)n.; Feschder, pl.; 2.Schmaus (der)n.; 3.schmause, v.; gschmaust, pp.

feat Daat (die)n.; Daade, pl.

feather 1.Fedder (die)n.; Feddre, pl.; 2.feddere, v.; gfeddert, pl.; **case** (for bed) Bettziech (die)n.; **duster** 1.Fedderwisch (der)n.; 2.Fledderwisch (der)n.

featherbed 1.Deckbett (es)n.; 2.Fedderbett (es)n.; **(cover)** Fedderdeck (die)n.

feathered fedd(e)rich, adj.

featherfew Meederle (es)n.

February 1.Febrewaar (der)n.; 2.Hanning (der)n.

fee Bezaahling (die)n.

feeble schwach, adj.

feed fiedere, v.; gfiedert, pp.; **(of horses and poultry)** Fresse (es)n.; **a threshing machine** nei/fiedere, v.; neigfiedert, pp.; **cutter** Fuderbank (die)n.; **entry** Fudergang (der)n.; **for animals** Fuder (es)n.; **from cut straw** Heckselfuder (es)n.

feel 1.fiehle, v.; gfiehlt, pp.; 2.gschpiere, v.; gschpiert, pp.; 3.schpiere,v.; schpiert,pp.; **a sensation** (as of crawling insect) griwwle, v.; gegriwwelt, pp.; **about** rum/fiehle, v.; rumgfiehlt, pp.; **at aa/fiehle, v.; aagfiehlt, pp.; **at home** heem(e)le, v.; gheemelt, pp.; **disgust** widdere, v.; gewiddert, pp.; **of** befiehle, v.; befiehlt, pp.; **one's way about** (in the dark) fischble, v.; gfischbelt, pp.

feeling (sense of touch) Gfiehl (es)n.; **for** Aafehles (es)n.

felloe (of a wagon wheel) Felg (die)n.; Felge, pl.

fellow 1.Dingrich (der)n.; 2.Dropp (der)n.; 3.Kall (der)n.; Kalls, pl.; **feeling** (sympathy) Mitgfiehl (es)n.; **man** 1.Menschebruder (der)n.; Menscherbrieder, pl.; 2.Mitbruder (der)n.; 3.Mitmensch (der)n.

fellowship Gemeinschaft (die)n

felon 1.Beesding (es)n.; 2.Naggelfluss (der)n.; 3.Verbrecher (der)n.; Verbrecher, pl.

female 1.weiblich, adj.; 2.Weibsbild (es)n.; 3.Weibsmensch (es)n.; Weibsleit, pl.; **(of birds)** Weibche (es)n.; **bumblebee** (so called because its face is black while that of the male is white) 1.Schwarzkopp (der)n.; 2.Schwatzkopp (der)n.; **cat** 1.Kitz (die)n.; 2.Kitzn (die)n.; **deer** 1.Haschkuh (die) n.; 2.Haschkuh (die)n.; **hatmaker** Hutmachern (die) n.; **nurse** Abwaarden (die)n. **pudendum** 1.Bix (die)n.; 2.Bussi (die)n.; 3.Fetzel (die)n.; 4.Fotz (die)n.; 5.Zott (die)n.; **rabbit** Kitz (die)n.; **singer** Singern (die)n.; **woodchuck** Grunddachskitz (die)n.

Ff

fence ... find

fence Fens (die)n.; Fense, pl.; **in** ei/fense, v.; eigfenst, pp.
    panel Gfach (es)n.; **rail** Fenseriggel (der)n.; Fenseriggel, pl.

fennel Fennichel (der)n.

Ferdinand Faerdinand (der)n.

ferment 1.gaehre, v.; gegaehrt; gegohre, pp.; 2.gehre, v.; gegehrt, pp.; 3.schaffe, v.; gschafft, pp.; 4.yaehre, v.; geyaehrt, pp.; 5.yehre, v.; geyehrt, pp.; 6.yohre, v.

fern Faaraan (der)n.

ferryboat 1.Ferri (die)n.; 2.Ferriboot (die)n.

fertile fruchtbaar, adj.

fertilize 1.dinge, v.; gedingt, gedunge, pp.; 2.mischde, v.; g(e)mischt, pp.

fervent hitzich, adj.

festal festlich, adj.

festival Fescht (es)n.; Feschder, pl.; **or anniversary day, September 24** (Schwenkfelder) Yohrsdaag (der)n.

fetch 1.ab/hole, v.; abgholt, pp.; 2.bei/griege, v.; beigrickt, pp.; 3.bei/hole, v.; beigholt, pp.; 4.bringe, v.; gebrocht, pp.; 5.hol(l)e, v.; gholt, pp.; 6.rum/ hole, v.; rumgholt, pp.; **away** weck/hole, v.; weckgholt, pp.; **back** zerick/hole, v.; zerickgholt, pp.; **down** runner/hole, v.; runnergholt, pp.; **here** haer/hole, v.; haergholt, pp.; **fetch home** heemhole, v.; **in** 1.nei/hole, v.; neigholt, pp.; 2.rei/hole, v.; reigholt, pp.; **or take up** nuff/hole, v.; nuffgholt, pp.; **out** raus/hole, v.; rausgholt, pp.; **over** riwwer/hole, v.; riwwergholt, pp.; **up** ruff/hole, v.; ruffgholt, pp.

fetlock Hufhaar (die)n., pl.; **joint of a horse** Filsglaech (der)n.

fever 1.Fiewer (es)n.; 2.Hitz (die)n.; **and agu** Kaltfiewer (es)n.

feverfew Meederle (es)n.

feverish fiewerisch, adj.

feverwort Fiewergraut (es)n.

few paar, pron., adj.; **times** paarmol, adv.

fib liege, v.; geloge, pp.

fiber Faade(m) (der)n.

fibers Fassere (die)n., pl.

fibrous faedmich, adj.

fibs Schnitz (die)n.; Schnitz, pl.

fickle wankelmiedich, adj.; **girl** Fladderwisch (der)n.

fiddle 1.Fiedel (die)n.; 2.Geig (die)n.; Geige, pl.; 3.geige, v.; gegeigt, pp.

fiddler Geiger (der)n.

fiddlestick Fiddelboge (der)n.; Fiddelboge, pl.

fiddling Gegeik (es)n.

fidget 1.geige, v.; gegeigt, pp.; 2.yucke, v.; geyuckt, pp. **(a horse)** dabbele, v.; gedabbelt, pp.; **with impatience-** Waermche (es)n. (en horrich --)

fidgeting 1.Gegeik (es)n.; 2.Geyuck (es)n.

fidgety 1.gafflich, adj.; 2.haschblich, adj.; **over something** bedroddle (sich --)v.; bedroddelt, pp.

field Feld (es)n.; Felder, pl.; **bindweed** Winne (die)n.; **grown up in brush** Grubbsefeld (es)n.; **in grass** Graasfeld (es)n.; **lark** Sootlaerrich (die)n.; **mouse**

Feldmaus (die)n.; Feldmeis, pl.; **or part of a field when plowed by making all turns to the left** Haaland (es)n.; **pumpkin** Seikaerbs (die) n.

fiery feierich, adj.

fife 1.Peif (die)n.; Peife, pl.; 2.Zwaerichpeif (die)n.; Zwaerichpeife, pl.

fifteen fuffzeh, adj.; pron.

fifth (part) Fimftel (es)n.

fifty fuffzich, adj.; pron.

fig Feik (die)n.; **tree** Feigebaam (der)n.

fight 1.aa/fechde, v.; aagfochde, pp.; 2.fechde, v.; gfochde, pp.; 3.Fecht (der)n.; 4.Schlaegerei (die)n.; **fight it out** aus/fechde, v.; ausgfochde, pp.

fighter 1.Fechder (der)n.; 2.Schlaeger (die)n.

figure 1.Figur (die)n.; 2.Nummer (die)n.; Nummere, pl.; 3.Zaahlwatt (es)n.; 4.Ziffer (der)n.; Ziffere, pl.

figure out 1.aus/figgere, v.; ausgfiggert, pp.; 2.ausrechle, v.; ausgrechelt,pp.; 3.figgere, v.; gfiggert, pp.

figwort Brau(n)watzel (die)n.

filch 1.weck/flause, v.; weckgflaust, pp.; 2.weck/lause, v.; weckgelaust, pp.

file 1.Feil (die)n.; Feile, pl.; 2.feile, v.; gfeilt, pp.; **off** ab/feile, v.; abgfeilt, pp.; **open** uff/feile, v.; uffgfeilt, pp.; **out** aus/feile, v.; ausgfeilt, pp.

fill 1.aa/fille, v.; aagfillt, pp.; 2.Fill (die)n.; 3.fille, v.; gfillt, pp.; 4.Filli (die)n.; 5.voll/mache, v.; vollgemacht, pp.; **a place with vehicles parking** zufaahre, v.; zugfaahre, pp.; **an office** 1.bediene, v.; bedient, pp.; 2.begleede, v.; begleedt, pp.; **in** nei/fille, v.; neigfillt, pp.; **out or up** aus/fille, v.; ausgfillt, pp.; **up** 1.eifille, v.; eigfillt, pp.; 2.no(och)fille, v.; no(och)gfillt, pp.; 3.zuschmeisse, v.; zugschmisse, pp.; **with secret joy** kitzle, v.; gekitzelt, pp.; **to the utmost capacity** gschtoppevoll, adv.

filling 1.Brotfilsel (es)n.; 2.Filling (die)n.; 3.Fil(l)sel (es)n.; 4.Filsing (der)n.

fillip 1.schnelle, v.; gschnellt, pp.; 2.Schneller (der)n.

filly 1.Fill (es)n.; Filler, pl.; 2.Filli (es)n.; Filler, pl.

film 1.Heitche (es)n.; 2.Heitel (es)n.; 3.Heitli (es)n.; **on milk** 1.Heitche (es)n.; 2.Heitel (es)n.; 3.Heitli (es)n.

filter 1.seene, v.; gseent, pp.; 2.Seener (der)n.; 3.Seih (die)n.; 4.seihe, v.; gseiht, pp.

filth 1.Dreck (der)n.; 2.Schmutz (der)n.

filthy dreckich, adj.; **person** 1.Dreckhammel (der)n.; 2.Drecksack (der)n.; 3.Drecksau (die)n.

fin (of a fish) Flussfedder (die)n.

finally 1.endlich, adv.; 2.letscht, adj. (-- zu guter); 3.vollschder, adj.; 4.zeletscht, adv.; 5.zuletscht, adv.

finch Fink (der)n.

find finne, v.; gfunne, pp.; **a partner** (for another in matrimony) kupple, v.; gekuppelt, pp.; **fault** 1.fuddre, v.; gfuddert, pp.; 2.griwwle, v.; gegriwwelt, pp.; 3.rum/gnickse, v.; rumgegnickst, pp.; 4.taadle, v.; getaadelt,pp.; 5.uff/reisse, v.; uffgerisse, pp. (es Maul --); **out** 1.aus/finne, v.; ausgfunne, pp.; 2.ergrinde, v.; ergrindt, pp.; 3.innewaerre, v.; innewaerre, pp.; **out by reckoning** no(och)rechle, v.; no(och) gerechelt, pp.

Ff

finder   flap

finder Finner (der)n.; Finner, pl.

fine 1.fei(n), adj.; 2.feischtielich, adj.; 3.scharmand, adj.; 4.scharmant, adj.; 5.Schtrof (die)n.; 6.schtrofe, v.; gschtroft, pp.; **(literally and figuratively)** feischtenglich, adj.; **tracery work** 1.Grickselfixel (es) n.; 2.Gritzelfixel (es)n.; 3.Kritzelfixel (es)n.

finest of all allerfeinscht, adj.

finger 1.Finger (der)n.; Finger, pl.; 2.fingere, v.; gfingert, pp.; 3.fingeriere, v.; gfingeriert, pp.; **fingers** Tatz (die)n.

finger bandage Fingerling (der)n.; Fingerling, pl.; **grass** 1.Gawwelgraas (es)n.; 2.Hinkelfuss(graas) (es)n.; 3.Zinkegraas (es)n.; **or hunt in the dark** fussle, v.; gfusselt, pp.; **stall** Fingerling (der)n.; Fingerling, pl.

fingernail Fingernaggel (der).; Fingerneggel, pl.

finical absenaat, adj.

finish 1.aus/fiehre, v.; ausgfiehrt, pp.; 2.b(e)schliesse, v.; b(e)schlosse, pp.; 3.faddich mache, v.; faddichgemacht, pp.; 4.vollende, v.; vollendet, pp.; **burning** aus/brenne, v.; ausgebrennt, pp.; **complaining** aus/greckse, v.; ausgegreckst, pp.; **giggling** aus/gickle, v.; ausgegickelt, pp.; **talking** aus/blaudre, v.; ausgeblaudert, pp.; **teething** aus/zaahe, v.; ausgezaaht, pp.; **threshing** aus/dresche, v.; ausgedrosche, pp.; **finish with** ab/zettle, v.; abgezettelt, pp.

finished 1.faddich, adj.; 2.faerdich, adj.; 3.reddi, adj.; 4.verbei, adv.; 5.veriwwer, adv.; 6.vollschder, adj.; 7.vollschder, adj.; **with something or someone** faddich, adj. (ebbes odder ebber -- sei mit); **one's education** 1.ausgelearnt, adj. 2.ausgschtudiert, adj.

fipenny bit Fipp (der)n.; Fippe, pl.

fir Tanne (die)n.

fire Feier (es)n.; **a gun** 1.ab/dricke, v.; abgedrickt, pp.; **eater** Feierfresser (der)n.; **fly** Feierfliek (die)n.; **off** ab/schiesse, v.; abgschosse, pp.; **red** feierrot, adj.; **shovel** Feierschipp (die)n.; **tongs** Feierzang (die)n.; Feierzange, pl.; **wood** Brennhols (es)n.

firefly Feiervoggel (der)n.; Feierveggel, pl.

fireman Feiermann (der)n.

fireplace 1.Feiereck (es)n.; Feierecke, pl.; 2.Feierhard (der)n.; Feierhard, pl.; 3.Feierplatz (der)n.; Feierbletz, pl.; **crane** Feierblotzgrone (der)n.

firewood Feierholz (es)n.; **for the winter** Winterhols (es)n.

fireworks Feierwaerrick (es)n.

firm 1.fescht, adv.; 2.hart, adj.; 3.schtandhaft, adj.; **(against something) by treading** wedder/drede, v.; weddergedrede, pp.; **in** bschteh, v.; bschtanne, pp. (debei --)

firmament Schtaernehimmel (der)n.

first 1.erscht, adj.; adv.; 2.vedderscht, adj.; 3.zuerscht, adv.; **bid (at public sale)** Aagebot (der)n.; **class** nummereens, adj.; **line of a nursery rhyme** Dross (es)n.; **rate** nummereens, adj.; **first run of spirits when distilling** Vorlaaf (der)n.; **stomach (of cattle)** ledrich (der)n.

firstly erschdens, adv.

fish 1.angle, v.; geangelt, pp.; 2.Fisch (der)n.; Fisch, pl.; 3.fische, v.; gfischt, pp.; **dam** Weiher (der)n.; **eggs** Fischoier (die)n., pl.; **pond** Fischwieher (der)n.; **scale** Schuppe (die)n.; **scales** 1.Fischschippe (die)n., pl.;

2.Fischschubbe (die)n.; Fischschibbe, pl.

fishbone Fischgraan (die)n.; Fischgranne, pl.

fisherman Fischer (der)n.

fishery Fischerei (die)n.

fishhook 1.Angel (die)n.; 2.Fischangel (die)n.; 3.Fischhoge (der)n.; Fischhoge, pl.

fishing loop of wire Fischschlupp (der)n.; **pole** 1.Gatt(die) n.; Gadde, pl.; 2.Geart (die)n.

fishnet Fischgaarn (es)n.; Fischgaarne, pl.

fishoil 1.Drun (der)n.; 2.Fischeel (es)n.

fishpole Fischgatt (die)n.; Fischgadde, pl.

fishrod Fischgatt (die)n.; Fischgadde, pl.

fissure Riss (der)n.

fist Fauscht (die)n.; Feischt, pl.

fit 1.aa/basse, v.; aagebasst, pp.; 2.basse, v.; gebasst, pp.; 3.faehich, adj.; 4.fehich, adj.; 5.kummbaawel, adj.; **In** 1.hie/basse, v.; hiegebasst, pp.; 2.nei/basse, v.; neigebasst, pp.; **out for housekeeping** aus/schteiere, v.; ausgschteiert, pp.; **together** 1.inennanner/mache, v.; inenannergmacht, pp.; 2.zamme/basse, v.; zammegebasst, pp.; 3.zamme/fidde, v.; zammegfitt, pp.; 4.zamme/fiege, v.; zammegfiegt, pp.; **well** verdraage, v.; verdraage, pp.; **well (of a garment)** bekumme, v.; is bekumme, pp.

fitted out gschtiwwelt, adj.

fitting 1.basslich, adj.; 2.bequem, adj.

five fimf; fimfe, adj.; **cornered** fimfeckich, adj.; **dollar bill** Fimfdaalernot (die)n.; **fold** fimf-feldich, adj.; **leaved** Fimfblettrich, adj.; **storied** fimfschtsckich, adj.; **times** fimfmol, adj.

fix 1.bessere, v.; gebessert, pp.; 2.ei/richde, v.; eigericht, pp.; 3.fascht/mache, v.; faschtgemacht, pp.; 4.verzimmere, v.; verzimmert, pp.; 5.zerechtmache, v.; zerechtgemacht, pp.; **(in a --)** 1.Greid (es)n. (in der -- sei); 2.Kreid (es)n. (in der -- sei); **conditions** b(e)schtimme, v.; b(e)schtimmt, pp.

fixed 1.gsetzt, adj.; 2.schtarr, adj.

flabbergasted vergelschdert, adj.

flag 1.Faahne (die)n.; Faahne, pl.; 2.Schwaartli (es)n.; 3.Schwertli (es)n.

flagstaff Faahneschtock (der)n.

flail 1.Dreschfleggel (der)n.; Dreschfleggel, pl.; 2.Fleggel (der)n.; Fleggel, pl.

flake Flocke (der)n.; Flocke, pl.; **ice (forming on wet ground)** Grundeis (es)n.

flaky flockich, adj.

flame 1.Flamm (die)n.; Flamme, pl.; 2.flamme, v.; gflammt, pp.; **up** 1.uff/flackere, v.; uffgflackert, pp.; 2.uff/flamme, v.; uffgflammt, pp.

flaming star 1.Deifelsabbisswarzel (die)n.; 2.Deiwelsabbis (watzel) (die)n.

flank 1.Flaehm (die)n.; 2.Flank (die)n.

flannel Flannel (der)n.

flap 1.fladdre, v.; gfladdert, pp.; 2.Flapp (der)n.; 3.flappe, v.; gflappt, pp.; 4.Latz (der)n.; **down** nunner/flappe, v.; nunnergflappt, pp.; **up** nuff/flappe, v.; nuffgflappt, pp.

Ff

flapping

flapping flappich, adj.

flare flack(e)re, v.; gflackert, pp.

flaring 1.flack(e)rich, adj.; 2.flickrich, adj.

flash 1.Blitz (der)n.; 2.blitze, v.; geblitzt, pp.; 3.flitze, v.; gflitzt, pp.

flashlight 1.Blitzlicht (es)n.; Blitzlichder, pl.; 2.Flaeschlicht (es)n.; Flaeschlichder, pl.

flask 1.Boddelche (es)n.; 2.Flasch (die)n.

flat flach, adj.; **footed** blattfiessich, adj.; **nosed** 1.breetnaasich, adj.; 2.breednaesich, adj.

flatiron Biggeleise (es)n.; Biggeleise, pl.

flatten out (with a roller) walze, v.; gewalzt, pp.

flatter 1.aa/schmeechle, v.; aagschmeechelt, pp.; 2.glinsle, v.; geglinselt, pp.; 3.schmeechle, v.; gschmeechelt, pp.

flatterer Schmeechler (der)n.

flattering schmeelich, adj.

flattery Schmeichelei (die)n.

flaw Undaedeli (es)n.

flax Flax (der)n.; **before it is broken** Boll (die)n.; **break** Flaxbrech (die)n.; **culture** Flaxbaue (es)n.; **wound round the distaff** Wickel (der)n.

flay 1.ab/schinne (sich --)v.; abgschunne, pp.; 2.ab/ziehe, v.; abgezoge, pp.

flea Floh (der)n.; Fleh, pl.; **beetle** Erdfleh (der)n.

flecked dubblich, adj.

flee 1.ab/schpringe, v.; abschprunge, pp.; 2.fatt/schpringe, v.; fattgschprunge, pp.; 3.weck/schpringe, v.; weckgschprunge, pp.

fleece (financially) baschde, v.; gebascht, pp.; **someone** schtriggle, v.; gschtriggel, pp.

fleshy fleeschich, adj.

flicker 1.flack(e)re, v.; gflackert, pp.; 2.Schpaech(t) (der)n.; 3.Schpechthaahne(der)n.; **(bird)** Gehlschpeecht (der)n.

flickering 1.flack(e)rich, adj.; 2.flickrich, adj.; 3.Gflacker (es)n.

flight 1.Abreissing (die)n.; 2.Flucht (die)n.; 3.Fluck (der)n.

flinch flinsche, v.; gflinscht, pp.

fling 1.schlenkere, v.; gschlenkert, pp.; 2.schnelle, v.; gschnellt, pp.; **away** weck/schlenkere, v.; weckgschlenkert, pp.; **off** ab/schnelle, v.; abgschnellt, pp.; **out** 1.naus/schlenkere, v.; nausgschlenkert, pp.; 2.naus/schnelle, v.; nausgschnellt, pp.; **up** nuff/schnelle, v.; nuffgschnellt, pp.

flint 1.Feierschtee (der)n.; Feierschtee, pl.; 2.Wacheschtee (der)n.

flip flap! klipp klapp!

flit flitze, v.; gflitzt, pp.

flitch (of bacon) 1.Schpeckseit (die)n.; 2.Seidefleesch (es) n.; 3.Seideschtick (es)n.

float 1.schwewe, v.; gschwebt, pp.; 2.schwimme, v.; gschwumme, pp.; **about** rum/schwewe, v.; rumgschwebt, pp.

flock 1.Drupp (die)n.; 2.Fluck (der)n.; 3.Haerd (die)n.

flog 1.ab/dachdle, v.; abgedachdelt, pp.; 2.ab/gaerwe, v.; abgegaerbt, pp.; 3.ab/gloppe, v.; abgegloppt; 4.ab/ wichse, v.; abgewichst, pp.; 5.belse, v.; gebelst, pp.; 6.britsche, v.; gebritscht, pp.; 7.dachdle, v.; gedachdelt, pp.; 8.Fitzeel (es)n.(mit -- schmiere); 9.flachse, v.; gflachst, pp.; 10.leddere, v.; geleddert, pp.; 11.schwaarte, v.;

flutter

gschwaart, pp.; 12.schwinge, v.; gschwunge, pp.; 13.schworte, v.; gschwort, pp.; 14.sohle, v.; gsohlt, pp.; 15.wamsche, v.; gewamscht, pp.; 16.weeche, v.; geweecht, pp. (der Buckel --); **in** nei/gaerwe, v.; neigegaerbt, pp.; **out** (of a place) 1.naus/dresche, v.; nausgedrosche, pp.; 2.naus/gaerwe, v.; nausgegaerbt, pp.; **soundly** 1.ab/dresche, v.; abgedrosche, pp.; 2.darich/dresche, v.; darichgedrosche, pp.; **thoroughly** versohle, v.; versohlt, pp.

flogging 1.Briggelsupp (die)n.; 2.Schlaek (die)n., pl.; 3.Waerming (die)n.; 4.Wichs (die)n.

flood 1.Fluss (der)n.; 2.Flut (die)n.; 3.Gewesser (es)n.; 4.Hochwasser (es)n.; 5.iwwer/laafe, v.; is iwwergeloffe,pp.; 6.iwwerschwemme, v.; iwwerschwemmt, pp.; 7.Iwwerschwemming (die)n.; **out** raus/schwemme, v.; rausgschwemmt, pp.

floor Bodde(m) (der)n.; **of a bakeoven** Backoffehaerd (der)n.

flop 1.Flapp (der)n.; 2.flappe, v.; gflappt, pp.; **away** weck/flappe, v.; weckgflappt, pp.; **down** plumpe, v.; geplumpt, pp.; **flop!** plumps!, interj.

flounce Falbel (die)n.

flour Mehl (es)n.; **and lard** (and sometimes sugar) **mixed and rubbed to the consistency of small lumps used as a covering** Riwwel (die)n.; Riwwele, pl.; **bag** Mehlsack (der)n.; Mehlseck, pl.; **chest** Mehlkischt (die)n.

flourish one's fists feischdle, v.; gfeischdelt, pp.

flourishing wexich, adj.

floury mehlich, adj.

flow fliesse, v.; gflosse, pp.; **(as water)** laafe, v.; g(e)loffe, pp.; **off** ab/fliesse, v.; abgflosse, pp.; **out** aus/fliesse, v.; ausgflosse, pp.; **towards** zuschtreeme, v.; zugschtreemt, pp.

flower 1.Blumm (die)n.; Blumme, pl.; 2.blimme, v. (Montgomery County, PA); **(name)** Hochzichblumm (die) n.; **bed** 1.Bliehknopp (der)n.; 2.Blummebett (es)n.; 3.Blummeland (es)n.; Blummelenner, pl.; **bud** Blumme(r)knopp (der)n.; **often** (plant) Scharnschderuss (die)n.; **seed** 1.Blummesome (der)n.; 2.Blummesume(der) n.; **stalk** Blummeschtock (der)n.; Blummerschteck, pl.

flowered 1.blummich, adj.; 2.geblumm, adj.

flowering plant Blummeschtock (der)n.; Blummerschteck, pl.

flowerpot Blummehaffe (der)n.; Blummeheffe, pl.

flowers of sulphur Schwewwelbliet (die)n.

flowery blummich, adj.

flowing fliessend, adj.

flue Zuckloch (es)n.

fluent fliessend, adj.

flummery 1.Gegramansel (es)n.; 2.Gramansel (es)n.

flurry 1.Gschtiwwer (der)n.; 2.Schtiwwer (der)n.; **of temper** yess!

flush iwwerschiesse, v.; iwwergschosse, pp.; **a bird** uff/schtiwwre, v.; uffgschtiwwert, pp.

flute Fleet (die)n.

flutter fladdre, v.; gfladdert, pp.; **away** weck/fladdre, v.; weckgfladdert, pp.; **in** nei/fladdere, v.; neigfladdert, pp.; **up** 1.nuff/fladdere, v.; nuffgfladdert, pp.; 2.uff/flattre,v.; uffgflattert, pp.

Ff

flux   for

flux Fluss (der)n.

Fly Week 1.Mickewoch (die)n.; 2.Muckewoch (die)n.

fly 1.Flieg (die)n.; Fliege, pl.; 2.fliege, v.; gfloge, pp.; **(insect)** 3.Mick (die)n.; Micke, pl.; 4.Muck (die)n.; Mucke, pl.; **about** rumhaer/fliege, v.; rumhaergfloge, pp.; **after** no(och)fliege, v.; no(och)gflogge, pp.; **against** wedder/fliege, v.; weddergflogge, pp.; **around** rum/fliege, v.; rumgfloge,pp.; **away** 1.fatt/fliege, v.; fattgflogge, pp.; 2.weck/fliege, v.; weckgflogge, pp.; **away slowly** abfladdre, v.; abgfladdert, pp.; **back** zerick/fliege, v.; zerickgfloge, pp.; **chaser;** 1.Mickeweddel (der)n.; 2.Mickewehrer (der)n.; 3.Wedel (der)n.; **down** nunner/fliege, v.; nunnergfloge, pp.; **hither** haer/fliege, v.; haergflogge, pp.; **in** 1.nei/fliege, v.; neigfloge, pp.; 2.rei/fliege, v.; reigflogge, pp.; **into a passion** raus/faahre, v.; rausgfaahre, pp.; **net** 1.Mickegaarn (es)n.; 2.Mickegschar (es)n.; **of a man's pants** 1.Latz (der)n.; 2.Hosselatz (der)n.; 3.Hosseschlitz (der)n.; **off** 1.ab/fliege, v.; abgflogge, pp.; 2.(as an ax or a stone from the surface of water) ab/flitsche, v.; abgflitscht, pp.; **open** uff/klappe, v.; uffgeklabbert, pp.; **out** raus/fliege, v.; rausgflogge, pp.; **over** niwwer/fliege, v.; niwwergflogge, pp.; **paper** Mickebabier (es)n.; **past** verbei/fliege, v.; verbeigfloge, pp.; **to a place** hie/fliege, v.; hiegflogge, pp.; **together** zamme/fiege, v.; zammegfiegt, pp.; **trap** Mickefall (die)n.; **up** 1.faahre, v.; gfaahre, pp. (in die hee --); 2.nuff/fliege, v.; nuffgflogge, pp.; **up in anger** uff/faahre, v.; uffgfaahre, pp.

flying fliegend, adj.

flyspeck Mickeschiss (der)n.

flytrap (facetious) Schlappmaul (es)n.

foal fille, v.; gfillt, pp.

foam 1.Schaam (der)n.; 2.schaame, v.; gschaamt, pp.; 3.Schaum (der)n.; 4.schaume, v.; gschaumt, pp.

foamy schaumich, adj.

fodder for cattle Kiehfuder (es)n.

foe Feind (der)n.; Feind, pl.

fog Newwel (der)n.

foggy 1.newwelich, adj.; 2.newwle, v.; genewwelt, pp.; 3.suddle, v.; gsuddelt, pp.

fold 1.Falt (die)n.; Falde, pl.; 2.zamme/lege, v.; zammeglegt, pp.; **back** zerick/falte, v.; zerickgfalte, pp.; **over** umschlagge, v.; umgschlagge, pp.

folds False (die)n., pl.

foliage 1.Bledder (die)n.; 2.Laab (es)n.

folk Volk (es)n.

folklore Volksaage (die)n.

follow 1.folye, v.; gfol(i)gt, pp.; 2.no(och)dappe, v., no(och) gedappt, pp.; 3.no(och)drachte, v.; no(och)gedrascht, pp.; 4.no(och)folge, v.; no(och)gfolgt, pp.; 5.no(och)folye, v.; no (och)gfoligt, pp.; 6.no(och)geh, v.; no(och)gange, pp.; 7.no (och)kumme, v.; no(och)kumme, pp.; 8.no(och)laafe; v.; no (och)gloffe, pp.; **a model in writing** no(och)schreiwe, v.; no (och)gschriwwe, pp. **closely** 1.hinnerdreigeh, adv.; 2.hinnerdreikumme, adv. **in a rage** no(och)schtaerme, v.; no(och)gschtaermt, pp.; **in a stiff manner** no(och)dapple, v.; no(och)gedappelt, pp.; **in mowing** no(och)maehe, v.; no (och)gemaeht, pp.; **in singing** no(och)singe, v.; no(och) gsunge, pp.; **instructions** schpure, v.; gschpurt, pp.; **someone** no(och)fege, v.; swiftly no(och)schiesse, v.; no(och) gschosse, pp.; **the track** schpure, v.; gschpurt, pp.; **the tracks** (of games) schpiere,v.;schpiert, pp.; **up**

1.hinnerdreischlagge, adv.; 2.no(och)drachde, v.; no (och)gedracht, pp.; 3.uff/folge, v.; uffgfolkt, pp.; **up a matter** hinnich, prep.; **with difficulty** no(och) graddle, v.; no(och)gegraddelt, pp.

follower 1.Aahenger (der)n.; 2.Folger (der)n.; 3.Noochfolyer (der)n.; 4.Noochmacher (der)n.

followers of Jacob Albright later known as the Evangelical Association Albrechtsleit (die)n., pl.

following hinnerhaer, adv.

folly 1.Dorheet (die)n.; 2.Dorheit (die)n.; 3.Narreschtreech (die)n., pl.; 4.Narrheet (die)n.

fond of gaern, adv. (-- esse); (-- hawwe)

fondle 1.gnootsche, v.; gegnootscht, pp.; 2.knootsche, v.; gegknootscht, pp.; 3.vergnootsche, v.; vergnootscht, pp.

food 1.Esse (es)n.; 2.Schpeis (die)n.; **(of dogs)** Fresse (es) n.; **trough** Fuderdrog (der)n.; Fuderdreeg, pl.

foodstuff Lewesmiddel (es)n.

fool 1.aa/fiehre, v.; aagfiehrt, pp.; 2.bedriege, v.; bedroge, pp.; 3.faxe, v.; gfaxt, pp.; 4.foppe, v.; gfoppt, pp.; 5.Hanswascht (der)n.; 6.Narr (der)n. (fer en -- halde); 7.Narr (der)n.; Narre, pl.; 8.vernarre, v.; vernarrt, pp.; 9.Zwickel (der)n.; Zwickel, pl.; **away** 1.verbamble, v.; verbambelt, pp.; 2.verbemble, v.; verbembelt, pp.; **away time** bemble, v.; gebembelt, pp.

foolery Narrheet (die)n.

foolish 1.deerich(t), adj.; 2.eefeldich, adj.; 3.lidderlich, adj.; 4.narrisch, adj.; 5.ungscheit, adj.; 6.unverninfdich, adj.; 7.uugscheit, adj.; **person** 1.Kalb (es)n, Kelwer, pl.; 2.Zippel (der)n.; **prank** Narreboss (die)n.; **talk** 1.Narreschwetz (es)n.; 2.narrisch, adj. (-- gschwetz)

foot Fuus (der)n.; Fiess, pl.; **bath** Fuusbaad (es)n.; **end** Fuusend (es)n.; **hold** Fuushald (die)n.; **measure** Messraahm (der)n.; **of a chair or bedstead** Schtolle (der)n.; **of a stocking** 1.Schtrumpsocke (der)n.; 2.Socke (der)n.; **print** Fuusdappe (der)n.; **sore** 1.boddegraemisch, adj.; 2.boddegrempisch, adj.; **sore** grempisch, adv.;

footbridge 1.Fuusbrick (die)n.; Fuusbricke, pl.; 2.Schteeg (die)n.; Schteege, pl.

foothill Hun(d)srick (der)n.; **in Lynn Township, Lehigh County, PA** Schocheri (der)n.

footmark 1.Drapp (der)n.; 2.Trapp (der)n.

footpath Fuuspaad (der)n.

footprint Dappe (der)n.

footrule 1.Zollschtaab (der)n.; 2.Zollschtaag (der)n.

fop 1.Fratzhans (der)n.; 2.Haehnche (es)n.

foppish fratzich, adj.

for 1.denn, conj. (rare usage;) 2.far, prep.; 3.fer, prep.; **a time** zeiteweis, adv.; **all** soviel, conj.; **all I care** mein(e)twege, adv.; **appearances' sake** schandeshalwer, adv.; **ever** ewichlich, adj.; **ever and ever** immer, adv. (-- un ewich); **her sake** um, prep. (-- ihr Wille); **love's sake** lieweshalwer; **miles** meileweis, adv.; **my sake** mein(e)twege, adv.; **riwwelkuche** Riwwel (die)n.; Riwwle, pl.; **sale** 1.feel, adv.; 2.fehl, adv.; **some time now** Zeithaer (en); **that** dattdefor, adv.; **that reason** 1.dahaer, adv.; 2.deswege, adv.; 3.drumm, adv.; **the benefit of** 1.far, prep.; 2.fer, prep.; **the sake of** lieweshalwer; **this** dodefor, adv.; **weeks** wochelang, adv.; **years** yohre lang, adj.

Ff

forbearance / four

forbearance 1.Langmut (der)n.; 2.langmiedich, adj.

forbid 1.eischtelle, v.; eigschtellt, pp.; 2.verbiede, v.; verbodde, pp.

force 1.bezwenge, v.; bezwengt, pp.; 2.Zwang (der)n.; 3.zwenge, v.; gezwengt, pp.; 4.zwinge, v.; gezwunge, pp.

force (an object) **through** darich/zwenge, v.; darichzwengt, pp.; **a plan through** darich/zwinge, v.; darichgezwunge, pp.; **in** eischiewe, v.; eigschowe, pp.; **off** ab/schprenge, v.; abgschprengt, pp.; **on** (some one) aazwinge, v.; aagezwunge, pp.; **one to swallow** eizwinge, v.; eigezwunge, pp.; **one's way in** rei/schaffe (sich --)v.; reigschafft, pp.; **or gallop or run around** rum/schprenge, v.; rumgschprengt, pp.; **out** aus/drenge, v.; ausgedrengt, pp.; **out by biting** aus/beisse, v.; ausgebisse, pp.; **to run** schprenge, v.; gschprengt, pp.; **to run down** nunner/schprenge, v.; nunnergschprengt, pp.; **together** 1.zamme/zwenge, v.; zammegezwengt, pp.; 2.zamme/zwinge, v.; zammegezwunge, pp.; **upon** uff/zwinge, v.; uffgezwunge, pp.

forcemeat Fil(l)sel (es)n.

forcing Drang (der)n.

ford Faahrt (die)n.

fore vedder, adj.; **flusher** Schippesiwweter (der)n.

forebay 1.Vorbau (der)n.; 2.Vorschuss (der)n.; Vorschuss, pl.

forecast 1.brofesseihe, v.; gebrofesseiht, pp.; 2.vor/saage, v.; vorgsaat, pp.; 3.weis/saage, v.

forefather Urvatter (der)n.

forefathers Vorvedder (die)n., pl.

forefeet Vedderfiess (die)n.

foreground Vorgrund (der)n.

forehead Schtaern (die)n.; Schtaerne, pl.; **strap** (of a bridle) Schtaernband (es)n.

foreign 1.auslendisch, adj.; 2.auslenn(er)isch, adj.; **country** Ausland (es)n.; **substance in the eye** Aag (es)n. (ebbes im -- hawwe)

foreigner Auslenner (der)n.; Auslenner, pl.

foreleg Vedderbeh (es)n.; Vedderbeh, pl.

foreman Vormann (der)n.

foremost vedderscht, adj.; **of all** allervedderscht, adj.

forename Vornaame (der)n.; Vorneeme, pl.

forenoon 1.Vammiddaag (der)n.; 2.Vormiddaag (der)n.

forerunner Vorlaafer (der)n.; Vorlaafer, pl.

foresee 1.vannenaus/sehne, v.; vannenausgsehne, pp.; 2.vor/sehne, v.; vorgsehne, pp.

foresight 1.Vorsarig (die)n.; 2.Vorsehnes (es)n.; 3.Vorsicht (die)n.

forest 1.Busch (der)n.; Bisch, pl.; 2.Wald (der)n. (rare usage); **fly** 1.Buschmick (die)n.; 2.Schtechmick (Die)n.; **moss** Buschwaasem (der)n.; **tree** Buschbaam (der)n.

forestall 1.Bass abschneide (der)v.; 2.vor/kumme, v.; vorkumme, pp.

forever 1.allfatt, adv.; 2.ewich, adj.; adv.; 3.immer, adv.

forewarn 1.verwarne, v.; verwarnt, pp.; 2.wanne, v.; gewarnt; gwannt, pp.; 3.warne, v.; gewarnt, pp.

forfeit verwaerricke, v.; verwaerrickt, pp.

forge 1.Eisehammer (der)n.; 2.Fortsch (der)n.; **records** felsche, v.; gfelscht, pp.

forged nail Naggel (der)n. (en gschnittner --)

forgery Felsching (die)n.

forget 1.vergesse, v.; vergesse, pp.; 2.verlaerne, v.; verlaernt, pp.; 3.verschmaerze, v.; verschmaerzt, pp.; **me-not** Vergessmichnet (die)n.

forgetful vergesslich, adj.

forgive 1.vergewwe, v.; vergewwe, pp.; 2.verzeihe, v.; verzeiht, pp.

forgiveness Vergewwing (die)n.

forgotten verdrickle, v.; verdrickelt, pp.

fork Gawwel (die)n.; Gawwle, pl.; **handle** Gawwelschtiel (der)n.; **(hay)** gawwele, v.; gegawwelt, pp.; **in a road** Gawwelweeg (der)n.

form 1.bilde, v.; gebild(e)t, pp.; 2.bschaffe, v.; bschaffe, pp.; 3.Form (die)n.; 4.Gschtalt (die)n.; 5.Puschduur (die)n.; **(as butter in the churn)** 1.glumpe; v.; geglumpt, pp.; 2.glimple, v.; geglimpelt, pp.; 3.klimple, v.; geklimpelt, pp.; **(as fruit on a tree or vine or potatoes on the roots)** aa/henke, v.; aaghenkt; aaghonke, pp.; **a habit** aagewehne, v.; aagewehnt, pp. (sich ebbes --); **a mist on a surface** aa/laafe, v.; aageloffe, pp.; **a scab** ab/heele, v.; abgheelt, pp.; **in a ball** zamme/balle, v.; zammegeballt, pp.; **in a ball** (of snow) balle, v.; geballt, pp.

formal schteif, adj.; **room** Offeschtupp (die)n.

formed gformt, adj.; **facetiously** (meaningless) blitzeblo un dunnergrie

former vorich, adj.

formerly 1.emol, adv; 2.frieher, adv.; 3.geborni, adj.; 4.veralders, adv.; 5.verzeite, adv.; 6.vordem, adv.; 7.vorher, adv.; 8.zuvor, adv.

fornicate hure, v.; ghurt, pp.

forsake verlosse, v.; verlosse, pp.

fortunate glicklich, adj.

fortunately glicklichweis, adv.

fortune Glick (es)n.; **teller** 1.Waahretsaager (der)n.; 2.Waahrsaager (der)n.; 3.Wohrsaager (der)n.

forty vatzich, adj.; pron.

forward 1.vaerri, prep.; 2.vaers(ch)ich, adj.; 3.voraa, adv.; 4.vorwaerts, adv.; 5.Vorwart (es)n.; 6.vorwitzich, adj.; 7.vorzus, adv.; 8.vurrand = voraa; **(here)** dovaerri, adv.; **(there)** dattvaerri, adv.

foster pflege, v.; gepflegt, pp.

fostering care Pfleech (die)n.

foul 1.luderich, adj.; 2.schtinkich, adj.

found 1.gfunne, adj.; 2.grinde, v.; gegrindt, pp.

foundation 1.Fundament (es)n.; Fundamender, pl.; 2.Grund (der)n.; **stone** Fundementschtee (der)n.; **wall** Fundementmauer (die)n.

founder 1.Grinder (der)n.; 2.Rehichkeet (es)n.

foundered ze reh

foundling Gefunnenes (en)

foundry Eisegiesserei (die)n.; Eisegiessereie, pl.

four 1.vier, adj.; pron.; 2.viere, adj.; pron.; **handed** vierhendich, adj.; **horse team** Viergeilsfuhr (die)n.; **hundred**

(Continued on page 281)

Ff

four (continued)   frothy

(Continued from page 280)

vierhunnert, adj., pron.; **leafed** vierblettrich, adj.; **o'clock**
  Nachtschadde (der)n.; **ply** vierdraehdich, adj.; **seated**
  viersitzich, adj.; **spot in cards** vierter (en --); **storied**
  vierschtechich, adj.; **thousand** vierdausend, adj., pron.;
  times viermol, adv.; **voices or parts** vierschtimmich, adj.;
  wheeled vierreddich, adj.; **years old** vieryaehrich, adj.

fourteen vatzeh, adj.; pron.

Fourth of July Viert Yuli (der)n.

fourth viert, adj.

fourthly viertens, adj.

fowl without a tail 1.Baarzer (der)n.; 2.Batzert (der)n.

fowling piece Schiessbriggel (der)n.

fox Fux (der)n.; Fix, pl.; **boots** aa/schuhe, v.; aagschuht,
  pp.; **and geese** Greizmiehl (die)n.; **grape**
  Schpeckdraub (die)n.; Schpeckdrauwe, pl.

fractious (of a horse) uffriehrisch, adj.

fragile 1.schprock, adj.; 2.verbrechlich, adj.

fragment Huddel (der)n.; **of crockery or pottery** Schaerb
  (die)n.; Schaerwe, pl.

fragrant 1.gutriechend, adj.; 2.gutriechich, adj.

frame 1.Gschtalt (die)n.; 2.Gschtell (es)n.; **on posts in
  which plants, especially cabbage, were raised from
  seed for transplanting** Grautkutsch (die)n.; **on which
  a churn sets** Butterbock (der)n.; **on which a log lies
  in sawing** Schemel (der)n.; **on which something is
  carried** Draag (die)n.

framing (of a structure) Gebelk (es)n.

France Frankreich (es)n.

franchise Schtimmrecht (es)n.

frantic doll, adj.

fraternity Briederlichkeet (die)n.

fratricide 1.Brudermaerder (der)n.; 2.Brudermard (der)n.

fraud 1.B(e)schisser (der)n.; 2.Bedruch (der)n.; 3.Bsch(e)
  isser (der)n.; 4.Bscheisserei (die)n.; 5.Schwindlerei
  (die)n.

freckle 1.Summerfleck (die)n.; Summerflecke, pl.;
  2.Sunnefleck (die)n.

freckled summerfleckich, adj.

Frederica Fridricke (die)n.

Frederick 1.Fridder (der)n.; 2.Fridderich (der)n.; 3.Fritz
  (der)n.

Free Mason Freimaurer (der)n.

free 1.befreie, v.; befreit, pp.; 2.frei, adj.; **of cost** koschdefrei, adj., adv.; **thinker** Freidenker (der)n.

freedom Freiheit (die)n.

freely freiwillich, adv.

freeze 1.friere, v.; gfrore, pp.; 2.gfriere, v.; gfrore, pp.;
  3.verfriere, v.; verfrore, pp.; **fast to** aa/(g)friere, v.;
  aagfrore, pp.; **out** aus/(g)friere, v.; ausgfrore, pp.;
  together zamme/gfriere, v.; zammegfrore, pp.; **up**
  1.uff/gfriere, v.; uffgfrore, pp.; 2.zu(g)friere, v.;
  zugfrore, pp.; 3.(for the winter) ei(g)friere, v.;
  eigfrore, pp.

French 1.franseesich, adj.; 2.franzeesisch, adj.; **clover**
  1.Haaseglee (der)n.; 2.Haaseglee (der)n.

frequently efters, adv.

fresh frisch, adj.; **sausage** Wascht (die)n. (frischi --); **young
  person** Rotznaas (die)n.; Rotznaas, pl.

freshen (of a cow) eikumme, v.; eikumme, pp.

fret 1.ab/quaele (sich --)v.; abgequaelt, pp.; 2.brutze, v.;
  gebrutzt, pp.

fretful 1.brutzich, adj.; 2.mutsich, adj.; 3.mutzich, adj.

friction Reiwerei (die)n.

Friday Freidaag (der)n.

friend Freind (der)n.; Freind, pl.

friendly 1.blauderich, adj.; 2.freindlich; 3.plauderich, adj.

friendship Freindschaft (die)n.

fright 1.Engschde (die)n.; Engschde, pl.; 2.Farich (die)n.;
  3.Schrecke (der)n.

frighten 1.schrecke, v.; gschreckt, pp.; 2.vergelschdere,
  v.; vergelschdert, pp.; 3.verschrecke, v.; verschrocke,
  pp.; 4.verschteere, v.; verschteert, pp.; **away**
  verscheeche, v.; verscheecht, pp.

frightened scheie, v.; gscheit, pp.

frightful 1.faerrichderlich, adj.; 2.schauderhafdich, adj.;
  3.schauderhaft, adj.

frightfully 1.madderonisch, adj.; 2.maerderlich, adj.;
  3.mardunisch, adj.

fringe 1.Fransel (die)n.; Fransle, pl.; 2.Taasel (die)n.

fringed 1.franslich, adj.; 2.verfranselt, adj.

fritter Pannekuche (der)n.; Pannekuche, pl.; **away**
  weck/bemble, v.; weckgebembelt, pp.

frivolity 1.Leichtsinn (der)n.; 2.Leichtsinnichkeit (die)n.

frivolous leichsinnich, adj.

fro devun, adv.

frock Gaund (der)n.; Geinder, pl.

frog 1.Bullirum (der)n.; 2.Frosch (der)n.; Fresch, pl.

frolic 1.Gruscht (die)n.; 2.kalfaktre, v.; gekalfaktert, pp.;
  3.Kruscht (die)n.; 4.rose, v.; gerost, pp.

frolicing 1.Geros (es)n.; 2.Roserei (die)n.

from 1.ab, adv., prep.; 2.vun, prep.; **above** 1.owwebie, adv.;
  2.owwerei, adv.; 3.owwerunner, adv.; 4.runner, adv.
  (vun owwe --); **afar** weithaer, adv.; **along there**
  datthaerzus, adv.; **below** unnebei, adv.; **down country**
  ruff, adv.(es land --); **her** vunre = vun re; **memory**
  aus(e)wennich, adj.; **of old** vun Alders her; **that direction** dattrei, adv.; **the beginning** urschpringlich, adv.;
  the foundation grundsboddem (vum); **the remotest
  time** yehaer, adv. (vun --); **the side** newebei, adv.
  (vun --); **there** datthaer, adv. (vun --); **today** aa, adv.
  (vun heit --); **up country** owwerei, adv.; **upstairs**
  owwerunner, adv.; **within** inneraus, adv.; **without**
  aussehaer, adv.

front 1.Frant (die)n.; 2.Front (die)n.; 3.vedder, adj.;
  4.vedderscht, adj.; **(in a vehicle, room or crowd with a
  verb of motion)** vaerri, prep.; **body bolster** (of a wagon)
  Reischemel (der)n.; **of an oven** Backoffeloch (es)n.

frost 1.Froscht (der)n.; 2.Reife (der)n.; **grape** Reifdraub
  (die)n.; Reifdrauwe, pp.

frosty reifich, adj.

froth 1.Schaam (der)n.; 2.schaame, v.; gschaamt, pp.;
  3.Schaum (der)n.; 4.schaume, v.; gschaumt, pp.

frothy schaumich, adj.

Ff

frown   fuzzy

frown Schtann (die)n. (-- runsle)

frozen blue blitzeblo verfrore

frozen delicacies Gfrornes (es)n.

frugal 1.haushalte, adj. 2.maessich, adj.; 3.schpaarsam, adj.

frugality Schpaarsamkeit (die)n.

fruit of a tree Frucht (die)n. (rare usage); **spur** 1.Schpore (der)n.; 2 Zacke (der)n.; **tree** Obschtbaam (der)n.;

fruit(s) 1.Obscht (es)n.; 2.Obs(t) (es)n.

fruitful fruchtbaar, adj.

fry 1.brode, v.; gebrode, pp.; 2.schmore, v.; **through** darich/brode, v.; darichgebrode, pp.

frying pan 1.Brodpann (die)n.; Brodpanne, pl.; 2.Brotpann (die)n.

fuchsia 1.Ohredroppe (die)n., pl.; 2.Ohreglocke (die)n.; 3.Ohrering (der)n.

fulfill 1.erfille, v.; erfillt, pp.; 2.vollfille, v.; vollfillt, pp.

fulfillment Erfilling (die)n.

full voll, adj.; **cheeked** dickbackich, adj.; **fledged** flick, adj.; **grown** ausgewaxe, adj.; **moon** 1.Vollicht (es)n.; 2.Vollmoond (der)n.; **of bedbugs** wansich, adj.; **of big holes** grosslecherich, adj.; **of care** sarrickvoll, adj.; **of cracks** rissich, adj.; **of holes** lecherich, adj.; **of roots** warzlich, adj.; **of seeds** kaernich, adj.

fuller's teasel 1.Bollhoke (der)n.; 2.Kardedischdel (die)n.

fully 1.fellich, adv.; 2.vellich, adj.; 3.vollens, adj.

fumble dappe, v.; gedappt, pp.

fun 1.Gschpass (der)n.; 2.Luschtbaarkeit (die)n.; 3.Rumbel (der)n.; 4.Schpass (der)n.

function funggiere, v.; gfunggiert, pp.

fund Geldsumm (die)n.

funeral Leicht (die)n.; Leichde, pl.; **cortege** Leicht (die)n.; Leichde, pl.; **director** 1.Begrawwer (der)n.; 2.Eibalsamierer (der)n.; 3.Laademacher (der)n.; Laademacher, pl.; 4.Laademesser (der)n.; 5.Leichde(n)berichder (der)n.; 6.Leichenbefaahrer (der)n.; 7.Leichtmann (der)n.; 8.Leichtversaryer (der)n.; **expenses** Leichtkoschde (die)n., pl.; **sermon** Leichtbreddich (die)n.

fungus haematodes Blutschwamm (der)n.

funnel cake Drechderkuche (der)n.; Drechderkuche, pl.

funny 1.gschpassich, adj.; 2.lecher(l)ich, adj.; 3.Schpass (der)n. (voll --); (-- mache); 4.schpassich, adj.; **business** Hokespokes (der)n.; **chap** Gschpassvoggel (der)n.; **fellow** 1.Faxemacher (der)n.; 2.Witzbold (der)n.; **person** Kaschber (der)n.; **saying** Schnaerkel (der)n., **stories** Schpichde (die)n.,pl.

fur Belz (der)n.; **cap** Belskapp (die)n.

furbelow Falbel (die)n.

furious 1.raasend, adj.; 2.raasich, adj.; 3.wiedich, adj.

furnace 1.Fanness (die)n.; Fannesse, pl.; 2.Farness (die)n.; 3.Schmelzoffe (der)n.

furnish 1.ei/richde, v.; eigericht, pp.; 2.liffere, v.; geliffert, pp.; **(food, board)** 1.bekeschdiche, v.; bekeschdicht, pp.; 2.verkeschdiche, v.; verkeschdicht, pp.; **or put on the ironwork of a wheel or wagon** ab/binne,v.; abgebunne,pp.

furniture Hausrod (es)n.

furrow Farrich(t) (die)n.; Farrichde, pl.; out aus/farichde, v.; ausgfaricht, pp.

further weider, adv.

fury 1.Aeyer (der)n.; 2.Raaserei (die)n.; 3.Wut (die)n.

future 1.Noochkunft (die)n. 2.Zukumft (die)n.

fuzz 1.Flies (es)n.; 2.Fusser (es)n.; 3.Fussre (die)n., pl.; 4.Gfusser (es)n.

fuzzy fuss(e)rich, adj.

Gg

gabble ... gauge

gabble schnattre, v.; gschnaddert, pp.

gabbler Babbler (der)n.

gable 1.Gewwel (der)n.; 2.Giwwel (der)n.; **end of the house** 1.Gibbelend (es)n. (-- vum Haus); 2.Giwwelend (es)n. (-- vum Haus)

Gabriel Gaawrel (der)n.

gad 1.Geart (die)n.; 2.rum/laafe, v.; rumg(e)loffe, pp.; 3.rum/schpringe, v.; rumgschprunge, pp.; 4.umher/laafe, v.; is umhergeloffe, pp.

gadabout 1.Droll (die)n.; 2.fek, adj. (en alti --); 3.Ritsch (die)n.; 4.Rutsch (die)n.; 5.rum/flankiere, v.; rumgflankiert, pp.; 6.rum/hammle, v.; rumghammelt, pp.; 7.rum/zoddle, v.; rumgezoddelt, pp.

gadding 1.Gedratsch (es)n.; 2.Gezacker (es)n.; 3.Katzeyammer (der)n.

gadfly Nisschisser (der)n.; Nisschisser, pl.

gag 1.Gnewwel (der)n.; 2.gnewwle, v.; gegnewwelt, pp.; 3.Gnupse (der)n.; 4.Knew(w)el (der)n.; 5.Maul (es)n. (es -- zu/binne; [zugebunne], pp.); 6.warixe, v.; gewarixt, pp.

gage messe, v.; gemesse, pp.

gain 1.Brofit(t) (der)n.; 2.Gewinn (der)(es) n.; 3.gewinne, v.; gewunne, pp.; 4.Vaddel (es)n.; 5.Vaddle (es)n.; 6.Vordeel (es)n.

gain (weight) zu/nemme, v.; zugnumme, pp.

gain a thing by craft or sharp practice ab/lause, v.; abgelaust, pp.; **the upper hand** Iwwerhand (die)n. (-- gewinne)

gainer Gewinner (der)n.

gale Schtarmwind (der)n.

gallbladder Gall(e)blos (der)n.

gallery (in a church) Bordkarich (die)n.

gallnuts Gallebbel (die)n., pl.

gallon 1.Gall (die)n.; 2.Gall(uun) (die)n.; Gall(uun)e, pl.; 3.Gallun (die)n.; **measure** Galleblech (es)n.

gallop (nursery rhyme) 1.Galopp (der)n.; 2.Golopp (der)n.; **about** rum/yaage, v.; rumgeyaagt, pp.

gallows 1.Galge (der)n.; 2.Galye (der)n.; Galye, pl.; **wood** Galgeholz (es)n.

gallstone Gall(e)schtee (der)n.; Gall(e)schtee, pl.

gamble 1.gammel, v.; gegammelt, pp.; 2.veryuxe, v.; veryuxt, pp.; 3.wedde, v.; g(e)wett, pp.; **away** verschpiele, v.; verschpielt, pp.

gambler 1.Gammler (der)n.; Gammler, pl.; 2.Schpieler (der)n.

gambol Bockschprung (der)n.

gambrel 1.Heese (der)n.; 2.Heesehols (es)n.; 3.Heeseholz (es)n.

game 1.Gewilbert (es)n.; 2.Schpiel (es)n.; (played with a knotted handkerchief with which blows are dealt) Blumpsack (der)n.; **cock** Fechthaahne (der)n.; **of ball** 1.Ballewiesals (es) n.; 2.Lochballe (der)n.; 3.Sauballe (der)n.; **of cards** 1.Haasenpeffer (der)n.; 2.Haasimpeffer (der)n.; **of cards** (localized in Allentown, PA) Datte

gander 1.Gansert (der)n.; Gansert, pl.; 2.Genserich (der)n.

gang 1.Rott (die)n.; 2.S(ch)ippschaft (die)n.

gangrene Brand (der)n.

gap 1.Effning (die)n.; 2.Lick (die)n.

gape 1.Aaschlaek (die)n., pl. (-- fresse); 2.gaffe, v.; gegafft, pp.; 3.Maul (es)n. (es -- uff/schparre; uffgschpatt), pp.; **across** niwwer/gaffe, v.; niwwergegafft, pp.; **after** no(och)gaffe, v.; no(och)gegafft, pp.; **around** 1.rum/gaffe, v.; rumgegafft, pp.; 2.rumhaer/gaffe, v.; rumhaergegafft, pp.; **at** aa/gaffe, v.; aagegafft, pp.; **back** zerick/gaffe, v. zerickgegafft, pp.; **in** 1.nei/gaffe, v.; neigegafft, pp.; 2.rei/gaffe, v.; reigegafft, pp.

gaps (in chicks) Biebser (der)n.

garbage Abfall (der)n.

garde Balsem (der)n. (rotschtenglicher --)

garden 1.Gaarde (der)n.; Gerde, pl.; 2.gaerdle, v.; gegaerdelt, pp.; **balm** Melisse (die)n.; **bed** Land (es)n.; Lenner, pl.; **fence** Gaardezau (die)n.; **hoe** Gaardehack (die)n.; **hydrangea** Neinmonetros (die)n.; **orpine** Hauswachs (der)n.; **path** Gaardeweg (der)n.; **rhubarb** 1.Babraa (der) n.; 2.Barbaraa (der)n.

gardener 1.Gaerdler (der)n.; 2.Gaerdner (der)n.; 3.Gerdler (der)n.; 4.Gerdner (der)n.

garget (a hog disease) 1.Millichfewer (es)n.; 2.Finne (die)n., pl.

gargle 1.aus/gargle, v.; ausgegargelt, pp.; 2.aus/schwenke, v.; ausgschwenkt, pp. (der Hals --); 3.garigle, v.; gegarigelt, pp.; 4.Garyel (die)n.

garland 1.Blumme(r)krans (der)n.; 2.Grans (der)n.; 3.Krans (der)n.

garlic 1.Gnoww(el)loch (der)n.; 2.Gnowwlich (der)n.; 3.Knoww(e)lich (der)n.; 4.Knowwelloch (der)n.; **mustard** Knowwlichgraut (es)n.

garments Gleeder (die)n., pl.

garret Garret (der)n.; **stairs** Schpeicherschteeg (die)n.

garter Schtrumpbendel (der)n.; Schtrumpbendle, pl.; **snake** Hausschlang (die)n.

gasp schnappe, v.; gschnappt, pp. (noch luft --)

gate 1.Dor (es)n.; Dore, pl.; 2.Falder (die)n.; **of a yard fence** Hofdeerle (es)n.

gatepost 1.Dierli-Poschde (der)n.; Dierli-Poschde, pl.; 2.Doreposchde (der)n.; Doreposchde, pl.

gateway Eifaahrt (die)n.

gather 1.sammle, v.; gsammelt, pp.; 2.uff/packe, v.; uffgepackt, pp.; 3.uff/picke, v.; uffgepickt, pp.; 4.zamme/bringe, v.; zammegebrocht, pp.; 5.zamme/lese, v.; zammegelese, pp.; 6.zamme/mache, v.; zammegemacht, pp.; 7.zamme/sammle, v.; zammegsammelt, pp.; 8.zamme/schaffe, v.; zammegschaft, pp.; **hastily** zamme/raffe, v.; zammegerafft, pp.; **in** eisammle, v.; eigsammelt, pp.; **in a hasty manner** zamme/huddle, v.; zammeghuddelt, pp.; **in hurriedly** nei/raffe, v.; neigerafft, pp.; **in one gathering-place** zammenannergeh, v.; zammenannergange, pp.; **up** 1.zamme/fasse, v.; zammegfasst, pp.; 2.zamme/nemme, v.; zammegenumme, pp.; **up hastily** raffe, v.; gerafft, pp.

gathering Sammlung (die)n.

gauge aus/messe, v.; ausgemesse, pp.

Gg

gawk — giggle

gawk Haschbel (der)n.; **about** schlendere, v.; gschlendert, pp.

gay 1.lebhaft, adj.; 2.luschdich, adj.

gazing or gaping Geguck (es)n.

gear 1.Geilschar (es)n.; 2.Schtrang (der)n.; Schtreng, pl.; **pole** Geilsgscharrschtang (die)n.

gee whiz! 1.dausendsapperlott! interj.; 2.dunnerkei(de)l, interj.

gee! (call to horses) hott!

gelatinous glewerich, adj.

geld 1.schneide, v.; gschnidde, pp.; 2.vergelse, v.; vergelst, pp.

gelded boar pig Barick (der)n.

gelder 1.Gelser (der)n.; 2.Schnitter (der)n.; 3.Seigelser (der)n.; 4.Seischneider (der)n.

gem Edelschtee (der)n.

Gemini (3rd sign of the zodiac) Zwilling (der)n.; Zwilling, pl.

general Feldhaerr (der)n.

generally 1.allgemee, adv.; 2.gebreichlich, adv.

generate zeige, v.; gezeikt, pp.

generation 1.Gschlecht (es)n.; 2.Menschealter (es)n.

generosity 1.Edelmut (der)n.; 2.Grossmut (der)n.

generous 1.freigew(w)ich, adj.; 2.grosshatzich, adj.; 3.hatzich, adj. (gut --)

genteel manierlich, adj.

gentian Dausendgildegraut (es)n.

gentle 1.gelind, adj.; 2.glimblich, adj.; 3.mild, adj.; 4.sanft, adj.; 5.sanftmiedich, adj.; **(of animals)** geduldich, adj.; **or tractable** (of animals) frumm, adj.

gentleman's coat Mannsrock (der)n.

gentleness Sanftmut (der)n.

genuflect Gnie biege (die)n. (Old Order Amish term)

George 1.Yarick (der)n.; 2.Yorch (der)n.

geranium Gerranne (die)n.; **(with scented leaves)** Weschpegerranne (die)n.

germ Keim (die)n.; Keime, pl.

German 1.deitsch, adj.; 2.deitschlennerisch, adj.; **born in Germany** Deitschlenner (der)n.; **scythe** (broad-bladed) Sens (die)n. (deitschi --)

germander G(a)mander (der)n.

Germany Deitschland (es)n.

germinate keime, v.; gekeimt, pp.

Gertrude's Day (March 17) Gertrudsdaag (der)n.

get 1.bei/griege, v.; beigrickt, pp.; 2.griege, v.; grickt, pp.; 3.warre, v.; is warre, pp.; **(a woman) in the family way** uff/bindle, v.; uffgebindelt, pp.; **get** (one) **to believe** (something) eiblaudre, v.; eigeblaudert, pp.; **(some one) away** 1.devungriege, v.; 2.weck/griege, v.; weckgrickt, pp.; **(someone) to do (something)** draagriege, v.; draagrickt, pp.; (something) **down** runner/griege, v.; runnergrickt, pp.; **a battered head** grindkopp, v. (sich en -- aaschwetze); **a blow** (slap) **in the face** griege, v.; grickt, pp. (eens ins Gsicht --); **a wrong impression from looking** vergucke (sich --)v.; verguckt, pp.; **against** wedder/kumme, v.; wedderkumme, pp.; **along** waertschafte, v.; gewaertschaft, pp.; **along on** bschteh, v.; bschtanne, pp.(debei --); **along together** schtalle, v.; gschtallt, pp.; **along well together** haermeniere, v.; haermeniert, pp.; **along with** gschtalle, v.; gschtallt, pp.; **along with others** mit/mache, v.; mitgemacht, pp.;

an idea eileichde, v.; eigeleicht, pp.; **away** weck/packe (sich --)v.; weckgepackt, pp.; **black** verschwaerze (sich --)v.; verschwaerzt, pp.; **blows** druffgriege, v.; druffgrickt, pp.; **busy** Heck (die)n.; Hecke, pl. (sich an die --e mache); **by trickery or cheating** ablusche, v.;abgeluchst, pp.; **dirty** ei/schmiere, v.; eigschmiert, pp.; **down from** runner/geh, v.; runnergange, pp.; **entangled** verhaschble (sich --)v.; loskumme, pp.; **free** los/kumme, v.; loskumme, pp.; **from** 1.haer/griege, v.; haergrickt, pp.; 2.haer/griege, v.; haergrickt, pp.; **in** rei/schaffe, v.; reigschafft, pp.; **in the house** nei/packe (sich --)v.; neigepackt, pp.; **information** aus/fische, v.; ausgfischt, pp.; **into** eischteige, v.; eigschtigge, pp.; **into someone'sgood graces** aa/mache, v.; aagemacht, pp.; (sich -- bei ebber); **into trouble** grindkopp, v. (sich en -- aaschwetze); **loose** los/warre, v.; loswarre, pp.; **off** ab/kumme, v.; is abkumme, pp.; **off by lying** raus/liege (sich --)v.; rausgelogge, pp.; **on an article of clothing** aa/griege, v.; aagrickt, pp.; **one's feet entangled** verhopple (sich --)v.; verhoppelt, pp.; **or cause to enter** nei/griege, v.; neigrickt, pp.; **out** 1.naus/mache (sich --) v.; nausgemacht, pp.; 2.naus/packe (sich --)v.; nausgepackt, pp.; 3.raus/griege, v.; rausgrickt, pp.; **out of** raus/ schaffe (sich --)v.; rausgschafft, pp.; **out of bed** raus/ graddle, v.; rausgegraddelt, pp.; **out of doing something** ab/scheele (sich --)v.; abgscheelt, pp.; **out of perpendicular**; aus/weiche, v.; ausgewiche, pp.; **out!** herraus! interj.; **ready** Aagschtalt (der)n. (so'n -- mache) **rid of**; 1.ab/schaffe, v.; abgschafft, pp.; 2.fatt/schaffe, v.; fattgschafft, pp.; 3.schaffe, v.; gschafft, pp. (aus em weg --); 4.weck/schaffe, v.; weckgschafft, pp.; **rid of them** aawaerre, v.; aawaerre, pp.; **through as best as one can** darich/schlagge (sich --)v.; darichgschlacht, pp.; **tipsy** gsoffe, v.; **to a place** 1.hie/kumme, v.; is hiekumme; 2.hie/schaffe (sich --)v.; hiegschafft, pp.; **to close** (a door) zugriege, v.; zugrickt, pp.; **to do something** draakumme, v.; is draakumme, pp.; **together** 1.versammle (sich --)v.; versammelt, pp.; 2.zamme/kumme, v.; is zammekumme, pp.; 3.zamme/laafe, v.; zummegeloffe, pp.; **up** (to a place) nuff/kumme, v.; nuffkumme, pp.; **up ahead** vorschaffe (sich --)v.; vorgschafft, pp.; **up with difficulty** uff/graddle, v.; uffgegraddelt, pp.; **wind of something** Wind (der)n. (-- griege vun ebbes)

gherkin Schtachelgummer (die)n.

ghost 1.Geischt (der)n.; Geischder, pl.; 2.Gschpuck (der) (es)n.; Gschpucker, pl.; 3.Schpuck(s) (es)n.; Schpucke, pl.; 4.Schpunk (der)n.

ghostly manifestations schpucke, v.; gschpuckt, pp.

giant Ries (der)n.

giddap (call to horses) Hepp!; **(nursery rhyme)** Hoss!

giddiness 1.Darmel (der)n.; 2.Schwindel (der)n.

giddy daremlich, adj.

gift Gschenk (es)n.; Gschenker, pl. **(of liver pudding, sausage, etc. made at butchering time)** Metzelsupp (die)n.

gig Fisch-schtecher (der)n.

giggle 1.gickere, v.; gegickert, pp.; 2.gickle, v.; gegickelt, pp.; 3.kickere, v.; gekickert, pp.

giggler   glimmer

giggler Kischbel (der)n.

giggling 1.Gegicker (es)n.; 2.kischblich, adj.

gild vergolde, v.; vergoldt, pp.

gill 1.Fischohr (es)n.; 2.Grundelraawer (die)n.;
   3.Grundelrewe (die)n.

gillyflower 1.Logeige (die)n.; 2.Lovgeige (die)n. (v=f Lofgeige)

gimlet Naggelbohre (der)n.; Naggelbohre, pl.

ginger Imber (der)n.; **bread** 1.Hunnichbrot (es)n.;
   2.Hunnichkuche (der)n.

gingercake Lebkuche (der)n.; Lebkuche, pl.

girder Balge (der)n.; Balge, pl.

girdle Gaerdel (der)n.; **(a tree)** gaerdle, v.; gegaerdelt, pp.

girl 1.Maed(s)che (es)n.; Maed(s)cher, pl.; 2.Meedel (es)
   n.; Meed, pl.; **friend** 1.Aldi (es)n. (mei --); 2.Meedel
   (es)n.; Meed, pl.; **from the farm** Bauersmeedel (es)n.

girl's game 1.Gensfuss (der)n.; 2.Katzekopp (der)n.;
   3.Ringmiehl (die)n.

girth 1.Gaerdel (der)n.; 2.Gart (die)n.; 3.Gatt (die)n.; Gadde, pl.

give 1.gewwe, v.; gewwe, pp.; 2.hie/gewwe, v.; hiegewwe,
   pp.; **(one a blow)** 1.hie/halde, v.; hieghalde, pp.
   (eens --); 2.hie/schlagge, v.; hiegschlagge, pp. (eens --);
   3.nei/brenne, v.; neigebrennt, pp. (eens --); 4.nei/halde,
   v.; neighalde, pp. (eens --); 5.nei/leichte, v.; neigeleicht,
   pp. (eens --); 6.eibrenne, v.; eigebrennt, pp. (eens --);
   7.eihalde, v.; eighalde, pp. (eens --); 8.eileichde, v.;
   eigeleicht, pp. (eens --); **a beating** 1.ab/schwaarde, v.;
   abgschwaart, pp.; 2.gaerwe, v.; gegaerbt, pp.; **a business
   order** addere, v.; geaddert, pp.; **a curt reply**
   ab/schnaebbe, v.; abgschnaeppt, pp.; **a feeling of**
   iwwerlaafe, v.; iwwerloffe, pp.; **a good flogging**
   ab/leddre, v.; abgeleddert, pp.; **a hearing** verheere, v.;
   verheert, pp.; **a lift** uff/helfe, v.; uffgholfe, pp.; **a name**
   benaame, v.; benaamt, pp.; **a person a calling down**
   runner/leese, v.; runnergeleest, pp.; **a quick retort**
   ab/kabbe, v.; abgekappt, pp.; **a rap** hie/basse, v.
   (eens --); **a reminder** no(och)schaerfe, v.;
   no(och)gschaerft, pp.; **a report** blatsche, v.; geblatscht,
   pp.; **a right** berechtiche, v.; berechticht, pp.; **a sharp
   rejoinder** zerick/hacke, v.; zerickghackt, pp.; **a smack in
   the face** Maul (es)n. (eens uffs -- schlagge); **a surly answer** zerick/gnarre, v.; zerickgegnarrt, pp.; **a tingling
   sensation** zingle, v.; gezingelt, pp.; **a tip** schtecke, v.;
   gschtocke, pp. (ebber, ebbes --); **a tongue-lashing**
   1.ab/balsamiere, v.; abgebalsamiert, pp.; 2.hechle, v.;
   ghechelt, pp.; **a whack** druffbuffe, v.; druffgebuffe, pp.;
   an enema grischdiere, v.; grischdiert, pp.; **assent by
   nodding** 1.nucke, v.; genuckt, pp.; 2.schnabble, v.;
   gschnappt, pp.; **away** 1.naus/schenke, v.; nausgschenkt,
   pp.; 2.verschenke, v.; verschenkt, pp.; 3.weck/gewwe, v.;
   weckgewwe, pp.; 4.weck/schenke, v.; weckgschenkt,
   pp.; **back** 1. heemgewwe, v.; heemgewwe, pp.;
   2.zerick/gewwe, v.; zerickgewwe, pp.; **back talk**
   zerick/blaudre, v.; zerickgeblaudert, pp.; **birth** 1.bobble,
   v.; gebobbelt, pp.; 2. gebaere, v.; gebore, pp.; **blows**
   druffbeitsche, v.; druffgebeitscht, pp.; **clandestinely**
   zu/schtecke, v.; zugschteckt, pp.; **credit** 1.barge, v.;
   gebarkt, pp.; 2.barye, v.; gebarigt, pp.; **ear** uff/harriche,
   v.; uffgharricht, pp.; **give evidence of pain or soreness**

autsche, v.; geautscht, pp.; **free scope** gewaehre losse,
v.; **full vent to one's devilishness** aus/deiwle (sich --)v.;
ausgedeiwelt, pp.; **here (to some one)** haer/gewwe, v.;
haergewwe, pp.; **in** 1.ei/gewwe, v.; eigewwe, pp.;
2.nei/gewwe, v.; neigewwe, pp.; 3.no(och)gewwe, v.;
no(och)gewwe, pp.; **information of** berichte, v.; bericht,
pp.; **information secretly** aadraage, v.; aagedraage, pp.;
light leichte, v.; geleicht, pp.; **me a kiss** mern = mer en
(geb -- boss); **notice of leaving** uff/kinne, v.; **off dust**
schtaawe, v.; gschtaabt, pp.; **on credit** verbarge, v.;
verbarkt, pp.; **one a piece of one's mind** Meening (die)n.
(die -- saage); **one a set back** zerick/setze, v.;
zerickgsetzt, pp.; **oneself away** verdappe (sich --)v.;
verdappt, pp.; **oneself free course in rage** aus/dowe
(sich --)v.; ausgedobt, pp.; **or hand over** riwwer/gewwe,
v.; riwwergewwe, pp.; **out** naus/gewwe, v.; nausgewwe,
pp.; **over** niwwer/gewwe, v.; niwwergewwe, pp.; **redress** ab/helfe, v.; abgholfe, pp.; **relief** batte, v.; gebatt,
pp.; **someone a lecture** Lefidde (die)n., pl. (ebber
die -- ablese); **someone a piece of mind** saage, v. gsaat,
pp. (ebber die Meening --); **the finishing touch**
ab/faddiche, v.; abgfaddicht, pp.; **tit for tat** 1.vergelde,
v.; vergolde, pp.; 2.vergelte, v.; vergolte, pp.; **to take
along with** mit/gewwe, v.; is mitgewwe, pp.; **up**
uff/gewe, v.; uffgewwe, pp.; **vent to one's opinion or
feelings** ab/blose, v.; abgeblost, pp.; **way** no(och)gewwe,
v.; no(och)gewwe, pp.

given name Vornome (der)n.; **to crying** verbrillt, adj.; **to
irritable complaining** vermaunst; **to laughing or
giggling** verlechert, adj.

glad froh, adj.

gladly 1.freedich, adj.; 2.gaern, adv.; 3.garn, adv.; 4.gern,
adv.; 5.gutwillich, adj.; 6.gutwillicherweis, adj.; **wish
another's good luck** gunne, v.; gegunnt, pp.
(gaern --)

glance Blick (der)n.; **around** rum/blicke, v.; rumgeblickt, pp.;
away weck/blicke, v.; weckgeblickt, pp.; **down**
nunner/blicke, v.; nunnergeblickt, pp.; **in or into**
nei/blicke, v.; neigeblickt, pp.; **off** 1.ab/glense, v.;
abgeglenst, pp.; 2.flitsche, v.; gflitscht, pp.; **out**
raus/blicke, v.; rausgeblickt, pp.; **glance up** nuff/blicke,
v.; nuffgeblickt, pp.

gland Dries (die)n.

glanders Ewichrotzer (der)n.; Ewichrotzer, pl.; **(in horses)**
Rotzer (der)n.

glare Schein (der)n.

glass Glaas (es)n.; Glesser, pl.; **bead** Glaaskarrell (die)n.;
eye Glaasaag (es)n.; **full** Glaasvoll (es)n.; **with a lid**
Deckelglaas (es)n.

glaze glessure, v.; geglessurt, pp.

glazed ice on the ground and on trees Glatteis (es)n.

glazing 1.Glansing (die)n.; 2.Glessur (die)n.

gleam glitzere, v.; geglitzert, pp.

glee Luschdichkeet (die)n.

glide schwewe, v.; gschwebt, pp.; **from** ab/ritsche, v.; abgeritscht, pp.; **off or slip** ab/witsche, v.; abgewitscht, pp.

glimmer schimmere, v.; gschimmert, pp.; **through**
darich/ schimmere, v.; darichgschimmert, pp.

Gg

glisten   golden

glisten funkle, v.; gfunkelt, pp.

glistening 1.glitzerich, adj.; 2.zwiterich, adj.

glitter 1.Glanz (der)n.; 2.glense, v.; geglenst, pp.; 3.glitzere, v.; geglitzert, pp.; 4.Schein (der)n.; 5.scheine, v.; gscheint, pp.

glittering glitzerich, adj.

globe 1.Erdballe (der)n.; 2.Erdreich (es)n.; **amaranth** Gleeblumm (die)n.

glorious 1.harlich, adj.; 2.herrlich, adj.

glory 1.Harrlichkeit (die)n.; 2.Herrlichkeit (die)n.

glove 1.Fingerhensching (der)n.; 2.Hensching (der)n.; Hensching, pl.

glow Gluut (die)n.

glue 1.Leim (der)n.; 2.leime, v.; gleimt, pp.; **pot** Leimkessel (die)n.

glutton 1.Fressdier (es)n.; 2.Fresser (der)n.; Fresser, pl.; 3.Fresshals (der)n.; 4.Vielfrass (der)n.

gluttonizing Fresserei (die)n.

gluttonous 1.seii(s)ch, adj.; 2.verfresse, adj.

gluttony Fressgranket (die)n.

gnarl Gnarre (der)n.; Gnarre, pl.; **or knot** (in wood) Gemasser (es)n.

gnarly 1.gnarrich, adj.; 2.knarrich, adj.; 3.mass(e)rich, adj.; **(of a tree, apple, or a roughly healed wound)** 1.gnarwlich, adj.; 2.gnaerwlich, adj.; 3.knarwlich, adj.

gnash 1.gna(r)schle, v.; gegnarschelt, pp.; 2.knaersche, v.; geknaerscht, pp.

gnashing of the teeth Zaehknaersche (es)n.

gnat Schnok (die)n.; Schnoke, pl.

gnaw 1.aa/gnawwere, v.; aagegnawwert, pp.; 2.gnawwere, v.; gegnawwert, pp.; 3.knawwere, v.; geknawwert, pp.; 4.naage, v.; genaagt, pp.; **at** 1.aa/fresse, v.; aagfresse, pp.; 2.Fresse (es)n. (am -- draa sei); 3.verbeisse, v.; verbisse, pp.; **off** ab/gnawwere, v.; abgegnawwert, pp.

gnome Erdgeischt (der)n.

gnomic song Schpruchlied (es)n.

go 1.geh, v.; gange, pp.; 2.laafe, v.; g(e)loffe, pp.; **about** rumhaer/geh, v.; rumhaergange, pp.; **about at uncanny times or places** rum/schpucke, v.; rumgschpuckt, pp.; **about boasting** rum/blose, v.; rumgeblose, pp.; **about complaining** rum/gnaunse, v.; rumgegnaunst, pp.; **about gossiping** rum/gackse, v.; rumgegackst, pp.; **about growling** rum/gnarre, v.; rumgegnarrt, pp.; **about raging** rum/raase, v.; rumgeraast, pp.; **against the grain** widdere, v.; gewiddert, pp.; **along at an easy trot** drolle, v.; gedrollt, pp.; **along haltingly** weck/zackere, v.; weckgezackert, pp.; **amiss** verunglicke, v.; verunglickt, pp.; **around fighting** rum/fechde, v.; rumgefochde, pp.; **around flourishing one's fists** rum/feischdle, v.; rumgfeischdelt, pp.; **around in shabby attire** rum/schlappe, v.; rumgschlappt, pp.; **around in wet weather or in wet grass** rum/hammle, v.; rumghammelt, pp.; **around noisely** rum/dunnere, v.; rumgedunnert, pp.; **around raising the devil** rum/deiwle, v.; rumgedeiwelt, pp.; **around scolding** rum/schelte, v.; rumgscholte, pp.; **around without any fixed purpose** rum/haschble, v.; rumghaschbelt, pp.; **as far as possible** aus/iewe, v.; ausgeiebt, pp.; **astray** 1.aerrgeh, v.; aerrgange, pp.; 2.veraerre (sich --)v.; veraerrt, pp.; **away** 1.fatt/geh, v.; fattgange, pp.; 2.weck/geh, v.; is weckgange, pp.; **back** zerick/geh, v.; zerickgange, pp.; **backward**

1.hinnerschich geh, v.; hinnerschichgange, pp.; 2.Grebsgang (der)n.; 3.Grebsgang (der)n. (in health) (-- geh); (-- hawwe) ; 4.uff, prep., adv. (-- em Grebsgang sei); **bankrupt** uff/breche, v.; uffgebroche, pp.; **bye-bye** (in speaking to children) daedae geh, v.; **courting** 1.schparige, v.; gschparigt, pp.; 2.schpatziere, v.; gschpatziert, pp.; **down** nunner/geh, v.; nunnergange, pp.; **down stairs** nunner/packe (sich --)v.; nunnergepackt, pp.; **home** heemgeh, v.; **in and out** geh, v.; gange, pp. (aus un ei --); **in the hole** (in datte) geh, v.; gange, pp. (beet --); **in with a will** 1.aa/lege, v.; aagelekt, pp.; 2.nei/schlagge, v.; neigschlagge, pp.; **into** nei/geh, v.; neigange, pp.; **into a decline** zerickzusgeh, adv.; **off** los/geh, v.; losgange, pp.; **on a journey or trip** ab/reisse, v.; abgereest, pp.; **on a still hunt** schpione, v.; gschpiont, pp.; **on up** nuff/packe (sich --) v.; nuffgepackt, pp.; **out** 1.aus/geh, v.; ausgange, pp.; 2.naus/geh, v.; nausgange, pp.; 3.naus/mache (sich --)v.; nausgemacht, pp.; **out of one's way** um/geh, v.; umgange, pp.; **over or across** 1.niwwer/geh, v.; niwwergange, pp.; 2.riwwer/geh, v.; riwwergange, pp. **pell mell** schtaawe, v.; gschtaabt, pp.; **through** darich/geh, v.; darichgange, pp.; **through with** erleewe, v.; erleebt, pp.; **to a place** hie/geh, v.; hiegange, pp.; **to a place by chance** hie/dappe, v.; hiegedappt, pp.; **to bed** 1.Bettlehem (es)n. (noch -- geh); 2.weck/lege (sich --)v.; weckgelegt, pp.; **to great trouble** aa/duh, v.; aageduh, pp. (sich viel Mieh --); **to hell** Deiwel (der)n. (geh zum --); **to meet** engegegeh, adj.; **to ruin** 1.Grund (der)n. (zu -- geh); 2.verfalle, v.; verfalle, pp.; 3.verlumbe, v.; verlumbt, pp.; 4.zerick/geh, v.; zerickgange, pp.; **to smash** zamme/fiege, v.; zammegfiegt, pp.; **to the dogs** Hund (der)n. (uff der -- kumme); **together** zammenannergeh, v.; zammenannergange, pp.; **too far** iwwerschritte, v.; iwwerschritt, pp.; **traveling** verreese, v.; verreest, pp.; **up** ruff/geh, v.; ruffgange, pp.; **uptown** Schteddel (es)n. (-- nuf/geh); **wandering about** rum/reese, v.; rumgereest, pp.; **with** mit/geh, v.; mitgange, pp.; **wrong** Schnur (die)n. (iwwer die -- hacke)

goad on aaretze, v.; aageretzt, pp.

goal Ziel (es)n.; **of life** Lewe(n)sziel (es)n.

goat Gees (der)n.; Gees, pl.

goatee Geesbaart (der)n.

goatskin 1.Geeshaut (die)n.; Geesheit, pl.; 2.Geesledder (es)n.

gobble (of a turkey) gullere, v.; gegullert, pp.

goblet 1.Becher (der)n.; 2.Henkeglaas (es)n.; Henkeglesser, pl.

God 1.Gott (der)n.; Gedder, pl.; 2.gut, adj. (-- mann); 3.Haerrgott (der)n.

godfather Pedder (der)n.

godlessness Gottlosichkeet (die)n.

godly gettlich, adj.

godmother 1.Geedel (die)n.; 2.God (die)n.

godsend Glicksfall (der)n.

goggles used by threshers Dreschbrill (die)n.

going Gang (der)n.(im --); **to church** Karrichgang (der)n.

goings on 1.du ens; 2.Gedu(ns) (es)n.

goiter 1.Gewex (es)n.; 2.Gropp (der)n.

gold Gold (es)n.; **piece** Goldschtick (es)n.; **thread** Goldwarzel (die)n.

golden 1.golde, adj.; 2.goldni(ch), adj.; **root** Deiwelsabbis (watzel) (die)n.; **tincture** Goldendur (die) n.; **willow** Gehlweide (der, die)n.; **yellow** goldegehl, adj.

Gg

goldenrod

goldenrod 1.Teegraut (es)n.; 2.Wundgraut (es)n.

goldfinch 1.Dischdelfink (die)n.; 2.Zelaatvoggel (der)n.; Zelaatveggel, pl.

goldsmith Goldschmitt (der)n.

gone 1.fart, adv.; 2.fatt/mache, v.; fattgemacht, pp. (mach dich fatt); 3.fatt/packe (sich --)v.; fattgepackt, pp.; 4.maschiere (sich --)v.; maschiert, pp. 5.naus/packe (sich --)v.; nausgepackt, pp.; **to seed** (of plants) gschosse, adj.

Good day! (How are you?) Wie geht's?; **evening!** 1.Guder Owed!; 2.Gut-n-Owed; **Friday** Karfreidaag (der)n.; **King Henry** (plant) 1.guter Heinrich (der)n.; 2.schtols Heinrich (der)n.; **Morning!** Gude(r) Mariye!; **night!** Gut Nacht!

good 1.braav, adj.; 2.gut, adj.; **eating** esse, v.; gesse, pp. (sich gut --); **for nothing** 1.nix nutz; 2.Nixnutz (der)n.; 3.unnitz(ich), adj.; 4.unnitz, adj.; **for-nothing fellow** Schlur(r)i (der)n.; **hearted** 1.gedrei, adj.; 2.hatzich, adj. (gut --); 3.meenich, adj. (gut --); **looking** guckich, adj. (gut --); **Lord!** 1.haerryaer(ru)m, interj.; 2.haerryammer!, interj.; 3.Troscht (der)n. (liewer --) **luck** 1.Glick (es)n. 2.glicke, v.; geglickt, pp.; **morals** moraalisch, adj.; **natured** gutmiedich, adj.; **time** blessiere (sich --)v.; blessiert, pp.; **view** rum/sehne, v.; rumgschne, pp.

goodbye 1.adge, int.; 2.faerriwell, adj.; 3.Hatge, interj.

goodness itself Schtunn (die)n. (die gut --); **knows!** Friede (der)n. (weiss der --)

goods 1.Schtoff(t) (es)n.; 2.Waar (die)n.

goose Gans (die)n.; Gens, pl.; **dung** Gensdreck (der)n.

goose's foot Gensfuss (der)n.; **neck** Genshals (der)n.

gooseberry Grusselbier (die)n.; Grusselbiere, pl.

goosefat Gensfett (es)n.

gooseflesh (from cold or fear) Genshaut (die)n.

goosefoot Melde (der)n. (wilder --)

gore 1.Schpeidel (der)n.; 2.Zwickel (der)n.; Zwickel, pl.

gorge eischtoppe, v.; eigschtoppt, pp.

gosling Gensli (es)n.; Genslin, pl.

gospel Evvengelium (es)n.

gossip 1.Babbel (die)n.; 2.Blatscher (der)n.; 3.dolmetsche, v.; gedolmetscht, pp.; 4.Dratsch (die)n.; 5.flatsche, v.; gflatscht, pp.; 6.Gschwetz (es)n.; 7.Retch (die)n.; 8.retsche, v.; geretscht, pp.; 9.verschwetze (sich --)v.; verschwetzt, pp.; **about** no(och)blaudre, v.; no(och)geblaudert, pp.; **across** (the fence) niwwer/gackse, v.; niwwergegackst, pp.

gossiping 1.Katzeyammer (der)n.; 2.Retscherei (die)n.; **(coffee party)** Kaffieklatsch (der)n.; **tour** 1.Babbelyacht (die)n.; 2.Blauderyacht (die)n.; **woman** Glatsch (die)n.

Gothic letters or figures Fraktura (die)n., pl.

Gottfried Gottfri (der)n.

gouge 1.Rundmeesel (der)n.; Rundmeesle, pl.; 2.Schpund (e)bohre (der)n.; Schpund(e)bohre, pl.

gourmand's delight Bauchgott (der)n.

gout Gicht (die)n.

govern 1.goweniere, v.; goweniert, pp.; 2.regiere, v.; regiert, pp.; 3.walte, v.; gewaltet, pp.

grass

government 1.Owwerichkeit (die)n.; 2.Regierung (die)n.

governor Gowe(r)nier (der)n.

gown Kutt (die)n.

grab 1.ergreife, v.; ergriffe, pp.; 2.greife, v.; gegriffe, pp.

grace (prayer) Gnaad(e) (die)n.

gracious 1.gnaedich, adj.; 2.gneedich, adj.

gradually 1.schriddich, adv.; 2.schrittweis(s), adv.

graft Zweig (die)n.; Zweige, pl.; **(a tree)** zweige, v.; gezweigt, pp.

grafting wax 1.waxschmier (die)n.; 2.Zweikschmier (die)n.

grain Fruchtkaern (die)n.; **(maturing on the field or after it is threshed)** Frucht (die)n.; **cradle** 1.Fruchtreff (es)n.; 2.Reff (es)n.; Reffer, pl.; **elevator** Fruchthaus (es)n.; **field** Fruchtfeld (es)n.; **of sand** 1.Sandkaern (die)n.; 2.Somekaern (die)n.; **of wheat** Weezekaern (die)n.

grain sown in fall and the resulting growth Winterfrucht (die)n.

granary (in the barn) Fruchtkammer (die)n.

grand 1.grossordich, adj.; 2.schtaatlich, adj.; **feast** Fresse (es)n. (en Fress)

grandchild Kinskind (es)n.; Kinskinner, pl.

granddaughter 1.Grossdochder (die)n.; 2.Enkelin (die)n. (rare usage)

grandfather 1.Graenpaep (der)n.; 2.Grossdaadi (der)n.; 3.Grossvadder (der)n.; 4.Daadi (der)n. (Amish usage); 5.Daed (der)n. (Amish usage)

grandmother 1.Grememm (die)n.; 2.Grossmammi (die)n.; 3.Grossmudder (die)n.; 4.Mammi (die)n.

grandparents Grosseldre (die)n., pl.

grandson 1.Enkel (der)n.; 2.Gross-soh(n) (der)n. 3.Kindsbu (der)n.; 4.Kindssuh (der)n.

granny's belief Alderweiwerglaawe (der)n.

grant 1.billiche, v.; gebillicht, pp.; 2.verwilliche, v.; verwillicht, pp.; **a favor** begnaadiche, v.; begnaadicht, pp.; **a hearing** ab/heere, v.; abgheert, pp.; **credit** 1.Buch (es)n. (ins -- schreiwe); 2.Eis (es)n. (uffs --schreiwe); 3.Greditt (der)n. (-- gewwe)

granulated kaernich, adj.

grape Draub (die)n.; Drauwe, pl.; **arbor** 1.Drauwegrischder (es)n.; 2.Drauwegrischt (es)n.; **hyacinth** 1.Blobottlicher (die)n., pl.; 2.Weiblumm (die)n.; 3.Weibottel (die)n.; 4.Weiglessli (es)n.; 5.Weiglessliche (es)n.; **juice** Drauwebrieh (die)n.; **or wine press** Drauwekelter (die)n.; **seed** Drauwekaern (die)n.

grapevine 1.Drauwerank (die)n.; 2.Drauweschtock (der)n.; Drauweschteck, pl.

grapewine Drauwewei (der)n.

grasp 1.fasse, v.; gfasst, pp.; 2.grabsche, v.; gegrabscht, pp.; 3.greife, v.; gegriffe, pp.; 4.zamme/fasse, v.; zammegfasst, pp.; **away** (from someone) weck/raffe, v.; weckgerafft, pp.; **for** dappe, v.; gedappt, pp. **hold on** aa/greife, v.; aagegriffe, pp.; **roughly** 1.aa/packe, v.; aagepackt, pp.; 2.halt/nemme, v.; haltgnumme, pp.; **up** uff/grapsche, v.; uffgegrapscht, pp.

grasping or miserly zwacke, v.; gezwackt, pp.

grass (applied to several varities of) 1.Graas (es)n.; 2.Schmelme; 3.Schwelme; **seed** 1.Graassome (der)n.; 2.Graassume (der)n.; **shears** Graasschier (die)n.; **snake** Graas-schlang (die)n.; Graas-schlange, pl.; **widow** scheede, v.; gscheede, pp. (en gscheedni fraa)

Gg

grasshopper

grasshopper 1.Hoischreck (die)n.; Hoischrecke, pl.; 2.Hoischrecker (der)n.; Hoischrecke, pl.; 3.Schrecke (die)n., pl.

grassland Graasland (es)n.; Grasslenner, pl.

grassy graasich, adj.

grate 1.aa/reiwe, v.; aageriwwe, pp.; 2.knaersche, v.; geknaerscht, pp.; 3.reiwe, v.; g(e)riwwe, pp.

grater Reiwise (es)n.

grave Graab (es)n.; Greewer, pl.; **digger** Dodegraawer (der)n.

gravedigger (and formerly also pallbearer) Graabmacher (der)n.; Greewermacher, pl.

gravel 1.grewwelich, adj.; 2.Kiss (der)n.; **plant** Grundschtrauss (der)n.

gravelly schiwwerich, adj.; **soil** Kissboddem (der)n.

gravestone Graabschtee (der)n.; Graabschtee, pl.

graveyard 1.Graabhof (der)n.; Graabhef, pl.; 2.Karichof (der)n.; Karrichhef, pl.

gravy Brieh (die)n.

gray gro(h), adj.; **haired** grohoorich, adj.; **headed** grokeppich, adj.; **plaided** groeckschteenich, adj.; **squirrel** Eechhaas (der)n.; Eechhaase, pl. (groher --)

graybeard Grobaart (der)n.

grayhead Grokopp (der)n.

grayish grolich, adj.

graze graase, v.; gegraast, pp.; **(cattle)** weede, v.; gweedt, pp.; **on** ab/weede, v.; abgeweedt, pp.

grease 1.aa/schmiere, v.; aagschmiert, pp.; 2.Fett (es)n.; 3.Schmier (die)n.; 4.Schmutz (der)n.; **spot** 1.Fettblacke(der)n.; 2.Schmutzblacke (der)n.

greasy 1.feddich, adj.; 2.fettich, adj.; 3.schmutzich, adj.

great 1.gross, adj.; 2.grossordich, adj.; 3.riesich, adj.; **aunt** Grossendi (die)n.; **bullrush** Binse (die)n.; **deal** 1.rechtschaffe, adj.; 2.reschaffe, adj.; **feed** Fresse (es)n. (en Fress); **goodness!** Friede (der)n. (du liewer --); **grandchild** 1.Grosskinskind (es)n.; Grosskinskinner, pl.; 2.Urenkel (der)n.; **grandfather** 1.Urgrossdaddi (der)n.; 2.Urgrossvadder (der)n.; **grandmother** Urgrossmutter (die)n.; **guns!** Gnalleise (es)n. (dunner uns --); **number** Unzaahl (die)n.; **ragweed** Bittreschtengel (der)n.; **shakes** wunners, adv.; **uncle** Grossonkel (der)n.

greaves Griewe (die)n., pl.

greediness 1.Begierichkeet (die)n.; 2.Raachgier (dle)n.

greedy 1.begierich, adj.; 2.geizich, adj.; 3.grabschich, adj.; 4.haabsichdich, adj.; 5.raachgier(s)ch, adj.; 6.rabschich, adj.; 7.wolfich, adj.

green grie(n), adj.; **as gall** gallegrie, adj.; **as grass** graas(e) grie, adv.; **briar** Dann (die)n. (grieni --); **cabbage worm** Grautwarm (der)n.; **foxtail** Kolwegraas (es)n.; **hellebore** (helleborus viridis) Niesgraut (es)n.; **or yellow foxtail** Haschgraas (es)n.

greenhouse Grie(n)haus (es)n.; Grienheiser, pl.

greenish grielich, adj.

greensward for bleaching Bleech (die)n.

greet 1.begegne, v.; begegnet, pp.; 2.bewil(l)kumme, v.; bewil(l)kummt, pp.; 3.griesse, v.; gegriesst, pl.

griddle Kucheblatt (die)n.

grow

grief 1.Drauer (die)n.; 2.Graam (der)n.; 3.Kummer (der)n.; 4.Leed(e) (der)n.; **stricken** drauerich, adj.

grieve 1.grenke, v.; gegrenkt, pp.; 2.kimmere (sich --)v.; gekimmert, pp.; 3.krenke, v.; gekrenkt, pp.; 4.Trau(e)re, v.; getrauert, pp.

grin 1.grinse, v.; gegrinst, pp.; 2.schmunsle, v.; gschmunselt, pp.

grind 1.knaersche, v.; geknaerscht, pp.; 2.schleife, v.; gschliffe, pp.; 3.zamme/maahle, v.; zammegemaahle, pp.; **(grain)** maahle, v.; g(e)maahle, pp.; **coarsely** schrode, v.; gschrot, pp.; **into chop** schrode, v.; gschrot, pp.; **off** ab/schleife, v.; abschliffe, pp.; **organ** Drehariyel (die)n.; **up** uff/maahle, v.; uffgemaahlt, pp.

grinder 1.Maahler (der)n.; Maahler, pl.; 2.Menscheschinner (der)n.

grinding (usually depreciatory) Maahlerei (die)n.

grindstone 1.Schleifschtee (der)n.; Schleifschtee, pl.; 2.Schtee (der)n.; Schtee, pl.

grinning Gschmunsel (es)n.

grip 1.aa/greife, v.; aagegriffe, pp.; 2.Griff (der)n. 3.halt/nemme, v.; haltgnumme, pp.; **(of hand) handle** Handgriff (der)n.; **hard** zuklemme, v.; zugeklemmt, pp.

gripes Griwwles (es)n.

griping in the bowels Bauchgriwwles (es)n.

grist mill Maahlmiel (die)n.

gristle 1.Gnaerwel (der)n.; 2.Gnarwel (der)n.; Gnarwel, pl.; 3.Knarwel (der)n.

gristly 1.gnaerwlich, adj.; 2.gnarwlich, adj.; 3.grusslich, adj.; 4.knarwlich, adj.

gristmill Schrotmiehl (die)n.; Schrotmiehle, pl.; **(grinding for toll)** Kunnemiehl (die)n.

groan 1.graahne, v.; gegraahnt, pp.; 2.grexe, v.; gegrext, pp.; 3.wimmele, v.; gewimmelt, pp.; 4.yammere, v.; geyammert, pp.; 5.yeemere, v.; geyeemert, pp.; 6.yomere, v.; geyomert, pp.

groaner Grauns (die)n.

groaning 1.Gegrauns (es)n.; 2.Gegrex (es)n.

groove Eischnitt (der)n.

grouchy person 1.Gretz (der)n.; 2.Kretz (der)n.; 3.Wandlaus (die)n. (so griddlich as en --)

ground 1.Bodde(m) (der)n.; 2.Grund (der)n.; **cherry** Yuddekasch (die)n.; Yuddekasche, pl.; **corn** (for young chickens) Griess (der)n.; **itch** Grundgretz (der)n.; **ivy** 1.Grundelraawer (die)n.; 2.Grundelrewe (die)n.; **pine** 1.Baerefuss (der)n.; 2.Wie-lenger-wie-lenger, n.; 3.Wie-lenger-wie-liewer (die)n.; **plate** 1.Schwell (die)n.; 2.Sohl (die)n.; **sausage meat** Waschdeeg (der)n.

Groundhog Lodge Grundsau Lodsch (der)n.

groundhog 1.Dachs (der)n. 2.Grund(d)ax (der)n.; Grund(d)axe, pl.; 3.Grundsau (die)n.; Grundsei, pl.

grounds of coffee Satz (der)n.

groundsel Grudelrewe (die)n., pl.

group 1.Drupp (die)n.; 2.Grupp (die)n.; 3.Hard (die)n.

grove Busch (der)n.; Bisch, pl.

grow waxe, v.; gewaxe, pp.; **again** no(och)wachse, v.; no(och) gewachst, pp.; **in different places** rumhaer/wachse, v.; rumhaergewachst, pp.; **into** nei/wachse, v.; neigewachst, pp. **out** raus/wachse, v.; rausgewachst, pp.

Gg

grow together — Gypsy

grow together 1.aa/waxe, v.; aagewaxe, pp.; 2.zamme/wachse, v.; zammegewachst, pp.; **up** 1.aa/waxe, v.; aagewaxe, pp.; 2.uff/waxe, v.; uffgwaxe, pp.; **up fast** uff/schiesse, v.; uffgschosse, pp.; **up to a certain point** nuff/wachse, v.; nuffgwachst, pp.

growing waxich, adj.; **cabbage** Grautschtock (der)n.

grain 1.Some (der)n.; 2.Soot (die)n.; **in clumps or bunches** ouschich, adj.

growl 1.grummle, v.; gegrummelt, pp.; 2.knarre, v.; geknarrt, pp.; 3.rum/maule, v.; rumgemault, pp.; **at** 1.aa/brumme, v.; aagebrummt, pp.; 2.aa/gnarre, v.; aa(ge)gnatt, pp.; 3.aaranne, v.; aagerannt, pp.

growling or grumbling Gegnarr (es)n.

grown uff/gewachse, v.; **up in weeds and brush** verwildert, adj.

growth Gewex (es)n.

grub grubbe, v.; gegrubbt, pp.; **into** nei/grubbe, v.; neigegrubbt, pp.

grubbing-hoe Grubbhack (die)n.

grudge 1.Grepp (der)n. (en --); 2.kipp

gruff schnarrich, adj.

grumble 1.brumme, v.; gebrummt, pp.; 2.brummle, v.; gebrumelt, pp.; 3.fuddre, v.; gfuddert, pp.; 4.gnaunse, v.; gegnaunst, pp.; 5.gnoddere, v.; gegnoddert, pp.; 6.graunse, v.; gegraunst, pp.; 7.grummle, v.; gegrummelt, pp.; 8.knarre, v.; geknarrt, pp.; 9.maule, v.; gemault, pp.; 10.rum/maule, v.; rumgemault, pp.; 11.yaunse, v.; geyaunst, pp.

grumbler Grauns (die)n.

grumbly gnodderich, adj.

grunt 1.gnarre, v.; gegnarrt, pp.; 2.greckse, v.; gegreckst, pp.

grunting 1.Gegrex (es)n.; 2.grecksich, adj.

guano Veggelmischt (der)n.

guarantee Versichering (die)n.

guard 1.behiede, v.; behiet, pp.; 2.bewaare, v.; bewaart, pp.; 3.hiete, v.; ghiet, pp.; **against** freihalte (sich --)v.

guardian 1.Gardien (der)n.; Gardiens, pl.; 2.Verweser (der)n.

guess 1.rode, v.; gerode, pp.; 2.Rot (der)n. (-- gewwe)

guest Gascht (der)n.

guide Fiehrer (der)n.

guidepost Wegweiser (der)n.; Wegweiser, pl.

guileless 1.unschuldich, adj.; 2.umschuldich, adj.

guilt Schuld (die)n.; Schulde, pl.

guilty schuldich, adj.

guinea hen Ginnihinkel (es)n.; Ginnihinkel, pl.; **pig** Ginniseiche (es)n.

guitar Gitar (die)n.

gull Seevoggel (der)n.

gullet Schlund (der)n.

gulp schlucke, v.; gschluckt, pp.; **down** 1.nunner/fresse, v.; nunnergfresse, pp.; 2.verschlinge, v.; verschlunge, pp.

gum berry Gummebeer (die)n.; **tree** 1.Gumme (der)n.; 2.Gummebaam (der)n.; Gummebeem, pl.

gum(s) 1.Zaahfleesch (es)n.; 2.Zohfleesch (es)n.

gun 1.Flint (die)n.; Flinde, pl.; 2.Gewehr (es)n.; 3.Schiessbriggel (der)n.; 4.Schiessgewehr (es)n.; **barrel** 1.Flindelaaf (der)n.; Flindeleef, pl.; 2.Laaf (der) n.; Leef, pl.; **cotton** Schiessbaawoll (die)n.

gunner Schitz (der)n.

gunpowder 1.Schiesspulwer (es)n.; 2.Schussbulfer (es)n.

gunsmith Bixemacher (der)n.

gunstock 1.Bixsekolwe (der)n.; 2.Flindegscheft (es)n.; 3.Flindekolwe (der)n.

gurgle 1.gluckse, v.; gegluckst, pp.; 2.gluxe, v.; gegluxt, pp.; 3.kluckse, v.; gekluckst, pp.

gusset 1.Gossduch (es)n.; 2.Winkel (der)n.

gust 1.Schtoss (der)n.; 2.Windschtoss (der)n.

guts Kuddle (die)n., pl.

gutter Graawe (der)n.; Greewer, pl.

gypsum Gips (der)n.

Gypsy Zi(g)einer (der)n.; Zi(g)einer, pl.

Hh

habit — hang

habit 1.Aagewehnet (die)n.; 2.Gewehnet (die)n.; 3.Manier (die)n.

habitual sneaking or slow movement Gschleich (es)n.

hackle Hackel (die)n.

hacksaw Drillseeg (die)n.; Drillseeg, pl.

hades Unnerwelt (die)n.

haft of a knife Messerkolwe (der)n.

haggle yutte, v.; geyutt, pp.

hail 1.Haagel (der)n.; 2.haagele, v.; gehaagelt, pp.; 3.schlosse, v.; gschlosse, pl.; 4.zurufe, v.; zugerufe, pp.

hail-storm 1.Schlosseschtarm (der)n.; 2.Schlossewedder (es)n.

hailstone Schloss (die)n.

hair 1.Haar (es)n.; 2.Hoor (die)n.; **net** Hoornetz (es)n.; **ribbon** 1.Boge (der)n.; 2.Hoorband (es)n.

hair's breadth 1.Hoorbreeding (die)n.; 2.Hoordicking (die)n.

hairbrush 1.Haarbascht (die)n.; Haarbaschde, pl.; 2.Hoorbascht (die)n.

hairpin 1.Haarschpell (die)n.; Haarschpelle, pl.; 2.Hoorschpell (die)n.

hairy 1.haarich, adj.; 2.hoorich, adj.

halbred Schpiess (der)n.

hale 1.gsund, adv.; 2.munder, adj.

half 1.halb, adv.; 2.halwer, adv.; 3.Helft (die)n.; **a dozen or so** Schtick (es)n. (schticker sex); **a pound** Halbpund (es) n.; **and half** halb un halb, adv.; **baked** 1.halb gebacke, adj.; 2.halwer gebacke, adj.; **brother** Halbbruder (der) n.; Halbbrieder, pl.; **dead** (of beasts) halbverreckt, adj.; **dollar** 1.Halbdaaler (der)n.; 2.Halwe; (der)n.; 3.Halwerdaaler (der)n.; **dozen** Halbdutzend (es)n.; **fool** Wickel (der)n.; **frozen water in streams** Grundeis (es) n.; **grown** 1.halbwechsich, adj.; 2.halwer ausgwaxe, adj.; 3.halwer uffgewaxe, adj.; **grown boy** Schpringer (der)n. (en gleener --); **hour** Halbschtunn(d) (die)n.; **measure** Halbmos (es)n.; **sister** Halbschweschder (die) n.; Halbschweschdre, pl.; **witted** eefeldich, adj.

halfway 1.halbwegs, adv.; 2.mitweegs, adv.

hall Gank (der)n.; Geng, pl.

hallelujah Halleluya (es)n.

halloo kreische, v.; gekrische, pp.

hallway 1.Gang (der)n.; Geng, pl.; 2.Gank (der)n.; Geng, pl.

halo (of the moon) 1.Mondhof (der)n.; 2.Moongringel (der)n.

halt 1.schtobbe, v.; gschtoppt, pp.; 2.uff/heere, v.; uffgheert, pp.

halter Halfder (die)n.; Halfdere, pl.; **chain** Halfterkett (die) n.; **strap** (on a harness) Halfderrierne (der)n.

halve or quarter fruit schnitze, v.; gschnitzt, pp.

ham 1.Hinnerschunke (der)n.; 2.Schinke (der)n.; 3.Schunke (der) n.; Schinke, pl.; **shoulder** Vedderschunke (der)n.

hame (of a horse-collar) Kummetschpaa (der)n.; Kummetschpee, pl.; **cover** Kummetdeck (die)n.; **hook** Schtrupp (der)n.; **strap** Kummetschpaarieme (der)n.

hamlet 1.Schteddel (es)n.; 2.Schteddli (es)n.; 3.Schtedtche (es)n.

hammer 1.globbe, v.; geglobbt, pp.; 2.Hammer (der)n. Hemmer, pl.; 3.hammere, v.; ghammert, pp.; 4.hemmere, v.; ghemmert, pp.; 5.kloppe, v.; gekloppt, pp.; (for sharpening scythes) Dengelhammer (der)n.; Dengelhemmer, pl.; **against** wedder/ gloppe, v.; weddergegloppt, pp.; **down**

nunner/gloppe, v.; nunnergegloppt, pp.; **in** 1.eigloppe, v.; eigegloppt, pp.; 2.nei/globbe, v.; neigeglobbt, pp.; **lightly** 1.gnuffe, v.; gegnufft, pp.; 2.knuffe, v.; geknufft, pp.; **or cock of a gun** 1.Haahne (der)n.; **out** 1.aus/ hammere, v.; ausghammert, pp.; 2.raus/gloppe, v.; rausgegloppt, pp.; **to pieces** verhammere, v.; verhammert, pp.; **together** zammegloppe, v. zammegegloppt, pp.

hammering Geglopp (es)n.

hand 1.Hand (die)n.; Hend, pl.; 2.reeche, v.; gereecht, pp.; **about** rum/lange, v.; rumglangt, pp.; **and kiss** (the kiss of peace in the plain churches) Hand un Kuss (der) n.; **around** 1.rum/gewwe, v.; rumgewwe, pp.; 2.rum/reeche, v.; rumgereecht, pp.; **brush** Handbascht (die)n.; **down** nunner/gewwe, v.; nunnergewwe, pp.; **fire pump** Schpritz (die)n.; **in** rei/gewwe, v.; reigewwe, pp.; **in a bid** ei/gewwe, v.; eigewwe, pp.; **made** handgemacht, adj.; **net** Fischhammer (der)n.; **of a clock** 1.Zeeche (es)n.; 2.Zoiger (der)n.; 3.Uhrezeeche (es)n.; Uhrezeeche, pl.; **or Dutch cheese** Schtinkkees (der)n.; **out** 1.naus/lange, v.; nausgelangt, pp.; 2.raus/reeche, v.; rausgereecht, pp.; 3.reeche, v.; gereecht, pp.; **over** 1.ab/reeche, v.; abgereecht, pp.; 2.haer/lange, v.; haergelangt, pp.; 3.iwwerlief(f)ere, v.; iwwerlieft, pp.; 4.iwwerliwwere, v.; iwwerliefert, pp.; **to someone** lange, v.; gelangt, pp.; **up** 1.ruff/gewwe, v.; ruffgewwe, pp.; 2.ruff/lange, v.; ruffgelangt, pp.; **breadth** Handbreeding (die)n.

handball Handballe (der)n

handful 1.garsche, adj.; 2.Handvoll(die)n.; **of finished flax** Waergel (es)n.

handkerchief 1.Duch (es)n.; Dicher, pl.; 2.Schnuppduch (es)n.; Schnuppdicher, pl.

handle 1.aa/fingere, v.; aagfingert, pp.; 2.handle, v.; g(e)handelt, pp.; 3.hendle, v.; ghendelt, pp.; 4.hotzele, v.; ghotzelt, pp.; 5.um/geh, v.; umgange, pp.; 6.verfaahre, v.; verfaahre, pp.; (of a basket) Heb (die)n.; (of a flail) Fleggelruut (die)n.; (of a hammer) Hammerschtiel (der)n.; (of a scythe) 1.Sensewar(e)f (der)n.; 2.Warf (der)n.; 3.Warref (der)n.; (of a tool or object) 1.Helm (der)n. 2.Hemmerhendel (der)n.; 3.Henk (die)n.; Henke, pl.; 4.Schtiel (der)n.; Schtiel, pl.; **over much** knootsche, v.; gegknootscht, pp.; **roughly** flachsiere, v.; gflachsiert, pp.

handrail 1.Handgelender (es)n.; 2.Handriggel (der)n.

hands 1.Gluppe (die)n.; 2.Kluppe (die)n.

handsaw Handseeg (die)n.

handsome 1.aasehnlich, adj.; 2.hibsch, adj.; 3.schee, adj.

handwork Handarewett (die)n.

handwriting 1.Handschreiwes (es)n.; 2.Handschrift (die) n.; 3.Schrift (die)n.

handy 1.gewandt, adj.; 2.gschickt, adj.; 3.hendich, adv.; **rag** (in the kitchen) Handlumbe (der)n.

hang henke, v.; ghenkt, g(e)honke, pp.; (something) at it draahenke, v.; draaghenkt, pp.; (something) inside rei/henke, v.; reighenkt, pp.; **around** rum/henke, v.; rumghenkt, pp.; **away** weck/henke, v.; weckghenkt, pp.; **down** runner/henke, v.; runnerghenkt, pp.; **in a place**

(Continued on page 291)

Hh

hang (continued)   haul

(Continued from page 290)

hie/henke, v.; hieghenkt, pp.; **loosely** bemble, v.;
gebembelt, pp.; **on** 1.aa/halde, v.; aaghalde, pp.;
2.aa/henke, v.; aaghenkt; aaghonke, pp.; **out**
raus/henke, v.; rausghenkt, pp.; **the feathers**
maudere, v.; gemaudert, pp.; **the lip** 1.Leffermaul
(es)n.; 2.Schippsche (es)n. (en -- mache);
3.Schlappmaul (es)n.; **together** zamme/henke, v.;
zammeghenkt, pp.; **up** 1.nuff/henke, v.; nuffghenkt,
pp.; 2.nuff/mache, v.; nuffgemacht, pp.; 3.uff/henke,
v.; uffghenkt, pp.

hank 1.Gnewwel (der)n.; 2.Gnupse (der)n.; 3.Knew(w)el (der)n.

hanker after continually nengere, v.; genengert, pp.

haphazard Graad(e)wohl (es)n. (uff --)

haphazard(ly) uff, prep., adv. (-- graad(e)wohl)

happen 1.bassiere, v.; bassiert, pp.; 2.bedreffe, v.; bedroffe, pp.;
3.befalle, v.; befalle, pp.; 4.dreffe (sich --)v.; gedroffe, pp.;
5.gschehe, v.; is gschehe, gschehne, pp.; 6.hafte, adj.;
7.vor/kumme, v.; vorkumme, pp.; 8.vorfalle, v.; vorgfalle,
pp.; 9.wedder/faahre, v.; wedderfaahre, pp.; 10.zu/dreffe
(sich --)v.; zugedroffe, pp.; 11.zudraage (sich --)v.;
zugedraage, pp.; 12.zufalle, v.; zugfalle, pp.; 13.zugeh, v.;
zugange, pp.; **twice** zwette (sich --)v.; gezwett, pp.

happening Vorgang (der)n.

Happy New Year! 1.Freihlich Neiyaahr!, interj.; 2.Hallich
Neiyaahr!, interj.

happy 1.frehlich, adj.; 2.froh, adj.; 3.glickselich, adj.;
4.haerlich, adj.; 5.hallich, adj.; 6.harlich, adj.;
7.luschtunfreehlich, adj.; 8.selich, adj.

harangue wildly dolmetsche, v.; gedolmetscht, pp.

harass gweele, v.; gegweelt, pp.

harassing gweelich, adv.

harbinger Vorlaafer (der)n.; Vorlaafer, pl.

hard drinking Gsauf (es)n.; **mouthed** (of horses)
hattmeilich, adj.; **smoked sausage** 1.Gnackwascht
(die)n.;   2.Knackwa(r)scht (die)n.; **soap** Laagseef
(die)n.; **working** hattschaffich, adj.

harden 1.backe, v.; gebacke, pp.; 2.eihaerte, v.; eighaert,
pp.; 3.haerde, v.; ghaert, pp.; 4.harde, v.; ghardt, pp.;
5.schtaahle, v.; gschtaahlt, pp.; 6.verhaerte, v.;
verhaert, pp.; 7.verharde, v.; verhardt, pp.

hardened mucose removed from the nose Bucker (der)n.

hardhearted hatthatzich, adj.

hardly 1.haerli, adv.; 2.kaum, adv.; 3.schier net, adv.;
4.schwerlich, adj.

hardness 1.Hadding (die)n.; 2.Haerding (die)n.

hardship Schtrapatze (die)n., pl.

hardware store Eiseschtor (der)n.; Eiseschtore, pl.

harelip 1.Haasemaul (es)n.; 2.Schaademaul (es)n.;
3.Schaartmaul (es)n.

harken lausche, v.; gelauscht, pp.

harlot Hur (die)n.; Hure, pl.

harm 1.Schaade (der)n.; 2.schaediche, v.; gschaedicht,
pp.; 3.Unheel (es)n.

harmful 1.schaadlich, adv.; 2.schaedlich, adj.;
3.scheedlich, adj.; 4.scheedlich, adv.

harmless 1.schaadlos, adv.; 2.unschaedlich, adj.

harmonica Maularigel (die)n.

harmonious mitschtimmich, adj.

harmonize iwwereischtimme, v.; iwwereigschtimmt, pp.

harness 1.Geilschar (es)n.; 2.Gscha(rr) (es)n.; Gscharre, pl.;
(horses) together zamme/schpanne, v.; zammegschpannt,
pp.; **leather** Harnischledder (es)n.; **of the lead horse**
Veddergschar (es)n.

harp Harf(e) (die)n.; Harfe, pl.

harrow 1.Eeg (die)n.; Eege, pl.; 2.eege, v.; geegt, pp.; 3.Eek
(die)n.; Eege, pl.; 4.nei/gratze, v.; neigegratzt, pp.

harrow before sowing voreege, v.; voreeekt, pp.; **in**
(seed)eieege, v.; eige-eekt, pp.

harry bloge, v.; geblogt, pp.

hart's tongue Haschzung (die)n.

hartshorn Haerschharngeischt (der)n.

harum-scarum woman Feger (der)n.

Harvest Home 1.Ernbreddich (die)n.; 2.Ern(d)karrich (die)
n.; 3.Erntfescht (es)n.; 4.Ern-Versammling (die)n.
(plain churches)

harvest 1.aernde, v.; geaernt, pp.; 2.Arn (die)n.;
3.eiaernde, v.; eigeaernt, pp.; 4.Ern (die)n.; **apple**
1.Aernabbel (der)n.; 2.Friehabbel (der)n.; Friehebbel,
pl.; **field** Aernfeld (es)n.; **time** Aernzeit (die)n.

harvesters Aernsleit (die)n., pl.

haslet Geling (es)n.; **of a calf** Kalbsgeling (es)n.

haste Eil (die)n.; Eile, pl.

hasten 1.dummle (sich --)v.; gedummelt, pp.; 2.eile, v.;
ge-eilt, pp.; 3.schaerre, v.; gschaerrt, pp.; **away**
weck/eile, v.; weckgeeilt, pp.

hasty 1.eilich, adj.; 2.iwwereilt, adj.

hat 1.Hut (der)n.; Hiet, pl.; 2.Schlapphut (der)n.; Schlapphiet, pl. (soft felt man's)

hatband Hutband (es)n.

hatch 1.briee, v.; gebriet, pp.; 2.briehe, v.; gebrieht, pp.;
an intrigue aa/schpinne, v.; aagschpunne, pp.; **out**
1.raus/briee, v.; rausgebriet, pp.; 2.raus/kumme, v.;
is rauskumme, pp.

hatchel 1.Flaxhatchel (die)n.; 2.hackle, v.; ghackelt, pp.;
3.Hechel (die)n.

hatchet 1.Beil (es)n.; Beiler, pl.; 2.Exel (es)n.

hatchway (of a roof) Dachlaade (der)n.; Dachlaade, pl.

hate Hass (der)n.

hated verhasst, adj.

hateful 1.abscheilich, adj.; 2.hesslich, adv.; adj.

hatred Abschei (der)n.

hatter Hutmacher (der)n.; Hietmacher, pl.

haughtiness Hochmut (der)n.

haughty 1.batzich, adj.; 2.gross feihlich, adj.; 3.hochmiedich,
adj.; 4.hochnaasich, adj.; 5.schtolz, adj.

haul faahre, v.; gfaahre, pp.; **away** ab/faahre, v.; abgfaahre, pp.;
in nei/faahre, v.; neifaahre, pp.; **into the barn** 1.eifaahre, v.;
eigfaahre, pp.; 2.rei/duh, v.; reigeduh; **or drive out** naus/
faahre, v.; nausgfaahre, pp.; **over the coals** 1.verhechle, v.;
verhechelt, pp.; 2.verhensle, v.; verhenselt, pp.; **someone
over the coals** los/ziege, v.; losgezoge, pp. (iwwer ebber --);
to a certain place bei/faahre, v.; beigfaahre, pp.; **together**
zamme/faahre, v.; is zammegfaahre, pp.

291

Hh

haulage — hearth

haulage Furhloh (der)n.

haunted schpucke, v.; gschpuckt, pp.

have hawwe, v.; ghat, ghadde, pp; **(something) at heart**
aa/leie, v.; aagelegge, pp.; **a birthday** yaehre (sich --)
v.; geyaehrt, pp.; **a lark** yuxe, v.; geyuxt, pp.; **a rash**
aus/faahre, v.; aus(g)faahre, pp.; **back** (return)
zerick/hawwe, v.; zerickghatt, pp.; **closed** zuhawwe,
v.; zughatt, pp.; **dealings with** umgeh, v.; umgange,
pp. (-- mit); **in mind** vorhawwe, v.; vorghatt, pp.; **it**
out aus/fechde, v.; ausgfochde, pp.; **one's face**
covered with pimples aus/faahre, v.; aus(g)faahre,
pp.; **someone arrested** fange, v.; gfange, pp.
(-- losse); **the upper hand** Iwwerhand (die)n.
(die -- hawwe; **to** misse, v.; gemisst, pp.; **you got it?**
hoschdes (hoscht du es)

haversack Schnappsack (der)n.; Schnappseck, pl.

having the heaves windgebroche, adj.

hawk 1.warixe, v.; gewarixt, pp.; 2.Woi (der)n.; Woi, pl.

hawkeyed scharfaagich, adj.

hawkweed Habbichgraut (es)n.

hawthorn 1.Schpellebaam (der)n.; 2.Weissdarn (der)n.

hay 1.Hoi (es)n.; 2.Hei (es)n. (rare usage); **hook** Hoirobber
(der)n.; **rack** (on a wagon) Waggeleeder (die)n.; **shed**
Hoischtall (der)n.

haycock 1.Hoihaufe (der)n.; 2.Hopihaufe (der)n.; Hopihaufe, pl.

hayfield Hoifeld (es)n. Hoifelder, pl.

hayflats Hoileedere (die)n.

hayfork Hoigawwel (die)n.; Hoigawwle, pl.

hayhole 1.Hoiloch (es)n.; Hoilecher, pl.; 2.Hoirechder (es)n.

hayloft 1.Hoibohre (der)n.; Hoibohre, pl.; 2.Hoidenn (es)
n.; Hoidenner, pl.

haymaking Hoiet (die)n.

haymow 1.Baare (der)n.; 2.Hoibaare (der)n.

hayrack Hoireff (es)n.; Hoireff, pl.

hayrake Hoireche (der)n.

haystack Hoischtock (der)n.; Hoischteck, pl.

haywagon Hoiwagge (der)n.

hazel bush Hasselheck (die)n.

hazelnut Hasselnuss (die)n.

hazy dufdich, adj.

He won't talk me into it! Er schwetzt mir kenn Loch hie
wu ich eens hab!

he er, pron.; **can't sit still** Sitzfleesch (es)n. (er hot kenn --);
did it after all doch, conj. (er hut's -- gedu); **did not**
breathe a word (about it) biebse, v.; gebiebst, pp. (er
hot kenn watt gebiebst); **did not succeed** gerode, v.;
gerode, pp. (es is ihm net --); **has it in his power** Versatz
(der)n. (er hut's im --); **has no property** waert, adv. (er is
nix --); **has recovered** driwwer, adv. (er is --); **has sev-**
ered relations ab, prep. (er is gans --); **hasn't quite got**
the knack Gschick (der)n. (er kann sich kenn
rechder -- gewwe); **is a bit off in the head** 1.Schparre
(der)n. (er hut en -- los); 2.Schparre (der)n.; (er hut
en -- zu viel odder eener zu wennich); 3.ab, prep. (er is
wennich --); **is always contrary** Gegedeel (es)n. (er is
immer's --); **is angry with me** iwwer, prep. (er is
bees -- mich); **is cautious** Wedder (es)n. (er draut

dem -- net recht); **is doing poorly** hinnerlich, adj. (es geh
ihm --); **is getting saucy** Hawwer (der)n.(-- schteckt 'n);
is good for nothing waert, adv. (er is nix --); **is hard at**
work schtarrick, adj. (er is -- draa); **is in poor circum-**
stances hinnerlich, adj. (es geh ihm --); **is so weak that**
he is not able to walk Wegschdeier (der)n. (er hot
der -- nimmi); **is suspicious** Wedder (es)n. (er draut
dem -- net recht); **is undecided** Schnepp (die)n. (er is uff
der --); **laid the blame on me** gewwe, v.; gewwe, pp. (er
hot mer sei schuld --); **raised Cain** wiescht, adj. (er
hut -- gemacht); **ran like the devil** Hollenner (der)n. (er
is gschprunge wie en --); **sheep** Schofbock (der)n.;
Schofbeck, pl.; **suffered not the slightest harm** Hoor
(die)n. (es hot em kenn -- geduh); **was a sight!**
dreisehne, v. (er hut arrig --) **he'll be sure to see it**
schunn, adv. (er waerd -- dezu sehne)

head 1.Bal (der)n.; 2.Blottschaal (die)n.; 3.Kabesch (die)n.;
4.Kalbascht (die)n.; 5.Kaschde (der)n.; Kaschde, pl.;
6.Kellebasch (die)n.; 7.Kopp (der)n.; Kepp, pl.; 8.Schaal
(die)n.; Schaale, pl.; **(of cattle)** Rinschtickvieh (es)n.;
(taller) koppsleng, adj.; **first** koppsvedderscht, adv.;
lettuce Haepterselaat (der)n.; **of grain** 1.Aehr (die)n.;
2.Ehr (die)n.; **of rye** Kannaehr (die)n.; **of wheat**
Weezeaehr (die)n.; **off** Bass abschneide (der)v.; **over**
heals iwwer, prep. (-- kopp un ohre); **piece of a bridle**
Schtaernríeme (der)n.; **plane** Leischhowwel (die)n.;
Leischhowwle, pl.

headache Koppweh (es)n.

headdress Koppputz (der)n.

headlong 1.Hobbertibobb(erti) (der)n.; 2.koppsvedderscht, adv.

heads (of cabbage or lettuce) Haepter (die)n., pl.

headstall Koppschtell (die)n.

headstone Graabschtee (der)n.; Graabschtee, pl.

headstrong 1.absenaat, adj.; 2.haeroisch, adj.; 3.Kopp
(der)n. (sei -- setze); **person** Trotzkopp (der)n.

heal 1.aa/heele, v.; aagheelt, pp. (together;) 2.ab/heele, v.;
abgheelt, pp.; 3.zamme/heele, v.; zammegheelt, pp.
(together); **all** Prunellegraut (es)n.; **perfectly** aus/heele,
v.; ausgheelt, pp.; **up** zuheele, v.; zugheelt, pp.

health 1.Gsundheet (die)n.; 2.Gsundtheit (die)n.

healthy 1.geraascht, adj.; 2.gsund, adj., adv.; 3.gut, adv.;
4.munder, adv.; 5.wohl, adj., adv.

heap 1.Glumbe (der)n.; 2.Haufe (der)n.; Heife, pl.;
3.Klumpe (der)n.; **up** (earth around plants) 1.heifle,
v.; gheifelt, pp.; 2.schgoffle, v.

heaped kauftich, adj.

heaping full kaufdevoll, adv.; **measure** kaufdevoll, adv.

hear 1.hariche, v.; gharicht, pp.; 2.heere, v.; gheert, pp.

hearsay 1.Geschwetz (es)n.; 2.Heersaage (es)n.

hearse 1.Dodekutsch (die)n.; 2.Dodewaage (der)n.;
Dodeweege, pl.

heart 1.Geling (es)n.; 2.Hatz (es)n.; Hatzer, pl.; **attack**
Hatzschlack (der)n.; **of cabbage** Grautda(r)sch (die)
n.; **trouble** Fehler (der)n. (-- am Hatz hawwe); **wood**
Hatzhols (es)n.

heartache 1.Graam (der)n.; 2.Hatzweh (es)n.

heartburn Sodbrenne(s) (es)n.

hearth 1.Feierhard (der)n.; Feierhard, pl.; 2.Haerd (der)n.

Hh

heartsick — herself

heartsick hatzgrank, adj.

hearty 1.hatz(h)aftich, adj.; 2.hatzhafdich, adv.; 3.hatzlich, adj.; 4.raschdich, adj.; **kiss** 1.Schmatz (der)n.; Schmatze, pl.; 2.Schmutz (der)n.

heat 1.aa/hitze, v.; aaghitzt, pp.; 2.Gluut (die)n.; 3.hitze, v.; ghitzt, pp.; 4.Waerming (die)n.; **(in --)** bocke, v.; gebockt, pp.; **over** iwwer hitze, v.; iwwerhitzt, pp.; **up** uff/hitze, v.; uffghitzt, pp.

heath aster Besereis (es)n.

heathen Heid(e) (der)n.; Heide, pl.

heathendom Heideland (es)n.

heathenish heidisch, adj.

heatstroke 1.Hitzschtreech (der)n.; 2.Sunneschtreech (der)n.

heaven Himmel (der)n.

heavenly himmlisch, adj.

heavenward himmelwaerts, adv., adj.

heavy 1.schwer, adj.; 2.windgebroche, adj.; **work** mannsaerwet (die)n.

heckle 1.schtumbiere, v.; schtumbiert, pp.; 2.verhechle, v.; verhechelt, pp.

hedge 1.Heck (die)n.; Hecke, pl.; 2.Heckefens (die)n.; **bindweed** Winne (die)n.; **hog cactus** 1.Baapscht (der)n.; Baapschde, pl.; 2.Baapschtkopp (der)n.

heed 1.aa/hariche, v.; aagharicht, pp.; 2.aa/heere, v.; aagheert, pp.; 3.achde, v.; geacht, pp.; 4.acht/gewwe, v.; achtgewwe, pp.

heedful achtsam, adj.

heel 1.Absatz (der)n.; Absetz, pl.; 2.Absetz (der)n.; 3.Faerschde (der)n.; 4.Farschde (der)n.

heifer Rinn (es)n.; Rind; Rinner, pl.; **(that calves for the first time)** Erschtling (der)n.

height 1.Grees (die)n.; 2.Heech (die)n.; 3.Heeh (die)n.; 4.Hen (die)n.

heir Erewer (der)n.; Erewer, pl.

held indoors by rain eireggne, v.; eigereggent, pp.

hell Hell (die)n.; **and damnation!** Mord (der)n. (zum --sackerment); **cat** Deiwelskatz (die)n.

helleborus viridis 1.Gnieswatzel (die)n.; 2.Grischtwatzel (die)n.

hellish hellisch, adj.

helmsman Schteiermann (der)n.

help 1.aa/helfe, v.; aagholfe, pp.; 2.aus/helfe, v.; ausgholfe, pp.; 3.batte, v.; gebatt, pp.; 4.bei/schteh, v.; beischtanne, pp.; 5.helfe, v.; gholfe, pp.; 6.Hilf (die)n.; 7.kumme, v.; kumme, pp. (zu Hilf --); **(one) around** rum/helfe, v.; rumgholfe, pp.; **(someone) away** weck/helfe, v.; weckgholfe, pp.; **help a person to get loose** los/helfe, v.; losgholfe, pp.; **help across** 1.niwwer/helfe, v.; niwwergholfe, pp.; 2.riwwer/helfe, v.; riwwergholfe, pp.; **along** 1.fatt/helfe, v.; fattgholfe, pp.; 2.mit/helfe, v.; mitgholfe, pp.; 3.no(och)helfe, v.; no(och)gholfe, pp.; **away** fatt/helfe, v.; fattgholfe, pp.; **down** 1.nunner/helfe, v.; nunnergholfe, pp.; 2.runner/helfe, v.; runnergholfe, pp.; **in** 1.rei/helfe, v.; reigholfe, pp.; 2.nei/helfe, v.; neigholfe, pp.; **in return** zerick/helfe, v.; zerickgholfe, pp.; **on the way** voraahelfe, v.; voraagholfe, pp.; **out** 1.raus/helfe, v.; rausgholfe, pp.; 2.naus/helfe, v.; nausgholfe, pp.; **to get together**

zamme/helfe, v.; zammegholfe, pp.; **up** 1.nuff/helfe, v.; nuffgholfe, pp.; 2.uff/helfe, v.; uffgholfe, pp.

helper 1.Handlanger (der)n.; Handlanger, pl.; 2.Helfer (der)n.; 3.Hilfer (der)n.; Hilfer, pl.

helpful behilf(l)ich, adj.

helpless 1.hilflos, adj.; 2.machtlos, adj.; 3.ubeholfe, adj.; 4.umbehilfich, adj.; 5.umbeholfe, adj.; 6.unbehilf(l)ich, adj.; 7.unbeholfe, adj.; 8.uubeholfe, adj.; **babe** Zeppelche (es)n.

helter-skelter 1.darich(e)nanner, adj.; 2.hollerboller, adv.

helve 1.Helm (der)n.; 2.Schtiel (der)n.; Schtiel, pl.

hem 1.ei/bendle, v.; eigebendelt, pp.; 2.Noht (die)n.; Neht, pl.; 3.Saam (der)n.; Saame, pl.; 4.saame, v.; gsaamt, pp.; 5.uff/saame, v.; uffgsaamt, pp.

hemisphere Halbkuggel (die)n.

hemorrhage Blutschtaerz (der)n.

hemp 1.Hanf(t) (der)n.; 2.Hannef (der)n.; **seed** Hannefsume (der)n.

hen Hinkel (es)n.; Hinkel, pl.; **(when with chicks)** 1.Gluck (die)n.; Glucke, pp.; 2.Kluck (die)n.; **egg** Hinkeloi (es)n. **house** Hinkelhaus (es)n.; **nest** Hinkelnescht (es)n. **roost** Hinkelsaddel (der)n.

hence dohaer, adv.

henceforth nau, adv. (vun -- aa)

Henry 1.Heinrich (der)n.; 2.Henner(i) (der)n.; 3.Henni (der)n.

hepatica Lewwergraut (es)n.

her 1.ihr, possessive adj.; 2.sie, pron.

herb 1.Blanz (die)n.; Blanze, pl.; 2.Graut (es)n.; Greider, pl.; 3.Kraut (es)n.; **tea** Kreidertee (der)n.

herbivorous graasfressend, adj.

herbs 1.Gegreider (die)n., pl.; 2.Gekreider (die)n., pl.; 3.Greider (die)n., pl.; 4.Kreider (die)n., pl.

herd 1.Drupp (die)n.; 2.haerde, v.; ghaerdt, pp.; 3.Hard (die)n.; 4.Meng(e) (die)n.; **together** zamme/haerde, v.; zammeghaerdt, pp.

herdgrass Haerdgraas (es)n.

here 1.do, adv.; 2.dohie, adv.; 3.haer, prep.; **and there** 1.do un datt, adv.; 2.iwwerletzich, adv.; **in front** do-vanne, adv.; **of late** letscht, adv. (es -- her)

hereabouts dorum, adv.

hereafter nochdem, adv.

hereditary 1.aagebore, adj.; 2.aerblich, adj.; 3.no(och)aerwe (sich --)v.; no(och)geaerbt, pp.

heresy Ketzerei (die)n.

heretic 1.Bucker (der)n.; 2.Fratzel (es)n.; 3.Galgevoggel (der)n.; 4.Hallunk (der)n.; 5.Hutzer (der)n.; 6.Kanallye (es)n.; 7.Ketzer (der)n.; Ketzer, pl.; 8.Lump (der)n.; 9.Schpitzbu(h) (der)n.; 10.Schuft (der)n.

Herman Haermann (der)n.

hermit Eensler (der)n.

hernia 1.Bruch (der)n.; Brich, pl.; 2.Schteebruch (der)n.; Schteebrich, pl.

hero Held (der)n.

heron Fischroiger (der)n.

herring Her(r)ing (der)n.

herself sie selwer, pron.

Hh

hesistate | **hoggishness**

hesitate 1.schteibere (sich --)v.; gschteibert, pp.; 2.schtutze, v.; gschtutzt, pp.; 3.waahle, v.; gewaahlt, pp.; 4.zaage, v.; gezaakt, pp.; 5.zaudere, v.; gezaudert, pp.

hesitation Gezaak (es)n.

Hessian Hess (der)n.; **fly** Weezelaus (die)n.

hestiation or evasion Gschraub (es)n.

hew beile, v.; gebeilt, pp.; **a log** bschlagge, v.;bschlagge,pp.; **away** weck/beile, v.; weckgebeilt, pp.; **logs** bschlagge, v.; bschlagge, pp. (holz --) **logs roughly** ab/schpaale, v.; abgschpaalt, pp.

hexagonal 1.sechseckich, adj.; 2.sexeckich, adj.

hiccough 1.Gickser (der)n.; 2.Schlickser (der)n.; 3.schlicksere, v.; gschlicksert, pp.; 4.Schlixer (der)n.; 5.Schluckse (es)n.; 6.Schluckser (der)n.

hickory Hickeri (es),n.; **splint broom** Schienebese(m) (der) n.; **storm** (a brisk wind which causes the hickory nuts to fall) Hickernis-Schtarm (der)n.

hickorynut Hickerinis (der)n.

hidden 1.schtecke, v.; gschteckt, pp.; 2.verschteckelt, adj.; 3.verschluppe (sich --)v.; verschluppt, pp.

hide 1.verschtecke, v.; verschteckt, pp.; 2.verschteckle (sich --) v.; verschteckelt, pp.; 3.verschteckle, v.; verschteckelt, pp.; **and-seek** 1.Schteckle (es)n.; 2.Schteckli (es)n.

hideous 1.greislich, adj.; 2.schrecklich, adj.

hieroglyphic Fiddelboge (der)n.; Fiddelboge, pl.

high hoch; heecher; heechest, adj.; **and low** Eck (es)n. (in alle --e); **blackberry** Dann (die)n. (hochi --); **in price** salzich, adj.; **mass** Hochamt (es)n.; **school** Hochschul (die)n.; Hochschule, pl.; **water** Flut (die)n.

highway Landschtross (die)n.; Landschtrosse, pl.

hill 1.Baerrick (der)n.; 2.Hiwwel (der)n.; Hiwwle, pl.; **road** Baerrickschtross (die)n.

hillside-plow Baerrickblug (der)n.

hilly 1.baergich, adj.; 2.bucklich, adj.; 3.grummbucklich, adj.; 4.hiwwlich, adj.

hilt Heft (es)n.

him 1.ihm, pron.; 2.'n, pron.

himself Nummereens (der)n.

hind foot Hinnerfuss (der)n.; **foremost** 1.hinnerscht, adj. ('s -- 's vedderscht); 2.hinnerscht-vedderscht, adv.; **leg** Hinnerbee (es)n.; **part** Hinnerdeel (es)n.; **quarter** (of beef) Hinnervaddel (es)n.; **wheel** Hinnerraad (es)n.

hinder 1.hinnere, v.; ghinnert, pp.; 2.uff/halde, v.; uffghalde, pp.; 3.verhinnere, v.;   verhinnert, pp.

hindmost 1.allerhinnerscht, adj.; 2.hinnerscht, adj.

hindrance Hinnernis (der)n.

hinge Band (es)n.; Benner, pl.; **of a door** 1.Angel (die)n.; 2.Deereband (es)n.

hint 1.aadeite, v.; aagedeit, pp.; 2.Eiblick (der)n.; 3.eiriwwle, v.; eigeriwwelt, pp.; 4.schtichele, v. gschtichelt, pp.

hip 1.Hift (die)n.; Hifde, pl.; 2.Hifts (die)n.; Hiftse, pl.

hipbone Hiftgnoche (der)n.; Hiftgnoche, pl.

hipshot 1.greizlaahm, adj.; 2.hifdelaahm, adj.

hire dinge, v.; gedingt, gedunge, pp.; **out** 1.naus/dinge, v.; nausgedingt, pp.; 2.verdinge (sich --)v.; verdingt, pp.

hired (indentured) **boy** Serwebu (der)n.; **(indentured)**

man Serwemann (der)n.; **hired boy to help on the farm** Gnecht (der)n. (glee --); **man** 1.Gnecht (der)n.; Gnecht, pl.; 2.Knecht (der)n..; 3.Serwe (der)n.

his sei, poss. adj.; **posterior** hinner, adj. (sei hinners)

hiss 1.hetze, v.; ghetzt, pp.; 2.zische, v.; gezischt, pp.

history Gschicht (die)n.

hit 1.dreffe, v.; gedroffe, pp.; 2.schlagge, v.; gschlaage, pp.; 3.zu/haue, v.; zugehaut, pp.

hitch 1.to a post; 2.a team of horses to another wagon rum/henke, v.; rumghenkt, pp.; 3.**(horses)** ei/schpanne, v.; eigschpannt, pp.; 4.**additional horses in front** vorschpanne, v.; vorgschpannt, pp.; 5.**fresh horses to a vehicle** rum/schpanne, v.; rumgschpannt, pp.; 6.**horses to a wagon**; nei/schpanne, v.; neigschpannt, pp.; 7.**to a post** aa/binne, v.; aagebunne, pp.

hitching post Aabinnposchde (der)n.; Aabinnposchde, pl.; **weight** 1.Aabinngewicht (es)n.; 2.Aabinnschtee (der) n.; Aabinnschtee, pl.

hither 1.dohaer, adv.; 2.her, adv.; 3.hin, adv.

hitherto bishaer, adv.

hives Heifts (die)n.

hoard 1.uff/haufe, v.; 2.Vorrot (der)n.; 3.zamme/lause, v.; zammegelaust, pp.; 4.zamme/   schpaare, v.; zam-megschpaart, pp.

hoarfrost Reife (der)n.

hoarse 1.heescher, adj.; 2.heeser, adj.; 3.rauhelsich, adj.; 4.rauschperich, adj.

hoary altgro, adj.

hobble around rum/hickle, v.; rumghickelt, pp.; **in** nei/holpere, v.; neigholpert, pp.; **out** naus/hickle, v.; nausghickelt, pp.

hobbling along Gschtolper (es)n.

hobbly hopplich, adj.

hobby horse Schteckegaul (der)n.

hobgoblin 1.Bautz (der)n.; 2.Gschpuck(s) (es)n.; 3.Wautz (der)n.

hobnail Hufnaggel (der)n.; Hufneggel, pl.

hock Gniekehl (die)n.; **(of animals)** Scheisshoke (der)n.

hocus-pocus Hokespokes (der)n.

hod Maa(r)tervoggel (der)n.

hoe 1.Hack (die)n.; Hacke, pl.; 2.hacke, v.; ghackt, pp.; 3.uff/hacke, v.; uffghackt, pp.; **down** Hosseschittler (der) n.; **out** raus/hacke, v.; rausghackt, pp.; **up** rum/hacke, v.; rumghackt, pp.; **vegetables** aa/hacke, v.; aaghackt, pp.

hoeing (a horse) vernaggle, v.; vernaggelt, pp.

hoer Hacker (der)n.

hog 1.Sau (die)n.; Sei, pl.; 2.Wutz (die)n.; 3.Wutzsau (die)n.; **(of a person)** Sau (die)n. (en gemachti --) **bladder** (when dried, used as a purse or tobacco pouch) Seiblos (die)n.; **cholera** Seigranket (die)n. **excrement** Seidreck (der)n.; **head** Saukopp (der)n.; **pen** Seischtall (der)n.; **skin** Seiledder (es)n.; **stomach** (cleaned and filled as an edible) Seimaage (der)n.; **trough** Seidrog (der)n.; **weed** 1.Bitterschtenge(l) (der)n.; 2.Bitterwaermet (der)n.; 3.Bolleryockel (der)n.

hoggish seii(s)ch, adj; **man** Ewwer (der)n.; Ewwer, pl.

hoggishness 1.Sauerei (die)n.; 2.Seierei (die)n.

Hh

Hognose snake — horseradish

hognose snake Bleeser (der)n.; Bleeser, pl.

hogs (above the size of suckling piglets and smaller than butcher hogs) Leefersei (die)n.

hold 1.Halt (die)n.; 2.hewe, v.; ghowe, pp.; 3.messe, v.; gemesse, pp.; **(as court)** ab/halte, v.; abghhalt, pp.; **(under bond or bail)** iwwerbinne, v.; iwwerbunne, pp.; **back** 1.uff/hewe, v.; uffghowe, pp.; 2.verzwenge, v.; verzwengt, pp.; 3.zerick/halde, v.; zerickghalde, pp.; 4.zerick/hewe, v.; zerickghowe, pp.; **fast** fescht/hewwe, v.; feschtghowe, pp.; **low** nidder/halde, v.; nidderghalde, pp.; **on** aa/hewe, v.; aaghowe, pp.; **out** reeche, v.; gereecht, pp.; **shut** zuhewe, v.; zughowe, pp.; **to the other side** niwwer/halde, v.; niwwerghalde, pp.; **together** 1.zamme/halte, v.; zammeghalte, pp.; 2.zamme/ hewe, v.; zammeghowe, pp.; **under** unner/hewe, v.; unnerghowe, pp.

holder (for berries improvised from chestnut bark) Keschdetutt (die)n.

hole 1.eiyaage, v.; eigeyaakt, pp.; 2.Loch (es)n.; Lecher, pl.; 3.Schlitz (der)n.; 4.Schlupploch (es)n.; **in which the stake of a worm fence is placed** Schtaakeloch (es)n.

holiday 1.Feierdaag (der)n.; Feierdaage, pl.; 2.Feschtdaag (der)n.; 3.Ruhzeit (die)n.

hollow 1.Daal (es)n.; Daale; Daaler, pl.; 2.Hehl (die)n.; 3.Hehling (die)n.; 4.Hiehling (die)n.; **(enclosed by hills or mountains)** Kessel (der)n.; Kessele, pl.; **cylinder** (for heating a room) Drumm (die)n.; **eyed** hohlaagich, adj.; **out** aus/hiehle, v.; ausghiehlt, pp; 2.aus/hieliche, v.; auskiehlicht, pp.

hollyhock Maulros (die)n.

Holy Communion 1.Nachtmol (es)n.; 2.Liewesmahl (es)n. (Dunker usage); **Kiss** Kuss (der)n.; **Week** Karwoch (die)n.

holy heilich, adj.; **smoke** Gnalleise (es)n. (dunner uns --); **water** Weihwasser (es)n.; **wate r font** Weiwasserkessel (der)n.

home 1.daheem, adv.; 2.heem, adv.; 3.Heemet (die)n.; Heemede, pl.; **baked** Heemgebacknes (es)n.; **feeling** Heemgfiehl (es)n.; **remedy** Hausmittel (es)n.; **with you** (call to a dog) heem, adv. (gehschde --)

homeless heemetlos, adj.

homelike 1.aaheemlich, adj.; 2.heem(e)le, v.; gheemelt, pp.; 3.heemlich, adj.

homeliness Unscheeheet (die)n.

homeopathic hommobaadisch, adj.

homesickness 1.heemgrank, adj.; 2.Heemweh (es)n.

homeward heemzus, adv.

honest 1.braav, adj.; 2.ehrlich, adj.; 3.rechtschaffe, adj.; 4.reschaffe, adj.

honestly 1.ehrlicherweis, adv.; 2.redlich, adj.

honesty Ehrlichkeet (die)n.; **(plant)** Moondraude (die)n.

honey Hunnich (der)n.; **locust tree** Schpellebaam (der)n.

honeybee Iem (die)n.; Ieme, pl.

honeycake Lebkuche (der)n.; Lebkuche, pl.

honeycomb 1.Hunnichros (die)n.; 2.Iemeros (die)n.

honeymoon 1.Bossdaage (die)n., pl.; 2.Flitterwoch (die)n., pl.

honeysuckle Hunnichsuckel (es)n.

honor 1.Ehr (die)n.; 2.ehre, v.; ge-ehrt, pp.; 3.Gunn (die)n.; 4.verehre, v.; verehrt, pp.

honorable 1.ehrbaar, adj.; 2.ehrwaerdich, adj.

hood Kapp (die)n.; Kappe, pl.; **wort** Kappegraut (es)n.

hoof Huf (der)n.; Hufe, pl.

hook Hoke (der)n.; Hoke, pl.; **(of cattle)** schtoose, v.; gschtoose, pp; **in** 1.ei/henke, v.; eighanke; eighenkt, pp.; 2.eihaekle, v.; eighaekelt, pp.; 3.nei/hokle, v.; neighokelt, pp.

hooked stick (used in pulling in limbs of cherry trees when picking) Kaschehoke (der)n.

hooks and eyes Hafte (die)n., pl. (-- un hoke)

hoop 1.ab/binne,v.; abgebunne,pp.; 2.Reef (der)n.; Reef, pl.; 3.Waagereef (der)n.; Waagereef, pl.; **iron** Reefeise (es) n.; **maker** Reefschneider (der)n.; **pole** Reefschtecke (der)n.; **skirt** Reefrock (der)n.; **snake** Reefschlang (die)n.

hop hupse, v.; ghupst, pp.; **about** rum/hupse, v.; rumghupst, pp.; **across** niwwer/hupse, v.; niwwerghupst, pp.; **away** weck/hupse, v.; weckghupst, pp.; **down** nunner/hupse, v.; nunnerghupst, pp.

hornbeam 1.Eiseholz (es)n.; 2.Hattriggel (der)n.; 3.Hoppehols (es)n.; **off or away** ab/hupse, v.; abghupst, pp.; **on one leg** hickle, v.; ghickelt, pp.; **out** naus/hupse, v.; nausghupst, pp.; **over** riwwer/hupse, v.; riwwerghupst, pp.; **pole** Hoppeschtang (die)n.

hope hoffe, v.; ghofft, pp.; **for the best** Hoffning (die)n. (uff der -- lewe)

hopeful hoffningsvoll, adj.

hopeless hoffnungslos, adj.

hopper Drechder (der)n.

hopple 1.Hoppel (die)n.; 2.hopple, v.; ghoppelt, pp.

hops Hoppe (die)n.

horehound 1.Adarn (der)n.; 2.Edann (der)n.; 3.Edarn (der)n.; 4.Edorn (der)n.

horizontal flax reel Wickelschtock (der)n.

horn Hann (es)n.; Hanner, pl.

horned snake Harnschlang (die)n.

hornet Hannesel (der)n.; Hannesel, pl.; **nest** Hannselnescht (es)n.

horrible 1.abscheilich, adj.; 2.erschrecklich, adj.; 3.grimmich, adj.; 4.grislich, adj.; 5.schrecklich, adj.

horrify verschrecke, v.; verschrocke, pp.

horror 1.Abschei (der)n.; 2.Schauder (der)n.; 3.Schrecke (der)n.

horse Gaul (der)n.; Geil, pl.; **balm** 1.Geilswatzel (die)n.; 2.Gschwaerewatzel (die)n.; **chestnut** Geilskescht (die) n.; Geilskeschde, pl.; **collar** 1.Kummet (es)n.; Kummede, pl.; 2.Kummetbloder (die)n.; **doctor** Geilsdokder (der)n.; **dung** Geilsdreck (der)n.; **feed** Geilsfuder (es)n.; **fiddle** Seigieg (die)n.; **fly** Buschmick (die)n.; **hair** Geilshoor (die)n.; **harnessed to the right** (of the saddle horse) Newegaul (der)n.; **head** Geilskopp (der)n.; **manure** Geilsmischt (der)n.; **meat** Geilsfleech (es)n.; **mint** Geilsbalsem (der)n.; **shoer** Huf(f)schmitt (der)n.; **stable** Geilsschtall (der)n.; Geilschtell, pl.; **tail** (plant) Schoftee (der)n.; **thief** Geilsdieb (der)n.; **whip** Fuhrmannsgeeschel (die)n.; **with a white forehead** Baalgaul (der)n.

horsebean Seibohn (die)n.

horsefly Breem (die)n.

horseplay Eselschtreech (die)n., pl.

horseradish Meerreddich (die)n.

Hh

horses / hydromel

horses Geilsfleech (es)n.
horseshoe Hufeise (es)n.; Hufeise, pl.
horsetail Geilsschwanz (der)n.; Geilsschwenz, pl.
horsewhip 1.ab/geeschle, v.; abgegeeschelt, pp.;
    2.Geilsgeeschel (die)n.
horsey 1.Geilche (es)n.; 2.Geili (es)n.
horticulture Gaardebau (der)n.
hosier Schtrimpmacher (der)n.
hospital 1.Haschbidaal (der)n.; 2.Haspittel (der)n.
hospitality Uffwaarting (die)n.
host Host (die)n.
hostile 1.feind, adj.; 2.feindlich, adj.; 3.feindselich, adj.
hostler Schtallgnecht (der)n.
hot 1.dumbich, adj.; 2.hees, adj.; **air** Luft (die)n. (heesi --);
    head Hitzkopp (der)n.; **punch** Schling (die)n.
hotel Wattshaus (es)n.; Wattsheiser, pl.; **business**
    Wattschaft (die)n.; **stand** Wattschaft (die)n.
hound 1.Hauns (der)n.; 2.Yaaghund (der)n.; Yaaghund, pl.; **(of a**
    wagon) 1.Backe (der)n.; Backe, pl.; 2.Deichselscher (die)n.
houndstongue 1.Hun(d)szung (die)n.; 2.Schoflaus (die)n.
hour 1.Schtund (die)n.; Schtunde, pl.; 2.Schtunn (die)n.;
    Schtunne, pl.; **hand** Schtunnezioger (der)n.; **of distress**
    Notschtunn (die)n.; **of mourning** Drauerschtunn (die)
    n.; **of prayer** Betschtunn (die)n.
hourglass Schtunneglaas (es)n.
house Haus (es)n.; Heiser, pl.; **furnishings** Haussache (die)
    n., pl.; **of mourning** 1.Drauerhaus (es)n.;
    2.Leichehaus (es)n.; 3.Leichthaus (es)n.; **of prayer**
    Bethaus (es)n.; **painter** Aaschtreicher (der)n.
housecleaning Hausbutze(s) (es)n.
housekeeper 1.Hauseldern (die)n.; 2.Hausheltern (die)n.; **(of a**
    family where the mother is dead) Hausfiehrer (der)n.
housewife Hausfraa (die)n.
housework Hausarewett (die)n.
housing Kummetdeck (die)n.
hovel Knallhitt (die)n.
How do you do! Wie bischt?
how wie, adv.; conj; **are things going with you** zugeh, v.;
    zugange, pp. (wie geht's zu bei eich); **is he doing** (of a
    sick person) befinne, v.; befunne, pp. (wie befinnter
    sich?); **is it that ...** kumme, v.; kumme, pp. (wie
    kummt's, dass ...); **many** 1.wieviel, adv.; 2.wiffel, adv.;
    much 1.wieviel, adv.; 2.wiffel, adv.; 3.Wie viel?; **the**
    deuce? grenket (wie dei --)
however yedoch, adv.
howling Gegrisch (es)n.
hub Naab (die)n.
hub ring Naawering (der)n.
huckster (at auctions) Mariyetender (der)n.
hug 1.armle, v.; gearmelt, pp.; 2.dricke, v.; gedrickt, pp.;
    3.gnootsche, v.; gegnootscht, pp.; 4.knootsche, v.;
    gegknootscht, pp.; 5.umarme, v.; umarmt, pp.
huge ungeheier, adj.
hull 1.ab/scheele, v.; abgscheelt, pp.; 2.Rumf (der)n.; **(of a**
    vessel) Rump (der)n.; Rumpe, pl.
hulling millstone Schaelschtee (der)n.

hum 1.brumme, v.; gebrummt, pp.; 2.summe, v.; gsummt,
    pp.; 3.sumse, v.; gsumst, pp.
human menschlich, adj.; **ability** Menschekunscht (die)n.;
    aid Menschehilf (die)n.; **being** 1.Mensch (der)n.;
    Mensche, pl.; 2.Menschekind (es)n.; **happiness** Men-
    scheglick (es)n.; **heart** Menschehatz (es)n.; **hermaph-**
    rodite Zwitter (der)n.; **kind** Menschheet (die)n.; **life**
    Menschelewe (es)n.; **speech** Menscheschproch (die)
    n.; **understanding** Menscheverschtand (der)n.
humble 1.deemiedich, adj.; 2.demiedich, adj.;
    3.erniedriche, v.; erniedricht, pp.; 4.niedrich, adj.
humbug 1.Flause (die)n., pl.; 2.Schwindel (der)n.
humdrum langweilich, adv.
humility Demut (die)n.
hummingbird 1.Blummevoggel (der)n.; 2.Brummvoggel
    (der)n.; 3.Hunnichvoggel (der)n.; 4.Schnaerrvoggel
    (der)n.; Schnaerrveggel, pl.; 5.Schnarveggelche (es)n.;
    6.Schnarvoggel (der)n.
humorous Schpass (der)n. (voll --)
hump Buckel (der)n.
humpback Grummbuckel (der)n.
humpbacked bucklich, adj.
hundred hunnert, adj.
hunger Hunger (der)n.
hungry hungerich, adj.
hunt 1.Yacht (die)n.; 2.yaegere, v.; geyaegert, pp.;
    3.hunde, v.; gehundt, pp.
hunter 1.Schitz (der)n.; 2.Yeeger (der)n.; Yeeger, pl.
hunting 1.geyaag, adj.; 2.Yaegerei (die)n.; **bag**
    Yackbautsch (der)n.
hurrah 1.hurraahe, v.; ghurraaht, pp.; 2.hurraah!, interj.
hurry 1.dummle (sich --)v.; gedummelt, pp.; 2.eile, v.; ge-eilt,
    pp.; **after** no(och)eile, v.; no(och)geeilt, pp.; **away** ab/fege,
    v.; abgfegt, pp.; **back** 1.zerick/dummle (sich --)v.;
    zerickgedummelt, pp.; 2.zerick/mache (sich --)v.;
    zerickgemacht, pp.; 3.grenke, v.; gegrenkt, pp.; 4.krenke, v.;
    gekrenkt, pp.
hurt (in speaking to children) Wewwi (es)n.; **(oneself)**
    1.schmatze, v.; gschmatzt, pp.; 2.weh/duh (sich --) v.;
    wehgeduh, pp.
husband 1.Ehemann (der)n.; 2.Mann (der)n.; Menner;
    Mansleit,pl.
hush-a-by 1.beilo, int.; 2.heiyo(bei)
hush! sch!, interj.
husk 1.baschde, v.; gebascht, pp.; 2.Bascht (die)n.;
    Baschde, pl.; **corn** schtrippe, v.; gschtrippt, pp.
    (welschkann --)
husking pin Baschtholz (es)n.; Baschthelzer, pl.
hussy Mensch (der)n.; Mensche, pl.
hustle after no(och)packe, v.; no(och)gepackt, pp.; **out**
    naus/wickle, v.; nausgewickelt, pp.
hut 1.Heisle (es)n.; 2.Hitt (die)n.
hyacinth 1.Schlisselblumm (die)n.; Schlisselblumme, pl.;
    2.Schtaernblumm (die)n.; Schtaernblumme, pl.;
    3.Schtannblumm (die)n.
hydromel Hunnichwasser (es)n.

Hh

hydrophobia   hysterics

hydrophobia Wasserschei (die)n.

hymn 1.Karrichelied (es)n.; Karrichelieder, pl.;
2.Karricheschtick (es)n.; Karricheschticker, pl.; 3.Lied
(es)n.; Lieder, pl.; 4.Lobgesang (der)n.; **book**
1.Gsangbuch (es)n.; 2.Liederbuch (es)n.;
Liederbicher, pl.; 3.Singbuch (es)n.; Singbicher, pl.

hyoscyamus Hunsfotzegraut (es)n.

hyphen Binnschtriche (der)n.

hypochondriac mellenkollisch, adj.

hypocrisy 1.Heichelei (die)n.; 2.Heichlerei (die)n.;
3.Scheiheilichkeet (die)n.

hypocrite 1.Heichler (der)n.; 2.Maulgrischt (der)n.;
3.Scheilheilicher (der)n.; Scheiheilicher, pl.

hypocritical 1.falschgsichtich, adj.; 2.heichlerisch, adj.;
3.langsichtich, adj.; 4.scheiheilich, adj.

hyssop Eisop (der)n.

hysteria 1.Schlicksergramp (der)n.; 2.Schlixergramp (der)n.

hysterics 1.Muddergichdre (die)n., pl.; 2.Mudderweh (es)n.

Ii

I

I ich, pron.; **am shivering** gfriere, v.; gfrore, pp. (es friert mich); **am sick at the stomach** iwwel, adj. (es is mer --); **am sure** aa, adv. (ich denk awwer --); **can't help it** defor (ich kann nix --); **don't care** drumm, adv. (ich geb nix --); **don't care a rap about it** 1.huder, adj. (ich geb kenn -- drum); 2.Hunsfotz (die)n. (ich geb kenn -- drum); **don't care for work** um, prep. (ich geb nix -- die aerwet); **don't concern myself about it** drumm, adv. (ich bekimmer mich nix --); **don't give a hang for what you say** scheisse, v.; gschisse, pp. (ich scheiss der druff); **don't mind work** um, prep. (ich geb nix -- die aerwet); **guess** deich; adv.; **hate to do it** 1.Greiz (es)n. (es is mer en --); 2.Kreiz (es)n. (es is mer en --); **have had enough** (to eat) satt, adj. (ich binn --); **have had enough of it** satt, adj. (ich hab's --); **have no objections** degege (ich hab nix --); **know what irks you** schaffe, v.; gschafft, pp.; (ich wees was dich schafft); **shuddered** (at the sight) 1.Grissel (die)n., pl. (die -- sinn mer ausgange); 2.Krissel (die)n., pl. (die -- sinn mer ausgange); **suppose** 1.deich; adv. 2.wull, adj.; **won't allow it** gewwe, v.; gewwe, pp. (do gebt's nix draus); **wonder** wunnere, v.; gewunnert, pp. (es wunnert mich)

I.H.S. Yesus (der)n. (-- Mensche Erleeser)

I'll be hanged 1.grenk (do will ich dei -- griege); 2.(damned) Damm (der)n. (do will ich iwwer der -- geh); **give him a tip** schtecke, v.; gschtocke, pp. (ich will's ihm --)

iagnis fatuus 1.Erdlichdel (es)n.; 2.Erdlicht (es)n.; Erdlichter, pl.

ice Eis (es)n.; **cold** eiskalt, adj.; **hook** 1.Eishoke (der)n.; 2.Schpiesshoke (der)n.; **pick** Eispick (die)n.; **saw** Eissaek (die)n.; **tongs** Eiszang (die)n.; **water** Eiswasser (es)n.

iceberg Eisbaerrick (der)n.

icehouse Eishaus (es)n.; Eisheiser, pl.

ichthyology Fischkunscht (die)n.

icicle Eiszabbe (der)n.; Eiszabbe, pl.

icy eisich, adj.

idea 1.Begriff (der)n.; 2.Eidie (die)n.; 3.Eifall (der)n.; Eifalle, pl.; 4.Gedanke (der)n.; Gedanke, pl.

identical leibhafdich, adv.

idiot Narr (der)n.; Narre, pl.

idle 1.miessich, adj.; 2.schlendere, v.; gschlendert, pp.; **talk** Geblabber (es)n.; **temporarily** ab/leie, v.; abgelegge, pp.

idleness 1.Miessichgang (der)n.; 2.Miessichkeet (die)n.

idler Faulenzer (der)n.; Faulenzer, pl.

idol Abgott (der)n.; Abgedder, pl.

idolatrous 1.abgeddisch, adj.; 2.abgettisch, adj., adv.

idolatry 1.Abgedderei (die)n.; 2.Abgetterei (die)n.

if 1.ob, conj.; 2.oob, conj.; 3.wann, conj.; **a person** wammer = wann mer; **he** 1.wammern = wammer en 2.wammer = wann mer; 3.wammerm = wammer em; **we** wammer = wann mer

ignite 1.aa/brenne, v.; aagebrennt, pp.; 2.aa/schtecke, v.; aagschteckt, pp.; 3.aa/zinde, v.; aagezindt, pp.; 4.zinde, v.; gezindt, pp.; **by rubbing** aa/reiwe, v.; aageriwwe, pp.

ignoble unedlich, adj.

ignominious schimp(er)lich, adj.

ignoramus Nixwisser (der)n.

ignorance 1.Unaerfaahring (die)n.; 2.Unvernunft (die)n.

ignorant 1.dumm, adj.; 2.unwissend, adj.

ill 1.fiehle, v.; gfiehlt, pp. (schlecht --); 2.grank, adj.; **(very)**

impiety

schlimm grank, adj.; **bred** ungezogge, adj.

illegal unrechtmaessich, adj.

illegible unleserlich, adj.

illegitimate leddicherweis, adj.; **(child)** 1.Baschdert (der) n.; 2.Beikind (es)n. 3.uff/gelese, v. (en --nes Kind)

illicit unaerlaabt, adj.

illiterate ungelaernt, adj.

illness 1.Granket (die)n.; 2.Grankheit (die)n.; Grankheide, pl.

illuminate erleichte, v.; erleicht, pp.

illusion Verblennerei (die)n.

image Bild (es)n.; Bilder, pl.

imagination 1.Eibildung (die)n.; 2.Vorschtelling (die)n.; 3.Vorschtellung (die)n.

imaginative eibildisch, adj.

imagine 1.ei/bilde (sich --)v.; eigebildt, pp.; 2.vorschtelle (sich --)v.; vorgschtellt, pp.

imbecility Bleedsinn (der)n.

imitate 1.no(och)affe, v.; no(och)geafft, pp.; 2.no(och)folge, v.; no(och)gfolgt, pp.; 3.no(och)mache, v.; no(och)g(e)macht, pp.; **in dancing** no(och)danse, v.; no(och)gedanst, pp.

imitating the bark of a dog buwu! interj.; **the sound of heavy steps** trapp, tripp, trapp!; **the sound of scissors in cutting** glitschiwippi; **the splashing sound of a water wheel** schlipp schlapp

immaterial ewweviel(ich),adv.

immature 1.gnetschich, adj.; 2.rotzich, adj.; 3.unreif, adj.; 4.unzeidich, adj.; **contemptible fellow** Bettschisser (der)n.

immeasurable 1.unaermesslich, adj.; 2.unermesslich, adj.

immediately 1.aagebletzlich, adv.; 2.blitzlich, adv.; 3.graadeweck, adv.; 4.neegscht am Dapeet, adv. ; 5.uff, prep., adv. (-- der Schtell);

immemorial undenklich, adj.

immense 1.iwwerweldich, adj.; 2.unermesslich, adj.; 3.ungeheier, adj.; **amount** Unsumm (die)n.; **number** Uuzaahl (die)n. **person** Gschtell (es)n. (marrickwardiches --)

immerse dunke, v.; gedunkt, pp.

immigrant Eiwandrer (der)n.

immoderate iwwermeesich, adj.

immoral unzichtich, adj.; **doings** Luderwese (es)n.

immortal 1.unschtaerblich, adj.; 2.uuvergenglich, adj.

immovable 1.naggelfascht, adj.; 2.naggelfescht, adj.; 3.unbewechlich, adj.; 4.unbeweklich, adj.

immure eimaure, v.; eigemauert, pp.

impart mit/deele, v.; mitgedeelt, pp.

impartial unbardeiisch, adj.

impatience 1.Umgeduld (die)n.; 2.Ungeduld (die)n.

impatiens (flowering plant) Yutt (der)n. (der ewiche --); sultans Allidaagsblumm (die)n.

impatient 1.umgeduldich, adj.; 2.ungeduldich, adj.

imperfect 1.fehlerhaft, adj.; 2.mangelhaft, adj.; 3.schewwetzich, adj.; 4.schiwwitzich, adj.; **specimen** Auswaerfling (der)n.

imperial crown Kaiserkron (die)n.

imperil Gfaahr (die)n. (in -- bringe)

impertinent 1.batzich, adj.; 2.fleggelhaft, adv.; 3.unmanierlich, adv.; adj.

impiety Gottlosichkeet (die)n.

298

Ii

implement

implement Waerkzeich (es)n.; **(any crooked)** Fiddelboge (der)n.; Fiddelboge, pl.; **shed** Waageschopp (der)n.; **used in beating flax from the stem** Britsch (die)n.

implements Geraetschaft (die)n.

implicate 1.ei/wickle, v.; eigewickelt, pp.; 2.nei/wickle, v.; neigewickelt, pp.; 3.verwickle, v.; verwickelt, pp.

implore flehe, v.; gfleht, pp.; **forgiveness or leniency, solicit or ask for something** ab/bitte, v.; abgebitt, pp.

impolite 1.unmanierlich, adv.; adj.; 2.unordich, adj.; 3.uumanieerlich, adj.

importance Bedeitung (die)n.

important wichdich, adj.

importune 1.bellere, v.; gebellert, pp.; 2.breble, v.; gebrebelt, pp.; **coaxing** Geleck (es)n.

impose uff/lege, v.; uffgelegt, pp.; **impossibility** 1.Unmeeglichkeet (die)n.; 2.Unmieglichkeet (die)n.; 3.Uumeeglichkeet (die)n.; 4.Uumieglichkeet (die)n.

impossible 1.ummieglich, adj.; 2.uumeeglich, adj.; 3.uumieglich, adj.

imprecate verwinsche, v.; verwinscht, pp.

impression 1.Dall(e) (die)n.; 2.Dell (die)n.; 3.Eidruck (der)n.

imprison 1.ei/schliesse, v.; eigschlosse, pp.; 2.ei/schparre, v.; eigschpatt, pp.; 3.eifange, v.; eigfange, pp.

improbable unwaahrscheinlich, adv.

improper unschicklich, adj.

improve 1.bessere (sich --)v.; gebessert, pp.; 2.uff/packe, v.; uffgepackt, pp.; 3.uff/picke, v.; uffgepickt, pp.; 4.verbessre, v.; verbessert, pp.; **by good feeding** 1.aa/fiedre, v.; aagfiedert, pp.; 2.uff/fiedre, v.; uffgfiedert, pp.; **(in health)** besser warre, adj.;

improve the occasion no(och)helfe, v.; no(och)gholfe, pp.

improvement 1.Bessering (die)n.; 2.Verbessring (die)n.

imprudent unkluch, adj.

impudent 1.frech, adj.; 2.unverschaemlich, adj.; 3.unverschaemt, adj.; **child** 1.Rotzer (der)n.; 2.Rotznaas (die)n.; Rotznaas, pl.; **little snip** Fratznaesel (es)n.; **person** Rotzkeffer (der)n.

in 1.an, prep.; 2.bei, prep.; 3.hinn, prep.; 4.im, prep.;5.in, prep.; 6.nei, prep.; **(here)** rei, adv.; **a faint** uumechdich, adj.; **a hurry** Knall (der)n. (uff -- und fall); **a jiffy** wuppsch, adv.; **a lower place** unne, adv.; **a serious condition** Iwwel zu Weg., adv.; **a trance** entzickt, adj.; **abundance** Hilli (die)n. (die -- un filli); **addition** 1.dezu, adv.; 2.zudem, adv.; **advance** 1.vadderhand, adv.; 2.vannenaus, adv.; 3.voraus, adv.; 4.vorderhand, adv.; 5.vorhaer, adv.; **all my life** Lebbdaag (der)n. (mei --); **all parts** alliwwer, adv.; **an agreeable manner** aagenehmlicherweiss, adj.; **arrears** 1.hinneno, adv.; 2.rickfellich, adj.; **at the side** (of something in motion) newenei, adv.; **below** 1.unnedrin, adv.; 2.unnenei, prep.; **between** 1.inzwische, prep.; 2.zwischedrin, adv.; **between** (in motion) zwischenei, adv.; **between there** dattdezwische, adv.; **bloom** blieh(i)ch, adj.; **bright daylight** Daag (der)n. (im helle --); **by the front way** 1.vannenei, adv.; 2.vannerei, adv.; **by way of the rear** hinnenei, adv.; **common** 1. gemeescheflich, adv.; 2.gemein, adj.; 3.gemeindlich, adj.; **company** 1. menanner, adv.; 2.mit(e)nanner, adv.; **conclusion** schliesslich, adj.; **confusion** 1.darich(e)nanner, adv.; 2. iwwernannernei, adj.;

incapacitated for work

3.verhuddelt, adj.; **exchange for** 1.far, prep.; 2.fer, prep.; **favor** beliebt, adj.; **favor of** 1.defor; 2.defor (-- sei); **first class style** Manier (die)n. (uff die verddderscht --); **flocks, herds or bevies** druppweis, adv.; **for it** 1.Greid (es)n. (in der -- sei); 2.Kreid (es)n. (in der -- sei); **from that direction** dattreizus, adv.; **front** 1.vanne, adv.; 2.vannedraus, adv.; **front of her** vannre = vane re; **front of him** vannrem = vanne em; **front of that** dattdevor, adv.; **general** iwwerhaapt, adv.; **good health** rischdich, adj.; **good order** zurecht, adv.; **good time** beizeit, adv.; **heat** (of horses) needlich, adj.; **heat** (of sows) rollich, adj.; **here** 1.dodrin, adv.; 2.donei, adv.; 3.dorei, adv.; **ignorance** uubewusst, adj.; **Indian file** hinnenannerno adv.; **justice** gerechterweis, adv.; **layers** schaalich, adj.; **less than no time** Gschwindichkeet (die)n. (inre --); **limited localities** blackeweis, adv.; **love** (with) verliebt, adj.; **low spirits** nidder/gschlagge, v.; niddergschlagge, pp.; **lump quantity** iwwerhaapt, adv.; **need** 1.aarem, adj.; adv.; 2.aarmseelich, adj.; adv.; 3.bedaerflich, adj.; 4.kimmerlich, adj.; 5.needich, adj.; 6.Not (die)n. (in --); **olden times** 1.veralders, adv.; 2.verzeite, adv.; **person** paerseenlich, adj.; **places** 1.blatzweis, adv.; 2.bletzweis, adj.; **plain terms** graadaus, adj.; **plenty** floribus, adv.; **pursuit** hinnerdrei, adv.; **rapid succession** nannerno, adv.; **rows** roigeweis, adv.; **short** katzum, adv.; **small lots** beim gleene, adv.; **spite of** trotz, prep.; **spots** blackeweis, adv.; **standing timber that part which is available for lumber** Nutzhols (es)n.; **store** vorraedich, adv.; **streaks** schtrichweis, adv.; **succession** 1.hinnenannerno adv.; 2.hinnernannerno, adv.; 3.nochenanner, adv.; **the afternoon** nummidaags, adv.; **the back country in** zerickzus, adv.; **the bottom** unnedrin, adv.; **the distance** weithie, adv.; **the environs** Bezaerrick (es)n. (im --); **the evening** oweds, adv.; **the first place** zuerscht, adv.; **the forenoon** vormiddaags, adv.; **the front part of** vannedrin, adv.; **the habit of** als, adv.; **the long run** 1.Leng (die)n. (uff die --); 2.uff, prep., adv. (-- die Leng); **the lower part** (geographically) unnedrauss, adv.; **the mean while** driwwer, adv.; **the middle of** midde(s), adv.; **the morning** mariyets, adv.; **the nick of time** 1.Haar (es)n. (in eem --); 2.wegs, adv. (graades --); **the rear** 1.hinne(s), prep.; 2.hinne, adv.; 3.hinnenooch, adv.; **the rear part of** hinnedrin, adv.; **the summer** summers, adv.; **the winter** winders, adv.; **there** 1.dattdrinn, adv.; 2.dattnei, adv.; **this place** (with a verb of motion) doanne, adv.; **this way** 1.dedarrich, adj.; 2.doreizus, adv.; **those times** sellemols, adv.; **through here** dodarrichnei, adv.; **through there** 1.dattdarichnei, adv.; 2.dattdarichrei, adv.; **time** 1.rechzeitich, adj.; 2.zeitlich, adj.; **times past** sellemols, adv.; **together** 1.zamme/schtosse, v.; zammegschtosse, pp.; 2.zammenei, adv.; **urgent need** bedaerfdich, adj.; **vain** 1.umsunscht, adv.; 2.vergebens, adv.; 3.vergeblich, adj.; 4.vergewens, adv.; **what way** 1.Aart (die)n. (uff was fern --); 2.Ort (die)n. (uff was fern --) **(to) one another** inenanner, adj.; **inaccuracy** Unrichdichkeet (die)n.; **inadvertently** uubedenkt, adj.; **inanimate** lablos, adj.; **inapproachable** unzugenglich, adj.

inattentive 1.faahrlessich, adj.; 2.gafflich, adj.

inaugurate eischweere,v.; eigschwore, pp.

inborn aagebore, adj.

incandescent weissgliedich, adj.

incapable unfaehich, adj.

incapacitated for work Britsch (die)n. (uff der -- sei)

Ii

incendiarism

incendiarism Mardbrennerei (die)n.

incendiary 1.Brandschtifder (der)n.; 2.Mardbrenner (der)n.

incense verzanne, v.; verzannt, pp.

incentive Ursach (die)n.; Ursache, pl.

incessant begging Gebettel (es)n.; **biting or itching** Gebeiss (es)n.; **cackling or chattering** Gegacks (es)n.; **chatter or babbling** Gebabbel (es)n.; **chattering** Gschnacker (es)n.; **coughing** 1.Ghuuscht (es)n.; 2.Kuscht (es)n.; **talker** Babbelmaul (es)n.; Babbelmeiler, pl.

incessantly 1.druffundewedder, adv.; 2.Schtick (es)n. (in eem -- fatt)

inch Zoll (der)n.; Zoll, pl.

incidentally newebei, adv.

incision Eischnitt (der)n.

incite 1.aa/hetze, v.; aaghetzt, pp.; 2.aaretze, v.; aageretzt, pp.; 3.aaschpore, v.; aagschport, pp.; 4.uff/schtachle, v.

inclement 1.rauh, adj.; 2.ungeschtiem, adj.

inclined geneicht, adj.; **to pilfer** Finger (der)n. (lange -- hawwe); **to roll** rollich, adj.; **to urinate** pisserich, adj.

include 1.ei/nemme, v.; eigenumme, pp.; 2.ei/schliesse, v.; eigschlosse, pp.; 3.eirechle, v.; eigerechelt, pp.; **in reckoning** nei/rechle, v.; neigerechelt, pp.

incoherent verkehrt, adj.

income Eikumme(s) (es)n.

incomparable umvergleichlich, adv.; adj.

incomplete eeseidich, adj.

incomprehensible unbegreiflich, adj.

inconsistent flack(e)rich, adj.

inconstant unschtaetich, adj.

inconvenient 1.unschicklich, adj.; 2.uuhendich, adj.

increase 1.Vermehrung (die)n.; 2.zu/nemme, v.; zugnumme, pp.; 3.Zunahm (der)n.; 4.zusetze, v.; zugsetzt, pp.; 5.Zuwachs (der)n.

incredible 1.unglaabich, adj.; 2.uuglablich, adj.

incredulous unglaawich, adj.

incriminate beschuldiche, v.; beschuldicht, pp.

incubate 1.aus/briehe, v.; ausgebrieht, pp.; 2.briehe, v.; gebrieht, pp.

incubator Briemaschien (die)n.

incur (debts) Schulde (die)n., pl. (-- mache)

indebted schuldich, adj.

indebtedness Schulde (die)n., pl.

indecent seftich, adj.

indeed 1.gewiss, adj.; 2.verhafdich, adv.

indefinite unbeschtimmt, adj.

indent 1.ei/dricke, v.; eigedrickt, pp.; 2.nei/dricke, v.; neigedrickt, pp.; 3.zamme/dricke, v.; zammegedrickt, pp.

indented gezackt, adj.

indentured servant Serwe (der)n.

independent unabhengich, adj.

indescribable uubeschreiblich, adj.

index 1.Noochweiser (der)n.; 2.Regischder (der)n.

index finger (in nursery rhyme) Lausknecker (der)n.

Indian 1.Insch (der)n.; Insche, pl.; 2.Insching (der)n.; Insching, pl.; **corn** 1.Feldwelschkann (es)n.; 2.Welschkann (es)n.;

inform

cress Gresse (die)n.; **paintbrush** Wibbe(r)willblumm (die)n.; **pipe** 1.Engelblimmli (es)n.; 2.Engelblumm (die)n.; **Summer** 1.Alt(er)weiwersummer (der)n.; 2. Inschingsummer (der)n.; 3.Noochsummer (der)n.; 4.Schmokwedder (es)n.; 5.Schmookdaage (die)n.; **turnip** 1.Araan (die)n.; 2.Araanszwiwwel (die)n.; 3.Arrentschzwiwwel (die)n.; **whoop** Yux (der)n.

indicate 1.aa/zeige, v.; aagezeicht, pp.; 2.bedeide, v.; bedeidt, pp.; 3.weisse, v.; g(e)wisse, pp.

indication Aaschein (der)n.

indicator Aazeiger (der)n.

indifference 1.gleichgiltichkeit, adj.; 2.Lappichkeet (die)n.

indifferent 1.achtlos, adj.; 2.ewweviel(ich),adv.; 3.lass, adj.; 4.lau, adj.; 5.leid(l)ich, adj.; 6.unbekimmert, adj.

indignant 1.bees, adj.; 2.verzannt, adj.; 3.zannich, adj.

indignation Zann (der)n.

indigo Indigo (der)n.

indirect middelbaar, adj.

indiscrete 1.unbedacht, adj.; 2.unbedenkt, adj.; 3.vorwitzich, adj.

indisposed 1.glaage, v.; geglaagt, pp.; 2.klaage, v.; geklaakt, pp.

indistinct 1.blass, adj.; 2.undeitlich, adj.

indistinctly welsch, adj.

individual Paerson (die)n.

indolence Faulheit (die)n.

induce (one) to change rum/hole, v.; rumgholt, pp.; **to leave** weck/griege, v.; weckgrickt, pp.

induct eifiehre, v.; eigfiehrt, pp.

industrious 1.emsich, adj.; 2.fleissich, adj.; 3.schaffich, adj.; 4.scheffich, adj.; **person** Scheffer (der)n.; Scheffer, pl.

industry Fleiss (der)n.

inevitably uuvermeidlich, adj.

inexperienced unaerfaahre, adj.

inexpressable 1.unaerschprechlich, adj.; 2.unausschprechlich, adj.

infancy Kindheit (die)n.

infant barn owl Scheiereili (es)n.; Scheiereilin, pl.

infanticide Kinnermard (der)n.

infatuated with vernaddert = vernarrt; **parsons** parrenaerrisch, adj.

infect aa/schtecke, v.; aagschteckt, pp.

infected aa/gschteckt, v. (past tense)

infectious aaschteckend, adj.

inferior plant or animal Baschdert (der)n.

infernal gottverdammt, adv.

infidelity Unglaawe (der)n.

infinite 1.unendlich, adv.; 2.unne End, adv.

infirm 1.grenk(er)lich, adj.; 2.schwach, adj.

infirmary Fehler (der)n.; Fehler, pl.; **of old age** Alderschwech (die)n.

inflammation 1.Fluss (der)n.; 2.Rotlaafe (es)n.

inflate uff/blose, v.; uffgebloost, pp.

inflict 1.uff/lege, v.; uffgelegt, pp.; 2.zufiege, v.; zugfliekt, pp.

inflorescence Blieh(t) (die)n.

influence Eifluss (der)n.; **over** aus/richde, v.; ausgericht, pp.

inform wisse losse, v.; wisse glosst (glesst = Amish usage); **on** 1.aadraage, v.; aagedraage, pp.; 2.verrode, v.; verrode, pp.

300

Ii

information

information Auskunft (die)n.
infrequently raar, adj.
infringe iwwer/dreede, v.; iwwerdrede, pp.
infuriated wiedich bees, adj.
ingenious kinschdlich, adj.
ingenuity Kundewidde (die)n.
ingratiate oneself 1.aaschmiere (sich --)v.; aagschmiert, pp.; 2.aasuckle, v.; aagsuckelt, pp.; 3.eischmeechle (sich --)v.; eigschmeechelt, pp.; 4.eischmiere (sich --) v.; eigschmiert, pp.
ingratiating aaschmeechlich, adj.
ingratitude 1.Undank (der)n.; 2.Uudank (der)n.
inhabit bewohne, v.; bewohnt, pp.
inhabitable bewohnbar, adj.
inhabitant 1.Bewohner (der)n.; 2.Eiwohner (der)n.; Eiwohner, pl.
inhale eihauche, v.; eighaucht, pp.
inherit erewe, v.; ge-erbt, pp.
inheritance 1.Erbschaft (die)n.; 2.Erebdeel (es)n.; 3.Erebschaft (die)n.
inhuman 1.ummenschlich, adj.; 2.unmenschlich, adj.
iniquitous doings Laschderwese (es)n.
iniquity 1.Beesheet (die)n.; 2.Beesheit (die)n.; 3.Boosheet (die)n.; 4.Bosheet (die)n.; 5.Bosheit (die)n.; 6.Laschder (es)n.; 7.Sindfrewel (der)n.
initial Buschdaag (der)n.; Buschdaawe, pl.
inject nei/schpritze, v.; neigschpritzt, pp.
injure 1.b(e)schaediche, v.; b(e)schaedicht, pp.; 2.b(e)scheediche, v.; b(e)scheedicht, pp.; 3.schaediche, v.; gschaedicht, pp.; 4.scheediche, v.; gscheedicht, pp.; 5.verletze, v.; verletzt, pp.; 6.weh/duh (sich --)v.; wehgeduh, pp.; **oneself by lifting too much** iwwerhewe (sich --)v.; iwwerhowe, pp.
injurious 1.schaedlich, adj.; 2.scheedlich, adj.
injury Schaade (der)n.
injustice 1.Unrecht (es)n.; 2.Uurecht (es)n.
ink Dinde (der)n.
inkling Ahning (die)n.
inkspot 1.Dindeblacke (der)n.; 2.Dindefleck (die)n.
inkstand 1.Dindeboddel (der)n.; Dindeboddle, pl.; 2.Dindefass (es)n.; 3.Dindeglaas (es)n.; Dindeglesser, pl.
innate aagebore, adj.
inner inner, adv.; **bark** Bascht (die)n.; Baschde, pl.; **most** innerscht, adv.
innkeeper Watt (der)n.; Wadde, pl.
innocence Unschuld (die)n.
innocent 1.umschuldich, adj.; 2.unschuldich, adj.; 3.uuschuldich, adj.
Innocents' Day (Dec. 28) Unschuldich Kindelsdaag (der)n.
inoculate (trees) bleedle, v.; gebleddelt, pp.
inquire 1.aasuche, v.; aagsucht, pp.; 2.erkindiche (sich --) v.; erkindicht, pp.; 3.umduh, v.; umgeduh, pp.; **about** no(och)froge, v.; gfrokt, pp.
inquiry 1.Frog (die)n.; 2.Froget (die)n.; 3.Unnersuchung (die)n.

intentionally

inquisitive 1.rum/schnuffle, v.; 2.rumgschnuffelt, pp.; 3.gwunnerich, adj.; 4.neigierich, adj.; 5.wunnerfitzich,adj.; 6.wunnerlich, adj.; 7.wunnernaasich, adj.; **person** 1.Wunnerfitz (der)n.; Wunnerfitz, pl.; 2.Wunnernaus (die)n.
insane 1.narrisch, adj.; 2.verrickt, adj.; **asylum** 1.Irrehaus (es)n.; 2.Narrehaus (es)n.
insect Insekt (es)n.; **which attacks smoked meat** Schneller (der)n.; 1.Geziffer (es)n.; 2.Ungeziffer (es)n.
insert nei/mache, v.; neigemacht, pp.
inside 1.drin, adv.; 2.inne, adv.; 3.innewennich, adv.; 4.inwendich, adv.; 5.inwennich, adv.; **out** 1.inwendich ausse, adv.; 2.letz, adv.; **wall** Wand (die)n.; Wend, pl.
insight 1.Eisehnes (es)n.; 2.Eisicht (die)n.
insignificant scheissich, adj.
insinuate eiriwwle, v.; eigeriwwelt, pp.
insinuating 1.glatt, adj.; 2.schmeelich, adj.
insinuatingly verdraulich, adj.
insipid leppisch, adj.
insist verdeffendiere (sich --) v.; verdeffendiert, pp.; **upon** 1.abselut(t), adv.; 2.dringe, v.; gedrunge, pp. (druff --)
insistently troublesome person 1.Grageeler (der)n.; 2.Krageeler (der)n.
insolent maulich, adj.
inspect visidiere, v.; visidiert, pp. (v = f)
inspire 1.aa/fei(e)re, v.; aagfeirt, pp.; 2.eihauche, v.; eighaucht, pp.
install 1.aa/schtelle, v.; aagschtellt, pp.; 2.ei/setze, v.; eigsetzt, pp.
instantly inschtand(l)ich, adj.
instead of 1.anschtatt(s), prep.; 2.im Blatz vun, prep.; 3.in schtatz, prep.; 4.schtatts, prep. (-- vun)
instep Reie (der)n.
instigate 1.aa/schtifde, v.; aagschtift, pp.; 2.schtifde, v.; gschtifde, pp.; 3.uff/schtifde, v.; uffgschtift, pp.
instigator 1.Aaschtifder (der)n.; 2.Urhewer (der)n.
instruct 1.aa/weis(s)e, v.; aagewisse, pp.; 2.ei/scharefe, v.; eigschareft, pp.; 3.lanne, v.; glannt, pp.; 4.lehre, v.; gelehrt, pp.
instruction Unnerricht (der)n.
instrument Inschdrument (es)n.; **used as a dinner horn** Schneckeharn (es)n.
insult 1.belei(ch)diche, v.; beleidicht, pp.; 2.Beleidichung (die)n.
insurance Versichering (die)n.
insurgent Uffriehrer (der)n.
intellect Verschtand (der)n.
intelligent 1.gluuch, adj.; 2.gscheit, adj.; 3.schmaert, adj.
intelligible begreiflich, adj.
intemperate unmaessich, adj.
intend 1.meene, v.; gemeent, pp.; 2.Sinn (der)n. (im -- hawwe) 3.welle, v.; gewellt, pp.; 4.wolle, v.; gewollt, pp.
intended to solle, v.; gsollt, pp.
intention Meening (die)n.
intentionally mutwillicherweis, adv.

Ii

inter | **it**

inter 1.beaerdiche, v.; beardicht, pp.; 2.begraawe, v.; begraawe pp.; 3.ei/graawe, v.; eigegraawe, pp.; 4.vergraawe, v.; vergraawe, pp.

intercept ab/fange, v.; abgfange, pp.

interchange ab/wechsle, v.; abgewechselt, pp.

intercourse 1.haer/nemme, v.; haergenumme, pp. (en fraa --); 2.peeke, v.; gepeekt, pp.; 3.Umgang (der)n.

interest (charge for the use of money) Indresse (die)n., pl.

interested indressiert, adv.

interesting indressant, adj.

interfere 1.Maul (es)n. (es -- neihenke); (es -- uffreisse); 2.nei/henke, v.; neighenkt, pp. (es maul --); 3.nei/middle (sich --)v.; neigemiddelt, pp.; 4.nei/mische (sich --)v.

interior 1.innerlich, adv.; 2.inwendich, adv.

interlarded zwischenei, adv.

intermeddle dezwischerede, v.

interment Beaerdichung (die)n.

intermittent fever Wexelfiewer (es)n.

internal innerlich, adv.

interpret 1.dolmetsche, v.; gedolmetscht, pp.; 2. verdolmetsche, v.; verdolmetscht, pp.

interpretation 1.Auslegung (die)n.; 2.Dolmetschung (die)n.

interpreter 1.Ausleger (der)n.; 2.Dolmetscher (der)n.

interrogate aus/froge, v.; ausgfrogt, pp.

interrupt 1.nei/blaerre, v.; neigeblaerrt, pp.; 2.nei/blaffe, v.; neigeblafft, pp.; 3.nei/henke, v.; neighenkt, pp. (es Maul --)

intersect darich/schneide, v.; darichgschnidde, pp.

intervals schuckweis, adv.

intervene dezwischekumme, v.

intestinal fat (of cattle) Daermfett (es)n.; (of hogs) Daermschmals (es)n.

intestine 1.Dar(re)m (die)n.; Daerm, pl.; 2.Endkeitel (der)n.; 3.Endkeitel (der)n.; 4.Engkeitel (der)n.

intimidate 1.ab/schrecke, v.; abgschreckt, pp.; 2.eischrecke, v.; eigschreckt, pp.; 3.schrecke, v.; gschreckt, pp.

into 1.in, prep.; 2.ins, prep.; 3.nei, prep.; **the front** vanne-nei, adv.

intolerable unaerdraeglich, adj.

intoxicate berausche, v.; berauscht, pp.

intoxicated 1.bedrunke, adj.; 2.bsoffe, adj.; 3.Buchs (der)n. (im -- sei); 4.gsoffe, adj.; 5.versoffe, adj.

intoxication 1.Rausch (der)n.; 2.Suff (der)n.

intrepid 1.unverzaacht, adj.; 2.unverzaakt, adj.

intriguer Munkler (der)n.

introduce 1.bei/bringe, v.; beigebrocht, pp.; 2.bekannt/mache, v.; bekanntgemacht, pp.; 3.eifiehre, v.; eigfiehrt, pp.; (in a conversation) 1.nei/bringe, v.; neigebrocht, pp.; 2.eibringe, v.; eigebrocht, pp.; (oneself) bekannt/mache (sich --)v.; bekanntgemacht,pp.

introduction Eileiding, (die)n.

intrude 1.eidrenge (sich --)v.; eigedrengt, pp.; 2.eimische (sich --)v.; eigemischt, pp.; 3.nei/dringe (sich --)v.

intuitive aagebore, adj.

inundate 1.iwwer/laafe, v.; is iwwergeloffe, pp.; 2. iwwerschwemme, v.; iwwerschwemmt, pp.

inundation Iwwerschwemming (die)n.

inure eihaerte, v.; eighaert, pp.

invalid 1.grenk(er)lich, adj.; 2.kraftlos, adj.

invent erfinne, v.; erfunne, pp.

invention Erfindung (die)n.

inventor Erfinder (der)n.

invert 1.um/kehre, v.; umgekehrt, pp.; 2.um/schtilbe, v.; umgschtilpt, pp.;

invest 1.aa/lege, v.; aagelekt, pp.; 2.aa/wende, v.; aagewendt, pp.; 3.nei/schtecke, v.; neigschteckt; neigschtocke, pp.; **money in something** schtecke, v.; gschtocke, pp. (Geld in ebbes --); **with** begleede, v.; begleedt, pp.

investigate 1.nei/faschle, v.; 2.no(och)faschdle, v.; no(och)gfaschdelt, pp.; 3.no(och)suche, v.; no(och)gsucht, pp.; 4.unner/suche, v.; unnergsucht, pp.

investigation Unnersuchung (die)n.

invigorate schtaerricke, v.; gschtaerrickt, pp.

invisible insichtbaar, adj.

invitation Eilaading (die)n.

invite 1.ei/laade, v.; eigelaade, pp.; 2.neediche, v.; geneedicht, pp.

invoke aa/rufe, v.; aagerufe, pp.

invulnerable kuggelfescht, adj.

inward 1.inwendich, adv.; 2.inwennich, adv.

ire Zann (der)n.

iris 1.Schwaartli (es)n.; 2.Schwaertli (es)n.; 3.Schwertli (es)n.

irk 1.grenkle, v.; gegrenk(h)elt, pp.; 2.krenkle, v.; gekrenkelt, pp.

iron 1.eis(n), adj.; 2.Eise (es)n.; 3.eise, adj.; **(for clothes)** Biggeleise (es)n.; Biggeleise, pl.; **bar with broad bit for digging post holes** Grundmeesel (der)n.; **clothes** biggle, v.; gebiggelt, pp.; **cookpot** 1.Eisehaffe (der)n.; Eisehaffe, pl.; 2.Kochhaffe (der)n.; 3.Eisekessel (der)n.; **ore** Eise-erz (es)n.; **out** 1.aus/biggele, v.; ausgebiggelt, pp.; 2.raus/biggele, v.; rausgebiggelt, pp.; **plow trace** 1.Blug(s)schtrang (der)n.; 2.Ketteschtrang (der)n.; 3.Plugs(s)chtrang (der)n. ; **used in splitting rails** Schpaldeise (es)n.; **wedge** Eisekeidel (der)n.; **works** Eisewarrick (es)n.

ironical verschenne, v.; verschennt, pp.

ironing Bigglerei (die)n.; **cloth** Biggelduch (es)n.

irregularly ball shaped pulschderich, adj.

irresolute wankelmiedich, adj.

irritable aeryerlich, adj.

irritation Aeryernis (die)n.

Isaiah Saees (der)n.

island 1.Eiland (es)n.; Eilender, pl.; 2.Insel (die)n.

Israel (given name) Isrel (der)n.

issue 1.Ausgang (der)n.; 2.raus/kumme, v.; is rauskumme, pp.

it 1.es, pron.; 2.'n, pron.; **has been threatening (rain) all day** drickse, v.; gedrickst, pp. (es drickst der ganse daag); **has served its purpose** Dienscht (der)n. (es hot sei --e gedu); **is a great pity** dauerunschaad (es is); **is a pity** schaad, adj. (es is --); **is freezing** gfriere, v.; gfrore, pp. (es gfriert); **is not a success** waerre, v.; warre; waerre,

(Continued on page 303)

it (continued)

Ii

ivy poisoning

(Continued from page 302)

pp. (es waerd net); **is true** wull, adj.; **is what you would expect** derno, adv. (es is aa --); **makes me laugh** lechere, v.; gelechert, pp. (es lechert mich); **seems to me** dinke, v.; gedinkt. pp. (es dinkt mich); **serves him right** schatte, v.; gschatt, pp. (es schatt ihm nix); **was unavailing** batte, v.; gebatt, pp. (es hot nix gebatt); **will come to nothing** gewwe, v.; gewwe, pp. (do gebt's nix draus); **would seem** 1.allemno, adv.; 2.scheins, adv.; **It's all gone to nothing!** Batsch (die)n. ('sis alles --); **It's not worthwhile** Sis net der Waert

itch 1.Beiss (der)n.; 2.beisse, v.; gebisse, pp.; 3.Gratz (der)n.; 4.Kretz (der)n.

itching 1.beissich, adj.; 2.gratzich, adj.; 3.kratzich, adj.

itchy 1.gretzich, adj.; 2.kretzich, adj.

ivy poisoning Gift (es)n.

Jj

jab — joker

jab (in the ribs) Ribbeschtoos (der)n
jabber welsche, v.; gewelscht, pp.
jabbering Gewelsch (es)n.; **person** Klabberdasch (die)n.
Jack 1.Hannes (der)n.; 2.Hans (der)n.; 3.Yockel (der)n.;
    4.Yockli (der)n.
jack Waggeschnepp (die)n.; **in a deck of cards** (singular
    form only) Bauer (der)n.; Bauere, pl.; **in-the-pulpit** 1.
    Aronszwiwwel (die)n.; 2.Arrentschzwiwwel (die)n.;
    3.Geilszwiwwel (die)n.; **o'lantern** Erdlicht (es)n.;
    Erdlichter, pl.
jackass Schtee-esel (der)n.; Schtee-esel, pl.; **colt**
    Schtee-eselfill (es)n.
jacket Wammes (der)n.; Wammes, pl.
jackknife Sackmesser (es)n.; Sackmessere, pl.
jackpudding Hanskaschber (der)n.
Jacob 1.Yakob (der)n.; 2.Yockli (der)n.; 3.Yokkob (der)n.
jade Schindmaerr (die)n.
jag 1.Kischt (die)n.; Kischde, pl.; 2.Rausch (der)n.;
    3.Schliwwer (der)n.; Schliwwere, pl.
jagging iron Kucheraedel (es)n.
jail Bressen(t) (die)n.; Bressende, pl.
Jakey 1.Yockel (der)n.; 2.Yockli (der)n.
jamb Peiler (der)n.; Peiler, pl.
January 1.Yanuaar (der)n.; 2.Yenner (der)n.
jar 1.Bumps (der)n.; 2.glebbre, v.; geglebbert, pp.;
    3.rassle, v.; gerasselt, pp.;4.schiddle, v.; gschiddelt,
    pp.; 5.Schtoss (der)n.
jargon Kauderwelsch (es)n.
jaundice Gehlsucht (die)n.
jaundiced gehlich, adj.
jaunt around rum/kessle, v.; rumgekesselt, pp.
jawbone 1.Kinnbacke (der)n.; 2.Zaahlaad (die)n.;
    3.Zohlaad (die)n.
jawbreaker 1.Gummebrecher (der)n.; 2.Rachebutzer
    (der)n.; Rachebutzer, pl.
jay 1.Haerrevoggel (der)n.; 2.Waldhaehr (der)n.
jealous 1.eifersichtich, adj.; 2.missdrauisch, adj.;
    3. missvergunnisch, adj.; 4.vergunnisch, adj.
jealousy Eifersucht (die)n.
jeer schpotte, v.; gschpott, pp.
jelly 1.Graftbrieh (die)n.; 2.Kraftbrieh (die)n.; 3.Seftle (es)n.
jerk 1.blotze, v.; geblotzt, pp.; 2.reisse, v.; gerisse, pp.;
    3.Schnaerr (der)n.; 4.schnaerre, v.; gschnaerrt, pp.;
    5.schnarre, v.; gschnatt, pp.; 6.schnelle, v.; gschnellt, pp.;
    7.yucke, v.; geyuckt, pp.; 8.Yux (der)n.; 9.zoppe, v.; gezoppt,
    pp.; 10.zucke, v.; gezucht, pp.; **apart** (or to pieces)
    verschnaerre, v.; verschnaerrt, pp.; **around** 1.rum/reisse, v.;
    rumgerisse, pp.; 2.rum/schnaerre, v.; rumgschnaerrt, pp.;
    away weck/schnelle, v.; weckgschnellt, pp.; **back**
    1.zerick/reisse, v.; zerickgerisse, pp.; 2.zerick/schnelle, v.;
    zerickgschnellt, pp.; 3.zerick/zoppe, v.; zerickgzoppt, pp.;
    down nunner/schnaerre, v.; nunnergschnaerrt, pp.; **line**
    Zopplein (der)n.; Zoppleine, pl.; **near to** hie/reide, v.;
    hiegridde, pp.; **out** 1.raus/schnaere, v.; rausgschnaert, pp.;
    2.raus/schnelle, v; rausgschnellt, pp.; 3.raus/zoppe, v.;
    rausgezoppt, pp.; **over** niwwer/schnelle, v.;
    niwwergschnellt, pp.; **up** 1.nuff/renne, v.; nuffgerennt, pp.;
    2.nuff/zoppe, v.; nuffgezoppt, pp.

jerking Geyuck (es)n.; **or fidgeting** Gschlenker (es)n.;
    young woman Schnaerr (die)n.
Jerusalem artichoke Erdabbel (der)n.
jest Schaerz (der)n.
jesting name for an infant beforeit has been baptized
    Panneschtielche (es)n.
jestingly of dust as thick as fog newwle, v.; genewwelt, pp.
Jesus 1.Yeesus (der)n.;2.Yeses(der)n.;**Christ** Yesus
    Grischdus(der)n.
Jew Yutt (der)n.; Yudde, pl.
Jew's Harp 1.Drumbel (die)n.; 2.Trommel (die)n.
jewel Kleinod (es)n.; **weed** Kehlgraut (es)n.
Jewish (aquiline) nose Yuttenaas (die)n.
jilt 1.iwwer/schmeisse, v.; iwwergschmisse, pp.; 2.sitze,
    v.; gsotze, pp. (-- losse)
jimsonweed 1.Geilskimmel (der)n.; 2.Hexekimmel (der)n.;
    3.Schtechabbel (der)n.
jingle glingle, v.; geglingelt, pp.
Job Hiob (der)n.
Job's comfort Hiobsdroppe (der)n.; **tears, the seed of**
    Coix lacaryma-jobi, an Asiatic grass Karelle, (die)n.
jockey Reider (der)n.; Reider, pl.
Joe Sepp (der)n.
Joel Yoel (der)n.
jog Schtoss (der)n.; **across to** niwwer/yackere, v.;
    niwwergeyackert, pp.; **after** 1.no(och)kessle, v.;
    no(och)gekesselt, pp.; 2.no(och)zackere, v.;
    no(och)gezackert, pp.; **along** 1.fatt/loddle, v.; fattgeloddelt,
    pp.; 2.haer/drolle, v.; haergedrollt, pp.; 3.yackere, v.;
    geyackert, pp.; 4.zackere, v.; gezackert, pp.; **around the**
    country rumhaer/kessle, v.; rumhaergekesselt, pp.; **or drive**
    around the country rum/yackere, v.; rumgeyackert, pp.; **out**
    naus/zackere, v.; nausgezackert, pp.
jogging or driving about Geyacker (es)n.
John Yohannes (der)n.; **George** Hansyarrick (der)n.;
Nicholas Hannickel (der)n.
Johnny cake Welschkannkuche (der)n.; Welschkannkuche, pl.;
    on the spot Heck (die)n.; Hecke, pl. (an (bei) die --e sei)
join 1.aa/schtosse, v.; aagschtosse, pp.; 2.aaschliesse (sich --
)v.; aagschlosse, pp.; 3.fiege, v.; gfiekt, pp.;
    4.wedder/schtosse; **another church which requires**
    rebaptism rum/daafe, v.; rumgedaaft, pp.; **by growing**
    aa/waxe, v.; aagewaxe, pp.; **by knitting** aaschtricke, v.;
    aagschtrickt, pp.; **in** mit/mache, v.; mitgemacht, pp.; **in**
    a dance mit/danse, v.; mitgedanst; **in eating** mit/esse,
    v.; mitgesse, pp.; **in marriage** 1.kop(u)liere, v.;
    kop(u)liert, pp.; 2.kopple, v.; gekoppelt, pp.; **in prayer**
    mit/bede, v.; mitgebet, pp.; **in the laugh** mit/lache, v.;
    mitgelacht, pp.; **the congregation** Gemee (die)n.
    (die -- aanemme) **joint** (in the human body) 1.Gewareb
    (es)n.; Gewarewe, pl.; 2.G(e)waerb (es)n.
jointer Sech (es)n.
jointly 1.menanner, adv.; 2.mit(e)nanner, adv.
joist Balge (der)n.; Balge, pl.
joke 1.Schaerz (der)n.; 2.Schnaerkel (der)n.; 3.Schtreech
    (der)n.; Schtreech, pl.
joker Schpassvoggel (der)n.

Jj

jokesmith | jut out

jokesmith Witzbold (der)n.

jolly 1.haerlich, adj.; 2.harlich, adj.; 3.herrlich, adj.;
4.luschdich, adj.; 5.luschtunfreehlich, adj.; 6.uff/gelebt, v.

jolt 1.Blotz (der)n.; 2.blotze, v.; geblotzt, pp.; 3.Bumps (der)n.;
4.Renn (der)n.; 5.schnarre, v.; gschnatt, pp.; 6.schtauche,
v.; gschtaucht, pp.; 7.verschtauche, v.; verschtaucht, pp.;
in passing over a rough surface 1.hobbere, v.; ghobbert,
pp.; 2.hubbere, v.; ghubbert, pp.

Jonas 1.Yones (der)n.; 2.Yoni (der)n.

Jonathan 1.Yones (der)n.; 2.Yoni (der)n.

Jordan Yordan (der)n.

Joseph or Joel (dim.) Yoli (der)n.

Josephine Seppi (die)n.

Josie Seppi (die)n.

jostle about rum/schtoose, v.; rumgschtoose, pp.

jounce blotze, v.; geblotzt, pp.

journal Daagbuch (es)n.; Daagbicher, pl.

journey 1.ab/reese, v.; abgereest, pp.; 2.Rees (die)n.; Reese,
pl.; 3.reese, v.; gereest, pp.; 4.Reis (die)n.; Reise, pl.

jowl Saukopp (der)n.

joy 1.Freede (die)n.; 2.Frehlichkeit (die)n.; 3.Freide (die)
n.; 4.Wonne (die)n.

joyful 1.frehlich, adj.; 2.luschdich, adj.; 3.vergniecht, adj.;
4.wohluff, adj.

joyfully freedich, adj.

Jubilee Yubelfescht (es)n.

Judas tree 1.Bohnebaam (der)n.; 2.Buhnebaam (der)n.

judge 1.richde, v.; gericht, pp.; 2.Richder (der)n.; Richder,
pl.; 3.urteile, v.; geurteilt, pp.

judgement Urteil (es)n.

jug 1.Grug (der)n.; Grieg, pl.; 2.Kruck (der)n.

juice 1.Brieh (die)n.; 2.Saft (die)n.; **exuded by
grasshoppers** 1.Melaasich (der)n.; 2.Melasses (der)n.

juicy 1.brie(h)ich, adj.; 2.safdich, adj.

July Yuli (der)n.

July 20 Eliasdaag (der)n.

jump 1.schpringe, v.; gschprunge, pp.; 2.Schprung (der)n.;
up uff/schpringe, v.; is uffgschprunge, pp.

Junco Schneevoggel (der)n.

junction Verbinnung (die)n.

June Yuni (der)n.

Juneberry 1.Korinne; 2.Wildkasch (die)n.; Wildkasche, pl.

juniper 1.Wachholder (der)n.; 2.Wachholler (der)n.; **berry**
Wachhollerbeer (die)n.

just 1.emol, ad;v 2.erscht, adv.; 3.ewwe, adj.; 4.gerecht,
adj.; 5.nerscht = erscht; 6.numme, adv.;
7.rechtmeesich, adv.; 8.(y)uscht, adv.; **about**
sozesaage, conj.; **now** 1.alleweil, adv.; 2.anneweil, adv.;
3.uscht, adv.; 4.yuscht, adv.

Justice of the Peace 1.Schgweier (der)n.; 2.Yuschdis (der)
n.; 3.Friedensrichter (der)n.

justice Gerechdichkeit (die)n.

justify rechfaertiche, v.; rechgfaerticht, pp.; **oneself**
1.verantwarte (sich --)v.; verantwart, pp.;
2.verdeffendiere (sich --) v.; verdeffendiert, pp.

jut out raus/schteh, v.; rausgschtanne, pp.

Kk

kaboodle — knife

kaboodle Lossement (es)n

Katie 1.(die)n.; 2.Kaet(i) (die)n.

katydid Hawwergees (der)n.; **(onomatopoetic)** Schrackack

keen 1.scharef, adj.; 2.schpitzohrich, adj.

keep 1.behalde, v.; 2.bewaare, v.; bewaart, pp.; 3.bhalde, v.; bhalde, pp.; 4.palde, v.; gepalde, pp.; **(a person) short in money** halde, v.; ghalde, pp. (Katz --); **a fire going** feiere, v.; gfeiert, pp.; **at it** 1.dewedermache, v.; dewedermacht, pp.; 2.draahalde (sich --)v.; draaghalde, pp.; **awake** 1.wache, v.; gwacht, pp.; 2.wachere = wache; **away** ab/warne, v.; abgewarnt, pp.; **away by biting** weck/beisse, v.; weckgebisse, pp.; **back** zerick/palde, v.; zerickgepalde, pp.; **carefully** verwaahre, v.; verwaahrt, pp.; **closed** zuhalte, v.; zughalte, pp.; **for future use** uff/hewe, v.; uffghowe, pp.; **hold of** faschthalde, v.; faschtghalde, pp.; **house** 1.hause, v.; ghaust, pp.; 2.haushalte, adj.; **in its lair** (of an animal) eihocke, v.; eighockt, pp.; **in place** bei/halde, v.; beighalde, pp.; **mum** schtill/schweige, v.; schtillgschweicht, pp.; **off** 1.ab/palde, v.; abgepalde, pp.; 2.wehre, v.; gewehrt, pp.; **off or away** ab/halte, v.; abghhalt, pp.; **on** uff/losse, v.; uffgelosst, pp.; **on** (as a coat) aapalde, v.; aagepalde, pp. ; **on** (one's hat) uff/palde, v.; uffgepalde, pp.; **on pratting** hie/gackse, v.; hiegegackst, pp.; **on using** fatt/brauche, v.; fattge-braucht, pp.; **on working** fatt/zackere, v.; fattgezackert, pp.; **safe** bewaare, v.; bewaart, pp.; **secret** 1.hehl halde, v.; 2.verduckle, v.; verduckelt, pp.; **silent** 1.schtill sei, v.; 2.schtill/schweige, v.; schtillgschweicht, pp; 3.verschweige, v.; verschweicht, pp.; **someone away** weck/halde, v.; weckgehalde, pp.; **to oneself** (as a se-cret) verschweige, v.; verschweicht, pp.; **together** zamme/ palde, v.; zammegepalde, pp.; **up** uff/halde, v.; uffghalde, pp.; **up with** no(och)halde, v.; no(och)ghaldt, pp.

keeping house in a slovenly manner glatt, adj. (net arrig -- haergeh)

keepsake Aadenke(s) (es)n.

keg 1.Ballfass (es)n.; Ballfesser, pl.; 2.Fass (es)n.; Fesser, pl.; 3.(es)n.; Fesslin, pl.

kerchief Koppduch (es)n.; Koppdicher, pl.

kernel 1.Fruchtkaern (die)n.; 2.Kann (die)n.; Kanne, pl.; **of large size** Mudderkaern (die)n.

kerosene Kohleel (es)n.; **can** Kohleelkann (die)n.; **lamp** Kohleellicht (es)n.

kettle Kessel (der)n.; Kessele, pl.

key 1.Schliess (die)n.; 2.Schlissel (der)n.; Schlissle, pl.; **(of a piano or organ)** Klaff (die)n.; **ring** Schlisselring (der)n.

keyhole Schlisselloch (es)n.; Schlissellecher, pl.; **guard** 1.Schlisselblettche (es)n.; 2.Schlissellochblettche (es)n.

kick 1.dredde, v.; gedredde, pp.; 2.Dreed (der)n.; 3.Fuusschtoss (der)n.; 4.v.; gschtrambelt, pp.; 5.schtrawwle, v.; gschtrawwelt, pp.; zapple, v.; gezappelt, pp.; 7.zawwle, v.; gezawwelt, pp.; **(of a horse)** 1.schlagge, v.; gschlaage, pp.; 2.zerick/hacke, v.; zerickghackt, pp.; **out** 1.naus/dredde, v.; nausgedredde, pp.; 2.raus/drede, v.; rausgedrede, pp.; **over the traces** 1.hacke, v.; ghackt, pp. (iwwer die Schtrang --); 2.Schnur (die)n. (iwwer

die -- hacke); **the bucket** 1.druffschnappe, v.; druffgschnappt, pp.; 2.grebiere, v.; grebiert, pp.; 3.verrecke, v.; verreckt, pp.; **up a row** rumore, v.; gerumort, pp.

kid (goat) Gees (der)n. (yunger --)

kidnapper Kinnerdieb (der)n.

kidney Nier (die)n.; Niere, pl.

kill 1.ausblose, v.; ausgeblose, pp. (eems Licht --); 2.deediche, v.; gedeedicht, pp.; 3.deete, v.; gedeet, pp.; 4.dod/mache, v.; dodgemacht, pp.; 5.schlachde, v.; gschlacht, pp.; 6.um/bringe, v.; umgebrocht, pp.

killdeer Gilleri (der)n.; Gilleri, pl.

killed um/kumme, v.; is umkumme, pp.

killing time Gebambel (es)n.

kin Freindschaft (die)n.

kind 1.Aart (die)n.; 2.freindlich, adj.; 3.gut, adj.; 4.liebreich, adj.; 5.Ort (die)n.; 6.Sart (die)n.; 7.Satt (die)n.; Sadde, pl.; **heartedness** Guthaerzichkeet (die)n.; **o'** 1.Aart (die)n. (uff en -- wie); 2.Ort (die)n. (uff en -- wie)

kindle zinde, v.; gezindt, pp.

kindling Feierholz (es)n.; **wood** Zindhols (es)n.

kindness Gutmeenichkeet (die)n.

king Keenich (der)n.; Keeniche, pl.; **and queen of trumps in datte** Bella (die)n.

king's evil Grankheet (die)n. (english --)

kingbird Iemefresser (der)n.; Iemefresser, pl.

kingdom 1.Keenichreich (es)n.; Keenichreicher, pl.; 2.Reich (es) n.; **of God** Gottesreich (es)n.; **of heaven** Himmelreich (es)n.

Kiss of Peace Kuss (der)n.

kiss 1.Boss (der)n.; Bosse, pl.; 2.bosse, v.; gebosst, pp.; 3.kisse, v.; gekisst, pp.; 4.schmutze, v.; gschmutzt, pp.

kissing Kisses (es)n.

kitchen Kich (die)n.; Kiche, pl.; **crockery** Kichegschar (es) n.; **cupboard** Kicheschank (der)n.; **door** 1.Kichedeer (die)n.; 2.Kichedier (die)n.; **paring knife** Kneip (der) n.; **table** Kichedisch (der)n.; **table for dishes** Aarichtdisch (der)n.; **utensils** 1.Kichegeraetschaft (die)n.; 2.Kitchegeraetschaft(die)n.

kite Drach (der)n.; Drache, pl.

kitten 1.Bussli (es)n.; Busslin, pl.; 2.Ketzel (es)n.

knack 1.Gschick (der)n.; 2.Va(e)rtel (der)n.

knapsack Schnappsack (der)n.; Schnappseck, pl.

knave 1.Schellem (der)n.; 2.Schelm (der)n.; 3.Schpitzbu(h) (der)n.

knead dough Deeg schaffe (der)n.; **trough** 1.Backdroog (der)n.; 2.Backmult (die)n.; Backmulde, pl.

knee 1.Gnie (es)n.; Gnie, pl.; 2.Knie (es)n.; **cap** 1.Gniekapp (die)n.; 2.Gniescheib (die)n.; **high** gniehoch, adv.

kneel 1.gnie-e, v.; gegniet, pp.; 2.kniee, v.; gekniet, pp.; **down** nunner/gniee, v.; nunnergegniet, pp.

kneepan Gniescheib (die)n.

kneesprung gnieschprunge, adj.

knell Dodeglocke (die)n.

knife Messer (es)n.; Messere, pl.; **edge** Messerschneid (die)n.; **for cutting hay in the stack** Hoimesser (es)n.; **handle** Mess-erschtiel (der)n.; **sheath** Messerschaed (die)n.

Kk

knifeblade

knifeblade 1.Messergling (die)n.; 2.Messerkling (die)n.

Knight of the Golden Circle (of Civil War times)
Scheierbruder (der)n.

knight Ritter (der)n.

knit schtricke, v.; gschtrickt, pp.

knitting 1.Gschtrick (es)n.; 2.Schtrickes (es)n.; **needle**
Schtricknoddel (die)n.

knob 1.Dierknopp (der)n.; Diergnepp, pl.; 2.Gnopp (der)
n.; Gnepp, pl.

knock 1.beitsche, v.; gebeitscht, pp.; 2.Gnicker (der)n.;
3.kloppe, v.; gekloppt, pp. **(at)** aa/globbe, v.;
aagegloppt, pp. **against** 1.wedder/schlagge, v.;
weddergschlagge, pp.; 2.wedder/schtosse, v.;
weddergschtosse, pp.; **around** rum/schlagge, v.;
rumgschlagge, pp.; **away** weck/schlagge, v.;
weckgschlagge, pp.; **down** 1.nidder/schlagge, v.;
niddergschlagge, pp.; 2.runner/schlagge, v,;
runnergschlagge, pp.; 3.umschlagge, v.; umgschlagge,
pp.; 4.umwische, v.; umgewischt, pp.;
5.zamme/schlagge, v.; zammegschlagge, pp.; **down the
price** handle losse (sich --)v.; **in** 1.nei/schlagge, v.;
neigschlagge, pp.; 2.rei/schlagge, v.; reigschlagge, pp.;
loose los/schlagge, v.; losgschlagge, pp.; **off**
1.ab/gloppe, v.; abgegllopp;t 2.ab/schlagge, v.;
abgschlagge, pp.; **off in running** ab/renne, v.;
abgerennt, pp.; **on** druffbeitsche, v.; druffgebeitscht,
pp. **out** naus/schlagge, v.; nausgschlagge, pp.; **over**
1.um/renne, v.; umgerennt, pp.; 2.um/schtosse, v.;
umgschtosse, pp.; **to pieces** zamme/schlagge, v.;
zammegschlagge, pp.

knoll on a mountain road Baerrickhiwwel (der)n.

knot 1.Gnack (der)n.; 2.gnibbe, v.; gegnippt, pp.; 3.Knack
(der)n.; 4.vergnibbe, v.; vergnippt, pp.; 5.verknippe,
v.; vergnippt, pp.; **(in a cord)** Gnipp (der)n.; **(in
lumber)** 1.Gnarre (der)n.; Gnarre, pl.; 2.Knarre (der)
n.; **(in woman's hair)** Haargnibbel (es)n.; **so it is difficult to undo** verknipp(l)e, v.; verknippelt, pp.; **together** zamme/gnippe, v.; zammegegnippt, pp.; **up**
vergnoddle, v.; vergnoddelt, pp.

knotgrass 1.Gneeterich (der)n.; 2.Silwergraas (es)n.;
3.Wegdred(d)er (der)n.

knothole Gnarreloch (es)n.; Gnarrelecher, pl.

knotted vergnoddelt, adj.

knotty 1.gnarrich, adj.; 2.gnarzich, adj.; 3.gnatzich, adj.;
4.knarrich, adj.; 5.knarzich, adj.

knotweed Gneeterich (der)n.

know wisse, v.; gwisst, pp. **in advance** 1.vannenaus/wisse,
v.; vannenausgewisst, pp.; 2.vorhaerwisse, v.;
vorhaergewisst, pp.; **nothing** Nixwisser (der)n.; **or understand something** kenne, v.; gekennt, pp.; **what to do**
seckendiere (sich --)v.; seckendiert, pp.

knowingly wissentlich, adj.

knowledge 1.Kunscht (die)n.; 2.Wissenschaft (die)n.

known bekannt, adj.

knuckle 1.Gnechel (der)n.; Gnechel, pl.; 2.Gneckel (der)n.

kochia 1.Baerrickfeier (es)n.; 2.Barigfeier (es)n.

kohlrabi 1.Golraabi (der)n.; 2.Golraawe (der)n.;

kohlrabi

3.Grautrieb (die)n.; 4.Kolraabi (der)n.

Ll

label — last

label Zettel (der)n.

labor Arewet(t) (die)n.

laborer 1.Schaffmann (der)n.; Schaffleit, pl.; 2.Scheffer (der)n.; Scheffer, pl.

labors (in childbirth) Kinsnoot (die)n.

lace 1.ei/bendle, v.; eigebendelt, pp.; 2.schniere, v.; gschniert, pp.; 3.Schnur (die)n.; **(as a corset)** schnure (sich --)v.; gschnurt, pp.

laced boot Schnierschtiwwel (der)n.; **shoe** Halbschtiwwel (der)n.

lacerate verschinne, v.; verschunne, pp.

lack 1.fehle, v.; g(e)fehlt, pp.; 2.Mangel (der)n.; 3.mangle, v.; gemangelt, pp.; 4.Not (die)n.; **of reason** Unvernunft (die)n.; **of sense** 1.Alwerheet (die)n.; 2.Unverschtand (der)n.; 3.Unverschtang (der)n.; 4.Unverschtennichkeit (die)n.

lackey Bedienter (der)n.

lacking common sense 1.alwer(n), adj. 2.ungebacke, adj.; 3.unmanierlich, adj.; 4.unverschtennich, adj.

lacteal vein Millichoder (die)n.

lad Bu (der)n.; Buwe, pl.

ladder Leeder (die)n.; Leedere, pl.; **(used in mounting the smoldering charcoal pile)** Kohlleeder (die)n.; **beam** Leederbaam (der)n.; Leederbeem, pl.; **wagon** Leederwaage (der)n.; Leederwegge, pl.

ladle 1.Kell (die)n.; Kelle,pl.; 2.Kochleffel (der)n.; 3.Leffel (der)n. (grosser --); 4.Schebber (der)n.; 5.Scheppleffel (der)n.

lady's handbag Kabbe, n.; **slipper** 1.Bullebeidel (der)n.; 2.Ewwergraut (es)n.; **thistle** Marien(s)dischdel (die)n.

lam belse, v.; gebelst, pp.

lamb 1.Lamm (es)n.; Lemmer, pl.; 2.Schaefel (es)n.; 3.Schaefli (es)n.; 4.Schippelche (es)n.; 5.Schippeli (es)n.; 6.Schippli (es)n.; Schipplin, pl.; 7.Schofli (es) n.; Schoflin, pl.

lamb's quarters Melde (der)n. (zaahmer --)

lambast flachsiere, v.; gflachsiert, pp.

lame laahm, adj.

lament 1.beweine, v.; beweint, pp.; 2.klaage, v.; geklaakt, pp.; 3.yammere, v.; geyammert, pp.

lamentable bedauerlich, adj.

lamenting 1.Gelammedier (es)n.; 2.Geyammer (es)n.; 3.Geyeemer (es)n.

lamp 1.Kohleellicht (es)n.; 2.Licht (es)n.; Lichder, pl.; **(in which a wick dipped in fat was used)** Fettlicht (es)n. **lampblack** Kehruus (der)n.

lamplight Lampehelling (die)n.

lampwick Weiche (der)n.; Weiche, pl.

lance Lans (die)n.

lancet Schpringschtock (der)n.; Schpringschteck, pl.

land 1.aa/lande, v.; aagelandt, pp.; 2.aus/messe, v.; 3.Land (es) n.; Lenner, pl.; **adapted for grains** Fruchtland (es)n.; **bird** Landvoggel (der)n.; **plate** (of a plow) Landseit (die)n.

landlady 1.Waddin (die)n.; 2.Wattin (die)n.; 3.Wattsfrau (die)n.

landlord Watt (der)n.; Wadde, pl.

landowner Landeegner (der)n.; Landeegner, pl.

landroller Walz (die)n.

landscape Landschaft (die)n.

lane Beiweg (der)n.; Beiwege, pl.

language Schprooch (die)n.; Schprooche, pl.

languish schmachde, v.; gschmacht, pp.

lanky (person) dinnleiwich, adj.

lantern 1.Ladann (die)n.; Ladanne, pl.; 2.Lutzer (die)n.; Lutzer, pl.

lap 1.lecke, v.; g(e)leckt, pp.; 2.Schoss (der)n.; **of the earth** Erdschoss (der)n.; **of the winding frame** schlecke, v.; gschleckt, pp.

lapel Aufschlack (der)n.

lard 1.Fett (es)n.; 2.Schmalz (es)n.; 3.Schmutz (der)n.; **burning lamp** Fettamschel (die)n.; **can** Schmalzschtenner (der)n.; **press** 1.Fettbress (die)n.; 2.Schmalsbress (die)n.

larder Esschank (der)n.

large gross, adj.; **(very)** grossmechtich, adj.; **boned** grossgnochich, adj.; **eyed** grossaagich, adj.; **flat stone** Schteeblatt (die)n.; **footed** grossfiessich, adj.; **intestine** 1. Aarschdaarem (der)n.; 2.Daarem (der)n. (gross --); 3. Grimmdar(e)m (der)n.; 4.Grossdarem (der)n.; **kettle** Kochkessel (der)n.; **lump** (resembling a cow's stomach) Wambe(r) (der)n.; **piece** 1.Ranse (der)n.; 2.schlarre (adj.); **piece of bread** Keidel (der)n.; **rake dragged by hand** Handschleefreche (der)n.; **wing feather** Schwingfadder (die)n.

largest of all allergreescht, adj.

lark 1.Larich (die)n.; 2.Yacht (die)n.

larkspur 1.Brinsebedaad (roder)n.; 2.Ridderschpor (der) n.; Ridderschpore, pl.; 3.Ritterschpor (der)n.

larva of carpet moth Schtaabfischel (es)n.

laryngitis Halsauszehring (die)n.

larynx 1.Halsreehr (es)n.; 2.Halsreehr (es)n.; 3.Kehlkopp (der)n.; 4.Schproochbax (die) n.

lascivious rammlich, adj.

lash 1.beitsche, v.; gebeitscht, pp.; 2.Fitz (die)n.; 3.fitze, v.; gfitzt, pp.; 4.fitzle, v.; gfitzelt, pp.; 5.Geeschel (die) n.; Geeschle, pl.; 6.geeschle, v.; gegeeschelt, pp.; 7.Hack (der)n.; 8.hacke, v.; ghackt, pp.; 9.Schnur (die)n.; **at** los/hacke, v.; losghackt, pp.; **until the skin breaks** darich/hacke, v.; darichghockt, pp.

lass Meedli (es)n.; Meedlin, pl.

lassitude Lassichkeit (die)n.

last 1.aus/dauere, v.; ausgedauert, pp.; 2.dauere, v.; gedauert, pp.; 3.fatt/dauere, v:; fattgedauert, pp.; 4.letscht, adj.; 5.waehre, v.; gewaehrt, pp.; 6.zeletscht, adv.; 7.zuletscht, adv.; **but two** drittelscht, adj.; **evening** geschderowed, adv.; **hook** Leeschthoke (der)n.; **of all** 1.allerhinnerscht, adj.; 2.allerlescht, adj.; **one to rise on New Year's Day** 1.Nei-Yaahr-Schitzli (es)n.; 2. Nei-Yaahr- Schlegel (der)n.; **one to rise on Shrove Tuesday** (day before Ash Wednesday) Esch(e)puddel (die)n.; **phase of the moon** Altlicht (es)n.; **year** vor(e)myaahr,adv.

Ll

last year's   leaping beetle

last year's letschtyaehrich, adv.

lasting dauerhaft, adj.

late 1.verewicht, adj.; 2.verschpaete (sich --)v.; verschpaet, pp.; 3.verstarwe, adj. (--ner, --ni, --nes); **cabbage** Schpotgraut (es)n.; **later; latest** schpot; schpeeder; es schpeedscht, adj.

lately katzlich, adv.

latent grudge Falschheet (die)n.

lath 1.Leddel (es)n.; 2.Leddelche (es)n.; 3.Lettche (es)n.; 4.Lettel (es)n.; 5.lettle, v.; gelettelt, pp.; 6.Lettli (es)n.; Lettlin, pl.; **nail** Lattenaggel (der)n.

lather 1.aa/seefe, v.; aagseeft, pp.; 2.ei/seefe, v.; eigseeft, pp.; 3.Schaum (der)n.; 4.Seefeschaum (der)n.

lathery schaumich, adj.

Latin ladeinisch, adj.

latter part of winter Noochwinter (der)n.

laugh 1.Lach (der)n.; 2.lache, v.; gelacht, pp.

laugh after no(och)lache, v.; no(och)gelacht, pp.; **at** aus/lache, v.; ausgelacht, pp.; **back or in return** zerick/lache, v.; zerickgelacht, pp.; **in one's sleeve** Fauscht (die)n. (sich die -- voll lache)

laughable 1.fannich, adj.; 2.lachlich, adj.; 3.lech(er)lich, adj.; 4.lecher(l)ich, adj.; 5.lecherich, adj.; 6.schpassich, adj.

laughing Gelach (es)n.

laughter 1.Gelach (es)n.; 2.Gelechter (es)n.

launch Schiffsboot (es)n.

laundry Wesch (die)n.

laundrywoman Weschfraa (die)n.; Weschweiwer, pl.

laurel 1.Buchs (der)n.; 2.Lorbeer (die)n.

lavender 1.Lafendel (der)n.; 2.Lavendal (der)n. (v=f Lafendal)

law 1.G(e)setz (es)n.; 2.Recht (es)n.; **suit** Rechschtreit (der)n.

lawful laamaeesich, adv.

lawfully rechtmeesich, adv.

lawn 1.Graasblatz (der)n.; 2.Hefli (es)n.; **mower** 1.Grasschneider (der)n.; 2.Heflimeher (der)n.

lax lass, adj.

laxative Laxiering (die)n.

lay lege, v.; g(e)legt, pp.; **(something)** under (as a stone under a wheel to hold a wagon on a slope) unner/lege, v.; unnergelekt, pp.; **alongside of each other** newenannerlege, adv.; **away** weck/lege, v.; weckgelegt, pp.; **back** zerick/lege, v.; zerickgelegt, pp.; **between** dezwischelege, v.; **by** 1.uff/lege, v.; uffgelegt, pp.; 2.zerick/lege, v.; zerickgelegt, pp.; **down** 1.hie/leie, v.; hiegelegge, pp.; 2.nidder/lege, v.; niddergelegt, pp.; 3.nunner/lege, v.; nunnergelegt, pp.; 4.runner/leege, v.; runnergeleegt, pp.; **down here** haer/lege, v.; haergelegt, pp.; **drain pipes** deich(l)e, v.; gedeich(el)t, pp.; **hold of** 1.aa/packe, v.; aagepackt, pp.; 2.glooe, v.; gegloot, pp. (sich fascht --); **in** 1.eikaafe, v.; eikaaft, pp. 2.nei/lege, v.; neigelegt, pp.; 3.rei/lege, v.; reigelekt, pp.; **in different places** rumhaer/lege, v.; rumhaergelekt, pp.; **in folds** 1.ei/falde, v.; eigfaldt, pp.; 2.eifalte, v.; eigfalt, pp.; **on** druffhalde, v.; druffghalde, pp.; **out** 1.aus/lege, v.; ausgelegt, pp.; 2.raus/lege, v.;

raugelekt, pp.; **out in order** zerechtlege, v.; zerrechtgelegt, pp.; **out separately** ausenanner/lege, v.; ausenannergelegt, pp.; **over** niwwer/ lege, v.; niwwergelegt, pp.; **over or on the side** umlege, v.; umgelekt, pp.; **up** ruff/lege, v.; ruffgelegt, pp.; **up** (stones) uff/lege, v.; uffgelegt, pp.; **up a wall** mauere, v.; gemauert, pp.; **up somewhere** nuff/lege, v.; nuffgelegt, pp.; **with** dezulege, v.; dezugeleegt, pp.

layer Gelek (es)n.; **(of hay)** G(e)leeg (es)n.; **of grain** (for one threshing by flail) Bett (es)n.; Bedder, pl.

laying hen 1.Leghinkel (es)n.; 2.Lekhinkel (es)n.

laziness 1.Faulheet (die)n.; 2.Faulheit (die)n.

lazy 1.faul, adj.; 2.faulense, v.; gfaulenst, pp.; **person** Faulenzer (der)n.; Faulenzer, pl.

leacherous man Hengscht (der)n.

lead 1.aa/fiehre, v.; aagfiehrt, pp.; 2.fiehre, v.; gfiehrt, pp.; **about** rum/fiehre, v.; rumgfirht, pp.; **astray** 1. verblaudere, v.; verblaudert, pp.; 2.verfiehre, v.; verfiehrt, pp.; 3.verschtifde, v.; verschtift, pp.; **away** 1.ab/fiehre, v.; abgfiehrt, pp.; 2.fatt/fiehre, v.; fattgfiehrt, pp.; 3.weck/fiehre, v.; weckgfiehrt, pp.; **back** zerick/fiehre, v.; zerickgfiehrt, pp.; **in** rei/fiehre, v.; reigfiehrt, pp.; **in or into** nei/fiehre, v.; neigfiehrt, pp.; **on behind** no(och)fiehre, v.; no(och)gfiehrt, pp.; **out** naus/fiehre, v.; nausgfiehrt, pp.; **over** niwwer/fiehre, v.; niwwergfiehrt, pp.; **past** verbei/fiehre, v.; verbeigfiehrt, pp.; **the mowers** 1.vormaehe, v.; vorgemaeht, pp.; 2.Vormaeher (der)n.; **the sicklers** vorschneide, v.; vorgschnidde, pp.; **the singing** 1.vorsinge, v.; vorgsunge, pp.; 2.Vorsenger (der)n.; **to hie/geh**, v.; hiegange, pp.; **to a place** hie/fiehre, v.; hiegfiehre, pp.; **up** 1.nuff/fiehre, v.; nuffgfiehrt, pp.; 2.ruff/ fiehre, v.; ruffgfiehrt, pp.

lead (metal) Blei (es)n.; **pencil** Bleipensil (der)n.

leader 1.Haaptkall (der)n.; 2.Haaptmann (der)n.; Hauptmenner, pl.; 3.Vorgenger (der)n.; **(of a gang)** Bellhammel (der)n.

leading rope or strap Halsreime (der)n.

leaf 1.Blaat (es)n.; Bledder, pl.; 2.Blatt (es)n.; Bledder, pl.; 3.Laab (es)n.; **bud** Laabknopp (der)n.; **lard** Niereschmals (es)n.; **of a table** Dischfliggel (der)n.

leafy blettrich, adj.

leak 1.raus/schweese, v.; rausgschweest, pp.; 2.rinne, v.; gerunne, pp.; 3.schwees(s)e, v.; gschwees(s)t, pp.; **away** weck/rinne, v.; weckgerunne, pp.; **in** rei/rinne, v.; reigerunne, pp.; **into** nei/rinne, v.; neigerunnt, pp.; **out** raus/rinne, v.; rausgerunne, pp.

lean 1.daerr, adj.; 2.darr, adj.; 3.lehne, v.; g(e)lehnt, pp.; **against** wedder/laahne, v.; weddergelaahnt, pp.; **and scurvy** (of cats) abgelumpt, adv.; **back** zerick/laahne, v.; zerickgelaahnt, pp.; **out** raus/laahne, v.; rausglaahnt, pp.; **to** Schuss-scheier (die)n.

leap Schprung (der)n.; **or start suddenly** ab/schpringe, v.; abschprunge, pp.; **year** Schalkyaahr (es)n.

leapfrog 1.Groddehupse (es)n.; 2.Grottehupse (es)n.

leaping beetle 1.Schneller (der)n.; Schneller, pl.; 2.Schnellkeffer (der)n.; Schnellkeffer, pl.

309

Ll

learn | lifelong

learn 1.erfaahre, v.; erfaahre, pp.; 2.innewaerre, v.; innewaerre, pp.; 3.laerne, v.; gelaernt, pp.; 4.lanne, v.; glannt, pp.; **by covert observation** ab/fange, v.; abgfange, pp.; **by looking on or by stealth** ab/gucke, v.; abgeguckt, pp.; **by observing** ab/sehne, v.; abgsehne, pp.

learned 1.gelaernt, adj.; 2.gelehrt, adj.

learnedness Gelehrsamkeit (die)n.

learning 1.Gelehrsamkeit (die)n.; 2.Lanning (die)n.; 3.Lehr (die)n.

lease verlehne, v.; verlehnt, pp.

leather 1.Ledder (es)n.; 2.leddere, v.; geleddert, pp.; **apron** Schatzfell (es)n.; **sheath on iron traces** der Schodde an der Keddeschtreng

leathern leddern, adj.

leathery ledderich, adj.

leave 1.ab/reisse, v. (sich -- vun); 2.raus/geh, v.;rausgange, pp.; 3.raus/packe (sich --)v.; rausgepackt, pp.; 4.weck/geh, v.; is weckgange, pp.; **(on a trip)** 1.fatt/geh, v.; fattgange, pp.; 2.verlosse, v.; verlosse, pp.; **away** weck/losse, v.; weckgelosst, pp.; **behind** 1.hinnerlosse, v.; hinnerlosse, pp.; 2.zerick/losse, v.; zerickgelosst, pp.; **by the front way** vannenaus/geh, v.; vannenausgange, pp.; **closed** zu/losse, v.; zuglosst, pp.; **hastily** ab/schiewe (sich --)v.; abgschowe, pp.; **in possession** losse, v.; g(e)losst, pp.; **off** 1.ab/losse, v.; abgelosst, pp.; 2.no(och)losse, v.; no(och)g(e)losst, pp.; **on a trip** ab/reese, v.; abgereest, pp.; **open** uff/losse, v.; uffgelosst, pp.; **out** haus/losse, v.; hausgelosst, pp.; **the nest** aus/fliege, v.; ausgflogge, pp.; **thoughtlessly** weck/haschble, v.; weckghaschbelt, pp.; **to the disposition of** (God) walte, v.; gewaltet, pp.; **undone** losse, v.; g(e)losst, pp.; **without notice** weck/laafe, v.; weck-geloffe, pp.

leaved blettrich, adj.

leaven Satz (der)n.

leavings Abfall (der)n.

lecherous rammlich, adj.

ledge Absatz (der)n.; Absetz, pl.

leech Blutsuckler (der)n.; Blutsuckler, pl.

leek Lauch (der)n.

left 1.iwwrich, adj.; 2.link, adj., prep.; **hand side** link, prep. (dei --); **handed** 1.links, adj.; 2.links-hendich, adj.

leftover 1.iwwerich, adj.; 2.Iwwerich (es)n.

leg 1.Bee (es)n.; Bee, pl.; 2.Schenkel (der)n.

legality Rechmaessichkeet (die)n.

legend Saag (die)n.

legislator Semmlimann (der)n.

legislature Semmli (es)n.

Lehigh lechaa; **Gap** Lechaa (die)n. (die -- kaft); **River** Lechaa (die)n.

lend 1.lehne, v.; g(e)lehnt, pp.; 2.naus/barge, v.; nausgebarkt, pp.; 3.weck/lehne, v.; weckglehnt, pp.; **a hand** raus/helfe, v.; rausgholfe, pp.; **out** weck/barge, v.; weckgebarkt, pp.

lender Lehner (der)n.

length Leng (die)n.; **of an arm** Armsleng (die)n.

lengthen 1.aaschtick(l)e, v,; aagschtickelt, pp.; 2.lengre, v.; gelengert, pp.; 3.verlengere, v.; verlengert, pp.; **a dress** bsetze, v.; bsetzt, pp.

lengthwise langweis, adv.

Lent 1.Faschde (die)n., pl.; 2.Faschtzeit (die)n.

lentil Kecherle (es)n.

Leo (5th sign of the zodiac) Leeb (der)n.; Leewe, pl.

Leonard Lennerd (der)n.

lessen erleichtere, v.; erleichtert, pp.

lesson Lehr (die)n.

let 1.losse, v.; g(e)losst, pp.; 2.verlehne, v.; verlehnt, pp.; 3.weck/lehne, v.; weckglehnt, pp.; **'er go** schliwwere, v.; gschliwwert, pp. (es -- losse); **alone** 1.bleiwe, v.; gebliwwe, pp. (-- losse;) 2.mit/fridde, v. (-- losse); **down** 1.nunner/losse, v.; nunnergelosst, pp.; 2.runner/ losse, v.; runnergelosst, pp.; **fly** schnelle, v.; gschnellt, pp.; **go** geh/losse; **go to ruin** verlause losse, v.; verlausegelosst, pp.; **have** losse, v.; g(e)losst, pp.; **in** rei/losse,v.; reiglosst, pp. (reiglesst = Amish usage); **know** wisse losse, v.; wisse glosst (glesst =Amish usage); **on** aa/losse, v.; aag(e)losst, pp.; **out** (a seem) aus/losse, v.; ausg(e)losst, pp.

letter Brief (der)n.; **(in the alphabet)** 1.Buschdaab (der)n.; Buschdaawe, pl.; 2.Buschdaag (der)n.; Buschdaawe, pl.; **carrier** 1.Briefdraager (der)n.;2.Briefdraeger (der) n.; 3.Meelmann (der)n.; Meelmenner, pl.; **of Jesus** (alleged) 1.Himmelsbrief (der)n.; 2.Yesesbrief (der) n.; **paper** Briefbabier (es)n.

lettuce 1.Selaat (der)n.; 2.Zelaat (der)n.

level 1.ewe, adj.; 2.ewene, v.; ge-ewent, pp.; **measure of grain** ab/schtreiche, v.; abgschtriche, pp.; **off** abeewene, v.; abgeewent, pp.; **space** Ewening (die)n.

lever Hebschtang (die)n.; **pump** Schnappgalye (der)n.

levity Leichtsinn (der)n.

lewd 1.dreckich, adj.; 2.lidderlich, adj.; 3.schmutzich, adj.; **woman** Zottel (der, die)n.

liable to decay verweslich, adj.

liar 1.Liegner (der)n.; 2.Lingner (der)n.; Lingner, pl.

liberal liberaal, adj.; **(in giving)** freigew(w)ich, adj.

liberate frei/setze, v.; freigsetzt, pp.

liberty Freiheit (die)n.

Libra (7th sign of the zodiac) Woog (die)n.; Wooge, pl.

licentious lidderlich, adj.

lick 1.lecke, v.; g(e)leckt, pp.; 2.Schleck (der)n.; 3.schlecke, v.; gschleckt, pp.; **all over** verschlecke, v.; verschleckt,, pp.; **off** ab/schlecke, v.; abscheckt, pp.; **out** aus/schlecke, v.; ausgschleckt, pp.; **out of** raus/schlecke, v.; rausgschlekt, pp.

lickspittle Leckaarsch (der)n.

licorice Lickerisch (der)n.; **root** Siessholz (es)n.; **stick** Siessholswatzel (die)n.

lid Deckel (der)n.

lie liege, v.; geloge, pp.; **(to someone)** eibrenne, v.; eigebrennt, pp. (eeni --); **against** wedder/leie, v.; weddergelegge, pp.; **around** rum/leie, v.;

(Continued on page 311)

lie (continued)

(Continued from page 310)

rumgelegge, pp.; **at full length** 1.aus/schtrecke (sich --)v.; ausgschtreckt, pp.; 2.hie/schtrecke (sich --)v.; hiegschtreckt, pp.; **back** zerick/leie, v.; zerickgelegge, pp.; **beside each other** newenannerleie, adv.; **down** 1.anne/lege (sich --)v.; anneglegt, pp.; 2.hie/leie (sich --)v.; hiegelegge, pp.; 3.kusche (sich --)v.; gekuscht, pp.; **flat** (after having been blown or knocked down) umleie, v.; umgelegge, pp.; **in ambush** uff/laure, v.; uffgelauert, pp.; **in wait** 1.ab/lauere, v.; abgelauert, pp.; 2.lauere, v.; gelauert, pp.; 3.no(och)drachde, v.; no(och)gedracht, pp.; **open** uff/leie, v.; uffgelegge, pp.

life Lewe (es)n.; Lewe, pl.; **insurance** Lewe(n)sversicherung (die)n.

lifelong 1.lewe(ns)lang, adv.; 2.leweslang, adv.

lifetime 1.Lewe(n)szeit (die)n.; 2.Leweszeit (die)n.

lift aa/hewe, v.; aaghowe, pp.; **(as a fog)** ab/newwle, v.; abgenewwelt, pp.; **around** rum/hewe, v.; rumgghowe, pp.; **away** 1.weck/hewe, v.; weckghowe, pp.; 2.weck/lifte, v.; **in** rei/hewe, v.; reighowe, pp.; **off** ab/hewe, v.; abghowe, pp.; **out** raus/hewe, v.; raughowe, pp.; **slightly** lippe, v.; gelippt, pp.; **up** 1.nuff/hewe, v.; nuffghowe, pp.; 2.ruff/hewe, v.; ruffghowe, pp.; 3.uff/hewe, v.; uffghowe, pp.; **with a lever** schnebbe, v.; gschneppt, pp.

lifter (for stove plates) 1.Offeeise (es)n.; 2.Hewer (der)n.

ligament Gliederband (es)n.

ligature Band (es)n.; Benner, pl.

light 1.aa/fei(e)re, v.; aagfeirt, pp.; 2.leicht, adj.; 3.Licht (es)n.; Lichder, pl.; **(a fire)** aa/mache, v.; aagemacht, pp.; **(a person) up stairs** nuff/leichte, v.; nuffggeleicht, pp.; **(of cake)** luck, adj.; **(of day)** hell, adj.; **(the lamp)** aa/schtecke, v.; aagschteckt, pp. (es Licht --); **blue** hellblo, adj.; **coat** Kittel (es)n.; **cover for horses in flying time** Geilsdeck (die)n.; **footed** leichtfiessich, adj. **gray** hellgro, adj.; **lunch** Imbiss (der)n.; **of day** Daageslicht (es)n.; **one's way** leichte, v.; geleicht, pp.; **one's way in** rei/leichte, v.; reigeleicht, pp.; **red** hellrot, adj.; **someone's way out** raus/leichte, v.; rausgeleicht, pp.; **the way across** niwwer/leichte, v.; niwwergeleicht, pp.; **the way after** (someone) no(och)leichte, v.; no(och)geleicht, pp.; **the way out** naus/leichte, v.; nausgeleicht, pp.; **up** uff/leichte, v.; uffgeleicht, pp.

lighten 1.blitze, v.; geblitzt, pp.; 2.erleichtere, v.; erleichtert, pp.; 3.leichte, v.; geleicht, pp.; 4.verleichtere, v.; verleichtert, pp.; 5.wedderleeche, v.; gewedderleecht, pp.; 6.wedderleichde, v.; gewedderleicht, pp.

lighter 1.Leichter (der)n.; 2.leichter, adv.

lightness Leichtichkeet (die)n.

lightning 1.Blitz (der)n.; 2.Wedderleech (der)n.; **bug** 1.Feierkeffer (der)n.; Feierkeffer, pl.; 2.Feiervoggel (der)n.; Feierveggel, pl.; **rod** 1.G(e)widderrut (die)n.; 2.Gwidderschtang (der)n.; Gwidderschtange, pl.; 3.Wedderrut (die)n.

like 1.aa/schteh, v.; aagschtanne, pp.; 2.gaern, adv.

linseed oil

(-- hawwe); 3.gfalle, v.; gfalle, pp.; 4.gleiche, v.; gegliche, pp.; 5.liewe, v.; geliebt, pp.; 6.wie, prep.; **everything** 1.Aart (die)n. (noch aller --); 2.Ort (die)n. (noch aller --); **her** ihresgleiche, adj. **likeable** leid(l)ich, adj.

liked beliebt, adj.

likelihood Waahrscheinlichkeet (die)n.

likely to gaern, adv.

likeminded gleichsinnt, adj.

liken vergleiche, v.; vergliche, pp.

likeness Bild (es)n.; Bilder, pl.

likewise gleicherweis, adv.

liking to eat gaern, adv. (-- esse)

lilac 1.Lelack (der)n.; 2.Pingschtblumm (die)n.; Pingschtblumme, pl.; 3.Pingschtnaggel (der)n.; 4.Pingschtblumm (die)n.; Pingschtblumme, pl.; **bush** Pingschtblummeschtock (der)n.; Pingschtblummeschteck, pl.

lily Lilye (die)n.; **of the valley** Moiblumm (die)n.; Moiblumme, pl.; **pads** Maerrebletter (die)n., pl.

lima bean Butterbohn (die)n.

limb Glied (es)n.; Glieder; Glidder, pl.; **(of a tree)** 1.Ascht (der)n. (rare usage;) 2.Briggel (der)n.; 3.Nascht (der)n.; Nescht, pl.; 4.Priggel (der)n.

limber lummerich, adj.

Limburger cheese Limbaeryer kees (der)n.

lime 1.Kallich (der)n.; 2.Kallick (der)n.; 3.kallicke, v.; gekallickt, pp.; **water** Kallichwasser (es)n.

limeburner Kallichbrenner (der)n.

limekiln Kallichhoffe (der)n.; Kallicheffe, pl.

limestone Kallichschtee (der)n.; **quarry** Kallichschteebruch (der)n.; **soil** Kallichschteebodde (der)n.

limit 1.End (es)n.; Ender, Enner, pl.; 2.Grens (die)n.; 3.Taermin (der)n.

limp 1.hickle, v.; ghickelt, pp.; 2.lummerich, adj.; 3.schnappe, v.; gschnappt, pp.; **about** rum/schnappe, v.; rumgschnappt, pp.; **after** no(och)hickle, v.; no(och)ghickelt, pp.; **back** zerick/schnappe, v.; zerickgschnappt, pp.; **over** niwwer/schnappe, v.; niwwergschnappt, pp.

limy kalkich, adj.

linchpin 1.Lone (der)n.; 2.Lune (der)n.

linden tree 1.Linne (die)n.; 2.Linnebaam (der)n.

line 1.Schtriche (der)n.; Schtriche, pl.; 2.Zeil (die)n. (rare usage;) **a garment** fudere, v.; gfudert, pp.; **out a hymn** vor/saage, v.; vorgsaat, pp.; **with a wall** aus/mauere, v.; ausgemauert, pp.

linen 1.flexe, adj.; 2.leine, adj.; 3.leinich, adj.

linger 1.rum/henke, v.; rumghenkt, pp.; 2.verweile, v.; verweilt, pp.

linguist Schprochkenner (der)n.

lining (of a garment) Fuder (es)n.

link 1.Glaech (der)n.; 2.Klaech (der)n.; **(in a chain)** Gleech (es)n.; Gleeche(r), pl.

linseed 1.Flaxsome (der)n.; 2.Flaxsume (der)n.; **oil** 1.Lei(n)olich (der)n.; 2.Olich (der)n.

Ll

linsey-woolsey / lock

linsey-woolsey 1.halbleine, adj.; 2.halbleinich, adj.

lint Gfusser (es)n.

lion Leeb (der)n.; Leewe, pl.; **cub** Leebli (es)n.

lion's foot 1.Deiwelsabbis (watzel) (die)n.;
    2. Rasselschlangwatzel (die)n.;
    3.Klapperschlangewatzel (die)n.

lip 1.Lefts (die)n.; Leftse, pl.; 2.Lipp (die)n.

liquid 1.brie(h)ich, adj.; 2.flissich, adj.; 3.wesserich, adj.;
    medicine Droppe (die)n., pl.

lisp 1.laerbse, v.; gelaerbst, pp.; 2.lischble, v.; gelischbelt,
    pp.; 3.schlarbse, v.; gschlarebst, pp.

list Lischt (die)n.

listen 1.folye, v.; gfol(i)gt, pp.; 2.lauschdere, v.;
    gelauschdert, pp.; 3.lausche, v.; gelauscht, pp.;
    4.uff/harriche, v.; uffgharricht, pp.; 5.zuharriche, v.;
    zugharricht, pp.; 6.zuheere, v.; zugheert, pp.; **surrep-**
    titiously no(och)lauschdere, v.; no(och)gelauschdert,
    pp.; **to** 1.aa/hariche, v.; aagharicht, pp.; 2.aa/heere,
    v.; aagheert, pp.; **to what is going on** (upon the
    other side) niwwer/harriche, v.; niwwergharricht, pp.

listener 1.Abharicher (der)n.; Abharicher, pl.; 2.Zuheerer
    (der)n.

listless saumselich, adj.

lit brennend, adj.

litany Litanei (die)n.

literal waertlich, adj.

litharge Silwerglett (die)n.

lithograph Schteedruck (der)n.

litigate schtreide, v.; gschtridde, pp.

litter (of pigs) 1.Brud (die)n.; 2.Brut (der)n.; 3.Bruud (die)
    n.; **(of sows)** waerfe, v.

little 1.bissel, adj.; 2.Bissli (es)n.; 3.glee, adj.; **(small**
    amount) Bissel (es)n.; **bag** 1.Seckche (es)n.; 2.Seckli (es)
    n.; Secklin, pl.; **basket** 1.Karebche (es)n.; 2.Karwel (es)
    n.; 3.Karwli (es)n.; **bench** Benkel (es)n.; **bird**
    1.Veggelche (es)n.; 2.Veggli (es)n.; Vegglin, pl.; **bit**
    Schleck (der)n.; **book** Bichelche (es)n.; **boy** 1.Biebche
    (es)n.; 2.Bubli (es)n.; 3.Buwli (es)n.; Buwlin, pl.; **boy's**
    trousers Hesselcher (die)n., pl.; **cake** Kichelche (es)n.;
    cap Keppsche (es)n.; **chicken** Hinkelche (es)n.; **drop**
    Dreppsche (es)n.; **fellow** 1.Grips(er) (der)n.; 2.Knaerps
    (der)n.; **fish** Fischel (es)n.; **flower** Blimmche (es)n.;
    garden 1.Gaerdli (es)n.; 2.Geardel (es)n.; **glass** (full)
    1.Glessel (es)n.; 2.Glessli (es)n.; **hat** Hietche (es)n.;
    heap 1.Heifel (es)n.; 2.Heifli (es)n.; **hole** 1.Lechel (es)n.;
    2.Lechli (es)n.; Lechlin, pl.; **hook** Heekel (es)n.; **house**
    Heisel (es)n.; **man** 1.Mennche (es)n.; 2.Mennli (es)n.;
    Mennlin, pl.; **meadow** Schwemmche (es)n.; **moustache**
    Schnurbaerdli (es)n.; **off in the head** kampes mentis
    (net gans --); **ox** Exli (es)n.; Exlin, pl.; **peg** Zebbche (es)
    n.; **piece of paper** Babierche (es)n.; **piece of wood**
    Helsel (es)n.; **pig** 1.Millichseiche (es)n.; 2.Seili (es)n.;
    3.Witzel (es)n.; 4.Wutzelche (es)n.; 5.Wutzi (es)n.;
    .Wutzlein (es)n.; **pitcher** 1.Grickche (es)n.; 2.Grickelche
    (es)n.; 3.Griggelche (es)n.; **porch** 1.Paertschli (es)n.;
    2.Schtuf (die)n.; **pot** 1.Heffel (es)n.; 2.Heffli (es)n.; **ras-**
    cal Zickel (es)n.; **sausage** waerschtche (es)n.; **screech**

---

owl Schteekeizli (es)n.; **shirt** 1.Hemmche (es)n.;
    2.Hemmli (es)n.; **spoon** Leffli (es)n.; Lefflin, pl.; **thing**
    Dingel(che) (es)n.; **tree** Beemche (es)n.; **wheel for cut-**
    ting out cake dough Reddel (es)n.; **woman** Weiwel (es)
    n.; **worm** Waermche (es)n.; **less; least** wennich;
    wennicher; es wennichscht, adj.

live 1.er(n)naehre (sich --)v.; ernaehert, pp.; 2.lewendich, adj.

live (reside) 1.wohne, v.; gwohnt, pp.; 2.wuhne, v.;
    gewuhnt, pp.; **at a distance** 1.ab/wohne, v.;
    abgewohnt, pp.; 2.ab/ wuhne, v.; abgewuhnt, pp.;
    for-ever Lewe(n)sgraut (es)n.; **in different places**
    rumhaer/wohne, v.; rumhaergewohnt, pp.; **on good**
    terms (with) aus/kumme, v.; is auskumme, pp.; **over**
    iwwerlewe, v.; iwwergelebt, pp.; **together**
    1.zamme/lewe, v.; zammegelebt, pp.;
    2.zamme/wohne, v.; zammegewohnt, pp.; **together**
    (man and wife) hause, v.; ghaust, pp. (-- menanner);
    within one's means aus/kumme, v.; is auskumme, pp.

livelihood 1.Lewe (es)n.; 2.Lewe(n)sunerhalt (der)n.

liveliness Munterkeet (die)n.

lively 1.flink, adj.; 2.lebhaft, adj.; 3.lewendich, adj.;
    4.lewich, adj.; 5.munder, adj.; 6.wusslich, adj.

liver Lewwer (die)n.; Lewwere, pl.; **grown** aagwaxe, adj.;
    pudding Lewwerwascht (die)n.; **spots** Lewwerflecke
    (die)n., pl.

liverwort Lewwergraut (es)n.

liverwurst 1.Lewwerfillsell (es)n.; 2.Liwwerwascht (die)n.

livid 1.schwarzunblo, adj.; 2.schwatzunblo, adj.

living 1.Lewe (es)n.; 2.lewendich, adj.

lizard 1.Eidechs (der)n.; 2.Ildechs (der)n.

Lizzie Liss(i) (die)n.

load 1.Laad (die)n.; Laade, pl.; 2.laade, v.; glaade, pp.;
    3.Lascht (die)n.; 4.uff/laade, v.; uffgelaade, pp.; **over**
    iwwerlaade, v.; iwwergelaade, pp.

loaf 1.bamble, v.; gebambelt, pp.; 2.faulense, v.;
    gfaulenst, pp.; 3.rum/henke, v.; rumghenkt, pp.;
    4.rum/hocke, v.; rumghockt, pp.; 5.rum/leie, v.;
    rumgelegge, pp.; **(of bread)** 1.Laeb (der)n.; 2.Leeb
    (der)n.; **around** 1.rumhaer/leie, v.; rumhaergelegge,
    pp.; 2.rum/lodle, v.; rumgelodelt, pp.; **sugar**
    Hutzucker (der)n.

loafer 1.Daagdieb (der)n.; 2.Faulenzer (der)n.; Faulenzer,
    pl.; 3.Rumleefer (der)n.; Rumleefer, pl.

loan 1.barge, v.; gebarkt, pp.; 2.barye, v.; gebarigt, pp.;
    3.lehne, v.; g(e)lehnt, pp.; 4.weck/lehne, v.;
    weckglehnt, pp.; **(to others)** verlehne, v.; verlehnt, pp.

loath unwillich, adj.

loathsomeness 1.Ekelhaftichkeit (die)n.;
    2.Ekelheftichkeet (die)n.

lobe of the lung Lungefliggel (der)n.

local ordlich, adj.

locate finne, v.; gfunne, pp.

location 1.Blatz (der)n.; Bletz, pl.; 2.Schtellung (die)n.

lock 1.schliesse, v.; gschlosse, pp.; 2.Schloss (es)n.;
    Schlesser, pl.; 3.Wischel (es)n.; 4.Wischli (es)n.;

(Continued on page 313)

Ll

lock (continued)

(Continued from page 312)

5.zuschliesse, v.; zugschlosse, pp.; **(of a canal of dam)** Schliess (die)n.; **(up)** verschliesse, v.; verschlosse, pp.; **in** 1.nei/schpaerre, v.; neigschpaert, pp.; 2.nei/ schparre, v.; neigschpatt, pp.; **of a rifle** Bixeschloss (es)n.; **of wool** Locke (der)n.; **out** 1.aus/schliesse, v.; ausgschlosse, pp.; 2.naus/schleese, v.; nausgschlosse, pp.;3.raus/schpaerre, v.; rausgschpaerrt, pp.; **up** 1.ei/schliesse, v.; eigschlosse, pp.; 2.ei/ schparre, v.; eigschpatt, pp.; 3.eischtecke, v.; eigschteckt, pp.; **with bolt** Riggelschloss (es)n.

locks lockich, adj.

locksmith Schlosser (der)n.; Schlosser, pl.

locomotive Inschein (der)n.; Inscheine, pl.

lodge loschiere, v.; loschiert, pp.; **information against** aa/gewwe, v.; is aagewwe, pp.

loft (above the barn floor) 1.Iwwerdenn (es)n.; 2.Owwerdenn (es)n.

log Block (der)n.; Bleck, pl.; **barn** Blockscheier (die)n.; Blockscheiere, pl.; **cabin** Blockhaus (es)n.; Blockheiser, pl.; **chain** 1.Blockkett (die)n.; Blockedde, pl.; 2.Schparkett (die)n.; Schparkedde, pl.; **hut** Blockheisli (es)n.; Blockheislin, pl.; **to be sawed up** Saegblock (der)n.

logging sled Blockschlidde (der)n.

logwood Blohols (es)n.

loin Rickmeesel (der)n.; **(roast)** Niereschtick (es)n.

loiter 1.bamble, v.; gebambelt, pp.; 2.rum/bamble, v.; rumgebambelt, pp.; 3.rum/schlaudere, v.; rumgschlaudert, pp.; 4.rum/schteh, v.; rumgschtanne, pp.; 5.rumher/schleiche, v.; rumhergschliche, pp.; 6.vergaffe (sich --)v.; vergafft, pp.; **about** rumher/schteh, v.; rumhergschtanne, pp.

loitering Gebembel (es)n.

Lombardy poplar 1.Hausbabble (die)n.; 2.Freiheitsbaam (der)n.

lonesome leedmiedich, adj.

long 1.lang, adj.; 2.langhi, adv.; 3.peine, v.; gepeint, pp.; 4.sehne (sich --)v.; gsehnt, pp.; 5.weit, adj.; **ago** lang zerick, adv.; **drawn out** langschichtich, adj.; **eared** langohrich, adj.; **faced** langsichtich, adj.; **footed** landfiessich, adj.; **for the bull** (of cows) bulle, v.; gebullt, pp.; **haired** langhoorich, adj.; **handled** langschtlelich, adj.; **illness** pehz, adj.; **in coming** aus/bliewe, v.; ausgebliwwe, pp.; **in happening** wedder/halte, v.; wedderghalte, pp. (hart --); **legged** langbeenich, adj.; **necked person** Genshals (der)n.; **nosed** langnaesich, adj.; **sleeper** Siwweschleafer (der)n.; **tailed** langschwensich, adj.; **wick end** (on a burning fat light Butze (der)n.; **winded** langwindich, adj.; **winded talk** 1.Briambel (der)n.; 2.Gebreddich (es)n.; **longer; longest** lang; lenger; lengscht, adj.

longing 1.Aalanges (es)n.; 2.Sehnsucht (die)n.; 3.Verlange (es)n.; 4.Zeitlang (es)n.; **desire** sehne (sich --)v.; gsehnt, pp.; **for home** aa/heemle, v.; aagheemelt, pp.; **longish** langlich, adj.

Lord's Prayer

look 1.aus/sehne, v.; ausgsehne, pp.; 2.Blick (der)n.; 3.dreisehne, v.; 4.Guck (der)n.; 5.gucke, v.; geguckt, pp.; 6.sehne, v.; gsehne, pp.; **(on)** dreigucke, adj.; **about** umduh, v.; umgeduh, pp.; **across** niwwer/gucke, v.; niwwergeguckt, pp.; **after** 1.no(och)blicke, v.; no(och)geblickt, pp.; 2.no(och)gucke, v.; no(och)geguckt, pp.; 3.no(och)sehne, v.; no(och)gsehnt, pp.; 4.umduh, v.; umgeduh, pp.; **around** 1.rum/gucke, v.; rumgeguckt, pp.; 2.rumhaer/gucke, v.; rumhaergeguckt, pp.; 3.um/sehne (sich --)v.; umgsehne, pp.; **at** 1.aa/blicke, v.; aageblickt, pp.; 2.aa/gucke, v.; aageguckt, pp.; 3.aa/ schaue, v.; aagschaut, pp.; 4.aa/seh(n)e, v.; aagsehne, pp.; **away** weck/gucke, v.; weckgeguckt, pp.; **back** 1.zerick/gucke, v.; zerickgeguckt, pp.; 2.zerick/sehne, v.; zerickgsehnt, pp.; **daggers** grinse, v.; gegrinst, pp.; **down** nunner/gucke, v.; nunnergeguckt, pp.; **for** suche, v.; gsucht, pp.; **forward to** schpitze, v.; gschpitzt, pp. (sich uff ebbes --); **in** 1.rei/gucke, v.; reigeguckt, pp.; 2.nei/gucke, v.; neigeguckt, pp.; **on** 1.druffgucke, v.; druffgeguckt, pp.; 2.zugucke, v.; zugeguckt, pp.; 3.zusehne, v.; zugsehne, pp.; **out** 1.naus/gucke, v.; nausgeguckt, pp.; 2.naus/sehne, v.; nausgsehne, pp.; 3.raus/gucke, v.; rausgeguckt, pp.; 4.raus/sehne, v.; rausgsehne, pp.; **over** 1.iwwergucke, v.; iwwerguckt; iwwergeguckt, pp.; 2.riwwer/gucke, v.; riwwergeguckt, pp.; **sheepish** schibbich gucke, v.; **there** hie/gucke, v.; hiegeguckt, pp.; **through** 1.darich/gucke, v.; darichgeguckt, pp.; 2.darich/sehne, v.; darichgsehne, pp.; **until one is tired** (in expecting some one or in staring) ausgucke, v.; ausgeguckt, pp. (sich die aage --); **up** 1.nuff/gucke, v.; nuffgeguckt, pp.; 2.ruff/gucke, v.; ruffgeguckt, pp.; 3.uff/blicke, v.; uffgeblickt, pp.; 4.uff/gucke, v.; uffgeguckt, pp.; 5.uff/suche, v.; uffgsucht, pp.

loom Webschtul (der)n.; Webschtiel, pl.

loop Schlupp (der)n.; Schlipp, pl.

loophole Schlupploch (es)n.

loose 1.lodd(e)rich, adj.; 2.lodder, adj.; 3.los, adj.; **girl** Buwerutsch (die)n.; **jointed** schlenkerich, adj.; **woman** 1.Glund (die)n.; 2.Ritsch (die)n.; 3.Rutsch (die)n.

loose strife Widderkumm (der)n.

loosen 1.los/mache, v.; losgemacht, pp.; 2.raus/loddle, v.; rausgeloddelt, pp.; 3.uff/lockere, v.; uffgelockert, pp.; **by blasting** los/schprenge, v.; losgschprengt, pp.; **by harrowing** uff/eege, v.; uffge-eekt, pp.; **by shaking or tapping** lockere, v.; gelockert, pp.; **by softening** los/weeche, v.; losgeweecht, pp.

lopsided 1.schepp, adj.; 2.scheppseidich, adj.

loquacious boberich, adj.

Lord 1.Harr (der)n.; 2.Herr (der)n.

Lord's Prayer Vadderunser (es)n.; **Supper** 1.Abendmahl (es)n.; 2.Awendmohl (es)n.

Ll

lordship

lordship (also used as an expletive) Haerrschaft (die)n.

lose 1.eibiesse, v.; eigebiesst, pp.; 2.verliere, v.; verlore, pp.; **all semblence** (of corpses) gucke, v.; geguckt, pp. (sich nix meh gleich --); **color** bleeche, v.; gebleecht, pp.; **flesh** 1.ab/falle, v.; abgfalle, pp.; 2.(as in illness) weck/falle, v.; weckgfalle, pp.; **in hauling or handling** verzottle, v.; verzottelt, pp.; **odor** verrieche, v.; verroche, pp.; **one's footing** aus/ritsche, v.; ausgeritscht, pp.; **one's money** um, prep. (-- sei geld kumme); **one's way** 1.verdappe (sich --)v.; verdappt, pp.; 2.verlaafe (sich --)v.; verloffe, pp.; **weight** ab/nemme, v.; abgenumme, pp.; **with age** verwaxe, v.; verwaxe, pp.

loss Verluscht (der)n.

lost color 1.ausgebleecht, adj.; 2.verschosse, adj.; **in amazement** verwatzle (sich --)v.; verwatzelt, pp.

lot 1.Lossement (es)n.; 2.Volk (es)n.; **(in derision)** 1.Blandaasch(e) (die)n.; 2.Plandaasch (die)n.

lottery Lodderie (die)n.

loud 1.hell, adj.; 2.laut, adj.; **report** 1.Gnall (der)n.; 2.Grach (der)n.; 3.Knall (der)n.

Louisa Luwies (die)n.

lounge 1.faulense, v.; gfaulenst, pp.;2.rumher/sitze, v.; rumhergsitzt, pp.; **around** rum/noddle, v.; rumgenodelt, pp.

louse Laus (die)n.; Leis, pl.

lovage 1.Liebgreitel (es)n.; 2.Liebschteckel (es)n.

love 1.Lieb (die)n.; 2.Liebschdi (die)n.; 3.liewe, v.; geliebt, pp.; **letter** Liewesbrief (der)n.; **powder** Liewespulwer (es)n.

lovely 1.herrlich, adj.; 2.lieblich, adj., adv.

lover Liebhawwer (der)n.; **of children** Kinnerfreind (der) n.; **of flowers** Blummaefreind (der)n.; **of horses** Geilsmann (der)n.

lovesick kaesich, adj.

Low German Blattdeitsch (es)n.

low 1.leis, adj.; 2.nidder, adj.; **(animal)** 1.blaerre, v.; geblaerrt, pp.; 2.blarre, v.; geblatt, pp.; **down** infaam(t), adj.; **mallow** Hemmerknepp (die)n., pl.; **mass** Mess (die)n. (en schtilli --); **murmuring** 1.Gebrummel (es)n.; 2.Grummel (es)n.

lower 1.nidder/losse, v.; nidderglosst, pp.; 2.unner, adj. **part** Unnerdeel (es)n.

lowliness Niddrichkeit (die)n.

lowly niddrich, adv.

lozenge 1.Kichelche (es)n.; 2.Kichli (es)n.; Kichlin, pl.

lubricate 1.eele, v.; ge-eelt, pp.; 2.ei/schmiere, v.; eigschmiert, pp.; 3.schmiere, v.; gschmiert, pp.; 4.schmutze, v.; gschmutzt, pp.

lucky glicklich, adj.

ludicrous lecherich, adj.

luggage Sack (der)n. (-- un Pack)

lukewarm 1.lauwaarm, adj.; 2.lo, adj.; 3.lowaarm, adv.

lullaby 1.Schockellied (es)n.; 2.Wiegelied (es)n.

lumbago 1.Buckelweh (es)n.; 2.Greiz (es)n. (im -- hawwe); 3. Greizweh (es)n.; 4.Kreiz (es)n. (im -- hawwe); 5.Rickweh (es)n.

lynx

lumber room Kemmerli (es)n.

lump 1.Glumbe (der)n.; 2.glumpe; v.; geglumpt, pp.; 3.Klumpe (der)n.; 4.Knopp (der)n.; 5.Schiwwel (der) n.; **(of earth)** Erdscholle (der)n.; **(of ice)** 1.Eisglumpe (der)n.; 2.Eisschiwwel (der)n.; **(of sugar)** 1.Gnolle (der)n.; 2.Zuckergnolle (der)n.

lumpy 1.glumbich, adj.; 2.gnoddlich, adj.; 3.gnollich, adj.; 4.klumpich, adj.; 5.knollich, adj.

lunatic 1.mondgrank, adj.; 2.Moondkalb (es)n.; 3.Narr (der)n.; Narre, pl.; 4.verrickt, adj.

lunch 1.Ess-schtick (es)n.; 2.Neweschtick (es)n.

lung Lung (die)n.; Lunge, pl.

lungwort Lungegraut (es)n.

lupine Wolfsbuhn (die)n.

lurk lauere, v.; gelauert, pp.

lurker Ufflauerer (der)n.

luscious luschderich, adj.

lustre Glanz (der)n.

Lutheran 1.ludderisch, adj.; 2.luderisch, adj.; 3.Lutteraaner (der)n.; 4.luttrisch, adj.

luxurious (of plants) mascht, adj.

lye Laag (die)n.

lympy Gliedwasser (es)n.

lynx Lucha (der)n.

Mm

mace — make

mace Muschkaadbliet (die)n.
machine Maschien (die)n.; Maschiene, pl.
machinery Maschienerie (die)n.
mad 1.bees, adj.; 2.doll, adj.; 3.haernwiedich,
adj.;4.narrisch, adj.; 5.verrickt, adj.; 6.wiedich, adj.;
mad-dog 1.Kappegraut (es)n.; 2.Wutgraut (es)n.; **dog**
Hund (der)n. (en beeser --) (en doller --)
mad-stone Wutschtee (der)n.
madder 1.Grapp (der)n.; 2.Krapp (der)n.
made of calico kaddunich, adj.; **of glass** glaase, adj.; **of**
gnoddelwoll gnoddelwolle, adj.; **of wool** wille, adj.
madly deiwelheftich, adj.
madness Raaserei (die)n.
madweed Wutgraut (es)n.
maggots Niss (die)n., pl.
maggoty lewendich, adj.
magic Hexerei (die)n.
magic bag (for curing a membrane over the pupil of the
eye) Fellgnopp (der)n.
magician 1.Banner (der)n.; 2.Hexemeeschder (der)n.
magnanimity Grossmut (der)n.
magnanimous grosshatzich, adj.
magnesia Bitteraerd (die)n.
magnet Magneet (es)n.
magnificence 1.Bracht (die)n.; 2.Pracht (die)n.
magnificent 1.brachtvoll, adj.; 2.prachtvoll, adj.
magnify vergreesere, v.; vergreesert, pp.
magnifying glass Vergreeseringsglaas (es)n.
maid Maad (die)n.; Maade, pl.
maiden 1.Meedche (es)n.; 2.Meedel (es)n.; Meed, pl.;
name Naame (der)n. (ledderlich --)
mail Meel (die)n.
maim vergripple, v.; vergrippelt, pp.
main beam (in a building) Darichzuck (der)n.; **building**
Haaptgebei (es)n.; **point or matter** Haaptwese (es)n.
mainly haaptsechlich, adv.
maintain 1.behaapde, v.; behaapt, pp.; 2.behapde, v.;
behapt, pp.; 3.erhalde, v.; erhalde, pp.
maintenance 1.Unnerhalt (der)n.; 2.Erhaltung (die)n.
majority 1.Mehrheet (die)n.; 2.Mehrheit (die)n.;
3.Mehrzaahl (die)n.
make mache, v.; gemacht, pp.; **(a garment) narrower or**
smaller einemme, v.; eigenumme, pp.; **(someone)**
believe something weis/mache, v.; weisgemacht,
pp.; **a big ado** rumpere, v.; gerumpert, pp.; **a big**
spread for someone uff/wische, v.; uffgewischt, pp.;
a blunder vergesse (sich --)v.; vergesse, pp.; **a com-**
plaint 1.aa/gewwe, v.; is aagewwe, pp.; 2.beglaage
(sich --)v.; beglaagt, pp. 3.verglaage, v.; verglaagt,
pp.; **a dash for** 1.druffloss/geh, v.; drufflossgange,
pp.; 2.los/geh, v.; losgange, pp. (druff --); **a detour**
1.um/faahre, v.; umgfaahre, pp.; 2.um/geh, v.;
ungange, pp.; **a face** Schnut (die)n. (en -- mache); **a**
fire better uff/feiere, v.; uffgfeiert, pp.; **a first bid**
aa/biede, v.; aagebodde, pp.; **a fool of** Narr (der)n.
(fer en -- halde); **a gurgling sound in the throat**

kollere, v.; gekollert, pp.; **a hole** (in a case or package) aa/breche, v.; aagebroche, pp.; **a hole by burn-**
ing darich/brenne. v.; darichgbrennt, pp.; **a labori-**
ous journey over niwwer/kessle, v.;
niwwergekesselt, pp.; **a laughing stock of** hensle, v.;
g(e)henselt, pp.; **a living** er(n)naehre (sich --)v.;
ernaehert, pp.; **a long, sour, distorted, terrible face**
Gsicht (es)n. (en lang, sauer, verdreht,
wiescht -- mache); **a loud report** 1.gnalle, v.;
gegnellt, pp.; 2.gnelle, v.; gegnellt, pp.; 3.knalle, v.;
geknallt, pp.; **a mark through** darich/schtreiche, v.;
darichgschtriche, pp.; **a mistake** fehl/greife, v.; fehlgegriffe, pp.; **a mistake in calculating** verrechle (sich
--)v.; verechelt, pp.; **a nest** 1.neschde, v.; genescht,
pp.; 2.nischde (sich --)v.; genischt, pp.; **a noise**
1.laerme, v.; gelaermt, pp. ; 2.rum/laerme, v.;
rumgelaermt, pp.; 3.rumore, v.; gerumort, pp.; **a**
noise in going around rum/glebbere, v.;
rumgeglebbert, pp.; **a note** aamarricke, v.;
aagemarrickt, pp.; **a present** 1.b(e)schenke, v.;
b(e)schenkt, pp.; 2.schenke, v.; gschenkt, pp.;
3.verschenke, v.; verschenkt, pp.; **a racket** haapere,
v.; ghaapert, pp.; **a report** 1.grache, v.; gegracht, pp.;
2.krache, v.; gekracht, pp.; **a rush** los/faahre, v.;
losgfaahre, pp.; **a shortcut** zu/schtrecke, v.;
zugschtreckt, pp.; **a show of oneself** ab/weise (sich --
)v.; abgewisse, pp.; **a smacking sound** schmatze, v.;
gschmatzt, pp.; **a specialty of** lege (sich --)v.; gelegt,
pp. (sich uff ebbes --); **a square turn in plowing**
rum/drehe, v.; rumgedreht, pp.; **a stack** schtocke, v.;
gschtockt, pp.; **a way or path through snow** baahne,
v.; gebaahnt, pp.; **an additional payment**
no(och)bezaahle, v.; no(och)bezaahlt, pp.; **an agree-**
ment 1.ab/schliesse, v.; abgschlosse, pp.;
2.abschliesse, v.; abgschlosse, pp.; **an arrangement**
aakediere, v.; aakediert, pp.; **awkward movements**
verhaschble (sich --)v.; **dirty** 1.dreckich mache, v.;
dreckich gemacht, pp.; 2.versaue, v.; versaut, pp.;
full of creases verrumple, v.; verrumpelt, pp.; **glad**
erfreie, v.; erfreit, pp.; **good** 1.gut/mache, v.;
gutgemacht, pp.; 2.raus/schlagge (sich --)n.;
rausgschlagge, pp.; **happy** beglicke, v.; beglickt, pp.;
hay Hoi mache, v.; gemacht, pp.; **inquiry about**
aa/froge, v.; aagfrogt, pp.; **inroads** 1.eigreife, v.;
eigegreifen, pp.; 2.eireisse, v.; eigerisse, pp.; **insinu-**
ating allusions schtichle, v.; gschtichelt, pp.; **it con-**
venient schicke mache, v.; gemacht, pp.; **it hot for**
someone schwewwle, v.; gschwewwelt, pp.; **known**
melde, v.; gemeldt, pp.; **less** verwenniche, v.;
verwennicht, pp.; **marks on** vermaericke, v.;
vermaerickt, pp.; **motions** rum/faawle, v.;
rumgfaawelt, pp.; **noise** yachde, v.; gyacht, pp.; **oath**
schweere, v.; gschwore, pp.; **one believe** eischwetze,
v.; eigschwetzt, pp.; **one feel at home** aa/heemle, v.;
aagheemelt, pp.; **one shudder** 1.grause, v.; gegraust,

(Continued on page 316)

Mm

make (continued)   March

(Continued from page 315)

pp.; 2.grissle, v.; gegrisselt, pp.; 3.krissle, v.;
gekrisselt, pp.; **one's computation too high**
iwwerrechle (sich --)v.; iwwerrechelt, pp.; **one's way
out** raus/schaffe (sich --)v.; rausgschafft, pp.; **one's
way under difficulties** 1.darich/fresse (sich --)v.;
darichfresse, pp.; 2.darich/schaffe (sich --)v.;
darichgschafft, pp.; **one's will** mache, v.; gemacht,
pp. (sei Wille --); **other arrangements**
1.rum/schtalle, v.; rumgschtallt, pp.; 2.um/schtalle,
v.; umgschtallt, pp.; **out** aus/mache, v.; ausgemacht,
pp.; **over** iwwer/mache, v.; iwwergemacht, pp.;
preparation 1.aaschtalle, v.; aagschtallt, pp.;
2.mache, v.; gemacht, pp. (aaschtalt --); **preparations for meals** (at funerals) uff/rischde, v.;
uffgerischt, pp.; **profit by** benutze, v.; benutzt, pp.;
public raus/gewwe, v.; rausgewwe, pp.; **ready**
1.aa/schicke (sich --)v.; aagschickt, pp.; 2.rischde
(sich --)v.; gerischt, pp.; 3.rischde, v.; g(e)rischt, pp.;
reparations gut, adj. (-- mache); **make room** Blatz
(der)n. (-- mache); **sausage** waerschde, v.;
gewaerscht, pp.; **sharp** schpitze, v.; gschpitzt, pp.;
shift behelfe (sich --)v.; beholfe, pp.; **smaller**
verglennere, v.; verglennert, pp.; **someone believe
something** weis/mache, v.; weisgemacht, pp.; **specialty** (of) lege, v.; gelegt, pp. (sich uff ebbes --);
straight for los/faahre, v.; losgfaahre, pp.; **the bubbling sound of boiling water** kollere, v.; gekollert,
pp.; **the end of the stroke of the scythe** (in mowing
low [high]) aus/hacke, v.; ausghackt, pp.
(nidder [hoch] --); **the rounds** rum/geh, v.;
rumgange, pp.; **untidy** verkutzle, v.; verkutzelt, pp.;
up (to become reconciled) uff/mache, v.;
uffgemacht, pp.; **up by working** no(och)schaffe, v.;
no(och)gschafft, pp.; **use of** aa/bringe, v.;
aagebrocht, pp.

making insinuating allusions Schtichlerei (die)n.
malaria Kaltfiewer (es)n.
male mennlich, adj.; **assistant in kitchen** (and waiter at
table at funerals) Kichedribbel (der)n.; **(of birds)**
1.Hehnli (es)n.; 2.Mennche (es)n.; **being** Mannskall
(der)n.; Mannsleit, pl.; **bumblebee** 1.Weisskopp (der)
n.; Weisskepp, pl.; 2.(which has a white forehead)
Baalhummel (der)n.; **mule** Gaulesel (der)n.; **nurse**
Abwaarder (der)n.; **pig** Ewwer (der)n.; Ewwer, pl.;
pigeon Daubert (der)n.; **servant** Knecht (der)n..;
sexual organs Gemech (es)n.
malevolence Iwwelwolle (es)n.
malice 1.Bo(o)sheet (die)n.; 2.Bosheit (die)n.; 3.Schpeit (der)n.
malicious 1.heemdickisch, adj.; 2.mutwillich, adj.;
3.schaadefroh, adj.; 4.schpeitvoll, adj.; 5.wiescht,
adj.; 6.wieschtgaschdich, adj.
maliciously mutwillicherweis, adv.
maliciousness 1.Beesheet (die)n.; 2.Beesheit (die)n.
mallard duck (male) Griekopp (der)n.; Griekepp, pl.
mallet 1.Hammer (der)n.; (en hilzner --); 2.Schleggel (der)n.

mallow Keesbabbel (die)n.; **seed pod** (in immature state
often eaten by children) 1.Hemmergnebbli (es)n.;
Hemmergnebblin, pl.; 2.Hemmergneppli (es)n.; Hemmergnepplin, pl.
malodorous dunnerschtinkich, adj.
mamma Mammi (die)n.
man 1.Mann (der)n.; Menner; Mansleit,pl.; 2.Mannskall
(der)n.; Mannsleit, pl.; 3.Menner (der)n.; **crazy** mannsleitnarrisch, adj.; **in the moon** Moondkalb (es)n.;
of-the-earth 1.Zaahrieb (die)n.; Zaahriewe, pl.;
2.Zohrieb (die)n.; **of-war** (ship) 1.Griegschiff (es)n.;
2.Grieksschiff (es)n.; **who hauls away dead animals**
Schinnerhannes (der)n.; **with a penchant for wearing
boots**; Schtiwwelmann (der)n.
manage 1.handhawwe, v.; handghat; handghadde,
pp.;2.um/ geh, v.; umgange, pp.; **on** aus/kumme, v.;
is auskumme, pp.; **to get** (oneself) **down** runner/
schaffe (sich --)v.; runnergschafft, pp.; **to get**
(something) **down** runner/schaffe, v.; runnergschafft, pp.; **to get in** rei/schaffe (sich --)v.;
reigschafft, pp.; **to get up** (to a place) nuff/griege, v.;
nuffgrickt, pp.; **with** bschteh, v.; bschtanne, pp.
(debei --)
mandrake 1.Buschabbel (der)n.; 2.Moiabbel (der)n.
mandrel 1.Bixeschtock (der)n.; 2.Ringschtock (der)n.
mane Maahne (die)n.
mangel-wurzel (root) 1.Mangelwazel (die)n.; 2.Mangold
(der)n.; 3.Dickwazel (die)n.; Dickwazle, pl. (Waterloo
Co. Ontario)
manger Fuderdrog (der)n.; Fuderdreeg, pl.
mangy raadich, adj.
manhood Mannheit (die)n.
manifest 1.aus/losse, v.; ausg(e)losst, pp.; 2.offenbaar, adj.
manifold 1.manchfalt, adj.; 2.vielfeldich, adj.
maniplication Vermehrung (die)n.
mankind Mensch (der)n.; Mensche, pl.
manly 1.mannhaft, adj.; 2.mennlich, adj.
manner Weis (die)n.; **of doing anything** Aagschtalt (der)
n.; **of living** Lewensweis (die)n.; **of working** Gschaff
(es)n.
mannerly mannierlich, adv.
manners 1.Manier (die)n.; 2.Mannier (die)n.; 3.Mores
(die)n., pl.
manservant Serwemann (der)n.
manslaughter 1.Do(o)dschlack (der)n.; 2.Ma(r)d (der)n.
mantel Mantel (der)n.
manual Handbuch (es)n.; **on powwowing** Brauchbuch (es)n.
manufacture oil from flaxseed or bitternuts Olich (der)n.
(-- schlagge)
manure 1.bedinge, v.; bedingt, pp.; 2.dinge, v.; gedingt,
gedunge, pp.; 3.mischde, v.; g(e)mischt, pp.;
4.Mischt (der)n.; **fork** Mischtgawwel (die)n.;
Mischtgawwele, pl.; **hook (for unloading manure)**
Mischthoke (der)n.; **juice** Mischtbrieh (die)n.; **pile**
Mischthaufe (der)n.; Mischtheife, pl.; **pile in the**

(Continued on page 317)

316

Mm

manure (continued) — maternal

(Continued from page 316)

barnyard Mischthof (der)n.; Mischthe(e)f, pl.; **sled** 1.Mischtschlidde (der)n.; 2.Schleef (die)n.; 3.Schteeboot (es)n.; Schteeboot, pl.; 4.Schteeschlidde (der)n.; Schteeschlidde, pl.; **spreader** (machine or person) 1.Mischtschpreeder (der)n.; 2.Mischtschpreher (der)n.; **wagon** Mischtwagge (der)n.

many 1.viel, pron; adj.; 2.mannich, adj.; **a time** manichmol, adv.; **kinds of** allerhand, adj.; **times** 1.en mannichmol, adv.; 2.manchmol, adv.; 3.manichmol, adv.

map Landkord (die)n.

maple 1.Meebel (der)n.; 2.Ahorn (der)n. (rare usage); **sap** Zuckerwasser (es)n.; **sap-catching-bucket** (wooden) Brengle (der)n.; Brengle, pl.

mar 1.uff/buckere, v.; uffgebuckert, pp.; 2.verbuckere, v.; verbuckert, pp.; 3.verschenne, v.; verschennt, pp.; **(by cutting)** 1.ab/grutze, v.; abgegrutzt, pp.; 2.vergratze, v.; vergratzt, pp.; 3.vergrutze, v.; vergrutzt, pp.

marble (toy) 1.Maarwel (die)n.; 2.Marbel (die)n.

marble(s) 1.Glicker (der)n.; Glicker, pl.; 2.Schneller (der)n.

March Matz (der)n.; 25 Eppeldaag (der)n.; **day** Matzdaag (der) n.; **foal** (person subjected to pranks on March 1) Matzfill(i) (es)n.; **hare** Matzhaas (der)n.; **weather** Matzwedder (es)n.; **march around** rum/maschiere, v.; rumgemaschiert, pp.; **out** raus/maschiere, v.; rausmaschiert, pp.; **up** nuff/maschiere, v.; nuffmaschiert, pp.

Marcus Markes (der)n.

mare 1.Ma(rr) (die)n.; Marre, pl.; 2.Maerr (die)n.; **(that is given to switching her tail)** schwenslich, adj.; **mule** Ma(rr)esel (der, die)n.; Ma(rr)esel, pl.

Margaret 1.Gret (die)n.; 2.Gretschel (es)n. (in a nursery rhyme) (Hansel un --)

Maria 1.Mareia (die)n.; 2.Maria (die)n.

marigold 1.Hoffart (der)n.; 2.Ringelblumm (die)n.; 3. Saametros (die)n.; 4.Sammetros (die)n.; 5.Schtinkblumm (die)n.; Schtinkblumme, pl.; 6.Schtinkbock (der)n.; Schtinkbeck, pl.; 7.Schtinker (die)n., pl.

maritime seeisch, adj.

mark 1.Maerrick (es)n.; 2.maerricke, v.; gemaerrickt, pp.; **by an ax on a tree** Hackmarrick (en)n.; **by stepping on** verdribble, v.; verdribbelt, pp.; **down** 1.aamarricke, v.; aagemarrickt, pp.; 2.nunner/maerricke, v.; nunnergemaerrickt, pp. 3.uff/maericke, v.; uffgemaerickt, pp.; **in** 1.nei/maricke, v.; neigmarickt, pp.; 2.rei/maerricke, v.; reigemaerrickt, pp.; **off** ab/maricke, v.; abgemarickt, pp.; **off with a pair of compasses** ab/zaerkle, v.; abgezaerkelt, pp.; **off with stakes** ab/schtecke, v.; abgschteckt, pp.; **out** raus/maerricke, v.; ausgemaerrickt, pp.; **up** 1.nuff/maerricke, v.; nuffgemaerrickt, pp.; 2.vermaericke, v.; vermaerickt, pp.

marker 1.Maerricker (der)n.; 2.Maricker (der)n.; 3.Mar(r)ickschtee (der)n.

market 1.March (der)n. (rare usage); 2.Maerrickzeeche (es) n.; 3.Marrick (der)(es)n.; Marrick, pl.; 5.marricke, v.; gemarrickt, pp.; 6.Marrickzeeche (es)n.; 7.Mol (die)n.; 8.Schrunn(e) (die)n.; **basket** Marrickkar(e)b (der)n.; **day**

Marrickdaag (der)n.; **house** Marrickhaus (es)n.; Marrickheiser, pl.; **price** Marrickbreis (der)n.; **produce** marricke, v.; gemarrickt, pp.; **wagon** 1.Marchwaagen (der)n. (rare); 2.Marrickwagge (der)n.; 3.Schtadtwagge (der)n.

marketplace 1.March (der)n.; 2.Marrick (der)n.

marksman Schitz (der)n.

marriage Heiraat (die)n.

marrow Marix (es)n.

marry 1.hei(e)re, v.; geheiert, pp.; 2.kopliere, v.; kopuliert, pp.; 3.verheiere (sich --)v.; verheiert, pp.

marsh Sump (der)n.; **marigold** Dotterblumm (die)n.

marshy sumpich, adj.

marsupial Pauschdier (es)n.

Martin 1.Maardi (der)n.; 2.Maert (der)n.; 3.Maerten (der) n.; 4.Mardi (der)n.

martingale Schprungrieme (der)n.

Martyrs Mirror Maretyrer Schpiggel (der)n.

marvelous 1.wunderbaar, adj.; 2.wunnerbaar, adj.

Mary 1.Mareia (die)n.; 2.Maria (die)n.; 3.Mariche (die)n.; **(nursery rhyme)** Maricheli (es)n.; **Ann** Ammeriele (es)n.

Maryland Ma(rr)land (es)n.

masculine mennlich, adj.

mash verdricke, v.; verdrickt, pp.

mashed potatoes 1.Grummbier (die)n. (gemaeschde --e); 2.Grummbiere (die)n. (gschtammde --); 3.Grummbiere Saess (es)n.

masher Schtamber (der)n.; Schtamber, pl.

mask 1.Affegsicht (es)n.; 2.Falschgsicht (es)n.; 3.Gfress (es)n.; 4.Raffelgsicht (es)n.; 5.Schlaraffegsicht (der) n.; 6.Schnarefeggelgsicht (es)n.

masked vermummt, adj.

mason Mauerer (der)n.; Mauerere, pl.

mason's hammer Mauerhammer (der)n.; **hawk** Schpatz (der)n.; **work** Maueraerwett (die)n.

masonary Maueraerwett (die)n.

masquerade vermuschdere (sich --)v.; vermuschdert, pp.

masquerader 1.Belznickel (der)n.; Belznickel, pl.; 2.Belznickler (der)n.; Belznickler, pl.

mass Mess (die)n.; **left after pressing the oil from flax-seed** Olichkuche (der)n.

massacre 1.metzle, v.; gemetzelt, pp.; 2.vermetzle, v.; vermetzelt, pp.

mast Mascht (der)n.

master 1.Baas (der)n.; 2.Me(e)schder (der)n.; Me(e)schder, pl.; 3.me(e)schdere, v.; geme(e)schdert, pp.

masterwort Meeschderwatzel (die)n.

masticate 1.kaue, v.; gekaut, pp.; 2.tschaae, v.; getschaat, pp.

mat Wischer (der)n.

match paare, v.; gepaart, pp.; **(for lighting a fire** 1.Schtreichholz (es)n.; Schtreichhelzer, pl.; 2.Schweffel-helzich (es)n.; Schweffel-helzicher, pl.; 3.Schweffel-schtecke (es)n.; Schweffel-schtecke, pl.; 4.Schwewwel-helzich (es)n.; Schwewwel-helzicher, pl.; 5.Schwewwel-schtecke (es)n.; Schwewwel-schtecke, pl.; 6.Zindhols (es)n. (rare usage)

mate paare (sich --), v.; gepaart, pp.

maternal mudderlich, adj.

Mm

mathmatician — melon

mathematician Rechler (der)n.
mathematics Rechelkunscht (die)n.
Matilda Metilde (die)n.
matricide Muddermard (der)n.
matrimony 1.Ehe (die)n.; 2.Eh(e)schtand (der)n.
matted growth of hair or grass Belz (der)n.
matter 1.aus/mache, v.; ausgemacht, pp.; 2.Madaerich
    (es)n.; 3.Madeering (der)n.; 4.Madering (der)n.;
    5.Sach (die)n.; Sache, pl.; **of no importance** Seidreck
    (der)n.
mattock 1.Greitzschpiggel (der)n.; 2.Grubbhack (die)n.;
helve Grubbhackehelm (der)n.
mattress Matratz (die)n.; Matratze, pl.
mature 1.reif, adj.; 2.uff/waxe, v.; uffgwaxe, pp.;
    3.zeidiche, v.; gezeidicht, pp.
maul 1.Holzschleggel (der)n.; 2.Schleggel (der)n.
Maundy Thursday Grie(ner)dunnerschdaag (der)n.
maw Wambe(r) (der)n.
maxim Grundsatz (der)n.
May Moi (der)n.
May apple 1.Buschabbel (der)n.; 2.Moiabbel (der)n.;
    Moiebbel, pl.; 3.Moiblumm (die)n.; Moiblumme, pl.
may 1.daerfe, v.; gedaerft, pp.; 2.meege, v.; gemeecht, pp.
maybe vielleicht, adv.
mayor Baergemeeschder (der)n.
Mayweed 1.Kamille (der)n. (wilder --); 2.Seikamille (der)n.
maze Verwicklung (die)n.
me 1.mer, pron.; 2.mich (accusative), pron.; 3.mir
    (dative), pron.
meadow 1.Schwamm (der)n.; 2.Wies (die)n.; 3.Wiss (die)
    n.; Wisse, pl.; **grass** Schwammgraas (es)n.; **lily**
    Feldlilye (die)n.;
mouse Wissemaus (die)n.; **sweet** Mehlgraut (es)n.
meal 1.Esse (es)n.; 2.Iems (der)n.; 3.Ims (der)n.; 4.Maahl
    (es)n.; 5.Mehl (es)n.; **(big)** Esse (es)n. (en gross --)
mealtime 1.Esszeit (die)n.; 2.Iem(s)zeit (die)n.; 3.Imszeit
    (die)n.; 4.Maahlzeit (die)n.
mealy mehlich, adj.
mean 1.bedeide, v.; bedeidt, pp.; 2.meene, v.; gemeent,
    pp.; 3.Middelmo(o)s (es)n.; **person** Schtinker (der)n.;
    Schtinker, pl.
meaning Meening (die)n.
meanness 1.Schlechdichkeit (die)n.; 2.Schlechtichkeet (die)n.
meantime 1.daereweil, adv.; 2.unnerweils, adv.
meanwhile 1.eweil, adv.; 2.unnerweils, adv.
measles Reedle (die)n., pl.
measure 1.ab/schtrecke, v.; abgschtreckt, pp.; 2.graad,
    adj.; 3.Maas (es)n.; 4.messe, v.; gemesse, pp.; 5.Mo
    (o)s (es)n.; **(grain)** uff/messe, v.; uffgemesse, pp.; **for**
    powder (in loading a gun) Laadmoos (es)n.; **into bags**
    fasse, v.; gfasst, pp.; **into other containers** um/fasse,
    v.; umgfasst, pp.; **off** ab/messe, v.; abgemesse, pp.;
    some out raus/fasse, v.; rausg(e)fasst, pp.; **very ex-**
    actly ab/zaerkle, v.; abgezaerkelt, pp.
measurement Messung (die)n.
meat Fleesch (es)n; **and vegetables** (cooked together)

G(e)miess (es)n.; **bench** (on which meat is worked
up) Fleeschbank (die)n.; **chopper**
1.Waerschtmaschien (die)n.; 2.Waschtmaschien (die)
n.; **for boiling** Kochfleesch (es)n.; **fork**
Fleeschgawwel (die)n.; **grinder** Fleeschmiehl (die)n.;
hook Fleeschhoke (der)n.; **pickling tub** Bauchzuwwer
(der)n.; **pot** (for preserving meat) Fleeschhaffe (der)
n.; **saw** 1.Fleeschseeg (die)n.; Fleeschseege, pl.;
2.Gnocheseeg (die)n.; Gnocheseege, pl.; **scraps left**
from butchering 1.Fil(l)sel (es)n.;
2.Lewwerwaschtfillsel (es)n.; 3.Pattwaschtfillsel (es)
n.
meatless potpie (Rev. C. Rahn) blinder Bottboi (der)n.
meaty fleeschich, adj.
mechanic Handwaricksmann (der)n.; Handswaricksleit, pl.
meddle 1.kimmere (sich --)v.; gekimmert, pp.; 2.middle
    (sich --)v.; gemiddelt, pp.; 3.mittle (sich --)v.; gemit-
    telt, pp.; 4.nei/middle (sich --)v.; neigemiddelt, pp.;
    5.nei/mische (sich --)v.; neigemischt, pp.; **with an-**
    other's property schnuppere, v.; gschnuppert, pp.
mediate middelbaar, adj.
mediation Bedrachdung (die)n.
mediator Mittler (der)n.
medical work Dokterbuch (es)n.
medicine 1.Arznei (die)n.; 2.Dokdersach (es)n.; 3.Droppe
    (die)n., pl. (any liquid); 4.Dokterschtofft (es)
    n.;5.Medizin (die)n.
medieval times Middelalder (es)n.
meditate 1.dief/denke, v.; diefgedenkt, pp.; 2.no(och)
    denke, v.; no(och)gedenkt, pp.; 3.simmeliere, v.;
    gsimmeliert,pp.; 4.sinne, v.; gsunne, pp.
meditative 1.dreeschtmiedich, adj.; 2.droschtmiedich,
    adj.; 3. treeschtmiedich, adj.; 4.trostmiedich, adj.
medium middelmaessich, adj., adv.; **height** Middelheech
    (die)n.
medley Gemisch (es)n.
meek 1.dreeschtmiedich, adj.; 2.droschtmiedich, adj.; 3.
    geduldich, adj.; 4.mild, adj.; 5.sanftmiedich, adj.;
    6.treeschtmiedich, adj.; 7.trostmiedich, adj.
meet 1.begegne, v.; begegnet, pp.; 2.versammle (sich --)
    v.; versammelt, pp.; 3.zamme/kumme, v.; is zamme-
    kumme, pp.; 4.zamme/laafe, v.; zummegeloffe, pp.;
    (by chance) zamme/dappe, v.; zammegedappt, pp.;
    secretly zamme/schleiche, v.; zammegschliche, pp.;
    unexpectedly zammernannerkumme, v.; zammer-
    nannergkumme, pp.; **with** aa/dreffe, v.; aagedroffe,
    pp.; **with an accident** verunglicke, v.; verunglickt, pp.
meeting 1.Versammling (die)n.; 2.Versammlung (die)n.;
    house Versammlinghaus (es)n.; with an accident
    unglicklich, adj.
melancholia 1.Milsgranket (die)n.; 2.Milsgrankheet (die)n.
melancholic 1.mellenkollisch, adj.; 2.milsich, adj.
melancholy 1.schwermiedich, adj.; 2.wunnerlich, adj.
mellow maer(e)b, adj.
melody 1.Melodei (die)n.; 2.Melodie (die)n.; 3.Weis (die)n.
melon 1.Melloon (die)n.; 2.Melluun (die)n.

Mm

melt — milkhouse

melt 1.aus/schmelze, v.; ausgschmolze, pp.; 2.daae, v.; gedaat, pp.; 3.schleffle, v.; gschleffelt, pp.; 4.schmelse, v.; gschmolse, pp.; 5.uff/daae, v.; uffgedaat, pp.; 6.uff/geh, v.; uffgange, pp.; 7.verschmelze, v.; verschmolze, pp.; **again** iwwer/schmelze, v.; iwwergschmolze, pp.; **away** weck/schmelze, v.; wechgschmolze, pp.; **off** ab/schmelze, v.; abgschmolze, pp.; **out** raus/schmelse, v.; rausgschmolse, pp.; **up** uff/schmelze, v.; uffgschmolze, pp.

member 1.Glied (es)n.; Glieder; Glidder, pl.; 2.Mitglied (es)n.; Mitglieder, pl.; **of a congregation** Gemeensglied (es)n.; **of a New Year's greeting party** Winscher (der)n.; Winscher, pl.

membrane Fell (es)n.

memento 1.Aadenke(s) (es)n.; 2.Erinnerung (die)n.

Memorial Day Gedechtnisdaag (der)n.

memorize aus(e)wennich lanne, v.; glannt, pp.

memory Gedechtnis (es)n.

mend 1.aa/flicke, v.; aagflickt, pp.; 2.flicke, v.; gflickt, pp.; 3.verschtickere, v.; verschtickert, pp.

mendacious verlogge, adj.

mending 1.Flickaerwet(t) (die)n.; 2.Gflick (es)n.; **(confounded)** Flickeri (die)n.; **material** Flickwese (es)n.

Mennonite 1.Mannischt (der)n.; 2.Mennischt (der)n.; Mennischde, pl.

menses 1.Blitz (der)n.; 2.Blumme (die)n.; 3.Granket (die) n.; 4.Krankheet (die)n. 5.Zeit (die)n.; Zeite, pl.

menstrual period unrein, adj. (--i zeit)

mental exertion Kopp-verreisses (es)n.; **grasp** Eiblick (der)n.

mention 1.biebse, v.; gebiebst, pp.; 2.nenne, v.; genennt, pp.; 3.piepse, v.; gepiebst, pp.

menu 1.Esszeddel (der)n.; 2.Fuderzeddel (der)n.

meow 1.Graunse, v.; gegraunst, pp.; 2.maunse, v.; gemaunst, pp.; 3.miau!

merchant 1.Kaafman (der)n.; Kaafleit, pl.; 2.Schtorkipper (der)n.; Schtorkipper, pl.

merciful 1.bar(e)mhatzich, adj.; 2.barmhaerzich, adj.

mercy 1.Bar(e)hatzichkeit (die)n.; 2.erbarme, v.; erbarmt, pp.; 3.erbaerme, v.; erbaermt, pp.; **seat (in church)** Gnaadebank (die)n.; Gnaadebenk, pp.

mere nothing Hun(d)strumpel (die)n.

merely 1.blos, adv.; 2.lauder, adv.

meritorious verdinschtlich, adj.

merriment 1.Frehlichkeet (die)n.; 2.Luscht (die)n.; 3. Luschtbaarkeit (die)n.

merry 1.luschdich, adj.; 2.vergniecht, adj.; 3.wohluff, adj.; **go-round** Schliffelmiehl (die)n.

mesh Gaarnschlupp (der)n.

mess 1.Gericht (es)n.; 2.Gschmier (es)n.; 3.Hutsch (der)n.; Hutsche, pl.; 4.Mar(r)asch(t) (der)n.; 5.Seierei (die)n.; 6.Wichs (die)n.; **by handling** zamme/gnootsche, v.; zammegegnootscht, pp.; **of peas** 1.Kochet (die)n.; 2.Kuchet Aerbse (en)n.; **up** versuddle, v.; versuddelt, pp.

message Bot(t)schaft (die)n.

messed uff/gepulschdert, v.

messuage Grundschtick (es)n.

metal Metaal (es)n.

meteor Drach (der)n.; Drache, pl.

Methodist 1.Maddedis (der)n.; 2.Maeddedist (der)n.; 3. Meddedischt (der)n.

metropolis Haaptschtadt (die)n.

mica Offeglaas (es)n.

Michael Michel (der)n.

Michaelmas daisy Besereis (es)n.

microscope Vergreeseringsglaas (es)n.

mid-afternoon snack 1.Drei-Uhr-Schtick, n.; 2.Vierhur-Schtick (es)n.

midday Middaag (der)n; **hour of rest** Rukschtunn (die)n.

middle 1.middelscht, adj.; 2.Mitt (die)n.; **age** 1.middeleldich, adj.; 2.Middelelt (die)n.; **age of life** Middelalder (es)n.; **finger** Langmann (der)n.; **man** Middelmann (der)n.; **name** Middelnaame (der)n.; **of the skull** Waerwel (der)n.; **ring** Middelring (der)n.

middling basslich, adj.

middlings 1.Bollmehl (es)n.; 2.Middelmehl (es)n.; 3. Schiebschtoff(t) (es)n.; 4.Schrot (die)n.

midge (spring peeper) Frosch (der)n.; Fresch, pl.

midnight 1.Halbnacht (die)n.; 2.Midde(r)nacht (die)n.; 3. Mitnacht (die)n.; 4.Mitte(r)nacht (die)n.

midway mitweegs, adv.

midwife Waartfraa (die)n.

miffed greppisch, adj.

might 1.Graft (die)n.; Grefde, pl.; 2.Macht (die)n.

mightily 1.gewaltichlich, adj.; 2.vollmechdich, adv.

mighty 1.gref(f)dich, adj.; 2.maessich, adj.; 3.mechdich, adj., adv.

migraine eeseidich, adj. (-- koppweh)

milch-cow Melkkuh (die)n.; Melkkieh, pl.

mild 1.gelind, adj.; 2.glimblich, adj.; 3.sanft, adj.

mildew Milldaa (der)n.

mildewed milldaaich, adj.

mildewy weeds Mildaagraut (es)n.

mile Meil (die)n.; Meile, pl.

miles away meileweit, adv.

milestone 1.Marrickschtee (der)n.; 2.Meilschtee (der)n..; Meilschtee, pl.

militia Militz (der)n.; **drill and the accompanying show** Bedallye (es)n.

milk 1.melke, v.; gemolke, pp.; 2.Millich (die)n.; **a cow dry (after calving)** ab/melke, v.; abgemolke, pp.; **can** Millichkann (die)n.; **cow** Millichkuh (die)n. Mellichkieh, pl.; **crock** Millichhaffe (der)n.; **fever** Millichfewer (es)n.; **pie** 1.Flitscher (der)n.; 2.Milichschlebbes (es)n.; 3.Millichboi (der)n.; 4.Raahmdaader (der)n.; 5.Millichflitscher (der)n. (Hamburg Versammling); **soup (with breadcrumbs)** Brockelsupp (die)n.; **strainer** Millichseih (die)n.; **tooth** Millichzaah (der)n.; Millichzeh, pl.; **tooth** Millichzoh (der)n. Millichzeh, pl.; **wagon** Millichwagge (der)n.; **whey** Millichmolge (die)n., pl.

milkhouse Millichhaus (es)n.; Millichheiser, pl.

Mm

milking — misstep

milking (in all its details) Melkerei (die)n.; **stool** Melkschtul(der)n.; Melkschtiel, pl.

milkmaid Melkern (die)n.

milkman Millichmann (der)n.

milkpail Melkeemer (der)n.

milkpan Blicki (es)n.

milkweed Millichgraut (es)n.

mill 1.maahle, v.; g(e)maahle, pp.; 2.Miehl (die)n.; Miehle, pl.; **dam** Miehldamm (der)n.; Miehldemmer, pl.; **for grinding bark** Lohmiehl (die)n.; **sweepings** Miehlschtaab (der)n.

millenial dausendyaehrich, adj.

millennium 1.Dausendreich (es)n.; 2.dausendyaehrich Reich (es)n.

miller Miller (der)n.; Miller, pl.; **(moth)** Lichteil (die)n.

miller's toll Mulder, (der)n.

milliner Hietmachern (die)n.

million 1.Mill(i)yoon (die)n.; 2.Mill(i)yuun (die)n.

millpond Miehldeich (der)n.

millstone Miehlschtee (der)n.; Miehlschtee, **cutter** Miehlschteehacker (der)n.

millwheel Miehlraad (es)n.; Miehlredder,

millwright Miehlmacher (der)n.; Miehlmacher, pl.

mimic 1.no(och)mache, v.; no(och)g(e)macht, pp.; 2.schpodde, v.; gschpott, pp.; 3.schpotte, v.; gschpott, pp.

mincemeat Minsfleesch (es)n.

mind 1.achde, v.; geacht, pp.; 2.Geescht (der)n.; 3.Gemiet (es)n.; 4.hiede, v.; ghiedt, pp.; 5.Meind (der, die)n.; 6.meinde, v.; gemeindt, pp.; 7.Sinn (der)n.

mine mei(n); meiner; meini, poss. pron.

miniature landscape (and other scenery used as a setting for the base of a Christmas tree) Putz (der)n.

minister 1.Breddicher (der)n.; Breddicher, pl.; 2.Preddicher (der)n.; 3.Diener zum Watt (Buch) (der) n. (Old Order Amish Usage); 4.Parre (der)n.; Parre, pl. (Lutheran and Reformed churches); **who reads sermons from manuscript** Babierschitz (der)n.

minister's wife Parre(s)fraa (die)n.

ministry 1.Breddicharnt (es)n.; 2.Preddichamt (es)n.

minority 1.Minderheet (die)n.; 2.Minderheit (die)n.

mint Balsem (der)n.

minute Minutt (die)n.; Minudde, pl.; **hand** Minuddezoiyer (der)n.

minutes (of a meeting) Nunnerschrift (die)n.

miracle Wunner (die, es)n.

mirasmus 1.Abnemmede (es)n.; 2.Abnemmes (es)n.

mire 1.Mar(r)asch(t) (der)n.; 2.Schlaam (der)n.; 3.Schlamm (der)n.

mirror Schpiggel (der)n.; Schpiggle, pl.

mirth 1.Frelichkeet (die)n.; 2.Luscht (die)n.

miry schmierich, adj.

misanthrope Menschefeind (der)n.

misanthropy Menschehass (der)n.

misbehave 1.bariere, v.; bariert, pp. (sich schlecht --); 2.bedraage, v.; bedraage, pp. (sich schlecht --);

3.schicke (sich net)v.; gschickt, pp.; 4.schlecht uff/fiehre, v.; schlecht uffgfiehrt, pp. (sich --); 5.uff/fiehre, v.; uffgfiehrt, pp. (sich schlecht --)

miscalculate letz rechle, v.; gerechelt, pp.

miscarriage 1.Fehlgebort (die)n.; 2.Miss(gebort) (die)n.

miscarry 1.fehl/geh, v.; fehlgange, pp.; 2.fehl/schlagge, v.; fehlgschlagge, pp.; 3.verdraage, v.; verdraage, pp.

miscellaneous 1.alle Aard, pron.; 2.eenichebbes, pron.; 3.eensichebbes, pron.; **article** 1.Gerebbelfress (es)n.; 2.Gfrees (es)n.

mischance Unfall (der)n.; Unfelle, pl.

mischievous 1.gnitz, adj.; 2.knitz, adj.; 3.lischdich, adj.; 4.mutwillich, adj.; 5.nixnutz(ich), adj.; 6.schlibberich, adj.; 7.schlau, adj.; 8.schlitzohrich, adj. 9.schniekich, adj.; 10.unaardich, adj.; 11.unflaet, adj.; 12.unflatt, adj.; 13.unnitz(ich), adj.; 14.verschmitzt, adj.; **boys** Buwescht(r)offt (des)n.; **child** 1.Nixnutz (der)n.; 2.Schnickelfritz (der)n.; 3.Unflaat (der)n.; **child(ren)** Keffer (der)n.; Keffer, pl.; **girls** Maedschtofft (es)n.

mischief 1.Mutwille (der)n.; 2.Nixnutz (der)n.; 3.Unheel (es)n.; 4.Unheil (es)n.

misconstruction Missdeitung (die)n.

miser 1.Bensepetzer (der)n.; 2.Geizhals (der)n.; 3.Geldsuckler (der)n.; Geldsuckler, pl.; 4.Gnickser (der)n.

miserable 1.ebaermlich, adj.; 2.elendich, adj.; 3.erbaermlich, adj.; 4.miseraawel, adj.

miserable (little) thing Elendsgweckel (es)n.; **(very)** hundsiwwel, adj.

miserably hundsiwwel, adv.

miserliness Gegnix (es)n.

miserly geizich, adv.

misery 1.Elend (es)n.; 2.Yammer (der)n.

misfortune 1.Kreiz (es)n.; 2.Umglick (es)n.; 3.Unglick (es)n.

mishap Unfall (der)n.; Unfelle, pl.

mislay 1.verlege, v.; verlegt, pp.; 2.verschleefe, v.; verschleeft, pp.

mislead verfiehre, v.; verfiehrt, pp.

misogynist Weiwerfeind (der)n.

misplace 1.verlege, v.; verlegt, pp.; 2.verschiewe, v.; verschowe, pp.; 3.verschleefe, v.; verschleeft, pp.

misrepresent weis/mache, v.; weisgemacht, pp.

miss 1.denewe/kumme, v.; denewekumme, pp.; 2.fehl/schiesse, v.; fehlgschosse, pp.; 3.fehle, v.; g(e)fehlt, pp.; 4.verfehle, v.; verfehlt, pp.; 5.verhopbasse, v.; verhopbasst, pp.; 6.verlabbe, v.; verlappt, pp.; 7.vermisse, v.; vermisst, pp.; 8.verseime, v.; verseimt, pp.; **(in shooting)** Fehlschuss (der)n.; **one's blow** fehl/(g)schlagge, v.; fehlgschlagge, pp.; **one's way** fehl/geh, v.; fehlgange, pp.

misshapen foot Dollfuus (der)n.

mission Mission (die)n.

missionary preacher Missionsbreddicher (der)n.

missionary sermon Missionsbreddich (die)n.

misstep Fehldritt (der)n.

Mm

mist 1.Duft (der)n.; 2.Newwel (der)n.

mistake 1.Fehler (der)n.; Fehler, pl.; 2.fiehl/schiesse,v.; fiehlgschosse, pp.; 3. Versehe (es)n.; 4.Versehne (es)n.

mistaken in vergaffe (sich --)v.; vergafft, pp.

mistreat 1.beyuuse, v.; beyuust, pp.; 2.missbrauche, v.; (ge)missbraucht, pp.; 3.misshandle, v.; misshandelt, pp.

mistreatment Misshandlung (die)n.

mistress 1.haerrin (die)n.; 2.Mee(s)chdern (die)n.

mistrust 1.missdraue, v.; (ge)missdraut, pp.; 2.net draue, v.; net gedraut, pp.

misty 1.dufdich, adj.; 2.neww(e)lich, adj.

misunderstand missverschteh, v.; missverschtanne, pp.

misunderstanding 1.Missverschtand (der)n.; 2.Missverschtendnis (es)n.; 3.Zwieschpalt (der)n.

misuse 1.beyuuse, v.; beyuust, pp.; 2.missbrauche, v.; (ge)missbraucht, pp.

mitten (with a separate thumb) Fauschthensching (der)n.

mix 1.aa/mache, v.; aagemacht, pp.; 2.eiriehre, v.; eigeriehrt, pp.; 3.menge, v.; gemengt, pp.; 4.zamme/mische, v. zammegemischt, pp.; **by stirring** 1.aa/riehre, v.; aageriehrt, pp.; 2.aa/schtarre, v.; aagschtarrt, pp.; 3.verriehre, v.; verriehrt, pp.; **dough** (with wooden paddle) satze, v.; gsatzt, pp.; **up** 1.uff/balixe, v.; uffgebalixt, pp.; 2.vermische, v.; vermischt, pp.; **up in an affair** dreimische (sich --)v.; **up with** nei/schmiere (sich --)v.; neigschmiert, pp. **mixed** gewaerrt, adv.; **up** verhuddelt, adj.; **up affair** 1.Lumberei (die)n.; 2.Schmiererei (die)n.

mixing ladle (kitchen) Riehrleffel (der)n.; Riehrleffel, pl.; **trough** (for feed) Fuderdrog (der)n.; Fuderdreeg, pl.

mixture 1.Gemasser (es)n.; 2.Gemisch (es)n.

moan 1.wimmele, v.; gewimmelt, pp.; 2.yammere, v.; geyammert, pp.; 3.yomere, v.; geyomert, pp.

moaning 1.Geyammer (es)n.; 2.Geyeemer (es)n.

mob Ungeziffer (es)n.

moccasin flower 1.Bullebeidel (der)n.; 2.Ewwergraut(es)n.

mock 1.aus/schpodde, v.; ausgschpott, pp.; 2.schpeddle, v.; gschpeddelt, pp.; 3.schpettle, v.; gschpeddelt, pp.; 4.schpodde, v.; gschpott, pp.; 5.schpotte, v.; gschpott, pp.

mocker 1.Schpedder (der)n.; 2.Schpetter (der)n.

mockery Schpott (der)n.

mocking Gschpott (es)n.; **bird** Schpottvoggel (der)n.

mockingly 1.schpettlich, adj., adv.; 2.schpoddich, adv.; 3.schpottich, adj.

mode of life Wandel (der)n.

model Moddel (die)n.; Moddle, pl.

moderate 1.maessich, adj.; 2.middelmaessich, adj.

moderation 1.Maessichkeet (die)n.; 2.Maessichkeit (die)n.; 3.Middelmo(o)s (es)n.

modest 1.bescheide, adj.; 2.sittsam, adj.

modesty Schamm (die)n.

Mohair yard Kameelgaarn (es)n.

moist 1.feicht, adj.; 2.nasslich, adj.; 3.nesslich, adj.

moisten 1.aa/feichde, v.; aagfeicht, pp.; 2.ei/feichde, v.; eigfeicht, pp.; 3.uff/feichde, v.; uffgfeicht, pp.; **and dry alternately** (as incuring flax) raetze, v.; geraetzt, pp.

moistness Feichdichkeit (die)n.

moisture 1.Feichtichkeet (die)n.; 2.Feichtichkeit (die)n.

molar Backezaah (der)n.

molasses 1.Melaasich (der)n.; 2.Melasses (der)n.; 3.Melassich (der)n.; **bread** Melaasich Brot (es)n.; **cake** Melassichkuche (der)n.

mold 1.Grooz (der)n.; 2.grooze, v.; gegroozt, pp.; 3.vergrooze, v.; vergroozt, pp.

moldy 1.groozich, adj.; 2.verschimmelt, adj.

mole (on skin) Muddermaerrick (es)n.; **(rodent)** 1.Beeskatz (die)n.; 2.Maulwar(re)f (der)n.; 3.Mol (die)n.; 4.Moondkalb (es)n.; 5.Schwammriesel (der)n.

molt (of chickens) feddere (sich --)v.; gfeddert, pp.

mom 1.Mamm (die)n.; 2.Memm (die)n.

moment Aageblick (der)n.; **ago** alleweil, adv.

momentarily 1.aageblicklich, adv.; 2.iwwerdem(m), adv.

Monday 1.Moondaag (der)n.; 2.Muundaag (der)n.

money Geld (es)n.; **(contributed to the support of the minister in the Lutheran and Reformed churches in earlier years)** Parregeld (es)n.; **box** Kass (die)n.; **for foreign missions** Missionsgeld (es)n.; **for taxes** Taxgeld (es)n.; **in coin** Hartgeld (es)n.; **making proposition or scheme** Geldmaschien (die)n.; **matters** Geldsache (die)n., pl.

moneywort Geldgraut (es)n.

monkey Aff (der)n.; Affe, pl.

monopoly Alleehandel (der)n.

monotonous musical performanc Gedudel (es)n.

monster 1.Ungeheier (es)n.; 2.Uumensch (der)n.

monstrous ungeheier, adj.

month 1.Monet (der)n.; 2.Munet (der)n.

monthly 1.monetlich, adv.; 2.Munet (alli --), adv.; 3.munetlich, adj., adv.

monument Denkmol (es)n.

moo! muh!

mood Gemiet (es)n.

mooley cow Muhlikuh (die)n; Muhlekieh, pl.

moon 1.Moon(d) (der)n.; Moon(d)e, pl.; 2.Muun(d) (der) n.; Muun(d)e, pl.

moonlight 1.Muunhelling (die)n.; 2.Muunlicht (es)n.

moonlit muunhell, adj.

moonshine Moondschei (der)n.

moosewood Oolehols (es)n.

mop Butzlumbe (der)n.

mope 1.Maul henke (es)v.; 2.Mops (der)n.; 3.Mopskopp (der)n.; 4.Moschkopp (der)n.

mopish 1.mopsich, adv.; 2.verdutzt, adj.; **reluctance** Grummelwasser (es)n.

moral morallisch, adj.; **duty** 1.Mensche(g)pflicht (die)n.; 2. Menschepflicht (die)n.

morality Moraal (die)n.

Moravian 1.Herrnhuder (der)n. Herrnhuder, pl.; 2. herrnhuderisch, adj.

morbid krankhaft, adj.

more 1.meh, adj.; 2.mehner, adj.; **and more** 1.immer mehr, adj.; 2.immermeh, adj.; **readily** liewer, adv.

321

Mm

morel

morel Marrichel (die)n.

morello (cherry) Amerelle (die)n.

morn Mariyeschtun(d) (die)n.

morning Mariye (der)n; **(hour)** Mariyeschtun(d) (die)n.;
chores Mariye-arewett (die)n.; **glory** Drechderblumm
(die)n.; **prayer** Mariyegebet (es)n.; **star** Mariyeschtann
(die)n.; **sun** Mariyesunn (die)n.

morocco Geesledder (es)n.

morsel Brocke (der)n.

mortal schtaerblich, adj.

mortality Schtaerblichkeit (die)n.

mortar Maa(r)der (der)n; **(apothecaries')** Maerscher (der)
n.; **(mixing) box** Maa(r)derbett (es)n.

mortification Brand (der)n.

mortify demiediche, v.; gedemiedicht, pp.

mortise Zabbeloch (es)n.; Zabbelecher, pl.

mosquito 1.Moschgieder (der)n.; Moschgieders, pl.;
2.Schnok (die)n.; Schnoke, pl.

moss Moos (es)n; **pink** Hiwwelblumm (die)n.;
Hiwwelblumme, pl.; **rose** Maasblumm (die)n.;
Maasblumme, pl.

most 1.mehrscht, adj.; 2.menschde, adj. (am --);
3.menscht, adj.; **assuredly** allemol, adv.; **likely**
allernaegscht, adv.; **of all** 1.allerliebscht, adj.;
2.liebschde (am;) 3.menschde, adj. (am --)

mostly 1.gemeenerhand, adj.; 2.greeschtdeels, adj.;
3. mehrschdens, adv.; 4.menschdens, adv.;
5.menschtdeel, adv.

moth 1.Fleddermaus (der)n.; Fleddermeis, pl.; 2.Schaab
(die)n.; **mullein** 1.Kaffigraut (es)n.; 2.Puttere
(schtengel) (der)n.

mother 1.Mamm (die)n.; 2.Mammi (die)n.; 3.Memm (die)
n.; 4.Mudder (die)n.; Midder; Middere, pl.; **in-law**
1. Schwaermudder (die)n.; 2.Schwermudder (die)n.;
3.Schwiegermudder (die)n.; 4.Schwiegern (die)n.; **of**
vinegar 1.Essichmutter (die)n.; 2.Mudder (die)n.;
tongue Mudderschprooch (die)n.

mother's milk Diddi (der)n.; **sister** (aunt) Mudder ihre
Schwescher (der)n.; **womb** Mudderleib (der)n.

motherwort Muddergraut (es)n.

motion Bewegung (die)n.

motto Motto (es)n.

mould 1.Form (die)n.; 2.Schimmel (der)n.;Schimmel,pl.;
(for tallow candles) Moddel (die)n.; Moddle, pl.

mouldboard 1.Wennbrett (es)n.; 2.Wenneise (es)n.; **side**
of a plow Wennseit (die)n.

moulder 1.Giesser (der)n.; 2.verweese, v.; verweest, pp.

moulding 1.Begleeding (die)n.; 2.Leescht (die)n.; 3.Leischt
(die)n.

mouldy schimm(e)lich, adj.

moult abfeddre (sich --)v.; abgfeddert, pp.

moulting season Mauszeit (die)n.

mount 1.Reitgaul (der)n.; 2.schtiege, v.; is gschtigge, pp.;
3.schtiege, v.; is gschtigge, pp.; **stairs noisily**
nuff/dunnere, v.; nuffgedunnert, pp.

mountain 1.Baerrick (der)n.; 2.Barig (der)n.; Bariye, pl.;

move

3.Beig (der)n.; Beiye, pl.; **mint** 1.Baerrickbalsem (der)
n.; 2.Barigbalsem (der)n.; **sage** Wollgemut (der)n.

mountainous baergich, adj.; **region** Gebaerricks (es)n.

mounted mail carrier Poschtreider (der)n.

mourn 1.drau(e)re, v.; gedrauert, pp.; 2.Trau(e)re, v.;
getrauert, pp.

mourners Drauerleit (die)n., pl.

mourning 1.Beschwerde (die)n.; 2.Drauer (die)n.; 3.Gwaal
(die)n.; 4.Haerzeleed (es)n.; 5.Leed(e) (der)n.; **garment** Drauergleed (es)n.; **veil** Schleier (der)n.

mouse Maus (die)n.; Meis, pl.; **hole** Mausloch (es)n.;
Mauslecher, pl.

mouser Mauskatz (die)n.

mousetrap Mausfall (die)n.

mousey 1.Meische (es)n.; 2.Meisel (es)n.; 3.Meisli (es)n.

moustache 1.Schnarrbaart (der)n.; 2.Schnauzbaart (der)
n.; 3.Schnurbort (der)n.

mouth 1.Bless (die)n.; 2.Gfress (es)n.; 3.Gosch (die)n.;
4.Kabesch (die)n.; 5.Maul (es)n.; Meiler, pl.; 6.Mund
(der)n.(rare); 7.Mundschtick (es)n.; 8.Rache (der)n.;
9.Raffel (die)n.; 10.Ranse (der)n.; 11.Reff (es)n.;
Reffer, pl.; 12.Riesel (der)n.; 13.Waffel (die)n.; **of the**
cave Maul (es)n. (es -- vum Drachloch) (es -- vun der
Hehling)

mouthful 1.Maulvoll (es)n.; 2.Schluck (der)n.

mouthpiece (of an instrument Mundschtick (es)n.

movable beweklich, adj; **circular wooden vat** (varying in
height from less than a foot to 4 feet) Schtiwwich
(der)n.

move 1.Aagschtalt (der)n.; 2.bewege, v.; bewekt, pp.;
3.grimme (sich --)v.; gegrimmt pp.; 4.krimme (sich--)v.;
gekrimmt, pp.; 5.mucke (sich --)v.; gemuckt, pp.; 6.rege
(sich --)v.; gerekt, pp.; 7.reisse, v.; gerisse, pp.; 8.ricke,
v.; gerickt, pp.; 9.robbe, v.; geroppt, pp.; 10.vermucke
(sich --)v.; vermuckt, pp.; 11.verrege (sich --)v.; verregt,
pp.; 12.verrege, v.; verregt, pp.; 13.verzucke, v.;
verzuckt, pp.; 14.wandle, v.; gewandelt, pp.; 15.ziege,
v.; gezoge, pp.; 16.ziehe, v.; gezoge, pp.; **(slowly)**
droddle, v.; gedroddelt, pp.; **about** rum/schtarre, v.;
rumgschtarrt, pp.; **after** no(och)ricke, v.;
no(och)gerickt, pp.; **along with** mit/ziege, v.;
mitgezogge, pp.; **around** rum/ricke, v.; rumgerickt, pp.;
away 1.weck/ziege, v.; weckgezogge, pp.;
2.weck/ziehe, v.; weckgezogge, pp.; **back and forth**
wischble, v.; gewischbelt, pp.; **down** nunner/ziege, v.;
nunnergezogge, pp.; **fast** schiesse, v.; gschosse, pp.;
frequently rum/rutsche, v.; rumgerutscht, pp.; **from**
place to place 1.rumhaer/rutsche, v.;
rumhaergerutscht, pp.; 2.rumhaer/ziege, v.;
rumhaergzogge, pp.; **here** 1.haer/ziege, v.; 2.her/ziege,
v.; hergezogge, pp.; **home** heemziege, v.;
heemgezogge, pp.; **in** 1.eiricke, v.; eigerickt, pp.;
2.nei/ziehe, v.; neigzoge, pp.; 3.rei/ricke, v.;
reigerickt, pp.; **in a jolting or uneven manner** hulpre,
v.; ghulpert, pp.; **into** 1.ei/nemme, v.; eigenumme, pp.;
2.ei/ziege, v.; eigezoge, pp.; 3.nei/ricke, v.; neigerickt,

(Continued on page 323)

Mm

move (continued)   mysterious

(Continued from page 322)

pp.; **into the same house** zamme/ziehe, v.; zammegezogge, pp. **near** 1.bei/ricke, v.; beigerickt, pp.; 2.hie/ricke, v.; hiegerickt, pp.; **one to pity** yammere (sich --)v.; geyammert, pp.; **out** 1.naus/ricke, v.; nausgerickt, pp.; 2.raus/ricke, v.; rausgerickt, pp.; 3.raus/ziege, v.; rausgezogge, pp.; **out of the way** aus/ricke, v.; ausgerickt, pp.; **over** 1.niwwer/ziege, v.; niwwergezoge, pp.; 2.niwwer/ziehe, v.; niwwergezoge, pp.; **precipitately** (of persons and horses) haschble, v.; ghaschbelt, pp.; **rapidly** flitze, v.; gflitzt, pp.; **to a place** hie/ziege, v.; hiegezogge, pp; **up** 1.nuff/ricke, v.; nuffgerickt, pp.; 2.nuff/ziege, v.; nuffgezogge, pp.; 3.ruff/ricke, v.; ruffgerickt, pp.; 4.ruff/ziege, v.; ruffgezoge, pp.; **up to each other** zamme/ricke, v.; zammegerickt, pp.; **with short steps** dripple, v.; gedrippelt, pp. **moving** (of household belongings) Zuck (der)n.; **alongside of each other** newenannerhaer, adv.;

moving day Ziegdaag (der)n.

mow 1.ab/mache, v.; abgemacht, pp.; 2.Baare (der)n.; 3.maehe, v.; gemaeht, pp.; 4.mehe, v.; gemeht, pp.; **(hay)** 1.Bore (der)n.; 2.Hoibohrer (der)n.; **around** (some obstruction in a field) raus/mehe, v.; rausgemeht, pp.; **around the field** (with the cradle to make way for the reaping machine) 1.aa/mehe, v.; aagemeht, pp. (es Feld --); 2.aamehe, v.; aagemeht, pp.; **down** 1.ab/mehe, v.; abgemeht, pp.; 2.nidder/mehe, v.; niddergemeht, pp.; 3.um/mehe, v.; umgemeht, pp.; 4.zamme/maehe, v.; zammegemaeht, pp.

mower 1.Maeher (der)n.; 2.Maehmaschien (die)n.; **(machine)** Mehmaschien (die)n.; **(person)** Meher (der)n.; Meher, pl.

much viel, pron; adj.; **(very)** 1.ewich, adj, adv. (gaar -- viel); 2.rechtschaffe, adj.; 3.reschaffe, adj.; **less** gschweige, conj.; **or continued eating** Esserei (die)n.; **reading** Geles (es)n.

mucilage Schleim (der)n.

mucus Schleim (der)n.

mud 1.Dreck (der)n.; 2.Marrasch(t) (der)n.; 3.Schlaam (der)n.; 4.Schlamm (der)n.; **(as used in red sky in the evening means fair weather the next day and red in the morning means mud by evening)** Kot (der)n. "Owedrot is mariyeschee un Mariyerot bis Owed, Dreck un Kot"; **swallow** Dreckschwallem (der, die)n.; **wasp** Dreckweschp (die)n.

muddy 1.drieb, adj.; 2.schmierich, adj.; 3.schmutzich, adj.

mudhole Dreckloch (es)n.; Drecklecher, pl.

muff verlabbe, v.; verlappt, pp.

mug 1.Gosch (die)n.; 2.Gruck (der)n.; Griek, pl.; 3.Kruck (der)n.; **in which coffee is served** (Moravian) 1.Griegel (es)n.; 2.Griggel (es)n.; **wort** Beifuus (der)n.

mulberry Maulbeer (die)n.; Maulbeere, pl.; **tree** Maulbeerebaam (der)n.; Maulbeerebeem, pl.

mule 1.Esel (der)n.; Esel, pl.; 2.Langohr (es)n.;3.Maulesel (der)n.; **colt** Eselhutsch (es)n.; **driver** Eseldreiwer (der)n.

mull (fabric) Schnupfharn (es)n.

mullein 1.Woll(e)graut (es)n.; 2.Wolleschtengel (der)n.; **leaf** Wolleblaat (es)n.; Wollebledder, pl.

multiplier onion 1.Gluckezwiwwel (die)n.; 2.Winderzwiwwel (die)n.; Winderzwiwwle, pl.

multiply vermehre (sich --)v.; vermehrt, pp.

multitude Schaar (die)n.

multure Mulder, (der)n.

mumble mummle, v.; gemummelt, pp.

mumbling Gemummel (es)n.

mumps Mumps (der)n.

mundane weltlich, adj; **pleasure** Weltluscht (die)n.

murder Dodmacherei (die)n.

murder 1.Ma(r)d (der)n.; 2.madde, v.; gematt, pp.; 3.maerde, v.; gemaerdt, pp.; 4.Maerderei (die)n.; 5.Marddaat (die)n.; 6.marde, v.; gemardt, pp.; 7.Mord (der)n.; **case** Maerdergschicht (die)n.; **story** Maerdergschicht (die)n.

murderer 1.Dodschlaeger (der)n.; 2.Madder (der)n.; Madder, pl.; 3.Maerder (der)n.; Maerder, pl.

murderous 1.madderlich, adv.; 2.maerderlich, adj.; **deed** Marddaat (die)n.

murmer 1.rabble, v.; gerabbelt, pp.; 2.rausche, v.; gerauscht, pp.; 3.wischble, v.; gewischbelt, pp.

muscilaginous schleimich, adj.

mush-meal Moschmehl (es)n.

mushroom 1.Erdschwamm (der)n.; 2.Marrichel (die)n.; 3.Schwamm (der)n.

music 1.Musik (die)n.; 2.Myusick (die)n.; **(as entertainment)** Schpieles (es)n.

musical musikaalisch, adj.

musician 1.Musikant (der)n.; 2.Schpielmann (der)n.

musk Moschk (der)n.

musket Muschkeet (die)n.

muskmelon Muschmelon (die)n.; Muschmelone, pl.

muskrat 1.Muschgratt (die)n.; 2.Muschgrott (die)n.; 3. Muschkratt (die)n.

muslin Musslien (der)n.

mussel Muschel (der)n.

must 1.misse, v.; gemisst, pp.; 2.Moscht (der)n.; **be procured** bei/misse, v.; beigemisst, pp.

mustard 1.Moschdert (der)n.; 2.Mostert (der)n.

mute schtumm, adj.; **person** Schtummer (der)n.

mutilate verschtim(m)le, v.; verschtimmelt, pp.

mutton 1.Hammelfleesch (es)n.; 2.Schooffleesch (es)n.

mutually unne(re)nanner, adv.

muzzle 1.Flindeloch (es)n.; Flindelecher, pl.; 2.Maulkar(e)b (der)n.; **for calves** (to prevent sucking cow) Schtachelband (es)n.; Schtachelbenner, pl.

my mei, poss. pron.; **beau** Alder (der)n. (mei --); **goodness** 1.meiner Seel!, interj.; 2.Ai!, interj.; 3.du liewer Zuschtand!, interj.; 4.Gott (der)n. (mei -- nochemol!); 5.Grund (der)n. (ei du --); 6.meiner Siwwe (noch eemol)!, interj.; **husband** (my old man) Alder(der)n. (mei --); **wife** Aldi (es)n. (mei --)

myopia Katzsichdichkeet (die)n.; Katzsichdichkeit, pl.

Mm

myopic

mysterious

(Continued from page 323)

myopic katzsichdich, adj., adv.

myself 1.mich (accusative), pron.; 2.Nummereens (der)n.

mysterious 1.geheem, adj.; 2.geheim, adj.

Nn

nag — neglected

nag 1.beb(b)ere, v.; gebeb(b)ert, pp.; 2.bobere, v.;
gebobert, pp.; 3.bohre, v.; gebohrt, pp.; 4.breble, v.;
gebrebelt, pp.; 5.knewwle, v.; geknewwelt, pp.;
(horse) 1.Geilche (es)n.; 2.Geili (es)n.; 3.Geilscher
(es)n.; 4.Maer (die)n.; 5.Maerr (die)n.

nagging 1.Gebeller (es)n.; 2.Gebrebel (es)n.

nail 1.aa/schlagge, v.; aagschlagge, pp.; 2.Naggel (der)n.;
3.naggel, v.; genaggelt, pp.; 4.Neggel (der)n.; Neggel,
pl.; **against** wedder/naggle, v.; weddergenaggelt, pp.;
down nunner/naggle, v.; nunnergenaggelt, pp.; **on**
aa/naggle, v.; aagenaggelt, pp.; **together**
zamme/naggle, v.; zammegenaggelt, pp.; **up**
1.nuff/naggle, v.; nuffgenaggelt, pp.; 2.zunaggele, v.;
zugenaggelt, pp.

naive nadierlich, adj.

naked 1.baar, adj.; 2.bloss, adj.; 3.nackich, adj.

name 1.benaame, v.; benaamt, pp.; 2.benenne, v.; benennt,
pp.; 3.heese, v.; gheese, pp.; 4.Naame (der)n.; Neeme,
pl.; 5.nenne, v.; genennt, pp.; 6.Nome (der)n.; Neeme,
pl.; **after** no(och)naame, v.; no(och)genaamt, pp.;
**(applied in colonial times to the northwestern part of
Lehigh Co. (PA) because of the dire need of the early
settlers)** Allemengel (der)n.

namely 1.naemlich, adj.; 2.neemlich, adj.; adv.

nap 1.dus(e)le, v.; geduselt, pp.; 2.leie, v.; gelege; geleye,
pp.; 3.schlummre, v.; gschlummert, pp.

nape (back of the neck) 1.Ankel (die)n.; 2.Gnick (es)n.;
3.Halsgnick (es)n.; 4.Nache (der)n.; 5.Zoppe (der)n.

napkin 1.Bauchduch (es)n.; Bauchdicher, pl.; 2.Halsduch
(es)n.; Halsdicher, pl.; 3.Rachebutzer (der)n.; Rachebutzer, pl.; 4.Schossduch (es)n.; Schossdicher, pl.

narcissus 1.Oschderblumm (die)n.; 2.Schtaernblumm
(die)n.; Schtaernblumme, pl.

narrate verzehle, v.; verzehlt, pp.

narration Erzehlung (die)n.

narrator Erzehler (der)n.

narrow 1.eng, adj.; 2.schmaal, adj.; **leafed plantain**
1.Schpitzewettrich (der)n.; 2.Kolweblaat (es)n.;
Kolwebledder, pl.; 3.Wegerich (der)n.; **minded**
enghaerzich, adj.; **path** Peedli (es)n.; Peedlin, pl.; **twisted
strip of dough** (on top of a pie) Schtreissel (es)n.

narrower enger, adj.

narrowing in the toe of a stocking; when knitting
eischtricke, v.; eigschtrickt, pp.

nary a red rot, adj. (kenn --er)

nasal darich die Naas, adv.; **bone** Naasbee (es)n.; **speech**
Naasegschwetz (es)n.

nasturtium(s) 1.Gresse (die)n.; 2.Paffekaffe (die)n., pl.;
3.Pafflekaffle (die)n., pl.

nasty 1.ga(r)schdich, adj.; 2.unflaet, adj.

nation Volk (es)n.

native 1.eigebore, adj.; 2.Lan(d)smann (der)n.

natural nadierlich, adj.; **gift** 1.Nadurgaab (die)n.; 2.Talent
(es)n. **quality** Nadurbeschaffenheet (die)n.

naturalist Nadurfarscher (der)n.

naturalize birgerhaft, v.

naturalized birgerhaft, adj.

naturally nadierlich, adv.

naturalness 1.Nadierlichkeet (die)n.; 2.Nadierlichkeit (die)n.

nature Naduur (die)n.

naught 1.nix, pron.; 2.Null (die)n.

naughtiness 1.Nixnutzichkeit (die)n.; 2.Unaart (die)n.;
3.Unzucht (die)n.

naughty 1.nixnutz(ich), adj.; 2.unaardich, adj.

nauseate 1.drehe, v.; gedreht, pp.; 2.grause, v.; gegraust,
pp.; 3.iwwele, v.; geiwwelt, pp.; 4.widderschteh, v.;
widderschtanne, pp.

nauseated 1.iwwel, adj.; 2.iwwelich, adj.; 3.kotzerich,
adj.; **by** ekle, v.; ge-ekelt, pp.

nauseating 1.iwwelich, adj.; 2.wedderlich, adj.;
3.widderlich, adj.

nave Naab (die)n.

navel Nawwel (der)n.; Nawwel; Newwel, pl.; **band**
Nawwelbinn (die)n.

navigation Schiffaahrt (die)n.

navy bean 1.Feldbohn (die)n.; Feldbohne, pl.;
2.Suppebohn (die)n.; Suppebohne, pl.

nay nee, adv.

Nazareth Naazrett (es)n.

near 1.gnapps, adv.; 2.naekscht, adv.; 3.rum/sei, v.; **(very)**
zimmlich naegscht, adj.; **by** dicht, adv.; **horse** (of a
two-horse team) Saddelgaul (der)n.; **sighted**
1.katzsichdich, adj.; adv.; 2.neegschtsichdich, adj.;
nearer; nearest neegscht; neecher; neegscht, adv.

nearest of all allernaegscht, adj., adv.

nearly 1.beinaah, adv.; 2.schnier, adv.; 3.zimmlich, adv.;
(very) 1.schier gaar, adv.; 2.schier gaarli, adv.; **dry** (of
cows) altmelkich, adj.

neat 1.nett, adj.; 2.niedlich, adj.

neat's foot oil Glooefett (es)n.; **leather** Rindledder (es)n.

neatness Niedichkeet (die)n.

necessary 1.brauchba(a)r, adv.; 2.needich, adv.; 3.nitzlich,
adv.; 4.notwendich, adv.; 5.notwennich, adv.

necessity 1.Bedaerfnis (es)n.; 2.Mangel (der)n.;
3. Notwendichkeit (die)n.

neck 1.Hals (der)n.; Helser, pl.; 2.Hels (der)n.; Helser, pl.; **(of
beef)** Halsschtick (es)n.; **(of violin)** Geigehals (der)n.

nee geborni, adj.

need 1.bedaerfe, v.; bedaerft, pp.; 2.brauche, v.; gebraucht,
pp.; 3.breiche, v.; gebreicht, pp.; 4.Mangel (der)n.;
5.Not (die)n.

needle Nodel (die)n.; Nodle, pl.

needy 1.aarem, adj.; adv.; 2.aar(e)mseelich, adj., adv.;
3.bedaerf(l)dich, adj.; 4.kimmerlich, adj.; 5.needich,
adj.; 6.Not (die)n. (in --)

negative term for minister 1.Paff (der)n.; 2.Seeledokder
(der)n.

neglect 1.verbamble, v.; verbambelt, pp.; 2.verbasse, v.;
verbasst, pp.; 3.verbemble, v.; verbembelt, pp.;
4.verhopbasse, v.; verhopbasst, pp.; 5.verlabbe, v.;
verlappt, pp.; 6.vernooclessiche, v.; vernooclessicht,
pp.; 7.verseime, v.; verseimt, pp.

neglected verlumpt, adj.

Nn

negligee — nimble

negligee Hausgleed (es)n.

negligence 1.Faahrlessichkeit (die)n.; 2.Lassichkeit (die)n.; 3.Lessichkeit (die)n.; 4.Noochlessichkeit (die)n.

negligent 1.faahrlessich, adj.; 2.labbich, adj.; 3.lappich, adj.; 4.lass, adj.; 5.nachlessich, adj.; 6.noochlessich, adj.; **person** 1.Lappaarsch (der)n.; 2.Lappes (der)n.; 3.Lapphund (der)n.; 4.Lappi (der)n.

negotiable verhandelbaar, adv.

Negro 1.Neger (der)n.; Neger, pl.; 2.Nieger (der)n.; 3.schwarz, adj.(en schwarzer); 4.Schwatzer (en)n.

neigh (of horses) 1.Greische, v.; gegrische, pp.; 2.hutschle, v.; ghutschelt, pp.; 3.lache, v.; gelacht, pp.; 4.nigre, v.; gnigert, pp.

neighbor 1.Lan(d)smann (der)n.; 2.Newemensch (der)n.; 3.Nochber (der)n.; Nochbere, pl.; **lady** Nochberin (die)n.

neighbor's house Nochbershaus (es)n.

neighborhood 1.Gegend (die)n.; 2.Naahe (die)n.; 3.Naeh (die)n.; 4.Nochberschaft (die)n.; 5.Umgegend (die)n.

neighborly nochberlich, adj.; **act** Nochberschtick (es)n.

neither one kem

neither...nor net...un aa net

nephew 1.Bruderskind (es)n.; 2.Gschwischderkind (es)n.; 3.Gschwischdersoh (der)n.

n'er-do-well Lump (der)n.

nerve 1.Naer(re)v (die)n.; 2.Naerf (die)n.; Naerfe, pl.

nervous 1.naerfich, adj.; 2.narefich, adj.; 3.zidderich, adj.; **fever** Naerfefiewer (es)n.; **wabble** Zidderwackel (der)n.

nest Nescht (es)n.; Neschder, pl.; **egg** 1.Leegoi (es)n.; Leegoier, pl.; 2.Neschtoi (es)n.; Neschtoier, pl.; **egg** (of glass) Glassoi (es)n.; Glassoier, pl.

nestle nischdle, v.; genischdelt, pp.

net 1.Gaarn (es)n.; 2.Gorn (es)n.; 3.Netz (es)n.

netting Netzwaerick (es)n.

nettle-rash Wiwwelsucht (die)n.

neuralgia Naerveweh (es)n.

neurosis Naerfefiewer (es)n.

neutral unbardeiisch, adj.

never 1.Daag (der)n. (sei [mei, dei] -- des lewes net); 2.keemols, adv.; 3.Lebbdaag (der)n. (sei -- net); 4.Lewe(es)n. (sei -- net); 5.nie net, adv.; 6.nie, adv.; 7.nie, adv. (er dutt -- nix); 8.niemols, adv.; 9.nimme, adv.; 10.nimmi, adv.; 11.seilewe(s), adv. (-- net); 12.selewe, adv. (-- net)

never (emphatic) 1.Daag des Lewes net!, adv.; 2.immer in ewich net!, interj.; 3.sei Lebbdaag net!, adv.; 4.sei Lewe(s) net!, adv.; **again** 1.nimmermeh, adv.; 2.nimmimeh, adv.; **any** nie, adv. (-- kenn); **to utter a cross word** schepp, adj. (en -- Watt gewwe)

nevermore 1.nimmermeh, adv.; 2.nimmimeh, adv.

nevertheless 1.netdesdewennicher, adv.; 2.nixdewennicher, adv.

New Mennonites (followers of Herr) Herreleit (die)n., pl.; **Testament** Nei Teschdement (es)n.; **Year** Nei Yaahr (es)n.; **Year's banter** Neiyaahrswetting (die)n.; **Year's Day** Neiyaahrsdaag (es)n.; **Year's Day late riser**

1.Silfeschder (der)n.; 2.Silli (der)n.; 3.Silweschder (der)n.; **Year's greeting** 1.Neiyaahrs-gruuss (der)n.; 2.Neiyaahrswinsch (der)n.; 3.Neiyaahrswunsch (der) n.; Neiyaahrswinsche, pl; 4.Winsching (die)n.; **Year's night** Neiyaahrnacht (die)n.; **York** Nei Yarick (der)n.

new 1.frisch, adj.; 2.nei, adj.; **comer** Aakemmling (der)n.; **convert** Neibekehrter (der, die)n.; **moon** 1.Neilicht (es)n.; 2.Neimoond (der)n.; 3.Neimuund (der)n.

newfangled 1.neimodisch, adj.; 2.neirunslich, adj.

newly neilich, adv.; **cleared land** Neiland (es)n.

news 1.Neiichkeede (die)n., pl.; 2.Noochricht (die)n.

newsboy Zeidingdrager (der)n.

newspaper 1.Zeiding (die)n.; Zeidinge, pl.; 2.Zeiting (die) n.; **reporter** Zeidingschreiwer (der)n.

next 1.naekscht, adv.; 2.negscht, adj.; **best** 1.naekschtbescht, adv.; 2.negschtbescht, adj.; **to him** 1.newem = newe em; 2.newes = newe es; 3.neweme = newe me; **to the largest** zwettgreescht, adj.; **to the oldest** zwetteltscht, adj.; **to the smallest** zwett-glennscht, adj.; **to the top rail** (in a worm fence) Reider (der)n.; Reider, pl.

nibble 1.gnawwere, v.; gegnawwert, pp.; 2.knawwere, v.; geknawwert, pp.; **at** 1.aa/gnawwere, v.; aagegnawwert, pp.; 2.vergnawwere, v.; vergnawwert, pp.

nibbler Schnippler (der)n.

nibbling Gegnawwer (es)n.

nice 1.abbedittlich, adj.; 2.fei(n), adj.; 3.kauscher, adj.; 4.nett, adj.; 5.niedlich, adj.; 6.sauwer, adj.; 7.schee, adj.

nicely zierlich, adj.

Nicholas 1.Nickel (der)n.; 2.Nickles (der)n.

nick 1.ei/schneide, v.; eigschnidde, pp.; 2.Kaft (die)n.; Kafde, pl.

nickel (coin) Finfsentschtick (es)n.; Finfsentschticker, pl.

nickname 1.Beinaame (der)n.; 2.Nicknaame (der)n.; 3.Schimpnaame (der)n.; 4.Schpottnaame (der)n.; 5.Unnaame (der)n.; **for members of the Evangelical denomination** Schtrawwler (der)n.; Schtrawwler, pl. **niece or nephew** 1.Bruderskind (es)n.; Bruderskinner, pl.; 2.Schweschderkind (es)n.; Schweschderkinner, pl.

niggardly grappschich, adj.

niggerhead Felsekopp (der)n.

night Nacht (die)n.; Nachde; Necht, pl.; **air** Nachtluft (die)n.; **blooming cereus** Nachtblumm (die)n.; Nachtblumme, pl.; **cap** Nachtkapp (die)n.; Schlofkapp (die)n.; **dress** Nachtgleed (es)n.; **hawk** Nachteil (die)n.; Nachteile, pl.; **light** Nachtlicht (es)n.; Nachtlichder, pl.; **stool** Kommood (die)n.; **sweat** Nachtschwitze (es)n.; **vigil** (with a corpse) Wach(t)nacht (die)n.; **watchman** Nachtwechder (der)n.; **work** Nachtaerwett (die)n.

nightgown 1.Nachthemm (es)n.; Nachthemmer, pl.; 2. Nachtkutt (die)n.; Nachtkudde, pl.

nightingale Nachtigaall (die)n.

nightly 1.alli Nacht, adv.; 2.nechtlich, adv.

nightmarish schlofschtermich, adv.

nightshirt Nachthemm (es)n.; Nachthemmer, pl.

nimble 1.fix, adj., adv.; 2.flink, adj.; 3.rasch(t), adj.; 4.wusslich, adj.

Nn

nimbus / not

nimbus Reggewolk (die)n.; Reggewolke, pl.

nine nein; neine, adj.; **bark** Neinheidichholz (es)n.; **eyed** neineegich, adj.; **o'clock snack** (served in the field to haying and harvesting hands) Neinuhrschtick (es)n.; **spot** (of cards) Neinder (es)n.

nineteen neinzeh, adj.

nineteenth neinzeht, adj.

ninetieth neinzischt, adj.

ninety neinzich, adj.

ninth 1.neint, adj.; 2.Neintel (es)n.

nip Nipp (es)n.

nippers Beisszang (die)n.

nipple 1.Bruchtwaarz (die)n.; Bruschtwaarze, pl.; 2.Schlotzer (der)n.; Schlotzer, pl.; 3.Waarz (die)n.; Waarze, pl.

nit 1.Niss (die)n.; 2.Nitz (die)n.; Nitze, pl.

nitric acid 1.Salpederfier (es)n.; 2.Schee(d)wasser (es)n.; 3.Scheewasser (es)n.

nitty nissich, adj.

no 1.kee, adj.; 2.kenn, adj.; 3.nee, adv.; **danger** Bang (die) n. (du brauscht kenn -- hawwe); **doubt** deich; **harm in trying** schatte, v.; gschatt, pp. (batt's nix, so schatt's nix); **harm meant** 1.Nix fer Ungut un gaar nix ver schpeit; 2.nix fer Ungut wann's regert; **longer** 1.nimme, adv.; 2.nimmi, adv.; **matter** schatte, v.; gschatt, pp. (nix --); **more** 1.nimme, adv.; 2.nimmi, adv. **offence I hope** ungut, adj. (nix fer --); **one** 1.niemand, pron.; 2.nimmand, pron.

Noah Nooi (der)n.

noble edel, adj.

nobody niemand, pron.

nocturnal nachtlich, adv.

nod 1.nucke, v.; genuckt, pp.; 2.schnabble, v.; gschnappt, pp.; 3.schnappe, v.; gschnappt, pp.

node (of a plant) G(e)waerb (es)n.

nodule Glimbel (es)n.

noise 1.Gedunner (es)n.; 2.Geglebber (es)n.; 3.Gelaerm (es)n.; 4.Gerumpel (es)n.; 5.Laerm(e) (der)n.; 6.Uuzucht (die)n.; 7.Uwing (die)n.; 8.Yacht (die)n.; 9.Zucht (die)n.; **(as in a factory or large gathering)** Dumor (es)n.; **(made by children)** Kinnerzucht (die)n.

noisy 1.laermich, adj.; 2.laermend, adj.; 3.yachdich, adj.; 4.yachtich, adj.; 5.zuchdich, adj.

nominate uff/nemme, v.; uffgenumme, pp.

non-Amish englisch, adj.; **essential** Newesach (die)n.; Newesache, pl.

nonagenarian Neinzichyaehricher (der)n.

none 1.kenner, adj.; pron.; 2.kenni, adj.; pron.; 3.kenns, adj.; pron.; **at all** gaar kenner; kenni; adj., pron.

nonplus 1.verbliffe, v.; verblifft, pp.; 2.verbluffe, v.; verblufft, pp.

nonsense 1.Faxe (die)n., pl.; 2.Hun(d)sbohne (die)n., pl.; 3.Hun(d)sbuhne (die)n., pl.; 4.Lapperei (die)n.; 5.Narreschtick (es)n.; 6.Schwoweschtreech (die)n., pl.; 7.Unsinn (der)n.

nonsensical unsinnich, adj.

noodle 1.Kaschde (der)n.; Kaschde, pl.; 2.Nudel (die)n.; Nudle, pl.; **soup** Nudelsupp (die)n.

nook Eck (es)n.; Ecke, pl.

noon Middaag (der)n.; **chores** Middaagarewett (die)n.; **time** Middaagszeit (die)n.

noose Schlupp (der)n.; Schlipp, pl.

nor noch (rare usage)

North Star Naddschtann (die)n.

north 1.nadd(e), adv.; 2.Nadde (die)n.; 3.Nard(e) (die)n.; 4.nard, adv.; **side** 1.Naddseit (die)n.; 2.Winderseit (die)n.; **wind** Naddwind (der)n.

northerly 1.naerdlich, adv.; 2.nardlich, adv.

northern polestar Nardschtaern (die)n.

northward 1.gege Naade, adv.; 2.naddlich, adv.

northwest wind 1.Naddweschtwind (der)n.; 2.Nardweschtwind (der)n.

northwest(erly) 1.naddewescht, adv.; 2.nardwescht, adv.

northwind Nardwind (der)n.

nose 1.Naas (die)n.; Nees, pl.; 2.Reicher (der)n.; 3.Reisel (der)n.; 4.Riecher (der)n.; 5.Riesel (der)n.; **(of animal)** Kolwe (der)n.; Kolwe, pl.; **around** rum/ries(e)le, v.; rumgerieselt, pp.; **cover** (of screen cloth for horse's nose, to protect against flies) Naaskaerwerli (es)n.; Naaskaerwerlin, pl.

nosegay Schtreissel (es)n.

nosey 1.geck, adj. (rare usage;) 2.naasich, adj.; 3.schnaflich, adj.; 4.schnawlich, adj.; **fellow** Schnaffler (der)n.; Schnaffler, pl.

nostril Naasloch (es)n.; Naaslecher, pl.

not net, adv.; **a cent** rot, adj. (kenn --er); **a single person was there** gotzich, adj. (kenn --er mensch warr datt); **a word** Wattche (es)n. (kenn --); **all there** Schparre (der) n. (-- los); **any** 1.kee, adj.; 2.kenner, adj.; pron.; 3.kenni, adj.; pron.; 4.kens, adj.; pron.; **appetizing** unabbeditlich, adj.; **appreciated** ungeeschdimiert, adj.; **as you value your life** beileiwe net!, interj.; **cordial** 1.gratzich, adj.; 2.kratzich, adj.; **double** eifach. adj.; **even** 1.net emol, adv.; 2.nettemol, adv.; **having all one's senses** gscheit, adj. (net gans recht --); **long ago** kaerzlich, adv.; **on your life!** bei Lewe net!, interj.; **once** 1.keemol, adv.; 2.kenmol, adv.; **one** 1.eensicher, adj.; 2.kee eener, pron.; 3.kenn eener, pron.; **permitted** 1.unaerlaabt, adj.; 2.unerlaabt, adj.; **produce true to breed or variety** ausorte, v.; ausgeort, pp.; **quite a quart** Gwaart (die)n. (en katzi --) **respect-ed** 1.unge-eschdimiert, adj.; 2.ungeeschdimiert, adj.; **so?** 1.Gell(e)?, interj.; 2.Gelte?, interj.; 3.Net waahr?; **straight** schepp, adj.; **thrive** 1.welle, v.; gewellt, pp. (net --); 2.wolle, v.; gewollt, pp. (net --); **to be able to do sufficient** Rot (der)n. (net -- du kenne); **to be endured** un(a)e(r)baermlich, adj.; **to have much regard for** druffhalde, v. (net viel --); **to look like the same person** gucke, v.; geguckt, pp. (sich nix meh gleich --); **to mention** 1.gschweige, conj.; 2.mol, adv. (-- gschwiege); **to tally** schtimme, v.; gschtimmt, pp. (net iwwer eens --); **wanted** iwwrich, adj.; **well** unwohl, adv.; **worth a damn** Fluch (der)n.; (kenn -- waert)

327

Nn

notable — nutritious

notable marickwaddich, adv.

notch 1.aus/schneide, v.; ausgschnidde, pp.; 2.Kaft (die)n.; Kafde, pl.; 3.kafte, v.; gekaft, pp.; 4.zackle, v.; gezackelt, pp.

notched 1.kaftich, adj.; 2.kefd(l)ich, adj.; 3.keft(l)ich, adj.

note 1.bemaricke, v.; bemarickt, pp.; 2.maericke, v.; gemaerickt, pp.; 3.maricke, v.; gemarickt, pp.; 4.Not (die)n.; 5.Zettel (der)n.

noted wohlbekannt, adj.

nothing nix, pron.

nothing (an idiomatic expres to children) = to return home empty handed with nothing for the children) en silwerich(G)Waardeweil un en goldich (G)Nixli mit heembringe; **at all** gaar nix, pron.; **but** 1.lauder, adj., adv.; 2.lauter, adj.; **doing!** Nix kumm raus!, interj.; **of the kind!** nixeso!, interj.; **special** nix Weiders; **suits him** brode, v.; gebrode, pp. (es is ihm nix rechts --); **to it!** Hohle Buhne!, interj.; **will come of it** draus, adv. (es waerd nix --)

notice 1.Acht (der, die)n. (-- uff ebbes hawwe); 2.Noochricht (die)n.

noticeable bemaerricklich, adj.

notification Meldung (die)n.

notify 1.aa/kindiche, v.; aagekindicht, pp.; 2.aa/saage, v.; aagsaat, pp.; 3.benoochrichde, v.; benoochrichdet, pp.

notorious allbekannt, adj.

noun 1.Naamewatt (es)n.; 2.Nomewatt (es)n.

nourish 1.n(a)ehre, v.; gen(a)ehrt, pp.

nourishment 1.Naahring (die)n.; 2.Naahrung (die)n.; 3.Naahrungsschtofft (es)n.; 4.Schpeis (die)n.

novelty 1.Nei-ichkeit (die)n.; Neiichkeide, pl.; 2.Neiheit (die)n.; Neiheide, pl.

November 1.Nofember (der)n.; 2.Nowember (der)n.

now 1.alleweil, adv.; 2.anneweil, adv.; 3.erscht, adv.; 4.nau, adv.; 5.yetz(t) nau, adv.; **and then** 1.dann un wann, adv.; 2.hie un widder, adv.; **and then a day** daageweis, adv.; **and then a month** monetweis, adv.; **it's about time** Nau is awwer ball Zeit!; **the business** (work, trouble) **begins** Dudel (der)n. (nau geht der -- aa)

nowadays 1.heidesdaags, adv.; 2.heidich(e)daags, adv.; 3.heidich, adv.; 4.heidzedaags, adv.; 5.heilichdaags, adv.; 6.heilichsdaags, adj.; 7.heitesdaags, adj.; 8.heitich(e)sdaags, adj.; 9.heitich, adj.; 10.heitzedaag, adj.

nowhere 1.naeryets, adv.; 2.naryets, adv.; 3.neiyets, adv.

noxious schaedlich, adj.

nubbin Knarze (der)n.

nubbins Seiwelschkann (es)n.

nude 1.bloos, adj.; 2.nackich, adj.

nudge in the rib 1.gickse, v.; gegickst, pp.; 2.giekse, v.; gegiekst, pp.

nudging Gschtubb (es)n.

nugget Glimbel (es)n.

nuisance 1.Druwwel (der)n. (en --); 2.Elend (es)n. (en --); 3.Greitz (es)n. (en --); 4.Gretz (der)n. (en --); 5.Unflaat (der)n.

number 1.Meng(e) (die)n.; 2.Nummer (die)n.; Nummere, pl.; 3.nummere, v.; nummeret, pp.; 4.Zaahl (die)n.; **one** Nummereens (der)n.

numberless 1.unzaehlich, adj.; 2.zaahllos, adj.

numbskull Dummkopp (der)n.; Dummkepp, pl.

numerable zaehlbaar, adj.

numeral 1.Zaahlwatt (es)n.; 2.Ziffer (der)n.; Ziffere, pl.

numerate zehle, v.; gezehlt, pp.

numeration Zaehlung (die)n.

numerous zaahlreich, adj.

numerous offspring Kinnersege (der)n.

nun 1.Glooschderfraa (die)n.; 2.Kloschderfraa (die)n.; 3. Schweschder (die)n.; Schweschdere, pl.

nuptial Hochzich (die)n.; Hochziche, pl.

nurse (a sick person) ab/waarde, v.; abgewaardt, pp; **or suck complacently** (of an infant) 1.nuddle, v.; genuddelt, pp.; 2.nusch(d)le, v.; genusch(d)elt, pp.

nursemaid Kinsmaad (die)n.

nursery (for trees) Baamschul (die)n.

nursing (a patient) 1.Abwarting (die)n.; 2.Abwartung (die)n.; 3.Waarting (die)n.; 4.Waartung (die)n.

nursing bottle Ditzboddel (die)n.; Ditzboddle, pl.

nut Nuss (die)n.; Niss, pl.; **(of a bolt)** Mudder (die)n.; **(silly person)** Schpundi (der)n.

nutmeg 1.Muschgaadnuss (die)n.; 2.Muschkaadnuss (die)n.

nutritious 1.naahrhafdich, adj.; 2.naahrhaft, adj.

Oo

oak ... of

oak Eeche (der, die)n.; **leaf** Eecheblaat (es)n.; **wood** Eecheholz (es)n.

oaken eeche, adj.

oaktree Eechebaam (der)n.; Eechebeem, pl.

oar Ruder (der)n.; Ruder, pl.

oat bin Hawwerkischt (die)n.; **chaff** Hawwerschprau (die) n. ; **field** Hawwerfeld (es)n.; Hawwerfelder, pl.; **grain** Hawwerkaern (die)n.; **harvest** Hawwerern (die)n.; **midge** Hawwerlaus (die)n.; Hawwerleis, pl.

oath 1.Eed (der)n.; 2.Schwur (der)n.

oatmeal Hawwermehl (es)n.

oats Hawwer (der)n.; **bag** Hawwersack (der)n.; **bug** Hawwerkeffer (der)n.; Hawwerkeffer, pl.

oatstraw Hawwerschtroh (es)n.

obdurate verschtockt, adj.

obedience 1.Gehorsam (der)n.; 2.Gehorsamkeit (die)n.

obedient 1.gehersam, adj.; 2.gehorsam, adj.

obey 1.bariere, v.; bariert, pp.; 2.befolge, v.; befolgt, pp.; 3.folye, v.; gfol(i)gt, pp.; 4.geharriche, v.; karricht, pp.; 5.meinde, v.; gemeindt, pp.; 6.no(och)folye, v.; no(och)gfoligt, pp.; 7.no(och)kumme, v.; no(och)kumme, pp.; 8.no(och)laafe; v.; no(och)gloffe, pp.; **the call of nature** speaking to children) ninkere, v.; geninkert, pp.

obituary Dodelischt (die)n.

object 1.Ardickel (der)n.; 2.dagege hawwe, v.; 3.Gegeschtand (der)n.; 4.Zweck (der)n.

objection 1.Eiwendung (die)n.; 2.Eiwenning (die)n.; 3. Gegehaldung (die)n.

obligate oneself verbinne (sich --)v.; verbunne, pp.

obligation 1.Pflicht (die)n.; 2.Verpflichtung (die)n.

oblige 1.verbinne, v.; verbunne, pp.; 2.verpflichde, v.; verpflicht, pp.

obliged to come in rei/misse, v.; reigemisst, pp.; **to cross over or pass over** niwwer/misse, v.; niwwergemisst, pp.; **to follow** no(och)misse, v.; no(och)gemisst, pp.; **to get out** raus/misse, v.; rausgemisst, pp.; **to go** fatt/misse, v.; fattgemisst, pp.; **to go down** nunner/misse, v.; nunnergemisst, pp.; **to go out** naus/misse, v.; nausgemisst, pp.; **to go to a place** hie/misse, v.; hiegmisst, pp.; **to return** zerick/misse, v.; zerickgemisst, pp.

obliging gfellich, adj.

oblique 1.iwwerecks, adj.; 2.schepp, adj.; 3.schraeks, adj.; 4.schreegs, adj.

obliterate 1.verdilye, v.; verdilgt, pp.; 2.verwische, v.; verwischt, pp.

oblong lenglich, adj.

obscene talk Seierei (die)n.

obscenities Gschwetz (es)n. (narrisch --)

obscure 1.undeitlich, adj.; 2.verfinschdere, v.; verfinschdert, pp.

observable bemarickbaar, adj.

observance 1.Befolgung (die)n.; 2.Beobachtung (die)n.

observe 1.aa/blicke, v.; aageblickt, pp.; 2.bedrachde, v.; bedracht, pp.; 3.befolge, v.; befolgt, pp.; 4.begucke, v.; beguckt, pp.

obstinate 1.absenaat, adj.; 2.bullkeppich, adj.; 3.glotzkebbich, adj.; 4.halsschtarrich, adj.; 5.Kopp (der)n. (sie is --s sei); 6.rabbelkebbi(s)ch, adj.; 7.schtarrkebbich, adj.; 8.schteifhalsich, adj.; 9.schtowwelich, adj.; 10.schtowwerich, adj.; 11.schtubbich, adj.; 12.uffsetzich, adj.; **cough** Gauzer (der)n.; **person** Glotzkopp (der)n.; Glotzkepp, pl.

obstreperous laermend, adj.

obstruct zuschtelle, v.; zugschtellt, pp.; **by building** zubaue, v.; zugebaut, pp.

obtain 1.erlange, v.; erlangt, pp.; 2.no(och)griege, v.; no(och)grickt, pp.; **a position by lying** nei/liege (sich --)v.; neigeloge, pp.; **by begging or persistency** ab/bettle, v.; abgebeddelt, pp.; **by marrying** erhiere, v.; erhiert, pp.; **by slow movements or delay** erschleiche, v.; erschliche, pp.

occasion Geleyeheit (die)n.

occasionally 1.allgebott, adj.; 2.alsemol, adv.; 3.ebmol(s), adv.

occupant B(e)sitzer (der)n.

occupation of a farmer Bauer(e)schtand (der)n.

occupied with trifles 1.gnuschdre, v.; gegnuschdert, pp.; 2.rum/gnuschdre, v.; rumgegnuschdert, pp.

occur schtattfinne, v.; schtattgfunne, pp.; **to** 1.ei/falle, v.; eigfalle, pp.; 2.eikumme, v.; eikumme, pp.

ocean See (der)n.

o'clock uhr, adv.

octagional achteckich, adj.

October 1.Oktober (der)n.; 2.Oktower (der)n.

oculist Aagedokder (der)n.; Aagedokder, pl.

odd 1.kariyos, adj.; 2.schpassich, adj.; 3.ungraad, adj.; **jobs** 1.Bambelaerwet (die)n.; 2.Bembelaerwet (die) n.; **or scattered years** yohrelang, adj.; **or scattering years** so yaahreweis, adv.

oddly acting person Kaschber (der)n.

odor Geruch (der)n.; **of bedbugs** Wansegeruch (der)n.

of 1.an, prep.; 2.vum, prep.; 3.vun, prep.; **(in telling time)** bis, prep.; **a (surly or bad) disposition** bees, adj. (genadurt --); **a bad color** iwwelguckich, adj.; **a certain build and stature** gepuschdurt, adj.; **a pleasing sensation** (mostly in a vulgar manner) schlau, adj.; **age** 1. vollyaarich, adj.; 2. vollyeahrich, adj.; **beech** buche, adj.; **blessed memory** verewicht, adj.; **brass** 1.messe, adj.; 2.messich, adj.; 3.messing, adj.; **brick** backeschteene, adj.; **calico** gedunich, adj.; **checkered cloth** kelschich, adj.; **course** 1.allerdings, adv.; 2.freilich, adv.; 3.woll, adj.; 4.wull, adj., adv.; **different mind** zweekeppich, adj.; **flannel** flannelle, adj.; **flax** 1.flachse, adj.; 2.waerricke, adj.; **her** vunre = vun re; **her kind** ihresgleiche, adj.; **his own kind** sein(e)sgleiche(s); **it** devun, adv.; **large build** grossglidderich, adj.; **man's stature** mannshoch, adv.; **old** 1.landhaer, adv.; 2.lang her, adv.; **one** vumme - vun me; **red silk** rotseide, adj.; **silver** silwer (n), adj. ; **steel** schtaahle, adj.; **stone** schteenich, adj.; **sugar** 1.zuckerich, adj.; 2.zuckern, adv.; **that**

(Continued on page 330)

329

Oo

of (continued)

(Continued from page 329)

1.dattdevun, adv.; 2.devun, adv.; **the length of a finger** fingerslang, adj.; **this** 1. dodevun, adv.; 2.dodewege, adv.; **three sorts** 1. dreierlee, adj.; 2.dreierlei, adj.; **tin** 1.bleche, adj.; 2. blechich, adj.; 3. zinne, adj.; 4.zinnich, adj. **today** 1.heidich, adj.; 2. hiedichdaagich, adj.; **two kinds** zweeaerlee, adv.; **use** nutz, adv.; **yore** 1.alders, adv. (ver --); 2.veralders, adv.

off 1.ab, adv.; 2.ab, prep.; 3.fatt, adv.; 4.fatt/maschiere, v.; fattmaschiert, pp. 5.weck, adv.; **and get back** zerick/packe (sich --)v.; zerickgepackt, pp.; **back in that direction** dattzerickzus, adv.; **back in this direction** dohinnriezus, adv.; **color** 1.dreckich, adj.; 2.schmutzich, adj.; **fall** Abfall (der)n.; **horse of the two leaders** Vannenewegaul (der)n.; **in the head** 1.backe, v.; gebacke, pp. (net gans recht gebacke); 2.Belskapp (die)n. (letz in der --); 3. kabiddelfescht, adv. (net gans --); 4.net gans kampes; **in this direction** doneizus, adv.; **over in that direction** doniwwerzus, adv.; **over in that direction** dattniwwerzus, adv.; **rear** (referring to a horse) hinnenewe, adj.; **to one side** newenaus, adv.

offence 1.Aaschtoss (der)n.; 2.Beleidichung (die)n.; 3.Eierniss (die)n.; 4.Verbreche (es)n.

offend 1.aa/schtosse, v.; aagschtosse, pp.; 2.belei(ch)diche, v.; beleidicht, pp.; 3.lege, v.; glegt, pp. (ebber ebbes in der Weg --); 4.verdriesse, v.; verdrosse, pp.

offended 1.bees, adj.; 2.kibbisch, adj.; 3.verdrosse, adj.

offender Iwwerdreder (der)n.

offer 1.aa/biede, v.; aagebodde, pp.; 2.Aabieting (die)n.; 3.Gebott (es)n.; **resistance** wedderschteh, v.; wedderschtanne, pp.; **thanks** dank/sage, v.; dankgsaat, pp.

offering 1.Opfer (es)n.; 2.Opfergeld (es)n.

office 1.Ambt (es)n.; 2.Amt (es)n.; 3.Bedienung (die)n.

official 1.Amtsmann (der)n.; 2.Beamter (der)n.

officious 1.ba(a)sich, adj.; 2.bassich, adj.

offspring 1.Noochkemmling (der)n.; 2.Noochkumme(r) (der)n.; Noochkumme(r), pl.

oft times 1.oftmols, adv. 2.oftzeide, adv.

often 1.efters, adv.; 2.oft, adv.; 3.oftmols, adv.

ogee-plane Leischhowwel (die)n.; Leischhowwle, pl.

Oh! 1.Aah!, interj.; 2.ach!, interj.; 3.Autsch!, interj.; 4.ei!, interj.; 5.O!, interj.; 6.oh!, interj.; **misery!** Yammer un Elend!; **my!** 1.Droscht (der)n. (liewer --); 2.Troscht (der)n. (liewer --); **ouch!** au!, interj.

oil 1.Eel (es)n.; 2.eele, v.; ge-eelt, pp.; 3.Eil (es)n.; **gland** (of fowl) 1.Barzel (der)n.; 2.Eelkennli (es)n.; 3.Eelkessli (es) n.; 4.Eelkewwich (es)n.; 5.Eelzeppli (es)n.; 6.Fettheffli (es)n.; 7.Fettpann (die)n.; Fettpanne, pl.; 8.Fettschnebbel (der)n.; 9.Puppnacker (der)n.; 10.Schmelzpann (die)n.; 11.Schmutzheffli (es)n.; 12.Schmutzkeidel (es)n.; 13.Schmutzkennli (es)n.; 14.Schnewwli (es)n.; 15.Schwanzgribs (es)n.; 16.Zibbel (der)n.; **of bitternuts** Nisseel (es)n.

oilcan 1.Eelkann (die)n.; 2.Schmierkann (die)n.

oilcloth Eelduch (es)n.; Eeldicher, pl.

oilstone Eelschtee (der)n.; Eelschtee, pl.

on

oily eelich, adj.

ointment 1.Salb (die)n.; 2.Schmier (die)n.; 3.Waxschmier (die)n.

Old Christmas, January 6 (celebrated by the Old Order Amish) Alt Grischtdaag (der)n.; **Nick** 1.Hollox (der)n.; 2.Hullox (der)n.; 3.Hullu (der)n.; 4.Hullux (der)n.; **Peter Tumbledown** Bummelhannes (der)n.

old alt, adj.; **(of a joke)** harrich, adj.; **(very)** 1.schtee-alt, adj.; 2.schteenalt, adj.; **country** (Germany) alt Land (es)n.; **crank** Kretz (der)n. (der alter --); **crank** (of a woman) Gretz (die)n. (die aldi --); **enough to die** dootzeidich, adj.; **fashioned** 1.altfrankisch, adj.; 2.altfrenkisch, adj.; 3.altguckich, adj.; 4.altmodisch, adj.; **look** altguckich, adj.; **maid** 1.Maed (die)n. (en aldi --); 2.Maedel (die)n. (en aldi --); **man** Grobaart (der)n.; **ruts** aldi Leier (die); **woman**; 1.Schachdel (die)n. (en aldi --); 2.Schaerwel (die)n.; **worn out cow** Schachdel (die)n. (en aldi --); **older; oldest** alt; **elder; es** elscht, adj.

olive 1.biddri Blaum (die)n.; biddri Blaume, pl.; 2.Eelbeer (die)n.; 3.Eelbier (die)n.; 4.Eelfrucht (die)n.; **leaf** Eelblaat (es)n.; **oil** Baamolich (der)n.; **tree** Eelbaam (der)n.; Eelbeem, pl.

omelet 1.Oierdotsch (es)n.; 2.Oierkuche (der)n.; 3.Oiermehl (es)n.

omen 1.Aazeeche (der, es)n.; 2.Vorbedeidung (die)n.; 3.Zeeche (es)n.

omentum Genetz (es)n.

omission Verseimung (die)n.

omit iwwerhuppe, v.; iwwerhuppt, pp.

omniscient allwissend, adj.

on 1.an, prep.; adv.; 2.auf, prep. (rare usage); 3.druff, prep.; 4.uff, prep; adv.; **a back road** newedrauss, adv.; **account of** 1.weeich, prep.; 2.wege, prep.; **account of it** dewege; **bad terms** aus/sei, v.; ausgewest, pp.; **behind** 1.hinne(r)draa, adv.; 2.hinne(r)her, adv.; 3.hinne(r)no, adv.; **both sides** hiwwe, adv. (-- un driwwe); **credit** uff barigs, adv.; **either side** hiwwe un driwwe, adv.; **foot** Fuus (der)n. (zu --); **hand** vorraedich, adv. **her** uffre = uff re; **here** dodruff, adv.; **it** uffs = uff es; **my account** mein(e)twege, adv.; **no account** 1.beileiwe net!, interj.; 2.darichaus, adv. (-- net); **one** uffme = uff me; **tenter-hooks** dottlich, adj.; **the alert** vorgucke, v.; vorgeguckt, pp.; **the average** 1.Darichschnitt (der)n. (so im --); 2.darichschnittlich, adv.; **the front part** vanne-druff, adv.; **the outside** 1.aus(e)wennich, adj.; 2.ausse, adv.; 3.aussewennich, adv.; **the outskirts** ausserum, adv.; **the point** (of) uff, prep., adv. (-- em Dapeet); **the rear part of** hinnedruff, adv.; **the right side** (in hitching horses) newehie, adv.; **the sly** hehling, adj.; **the spur of the moment** 1.Schtutz (der)n. (uff der --); 2.uff, prep., adv. (-- der Schtutz); **the strength of** dodruffhie, adv.; **the strength of it** druffhie, adj.; **the strength of that** dattdruffhie, adv.; **the surface** owwedruff, adv.; **the watch** Waart (die)n.; **the way** 1.uff, prep., adv. (-- em Weg); 2.unnerwegs, adv.; **the way** (coming) **across** riwwerzus, adv.; **the way** (coming) **up** ruffzus, adv.; **the**

(Continued on page 331)

Oo

on (continued)

(Continued from page 330)

way (going) across niwwerzus, adv.; the way (going) in neizus, adv.; the way back zerickzus, adv.; the way coming haerzus, adj.; the way coming in reizus, adv.; the way coming out rauszus, adv.; the way down 1.nunnerzus, adv.; 2.runnerzus, adv.; the way going 1.hizus, adv.; 2.weckzus, adv.; the way going out nauszus, prep.; the way up nuffzus, adv.; the whole darichaus, adv.; the wing Fluck (der)n.(im --); there dattdruff, adv.; this side 1.hiwwe, adv.; 2.hiwwich, adv.; top owwedruff, adv.; top of one another uffenanner, adv.

once e(e)mol, adv.; (upon a time) mol(i), adv.; before schunnemol, adv.; more 1.nochemol, adv.; 2.widder, adv.

one 1.ee, pron.; adj.; 2.eener, pron.; adj.; 3.eenes, adj.; 4.eeni, adj.; 5.eens, pron.; adj.; 6.mer, pron.; (of several) Eent (der, die, es)n.; above (over, on top of) another iwwer(e)nanner, prep.; after the other 1.eens, adj. (-- ums anner); 2.nochenanner, adv.; 3.ums = um es (eens -- anner); against the other weddernanner, adv.; one another nanner, pron.; armed ee-aermich, adj.; below the other unne(re)nanner, adv.; careless of his health Karichhofkandidaat (der)n.; eyed 1.Aag (es)n. (ee Aagich); 2.scheel, adj.; given to pouting Brutzkiwwel (der)n.; holding office Beamter (der)n.; horse wagon Eegeilswagge (der)n.; in pursuit of another nannerno, adv.; living in the back hills Hinnerbarriger (der)n.; person eener, pron.; adj.; seated eesitzich, adj.; sided eeseidich, adj.; who exercises power Banner (der)n.; who hammers out iron at a forge Dengler (der)n. (eisi --); who only nibbles at things (at the table) Schnippler (der)n.; who rakes Recher (der)n.; Recher, pl.; who rocks Schockler (der)n.; Schockler, pl.; who slanders his neighbors Nochbrebeitscher (der)n.; who spreads manure Mischtschpraehe (der)n.; who wakens Wecker (der)n.

onerous laschtbaar, adj.

onion Zwiwwel (die)n.; Zwiwwle, pl.; pie Zwiwwlekuche (der)n.; sets Zwiwwel (die)n.; Zwiwwle, pl. (gleeni Zwiwwle); soup Zwiwwelsupp (die)n.; top 1.Schlott (die)n.; 2.Zwiwwelschlott (die)n.; 3.Zwiwwelschuss (der)n.

onlooker Gucker (der)n.

only 1.blos, adv.; 2.eensichscht, adv.; 3.eenzich, adv.; 4.erscht, adv.; 5.lauder, adv.; 6.narre, adv.; 7.nerscht = erscht; 8.numme, adv.; 9.nur, adv.; 10.uscht, adv.; 11.yuscht, adv.

onomatopoetic for the clangor of bells kling klang!; to imitate the croak of a frog bullirum!

onward weider, adv.

ooze 1.raus/schweese, v.; rausgschweest, pp.; 2.rinne, v.; gerunne, pp.; 3.Schlamm (der)n.; 4.schwees(s)e, v.; gschwees(s)t, pp.; from a wound or abraded skin 1.eedere, v.; geeidert, pp.; 2.eidere, v.; geeidert, pp.;

orchard

3.odere, v.; geodert, pp.; out 1.gwelle, v.; gegwellt; gegwolle, pp.; 2.raus/suddre, v.; rausgsuddert, pp.

open 1.effne, v.; ge-effnet, pp.; 2.uff/geh, v.; uffgange, pp.; 3.uff/hawwe, v.; uffghat, pp.; 4.uff/mache, v.; uffgemacht, pp.; 5.uff/schlagge, v.; uffgschlagge, pp.; 6.uff, adv.; 7.uffe, adv.; 8.uffne, adj.; (an umbrella) uff/schpanne, v.; uffgschpannt, pp.; (snow) drifts Baa(h)n mache, v.; Baa(h)n gemacht, pp.; a package aus/packe, v.; ausgepackt, pp.; a vein oderlosse, v.; oddergelosst, pp.; by hammering uff/globbe, v.; uffgegloppt, pp.; doors Diere (die)n., pl. (offni --); link (for repairing chain) Notgleech (der)n.; the field uff/mache, v.; uffgemacht, pp. (es Feld --); wide 1.uff/reise, v.; uffgerisse, pp.; 2.uff/schpaerre, v.; uffgschpaerrt, pp.; 3.uff/schparre, v.; uffgschpatt, pp.; with a pointed instrument uff/schteche, v.;uffgschtoche, pp.

opened aagebroche, adj.

opening 1.Effning (die)n.; 2.Uffning (die)n.

openly 1.effentlich, adv.; 2.offentlich, adv.; 3.uffnich, adv.

operate schaffe, v.; gschafft, pp.

opiate 1.Schlo(o)fdrobbe (die)n., pl.; 2.Schloofmiddel (es)n.

opinion 1.Aasicht (die)n.; 2.Meening (die)n.

opodeldoc Opedildack (es)n.

opponent 1.Gegner (der)n.; 2.Wedderleger (der)n.

opportune gelege, adj.

opportunity 1.Gelegeheit (die)n.; 2.Geleyeheit (die)n.

oppose 1.gegehalde, adj.; 2.gegekalde, adj.; 3.wedderlege, v.; wedderlegt, pp.; 4.wedderschteh, v.;wedderschtanne, pp.; in an argument Wedderbatt (der)n. (ebber -- halde)

opposed 1.abwennich, adj.; 2.gegenanner, adv.

opposite 1.Gegedeel (es)n.; 2.gegeniwwer, adv.; of the literal meaning - a rotten egg guy fei, adj. (en feiner Kall); or towards each other or one another gegenanner, adv.

opposition Wedderbatt (der)n.

oppress unner/dricke, v.; unnergedrickt, pp.

oppression Unnerdrickung (die)n.

oppressor 1.Schinner (der)n.; 2.Unnerdricker (der)n.

opprobrious epithet Schimpnaame (der)n.

option Waahl (die)n.

opulent reich, adj.

or 1.adder, conj.; 2.odder, conj.; 3.schunscht, conj.; it odders = odder es

orach Melde (der)n. (zaahmer --)

orally mindlich, adv.

orange aarensch, adj.

orange Arrensch (die)n.

orate rede, v.; geredt, pp.

orator 1.Redner (der)n.; 2.Schprecher (der)n.; 3.Schwetzer (der)n.; Schwetzer, pl.

oratory Redekunscht (die)n.

orchard 1.Baamgaarde (der)n.; 2.Bammgaarde (der)n.; 3. Bungert (der)n.; 4.Bunnert (der)n.; grass 1. Baamgaardegraas (es)n.; 2.Bungertgraas (es)n.

331

Oo

orchid — overdo

orchid Gungelrieb (die)n.; Gungelriewe, pl.
ordain ei/setze, v.; eigsetzt, pp.
order 1.addere, v.; geaddert, pp.; 2.Addning (die)n.;
  3.Ardning (die)n.; 4.Befehl (der)n.; 5.befehle, v.;
  befohle, pp.; 6.bschtelle, v.; bschtellt, pp.; 7.Ordning
  (die)n.; 8.Ordnung (die)n.; 9.verardne, v.; verardent,
  pp.; 10.Verardning (die)n.; 11.Zucht (die)n.; **(in business)** Adder (die)n.; **(one) down** nunner/heese, v.;
  nunnergheese, pp.; **around** rum/addere, v.;
  rumgeaddert, pp.; **away** weck/addere, v.;
  weckgeaddert, pp.; **down from a place**
  runner/addere, v.; runnergeaddert, pp.; **from one
  place to another** rumhaer/addere, v.;
  rumhaergeaddert, pp.; **out** 1.naus/weise, v.;
  nausgwisse, pp.; 2.raus/addere, v.; rausgeaddert,
  pp.; **to a certain place** hie/bschtelle, v.; hiebeschtellt,
  pp.; **to come here** 1.haer/bschtelle, v.; haerbschtellt,
  pp.; 2.her/beschtelle, v.; herbschtellt, pp.
orderly 1.adentlich, adv.; 2.ordentlich, adv.;
  3.verschtendich, adv.
ordinarily 1.gewehnichlich, adv.; 2.gwehnlich, adj., adv.
ordination 1.Eisetzing (die)n.; 2.Eisetzung (die)n.
ore Erz (der)n.; **smelter** Schmelzoffe (der)n.
organic disease of the heart Hatzfehler (der)n.
organist Ariyelschpieler (der)n.; Ariyelschpieler, pl.
orient Mariyeland (es)n.
origin 1.Aafang (der)n.; 2.Beginn (der)n.; 3.Herkummes
  (es)n.; 4.Urschprung (der)n.
originally urschpringlich, adv.
originate 1.entschteh, v.; entschtanne, pp.; 2.uff/griege,
  v.; uffgrickt, pp.
originator Urhewer (der)n.
ornament 1.verzackere, v.; verzackert, pp.; 2.verzickere,
  v.; verzickert, pp.; 3.Zier (die)n.; 4.Zierraat (die)n.
orphan Waisekind (es)n.; Waisekinner, pl.
orphan's home Waisehaus (es)n.
orthodox kabbidelfescht, adj.; **(in belief)**
  1.Karricheglaawe (der)n.; 2.rechtglaawich, adj.;
  3.rechtgleibich, adj.
osier (willow) Karebweide (die)n.
ossified verknechert, v.
ossify vergnechere, v.; vernechert, pp.
ostensible vorgeblich, adj.
ostensibly scheinbaar, adj.
osteology 1.Gnochelehr (die)n.; 2.Knochelehr (die)n.
Oswego tea Muddergraut (es)n.
other anner, adj.; pron.
otherwise 1.annerschder, adj.; adv.; 2.annerscht, adv.;
  3.schunscht, adv.; 4.sunscht, adv.
Ouch! Autsch!, interj.
ought to go out naus/solle, v.; nausgsollt, pp.
our 1.unsrer, pron.; 2.unsri, pron.
ours 1.unsrer, pron.; 2.unsri, pron.
ourself 1.uns, pron.; 2.unsereem, pron.; 3.unsereens, pron.
oust 1.aus/beisse, v.; ausgebisse, pp.; 2.aus/dreiwe, v.;
  ausgedriwwe, pp.; 3.aus/schtosse, v.; ausgschtosse,

pp.; 4.naus/duh, v.; nausgeduh, pp.
out along here dodraanaus, adv.; **along there**
  1.dattdraanaus, adv.; 2.dattdraaniwwer, adv.; **back**
  1.hinnedraus(s), adv.; 2.hinnrizus, adv.; **behind**
  hinnenaus, adv.; **below** 1.unnenaus, prep.; 2.unner
  (r)aus, adv.; **by** newedrauss, adv.; **by the front way**
  vannenaus, adv.; **cast** Auswaerfling (der)n.; **from
  behind** hinneraus, adv.; **from that direction**
  dattrauszus, adv.; **from there** dattraus, adv.; **front**
  vannedraus, adv.; **here** 1.dodrauss, adv.; 2.dohaus,
  adv.; 3.doraus, adv.; **house** 1.Briwwi (es)n.; 2.Heisli
  (es)n.; Heislin, pl. 3.Nessi (es)n.; 4.Priwwi (es)n.;
  5.Scheisshaus (es)n.; Scheissheiser, pl.;
  6.Scheisskammer (die)n.; **in that direction** dattnauszus, adv.; **in this direction** donauszus, adv.; **of**
  1.aus, prep.; adv.; 2.naus, adv.; 3.raus, adv.; prep.; **of
  breath** Odem (der)n. (aus --); **of commission**
  Schtreech (der)n. (aus --); **of doors** haus(s), adv.; **of
  it** haus(s), adv.; **of joint** Fuuge (die)n. (aus -- sei); **of
  matrimony** leddicherweis, adv.; **of one's head** Heisel
  (es)n. (aus em -- [Heisli]); **of one's mind**
  1.verschowe, adv. (-- im haernkaschde); 2.verzickt,
  adj.; **of order** 1.fix, adj. (aus --); 2.nix meh waert,
  adj.; **of place** verrickt, adj.; **of shape** winnisch, adj.;
  of the way 1.newedrauss, adv.; 2.Weg (der)n. (aus
  em --); **of the way section** Eck (es)n.; Ecke, pl.; **of
  wack** 1.fix, adj.; 2.kaputt, adj.; 3.nix meh waert, adj.;
  there 1.dattdraus, adv.; 2.dattnaus, adv.; **this way**
  dorauszus, adv.; **through here** 1.dodarrichnaus, adv.;
  2.dodarrichraus, adv.; **through there**
  1.dattdarichnaus, adv.; 2.dattdarichraus, adv.; **up
  above** 1.owwedraus, adv.; 2.owwenaus, adv.; **with
  it!** raus mit!, interj.
outbid 1.ab/biede, v.; abgebodde, pp.; 2.iwwerbiede, v.;
  iwwerbodde, pp.
outbreak 1.Ausbrechung (die)n.; 2.Ausbruch (der)n.
outbuilding Newegebei (es)n.; Newegebeier, pl.
outcry Gelammedier (es)n.
outer eissaerscht, adv.
outfit 1.Ausscht(e)ier (der)n.; 2.Hausscht(e)ire (der)n.
outgrow verwaxe, v.; verwaxe, pp.
outlet Ausgang (der)n.
outlive 1.aus/lewe, v.; ausgelebt, pp.; 2.iwwerlewe, v.;
  iwwerlebt, pp.
outlook 1.Aablick (der)n.; 2.Aasicht (die)n.; 3.Sicht (die)n.
outrageous 1.frewelhaft, adj.; 2.laschderhaft, adj.
outside 1.aus(e)wennich, adj.; 2.ausewendich, adv.; 3.
  ausewennich, adv.; 4.ausse, adv.; 5.ausserum, adv.;
  6.aussewennich, adv.; 7.draus(s) prep.; adv.; 8.haus,
  adv. 9.hauss, adv.; **cellar door** Kellerhals (der)n.;
  Kellerhels, pl.; **door** (of a house) 1.Hausdeer (die)n.;
  2.Hausdier (die)n.
outstrip in driving vorfaahre, v.; vorgfaahre, pp.; **in riding**
  vor/reide, v.; vorgeridde, pp.
outwit aus/biede, v.; ausgebodde, pp.
ovary (in fowls) 1.Legschtock (der)n.; 2.Oierschtock (der)n.

Oo

oven

oven Offe (der)n.; Effe, pl; **door** Backoffeloch (es)n.; **scraper** Backoffekitsch (die)n.; **swab** 1.Huddellumbe (der)n.; 2.Huddelwisch (der)n.; **wood** Backholz (es)n.

over 1.iwwer, prep.; 2.iwwrich, adj.; 3.niwwer, adv.; 4.owwich, adj.; 5.owwich, prep.; 6.owwich, prep.; 7.verbei, adv.; verbei/sei, v.; verbeigewest, pp. 9.veriwwer, adv.; **(on this side)** riwwer, adv.; **along there** dattdraariwwer, adv.; **attentive to parsons** parrenaerrisch, adj.; **drink (booze)** schnuddle, v.; gschnuddelt, pp.; **exert oneself** iwwerduh (sich --)v.; iwwer(ge)du ; **here** 1dodriwwe, adv.; 2.dohiwwe, adv.; 3.hiwwe, adv.; 4.riwwer, adv.; **in the rear** hinneniwwer, adv.; **in this direction** dodarrichniwwer, adv.; **it** driwwer, adv.; **night** iwwer Nacht, adv.; **persuade** verblaudere, v.; verblaudert, pp.; **reckon** iwwerschiesse, v.; iwwergschosse, pp.; **smart** 1. iwwergscheit, adj.; 2.witzich, adj.; **that way** dattriwwer, adv.; **the back or rump** hinnedriwwer, adv.; **the top** owwedriwwer, adv.; **there** 1.dattniwwer, adv.; 2.driwwe, adv.; **this** dodriwwer, adv.; **through here** 1.dodarrichrei, adv.; 2.dodarrichriwwer, adv.; 3.dattdarichniwwer, adv.; 4.dattdarichriwwer, adv.; **yonder** niwwerzus, adv.

overall jacket 1.Kuddel (der)n.; Kiddel, pl.; 2.Iwwerkiddel (der)n.

overalls Iwwerhosse (die)n., pl.

overbid iwwerbiede, v.; iwwerbodde, pp.

overcast 1.drieb, adj.; 2.iwwerzoge, adj.

overcharging Yudderei (die)n.

overcoat Iwwerrock (der)n.

overcome 1.iwwerkumme, v.; iwwerkumme, pp.; 2. iwwerweldiche, v.; iwwerweldicht, pp.

overdo 1.iwwerdreiwe, v.; iwwerdriwwe, pp.; 2.iwwerduh, v.; iwwer(ge)duh, pp.; **(in plastering or the use of salve)** verbleschdere, v.; verbleschdert, pp.

overeat iwwerfresse (sich --)v.; iwwerfresse, pp.

overfatigue iwwerrechle, v.; iwwerrechelt, pp.

overflow 1.Ablaaf (der)n.; 2.iwwer/laafe, v.; is iwwergeloffe, pp.; 3.Iwwerfluss (der)n.; 4.iwwerschwemme, v.; iwwerschwemmt, pp.; **(of streams)** schwemme, v.; gschwemmt, pp.

overflowing 1.iwwerflissich, adv.; 2.schtiwwich voll, adv.

overgrow 1.iwwerwachse, v.; iwwerwachse, pp.; 2.iwwerwaxe, v.; iwwerwaxe, pp.

overgrown (with weeds) verwaxe, v.; verwaxe, pp.

overhang (of a P.G. barn) 1.Vorbau(er) (der)n.; 2.Vorschuss (der)n.; Vorschuss, pl.

overhaste (causing mistakes) Iwwereiling (die)n.

overhasty huddlich, adv.

overhead drowwe, adv.

overhear 1.ab/heere, v.; abgheert, pp.; 2.iwwerheere, v.; iwwerheert, pp.

overheat 1.iwwerhitze, v.; iwwerhitzt, pp.; 2.verhitze, v.; verhitzt, pp.

overload iwwerlaade, v.; iwwerlaade, pp.

overlook 1.verbasse, v.; verbasst, pp.; 2.verhopbasse, v.;

ox

verhopbasst, pp.; **(a matter)** iwwerseh(e) (sich --)v.; iwwersehne, pp.

overly curious schnausich, adj.; **nice (in eating)** nischble, v.; gnischbelt, pp.

overnight iwwernacht, adj.

overpower iwwerweldiche, v.; iwwerweldicht, pp.

overreach oneself iwwergreife (sich --)v.; iwwergriffe, pp.

overrun 1.Iwwerhand (die)n. (-- nemme); 2. iwwerhand/nemme, v.; iwwerhandgnumme, pp.; **with weeds or briers** zunischde, v.; zugenischt, pp.

overscald (a hog or fowl) verbriehe, v.; verbrieht, pp.

oversee 1.iwwersehe, v.; iwwersehne, pp.; 2.iwwersehne, v.; iwwersehne, pp.

overseer Iwwersehner (der)n.

overshoe Iwwerschuh (der)n.; Iwwerschuh, pl.

overshoot 1.Iwwerschuss (der)n.; 2.Vorschuss (der)n.; Vorschuss, pl.; **(mill wheel)** 1.iwwerschlechtich, adj.; 2.Iwwerschussraad (es)n.

oversleep verschlofe (sich --)v.; verschlofe, pp.

overspin (of the tent caterpillar) zunischde, v.; zugenischt, pp.

overstudy (and injure the health) iwwerschtudiere, v.; iwwerschtudiert, pp.

overtake 1.ei/hole, v.; eigholt, pp.; 2.iwwernemme, v.; iwwernumme, pp.

overthrow 1.schtaerze, v.; gschtaerzt, pp.; 2.um/schtosse, v.; umgschtosse, pp.

overturn 1.iwwer/schtilbe, v.; iwwergschtilpt, pp.; 2.iwwer/welse, v.; iwwergewelst, pp.; 3.um/schtaerze, v.; umgschtaertzt, pp.; 4.um/welse, v.; umgewelst, pp.

overweight Iwwergewicht (es)n.

overwhelm with iwwerheifle, v.; iwwerheifelt, pp.

overwork 1.ab/gwaele (sich --)v.; abgegwaelt, pp.; 2.ab/quaele (sich --)v.; abgequaelt, pp.; 3.ab/schinne (sich --)v.; abgschunne, pp.; 4.schinne, v.; gschunne, pp.

owe 1.Kreid (es)n. (in der -- sei); 2.schuldich, adj. (ebber -- sie) (dative); **to** verdanke, v.; verdankt, pp.

owing schuldich, adj.

Owlglass (a mythical person full of wisdom and pranks frequently lamenting the opposite of what is to happen) 1.Eil (die)n.; Eile, pl.; 2.Eideschpiggel (Till) (der)n.; 3.Eileschpiggel (Till) (der)n.; 4.Eireschpiggel (Till) (der)n.; 5.Eisehannes (Till) (der)n.

own 1.b(e)sitze, v.; b(e)sesse, pp.; 2.eege, adj.; 3.eeges, adj.; 4.eegne, adj.; 5.eegne, v.; ge-eegent, pp.; **up** uff/eegne, v.; uffge-eegnet, pp.

owner 1.B(e)sitzer (der)n.; 2.Eegner (der)n.; Eegner, pl.

ox Ox (die)n.; Oxe, pl.; **broken to work** Schaff-ox (der)n.; **cart** Oxekarich (der)n.; Oxekarich, pl.; **yoke**

333

Pp

pace — parade

pace 1.schridde, v.; gschritt, pp.; 2.Schritt (der)n.; Schridde, pl.

pace off ab/schridde, v.; abg(e)schritt, pp.; **(in plowing)** schlagge, v.; gschlagge, pp. (en Droot --); **over or off** 1. iwwer/schridde, v.; iwwergschritt, pp.; 2.iwwerschritte,v.; iwwergschritt, pp.

pacifier Schlotzer (der)n.; Schlotzer, pl.

pacify 1.beruhiche, v.; beruhicht, pp.; 2.dischdere, v.; gedischdert, pp.; 3.dischdre, v.; gedischdert, pp.;4.schtille, v.; gschtillt, pp.

pack 1.Pack (der)n.; Peck, pl.; 2.zamme/packe, v.; zammegepackt, pp.; **away** weck/packe, v.; weckgepackt, pp.; **bag and baggage** zamt(e), adv. (mit --); **in** 1.nei/packe, v; neigepackt, pp.; 2.rei/packe, v.; reigepackt, pp.; **over** iwwerpacke, v.; iwwergepackt, pp.; **the ground** (as by a heavy rain) zamme/blatsche, v.; zammegeblatscht, pp.; **up** uff/packe, v.; uffgepackt, pp.

package Pack (der)n.; Peck, pl.; **or paper** Brief (der)n.

pad 1.aus/schtobbe, v.; ausgschtoppt, pp.; 2.Gepulschder (es)n.; 3.polschdre, v.; gepolschdert, pp.

paddle 1.blet(s)che, v.; gebletscht, pp.; 2.Britsch (die)n.; 3. Ruder (der)n.; Ruder, pl.; 4.Weddel (der)n.; 5.Wedel (der)n.; **something down flat** britsche, v.; gebritscht, pp.; **wheel** Fledderraad (es)n.; Fledderredder, pl.

paddling Bletching (die)n.

padlock Henkeschloss (es)n.

page 1.Blaat (es)n.; Bledder, pl.; 2.Blatt (es)n.; Bledder, pl.

pail 1.Eemer (der)n.; 2.Scheppkiwwel (der)n.

pailful 1.Eemervoll (der)n.; 2.Kiwwelvoll (der)n.

pain 1.greppe, v.; gegreppt, pp.; 2.Pein (die)n.; 3.Schmaerze (die)n., pl.; 4.schmaerze, v.; gschmaerzt, pp.; 5.Schmatz (der)n.; Schmatze, pl.; 6.schmatze, v.; gschmatzt, pp.; 7.weh/duh, v.; wehgeduh, pp.; **in an old wound** Wundschmatze (die)n., pl.; **in the limbs** Gliederschmaerze (die)n., pl.

painful 1.peinlich, adj.; 2.schmaerzhaft, adj.; 3.schmaerzlich, adj.; 4.weh, adj. 5.weh/duh, v.;wehgeduh, pp.

pains Mieh (die)n.

paint 1.aa/schtreiche, v.; aagschtriche, pp.; 2.Far(r)eb (die)n.; Farewe, Farwe, pl.; 3.Farb (die)n.; Farwe; Farewe, pl.; **mill** Farbmiehl (die)n.; **with oils** mole, v.; gemolt, pp.

paintbrush 1.Aaschtreichpensil (der)n.; 2.Farbpensil (der)n.

paintbucket Farbkessel (der)n.

painted cup Wibbe(r)willblumm (die)n.

painter Moler (der)n.; Moler, pl.

painter's brush Pensil (der)n.

pair 1.Paar (es)n.; 2.paar, pron., adj.; 3.paare, v.; gepaart, pp.; **off** ab/paare, v.; abgepaart, pp.

pal Kummeraad (der)n.; Kummeraade, pl.

palace Palscht (der)n.

palatable schmackhaft, adj.

palate Gumme (der)n.

Palatinate 1.Pals (die)n.; 2.Palz (die)n.

Palatine 1.pelsich, adj.; 2.Pelzer (der)n.; Pelzer, pl.

palaver 1.breble, v.; gebrebelt, pp.; 2.Gebrebel (es)n.

pale 1.blass, adj.; 2.bleech, adj.; 3.Glabbord (es)n.; Glabbaerd, pl.; 4.scheech, adj.; **touch-me-not** Glaasgraut (es)n.

paling fence Zau (der)n. (rare usage)

pall widderschteh, v.; widderschtanne, pp.

pallbearer 1.Baahredraeger (der)n.; 2.Draeger (der)n.; Draeger, pl.

pallid bleech, adj.

Palm Sunday 1.Pallemsunndaag (der)n.; 2.Palmsundaag (der)n.

palm 1.Pallem (der)n.; 2.Palm (der)n.; **leaf** Palmblaatt (es) n.; **off on** 1.aa/basse, v.; aagebasst, pp.; 2.uff/blaudre, v.; uffgeblaudert, pp.; 3.uff/schwetze, v.; uffgschwetzt, pp.

palpitation (of the heart) Hatzglobbe(s) (es)n.

paltry 1.aaremseelich, adj.; 2.aarmseelich, adj.; adv.

pamper 1.bobble, v.; bobbelt, pp.; 2.verbobble, v.; verbobbelt, pp.

pampered 1.mascht, adj.; 2.verbobbelt, adj.

pamphlet 1.Babierbich(e)li (es)n.;Babierbich(e)lin,pl.; 2.Bichli (es)n.

pan Pann (die)n.; Panne, pl.; **cover** Pannedeckel (der)n.; **used in putting corncobs into a stove** Grutzeschaufel (die)n.

pancake 1.Flammkuche (der)n.; 2.Pannekuche (der)n.; Pannekuche, pl.

pane of glass 1.Fenschderscheib (die)n.; Fenschderscheiwe, pl.; 2.Scheib (die)n.

panegyric Lobreed (die)n.

panhandle Panneschtiel (der)n.

panicle Rischbel (die)n.

pannier Brotkareb (der)n.; Brotkareb, pl.

pant 1.hechze, v.; g(e)hechzt, pp.; 2.keich(l)e, v.; gekeiche (l)t, pp.; 3.lelle, v.; glellt, pp.; **(of humans)** bloose, v.; gebloose, pp.

panther Bender (der)n.; Bender, pl.

panting keich(l)ich, adj.

pantry 1.Brotschank (der)n.; 2.Esschank (der)n.; 3. Gscharrschank (der)n.; 4.Kellereck (es)n.; 5.Mehlkammer (die)n.; Mehlkammer, pl.

pants Hosse (die)n. **pants leg** Hossebee (es)n.; **pocket** Hossesack (der)n.; Hosseseck, pl.

pap 1.Brei (der)n.; 2.Mehlbrei (der)n.; 3.Millichbrei (der)n.; **(with horseradish and egg)** Meerreddichbrie (der)n.

papa 1.Baba (der)n.; 2.Babbe (der)n.; 3.Daadi (der)n.; 4.Daed (der)n.

paper 1.Babier (der)n.; Babiere, pl.; 2.Fabier (es)n.; Fabiere, pl. **bag** 1.Babiersack (der)n.; Babierseck, pl.; 2.Babierseckli (der)n.; Babiersecklin, pl.

paper taper 1.Leichder (der)n.; Leichder, pl.; 2.Leichter (der)n.; **wad** Babierschtobber (der)n.

par value Gleichewaert (es)n.

parable Gleichnis (es)n.

parade schtrutze, v.; gschtrutzt, pp.

Pp

paradise — patch

paradise 1.Paradies (es)n.; 2.Paredies (es)n.
paragraph Absatz (der)n.; Absetz, pl.
parallel gleichlaafend, adj.
paralyzing fear Dod(es)angscht (die)n.
paraphrase umschreiwe, v.; umschriwwe, pp.
parasite Suckler (der)n.
parasitic animal Mielikeffer (der)n.
parasitism Schmarotzerei (die)n.
parboil 1.ab/koche, v.; abgekocht, pp.; 2.briehe, v.;
  gebrieht, pp.; 3.gwelle, v.; gegwellt, pp.
parchment Bargement (es)n.
pardon 1.begnaadiche, v.; begnaadicht, pp.;
  2.Begnaadichung (die)n.; 3.vergewwe, v.; vergewwe,
  pp.; 4.verzeihe, v.; verzeiht, pp.
pare schaele, v.; gschaelt, pp.
parents 1.Eldre (die)n., pl.; 2.Eltre (die)n., pl.
paring Schaal (die)n.; Schaale, pl.; **knife** Schaelmesser (es)n.
parish Parreschtell (die)n.
parity 1.Gleichheet (die)n.; 2.Gleichheit (die)n.
park Park (der)n.
parochial school Karrichschul (die)n.
parrot Babbegoi (der)n.
parsley Peedrli (der)n.
parsnip 1.Baschnaad (die)n.; Baschnaade, pl.;
  2.Baschtnaad (die)n.
parson 1.Breddicher (der)n.; Breddicher, pl.;
  2.Kanselglopper (der)n.; (contemptious) 1.Brieschder
  (der)n.; 2.Prieschder (der)n.; 3.Preischder (der)n.
part 1.Aadeel (es)n.; 2.ab/reisse, v.; abgerisse, pp.; 3.Batt
  (der)n.; 4.deele, v.; gedeelt, pp.; 5.Paert (die)n.;
  6.scheide, adj.; 7.scheide, v.; gscheide, pp.; 8.Schtick
  (es)n.; 9. verdeele, v.; verdeelt, pp.;
  10.vunenanner/geh,v.; vunenannergange, pp.; **(of
  hair)** 1.Lauspaad (der)n. (humorous); 2.scheedle, v.;
  gscheedelt, pp.; 3.Scheedel (der)n.
part of the earth 1.Erddeel (es)n.; 2.Weltdeel (es)n.; **of
  the wall** (between the roof and the floor of a garret)
  Gniewand (die)n.; **of the way** Schtick Wegs, adv.;
  with foolishly weck/narre, v.; weckgenaart, pp.
partially deel (weis), adv.
participate mit/mache, v.; mitgemacht, pp.
particle (of the outer coat in the flax plant separated in
  process of breaking) Brechaggel (die)n.
particular(ly) 1.abaddich, adv., adj.; 2.abard, adv.;
  3.abbardich, adv., adj.; 4.baddich, adv.; 5.besonders,
  adv.; 6.besonner(s), adv.; 7.bsonders, adv.;
  8.bsunders, adv.; 9.vornemlich, adj.
partition wall Middelwand (die)n.
partly deels, adv.; **fermented** (of cider) 1.gratzich, adj.; 2.
  kratzich, adj.
partner Paertner (der)n.
partridge 1.Badries(e)li (es)n.; 2.Badriesel (es)n.; 3.
  Badrieselche (es)n.; **berry** (Matchella repens)
  1.Budderbeer (die)n.; 2.Butterbeer (die)n.;
  3.Fersandebeer (die)n.; 4.Windergrie (die)n.
party Partei (die)n.

pass verbei/geh, v.; verbeigange, pp.; **(at the table)** lange,
  v.; gelangt, pp.; **amount** 1.gelde, v.; gegolde, pp.;
  2.gelte, v.; gegolte, pp.; **(in cards)** 1.basse, v.;
  gebasst, pp.; 2.verbasse, v.; verbasst, pp.; **(time)**
  1.verfliesse, v.; verflosse, pp.; 2.zu/bringe, v.;
  zugebrocht, pp.; **by** 1.iwwerhuppe, v.; iwwerhuppt,
  pp.; 2.verbei/kumme, v.; verbeikumme, pp.; **into
  oblivion** verschalle, v.; verschallt, pp.; **off** 1.ab/geh,
  v.; abgange, pp.; 2.haer/geh, v.; haergange, pp.; **over**
  1.verblosse, v.; verblosse, pp.; 2.vergeh, v.;
  vergange, pp.; 3.veriwwergeh, v.; veriwwergange,
  pp.; 4.weck/geh, v.; is weckgange, pp.; **rapidly over**
  iwwerschiesse, v.; iwwergschosse, pp.; **the time**
  verweile (sich --)v.; verweilt, pp.; **the time of day** Zeit
  (die)n. 1.(die -- biete); 2.(-- verdreiwe); **through** (like
  a shudder) darich/faahre, v.; darichgfaahrt, pp.
passable gangbaar, adv.
passageway Gang (der)n.; Geng, pl.
passageway in barn Scheiergang (der)n.
passing verbeigehend, adj.; **away** 1.verfliege, v.;
  verflogge, pp.; 2.Vergang (der)n. (im --); **excitement**
  Schtrohfeier (es)n.
passion flower Passionsblumm (die)n.
passionate schpielich, adj.
Passover Oschderfescht (es)n.
past 1.iwwer, adv.; 2.verbei, adv.; 3.Vergange(n)heit (die)
  n.; 4.vergange, adv.; 5.veriwwer, adv.; 6.verloffe,
  adv.; **(in telling time)** 1.iwwer, adv.; 2.nooch, adv.;
  3.verbei, adv.; **evening** denowed, adv.; **morning**
  demaiye, adv.
paste 1.babbe, v.; gebappt, pp.; 2.Bapp (die)n.; 3.bappe,
  v.; gebappt, pp.; 4.Wichs (die)n.; 5.Wix (die)n.;
  against wedder/bappe, v.; weddergebappt, pp.; **on**
  1.aa/gle(e)we, v.; aageglebt, pp.; 2.aa/klewe, v.;
  aageklebt, pp.
pasteboard Babbedeckel (der)n.
pastime 1.Basseltang, n.; 2.Zeitverdreib (der)n.
pastor 1.Paschdor (der)n.; 2.Seelsaryer (der)n.
pastries Backsach (es)n.
pastry dough (with meringue) covering baked in shape of
  a pie) Schaumkuche (der)n.
pasture 1.Weed (die)n.; 2.Weedland (es)n.; 3.Wiss (die)n.;
  Wisse, pl.; **field** Weedfeld (es)n.
pat 1.bletschle, v.; gebletschelt, pp.; 2.detschle, v.;
  gedetschelt, pp.; 3.schtreiche, v.; gschtriche, pp.;
  4.schtreichle, v.; gschtreichelt, pp.; **a-cake** betschle,
  v.; gebetschelt, pp.; **down** nunner/betschle, v.;
  gebetschelt, pp.
patch 1.aa/flicke, v.; aagflickt, pp.; 2.Blacke (der)n.;
  3.Fleck(e) (der)n.; Flecke, pl.; 4.Flick (es)n.; Flick, pl.;
  5.flicke, v.; gflickt, pp.; 6.Lappe (der)n.; 7.Schtick (es)
  n.; 8. verschtickere, v.; verschtickert, pp.; **in woods**
  (where timber has been cut and new timber is growing)Holzschlack (der)n.; **of corn** Welschkannschtick
  (es)n.; **on a boot or shoe** 1.Reischder (der)n.; **up**
  uff/blaschdere, v.; uffgeblaschdert, pp.

335

Pp

patching

patching Flickaerwet(t) (die)n.
patchwork Flickaerwet(t) (die)n.; **quilt** Schtickeldebbich (der)n.
paternoster 1.Vaddernaus (es)n.; 2.Vadderunser (es)n.
path 1.Paad (der)n.; 2.Paedche (es)n.; 3.Paedel (es)n.;
    4.Peedche (es)n.; 5.Peedel (es)n.; 6.Wegli (es)n.;
    (through snow) 1.Baa (der)n.; 2.Boo (der)n.
pathetic bedauerlich, adj.
pathway Fuusweg (der)n.; Fuusswege, pl.
patience 1.Geduld (die)n.; 2.Geduldichkeet (die)n.;
    3.Langmut (der)n.
patient 1.Granker (der)n.; Granke, pl.; 2.langmiedich, adj.;
    3.Pazient (der)n.
patricide Vaddermard (der)n.
patriot Patrioot (der)n.
patriotic patrioodisch, adj.
patron Beschitzer (der)n.
patronize 1.unner/schtitze, v.; unnergschtitzt, pp.;
    2. unnerschtitze, v.; unnerschtitzt, pp.
patter blatsche, v.; geblatscht, pp.
pattern 1.Moddel (die)n.; Moddle, pl.; 2.Muschder (es)n.;
    book Muschderbuch (es)n.
patty cake, patty cake Batsche, batsche, Kicheli!
Paul Paul (der)n.
paunch 1.Henkbauch (der)n.; 2.Leib (der)n.; 3.Sack (der)
    n.; Seck, pl.
paunchy 1.dickseckisch, adj.; 2.rundleiwich, adj; **person**
    Dickbauch (der)n.
pauper Aarmer (en)n.
pause 1.Absatz (der)n.; Absetz, pl.; 2.schtutze,
    v.;gschtutzt, pp.
paw 1.Dobe (die)n.; 2.Klooe (die)n.; 3.Tatz (die)n.; **(of a**
    horse) hacke, v.; ghackt, pp. ; **across** (of horses)
    niwwer/hacke, v.; niwwerghackt, pp.
pay 1.Bezaahling (die)n.; 2.Bezaahlung (die)n.; 3.bezaale, v.;
    bezaalt, pp.; 4.bleche, v.; geblecht, pp.; 5.Loh (der)n.; 6.Luh
    (der)n.; 7.Verdi(e)nscht (der)n.; **(fine)** beche, v.; gebecht,
    pp.; **at a certain place** hie/bezaahle, v.; hiebezaahlt, pp.;
    attention 1.acht/gewwe, v.; achtgewwe, pp.; 2.uff/basse,
    v.; uffgebasst, pp.; **attention to** in acht nemme, v.; **atten-**
    tion to a thing Acht (der, die)n. (-- uff ebbes hawwe); **back**
    zerick/bezaahle, v.; zerickbezaahlt, pp.; **day** Bezaahlsdaag
    (der)n.; **down** 1.hie/bezaahle, v.; hiebezaahlt, pp.;
    2.nunner/bleche, v.; nunnergeblecht, pp.; **in advance**
    vannenaus/bezaa(h)le, v.; vannenausbezaa(h)lt, pp.; **later**
    no(och)bezaahle, v.; no(och)bezaahlt, pp.; **no attention to a**
    thing Acht (der, die)n. (kenn -- hawwe uff ebbes); **off**
    ab/bezaale, v.; abbezaalt, pp.; **off a bill with labor**
    aus/schaffe, v.; ausgschafft, pp.; **out** aus/bezaahle, v.;
    ausbezaahlt, pp.; **over** niwwer/bezaahle, v.;
    niwwerbezaahlt, pp.; **up** (reluctantly) raus/bleche, v.;
    rausgeblecht, pp.
payment 1.Bezaahling (die)n.; 2.Bezaahlung (die)n.
pea 1.Aerbs (die)n.; Aerbse, pl.; 2.Aerebe (die)n.;
    Aerebse, pl.; 3.Blickaerbs (die)n. (grown for the pea
    as distinguished from sugar peas grown for the pod);
    pod 1.Aerbseschef (die)n.; Aerbseschefe, pl.;
    2.Ar(e)bseschood (die)n.; Arebseschoode, pl.; **soup**
    Aerbsesupp (die)n.

pendent

peace 1.Eenichkeit (die)n.; 2.Friede (der)n.; 3.Ruh (die)n.
peaceable friedlich, adj.
peaceful friedlich, adj.
peach 1.Pae(r)sching (der)n.; 2.Pasching (der)n; **orchard**
    Paerschingbungert (der)n.; **stone** 1.Paerschingschtee
    (der)n.; Paerschingschtee, pl.; 2.Paschingsaame (der)
    n.; Paschingsaame, pl.; **tree** Paerschingbaam (der)n.;
    Paerschingbeem, pl.
peacock Pohaahne (der)n.; Pohinkel, pl.
peacock's feather Pohaahnefedder (die)n.
peahen Pohinkel (es)n.; Pohinkel, pl.
peak 1.Gibbel (der)n.; Gibbel, pl.; 2.Punkt (der)n.; Punkde,
    pl.; 3.Schpitz(e) (der)n.
peaked schpitzich, adj.; **(woolen) cap** Zibbelkapp (die)n.;
    Zibbelkabbe; Zibbelkepp, pl.
peal Schaal (die)n.; Schaale, pl.
peanut Grundniss (die)n.
pear 1.Beer (die)n.; Beere, pl.; 2.Bier (die)n.; Biere, pl.;
    tree 1.Beerebaam (der)n.; Beerebeem, pl.;
    2.Bierebaam (der)n.; Bierebeem, pl.
peas 1.gleener griener Gnoodle (der)n.;
    2.grieni Schoofgnoodle (die)n.
pebble 1.Kissel (der)n.; 2.Schteeche (es)n.
peck Beck (der)n.; **at** aa/picke, v.; aagepickt, pp.
peculiar 1.eigediemlich, adj.; 2.sunderbaar, adj.;
    3.sunnerbaar, adj. 4.wild, adj.
pedant Philischder (der)n.
peddle 1.graemere, v.; gegraemert, pp.; 2.greemere, v.;
    gegreemert, pp.; 3.kraemere, v.; gekraemert, pp.;
    out aus/zeddle, v.; ausgezeddelt, pp.
peddler 1.Graemer (der)n.; 2.Greemer (der)n.; Greemer,
    pl.; 3.Kraemer (der)n.
pedestrian 1.Fuusgenger (der)n.; 2.Laafer (der)n.; Laafer, pl.
peel 1.aa/scheele, v.; aagscheelt, pp.; 2.aus/schaale, v.; aus-
    gschaalt, pp.; 3.aus/scheele, v.; ausgscheelt, pp.; 4.schaele,
    v.; gschaelt, pp.; **off** 1.ab/scheele, v.; abgscheelt, pp.;
    2.weck/scheele, v.; weckgscheelt, pp.
peep (of chickens) 1.biebse, v.; gebiebst, pp.; 2.piepse, v.;
    gepiepst, pp.; **(of the sun)** blicke, v.; geblickt, pp.;
    through darich/blicke, v.; darichgeblickt, pp.
peevish 1.brutzich, adj.; 2.zannich, adj.
peewee (small bird) Piewie (der, es)n.; Piewie, pl.
peg Zabbe (der)n.; Zabbe, pl.; **hole** Zabbeloch (es)n.;
    Zabbelecher, pl.
pegging awl 1.Pinbohre (der)n.; Pinbohre, pl.;
    2.Pinnbohre(der)n.
pell-mell iwwernannernei, adj., adv.
pelt 1.Belz (der)n.; 2.bschmeisse, v.; bschmisse, pp.;3.Fell
    (es)n.
pen Fedder (die)n.; Feddre, pl.; **in** 1.nei/schparre, v.;
    neigschpatt, pp.; 2.rei/schparre, v.; reigschpatt, pp.;
    out naus/schpaerre, v.; nausgschpaert, pp.; **up**
    1.eifange, v.; eigfange, pp.; 2.nei/schpaerre, v.;
    neigschpaert, pp.; **up together** zamme/schpaerre, v.;
    zammegschpaerrt, pp.
pendent flappich, adj.

336

Pp

pendulum ... personal

pendulum (of a clock) 1.Baermedickel (der)n.; 2.Zengel (der)n.; Zengel, pl.

penetrable darichdringlich, adj.

penetrate darich/dringe, v. darichgedrunge, pp.

penholder 1.Fedderrohr (es)n.; 2.Fedderschtiel (der)n.

peninsula Halbinsel (die)n.

penis 1.Bibbeli (der)n.; 2.Bibs (der)n.; 3.Schnickel (der)n.; 4.Schpitz (der)n.; 5.Wetzer (der)n.

penitentiary Zuchthaus (es)n.

penknife 1.Feddermesser (es)n.; 2.Messerli (es)n.; 3. Sackmesser (es)n.;Sackmessere,pl.

penman Schreiwer (der)n.; Schreiwer, pl.

Pennsylvania 1.Pennsilfaani, n.; 2.pennsilfaanisch, adj.; 3.Pennsilweeni, n.; 4.Pennsylvaani, n.

Pennsylvania Dutch (German) 1.Pennsilfaanisch Deitsch, adj.; 2.Pennsilweeni Deitsch, adj.

Pennsylvanian 1. Pennsylfaanier, (der)n.; Pennsylvaanier (der)n.

penny 1.Bens (der)n.; Bense, pl.; 2.kupfer (en)

pennyroyal 1.Ballei, n.; 2.Balloi, n.; 3.Grod(d)ebalsem (der)n.

pensive noochdenklich, adj.

pentagonal fimfseidich, adj.

Pentateuch fimf Bicher Mosis (die)n.

Pentecost Pingschde (die)n., pl.

peony 1.Gichtros (die)n.; Gichtrosse, pl.; 2.Peinis (die)n., pl.; **plant** Gichtroschtock (der)n.

people 1.Leit (die)n.; 2.Mensche (die)n., pl.; **going to or from church** Karichleit (die)n., pl.

pepper 1.Peffer (der)n.; Peffer, pl.; 2.peffere, v.; gepeffert, pp.; **and salt** (colored) greel, adj.

peppermint 1.Balsem (der)n.; 2.Balsem (der)n. (rotschtenglicher --); 3.Peffermins (der)n.; **tea** 1.Balsemtee (der)n.; 2.bloschtengicher Tee (der)n.; 3.Maagebalsem (der)n.; 4.Maagetee (der)n.; 5.weisschtengicher Tee (der)n.

perambulator Messraad (es)n.; Messredder, pl.

perceive by listening aa/heere, v.; aagheert, pp.

perceptibly sichtbarlich, adj.

perfect 1.fehlerfrei, adj.; 2.vollkumme, adj.;

perforate darich/bohre, v.; darichgebohrt, pp.

perform 1.aus/fiehre, v.; ausgfiehrt, pp.; 2.aus/richde, v.; ausgericht, pp.; 3.duh, v.; geduh, pp.; **magic** hexe, v.; ghext, pp.; **the marriage ceremony** 1.kop(u)liere, v.; kop(u)liert, pp.; 2.kopliere, v.; kopuliert, pp.

perfume 1.ei/balsamiere, v.; eigebalsamiert, pp.; 2.Reichdrobbe (die)n., pl.; 3.Wohlgeruch (der)n.

perfumery Riechdroppe (die)n., pl.

perhaps 1.deich; 2.velleicht, adv.; 3.verleicht, adv.; 4.vielleicht, adv.

pericranium 1.Haernschaedelhaut (die)n.; 2.Schaedelhaut (die)n.

peril Gfaahr (die)n.

perilous gfehrlich, adj.

period 1.Duppe (der)n.; 2.Punkt (der)n.; Punkde, pl.

periodically zeideweis, adv.

periphery Umgrees (die)n.

perish 1.Grund (der)n. (zu -- geh); 2.um/kumme, v.; is umkumme, pp.; 3.zugrund/geh, v.; zugrundgange, pp.; 4.zuschand/geh, v.; zuschandgange, pp; **from freezing** aus/(g)friere, v.; ausgfrore, pp.

peritoneum Netz (es)n.

peritonitis Brand (der)n.

perjure oneself falsch, adj. (-- schweere)

permanence Fattdauer (die)n.

permission 1.Erlaawing (die)n.; 2.Erlabnis (die)n.

permit erlaawe, v.; erla(a)bt, pp; **oneself to be persuaded** 1.verblaudre losse (sich --)v.; 2.verschwetze losse (sich --)v.; **to come to the front** vor/losse, v.; vorgelosst, pp.; **to come together** zamme/losse, v.; zammegelosst, pp.; **to enter** rei/losse,v.; reiglosst, pp. reiglesst = Amish usage; **to get up** uff/losse, v.; uffgelosst,pp.; **to go back** zerick/losse, v.; zerickgelosst, pp.

pernicious verdaerblich, adj.

perpendicular 1.kaerzegraad, adj.; 2.kerzegraad, adj.; 3. senkrecht, adj.

perpetual immerwaehrend, adj.; **motion** ewich Unruh (die)n.

perpetuate 1.vereewiche, v.; vereewicht, pp.; 2.verewiche, v.; verewicht, pp.

perplexed 1.verwart, adj.; 2.verwatt, adj.

persecute 1.drackdiere, v.; gedrackdiert, pp.; 2.verfolge, v.; verfolgt, pp.

perserverance Ausdauer (die)n.

persimmon 1.Mischbel (die)n.; 2.Schpaerwel (die)n.; 3.Schparwel (die)n.; 4.Wischpel (die)n. wischpel = mischpe; **tree** 1.Mischblebaam (der)n.; Mischble-beem, pl.; 2.Schparwelbaam (der)n.; **wood** 1.Mischbleholz (es)n.; 2.Wischbleholz (es)n.

persist 1.dezuschticke, v.; dezugschtickt, pp.; 2.schticke, v.; gschtickt, pp.

person Paerson (die)n; (as a term of opprobrium) Kiehdrechroller (der)n.; **addicted to complaining** Grecksmiehl (die)n.; **born in January** Yennerkalb (es)n.; Yennerkelwer, pl.; **(in quoits) who makes a score of less than 6** (bockseckel) (en -- aahenge); **living on or near the Blue Mountain** 1.Blobarricker (der)n.; 2.Blobarriger (der)n.; **living on the other side of the Blue Mountain** Iwwerbarryer (der)n.; **or horse given to abrupt or rapid movements** Schussel (der)n.; **or horse that rushes like mad** Renndler (es)n.; **walking with a shambling gait** 1.Schlotterfuss (der)n.; 2.Schlodderfuss (der)n.; **who drops in** (with heavy steps) Beigdappter (en)n.; **who holds off** Drickser (der)n.; **who makes insinuating allusions** Schtichler (der)n.; **who raked and bound the grain** (after the man with grain-cradle) Uffnemmer (der)n.; **who shoots in the New Year** Neiyaahrschnitz (der)n.; Neiyaahrschnitz, pl.; **who slobbers** Schlawwermaul (es)n.; **who tasted the sausage meat for condiments** Schmackwaerscht (der)n.; **with a sweet tooth** Zuckermaul (es)n.; **with disheveled hair** Schtruwwelkopp (der)n.; **with white hair** Weisskopp (der)n.; Weisskepp, pl.

personal paerseenlich, adj.

Pp

personate — pierced

personate vorschtelle, v.; vorgschtellt, pp.

persuade 1.berede, v.; beredt, pp.; 2.eischwetze, v.; eigschwetzt, pp.; 3.nei/blaudre, v.; neigeblaudert, pp.; 4.nei/schwetze, v.; neigschwetzt, pp.; 5.uff/blaudre, v.; uffgeblaudert, pp.; 6.verschwetze, v.; verschwetzt, pp.; 7.zwinge, v.; gezwunge, pp.; **(someone) to buy or accept** (something) aa/blaud(e)re, v.; aageblaudert, pp.

persuasion Iwwerzeigung (die)n.

pert keck, adj.; **child** 1.Rotzer (der)n.; 2.Rotznaas (die)n.; Rotznaas, pl.; **young fellow** Rotzhoge (der)n.; Rotzhoge,pl.

pertain 1.aageheere, v.; aageheert, pp.; 2.geheere, v.; gegheert, pp.; 3.gheert, v.; gheert, pp.

perverse 1.verkehrt, adj.; 2.verkehrt, adj.

pest Pescht (die)n.; Peschde, pl.; **of flies** Mickevieh (es)n.

pester 1.bellere, v.; gebellert, pp.; 2.bloge, v.; geblogt, pp.; 3.gweele, v.; gegweelt, pp.

pestiferous peschthaft, adj.

pestilence Pescht (die)n.; Peschde, pl.

pet 1.glinsle, v.; geglinselt, pp.; 2.Liebling (der)n.

petal Blummeblaat (es)n.; Blummebledder, pp.

Peter 1.Peeder (der)n.; 2.Pidder (der)n.; 3.Pitt(er) (der)n.

Peter and Paul Day (June 29) Peeder un Paul (der)n.; **in Chains' Day** (August 1) Peederkett (der)n.

petiole Blummeschtiel (der)n.; Blummeschtiel, pl.

petition Bittschrift (die)n.

petroleum barrel Kohleelfass (es)n.

petticoat Unnerrock (der)n.; Unnerreck, pl.

petty glee, adj.; **fault-finder** Schindeldecker (der)n.; Schindeldecker, pl.

petunia Drechderblumm (die)n.

pew 1.Bank (die)n.; Benk, pl.; 2.Karricheschtul (der)n.; Karricheschtiel, pl.; 3.Karrichesitz (der)n.

pews Karichebenk (die)n., pl.

pewter Zinn (es)n.; **sand** Silwersand (der)n.

Pharisee Pharisaer (der)n.; Pharisaer, pl.

pharmaceutics Abbedeekerkunscht (die)n.

pharmacy Abbedeek (die)n.; Abbedeek, pl.

pheasant 1.Fassant (die)n.; Fassande, pl.; 2.Fersant (die)n.

phenomenon 1.aageschpickel (der)n.; 2.Aageschpiggel (der)n.; 3.Aggeschpiel (der)n; **(any)** 1.Aageschpickel (der)n.; 2.Aageschpiggel (der)n.; 3.Aggeschpiel (der)n.

philanthrope Menschefreind (der)n.

Philip 1.Phillipp (der)n. 2.Philp (der)n.

Philippine 1.Philibbine (die)n.; 2.Philippine (die)n.

Philopena Philepiene (es)n.

philosopher Philosoph (der)n.

phiz Bless (die)n.

phlegm Rotz (der)n.

photograph 1.ab/nemme, v.; abgenumme, pp.; 2.Pickder (es)n.; Pickder, pl.

photographer Abnemmer (der)n.; Abnemmer, pl.

physic 1.bar(r)iere, v.; bar(r)iert, pp.; 2.Laxiering (die)n.

physical nadierlich, adj.

physician Dokder (der)n.; Dokder, pl.

piano 1.Glabberbax (die)n.; Glabberbaxe, pl.; 2.Glaffier (es)n.; Glaffiere, pl.; 3.Glavier (es)n; **key** Glaff (die)n.; Glaffe, pl.

piccolo Zwaerichpeif (die)n.; Zwaerichpeife, pl.

pick 1.ab/robbe, v; abgeroppt, pp.; 2.eisammle, v.; eigsammelt, pp.; 3.picke, v.; gepickt, pp.; 4.robbe, v.; geroppt, pp.; 5.zoppe, v.; gezoppt, pp.; **(apples)** Ebbel (der)n. (-- breche); **away** weck/lese, v.; weckglese, pp.; **ax** Pick (die)n.; **flaws in a person** naus/mache, v.; nausgemacht, pp. (iwwer ebber --); **off** 1.ab/lese, v.; abgelese, pp.; 2.ab/robbe, v; abgeroppt, pp.; **or read after** (someone) no(och)lese, v.; no(och)glese, pp.; **out** 1.aus/picke, v.; ausgepickt, pp.; 2.raus/lese, v.; rausglese, pp.; 3.raus/picke, v.; rausgepickt, pp.; 4.raus/suche, v.; rausgsucht, pp.; 5.wehle, v.; gewehlt, pp.; **over** darich/lese, v.; darichgelese, pp.; **up** 1.lese, v.; glese, pp.; 2.uff/hewe, v.; uffghowe, pp.; 3.uff/picke, v.; uffgepickt, pp.; **up** (potatoes, stones) uff/lese, v.; uffglese, pp.; **up** (with a fork) uff/gawwle, v.; uffgegawwelt, pp.

picked up uff/gelese, v.

picker Leser (der)n.

pickerel Hecht (der)n; **weed** Hechtgraut (es)n.

picket Glabbord (es)n.; Glabbaerd, pl.

picketfence Glabbordfens (die)n.; Glabbordfense, pl.

pickle 1.Bickel (die)n.; Bickels, pl.; 2.Gummer (die)n.; Gummere, pl.; 3.Gummerche (es)n.; Gummercher, pl.; 4.pickle, v.; gepickelt, pp.; 5.Salzlaag (die)n.; 6.Salzlack (die)n; **salad** (cucumber) Gummreselaat (der)n.

pickled meat Pickelfleesch (es)n.

picnic Picknick (die)n; **on May 1** moiye, v.; gemoit, pp.

picture 1.Bild (es)n.; Bilder, pl.; 2.Gleichnis (es)n.; 3.Pichder (es)n.; Pichder, pl.; 4.Vergleichnis (es)n.; **book** Bilderbuch (es)n.; Bilderbicher, pl.; **of life** Lewensbild (es)n.

piddle piddle, v.; gepiddelt, pp.

pie 1.Boi (der, es)n.; 2.Pei (es)n.; **covered with crumbs of flour, lard and sugar** Grimmelboi (der)n.; **made of schnitz** Schnitzkuche (der)n.; **paddle** 1.Boibritsch (die)n.; 2.Peibritsch (die)n.; **plant** 1.Babraa (der)n.; 2.Barbaraa (der)n.; **bald** scheckich, adj.

piece 1.Schtick (es)n.; 2.uff/schtickere, v.; uffgschtickert, pp.; **of land** (plowed by making either all right or all left turns) Land (es)n.; Lenner, pl.; **of paper** (floating in a cup or saucer filled with fat and lit to furnish light) Schwimmlichdel (es)n.; **of slate** Schiwwer (der)n.; Schiwwere, pl.

piecemeal schtickweis, adv.

pied-billed grebe 1.Dreckschlibber (der)n.; 2.Wasserschlibber (der)n.; Wasserschlibber, pl.

pier 1.Brickepeiler (der)n.; 2.Peiler (der)n.; Peiler, pl.

pierce 1.nei/schteche, v.; neigschtoche, pp.; 2.nei/schtecke, v.; neigschteckt; neigschtocke, pp.; 3.schteche, v.; gschtoche, pp; **the roof of a horse's mouth** (to relieve blind staggers) Gumme (der)n. (der -- schtecke)

pierced verschtoche, adj.

338

Pp

piety — Pius' Day

piety 1.Frommichkeet (die)n.; 2.Frommichkeit (die)n.

piffling talk Baeffzes (es)n.

pig 1.Wutz (die)n.; 2.Wutzsau (die)n; **ball** (Amish game, "Stay pig"!) Seiballe (der)n.; **call** Huss, Sau!

pig's ear Seiohr (es)n.; **feet jelly** Galleri(ch) (es)n.; **litter** Seinescht (es)n.; **stomach filled and pressed** Schwortemaage (der)n. **tail** Seischwans (der)n.

pigeon Daub (die)n.; Dauwe, pl.; **droppings** Dauwemischt (der)n.

pigeon's crop Dauwegropp (der)n; **milk** Dauwemillich (die)n.

piggish seii(s)ch, adj.

piggy 1.Wutzelche (es)n.; 2.Wutzi (es)n.; 3.Wutzlein (es)n.

piglet Wutzli (es)n.; Wutzlin, pl.

piglets of suckling age Suckelsei (die)n.

pigtail Hoorschwanz (der)n.

pigweed Haahnekamm (der)n.

pike Schpiess (der)n;

pile of junk or trash Gegnuschel (es)n.; **of stones** Schteehaufe (der)n.; **up** uff/heifle, v.; uffgheifelt, pp.

pilfer weck/butze, v.; weckgebutzt, pp.

pilgrim Pilyer (der)n.; Pilyer, pl.

Pilgrim's Progress Pilyerrees (die)n.

pill Pill (die)n.; Pille, pl.

pillar 1.Peiler (der)n.; Peiler, pl.; 2.Poschde (der)n.; Poschde, pl; **of the church** 1.Gmeesposchde (der)n.; 2.Karichposchde (der)n.

pillion Saddelkisse (es)n.

pillow 1.Kisse (es)n.; Kissin, pl.; 2.Kissi (es)n.; Kissin, pl.; 3.Kobbekisse (es)n.; Kobbekissi, pl.; 4.Kobbekissi (es)n.; 5.Pilwe (die)n.; **case** 1.Koppeziech (die)n.; 2.Pilweziech (die)n.; **stuffed with feathers** Fedderkissi (es)n.

pilot Schteiermann (der)n.

pimpernel Pimpernell (der)n.

pimple 1.Peckche (es)n.; 2.Pock (die)n.; Pocke, pl.

pimpled pockich, adj.

pimply pockich, adj.

pin 1.Schpell (die)n.; 2.schpelle, v.; gschpellt, pp.; 3.Zabbe (der)n.; Zabbe, pl; **cushion** Schpellekisse (es)n.; **or bolt of a doubletree** 1.Waagenaggel (der)n.; 2.Wogenaggel (der)n.; **to** aa/schpelle, v.; aagschpellt, pp.; **together** 1.zamme/schpelle, v.; zammegschpellt, pp.; 2.zu/schpelle, v.; zugschpellt, pp.; **up** nuff/schpelle, v.; nuffschpellt, pp.

pince-nez Naasepetzer (der)n.

pincers Beisszang (die)n.

pinch 1.glemme, v.; geglemmt, pp.; 2.gwetsche, v.; gegwetscht, pp.; 3.Klemm (die)n.; 4.Petz (die)n.; 5.petze, v.; gepetzt, pp. 6.Petzer (der)n.; Petzer, pl.; **(in cooking)** Messerschpitze (der)n.; **a top crust on pie** petze, v.; gepetzt, pp.; **in** nei/glemme, v.; neigeglemmt, pp.; **in** (of flower buds) ab/gnicke, v.; abgegnickt, pp.; **off** ab/petze, v.; abgepetzt, pp.; **one's finger** glemme, v. (sich der Finger --); **open** uff/petze, v.; uffgepetzt, pp.; **shut** zamme/petze, v.; zammegepetzt, pp.

pine (tree) Beint (baam) (der)n.; **away in misery** verelende, v.; verelendt, pp.

pink (swamp --) 1.Pingschtblumm (die)n.;

Pinschtblumme, pl.; 2.Pingschtnaggel (der)n.

pinnacle Gibbel (der)n.; Gibbel, pl.

pinned (on) aagschpellt, adj.

pint Beint (die)n.; **measure** Beintblech (es)n.

pintle (of a hinge) Glooe (der)n.

pinxter flower 1.Pingschdeblumm (die)n.; 2.Pingschtblumm (die)n.; Pinschtblumme, pl.; 3.Wibberwillschtock (der)n.; Wibberwillschteck, pl.

pious 1.fromm, adj.; 2.frumm, adj.

pip Pipser (der)n.

pipe 1.Peifel (es)n.; 2.Reehr (die)n.; 3.Rehr (die)n.; **(conduit)** Deichel (es)n.; Deichle, pl.; **(tobacco)** Peif (die)n.; Peife, pl.; **hole** 1.Rohrloch (es)n.; 2.Ziegloch (es)n.; **hole into a chimney** Scharnschteeloch (es)n.; **organ** 1.Ariyel (die)n.; Ariyle, pl.; 2.Karricharyel (die)n.; 3.Peifarigel (die)n.; Peifarigele, pl.; **stem** 1.Peifrehe (die)n.; 2.Peifreehr (die)n.; **wrench** Deichelschneider (der)n.; Deichelschneider, pl.

piper Peifer (der)n.; Peifer, pl.

pippin Notabbel (der)n.

pipsissema Gehlwassergraut (es)n.

piquant (of persons) safdich, adj.

pirate Seeraawer (der)n.

Pisces (12th sign of the zodiac) Fisch (der)n.; Fisch, pl.

pismire Imens (die)n.; Imense, pl.

piss pisse, v.; gepisst, pp; **a-bed** 1.Bettpisser (der)n.; 2.Bettseecher (der)n.; **oak** (hisses when it burns) Pisseeche (der, die)n.

pistol 1.Pischdol (die)n.; Pischdole, pl.; 2.Rewollwer (der)n.; Rewollwer, pl.

pit 1.Grub (die)n.; Gruwe, pl.; 2.Grundloch (es)n; **a-pat** (of feet) Gedribbel (es)n.

pitch 1.Bech (es)n.; 2.Beinthaarz (der)n; **(hay)** gawwele, v.; gegawwelt, pp.; **away** (with a fork) weck/gawwle, v.; weckgegawwelt, pp.; **dark** 1.schtichdunkel, adv.; 2.schtockdunkel, adj.; **down** nunner/gawwele, v.; nunnergegawwelt, pp.; **hay or straw in** eigawwle, v.; eigegawwelt, pp.; **in** 1.dreischlagge, v.; 2.Hand aa/schlagge, v.; Hand aaschlagge, pp.; **into** (a person) hergeh, v.; hergange, pp. (iwwer ebber --); **into him** (verbally) haer/geh, v.; haergange, pp. (iwwer ihn --);**up** ruff/gawwle, v.; ruffgegawwelt, pp.; **up** (with a fork) nuff/gawwele, v.; nuffgegawwelt, pp.

pitcher 1.Gruck (der)n.; Griek, pl.; 2.Kruck (der)n.

pith Marix (es)n.

pithy belsich, adj.; **(of radishes)** punkich, adj.

pitiable 1.bedeierlich, adj.; 2.bedierlich, adj.

pitiful 1.aaremseelich, adj.; 2.bedauerlich, adj.; 3. bekimmerlich, adj.; 4.ebaermlich, adj.; 5.elendich, adj.; 6.schendlich, adj.; 7.yemmerlich, adj.

Pitman rod (on a mower) Messerschtang (die)n.; Messerschtange, pl.

pity 1. bedaure, v.; bedauert, pp.; 2.erbaerme, v.; erbaermt, pp.; 3.erbarme, v.; erbarmt, pp.; **(to excite pity)** dauere, v.; gedauert, pp.

Pius' Day (July 11) Piusdaag (der)n.

Pp

placard — pleasure

placard Aaschlack (der)n.

place 1.Blatz (der)n.; Bletz, pl.; 2.Bletzel (es)n.; 3.hie/mache, v.; hiegemacht, pp.; 4.lege, v.; g(e)legt, pp.; 5.Ort (der)n.; 6.Platz (der)n.; Pletz, pl.; 7.Pletzel (es)n.; 8.Schtell (die)n.; 9.schtelle, v.; gschtellt, pp.; **at different points** rumher/schtelle, v.; rumherschtellt, pp.; **for an iron kettle** (under covered front of old style bakeoven) Kesselloch (es)n.; **for chopping wood** Holsblatz (der)n.; **for drying vegetables and fruit** Daerr (die)n.; **of dwelling** 1.Wohning (die)n.; 2.Wohnung (die)n.; **of safety** nummero sicher, adv.; **or push forward** vor/ricke, v.; vorgerickt, pp.; **or set under** unner/schtelle, v.; unnergschtellt, pp.; **or set up somewhere** nuff/schtelle, v.; nuffgschtellt, pp.; **something for drying** uff, prep., adv. (ebbes -- die Daerr duh); **where mowing is done** Maehd (die)n.; **where pomace was piled in old cider mills** Kelder (die)n.

placenta 1.Butze (die)n.; 2.Butzing (die)n.; 3.Noochgebort (die)n.; 4.Noochgeburt (die)n. (animals) 5.Seiwering (die)n. (animals)

placid mild, adj.

placket Schlitz (der)n.

plague 1.ab/maertre, v.; abgemaertert, pp.; 2.Blog (die)n.; 3. Blok (die)n.; 4.Peinich (die)n.; 5.peiniche, v.; gepeinicht, pp.; 6.Pescht (die)n.; Peschde, pl.; 7.Plok (die)n.; 8.Sucht (die)n.

plaid dobbel-schteenich, adj.

plain 1.bleen, adj.; 2.deitlich, adj.; 3.eifach. adj.; 4.flach, adj.; **(comprehensible)** handgreiflich, adj.; **truth** Wahret (die)n.(deitschi --)

plainly katzab, adv.

plaintiff 1.Glaeger (der)n.; Glaeger, pl.; 2.Klaeger (der)n.

plait 1.flechde, v.; g(e)flochde, pp.; 2.zebbe, v.; gezeppt, pp.

plan 1.Abriss (der)n.; 2.aus/lege, v.; ausgelegt, pp.; 3.aus/mache, v.; ausgemacht, pp.; 4.Blaan (der)n.; 5.blaane, v.; geblaant, pp.; **an April fool prank** Abrill (der)n. (in -- schicke)

plane 1.Howwel (die)n.; Howwle, pl.; 2.howwle, v.; ghowwelt, pp.; **bit** (iron) Howweleise (es)n.; **off** ab/howwle, v.; abghowwelt, pp.

planet 1.Blaneet (der)n.; 2.Planet (der)n.

plank 1.Blank (die)n.; Blanke, pl.; 2.Plank (die)n.

plant 1.aa/blanze, v.; aageblanzt, pp.; 2.Blanz (die)n.; Blanze, pl.; 3.blanze, v.; geblanzt, pp.; 4.planse, v.; geplanst, pp.; 5.schtecke, v.; gschteckt, pp.; 6.Schtock (der)n.; Schteck, pl.; **corn in checkerboard fashion** zackere, v.; gezackert, pp.; **in a certain place** hie/blanze, v.; hiegeblanzt, pp.; **in another place** rum/blanze, v.; rumgeblanzt, pp.; **in different places** rumher/blanze, v.; rumhergeblanzt, pp.; **in or into** nei/blanze, v.; neigeblanzt, pp.; **louse** Erdfloh (der)n.; Erdfleh, pl.; **out** aus/setze, v.; ausgsetzt, pp.; **together** zamme/blanze, v.; zammegeblanzt, pp.; **up** nuff/blanze, v.; nuffgeblanzt, pp.

plantain leaf Seiohreblaatt (es)n.

planting Blanset (die)n.

plash rausche, v.; gerauscht, pp.

plaster 1.Blaschder (es)n.; 2.Bleschder (die)n.; 3.bleschdere, v.; gebleschdert, pp.; 4.Plaschder (die)n.; **(for drawing)** 1.Zuckblaschder (es)n.; 2.Ziegblaschder (es)n.; **of Spanish fly** 1.Mickeblaschder (es)n.; 2.Muckeblaschder (es)n.; **up** 1.verbleschdere, v.; verbleschdert, pp.; 2.zubleschdre, v.; zugebleschdert, pp.

plasterer Bleschderer (der)n.; Blechderer, pl.

plate Deller (der)n.; Deller, pl.; **(at front of cook-stove)** Offeblatt (die)n.; **(of a stove)** 1.Blatt (die)n.; 2.Platt (die)n.

plateful Dellervoll (der)n.

Plattdeutsch (Low German) Blattdeitsch (es)n.

plausible 1.glaablich, adj.; 2.scheinbaar, adj.

play 1.rose, v.; gerost, pp.; 2.schpiele, v.; gschpielt, pp.; **a prank** Dummheet (die)n. (dummheete mache); **a sharp trick upon** uff/zwacke, v.; uffgewackt, pp.; **along with** mit/schpiele, v.; mitgschpielt, pp.; **an instrument badly** dudle, v.; gedudelt, pp.; **around** rum/schpiele, v.; rumgschpielt, pp.; **ball** schpiele, v.; gschpielt, pp. (Balle --); **cards**; schpiele, v.; gschpielt, pp.; **enchantingly well** (He plays so enchantingly that the chickens would die because of it.) Er kann so gut schpiele, as die Hinkel doot gehne.; **in the water puddles** gsuddle, v.; gsuddelt, pp.; **innocent** 1.aaschtelle, v.; aagschtellt, pp. (sich dumm --); 2.dumm aa/schtelle (sich --)v.; aagschtellt, pp.; **off** ab/schpiele, v.; abgschpielt, pp.; **on the Jew's harp** drummble, v.; gedrummbelt, pp.; **or other activity** aus/dowe (sich --)v.; ausgedobt, pp.; **pranks** 1.aa/dreiwe, v.; aagedriwwe, pp.; 2.Gschpichte (die)n., pl. (-- mache); 3.narre, v.; genatt; gnaart, pp.; 4.verrobbe, v.; verroppt, pp.; **ring tag** Ring (der)n. (-- schpiele); **see-saw** riggelreide, v.; riggelgeridde, pp.; **the clown** hanswarschtle, v.; gehanswarschtelt, pp.; **the parasite** suckle, v.; gsuckelt, pp.; **tip-cat** schpiele, v.; gschpielt, pp. (Nepsel --); **up** uff/schpiele, v.; uffgschpielt, pp.;

played out ausgschpielt, adj.

player Schpieler (der)n.

playful mutwillich, adj.; **nickname** Haahnewackel (der)n.

playground Schpielblatz (der)n.

playing Gschpiel (es)n.; **card** Schpielkord (die)n.; **in the water puddles** (of children) Gsuddel (es)n.

playmate Schpielkummeraad (der)n.

plea Bitt (die)n.; Bidde, pl.

plead excuses raus/schtreiche (sich --)v.; rausgschtriche, pp.

pleasant 1.aagenehmlicherweiss, adj.; 2.blessierlich, adj.; 3.freindlich, adj.; 4.lieblich, adj.

please aa/schteh, v.; aagschtanne, pp.

pleasing aaschmeechlich, adj.

pleasurable 1.aagenehm, adj.; 2.blessierlich, adj.

pleasure 1.Blessier (die)n.; 2.Frehlichkeit (die)n.; 3.Gschpass (der)n.; 4.Luscht (die)n.; 5.Luschtbaarkeit (die)n.; 6.Schpass (der)n.; 7.Vergniege (der)n.

Pp

pleat — polish

pleat Falt (die)n.; Falde, pl.

pledge 1.Verschpreche(s) (es)n.; 2.verschpreche, v.;
verschproche, pp.

plentiful reichlich, adv.

plenty 1.blendi, adj.; 2.Iwwerfluss (der)n.

pleura 1.Ribbefell (es)n.; 2.Rippefell (es)n.

pleurisy root 1.Millichgraut (es)n.; 2.Rhummedisgraut (es)
n.; 3.Rummedissgraut (es)n.

pliable biegsam, adj.

pliers Petzer (der)n.; Petzer, pl.

plight Zuschtand (der)n.; Zuschtende, pl.

plod somewhere with a cane naus/schtocke, v.;
nausgschtockt, pp.

plover 1.Feldhinkel (es)n.; 2.Gilderi (der)n.; 3.Gilleri (der)
n.; Gilleri, pl.; 4.Reg(g)evoggel (der)n.

plow 1.Blug (der)n.; Blieg, pl.; 2.bluge, v.; geblugt, pp.; 3.Plug
(der)n.; Plieg, Pliek, pl.; 4.pluge, v.; geplu(g)kt, pp.;
5.rum/bluge, v.; rumgeblugt, pp.; 6.rum/mache, v.;
rumgemacht, pp.; 7.rum/schaffe, v.; rumgschafft, pp.;
8.zackere, v.; gezackert, pp.; **after** no(och)bluge, v.;
no(och)geblugt, pp.; **between the rows of growing plants**
aus/bluge, v.; ausgeblugt, pp.; **drag** 1.Blugschleef (es)n.;
2.Plug(s)schleef (die)n.; **for different persons**
rumher/bluge, v.; rumhergeblugt, pp.; **handle** 1.Blug(s)
hendel (der)n.; 2.Plug(s)hendel (der)n.; **in** (seed) eibluge, v.;
eigeblugt, pp.; **in a clockwise direction** nei/bluge, v.;
neigeblugt, pp.; **in a counter- clockwise direction**
naus/bluge, v.; nausgeblugt, pp.; **in partnership**
zamme/bluge, v.; zammegeblugt, pp.; **out** (as potatoes)
1.aus/bluge, v.; ausgeblugt, pp.; 2.raus/bluge, v.;
rausgeblugt, pp.; **poorly** 1.rum/bluge, v.; rumgeblugt, pp.;
2.rum/schinne, v.; rumgschunne, pp.; 3.weck/schinne, v.;
weckgschunne, pp.; **shoe** 1.Blugschleef (es)n.; 2.Plug(s)
schleef (die)n.; **under** (as a cover crop) unner/bluge, v.;
unnergeblugt, pp.; **under** (as potatoes) zufaerrichde, v.;
zugfaerricht, pp.; **up** uff/bluge, v.; uffgeblugt, pp.; **with a
jointer** Sechbluk (der)n.

plowable land Bau (der)n.

plowbeam 1.Blug(s)grendel (der)n.; 2.Grandel (der)n.;
3.Grendel (der)n. (blug[s] --) 4.Plugsgrendel (der)n.

plowed field (all turns made to the left) Haaschemel (der)n.

plowshare 1.Blugschaar (es)n.; Blugschaare, pl.;
2.Plugschaar (es)n.; 3.Schaar (es)n.

pluck 1.ab/robbe, v; abgeroppt, pp.; 2.robbe, v.; geroppt,
pp.; 3.uff/robbe, v.; uffgeroppt, pp.; **(to pieces)**
verblicke, v.; verblickt, pp.; **leaves from** 1.ab/blaade, v.;
abgeblaadt, pp.; 2.ab/bleddere, v.; abgebleddert, pp.

pluckable (of goose feathers at certain seasons) flick, adj.

plug 1.schtoppe, v.; gschtoppt, pp.; 2.verschtobbe, v.;
verschtoppt, pp.; 3.Zabbe (der)n.; Zabbe, pl.; 4.zu/schtecke,
v.; zugschteckt, pp.; 5.zu/zabbe, v.; zugezappt, pp.

plum 1.Blaum (die)n.; Blaume, pl.; 2.Gwetsch (die)n.;
Gwetsche, pl.; **stone** Blaumeschtee (der)n.; **tree**
1.Blaumebaam (der)n.; 2.Gwetschebaam (der)n.;
Gwetschebeem, pl.

plumb 1.ab/senkle, v.; abgsenkelt, pp.; 2.Senkblei (es)n.;
3. senkle, v.; gsenkelt, pp.; **line** 1.Mauersenkel (der)
n.; 2.Sankelschnur (die)n.; 3.Senkblei (es)n.;

4.Senkelschnur (die)n.

plumber Bleischaffer (der)n.

plumes on a lady's hat Schtreiss (die)n., pl.

plummet 1.Sankel (der)n.; 2.Senkel (der)n.; 3.Zenkel (der)
n.; Zenkel, pl.

plump 1.dick, adj.; 2.fett, adj.; 3.plurmp, adj.; 4.plumpe, v.;
geplumpt, pp.; 5.bumm! interj.

plunder plindere, v.; geplindert, pp.

plurality Mehrheet (die)n.

ply the needle no(o)dle, v.; geno(o)delt, pp.

pneumonia 1.Bruschtfiewer (es)n.; 2.Lungefiewer (es)n.

pocket 1.Dasch (die)n. (rare usage); 2.Sack (der)n.
(in -- schtecke); 3.Sack (der)n.; Seck, pl.

pocketbook Backebuch (es)n.; Backebicher, pl.

pocketknife Sackmesser (es)n.; Sackmessere,pl.

pod 1.Schef (die)n.; Schefe, pl.; 2.Schot (die)n.; **bean**
Schotebohn (die)n.

poem Gedicht (es)n.; Gedichde, pl.

poet Dichder (der)n.; Dichder, pl.

point 1.deide, v.; gedeidt, pp.; 2.deite, v.; gedeit, pp.;
3.Punkt (der)n.; Punkde, pl.; 4.Schpitz(e) (der)n.; **of a
knife** Messerschpitze (der)n.; **of a needle**
Noodelschpitze (die)n.; **of a plowshare** 1.Blug(s)naas
(die)n.; 2.Plug(s)naas (die)n.; **of the roof at the gable-end** Dachgiwwel (der)n.; **out** weise, v.; gewisse,
pp.; **out in reading** no(och)weise, v.; no(och)gewisse,
pp.; **to** hie/weise, v.; hiegewisse, pp.

pointed 1.schpitzich, adj.; 2.zachich, adj.; 3.zackich, adj.;
4.zacklich, adj.; **cap** 1.Schnawwelkeppli (es)n.;
2.Zibbelkapp (die)n.; Zibbelkabbe; Zibbelkepp, pl.

pointer Deiter (der)n.

poison 1.Gift (es)n.; 2.vergifte, v.; vergift, pp.; **berry** Giftbeer
(die)n.; **ivy** 1.Gift (der)n. (ranklich --); 2.Rankegift (es)n.

poisonous 1.gifdich, adj.; 2.giftich, adj.

poke 1.nuff/schtarre, v.; nuffgschtatt, pp.; 2.poke, v.; gepokt,
pp.; 3.schtarre, v.; gschtarrt, pp.; 4.schtoose, v.; gschtoose,
pp.; **along** leiere, v.; geleiert, pp.; **around** rum/poke, v.;
rumgepokt, pp.; **down** nunner/renne, v.; nunnergerennt,
pp.; **off** (with a stick) ab/schtubbe, v.; abschtuppt, pp.;
one's nose in everybody's business 1.Naas (die)n. (-- in
alles schtecke); 2.schtecke, v.; gschtocke, pp. (die Naas in
alles --); **one's nose into a matter** nei/schnuffle, v.;
neigschnuffelt, pp.; **out** raus/poke, v.; rausgepokt, pp.

pokeberry Pokbeer (die)n.; Pokbeere, pl.

poker Poker (der)n.

pokeweed Dindebeer (die)n.

poking pokich, adv.

pole 1.Deichsel (die)n.; 2.Schtang (die)n.; Schtange, pl.;
3.Schwing (die)n.; **bean** 1.Graddelbohn (die)n.;
Graddelbohne, pl.; 2.Graddelbuhn (die)n.;
Graddelbuhne, pl.; 3.Schteckebohn (die)n.; **chain**
1.Deichselkett (die)n.; 2.Deixelkett (die)n.; Deixelkedde,
pl.; **pin** 1.Bogehammer (der)n.; Bogehemmer, pl.;
2.Deichselnaggel (der)n.; 3.Deixelnaggel (der)n.

polecat Bisskatz (die)n.; Bisskatze, pl.

polish 1.ab/schleife, v.; abschliffe, pp.; 2.wichse, v.; gewichst, pp.; 3.wixe, v.; gewixt, pp.

Pp

polite — potpie

polite manierlich, adj.

politeness Manierlichkeet (die)n.

politics 1.Balledicks (die)n.; 2.Palledix (die)n.; 3.Politik(s) (die)n.

polka-dotted dibbeldunich, adj.

pollen 1.Blummeschtaab (der)n.; 2.Someschtaab (der)n.; 3.Sumeschtaab (der)n.

polygamy Vielweiwerei (die)n.

polygon Vieleck (es)n.

pomace Dreschder (der)n.

pomade Hoorschmier (die)n.

pomegranate Granaadabbel (der)n.

pommel 1.Knoffe (der)n.; 2.Saddelgnopp (der)n.; 3.verbelze, v.; verbelzt, pp.

pommeling Gegnuff (es)n.

pond 1.Daal (es)n.; Daale; Daaler, pl.; 2.Deich (es)n.; Deicher, pl.; 3.Wasserloch (es)n.; Wasserlecher, pl.; **grass** Dammgraas (es)n.; **lily** Wasserlilye (die)n.

ponder 1.bedeide, v.; bedeidt, pp.; 2.bedenke, v.; bedenkt, pp.; 3.iwwer/denke, v.; iwwergedenkt, pp.; 4.iwwerlege, v.; iwwerlekt, pp.

poodle Pudelhund (der)n.; Pudelhund, pl.

pooh! puh!, inter.

pool 1.Deich (es)n.; Deicher, pl.; 2.Dreckloch (es)n.; Drecklecher, pl.; 3.Wasserloch (es)n.; Wasserlecher, pl.

poor 1.aarem, adj.; adv.; 2.aaremseelich, adj.; 3.aarmseelich, adj.; adv.; 4.bedaerfdich, adj.; 5.elendich, adj.; 6.maager, adj.; 7.miseraawel, adj.; **(in health)** gribblich, adj.; **devil** Schlucker (der)n. (aarmer --); **director** Arem(p)fleger (der)n.; **farmer** Schtengelbauer (der)n; **house** Aremhaus (es)n.; **in quality** (of apples) wassersichdich, adj.; **pocket knife** Grottegicker (der)n.; **sickler** Grutzer (der)n.; **wretch** aaremer Schlucker, (der)n.; **poorer; poorest** 1.aarm; aarmer; aarmscht, adj.; 2.aerm; aermer; aermscht, adj.

poorhouse Aarmehaus (es)n.

poorly 1.aermlich, adv.; 2.bekimmerlich, adj.; 3. bekimmerlich, adv.; 4.hinnerlich, adv.

pop-corn Biebliwelschkaan (es)n.

Pope 1.Baapscht (der)n.; Baapschde, pl.; 2.Paabscht (der)n.

popgun (made of hollowed out elder stem) 1.Hollerbix (die)n.; 2.Hollerflint (die)n.

poplar Babble (der)n.; Babble, pl.

poppy 1.Flatterros (die)n.; 2.Maach (der)n.; 3.Maag (der) n.; 4.Fadderros (die)n.

popular 1.beliebt, adj.; 2.paplaer, adj.

populous volkreich, adj.

porch Bortsch (die)n.; **railing** Portschgelender (es)n.

porcupine 1.Iegel (der)n.; 2.Igel (der)n.; 3.Schtachelsau (die)n.; 4.Schtachelschwein (es)n.

pork Seifleesch (es)n.; **chops** Rickmeesel (es)n.

porous 1.luck, adj.; 2.rosich, adj.

porridge Mehlsupp (die)n.

porringer Blechel (es)n.

portend vorbedeite, v.; vorbedeit, pp.

portent Vorbedeidung (die)n.

porter 1.Deerhieter (der)n.; 2.Draeger (der)n.; Draeger, pl.

portulaca Maasblumm (die)n.; Maasblumme, pl.

position Schtell (die)n.

position in life Lewe(n)sschtand (der)n.

positively 1.ausdricklich, adv.; 2.darichaus, adv.; 3.positiv,adj.

possess 1.b(e)sitze, v.; b(e)sesse, pp.; 2.eegne, v.;ge-eegent, pp.

possession 1.Eegedum (es)n.; 2.Versatz (der)n.

possessor B(e)sitzer (der)n.; B(e)sitzer, pl.

possible 1.meechlich, adv.; 2.meeglich, adv.; 3.mieglich, adv.

possibly 1.eischt, adj.; 2.meeglicherweis, adj.; 3. meeylicherweis, adv.

post 1.aa/schlagge, v.; aagschlagge, pp.; 2.Poschde (der) n.; Poschde, pl.

post advance in price uff/schlagge, v.; uffgschlagge, pp.

post-auger Poschdebohre (der)n.

post-ax Poschde-ax (die)n.; Poschde-ex, pl.

post dog (of iron) Poschdehund (der)n.

post fence Riggelfen (die)n.;Riggelfense, pp.

post hole Poschdeloch(es)n.; Poschdelecher, pl.

post office Poschtaffis (die)n.

post with holes (for making fence) Lochposchde (der)n.; Lochposchde, pl.

postage Poschtgeld (es)n.

posted-statement Aaschlack (der)n.

posterior 1.Aarsch (der)n.; 2.After (es)n.; 3.Baerzel (der)n.; 4.Hinners (der)n.; **part of the knee joint** Gniekehl (die)n.

posterity 1.Noochkummenschaft (die)n.; 2.Noochkunft (die)n.

postfence Poschdefens (die)n.

postmaster Poschtmeeschder (der)n.; Poschtmeeschder, pl.

postpone 1.ab/bschtelle, v.; abbschtellt, pp.; 2.ab/duh, v.; abgeduh, pp.; 3.ab/schiewe, v.; abschowe, pp.; 4.ab/schtelle, v.; abgschtellt, pp.; 5.iwwerlege, v.; iwwergelekt, pp.; 6.naus/schiewe, v.; nausgschowe, pp.; 7.uff/schiewe, v.; uffgschowe, pp.

postscript Noochschrift (die)n.

posture Puschduur (die)n.

posy Blummeschtrauss (der)n.

pot 1.Haffe (der)n.; Heffe, pl.; 2.Kessel (der)n.; Kessele, pl.; **bellied** dickleiwich, adj.; **cheese** Faulerkees (der) n.; **cover** Haffedeckel (der)n.

potash Bottesch (die)n.

potato 1.Grummbeer (die)n.; Grummbeere, pl.; 2.Grummbier (die)n.; Grummbiere, pl.; 3.Kadoffel (die) n. (rare usage); **bug** Grummbierekeffer (der)n.; Grummbierekeffer, pl.; **patch** Grumbeereschtick (es)n.; **picker** Grumbeereleser (der)n.; **pie** Grummbeereboi (der)n.; **shovel** Grummbeereschaufel (die)n.; Grummbeereschaufle, pl.; **soup** Grumbeeresupp (die) n.; **stalk** Grumbeereschtengle (der)n.; **top** Grumbeereschtengle (der)n.

potbelly Dicksack (der)n.; Dickseck

potpie Bottboi (der)n.

Pp

potsherd

potsherd Haffeschaerb (die)n.

potter 1.Heffemacher (der)n.; Heffemacher, pl.; 2.Heffner (der)n.; Heffner, pl.

pottery Heffnerei (die)n.

pouch cheek Heckbacke (der)n.; Heckbacke, pl.

poultry Feddervieh (es)n.

pound 1.globbe, v.; geglobbt, pp.; 2.kloppe, v.; gekloppt, pp.; 3.Pund (es)n.; Pund, pl.; **apple** 1.Falliwalder (der) n.; 2.Pundabbel (der)n.; **in** nei/belse, v.; neigebelst, pp.; **out** raus/belse, v.; rausgebelst, pp.

pounder Schtembel (der)n.

pour 1.giesse, v.; gegosse, pp.; 2.leere, v.; gleert, pp.; 3.schitte, v.; gschitt, pp; **away** (of liquids) weck/schidde,v.; weckgschitt, pp.; **back** zerick/schitte, v.; zerickgschitt, pp.; **down** 1.hie/schidde, v.; hiegschidt, pp.; 2.runner/schidde, v.; runnergschitt, pp.; **from one vessel into another** zamme/leere, v.; zammegeleert, pp.; **in** eischenke, v.; eigschenkt, pp.; **into** nei/schidde, v.; neigschitt, pp.; **into** (of beverages at table) nei/schenke, v.; neigschenkt, pp.; **into** (of grain) nei/leere, v.; neigleert, pp.; **medicine down** throat eischitte, v.; eigschitt, pp.; **off** 1.ab/giese, v.; abgschitt (abgegosse - rare usage) pp.; 2.ab/schidde, v.; abgschitt, pp.; 3.ab/schitte, v.; abgschitt, pp.; **out** 1.aus/schidde, v.; ausgschitt, pp.; 2.eischenke, v.; eigschenkt, pp.; 3.naus/schidde, v.; nausgschitt, pp.; 4.raus/schidde, v.; rausgschitt, pp.; 5.verleere, v.; verleert, pp.; **out** (coffee, milk, etc.) 1.aus/schenke, v.; ausgschenkt, pp.; 2.raus/schenke, v.; rausgschenkt, pp.; **over** niwwer/ schidde, v.; niwwergschitt, pp.

pout 1.brutze, v.; gebrutzt, pp. (es Maul --); 2.henke, v.; ghenkt, pp. (es Maul --); 3.Schippsche (es)n. (en -- mache); 4.Schnippche (es)n. (en -- mache); 5.Schnut (die)n. (en -- mache); 6.uff, prep. adv. (-- der Brutzbank sitze)

pouter 1.Brunsbank (die)n.; 2.Brutzbank (die)n.

pouting Gebrutz (es)n; **bench** Brutzbank (die)n.; **corner** (corner into which pouting children retire) Brutzeck (es)n.

pouty brutzich, adj.

pouty 1.Aarmut (die)n.; 2.Armedei (die)n.; **grass** Baerschdegraas (es)n.

powder 1.Bulfer (es)n.; 2.Bulver (es)n.; 3.Bulwer (es)n.; 4.Pilverlin (es)n.; 5.pudre, v.; gepudert, pp.; 6.Pulfer (es)n.; 7.Pulver (es)n.; 8.Pulwer (es)n.; **(to be taken)** Briefelche (es)n.; **horn** Pulwerhann (es)n.; **mill** Pulwermiehl (die)n.; **used for blasting** 1.Felsebulwer (es)n.; 2.Felsepulfer (es)n.

powdered vermaahle, adj.

power 1.Allergwalt (die)n.; 2.Gewalt (die)n.; 3.Graft (die) n.; Grefde, pl.; 4.Kraft (die)n.; 5.Macht (die)n.; **of speech** Schprooch (die)n.

powerful 1.gewaltich, adj.; 2.mechdich, adj.

powwow brauche, v.; gebraucht, pp.; **doctor**

pregnant

1.Brauchdokder (der)n.; 2.Braucher (der)n.; 3.Brauchfraa (die)n.; **word** (used in formula rheumatism) Hexeschuss (der)n.

powwowing 1.Braucherei (die)n.; 2.Kinschdlerei (die)n.

practice 1.aus/iewe, v.; ausgeiebt, pp.; 2.Iebing (die)n.; 3.Iewing (die)n.; **medicine** 1.Dekterei (die)n.; 2.doktere,v.; gedoktert, pp.

praise 1.belowe, v.; belobt, pp.; 2.Lob (es)n.; 3.lowe, v.; gelobt, pp.; 4.riehme, v.; geriehmt, pp.; 5.uff/lowe, v.; uffgelobt, pp.

prance (of a horse) densle, v.; gedenselt, pp.

prank 1.Schabernack (der)n.; 2.Schtreech (der)n.; Schtreech, pl.; 3.Aaschlaek (die)n., pl.; 4.Aaschtreech (die)n., pl.

prairie chicken Feldhinkel (es)n.

prate 1.beb(b)ere, v.; gebeb(b)ert, pp.; 2.hie/babble, v.; hiegebabbelt, pp.

prattle baple, v.; gebabbelt, pp.

pray 1.bede, v.; gebet, pp.; 2.bitte, v.; gebitt, pp.; **(silently into one's hat before taking seat in church)** Hut (der)n.(in -- bede)

prayer 1.Bede(s) (es)n.; 2.Gebet (es)n.; Gebeder, pl.; **book** 1.Betbuch (es)n.; Betbicher, pl.; 2.Gebetbuch (es)n.; Gebetbicher, pl.; **meeting** 1.Betschtund (die)n.; 2.Betschtunn (die)n.

preach 1.breddiche, v.; gebreddicht, pp.; 2.preddiche, v.; gepreddicht, pp.; **to the weariment of the congregation** ausbreddiche (sich --)v.; ausgebreddicht, pp.

preacher 1.Breddicher (der)n.; Breddicher, pl.; 2.Diener (der)n.; Diener, pl.; 3.Preddicher (der)n.; 4.Redner (der)n.

preaching Gebreddich (es)n.

precarious unsicher, adj.

precaution Vorsicht (die)n.

precede 1.vor/geh, v.; vorgange, pp.; 2.voraa/geh, v.; voraagange, pp.; 3.vorhaergeh, v.; verhaergange, pp.; 4.vorher/geh, v.; vorhergange, pp.

preceptor Lehrer (der)n.

precipice Abgrund (der)n.

precipitate Ghaschbel (es)n.; **thoughtless movement** Kaschbel (es)n.

precipitate(ly) 1.haschblich, adv.; 2.rasch, adv.; 3.vorwitzich, adv.; 4.yaehlings, adv.

precocious youngster 1.Hocheschisser (der)n.; 2.Hoseschisser (der)n.

predict 1.brofesseihe, v.; gebrofesseiht, pp.; 2.vannenaus/saage, v. vannenausgsaat, pp.; 3.vor/saage, v.; vorgsaat, pp.; 4.vorhaersaage, v.; vorhaergsaat, pp.; 5.vorher/saage, v.; vorhersaagt, pl.

prediction Brophezeiung (die)n.

preface 1.vanneher, adv.; 2.Vorreed (die)n.; 3.Vorwart (es)n.

prefer vor/ziege, v.; vorgezogge, pp.

preference Vorzuck (der)n.

pregnant 1.Familye (die)n. (im e -- weg); 2.schwanger, adj.; 3.uffgebindelt, adj.; 4.uffgeblosse, adj.

343

Pp

prejudice

prejudice Vorurteil (es)n.; **against** (another) verschtifde, v.; verschtift, pp.

premature birth Miss (die)n.

prematurely 1.freihzeidich, adv.; 2.friehzeitich, adj.

premonition Aageschpiegel (der)n.

preparation 1.Eirichding (die)n.; 2.Rischderei (die)n.; 3. Rischding (die)n.

preparatory service (prior to Communion) 1.Vorb(e)reiding (die)n. (Lutheran and Reformed); 2.Adningsgmee (die)n. (Amish;) 3.Zubreiding (die)n. (Mennonite)

prepare 1.Aagschtalt (der)n. (so'n -- mache); 2.ei/richde, v.; eigericht, pp.; 3.rischde (sich --)v.; gerischt, pp.; 4.vorbereide, v.; vorbereidt, pp.; 5.zerechtmache, v.; zerechtgemacht, pp.; 6.zu/richde, v.; zugericht, pp.; 7.zu/rischde, v.; zugerischt, pp.; **a corpse for the coffin** aus/lege, v.; ausgelegt, pp.

prepared 1.bereit, adj.; 2.zugerischt, adj.

prerogative Vorrecht (es)n.

prescribe 1.verschreiwe, v.; verschriwwe, pp.; 2.vor/setze, v.; vorgsetzt, pp.

prescription Rezept (die)n.

presence Gegewart (die)n.; **of mind** bsunne, adj.

present 1.bei/wohne, v.; beigewohnt, pp. 2.b(e)schenke, v.; b(e)schenkt, pp.; 3.Bressent (es)n.; 4.gege(n)waertich, adj.; 5.G(e)schenk (es)n.; Gschenker, pl.; 6.eifinne (sich --)v.; eigfunne, pp.; 7.Mitgift (die)n.; 8.Pressent (es)n.; 9.Schenkaasche (die)n.; 10.vor/draage, v.; vorgedraage, pp.

present (time) 1.Gegewart (die)n.; 2.yetzich, adj.

presently 1.graadeweck, adj.; 2.iwwerdem(m), adv.

preservation Erhaltung (die)n.

preserve 1.aa/halde, v.; aaghalde, pp.; 2.aus/dauere, v.; ausgedauert, pp.; 3.behalde, v.; 4.behiede, v.; behiet, pp.; 5.bewaare, v.; bewaart, pp.; 6.erhalde, v.; erhalde, pp.; **(fruit)** 1.ei/mache, v.; eigemacht, pp.; 2.uff/duh, v.; uffgeduh, pp.

preserves 1.Eigemachdes (es)n.; 2.eimache, v.; eigemacht, pp. (eigemacht Sach); 3.Psaref (es)n.; 4.Pserfs (es)n.; 5.Sach (die)n. (gekennt --)

president 1.Bresident (der)n.; Bresidende, pl.; 2.Vorsitzer (der)n.; Vorsitzer, pl.

press 1.Bress (die)n.; 2.dricke, v.; gedrickt, pp.; 3.Press (die)n.; 4.presse, v.; gepresst, pp.; 5.verdricke, v.; verdrickt, pp.; **against** bei/dricke, v.; beigedrickt, pp.; **down** nunner/dricke, v.; nunnergedrickt, pp.; **or pinch off** ab/dricke, v.; abgedrickt, pp.; **out** aus/dricke, v.; ausgedrickt, pp.; **through** darich/dricke, v.; darichgedrickt, pp.; **together** zuklemme, v.; zugeklemmt, pp.; **together hard** 1.ei/dricke, v.; eigedrickt, pp.; 2.zamme/dricke, v.; zammegedrickt, pp.; **with the thumb** deimele, v.; gedeimelt, pp.

pressing Drickes (es)n. (so'n --)

pressings from flaxseed ground cattle fee Olichmehl (es)n.

prestige Vorrang (der)n.

presumably 1.allernaegscht, adv.; 2.an dem, adv.;

priest's

3.andem, adj.; 4.andem, adj.; 5.vermutlich, adv.

presume 1.iwwerhewe (sich --)v.; iwwerhowe, pp.; 2.mutmaase, v.; gemutmaast, pp.; 3.mutmoos(s)e, v.; gemutmoost, pp.; 4.unner/schteh (sich --)v.; 5.unnerschteh, v.; 6.vermude, v.; vermut, pp.; 7.zehle, v.; gezehlt, pp.

presumption 1.Mutmaasing (die)n.; 2.Mutmoosing (die)n.

pretend 1.aa/losse, v.; aag(e)losst, pp.; 2.ab/schpiele, v.; abgschpielt, pp.; 3.haer/schtelle (sich --)v.; haergschtelle, pp.; 4.haer/schtelle (sich --)v.; haergschtelle, pp.; 5.her/ schtelle (sich --)v.; hergschtellt, pp.; 6.verschtelle (sich --)v.; verschtellt, pp.; 7.vor/gewwe, v.; vorgewwe, pp.; 8.wann, adv. (mach as --)

pretending Christian 1.Maulgrischt (der)n.; 2.Naamegrischt (der)n.; 3.Nomegrischt (der)n.

pretense Verschtelling (die)n.

pretext 1.Ausrett (die)n.; Ausredde, pl.; 2.Eiwendung (die)n.; 3.Eiwenning (die)n.; 4.vor/gewwe, v.; vorgewwe, pp.

prettily zier, adj.

pretty 1.nett, adj.; 2.niedlich, adj.; 3.schee, adj.; 4.zimmlich, adv.; **good** zimmlich, adv.

pretzel 1.Bretzel (es)n.; 2.Pretzel (es)n.; 3.Schtreichler, n.; 4.Schtreissel (es)n; **covered with sugar instead of salt** Zuckerbretzel (es)n.

prevail 1.iwwerkumme, v.; iwwerkumme, pp.; 2.iwwerwinde, v.; iwwerwunne, pp.; 3.iwwerwinne, v.; iwwerwunne, pp.; 4.meeschdere, v.; gemeeschdert, pp.; **on someone to accept** (something) aa/schwetze, v.; aagschwetzt, pp.

prevaricate (in a matter) ab/munkle, v.; abgemunkelt, pp.

prevent 1.hinnere, v.; ghinnert, pp.; 2.verheide, v.; verheit, pp.; 3.verhiete, v.; verhiet, pp.; 4.verhinnere, v.; verhinnert, pp.; 5.verwehre, v.; verwehrt, pp.

prevention Verhinnerung (die)n.

previously 1.vadderhand, adv.; 2.vadem, adv.; 3.vordem, adv.; 4.vorderhand, adv.; 5.vorhaer, adv.; 6.vorher, adv.

prey Raab (die)n.

price 1.Breis (der)n.; 2.Preis (der)n.

prick 1.nei/schteche, v.; neigschtoche, pp.; 2.schteche, v.; gschtoche, pp.; **or sting full of holes** verschteche, v.; verschtoche, pp.; **the ears** 1.Ohre (die)n., pl. (-- schpitze); 2.schpitze, v.; gschpitzt, pp. (die ohre --)

prickle Schtachel (die)n.

prickly schtachlich, adj.; **ash** 1.Brockelesche (die)n.; 2.Brocklesche (die)n.; **heat** Hitzpocke (die)n.,pl.; **lettuce** 1.Schtechgraut; 2.Schechselaat; **pear** Deifelszung (die)n.

pride 1.Schtaat (der)n.; 2.Schtolz (der)n.

priest 1.Baapscht (der)n.; Baapschde, pl.; 2.Breischder (der)n.; Breischder, pl.; 3.Brieschder (der)n.; 4.Preischder (der)n.; 5.Prieschder (der)n.; **who is a member of an order** Adderbreischder (der)n.

priest's (minister's) **pocket** Paffesack (der)n.

Pp

priestly — protrude

priestly geischtlich, adj.

primer A-b-c-buch (es)n.

priming Zindpulwer (die)n.

primrose Schlisselblumm (die)n.; Schlisselblumme, pl.

princes' feather 1.Fleehgraut (es)n.; 2.Flehgraut (es)n.; 3.Schwenz (die)n., pl. (rodi --)

principle Grundsatz (der)n.; **(drawing interest)** Haaptsumm (die)n.; **part** Haaptschtick (es)n.; **place** Haaptblatt (der)n.; **thing** 1.Haapt (es)n.; 2.Haaptsach (die)n.

print 1.Druck (der)n.; 2.drucke, v.; gedruckt, pp.; 3.Gedruckes (es)n.

printed matter Drucksache (die)n., pl.

printer Drucker (der)n.; Drucker, pl.

printer's ink Druckdinde (der)n.

printing Gedruckes (es)n.

printshop Druckerei (die)n.

prismire 1.Iemens (die)n.;Iemense,pl.; 2.Umens (die)n.; Umense, pl.

prison 1.Bressen(t) (die)n.; Bressende, pl.; 2.Gfengnis (es)n.

prisoner Gfangner (der)n.; Gfangne, pl.

privilege Vorrecht (es)n.

privy 1.Abdritt (der)n.; 2.Briwwe (es)n.; 3.Briwwi (es)n.

prize 1.Breis (der)n.; 2.Dreffer (der)n.; 3.schetze, v.; gschetzt, pp.

probability Waahrscheinlichkeet (die)n.

probable mieglich, adv.

probably 1.meechlich, adv.; 2.meeglich, adv.; 3.meiglich, adv.; 4.vermutlich, adv.; 5.waahrscheinlich, adv.

proboscis 1.Reisel (der)n.; 2.Riesel (der)n.

proceed 1.verfaahre, v.; verfaahre, pp.; 2.voraa/geh, v.; voraagange, pp.

proclaim 1.ab/rufe, v.; abgerufe, pp.; 2.aus/rufe, v.; ausgerufe, pp.; 3.aus/schreiwe, v.; ausgschriwwe, pp.

proclamation Ausruuf (der)n.

procrastinate 1.ab/duh, v.; abgeduh, pp.; 2.ab/schiewe, v.; abschowe, pp.; 3.uff/schiewe, v.; uffgschowe, pp.

procure 1.aa/schaffe, v.; aagschafft, pp.; 2.bei/griege, v.; beigrickt, pp.; 3.bei/schaffe, v.; beigschafft, pp.; 4.verschaffe, v.; verschafft, pp.; 5.zuschaffe, v.; zugschafft, pp.; **by trading** eihandle, v.; eighandelt, pp.

prod out of raus/schtuppe, v.; rausgschtuppt, pp.

prodigy Wunner (die, es)n.;

produce 1.Produkte (die)n., pl.; 2.vor/bringe, v.; vorgebrocht, pp.; **effect** aa/schlagge, v.; aagschlagge, pp.

product Ardickel (der)n.

profanity 1.Flucherei (die)n.; 2.Gefluch (es)n.

profess bekenne, v.; bekennt, pp.

professor 1.Brofesser (der)n.; 2.Professer (der)n.; 3. Brotfresser (der)n. (humorous)

profit 1.Brofit(t) (der)n.; 2.Nutze (der)n.; 3.Schpeck (der)n.

profitable 1.brofitlich, adj.; 2.nitzlich, adj.

profound dief, adj.

profoundly still meiseschtill, adv.

progosticgate vorher/saage, v.; vorhersaagt, pl.

progress 1.Fattschritt (der)n.; 2.Rees (die)n.; Reese, pl.; 3.voraa/geh, v.; voraagange, pp.; 4.voraa/kumme, v.;

voraakumme, pp.

prohibit 1.verbiede, v.; verbodde, pp.; 2.verwehre, v.; verwehrt, pp.

project 1.raus/schteh, v.; rausgschtanne, pp.; 2.raus/schtoose, v.; rausgschtoose, pp.; 3.vor/schteh, v.; vorgschtanne, pp.

projection Zacke (der)n.

prolong verlengere, v.; verlengert, pp.

prolonged 1.glingich, adj.; 2.zinkich, adj.

promenade schpatziere, v.; gschpatziert, pp.

promise 1.Verschpreche(s) (es)n.; 2.verschpreche, v.; verschproche, pp.; 3.Watt (es)n.; Wadde, pl.

prompt bereit, adj.

promptly in eens, zwee, drei, adv.

promulgate aus/saage, v.; ausgsaat, pp.

prone to bite beissich, adj.; **to cry** verheilt, adj.; **to grumble** 1.grummlich, adj.; 2.knarrich, adj.; **to pout** verbrutzt, adj.; **to scream** (or cry) vergrische, adj.; **to stumble** schtolperich, adj.

prong Zacke (der)n.; **(of a fork)** Gawwelzinke (die)n.; of (wooden) **grain cradle** Reffzaah(n) (der)n.; Reffzeh, pl.

pronounce aus/schpreche, v.; ausgschproche, pp.; **an article sold at auction** ab/schlagge, v.; abgschlagge, pp.

pronunciation Ausschproch (die)n.

proof 1.Beweis (der)n.; 2.Beweisung (die)n.; 3.Noochweis (der)n.

prop Schteiber (der)n.; Schteiber, pl.; **open or up** uff/schteibere, v.; uffgschteibert, pp.

propagate vermehre (sich --)v.; vermehrt, pp.

proper 1.kauscher, adj.; 2.kummbaawel, adj.; **name** Grischbel (der)n.

property 1.Eegedum (es)n.; 2.Eigendum (es)n.; 3.Vermeege (es)n.

prophecy 1.Brophezeiung (die)n.; 2.Weissaaging (die)n.; 3.Weissaayung (die)n.; 4.brofesseihe, v.; gebrofesseiht, pp.; 5.vor/saage, v.; vorgsaat, pp.; 6.weissaage, v.

prophet 1.Brofeet (der)n.; Brofeede, pl.; 2.Brophet (der)n.

proposal Vorschlack (der)n.

propose 1.vor/bringe, v.; vorgebrocht, pp.; 2.vor/schlagge, v.; vorgschlagge, pp.

proprietor Eegner (der)n.; Eegner, pl.

prosecute aaglaage, v.; aageglaagt, pp.

prospect Aussicht (die)n.

prosper 1.aa/kumme, v.; is aakumme, pp. (gut --); 2.aus/mache, v.; ausgemacht, pp. (gut --); 3.gedeihe, v.; gediehe, pp.; 4.uff/kumme, v.; is uffkumme, pp.

protect 1.behiede, v.; behiet, pp.; 2.beschitze, v.; beschitzt, pp.; 3.schitze, v.; gschitzt, pp.

protection 1.Schirm (der)n.; 2.Verwaahring (die)n.

protest uff/lege (sich --)v.; uffgelegt, pp.

Protestant Proteschdant (der)n.

prothonotary Waesevadder (der)n.

protracted (prayer) **meeting** 1.Langversammling (die)n.; 2.Versammling (die)n. (lang --)

protrude naus/schtecke, v.; nausgschteckt, pp.

Pp

proud

proud 1.batzich, adj.; 2.brotzich, adj.; 3.grossmeenich, adj.; 4.grossmiedich, adj. 5.Naas (die)n. (-- hoch draade); 6.Schtaat (der)n. (en grosser -- draus/ mache); **(very)** wunnerschtolz, adj.; **flesh** Wildfleesch (es)n.

prove beweise, v.; bewisse, pp.; **(a matter)** iwwerweise, v.; iwwerwisse, pp.; **a statement** gut, adj. (-- mache)

proverb Schprichwart (es)n.

provide 1.aa/schaffe, v.; aagschafft, pp.; 2.bei/schaffe, v.; beigschafft, pp.; 3.her/schaffe, v.; hergschafft, pp.; 4.sarge, v.; gsarrickt, pp.; 5.verschaffe, v.; verschafft, pp; **for** 1.bsarge, v.; bsarkt, pp.; 2.versehe, v.; versehne, pp.; 3.versehne, v.; versehne, pp.; **for one-self** vor/sehne (sich --)v.; vorgsehne, pp.; **with strips or laths** schtrippe, v.; gschtrippt, pp.

provided for bsarkt, adj.

provident vorsichdich, adj.

provision 1.Vorrot (der)n.; 2.Vorsarig (die)n.

provisions 1.Lewesmiddel (es)n.; 2.falsch, adj. (-- mache); 3.uff/schtifde, v.; uffgschtift, pp.; 4.verzanne, v.; verzannt, pp.

provoked uffschtennich, adj.

provoking 1.aeryerlich, adj.; 2.veraeryerlich, adj.; 3. verdriesslich, adj.

prowl 1.rum/lause, v.; rumgelaust, pp.; 2.rumher/schleiche, v.; rumhergschliche, pp.

prudence 1.Kluuchheet (die)n.; 2.Kluuchheit (die)n.

prudent klu(u)ch, adj.

prune 1.aus/butze, v.; ausgebutzt, pp.; 2.Gwetsch (die)n.; Gwetsche, pl; **the orchard** Bungert (der)n. (-- aus/ butze)

pruning hook Baammesser (es)n.

pry 1.nei/dringe (sich --)v.; 2.nei/schnubbere, v.; neigschnubbert, pp.; 3.no(och)faschdle, v.; no(och)gfaschdelt, pp.; 4.rum/faschle, v.; rumgfaschelt, pp.; 5.schnubbere, v.; gschnubbert, pp.; 6.schnuffle, v.; gschnuffelt, pp.; 7.schnuppere, v.; gschnuppert, pp.; **into** aus/schniffle, v.; ausgschniffelt, pp.; **up** uff/schnebbe, v.; uffgschneppt, pp.

prying 1.geck, adj. (rare usage;) 2.schnupperich, adj.; 3. wunnerfitzich, adj.

psalm 1.Psallem (der)n.; 2.Psalm (der)n.

psalter Psalter (der)n.

pseudo-Christian 1.Naamegrischt (der)n.; 2.Nomegrischt (der)n.

pubescent flick, adj.

public notice Bekanntmachung (die)n.; **sale** Fend(y)u (die) n.; **school** Freischul (die)n.

publicly 1.effentlich, adv.; 2.offentlich, adv.

publish 1.bekannt/mache, v.; bekanntgemacht, pp.; 2.raus/gewwe, v.; rausgewwe, pp.; **marriage bans** aus/rufe, v.; ausgerufe, pp.

pudding 1.Lewwerwaschtfillsel (es)n.; 2.Pattwaschtfillsel (es)n.

puddle 1.Deich (es)n.; Deicher, pl.; 2.Dreckloch (es)n.;

pump

Drecklecher, pl.; 3.Puddel (der)n.; 4.puddle, v.; gepuddelt, pp.; 5.Wasserloch (es)n.; Wasserlecher, pl.

puerperal convulsions Muddergichdre (die)n., pl.

puff 1.keich(l)e, v.; gekeiche(l)t, pp.; 2.keiche, v.; gekeicht, pp.; **adder** 1.Blaeser (der)n.; 2.Bleeser (der)n.; Bleeser, pl.

puffery Gepulschder (es)n.

pugnosed schtumpnaasich, adj.

puke kotze, v.; gekotzt, pp.

pull 1.reisse, v.; gerisse, pp.; 2.robbe, v.; geroppt, pp.; 3.ziege, v.; gezoge, pp.; 4.ziehe, v.; gezoge, pp.; 5.zoppe, v.; gezoppt, pp. 6.Zuck (der)n.; **(draw) out** raus/ziege, v.; rausgezogge, pp.; **against** wedder/ziehe, v.; weddergezogge, pp.; **along with** mit/ziehe, v.; mitgezogge, pp.; **apart** verrobbe, v.; verroppt, pp.; **around** rum/ziehe, v.; rumgezoge, pp.; **away** 1.fatt/ziehe, v.; fattgezogge, pp.; 2.weck/ziege, v.; weckgezogge, pp.; 3.weck/ziehe, v.; weckgezogge, pp.; **back** zerick/ziehe, v.; zerickgezoge, pp.; **down** 1.nunner/ ziege, v.; nunnergezogge, pp.; 2.runner/ziehe, v.; runnergezogge, pp.; **ear** 1.ziwwele, v.; geziwwelt, pp.; 2.zowwele, v.; gezowwelt, pp. ; **in** 1.ei/ziehe, v.; eigezogge, pp.; 2.nei/ziehe, v.; neigezoge, pp.; 3.rei/zehe, v.; reigezoge, pp.; **in by jerks** rei/zobbe, v.; reigezoppt, pp.; **off by light jerks** ab/zobbe, v.; abgezoppt, pp.; **or drag through** darich/ziehe, v.; darichgezoge, pp.; **or move after** 1.no(och)ziege, v.; no(och)gzogge, pp.; 2.no(och)ziehe, v.; no(och)zoge, pp.; **out** 1.aus/robbe, v.; ausgeroppt, pp.; 2.aus/zobbe, v.; ausgezoppt, pp.; 3.raus/robbe, v.; rausgeroppt, pp.; **over** 1.niwwer/reisse, v.; niwwergerisse, pp.; 2.niwwer/ziege, v.; niwwergezoge, pp.; 3.niwwer/ziehe, v.; niwwergezoge, pp.; **shut** zureisse, v.; zugerisse, pp.; **the trigger** 1.ab/dricke, v.; abgedrickt, pp.; 2.los/ dricke, v. losgedrickt, pp.; **tight** zu/ziehe, v.; zugezoge, pp.; **to pieces** verzobbe, v.; verzoppt, pp.; **together** zamme/ziehe, v.; zammegezogge, pp.; **up** 1.nuff/ziehe, v.; nuffgezogge, pp.; 2.ruff/ziege, v.; ruffgezoge, pp.; 3.ruff/ziehe, v.; ruffgezoge, pp.; 4.uff/robbe, v.; uffgeroppt, pp.

pulley Winn (die)n.; Winne, pl.

pulpit Kansel (die)n.

pulpit Breddicherschtul (der)n. (Montgomery Co. Mennonites)

pulpit orator Kanselredner (der)n.

pulse 1.Bols (die)n.; 2.Puls (der)n.

pulverized vermaahle, adj.

pumice Bimschtee (der)n.

pummel 1.gnuffe, v.; gegnufft, pp.; 2.knuffe, v.; geknufft, pp.

pump 1.bumbe, v.; gebumbt, pp.; 2.Bump (die)n.; Bumpe, pl.; 3.Bumpeschtock (der)n.; **away** weck/bumbe, v.; weckgebumpt, pp.; **dry** aus/bumbe, v.; ausgebumpt,

(Continued on page 347)

346

Pp

pump (continued)　　　　　　　　　　　　　　　　　　　　put

(Continued from page 346)

pp.; **floor** Bumpebett (es).; **handle** 1.Bumbehandel (der)n.; 2.Bumbeschwengel (der)n.; 3.Bumpeschtiel (der)n.; **house** Bumbehaus (es)n.; Bumbeheiser, pl.; **maker** Bumpemacher (der)n.; **off** ab/bumbe, v.; abgebumpt, pp.; **out** raus/bumpe, v.; rausgebumpt, pp.; **piston** 1.Bumpekiwwel (der)n.; 2.Kiwwel (der)n.; Kiwwel, pl.; **spout** Bumbezott (die)n.; **trough** Bumpedrog (der)n.; **up** 1.ruff/bumbe, v.; ruffgebumpt, pp.; 2.ruff/bumpe, v.; ruffgebumpt, pp.

pumpkin 1.Kaer(r)bs (die)n.; Kaer(r)bse, pl.; 2.Karrebs (die)n.; Karrebse, pl.; **patch** 1.Kaerbseschtick (es)n.; 2.Karebseschtick (es)n.; **pie** 1.Kaerbsekuche, (der)n.; 2.Karebsekuche (der)n.; **porridge** Kaerbsebrei (der) n.; **seed** Kaerbsekann (die)n.; **vine** Kaerbseschtock (der)n.

pun Wartschpiel (es)n.

punch Petzer (der)n.; Petzer, pl.

punctual 1.pink(t)lich, adv.; 2.zeitlich, adj.

puncture 1.darich/renne, v.; darichgerennt, pp.; 2.darich/schtecke, v.; darichgschteckt; darichgschtocke, pp.

pungent 1.beisse, v.; gebisse, pp.; 2.beissich, adj.; 3.gratzich, adj.; 4.kratzich, adj.

punish 1.ab/schtrofe, v.; abgschtroft, pp.; 2.beschtrofe, v.; beschtroft, pp.; 3.gewwe, v.; gewwe, pp. (feng --); 4.schtrofe, v.; gschtroft, pp.

punishable schtrofbaar, adj.

punishment 1.Peinich (die)n.; 2.Schtrof (die)n.

punk Schwamm (der)n.

puny pinsich, adj.

pup 1.Hundel (es)n.; 2.Hundli (es)n.; Hundlin, pl.

pupil Schuler (der)n.; Schieler, pl.; **(of the eye)** 1.Aageabbel (der)n.; 2.Kindel (es)n.

puppe Waermche (es)n. (en horrich --)

puppet Bobb (die)n.

pur zwaerne, v.; gezwaernt, pp.

purchase 1.ab/handle, v.; abghandelt, pp.; 2.eihandle, v.; eighandelt, pp.; 3.eikaafe, v.; eikaaft, pp. 4.Kaaf (der) n.; 5.kaafe, v.; kaaft, pp.; **money** Kaafgeld (es)n.

purchaser 1.Kaafer (der)n.; 2.Kaefer (der)n.; Kaefer, pl.

pure 1.gereinicht, adj.; 2.rei, adj.; 3.rein, adj.

purgation 1.Barrierung (die)n.; 2.Reiniching (die)n.

purgative Laxiering (die)n.

purgatory Fekfeier (es)n.

purge bariere, v.; bariert, pp.

purge (for constipation) 1.ab/fiehre, v.; abgfiehrt, pp.; 2.aus/butze, v.; ausgebutzt, pp.; 3.barriere, v.; barriert, pp.; 4.laxiere, v.; gelaxiert, pp; **thoroughly** aus/laxiere, v.; ausgelaxiert, pp.

purify reiniche, v.; gereinicht, pp.

purline 1.Dachpett (die)n.; 2.Dachrut (die)n.; 3.Pett (die)n.

purloin schnause, v.; gschnaust, pp.

purple amaranth Kolwemelde (der)n.

purpose 1.Absicht (die)n.; 2.vor/nemme (sich --)v.; vorgenumme, pp.; 3.Zweck (der)n.

purposely 1.fer Parebes, adv.; 2.parebes, adv.; 3.parebislich, adv.; 4.uff, prep., adv. (-- Parebes)

purr schpinne, v.; gschpunne, pp.

purse 1.Beidel (der)n.; 2.Geldsack (der)n.; Geldseck, pl.

purslane Seibaerzel (der)n.

pursue 1.no(och)geh, v.; no(och)gange, pp.; 2.schprenge, v.; gschprengt, pp.; 3.trachte, v.; getracht, pp.

pus 1.Madaerich (es)n.; 2.Madaering (es)n.; 3.Made(e)ring (der)n.

push 1.Renn (der)n.; 2.schiewe, v.; gschowe, pp.; 3.schtoose, v.; gschtoose, pp.; 4.Schtoss (der)n. **about** rum/schiewe, v.; rumgschowe, pp.; **after** no(och)schiewe, v.; no(och)gschowe, pp.; **against** wedder/schiewe, v.; weddergschowe, pp.; **away** 1.fatt/schiewe, v.; fattgschowe, pp.; 2.weck/schtosse, v.; weckgschtosse, pp.; **down** nunner/schtosse, v.; nunnergschtosse, pp.; **forward** vor/schiewe, v.; vorschowe, pp.; **in** 1.eischiewe, v.; eigschowe, pp.; 2.rei/schiewe, v.; reigschowe, pp.; 3.rei/schtoose, v.; reigschtoose, pp.; **into** nei/schiewe, v.; neigschowe, pp.; **off (the sheaf from a dro or self-rake reaper)** ab/schiewe, v.; abschowe, pp.; **out** naus/schiewe, v.; nausgschowe, pp.; **over** um/schiewe, v.; umgschowe, pp.; **past** verbei/schiewe, v.; verbeigschowe, pp.; **shut** zu/schiewe, v.; zugschowe, pp.; **together** zamme/schiewe, v.; zammegschowe, pp.; **towards** hie/schiewe, v.; hiegschowe, pp.; **under** unner/schiewe, v.; unnergschowe, pp.; **up** ruff/schiewe, v.; ruffgschowe, pp.

pussy 1.Bussi (die)n.; 2.Bussli (die); **cat** Bussikatz (die)n.; **willow** 1.Kitzelweide (die)n.; 2.Schwammweide (die) n.

put 1.lege, v.; g(e)legt, pp.; 2.schtelle, v.; gschtellt, pp.; **(flax) into bundles spinning** dock(e), v.; gedockt, pp.; **(sausage) into the pan** Brotwascht (die)n. (-- in die Pann leere); **(some one to doing something)** draaduh, v.; draageduh, pp.; **(something) into a for position** vorschaffe, v.; vorgschafft, pp.; **a cake in the oven** Kuche (der)n. (en -- setze); **a high price on something** peffere, v.; gepeffert, pp.; **a hoop on a barrel or cask** ab/binne,v.; abgebunne,pp.; **a new steel edge on a tool** aa/schtaahle, v.; aagschtaahlt, pp.; **a patch on** verflicke, v.; verflickt, pp.; **a point on** schpitze, v.; gschpitzt, pp.; **a ring through the snout (pig)** ringe, v.; geringt, pp.; **across** niwwer/duh, v.; niwwergeduh, pp.; **an end to** eischtelle, v.; eigschtellt, pp.; **away** weck/duh, v.; weckgeduh,pp.; **crumbs in soup** aabrockle, v.; aagebrockelt, pp. (die Supp --); **dinner on the table** aa/richde, v.; aagericht, pp.; **down** nunner/duh, v.; nunnergeduh, pp.; **forth leaves** dreiwe, v.; gedriwwe, pp.; **forth vines** ranke, v.; gerankt, pp.; **grain in place preparatory to threshing** aa/lege, v.; aagelekt, pp.; **harness on a horse** 1.uff/gscha(e)rre, v.; uffgscha(e)rrt;

(Continued on page 348)

347

Pp

put (continued)

(Continued from page 347)

uffgschatt, pp.; 2.uff/ziggele, v.; uffgeziggelt, pp.; **holes in** (a post) aus/loche, v.; ausgelocht, pp. (Poschde --); **holes in slate, tin, etc.** lechere, v.; gelechert, pp.; **horses to** aa/schpanne, v.; aagschpannt, pp.; **in** 1.ei/setze, v.; eigsetzt, pp.; 2.kumme, v.; is kumme, pp. 3.nei/duh, v.; neigeduh, pp.; 4.rei/duh, v.; reigeduh; **in a safe place** weck/schtecke, v.; weckgschtocke, pp.; **in addition** dezuduh, v.; dezugeduh, pp.; **in disorder** zamme/ rumple, v.; zammegerumpelt, pp.; **in motion with the feet** aa/drede, v.; aagedrede, pp.; **in order** 1.ei/richde, v.; eigericht, pp.; 2.uff/raahme, v.; uffgeraahmt, pp.; **in place** nei/mache, v.; neigemacht, pp.; **into alignment** richde, v.; gericht, pp.; **into hives** (bees) fasse, v.; gfasst, pp.; **into one's pocket** eischtecke, v.; eigschteckt, pp.; **into place** hie/duh, v.; hiegeduh, pp.; **iron on** (a wagon) bschlagge, v.; bschlagge, pp.; **off** ab/duh, v.; abgeduh, pp.; **on** 1.aa/duh, v.; aageduh, pp.; 2.aa/griege, v.; aagrickt, pp.; 3.aa/henke, v.; aaghenkt; aaghonke, pp.;rumhaeruffgschtellt, pp.; **up or stick up** nuff/schtecke, 4.aa/ziehe, v.; aagezoge, pp.; **on** (a hat) 1.uff/duh, v.;uffgeduh, pp.; 2.uff/setze, v.; uffgsetzt, pp.; **on an article of clothing** aa/helfe, v.; aagholfe, pp.; **on the bum** Hund (der)n. (uff der -- kumme); **on the stove to boil** iwwer/duh, v.; iwwergeduh, pp.; **on trinkets or jewelry for ornament** behenge (sich --)v.; behenkt, pp.; **one on short rations** ee, adj., adv. (eem der Brotkareb heecher henge); **put or place here** haer/duh, v.; haergeduh, pp.; **or set back** zerick/duh, v.; zerickgeduh, pp.; **or transport over** niwwer/schaffe, v.; niwwergschafft, pp.; **out** 1.naus/duh, v.; nausgeduh, pp.; 2.raus/duh, v.; rausgeduh, pp.; **out** (a fire) lesche, v.; gelescht, pp.; **out of the way** 1.Weg (der)n. (aus em -- schaffe); **over** riwwer/duh, v.; riwwergeduh, pp.; **roof on** decke, v.; gedeckt, pp.; **saddle on** uff/saddle, v.; uffgsaddelt, pp.; **teeth in a rake** aus/zaahne, v.; ausgezaahnt, pp.; **to a vote** ab/schtimme, v.; abgschtimmt, pp.; **tobacco up on the laths** uff/schpitze, v.; uffgschpitzt,pp. (Duwack --); **together** 1.inennanner/ mache, v.;inenannergmacht, pp.; 2.zamme/duh, v.; zammegeduh,pp.; **trust in someone** aa/verdraue, v.; aaverdraut, pp.; **up** 1.nuff/duh, v.; nuffgeduh, pp.; 2.ruff/duh, v.; ruffgeduh, pp.; 3.uff/schtecke, v.; uffgschteckt; uffgschtocke, pp.; 4.uff/schtelle, v.; uffgschtellt, pp.; **up (cattle) for fattening** eischtelle, v.; eigschtellt, pp.; **up (hay)** uff/duh, v.; uffgeduh, pp.; **up (the hair)** nuff/drehe, v.; nuffgedreht, pp.; **up a line** uff/schpanne, v.; uffgschpannt, pp.; **up at (an inn)** ei/kehre, v.; eigekehrt, pp.; **up at different inns** rumhaer/ uffschtelle, v.; v.; nuffgschtocke, pp.; **up with** 1.aa/nemme, v.; aag(e)numme, pp.; 2.verschmaerze, v.; verschmaerzt, pp.; **warp on a**

puzzled

loom for weaving aa/zettle, v.; aagezettelt, pp.

putlog (one of the short timbers that support the flooring of a scaffold) Gerischtholz (es)n.

putrid faul, adj.

putty 1.Fenschderkitt (der)n.; 2.kidde, v.; gekitt, pp.; 3.Kitt (der)n.; 4.kitte, v.; gekitt, pp.; **knife** Kittmesser (es)n.

puttyroot Adem-un-Eva, n.

puzzle grass schtreefich Grass (es)n.

puzzled faschtwarre, v.; faschtwarre, pp.

Qq

quack — quote

quack 1.grexe, v.; gegrext, pp.; 2.gwaxe, v.; gegwaxt, pp.; **(of ducks)** schnattre, v.; gschnaddert, pp.

quacking Gegwacker (es)n.

quadrangle Viereck (es)n.

quadrangular viereckich, adj.

quadruped 1.vierbeenich, adj.; 2.vierfiessich, adj.

quadruple vierfeldich, adj.

quaggy schwammich, adj.

quagmiry boddemlos, adj.

quail 1.Badderiesle (es)n.; Badderieslin, pl.; 2.Badries(e)li (es)n.; 3.Badriesel (es)n.; 4.Badrieselche (es) n.;5.Feldhinkel (es)n.

quaint sunderbaar, adj.

qualifications Faehichkeet (die)n.

quality 1.Aart (die)n.; 2.Ort (die)n.

qualm Gezwacker (es)n.

quandry 1.Glemm (die)n.; 2.Klemm (die)n.

quarrel 1.aa/fechde, v.; aagfochde, pp.; 2.aafechding (die) n.; 3.aus/falle, v.; ausgfalle, pp.; 4.baefze, v.; gebaefzt, pp.; 5.baffze, v.; gebaffzt, pp.; 6.beffze, v.; gebeffzt, pp.; 7.befze, v.; gebefzt, pp.; 8.gnafze, v.; gegnafzt, pp.; 9.gneffere, v.; gneffert, pp.; 10.gnefze, v.; gegnefzt, pp.; 11.grageele, v.; grageelt, pp.; 12.kibbe, v.; gekippt, pp.; 13. knuffe, v.; geknufft, pp.; 14.krageele, v.; grakeelt, pp.; 15.renkle, v.; gerenkelt, pp.; 16.schtreide, v.; gschtridde, pp.; 17.schtreidich warre, adj.; 18.Schtreit (der)n.; 19.zaerife, v.; gezaerift, pp.; 20.zarfe, v.; gezareft, pp.; **due to slander** Liegeschtreit (der)n.

quarreling 1.Geblaff(z) (es)n.; 2.Gegnuff (es)n.; 3.Gschtreit (es)n.; 4.schtreidich,

quarrels Fechderei (die)n.

quarrelsome verfochde, adj; **person** 1.Fechthaahne (der) n.; 2.Gnefzer (der)n.; 3.Grageeler (der)n.; 4.Krageeler (der)n.

quarry Bruch (der)n.; Brich, pl.; **(stone)** Schtee (der)n. (-- breche); **or hole in which flax roasted and broken** Brechloch (es)n.

quart Gwaart (die)n.; Gwaart, pl.; **measure** Gwaartmos (es)n.

quarter ($0.25) 1.Vaddel (der) (-- Daaler)n.; 2.Vaerdel (der) (-- Daaler)n.

quarter (1/4) 1.Vaddel (es)n.; 2.Vaerdel (es)n.; **of a pound** Vaddelpund (es)n.; **of an hour** Vaddelschtunn (die)n.

quarterly vaddelyaerich, adv.

quartz 1.Gwarz (der)n.; 2.Wacke (der)n.; 3.Weisswacke (der)n.

quash gwatsche, v.; (ge)gwatscht, pp.

queen Keenichen (die)n.

Queen Anne's pocket melon (grown for its fragrance) 1. Granaatabbel (der)n.; 2.Grenaadeppli (es)n.

queen bee Keenich (der)n.; Keeniche, pl.;

queen of clubs Greizhur (die)n.

queen king and ace, or jack queen and king of trumps in the game of Datte dattebella

queer 1.eefeldich, adj.; 2.karyos, adj.; 3.ordlich, adv.; 4.sunderbaar, adj.; 5.verzwickt, adj.; **duck** 1.Kauz (der)n.; 2.Kiyoon (der)n.

quench lesche, v.; gelescht, pp.; **querulous** boberich, adj.

question 1.befroge, v.; befrogt, pp.; 2.Frog (die)n.; 3.Froget (die)n.; **minutely** aus/froge, v.; ausgfrogt, pp.

queue Haarschwanz (der)n.

quick 1.fix, adj.; 2.flink, adv.; 3.gschwind, adv.; 4.rasch(t), adj.; 5.schwind, adj.; **grass** Gwecke (die)n.; **(of a nail or horse's hoof)** Lewe (es)n.

quicken erquicke, v.; erquickt, pp.

quick(ly) 1.dabber, adv.; 2.dapper, adv.; 3.hardich, adj.; adv.; 4.schnell, adj.; adv.

quickness Gschwindichkeet (die)n.

quicksand 1.Gfleeztersand (der)n.; 2.Sand (der)n. (gfleetzter --)

quicksilver Gwecksilwer (es)n.

quid 1.Kau (der)n.; 2.Widder(ver)kau (der)n.

quiet 1.beruhiche, v.; beruhicht, pp.; 2.Friede (der)n.; 3.ruhich, adj.; 4.sachde, adv.; 5.schtill, adj.; 6.schtille, v.; gschtillt, pp.; **as a mouse** mauseschtill, adj.

quill 1.Fedderkeidel (der)n.; 2.Gensfedder (die)n.

quilor harness (the distinct parts of which were a breeching and side or under-belly straps connected with the collar so as to enable horses to hold back a load better in going down hill) Aftergschaerr (es)n.

quilt 1.Debbich (der)n.; 2.gwilde, v.; gegwillt, pp.; 3.Gwilt (die)n.; 4.schtebbe, v.; gschteppt, pp.; 5.schteppe, v.; gschteppt, pp.; 6.schtickere, v.; gschtickert, pp.; 7.schtickle, v.; gschtickelt, pp.; **pattern** Sunnedebbich (der)n.

quilting Schtickerei (die)n.

quince Gwitt (die)n.; Gwidde, pl; **seed** Gwiddekaern (die) n.; Gwiddekaerne, pl.; **tree** Gwiddebaam (der)n.; Gwiddebeem, pl.

quinquennial fimfyaahrich, adj.

quinsy 1.Gwiddebaam (der)n.; Gwiddebeem, pl.; 2.Gwinsi (die)n.; 3.Halsweh (es)n.

quintruple fimf-feldich, adj.

quit 1.meide, v.; gemeidt, pp.; 2.schtobbe, v.; gschtoppt, pp.; 3.uff/gewe, v.; uffgewwe, pp.; **notice** Ausbeitzettel (der)n.

quitch grass Hun(d)sgraas (es)n.

quite 1.gaar, adv.; 2.ganz, adv.; 3.ordlich, adv.

quiver ziddere, v.; geziddert, pp.; **(of arrows)** Peilesack (der)n.

quote aa/fiehre, v.; aagfiehrt, pp.

Rr

rabbit ... rare

rabbit 1.Fuug (die)n.; 2.Haas (der)n.; Haase, pl.; **grease** Haasefett (es)n.; **hound** Haasehund (der)n.; **hunting** Haaseyacht (die)n.; **meat** Haasefleesch (es)n.; **snare** Haaseschlupp (der)n.; **tea** Haasetee (der)n.; **trap** Haasefall (die)n.

rabble 1.Gschmees (es)n.; 2.Gsindel (es)n.; 3.Lumbegsindel(es)n.; 4.Schtoff(t) (es)n.; 5.Ungeziffer (es)n.; **(confounded)** 1.Viech (es)n.; 2.Vieh (es)n.

rabid 1.bees, adj.; 2.doll, adj.; 3.raasend, adj.; 4.wiedich, adj.

raccoon (a misapprehension where used) Dachs (der)n.

race 1. Laaf (der) n.; Leef, pl.; 2. Schtamm (der) n.; **after** no(och)yaage, v.; no(och)g(e)yaagt, pp.; **along** schussele, v.; gschusselt, pp.

rack Reff (es)n.; Reffer, pl.; **down** verschittle, v.; verschiddelt, pp.

racket 1.Gedunner (es)n.; 2.Geraebbel (es)n.; 3.Lerm(e) (der)n.

radiant schtraallich, adj.

radiate schtraale, v.; gschtraalt, pp.

radish Reddich (die)n.; Reddiche, pl.; **seed** 1.Reddichsaame (der)n.; 2.Reddichsome (der)n.; 3.Reddichsume (der)n.

raffle hossle, v.; ghosselt, pp.

rafter Schparre (der)n.; Schparre, pl.

rag 1.Labbe (der)n.; 2.Lumbe (der)n.; Lumbe, pl.; 3.Zoppe (der)n.; 4.Zottel (der, die)n.; **and bone collector** Gnocheyockel (der)n.; **carpet** Lumbekarrebet (der)n.; **doll** Lumbebopp (die)n.; **picker** Lumbesammler (der) n.

ragbag Lumbesack (der)n.; Lumbeseck, pl.

rage 1.arig mache, v.; ariggemacht, pp.; 2.dowe, v.; gedopt, pp.; 3.hause, v.; ghaust, pp.; 4.raase, v.; g(e)raast, pp.; 5.Wut (die)n.; 6.Zann (der)n.; **around** 1.rum/dowe, v.; rumgedopt, pp.; 2.rum/hause, v.; rumghaust, pp.

ragged 1.kaflich, adj.; 2.lumbich, adj.; 3.verhutzelt, adj.; 4.verlumpt, adj.; 5.zoddlich, adj.; 6.zoppich, adj.; **robin** schtruwwlich Nans (die)n.

raging raasend, adj.

ragman 1.Lumbemann (der)n.; Lumbemenner, pl.; 2. Zoddelmann (der)n.; Zoddelmenner, pl.

ragweed 1.Bolleryockel (der)n.; 2.Flehgraut (es)n.; 3.Warmet (der)n. (wilder --); 4.Warmut (es)n. (wilder --)

raid Eifall (der)n.; Eifalle, pl.

rail 1.Riggel (der)n.; 2.schpotte, v.; gschpott, pp.; **at** 1. verschenne, v.; verschennt, pp.; 2.verschimbiere, v.; verschimbiert, pp.; **fence** Riggelfens (die)n.; Riggelfense, pp.; **section** Gfach (es)n.

railing 1.G(e)lender (es)n.; 2.Gelander(es)n.; **(of a stair)** Schteeglone (der)n.; Schteeglone, pl.

railroad Riggelweg (der)n.; **ticket** Faahrzeddel (der)n.

rails (of a railroad) Schiene (die)n., pl.

rain 1.nass adj. (-- mache); 2.reg(g)ne, v.; gereg(g)net, pp.; 3.Reg(g)e (der)n.; 4.reg(g)e, v.; gereg(g)ert, pp.; 5.Reger (der)n.; 6.regere, v.; gereg(g)ert, pp.; 7.Regge (der)n.; **a few drops** 1.dropse, v.; gedropst, pp. 2.dropsle, v.; gedropselt, pp.; **barrel** Reg(g)efass (es)n.;Reg(g)efesser, pl.; **gauge** Reg(g)emesser (der) n.; **in** rei/reg(g)ere, v.; reigereg(g)ert, pp.; **on and on** fatt/reg(g)ere, v.; fattgreg(g)ert, pp.; **or snow slightly** runner/mache, v.; rummergemacht, pp.

rainbow 1.Reggeboge (der)n.; 2.Reggebowe (der)n.

raindrop 1.Reggedrobbe (der)n.; 2.Reggedropp(s) (der)n.; 3.Reggedroppse (der)n.

rainspout 1.Dachkandel (der)n.; 2.Kandel (der)n.; Kandle, pl.

rainstorm Reggeschtarem (der)n.

rainwater Reggewasser (es)n.

rainy 1.raerrich, adj.; 2.reggerich, adj.; 3.reggnich, adj.; 4.suddlich, adj.; **day** Reggedaag (der)n.; Reggedaage, pl.; **weather** Reggewetter (es)n.

raise 1.bauere, v.; gebauert, pp.; 2.nuff/mache, v.; nuffgemacht, pp.; 3.uff/richde, v.; uffgericht, pp.; 4.uff/ziege, v.; uffgezoge, pp.; 5.uff/ziehe, v.; uffgezoge, pp; **(money)** uff/mache, v.; uffgemacht, pp.; **(the frame of a building)** uff/schlagge, v.; uffgschlagge, pp.; **a disturbance** haermeniere, v.; haermeniert, pp.; **a racket** 1.haabere, v.; ghaabert, pp.; 2.Zucht (die)n. (en -- verfiehre); **the head or body suddenly** uff/ducke, v.; uffgeduckt, pp.; **the price of** nuff/handle, v.; nuffg(e)handelt, pp.

raised cake Schtieber (der)n.; Schtieber, pl; **platform for raising plants** Kutsch (die)n.; Kutsche, pl.; **platform in a blacksmith's shop where the fire and tools are found** Ess (die)n.; **potato cake** Gangnerkuche (der)n.

raisin 1.Resein (die)n.; Reseine, pl.; 2.Rosein (die)n.

rake 1.Kitsch (die)n.; Kitsche, pl.; 2.Reche (der)n.; 3.reche, v.; gerecht, pp.; 4.Recher (der)n.; Recher, pl.; 5.rechere, v. (Waterloo Co., Ont.); **after** no(och)reche, v.; no(och)gerecht, pp.; **and bind** 1. no(och)reche, v.; no(och)gerecht, pp.; 2.uff/binne, v.; uffgebunne, pp.; **and bind oats** Hawwer uff/nemme, v.; **handle** Recheschtiel (der)n.; **off** ab/reche, v.; abgerecht, pp.; **out of** raus/reche, v.; rausgerecht, pp.; **up** 1.uff/reche, v.; uffgerecht, pp.; 2.zamme/reche, v.; zammegerecht, pp.

ram 1.Bock (der)n.; Beck, pl.; 2.Schofbock (der)n.; Schofbeck, pl.

ramrod Laadschtecke (der)n.

rancid ransich, adj.

randlebar Kesselschtang (die)n.

range rum/wandre, v.; rumgewandert, pp.; **(stove)** Kochoffe (der)n.; Kocheffe, pl.; **around** ranse, v.; geranst, pp.

rank 1.ransich, adj.; 2.Schtand (der)n.; **(odor)** schtinkich, adj.

ransome los/kaafe, v.; loskaaft, pp.

rap 1.globbe, v.; geglobbt, pp.; 2.huder, adj.; 3.huder, adj.; 4.Hunsfotz (die)n.; 5.kloppe, v.; gekloppt, pp.; 6.Piff (der)n.

rapid(ly) 1.schnell, adj.; adv.; 2.reissend, adv.; 3.zwiterich, adj.

rare raar, adj.

Rr

rarely — rear

rarely wunnerselde, adv.

rarity 1.Raarichkeet (die)n.; 2.Rirarridaed (die)n.

rascal 1.Bucker (der)n.; 2.Fratzel (es)n.; 3.Galgevoggel (der) n.; 4.Kanallye (es)n.; 5.Ketzer (der)n.; Ketzer, pl.; 6.Lump (der)n.; 7.Schpitzbu(h) (der)n.; 8.Schuft (der)n.

rascality Nidderdrechdichkeit (die)n.

rascally 1.nidderdrechdich, adv.; 2.schliwwerich, adv.

rash 1.Frissel (es)n.; 2.Summerpocke (die)n., pl; **like** 1.ausfaahrisch, adj.; 2.ausfiehrich, adj.

rasp 1.Holzfeil (die)n.; 2.Raschbe(l) (der)n.; Raschbe(l), pl.; 3.raschble, v.; geraschbelt, pp.

raspberry 1.Hembeer (die)n.; Hembeere, pl.; 2.Hembier (die)n.; Hembiere, pl.; **bug** Hemmbierekeffer (der)n.

rat Ratt (die)n.; Ratte, pl.; **nest** Raddenescht (es)n.

ratchet Glebberraad (es)n.; Glebberredder, pl.

ratgut Raddegift (es)n.

rather 1.eher, adv.; 2.ehnder, adj.; adv. 3.ender, adj.; 4. erschder, adv.; 5.liewer, adv.; 6.neecher, adv.; 7.ordlich, adv.; 8.sadde, adv.; 9.zimmlich, adv.; **like** leide, v.; gelidde, pp. (gut --)

ratify b(e)schtaetiche, v.; b(e)schtaeticht, pp.

rattail Raddeschwanz (der)n.

rattan (cane) Rohrschtock (der)n.

rattle 1.glebbere, v.; geglebbert, pp.; 2.gleppre, v.; gegleppert, pp.; 3.kleppre, v.; gekleppert, pp.; 4.Rabbel (es)n.; Rabble, pl.; 5.rapple, v.; gerabbelt, pp.; 6.Rassel (die)n.; 7.rassle, v.; gerasselt, pp.; 8.rischble, v.; gerischbelt, pp; **in the throat** haerchle, v.; ghaerchelt, pp.; **off** 1.ab/rapple, v.; abgerappelt, pp.; 2.ab/zeehle, v.; abgezeehlt, pp.; **wheel** Glebberraad (es)n.; Glebberredder, pl.

rattlesnake Rasselschlang (die)n.; **plantain** 1.Aerrgraut (es)n.; 2.Ergraut (es)n.; **root** Deiwelsabbis (watzel) (die)n.; **weed** 1.Odergraut (es)n.; 2.Rasselschlangebledder (die), pl.

rattletrap Rabbelkaschde (der)n.

rattling 1.Gerassel (es)n.; 2.glepprich, adj.; 3.klepprich, adj.; 4.rabblich, adj.; 5.rapplich, adj.

rattrap Raddefall (die)n,.; Raddefalle, pl.

raucous 1.rauh, adj.; 2.rauschberich, adj.; 3.rauschperich, adj.

rave 1.aa/geh, v.; aagange, pp.; 2.aageh, v.; aagange, pp.; 3. raase, v.; g(e)raast, pp.; 4.schtaerme, v.; gschtaermt, pp.; 5.wiede, v.; gewiet, pp.; 6.wiete, v.; gewiet, pp.

ravel verwickle, v.; verwickelt, pp.

raven 1.Grabb (die)n.; Grabbe, pl.; 2.Krabb (die)n.; 3.Raabe (der)n.

ravine Hohl (es)n.

raving 1.raasend, adj.; 2.wiedich, adj.

ravish 1.raawe, v.; geraabt, pp.; 2.schende, v.; gschendt, pp.

ravisher Schender (der)n.

raw 1.rauh, adj.; 2.roh, adj.; **fellow** Grauthammel (der)n.

ray Schtrohl (der)n.

raylike schtraallich, adj.

raze nidder/reisse, v.; niddergerisse, pp.

razor 1.Balmiermesser (es)n.; Balmiermesser, pl.; 2.Balwier(e)messer (es)n.; Balwier(e)messer, pl.;

3.Kneip (der)n. (used jokingly); **sheath** Balwierscheed (die)n.

re-echo zerick/schalle, v.; zerickgschallt, pp.

reach 1.erlange, v.; erlangt, pp.; 2.her/lange, v.; heregelangt, pp.; 3.lange, v.; gelangt, pp.; 4.reeche, v.; gereecht, pp.; **(to a place)** hie/hewe, v.; hieghowe, pp.; **back** zerick/reeche, v.; zerickgereecht, pp.; **down** runner/reeche, v.; runnergereecht, pp.; **in** 1.nei/lange, v.; neigelangt, pp.; 2.rei/lange, v.; reigelangt, pp.; 3.rei/reeche, v.; reigereecht, pp.; **or hand down** nunner/reeche, v.; nunnergereecht, pp.; **or hand up** nuff/reeche, v.; nuffgereecht, pp.; **out** 1.naus/lange, v.; nausgelangt, pp.; 2.naus/reeche, v.; nausgereecht, pp.; 3.raus/lange, v.; rausgelangt, pp.; 4.raus/reeche, v.; rausgereecht, pp.; **over** niwwer/reeche, v.; niwwergereecht, pp.; **together** zamme/reeche, v.; zammegereecht, pp.; **up** nuff/lange, v.; nuffgelangt, pp.

read 1.darich/lese, v.; darichgelese, pp.; 2.laute, v.; gelaut, pp.; 3.lese, v.; glese, pp.; **aloud** vor/lese, v.; vorgelese, pp.; **before singing** vor/lese, v.; vorgelese, pp.; **lines for repitition in singing** aus/leine, v.; ausgeleint, pp.; **lips** ab/nemme (dative)v. (ebber an der Libbe --); **off** 1.ab/lese, v.; abgelese, pp.; 2.haer/lese, v.; haergelese, pp.; 3.her/lese, v.; hergelese, pp.; 4.her/lese, v.; hergelese, pp.; 5.runner/leese, v.; runnergeleest, pp.; 6.verlese, v.; verlese, pp.

reader Leser (der)n.

reading Leses (es)n.; **(of something out loud)** Vorleses (es)n.; **selection** Leseschtick (es)n.; **writing and arithmetic** Schreiwes (es)n. (-- un es Rechles)

ready 1.bereit, adj.; 2.faddich, adj.; 3.faerdich, adj.; 4.fix, adj.; 5.gerischt, adj.; 6.reddi, adj.; 7.zurecht, adj.; 8.zurecht, adv.; **for the stallion** rossich, adj.; **money** Geld (es)n.(-- leie hawwe)

real reel, adj.

reality Waerklichkeet (die)n.

really 1.behiedes, adv.; 2.eegentlich, adv.; 3.gewiss, adj. (so -- as alles); 4.verhafdich, adv.; 5.verhaffdich, adj.; 6.verhaftich, adj.; 7.Waahret (die)n. (fer -- saage); 8. waahrhafdich, adv.; 9.waerecklich, adv.; 10.waericklich, adv.; 11.waerklich, adv.; 12.waricklich, adv.; 13.weiss der Zuschtand, adv.; 16.wohrhafdich, adv.; 17.wohrhaftich, adj.

reap mehe, v.; gemeht, pp; **grain with a sickle** schneide, v.; gschnidde, pp.

reaper 1.Fruchtmaschien (die)n.; 2.Maehmaschien (die) n.; 3.Mehmaschien (die)n.; 4.Schnidder (der)n.; Schnidder, pl.; 5.Schnitter (der)n.

rear 1.Hinnerdeel (es)n.; 2.uff/ziege, v.; uffgezoge, pp.; **(a child)** uff/bringe, v.; uffgebrocht, pp.; **axle** Hinnerax (die)n.; **bolster** (of a wagon) Hinnerschemel (der)n.; Hinnerschemel, pl.; **end** Hinnerbacke (der)n.; Hinnerbacke, pl.; **near horse** (of a four horse team) Saddelgaul (der)n.

Rr

reason 1.Ursach (die)n.; Ursache, pl.; 2.Verschtand (der)n.
reasonable verninfdich, adj.
rebate 1.ab/losse, v.; 2.ab/losse, v.; abgelosst, pp.
Rebecca 1.Becki (die)n.; 2.Rebekka (die)n.; 3.Rebekka (die)n.
rebel Schtrang (der)n. (iwwer -- hacke)
rebellious 1.rabbelkebbi(s)ch, adj.; 2.uffriehrisch, adj.
rebuff ab/faddiche, v.; abgfaddicht, pp.
rebuild iwwer/baue, v.; iwwergebaut, pp.
rebuke 1.schelde, v.; gscholde, pp.; 2.schimfe, v.; gschimft, pp.
recall 1.b(e)sinne (sich --)v.; b(e)sunne, pp.; 2.eikumme, v.; eikumme, pp.; 3.zerick/rufe, v.; zerickgerufe, pp.
recede 1.no(och)gewwe, v.; no(och)gewwe, pp.; 2.nunner/geh, v.; nunnergange, pp.; 3.zerick/geh, v.; zerickgange, pp.
receipt Reseet (es)n.; Reseede, pl.
receive 1.aa/nemme, v.; aag(e)numme, pp.; 2.eigriege, v.; eigrickt, pp.; 3.griege, v.; grickt, pp.; 4.nemme, v.; gnumme, pp; **(into the fellowship) a handshake and kiss** (the ritual greeting of the plain churches) uffnemme mit Hand und Kuss
receiver Nemmer (der)n.; Nemmer, pl.
recently 1.do yetz, adv.; 2.kaerzlich, adv.; 3.katzlich, adv.; 4.neilich, adv.; 5.unnilengscht, adv.
receptacle Gfess (es)n.
reception Aufnahm, (die)n.
recipe 1.Reseet (es)n.; Reseede, pl.; 2.Rezept (die)n.
recite uff/saage, v.; uffsaat, pp.
reckon 1.figgere, v.; gfiggert, pp.; 2.hie/rechle, v.; hiegrechelt; 3.rechne, v.; gerechent, pp.; **again** no(och)rechle, v.; no(och)gerechelt, pp.; **in** 1.dezurechle, v.; dezugerechelt, pp.; 2.nei/rechle, v.; neigerechelt, pp.
reckoning 1.Rechenschaft (die)n.; 2.Zech (die)n.
recline 1.lehne, v.; g(e)lehnt, pp.; 2.ruh(g)e, v.; geru(h)gt, pp.; 3.zerick/lege (sich --)v.; zerickglegt, pp.; 4.zerick/lehne, v.; zerickgelehnt, pp.
recognize 1.aakenne, v.; aakennt, pp.; 2.erkenne, v.; erkennt, pp.; 3.kenne, v.; gekennt, pp.
recollect 1.bei/falle, v.; beigfalle, pp. (dat. of the pronoun); 2.ei/bilde (sich --)v.; eigebildt, pp.; 3.erinnere (sich --) v.; erinnert, pp.
recollection Erinnerung (die)n.
recommend aab(e)fehle, v.; aab(e)fohle, pp.
recommended ironically to a person who is finicky in eating Gumme (der)n. (der -- schaawe)
recompense 1.belohne, v.; belohnt, pp.;2.beluhne, v.; beluhnt, pp.
record 1.nunner/schreiwe, v.; nunnergschriwwe, pp.; 2.Regischder (der)n.; 3.uff/maericke, v.; uffgemaerickt, pp.; 4.uff/schreiwe, v.; uffgschriwwe, pp.; 5.verzeichne, v.; verzeichent, pp.
recoup raus/fresse (sich --)v.; rausgfresse, pp.
recover 1.erhole (sich --)v.; erholt, pp.; 2.fresse (sich --), v.; 3.mache (sich --)v.; gemacht, pp.; 4.raus/fresse

(sich --)v.; rausgfresse, pp.; 5.raus/mache (sich --)v.; rausgemacht, pp.; 6.rum/kumme, v.; is rumkumme, pp.; 7.zerick/griege, v.; zerickgrickt, pp.; **from an illness** uff/kumme, v.; is uffkumme, pp.
recovery Erholung (die)n.
recreation 1.Erfrischung (die)n.; 2.Erquickung (die)n.
rectangle Viereck (es)n.
rectangular viereckich, adj.
rectified geleitert, adj.
rectify recht mache, v.; recht gemacht, pp.
rectum 1.Maschtdarem (der)n.; 2.Orschdarem (der)n.
recuperate davun/kumme, v.; davunkumme, pp.
red rot, adj.; **as blood** blutrot, adj.; **ash** Rotesche (die)n.; **beet** Rotrieb (die)n.; Rotriewe, pl.; **berried elder** Holler (der)n. (roter --); **cedar** Rotzedre (der)n.; **chalk** 1.Reddel (es)n.; 2.Reedel (es)n.; **chickweed** 1.Hinkeldarm (der)n. (roder --); 2.Hinkeldarm (der)n. (roder --); **hot** 1.gliedich, adj.; 2.rotgliedich, adj.; **poker plant** Feierflamm (die)n.; **morning sky** Maryerot (es)n.; **mulberry** 1. Schwarzmaulbeer (die)n.; 2.Schwatzmaulbeer (die)n.; **nose** Feierkolwe (der)n.; **oak** Eeche (die)n. (rot --); **pimpernel** rot, adj. (--er hinkeldarm); **precipitate** 1.Bresibedaat (es)n. (rot --); 2.Prinsipidaat (es)n. (rot --); **raspberry** 1.Hembeer (die) n. (roder --); 2.Hembier (die)n. (rodi --); **seeded dandelion** Hinkelselaat (der)n.; **squirrel** Eechhaas (der)n. (roder --); **stemmed** rotschtenglich, adj.; **tailed hawk** Hinkelwoi (der)n. (rotschwensicher --)
redbird Rotvoggel (der)n.; Rotveggel, pl.
redd up uff/raahme, v.; uffgeraahmt, pp.
reddish 1.rotachdich, adj.; 2.rotlich, adj.
reddle Reedel (es)n.
redeem erleese, v.; erleest, pp.
Redeemer Erleeser (der)n.
redeemer Heiland (der)n.
redemption Erleesung (die)n.
redfin Rotfisch (der)n.
redheaded 1.rothaarich, adj.; 2.rotkebbich, adj.; **person** Rotkopp (der)n.; Rotkepp, pl.; **woodpecker** Rotkopp (der)n.; Rotkepp, pl.
reduce the rations Hawwersack (der)n. (-- heecher henke)
reduced in circumstances runner/kumme, v.; runnerkummer, pp.
reduplicate verdopple, v.; verdoppelt, pp.
redwood Rothols (es)n.
reed Rohr (es)n.
reedbird 1.Buddervoggel (der)n.; 2.Buttervoggel (der)n.
reel haschble, v.; ghaschbelt, pp.; **along** hie/dargele, v.; hiegedaregelt, pp.; **in** nei/dargele, v.; neigedargelt, pp.
refer (back) zerick/weise, v.; zerickgewisse, pp.
reference Beweisung (die)n.
refined geleitert, adj.
refinement Bildung (die)n.
reflect 1.no(och)denke, v.; no(och)gedenkt, pp.; 2.schpiggle, v.; gschpiggelt, pp.
reform verbessre, v.; verbessert, pp.

Rr

Reformed — reminder

Reformed 1.Reffemiert (der)n.; 2.Reformiert, adj.

refractory schtrawwatzich, adj.

refrain verhalde (sich --)v.; verhalde, pp; **from** unnerwege losse, v.; unnerwege gelosst, pp.

refresh 1.erfrische, v.; erfrischt, pp.; 2.erquicke, v.; erquickt, pp.; 3.laabe, v.; gelaabt, pp.; 4.laawe, v.; gelaabt, pp.; 5.uff/frische, v.; uffgfrischt, pp.

refreshment 1.Erfrischung (die)n.; 2.Erquickung (die)n.; 3. Uff-frischung (die)n.

refrigerate 1.ab/kiehle, v.; abgekiehlt, pp.; 2.kiehle, v.; gekiehlt, pp.

refuge 1.Schutz (der)n.; 2.Zuflucht (die)n.

refund zerick/bezaahle, v.; zerickbezaahlt, pp.

refuse 1.ab/lehnt, v.; abgelehnt, pp.; 2.ab/saage, v.; abgsaat, pp.; 3.ab/schpreche, v.; abschproche, pp.; 4.Abfall (der)n.; 5.Dreck (der)n.; 6.verweigere, v.; verweigert, pp.

regain 1.erhole (sich --)v.; erholt, pp.; 2.fresse (sich --), v.; 3.mache (sich --)v.; gemacht, pp.; 4.rum/kumme, v.; is rumkumme, pp.; 5.zerick/griege, v.; zerickgrickt, pp.; **consciousness** zukumme, v.; zukumme, pp.

regal keenichlich, adj.

regard 1.aa/seh(n)e, v.; aagsehne, pp.; 2.achde, v.; geacht, pp.; 3.eschdimiere, v.; ge-eschdimiert, pp.; 4.eschtimiere, v.; ge-eschtimiert, pp.; 5.Hiesicht (die)n.; 6.Hiesicht (die)n.; **consideration** (of) Ricksicht (die)n.

regeneration Widdergebort (die)n.

regiment Reggiment (es)n.

Regina Regine (die)n.

region Gegend (die)n.

register 1.ei/schreiwe, v.; eigschriwwe, pp.; 2.uff/schreiwe, v.; uffgschriwwe, pp.

regret 1.bedauere, v.; bedauert, pp.; 2.gereie, v.; gereit, pp.; 3.greppe, v.; gegreppt, pp.; 4.krenke, v.; gekrenkt, pp.; 5.Rei (die)n.; 6.reie, v.; gereit, pp.

regular regelmaessich, adj.

regularity Regelmaessichkeet (die)n.

regulate 1.reggeliere,v.; reggeliert, pp.;2.reggle, v.; gereggelt, pp.

regulation Verardning (die)n.

regurgitate 1.kotze, v.; gekotzt, pp.; 2.woxe (sich --)v.; gewoxt, pp.

reign regiere, v.; regiert, pp.

rein 1.Lein (die)n.; 2.Rieme (der)n.; **up** zerick/henke, v.; zerickghenkt, pp.

reins 1.Zaam (der)n.; 2.Zaamziggel (der)n.

reiterate widderhole, v.; widderholt, pp.

reject 1.ab/saage, v.; abgsaat, pp.; 2.verschtosse, v.; verschtosse, pp.; 3.verwaerfe, v.; verworfe, pp.; 4.zerick/schtelle, v.; zerickschtellt, pp.

rejoice frehe (sich --), v.; gfreht, pp.; **along with** mit/yuwele, v.; mitgeyuwelt, pp.

relapse Zerickfall (der)n.

relate 1.haer/saage, v.; haergsaagt, pp.; 2.haer/saage, v.; haergsaagt, pp.

related to Freinschaft (der)n. (im -- sei)

relation Verheltnis (es)n.

relations Freind (die)n., pl.

relative 1.Aaverwandter (der)n.; 2.Aaverwandti (die)n.; 3.Blutsfreind (der)n.; Blutsfreind, pl.; 4.Freind (der) n.; Freind, pl.; 5.Verwandte(r) (der)n.

relatives 1.Freind (die)n., pl.; 2.Freindschaft (die)n.; 3.Verwandschaft (die)n.

release 1.Befreiung (die)n.; 2.frei/gewwe, v.; freigewwe, pp.; 3.frei/losse, v.; freeglosst, pp.; 4.los/losse, v.; losgelosst, pp.

released frei/geh, v.; freigange, pp.

relent no(och)losse, v.; no(och)g(e)losst, pp.

relentless unbaremhartzich, adj.

reliable 1.rechschaffich, adj.;2.rechtschaffe, adj.; 3.reschaffe, adj.; 4.verdrauensvoll,adj.; 5.verdraulich,adj.; 6.verlessich, adj.

reliance Zuverdraue (es)n.

relict Wittfraa (die)n. (hinnerlossni --)

religion Relichion (die)n.

relinquish 1.iwwerlosse, v.; iwwerlosse, pp.; 2.uff/schmeisse, v.; uffschmisse, pp.

rely on druff verlosse (sich --)v.; verlosse, pp.

remain bleiwe, v.; gebliwwe, pp.; **at a distance** ab/bleiwe, v.; abgebliwwe, pp.; **away** 1.fatt/bleiwe, v.; fattgebliwwe, pp.; 2.weck/bleiwe, v.; weckgebliwwe, pp.; **behind** zerick/bleiwe, v.; zerickgebliwwe, pp.; **closed** zubleiwe, v.; zugebliwwe, pp.; **in place** aa/bleiwe, v.; aagebliwwe, pp.; **off** ab/bleiwe, v.; abgebliwwe, pp.; **in open** uff/bleiwe, v.; uffgebliwwe. pp.; **seated** hocke bleiwe, v.; hockegebliwwe, pp.; **together** zamme/bleiwe,v.; zammegebliwwe, pp.

remainder 1.Iwwerbleibsel (es)n.; 2.Iwwerrescht (der)n.

remaining iww(e)rich, adj.

remains of woven goods Socke (der)n.

remand vor/halde, v.; vorghalde, pp.

remark 1.Bemaerrickung (die)n.; 2.bemaricke, v.; bemarickt, pp.

remarkable 1.maerickunswaerdich, adj.; 2.maerrickwaerdich, adj.; 3.marickwaddich, adj.

remedy 1.Heilmittel (es)n.; 2.Middel (es)n.

remember 1.b(e)sinne (sich --)v.; b(e)sunne, pp.; 2.bei/falle, v.; beigfalle, pp. (dat. of the pronoun); 3.ei/falle, v.; eigfalle, pp.; 4.erinnere (sich --)v.; erinnert, pp.; 5.meinde, v.; gemeindt, pp.; **to** 1.begegne, v.; begegnet, pp.; 2.bewil(l)kumme, v.; bewil(l)kummt, pp.; 3.griesse, v.; gegriesst, pl.

rememberance 1.Aadenke(s) (es)n.; 2.Denkzeige (es)n.; 3.Gedechtnis (es)n.

remind 1.ermaahne, v.; ermaahnt, pp.; 2.gegehalde, adj.; 3. gegekalde, adj.; 4.gemaahne, v.; gemaahnt, pp.; 5. gmaahne, v.; gmaahnt, pp.; **emphatically** aab(e)fehle, v.; aab(e)fohle, pp.; **one of home** aa/heemle, v.; aagheemelt, pp.

reminder 1.Dankzeige (es)n.; 2.Denkseckli (es)n.; Denksecklin, pl.; 3.Denkzeddel (der)n.; 4.Denkzeeche (es)n.

Rr

reminiscence

reminiscence Erinnerung (die)n.

remissness Noochlessichkeit (die)n.

remit erlosse, v.; erlosst, pp.

remnant 1.Abfall (der)n.; 2.Iwwerbleibsel (es)n.;
3. Iwwerrescht (der)n.; 4.Reschdel (es)n.; 5.Rescht (es)n.

remnants iwwerletzich, adv. (-- schtofft)

remodel rum/moddle, v.; rumgemoddelt, pp.

remonstrance Ermaahnung (die)n.

remonstrate fuddre, v.; gfuddert, pp.

remote faern, adv.

remove 1.ab/ziehe, v.; abgezoge, pp.; 2.aus/heewe, v.;
ausghowe, pp.; 3.weck/duh, v.; weckgeduh,pp.;
4.weck/mache, v.; weckgemacht, pp.;
5.weck/nemme, v.; weckgenumme, pp.;
6.weck/raahme, v.; weckgeraahmt, pp.;
7.weck/schaffe, v.; weckgschafft, pp.; **by digging**
ab/graawe, v.; abgegraawe, pp.; **by mowing**
weck/maehe, v.; weckgemaeht, pp.; **by plucking**
weck/roppe, v.; weckgeroppt, pp.; **by pumping** (to
get fresh water) ab/bumbe, v.; abgebumpt, pp.; **by
tying** (a wart) ab/binne,v.; abgebunne,pp.; **dust from**
ab/schtaawe, v.; abgschtaapt, pp.; **from a kettle
with a fork** raus/schteche, v.; rausgschtoche, pp.;
sprouts 1.ab/keime, v.; abgekeimt, pp.; 2.keime, v.;
gekeimt, pp.; **strings** (of beans) feede, v.; gfeedt, pp.;
the stones (from cherries) schteene, v.; gschteent,
pp.; **to the rear** (as straw threshing) zerick/mache, v.;
zerickgemacht, pp.

remunerate 1.belohne,v.; belohnt, pp.;2.beluhne,v.;
beluhnt, pp.

remuneration 1.Loh (der)n.; 2.Luh (der)n.

rend verreisse, v.; verrisse, pp.; **asunder** 1.verschoddere, v.;
verschoddert, pp.; 2.verschottere, v.; verschottert, pp.

render (lard) aus/schmelze, v.; ausgschmolze, pp.

renew erneire, v.; erneiert, pp.

renounce 1.ab/saage, v.; abgsaat, pp.; 2.ab/schweere, v.;
abgschwore, pp.

renowned beriehmt, adj.

rent 1.Loch (es)n.; Lecher, pl.; 2.Riss (der)n.; 3.verlehne,
v.; verlehnt, pp.; 4.weck/lehne, v.; weckglehnt, pp.

rented place Lehnsblatz (der)n.

repack rum/packe, v.; rumgpackt, pp.

repair 1.bessere, v.; gebessert, pp.; 2.fascht/mache, v.; faschtgemacht, pp.; 3.verzimmere, v.; verzimmert, pp.; **roads**
Weg (der)n. (-- mache); **shoes** schuhflicke, v.; gflickt, pp.;
something uff/duh, v.; uffgeduh, pp. (ebbes --)

repay 1.vergelte, v.; vergolte, pp.; 2.zerick/gewwe, v.;
zerickgewwe, pp.

repeal ab/schaffe, v.; abgschafft, pp.

repeat 1.her/saage, v.; hergsaat, pp.; 2.iwwer/hole, v.;
iwwerholt, pp.; 3.iwwer/mache, v.; iwwergemacht,
pp.; 4. iwwerhole, v.; iwwerholt, pp.; 5.widderhole,
v.; widderholt, pp.; **another's words** no(och)saage,
v.; no(och)gsaat, pp.; **the words of another in
prayer** no(och)bede, v.; no(och)gebet, pp.

repeated act of feeling Gfiehl (es)n.; **innuendos**

resent

Gschtichel (es)n.; **or continued lying** Liegerei (die)n.;
pouring Gschitt (es)n.; **stumbling** Gschtolper (es)n.

repeatedly 1.iwwer un iwwer, adv.; 2.iwwer, prep.
(-- un --)

repeating the same old story or complaint Geleier (es)n.

repel zerick/schtosse, v.; zerickgschtosse, pp.

repent 1.bereie, v.; bereit, pp.; 2.Buss(e) (die)n. (Busse
duh)

repentance 1.Rei (die)n.; 2.Buss(e) (die)n.

repentant reimiedich, adj.

repetition Widderholung (die)n.

repine begraeme (sich --)v.; begraemt, pp.

replant no(och)blanze, v.; no(och)geblanzt, pp.

replete voll, adj.

reply 1.antwadde,v.; geantwatt, pp.;2.Antwatt (die)n.;
Antwadde, pl.

report 1.aa/bringe, v.; aagebrocht, pp.; 2.aa/gewwe, v.; is
aagewwe, pp.; 3.Bericht (der)n.; 4.berichte, v.;
bericht, pp.; 5.Gegrisch (es)n.; 6.Gnelle (der)n.;
7.Krach (der)n.

repose Ruh (die)n.

represent verdrede, v.; verdrede, pp.

repress 1.ei/halde, v.; eighalde, pp.; 2.unner/dricke, v.;
unnergedrickt, pp.

reprimand 1.ab/kabbe, v.; abgekappt, pp.; 2.ab/schiesse,
v.; abgschosse, pp.; 3.ab/schtrofe, v.; abgschtroft,
pp.; 4.aus/butze, v.; ausgebutzt, pp.; 5.aus/schenne,
v.; ausgschennt, pp.; 6.schelde, v.; gscholde, pp.;
7.Verheer (es)n.; 8.verheere, v.; verheert, pp.

reproach vor/halde, v.; vorghalde, pp.; **(with)**
vor/schmeisse, v.; vorg(e)schmisse, pp.

reproof Schtrofing (die)n.

reprove 1.ab/schtrofe, v.; abgschtroft, pp.; 2.vermaahne,
v.; vermaahnt, pp.

reptile Schlang (die)n.; Schlange, pl.

Republican 1.Republikaaner (der)n.; Republikanner, pl.;
2.republikannisch, adj.

repulse zerick/dreiwe, v.; zerickgedriwwe, pp.

reputable aasehnlich, adj.

reputation 1.guder Naame (der)n.; 2.Lob (es)n.; 3.Naame
(der)n. (schlechder --)

request 1.aab(e)fehle, v.; aab(e)fohle, pp.; 2.Aaschpruch
(der)n.; 3.Begehr (der)n.; 4.Fodderes (es)n.; 5.heese,
v.; gheese, pp.

require 1.erfoddre, v.; erfoddert, pp.; 2.verlange, v.;
verlangt, pp.

requirement Foddrung (die)n.

rescue 1.befreie, v.; befreit, pp.; 2.Befreiung (die)n.;
3.erredde, v.; errett, pp.; 4.redde, v.; gerett, pp.

research unnersuche, v.; unnersucht, pp.

resemblance Aehnlichkeit (die)n.

resemble no(och)aarde, v.; no(och)geaart, pp.; **(act like)
one's mother** muddere (sich --)v.; gemuddert, pp.;
(act like) one's father vaddere (sich --)v.

resent 1.faahre, v.; gfaahre, pp (in die hee --); 2.in die Heh
faahre, v.; 3.iwwel/nemme, v.; iwwelgnumme, pp.

353

Rr

resentful — revolve

resentful uffschtennich, adj.

resentment Falschheet (die)n.

reservation for life (in house, room, firewood, etc. in old deeds) 1.Aus(en)palt (der)n.; 2.Ausbehalt (der)n.; 3.Ausverhalt (der)n.

reserve zerick/halde, v.; zerickghalde, pp.

reside 1.uff/halde (sich --)v.; ufghalde, pp.; 2.wohne, v.; gwohnt, pp.; 3.wuhne, v.; gewuhnt, pp.

residence 1.Wohnblatz (der)n.; 2.Wuhnblatz (der)n.; Wuhnbletz, pl.

resident 1.Eiwuhner (der)n.; Eiwuhner, pl.; 2.wohnhaft, adj.; 3.wuhnhaft, adj.

residue Iwweriches (es)n.

resign uff/schmeisse; **(from an office)** ab/danke, v.; abgedankt, pp.

resigned ergewwe (sich --)v.; ergewwe, pp.

resin 1.Beinthaarz (der)n.; 2.Haarz (der)n.

resinous haarzich, adj.

resist 1.Feddre schtraube (die)n.; 2.schteibre (sich --),v.; 3.schtraube (sich --), v.; 4.wedder/halde, v.; wedderghalde, pp.; 5.wedder/schteh, v.; weddergschtanne, pp.; 6.wehre (sich --)v.; g(e)wehrt, pp.; 7.widderschteh, v.; widderschtanne, pp.

resistance 1.Wedderschtand (der)n.; 2.Widderschtand (der)n.

resolute resolutt, adj.

resolution B(e)schluss (der)n.

resolve b(e)schliesse, v.; b(e)schlosse, pp.

respect 1.aa/seh(n)e, v.; aagsehne, pp.; 2.eschdimiere, v.; ge-eschdimiert, pp.; 3.reschpekdiere, v.; reschpekdiert, pp.; 4.Reschpekt (der)n.

respectable 1.aaschtennich, adj.; 2.aasehnlich, adj.; 3. reschpeckdaawel, adj.

respected aagsehne, adv.

resplendent glensend, adj.

respond antwadde, v.; geantwatt, pp.

response Antwatt (die)n.; Antwadde, pl.

responsible 1.antwattlich, adj.; 2.gutschteh, adj.; 3. pflichdich, adj; **for** eischteh, v.; eigschtanne, pp.

rest 1.leie, v.; gelege; geleye, pp.; 2.Rascht (die)n.; 3.Ruh (die)n.; 4.ruh(g)e, v.; geru(h)gt, pp.; **heavily** (upon) nacke, v.; genackt, pp.; **upon** uff/leie, v.; uffgelegge, pp.

resting Rugerei (die)n.; **place** Ruhblatz (der)n;

restless 1.umruhich, adj.; 2.unruhich, adj.; 3.unschtaetich, adj.; 4.zawwlich, adj.

restlessness 1.Umruh (die)n.; 2.Unruh (die)n.

restorative balsam Lewesbalsam (der)n.

restore 1.gut/mache, v.; gutgemacht, pp.; 2.widderher/schtelle, v.; widderhergschtellt, pp; **(a sick person)** uff/bringe, v.; uffgebrocht, pp.; **peace** Friede (der)n. (-- schtifde)

restrain 1.eischrenke, v.; eigschrenkt, pp.; 2.halde, v.; ghalde, pp.; 3.verzwenge, v.; verzwengt, pp.; 4.zerick/halde, v.; zerickghalde, pp.

restrict ei/halde, v.; eighalde, pp.

result 1.aus/geh, v.; ausgange, pp.; 2.ende, v.; geendt, pp.; 3.Erfolk (der)n.; 4.raus/kumme, v.; is rauskumme, pp.

resume 1.uff/nemme, v.; uffgenumme, pp.; 2.widder, adv. (-- draa gehne)

resurrection Auferschtehing (die)n.

resuscitate aufaerwecke, v.; aufaerweckt, pp.

retail schtickweis, adv.

retain an undue proportion iwwergrabsche (sich --)v.; iwwergrabscht, pp.

retainer Aageld (es)n.

retaliate zerick/gewwe, v.; zerickgewwe, pp.

retard uff/halde, v.; uffghalde, pp.

retch 1.iewe (sich --)v.; geiebt, pp.; 2.kotze, v.; gekotzt, pp.

reticent verschwiche, adj.

reticulum Netz (es)n.

retina (of the eye) Netzhaut (die)n.

retire Ruh (die)n. (sich in -- setze)

retort zerick/saage, v.; zerickgsaagt, pp.

retreat 1.Aufenthalt (der)n.; 2.weiche, v.; gewiche, pp.; 3.zerick/falle, v.; zerickgfalle, pp.; 4.zerick/geh, v.;zerickgange, pp.; 5.zerick/ziehe, v.; zerickgezoge, pp.

return 1.zerick/bringe, v.; zerickgebrocht, pp.; 2.zerick/geh, v.; zerickgange, pp.; 3.zerick/kumme, v.; zerickkumme, pp.; 4.zerick/nemme, v.; zerickgnumme, pp; **(things borrowed)** heembringe, v.; heemgebrocht, pp.; **home empty handed with nothing for the children of the house** (no candy, etc.) Nixli mit heembringe; **hoe stealthily** heemschtehle (sich --)v.; heemgschtohle, pp.

returned redour, adv.

reveal offenbaare, v.; (ge)offenbaart, pp.; **a secret** babble, v.; gebabbelt, pp.

revel schmause, v.; gschmaust, pp.

revenge 1.Ewekummes (es)n.; 2.Raache (die)n.; 3. Zerickbezaahling (die)n.

revengeful raachgierisch, adj.

revengefulness Raachgier (die)n.

reverberate 1.klange, v.; geklangt, pp.; 2.klinge, v.; geklingt, pp.; 3.schalle, v.; gschallt, pp.; 4.schelle, v.; gschellt, pp.

revere verehre, v.; verehrt, pp.

reverence ehrwaerdiche, v.; geehrwaerdicht, pp.

reverse 1.rum/drehe, v.; rumgedreht, pp.; 2.um/kehre, v.; umgekehrt, pp.

reversed hinnerschich, adj.

revert zerick/schlagge, v.; zerickgschlagge, pp.

revile 1.schimbe, v.; gschimbt, pp.; 2.schmaehe, v.; gschmaeht, pp.

revive kumme, v.; kumme, pp. (zu sich --)

revoke 1.ab/saage, v.;abgsaat,pp.;2.widderrufe, v.; widderrufe, pp.

revolve 1.um/drehe, v.; umgedreht, pp.; 2.um/welse, v.; umgewelst, pp.

Rr

reward — riotous living

reward 1.belohne, v.; belohnt, pp.; 2.Belohning (die)n.; 3.Belohnung (die)n.; 4.beluhne, v.; beluhnt, pp.; 5.Dank(der)n.; 6.Verdi(e)nscht (der)n.; 7.vergelde, v.; vergolde, pp.; 8.vergelte, v.; vergolte, pp.

rewrite iwwerschreiwe, v.; iwwergschriwwe, pp.

rheum Schnubbe (der)n.

rheumatic pains Gliederschmaerze (die)n., pl.

rheumatism 1.Fluss (der)n.; 2. Rhummedis (die)n.; 3. Rummedis (die)n.

rheumy flussich, adj.

rhinoceros Naasharn (es)n.

Rhode Island Red (chicken) Fasandehinkel (es)n.

rhubarb 1.Rhabarbraa (der)n.; 2.Weiblanz (die)n.

rhyme 1.Reim (der)n.; Reime, pl.; 2.reime, v.; gereimt, pp.

rhythm Takt (der)n.

rib Ripp (die)n.; Ribbe, pl; **roast** 1.Rippeschtick (es)n.; 2.Ribbeschtick (es)n.

ribbed 1.ribbich, adj.; 2.ribbich, adv.

ribbon 1.Band (es)n.; Benner, pl.; 2.Schlupp (der)n.; Schlipp, pl.

ribgrass Schpitzewettrich (der)n.

ribs with meat on them 1.Ribbefleesch (es)n.; 2.Rippefleesch (es) n.

rice Reis (der)n.; **boiled in milk** Reisbrei (der)n.; **soup** Reissupp (die)n.

rich 1.reich, adj.; 2.wohlhaabend, adj.; **(soil)** fett, adj.; **pickings** Fresse (es)n.

riches Reichdum (der)n.

richweed Glaasgraut (es)n.

rickets Rickgrankheit (die)n.

rickety 1.ausgeloddert, adj.; 2.gnackrich, adj.; 3.lodd(e) rich, adj.; 4.lodder, adj.; 5.noddlich, adj.; 6.wabblich, adj; **vehicle** Klabberdasch (die)n.

rid fatt/schaffe, v.; fattgschafft, pp.

riddle Raetsel (es)n.; **by shooting** verschiesse, v.; verschosse, pp.

ride (a horse) reide, v.; gridde, pp.; **(drive) along with** mit faahre, v.; mitgfaahre, pp.; **(on a vehicle)** faahre, v.; gfaahre, pp.; **(one) on a rail** riggelreide, v.; riggelgeridde, pp.; **after** no(och)reide, v.; no(och)geridde, pp.; **along with** mit/reide, v.; mitgeridde, pp.; **around** rum/reide, v.; rumgeridde, pp.; **away** 1.fatt/reide, v.; fattgridde, pp.; 2.weck/reide, v.; weckgeridde, pp.; **back** zerick/reide, v.; zerickgeridde, pp.; **from place to place** rumhaer/reide, v.; rumhaergeridde, pp.; **here** (a horse) haer/reide, v.; haergeridde, pp.; **in** 1.nei/reide, v.; neigeridde, pp.; 2.rei/ reide, v.; reigeridde, pp.; **in advance** vannenaus/reide, v.; vannenausgeridde, pp.; **out** naus/reide, v.; nausgridde, pp.; **past** verbei/reide, v.; verbeigeridde, pp.; **past another** (in the same direction) vor/reide, v.; vorgeridde, pp.; **the bakeoven** (said of a young man or woman if, for the second time, a younger brother or sister married) Backoffe reide (der) n.; **through** darich/reide, v.; darichgeridde, pp.; **together** zamme/reide, v.; zammegeridde, pp.; **up** 1.nuff/reide, v.; nuffgeridde, pp.; 2.ruff/reide, v.;

ruffgeridde, pp.

rider 1.Reider (der)n.; Reider, pl.; 2.Ritter (der)n.

ridge Hun(d)srick (der)n.; **or heaped row** (in which sweet potatoes are planted) Wallem (die)n.; Walme, pl.

ridgepole 1.Dachf(a)erscht (der)n.; 2.Faerscht (der)n.; 3.Farscht (der)n.

ridicule 1.aus/hensle, v.; ausghenselt, pp.; 2.aus/lache, v.; ausgelacht, pp.; 3.lecherlich, adj. (-- mache); 4.verlache, v.; verlacht, pp.; 5.verschpodde, v.; verschpott, pp.

ridiculous 1.lecher(l)ich, adj.; 2.lecherich, adj.; 3.schpassich, adj.

ridicuously cheap schpottwolfel, adj.

riding a hobby-horse Schteckereide (es)n.; **horse** Reitgaul (der)n.

riff-raff Schtoff(t) (es)n.

riffle Riffel (die)n.

rifle 1.Bix (die)n.; 2.Kuggelbix (die)n.; 3.Kuggleflint (die) n.; **barrel** Bixelaaf (der)n.

rifled gun Flint (die)n. (gezogni --)

right 1.kauscher, adj.; 2.Recht (es)n.; 3.recht, adj.; 4.rechts, adj.; **(sane)** gnedst, adj.; **angled corner** Winkeleck (es)n.; **away** 1.graad, adv.; 2.wegs, adv. (graades --); **handed** 1.Recht (Hand) (die)n.; 2.rechts, adj.; 3.rechtshandich, adj.; **through** midde darrich, adv.

righteous gerechdich,

righteousness Gerechdichkeit (die)n.

rightly gerechterweis, adv.

rigid schteif, adj.

rigorous schtreng, adj.

rim (of a hat) Ran(e)ft (der)n.; **(of wheel)** Reef (der)n.; Reef, pl.

rind Schaal (die)n.; Schaale, pl.; **(of bacon or ham)** 1.Rinn (die)n.; 2.Schpeckschwaart (die)n.; 3.Schwaart (die) n.; 4.Schwort (die)n.

ring 1.glingle, v.; geglingelt, pp.; 2.Klang (der)n.; 3.klange, v.; geklangt, pp.; 4.klinge, v.; geklingt, pp.; 5.klingle, v.; geklingelt, pp.; 6.laute, v.; gelaut, pp.; 7.ringe, v.; grunge, pp.; 8.schelle, v.; gschellt, pp.; **(a bell)** 1.belle, v.; gebellt, pp.; 2.laude, v.; gelaut, pp.; **(finger ring)** Ring (der)n.; **(jewelry)** Fingerring (der) n.; **tag** Ringausschlagge (es)n.

ringbone Ringbon (der)n.

ringer (at quoits) Ringler (der)n.

ringlet 1.Groll (die)n.; Grolle, pl.; 2.Kroll (die)n.; 3.Ringel (es)n.

ringworm Ringwarem (der)n.; Ringwaerm, pl.

rinse 1.ab/schwenke, v.; abgschwenkt, pp.; 2.schpiele, v.; gschpielt, pp.; 3.schpiele, v.; gschpielt, pp.; 4.schwenke, v.; gschwenkt, pp.; **out** 1.aus/schwenke, v.; ausgschwenkt, pp.; 2.raus/schwenke, v.; rausgschwenkt, pp.

rinsing tub (for family washing) Schwenkzuwwer (der)n.; Schwenkziwwer, pl.

riotous living Luschtlewe (es)n.

355

Rr

rip — Roman

rip 1.trenne, v.; detrennt, pp.; 2.uff/drenne, v.; uffgedrennt, pp; **off** ab/drenne, v.; abgedrennt, pp.

ripe 1.maer(r)b, adj.; 2.marb, adj.; 3.mareb, adj.; 4.reif, adj.; 5.zeidich, adj.

ripen zeidiche, v.; gezeidicht, pp.

ripple Riffel (die)n.

rise 1.schteige, v.; gschtigge, pp.; 2.uff/kumme, v.; is uffkumme, pp.; 3.uff/schteige, v.; uffgschtigge, pp.; **abruptly** uff/faahre, v.; uffgfaahre, pp.; **from the dead** aufaerschteh, v.; aufaerschtanne, pp.; **in anger** uff/schtaerme, v.; uffgschtaermt, pp.; **in price** nuff/geh, v.; nuffgange, pp.; **like a spray** (from the ground in a heavy rain) newwle, v.; genewwelt, pp.

rising of the moon Moon(d)uffgang (der)n.

risk 1.fendere, v.; gfendert, pp.; 2.vendere, v.; gvendert, pp.; 3.woge, v.; gewogt, pp.

rival Mitschtreiter (der)n.

river Rewwer (der)n.; Rewwer, pl.; **birch** Wasserbaerke (die)n.

rivet 1.aa/niede, v.; aageniet, pp.; 2.Niet (der)n.; 3.niete, v.; geniet, pp.; 4.Nietnaggel (der)n.; 5.um/niede, v.; umgeniet, pp.

riwwelsoup Gnoddelsupp (die)n.

road 1.Faahrweg (der)n.; Faahrwege, pl.; 2.Schtross (die) n.; Schtrosse, pl.; 3.Weg (der)n.; Wege, pl.; **repairer** Wegmacher (der)n.; **supervisor** Wegmeeschder (der)n.; **through a forest** (for hauling wood) 1.Buschweg (der)n.; 2.Holzweg (der)n.; **toll house** Zollhaus (es)n.

road supervisor Wegmeeschder (der)n. gewandert, pp.;

roam 1.droddle, v.; gedroddelt, pp.; 2.wandere, v.; **about** rum/flankiere, v.; rumgflankiert, pp.; **after** no(och)flankiere, v.; no(och)gflankiert, pp.; **around** (especially evenings Sunday afternoon) rum/eesle, v.; rumge-eeselt, pp.; **at large** (of cattle) frei/laafe, v.; freigloffe, pp.

roar 1.Braus (der)n.; 2.brause, v.; gebraust, pp.; 3.brille, v.; gebrillt, pp; **at** aaranne, v.; aagerannt, pp.

roaring 1.Gebraus (es)n.;2.Gedob (es)n.; **or rustling** Gerausch (es)n.

roast reeschde, v.; gereescht, pp; **(thoroughly)** darich/rooschde, v.; darichgerooscht, pp.

roasting ear Rooschtnier (der)n.; Rooschtniers, pl.

rob 1.beraawe, v.; beraabt, pp.; 2.bockseckle, v.; gebockseckelt, pp.; 3.bschtehle, v.; bschtellt; bschtohle, pp.; 4.raawe, v.; geraabt, pp.

robbed (of the soil) ausgebauert, adj.

robber 1.Dieb (der)n.; Dieb, pl.; 2.Raawer (der)n.; Raawer, pl.

robber's den Raabnescht (es)n.

robbery Raawerei (die)n.

Robert Rawwert (der)n.

robin Amschel (die)n.; Amschle, pl.

robust 1.raubaschdich, adj.; adv.; 2.rischdich, adj.; 3.schtarick, adj.; 4.schtarrick, adj.

rock Felse (der)n.; Felse, pl; **(on a chair)** schockle, v.; gschockelt, pp.; **(to sleep)** baie, v.; gebait, pp.; **candy** Kandelzucker (der)n.; **chestnut oak** Keschd(an)eeche (der)n.; **hammer** Schlackhammer (der)n.; Schlackhemmer, pl.; **moss** Felsemoos (es)n.; **salt** Viehsalz (es)n.

rocker Schockler (der)n,; Schockler, pl.

rocket Rageet (die)n.

rocking Gschockel (es)n.; **chair** 1.Schockelschtul (der)n.; Schockelschtiel, pl.; 2.Schockler (der)n,; Schockler, pl.

rocks 1.Gliftse (die)n., pl.; 2.Kliftse, (die)n., pl.

rocky felsich, adj.; **cliff** Wand (die)n.; Wend, pl.; **summit** Felsekopp (der)n.

rod 1.Schtang (die)n.; Schtange, pl.; 2.Schwing (die)n.; **of a flail** Rut (die)n.

roe Fischoier (die)n., pl.

rogue 1.Fuggadivus (der)n.; 2.Ketzer (der)n.; Ketzer, pl.; 3.Schalk (der)n.; 4.Schallack (der)n.; 5.Schallicks (der) n.; 6.Schellem (der)n.; 7.Schellix (der)n.; 8.Schelm (der)n.; 9.Schlem (der)n.; 10.Schlingel (der)n.

roguery 1.Bedriegerei (die)n.; 2.Schalkheet (die)n.; 3.Schelmerei (die)n.

roguish song Schelmlied (es)n.; Schelmlieder, pl.

roll 1.Roll (die)n.; 2.rolle, v.; gerollt, pp.; 3.Weck (der)n.; Weck, pl.; 4.welse, v.; gewelst, pp.; 5.Wickel (der)n.; 6.wickle, v.; gewickelt, pp.; **(earth)** 1.walze, v.; ge-walzt, pp.; 2.welze, v.; gewelzt, pp.; **(of butter)** Klumpe (der)n.; **(of horses)** rolle (sich --)v.; gerollt, pp.; **(something) to a place** haer/welse, v.; **around** rum/rolle, v.; rumgerollt, pp.; **away** 1.fatt/rolle, v.; fattgerollt, pp.; 2.weck/rolle, v.; weckgerollt, pp.; **back** zerick/rolle, v.; zerickgerollt, pp.; **butter** Balle-budder (der)n.; **down** nunner/rolle, v.; nunnergerollt, pp.; **from or off** ab/rolle, v.; abgerollt, pp.; **in** 1.nei/rolle, v.; neigerollt, pp.; 2.nei/welze, v.; neigewelzt, pp.; 3.rei/rolle, v.; reigerollt, pp.; **into balls** (butter) eiballe, v.; eigeballt, pp.; **of dirt** (formed on body by rubbing) 1.Dreckriwwel (die)n.; 2.Riwwel (die)n.; Riwwle, pl.; **or tumble over and over** rum/batzle, v.; rumgebatzelt, pp.; **out** 1.aus/dreele, v.; ausgedreelt, pp.; 2.naus/rolle, v.; nausgerollt, pp.; 3.raus/ rolle, v.; rausgerollt, pp.; **out thin** aus/rolle, v.; ausgerollt, pp.; **over** 1.iwwer/welse, v.; iwwergewelst, pp.; 2.um/rolle, v.; umgerollt, pp.; **this way** haer/rolle, v.; haergerollt, pp.; **to** hie/rolle, v.; hiegerollt, pp.; **up** 1.nuff/rolle, v.; nuffgerollt, pp.; 2.nuff/welse, v.; nuffgewelst, pp.; 3.nuff/wickle, v.; nuffgewickelt, pp.; 4.uff/rolle, v.; uffgerollt, pp.; 5.zamme/rolle, v.; zammegerollt, pp.

roller 1.Roller (der)n.; Roller, pl.; 2.Walz (die)n.

rolling mill Rollmiehl (die)n.; **pin** 1.Dreegholz (es)n.; Dreeghelzer, pl.; 2.Dreelholz (es)n.; Dreelhelzer, pl.; 3.Drehholz (es)n.; 4.Drollholz (es)n.; Drollhelzer, pl.; 5.Roller (der)n.; Roller, pl.; 6.Rollhols (es)n.; 7.Waerkelholz (es)n.

Roman 1.Reemer (der)n.; Reemer, pl.; 2.reemisch, adj; **wormwood** 1.Bitterschtenge(l) (der)n.; 2.Bitterwaermet (der)n.

Rr

romp — rubbing

romp kalfaktre, v.; gekalfaktert, pp.

rone Roon (die)n.; Raane, pl.

roof Dach (es)n.; Decher, pl.; **of a house** Hausdach (es)n.; Hausdecher, pl.; **support** Dachschtul (der)n.; Dachschtiel, pl.

roofing lath Latt (die)n.; Ladde, pl.

room (in a house) 1.Schtupp (die)n.; Schtuwwe, pl.; 2.Zimmer (es)n. (rare usage); **(space)** Blatz (der)n.; Bletz, pl.; **for hanging clothes** Gleederschtubb (die)n.; **not regularly used** Kammer (die)n.; Kemmer, pl.

roomful Schtuppvoll (der)n.

rooster 1.Gickerigi (der)n.; 2.Gickerigu (der)n.

root Warzel (die)n.; **(of a decayed tooth)** Schtarze (der)n.; **(of a plant)** Watzel (die)n.; Watzle, pl.; **(of hogs)** 1.schtubbe, v.; gschtuppt, pp.; 2.wiehle, v.; gewiehlt, pp.; **and branch** rumps un schtumps, adv.; **cellar** Riewekeller (der)n.; Riewekeller, pl.; **out** 1.aus/rodde, v.; ausgerott, pp.; 2.raus/wiehle, v.; rausgewiehlt, pp.; **over** (a field) verwiehle, v.; verwiehlt, pp.; **up** uff/wiehle, v.; uffgewiehlt, pp.

rooting or rummaging Gewiehl (es)n.

rootlet 1.Wa(e)rzelche (es)n.; 2.Watzelche (es)n.; Watzelcher, pl.

roots (intertwined) zamme/warzle, v.; zammegewarzelt, pp.

rope Schtrich (der)n.; **halter** Schtrickhalfder (die)n.; Schtrickhalfder, pl.

rosary Rosegranz (der)n.

rose Ros (die)n.; Rose, pl; **of heaven** Himmelros (die)n.; **of Sharon** 1.Blummebaam (der)n.; 2.Holzros (die)n.; **plant** Schtockros (die)n.; **willow** 1.Reefweide (der)n.; 2.Rotweide (der, die)n.

rosebush Roseschtock (der)n.

rosemary Rosmarei (die)n.

rosey rosich, adj.

Rosie Reesel (es)n.

rosin Rasem (der)n.

rot 1.faule, v.; gfault, pp.; 2.verfaule, v.; verfault, pp; **away** weck/faule, v.; weckgfault, pp.; **down** nunner/faule, v.; nunnergfault, pp.; **off** ab/faule, v.; abgfault, pp.; **out** raus/faule, v.; rausgfault, pp.; **through** darich/faule, v.; darichgfault, pp.

rotation Umdrehung (die)n.

rotten 1.aagfault, adj.; 2.faul, adj.; 3.verfault, adj.; **affair** Lumbegschicht (die)n.

rotund rund, adj.

rough 1.holbrich, adj.; 2.hulbrich, adj.; 3.hulbrich, adj.; 4.raubaschdich, adj.; adv.; 5.rauh, adj.; 6.roh, adj.; 7.schtrubbich, adj.; 8.zoppich, adj; **(of a road or the cross terrain of a potato or corn field)** 1.hob(b)rich, adj.; 2. rubbich, adj.; 3. ruppich, adj.; 4.rubbich,adj.; 5.rub(b)lich, adj.; **carpenter** Zimmermann (der)n.; **coated** schtrubbich, adj.; **fellow** 1.Mannsvieh (es)n.; 2.Rauschebeidel (der)n.; 3.Rilps (der)n.; 4.Schwaart (die)n.; **pranks** Eselschtreech (die)n., pl.; **shelled** (pear) rauhschaalich, adj.

roughest 1.grebbscht, adj.; 2.grobbscht, adj.

round 1.haerum, adv.; 2.Roiyet (die)n.; 3.rollich, adj.; 4.rum, adv.; 5.rumher, adv.; 6.Rund (die)n.; 7.rund, adj.; 8. Schprosse (der)n.; 9.Schtaffel (die)n.; 10.umher, adv.; **(about) in front** vannerum, adv.; **about** 1.ausserum, adv.; 2.haerum, adv.; 3.rumher, adv.; **of a rack** Reffschprosse (der)n.; **off** ab/runde, v.; abgerundt, pp.; **rung** Schtachel (die)n.

roundish rundlich, adj.; **stone placed on fence posts** Rukschtee (der)n.

roundness Runding (die)n.

rouse 1.erwecke, v.; erweckt, pp.; 2.uff/riehre, v.; uffgriehrt, pp.; 3.uff/schtiwwre, v.; uffgschtiwwert, pp.; 4.uff/wecke, v.; uffgeweckt, pp.

rouser Rauscher (der)n.

rousing rauschend, adj.

roustabout Rabbelkaschde (der)n.

rout 1.schprenge, v.; gschprengt, pp.; 2.veryaage, v.; veryaagt, pp.

rove flankiere, v.; gflankiert, pp.

row 1.Reih (die)n. = Roi (die;) 2.Roi (die)n.; Roie, pl.; 3.Roiet (die)n.; 4.rudere, v.; gerudert, pp.; 5.Schtraw (w)atz (der)n.; 6.Schtruwutz (der)n.; 7.Schtruwwertz (der)n.; 8.Wese(s) (es)n.; **back** zerick/rudere, v.; zerickgerudert, pp.; **in** rei/rudre, v.; reigerudert, pp.; **into** nei/rudere, v.; neigerudert, pp.; **to a place** hie/rudre, v.; hiegerudert, pp.

rowboat Baedi (die)n.

rowdy 1.Raubelz (der)n.; 2.Raubengel (der)n.; 3.Schliffel (der)n.

rowdyish 1.raubeenich, adj.; 2.raubelzich, adj.; 3.ungebascht, adj.

royal keenichlich, adj.

rub reiwe, v.; g(e)riwwe, pp.; **down** nunner/reiwe, v.; nunnergeriwwe, pp.; **fine** verriwwle, v.; verriwwelt, pp.; **in** 1.eireiwe, v.; eigeriwwe, pp.; 2.nei/reiwe, v.; neigeriwwe, pp.; **in grease** ei/schmiere, v.; eigschmiert, pp.; **into as crumbs** nei/riwwle, v.; neigeriwwelt, pp.; **off** ab/reiwe, v.; abgeriwwe, pp.; **off dirt in rivels** (rolls) ab/riwwle, v.; abgeriwwelt, pp.; **open** uff/reiwe, v.; uffgeriwwe, pp.; **out** 1.aus/reiwe, v.; ausgeriwwe, pp.; 2.aus/riwwle, v.; ausgeriwwelt, pp.; 3.aus/wische, v.; ausgewischt, pp.; 4.verreiwe, v.; verriwwe, pp.; **through** darich/reiwe, v.; darichgeriwwe, pp.; **to powder** verreiwe, v.; verriwwe, pp.; **together** zamme/reiwe, v.; zammegeriwwe, pp.; **together with a swishing sound** (of corduroy trousers) 1.gwetzt, v.; gegwetzt, pp.; 2.wetze, v.; gewetzt, pp.; **with linament** aa/reiwe, v.; aageriwwe, pp.; **with ointment** schmiere, v.; gschmiert, pp.

rubber 1.Gamm (der)n.; 2.Iwwerschuh (der)n.; Iwwerschuh, pl.; **ball** Gammballe (der)n.; **boots** Gammschtiwwel (der)n.; **hose** Gammdeichel (der, es)n.; **nipple** Gammditz (der)n.; **overshoe** Gammschuh (der)n.

rubbing Reiwing (die)n.

357

Rr

rubbish

rubbish Unrot (der)n.
rubble Rollschtee (der)n.
rudder 1.Ruder (der)n.; Ruder, pl.; 2.Schteirruder (der)n.
ruddy rot, adj.
rude 1.grob(b), adj.; adv.; 2.grobb, adj.; 3.rau, adj.; adv.;
    4.raubaschdich, adj.; adv.; 5.raubauzich, adj.; adv.;
    6.rilpisch, adj.; adv.
rudely 1.grob(b), adj.; adv.; 2.rau, adj.; adv.;
    3.raubaschdich, adj.; adv.; 4.raubauzich, adj.; adv.;
    5.rilpisch, adj.; adv.
rudeness Grobbheet (die)n.
Rudolph Rudi (der)n.
rue 1.gereie, v.; gereit, pp.; 2.Raude (die)n.
ruffian 1.Grobbnickel (der)n.; 2.Raubelz (der)n.;
    3.Raubengel (der)n.
ruffle schtraube, v.; gschtraubt, pp.; **the feathers**
    schtraube, v.; gschtraubt, pp. (die feddre --); **(of a**
    turkey) 1.gschpruuze, v.; gschpruuzt, pp.;
    2.schpreize, v.; gschpreizt, pp.; 3.schproose (sich --)
    v.; gschproozt, pp.; 4.uff/schpraue (sich --)v.;
    uffgschpraut, pp.
ruin 1.haer/richde, v.; haergericht, pp.; 2.haer/richde, v.;
    haergericht, pp.; 3.her/richde, v.; hergericht, pp.;
    4.hie/richde, v.; hiegericht, pp.; 5.rumeniere, v.;
    rumgeniert, pp.; 6.ruminere, v.; geruminiert, pp.;
    7.rungeniere, v.; rungeniert, pp.; 8.verbuckere, v.;
    verbuckert, pp.; 9.verdarewe, v.; verdarewe, pp.;
    10.verdutze, v.; verdutzt, pp.; 11.Verfall (der)n.;
    12.verhause, v.; verhaust, pp.; 13.verhunse, v.;
    verhunst, pp.; 14.verletze, v.; verletzt, pp.;
    15.verrumeniere, v.; verrumeniert, pp.;
    16. verrungeniere, v.; verrungeniert, pp.;
    17.verschtimmle, v.; verschtimmelt, pp.;
    18.versuddle, v.; versuddelt, pp.; 19.verummeniere,
    v.; verummeniert, pp.; 20. verungeniere, v.;
    verungeniert, pp.
ruination Unnergang (der)n.
ruined 1.fix, adj. (aus --); 2.kabutt, adj.; 3.nix meh waert,
    adj.; 4.verschtutzt, adj.
rule 1.haerrsche, v.; ghaerrscht, pp.; 2.herrsche, v.;
    gherrscht, pp.; 3.Regel (die)n.; 4.regiere, v.; regiert,
    pp.; **of action** Richtschnur (die)n.
rum Dramm (der)n.
rumble 1.bollere, v.; gebollert, pp.; 2.bummere, v.;
    gebummert, pp.; 3.haabere, v.; ghaabert, pp.;
    4.haapere, v.; ghaapert, pp.; 5.rassle, v.; gerasselt,
    pp.; 6.rumble, v.; gerumbelt, pp.
rumbling Gerumpel (es)n.; **noise** Geboller (es)n.
rummage 1.aus/suche, v.; ausgsucht, pp.; 2.rum/wiehle,
    v.; rumgewiehlt, pp.; 3.schnuffle, v.; gschnuffelt, pp.;
    4.wiehle, v.; gewiehlt, pp.
rumor 1.Gebrummel (es)n.; 2.Grummel (es)n.
rump 1.Batzel (der)n.; 2.Niereschtick (es)n.; **steak**
    Baerzelschtick (es)n.
rumpus Uuzucht (die)n.
run 1.Grick (die)n.; Grecke; Gricke, pl.; 2.Rannli (es)n.;

run

3.renne, v.; gerennt, pp.; 4.Runn (die)n.; 5.schpringe,
v.; gschprunge, pp.; **(for office)** laafe, v.; g(e)loffe,
pp.; **(of contracts)** laafe, v.; g(e)loffe, pp.; **(off)** Laaf
(der)n.; Leef, pl.; **about** 1.rum/schpringe, v.;
rumgschprunge, pp.; 2. rumher/schpringe, v.;
rumhergschprunge, pp.; **against** wedder/schpringe,
v.; weddergschprunge, pp.; **ahead of** vor/schpringe,
v.; vorschprunge, pp.; **an errand** Schpringarwet duh
(die)v.; **around** Middel (es)n.; **around** rum/schpringe,
v.; rumgschprunge, pp.; **around** (all over)
rum/demmere, v.; rumgedemmert, pp.; **away**
1.ab/schpringe, v.; abschprunge, pp.;
2.darich/brenne. v.; darichgebrennt, pp.;
3.darich/geh, v.; darichgange, pp.; 4.fatt/schpringe,
v.; fattgschprunge, pp.; 5.fege, v.; gfegt, pp.;
6.weck/schpringe, v.; weckgschprunge, pp.; **away** (of
liquids) weck/laafe, v.; weckgeloffe, pp.; **back**
zerick/schpringe, v.; zerickgschprunge, pp.; **down**
1.ab/laafe, v.; abgeloffe, pp.; 2.nunner/schpringe, v.;
nunnergschprunge, pp.; 3. verlumbe, v.; verlumbt,
pp.; 4.verlumpt, adj.; **from place to place**
rumher/schpringe, v.; rumhergschprunge, pp.; **hel-**
ter-skelter Weisskopp (der)n. (wie en -- schpringt);
hither haer/schpringe, v.; haergschprunge, pp.; **in**
rei/schpringe, v.; reigschprunge, pp.; **in** (of liquids)
nei/laafe, v.; neigeloffe, pp.; **like the Old Scratch**
1.Baerschdebinner (schpringe wie'n --);
2.baerschdebinner, adj.; (wie en -- schaffe [saufe,
schpringe]); **of four of the same suit** (above the
seven spot in the game of datte) fuffzich, adj.; pron.;
of three cards of the same suit (the seven spot being
the lowest card in the deck) in the game of datte
Datte (en --); **off** 1.ab/laafe, v.; abgeloffe, pp.;
2.ab/rinne, v.; abgerunne, pp.; **off** (of liquids)
verlaafe, v.; verloffe, pp.; **or rage to exhaustion**
ab/dowe (sich --)v.; abgedobt, pp. **out** 1.aus/fliesse,
v.; ausgflosse, pp.; 2.aus/laafe, v.; is ausgeloffe, pp.;
3.naus/schpringe, v.; nausschprunge, pp.;
4.raus/schpringe, v.; rausgschprunge, pp.; **out** (of
liquids) 1.naus/laafe, v.; nausgeloffe, pp.;
2.raus/laafe, v.; rausgeloffe, pp.; **over**
niwwer/schpringe,v.; niwwerschprunge, pp.; **over** (of
liquids) niwwer/laafe, v.; niwwergeloffe, pp.; **there**
hie/schpringe, v.; hiegschprunge, pp.; **to** (of liquids)
hie/laafe, v.; hiegeloffe, pp.; **to seed** schiesse, v.;
gschosse, pp.; **to the head of** vor/schpringe, v.;
vorschprunge, pp.; **together** zamme/schpringe, v.;
zammegschprunge, pp.; **up** nuff/schpringe, v.;
nuffgschprunge, pp.; **up against** wedder/renne, v.;
weddergerennt, pp.; **up against a snag in one's plans**
wedder/laafe, v.; weddergeloffe, pp.; **up to**
1.bei/schpringe, v.; beischprunge, pp.;
2.zu/schpringe, v.; zugschprunge, pp.; **weather**
Schpringwedder (es)n.; **wildly** 1.drufflos/schpringe,
v.; drufflossgschprunge, pp.; 2.los/schpringe, v.;
losgschprunge, pp. (druff --)

Rr

runagate ... ryegrass

runagate Schwammkaader (der)n.

rune Roon (die)n.; Raane, pl.

rung 1.Schprosse (der)n.; 2.Schtaffel (die)n.; **of a ladder** Leederschpross(e) (der)n.; Leederschprosse, pl.

runnel Schpringegraawe (der)n.

runner (of a rocking chair) Schockelleefer (der)n.; Schockelleefer, pp.; **(of a sleigh)** 1.Laefer (der)n.; 2.Leefer (der)n.; Leefer, pl.; 3.Schliddeleefer (der)n.

running fliessend, adj.; **bean** Rankelbohn (die)n.; **brier** Rankeldanne (die)n.,pl.

runt 1.Grutzer (der)n.; 2.Kaschde (der)n.; Kaschde, pl.

rupture 1.Bruch (der)n.; Brich, pl.; 2.Schteebruch (der)n.; Schteebrich, pl.

rural lendlich, adj.

rush 1.Bensegraas (es)n.; 2.renne, v.; gerennt, pp.; **about** raase, v.; g(e)raast, pp.; **about aimlessly** rum/renne, v.; rumgerennt, pp.; **after** 1.no(och)haschble, v.; no(och)ghaschbelt, pp.; 2. no(och)renne, v.; no(och)gerennt, pp.; **away** weck/renne, v.; weckgerennt, pp.; **back** zerick/renne, v.; zerickgerennt, pp.; **from place to place** rumhaer/renne, v.; rumhaergerennt, pp.; **in** rei/schtaerme, v.; reigschtaermt, pp.; **out** raus/renne, v.; rausgerennt, pp.; **over** niwwer/renne, v.; niwwergerennt, pp.; **past** 1.verbei/renne, v.; verbeigerennt, pp.; 2.verbei/schiesse, v.; verbeigschosse, pp.; **up** 1.nuff/haschble, v.; nuffghaschbelt, pp.; 2.nuff/schiesse, v.; nuffgschosse, pp.; 3.ruff/renne, v.; ruffgerennt, pp.

rusk Weck (der)n.; Weck, pl.

russet brau(n), adj.

rust 1.roschde, v.; geroscht, pp.; 2.Roscht (der)n.; 3.verroschde, v.; verroscht, pp.; **away** 1.uff/roschde, v.; uffgeroscht, pp.; 2.weck/roschde, v.; weckgeroscht, pp.; **fast** aa/roschde, v.; aageroscht, pp.; **off** ab/roschde, v.; abgeroscht, pp.; **out** raus/roschde, v.; rausgeroscht, pp.

rusted 1.ausgeroscht, adj.; 2.geroscht, adj.; 3.verroscht, adj.

rustic 1.Buschgnibbel (der)n.; 2.Karebseroller (der)n.; 3.Schollehupser (der)n.

rustle 1.rabble, v.; gerabbelt, pp.; 2.rassle, v.; gerasselt, pp.; 3.rausche, v.; gerauscht, pp.; 4.rischble, v.; gerischbelt, pp.; 5.wischble, v.; gewischbelt, pp.

rustling Gebraus (es)n.

rusty roschdich, adj.

rut 1.bocke, v.; gebockt, pp.; 2.Glees (es)n.; Gleeser, pl.

rutabaga 1.Gallrieb (die)n.; Gallriewe, pl.; 2.Golrieb (die) n.; 3.Schweedrieb (die)n. (Waterloo Co., Ontario, Canada)

rutting season Laafzeit (die)n.

rye 1.Kann (es)n.; 2.Rocke (der)n.; **blossom** Kannbliet (die)n.; **bread** 1.Kannbrot (es)n.; 2.Rockebrot (es)n.; **field** Kannfeld (es)n.; Kannfelder, pl.; **flour** 1.Kannmehl (es)n.; 2.Rockemehl (es)n.; **stalk** Kannschtock (der)n.; **straw** 1.Kannschtroh (es)n.; 2.Langschtroh (es)n.; **whiskey** Kanndramm (der)n.

ryegrass 1.Rehgraas (es)n.; 2.Rockegraas (es)n.

Ss

saccharine

saccharine zuchrich, adj.

sack Sack (der)n.; Seck, pl.

sack (a beau) ab/schicke, v.; abgschickt, pp.

sackcloth Sackduch (es)n.

sacrament 1.Sackrament (es)n.; 2.Sakremant (es)n.

sacred sabbaatvoll, adj.

sacrifice Opfer (es)n.

sacristy Sakrischdei (es)n.

sad 1.bedauerlich, adj.; 2.bedreibt, adj.; 3.drauerich, adj.; 4.leedmiedich, adj.; 5.traurich, adj.

sadden bedriewe, v.; bedriebt, pp.

saddle 1.Saddel (der)n.; Saddel, pl.; 2.saddle, v.; gsaddelt, pp; **(someone) with** uff/saddle, v.; uffgsaddelt, pp.; **girth** Saddelgatt (die)n.; Saddelgadde, pl.; **on the saddle horse** Waggesaddel (der)n.; Waggesaddel, pl.

saddlebag Zwaerichsack (der)n.

saddlecloth Saddeldeck (die)n.

saddler Saddler (der)n.; Saddler, pl.

saddletree Saddelbank (die)n.

sadiron 1.Biggeleise (es)n.; Biggeleise, pl.; 2.Gletteise (es)n. (rare usage)

sadness 1.Bedriebung (die)n.; 2.Drauerichkeet (die)n.

safe sicher, adj.

safe(ly) sicher, adj.; adv.

safeguard schutze, v.; schutzt, pp.

safety pin Windelschpell (die)n.

safflower 1.Saff(e)rich (der)n.; 2.Saffran (der)n.

saffron 1.Saff(e)rich (der)n.; 2.Saffran (der)n.

sag 1.sacke, v.; gsackt, pp.; 2.senke, v.; gsenkt, pp.

sagacious 1.scharefsichdich, adj.; 2.scharfsichdich, adj.

sagacity Scharefsinn (der)n.

sage (tea) 1.Grod(d)ebalsem (der)n.; 2.Groddetee (der)n.; 3.Sal(l)we(i) (der)n.; 4.Salbtee (der)n.; **(wise)** 1.gluch, adj.; 2.gscheid, adj.

Sagittarius (9th sign of the zodiac) Schitz (der)n.

said to solle, v.; gsollt, pp.

sail 1.Segel (es)n.; 2.segle, v.; gsegelt, pp.

sailcloth Segelduch (es)n.

sailor Schiffmann (der)n.; **pants** Labberhosse (die)n., pl.

saint 1.Heilicher (en)n.; 2.Heilichi (en)n.

salad 1.Selaat (der)n.; 2.Zelaat (der)n.; **dressing** Selaatbrieh (die)n.

sale of goods Absatz (der)n.; Absetz, pl.

saline salzich, adj.

saliva 1.Schlawwer (es)n.; 2.Schpau (der)n.; 3.Schpautz, (der)n.; 4.Schpauz (der, es)n.

sallow 1.bleech, adj.; 2.gehl, adj.

salmagundi (salad plate of meats, anchovies, eggs and vegetables arranged in rows with salad dressing) Salma(n)gundi (es)n.

saloon Baerschtubb (die)n.; Baerschtuwwe, pl.

Salt River Salz Rewwer (der)n.

salt 1.pickle, v.; gepickelt, pp.; 2.Salz (es)n.; 3.salze, v.; gsalze, pp.; **down** 1.ei/lege, v.; eiglegt, pp.; 2.eisalse, v.; eigsalse, pp.; 3.nunner/salze, v.; nunnergsalze, pp.; **lick** Salzschleck (die)n.; **rheum** Salzfluss (der)n.

sausage

saltcellar Salzbix (die)n.

salting Salzing (die)n.; **trough** (for salting meat in preparation for curing) or for cattle Salzdroog (der)n.; Salzdreeg, pl.

saltpeter Salpeeder (der)n.

saltwater Salzwasser (es)n.

salty salzich, adj.

salute Zeit (die)n. (die -- biete)

salvation Selichkeet (die)n.

salve 1.Blaschder (es)n.; 2.Plaschder (die)n.; 3.Salb (die)n.; 4.Schmier (die)n.; 5.Waxschmier (die)n.; 6.Wundblascher (es)n.

same 1.gleich, adv.; 2.naemlich, adj.; **kind** desgleiches, pron.; **old story** 1.Gschlauder (es)n.; 2.Leier (die)n. (die alt --); 3.Schlauder (es)n.

sanctify heiliche, v.; gheilicht, pp.

sanctuary Heilichtum (es)n.

sand Sand (der)n; **screen** 1.Sandsibb (die)n.; 2.Sandsieb (die)n.; **sieve** 1.Sandsibb (die)n.; 2.Sandsieb (die)n.

sandman 1.Sandmann (der)n.; 2.Schlofleis (die)n., pl.

sandpaper Sandbabier (es)n.

sandpile Sandhaufe (der)n.

sandpit Sandloch (es)n.

sandstone Sandschtee (der)n.

sandy 1.sandfarwich, adj.; 2.sandich, adj.; 3.wettschteenich, adj.; **soil** Sandboddem (der)n.

sanicle 1.Sanickel (die)n.; 2.Sanickelwatzel (die)n.

Santa Claus 1.Belznickel (der)n. Belznickel, pl.; 2.Grischtkindli (es)n.; 3.Krischkindel (es)n.; 4.Sanda Klaas (der)n.

sap 1.Saft (die)n.; 2.Schpundi (der)n.

sappy safdich, adj.

sapwood Schpundholz (es)n.

sarcastic 1. hensle, v.; g(e)hensel pp.; 2.scheppmeilich, adj.

sarsaparilla Sassafrill (die)n.

sash-window Schiebfenschder (es)n.

sassafras Sassefra(a)s (es)n.

Satan 1.Saadan (der)n.; 2.Saatan (der)n.

satanical 1.saadanisch, adj.; 2.saatanisch, adj.

satisfaction 1.Befriedichung (die)n.; 2.Zufriddeheet (die)n.

satisfied 1.droschtmiedich, adj.; 2.satt, adj.; 3.trostmiedich, adj.; 4.zufridde, adj.

satisfy 1. aa/schteh, v.; aagschtan pp.; 2. befriediche, v. befreidicht, pp.; 3.seddich, v.; gseddicht, pp.; 4.settiche, v.; gsetticht, pp.; **one's desire** (both good and a bad sense) Luschde (der) (sei -- biesse)

Saturday Samschdaag (der)n.; **before Easter** (Moravian) Sabbaat (der)n (der grosse --); **child** (child born on Saturday) Samschdaagskind (es)n.

sauce Dunkes (es)n.

saucepan Kochpann (die)n.

saucer 1.Blettche (es)n.; Blettche pl.; 2.Blettli (es)n.; Blettli pl.; 3.Schaelche (es)n Schaelcher, pl.; 4.Schaeli (es)n.; 5.Teeblettche (es)n.; 6.Teebletti (es)n.

saucy 1.batzich, adj.; 2.frech, adj.; 3.maulich, adj.

sauerkraut Sauergraut (es)n.; **stamper** Sauergrautschtembel (der)n.

Ss

sausage | **scavenger**

sausage 1.Brotwascht (die)n.; 2.Fil(l)sel (es)n.; 3.Warscht (die)n.; 4.Wascht (die)n.; **in casing** Daermwascht (die) n.; **meat** 1.Waerschtfleesch (es)n.; 2.Waschtfleesch (es) n.; **stuffer** 1.Schaawer (der)n.; Schaawer, pl.; 2. Waerschtdrechder (der)n.; 3.Waerschtschiesser (der) n.; 4.Waschdrechder (der)n.; 5.Waschschtobber (der)n.

savage wild, adj.

savagely reissend, adv.

save 1.bei/lege, v.; beigeleg pp.; 2.devunbringe, v.; 3.erleese, v.; erleest, pp.; 4.erredde, v.; errett, pp.; 5.erschpare, v.; erschpar pp.; 6.redde, v.; gerett, pp.; 7.rette, v.; gerett, pp.; 8.schpaare, v.; gschpaar pp.; 9.uff/hewe, v.; uffghowe, pp.; 10.uff/lege, v.; uffgeleg pp.; 11.uff/schpaare, v uffgschpaart, pp.; 12.uff/schparre, vuffgschpatt, pp.; 13.zerick/lege, v zerickgelegt, pp.; **for the future** verschpaare, v.; verschpaart, pp.

saved (religious sense) seelich, adj.

saveloy Knackwa(r)scht (die)n.

saving schpaarsam, adj.

Savior Erleeser (der)n.

savory lieblich, adj.

saw 1.Saeg (die)n.; Saege, pl.; 2.saege, v.; gsaegt, pp;

clamp Saegeglamm (die)n.; Saegeglamme, pl.; **down** um/saege, v.; umgsaegt, pp.; **file** Saegfeil (die)n.; **into** 1.eisaege, v.; eigsaekt, pp.; 2.nei/saege, v.; neigsaekt, pp.; **into pieces** versaege, v.; versaegt, pp.; **off** 1.ab/saege, v.; absaegt, pp.; 2.weck/saege, v.; weckgsaegt, pp.; **out** raus/saege, v.; rausgsaegt, pp.; **rest** Saegmachter (der)n.; **slabs from a log** ab/schwaarde, v.; abgschwaart, pp.; **truer** Saegrichder (der)n.; **up** uff/saege, v.; uffgsaegt, pp. **sawbuck** 1.Holzbock (der)n.; Holzbec pl.; 2.Holzbock (der)n.; Holzbec pl.; 3.Saegbock (der)n.; Saegbec pl.

sawdust Saegmehl (es)n.

sawhorse 1.Saegbock (der)n.; Saegbec pl.; 2.Schemel (der)n.

sawmill Saegmiehl (die)n.

sawtooth 1.Saegezaah (der)n.; 2.Saegezoh (der)n.

sawyer Saeger (der)n.

saxifrage Mausohr (es)n.

say saage, v.; gsaat, pp.; **"yes" to** beyaae, v.; beyaat, beyat pp.; **how many** (in game of datte) aa/saage, v.; aagsaat, pp.

saying 1.Saag (die)n.; 2.Schpruch (der)n.; Schpric pl.

scab Grind (der)n.; **of small pox or vaccinatio** Parblegrind (der)n.

scabbard Scheed (die)n.

scabby 1.grindich, adj.; 2.raadich, adj.

scablous kretzich, adj.

scabrous 1.schewwetzich, adj.; 2.schiwwitzich, adj.

scaffold 1.Galye (der)n.; Galye, pl.; 2.Gerischt (der)n.

scald 1.aa/briehe, v.; aagebrieh pp.; 2.ab/briehe, v.; abgebrieh pp.; 3.aus/seefe, v.; ausgseef pp.; 4.briehe, v.; gebrieht, pp.; 5.verbriehe, v.; verbrieh pp.; **(a vessel)** aus/briehe, v.; ausgebrieh pp.

scalding trough (in butchering) Briehdrog (der)n.; **vat** Briehfass (es)n.

scale 1.erschteige, v.; erschteigg pp.; 2.Schaal(e)woog (die)n.; 3.Woog (die)n.; Wooge, pl.

scales of fish Schibbe (die)n., pl.

scallop 1.aus/zacke, v.; ausgezack pp.; 2.Kaft (die)n.; **school** Kafde, pl.; **edge** Zacke (der)n.scalloped kafdich, adj.

scaly 1.schaalich, adj.; 2.schibbich, adj.

scamp 1.Daagdieb (der)n.; 2.Dreckhund (der)n.; 3.Fuggadivus (der)n.; 4.Galgeschtrick (der)n.; 5.Kanallye (es)n.; 6.Laushund (der)n.; 7.Scheisspog (der)n.; 8.Schindluder (der)n.; 9.Schinnluder (der)n.; 10.Schwaerneeter (der)n.; 11.Schwerneeder (der)n.; 12.Seckelwetzer (der)n.

scandal Aaschtoss (der)n.

scandalous 1.aaschteesich, adj.; 2.schendlich, adj.; **affair** Schandwese (es)n.

scantily 1.gnapps, adv.; 2.kaum, adv.

scantling Greizhols (es)n.

scanty kaum, adv.

scapegoat Sindebock (der)n.

scar 1.Mol (die)n.; 2.Moler (der)n.; Moler, pl.; 3.Narb (die)n.; 4.Schramm (die)n.; 5.Schrume (die)n.; 6.Schrumm (die)n.; 7.Schrunn(e) (die)n.; 8.Wundnarb (die)n.

scarce 1.raar, adj.; 2.schpaerlich, adj.

scarcely 1.gnapps, adv.; 2.kaum, adv.; 3.knapps, adj.; 4.schwerlich, adj.; 5.schwerlich, adv.

scarcity Raarichkeet (die)n.

scare 1.eischrecke, v.; eigschreck pp.; 2.Schrecke (der)n.; 3.schrecke, v.; gschreck pp.; 4.verschrecke, v. verschrocke, pp; **(someone)** eigelschdere, v.; eigegelschdert, pp.; **off** ab/schrecke, v.; abgschreck pp.

scarecrow 1.Butzemann (der)n.; 2.Lumbemann (der)n Lumbemenner, pl.

scared gelschderich, adj.

scarf Schubbe (die)n.

scarlet fever 1.Schallach (es)n.; 2.Schallachfiewer (es)n.; **rash** Schallachfrissel (es)n.; **runner** 1.Feierbohn (die) n Feierbohne, pl.; 2.Feierbuhn (die)n Feierbuhne, pl.; **sage** Saldaadeschtreiss (die)n., pl.; **sumac** Essichhols (es)n.; **tanager** 1.Blutfink (der)n.; 2.Blutvoggel (der) n.; 3.Flicker (es)n.; Flicker, pl.; **thorn** 1.Danneschpell (die)n.; 2.Darneschpell (die)n.

scat! 1.katz!, interj.; 2.Kss!

scatter 1.ausenanner/geh, v.; ausenannergange, pp.; 2.schprettle, v.; gschpreddelt, pp.; 3.schtewwere, v.; gschtewwer pp.; 4.verschittle, v verschiddelt, pp.; 5.verschtewwere, v.; verschtewwert, pp.; 6.zoddele, v.; gezoddelt, pp.; **about** 1.rum/schtiere, v.; rumgschtiert, pp.; 2.rum/schtraae, v.; rumgschtraet, pp.; 3.rum/zoddle, v.; rumgezoddelt, pp.; **by scratching** verschaere, v.; verschaert, pp.; **grass in a swath** verschmeisse, v.; verschmisse, pp.

scatterbrained 1.gedankelos, adj.; 2.Schussel (der)n.

scattered verschtiwwert, adj.

scatteringly 1.blatzweis, adj.; 2.bletzweis, adj.

scavanger's team and wagon Luderfuhr (die)n.

scavenger 1.Feger (der)n.; 2.Ludermann (der)n.; 3.Schinn (der)n.; 4.Schinnerhannes (der)n.

Ss

scent | **screwing**

scent 1.Schmack (der)n.; 2.widdere, v.; gewiddert, pp.; **(of horses)** wittere, v.; gewittert, pp.

schell Schaal (die)n.; Schaale, pl.

scholar 1.Gelehrter (der)n.; 2.Schuler (der)n.; Schieler, pl.

school Schul (die)n.; **bench** Schulhausbank (die)n.; **book** Schulbuch (es)n.; Schulbicher, pl.; **boy** Schulbu (der) n.; Schulbuwe, pl.; **day** Schuldaag (der)n.; Schuldaage, pl.; **director** Schulkorreggder (der)n.; **girl** Schulmaedel (es)n.; Schulmaed, pl.; **has been called to order** aa, adv. (die Schul is --); **superintendent** Schulbaas (der)n.; **tax** Schultax (der)n.

schoolhouse Schulhaus (es)n.; Schulheiser, pl.

schooling 1.Lanning (die)n.; 2.Schuling (die)n.

schoolmaster 1.Schulmann (die)n.; 2.Tieschern (die)n.

schoolmate Schulkummeraad (der)n.; Schulkummeraade, pl.

schoolroom Schulschtubb (die)n.; Schulschtubbe, pl.

schoolyard Schulhof (der)n.; Schulheef, pl.

schoolyear Schulyaahr (es)n.; Schulyaahre, pl.

Schwenckfelder Schwenckfelder (der)n. - member of the religious sect founded by Kaspar Schwenckfeld

science 1.Kunscht (die)n.; 2.Wissenschaft (die)n.

scion Zweig (die)n.; Zweige, pl.

scissors Scher (die)n.; Schere, pl.

scold 1.aa/schnarre, v.; aagschnatt, pp.; 2.ab/hechle, v.; abghechelt, pp.; 3.ab/zanke, v.; abgezankt, pp.; 4.aus/schelde, v.; ausgscholde, pp.; 5.blose, v.; geblose, pp.; 6.gnoddere, v.; gegnoddert, pp.; 7.gnuddere, v.; gegnuddert, pp.; 8.knarre, v.; geknarrt, pp.; 9.knewwle, v.; geknewwelt, pp.; 10.maule, v.; gemault, pp.; 11.schelde, v.; gscholde, pp.; 12.verschelde, v.; verscholde, pp.; 13.verschimfe, v.; verschimft, pp.; 14.zanke, v.; gezankt, pp.; 15.Zenkrin (die)n.; **after (someone)** no(och)maule, v.; no(och)gemault, pp.; **in an undertone** brummle, v.; gebrumelt, pp.; **in return** zerick/schelte, v.; zerickgscholte, pp.

scolding 1.Gezank (es)n.; 2.Gschelt (es)n.; 3.zankich, adj.; 4.Zanking (die)n.; **person** Zeck (die)n.; Zecke, pl.

scoop 1.Schipp (die)n.; 2.Wurfschaufel (die)n.; **out** aus/leffle, v.; ausgeleffelt, pp.; **shovel** 1.Schaufel (die)n.; 2.Warfschaufel (die)n.

scorch 1.aa/brenne, v.; aagebrennt, pp.; 2.brenne, v.; gebrennt, pp.; 3.versenke, v.; versenkt, pp.; **(by the sun)** brode, v.; gebrode, pp.

score 1.hie/rechle, v.; hiegrechelt, 2.Zech (die)n.

scorn Schpott (der)n.

Scorpio (8th sign of the zodiac) Skorpion (der)n.

scoundrel 1.Galgedieb (der)n.; 2.Ketzer (der)n.; Ketzer, pl.; 3.Lump (der)n.

scour scheiere, v.; gscheiert, pp.

scourage geeschle, v.; gegeeschelt, pp.

scout Schpion (der)n.

scramble reisse (sich --) v.; gerisse, pp.

scrap Brocke (der)n.

scrape 1.Glemm (die)n.; 2.Klemm (die)n.; 3.schaawe, v.; gschaabt, pp.; 4.schaere, v.; gschaert, pp.; 5.schaerre, v.; gschaerrt, pp.; 6.schaerre, v.;

gschaerrt, pp.; **into** nei/gratze, v.; neigegratzt, pp.; **off** ab/schaawe, v.; abgschaabt, pp.; **with a "Kitsch"** kitsche, v.; gekitscht, pp.

scraper (for removing ashes) Kitsch (die)n.; Kitsche, pl.; **(used for scraping out a kneeding trough)** Backmulgratzer (der)n.; Backmulgratzer, pl.

scraping Gschaerr (es)n.

scrapings of the kneading trough Sauerdeeg (der)n.

scrapple Pannhaas (der)n.

scraps of leather Leimledder (es)n.

scratch 1.Gratz (der)n.; 2.gratze, v.; gegratzt, pp.; 3.Gritz (der)n.; 4.kratze, v.; gekratzt, pp.; 5.schaere, v.; gschaert, pp.; 6.schaerre, v.; gschaerrt, pp.; 7.scharre, v.; gschatt, pp.; 8.vergratze, v.; vergratzt, pp.; **around** 1.rum/schaere, v.; rumgschaert, pp.; 2.rum/scharre, v.; rumgschatt, pp.; **away** 1.weck/gratze, v.; weckgegratzt, pp.; 2.weck/scharre, v.; weckgschatt, pp.; **back** zerick/schaerre, v.; zerickgschaerrt, pp.; **in** eischaerre, v.; eigschaerrt, pp.; **off or away** ab/schaere, v.; abgschaerrt, pp.; **open** 1.uff/gratze, v.; uffgegratzt, pp.; 2.uff/schaerre, v.; uffgschaerrt, pp.; **or scrape off** ab/gratze, v.; abgegratzt, pp.; **out** 1.aus/gratze, v.; ausgegratzt, pp.; 2.naus/schaere, v.; nausgschaert, pp.; 3.raus/gratze, v.; rausgegratzt, pp.; 4.raus/scharre, v.; rausgschatt, pp.; **over** iwwergratze, v.; iwwergegratzt, pp.; **together** 1.zamme/gratze, v.; zammegegratzt, pp.; 2.zamme/schaerre, v.; zammegschaerrt, pp.

scratched 1.vergratzt, adj.; 2.verschunne, adj.

scratcher (for gardening) Heegel (der)n.; Heegel, pl.

scratching 1.Gegratz (es)n.; 2.Gschaerr (es)n.

scrawl or scribble over aus/gritzle, v.; ausgegritzelt, pp.

scrawly gritzlich, adj.

scream 1.Grisch (der)n.; 2.kreische, v.; gekrische, pp.; 3.Krisch (der)n.; 4.Mardgrisch (der)n.; **across** niwwer/greische, v.; niwwergegrische, pp.; **at** aa/greische, v.; aagegrische, pp.; **oneself hoarse** ab/greische; abgegrischt, pp. (sich der Hals --)

screaming Gschrei (es)n.

screech owl Nachteil (die)n.; Nachteile, pl.

screen 1.sibbe, v.; gsibbt, pp.; 2.Sieb (die)n.; Siewe(r), pl.; **(for window)** 1.Mickefenschder (es)n.; 2.Muckefenschder (es)n.; **door** 1.Mickedeer(e) (die) n.; 2.Mickedier (die)n.; 3.Muckedeer (die)n.; 4.Muckedier (die)n.; 5.Siebdeer (die) n.

screw 1.Schraub (die)n.; Schrauwe, pl.; 2.schrauwe, v.; gschraubt, pp.; 3.Winn (die)n.; Winne, pl.; **fast** aa/schrauwe, v.; aagschraubt, pp.; **jack** 1.Waggewinn (die)n.; 2.Winn (die)n.; Winne, pl.; **of a vice** Schtockschraub (die)n.; **open** uff/drehe, v.; ufgedreht, pp.; **out** raus/schrauwe, v.; rausgschraubt, pp.; **tap** Schneideise (es)n.; **thread** G(e)winn (die)n.; **up** nuff/schrauwe, v.; nuffgschraubt, pp.

screwdriver 1.Schrauwedreher (der)n.; 2.Schrauwezieher (der)n.

screwing Gschraub (es)n.

362

Ss

scrible   seedling

scribble 1.gritzle, v.; gegritzel, pp.; 2.kritzle, v.; gekritzelt, pp.; **a copy of** ab/gritzle, v.; abgegritzelt, pp.

scribble down hie/gritzle, v.; hiegegritzelt, pp.; **in** nei/gritzle, v.; neigegritzelt, pp.; **on** aa/gritzle, v.; aagegritzelt, pp.

scribbler 1.Gritzler (der)n.; 2.Kritzler (der)n.

scribbling 1.Gegritzel (es)n.; 2.Grickselfixel (es)n.; 3.Gritzelfixel (es)n.; 4.Hoke (der)n.; Hoke, pl.; 5.Kritzelfixel (es)n.

scribblingly gritzlich, adj.

scribe Schreiwer (der)n.; Schreiwer, pl.

scrimp geize, v.; gegeizt, pp.

scriptual schriftmeesich, adj.

scripture 1.Gotteswatt (es)n.; 2.Schrift (die)n.; **text** 1.Biwelschpruch (der)n.; 2.Schpruch (der)n.; Schprich, pl.

scritch-scratch (imitating the sound of a pen in rapid writing) 1.kriksel dei krix!; 2.kriksel fixel!

scrofulous flussich, adj.

scrotum 1.Beidel (der)n.; 2.Seckel (der)n.

scrub Grubbs (der)n.; **(a floor)** uff/wesche, v.; uffgewesche, pp.; **oak** Grundeeche (die)n.; **off** ab/fege, v.; abgfegt, pp.; **out** naus/fege, v.; nausgfegt, pp.

scrubbing Reiwing (die)n.; **brush** Reibbascht (die)n.

scruff of the neck Grips (der)n.

scrutinize 1.begucke, v.; beguckt, pp.; 2.eiblicke, v.; eigeblickt, pp.

scum 1.Schaam (der)n.; 2.Schaum (der)n.

scurf Schuppe (die)n.

scurvy Scharbock (der)n.

scutch 1.Flaxschwing (die)n.; 2.schwinge, v.; gschwunge, pp.; 3.Schwingmiehl (die)n.; 4.Schwingraad (es)n.

scythe 1.Graassens (die)n.; 2.Sens (die)n.; Sense, pl.; **(for cutting briers)** Heckesens (die)n.; **anvil** Dengelschtock (der)n.; Dengelschteck, pl.

sea See (der)n.**; onion** Seezwiwwel (die)n.

seal 1.Seehund (der)n.; 2.Siegel (es)n.; 3.Siggel (es)n.; 4.siggele, v.; gsiggelt, pp.

sealing wax Siggelwachs (der)n.

seam 1.Noht (die)n.; Neht, pl.; 2.Saam (der); Saame, pl.

seamstress 1.Frackmachern (die)n.; 2.Naehern (die)n.; 3.Schneidern (die)n.

search around rum/suche, v.; rumgsucht, pp.; **for** 1.suche, v.; gsucht, pp.; 2.uff/suche, v.; uffgsucht, pp.; **in every**

part darich/schtewwere, v.; darichgschtewwert, pp.; **thoroughly** aus/suche, v.; ausgsucht, pp.; **through** darich/suche, v.; darichgsucht, pp.

searching or rummaging Gsuch (es)n.

seashell Seeschaal (die)n.

seasick seegrank, adj.

seasickness Seegranket (die)n.

season 1.Yaahreszeit (die)n.; 2.Yaahrgang (der)n.; 3.Yaahrszeit (die)n.; 4.Yohr(e)zeit (die)n.; 5.yohrgang (der)n.; **for sowing winter cereals** Soot (die)n.

seasonable zeidich, adj.

seat 1.hocke, v.; ghockt, pp.; 2.hocke, v.; ghockt, pp.; 3.Sitz (der)n.; Sitze, pl.; **(oneself)** 1.hie/hocke, v.; hieghockt, pp. ; 2.hocke (sich --)v.; ghockt, pp.; 3.setze (sich --), v.; gsetzt, pp.; **of pants or trousers** 1.Hosseaarsch (der)n.; 2.Hossesitz (der)n.

seaweed Seegraas (es)n.

secede 1.devungeh, v.; 2.zerick/ziehe, v.; zerickgezoge, pp.

Second Christmas, Dec. 26 Zwedde Grischtdaag (der)n.

second zwett, adj.; **(measure of time)** Segund (die)n.; Segunde, pl.; **crop** 1.Aamet (es)n.; 2.Ohmet (es)n.; 3.Ohmet (es)n.; 4.Omet (es)n.; 5.Uhmet (es)n.; **hand (of a clock)** 1.Segundezeeche (es)n.; 2.Segundezoier (es)n.; **quality flour** Middelmehl (es)n.; **story** (in a dwelling) Schpeicher (der)n.; **time** zwett Mol (es)n.

secondly zweddens, adv.

secret 1.Geheemnis (es)n.; 2.Geheimnis (es)n.; 3.Verborge (es)n.; **rummaging** Gschnuffel (es)n.

secretary Sekritaer (der)n.

secretly 1.gheem, adv.; 2.heemlich, adv.; 3.heemlicherweis, adv.; 4.hehling(s), adv.; 5.hehlingerweis, adj.; 6.hehlingerweis, adv.;7.hinnerum, adv.

sect Sekt (die)n.

section 1.Abschnitt (der)n.; 2.Gezaerrick(s) (es)n.; 3.Landschaft (die)n.; 4.Weltdeel (es)n.

sections of (dried) **fruit** Schnutz (der)n.; **of apple** Schnitz (die)n.; Schnitz, pl.

secular weltlich, adj.; **priest** Weltbrieschder (der)n.

secure 1.sicher, adj.; 2.versichere, v.; versichert, pp.;

eatables by stealth schnause, v.; gschnaust, pp.

sedge Sauergraas (es)n.

seduce verfiehre, v.; verfiehrt, pp.

seducer Verfiehrer (der)n.

see sehne, v.; gsehne, pp.; **as far as** hie/sehne, v.; hiegsehne, pp.; **back** zerick/sehne, v.; zerickgsehnt, pp.; **down** nunner/sehne, v.; nunnergsehne, pp.; **into** nei/sehne, v.; neigsehne, pp.; **off** (to a distance) weck/sehne, v.; weckgsehne, pp.; **the point** eisehne, v.; eigsehne, pp.; **through** darich/sehne, v.; darichgsehne, pp.; **to** no(och)gucke, v.; no(och)geguckt, pp.

seed 1.Kaern (die)n.; Kaerne, pl.; 2.naus/saee, v.; nausgsaet, pp.; 3.naus/saehe, v.; nausgsaeht, pp.; 4.Saame (der)n.; 5.schiesse, v.; gschosse, pp.; 6.Some (der)n.; 7.Soot (die)n.; 8.Sume (der)n.; **(a field)** rum/schaere, v.; rumgschaert, pp.; **a stubble-field in the same crop** schtopple, v.; gschtobbelt, pp.; **ball of the potato** Grumbeereglicker (der)n.; **corn** 1.Blanswelschkaan (es)n.; 2.Saamewelschkann (es)n.; 3.Somewelschkann (es)n.; 4.Sootwelschkann (es)n.; **grain** Sootfrucht (die)n.; **potato** 1.Blansgrumbeer (die)n.; 2.Sootgrummbeer (die)n.; **rye** Sootkarn (es)n.; **wheat** Sootweeze (der)n.

seeding (of wheat and rye) naus/mache, v.; nausgemacht, pp. (Soot --)

seedling Blenselche (es)n.

Ss

seedpod — sermon

seedpod Somekopp (der)n.

seek 1.suche, v.; gsucht, pp.; 2.um/sehne (sich --)v.; umgsehne, pp.

seem 1.dinke (sich --)v.; gedinkt, pp.; 2.dinke, v.; gedinkt, pp.; 3.scheine, v.; gscheint, pp.; 4.vor/kumme, v.; vorkumme, pp.

seemingly 1.demno, adv.; 2.demnooch, adv.; 3.scheinbaar, adj.; 4.scheinbaar, adv.; **dead** scheidoot, adj.

seep away 1.versoddere, v.; versoddert, pp.; 2.versuddere, v.; versuddert, pp.; **through** darich/suddre, v.; darichgsuddert, pp.

seesaw 1.geige, v.; gegeikt, pp. (uff un ab --); 2.uff, prep., adv. (-- und ab geige)

seethe koche, v.; gekocht, pp.

seething kochich, adv.

segment of a tree trunk Klotz (der)n.

seine 1.Schleefgaarn (es)n.; 2.Schtarichelgaarn (es)n.

seize 1.aa/packe, v.; aagepackt, pp.; 2.fange, v.; gfange, pp. ergreife, v.; ergriffe, pp.; 3.greife, v.; gegriffe, pp.; 4.halt/nemme, v.; haltgnumme, pp.; 5.halt/nemme, v.; haltgnumme, pp.; 6.packe, v.; gepackt, pp.

seldom selde, adv.

select 1.abaddich, adv., adj.; 2.abbardich, adv., adj.; 3.aus/lese, v.; ausg(e)lese, pp.; 4.baddich, adv.; 5.raus/lese, v.; rausglese, pp.; 6.raus/suche, v.; rausgsucht, pp.; 7.wehle, v.; gewehlt, pp.

selection Waahl (die)n.

self 1.selbscht, pron.; 2.selwer(t), pron.; **heal** 1.Brunelle (die)n.; 2.Brunellegraut (es)n.; 3.Greidliwidderbring (der)n.; 4.Greitliwidderbring (der)n.; 5.Heelgraut (es) n.; 6.Kreidliwidderbring (der)n. 7.Prunellegraut (es) n.; **important** 1.grossmiedich, adj.; 2.hocheibildich, adj.; **praise** Eegelob (der)n.; **willed** eegemechtich, adj.; **willed person** Dickkopp (der)n.

selfish eegesinni(s)ch, adj.

sell verkaafe, v.; verkaaft, pp.; **at auction** 1.verschteege, v.; verschteekt, pp.; 2.verschteeye, v.; verschteegt, pp.; **by forced sale** aus/verkaafe, v.; ausverkaaft, pp.; **by persuasion** aa/henke, v.; aaghenkt; aaghonke, pp.; **off** verhandle, v.; verhandelt, pp.; **out** aus/verkaafe, v.; ausverkaaft, pp.; **them** aawaerre, v.; aawaerre, pp.

seller 1.Verkaafer (der)n.; 2.Verkeefer (der)n.

selvedge 1.Salwen (die)n.; 2.Selwen (die)n.

semaphore Erdschpigge (der)n.

semi annual halbyaehrich, adj.; **centennial** fuffzichyaehrich, adj.; **circle** Halbkreis (der)n.

seminary Seminaar (es)n.

senate Senaat (der)n.

senator Senaador (der)n.

send schicke, v.; gschickt, pp.; **about one's business** ab/faddiche, v.; abgfaddicht, pp.; **after** no(och)schicke, v.; no(och)gschickt, pp.; **along with** mit/schicke, v.; mitgschickt, pp.; **around** rum/schicke, v.; rumgschickt, pp.; **away** 1.fatt/schicke, v.;

fattgschickt, pp.; 2.weck/schicke, v.; weckgschickt, pp.; **back** zerick/schicke, v.; zerickgschickt, pp.; **forth shoots or sprouts** 1.aus/schlagge, v.; ausgschlagge, pp.; 2.aus/waxe, v.; ausgewaxe, pp.; **hither** 1.haer/shicke, v.; haergschickt, pp.; 2.her/schicke, v.; hergschickt, pp.; **home** heemschicke, v.; heemgschickt, pp.; **in** 1.eischicke, v.; eigschickt, pp.; 2.nei/schicke, v.; neigschickt, pp.; **on before** vannenaus/schicke, v.; vannenausgschickt, pp.; **out** 1.aus/schicke, v.; ausgschickt, pp.; 2.naus/schicke, v.; nausgschickt, pp.; **out shoots** aus/schiesse, v.; ausgschosse, pp.; **over** 1.niwwer/schicke, v.; niwwergschickt, pp.; 2.riwwer/schicke, v.; riwwergschickt, pp.; **regards** griesse, v.; gegriesst, pl.; **regards to** 1.begegne, v.; begegnet, pp.; 2.bewillkumme, v.; bewillkummt, pp.; **to a place** 1.ammenent/schicke, v.; 2.ammenot/schicke, v.; 3.anne/schicke, v. annegschickt, pp.; 4.hie/schicke, v.; hiegschickt, pp.; **up** ruff/schicke, v.; ruffgschickt, pp.; **up ahead** vor/schicke, v.; vorgschickt, pp.

seneca snakeroot 1.Gleenischlangewatzell (die)n.; 2.Klapperschlangewatzel (die)n.

sensation of crawling insects Gegrawwel (es)n.

sense Sinn (der)n.; **of hearing** Keer (es)n.

senseless 1.ochsich, adj.; 2.ochsich, adj.; 3.unsinnich, adj.; **person** Unverschtand (der)n.

sensible 1.verdinfdich, adj.; 2.verschtendich, adj.; 3. verschtennich, adj.; **of** 1.gschpiere, v.; gschpiert, pp.; 2. schpiere, v.;schpiert,pp.

sensual living Luschtlewe (es)n.

sentence 1.Urteil (es)n.; 2.urteile, v.; geurteilt, pp.

sentinel Wechder (der)n.;Wechder,pl.

separable prefix of verbs (adding the idea of pellmell, crowding, precipitately, abruptly, voraciously) 1.zammenunner, adv.; 2.zammenei, adv.

separate 1.ab/deele, v.; abgedeelt, pp.; 2.ab/reisse, v.; abgerisse, pp.; 3.ausenanner/geh, v.; ausenannergange, pp.; 4.ausenanner/mache, v.; ausenannergemacht, pp.; 5.ausenanner, adj.; 6.drenne, v.; gedrennt, pp.; 7. scheede, v.; gscheede, pp.; 8.scheide, adj.; 9.scheide, v.; gscheide, pp.; 10.trenne, v.; detrennt, pp.; 11. vunenanner/geh, v.; vunenannergange, pp.; 12.vunenanner, adv.; **cream from milk** ab/raahme, v.; abgeraahmt, pp.; **from** verdeele, v.; verdeelt, pp.; **into crumbs** krimmle (sich --)v.; gekrimmelt, pp.; **into sorts** aus/lese, v.; ausg(e)lese, pp.

separation 1.Drennung (die)n.; 2.Trennung (die)n.

September September (der)n.

seranade a newly married couple belle, v.; gebellt, pp.

serious 1.aernschthaft, adj.; 2.anscht, adj.; 3.schlimm, adj.; 4.schlimm, adj.

seriously aernschtlich, adv.

seriousness Ernscht (der)n.

sermon 1.Breddich (die)n.; Breddiche, pl.; 2.Preddich (die)n.; 3.Aernbreddich (die)n. (harvest thanksgiving)

Ss

serum | shaft

serum blutwasser, adj.

servant Bedienter (der)n.; **girl** 1.Dinschtmeedel (es)n.; 2.Maad (die)n.; Maade, pl.; 3.Serwenmaedechen (die)n.

serve 1.bediene, v.; bedient, pp.; 2.diene, v.; gedient, pp.; 3.uff/draage, v.; uffgedraage, pp.; **a quit notice** 1.aus/biede, v.; ausgebodde, pp.; 2.uff/kinne, v.; **one's apprenticeship** Zeit (die)n. (sei -- schteh); **one's time** aus/diene, v.; ausgedient, pp.; **or handle roughly** salwiere, v.; gsalwiert, pp.; **subsequently** no(och)schteh, v.; no(och)gschtanne, pp.

served (of sows) rolle, v.; gerollt, pp.

service Bedienung (die)n.; **for children** Kinnerfescht (es)n.

serviceable 1.brauchbaar, adj.;2.dinschdlich, adj.; 3.nitzlich, adj.

serviette 1.Bauchduch (es)n.; Bauchdicher, pl.; 2.Dellerduch (es) n.; Dellerdicher, pl.; 3.Rachebutzer (der)n.; Rachebutzer, pl.

set 1.S(ch)ippschaft (die)n.; 2.setze, v.; gsetzt, pp.; 3.Volk (es)n.; **(dogs) on** no(och)hetze, v.; no(och)ghetzt, pp.; **(machines) so as to mow lower** nidder/schtelle, v.; niddergschtellt, pp.; **(of the sun)** unner/geh, v.; unnergange, pp.; **a date for** b(e)schtimme, v.; b(e)schtimmt, pp.; **a gore in a garment** schpeidele, v.; gschpeidelt, pp.; **apart** ausenanner/setze, v.; ausenannergsetzt, pp.; **away** 1.weck/schtelle, v.; weckgschtellt, pp.; 2.weck/setze, v.; weckgsetzt, pp.; **beside each other** 1.newenanner/setze, v.; newenannergsetzt, pp.; 2.newenannerschtelle, adv.; **down** 1.hie/setze, v.; hiegsetzt, pp.; 2.nunner/setze, v.; nunnergsetzt, pp.; 3.runner/schtelle, v.; runnergschtellt, pp.; **fire to** aa/schtecke, v.; aagschteckt, pp.; **free** 1.frei/gewwe, v.; freigewwe, pp.; 2.frei/mache, v.; freigemacht, pp.; 3.frei/schpreche, v.; freischproche, v.; 4.los/losse, v.; losgelosst, pp.; **in** 1.nei/setze, v.; neigsetzt, pp.; 2.rei/schtelle, v.; reigschtellt, pp.; **in order** zerechtschtelle, v. zerechtgschtellt, pp.; **of artifical teeth** 1.Gebiss (es)n.; Gebisser, pl.; 2.Reff (es)n.; Reffer, pl.; **on fire** aa/fei(e)re, v.; aagfeirt, pp.; **or place here** haer/schtelle, v.; haergschtellt, pp.; **or put ahead** vorduh, v.; vorgeduh, pp.; **or put down** hie/schtelle, v.; hieschtellt, pp.; **or put in a place** nei/schtelle, v.; neigschtellt, pp.; **out** 1.naus/schtelle, v.; nausgschtellt, pp.; 2.naus/setze, v.; nausgsetzt, pp.; **out**(plants) 1.aus/schtecke, v.; ausgschteckt, pp.; 2.raus/schtelle, v.; rausgschtellt, pp.; 3.raus/setze, v.; rausgsetzt, pp.; **over** 1.iwwer/setze, v.; iwwergsetzt, pp.; 2.niwwer/schtelle, v.; niwwergschtellt, pp.; 3.niwwer/setze, v.; niwwergsetzt, pp.; 4.riwwer/schtelle, v.; riwwergschtellt, pp.; 5.riwwer/setze, v.; riwwergsetzt, pp.; **stakes** ab/schtickle, v.; abgschtickelt, pp.; **the table** rischde, v.; g(e)rischt, pp.; **to rise** aa/setze, v.; aagsetzt, pp.; **under** unner/setze, v.; unnergsetzt, pp.; **up** 1.ruff/schtelle, v.; ruffgschtellt, pp.; 2.schtelle, v.; gschtellt, pp.; 3.uff/schteh, v.; uffgschtanne, pp.; 4.uff/setze, v.; uffgsetzt, pp.; **up in shocks** (grain)

schacke, v.; gschackt, pp.; **up the drinks** aa/setze, v.; aagsetzt, pp.; **with a fringe** aa/fransle, v.; aagfranselt, pp.

setting Unnergang (der)n.; **(of eggs)** Setzet (die)n.; **of the moon** Moon(d)unnergang (der)n.

settle 1.aus/mache, v.; ausgemacht, pp.; 2.schlichde, v.; gschlicht, pp.; 3.schlichte, v.; gschlicht, pp.; 4.senke, v.; gsenkt, pp.; **a difference** 1.aus/fechde, v.; ausgfochde, pp.; 2.bei/lege, v.; beigelegt, pp.; **a matter** (offhand) Wese(s) (es)n. (net viel -- mache); **down in a certain place**; hie/blanse (sich --)v.; hiegeblanst; **one's hash** (in an argument) balsamiere, v.; gebalsamiert, pp. **settled** gsetzt, adj.

settlement Richtichkeet (die)n.

seven siwwe, adj,; pron.; **spot in cards** siwweter (en), adj.

sevenfold siwwefach, adj.

seventeen siwwezeh, adj.; pron.

seventeenth siwwezeht, adj.

seventh siwwet, adj.

seventieth siwwezichscht, adj.

seventy siwwezich, adj.; pron.

sever 1. drenne, v.; gedrennt, pp.; 2.trenne, v.; detrennt, pp.

several 1.ettlich, adj.; 2.wisch, adj. (en --); **days** daageweis, adv.; **years** yaahreweis, adv.; **years in succession** yohrelang, adj.

severe 1.schtreng, adj.; 2.schtrikt, adj.

severely 1.gedichdich, adv.; 2.gedicht, adj.; 3.geheerich, adv.; 4.grindlich, adv.; 5.kindlich, adv.; 6.salwiers, adv.

sew naehe, v.; genaeht, pp.; **fast** nodle, v.; genodelt, pp.; **on** aa/naehe, v.; aagenaeht, pp.; **over again** iwwer/ nehe, v.; iwweregenaeht, pp.; **together** 1.zamme/naehe, v.; zammegenaeht, pp.; 2.zamme/schteppe, v.; zammegschteppt, pp.; **up** zunaehe, v.; zugenaeht, pp.; **up in** einaehe, v.; eigenaeht, pp.

sewed articles Genaeh (es)n.

sewing 1.Genaeh (es)n.; 2.Naehes (es)n.; **basket** Naehkaerwel (es)n.; **machine** Naehmaschien (die)n.; Naehmaschiene, pl.; **silk** Naehseide (der)n.; **table** Nae(h)disch (der)n.

sex Geschlecht (es)n.

sexton Kischder (der)n.

sh! sch!, interj.

shack Wansenescht (es)n.

shackle (to tie with chains) Kett (die)n.; Kedde, pl. (mit Kedde binne)

shade 1.Schadde (der)n.; 2.Schatte (der)n.; **tree** 1. Schaddebaam (der)n.; Schaddebeem, pl.; 2.Schattebaam (der)n.

shadow 1.Schadde (der)n.; 2.Schatte (der)n.; **picture** 1. Schaddebild (es)n.; 2.Schattebild (es)n.

shady 1.halbdunkel, adj.; 2.schaddich, adj.; 3.schattich, adj.; **side** 1.Schaddeseit (die)n.; 2.Schatteseit (die)n.

shaft Schaft (der)n.; Schafde, pl.; **(of a horse-drawn carriage)** Lann (die)n.; Lanne, pl.

Ss

shaggy — shelf

shaggy zoddlich, adj.

shake 1.riddle, v.; geriddelt, pp.; 2.schiddle, v.; gschiddelt, pp.; 3.schoddre, v.; gschoddert, pp.; 4.schottere, v.; gschottert, pp.; 5.wabble, v.; gewabbelt, pp.; 6.wibble, v.; gewibbelt, pp.; **around** rum/schiddle, v.; rumgschiddelt, pp.; **down** runner/schiddle, v. runnergschiddle, pp.; **from cold** schnaddre, v.; gschnaddert, pp.; **hands** 1.Batsch (die)n. (die -- gewwe); 2.Hand (die)n. (ebber -- gewwe); 3.schiddle, v.; schiddelt, pp. (Hend --); **loose** loddle, v.; geloddelt, pp.; **off** 1.ab/schiddle, v.; abgschiddelt, pp.; 2.ab/schlenkere, v.; abgschlenkert, pp.; 3.ab/schliddle, v.; abgschiddelt, pp.; **out** 1.ab/schliddle, v.; abgschiddelt, pp.; 2.aus/schiddle, v.; ausgschiddelt, pp.; 3.naus/schiddle, v.; nausgschiddelt, pp.; 4.raus/schittle, v.; rausgschittelt, pp.; 5.raus/schliddle, v.; rausgschiddelt, pp.; **out** (a rug) ab/schiddle, v.; abgschiddelt, pp.; **up** 1.uff/riddle, v.; uffgeriddelt, pp.; 2.uff/schiddle, v.; uffgschiddelt, pp.; **vigorously** schlenkere, v.; gschlenkert, pp.

shaker of a threshing machine Schiddler (der)n.

shaking Gschittel (es)n.

shaky 1.lodd(e)rich, adj.; 2.lodder, adj.; 3.wabblich, adj.; 4.wacklich, adj.; 5.wanklich, adj.

shale 1.Schifferschtee (der)n.; 2.Schiwwerschtee (der)n.; **(formation)** Schiwwer (der)n.; Schiwwere, pl.

shall waerre, v.; warre; waerre, pp.

shallow 1.eefeldich, adj.; 2.flach, adj.; 3.net dief, adj.; **ditch across a road** 1.Abloos (der)n.; 2.Abweiser (der)n.; **pool** (in woods or in low ground) Wasserpann (die)n.

shaly 1.schifferich, adj.; 2.schifferschteenich, adj.; 3. schiwwer-schteenich, adj.; 4.schiwwerich, adj.; 5. schiwwerschteenich, adj.

shamble 1.schlodere, v.; gschlodert, pp.; 2.schlodle, v.; gschlodert, pp.; 3.schloidere, v.; gschlodert, pp.

shame 1.aus/schemme, v.; ausgschemmt, pp.; 2.Schaam (die)n.; 3.Schan(d) (die)n.; 4.verhensle, v.; verhenselt, pp.; **on you** schemme, v.; gschemmt, pp. (schemm dich)

shameful 1.schandbaar, adj.; 2.schandlich, adj.; 3.schendlich, adj.; 4.schimb(er)lich, adj.; 5.schimp(er)lich, adj.

shamefully schandbaarlich, adj.

shameless schandlos(ich), adj.

shampoo Koppwesching (die)n.

shanty Heisli (es)n.; Heislin, pl.

shape 1.bilde, v.; gebild(e)t, pp.; 2.bschaffe, v.; bschaffe, pp.; 3.Puschduur (die)n.

shaped gformt, adj.; **notes** Buchweezenode (die)n., pl.

shapely gepuschdurt, adj. (gut --)

share 1.Aadeel (es)n.; 2.ab/deele, v.; abgedeelt, pp.; 3.Batt (der)n.; 4.Blugschaar (es)n.; Blugschaare, pl.; 5.Deel (es)n., pl.; 6.deele, v.; gedeelt, pp.; 7.Deeler (die)n.; 8.mit/deele, v.; mitgedeelt, pp.; 9.Paert (die)

n.; 10.Schier (es)n.; 11.verdeele, v.; verdeelt, pp.

sharing dalehafdich, adj.

shark 1.Bedrieger (der)n.; 2.Hoifisch (der)n.

sharp 1.schaef, adj.; 2.scharef, adj.; 3.scharf, adj.; **(to the taste)** beissich, adj.; **eyed** scharefsichdich, adj.; **pains** Reisses (es)n.; **rejoiner** Hack (der)n.

sharpen 1.aa/schtaahle, v.; aagschtaahlt, pp.; 2.schaerfe, v.; gschaerft, pp.; 3.scharefe, v.; gschareft, pp.; 4.schleife, v.; gschliffe, pp.; 5.schpitze, v.; gschpitzt, pp.; **by hammering out** dengle, v.; gedengelt, pp.

shave 1.balwiere (sich --)v.; (ge)balwiert, pp.; 2.balwiere, v.; gebalwiert, pp.; 3.rasiere (sich --)v.; gerasiert, pp.; **off** ab/balwiere, v.; abgebalwiert, pp.

shaver 1.Schisser (der)n.; Schisser, pl.; 2.Zickel (es)n.

shaving Howwelschpaa (der)n.; Howwelschpae, pl.; **brush** Balwierpensil (der)n.; **soap** Balwierseef (die)n.

shawl Koppduch (es)n.; Koppdicher, pl.

she sie, pron.; **is** sies = sie es; sie is; **wears the breeches** Hosse (die)n., pl. (sie hot die -- aa)

sheaf 1.Bundel (der)n.; Bindel, pl.; 2.Garb (die)n.; Garwe, pl.; 3.Schaep (der)n.; **covering of a shock of grain** Kapp (die)n.; Kappe, pl.

shear 1.ab/schneide, v.; abgschnidde, pp.; 2.schare, v.; gschart, pp.; 3.schere, v.; gschore, pp.; **off** 1. ab/schere, v.; abgschore, pp.; 2.weck/schere, v.; weckgschore, pp.

shears Scheer (die)n.

sheath Scheed (die)n.; **of a hog** (hung up for the birds in winter) Seinawwel (der)n.; **of a horse** Schlauch (der)n.

sheaves of grain for one threshing by machine Bett (es) n.; Bedder, pl.

shed Schopp (der)n.; Schepp, pl.; **barn** 1.Schoppscheier (die)n.; 2.Schottscheier (die)n.; Schottschiere, pl.;3.Schuss-scheier (die)n.; **blood** Blut (es)n. (-- vergiesse); **leaves** laawe (sich --)v.; gelaabt, pp.; **the coat** 1.ab/heere (sich --)v.; abgheert, pp.; 2.abhoore (sich --)v.; abgehoort, pp.; 3.haere (sich --)v.; ghaert, pp.; 4.heere (sich --)v.; gheert, pp.; **the milk teeth** ab/zaahne, v.; abgzaahnt, pp.

sheep Schof (es)n.; Schof, pl.; **dog** Schofhund (der)n.; **excrement** 1.Schofgnoddel (der)n.; 2.Schofknoddel (der)n.; **manure** Schofmischt (der)n.; **shears** Schofscher (die)n.

sheep's nose Schofnaas (die)n.; **skin** 1.Schofbelz (die)n.; 2.Schofhaut (die)n.; 3.Wollfell (es)n.

sheepberry 1.Schofbeer (die)n.; 2.Schofgnoddelbeer (die) n.; 3.Schofkasch (die)n.

sheepfold Schofschtall (der)n.

sheepish 1.schofisch, adj.; 2.verdutzt, adj.

sheer 1.lauder, adj.; 2.lauter, adj.; **down** yaehlings, adv.

sheet iron Rohrblech (es)n.; **of paper** Boge (der)n.

shelf 1.Laade (der)n.; Laade, pl.; 2.Schelf (es)n.; Schelfer, pl.; 3.Sims (der)n.; **(hanging type)** Henklaade (der)n.; Henklaade, pl.; **on kitchen stove** Offelaade (der)n.; Offelaade, pl.

Ss

| shell | short |

shell 1.ab/scheele, v.; abgscheelt, pp.; 2.aus/schaale, v.; ausgschaalt, pp.; 3.aus/scheele, v.; ausgscheelt, pp.; 4.Muschel (der)n.; 5.scheele, v.; gscheelt, pp.; 6.Schef(die)n.; Schefe, pl.; 7.Schot (die)n.; **(a nut)** aus/globbe, v.; ausgeglobbt, pp.; **(beans or peas)** blicke, v.; geblickt, pp.; **(corn)** aus/mache, v.; ausgemacht, pp.; **(on single tree)** Schaal (die)n.; Schaale, pl.; **(peas or beans)** aus/picke, v.; ausgepickt, pp.; **bean** Blickbohn (die)n.

shellbarks Hickerniss (die)n., pl.

shelly schaalich, adj.

shelter 1.Obdach (es)n.; 2.Obdach (es)n.; 3.Schutz (der)n.; 4.schutze, v.; schutzt, pp.

shepherd 1.Haert (der)n.; 2.Schaefer (der)n.; Schaefer, pl.; 3.Schofheider (der)n.

shepherd's purse 1.Bockseckel (es)n.; 2.Dodder (der)n.; 3.Schofseckel (der)n.; **purse (also false flax from the similarity of the two plants)** Deschelgraut (es)n.

sherd Schaerb (die)n.; Schaerwe, pl.

sheriff Schrief (der)n.

sheriff's return Retour (es)n.

shield 1.raus/schtreiche, v.; rausgschtriche, pp.; 2.Schild (es)n.

shift blame to another ab/leegele, v.; abgeleegelt, pp.

shiftless helflos, adj.; **person** 1.Lappaarsch (der)n.; 2.Lapphund (der)n.; 3.Lodel (der)n.

shilling Schilling (der)n.

shimmer tremulously zwitzere, v.; gezwitzert, pp.

shimmering schimmerich, adj.; **tremulously** 1.zwiterich, adj.; 2.zwitscherich, adj.

shinbone Schinnbee (es)n.

shine 1.flinke, v.; gflinkt, pp.; 2.glense, v.; geglenst, pp.; 3.scheine, v.; gscheint, pp.; 4.schimmere, v.; gschimmert, pp.; **in** rei/scheine, v.; reigscheint, pp.; **out** raus/scheine, v.; rausgscheint, pp.; **through** 1.darich/leichde, v.; darichgeleicht, pp.; 2.darich/scheine, v.; darichgscheint, pp.

shingle 1.Schindel (die)n.; Schindle, pl.; 2.Schindel (die)n.; Schindle, pl. (mit Schindle decke); 3.schindel, v.; gschindelt, pp.; 4.schindle, v.; gschindelt, pp.; **maker** Schindelmacher (der)n.; Schindelmacher, pl.; **nail** Schindelnaggel (der)n.; **roof** Schindeldach (es)n.; Schindeldecher, pl.

shingler Schindeldecker (der)n.; Schindeldecker, pl.

shining glensend, adj.

ship Schiff (es)n.; Schiffer, pl.

shipwreck Schiffbruch (der)n.

shirk ab/schpiele, v.; abgschpielt, pp.

shirker (man who goes to town and neglects his farm work) Yaeger (der)n.

shirt Hemm (es)n.; Hemmer, pl.; **bosom** Hemmerbussem (der)n.; **collar** Hemmergraage (der)n.; **sleeve** Hemmaermel (der)n.

shirttail Hemmerschwanz (der)n.; Hemmerschwenz, pl.

shit scheisse, v.; gschisse, pp.; **breech** Hoseschisser (der)n.; **in one's pants** verdotte (sich --)v.; verdottelt, pp.; **into** nei/scheisse, v.; neigschisse, pp.

shiver 1.Schauder (der)n.; 2.schaudere, v.; gschaudeert, pp.; 3.schiddle, v.; gschiddelt, pp.; **to pieces** 1.verschoddere, v.; verschoddert, pp.; 2.verschottere, v.; verschottert, pp.

shoat 1.Laefer (der)n.; 2.Laefersau (die)n.; **butchered in fall** 1.Fiehseiche (es)n.; 2.Friehseiche (es)n.

shock of grain Schack (der)n.

shocking 1.schauderhafdich, adj.; 2.schauderhaft, adj.

shoe 1.Schuck (der)n.; 2.Schuh (der)n.; Schuh, pl.; **(a horse)** 1.bschlagge, v.; bschlagge, pp.; 2.uff/schlagge, v.; uffgschlagge, pp. (en eise --); **blacking** Schuhbla(e)cke (der)n.; **brush** Schuhbascht (die)n.; **buckle** Schuhschnall (die)n.; **button** Schuhgnopp (der)n.; **mat** 1.Hauslumbe (der)n.; 2.Schuhbutzer (der)n.; 3.Schuhgratzer (der)n.; **peg** Pinnaggel (der)n.; **provided with a strap for pulling on it** Ohreschuh (der)n.; **sole** Schuhsohl (der)n.

shoelace 1.Schuhbendel (der)n.; 2.Schuhreime (der)n.

shoemaker 1.Schuhmacher (der)n.; Schuhmacher, pl.; 2.Schuschder (der)n.; 3.Schuster (der)n.

shoemaker's blacking Schuhdinde (der)n.; **knife** Kneip (der)n.; **last** Leescht (der)n.; **pliers** Ledderzang (die)n.; Ledderzange, pl.; **sleeking stick** 1.Schlichthols (es)n.; 2.Schlitzholz (es)n.; **stirrup or strap** Gnieriem(e) (der)n.; Genierieme, pl.; **strap or stirrup** 1.Knierem (der)n.; 2.Knierieme (der)n.; **thread** 1.Drohtgaarn (es)n.; 2.Schuhmacherdrott (der)n.; **wax** Bech (es)n.

shoo! schu!, interj.

shoofly cake Melassichriwwelkuche (der)n.; **pie** Melassichriwwelboi (der)n.

shoot 1.schiesse, v.; gschosse, pp.; 2.Schuss (der) n.; **after** no(och)schiesse, v.; no(och)gschosse, pp.; **away** druffloss/schiese, v.; drufflossgschosse, pp.; **crap** waerfle, v.; gewaerfelt, pp.; **down** 1.nidder/schiesse, v.; niddergschosse, pp.; 2.nunner/gnalle, v.; nunnergegnellt, pp.; 3.nunner/knalle, v.; nunnerknallt, pp.; 4.runner/schiesse, v.; runnergschosse, pp.; 5.um/gnalle, v.; umgegnallt, pp.; 6.um/schiesse, v.; umschosse, pp.; 7.zamme/schiesse, v.; zammegschosse, pp.; **into** nei/schiesse, v.; neigschosse, pp.; **or gush out** naus/schiesse, v.; nausgschosse, pp.; **over** niwwer/schiese, v.; niwwergschosse, pp.; **through** darich/schiesse, v.; darichgschosse, pp.; **up** 1.nuff/schiesse, v.; nuffgschosse, pp.; 2.uff/schiesse, v.; uffgschosse, pp.

shooting Gschiess (es)n.; **iron** Schiessgewehr (es)n.

shore Ufer (es)n.

short 1.butzich, adj.; 2.katz, adj.; 3.zaart, adj.; **(of breath)** schnaufe, v.; gschnauft, pp.; **address (to the relatives of the deceased at a funeral)** Vermaahning (die)n.; **coat** Wammes (der)n.; Wammes, pl.; **downpour of rain or gust of wind** Schuck (der)n.; **fat person** Gwaddi (der)n.; **haired** katzhaarich, adj.; **handled** katzschtielich, adj.; **jump** Bockschprung (der)n.;

(Continued on page 368)

Ss

short (continued)

(Continued from page 367)

legged katzbeenich, adj.; **legged dog** 1.Dachs (der)n.; 2.Dax (der)n.; **letter** Zettel (der)n.; **of breath** 1.katzo(o)demich, adj.; 2.katzodem, adj.; 3.keich(l)ich, adj.; 4.leilich, adj.; **off** masch, adj.; **row** (at one end of a field) 1.Schtimbelroi (die)n.; 2.Schtimpelroi (die)n.; **run before leaping** Aaschprung (der)n.; **stout person** Gnibbel (der)n.; Gnibbel, pl.; **sudden prayer** Katzgebet (es)n.; **tailed** katzschwenzich, adj.; **time** Schuck (der)n.; **way** 1.Schtickel (es)n.; 2.Schtickli (es)n.; **while** 1.Bissel (es)n.; 2.Bissli (es)n.; **winded** katzo(o)chd(e)mich, adj.

shorten 1.ab/katze, v.; abgekatzt, pp.; 2.katze, v.; gekatzt, pp.; 3.verkatze, v.; verkatzt, pp.

shorthand writer Schnellschreiwer (der)n.

shortly 1.katzlich, adv.; 2.zimmlich glei, adv.; **after** druff, adv. (katz --)

shortness 1.Kaerzing (die)n.; 2.Kirz (die)n.

shorts 1.Gleie (die)n.; 2.Kleie (die)n.

shortsighted dichtsichdich, adj.

shorty 1.Dachsi (der)n.; 2.Daxi (der)n. (glee --)

shot 1.Middelmehl (es)n.; 2.Schiebschtoff(t) (es)n.; 3.Schitz (der)n.; 4.Schrot (die)n.; 5.Schuss (der)n.; **away** verschosse, adj.; **fired to kill or drive out a witch** Hexeschuss (der)n.; **pouch** Schrotsack (der)n.; **to pieces** verschosse, adj.

shotgun Schrotflint (die)n.; Schrotflinde, pl.

shoulder 1.Nacke (der)n.; 2.schuldere, v.; gschuldert, pp.; 3.Schulter (die)n.; 4.schultere, v.; gschultert, pp.; **(ham)** 1.Schunkefleesch (es)n.; 2.Vedderschunkefleesch (es) n.; **(human)** 1.Axel (die)n.; Axele, pl.; 2.Schulder (die)n.; **bag** Zwa(e)richsack (es)n.; **blade** Schulderblaat (es)n.; **bone** Axelgnoche (der)n.

shout 1.Gegreisch (es)n.; 2.Geschrei (es)n.; 3.gilbse, v.; gegilbst, pp.; 4.Greische, v.; gegrische, pp.; 5.Krisch (der)n.; 6.schreie, v.; gschreit, pp.; 7.yauchze, v.; geyauchzt, pp.; 8.yautze, v.; geyautzt, pp.; 9.yohle, v.; geyohlt, pp.; 10.yubele, v.; geyubelt, pp.; 11.Yux (der) n.; 12.yuxe, v.; geyuxt, pp.; **across** niwwer/yohle, v.; niwwergeyohlt, pp.; **after** no(och)greische, v.; no(och)gegrische, pp.; **around** rum/yohle, v.; rumgeyohlt, pp.; **at** no(och)halde, v.; no(och)ghaldt, pp.; **In** nei/yohle, v.; neigeyohlt, pp.; **up** nuff/yohle, v.; nuffgeyolt, pp.

shouting Geyux (es)n.

shove 1.schiewe, v.; gschowe, pp.; 2.schtoose, v.; gschtoose, pp.; 3.Schub (der)n.; **away** weck/schiewe, v.; weckgschowe, pp.; **back** zerick/schiewe, v.; zerickgschowe, pp.

shovel 1.Grundschaufel (die)n.; Grundschaufel, pl.; 2.schaufle, v.; gschaufelt, pp.; 3.scheppe, v.; gscheppt, pp.; 4.Schipp (die)n.; **away** 1.weck/schaufle, v.; weckgschaufelt, pp.; 2.weck/scheppe, v.; weckgscheppt, pp.; **handle** Schaufelhaendel (der)n.; Schaufelhaendle, pl.; **in**

eischeppe, v.; eigscheppt, pp.; **into** nei/scheppe, v.; neigscheppt, pp.; **off** ab/scheppe, v.; abgscheppt, pp.; **or dip** (from one place to another) rum/scheppe, v.; rumgscheppt, pp.; **or dip in** rei/schebbe, v.; reigscheppt, pp.; **or dip up**; ruff/scheppe, v.; ruffgscheppt, pp.; **out** naus/scheppe, v.; nausgscheppt, pp.; **over** niwwer/scheppe, v.; niwwergscheppt, pp.; **plow** 1.Hokeblug (der)n.; 2.Schaufelblug (der)n.; Schaufelblieg, pl.; **up** uff/scheppe, v.; uffgscheppt, pp.; **up somewhere** nuff/scheppe, v.; nuffgscheppt, pp. **show** 1.aa/weis(s)e, v.; aagewisse, pp.; 2.Guckkaschde (der)n.; 3.Kuckkaschde (der)n.; 4.uff/weise, v.; uffgeweist, pp.; 5.weise, v.; gewisse, pp.; 6.weisse, v.; g(e)wisse, pp.; (another) **how to do something** vor/mache, v.; vorgemacht, pp. (ebber ebbes --) **about** rum/weise, v.; rumgewisse, pp.; **around** rum/nemme, v.; rumgnumme, pp.; **away** weck/weise, v.; weckgewisse, pp.; **off** ab/weise (sich --)v.; abgewisse, pp.; **out** naus/weise, v.; nausgwisse, pp.; **the teeth** blicke, v.; geblickt, pp. (die Zeh --); **the teeth** (in smiling or anger) 1.blecke, v.; gebleckt, pp.; 2.blecke, v.; gebleckt, pp. (die Zeh --); **the way down** nunner/weise, v.; nunnergewisse, pp.; **the way up** nuff/weise, v.; nuffgewisse, pp.

shower 1.Rege (der)n.; 2.Reg(g)eschauer (der)n.; 3.Schauer (der)n.; 4.schauere, v.; gschauert, pp.; 5.Schpritzer (der)n.; 6.Schuer (der)n.; 7.schuere, v.; gschuert, pp.; **(downpour)** Blatzrege (der)n.

showery schuerich, adj.

showing signs of decay (as a tree) ab/schtennich, v.; **the ribs** (of a lean horse) ribbich, adj.

shred Fetze (der)n.

shrew Leschdermaul (es)n.

shrewd 1.schar(e)f, adj.; 2.scharfsinnich, adj.; **one in pressing a bargain** Drickser (der)n.

shrewdness Lischt (die)n.

shriek 1.Greische, v.; gegrische, pp.; 2.Mardgrisch (der)n.

shrill whistle Piff (der)n.

shrink 1.ei/geh, v.; eigange, pp.; 2.eischnaerre, v.; eigschnaerrt, pp.; 3.eischrenke, v.; eigschrenkt, pp.;4.zamme/faahre, v.; is zammegfaahre, pp.; 5.zamme/geh, v.; zammegange, pp.; **(a tire, cloth)** schrenke, v.; gschrenkt, pp.; **from** scheie (sich --)v.; **in drying** eidaerre, v.; eigedaerrt, pp.

shrivel 1.uff/drickle, v.; uffgedrickelt, pp.; 2.uff/hutzle, v.; uffghutzelt, pp.; 3.zamme/schrumble, v.; zammegschrumbelt, pp.; **up** zamme/schnaerre, v.; zammegschnaerrt, pp.

shriveled 1.hutzlich, adj.; 2.verschrumbelt, adj.

shroud 1.Dodegleed (es)n.; 2.Dodesduch (es)n.; Dodesdicher, pl.; 3.Dodesgleeder (es), pl.

Shrove Tuesday 1.Faas(e)nacht (die)n.; 2.Faschtnacht (die)n.; 3.Fassenacht (die)n.; 4.Pannekuchedaag (der)n.

shrug verzucke, v.; verzuckt, pp.

Ss

shudder — since

shudder 1.schaudere, v.; gschaudeert, pp.; 2.ziddere, v.; geziddert, pp.

shuddering 1.schauderlich, adj.; 2.schauer(l)ich, adj.; 3.schauerich, adj.

shuffle the cards 1.Kard (die)n. (--e mixe); 2.Kord (die)n. (--e mixe)

shun 1.meide, v.; gemeidt, pp.; 2.Meinding halde (die)v.; Meinding ghalde, pp.

shunning Meinding (die)n.

shut 1.zu/mache, v.; zug(e)macht, pp.; 2.zu, adj.; **off** 1.ab/schtobbe, v.; abgschtoppt, pp.; 2.zudrehe, v.; zugedreht, pp.; **up** 1.Maul halde (es)v.; 2.schtill sei, v.

shutter 1.Fenschderlaade (der)n.; 2.Finschderlaade (der) n.; 3.Laade (der)n.; Leede, pl.

shy 1.bang, adj.; 2.bleed, adj.; 3.faerichbutzich, adj.; 4.leitschei, adj.; 5.menscheschei, adj.; 6.schei, adj.; 7.scheie, v.; gscheit, pp.; 8.schichder, adj.; 9.schichderich, adj.; 10.verzaacht, adj.

sick 1.biebse, v.; gebiebst, pp.; 2.grank, adj.; 3.krank, adj.; 4.peipse, v.; gepiebst, pp.; 5.unwohl, adj.; **'em!** (to a dog) 1.Hullu!; 2.Kss!; **abed** leie, v.; gelege; geleye, pp.; **bed** 1.Grankebett (es)n.; 2.Krankebett (es)n.; **in bed**; bettgrank, adj.; **person** 1.grank, adj. (en --es); 2.krank, adj. (en --es)

sicken iwwele, v.; geiwwelt, pp.

sickle Sichel (die)n.; Sichle, pp.

sickler 1.Schnidder (der)n.; Schnidder, pl.; 2.Schnitter (der)n.; 3.Sichler (der)n.; Sichler, pl.

sickliness 1.Schwechlichkeet (die)n.; 2.Schwechlichkeit (die)n.

sickly 1.biebsich, adj.; 2.grenkle, v.; gegrenkelt, pp.; 3.gniblich, adj.; 4.grenklich, adj.; 5.grenklich sie, v.; grenklich gewest, pp.; 6.krenkle, v.; gekrenkelt, pp.; 7.Piens (die)n.; 8.piense, v.; gepienst, pp.; 9.rum/pehze, v.; rumgepehzt, pp.; 10.rum/piense, v.; rumgepienst, pp.; 11.schlecht fiehle, v.; gfiehlt, pp.

sickness 1.Blog (die)n.; 2.Blok (die)n.; 3.Grankheet (die)n.; 4.Krankheet (die)n.; 5.Plok (die)n.

side Seit (die)n.; Seide, pl.; **passage** Abgang (der)n.; **street** Seitschtross (die)n.; **trace** Seideblatt (es)n.; **tree** Seideblatt (es)n.; Seidebledder, pl.; **wages** Seitloh (der) n.; **with someone** Batt (der)n. (ebber sei -- nemme)

sidestreet Seidschtross (die)n.

sideways 1.seidlings, adj., adv.; 2.seidwaerts, adj., adv.; 3.seidweks, adj., adv.; 4.seitlings, adv.; 5.seitwaerts, adv.; 6.seitwegs, adv.

sieve 1.raede, v.; geraedt, pp.; 2.riddle, v.; geriddelt, pp.; 3.Sebb (die)n.; 4.Seiner (der)n.; Seiner, pl.; 5.Sibb (die) n.; 6.sibbe, v.; gsibbt, pp.; 7.sichde, v.; gsicht, pp.; 8.sichte, v.; gsicht, pp.; 9.Sieb (die)n.; Siewe(r), pl.

sift 1.seine, v.; gseint, pp.; 2.sibbe, v.; gsibbt, pp.

sifter (for flour) Reeder (der)n.; Reeder, pl.

sigh 1.schluchze, v.; gschluchzt, pp.; 2.seifze, v.; gseifzt, pp.; 3.Seifzer (der)n.; Seifzer, pl.

sighing 1.seiferich, adv.; 2.seifzerich, adj.

sight 1.Aablick (der)n.; 2.Aasicht (die)n.; **(of a rifle)** Visier (es)n.

sign 1.Aazeeche (der, es)n.; 2.Maerrick (es)n.; 3.Schild (es) n.; 4.unner/schreiwe, v.; unnergschriwwe, pp.; 5.unner/zeichne, v.; 6.unnerschreiwe, v.; unnerschriwwe, pp.; 7.unnerzeiche, v.; 8.Wink (der)n.; 9.Zeeche (es)n.; **of distress** Notzeeche (es)n.; **of the zodiac** Zeeche (es)n.; **off** ab/seine, v.; abgseint, pp.

signal Lock (der)n.

signature Unnerschrift (die)n.

signboard Wegweiser (der)n.; Wegweiser, pl.

signer Unnerschreiwer (der)n.

significance Bedeitung (die)n.

significant bedeitlich, adj.

signify 1.aa/deide, v.; aagedeit, pp.; 2.aadeite, v.; aa- gedeit, pp.; 3.bedeide, v.; bedeidt, pp.

signpost 1.Schildposchde (der)n.; 2.Wegweiser (der)n.; Wegweiser, pl.

silence 1.Ruh (die)n.; 2.schtille, v.; gschtillt, pp.; 3. Schtillschweige (es)n.

silent 1.schtill, adj.; 2.schweige, v.; gschweicht, pp.; 3.schweiyend, adj.; 4.verschwiche, adj.; **fart** 1.Schleicher (der)n.; 2.Schtinker (der)n.; Schtinker, pl.

silk Seide (der)n.; **mill** Seidemiehl (die)n.

silken seidich, adj.

silkworm Seidewar(e)m (der)n.

sill Schwell (die)n.

silly 1.eefeldich, adj.; 2.gegisch, adj.; 3.halbscheit, adj.; 4.iwwerecks, adj.; 5.kaesich, adj.; 6.kalwerich, adj.; 7.keesich, adj.; 8.kischblich, adj.; 9.labbich, adj.; 10.lappich, adj.; 11.verkiddert, adj.; **child** (usually applied playfully) Bensel (es)n.; **person** 1.Aff (der)n.; Affe, pl.; 2.Fill (es)n.; Filler, pl.; 3.Gans (die)n.; Gens, pl.; 4.Hanswascht (der)n.; 5.Mensch (der)n. (en leb- bischer --); 6.Simbel (der)n.; 7.Simpel (der)n.

Silvanus Silvaanus (der)n.

silver Silwer (es)n.; **coin** Silwerschtick (es)n.

silverfish Silwerfisch (der)n.; Silwerfisch, pl.

silversmith Silwerschmitt (der)n.

Simeon Sim (der)n.

similar 1.aehnlich, adj.; 2.gleich, adj.; 3.vergleichlich, adj.

simmer 1.brutzle, v.; gebrutzelt, pp.; 2.koche, v.; gekocht, pp.; 3.siede, v.; 4.soddere, v.; gsoddert, pp.; 5.suddere, v.; gsuddert, pp.

Simon Sim (der)n.

simple 1.eefach, adj.; 2.eefeldich, adj.; 3.eifach. adj.; 4.glorensich, adj.; 5.leicht, adj.; 6.schlicht, adj.; **hearted** treihaerzich, adj.; **person** Dottel (der)n.

simpleton 1.Eefachtsbensel (es)n.; 2.Eefachtspensil (es)n.; 3.Schnepp (die)n.; 4.Simbel (der)n.; 5.Simpel (der)n.

simply 1.bloos, adj.; 2.ewwe, adj.

simultaneous gleichzeitich, adj.

sin 1.Sin(d) (die)n.; Sin(d)e,pl.; 2.sindiche, v.; gsindicht, pp.; 3.versindiche (sich --)v.; versindicht, pp.

since 1.as, conj.; 2.das, conj.; 3.dizeit, conj. (-- as); 4.seiddem, prep.; 5.seider, prep. 6.seit, prep.; 7.sidder, prep.; 8.sinter, adv. 9.vunwege, conj.; 10.vunwege, prep.; 11.zidder, prep.; 12.zinter, adv.; 13.zitter, adv.; **one** zitterm = zitter em; **then** diezeit, adv.

Ss

sincere

sincere 1.aernschthaft, adj.; 2.uffrichdich, adj.

sinew Flex (die)n.

sinewy 1.flexich, adj.; 2.naerfich, adj.

sinful 1.sindhafdich, adj.; 2.sindhaft, adj.

sinfulness Sindhafdichkeit (die)n.

sing singe, v.; gsunge, pp.; **(a tune)** ab/singe, v.; absunge, pp. (eens --); **(of birds)** zwitschere, v.; gezwitschert, pp.; **along** mit/singe, v.; mitgsunge, pp.; **or trill** (only of the singing or trilling of hens) zeedre, v.; gezeedert, pp.

singe 1.senke, v.; gsenkt, pp.; 2.versenke, v.; versenkt, pp.; **off** ab/senke, v.; abgsenkt, pp.

singer 1.Senger (der)n.; 2.Singer (der)n.; Singer, pl.

singing 1.G(e)sang (der)n.; 2.Gsang (der)n.; **or buzzing** Gsing (es)n.; **school** Singschul (die)n.

single 1.eensel, adj.; 2.eenzel, adj.; 3.gotzich, adj.; **(not double)** eefacht(ich), adj.; **(unmarried)** 1.eens, adj.; 2.eenzich, adj.; 3.leddich, adj.; **barreled** eelaafich, adj.

singletree 1.S(ch)illscheit (es)n.; S(ch)illscheider, pl.; 2.Sillscheit (es)n.; Sillscheider, pl.; **hook** Sillscheidhoke (der)n.; Sillscheidhoke, pl.

singly 1.eeletzich, adj., adv.; 2.eensel, adj.; 3.eensicherweis, adj.; 4.eenzel, adj.; 5.eezechtich, adj.; 6.schtickweis, adv.

sink 1.no(och)gewwe, v.; no(och)gewwe, pp.; 2.nunner/geh, v.; nunnergange, pp.; 3.sacke, v.; gsackt, pp.; 4.Schpielbank (die)n.; Schpielbenk, pl.; 5.senke, v.; gsenkt, pp.; 6.sinke, v.; gsunke, pp.; 7.Uffschpielbank (die)n.; 8.unner/geh, v.; unnergange, pp.; 9.versinke, v.; versunke, pp.; 10.Wasserbank (die)n.; Wasserbenk, pl.; 11.Zoddelbank (die)n.; **down** nidder/sinke, v.; niddergsunke, pp.; **in** 1.eisinke, v.; eigsanke, pp.; 2.nei/sinke, v.; neigsunke, pp.; **out of sight** versinke, v.; versunke, pp.

sinkhole Sinkloch (es)n.; Sinklecher, pl.

sinner Sinder (der)n.; Sinder, pl.

sip 1.lebbere, v.; gelebbert, pp.; 2.leppere, v.; geleppert, pp.; 3.Nipp (es)n.; 4.siffe, v.; gsifft, pp.; 5.suckle, v.; gsuckelt, pp.

Sister Service (annual, for women and girls, Moravian) Schwester(n)fescht (es)n.

sister Schweschder (die)n.; Schweschdere, pl.; **in-law** 1.Gschwei (die)n.; 2.Schwaegern (die)n.; 3.Schwei (die)n.; 4.Schwerschweschder (die)n.

sisterly schweschderlich, adj.

sit sitze, v.; gsitzt, gsotze, pp.; **(in) back** zerick/hocke, v.; zerickghockt, pp.; **about** rumher/sitze, v.; rumhergsitzt, pp.; **alongside of each other** newenanner/hocke, v.; newenannerghockt, pp.; **around** rum/hocke, v.; rumghockt, pp.; **at a distance** ab/sitze, v.; abgsotze, pp.; **by** 1.dabei/sitze, v.; 2.debeisitze, v.; debeigsitzt, pp.; **down** 1.anne/hocke (sich --), v.; 2.anne/sitze (sich --)v.; annegsitzt, pp.; 3.hie/hocke (sich --)v.; hieghockt, pp.; 4.hie/setze (sich --)v.; hiegsetzt, pp.; 5.setze (sich --), v.; gsetzt, pp.; **on the other side** niwwer/hocke (sich --)v.; niwwerghockt, pp.; **together** zamme/hocke, v.; zammeghockt, pp.; **up** uff/sitze, v.; uffgsotze, pp.; **up** (especially with a sick person) uff/hocke, v.; uffghockt, pp.

skin

situation 1.Schtell (die)n.; 2.Zuschtand (der)n.; Zuschtende, pl.

six 1.sechs, adj.; 2.sechse, adj.; 3.sex; sexe, pron.; **hundred** sechshunnert, adj.; **months old** halbyaehrich, adj.; **or so** Schtick (es)n. (Schticker sex); **spot of cards** sechsder, adj. (en sechsder); **times** 1.sechsmol, adj.; 2.sexmol, adv.; **weeks or so** Woch (die)n. (en --ner sex); **years old** 1.sechsyaehrich, adj.; 2.sexyaerich, adj.

sixteen sechzeh, adj.; pron.

sixteenth sechzeht, adj.

sixth sechst, adj.; **of a barrel** 1.Sechsdel (es)n.; 2.Sexdel (es)n.; **part** 1.Sechsdel (es)n.; 2.Sexdel (es)n.

sixtieth sechzichscht, adj.

sixty sechzich, adj.; pron.

size Grees (die)n.

sizing (put on wagon covers to weather proof them) Schlicht (der)n.

sizz (sound made when wetting hot iron) piesse, v.; gepiesst, pp.

sizzle 1.bradsle, v.; gebradselt, pp.; 2.bredsle, v.; gebredselt, pp.; 3.brodsle, v.; gebrodselt, pp.

skate schleife, v.; gschliffe, pp.

skein 1.Gnack (der)n.; 2.Gnewwel (der)n.; 3.Gnupse (der)n.; 4.Knack (der)n.; **(of spun flax)** Schtrang (der)n.; Schtreng, pl.

skeleton 1.Gnochemann (der)n.; 2.Gnocheyarrigel (der)n.; 3.Gnocheyockel (der)n.; 4.Knocheyarrigel (der)n.; **(bony) horse** 1.Gnochegaul (der)n.; 2.Knochegaul (der)n.

skeptical hattglaawich, adj.

sketch 1.ab/mole, v.; abgemolt, pp.; 2.mole, v.; gemolt, pp.

skill Kunscht (die)n.

skim 1.ab/raahme, v.; abgeraahmt, pp.; 2.ab/zebbe, v.; ab(ge)zeppt, pp.; **off** ab/scheppe, v.; abgscheppt, pp.; **off scum** (from boiling liquids) 1.ab/schaame, v. abgschaamt, pp.; 2.ab/schaume, v.; abgschaumt, pp.; **over** driwwergeh, v.; driwwergange, pp.; **over** (do something perfunctorily) iwwer/schinne, v.; iwwergschunne, pp.

skim(med) milk Millich (die)n. (maageri --)

skimmer 1.Raahmleffel (der)n.; 2.Rahmleffel (der)n.; 3.Schaumkel (die)n.; Schaumkele, pl.; 4.Schaumleffel (der)n.; Schaumleffele

skimming ladle 1.Raahmleffel (der)n.; 2.Schaumkel (die)n.; Schaumkele, pl.; 3.Schaumleffel (der)n.; Schaumleffele

skimp 1.driwwergeh, v.; driwwergange, pp.; 2.iwwer/schinne, v.; iwwergschunne, pp.; 3.schinne, v.; gschunne, pp.; **in seed** nei/schinne, v.; neigschunne, pp.

skin 1.ab/belze, v.; abgebelzt, pp.; 2.ab/ziehe, v.; abgezoge, pp.; 3.Belz (der)n.; 4.bschinne, v.; bschunne,pp.; 5.Fell (es)n.; 6.schinne, v.; gschunne, pp.; **(animals)** ab/schinne, v.; abgschunne, pp.; **disease** Hautgranket (die)n.; **eruption** 1.Ausfaahres (es) n.; 2.Ausfaahring (die)n.; **through** (get through with difficulty) darich/schinne, v.; darichschunne, pp.

Ss

skinny   slide

skinny 1.darr, adj.; 2.maager, adj.; **(of horses)** ribbich, adj.

skip 1.iwwerhubbe, v.; iwwerhuppt, pp.; 2.iwwerhuppe, v.; iwwerhuppt, pp.; 3.schpringe, v.; gschprunge, pp.; **stones over water surface** flitsche, v.; gflitscht, pp.

skipper Schiffer (der)n.

skirt (of a dress) 1.Iwwerschtock (der)n.; 2.Schtock (der)n.; Schteck, pl.

skull 1.Haernschaal (die)n.; 2.Haernschaedel (der)n.; 3.Hannschaedel (der)n.; 4.Schaal (die)n.; Schaale, pl.; 5.Schaedel (der)n.

skullcap 1.Kappegraut (es)n.; 2.Paffekapp (die)n.; 3.Schildgraut (es)n.

skunk Bisskatz (die)n.; Bisskatze, pl.; **cabbage** Bisskatzegraut (es)n.

skunk oil Bisskatzefett (es)n.

skunk's pelt Bisskatzehaut (die)n.

sky Luft (die)n.; **blue** himmelblo, adj.

skylarking Geyux (es)n.

skylight Dachfenschder (es)n.; Dachfenschdere, pl.

slab 1.Schwaart (die)n.; 2.Schwaart (die)n.; 3.Schwort (die)n.; 4.Schwort (die)n.

slack schlaff, adj.

slacken 1.ei/halde, v.; eighalde, pp.; 2.no(och)losse, v.; no(och)g(e)losst, pp.

slake lesche, v.; gelescht, pp.

slam zu/schlagge, v.; zugschlagge, pp.; **shut** zuglappe, v.; zugeglappt, pp.; **together** zamme/belse, v.; zammegebelst, pp.

slander 1.ei/hacke, v.; eighackt, pp.; 2.leschdere, v.; geleschdert, pp.; 3.no(och)liege, v.; no(och)geloge, pp.; 4.Schandfleck (die)n.; 5.verretsche, v.; verretscht, pp.

slanderer Laschdermaul (es)n.

slandering Liegerei (die)n.

slanderous verretscht, adj.; **gossip** Geretsch (es)n.

slant schlaamse, v.; gschlaamst, pp.; **off** schraekse, v.; gschraekst, pp.

slanting schlaams, adj.

slap Schlack (der)n.; **on the cheek** Backeschtreech (der)n.;

slap! buff!, interj.

slapdash 1.hibberdiglibb, adv.; 2.plitsch platsch, adv.

slash 1.schlitze, v.; gschlitzt, pp.; 2.Schmarre (der)n.

slat 1.Leddche (es)n.; 2.Leddel (es)n.; 3.Leescht (die)n.; 4.Leischt (die)n.; 5.Lettche (es)n.; 6.Lettel (es)n.

slate 1.Schifferschtee (der)n.; 2.Schiwwerschtee (der)n.;

colored 1.schifferich, adj.; 2.schiwwerich, adj.

slater's stake 1.Deifel (der)n.; 2.Deiwel (der)n.

slattern 1.Glund (die)n.; 2.Rabbelzott (die)n.; 3.Schlump (die)n.

slatternly 1.schlumbich, adj.; 2.schlumpich, adj.; 3.schlumsich, adj.

slaty 1.schifferich, adj.; 2.schifferschteenich, adj.; 3.schiwwer-schteenich, adj.; 4.schiwwerich, adj.; 5.schiwwerschteenich, adj.; 6.schlifferschteenich, adj.

slaughter 1.ab/schlachde, v.; abgschlacht, pp.; 2.schlade, v.; gschlacht, pp.

slaughterhouse Schlachthaus (es)n.; Schlachtheiser, pl.

slave 1.Gschlaaf (der)n.; 2.Kschlaav (es)n.; 3.kschlaave, v.; kschlaavt, pp.; 4.negere, v.; gnegert, pp.; 5.niegere, v.; gniegert, pp.; 6.Schklaaf (der)n.; 7.schklaafe, v.; gschlaaft, pp.

slavery 1.Gschlaaferei (die)n.; 2.Kschlaaverei (die)n.; 3.Schklaaferei (die)n.

slay 1.dodschlagge, v.; dodgschlagge, pp.; 2.dood/mache, v.; doodgemacht, pp.; 3.dood/schlaage, v.; doodgschlaage, pp.

sled 1.Blockschlidde (der)n.; 2.Schlidde (der)n.; 3.Schteeschlidde (der)n.; Schteeschlidde, pl.

sledge Schteeschleegel (der)n.; **(on runners)** 1.Mischtschlidde (der)n.; 2.Schleef (die)n.; 3.Schteeboot (es)n.; Schteeboot, pl.; 4.Schteeschlidde (der)n.; Schteeschlidde, pl.

sledgehammer 1.Schleggel (der)n.; 2.Schleggelhammer (der)n.; Schleggelhemmer, pl.; 3.Zuschlackhammer (der)n.

sleek glatt, adj.; **up** uff/schmutze, v.; uffgschmutzt, pp.

sleep 1.ruh(g)e, v.; geru(h)gt, pp.; 2.Schlof (der)n.; 3.schlofe, v.; gschlofe, pp.; **beside each other** newenanner/schlofe, v.; newenannergschloft, pp.; **like a log** Block (der)n. (wie en -- schlofe); **off** (the effects of drink) ab/schlofe, v.; abgschlofe, pp.; **on** fatt/schlofe, v.; fattgschlofe, pp.; **unsoundly** (of ill people) faable, v.; gfaabelt, pp.

sleeper Schlaefer (der)n.

sleepiness Schlofleis (die)n., pl.

sleepwalker Nachtwandler (der)n.

sleepy schlaeferich, adj.; **catchfly** Darrschtengel (der)n.; **head** 1.Schlofkopp (der)n.; 2.verschlofe, v. (-- sei)

sleet 1.Kissel (der)n.; 2.kissle, v.; gekisselt, pp.; **storm** Kisselwedder (es)n.

sleety kisslich, adj.; **weather** Kisselwedder (es)n.

sleeve Aermel (der)n.; **hole** Aermelloch (es)n.

sleigh Schlidde (der)n.; **bell** 1.Klingel (die)n.; 2.Schliddebell (die)n.; **riding** Schliddefaahre (es)n.

sleighing Schliddebaah (die)n.

slender 1.dinn, adj.; 2.graad, adj.; 3.gschmeidich, adj.; 4.maager, adj.; 5.schlank, adj.; 6.schnackerich, adj.; 7.schneckerich, adj.; 8.schnurschtracks, adj.; 9.schpindlich, adj.; 10.schtrack(s), adj.; **cyperus** Ochsegraas (es)n.; **dog** (also applied to other animals and even to persons) Windhund (der)n.; **galingale** Ochsegraas (es)n.

slice 1.bledle, v.; gebledelt, pp.; 2.blettlich schneide, v.; 3. Schtick (es)n.

slide 1.ab/witsche, v.; abgewitscht, pp.; 2.glitsche, v.; geglitscht, pp.; 3.klitsche, v.; gegklitscht, pp.; 4.Rutsch (die)n.; 5.rutsche, v.; gerutscht, pp.; 6.Schiewer (der)n.; Schiewer, pl.; 7.schleife, v.; gschliffe, pp.; **ahead** vor/rutsche, v.; vorgerutscht, pp.; **away** weck/rutsche, v.; weckgerutscht, pp.; **back** zerick/rutsche, v.; zerickgerutscht, pp.; **down** 1.nunner/rutsche, v.; nunnergerutscht, pp.; 2.nunner/schleife, v.; nunnergschliffe, pp.; 3.runner/rutsche, v.;

(Continued on page 372)

slide

(Continued from page 371)

runnergerutscht, pp.; **in** rei/rutsche, v.; reigerutscht, pp.; **into** nei/rutsche, v.; neigerutscht, pp.; **off** 1. ab/glitsche, v.; abgeglitscht, pp.; 2.abglitsche, v.; abgeglitscht, pp.; **or fidget around** rum/rutsche, v.; rumgerutscht, pp.; **out** 1.naus/rutsche, v.; gerutscht, pp.; 2.raus/rutsche, v.; rausgerutscht, pp.; 3.raus/schleife, v.; rausgschliffe, pp.; **to a place** hie/rutsche, v.; hiegerutscht, pp.; **toward or near** (one) haer/rutsche, v.; haergerutscht, pp.

sliding bolt (of a door) Schiewer (der)n.; Schiewer, pl.

sliding door (on barn) Schiebdor (es)n.; Schiebdore, pl.

slight gering, adj.; **blow** Schlack (der)n.; **crack of whip** Flitscher (der)n.; **elevation of ground** Buckel (der)n.; **noise** Gereisch (es)n.

slightly intoxicated benewwelt, adj.

slim 1.schnackerich, adj.; 2.schneckerich, adj.

slime 1.Schlaam (der)n.; 2.Schlamm (der)n.; 3.Schleim (der)n.

slimy schleimich, adj.

sling 1.Schlenk (die)n.; 2.Schling (die)n.

slink schleiche, v.; gschliche, pp.

slip 1.ab/ritsche, v.; abgeritscht, pp.; 2.aus/glitsche, v.; ausgeglitscht, pp.; 3.aus/ritsche, v.; ausgeritscht, pp.; 4.aus/rutsche, ausgerutscht, pp.; 5.glitsche, v.; geglitscht, pp.; 6.klitsche, v.; gegklitscht, pp.; 7.rutsche, v.; gerutscht, pp.; 8.schlibbe, v.; gschlippt, pp.; 9.Schlipp (der)n.; 10.Schnittling (der)n.; **(in speaking)** verschnabbe (sich --)v.; verschnappt, pp.; **(of plants)** Neschtelche (es)n.; **ahead** vor/rutsche, v.; vorgerutscht, pp.; **away** 1.ab/witsche, v.; abgewitscht, pp.; 2.aus/witsche, v.; ausgewitscht, pp.; **from** ab/ritsche, v.; abgeritscht, pp.; **in** 1.ei/schluppe, v.; eigschlupt, pp.; 2.eirutsche, v.; eigerutscht, pp.; 3.eischlippe, v.; eigschlippt, pp.; 4.eiwitsche, v.; eigewitscht, pp.; 5.nei/schlibbe, v.; neigschlippt, pp.; **near** haer/schlippe, v.; haergschlippt, pp.; **of paper** 1.Babierche (es)n.; 2.Babierli (es)n.; 3.Zettel (der)n.; **off** 1.ab/glitsche, v.; abgeglitscht, pp.; 2.ab/rutsche, v.; abgerutscht, pp.; 3.ab/schlibbe, v.; abgschlippt, pp.; 4.abglitsche, v.; abgeglitscht, pp.; 5.flitsche, v.; gflitscht, pp.; **on** aa/schlibbe, v.; aagschlippt, pp.; **out** 1.aus/witsche, v.; ausgewitscht, pp.; 2.naus/schlippe, v.; nausgschlippt, pp.; 3.raus/schlippe, v.; rausgschlippt, pp.; 4.raus/witsche, v.; rausgewitscht, pp.; **out of the ground** (by the plow in plowing) Ritscher (der)n.; Ritscher, pl.; **the mind** aus/falle, v.; ausgfalle, pp.; **through** 1.darich/schlibbe, v.; darichgschlippt, pp.; 2.darich/witsche, v.; darichgewitscht, pp.

slipper Pantoffel (der)n. (rare usage)

slippery 1.glitschich, adj.; 2.klitschich, adj.; 3.rutschich, adj.; 4.schlibberich, adj.; 5.schlibbich, adj.; **elm** 1.Rotzholz (es)n.; 2.Rusch(d)e (die)n. (rote --)

slit 1.aus/schlitze, v.; ausgschlitzt, pp.; 2.eischlitze, v.; eigschlitzt, pp.; 3.Schlitz (der)n.; **open** uff/schlitze, v.; uffgschlitzt, pp.; **through** darich/schlitze, v.;

small

darichgschlitzt, pp.; **up** verschlitze, v.; verschlitzt, pp.

sloathful and procrastinating person Bummelhannes (der)n.

slobber 1.schlawwere, v.; gschlawwert, pp.; 2.vernuddle, v.; vernuddelt, pp.; **over oneself** verschlawwere (sich --)v.; verschlawwert, pp.

slobbering 1.Gschlawwer (es)n.; 2.schlawwerich, adj.

slop 1.Brieh (die)n.; 2.schlabbe, v.; gschlappt, pp.; 3.schlappe, v.; gschlappt, pp.; **barrel** 1.Schlappfass (es)n.; Schlappfesser, pl.; 2.Seifass (es)n.; Seifesser, pl.; **bucket** Schlappeemer (der)n.

slope 1.ab/henke, v.; abghonke, pp.; 2.ab/schlaamse, v.; abgschlaamst, pp.; 3.Hank (der)n.; 4.Hank (der)n.; 5.schlaamse, v.; gschlaamst, pp.

sloping 1.abhenki(s)ch, adj.; 2.schlaams, adj.

sloppy 1.kutslich, adj.; 2.schlabbich, adj.; **work** Suddelarewett (die)n.

sloth Vielfrass (der)n.

sloven Schlamp (die)n.

slovenly schlambich, adj.; **person** 1.Schlabbes (der)n.; 2.Schlappes (der)n.; 3.Seikaschde (der)n.; **walker** Schlappfuuss (der)n.; **woman** Kaddel (die)n.

slow langsam, adj.; **about** zaudere, v.; gezaudert, pp.

slowly 1.sachde, adv.; 2.sachdiche, adv.; 3.safdich, adv.; 4.saftich, adj.

slowpoke Schleich (die)n.

sluggard Faulenzer (der)n.; Faulenzer, pl.

sluice Ablaaf (der)n.

slumber 1.leie, v.; gelege; geleye, pp.; 2.Schlummer (der) n.; 3.schlummere, v.; gschlummert, pp.;4.schlummre, v.; gschlummert, pp.

slumbering Gschlummer (es)n.

slush 1.Marasch(t) (der)n.; 2.Marrasch(t) (der)n.

sly 1.darichdriwwe, adj.; 2.fuxich, adj.; 3.gewixt, adj.; 4. lischdich, adj.; 5.schlau, adj.; 6.schlibberich, adj.; 7. schlitzohrich, adj.; 8.schniekich, adj.; 9.verschmitzt, adj.

smack 1.Schmatz (der)n.; Schmatze, pl.; 2.schmatze, v.; gschmatzt, pp.; 3.Schmutz (der)n.; 4.Schnutz (der)n.; **(on the face or behind)** Blatsche (es)n.; **the lips** blatsche, v.; geblatscht, pp.

smacking (of the lips in eating or kissing) Gschmatz (es)n.

small 1 grubbich, adj.; 2.klee, adj.; 3.wuns(l)ich, adj.; 4.wunz(l)ich, adj.; **(immature) bull** Bulli (es)n.; **animal** 1.Dierche (es)n.; 2.Dierli (es)n.; Dierlin, pl.; **ax** Exel (es)n.; **bag with a long handle** (in taking up the collection in church) 1.Klingelsack (der)n.; 2.Klingelseckel (es)n.; 3.Klingelseckli (es)n.; **barking cur** Gnefzer (der)n.; **bed** Gribb (die)n.; **blockhouse** 1.Blockheisel (es)n.; Blockheisli, pl.; 2.Blockheisli (es) n.; lockheislin, pl.; **boned** feignochich, adj.; **bottle** 1.Boddelche (es)n.; 2.Flasch (die)n.; **bunch or wisp** (of hay) Wischbel (der)n.; **calabash** Beschtli (es)n.; **cellar window** Daagloch (es)n.; **child** glee, adj.

(Continued on page 373)

Ss

small

(Continued from page 372)

(en gleenes); **chores** Gnoddelaerwet (die)n.; **cloth** Dichelche (es)n.; **clothes room** Kemmerli (es)n.; **cloud** Welkche (es)n.; **debts** 1.Lebberschulde (die) n.,pl.; 2.Lepperschulde(die)n., pl.; **flowered crowfoot** Haahnefuuss (der)n.; **gate** 1.Daerche (es)n.; 2.Daerli (es)n.; 3.Deerche (es)n.; 4.Deerli (es)n.; 5.Dierche (es)n.; **handful** (of grass, weeds) Bischel (es)n.; **head** (as of a baby) Keppsche (es)n.; **holes** lickich, adj.; **house** Heisli (es)n.; Heislin, pl.; **jug** Griegel (es)n.; **keg** 1.Fesse (es)n.; 2.Fessel (es)n.; **light-cake** Weck (der) n.; Weck, pl.; **limbed** gleeglidderich, adj.; **limbs of trees cut up for firewood** Briggelhols (es)n.; **load** Schleppche (es)n.; **lump** 1.Gnoddel (der)n.; 2.Klimpel (es)n.; 3.Knoddel (der)n.; **nail** 1.Negg(e)li (es)n.; 2.Neggelche (es)n.; Neggelcher, pl.; **lumber** wisch, adj. (en --); **of the back** 1.Greitz (es)n.; Greitzer, pl.; 2.Kreiz (es)n.; **parcel** Peckche (es)n.; **patch** 1.Bleche (es)n.; 2.Blechli (es)n.; 3.Bleckche (es)n.; 4.Bleckli (es) n.; **piece** 1.Schtickel (es)n.; 2.Schtickli (es)n.; **piece of cloth** 1.Blacke (der)n.; 2.Fleck(e) (der)n.; Flecke, pl.; 3.Lappe (der)n.; **pieces of beef** (stuffed in bags of tripe, pickled in dilute vinegar, sliced, fried and served with gravy) 1.Rolitsch (die)n.; 2.Rolliche (die) n.; **plant** Blenselche (es)n.; **pot** Haefel (es)n.; **pox** schwarz, adj. (schwarze parble); **quart** Gwaart (die)n. (en katzi --); **remainder** 1.Schtimbel (der)n.; 2.Schtimpel (der)n.; **roll** (of butter)1.Glimbel (es)n.; 2.Klimpel (es)n.; **room** 1.Schtibbche (es)n.; 2.Schtippche (es)n.; **round cakes** Schtreissel (es)n.; **round glacial stone** (believed to have been hurled in a bolt of lightning) Gewidderschtee (der)n.; **shoe** Schickelche (es)n.; **spool** 1.Schpielche (es)n.; 2.Schpulche (es)n.; **spot** 1.Bleche (es)n.; 2.Blechli (es) n.; 3.Bleckche (es)n.; 4.Bleckli (es)n.; **stream** Rannli (es)n.; **tassel** Schtreissel (es)n.; **thin book** Bichli (es) n.; **tin kettle** Blicki (es)n.; **tub** Ziwwerche (es)n.; **wooden dish or goblet** Helzich (es)n.; **wooden pail with one long stave for a handle** Kiwwel (der)n.; Kiwwel, pl.; **wooden vessel used in carrying water to workmen** Schtitz (der)n.; Schtitze, pl.; **woods** Bischel (es)n.

smallpox 1.Parble (die)n.; 2.Schwatze (die)n.

smart 1.gluch, adj.; 2.schmaert, adj.; 3.schmatze, v.gschmatzt, pp.

smartly zier, adj.; **dressed young fellow** Baerschdelche (es)n.

smartweed Bitterkneeterich (der)n.

smarty 1.Naaseweis (die)n.; 2.Nasseweis (die)n.

smash 1.verschlagge, v.; verschlagge, pp.; 2.verschmeisse, v.; verschmisse, pp.; 3.flatsch!, interj.

smear 1.Salb (die)n.; 2.saue, v.; gsaut, pp.; 3.schmiere, v.; gschmiert, pp.;

smear all over verblaschdert , pp. verblaschdert; **shut** zu/schmiere, v.; zugschmiert, pp.

smearing Gschmier (es)n.

smeary schmierich, adj.; **or greasy work** 1. Schmiererei

snare

(die)n.; 2.Schmierwese (es)n.

smell 1.Geruch (der)n.; 2.rieche, v.; groche, pp.; 3.rum/rieche, v.; rumgeroche, pp.; 4.widdere, v.; gewiddert, pp.; 5. wittere, v.; gewittert, pp.; **(in certain areas)** 1.schmacke, v.; gschmackt, pp.; 2.schmecke, v.; gschmeckt, pp.; **a rat** 1.Ratt (die)n. (en -- schmacke); 2.schmacke, v.; gschmackt, pp. (en Ratt --); **at** aa/ rieche, v.; aageroche, pp.

smelly schtinkich, adj.

smelt schmelse, v.; gschmolse, pp.

smile 1.aa/lache, v.; aagelacht, pp.; 2.lechle, v.; gelechelt, pp.; 3.schmunsle, v.; gschmunselt, pp.

smiling 1.Gschmunsel (es)n.; 2.schmunslich, adj.

smithy Schmittschapp (der)n.; Schmittschepp, pl.

smoke 1.Rauch (der)n.; 2.Schmok (der)n.; 3.schmoke, v.; gschmokt, pp.; **pipe** Schmokpeif (die)n.

smoked jowl 1.Kiehbacke (der)n.; 2.Kinnbacke (der)n.;

sausage Wascht (die)n. (gschmokdi --)

smokehouse Schmokhaus (es)n.; Schmokheiser, pl.

smoky schmokich, adj.

smooth 1.ab/gledde, v.; abgeglett, pp.; 2.ewe, adj.; 3.glatt mache, v.; **and even** blatt, adj.; **bore rifle** Glattbix (die)n.; **chaff** (wheat) 1.Schprau (die)n. (gladdi --e); 2. glattschprauich, adj.; 3.glattschprei-ich, adj.

smoothing plane Schlichthowwel (die)n.

smother 1.dambe, v.; gedampt, pp.; 2.schmoddere, v.; gschmoddert, pp.; 3.verschmoddere, v.; verschmoddert, pp.; 4.verschticke, v.; verschtickt, pp.

smuggle in 1.eischmuggle, v.; eigschmuggelt, pp.; 2.rei/ schmuggle, v.; reigschmuggmelt, pp.

smutty 1.lebbisch, adj.; 2.leppisch, adj.; 3.safdich, adj.; 4.schmutzich, adj.

snail Schneck (die)n.; Schnecke, pl.; **shell** Schneckehaus (die)n.

snake Schlang (die)n.; Schlange, pl.; **fence** Schtaagefens (die)n.; Schtaagefense, pl.

snakebite Schlangebiss (der)n.

snakeroot Schlangewatzel (die)n.

snakeskin Schlangehaut (die)n.

snap 1.schnabbe, v.; gschnappt, pp.; 2.Schnapp (die)n.; 3.schnappe, v.; gschnappt, pp.; 4.Schnepp (die)n. 5.Schnupp (die)n.; **(fastener)** Schloss (es)n.; Schlesser, pl.; **a person off** Maul (es)n. (iwwer's -- faahre); **at someone** (as a vicious dog) gnappe, v.; gegnappt, pp.; **in two** ab/breche, v.; abgebroche, pp. (masch --); **off** ab/ schnaebbe, v.; abgschnaeppt, pp.; **the chalk line** (in hewing timber) ab/schnelle, v.; abgschnellt, pp.

snapdragon 1.Lewemaul (es)n.; 2.Freschmeiler (die)n., pl.

snapping turtle Schnebber (der)n.

snappish 1.bissich, adj.; 2.schnauzich, adj.;3.verdriesslich, adj.

snare 1.Fallschtrick (der)n.; 2.schnebbe, v.; gschneppt, pp.; **drum** Gleedrumm (die)n.; **game** 1.schlebbe, v.; gschleppt, pp.; 2.schleppe, v.; gschleppt, pp.; 3.schlibbe, v.; gschlippt, pp.

Ss

snarl — snuffling

snarl 1.aa/gnarre, v.; aa(ge)gnatt, pp.; 2.knarre, v.; geknarrt, pp.; 3.schnarre, v.; gschnarrt, pp.; 4.schnarre, v.; gschnatt, pp.

snatch raffe, v.; gerafft, pp.; **away** 1.weck/fange, v.; weckgfange, pp.; 2.weck/grabsche, v.; weckgegrabscht, pp.; 3.weck/reisse, v.; weckgerisse, pp.;4.weck/schnabbe, v.; weckgschnappt, pp.; 5.weck/schnaerre, v.; weckgschnaerrt, pp.; **up** 1. uff/fange, v.; uffgfange, pp.; 2.uff/raffe, v.; uffgerafft, pp.

snathe 1.Sensewar(e)f (der)n.; 2.Warf (der)n.; 3.Warref (der)n.

sneak 1.Duppmeiser (der)n.; 2.Munkler (der)n.; 3. schleiche, v.; gschliche, pp.; **after** no(och)schleiche, v.; no(och)schleiche, pp.; **along** hie/schleiche, v.; hiegschliche, pp.; **around** 1.rum/lause, v.; rumgelaust, pp.; 2.rum/schleiche, v.; rumgschliche, pp.; 3.rumher/lause, v.; rumhergelaust, pp.; 4.rumher/schleiche, v.; rumhergschliche, pp.; **away** 1.ab/schleiche, v.; abgschliche, pp.; 2.ab/schtehle, v.; abschtohle, pp.; 3.fatt/schleiche, v.; fattgschliche, pp.; 4.weck/schleiche, v.; weckgschliche, pp.; **hither** 1.haer/schleiche, v.; haergschliche, pp.; 2.her/schleiche, v.; hergschliche, pp.; **in** 1.nei/schleiche, v.; neigschliche, pp.; 2.rei/schleiche, v.; reigschliche, pp.; **out** naus/schtehle (sich --), v.; nausgschtole,pp.; **past** 1.verbei/schleiche, v.; verbeigschliche, pp.; 2.vorbei/schleiche, v. vorbeigschliche, pp.; **together** zamme/schleiche, v.; zammegschliche, pp.; **up** 1.nuff/schleiche, v.; nuffgschliche, pp.; 2.nuff/schluppe, v.; nuffgschluppt, pp.

sneaking 1.duckmeisich, adj.; 2.duppmeisich, adj.; 3.schnubbich, adj.; 4.schnuppich, adj.; **person** Schleich(die)n.

sneakingly bschtohlnerweis, adv.

sneaky 1.schnackich, adj.; 2.schniekich, adj.; 3.schniekisch, adj.

sneer schpettle, v.; gschpeddelt, pp.

sneering Gschpettel (es)n.

sneeringly schpettlich, adj.

sneeze niesse, v.; geniesst, pp.

sneezewort Nieregraut (es)n.

snicker 1.gickere, v.; gegickert, pp.; 2.kickere, v.; gekickert, pp.

sniff 1.schnubbe, v.; gschnuppt, pp.; 2.schnuppe, v.; gschnuppt, pp.; 3.schuffle, v.; gschuffelt, pp.

sniffle 1.schnubbe, v.; gschnuppt, pp.; 2.schnubbere, v.; gschnubbert, pp.; 3.schnuffle, v.; gschnuffelt, pp.; 4.schnuppere, v.; gschnuppert, pp.; 5.schuffle, v.; gschuffelt, pp.

snip 1.Schnibbelche (es)n.; 2.Schnippelche, (es)n.; 3.schnipple, v.; gschnippelt, pp.; 4.Schnipsel (es)n.; **(of a boy)** Kaschde (der)n.; Kaschde, pl.

snipe (game bird) Schnepp (die)n.

snipe (mystical animal hunted with a sack on cold winter's night) 1.Elbedritsch (es)n.; Elbegritsche, pl.; 2.Elbedritschel (es)n.; Elbedritschelcher, pl.; 3.Elbedritschelche (es)n.; Elbedritschelcher, pl.; 4.Elbedritschli (es)n.; Elbedritschlin, pl.; 5.Elbegrixel (es) n.; Elbegrixelcher, pl.; 6.Elderbritsch (es)n.; Elderbritsche, pl.; 7.Elderdritsch (es)n.; Elderdritsche, pl.; 8.Eldertwitsch (es)n.; Eldertwitsche, pl.; 9.Elefantdritsch (es)n.; Elefantdritsche, pl.; 10.Elefantgrixel (es)n.; Elefantgrixelcher, pl.; 11.Elfedritsch (es)n.; Elfedritsche, pl.; 12.Elfedritschel (es)n.; Elfedritschelcher, pl.; 13.Elfedritschelche (es)n.; Elfedritschelcher, pl.; 14.Elfedritschli (es)n.; Elfedritschlin, pl.; 15.Elfegrixel (es)n.; Elfegrixelcher, pl.

snitz pie Schnitzboi (der)n.; Schnitzboi, pl.

snobbish 1.feihaerich, adj.; 2.yungleidisch, adj.

snoop through 1.aus/schnausse, v.; ausgschnausst, pp.; 2.darich/schnuffle, v.; darichgschnuffelt, pp.

snoopy 1.schnubbich, adj.; 2.schnuppich, adj.; 3.vorwitzich, adj.

snoot Schnut (die)n.

snooty yungleidisch, adj.

snore 1.schnaixe,v.; gschnaixt, pp.; 2.schnarixe, v.; gschnarixt, pp.

snorer Schnarixer (der)n.

snoring Gschnarricks (es)n.

snort 1.schnaube, v.; 2.schnauze, v.; gschnauzt, pp.;3.schnobe, v.; gschnobt, pp.

snot 1.Rotz (der)n.; 2.rotze, v.; grotzt, pp.; 3.Kod(d)er (der) n.; **eater** (child) Rotzfresser (der)n.; Rotzfresser, pl.

snotty rotzich, adj.

snout (hog) 1.Riesel (der)n.; 2.Schnut (die)n.

snow 1.Schnee (der)n.; 2.schnee-e, v.; gschneet, pp.; **in** 1.rei/schnee-e, v.; reigschneet, pp.; 2.zu-schnee-e, v.; zugschneet, pp.; 3.zuschneee, v.; zugschneet, pp.; **shovel** Schneeschaufel (die)n.; **squall** Schneeschtiwwer (der)n.; **storm** Schneeschtar(e)m (der)n.; **water** Schneewasser (es)n.; **white** schneeweiss, adj.

snowball Schneeballe (der)n.; **tree** Schneeballebaam (der)n.

snowbird Schneevoggel (der)n.

snowbound verschnee-e, v.; verschneet, pp.

snowdrop Schneeblumm (die)n.; Schneeblumme, pl.

snowflake 1.Schneebrocke (der)n.; 2.Schneeflocke (der)n.

snowplow Schneeblug (der)n.; Schneeblieg, pl.

snowstorm 1.Schneegschtiwwer (der)n.; 2.Schneeschtiwwer (der)n.

snowy schneeich, adj.

snuff 1.Schnupf (der)n.; 2.Schnuppduwack (der)n.

snuffer(s) 1.Lichtbutzer (der)n.; 2.Lichtbutzscheer (die)n.; 3.Lichtbutzscher (die)n.

snuffle 1.schnubbe, v.; gschnuppt, pp.; 2.schnuppe, v.; gschnuppt, pp.; **around** rum/schnuffle, v.; rumgschnuffelt, pp.

snuffling Gschnuffel (es)n.

Ss

snug

snug begweem, adj.

snuggle 1.nei/kuschle (sich --),v.; 2.nischdle, v.;
genischdelt, pp.

So long! Hatyee!, interj.

so 1.Kutterments (die)n., pl.; 2.so, adj.; adv.; conj.; **at this
time** dies, adj. (so um -- Zeit); **me** some = so me;
much the (better) desde (besser); **one** sore = so
eenre (dative sing fem); **so** 1.middelmaessich, adj.;
2.middelmaessich, adv.; **'n** Reisses (es)n.

soak 1.ei/weeche, v.; eigeweecht, pp.; 2.uff/weeche, v.;
uffgeweecht, pp.; **through** 1.darich/schlagge, v.;
darichgschlagge, pp.; 2.darich/weeche, v.;
darichgweecht, pp.

soaked lachdich, adj.

soaking wet 1.puddelnass, adj.; 2.weschnass, adj.;
3.weschpuddelnass, adj.

soap 1.aa/seefe, v.; aagseeft, pp.; 2.Seef (die)n.; 3.seefe,
v.; gseeft, pp.; **dish** Seefschissel (die)n.; **fat** Seefefett
(es)n.; **making vat** Schtenner (der)n.; Schtenner, pl.

soapsuds Seef(e)wasser (es)n.

soapy seefich, adj.

sob 1.schluchze, v.; gschluchzt, pp.; 2.schnippse, v.;
gschnippst, pp.; 3.seifze, v.; gseifzt, pp.

sober nichdern, adj.

sociable 1.blauderich, adj.; 2.gsellich, adj.; 3.plauderich,
adj.; 4.umgenglich, adj.

social gathering Zammelaaf (der)n.

society Gesellschaft (die)n.

sock 1.Schtrump (der)n.; Schtrimp, pl.; 2.Socke (der)n.

sod 1.Gseedes (es)n.; 2.Wassem (der)n.; **filled with
couch-grass** Gweckewasem (der)n.

soda Sode (die)n.

sofa Sofe (es)n.

soft 1.feischtielich, adj.; 2.leis, adj.; 3.mareb, adj.; 4.sanft,
adj.; 5.schwammich, adj.; 6.weech, adj.; **and low**
dus, adj.; **boiled eggs** briehe, v.; gebrieht, pp.
(Oier --); **felt man's hat** Schlapphut (der)n.;
Schlapphiet, pl.; **hearted** weechhatzich, adj.;
mouthed (of horses) weechmeilich, adj.; **soap**
Schmierseef (die)n.

soften weech/mache, v.; weechgemacht, pp.; **by soaking**
uff/weeche, v.; uffgeweecht, pp.

softly 1.sachde, adv.; 2.sachdich, adv.; 3.safdich, adv.;
4.saftich, adj.; 5.sietsam, adj.

soggy 1.delkich, adj.; 2.gnetschich, adj.; 3.schlumblich,
adj.; (of bread) wasserschtraemich, adj.; (of ground
too wet to plow) glodsich, adj.; **streak in bread**
Wasserschtraehme, n. **soil** 1.Bau (der)n.; 2.Bodde(m)
(der)n.; 3.Grund (der)n.; 4.Land (es)n.; Lenner, pl.;
5.verdrecke, v.; verdreckt, pp.; 6.verflecke, v.;
verfleckt, pp.; 7.verhause, v.; verhaust, pp.;
8.verkaffle, v.; verkaffelt, pp.; 9.vernuddle, v.;
vernuddelt, pp.; 10.versaue, v.; versaut, pp.;
11.verschlabbe, v.; verschlappt, pp.; 12.verschmiere
(sich --)v.; verschmiert, pp.; 13.verschmiere, v.;
verschmiert, pp.; 14.versuddle, v.; versuddelt, pp.;

son

(by slopping) verschnuddle, v.; verschnuddelt, pp.;
adapted for growing wheat Weezebodde(m) (der)n.;
covered with small boulders wackich, adj.; **diapers**
verhause, v.; verhaust, pp.; **one's person or clothes**
verdrecke (sich --)v.; verdreckt, pp.; **or mess by handling** vergnootsche, v.; vergnootscht, pp.; **or spoil by
sweating** verschwitze, v.; verschwitzt, pp.; **the diaper** (of infants) wiescht mache (sich --)v.;
wieschtgemacht, pp.; **with grease** verschmutze, v.;
verschmutzt, pp.

soiled 1.dreckich, adj.; 2.fleckich, adj.; 3.verschmiert, adj.;
by sweating verschwitzt, adj.

solace Droscht (der)n.

sold out ausverkaaft, adj.

Sold! (said the auctioneer) Abschlaage!, interj.

solder 1.leede, v.; gleede, gleed, pp.; 2.liede, v.; gelied,
pp.; 3.liete, v.; geliet, pp.

soldering iron 1.Leedkolwe (der)n.; 2.Leitkolwe (der)n.;
Leitkolwe, pl.

soldier 1.Saldaat (der)n.; 2.Soldaat (der)n.; Soldaade, pl.

soldier's cap Saldaatekapp (die)n.; **coat** Saldaaterock
(der)n.

sole 1.Sohl (die)n.; 2.sohle, v.; gsohlt, pp.; **leather**
Sohlledder (es)n.; **of foot** Fuusohl (die)n.

solemn feierlich, adj.

solemnity Feierlichkeet (die)n.

solicitous 1.aa/leie, v.; aagelegge, pp; 2.aagelegge, adj.;
3.besarickt, adj.; 4.bsarkt, adj.; 5.sarickfeldich, adj.

solid fascht, adj.

solitary 1.einsam, adj.; 2.eisam, adj.; 3.menscheschei,
adj.; **rock** (from glacial period) Felsekopp (der)n.

solitude Eisamkeet (die)n.

Solomon Sallemann (der)n.

soluble vergenglich, adj.

some 1.deel, adj.; pron.; 2.Deele (es)n.; 3.ebbes, adj.;
pron.; 4.en paar, adj.; 5.etliche, adj.; pron.; 6.paar,
pron., adj.; 7.wennich, adj.; pron.; **time ago** do
vergange, adv.; **what long** lenglich, adj.

somebody 1.ebber, pron.; 2.eener, pron.; adj.

someone ebber, pron.

somersault 1.Barzelbaam (der)n.; 2.Batzelbaam (der)n.;
3.kopp/ schtatze, v.; koppgschtatzt, pp.

something ebbes, adj.; pron.; **in view** Aag (es)n.; (ebbes
im -- hawwe); **like** ebbes, adj. (-- gleich); **to hammer
with** gloppiches (ebbes); **worth while** ebbes, adj.
(-- gleich); **wrong** faul (ebbes)adv.

sometimes 1.alsemol, adv.; 2.deelmol, adv.;
3.manichmol, adv.

somewhat atlich, adj.; **heavy** schwerlich, adj.; **helpless**
1.boddegraemisch, adj.; 2.boddegrempisch, adj.

somewhere 1.aeryets, adv.; 2.ammenent, adv.;
3.ammenot, adv.; 4.ariyets, adv.; 5.eicks wo, adv.;
6.eiyets (wo), adv.

somnambular moondsichdich, adj.

son 1.Soh (der)n.; 2.Suh (der)n.; Seh, pl.; **in-law**

(Continued on page 376)

Ss

son (continued)

(Continued from page 375)

1.Dochdermann (der)n.; 2.Schwiegersoh (der)n.;
3.Schwiegersuh (der)n.; **of-a-gun** 1.Fratzel (es)n.;
2. Schwerneeder (der Schwaerneeter (der)n.; **who
turned out well** gerode, v.; gerode, pp. (en gut
gerodner Soh)

Song of Solomon Hohelied (es)n.

song 1.Lied (es)n.; Lieder, pl.; 2.Liedel (es)n.; 3.Liedli (es)n.;
song Schnitzelbank (die)n; 4.Singschtick (es)n.;
Singschticker, pl.; **leader** 1.Vorschtimmer (der)n.;
2. Vorsinger (der)n.; Vorsinger, pl.; **service** Singing (die)n.

songbook Liederbuch (es)n.; Liederbicher, pl.

soon 1.ball, adv.; 2.ballemol, adv.; 3.beinaegschdem,
adv.; 4.glei, adv.; 5.glie, adv.; 6.gschwind, adv.;
7.in eens, zwee, drei, adv.; 8.iwwerdem(m), adv.;
9.iwwerweil, adv.; 10.iwwreweil, adv.; 11.lieb, adv.;
adj.; **(very)** 1.mit naegschdem, adv.; 2.naekscht, adv.
(mit [bei] naekschtem); 3.zimmlich glei, adv.

sooner 1.eher, adv.; 2.ehnder, adv.; 3.erschder, adv.;
4.neecher, adv.; **or later** emol, adv; **than** eb, conj.; prep.

soot Russ (der)n.

soothe 1.dischdere, v.; gedischdert, pp.; 2.dischdre, v.;
gedischdert, pp.; 3.schmeechle, v.; gschmeechelt,
pp.; 4. schtille, v.; gschtillt, pp.

soothsayer 1.Waahretsaager (der)n.; 2.Waahrsaager (der)
n.; 3.Wohrsaager (der)n.

sooty russich, adj.

sophisticated freihaerich, adj.; **fellow** Wix (der)n.

soporific Schlofdrobbe (die)n., pl.

sorceress 1.Hex (die)n.; Hexe, pl.

sordid schmutzich, adj.

sore 1.bleed, adj.; 2.roh, adj.; 3.schmaerzhaft, adj.; 4.weh,
adj.; 5.weh, adj. (ebbes --es); 6.Wewwi (es)n.; 7.wund,
adj.; **(as punishment for sin)** Sindeschuld (die)n.;
Sindeschulde, pl.; **throat** 1.Gwinsi (die)n.; 2.Wehhals
(der)n.; Wehhels, pl.

sorrel Sauerrambel (der)n.; **horse** 1.Fuxgaul (der)n.; 2.
Schweesfux (der)n.

sorrow 1.Beschwerde (die)n.; 2.Driebsaal (der)n.; 3.Gwaal
(die)n.; 4.Leed(e) (der)n.; 5.Sarig (die)n.; 6.Sarye (die,
es)n.

sorrowful 1.bedauerich, adj.; 2.bedreibt, adj.;
3.drauerich, adj.; 4.leedmiedich, adj.

sorry 1.ee, adj., adv.; 2.(eem [dative singular] leed duh)

sort 1.Aart (die)n.; 2.aus/saarde, v.; aussaart, pp.;
3.aus/sorde, v.; ausgsort, pp.; 4.Ort (die)n.; 5.sarde,
v.; gsart, pp.; 6.Sart (die)n.; 7.sarte, v.; gsart, pp.;
8.Satt (die)n.; Sadde, pl.; **of** 1.Aart (die)n. (uff
en -- wie); 2.Ort (die)n. (uff en -- wie) 3.sadde, adv.;
over rum/lese, v.; rumgelese, pp.

sot Schtinkbock (der)n.; Schtinkbeck, pl.

soul 1.Seel (die)n.; Seele, pl.; 2.soul satisfying;
3.gemietlich, adj.

sound 1.Klang (der)n.; 2.klange, v.; geklangt, pp.; 3.klinge,
v.; geklingt, pp.; 4.laude, v.; gelaut, pp.; 5.Laut (der)
n.; 6.laute, v.; gelaut, pp.; 7.Schall (der)n.; Schalle,

sow

pl.; 8.schalle, v.; gschallt, pp.; 9.schelle, v.; gschellt,
pp.; 10.Ton (der)n.; **across** 1.niwwer/schalle, v.;
niwwergschallt, pp.; 2.niwwer/schtimme, v.;
niwwergschtimmt, pp.; **after** no(och)schalle, v.;
no(och)gschallt, pp.; **at a distance** weck/schalle, v.;
weckgschallt, pp.; **in** rei/schalle, v.; reigschallt, pp.;
into (a place) nei/schalle, v.; neigschallt)n.; 3., pp.;
made to imitate ducks Gwack!; **of disgust** (uttered
by mothers to cause a child to desist from taking up
or from; taking some object into the mouth)
1.baetschi!, interj.; 2.Baex(i)!, interj.; 3.bax(i)!,
interj.; **one's own praises** 1.raus/schtreiche (sich --)
v.; rausgschtriche, pp.; 2.schtreiche (sich --)v.; **out
from** raus/schalle, v.; rausgschallt, pp.; **up**
ruff/schalle, v.; ruffgschallt, pp.; **up** (to a place)
nuff/schalle, v.; nuffgschnallt, pp.

sounding board Schallbrett (es)n.

soup Supp (die)n.; **bone** 1.Gnochefleesch (es)n.;
2. Subbegnoche (der)n.; **dish** Subbeschissel (die)n.;
ladle Subbekell (die)n.; Subbekelle, pl.; **made of
bread, water, salt and pepper** 1.penede =
wassersupp (contemptuous for any soup)
2.Wassersupp (der)n.; **made with "Riwwle"**
Riwwelsupp (die)n.; **meat** Subbefleesch (es)n.; **of
left-overs** Schpatzesupp (die)n.; **with rum in it**
Drammsupp (die)n.

sour 1.sauer, adj.; 2.unfrehlich, adj.; **(of milk)** kaesich,
adj.; **(tart) apple** Sauerabbel (der)n.; **cherry**
Sauerka(e)sch (die)n.; Sauerka(e)sche, pl.; **cream
cake** 1.Sauereraahmkuche (der)n.;
Sauereraahmkuche, pl.; 2.Sawereraahmkuche (der)
n.; Sawereraahmkuche, pl.

source Urschprung (der)n.

souse 1.Galleri(ch) (es)n.; 2.Gallrich (der)n.; 3.Shnadderli
(es)n.; 4.Zidderli (der)n.

south 1.saut, adv.; 2.Sudd(e) (die)n.; 3.sudde, adv.; **side**
Middaagseit (die)n.

southerly 1.siddlich, adj.; 2.siddlich, adv.; 3.siedlich, adv.

southern 1.siddlich, adj.; 2.siedlich, adj.; 3.suddlich, adv.;
wood Aldermann (Schtock) (der)n.

southward noch Middaag zu, adv.

southwest suddwescht, adv.

sow (a field) 1.aus/saehe, v.; ausgsaeht, pp.; 2.eisaee, v.;
eigsaet, pp.; 3.naus/mache, v.; nausgemacht,
pp;4.naus/saee, v.; nausgsaet, pp.; 5.naus/saehe, v.;
nausgsaeht, pp.; 6.sae-e, v.; gsaegt, pp.; 7.saehe, v.;
gsaeht, pp.; **(a field) with gypsum** gipse, v.; gegipst,
pp.; **in dust** eischtaawe, v.; eigschtaabt, pp.; **poorly**
1.naus/schaere, v.; nausgschaert, pp.; 2.nei/schaere,
v.; neigschaert, pp.; **with a drill** drille, v.; gedrillt, pp.

sow (female pig) 1.Loos (die)n.; Loose, pl.; 2.Sau (die)n.;
Sei, pl.; **bug** 1.Kelleresel (der)n.; 2.Kellerhaasli (es)n.;
Kellerhasslin, pl.; 3.Kellerkeffer (der)n.; Kellerkeffer,
pl.; 4.Kellerlaus (die)n.; Kellerleis, pl.; 5.Kellermaus
(die)n.; Kellermeis, pl.; 6.Kellermeisli (es)n.; Kellermeislin, pl.; 7.Kellerox (der)n.; Kelleroxe, pl.

376

Ss

sowed field in wheat or rye — spike

sowed field in wheat or rye 1.Somefeld (es)n.;2.Sootfeld (es)n.

sower Saehmann (der)n.

soybean 1.Kecherli (es)n.; 2.Kiehbohn (die)n.; Kiehbohne, pl.

space in a building (immediately under the ridge pole) Faerscht (der)n.; **of time** Weil (die)n.

spacious scheinbaar, adj.

spade 1.rum/graawe, v.; rumgegraawe, pp.; 2.rum/mache, v.; rumgemacht, pp.; 3.rum/schpaade, v.; rumgschpaade, pp.; 4.Schaufel (die)n.; 5.Schipp (die)n.; 6.Schiwwel (die)n.; 7.schpaade, v.; gschpaade, pp.; 8.Schpaat (die)n.; **(in cards)** Schipp (die)n.

spadix of calamus Kalmusschwanz (der)n.

spall Schpaal (der)n.; Schpaale; Schpalde, pl.

span Schpann (der)n.

Spanish schpanisch, adj.; **needle** 1.Buweleis (die)n., pl.; 2. Maedleis (die)n., pl.; 3.Schpanodel (die)n.; Schpanodle, pl.

spank 1.blet(s)che, v.; gebletscht, pp.; 2.flabbe,v.; gflabbt, pp.; 3.flappe, v.; gflappt, pp.

spare 1.schone, v.; gschont, pp.; 2.schpaare, v.; gschpaart, pp.; 3.schune, v.; gschont, pp.; 4.schune, v.; gschunt, pp.; 5.verschone, v.; verschont, pp.; 6.verschpaare, v.; verschpaart, pp.; 7.verschune, v.; verschont, pp.; **ribs** Ribbefleesch (es)n.

sparing with gnappse, v.; gegnappst, pp.

spark 1.Feierfunke (der)n.; 2.Funke (der)n.; Funke, pl.; **plug** Funkezabbe (der)n.

sparkle 1.finkle, v.; gfinkelt, pp.; 2.flinke, v.; gflinkt, pp.; 3. flunke, v.; gflunkelt, pp.; 4.funkle, v.; gfunkelt, pp.

sparrow 1.Schpaerling (der)n.; 2.Schpatz (der)n.; 3.Schpetzel (es)n.

spavin Schpaade (der)n.

spawn Fischbrud (die)n.

spay schneide, v.; gschnidde, pp.

spayed sow 1.Geld (die)n.; Gelde, pl.; 2.Gelds (die)n.; Geldse, pl.; 3.Gelsd (die)n.; Gelsde, pl.

Speak out! Raus mit der Fareb!

speak 1.rede, v.; geredt, pp.; 2.schpreche, v.; gschproche, pp.; 3.schwetze, v.; gschwetzt, pp.; **freely** 1.raus/saage, v.; rausgsaat, pp.;2.raus/schwetze, v.; rausgschwetzt, pp.; **gruffly** 1.aa/faahre, v.; aagfaahre, pp.; 2.aa/ranse, v.; aageranst, pp.; 3.schnarre, v.; gschnarrt, pp.; **ill of one** 1.(behind his back) no(och)saage, v.; no(och)gsaat, pp.; 2.naus/mache, v.; nausgemacht, pp. (iwwer ebber --) **indistinctly** 1.laerbse, v.; gelaerbst, pp.; 2.larbse, v.; gelarbst, pp.; 3.muffle, v.; gmuffelt, pp.; 4.schtruddle, v.; gschtruddelt, pp.; **out** 1.aus/schpreche, v.; ausgschproche, pp.; 2.aus/schwetze, v.; ausgschwetzt, pp.; **roughly to** aa/schnarre, v.; aagschnatt, pp.

speaker 1.Reeder (der)n.; 2.Schprecher (der)n.; 3.Schwetzer (der)n.; Schwetzer, pl.

speaking trumpet Schallhann (es)n.

spear 1.Schpiess (der)n.; 2.schpiesse, v.; gschpiesst, pp.; **with a fork** nei/schpiesse, v.; neigschpiesst, pp.

spearmint 1.Balsem (der)n. (wilder --); 2.grieschtenglich Balsem (der)n.

special(ly) 1.abaddich, adv., adj.; 2.abard, adv.; 3.abbardich, adv., adj.; 4.baddich, adv.; 5.weiders, adv.

specie Hartgeld (es)n.

species of apple Hunnichabbel (der)n.; **of lily** Kaiserskron (die)n.

specification Bezeigung (die)n.

specify bezeige, v.; bezeikt, pp.

speck (of flies) Schiss (der)n.

specked verduppt, adj.

speckled 1.kipprich, adj.; 2.schifferich, adj.; 3. schifferschteenich, adj.; 4.schiffrich, adj.; 5.schiwwer-schteenich, adj.; 6.schiwwerich, adj.; 7.schiwwerschteenich, adj.; **bean** Voggelsbohn (die) n.; **red** rot scheckich, adj.

spectacle 1.Aageschpickel (der)n.; 2.Aageschpiel (der)n.; 3.Aageschpiggel (der)n.; 4.Aasicht (die)n.; 5.Schpeckdaagel (der)n.; 6.Schpeckdaakel (der)n.; 7.Schpekdaagel (der)n.; 8.Schpektakel (der)n.; 9.Aageglesser (die)n., pl.; 10.Brill (die)n.; Brille, pl.

spectacles-case Brillescheed (die)n.; Brillescheede, pl.

specter Schpunk (der)n.

speculate 1.schpeckeliere, v.; gschpeckeliert, pp.; 2. schpekeliere, v.; gschpekeliert, pp.

speech 1.Reed (die)n.; 2.Retschrett (die)n.; 3.Rett (die)n.; 4. Schprooch (die)n.; **(at a meeting, banquet)** Feschtred (es)n.

spell 1.aus/schlagge, v.; ausgschlagge, pp.; 2.Lick (die)n.; 3.Schtiwwer (der)n.; 4.Zauber (der)n.

spell-book Brauchbuch (es)n.

spelt Schpels (der)n.

spend 1.darich/blose, v.; darichgeblose, pp.; 2.schpende, v.; gschpendt, pp.; 3.uff/lewe, v.; uffglebt, pp.; 4.verlewe, v.; verlebt, pp.; 5.verwenne, v.; verwennt, pp.; 6.weck/balke, v.; weckgebalkt, pp.; 7.zehre, v.; gezehrt, pp.; 8.zu/bringe, v.; zugebrocht, pp.; **(time)** rum/bringe, v.; rumgebrocht, pp.; **for dainties** verfresse, v.; verfresse, pp.; **in drink** 1.uff/saufe, v.; uffgsoffe, pp.; 2.versaufe, v.; versoffe, pp.; **money lavishly** Geld (es)n. (-- verschpritze); **money with doctors** verdokdere, v.; verdokdert, pp.

spending money 1.Zehrgeld (es)n.; 2.Zehring (die)n.

spendthrift Darichbringer (der)n.; Darichbringer, pl.

spice Gewaerz (es)n.; Gewaerzer, pl.; **cooky** Kiehzung (die)n.; **wood** Pefferholz (es)n.

spider Schpinn (die)n.; Schpinne, pl.

spiderweb Schpinneweb (es)n.; Schpinnewewer, pl.

spiderwort Schpinnegraut (es)n.

spigot 1.Graahne (der)n.; 2.Grone (der)n.; 3.Kraander)n.; 4.Zabbe (der)n.; Zabbe, pl.

spike (of yellow or green foxtail) Rischbel (die)n.; **of timothy** Kolwe (der)n.; Kolwe, pl.; **toothed harrow** Schpeikeeg (die)n.

Ss

spikenard

spikenard (herb of ginseng family) Sassefrill (die)n. (zaahmi --)

spill 1. us/leere, v.; ausgeleert, pp.; 2.verleere, v.; verleert, pp.; 3.verschidde, v.; verschitt, pp.; 4.verschitte, v.; verschitt, pp.; 5.verschlabbe, v.; verschlappt, pp.; **water** (all over the floor) 1.verdriele, v.; verdrielt, pp.; 2.verdrillt, v.; verdrillt, pp.

spin schpinne, v.; gschpunne, pp.; **off** ab/schpinne, v.; abgschpunne, pp.

spinach Schpinaat (der)n.

spindle Schpindel (der)n.

spindling schpindlich, adj.

spine 1.Richschtrang (der)n.; Richschtreng, pl.; 2.Rick (der)n.; Ricke, pl.

spinning wheel (for wool) Wollraad (es)n.; **wheel** Schpinnraad (es)n.; Schpinnredder, pl.

spire 1.Tann (der)n.; 2.Tarm (der)n.; 3.Tarn (der)n.; 4.Turm (der)n.

spirit Geischt (der)n.; Geischder, pl.; **hunter** 1.Ewichyaeger (der)n.; 2.Siwweyaeger (der)n.; **of the times** Zeitgeischt (der)n.

spirited mudich, adj

spirits 1.(drink) Schnapps (der)n.; 2.Schpaerrit (der)n.

spiritual geischtlich, adj.

spiritualistic performances Kinschdlerei (die)n.

spirting Gschpritz (es)n.

spit 1.Schpau (es)n.; 2.schpaue, v.; gschpaut, pp.; 3.schpautze, v.; gschpautzt, pp.; 4.schpauze, v.; gschpauzt, pp.; 5.schpucke, v.; gschpuckt, pp.; 6.schpuuze, v.; gschpuuzt, pp.; **in** nei/schpaue, v.; neigschpaut, pp.; **out** 1.aus/schpauze, v.; ausgschpauzt, pp.; 2.naus/schpaue, v.; nausgschpaut, pp.; 3.weck/schpaue, v.; weckgschpaut, pp.

spite 1.Beesheet (die)n.; 2.Beesheit (die)n.; 3.Groll (der) n.; 4.reie, v.; gereit, pp.; 5.schpeide, v.; gschpeidt, pp.; 6.Schpeit (der)n.; 7.(Montgomery Co., PA) schpidde, v.; gschpitt, pp.

spiteful 1.boshaft, adj.; 2.schpeitvoll, adj.; 3.trotzich, adj.

spitting Gschpautz (es)n.

spittle 1.Schpau (der)n.; 2.Schpautz, (der)n.; 3.Schpauz (der, es)n.

spittoon Schpaubax (die)n.; Schpaubaxe, pl.

splash 1.aa/schpritze, v.; aagschpritzt, pp.; 2.blatsche, v.; geblatscht, pp.; 3.raus/schtritze, v.; rausgschtritzt, pp.; 4.rausche, v.; gerauscht, pp.; 5.schpritze, v.; gschpritzt, pp.; 6.schtritze, v.; gschtritzt, pp.; **around** rum/puddle, v.; rumgepuddelt, pp.; **in** nei/schpritze, v.; neigschpritzt, pp.; **in water** 1.flatsche, v.; gflatscht, pp.; 2.suddle, v.; gsuddelt, pp.; **into** nei/blatsche, v.; neigeblatscht, pp.; **out** raus/ schpritze, v.; rausgschpritzt, pp.; **up** nuff/schpritze, v.; nuffgschpritzt, pp.; **with mud** verblatsche, v.; verblatscht, pp.

splashing Gschpritz (es)n.; **(of a downpour)** blatschich, adj.

splay mouthed 1.Breedmaul (es)n.; 2. Breetmaul (es)n.

spool

spleen 1.Mils (die)n.; 2.Milz (die)n.

splendid 1.brechdich, adj.; 2.hallich, adj.; 3.harlich, adj.; 4.herrlich, adj.

splendidly 1.Aart (die)n. (das es en -- hot); 2.Ort (die)n. (das es en -- hott)

splendor 1.Bracht (die)n.; 2.Glanz (der)n.; 3.Pracht (die)n.

splenetic 1.milsich, adj.; 2.milzich, adj.

splint 1.Schpund (der)n.; **(used in making baskets, brooms and chair-seats)** Schiene (die)n.

splint basket Schien(e)kar(e)b (der)n.

splint (for setting bones) Schindel (die)n.; Schindle, pl.

splinter 1.Schliffer (der)n.; Schliffere, pl.; 2.Schliwwer (der) n.; Schliwwere, pl.; 3.schliwwere, v.; gschliwwert, pp.; 4.verschliwwere, v.; verschliwwert, pp.

splintery 1.schlifferich, adj.; 2.schliwwerich, adj.

split 1.schpalde, v.; gschpalt, pp.; 2.schplidde, v.; gschplitt, pp.; 3.Schplitt (der)n.; 4.schplitte, v.; gschplitt, pp.; 5.verschpalde, v.; verschpalt, pp.; 6.verschplidde, v.; verschplitt, pp.

split ring (joining the singletree to the doubletree) Middelring (der)n.; **up** uff/schplidde, v.; uffgschplitt, pp.

splitting axe Schpaltax (die)n.; Schpaltex, pl.

spoil 1.her/richde, v.; hergericht, pp.; 2.hie/richde, v.; hiegericht, pp.; 3.verbuckere, v.; verbuckert, pp.; 4.verdarewe, v.; verdarewe, pp.; 5.verhunse, v.; verhunst, pp.; 6.verletze, v.; verletzt, pp.; 7.verschtimmle, v.; verschtimmelt, pp.; verschtimple, v.; verschtimmelt, pp.; **(a child)** verwehne, v.; verwehnt, pp.; **by abuse** verkollebiere, v.; verkollebiert, pp.; **by notching** verkefdle, v.; verkefdelt, pp.; **by raining** nei/regge, v.; neigeregert, pp.; **by rainy weather** verreggere, v.; verreggert, pp.; **by scratching** 1.vergratze, v.; vergratzt, pp.; 2.verschaere, v.; verschaert, pp.; **by snowing** verschnee-e, v.; verschneet, pp.; **by urinating on** 1.verpisse, v.; verpisst, pp.; 2.verseeche, v.; verseecht, pp.; **in making** verpusche, v.; verpuscht, pp.; **or damage by weathering** verraeze, v.; verraezt, pp. **with too much**

salt versalze, v.; versalzt, pp.

spoiled 1.verdarewe, adj.; 2.verdutzt, adj.; 3.verkollebiert, adj.; 4.verschtimmelt, adj.; **(of an egg that has been set too long)** verbriet, adj.; **(of canned fruits)** gruuscht, adj.; **(of plants)** verschtutzt, adj.; **(or over- indulged) child** Ding (es)n. (verglinselt --); **with too much pepper** verpeffert, adj.

spoke (in a wheel) 1.Schpacht (der)n.; Schpachde, pl.; 2.Schpeech (der)n.; Schpeeche, pl.

sponge Schwamm (der)n.; **cake** 1.Oierkuche (der)n.

spongy (of fruit, radishes) 1.belsich, adj.; 2.punkich, adj.

sponsors (at baptismal) 1.Daafzeige (die)n., pl.; 2.Pedder (der)n. (-- un god)

spook 1.Gschpuck (der)n.; Gschpucker, pl.; 2.Schpuck(s) (es)n.; Schpucke, pl.

spool Schpule (der)n.

378

Ss

spoon

spoon Leffel (der)n.; Leffle, pl.
spoonful Leffelvoll (der)n.
sporatic weitleftich, adj.
spores (of the ground pine) Hexemehl (es)n.
sportive yuxich, adj.
spot 1.Blacke (der)n.; 2.Duppe (der)n.; 3.Fleck(e) (der)n.;
    Flecke, pl.; 4.flecke, v.; gfleckt, pp.; 5.Lappe (der)n.;
    6.verflecke, v.; verfleckt, pp.
spots on the skin (liver spots?) Karichhofflecke (die)n.
spotted 1.blackich, adj.; 2.dibbeldunich, adj.; 3.dipplich,
    adj.; 4.dupplich, adj.; 5.fleckich, adj.; 6.scheckich,
    adj.; 7.scheel, adj.; 8.schprechlich, adj.; **cow** 1.Scheck
    (die)n.; 2.Scheckikuh (die)n.; **cranesbill** 1.Grabbefuss
    (der)n.; 2.Grabbeschnawwel (der)n.; **geranium**
    1.Grabbefuss (der)n.; 2.Grabbeschnawwel (der)n.;
    sandpiper Yuckschnepp (die)n.; **wintergreen**
    1.R(h)ummedisgraut (es)n.;
spout 1.Kandel (der)n.; Kandle, pl.; 2.Rohr (es)n.;
    3.schtrudle, v.; gschtrudelt, pp.; **(of coffee or tea
    pot)** 1.Schnawwel (der)n.; Schnewwel, pl.; 2.Zott
    (die)n.
sprain 1.Verrengt (es)n.; 2.verrenke, v.; verrenkt, pp.;
    3.verschtauche, v.; verschtaucht, pp.
sprawl hie/blatsche, v.; hiegeblatscht, pp.; **out** schprauze,
    v.; gschprauzt, pp.
spray of leaves Labbwisch (der)n.
spread 1.aus/breede, v.; ausgebreet, pp.; 2.Schprae (die)n.;
    3.schpraehe, v.; gschpraet, pp.; 4.schprettle, v.;
    gschpreddelt, pp.; 5.schtraee, v.; gschtraet, pp.;
    6.verbreede, v.; verbreet, pp.; 7.verbreite, v.; verbreit,
    pp.; 8.verschpaehe, v.; verschpraet, pp.; 9.verschpraee,
    v.; verschpraet, pp.; **(bed a stable or cattle)** schtraehe,
    v.; gschtraet, pp.; **(of colors)** darich/schiesse, v.;
    darichgschosse, pp.; **(something) over** iwwer/decke, v.;
    iwwergedeckt, pp.; **by telling** rum/saage, v.; rumgsaat,
    pp. **evil reports about someone** aus/greische, v.;
    ausgegrische, pp. (ebber --); **oneself** ausbreede (sich --)
    v.; ausgebreet, pp.; **out** 1.aus/schpraehe, v.;
    ausgschpraet, pp.; 2.schpraddlich, adj.;
    3.verschpraddelt, adj.; **out (like a plant)** schpraddle, v.;
    gschpraddelt, pp.; **reports** 1.naus/blaere, v.;
    nausgeblaert, pp.; 2.naus/blaffe, v.; nausgeblafft, pp.;
    3.rum/blaudre, v.; rumgeblaudert, pp.;
    4.rumher/blaudre, v.; rumhergeblaudert, pp.;
    5.rumher/greische, v.; rumhergegrische, pp.; **some-
    thing on bread** schmiere, v.; gschmiert, pp.; **tales**
    1.aus/babble, v.; ausgebabbelt, pp.; 2.greische, v.;
    gegrische, pp.; **upwards** (of vines) nuff/ranke, v.;
    nuffgerankt, pp.
spreading dogbane Hun(d)sgraut (es)n.
sprig Schtreissel (es)n.
sprightly 1.lebhaft, adj.; 2.wusslich, adj.
spring 1.Fedder (die)n.; Feddre, pl.; 2.Schneller (der)n.;
    (of lumber) schpringe, v.; gschprunge, pp.; **(of wa-
    ter)** 1.Brunne (die)n.; 2.Gwell (die)n.; 3.Schpring
    (die)n. **(season)** 1.Friehling (der)n.; 2.Friehyaahr (es)
    n; **day** Friehyaahrsdaag (der)n.; **halted**

squeeze

    schnaerrfiessich, adj.; peepers 1.Fresch (die)n., pl.;
    2.Friehling (die)n., pl.; **up** 1.uff/gwelle, v.;
    uffgegwellt, pp.; 2.uff/kumme, v.; is uffkumme, pp.;
    3.uff/quelle, v.; uffgequellt, pp.; **up and down**
    gaunsche, v.; gegaunscht, pp.; **weather**
    1.Friehyaarhswedder (es)n.; 2.Schpringwedder (es)n.
springhouse Schpringhaus (es)n.
springwater Schpringegewasser (es)n.
sprinkle 1.aa/schpritze, v.; aagschpritzt, pp.; 2.netze, v.;
    genetzt, pp.; 3.raus/schtritze, v.; rausgschtritzt, pp.;
    4.schpritze, v.; gschpritzt, pp.; 5.schtritze, v.;
    gschtritzt, pp.; **(of rain)** Schpritzer (der)n.; **wash**
    (before ironing) 1.eischpritze, v.; eigschpritzt, pp.;
    2.Wesch (die)n. (-- aaschpritze)
sprinkler of a sprinkling can Giesskannekopp (der)n.
sprinkling can 1.Giesskann (die)n.; 2.Schtitz (der)n.;
    Schtitze, pl.
sprout 1.Keim (die)n.; Keime, pl.; 2.Schuss (der)n.;3.uff/geh,
    v.; uffgange, pp.; 4.uff/kumme, v.; is uffkumme, pp.
sprouted ausgewaxe, adj.
sprung (of a window, door) verschprunge, adj.
spry supel, adj.
spunk Schpank (der)n.
spunky 1.batzich, adj.; 2.schpankich, adj.
spur Schpore (der)n.
spurn weck/schtosse, v.; weckgschtosse, pp.
sputter schtruddle, v.; gschtruddelt, pp.; **(of boiling
    mush)** schpratzle, v.; gschpratzelt, pp.
spy 1.nei/faschle, v.; 2.Schnuffler (der)n.; Schnuffler, pl.;
    3. Schpion (der)n.; **glass** Schpekdief (es)n.; **out**
    1.aus/faschle, v.; ausgfaschelt, pp.; 2.aus/fische, v.;
    ausgfischt, pp.; 3.aus/fischle, v.; ausgfischelt, pp.;
    4.rum/ rieche, v.; rumgeroche, pp.; 5.schpione, v.;
    gschpiont, pp.
squab Daub (die)n. (yungi --)
squall Schtiwwer (der)n.; **(of snow)** Gschtiwwer (der)n.
squander 1.darich/bringe, v.; 2.darich/yaage, v.;
    darichgeyaagt, pp.; 3.schpende, v.; gschpendt, pp.;
    4. verbamble, v.; verbambelt, pp.; 5.verbemble, v.;
    verbembelt, pp.; 6.verbringe, v.; verbrocht, pp.;
    7.verduh, v.; verduh, pp.; 8.verfuggere, v.;
    verfuggert, pp.; 9.verzackere, v.; verzackert, pp.; **on
    food** verfresse, v.; verfresse, pp.
squandering verdunisch, adj.
square 1.viereckich, adj.; 2.Winkel (der)n.; 3.winkel, adj.;
    (carpenter's tool) Winkeleise (es)n.; **accounts**
    ab/rechle, v.; abgerechelt, pp.
squash Kaer(r)bs (die)n.; Kaer(r)bse, pl.; **beetle**
    Kaerbsekeffer (der)n.; Kaerbsekeffer, pl.
squeak (of mice) gwieke, v.; gegwiekt, pp.
squeal kreische, v.; gekrische, pp.
squealing Gschrei (es)n.
squeamish 1.eklich, adj.; 2.kotzerich, adj.
squeeze 1.dricke, v.; gedrickt, pp.; 2.presse, v.; gepresst,
    pp.; 3.rum/dricke, v.; rumgedrickt, pp.; 4.verdricke,

(Continued on page 380)

379

Ss

squeeze (continued)

(Continued from page 379)

v.; verdrickt, pp.; **open** uff/dricke, v.; uffgedrickt, pp.;
out raus/dricke, v.; rausgedrickt, pp.

squill 1.Saezwiwwel (die)n.; 2.Seezwiwwel (die)n.

squint schiele, v.; gschielt, pp.

squirm 1.rutsche, v.; gerutscht, pp.; 2.schrauwe,v.;
gschraubt, pp.

squirming (child) rutschich, adj.

squirrel 1.Eecherli (es)n.; 2.Eechhaernche (es)n.;
3.Eechhaesel (es)n.; 4.Gschgwall (der)n.; Gschgwalle,
pl.

squirt 1.aa/schpritze, v.; aagschpritzt, pp.;
2.raus/schtritze, v.; rausgschtritzt, pp.; 3.schpritze,
v.; gschpritzt, pp.; 4.schtritze, v.; gschtritzt, pp.;
5.Wasserschpritz (die)n.

squirt gun Schtritzbix (die)n.

squish (in mud) gwatsche, v.; (ge)gwatscht, pp.

St. Andrew's Day, Nov 30. Andreasdaag (der)n.; **Bartholomew's Day**, August 24 Baardelmae (der)n.; **James
Day**, July 25 Yakobus (der)n.; **John's wort**
1.Gottesblut (das)n.; 2.Hexegraut (es)n.; 3.Kansgraut
(es)n.; 4.Yohannsgraut (es)n.; **Lawrence Day**, August
10.Laarenzius (der)n.; **Nicholas** Belznickel (der)n.;
Belznickel, pl.

stab schteche, v.; gschtoche, pp.

stable 1.Schtall (der)n.; Schtell, pl.; 2.schtalle, v.; gschtallt,
pp.; **door** Schtalldier (die)n.

stabling Schtalling (die)n.

stack Schtock (der)n.; Schteck, pl.; **of rye** Kannschtock
(der)n.

staff Schtaab (der)n.; Schtaawe, pl.

stag's head Haschkopp (der)n.

stagger 1.darigle,v.; gedarigelt,pp.;2.wanke, v.; gewankt,
pp.; **after** no(och)darigle,v.;no(och)gedarigelt,
pp.;**around** 1.rum/dargele,v.; rumgedargelt,
pp.;2.rumdarigle,v.; rumgedarigelt,pp.

stagnation Schtillschtand (der)n.

stain 1.Fleck(e) (der)n.; Flecke, pl.; 2.flecke, v.; gfleckt, pp.

stair Schtuf (die)n.

stairs Schteeg (die)n.; Schteege, pl.

stairway Schteeg (die)n.; Schteege, pl.

stake 1.Schtaake (der)n.; 2.Schtickel (der)n.; **fence**
(zig-zag) Schtaakefens (der)n.; Schtaagefense, pl.

stale 1.abgschtanne, adj.; 2.alt, adj.; **(of a joke)** harrich, adj.

stalk 1.Hallem (der)n.; 2.Halm (der)n.; Halme, pl.;
3.Schtengel (der)n.; 4.Schtengli (es)n.; **with a flower**
Blummeschtrauss (der)n.

stalker (kind of fish net) Schtellgaarn (es)n.

stall Schtall (der)n.; Schtell, pl.

stalled (with a load) schtecke, v. (-- bleiwe)

stallion Zuchthengscht (der)n.; **with retained testicles**
Glopphengscht (der)n.

stammer 1.schtoddere, v.; gschtoddert, pp.; 2.schtottere,
v.; gschtottert, pp.

stammering schtotterich, adj.

stamp schtambe, v.; gschtampt, pp.; **into** nei/schtambe,

v.; neigschtumpt, pp.; **off** ab/schtambe, v.;
abgschtambt, pp.; **beat out** aus/schtambe, v.;
ausgschtampt, pp.; **out cookies** (with a cookie cutter)
aus/schtecke, v.; ausgschteckt, pp. (Kichelcher --); **to
pieces** verschtambe, v.; verschtampt, pp.

stampede Flucht (die)n.

stamper 1.Schtamber (der)n.; Schtamber, pl.;
2.Schtembel (der)n.; 3.Schtember (der)n.; **used in
making sauerkraut** Grautschtamper (der)n.

stamping Gschtamp (es)n.; **hole** (made by horses in chasing flies) Schtamploch (es)n.

stand 1.Schtand (der)n.; 2.schteh, v.; gschtanne, pp.;
3. schtende, v.; **(by one's contentions)** debeischteh,
v.; debeigschtanne, pp.; **around** 1.rum/schteh, v.;
rumgschtanne, pp.; 2.rumher/schteh, v.;
rumhergschtanne, pp.; **at a distance** 1.ab/schteh, v.;
abgschtanne, pp.; 2.ab/ schtelle (sich --), v.;
abgschtellt, pp.; **back** zerick/schteh, v.;
zerickgschtanne, pp.; **between** dezwischeschteh, v.;
by one's guns 1.dabei/schteh, v.; 2.uff/halde, v.;
uffghalde, pp.; **firm** (in an altercation) nemme, v.;
genumme, pp. (sei Hinnerbart --) (sei
Hinnerbatt --); **for beehives** lemeschtand (der)n.; **for
salting meat** Schtenner (der)n.; Schtenner, pl.; **idle**
hie/schteh, v.; hiegschtanne, pp.; **in need of**
brauche, v.; gebraucht, pp.; **open** 1.schparre, v.;
gschpatt, pp.; 2.uff/schteh, v.; uffgschtanne, pp.;
ready for attack schtelle (sich --)v.; **still**
schtill/schteh, v.; schtillgschtanne, pp.; **superior**
grossschteh, adv.; **together** zamme/schteh, v.;
zammegschtanne, pp.; **up** uff/schteh, v.;
uffgschtanne, pp.; **up against** seckendiere (sich --)v.;
seckendiert, pp.; **well** gutschteh, adj.

Standard Time ("slow time") 1.Gottszeit (die)n.; 2.Zeit
(die)n. (langsami --);

standard (of a wagon) 1.Runge (der)n.; 2.Runne (der)n.

standing with one's legs far apart 1.breedbeenich, adj.;
2.breetbeenich, adj.

standstill Schtillschtand (der)n.

stanza Vaersch(t) (der)n.

star 1.Schtaern (die)n.; Schtaerne, pl.; 2.Schtann (der)n.;
Schtanne, pp.; **of Bethlehem** Schtaernblumm (die)n.;
Schtaernblumme, pl.

starch 1.blehe, v.; gebleet, pp.; 2.Schtaerick (die)n.;
3.schtaericke, v.; gschtaerickt, pp.; 4.Schtaerrick (die)n.;
5.schtaerricke, v.; gschtaerrickt, pp.; 6.Schtaik (die)n.;
7.schtaike, v.; gschtaikt, pp.; 8.Schtarick (die)n.

starched wash gschtaerickdi Wesch (die)n.

stare gaffe, v.; gegafft, pp.; **at** vergaffe (sich --)v.; vergafft, pp.

staring schtarr, adj.

starlit schtaernehell, adj.

starry 1.schtaernich, adj.; 2.schtannich, adj.

start 1.aa/fange, v.; aagfange, pp.; 2.aa/setze, v.; aagsetzt,
pp.; 3.ab/geh, v.; abgange, pp.; 4.schterde, v.;
gschter(d)t, pp.; **(from fright)** zamme/faahre, v.; is
zammegfaahre, pp.; **(out)** aus/setze, v.; ausgsetzt, pp.;

Ss

start (continued)   stick

a fire 1.aa/lege, v.; aagelekt, pp.; 2.feiere, v.; gfeiert, pp.; 3.uff/feiere, v.; uffgfeiert, pp.; **a matter** aa/zettle, v.; aagezettelt, pp.; **brooding** (of a hen) setze (sich --), v.; gsetzt, pp.; **by blowing** aa/blose, v.; aageblose, pp.; **driving** aa/dreiwe, v.; aagedriwwe, pp.; **off** ab/laafe, v.; abgeloffe, pp.; **off suddenly** uff/gratze, v.; uffgegratzt, pp.; **on a reel** aa/ wickle, v.; aagewickelt, pp.; **on a spree** aa/saufe (sich --)v.; aagsoffe, pp.; **something** aa/fackle (ebbes), v.; aagfackelt, pp.; **spinning** aa/schpinne, v.; aagschpunne, pp.; **the fire in a blast furnace** ei/blose, v.; eigeblose, pp.; **to drive away** ab/faahre, v.; abgfaahre, pp.; **to lift** aa/hewe, v.; aaghowe, pp.; **up** faahre, v.; gfaahre, pp.; (in die hee --)

starting a run Aalaaf (der)n.

starve 1.aus/hungere, v.; ausghungert, pp.; 2.verhungere, v.; verhungert, pp.

starved aushungert, adj.

starwort Hinkeldarm (der)n.

state 1.Adder (die)n.; 2.Schtaat (der)n.; 3.Schtand (der)n.; 4.Zuschtand (der)n.; Zuschtende, pl.; **of being alone** Alleesei (es)n.; **of growing old** Altwarre (es)n.

statute Gsetz (es)n.

stave (of a barrel, cask) 1.Fassdaub (die)n.; Fassdauwe, pl.; 2.Daub (die)n.; Dauwe, pl.

stay 1.bleiwe, v.; gebliwwe, pp.; 2.schtecke, v.; gschteckt, pp.; 3.schticke, v.; gschtickt, pp.; 4.verweile, v.; verweilt, pp.; 5.waarde, v.; **away** 1.fatt/bleiwe, v.; fattgebliwwe, pp.; 2.weck/bleiwe, v.; weckgebliwwe, pp.; **chain** Schtiefkett (die)n.; **for the night** 1.bleiwe, v. gebliwwe, pp. (iwwer Nacht --); 2.loschiere, v.; loschiert, pp.; **here** dobleiwe, v.; dogebliwwe, pp.; **on behind** zerick/henke, v.; zerickghenkt, pp.; **under** (water) unner/bleiwe, v.; unergebliwwe, pp.; **up** uff/bleiwe, v.; uffgebliwwe, pp.

steadfast 1.schtandhafdich, adj.; 2.schtandhaft, adj.; 3.schtarick, adj.

steadily 1.schtaedich, adv.; 2.schtaetich, adj.

steady schtandhaft, adj.; **by holding an ax against** wedder/halte, v.; wedderghalte, pp. (die ax --); **drinker** leppere, v.; geleppert, pp.; **rain** Landregge (der)n.

steal 1.schleiche, v.; gschliche, pp.; 2.schlibbe, v.; gschlippt, pp.; 3.schtehle, v.; gschtohle, pp.; 4.weck/lause, v.; weckgelaust, pp.; **away** 1.ab/schlibbe, v.; abgschlippt, pp.; 2.weck/schlibbe, v.; weckgschlippt, pp.; 3.weck/schtehle, v.; weckgschtohle, pp.; **from** 1.ab/schtehle, v.; abschtohle, pp.; 2.beschtehle, v.; beschtohle, pp.; 3.bschtehle, v.; bschtellt; bschtohle, pp.; 4.heemschleiche, v.; heemgschliche, pp.

stealth Heemlichkeet (die)n.

stealthily verschtohlenerweis, adv.

steam dambe, v.; gedampt, pp.

steamed dumpling Dampgnopp (der)n.; Dampgnepp, pl.

steel Schtaal (der)n.; **bit** Eisibohre (der)n.

steelyard Schnellwoog (die)n.

steep 1.aa/briehe, v.; aagebrieht, pp.; 2.abschissich, adj.; 3.gaeh(e), adj.; **(of hills)** gege, adj.; **slope** Abhang (der)n.; **stretch** of road Schtich (der)n.

steeple 1.Dann (der)n.; 2.Tann (der)n.; 3.Tarm (der) n.;4.Tarn (der)n.; 5.Turm (der)n.

steer 1.Ox (der)n.; 2.Rinnsvieh (es)n.; 3.schteiere, v.; gschteiert, pp.; 4.Schtier (der)n.; **(fat or fattening)** Maschtox (der)n.

steering wheel Schteierraad (es)n.

stellate sedge Bocksbaart (der)n.

stem 1.Schtamm (der)n.; 2.Schtengel (der)n.; 3.Schtengli (es)n.; **from** 1.her/schtamme, v.; hergschtammt, pp.; 2.her/schtamme, v.; hergschtammt, pp.

stench Gschtank (der)n.

stenographer Schnellschreiwer (der)n.

step 1.dredde, v.; gedredde, pp.; 2.schridde, v.; gschritt, pp.; **(from one floor level to another)** 1.Absatz (der) n.; Absetz, pl.; 2.Uffsatz(der)n.; Uffsetz, pl.; **(heavily)** 1.dappe, v.; gedappt, pp.; 2.trappe, v.; getrappt, pp.; **(on stair)** 1.Schtuf (die)n.; 2.Drepp (die)n.; Drebbe, pl.; **(walking)** Schritt (der)n.; Schridde, pl.; **across** niwwer/schridde, v.; niwwergschritt, pp.; **away** weck/schridde, v.; weckgschritt, pp.; **back** zerick/schritte, v.; zerickgschritt, pp.; **box** Schpindelpann (die)n.; **brother** Schtiefbruder (der)n.; Schtiefbrieder, pl.; **by step** 1.schriddich, adv.; 2.schrittweis(s), adv.; **child** Schtiefkind (es)n.; Schtiefkinner, pl.; **daughter** Schtiefdochder (die)n.; **down** nunner/schteige, v.; nunnergschtigge, pp.; **father** 1.Schtiefdaadi (der)n.; 2.Schtiefvadder (der)n.; **grandmother** Schtiefgrossmammi (die)n.; **in a certain place** hie/drede, v.; hiegedrede, pp.; **into** 1.eischteige, v.; eigschtigge, pp.; 2.nei/drede, v.; neigedrede, pp.; **into unexpectedly** nei/dabbe, v.; neigedappt, pp.; **mother** 1.Schtiefmammi (die)n.; 2.Schtiefmudder (die)n.; **off** ab/schtrecke, v.; abgschtreckt, pp.; **on** uff/drede, v.; gedredde, pp.; **sister** Schtiefschweschder (die)n.; **son** Schtiefsohn (der)n.

sterile unfruchtbaar, adj.

stern Hinnerdeel (es)n.

stew 1.dambe, v.; gedampt, pp.; 2.dempe, v.; gedempt, pp.; 3.schmore, v.

stick 1.babbe, v.; gebappt, pp.; 2.bappe, v.; gebappt, pp.; 3.Briggel (der)n.; 4.gickse, v.; gegickst, pp.; 5.giekse, v.; gegiekst, pp.; 6.glewe, v.; geglebt, pp.; 7.schteche, v.; gschtoche, pp.; 8.Schtecke (der)n.; 9.schtecke, v.; gschteckt, pp.; 10.schticke, v.; gschtickt, pp.; **(of candy)** 1..Schtengel (der)n.; 2.Schtengli (es)n.; **a drink** 1.Mick (die)n. (en -- nei/duh); 2.Muck (die)n. (en -- nei/duh); **fast** faschtschtecke, v.; faschtgschtocke, pp.; **game** ("sticking the stick") (Amish) Schteckli (es)n. (-- schtecke); **in place**

(Continued on page 382)

Ss

stick (continued)

(Continued from page 381)

hie/schtecke, v.; hiegschteckt, pp.; **insect** 1.Buscheesel (der)n.; Buscheesel, pl.; 2.Schteckedier (es)n.; Schteckediere, pl.; **of candy** 1.Zuckerschtengel (es)n.; 2. Zuckerschtengelche (es) n.; 3.Zuckerschtengli (es)n.; **or put in a place** nei/schtecke, v.; neigschteckt; neigschtocke, pp.; **out** 1.naus/schtecke, v.; nausgschteckt, pp.; 2.raus/ schtecke, v.; rausgschteckt, pp.; **through** darich/schtecke, v.; darichgschteckt; darichgschtocke, pp.; **to** dabei/bleiwe, v.; **to the house** eihocke, v.; eighockt, pp.; **to the pan in frying** aa/brode, v.; aagebrode, pp.; **together** 1.zamme/babbe, v.; zammegebappt, pp.; 2.zamme/schtecke, v.; zammegschtocke, pp.; 3.zamme/schticke, v.; zammegschtickt, pp.; **together in baking** zamme/backe, v.; zammegebackt, pp.; **used for twisting a rope of strawband** 1.Gnupse (der)n.; 2.Gnewwel (der)n.; 3.Knew(w)el (der)n.; **with** debeibliewe, v.; debeigebliwwe, pp.

stickseed Bettellaus (die)n.

sticky 1.aahen(k)sich, adj.; 2.aahenkisch, adj.; 3.babbich, adj.; 4.glebich, adj.; 5.gleewich, adj.; 6.schmierich, adj.; 7. schtickich, adj.

stiff 1.schteif, adj.; 2.schtraff, adj.

stiffness Schteifheit (die)n.

still 1.als, adv.; 2.noch, adv.; 3.ruhich, adj.; 4.schtill, adj.; **as a mouse** meiseschtill, adv.; **born** dodgebore, adj.

still! psch!, interj.

stilt Schtels (die)n.

sting 1.Biss (der)n.; 2.gickse, v.; gegickst, pp.; 3.giekse, v.; gegiekst, pp.; 4.schteche, v.; gschtoche, pp.; 5.Schtich (der)n.; **(of a bee)** Schtachel (der)n.; Schtachle, pl.; **of a wasp** Weschbeschtich (der)n.; **of an insect** 1.Gickser (der)n.; 2.Schtecher (der)n.; Schtecher, pl.

stinger (of a bee) Schtecher (der)n.; Schtecher, pl.

stinging nettle Brennes(s)el (der)n.

stingy 1.geize, v.; gegeizt, pp.; 2.geizich, adj.; 3.gnickse, v.; gegnickst, pp.; 4.knapps, adj.

stink 1.Gschtink (es)n.; 2.ludre, v.; gludert, pp.; 3.schtinke, v.; gschtunke, pp.

stinkbug Schtinkkeffer (der)n.; Schtinkkeffer,pl.

stinker Schtinker (der)n.; Schtinker, pl.

stinking camomile Seikamille (der)n.; **eryngo** Schlangegraas (es)n.

stint gnappse, v.; gegnappst, pp.

stipulate 1.bedinge, v.; bedingt, pp.; 2.Bedingung (die)n.

stir 1.bewege, v.; bewekt, pp.; 2.mucke (sich --)v.; gemuckt, pp.; 3.nuff/schtarre, v.; nuffgschtatt, pp.; 4.poke, v.; gepokt, pp.; 5.rege (sich --)v.; gerekt, pp.; 6.rege, v.; geregt, pp.; 7.riehre, v.; geriehrt, pp.; 8.rum/riehre, v.; rumgeriehrt, pp.; 9.sch(i)ere, v.; gschiert, pp.; 10.schtarre, v.; gschtarrt, pp.; 11.verrege (sich --)v.; verregt, pp.; 12.verrege, v.; verregt, pp.; **(always with a negative)** vermucke

stooped

(sich --)v.; vermuckt, pp.; **(fire)** raede, v.; geraedt, pp.; **in** eiriehre, v.; eigeriehrt, pp.; **out** 1.aus/schtarre, v.; ausgschtarrt, pp.; 2.raus/schtarre, v.; rausgschtarrt, pp.; **up** 1.aa/richde, v.; aagericht, pp.; 2.aa/schtarre, v.; aagschtrrt, pp.; 3.rum/riehre, v.; rumgeriehrt, pp.; 4.rum/ schtarre, v.; rumgschtarrt, pp.; 5.schtifde, v.; gschtifde, pp.; 6.uff/hetze, v.; uffghetzt, pp.; 7.uff/poke, v.; uffgepokt, pp.; 8.uff/rege, v.; uffgeregt, pp.; 9.uff/riege, v.; uffgeregt, pp.; 10.uff/riehre, v.; uffgriehrt, pp.;11.uff/schtachle, v.; 12.uff/schtarre, v.; uffgschtarrt, pp.

stirrer 1.Reihrer (der)n.; 2.Riehrer (der)n.; **fastened on to the copper kettle** (in which applebutter is made) Lattwarrickriehrer (der)n.

stirrup 1.Schteibiggel (der)n.; 2.Schteigbiggel (der)n.

stitch 1.aus/n(a)ehe, v.; ausgen(a)eht, pp.; 2.reihe, v.; gereiht, pp.; 3.schtebbe, v.; gschteppt, pp.; 4.schteppe, v.; gschteppt, pp.; **in one's side** Seideschteche (es)n.

stock 1.Logeige (die)n.; 2.Lovgeige (die)n. (v=f Lofgeige); **(of a gun)** 1.Schaft (der)n.; Schafde, pl.; 2.Scheft (der)n.

stocking Schtrump (der)n.; Schtrimp, pl.

stocklock Riggelschloss (es)n.

stocky schtumbich, adj.

stole Schtol (die)n.

stomach 1.Bauch (der)n.; Beich, pl.; 2.Leib (der)n.; 3.Maage (der)n.; **(of cattle)** Wambe(r) (der)n.; **bitters** Maagebidders (es)n.; **cramps** Maagegramp (der) n.; **fever** Maagefiewer (es)n.; **tooth** (lower canine) Maagezaah (der)n.

stomachache 1.Bauchweh (es)n.; 2.Leibschmatze (die)n.,pl.

stone 1.Schtee (der)n.; Schtee, pl.; 2.schteeniche, v.; gschteenicht, pp.; **(of fruit)** Kann (die)n.; Kanne, pl.; **blind** schtockblind, adj.; **clover** Schteeglee (der)n.; **crusher** Schteebrecher (der)n.; Schteebrecher, pl.; **deaf** schtockdaub, adj.; **fence** Schteefens (die)n.; Schteefense, pl.; **from the Blue Mountain** Baerrickschtee (der)n.; **jug** Schteegruck (der)n.; **quarry** Schteebruch (der)n.; Schteebrich, pl.; **row** (often as a fence between two fields) Schteeroi (die) n.; **sledge** Schteehammer (der)n.; Schteehemmer, pl.; **step** Schteedrepp (die)n.; Schteedrebbe, pl.; **used in crushing flaxseed** (or butternuts in making oil) Olichschtembel (der)n.; **wall** Schteemauer (die) n.; **boat** 1.Schteeboot (es)n.; Schteeboot, pl. 2.Schteeschlidde (der)n.; Schteeschlidde, pl.

stonecutter Schteehacker (der)n.; Schteehacker, pl.;

stonemason Raumaurer (der)n.

stony schteenich, adj.

stool Schtulgang (der)n.; **pigeon** Schtuhldaub (die)n.

stoop 1.bicke (sich --), v.; gebickt, pp.; 2.Schtuf (die)n.; **shouldered** bucklich, adj.

stooped 1.dachsich, adj.; 2.daxich, adj.; **(bent from age)** gedaucht, adj.

Ss

stop

stop 1.aa/halde, v.; aaghalde, pp.; 2.ab/breche, v.;
abgebroche, pp.; 3.ab/schtobbe, v.; abgschtoppt,
pp.; 4.Absatz (der)n.; Absetz, pl.; 5.ei/halde, v.;
eighalde, pp.; 6.halde, v.; ghalde, pp.;
7.schtill/schteh, v.; schtillgschtanne, pp.; 8.schtobbe,
v.; gschtoppt, pp.; 9.uff/ heere, v.; uffgheert, pp.;
10.uff/losse, v.; uffgelosst, pp.; 11.unnerwege losse,
v.; unnerwege gelosst, pp.; **(at an inn)** uff/schtelle,
v.; uffgschtellt, pp.; **a hole or leak** 1.verschtobbe, v.;
verschtoppt, pp.; 2.zu/schtecke, v.; zugschteckt, pp.;
3.zu/zabbe, v.; zugezappt, pp.; **at ei/kehre, v.;**
eigekehrt, pp.; **blood** Blut (es)n. (-- schtille); **blooming** verbliehe, v.; verblieht, pp.; **off** ab/schtobbe, v.;
abgschtoppt, pp.; **short** schtecke, v. (-- bleiwe); **up**
1.schtobbe, v.; gschtoppt, pp.; 2.zu/schtobbe, v.;
zugschtoppt, pp.; 3.zuschtoppe, v.; zugschtoppt, pp.;
up cracks (with plaster, etc.) zu/schmiere, v.;
zugschmiert, pp.

stopcock 1.Graan (der)n.; 2.Kraan (der)n.; 3.schtoppe, v.;
gschtoppt, pp.

stopped verschtoppt, adj.

stopper 1.Garrick (der)n.; 2.Schtobber (der)n.;
3.Schtopper (der)n.; 4.Zabbe (der)n.; Zabbe, pl.

storage place for grain, hay, straw (out building)
1.Schutzscheier (die)n.; Schutzscheiere,
pl.; 2.Schottscheier (die)n.; Schottschiere, pl.

store Schtor (der)n.; Schtore, pl.; **up** ei/lege, v.; eiglegt, pp.

storekeeper Schtorkibber (der)n.; Schtorkibber, pl.

stork 1.Schtarich (der)n.; 2.Schtarrich (der)n.

storm 1.Schtaerm (der)n.; 2.Schtar(e)m (der)n.;
3.Schtarmwind (der)n.; 4.Schtorm (der)n.;
5.Unwedder (es)n.; 6.Uuwedder (es)n.; 7.Wedder
(es)n.; **out** raus/schtaerme, v.; rausgschtaermt, pp.

stormy 1.schtaremich, adj.; 2.schtarme, v.; gschtarmt,
pp.; 3.schtarmich, adj.; **weather** Unwedder (es)n.

story Schtori (die)n.; Schtories, pl.; **(of a building)** Schtock
(der)n.; Schteck, pl.

stout 1.dick, adj.; 2.fett, adj.; 3.Lammel (der)n.; 4.Lemmel
(der)n.; 5.schtandhaft, adj.; 6.schtarick, adj.;
7.schtarrick, adj.; 8.Waddel (der)n.; **lad** Bengel (der)n.

stove 1.Offe (der)n.; Effe, pl.; 2.Offe (der)n.; Effe, pl.;
block (placed under stove legs) Fuus (der)n.; Fiess,
pl.; **brush** Offebascht (die)n.; **door** Offedeer (die)n.;
for heating Hitzoffe (der)n.; **leg** Offebee (es)n.; **lid**
Offedeckel (der)n.; **pipe** Rohr (es)n.; **polish**
Offeschwaerz (die)n.; **room** Offeschtupp (die)n.

stovepipe Offerohr (es)n.; **elbow** Offe-elboge (der)
n.;Offe-elboge, pl.; **hat** Schtitzhut (der)n.

stow away hie/schtecke, v.; hiegschteckt, pp.

straight 1.graad, adj.; 2.schnurschtracks, adj.;
3. schnurschtracks, adv.; 4.schtrack(s), adj.; **line**
Richtschnur (die)n.; **(perfectly)** 1.kaerzegraad, adj.;
2.kerzegraad, adj.

straightaway schtrack(s), adj.

straightway eenes Gangs, adv.

strain 1.schtauche, v.; gschtaucht, pp.; 2.schtrenge, v.;

strength

gschtrengt, pp.; **(food)** darich/dreiwe, v.;
darichdriwwe, pp.; **(liquids)** 1.darich/seihe, v.;
darichgseiht, pp.; 2.seene, v.; gseent, pp.; 3.seihe, v.;
gseiht, pp.; 4.siene, v.; gsient, pp.; **out** raus/seihe, v.;
rausgseiht, pp.; **through** 1.darich/seihe, v.;
darichgseiht, pp.; 2.seihe, v.; gseiht, pp.

strained cranberries darichdriwwne Schwammbeere (die)n.

strainer 1.Seener (der)n.; 2.Seih (die)n.; 3.Sienerli (es)n.;
Sienerlin, pl.

stramonium 1.Geilskimmel (der)n.; 2.Schtechabbel (der)n.

strange 1.fremm, adj.; 2.kariyos, adj.; 3.seldsam, adj.;
4.seltsam, adj.; 5.sunderbaar, adj.; 6.sunnerbaar,
adj.; 7.unbekannt, adj.; 8.wunnerlich, adj.; **person**
1.Kauz (der)n.; 2.Kiyoon (der)n.; 3.yoon (der)n.; **sight**
1.Schpekdaagel (der)n.; 2.Schpektakel (der)n.

stranger 1.Fremder (en)n.; 2.Fremmer (der)n.

strangers Leit (die)n., pl. (fremmi --)

strangle 1.iwwer/schlucke, v.; iwwergschluckt, pp.;
2.zuschniere, v.; zugschniert; pp.; **(a person)**
zuschniere, v.; zugschniert, pp. (die Kehl --)

strap 1.Band (es)n.; Benner, pl.; 2.Reime (der)n.; **of
leather** Rieme (der)n.; **or buckle back**
zerick/schnalle, v.; zerickgschnallt, pp.; **or buckle
together** zamme/schnalle, v.; zammegschnallt, pp.;
to rein up a horse's head Uffhebrieme (der)n.

straw 1.Piff (der)n.; 2.Schtroh (es)n.; **(cut fine) storage
room** (in a barn) Hexelkammer (die)n.; **as it comes
from the thresher** gewaerrt, adv. (-- schtroh); **band**
(for tying sheaves) 1.Seel (es)n.; 2.Schtrohseel (es)n.;
bolster (pillow) Schtrohkisse (es)n.; **bundle** (used in
burning hornet's nests, etc.) Schtrohfackel (die)n.;
cut fine for feed 1.Hecksel (es)n.; 2.Hexel (es)n.;
cutter Schtrohbank (die)n.; **hat** Schtrohhut (der)n.;
Schtrohhiet,pl.; **haulm** Schtrohhalm (der)n.; **heap**
Schtrohhaufe (der)n.; **hook** (pitchfork with bent
tines) Schtrohhoke (der)n.; Schtrohhoke, pl.; **mattress** Schtrohsack (der)n.; Schtrohseck, pl.; **mow**
1.Schtrohbohre (der)n.; 2.Schtrohdenn (es)n.;
Schtrohdenner, pl.

strawberry 1.Abeer (die)n.; 2.Aebeer (die)n.; Aebeere, pl.;
3.Aebier (die)n.; Aebiere, pl.; 4.Aer(e)bel (die)n.;
Aerebel, pl.; 5.Erbeer (die)n.; 6.Erbel (die)n.; 7.Errebbel
(die)n.; **cleaning** Butz(e)li(es)n.; Butz(e)lin, pl.

strawflower Schtrohblumm (die)n.

strawstack Schtrohschtock (der)n.; Schtrohschteck, pl.

stray 1.ab/weiche, v.; abgeweicht, pp.; 2.beigeloffe, v. (pp. of
beilaafe) (so en -- Katz); 3.verlaafe (sich --)v.; verloffe, pp.

streak 1.Schtreef(e) (der)n.; 2.Schtrich (der)n.; **of light**-
Lichtschtraahl (der)n.

streaked 1.schlachtich, adj.; 2.schtraehmich, adj.
3.schtriebich, adj.

streaky schlachtich, adj.

stream Schtrom (der)n.

street Schtross (die)n.; Schtrosse, pl.

strength 1.Gwalt (die)n.; 2.Kraft (die)n.; 3.Lewe(n)skraft (die)
n.; 4.Schtaerrick (die)n.; 5.Schtarick (die)n.

Ss

strengthen

strengthen 1.befeschdiche, v.; befeschdicht, pp.;
2.schtaerricke, v.; gschtaerrickt, pp.;
3.verschtaerricke, v.; verschtaerrickt, pp.

stretch 1.aa/schtrenge, v.; aagschtrengt, pp.; 2.aa/ziehe, v.;
aagezoge, pp.; 3.schpanne, v.; gschpannt, pp.; 4.Schtick
(es)n.; 5.Schtreck (die)n.; 6.schtrecke, v.; gschtreckt,
pp.; **(onself)** aus/schtrecke (sich --)v.; ausgschtreckt,
pp.; **down** nunner/schtrecke, v.; nunnergschtreckt, pp.;
or put up (a rope) naus/schpanne, v.; nausgschpannt,
pp.; **out** 1.aus/schtrecke, v.; ausgschtreckt, pp.; 2.hie/
schtrecke, v.; hiegschtreckt, pp.; 3.raus/schtrecke, v.;
rausgschtreckt, pp.; **taut** aa/schpanne, v.; aagschpannt,
pp.; **up** 1. aaschtrecke, v.; aagschtreckt, pp.;
2.nuff/schtrecke, v.; nuffgschtreckt, pp.;
3.uff/schtrecke, v.; uffgschtreckt, pp.

strew schtraee, v.; gschtraet, pp.

stricken measure gschtriche, adj. (-- Mos)

strickle Schtreichholz (es)n.; Schtreichhelzer, pl.

strict 1.schtreng, adj.; 2.schtrikt, adj.

stride Schtritt (der)n.; Schtridde, pl.

strife 1.Haader (der)n.; 2.Schtreit (der)n.; 3.Zank (der)n.;
4.Zankerei (die)n.

strike 1.dreffe, v.; gedroffe, pp.; 2.gewwe, v.; gewwe, pp.
(feng --); 3.globbe, v.; geglobbt, pp.; 4.schlagge, v.;
gschlaage, pp.; 5.schtreiche, v.; gschtriche, pp.;
6.schwuppe, v.; gschwuppt, pp.; 7.zu/haue, v.;
zugehaut, pp.; **(of lightning)** ei/schlagge, v.;
eigschlagge, pp.; **at something** hie/schlagge, v.;
hiegschlagge, pp.; **at wildly** los/schlagge, v.;
losgschlagge, pp. (druff --); **back** zerick/ schlagge, v.;
zerickgschlagge, pp.; **or hammer on** druffbelse, v.;
druffgebelst, pp.; **out** aus/schtreiche, v.; ausgschtriche,
pp.; **up** (a hymn) aaschtimme, v.; aagschtimmt, pp.;
with an open hand blet(s)che, v.; gebletscht, pp.

striker Schlaeger (die)n.

string 1.Bendel (der)n.; 2.Faade(m) (der)n.; 3.Saet (die)n.;
4.Schnur (die)n.; **(apron)** Schatzbendel (die)n., pl.; **(fish)**
Hengel (der)n.; **(violin)** Seet (die)n.; **bean** Kochbohn
(die)n.; **used in tying a bag** Sackbendel (der)n.

stringent schtrikt, adj.

stringy faedmich, adj.

strip 1.aus/ziehe (sich --)v.; ausgezoge, pp.; 2.Leescht (die)
n.; 3.Schtraeme (der)n.; 4.Schtreef(e) (der)n.; 5.Schtrich
(der)n.; 6.Schtriehme (der)n.; 7.Schtripp (der)n.;
8.schtrippe, v.; gschtrippt, pp.; 9.schtruppe, v.;
gschtruppt, pp.; **of** 1.beraawe, v.; beraabt, pp.;
2.ab/schtrippe, v.; abgschtrippt, pp.; **off** (clothing)
1.ab/blaade, v.; abgeblaadt, pp.; 2.aus/duh (sich --)v.;
ausgeduh, pp.; 3.schtribbe (sich --)v.; gschtrippt, pp.

stripe 1.Schtreef(e) (der)n.; 2.Schtrich (der)n.

striped 1.schtraehmich, adj.; 2.schtreefich, adj.;
3.schtreemich, adj.

stripes Rune (die)n., pl.

strive browiere, v.; (ge)browiert, pp.; **after** 1.drachde, v.;
gedracht, pp.; 2.trachte, v.; getracht, pp.

stroke 1.Hannschlack (der)n.; 2.Hannschtreech (der)n.;
3.Schlaag (der)n. 4.Schlack (der)n.; 5.Schtreech (der)

stumble

n.; Schtreech, pl.; 6.schtreiche, v.; gschtriche, pp.;
7.schtreichle, v.; gschtreichelt, pp.; 8.Schtriche (der)
n.; Schtriche, pl.

strong 1.dauerhaft, adj.; 2.kreftich, adj.; 3.mechdich, adj.;
4.schtarick, adj.; 5.schtarrick, adj.; **(of an odor)** laut,
adj.; **drink** Drinke (es)n.

strongly hefdich, adj.

strop Schtreichrieme (der)n.

stroped schtriebich, adj.

structure Gebei (es)n.; Gebeier, pl.

struggle 1.reisse (sich --) v.; gerisse, pp.; 2.reisse, v.;
gerisse, pp.; 3.schleggele, v.; gschleggelt, pp.;
4.schtramble, v.; gschtrambelt, pp.; 5.schtrawwle, v.;
gschtrawwelt, pp.; 6.zapple, v.; gezappelt, pp.;
7.zawwle, v.; gezawwelt, pp.

struggling or wriggling about Gezawwel (es)n.

strut 1.ranse, v.; geranst, pp.; 2.schpranze, v.; gschpranzt,
pp.; 3.Schtratz (der)n.; 4.schtratze, v.; gschtratzt, pp.;
5.schtrutze, v.; gschtrutzt, pp.

stub Schtarze (der)n.; **one's toe** schtubbe, v.; gschtuppt, pp.

stubbing Gschtubb (es)n.

stubble Schtoppel (die)n.; **field** 1.Schtobbelfeld (es)n.;
2.Schtoppelfeld (es)n.

stubbly 1.schtopplich, adj.; 2.schtublich, adj.

stubborn 1.absenaat, adj.; 2.eegesinni(s)ch, adj.;
3.hattneckich, adj.; 4.obsenaat, adj.; 5.rabbelkebbi(s)ch,
adj.; 6.schtarnkebbich, adj.; 7.schtarrkebbich, adj.;
8. schtockebbich, adj.; 9.schtowwerich, adj.;
10.schteibere (sich --)v.; gschteibert, pp.;11.schtubbich,
adj.; 12.schtupprich, adj.; 13.widderbaerschdich, adj.;
person 1.Rinskopp (der)n.; 2.Schtarrkopp (der)n.

stuck halde, v.; ghalde, pp. (-- bleiwe); **up** 1.brotzich, adj.;
2.fei, adj.; 3.hochneesich, adj.

student Schtudent (der)n.; Schtudende, pl. ;Schuler (der)n.

study schtudiere, v.; gschudiert, pp.; **out** aus/schtudiere,
v.; ausgschtudiert, pp.; **thoroughly** aus/schtudiere,
v.; ausgschtudiert, pp.

stuff 1.aus/schtobbe, v.; ausgschtoppt, pp.; 2.polschdre,
v.; gepolschdert, pp.; 3.schtobbe, v.; gschtoppt, pp.;
4.Schtoff(t) (es)n.; 5.schtoppe, v.; gschtoppt, pp.; **in**
eischtoppe, v.; eigschtoppt, pp.; **into** nei/schtobbe,
v.; neigschtoppt, pp.

stuffed flank Flaehm (die)n. (en gfilldi --); **olives** Blaume
(die)n., pl. (rotbrutziche biddre --)

stuffing 1.Brotfilsel (es)n.; 2.Filling (die)n.; 3.Fil(l)sel (es)
n.; 4.Filsing (der)n.

stuffy 1.schtickich, adj.; 2.schtinkich, adj.

stumble 1.bei/dabbe, v.; beigedappt, pp.; 2.dohiefalle, v.;
3.kalware, v.; gekalwart, pp.; 4.schtolbere, v.;
gschtolbert, pp.; 5.schtolpere, v.; gschtolpert, pp.;
about rum/schtolbere, v.; rumgschtolbert, pp.; **after**
1. hinnerdreischtolbere, v.; 2.hinnerdreischtolbere,
v.; 3.no(och)schtolbere, v.; no(och)schtolbert, pp.;
around rumhaer/schtolpere, v.; rumhaergschtolpert,
pp.; **away** 1.ab/schtolbere, v.; abgschtolbert, pp.;

(Continued on page 385)

Ss

stumble (continued)   sugar

(Continued from page 384)

2.weck/schtolpere, v.; weckgschtolpert, pp.; **in**
1.nei/renne, v.; neigerennt, pp.; 2.nei/schtolpere, v.;
neigschtolpert, pp.; **out** 1.naus/schtolbere, v.;
nausgschtolbert, pp.; 2.raus/schtolpere, v.;
rausgschtolpert, pp.; **over** iwwerschtolpere,
iwwerschtolpert, pp.; **past** verbei/schtolpere, v.;
verbeigschtolpert, pp.

stump 1.Schtarze (der)n.; 2.schtumbe, v.; gschtumpt, pp.;
(of a tree, tooth, limb) Schtumbe (der)n.; **about**
gnabbere, v.; gegnabbert, pp.; **fence** Schtumbefens
(die)n.; **puller** Schtumberobber (der)n.

stumpy 1.abgschtumpt, adj.; 2.schtumbich, adj.; **old tree**
1.Gnarze (der)n.; 2.Gnazze (der)n.; 3.Knarze (der)n.

stunted 1.butzich, adj.; 2.grubbich, adj.; 3.verbutzt, adj.;
fruit Gnickerli (es)n.; Gnickerlin, pl.; **human being or
animal** Grubbes (es)n.

stupid 1.dumm, adj.; 2.hattlannich, adj.; 3.mupsich, adj.;
4.schtupid, adj.; **fellow** 1.Kaeskopp (der)n.;
2.Mopskopp (der)n.; 3.Moschkopp (der)n.

stupidity 1.Dummheet (die)n.; 2.Dummheit (die)n.;
Dummheide, pl.

sturdy 1.gsetzt adj. (gut --); 2.schtandhafdich, adj.;
3.schtarick, adj.

stutter 1.schtoddere, v.; gschtoddert, pp.; 2.schtottere,
v.; gschtottert, pp.

stuttering 1.Gschtotter (es)n.; 2.schtodderich, adj.;
3.schtotterich, adj.

sty (on the eyelid) 1.Schussbloder (die)n.; 2.Wegschisser
(der)n.

stylish schtolzich, adj.

Suabia Schwoweland (es)n.

Suabian 1.schaewisch, adj.; 2.schwaewisch, adj.;
3.Schwob (der)n.; Schwowe, pl.

subdue 1.benniche, v.; gebennicht, pp.; 2.iwwerweldiche,
v.; iwwerweldicht, pp.; 3.iwwerwinne, v.;
iwwerwunne, pp.; 4.nunner/duh, v.; nunnergeduh,
pp.; **by secret power** banne, v.; gebannt, pp.

subdued noise 1.dummel, adj.; 2.Gedummel (es)n.; **or
unintelligable grumbling** Gemunkel (es)n.

subject Gegeschtand (der)n.; **to** behaft, adj.

submissive 1.gehorsam, adj.; 2.gerhersam, adj.

submit kusche (sich --)v.; gekuscht, pp.

subsequently 1.dennord, adv.; 2.dennort, adv.; 3.derno,
adv.; 4.noochhaerich, adj.

subservient unnerdaenich, adj.

subside 1.kusche (sich --)v.; gekuscht, pp.; 2.lege (sich --)
v.; gelegt, pp.

subsist er(n)naehre (sich --)v.; ernaehert, pp.

subtract ab/nemme, v.; abgenumme, pp.

succeed 1.fatt/kumme, v.; is fattkumme, pp.; 2.gedeihe, v.;
gediehe, pp.; 3.mache (sich --) v.; gemacht, pp.; 4.
no(och)folge, v.; no(och)gfolgt, pp.; 5.raus/mache (sich --
)v.; rausgemacht, pp.; 6.raus/schlagge (sich --)n.;
rausgschlagge, pp.; 7.schlagge (sich --), v.; **in** glicke, v.;
geglickt, pp.

success Glick (es)n.

succession 1.Reih (die)n. = Roi (die;); 2.Roi (die)n.; Roie, pl.

successor Noochfolger (der)n.

succor 1.bei/schpringe, v.; beischprunge, pp.; 2.bei/schteh,
v.; beischtanne, pp.; 3.helfe, v.; gholfe, pp.

succory Kaffigraut (es)n.

such 1.so eens, adj.; adv.; pron.; 2.so, adj.; adv.; conj.;
3. soddich, adj.; adv.; pron.; 4.soich, adj.; adv.; pron.;
5.sollich, adj.; adv.; pron.; **a one** eener, adv. (so --);
as he sein(e)sgleiche(s); **as we** 1.unsereems, pron.;
2.unsereens, pron.; **like** sodegleiche, adj.; **things**
1.Kudderments (die)n., pl. (so --); 2.Kutterments
(die)n., pl.

suck 1.lutsche, v.; gelutscht, pp.; 2.saufe, v.; gsoffe, pp.;
3. schlotze, v.; gschlotzt, pp.; 4.suckle, v.; gsuckelt,
pp.; 5. vernuddle, v.; vernuddelt, pp.; **in** eisuckle, v.;
eigsuckelt, pp.; **off** ab/suckle, v.; absuckelt, pp.; **out**
1.aus/suckle, v.; ausgsuckelt, pp.; 2.raus/suckle, v.;
rausgsuckelt, pp.

sucker Ausschlack (der)n.; **(person)** Suckler (der)n.

suckle 1.drenke, v.; gedrenkt, pp.; 2.nutsche, v.; genutscht,
pp.

suckling filly Suckelfill (es)n.; **pig** 1.Seiche (es)n.; 2.Seili
(es)n.; 3.Suckelsau (die)n.

sudden pain in the hip Hexeschuss (der)n.; **turn** Wexel
(der)n.

suddenly 1.bletzlich, adv.; 2.eemol, adv. (uff --); 3.Schtutz
(der)n. (uff der --); 4.uff, prep., adv. (-- der Schtutz);
5.uff, prep., adv. (-- emol); 6.uffe(e)mol, adv.; 7.unni
Verseimes, adv.

sudorific herbs Schwitzgegreider (die)n., pl.

Sue Suss (die)n.

sue at court verglaage, v.; verglaagt, pp.

suet 1.Fett (es)n.; 2.Nierefett (es)n.; 3.Niereinschlich (es)
n.; 4.Rinsfett (es)n.

suffer 1.aus/schteh, v.; ausgschtanne, pp.; 2.erleide, v.;
erlidde, pp.; 3.leide, v.; gelidde, pp.; 4.Not (die)n.
(-- leide); 5.schwitze, v.; gschwitzt, pp.; **(for)** bleche,
v.; geblecht, pp.; **bodily harm** (in an accident)
eibiesse, v.; eigebiesst, pp.; **from burning** verbrenne,
v.; verbrennt, pp.; **with others** mit/leide, v.;
mitgelidde, pp.

suffering Leid (es)n.

sufferings Schtrapatze (die)n., pl.

suffice 1.aus/lange, v.; ausgelangt, pp.; 2.aus/reeche, v.;
ausgereecht, pp.; 3.hie/lange, v.; hieglangt, pp.;
4.hie/reeche, v.; hiegereecht, pp.; 5.lange, v.; gelangt,
pp.; 6.reeche, v.; gereecht, pp.; 7.rum/lange, v.;
rumglangt, pp.; 8.rum/reeche, v.; rumgereecht, pp.

sufficient 1.genunk, adj.; 2.heilenglich, adv.; 3.hielenglich,
adj.; 4.hinlenglich, adj.

suffocate 1.erschticke, v.; erschtickt, pp.; 2.verschticke,
v.; verschtickt, pp.

suffuse iwwergiesse, v.; iwwer(ge)gosse, pp.

sugar 1.Siesses (es)n.; 2.Zucker (der)n.; **applebutter**

(Continued on page 386)

Ss

sugar (continued)

(Continued from page 385)

(made with sugar, not boiled down) Zuckerlattwarick (der)n.; **barrel** Zuckerfass (es)n.; **beet** Zuckerrieb (die)n.; **bowl** Zuckerbool (die)n.; **candy** (hard, made of maple sugar) Zuckerscheifli (es)n.; Zuckerscheiflin, pl.; **maple** Zuckerbaam (der)n.; **maple grove** Zuckerbusch (der)n.; Zuckerbisch, pl.; **of lead** Bleizucker (der)n.; **peas** (pod peas) Zuckerarebse (die)n.; Zuckerarebse, pl.; **teat** (baby's pacifier of bread and sugar) Schlutzer (der)n.

sugarless (of coffee without milk and sugar) baarfiessich, adj.

sugary zuckerich, adj.

suggest 1.aa/gewwe, v.; is aagewwe, pp.; 2.aa/rode, v.; aagerode, pp.; 3.aa/schtifde, v.; aagschtift, pp.; 4.rode, v.; gerode, pp.

suicide Selbschtmard (der)n.

suit 1.Aazuck (der)n.; 2.basse, v.; gebasst, pp.; 3.gfalle, v.; gfalle, pp.; 4.recht sei (dative); **of clothes** (given an apprentice, servant, hired boy at the end of service) Freigleeder (die)n.,pl.

suitable 1.leere (sich --), v.; geleert, pp.; 2.keere (sich --) v.; gekeert, pp.; 3.schicklich, adj.

suited to each other zamme/basse, v.; zammegebasst, pp.

sulk 1.drotze, v.; gedrotzt, pp.; 2.maudere, v.; gemaudert, pp.; 3.moopse, v.; gmoopst, pp.; 4.mopse, v.; gemopst, pp.; 5.mupse, v.; gemupst, pp.; 6.trotze, v.; getrotzt, pp.; 7.uff, prep. adv. (-- der Brutzbank sitze)

sulker Brutzkiwwel (der)n.

sulking Gebrutz (es)n.

sulky 1.brutsich, adj.; 2.brutzich, adj.; 3.gnodderich, adj.; 4.moobsich, adj.; 5.mupsich, adj.; 6.mutsich, adj.; 7.mutzich, adj.; 8.Schnepp (die)n.; **(vehicle)** Gick (die)n.; Gicke, pl.; **person** Mupskoop (der)n.

sullen brutsich, adj.

sullenness (with suppressed crying) Grummelwasser (es)n.

sulphur Schwewwel (der)n.

sulphuric acid Schwewwelsauer (die)n.

sultry 1.schmodderich, adj.; 2.schmodich, adj.; 3.schmudich, adj.; 4.schwiel, adj.

sum Summ (die)n.; **of money** Geldsumm (die)n.

sumac 1.Schum(a)eck (es)n.; 2.Schumack (es)n.; **tree** Schuhmacherbaam (der)n.; Schuhmacherbeem, pl.

summer Summer (der)n.; **complaint** 1.Summerblog (die)n.; 2.Summergranket (die)n.; **cypress** 1.Baerrickfeier (es)n.; 2.Barigfeier (es)n.; **heat** Summerhitz (die)n.; **kitchen** 1.Kochhaus (es)n.; 2.Summerheisel (es)n.; 3.Summerheisli (es)n.; 4.Summerkich (die)n.; **like** summerich, adj.; **pear** Summerbeer (die)n.; **savory** 1.Bohnegraut (es)n.; 2.Bohnegreidel (es)n.; 3.Bohnegreitle (es)n.; 4.Buhnegraut (es)n.; 5.Buhnegreidel (es)n.; 6.Buhnegreitel (es)n.; 7.Buhnegreitle (es)n.; **school** Summerschul (die)n.; **weather** Summerwedder (es)n.; **house** Summerheisli (es)n.

summit Gippel (der)n.; **on the Blue Mountain** (west of the Lehigh Gap, PA) Backeffel (es)n. (dem. of Backoffen)

summon vor/laade, v.; vorgelaade, pp.

sumptuous 1.brachtvoll, adj.; 2.prachtvoll, adj.; **feast**

suppose

Parrefresse (es)n.

sun Sunn (die)n.; **bonnet** Schtrupphut (der)n.; **glass** Brennglaas (es)n.

sunbeam Sunneschtraahl (der)n.

sunbonnet Schlapphut (der)n.; Schlapphiet, pl.

sunburned sunnverbrennt, adj.

Sunday 1.Sunndaag (der)n.; 2.sunndaagsich, adj.; **child** (child born on Sunday) Sunndaagskind (es)n.; **clothes** Sunndaagsgleeder (die)n.,pl.; **go-to-meeting coat** (Mennonite) Mutse (die)n., pl.; **school** Sunndaagschul (die)n.

sundial Sunneuhr (die)n.

sunfish Sunnefisch (der)n.

sunflower Sunneblumm (die)n.; Sunneblumme, pl.

sunglass Sunneglaas (es)n.

sunken road Hohlweg (der)n.

sunlight Sunnelicht (es)n.

sunny sunnich, adj.

sunrise 1.Sunneuffgang (der)n.; 2.Sunnuff (der)n.

sunset 1.Sunneunnergang (der)n.; 2.Sunnunner (der)n.

sunshine Sunneschei(n) (der)n.

sunstroke Sunneschtich (der)n.

superabundance Iwwerfluss (der)n.

superabundant iwwermeesich, adj.

superficially 1.owwedriwwer, adj.; 2.owwerflechlich, adj.

superfluous 1.iwwerflissich, adj.; 2.iwwrich, adj.

superhuman iwwermenschlich, adj.

superintend baase, v.; gebasst, pp.

superintendent 1.Baas (der)n.; 2.Seperdent (der)n.; 3. Superdent (der)n.; 4.Superintend (der)n.; **of schools** Schulsuperintend (der)n.

superior to that 1.datt-driwwer-draus, adv.; 2.dattdriwwerdraus, adv.

superiority Owwerhand (die)n.

superscription Iwwerschrift (die)n.

superstition 1.Aawerglaawe (der)n.; 2.Alderweiwerglaawe (der)n.; 3.Hexeglaawe (der)n.; 4.Kalennerglaawe (der)n.

superstitious 1.aawerglaawisch, adj.; 2.awwerglaawi(s)ch, adj.

supervisor (of roads) Wegmeeschder (der)n.

supper 1.Mattsait (es)n.; Mattsaide, pl.; 2.Nachtesse (es) n.; 3.Owedesse (es)n.

supplant 1.aus/beisse, v.; ausgebisse, pp.; 2.aus/drenge, v.; ausgedrengt, pp.; 3.raus/beisse, v.; rausgebisse, pp.

supple 1.lummerich, adj.; 2.supel, adj.

supply versar(i)ye, v.; versarigt, pp.

support 1.aa/nemme, v.; aag(e)numme, pp.; 2.annaehre, v.; annaehrt, pp.; 3.er(n)naehre, v.; ernaehert, pp.; 4.erhalde, v.; erhalde, pp.; 5.ernaehre, v.; ernaehrt, pp.; 6.Loone (der)n.; 7.unner/schtitze, v.; unnergschtitzt, pp.; 8.unnerschtitze, v.; unnerschtitzt, pp.; 9.voraus/setze, v.; vorausgsetzt, pp.

suppose 1.aa/nemme, v.; aag(e)numme, pp.; 2.voraus/setze, v.; vorausgsetzt, pp.

386

Ss

supposed cause of rabies ...
sweep

supposed cause of rabies in dog located under the tongue Mudderwaerm (die)n., pl.

supposition 1.Mutmaasing (die)n.; 2.Mutmoosing (die)n.

suppress unner/dricke, v.; unnergedrickt, pp.

surcingle 1.Bauchgart (die)n.; 2.Bauchgatt (die)n.

sure 1.doch, adv.; 2.freilich, adj.; 3.schur, adj.; 4.sicher, adj.; **as fate** 1.Deiwel (der)n. (hols der --); 2.hole, v.; gholt. pp. (hol's der deiwel) (hol's der schinner); **as I'm alive** 1.gewiss, adj. (so -- as alles); 2.wisse, v.; gewisst, pp. (weiss der Himmel); **as you're alive!** Friede (der)n. (weiss der --); **enough** allerdings, adv.

surely 1.beschur, adv.; 2.doch, adv.; 3.fer schur, adv.; 4.freilich, adv.; 5.hunnemol, adv.

surfeit iwwerlaade, v.; iwwerlaade, pp.

surgeon Wunddokder (der)n.

surmise 1.mutmaase, v.; gemutmaast, pp.; 2.Mutmaasing (die)n.; 3.mutmoos(s)e, v.; gemutmoost, pp.; 4.Mutmoosing (die)n.

surmount iwwerschteh, v.; iwwerschtanne, pp.

surname 1.Familyenaame (der)n.; 2.Zunaame (der)n.; 3.Zunome (der)n.

surpass 1.biede, v.; gebodde, pp.; 2.iwwerdreffe, v.; iwwerdroffe, pp.

surplice Korhemm (es)n.

surplus 1.Iwwerfluss (der)n.; 2.Iwwerschuss (der)n.

surprise 1.iwwerfalle, v.; iwwerfalle, pp.; 2.iwwerrasche, v.; iwwerrascht, pp.; 3.iwwerschlagge, v.; iwwerschlagge, pp.; 4.verschtaune, v.; verschtaunt, pp.

surprised 1.erschtaune (sich --)v.; 2.verschtaune (sich --) v.; verschtaunt, pp.

surprising 1.erschtaunlich, adj.; adv.; 2.verschtaunlich, adv.; adj.

surrender 1.ergewwe (sich --)v.; ergewwe, pp.; 2.iwwergewwe (sich --)v.; iwwergewwe, pp.

surround umringe, v.; umringt, pp.

surrounding country Umgegend (die)n.; **section** Umgrees (die)n.

survey 1.iwwersehe, v.; iwwersehne, pp.; 2.iwwersehne, v.; iwwersehne, pp.; **(land)** 1.ab/messe, v.; abgemesse, pp.; 2.aus/messe, v.; ausgemesse, pp.

surveyor Landmesser (der)n.; Landmesser, pl.

survive 1.devunkumme, v.; 2.driwwerkumme, v.; is driwwerkumme, pp.; 3.iwwerschteh, v.; iwwerschtanne, pp.

Susanna Sussanne (die)n.

Susie Suss (die)n.

suspect ahne, v.; geahnt, pp.

suspend uff/henke, v.; uffghenkt, pp.

suspenders 1.Ga(e)llesse (die)n.; 2.Hossedraeger (die)n., pl.

suspension Schtillschtand (der)n.

suspicion Verdacht (der)n.

suspicious 1.missdrauisch, adj.; 2.verdechdich, adj.

sustain naehre, v.; genaehrt, pp.; **one's part** 1.hie/halde, v.; hieghalde, pp.; 2.wedder/halde, v.; wedderghalde, pp.

sustenance Lewe(n)sunerhalt (der)n.

svelte 1.gschmeidich, adj.; 2.schlank, adj.

swaddling clothes Windel (der)n.; Windle, pl.

swallow 1.schlucke, v.; gschluckt, pp.; 2.verschlinge, v.; verschlunge, pp.; **(bird)** 1.Schwal(le)m (der)n.; Schwalme, pl.; 2.Schwalme (der)n.; Schwalme, pl.; **(food or liquid)** Schluck (der)n.; **down** nunner/schlucke, v. nunnergschluckt, pp.

swallow's nest Schwalmenescht (es)n.

swallowtail Mutze (der)n.; Mutze, pl.; **coat** Fliggelrock (der)n.

swamp 1.Marasch(t) (der)n.; 2.Marrasch(t) (der)n.; 3.Schwamm (der)n.; 4.Sump (der)n.; **pink** 1.Pingschtblumm (die)n.; Pinschtblumme, pl.; 2.Pingschtnaggel (der)n.

swamp thistle Schwammdischdel (die)n.; **white oak** 1.Schwammeeche (die)n.; 2.Zappeeche (die)n.

swampy 1.schwammich, adj.; 2.sumbich, adj.; **spot** Sumploch (es)n.

swan 1.Schwaan (der)n.; 2.Schwann (der)n.

swarm 1.Schwaarm (der)n.; 2.schwaerme, v.; gschwaermt, pp.; 3.Schwarm (der)n.; 4.schwarme, v.; gschw(a)ermt, pp.; 5.wewwere, v.; gewewwert, pp.; 6.wimmle, v.; gewimmelt, pp.; 7.wiwwle, v.; gewiwwelt, pp.; **of bees** lemeschwarm (der)n.; **out** raus/schwaerme, v.; rausgschwaermt, pp.

swarming Gewimmer (es)n.

swash rausche, v.; gerauscht, pp.

swath 1.Gemaad (die)n.; 2.Schwaad (die)n.

swathe eiwindle, v.; eigewindelt, pp.

sway 1.schwanke, v.; gschwankt, pp.; 2.schwenke, v.; gschwenkt, pp.; **bar** Reischeit (es)n.; **to and fro** dardle, v.; gedardelt, pp.

swaying schwankich, adj.

swear 1.fluche, v.; gflucht, pp.; 2.schweere, v.; gschwore, pp.; 3.verfluche, v.; verflucht, pp.; **in** eischweere,v.; eigschwore, pp.; **off** ab/schweere, v.; abgschwore, pp.; **out (a warrant)** raus/schwe(e)re, v.; rausgschwore, pp.; **with an oath** bschweere, v.; bschwore, pp.

swearer Flucher (der)n.

swearing 1.Flucherei (die)n.; 2.Gefluch (es)n.

sweat 1.Schwees (der)n.; 2.Schwitz (der)n.; 3.schwitze, v.; gschwitzt, pp.; **drop** Schweesdrobbe (der)n.; **out** aus/ schwitze, v.; ausgschwitzt, pp.

sweated schwitzich, adj.

sweating 1.Gschwitz (es)n.; 2.Schwitzing (die)n.

sweaty schwitzich, adj.

sweeny 1.Schweini(ng) (die),n.; 2.Schwinne (die)n.

sweep 1.fege, v.; gfegt, pp.; 2.kehre, v.; gekehrt, pp.; 3.Schwung (der)n.; **away** weck/kehre, v.; weckgekehrt, pp.; **down** nunner/kehre, v.; nunnergekehrt, pp.; **off** ab/kehre, v.; abgekehrt, pp.; **out** 1.aus/kehre, v.; ausgekehrt, pp.; 2.raus/kehre, v.; rausgekehrt, pp.; **over** niwwer/kehre, v.; niwwergekehrt, pp.; **up** 1.uff/kehre, v.; uffgekehrt, pp.; 2.zamme/kehre, v.; zammegekehrt, pp.; **up ashes (in an oven)** huddle, v.; ghuddelt, pp.

Ss

sweepings

sweepings 1.Kehrdreck (der)n.; 2.Kehrich (der)n.; **(of a gristmill)** Mehlschtaab (der)n.

sweet siess, adj.; **apple** Siessabbel (der)n.; Siessebbel, pl.; **as honey** hunnichsiess, adj.; **as sugar** zuckersiess, adv.; **briar** Darneros (die)n.; **cake** Siesskuche (der)n.; Seisskuche, pl.; **cherry** Siesskasch (die)n.; Siesskasche, pl. **cicely** 1.Siesswatzel (die)n.; 2.Karnligraut (es)n.; 3.Karwligraut (es)n.; 4.Siessfennichel (der)n.; **corn** Siesswelchkann (es)n.; **cream cake** 1.Siesseraahmkuche (der)n.; Siessraahmkuche, pl.; 2.Siessroomkuche (der) n.; Siessroomkuche, pl.; **everlasting** (flower) 1.Reiblumm (die)n.; 2.Reinblumm (die)n.; **fern** 1.Faaraan (der)n.; 2.Faare (der)n.; 3.Geilstee (der)n.; 4.Holzfaaran (der)n.; 5.Holzfaare (der)n.; **flag** Kalmus (es)n.; **marjoram** 1.Maaran (der)n.; 2.Maru(n) (der)n.; 3.Meiy(er)un (der)n.; **oil** Baamolich (der)n.; **pepper** 1.Gaardepeffer (der)n.; Gaardepeffer, pl.; 2. Peffer (der)n. (siesser --); **potato** 1.Karebsegrummbeer (die) n.; 2.Karebsegrummbier (die)n.; 3.Siessgrummbeer (die)n.; Siessgrumbeere, pl.; **pumpkin** 1.Kochaerbs (die) n.; 2.Kochkaerbs (die)n.; **scented fern** Wiederkau (die) n.; **scented goldenrod** 1.Baerricktee (der)n.; 2.Barigtee (der)n.; 3.Blobarrgertee (der)n.; 4.Blobarrick(ger)tee (der)n.; **vernal grass** Siessgraas (es)n.

sweetbread (thymus of a young animal used for food) Siessfleesch (es)n.

sweetbrier Danneros (die)n.

sweeten mache, v.; gemacht, pp. (siess --)

sweetheart 1.Hatzli (es)n.; 2.Liebschdi (die)n.; 3.Schatz (der)n.; Schatz, pl.; 4.Schetzel (es)n.; 5.Zier (die)n.

sweetish siesslich, adj.

sweets 1.Schleckerei (die)n.; 2.Schleckerwese (es)n.; 3. Schleckes (es)n.; 4.Siesses (es)n.; 5.Zuckersach (es)n.

swell 1.aa/gschwelle, v.; aagschwolle, pp.; 2.gschwelle, v.; gschwolle, pp.; 3.schwelle, v.; gschwolle, pp.; 4.schwiele, v.; gschwole, pp.; 5.uff/gwelle, v.; uffgegwellt, pp.; 6.uff/ quelle, v.; uffgequellt, pp.; 7.verschwelle, v.; verschwolle, pp.; **from moisture** 1.gegwolle, v.; 2.gwelle, v.; gegwellt, pp.; 3.uff/gwelle, v.; uffgegwellt, pp.; **the utter before calving** eidere, v.; geeidert, pp.; **up** 1.uff/gschwelle, v.; uffgschwolle, pp.; 2.uff/schwelle, v.; uffgschwolle, pp.

swelled-out cheek Pauschbacke (der)n.

swelling Gschwulscht (die)n.; **of the neck or throat** Dickhals (der)n.; Dickhels, pl.

swift 1.leichtfiessich, adj.; 2.schteik, adv. (Amish usage)

swift(ly) 1.leichtfiessich, adj.; adv.; 2.schnell, adj.; adv.; 3.schtaik, adj.; adv.; 4.schtarick, adj.; adv.

swiftness 1.Schnellichkeet (die)n.; 2.Schnellichkeit (die)n.

swill 1.Schlapp (die)n.; 2.Seisaufe (es)n.; **barrel** 1.Schlappfass (es)n.; Schlappfesser, pl.; 2.Seifass (es)n.; Seifesser, pl.; **bucket** 1.Seieemer (der)n.; 2.Seikiwwel (der)n.

swim schwimme, v.; gschwumme, pp.; **about** rum/schwimme, v.; rumgschwumme, pp.; **across** niwwer/schwimme, v.; niwwergschwumme, pp.; **after** no(och)schwimme, v.; no(och)schwumme, pp.; **out**

syrup

raus/schwimme, v.; rausgschwumme, pp.; **to a place** hie/schwimme, v.; hiegschwumme, pp.; **up** nuff/ schwimme, v.; nuffgschwumme, pp.

swimmer Schwimmer (der)n.; Schwimmer, pl.

swimming hole 1.Schwimmblatz (der)n.; Schwimmbletz, pl.; 2.Schwimmloch (es)n.; Schwimmlecher, pl.

swindle 1.bedriege, v.; bedroge, pp.; 2.bscheisse, v.; bschisse, pp.; 3.Geldmacherei (die)n.; 4.Schwindel (der)n.; 5.schwindle, v.; gschwindelt, pp.; 6.Schwindlerei (die)n.

swindler 1.Schwindler (der)n.; Schwindler, pl.; 2.Yauner (der)n.

swindling Schwindlerei (die)n.

swine 1.Rieselvieh (es)n.; 2.Sau (die)n.; Sei, pl.

swing 1.Gaunsch (die)n.; Gaunsche, pl.; 2.schlenkere, v.; gschlenkert, pp.; 3.Schwing (die)n.; 4.schwinge, v.; gschwunge, pp.; 5.Schwung (der)n.; 6.weddle, v.; geweddelt, pp.; **about** 1.rum/schwenke, v.; rumgschwenkt, pp.; 2.rum/schwewe, v.; rumgschwebt, pp.; **around** rum/ schlenkere, v.; rumgschlenkert, pp.; **beam** (used in raising a bucket out of a well) Schweb (die)n.; **out** raus/schwinge, v.; rausgschwunge, pp.

swinging schlenkerich, adj.; **shelf** Brothank (der)n.

swingle Schwingmesser (es)n.

swingle (of a flail) 1.Fleggelkilb (die)n.; 2.Kilb (der)n.

switch 1.gadde, v.; gegaddt, pp.; 2.gaerde, v.; gegaerdt, pp.; 3.Gatt (die)n.; Gadde, pl.

swollen 1.gschwolle, adj.; 2.verschwolle, adj.; **gland** Wachsgnopp (der)n.

swoon 1.Ummacht (die)n.; 2.ummechdich warre, v.; is ummechdich warre; 3.pp. Uumacht (die)n.

swooning uumechdich, adj.

swoop Schwupp (der)n.

sword 1.Dege (der)n.; 2.Schwaert (es)n.

sycamore 1.Gnopphols (es)n.; 2.Holzgnoppbaam (der)n.; 3.Wasserpitschbaam (der)n.

sycophant Schleppschlecker (der)n.

sympathize mit/leide, v.; mitgelidde, pp.

sympathy 1.Aafehles (es)n.; 2.Menschegfiehl (es)n.; 3.Mitgfiehl (es)n.; 4.Mitleid(es) (es)n.

synod Synod (die)n.

synonymous gleichdeitend, adj.

synovial fluid Gliedwasser (es)n.

syringe 1.Schpritz (die)n.; 2.Schtritz (die)n.

syrup Sirrop (der)n.

Tt

tabernacle — take

tabernacle Tabernaakel (der)n.

table Disch (der)n.; Disch, pl.; **crockery** Schaerb (die)n.; Schaerwe, pl.; **fork** Dischgawwel (die)n.; **knife** Dischmesser (es)n.; **leaf** Dischblaat (es)n.; **leg** Dischbee (es)n.; **with extensions** (drop-leaf table) Fliggeldisch (der)n.

tablecloth Dischduch (es)n.; Dischdicher, pl.

tablespoon 1.Essleffel (der)n.; 2.Subbeleffel (der)n.

tackle something (with might and main) aa/raffe, v.; aagerafft, pp.

tact Schicklichkeit (die)n.

tadpole 1.Dickkopp (der)n.; 2.Mollekopp (der)n.; 3.Molligropp (der)n.; Molligrobbe, pl.; 4.Mullikopp (der)n.

taffy 1.Mooschi (der)n.; 2.Nooschi (der)n.; 3.Schpatze (der)n.

tail 1.Schwanz (der)n.; Schwenz, pl.; 2.Weddel (der)n.; 3.Wedel (der)n.; **feather** Schwanzfedder (die)n.

tailboard 1.Schussbord (es)n.; 2.Schussbrett (es)n.

tailcoat Mutze (der)n.; Mutze, pl.

tailor 1.Schneider (der)n.; Schneider,pl.; 2.schneidere, v.; gschneidert, pp.

taint beflecke, v.; befleckt, pp.

take nemme, v.; gnumme, pp.; **(as paint)** aa/nemme, v.; aag(e)numme, pp.; **(good) aim** aa/ziele, v.; aagezielt, pp.; **a (thorough) rest** aus/ruh(g)e (sich --)v.; ausgeruugt, pp.; **a chance** aa/kumme, v.; is aakumme, pp. (druff -- losse); **a drink** 1.uff/schidde, v. (eens --); 2.uff/schitte, v.; uffgschitt, pp. (eens --); **a drink of whiskey** 1.ab/petze, v.; abgepetzt, pp. (eens --); 2.Schnapps (der)n. (en -- nemme); **a dust bath** (of fowls) puddre, v.; gepuddert, pp.; **a good hold of** (in nape of neck) Schoppe (der)n. (am -- nemme); **a part of a thing for use** aa/reisse, v.; aagerisse, pp.; **a seat near** bei/ricke, v.; beigerickt, pp.; **a seat up front** vor/sitze, v.; vorgsotze, pp.; **a taste of** verschmacke, v.; verschmackt, pp.; **a walk** aus/geh, v.; ausgange, pp.; **advantage of** iwwernemme, v.; iwwernumme, pp.; **advice** aa/hariche, v.; aagharicht, pp.; **after** 1.no(och)aarde, v.; no(och)geaart, pp.; 2.no(och)nemme, v.; no(och)gnumme, pp.; **ahold of** 1.aa/greife, v.; aagegriffe, pp.; 2.aa/packe, v.; aagepackt, pp.; 3.halt/nemme, v.; haltgnumme, pp.; **aim** aa/setze, v.; aagsetzt, pp.; **along with** mit/nemme, v.; mitgenumme, pp.; **amiss** verdenke, v.; verdenkt, pp.; **an interest in** kimmere (sich --)v.; gekimmert, pp.; **an oath** Eed (der)n. (en -- nemme); **apart** 1.ausenanner/mache, v.; ausenannergemacht, pp.;2.ausenanner/nemme, v.; ausenannergenumme, pp.; **away** 1.fatt/nemme, v.; fattgenumme; 2.weck/nemme, v.; weckgenumme, pp.; **away from** 1.ab/nemme, v.; abgenumme, pp.; 2.devunnemme, v.; **away from a liquid** ab/scheppe, v.; abgscheppt, pp.; **back** zerick/nemme, v.; zerickgnumme, pp.; **by storm** schtaerme, v.; gschtaermt, pp.; **by surprise** iwwerrumple, v.; iwwerrumpelt, pp.; **by the hair**

Wickel (der)n. (am -- nemme); **care** 1.acht/gewwe, v.; achtgewwe, pp.; 2.uff/basse, v.; uffgebasst, pp.; **care of** Acht (der, die)n. (in -- nemme); **care of** (someone) sarye, v.; gsarrickt, pp. (-- fer ebber); **charge of** iwwernemme, v.; iwwernumme, pp.; **counsel** berode, v.; berode, pp.; **down** nunner/nemme, v.; nunnergenumme, pp.; **down or off** ab/henke, v.; abghonke, pp.; **fire** 1.aa/geh, v.; aagange, pp.; 2.aageh, v.; aagange, pp. **for another** verwexle, v.; verwexelt, pp.; **from place to place** rumhaer/nemme, v.; rumhaergenumme, pp.; **heed** bemaricke, v.; bemarickt, pp.; **heed** (that) aus/sehne, v.; ausgsehne, pp.; **his part** nemme, v.; genumme, pp. (sei Batt --); **hold of** 1.aa/fasse, v.; aagfasst, pp.; 2.faschtnemme, v.; faschtgenumme, pp.; 3.fasse, v.; gfasst, pp.; 4.zugreife, v.; zugegriffe, pp.; **hold of by means of tendrils** aa/ranke, v.; aag(e)rankt, pp.; **home** heemnemme, v.; heemgnumme, pp.; **in** 1.ei/nemme, v.; eigenumme, pp.; 2.eigriege, v.; eigrickt, pp.; 3.rei/nemme, v.; reigenumme, pp.; **measurement for clothing** aa/messe, v.; aagemesse, pp.; **medicine** doktere, v.; gedoktert, pp.; **notice** 1.maericke, v.; gemaerickt, pp.; 2.maricke, v.; gemarickt, pp.; **off** 1.ab/duh, v.; abgeduh, pp.; 2.ab/nemme, v.; abgenumme, pp.; **off (change) one's clothes** aus/ziehe (sich --)v.; ausgezoge, pp.; **off from** ab/mache, v.; abgemacht, pp.; **offence** iwwel, adj. (-- nemme); **offense** uff/nemme, v.; uffgenumme, pp.; **one's own part** seckendiere (sich --)v.; seckendiert, pp.; **one's place or stand** hie/schtelle (sich --)v.; hiegschtellt, pp.; **out** raus/nemme, v.; rausgenumme, pp.; **out in trade** aus/nemme, v.; ausgenumme, pp.; **over** 1.iwwer/nemme, v.; iwwergenumme, pp.; 2.iwwernemme, v.; iwwergenumme, pp.; 3.niwwer/nemme, v.; niwwergenumme, pp.; **over the coals** hechle, v.; ghechelt, pp. (iwwer die -- ziehe); **part** 1.eigreife, v.; eigegreifen, pp.; 2.mit/mache, v.; mitgemacht, pp.; **place** 1.schtattfinne, v.; schtattgfunne, pp.; 2.vor/geh, v.; vorgange, pp.; **root** 1.warzle, v.; gewarzelt, pp.; 2.watzle, v.; gewatzelt, pp.; **short steps** fiessle, v.; gfiesselt, pp.; **sick** 1.grenkle, v.; gegrenkelt, pp.; 2.krenkle, v.; gekrenkelt, pp.; **snuff** 1.schnubbe, v.; gschnuppt, pp.; 2.schnuppe, v.; gschnuppt, pp.; **someone's part** Batt (der)n. (ebber sei -- nemme); **strong drink** schnuddle, v.; gschnuddelt, pp.; **the bonnet** (join church) Kapp (die)n. (die Kappe nemme); **the harness from a horse** 1.abschaere, v.; abschaert, pp.; 2.abscharre, v.; abgschatt, pp.; **the miller's toll** muldere, v.; gemuldert, pp.; **the rind from pork** ab/schwaarde, v.; abgschwaart, pp.; **the trouble** bemiehe (sich --)v.; bemieht, pp.; **through** darich/nemme, v.; darichgnumme, pp.; **to a place** 1.hie/bringe, v.; hiegebrocht, pp.; 2.hie/nemme, v.; hiegnumme, pp.; **to drink** schnuddle, v.; gschnuddelt, pp.; **to heart** behatziche, v.; behatzicht, pp.; **to one's bed** lege (sich

(Continued on page 390)

Tt

take (continued)

(Continued from page 389)

--) v.; gelegt, pp.; **together** zamme/nemme, v.; zammegenumme, pp.; **up** uff/nemme, v.; uffgenumme, pp.; **upon one's self** 1.iwwernemme, v.; iwwergenumme, pp.; 2.iwwernemme, v.; iwwernumme, pp.; **virginity** Kasch (die)n. (-- breche)

taken or collected in advance vanneweck, adv.

taker Nemmer (der)n.; Nemmer, pl.

tale 1.Gschicht (die)n.; 2.Schtori (die)n.; Schtories, pl.; **of being henpecked** Leffidde (die)n., pl.; **of murder** Mardgschicht (die)n.; **of woe** Leffidde (die)n., pl.

talebearer 1.Blatscher (der)n.; 2.Ohrebleeser (der)n.; 3.Retscher (der)n.

talent 1.Gaab (die)n.; Gaawa, pl.; 2.Talent (es)n.

tales 1.Gschpichte (die)n., pl.; 2.Schpichde (die)n.,pl.

talk 1.blaudere, v.; geblaudert, pp.; 2.plaudre, v.; geplaudert, pp.; 3.schwetze, v.; gschwetzt, pp.; **(of formal speech only)** schpreche, v.; gschproche, pp.; **(someone) into (something)** 1.eiblaudre, v.; eigeblaudert, pp.; 2.nei/schwetze, v.; neigschwetzt, pp.; 3.verschwetze, v.; verschwetzt, pp.; **about** (someone) schwetze, v.; gschwetzt, pp. (-- iwwer ebber); **at random** 1.drufflos/schwetze, v.; drufflossgschwetzt, pp.; 2.los/schwetze, v.; losgschwetzt, pp. (druff --); **back** 1.zerick/maule, v.; zerickgemault, pp.; 2.zerick/schwetze, v.; zerickgschwetzt, pp.; **boisterously** rum/blarre, v.; rumgeblatt, pp.; **fast or incessantly** 1.babble, v.; gebabbelt, pp.; 2.blabbere, v.; geblabbert, pp.; **fine** schwetze, v.; gschwetzt, pp. (feischtenglich --); **in a long and tiresome manner** 1.balaadsche, v.; gebalaadscht, pp.; 2.prolaatsche = ballaadsche; **incoherently** (in delirium or severe illness) faawle, v.; gfaawelt, pp.; **indiscreetly** iwwerschnappe (sich --) v.; iwwergschnappt, pp.; **into** zwinge, v.; gezwunge, pp.; **nonsense** Mann (der)n. (wie en -- unne Kopp schwetze); **on** fatt/blaudre, v.; fattgeblaudert, pp.; **one's head off** schwetze, v.; gschwetzt, pp. (ebber en Loch in der Kopp --) (dative); **someone into taking** uff/schwetze, v.; uffgschwetzt, pp.; **to one's heart's content** aus/blaudre (sich --),v.; ausgeblaudert, pp.; **together** 1.zamme/blaudre, v.; zammegeblaudert, pp.; 2.zamme/schwetze, v.; zammegschwetzt, pp.; **too long** 1.verbabble (sich --)v.; verbabbelt, pp.; 2.verblaudre (sich --)v.; verblaudert, pp.; **up** (to a person) uff/schwetze, v.; uffgschwetzt, pp.

talkative 1.babblich, adj.; 2.blauderich, adj.; 3.gackrich, adj.; 4.plauderich, adj.; 5.schnebberich, adj.; 6.vergaxt, adj.; 7.verschnawwelt, adj.; 8.windich, adj.

talker Schwetzer (der)n.; Schwetzer, pl.

talking Geblauder (es)n.

tall lang, adj.; **(very)** grossmechtich, adj.; **speedwell** (Culver's root) Ehrenpreis (der)n. (hocher --); **thin person** 1.Bohneschtecke (der)n.; 2.Buhneschtecke (der)n.; Buhneschtecke, pl.

tallow Inschlich (es)n.; **candle** Inschlichlicht(es)n.;

tar

Inschlichlichder, pl.

tally 1.klappe, v.; geklappt, pp.; 2.raus/kumme, v.; is rauskumme, pp.(eens --); 3.raus/kumme, v.; rauskumme, pp.(iwwer eens --); 4.reime (sich --)v.; gereimt, pp.; 5.reime, v.; gereimt, pp.; 6.verlese, v.; verlese, pp.

talon Glooe (die)n.; Glooe, pl.

tame 1.zaahm, adj.; 2.zaahme, v.; gezaahmt, pp.; 3.zehme, v.; **(an animal)** aa/zaahme, v.; aagezaahmt, pp.

tamp schtambe, v.; gschtampt, pp.

tamping tool Poschdeschtamber (der)n.

tan (beat) 1.gaerwe, v.; gegaerbt, pp.; 2.garewe, v.; gegarebt, pp.; 3.weeche, v.; geweecht, pp. (der Buckel --); **(skin)** ab/gaerwe, v.; abgegaerbt, pp.; **pit** Lohgrub (die)n.

tanbark 1.Gaerwerloh (die)n.; 2.Loh (die)n.; **color** lohrot, adj.

tandem hinnenanner, adv.

tangible fiehlba(a)r, adj.

tangle 1.verwickle, v.; verwickelt, pp.; 2.Verwicklung (die) n.; **of weeds or brush** Genischt (es)n. **tangled** 1.drin, adj.; 2.gewaerrt, adv.; 3.ghuddelt, adj.; 4.inenanner, adj.; 5.ranklich, adj.; 6.verwatt, adj.; **affair** Huddelwese (es)n.; **affairs** 1.Ketzerei (die)n.; 2.Kuddelwese (es)n.; **hair** Meislinescht (es)n.; Meislineschder, pl.; **straw** (out of the thresher) Huddelschtroh (es)n.; **threads** Kuddelwese (es)n.

tanner 1.Gaewer (der)n.; Gaewer, pl.; 2.Garewer (der)n.; Garewer, pl.

tanner's vat Gaerwergrub (die)n.

tannery 1.Gaerwerei (die)n.; 2.Garewerei (die)n.

tansy 1.Kiehbidders (es)n.; 2.Reefaa(re) (der)n.; 3.Reefaare (der)n.; 4.Reefart (der)n.; 5.Reifaare (der) n.; 6.Reinfart (der)n.; **bitters** 1.Reefaabidders (es)n.; 2.Reefaar(t)bidders (es)n.; **tea** Reefaa(rt)tee (der)n.

tantalize 1.bloge, v.; geblogt, pp.; 2.gweele, v.; gegweelt, pp.; 3.neck(s)e, v.; geneckt, pp.; 4.rum/zaere, v.; rumgezaert, pp.

tantalizing neck(s)ich, adj.

tantrum Yess (der)n.

tap 1.aa/bohre, v.; aagebohrt, pp.; 2.aa/zabbe, v.; aagezappt, pp.; 3.ab/zabbe, v.; abgezappt, pp.; 4.aus/zabbe, v.; ausgezappt pp.; 5.bohre, v.; gebohrt, pp.; 6.raus/zabbe, v.; rausgezappt, pp.; 7.zappe, v.; gezappt, pp.; **(out)** 1.verzabbe, v.; verzappt, pp.; 2.verzappe, v.; verzappt, pp.; **off vinegar** ab/moschdere, v.; abgemoschdert, pp.

tape 1.Bendel (der)n.; 2.Bennel (der)n.; **measure** Messband (es)n.

taper 1.ab/schaerfe, v.; abgschaerft, pp.; 2.ab/schlaamse, v.; abgschlaamst, pp.; **(candle)** Waxlicht (es)n.; Waxlichder, pl.

tapestry Wanddeppich (der)n.

tapeworm Bandwarem (der)n.

taproot Hatzwatzel (die)n.

tapster Zapper (der)n.

tar 1.Darr (der)n.; 2.darre, v.; gedarrt, pp.; **keg** (suspended

(Continued on page 391)

390

Tt

tar (continued)

(Continued from page 390)

from the axle of a wagon on long trips) 1.Darrlogel (der) n.; 2.Darrlokel (der)n.; 3.Darryockel (der)n.

tardy hinnerhand, adj.

target Scheib (die)n.

tarry 1.uff/halde, v.; uffghalde, pp.; 2.verweile, v.; verweilt, pp.; 3.verzeihe, v.; verzeiht, pp.; 4.verziege, v.; verzogge, pp.; 5.weile, v.; geweilt, pp.; **(of tar)** darich, adj.

tart seierlich, adj.; **(made of dried apples covered with sugared crumbs)** Schnitzriwwelkuche (der)n.

tarter Weisschtee (der)n.

tassel 1.Fransel (die)n.; Fransle, pl.; 2.Taasel (die)n.; **(of corn)** Faahne (die)n.; Faahne, pl.

tassels Schtreiss (die)n., pl.

taste 1.Schleck (der)n.; 2.schmacke, v.; gschmackt, pp.; 3.schmecke, v.; gschmeckt, pp.; 4.Versuch (der)n.; 5.versuche, v.; versucht, pp.; **(in some areas)** Gschmack (der)n.; **(in testing)** verschlecke, v.; verschleckt, pp.; **or eat with a smacking sound** schmatze, v.; gschmatzt, pp.

tasteless 1.lebbich, adj.; 2.lebbisch, adj.; 3.leppisch, adj. **tasting or eating dainties** Gschleck (es)n.

tatter 1.verrisse, adj.; 2.Zoppe (der)n.

tattered 1.lumbich, adj.; 2.zoddlich, adj.

tattle 1.babble, v.; gebabbelt, pp.; 2.belle, v.; gebellt, pp.; 3.blatsche, v.; geblatscht, pp.; 4.retsche, v.; geretscht, pp.

tattler 1.Blatscher (der)n.; 2.Neiichkeidedraeger (der)n.; 3.Ohrebleeser (der)n.; 4.Ohrebleeser (der)n.; 5.Retch (die)n.; 6.Retcher (der)n.

tattletale 1.Hambariyer (die)n.; 2.Retschbeddi (die)n.; 3.Retschbelli (die)n.; 4.Retschmaul (es)n.; 5.Schnellposcht (die)n.

taunt 1.aus/schpodde, v.; ausgschpott, pp.; 2.bschimpe, v.; bschimpt, pp.; 3.schmaehe, v.; gschmaeht, pp.; 4. schpedde, v.; gschpett, pp.; 5.schpeddle, v.; gschpeddelt, pp.; 6.schpettle, v.; gschpeddelt, pp.

Taurus (2nd sign of the zodiac) 1.Ox (der)n.; 2.Schtier (der)n.

tavern Wattshaus (es)n.; Wattsheiser, pl.

taverner Watt (der)n.; Wadde, pl.

tawny 1.gehlbrau(n), adj.; 2.lohrot, adj.

tax 1.Abdrack (der)n.; 2.Tax (der)n.; Taxe, pl.; 3.taxe, v.; getaxt, pp.; **exempt** taxfrei, adj.

taxable taxbaar, adj.

taxidermist Gediereausschtopper (der)n.

taxpayer Taxbezaahler (der)n.; Taxbezaahler, pl.

tea Tee (der)n.; **from downy mint** Balsemtee (der)n.; **towel** Abbutzlumbe (der)n.; Abbutzlumbe, pl.

teaberry Buchsbeer (die)n.

teach 1.laerne, v.; gelaernt, pp.; 2.lanne, v.; glannt, pp.; **animals tricks** ab/richde, v.; abgericht, pp.; **school** Schulhalde, v.; ghalde, pp.

teacher 1.Lehrer (der)n.; 2.Schulmann (die)n.; 3. Tieschern (die)n.; 4.Schulme(e)schder (der)n. (male;) 5. Schulme(e)schdern (die)n. (female)

teakettle Teekessel (der)n. Teekessele, pl.

tealeaf Teeblaat(es)n.; Teebledder, pl.

Team Mennonites Fuhreleit (die)n.

team (of horses, or horses and wagon) Fuhr (die)n.;

tell

Fuhre, pl.; **(of men)** Mannschaft (die)n.

teamster Fuhrmann (der)n.; Fuhrmenner, pl.

teamster's whip Faahrgeeschel (die)n.

teapot Teekann (die)n.; Teekanne, pl.

tear (drop) 1.Draen (die)n.; Draene, pl.;2.Traen (die) n.;Traene, pl.

tear 1.eischlitze, v.; eigschlitzt, pp.; 2.Loch (es)n.; Lecher, pl.; 3.reisse, v.; gerisse, pp.; 4.Riss (der)n.; 5.Schlitz (der)n.; **to pieces** verreisse, v.; verrisse, pp.; **a slit or hole in** nei/reisse, v.; neigerisse, pp.; **apart** vunanner/reise, v.; vunannergerisse, pp.; **down** 1.ab/reisse, v.; abgerisse, pp.; 2.nidder/reisse, v.; niddergerisse, pp.; 3.nunner/reisse, v.; nunnergerisse, pp.; 4.runner/reisse, v.; runnergerisse, pp.; 5.um/reisse, v.; umgerisse, pp.; 6.zamme/reisse, v.; zammegerisse, pp.; **down** (a building) weck/reisse, v.; weckgerisse, pp.; **in** rei/reisse, v.; reigerisse, pp.; **in two** darich/reisse, v.; darichgrisse, pp.; **into** aa/reisse, v.; aagerisse, pp.; **into small pieces** fei/reisse, v.; feigerisse, pp.; **loose** los/reisse, v.; losgerisse, pp.; **off** ab/reisse, v.; abgerisse, pp.; **open** uff/reise, v.; uffgerisse, pp.; **out** 1.aus/reisse, v.; ausgerisse, pp.; 2.raus/reisse, v.; rausgerisse, pp.; **thumb** 1.Mus(s)fress (es)n.; 2.Muusfress (es)n.; **to pieces** verrobbe, v.; verroppt, pp.

tears Aagewasser (es)n.

tease 1.bloge, v.; geblogt, pp.; 2.hensle, v.; g(e)henselt, pp.; 3.neck(s)e, v.; geneckt, pp.; 4.nexe, v.; genext, pp.; 5.reiwe, v.; g(e)riwwe, pp.; 6.retze, v.; geretzt, pp.; 7.rum/zaere, v.; rumgezaert, pp.; 8.zaere, v.; gezaert, pp.; 9.zarre, v.; gezatt, pp.

teasing Gezaerr (es)n.

teaspoon 1.Teeleffel (der)n.; Teeleffele, pl.; 2.Teeleffli (es)n.; Teelefflin, pl.

teaspoonful 1.Teeleffelvoll (der)n.; 2.Teelefflivoll (der)n.

teat 1.Diddi (der)n.; 2.Dittli (es)n.; 3.Ditz (der)n.; Ditze, pl.; 4.Ditzli (es)n.; Ditzlin, pl.; 5.Waarz (die)n.; Waarze, pl.; **(of a cow)** Schtriche (der)n.; Schtriche, pl.

ted wende, v.; gewennt, pp.; **hay** 1.uff/wenne, v.; uffgewennt, pp.; 2.wenne, v.; gewennt, pp.

tedder Wenner (der)n.

tedious 1.langwa(e)rich, adj.; 2.langweilich, adj.; 3.verdrisslich, adj.; **job** Gnoddelaerwet (die)n.

teeth 1.zaahne, v.; gezaahnt, pp.; 2.zohne, v.; gezohnt, pp.

telescope 1.Schpeckdief (es)n.; 2.Schpekdief (es)n.

tell 1.aa/bringe, v.; aagebrocht, pp.; 2.ab/zeehle, v.; abgezeehlt, pp.; 3.erzehle, v.; erzehlt, pp.(rare usage); 4.melde, v.; gemeldt, pp.; 5.saage, v.; gsaat, pp.; 6.verzehle, v.; verzehlt, pp.; **(someone) what is what** vor/zehle, v.; vorgezehlt, pp.; **a fib** schnitze, v.; gschnitzt, pp.; **a lie** 1.aa/basse, v.; aagebasst, pp. (eeni --); 2.aa/henke, v.; aaghenkt, aaghonke, pp. (eeni --); 3.liege, v.; geloge, pp.; 4.ab/schpinne, v.; abgschpunne, pp. (eens --); **fortune** 1.waahrsaage, v.; waahrgsaat, pp.; 2.wohrsaage, v.; wohrsaat, pp.; **in advance** 1.vannenaus/saage, v. vannenausgsaat, pp.; 2.vorhaersaage, v.; vorhaergsaat, pp.; 3.vorher/saage,

(Continued on page 392)

Tt

tell (continued)

v.; vorhersaagt, pl.; **lies behind one's back** no(och)retsche, v.; no(och)geretscht, pp.; **off** ab/schiesse, v.; abgschosse, pp.; **stories** dings mache, v.; **straight** graad (dative) saage, v.; **to one's face** Gsicht (es)n (ins -- saage)

teller 1.Zaehler (der)n.; 2.Zehler (der)n.

telltale 1.Gaffmaul (es)n.; 2.Ohrebleeser (der)n.; 3.Ohrebloser (der)n.

temper 1.hadde, v.; 2.schtaahle, v.; gschtaahlt, pp.; 3.Zann (der)n.; 4.Zann (der)n.; **(air in a room)** iwwerschlagge, v.; iwwerschlagge, pp.

temperance crank Wassersimpel (der)n.

temperate 1.maessich, adj.; 2.nichdern, adj.; 3.tempere (sich --)v.; getempert, pp.

template Pett (die)n.

temple Tempel (der)n.; **(side of the head)** Schlof (der)n.

temporal 1.weltlich, adj.; 2.zeitlich, adj.

temporarily Zeit (die)n. (farn --)

tempt versuche, v.; versucht, pp.; **(by the devil)** aa/fechde, v.; aagfochde, pp.

temptation Versuchung (die)n.

tempter Verfiehrer (der)n.

Ten Commandments Zehe Gebodde (die)n.

ten zehe, adj.; pron.; **foot pole** 1.Richtscheit (es)n.; 2.Zehefuusschtecke (der)n.; **spot** (in cards) Zeheder (en); **times** zehemol, adv.; **years old** zehejaahrich, adj.

tenable haltbaar, adj.

tenacious 1.aahen(k)sich, adj.; 2.aahenkisch, adj.

tenant Lehnsmann (der)n.; Lehnsleit, pl.; **farmer** Lehnsbauer (der)n.; **house** 1.Daaglehnerhaus (es)n.; 2.Lehnshaus (es)n.

tend 1.pflege, v.; gepflegt, pp.; 2.versar(i)ye, v.; versarigt, pp.

tender 1.maer(r)b, adj.;2.maereb,adj.;3.zaart,adj.;(skin) bleed, adj.

tenderloin 1.Bickelfleesch (es)n.; 2.Fisch (der)n.; Fisch, pl.; 3.Fischli (es)n.; 4.Fischlin (die)n., pl.

tendon Flex (die)n.

tendril 1.Finger (der)n.; Finger, pl.; 2.Rank (die)n.; Ranke, pl.; 3.Schpinner (der)n.; Schpinner, pl.

tenesmus Drang (der)n.

tenon Zabbe (der)n.; Zabbe, pl.

tent 1.Zelt (es)n.; Zelder, pl.; 2.Zelthaus (es)n.; **cloth** Zeltduch (es)n.

tenth 1.Zehed(e)l (es)n.; 2.zehet, adv.; **part** Zehe(de)deel (es)n.

tepid lauwaarm, adj.

term Taermin (der)n.; **applied to a person who guesses or judges correctly or who boasts of being able to do so** Dreffloch (es)n.; **applied to child who accompanies his parents to the harvest field and cut grain with the sickle as he was able** Gipser (der)n.; **applied to the sickling of grain by small children** gipse, v.; gegipst, pp.

term of contempt (usually for a callow youth) Rotzleffel (der)n.; **contempt for an ignorant bully** Bulle (der)n. (so een --); **of endearment** (applied to an infant in

thanksgiving

its cradle) Schnutz (der)n.; **of ridicule** Schwob (der) n.; Schwowe, pl.; **of vituperation** 1.Hellsackerment (der)n.; 2.Luder (es)n.

termagant Zenkrin (die)n.

terms Bedingung (die)n.; **of endearment** (applied to infant in its cradle) 1.Neschatgweckerli (es)n.; 2.Neschtgwackerli (es)n.

terrible 1.baremlich, adj.; 2.barmlich, adj.; 3.entsetzlich, adj.; 4.erschrecklich, adj.; 5.farichderlich, adj.; 6.greislich, adj.; 7.grislich, adj.; 8.kreislich, adj.; 9.schauderhafdich, adj.; 10.schauderhaft, adj.; 11.scheisslich, adj.; 12.schreckballisch, adj.; 13.schreckbollisch, adj.; 14.schrecklich, adj.; **St. Nicholas** (Santa Claus) **mask** Belsnickel (der)n. (wieschgaschdich -- gfress)

terribly 1.barbaarisch, adv.; 2.bummerisch, adj.; 3.ersetzlich, adv.; 4.fleggelhefdich, adv.; 5.gottsyemmerlich, adj.; 6.hesselborich, adv.; 7.hesseldannisch, adv.; 8.hesseldonisch, adv.; 9.hesselronisch, adv.; 10.un(a)e(r)baermlich, adj.; 11.unerbaermlich, adv.; **much** wiescht viel, adv.

terrified scheech, adj.

terrify 1.erschrecke, v.; erschreckt, pp.; 2.vergelschdere, v.; vergelschdert, pp.; 3.verschrecke, v.; verschrocke, pp.

terror 1.Engschde (die)n.; Engschde, pl.; 2.Furcht (die)n.; 3.Schrecke (der)n.

Testament Teschdament (es)n.

testator Erblosser (der)n.

testicles 1.Glicker (der)n.; Glicker, pl.; 2.Hode (der)n.; Hode, pl.

testify 1.Zeichnis (es)n. (-- gewwe); 2.Zeignis (es)n. (--gewwe)

testimony 1.Zeichnis (es)n.; 2.Zeignis (es)n.; 3.Zeiknis (es)n.

testy griddlich, adj.

tether Schpannseel (es)n.; Schpannseele, pl.

text Text (der)n.

than 1.als, adv., conj.; prep.; 2.as, conj.; prep.; 3.dann, conj.; prep.; 4.das, conj.; prep.; 5.wie, prep.

Thank you! (usually used by elders in reminding a small child to say Thank you!) saeddi!

thank 1.ab/schtadde, v.; abgschtatt, pp. (dank --); 2.ab/schtatte, v.; abgschtatt, pp.; 3.bedanke (sich --)v.; bedankt, pp.; 4.danke, v.; gedankt, pp.; 5.Danki (der)n. (-- saage); 6.Denki (der)n. (-- saage); **for** verdanke, v.; verdankt, pp.; **you-ma'am** 1.Abloos (der)n.; 2.Blotzer (der)n.; Blotzer, pl.; **you!** 1.Danki (schee)!, interj.; 2.Dankyaa! interj.; 3.Denki! interj.; 4.Ich saag Dank(i)!; 5.Ich saag Denki!

thankful dankbaar, adj.

thankfulness Dankbaarkeet (die)n.

thanks 1.Dank (der)n.; 2.Dankes (es)n.; 3.Danki (der)n.; 4.Denki (der)n.; 5.Ich saag Dank(i)!; 6.Ich saag Denki!

Thanksgiving 1.Betdaag (der)n.; 2.Dankfescht (es)n.; 3.Danksaagesdaag (der)n.; 4.Danksaagung (die)n.; **sermon** Dankbreddich (die)n.

Tt

that | thirtieth

that 1.as, pron.; adj.; conj.; 2.ass = dass, conj.; 3.das, pron.; adj.; conj.; 4.der, pron.; adj.; conj.; 5.des, pron.; adj.; conj.; 6.sell, pron.; adj.; conj.; 7.seller, pron.; adj.; conj.; 8.selli, pron.; adj.; conj.; **is** also, adv.; **is none of your business** 1.aageh, v.; aagange, pp. (sell geht dich nix --); 2.Scheissdreck (der)n. (des geht dich kenn -- aa); **one** 1.sell, pron.; 2.seller, pron.; 3.selli, pron.; **provokes me** falsch, adj. (des macht mich --); **time** sell(e)mol, adv.; **way** selleweg, adv.; **which** was, rel.pron.

thatch 1.Dachschtroh (es)n.; 2.decke, v.; gedeckt, pp.

thatched roof Schtrohdach (es)n.; Schtrodecher, pl.

thaw 1.aus/daae, v.; ausgedaat, pp.; 2.daae, v.; gedaat, pp.; 3.daue, v.; gedaut, pp.; 4.schleffle, v.; gschleffelt, pp.; 5.uff/daae, v.; uffgedaat, pp.; 6.uff/geh, v.; uffgange, pp.

thawing weather Schleffelwedder (es)n.

The Reformed Church (now The United Church of Christ) Reformiert Karich (die)n.

the 1.den, def.art.; 2.der, def. art.; 3.des, def. art.; 4.die, def. art.; 5.es, def. art.; **devil!** kotzsapperment!; **dickens!** ei der Dausich!, interj.; **fire is made** aa, adv. (es feier is --); **first** sercht = es erscht; **like** degleiche, dem. pronoun; **rain is passing to the south** Regge, (der)n. (der -- geht unnedarich); **rest is but a trifle** Hund (der)n. (kummt mer iwwer der --, so kummt mer iwwer der schwans); **whole business** Schipp (die)n. (-- an schtiel); **whole shebang** ganz Bedallye (es)n.; **whole thing** Mallifitz (die)n. (die gans --); **wine is strong** Grille (die)n., pl. 1.(-- im kopp); 2.(der wei hot --)

theft Diebschtaahl (der)n.

them sie, pron.

then 1.alsdann, adv.; 2.dann, adv.; 3.dennord, adv.; 4.derno, adv.; 5.derno, adv.; 6.dozumol, adv.; 7.no, adv.; 8.nooch sellem, adv.; 9.nooch sem, adv.; 10.nord, adv.; 11.sellem, adv.; 12.sell(e)mol, adv.; 13.sellemols, adv.; **lo!** nard

thence vun dann, adv.

Theodore Dori (der)n.

Theodoric Diedre (der)n.

theologue Schriftler (der)n.

Theophilus Gottlieb (der)n.

therapeutics Heilkunscht (die)n.

There was nothing good about it! S waar kenn Maulvoll gut!

there 1.daa, adv.; 2.dadde, adj.; 3.dart, adj.; 4.datt, adj.; 5. datte, adj.; **(motion thither)** 1.datthie, adv.; 2.hie, adv.; **by the side of** dattdenewe, adv.; **in front** dattvanne, adv.; **is no difficulty about this** Kunscht (die)n. (kenn --); **is nothing better** driwwer, adv. (es is nix --); **is nothing left** ausbacke, v.; ausgebacke, pp. (do iss ausgebacke); **is something suspicious (queer) about this** kauscher, adj. (do is aa ebbes net gans recht --); **on** druffanne, adv.; **was some row** schelle, v.; gschellt, pp. (des hot awwer gschellt);

were some high doings haer/geh, v.; haergange, pp. (do is es awwer haergange)

there's a difficulty somewhere Haas (der)n. (en -- im Peffer); **no telling** wisse, v.; gewisst, pp. (mer kennt net --); **the devil to pay** Deihenker (die)n. (der -- is los)

thereabout dattrum, adv.

thereafter 1.daarnooch, adv.; 2.dennooch, adv.; 3.derno, adv.; 4.dernooch, adv.

therefore 1.daarum, adv.; 2.deswege, adv.; 3.devun, adv.

therewith 1.damit, adv.; 2.demit, adv.

these boys 1.Buweschtofft (des;) 2.Buweschtrofft (des)n.; **girls** Maedschtofft (es)n. (des --)

they sie, pron.; **are always at odds** gegenanner, adv. (sie sinn immer --); **are having an altercation** 1.menanner, adv. (sie hen's --); 2.mit(e)nanner, adv. (sie hen's --); **get along well together** 1.menanner, adv. (sie kenne's --); 2.mit(e)nanner, adv. (sie kenne's --); **have an understanding** 1.menanner, adv. (sie hen's --); 2.mit(e)nanner, adv. (sie hen's --); **went in pell-mell** dezu, adv. (sie sinn -- nei)

thick 1.dick, adj.; 2.schteif, adj.; **as a finger** fingersdick, adj.; **as a thumb** daumesdick, adj.; **fleshy part of a quarter of bee** Gwalle (der)n.; **milk** Dickmillich (die)n.

thicket 1.Heck (die)n.; Hecke, pl.; 2.Heckes (die, es)n.

thickheaded dickkebbich, adj.

thickness Dicking (die)n.

thief 1.Dieb (der)n.; Dieb, pl.; 2.Schtehler (der)n.

thieving nature (to be of a) bschtohle, adj.

thigh Schenkel (der)n.

thighbone Schenkelgnoche (der)n.

thimble Fingerhut (der)n.; Fingerhiet, pl.

thin 1.dinn, adj.; 2.lang, adj.; **(out)** 1.dinne, v.; gedinnt, pp.; 2.dinne, v.; gedinnt, pp.; 3.dinnere, v.; gedinnert, pp.; **rope** Lein (die)n.; **skinned** 1.dinnschaalich, adj.; 2.dinnschaalich, adj.; **stemmed** 1.dinnschwensich, adj.; 2.dinnschwensich, adj.

thing 1.Ding (es)n.;Dinger, pl.;2.Sach (die)n.;Sache,pl.;3.Wese (es)n.

things like that dings; **look desperate** hutzlich, adj. (es guckt -- aus)

think 1.denke, v.; gedenkt, pp.; 2.glaawe, v.; geglaabt, pp.; 3.meene, v.; gemeent, pp.; 4.sinne, v.; gsunne, pp.; **back** zerick/denke, v.; zerickgedenkt, pp.; **of** ahne, v.; geahnt, pp.; **of it** draadenke, v.; draagedenkt, pp.; **out** 1.aus/denke, v.; ausgedenkt, pp.; 2.aus/sinne, v.; ausgsunne, pp.; **over** 1.b(e)sinne (sich --)v.; b(e)sunne, pp.; 2.iwwer denke, v.; iwwergedenkt, pp.; **up** uff/denke, v.; uffgedenkt, pp.

thinkable denkbaar, adj.

third dritt, adj.; **stomach of ruminants** Manchfalt (die)n.

thirdly drittens, adv.

thirst Da(r)scht (der)n.

thirsty 1.da(r)schdich, adj.; 2.daschdich, adj.

thirteen dreizeh, adj.; pron.

thirteenth dreizeht, adj.

thirtieth dreissichscht, adj.

Tt

thirty ... throw

thirty dreissich, adj.; pron.

this 1.daer, dem. adj.; 2.den, dem. adj.; 3.des, dem. adj.; 4.die, dem. adj.; 5.dies, adj. (rare usage); **book gives an account of things** lese, v.; gelese, pp. (des buch lest vun so sache); **day a week** Daag (der)n. (heit iwwer acht --); **evening** denowed, adv.; **is no concern of yours** Dreck (der)n. (des geht dich kenn -- aa); **is no good** Katz (die)n. (des is fer die --); **last week** diewoch, adv.; **morning** 1.demaiye, adv.; 2.den Mariye, adv.; **time** 1.des(s)emol, adv.; 2.desmol, adv.; **way** denneweg, adv.; **won't do** schaffe, v.; gschafft, pp. (des schafft net)

thither 1.dahie, adv.; 2.dattanne, adv.; 3.dehi, adv.

thong (of a flail) 1.Reime (der)n.; 2.Rieme (der)n.

thorn 1.Dann (die)n.; Danne, pl.; 2.Darn (die)n.; 3.Dorn (die)n.; 4.Schtachel (die)n.; **apple** 1.Schtachelgraut (es)n.; 2.Schtechabbel (der)n.; **bush** 1.Danneschtock (der)n.; 2.Darneschtock (der)n.; **in the flesh** Dann (die)n. (-- im Aag)

thorny 1.dannich, adj.; 2.darnich, adj.; 3.schtachlich, adj.

thorough dichtich, adj.

thoroughly 1.darich un darich, adv. 2.darich, adj. (-- un --); 3.dichtichlich, adj.; 4.gedichdich, adv.; 5.gedicht, adj.; 6.geheerich, adv.; 7.grindlich, adv.; 8.kindlich, adv.; 9.salwiers, adv.; **English** schtock Englisch adj.

thoroughwort Darichwax (der)n.

those selli, dem. adj.; **days** Daag (der)n. (seller --e); **who** die wu, pron.

though doch, adv.

thought 1.Gedanke (der)n.; Gedanke, pl.; 2.Kundewidde (die) n.; **of marriage** 1.Heiraats(ge)danke (der)n.; 2.Heiraschbelsgedanke (der)n.; **provoking** bedenklich, adj.

thoughtful 1.diefsinnich, adj.; 2.gedankevoll, adj.

thoughtless leichtsinnich,adj.;**movement** (continued) Ghaschbel (es)n.

thoughtless(ly) 1.unbedacht, adj.; 2.unbedenkt, adj.

thoughtlessness Leichtsinnichkeit (die)n.

thoughts of marriage Heiraatsdanke (der)n.

thousand 1.dause(n)d, adj.; pron.; 2.tausend, adj., pron.; **legger** Dausendfiesser (der)n.; **times** dausendmol, adv.

thrash 1.ab/gaerwe, v.; abgegaerbt, pp.; 2.dechsle, v.; gedechselt, pp.; 3.lause, v.; gelaust, pp.; **a spell** Lick (die)n. (en -- dresche); **soundly** darich/leddere, v.; darichgeleddert, pp., **with flail or machine** ab/dresche,v.; abgedrosche, pp.

thread 1.ei/feedle, v.; eigfeedelt, pp.; 2.Faade(m) (der)n.; 3.Neez (der)n.; 4.Neezfaadem (der)n.; 5.Neezfadde (der)n.; **a needle** 1.eifaedle, v.; eigfaedelt, pp.; 2.eifeddle, v.; eigfeddelt, pp.

threads Fassere (die)n., pl.

threat Drehing (die)n.

threaten 1.drehe, v.; gedreht, pp.; 2.drohe, v.; gedroht, pp.; 3.droie, v.; gedroit, pp.; **(with clenched fist)** Fauscht (die)n (en -- mache); **or promise without fulfilling** drickse, v.; gedrickst, pp.; **rain** 1.brutze, v.; gebrutzt, pp.; 2.drohe, v.; gedroht, pp.; **thunder**

storms 1.gewiddre, v.; gewiddert, pp.; 2.g(e)widdrich, adj.

three drei, adj.; pron.; **days or so** Daage drei, adv.; **horse team** Dreigeilswoog (die)n.; Dreigeilswooge, pl.; **leaved** dreiblettrich, adj.; **legged** dreibeenich, adj.; **ply** 1.dreidoppelt, adj.; 2.dreidraehich, adj.; **pronged** dreizinkich, adj.; **seated** dreisitzich, adj.; **sheets in the wind** gschwewwelt, adj.; **sided** dreiseidich, adj.; **year-old** dreiyaehrich, adj.

thresh dresche, v.; gedrosche, pp.; **out** 1.aus/dresche, v.; ausgedrosche, pp.; 2.raus/dresche, v.; rausgedroscht, pp.

thresher Drescher (der)n.; Drescher, pl.

threshing floor 1.Denn (die)n.; 2.Dreschdenn (die, es)n.; Dreschdenner, pl.; **floor wall** Dennwand (die)n.; **machine** Dreschmaschien (die)n.; Dreschmaschiene, pl.; **time** Dreschzeit (die)n.

threshold 1.Deer(e)schwell (die)n.; Deer(e)schwelle, pl.; 2. Diereschwell (die)n.

thrice dreimol, adv.

thrifty 1.schaffich, adj.; 2.wexich, adj.; **(of plants)** 1.wachsich, adj.; 2.waxich, adj.

thrill 1.darich/schaudre, v.; darichgschaudert, pp.; 2.Grissel (die)n., pl.; 3.Krissel (die)n., pl.

thrilling 1.greislich, adj.; 2.kreislich, adj.

thrive 1.gerode, v.; gerode, pp. (gut --); 2.voraa/kumme, v.; voraakumme, pp.; 3.waxe, v.; gewaxe, pp.

throat 1.Geigel (die)n.; Geigel, pl.; 2.Geigle (die)n.; 3.Kehl (die)n.; 4.Schlucker (der)n.; 5.Schluckerli (es)n.; 6.Schlund (der)n.; **band** Kehlband (es)n.; **latch** (on bridle) Kiehband (die, es)n.; Kiehbenner, pl.

throne Dron (der)n.

through and between zwischedarich, adv.; **below** unnedarich, adv.; **here** dattdarich, adv.; **the midst of** dezwischedarrich, adv.; **this** 1.dedarrich, adj.; 2.dodedarrich, adv.; 3.dodedarrich, adv.; **this section** dodarrich, adv.

throughout 1.darich, adv.; 2.darich(e)weck, adv.; 3.darichhaus, adv.

throw schmeisse, v.; gschmisse, pp.; **about** 1.rum/schmeisse, v.; rumgschmisse, pp.; 2.rumhaer/schmeisse, v.; rumhaergschmisse, pp.; **after** no(och)schmeisse, v.; no(och)gschmisse, pp.; **against** wedder/schmeisse, v.; weddergschmisse, pp.; **around** rum/schmeisse, v.; rumgschmisse, pp.; **at** bschmeisse, v.; bschmisse, pp.; **away** 1.los/warre, v.; loswarre, pp.; 2.weck/schmeisse, v.; weckgschmisse, pp.; **back** zerick/schmeisse, v.; zerickgschmisse, pp.; **down** 1.hie/schmeisse, v.; hiegschmisse, pp.; 2.runner/schmeisse, v.; runnergschmisse, pp.; 3.um/schmeisse, v.; umgschmisse, pp.; 4.zamme/schmeisse, v.; zammegschmisse, pp.; **in** nei/schmeisse, v.; neigschmisse, pp.; **off** ab/schmeisse, v.; abgschmisse, pp.; **out** 1.naus/schmeisse, v.; nausgschmisse, pp.; 2.raus/schmeisse, v.; rausgschmisse, pp.; **over** 1.iwwer/schmeisse, v.; iwwergschmisse, pp.;

Tt

throw (continued)　　　　　　　　　　　　　　timidity

2.niwwer/schmeise, v.; niwwergschmisse, pp.;
3.riwwer/schmeisse, v.; riwwergschmisse, pp.;
stones schteeniche, v.; gschteenicht, pp.; **up**
1.nuff/schmeisse, v.; nuffgschmisse, pp.;
2.ruff/schmeisse, v ruffgschmisse, pp.; **up** (vomit)
breche (sich --)v.; gebroche, pp.
throwing Gschmeiss (es)n.
thrum or drone an air leiere, v.; geleiert, pp.
thrush (bird) 1.Amschel (die)n.; Amschle, pl.;
2.Buschvoggel (der)n.; 3.Droschel (die)n.; 4.Drossel
(die)n.; 5.Heckedroschel (die)n.; Heckedroschle, pl.
thrust 1.Renn (der)n.; 2.renne, v.; gerennt, pp.; 3.Schtoss
(der)n.; **away** weck/renne, v.; weckgerennt, pp.;
back zerick/renne, v.; zerickgerennt, **thrust down**
runner/schtosse, v.; runnergschtosse, pp.; **in**
1.nei/renne, v.; neigerennt, pp.; 2.nei/schtosse, v.;
neigschtosse, pp.; 3.rei/renne, v.; **out** 1.naus/renne,
v.; nausgerennt, pp.; 2.naus/schtosse, v.;
nausgschtosse, pp.
thud Blotz (der)n.; **thud!** 1.blump(s)!; 2.plumps!, interj.
thumb Daume (der)n.; (in nursery rhyme)
Hawwerschtecher (es)n.; **latch** Schlenk (die)n.; **sucking child** Daumesuckler (der)n.; Daumesuckler, pl.
thumbnail Daumenaggel (der)n.
thumbstall 1.Daumling (der)n.; 2.Deimling (der)n.
thump in the ribs 1.Ribbebuffer (der)n.; 2.Rippebuffer (der)n.
thunder 1.Dimmel (es)n.; 2.dimmele, v.; gedimmelt, pp.;
3.Dunner (der)n.; 4.dunnere, v.; gedunnert, pp.;
5.gewiddre, v.; gewiddert, pp.; 6.Gwidder (es)n.;
7.gwiddere, v.; (ge)widdert, pp.; **and lighten**
weddere, v.; geweddert, pp.; **cloud** Gewidderwolk
(die)n.; **shower** Gewidderregge (der)n.
thunderation! schtaernriesel, interj.
thunderbolt 1.Dunnerschlack (der)n.;
2.Gewidderschtreech (der)n.; 3.Gwidderschtreech
(der)n.
thundering horses Gwiddergeil (die)n., pl.
thundershower Gwidderregge (der)n.
thunderstorm 1.Dimmelwedder (es)n.; 2.Dunnerwetter
(es)n. (rare;) 3.G(e)widder (es)n.; 4.Gewidderschtarm
(der)n.; 5.Gwidder (es)n.; 6.Gwidderschtarem (der)
n.; 7.Wedder (es)n.
Thursday Dunnerschdaag (der)n.
thwarting hinnerlich, adj.
tick 1.Barricks (der) (uff -- kaafe); 2.knacke, v.; geknackt,
pp.; 3.knecke, v.; gekneckt, pp.; 4.Meedleis (die)n.;
5.Schoflaus (die)n.; 6.Schofleis (die)n.; 7.ticke, v.;
getickt, pp.; 8.Zeck (die)n.; Zecke, pl.; **tock** gnick
gnock
ticket 1.Zettel (der)n.; 2.Zettel (der)n.
ticking (for feather bed) Drilling (der)n.
tickle kitzle, v.; gekitzelt, pp.
tickling 1.gratzich, adj.; 2.kratzich, adj.; **sensation**
1.gratzes (en;) 2.Kitzles (es)n.
ticklish 1.griddlich, adj.; 2.kitzlich, adj.
tickseed 1.Buweleis (die)n., pl.; 2.Maedleis (die)n., pl.;

3.Meedleis (die)n., pl.; 4.Schoflaus (die)n.
tidiness 1.Niedichkeet (die)n.; 2.Niedlichkeet (die)n.
tidy 1.nett, adj.; 2.sauwer, adj.; 3.seiwerlich, adj.; **up**
uff/raahme, v.; uffgeraahmt, pp.
tie binne, v.; gebunne, pp.; aa/binne, v.; aagebunne, pp.;
back (the of horse) zerick/binne, v.; zerickgebunne,
tie bundles (of rye straw) **with a "Gnewwel"**
ab/gnewwle, v.; abgegnewwelt, pp.; **down**
nunner/binne, v.; nunnergebunne; pp.; **fast**
1.aa/binne, v.; aagebunne, pp.; 2.binne, v.; gebunne,
pp. (fescht --); **in** nei/binne, v.; neigebunne, pp.; **in
another place** 1.rum/binne, v.; rumgebunne, pp.;
2.weck/binne, v.; weckgebunne, pp.; **inside**
rei/binne, v.; reigebunne, pp.; **knots in yarn**
ab/gnibbe, v.; abgegnippt, pp.; **on** aa/gnibbe, v.;
aagegnippt, pp.; **outside** 1.naus/binne, v.;
nausgebunne, pp.; 2.raus/binne, v.; rausgebunne,
pp.; **over** iwwerbinne, v.; iwwergebunne, pp.;
sheaves after a cradler no(och)binne, v.;
no(och)gebunne, pp.; **strap** Aabinnrieme (der)n.;
together zamme/binne, v.; zammegebunne, pp.; **up**
1.nuff/binne, v.; nuffgebunne, pp.; 2.ruff/binne, v.;
ruffgebunne, pp.; 3.uff/binne, v.; uffgebunne, pp.;
4.verbinne, v.; verbunne, pp.; 5.zubinne, v.;
zugebunne, pp.
tiger 1.Dicher (der)n.; 2.Ticher (der)n.; **lily** Dicherlilye (die)n.
tight 1.eng, adj.; 2.fascht, adj.; 3.fescht, adj.; 4.fescht, adv.;
5. geizich, adj.; 6.schpanne, v.; gschpannt, pp.; **place**
Petz (die)n.
tighten 1.aa/ziehe, v.; aagezoge, pp.; 2.eischnalle, v.;
eigschnallt, pp.; **(a screw)** nei/drehe, v.; neigedreht,
pp.
'til erscht, adv.
tile Ziggel (der)n.
Tilghman Till(i) (der)n.
till baue, v.; gebaut, pp.
Tillie Till(i) (die)n.
tilt 1.schneppe, v.; gschneppt, pp.; 2.uff/schnabbe, v.;
uffgschnappt, pp.; 3.um/schtaerze, v.; umgschtaertzt, pp.; **back** zerick/schneppe, v.;
zerickgschneppt, pp.; **down** nunner/schnappe, v.;
nunnergschnappt, pp.; **lath** Schpriggel (der)n.; **out**
raus/schneppe, v.; rausgschneppt, pp.; **over**
niwwer/schnebbe, v.; niwwergscheppt, pp.
timber Bauhols (es)n.; **raiser** (in building) Schwenkfelder
(der)n.
time 1.Mol (es)n.; 2.Zeit (die)n.; Zeite, pl.; **of grace**
gnaadezeit (die)n.; **of rest** Ruhzeit (die)n.; **when
birds of passage take their flight** Fliegzeit (die)n.;
when young birds can fly Fliegzeit (die)n.
timely zeitlich, adv.
timeworn veralt, adj.
timid 1.bang, adj.; 2.eigezogge, adj.; 3.faerichbutzich,
adj.; 4.schichder, adj.; 5.schichderich, adj.;
6.verzaacht, adj.
timidity Bangichkeet (die)n.

Tt

timorous

timorous faerichbutzich, adj.

tin 1.Blech (es)n.; 2.Zinn (es)n.; **cup** 1.Beintblech (es)n.; 2.Blech (es)n.; 3.Drinkblech (es)n.; 4.Zinn (es)n.; **cup-full** Blechvoll (es)n.; **foil** Blattzinn (es)n.; **roof** Blech(e)dach (es)n.; **vessel smaller than a pail** Blicki (es)n.

tincture Tinktur (die)n.

tinker 1.beschdle, v.; gebeschdelt, pp.; 2.Kesselflicker (der)n.; 3.Schpengler (der)n.; 4.zimmere, v.; gezimmert, pp.

tinkle klingle, v.; geklingelt, pp.

tinny 1.blechich, adj.; 2.zinnich, adj.

tinshears Blechscheer (die)n.

tinsmith 1.Blechschmitt (der)n.; 2.Schpengler (der)n.

tinted lachdich, adj.

tinware 1.Blechegschaerr (es)n.; 2.Blechwaar (es)n.

tip 1.Punkt (der)n.; Punkde, pl.; 2.Schpitz(e) (der)n.; 3.um/falle, v.; umgfalle, pp.; 4.Zippel (der)n.; **(on settling a bill)** Drinkgeld (es)n.; **over** kippe, v.; gekippt, pp.

tipsy 1.bedrinke (sich --), v.; bedrunke,pp.; 2.bedrunke, adj.; 3.benewwelt, adj.; 4.gschwewwelt, adj 5.Kopp (der)n. (en -- hawwe); 6.Naas (der)n. (zu viel im -- hawwe); 8.Tee(der)n. (im -- sei)

tire 1.ab/binne,v.; abgebunne,pp.; 2.mied adj. (-- warre); **(wheel)** 1.Waagereef (der)n.; Waagereef, pl.; 2.Waggereef (der)n.; **oneself walking** mied laafe (sich --)v.; **someone out** ab/madde, v.; abgematt, pp.

tired mied, adj.; **(of it)** Leed (der)n. (der -- hawwe draa); **of** 1.leedich, adj.; 2.verleede, v.; verleedt, pp.

tiredness 1.Miedichkeet (die)n.; 2.Miedichkeit (die)n.

tiresome 1.langweilich, adj.; 2.miehseelich, adj.; 3.verleedtsam, adj.; **talker** 1.Gacke (die)n.; 2.Gax (die)n.

'tis well! wohlaan!

tit-tat-toe Fickmiehl (die)n.

title 1.Recht (es) (-- dazu); 2.Tiddel (der)n.; 3.Titel (der)n.

titty Diddi (der)n.

to 1.an, prep.; 2.em, prep.; 3.gege, prep.; 4.noch, prep.; 5.se = zu; 6.ze = zu; 7.zu, prep.; **a hair** hoorgnapps, adj.; **be** sei, v.; is g(e)west, pp.; **be (as to one's health or condition)** befinne (sich --)v.; befunne, pp.; **be sure** allerdings, adv.; **beat the band** Ort (die)n (dass es en -- hott); **do** Gefucker (es)n.; **her** zure = zu re; **it** zus = zu es; **one** 1.zum = zu e;m 2.zume = zu me; **school** schule, v.; gschult, pp.; **set** aa/richde, v.; aagericht, pp ; **"sport" boots** schtiffle, v.; gschtiffelt, pp.; **that** 1.dattdazu, adv.; 2.dattdezu, adv.; 3.dezu, adv.; **the** ans = an es; **the front** vannehie, adv.; **the left** 1.linkerhand, adv.; 2.links, adj.; **the other side** doniwwer, adv.; **the right** rechts, adj.; **them** ne = ihne; **this place** dohie, adv.; **this side** riwwer, adv.; **want to** wolle, v.; gewollt, pp.; **what place** wu anne, adv.; **you** eich, pron.

toad 1.Groot (die)n.; Grodde, pl.; 2.Grott (die)n.; 3.Hupsgrott (die)n.; 4.Krott (die)n.; 5.Seechgrott (die)n.; **foot** Grottefuss (der)n.

toadflax 1.Hun(d)sblumm (die)n.; 2.Rosmarei (die)n. (wilder --)

toadstool 1.Giftschwamm (der)n.; 2.Grottefuss (der)n.;

tonic

3.Grotteschtuhl (der)n.; 4.Schwamm (der)n.

toast 1.baehe, v.; gebaeht, pp.; 2.Brot (es)n. (gebaeht --); 3.Brot (es)n. (gereescht --); 4.Drinkschpruch (der)n.

tobacco Duwack (der)n.; **cloth** Duwackduch (es)n.; Duwackdicher, pl.; **flower** Duwacksblumm (die)n.; Duwacksblumme, pl.; **juice** Duwacksbrieh (die)n.; **plant** Duwacksschtengel (der)n.; **rope** Duwackschtrick (der)n.; Duwackschtrick, pl.; **sieve** Duwacksieb (die)n.

Tobias Dowwes (der)n.

today heit, adv.; **noon** demiddaag, adj.

toddle after no(och)dradde, v.; no(och)gedratt, pp.

toddler Schpringer (der)n. (en gleener --)

toe Zehe (der)n.; Zehe, pl.; **cap** (of a shoe) Kapp (die)n.; Kappe, pl.

together 1.anenanner, adv.; 2.annenanner, adv.; 3.beinanner, adv.; 4.beisamme, adv.; 5.menanner, adv.; 6.mit(enanner, adv.; 7.mit(e)nenner, adv.; 8.samt, adv.; 9.zamme/petze, v.; zammegepetzt, pp.; 10.zamme, adv.; 11. zammenanner, adv.; 12.zammer, adv.; 13.zamme/sei, v.; zammegewest, pp.; **with** 1.mitsamde, prep.; 2.mitzamde(n), prep.; 3.mitzamte(n), prep.; 4.samde, prep.; 5.samt(e), prep.; 6.zamt(e), adv.

toil 1.Blok (die)n.; 2.Plok (die)n.

toilet 1.Briwwe (es)n.; 2.Briwwi (es)n.; 3.Heisli (es)n.; Heislin, pl.; **hole** Scheissloch (es)n.; Scheisslecher, pl.

toilsome mieseelich, adj.

token Aazeeche (der, es)n.

tolerable 1.ausschtehlich, adj.; 2.basslich, adj.; 3. middelmaessich, adj.; 4.zimmlich, adv.

tolerate 1.aus/schteh, v.; ausgschtanne, pp.; 2.dulde, v.; geduldet, pp.; 3.leide, v.; gelidde, pp.; 4.verschmaerze, v.; verschmaerzt, pp.

toll bell (at funerals) 1.Bell (die)n.(-- toole); 2.Glock (die)n. (-- toole)

tomato 1.Bommerans (die)n.; 2.Bummerans (die)n.; 3.Gummerans (die)n.; 4.Tamaet(i)s (die)n., pl.; **bug** Tomaetskeffer (der)n.; **juice** Tamaetsbrieh (die)n.

tomb Graab (es)n.; Greewer, pl.

tomboy Buweschmaga (der)n.; Buweschmaga, pl.

tombstone cutter Graabschteehacker (der)n.

tomcat Kaader (der)n.; Kaader, pl.

tomfoolery 1.Faxe (die)n., pl.; 2.Hanswaschtschtreech (die)n., pl.; 3.Narreschtreech (die)n., pl.; 4.Schwoweschtreech (die)n., pl.

tomorrow mariye, adv.; **morning** mariyefrieh, adv.

ton 1.Dann (die)n.; 2.Dunn (die)n.

tone 1.Grundfarb (die)n.; 2.Ton (der)n.

tongs Zange (die)n.

tongue (human) Zung (die)n.; Zunge, pl.; **(human)** (humorous) Deixel (die)n.; **(of shoe)** (humorous) Schlecker (der)n.; Schlecker, pl.; **and groove plane** Fedderhowel (die)n.; Fedderhowwle, pl.; **tied** schtumm, adj.

tonic Schtaerrickungsmittel (es)n.

Tt

tonsillitis

tonsillitis 1.Driese (die)n. pl. (-- brenne dreck); 2.Driese (die)n., pl. (wehe --); 3.Wehhals (der)n.; Wehhels, pl.

too 1.dazu, adv.; 2.dergleiche, adv.; 3.desgleiches, adv.; 4.zu, adv.

tool 1.Waerkzeich (es)n.; 2.Waerzeich (es)n.; **for scribing angle** Wedderhex (die)n.; **used by coopers** 1.Gargelreisser (der)n.; 2.Garyelreisser (der)n.; **used in digging graves to secure a straight edge** Schtosseise (es)n.; 1.Gscha(rr) (es)n.; Gscharre, pl.; 2.Handwarricksgschaer (es)n.

tooth 1.Zaah (der)n.; Zeh, pl.; 2.zackle, v.; gezackelt, pp.; 3.Zoh (der)n.; Zeh, pl.; **extractor** 1.Zaehropper (der) n.; 2.Zehrobber (der)n.; **powder** 1.Zaehpulwer (es)n.; 2.Zehpulwer (es)n.; **socket** 1.Zaahlaad (die)n.; Zehland, pl.; 2.Zohlaad (die)n.; **ulcer** Zaahgschwaere (der)n.

toothache 1.Zaahweh (es)n.; 2.Zohweh (es)n.

toothbrush 1.Zaehbascht (die)n.; 2.Zehbascht (die)n.

toothed 1.gezackt, adj.; 2.zackich, adj.; 3.zacklich, adj.

toothie 1.Zaehche (es)n.; 2.Zehche (es)n.

toothpick 1.Zaehbutzer (der)n.; 2.Zehblicker (der)n.; 3.Zehbutzer (der)n.; 4.Zehschtarer (der)n.; Zehschtarer, pl.

toothsome schmackhaft, adj.

top 1.Gibbel (der)n.; Gibbel, pl.; 2.Gippel (der)n.; 3.zerick/schneide, v.; zerickgschnidde, pp.; **(of a tree)** Dopp (der)n.; **(plants)** 1.kebbe, v.; gekeppt, pp.; 2.keppe, v.; gekeppt, pp.; **curl** (mostly on the heads of children) Kowwel (die)n.; **hat** 1.Schtitz (der)n.; Schtitze, pl.; 2.Schtitzhut (der)n.; **of a plant** Kraut (es) n.; **of a tree** Faerscht (der)n.; **sirloin** Rickschtick (es) n.; **tobacco** Duwack (der)n. (-- taape)

toper 1.Brandeweifass (es)n.; 2.Drammratt (die)n.; 3.Drinker (der)n.

topple 1.nunner/schtatze, v.; nunnergschtatzt, pp.; 2.runner/schtatze, v.; runnergschtatzt, pp.; 3.schtatze, v.; gschtatzt, pp.; **over** 1.kibbe, v.; gekippt, pp.; 2.kippe, v.; gekippt, pp.

topsy-turvey 1.unnerscht's ewwerscht, adv., adj.; 2.drunner un driwwe;r 3.verkehrt, adj.

torch Fackel (die)n.

torment 1.bellere, v.; gebellert, pp.; 2.bendere, v.; gebendert, pp.; 3.bloge, v.; geblogt, pp.; 4.deifle, v.; gedeifelt, pp.; 5.deiwle, v.; gedeiwelt, pp.; 6.Drangsaal (der)n.; 7.driwweliere, v.; gedriwwliert, pp.; 8.fiole, v.; gfiolt, pp.; 9.Gwael (die)n.; 10.Gwaelaarsch (der)n.; 11.gwaele, v.; gegwaelt, pp.; 12.Pein (die)n.; 13.peiniche, v.; gepeinicht, pp.; 14.Pescht (die)n.; Peschde, pl.; **(verbally)** 1.grageele, v.; grageelt, pp.; 2.krageele, v.; grakeelt, pp.

tormenting 1.gwaelich, adj.; 2.gweelich, adv.; 3.peinlich, adj.; **(nagging) child** Gwaeleise (es)n.; **or worrying** Gequael (es)n.

torn aagrisse, adj.

torpid gfiehllos, adj.

tortoise 1.Landschillgrott (die)n.; 2.Schillgrott (die)n.;

tract

Schillgrodde, pl.

torture 1.maerdere, v.; gemaerdert, pp.; 2.maerdere, v.; gemaerdert, pp.

toss schmeisse, v.; gschmisse, pp.; **(a ball)** schucke, v.; gschuckt, pp.; **to** hie/schnelle, v.; hiegschnellt, pp.

totally rumps un schtumps, adv.

totter (to shake, wobble) 1.wackle, v.; gewackelt, pp.; 2.wankle, v.; gewankelt, pp.

tottering gnackrich, adj.

touch 1.aa/fiehle, v.; aagfiehlt, pp.; 2.aa/fingere, v.; aagfingert, pp.; 3.aa/reeche, v.; aagereecht, pp.; 4.aa/rege, v.; aageregt, pp.; 5.aa/riehre, v.; aageriehrt, pp.; 6.befiehle, v.; befiehlt, pp.; **(glasses)** aa/schtosse, v.; aagschtosse, pp.; **base** (in playing hide seek) ab/detschle, v. abgedetschelt, pp.; **hole** 1.Zindloch (es)n.; 2.Zindpann (die)n.; **me-not** Schpringblumm (die)n.; Schpringblumme, pl.

touching riehrend, adj.

touchy 1.kitzlich, adj.; 2.mutsich, adj.; 3.mutzich, adj.; 4.needlich, adj.

tough 1.zaeh, adj.; 2.zeh, adj.; **one** Rachebutzer (der)n.; Rachebutzer, pl.

toughness 1.Zaehichkeet (die)n.; 2.Zehichkeet (die)n.

tousled schtrubbich, adj.

tow 1.Schwingwaerick (es)n.; 2.Waerick (es)n.; 3.Waerrick (es)n.; **haired child** Weisskopp (der)n.; Weisskepp, pl.; **of first hackling** Bollwaerrick (es)n.

toward 1.engege, prep.; 2.geeich, prep.; 3.geg(g)e, adv.; 4.gege, prep.; **morning** gege Mariye, adv.; **the east** gege Mariye, adv.; **the end** letscht, (es -- her); **the north** 1.nadd(e), adv.; 2.Nadde (die)n (gege --); 3.naerdlich, adv.

towards 1.geyich, adv.; 2.no, adv.; 3.no, prep.; 4.noch, prep.; 5.nooch, adv.; 6.nooch, prep.; **the end of** ausgangs, adv.; **the south** noch Middaag zu, adv.

towel 1.Abdrickellumbe (der)n.; 2.Handduch (der)n.; Handdicher, pl.; 3.Handlumbe (der)n.

towhead Flaxkopp (der)n.

towheaded flaxkebbich, adj.

town 1.Schtdadt (die)n.; Schtedt, pl.; 2.Schteddel (es)n. 3.Schtedtche (es)n.; 4.Schtedtli (es)n.; **girl** Schtedlermeedel (es)n.; Schtedlermeed, pl.; **resident** Schtedler (der)n.; Schtedler, pl.

toy 1.Kinnerschpielsach (die)n.; Kinnerschpielsache, pl.; 2.Schpielsach (die)n.; Schpielsache, pl.; 3.Tand (der)n.

trace 1.Gschpur (die)n.; Gschpure, pp.; 2.Schpur (die)n.; Schpure, pl.; 3.schpure, v.; gschpurt, pp.; **(part of harness)** 1.Schtrang (der)n.; Schtreng, pl.; 2.Keddeschtrang (der)n.; **chains** Halbschtreng (die)n., pl.

traceable (of animals) fromm, adj.

track 1.Gschpur (die)n.; Gschpure, pp.; 2.Schpur (die)n.; Schpure, pl.; **(of a wagon)** Glees (es)n.; Gleeser, pl.; **of ants in grass** 1.Iemensepaad (der)n.; 2.Umensepaad (der)n.

tract Schtreck (die)n.

Tt

trade

trade 1.ab/handle, v.; abghandelt, pp.; 2.aus/wechsle, v.; ausgewechselt, pp.; 3.aus/wexle, v.; ausgewexelt, pp.; 4.Handel (der)n.; 5.handle, v.; g(e)handelt, pp.; 6.Handwarricksgscheft (es)n.; 7.Kunnschaft (die)n., pl.; **off** verhandle, v.; verhandelt, pp.

tradesman Handelsmann (der)n.; Handelsleit, pl.

trading Handelwese (es)n.

tragic sight 1.aageschpickel (der)n.; 2.Aageschpiggel (der)n.

trail Priefing (die)n.

trailing arbutus 1.Erdschtreiss (die)n., pl.; 2.Grundschtrauss (der)n.

train 1.ab/richde, v.; abgericht, pp.; 2.uff/ziehe, v.; uffgezoge, pp.; 3.ziehe, v.; gezoge, pp.; **(railroad)** 1.Reiggelwegkaers (die)n.; 2.Riggelweg (der)n.;

training Zucht (die)n.

traitor Verraeter (der)n.

trammel Feierhohl (der)n.

tramp 1.dabbele, v.; gedabbelt, pp.; 2.Landlaafer (der)n.; 3.rum/laafe, v.; rumg(e)loffe, pp.; 4.Rumleefer (der)n.; Rumleefer, pl.; 5.Zoddelmann (der)n.; Zoddelmenner, pl.; **down** zamme/dripple, v.; zammegedrippelt, pp.; **out** raus/drede, v.; rausgedrede, pp.

trample 1.dripple, v.; gedrippelt, pp.; 2.nunner/drede, v.; nunnergedrede, pp.; 3.schtramble, v.; gschtrambelt, pp.; 4.verdabbe, v.; verdappt, pp.; **down** verdribble, v.; verdribbelt, pp.; **on** verdrede, v.; verdrede, pp.

tranquil 1.ruhich, adj.; 2.schtill, adj.

transcribe ab/schreiwe, v.; abgschriwwe, pp.

transcript Abschrift (die)n.

transfer 1.iwwer/draage,v; iwwergedraage, pp.; 2.iwwer/mache, v.; iwwergemacht, pp.; **a load** rum/laade, v.; rumglaade, pp.

transform um/wandle, v.; umgewandelt, pp.

transgress 1.iwwer/dreede, v.; iwwerdrede, pp.; 2.iwwer/ laafe, v.; iwwergelofe, pp.

transgressor Iwwerdreder (der)n.

transient vergenglich, adj.

translate iwwersetze, v.; iwwersetzt, pp.

translator 1.Iwwersatzer (der)n.; Iwwersatzer, pl.; 2.Iwwersetzer (der)n.

transmission Verwandlung (die)n.

transmit a disease aa/henke, v.; aaghenkt; aaghonke, pp.

transmute verwandle, v.; verwandelt, pp.

transparent darichsichdich, adj.

transplant 1.aus/blanze, v.; ausgeblanzt, pp.; 2.aus/schtecke, v.; ausgschteckt, pp.; 3.aus/setze, v.; ausgsetzt, pp.; 4.raus/blanze, v.; rausgeblanzt, pp.; 5.rum/blanze, v.; rumgeblanzt, pp.

transport commodities in a canal boat boote, v.; geboot, pp.

transposition Versetzung (die)n.

trap Fall (die)n.; Falle, pl.

trapdoor 1.Falldeer (die)n.; 2.Falldier (die)n.

trash 1.Gerebbelfress (es)n.; 2.Gfrees (es)n.; 3.Lumberei (die)n.

tried

trave Notschtall (der)n.

travel 1.reese, v.; gereest, pp.; 2.wandle, v.; gewandelt, pp.; **from place to place** rumhaer/reese, v.; rumhaergereest, pp.

traverse darich/reese, v.; darichgereest, pp.

tray (in cards) dritt, adj. (en --er)

treacherous 1.falsch, adj.; 2.hemdickisch, adj.

tread 1.dredde, v.; gedredde, pp.; 2.Dritt (der)n.; **down** 1.nidder/drede, v. niddergedrede, pp.; 2.nunner/drede, v.; nunnergedrede, pp.

treadle Dreeder (der)n.

treason Verrot (der)n.

treasure Schatz (der)n.; Schatz, pl.

treasurer Schatzmeeschder (der)n.

treasury 1.Kass (die)n.; 2.Schatzkammer (die)n.

treat 1.behandle, v.; behandelt, pp.; 2.Luscht (die)n.; 3.uff/setze, v.; uffgsetzt, pp.; **(oneself) with salve or ointment** blaschdere, v.; geblaschdert, pp.; **a horse with vapor** (from a rosin, tar, etc. for pneumonia and distemper) bereechere, v.; bereechert, pp.; **with forbearance** 1.schone, v.; gschont, pp.; 2.schune, v.; gschunt, pp.

treatise on botany Kreiderbuch (es)n.

treatment 1.Behandlung (die)n.; 2.Handlung (die)n.

treble dreifaechich mache, v.

tree 1.Baam (der)n.; Beem, pl.; 2.Boom (der)n.; **frog** 1.Frosch (der)n.; Fresch, pl.; 2.Laabfrosch (der)n.; 3.Laabgrott (die)n.; **kidney bean** 1.Feierbohn (die)n.; Feierbohne, pl.; 2.Feierbuhn (die)n.; Feierbuhne, pl.; **moss** Baamoos (es)n.; **toad** 1.Laabfrosch (der)n.; 2.Laabgrott (die)n.

tremble 1.schnaddre, v.; gschnaddert, pp.; 2.schnattre, v.; gschnaddert, pp.; 3.ziddere, v.; geziddert, pp.

trembly 1.engschderich,adj.;2.engschderlich,adj.;3. zidderich,adj.

tresspass iwwer/dreede, v.; iwwerdrede, pp.

trestle Schemel (der)n.

trial 1.Preifing (die)n.;2.Unnersuchung (die)n.; 3.Versuch (der)n.

triangle Dreieck (es)n.; **(musical instrument)** Dreiangel (der)n.

triangular dreieckich, adj.

tribe 1.Schlack (der)n.; 2.Schtamm (der)n.

tribulation Driebsaal (der)n.

trick 1.aa/schmiere, v.; aagschmiert, pp.; 2.Rumbel (der)n.; 3.Schabernack (der)n.; **performer** Kinschdler (der)n.; Kinschdler, pl.

tricks 1.Aaschtreech (die)n., pl.; 2.Flause (die)n., pl.; 3.Gnop(der)n.; Gnepp, pl. (gnepp im kopp); 4.Naube (die)n., pl.; 5.Nubbe (die)n.; 6.Nuppe (die)n., pl.

trickster 1.Bedrieger (der)n.; 2.Schpuli (der)n.

tricky 1.gnitz, adj.; 2.kniffisch, adj.; 3.kniffzich, adj.; 4.knitz, adj.; 5.schlau, adj.; **tricky** Gnopp (der)n.; Gnepp, pl. (gnepp hinnich die Ohre hawwe)

trident Dreischpitz (der)n.

tried probaat, adj.

Tt

trifle — tumble

trifle 1.Dreck (der)n.; 2.Gleenichkeet (die)n.; **(any)** Dreck (der)n. (eenicher --)

trifling matter Hinkeldreck (der)n.

trigger 1.Dricker (der)n.; 2.Schnebber (der)n.; 3.Schneller (der)n.

trill drillere, v.; gedrillert, pp.

trim 1.aus/schneide, v.; ausgschnidde, pp.; 2.aus/ziehe, v.; 3.besetze, v.; 4.bsetze, v.; bsetzt, pp.; 5.mache, v.; gemacht, pp. (zurecht --); 6.trimme, v.; getrimmt, pp.; 7.zerechtmache, v.; zerechtgemacht, pp.; **down** 1.dechsle, v.; gedechselt, pp.; 2.dexle, v.; gedexelt, pp.; **trees** butze, v.; gebutzt, pp. (Beem --)

trimmer used in cutting bushes Heckehoke (der)n.; Heckehoke, pl.

trimming Bsetzing (die)n.

trimmings (around hard soap) 1.Abfall (der)n.; 2.Brockeldings (die)n., pl.

trinity Dreieehnichkeit (die)n.

trip 1.Rees (die)n.; Reese, pl.; 2.Reis (die)n.; Reise, pl.; 3.Tour (die)n.

tripe 1.Kuddelfleck (der)n.; 2.Rindswambe(r) (der)n.

triple dreifach, adj.

tripletree Dreiwoog (die)n.

tripod Dreifuss (der)n.

triune dreieenich, adj.

trivet Dreifuss (der)n.

trivial matter Schiss (der)n.

trombone players (in Moravian ceremonies) Posaunerkor (der)n.

trooper Reider (der)n.; Reider, pl.

trot 1.dradde, v.; gedratt, pp.; 2.Dratt (der)n.; 3.dratte, v.; gedratt, pp.; **after** no(och)dradde, v.; no(och)gedratt, pp.; **along** hie/drolle, v.; hiegedrollt, pp.; **in** nei/drolle, v.; niegedrollt, pp.; **off** ab/dradde, v.; abgedratt, pp.; **up** nuff/drolle, v.; nuffgedrollt, pp.

troth Treie (die)n.

trotter 1.Dradder (der)n.; 2.Dratter (der)n.

trouble 1.Badder (der, die)n.; 2.bemiehe, v.; bemieht, pp.; 3. Beschwerde (die)n.; 4.Blog (die)n.; 5.Blok (die)n.; 6. Druwwel (der)n.; 7.druwwle, v.; gedruwwelt, pp.; 8.Elend (es)n.; 9.Lumberei (die)n.; 10.Mieh (die)n.; 11.Plok (die)n.; 12.Sarge, (die)n.; 13.Sarges (es)n.; 14.Sarick (die)n.; 15. Sarye (die, es)n.; 16.schteere, v.; gschteert, pp.; 17. Verleggeheet (die)n.; 18.Yammer (der)n.; **maker** 1.Zwaerrick (der)n. (en rechter --); 2.Zwieschpalt (der)n.; **oneself** bekimmere (sich --)v.; beklmmert, pp.

troubled verlegge, adj.

troublesome 1.beschwerlich, adj.; 2.hinnerlich, adj.; 3.iwwerleschdich, adj.; 4.verdriesslich, adj.

trough Drog (der)n.; Dreeg, pl.

trousers buckle Hosseschnall (die)n.; **button** Hossegnopp (der)n.; **leg** Hossebeh (es)n.

trout Forell (die)n.

trowel 1.Bleschderkell (die)n.; 2.Kaer (die)n.; Kaere, pl.; 3.Kell (die)n.; Kelle, pl.; 4.Mauerkell (die)n.

truant 1.Daagdieb (der)n.; 2.Schulschwenser (der)n.

trudge dratsche, v.; gedratscht, pp.; **after** no(och)basse, v.; no(och)gebasst, pp.; **away** weck/dabbe, v.; weckgedappt, pp.; **back** zerick/dappe, v.; zerickgedappt, pp.; **lazily over** niwwer/lodle, v.; niwwergeloddelt, pp.; **up** nuff/dappe, v.; nuffgedappt, pp.

true 1.gedreilich, adj.; 2.recht, adj.; 3.trei, adj.; 4.uffrichdich, adj.; 5.waahr, adj.; 6.wohr, adj.

truly 1.sogaar, adv.; 2.verhafdich, adv.; 3.verhaftich, adj.; 4.waahrhafdich, adv.; 5.waahrhafdich, adv.; 6.waericklich, adv.; 7.waerklich, adv.; 8.waricklich, adv.; 9.wohrhaftich, adj.; 10.zwaar, adv.

trump 1.Drump (der)n.; 2.drumpe, v.; gedrumpt, pp.; **up lies** erliege, v.; erlogge, pp.

trumpet Drumbet (die)n.

trundle bed 1.Bettleedel (es)n.; 2.Schiebbettlaedche (es) n.; 3.Schiewerli (es)n.

trunk Schtamm (der)n.

truss Bruchband (es)n.

trust 1.barge, v.; gebarkt, pp.; 2.Barricks (der)n. (uff -- kaafe); 3.draue, v.; gedraut, pp.; 4.Verdraue (es)n.; 5.verdraue, v.; verdraut, pp.

trusting 1.verdrauensvoll, adj.; 2.zudrauisch, adj.

truth 1.Waahret (die)n.; 2.Waahrheit (die)n.; 3.Wohret (die)n.

truthful 1.waahrhaft, adj.; 2.wohrhaft, adj.

try 1.browiere, v.; (ge)browiert, pp.; 2.versuche, v.; versucht, pp.; **all sorts of doctors medicines** rum/dokdere, v.; rumgedokdert, pp.; **especially** iewe, v.; geiebt, pp.

trying griddlich, adj.; **child** 1.Gwaelaarsch (der) n.;2.Gwaelholz (es)n.

tub 1.Schtenner (der)n.; Schtenner, pl.; 2.Zuwwer (der)n.; Ziwwer, pl.

tuba Basshann (es)n.

tube Reehr (die)n.

tuber Gnolle (der)n.

tuberculosis Auszehring (die)n.

tuck in nei/schtecke, v.; neigschteckt; neigschtocke, pp.; **under** (as the end of the band in binding grain) 1.unner/schrecke, v.; unnergschreckt, pp.; 2.unner/schtrecke, v.; unnergschtreckt, pp.

tucker (for goods) en (die) Howwel wu sie die False (tucks) ziege mit

tucks False (die)n., pl.

Tuesday Dinschdaag (der)n.

tuft 1.Pusch (der)n.; 2.Wischel (es)n.; 3.Wischli (es)n.

tug zaere, v.; gezaert, pp.

tuition Schulgeld (es)n.

tulip 1.Dollebaan (die)n.; 2.Dullebaan (die)n.; Dullebaane, pl.; 3.Dulleblumm (die)n.; **tree** 1.Babbel (der)n.; 2.Babble (der)n.; Babble, pl.

tumble 1.barzle, v.; gebarzelt, pp.; 2.Batzelbaam (der)n. (en -- schlagge); 3.batzle, v.; gebatzelt, pp.;

(Continued on page 400)

Tt

tumble (continued)

(Continued from page 399)

4.iwwer/schlagge, v.; iwwerschlagge, pp.;
5.schtaerze, v.; gschtaerzt, pp.; 6.Schtatz (der)n.;
7.schtatze, v.; gschtatzt, pp.; 8.um/schtaerze, v.;
umgschtaertzt, pp.; **about** rum/falle, v.; rumgfalle,
pp.; **away** weck/batzle, v.; weckgebatzelt, pp.; **down**
1.nunner/batzle, v.; nunnergebatzelt, pp.;
2.runner/batzle, v.; runnergebatzelt, pp.;
3.zamme/batzle, v.; zammegebatzelt, pp.; **off**
ab/batzle, v.; abgebatzelt, pp.; **out** 1.naus/schtaerze,
v.; nausgschtaerzt, pp.; 2.raus/batzle, v.;
rausgebatzelt, pp.; 3.raus/schtatze, v.; rausgschtatzt,
pp.; **over** um/batzle, v.; umgebatzelt, pp.

tumblebug Kiehdrechroller (der)n.

tumbler Glaas (es)n.; Glesser, pl.

tumult 1.Laerm(e) (der)n.; 2.Uffruhr (der, die)n.

tune 1.schtimme, v.; gschtimmt, pp.; 2.Weis (die)n.; **the
cow died on** Leier (die)n. (die aldi --)

tuning fork Schtimmgawwel (die)n.

turd 1.Gnoddel (der)n.; 2.Knoddel (der)n.; 3.Scheissdreck
(der)n.

tureen Subbeschissel (die)n.

turkey Welschhinkel (es)n.; Welschhinkel, pl.; **buzzard**
1.Aadler (der)n.; Aadler, pl.; 2.Ludergrabb (die)n.;
3.Ludergrapp (die)n.; 4.Ludervoggel (der)n.;
5.Ooshaahne (der)n.; Ooshaahne, pl.; 6.Ooshinkel
(es)n.; Ooshinkel, pl.; 7.Oosvog(g)el (der)n.; 8.Osswoi
(der)n.; **gobbler** Welschhaahne (der)n.;
Welschhaahne; Welschhinkel, pl.

turmeric 1.Blutwarzel (die)n.; 2.Blutwatzel (die)n.

turn 1.Dreh (die)n.; 2.drehe, v.; gedreht, pp.; 3.drehe, v.;
gedreht, pp. (ebbes --); 4.Reih (die)n. = Roi (die);
5.Roi (die)n.; Roie, pl.; 6.Roiet (die)n.; 7.Roiyet (die)
n.; 8.schwenke, v.; gschwenkt, pp.; 9.wende, v.;
gewennt, pp.; **(in road)** Kehr (die)n.; **a sommersault**
Batzelbaam (der)n. (en -- schlagge); **ahead** (a clock)
vor/drehe, v.; vorgedreht, pp.; **around** 1.rum/drehe,
v.; rumgedreht, pp.; 2.um/drehe, v.; umgedreht, pp.;
3.um/kehre, v.; umgekehrt, pp.; **aside** 1.ab/laafe, v.;
abgeloffe, pp.; 2.aus/wenne, v.; ausgewennt, pp.;
away 1.um/drehe, v.; umgedreht, pp.; 2.verdrehe,
v.; verdreht, pp.; **back** 1.um/kehre, v.; umgekehrt,
pp.; 2.zerick/drehe, v.; zerickgedreht, pp.; **button**
1.Driller (der)n.; 2.Waerwel (der)n.; **down**
nunner/drehe, v.; nunnergedreht, pp.; **down** (edges)
nunner/klempe, v.; nunnergeklempt, pp.; **first furrow** aa/bluge, v.; aageblugt, pp.; **flat** ab/schteh, v.;
abgschtanne, pp.; **for drying** 1.uff/wenne, v.;
uffgewennt, pp.; 2.wenne, v.; gewennt, pp.; **hay**
1.Hoi wende, v.; gewennt, pp.; 2.Hoi wenne, v.;
gewennt, pp.; **in** 1.eidrehe, v.; eigedreht, pp.;
2.nei/drehe, v.; neigedreht, pp.; **in a seem** eidrehe,
v.; eigedreht, pp.; **in plowing** (end of corner of field)
(Berks Co., PA) Auswenger (der)n.; Auswenger, pl.; **in
the edge in hemming** ei/bicke, v.; eigebickt, pp.;
inside out 1.letz mache (sich --)v.; 2.rum/drehe, v.;

twentieth

rumgedreht, pp.; **off** 1.ab/drehe, v.; abgedreht, pp.;
2.zudrehe, v.; zugedreht, pp.; **on** druff/drehe, v.;
druffgedreht, pp.; **on** (as a light) aa/drehe, v.;
aagedreht, pp.; **on a lathe** ab/drehe, v.; abgedreht,;
out 1.aus/drehe, v.; ausgedreht, pp.; 2.aus/weiche,
v.; ausgewiche, pp.; 3.gerode, v.; gerode, pp.;
4.raus/drehe, v.; rausgedreht, pp.; **out unsuccessful**
1.fehl/gschlagge, v.; fehlgschlagge, pp.;
2.fehl/schlagge, v.; fehlgschlagge, pp.; **out well**
gerode, v.; gerode, pp. (gut --); **over**
1.niwwer/drehe, v.; niwwergedreht, pp.;
2.riwwer/drehe, v.; riwwergedreht, pp.; 3.um/drehe,
v.; umgedreht, pp.; 4.um/kehre, v.; umgekehrt, pp.;
5.um/schtilbe, v.; umgschtilpt, pp.; **over by rooting**
rum/wiehle, v.; rumgewiehlt, pp.; **someone away**
ab/weise (sich --)v.; abgewisse, pp.; **the first furrow**
aa/faahre, v.; aagfaahre, pp.; **the furrow**
rum/wenne, v.; rumgewennt, pp.; **the leaves of a
book** 1.darich/blettre, v.; darichgeblettert, pp.;
2.rum/blettre, v.; rumgeblettert, pp.; **the pages of a
book** blettre, v.; geblettert, pp.; **the wrong way**
verdrehe, v.; verdreht, pp.; **things topsy-turvy**
1.darich/wiehle, v.; darichgewiehlt, pp.;
2.darichnanner/mache, v.; darichnannergemacht,
pp.; 3. darichnannerwiehle, v.; **this way** haer/drehe,
v.; haergedreht, pp.; **to hie/wenne** (sich --), v.;
hiegewennt, pp.; **to cheese** 1.kaese, v.; gekaest, pp.;
2.keese, v.; gekeest, pp.; **towards** hie/drehe, v.;
hiegedreht, **turn up** 1.ruff/drehe, v.; ruffgedreht,
pp.; 2.uff/drehe, v.; ufgedreht, pp.; **up** (collar)
nuff/schlagge, v.; nuffgschlagge, pp.; **up** (sleeves)
nuff/wenne, v.; nuffgewennt, pp.; **up edges of tin or
zinc** nuff/klempe, v.; nuffgeklempt, pp.; **up one's
nose** 1.Naas (die)n. (-- nuff/runsle) (-- ringle);
2.nuff/runsle, v.; nuffgerunselt, pp.; (die Naas --)
3.ringle, v.; geringelt, pp. (die Naas --); **with the
plow** um/bluge, v.; umgeblugt, pp.

turning lathe Drehbank (die)n.; Drehbenk, pl.

turnip Rieb (die)n.; Riewe, pl.; **patch** Riewschtick (es)n.;
salad Rieweselaat (der)n.; **seed** Riebsaame (der)n.;
soup Riewesupp (die)n.; **sowing day**, July 2
Riebsaehdaag (der)n.

turntable for front wagon wheels Fimftraad (es)n.;
Fimftredder, pl.

turpentine 1.Daerbedien (es)n.; 2.Darebedien (es)n.

turtle Schillgrott (die)n.; Schillgrodde, pl.; **dove**
1.Daddeldaub (die)n.; Daddeldauwe, pl.;
2.Dardeldaub (die)n.

tusk Fangzaah (der)n.; Fangzeh, pl.

tutor Unnerlehrer (der)n.

twaddle 1.faawle, v.; gfaawelt, pp.; 2.Lapperei (die)n.;
3.Wind (der)n.

twelfth zwelft, adv.; **(part)** Zwelfde (es)n.

twelve zwelf; zwelfe, adj.; pron.

Twelvetide, Dec 25 - Jan 6 Belsnickelzeit (die)n.

twentieth zwansichscht, adj.; **(part)** Zwansichschdel (es)n.

Tt

twenty zwansich, adj.; pron.

twibill Zwaerichax (die)n.

twice zweemol, adv.

twig 1.Neschtli (es)n.; Neschtlin, pl.; 2.Zweig (die) n.;Zweige, pl.

twilight 1.dauschber, adv.; 2.dauschder, adv.; 3.Demmerung (die)n.; 4.Duschber (die)n.; 5.duschber, adv.; 6.Duschder (die)n.; 7.duschder, adv.

twill 1.Zwillich (der)n.; 2.zwillichde, v.; gezwillicht, pp.

twilled gezwillicht, adj.

twin 1.Zwilling (der)n.; Zwilling, pl.; 2.Zwillingbobbli (es) n.; Zwillingbobblin, pl.

twine 1.Gaarn (es)n.; 2.Schnur (die)n.; **about** 1.um/fasse, v.; umgfasst, pp.; 2.umfasse, v.; umfasst, pp.; **around** rum/ranke, v.; rumgerankt, pp.; **in** nei/flechde, v.; neigflochde, pp.

twinge 1.Gezwacker (es)n.; 2.Schtich (der)n.

twinkle glitzere, v.; geglitzert, pp.

twirl um/drehe, v.; umgedreht, pp.

twist 1.Dreh (die)n.; 2.drehe, v.; gedreht, pp.; 3.rum/drehe, v.; rumgedreht, pp.; 4.verdrehe, v.; verdreht, pp.; 5.verrenke, v.; verrenkt, pp.; **(yarn)** zwaerne, v.; gezwaernt, pp.; **tight** gnewwle, v.; gegnewwelt, pp.; **tobacco** Roll(e)duwack (der)n.; **together** zamme/drehe, v.; zammegedreht, pp.

twisted up iwwerzwarich, adj.

twisting wheel (in spinning) Zwaernraad (es)n.

twit schtichle, v.; gschtichelt, pp.

twitch 1.Braems (der)n.; 2.darich/zucke, v.; darichgezucht, pp.; 3.Schtich (der)n.; 4.verzucke, v.; verzuckt, pp.; 5.zucke, v.; gezucht, pp.

twitchy zuckich, adj.

twitter 1.zwitschere, v.; gezwitschert, pp.; 2.zwitzere, v.; gezwitzert, pp.

two zwee, adj.; pron.; **faced** 1.zweegsichtich, adj.; 2.zweeseidich, adj.; **first furrows thrown against each other in plowing to the right** Grod (der)n.; **fold** zweefach, adj.; **horse wagon** Zweegeilswagge (der) n.; Zweegeilswegge, pl.; **legged** zweebeenich, adj.; **seated** zweesitzich, adj.; **storied** zweeschteckich, adj.; **weeks** Daag (die)n., pl. (varzeh --); **weeks from today** Daag (der)n. (heit iwwer vatzeh --); **wheeled** zweereddrich, adj.; **years old** 1.zweeyaahrich, adv.; 2.zweeyaehrich, adj.; **yolks** zweedoddrich, adj.

tying apron Binnschatz (der)n.

typhoid fever Beesfiewer (es)n.

tyrant 1.Menscheschinner (der)n.; 2.Tyrann (der)n.

Uu

U-shaped piece at the end of a flail — undertaker

U-shaped piece at the end of the handle of a flail 1.Kapp (die)n.; Kappe, pl.; 2.Fleggelkopp (der)n.

udder Eider (es)n.

ugh! Fui!, interj.

ugliest of all allerwiescht, adj.

ugly 1.Gfress (es)n.; 2.mupsich, adj.; 3.wiescht, adj.; **face** 1.Affegsicht (es)n.; 2.Riewegsicht (es)n.

ulcer Gschwier (es)n.; **on a tooth** Zohgschwaere (der)n.

umbilical cord Nawwelschnur (die)n.; **hernia** Nawwelbruch (der)n.

umbilicus Nawwel (der)n.; Nawwel; Newwel, pl.

umbrella 1.Amberell (die)n.; Amberelle, pl.; 2.Reggeschaerm (der)n.; 3.Schaerm (der)n.

umpire Richder (der)n.; Richder, pl.

unable unfaehich, adj.; **to chew the cud** ledrich (der)n. (der -- verliere); **to sleep** verwache, v.; verwacht, pp.

unacceptable 1.missfellich, adj.; 2.aanehmlich, adj.

unaccountable seldsam, adj.

unacquainted fremm, adj.

unanimous eeschtimmich, adj.

unavailing vergeblich, adj.

unaware unversehne, adj.

unawed unverdrosse, adj.

unbearable 1.unerbaermlich, adj.; 2.unleid(l)ich, adj.

unbecoming 1.unaschtendich, adj.; 2.ungeziemt, adj.

unbelief 1.Umglaawe (der)n.; 2.Unglaawe (der)n.; 3.Uuglaawe (der)n.

unbloody sacrifice of the cross Mess (die)n.

unborn ungebore, adj.

unbounded grenselos, adj.

unbridle ab/zaahme, v.; abgezaahmt, pp.

unbrushed ungebascht, adj.

unbuckle 1.los/schnalle, v.; losgschnallt, pp.; 2.uff/schnalle, v.; uffgschnallt, pp.

unbutton 1.ab/gnibbe, v.; abgegnippt, pp.; 2.uff/gnebbe, v.; uffgegneppt, pp.; 3.uff/gneppe, v. uffgegneppt, pp.; 4.uff/gnibbe, v.; uffgegnippt, pp.

uncanny 1.unfreindlich, adj.; 2.ungemietlich, adj.; 3. unheemlich, adj.; 4.uuheemlich, adj.

uncertain 1.misslich, adj.; 2.unbeschtimmt, adj.; 3. unbestimmt, adj.; 4.ungewiss, adj.; 5.unsicher, adj.

uncharitable 1.unvergunnisch, adj.; 2.uuvergunnisch, adj.

uncivil 1.uubaerschdich, adj.; 2.uubaerschtich, adj.

unclasp uff/hoke, v.; uffghokt, pp.

uncle 1.Ankel (der)n.; 2.Onkel (der)n.

unclean unrein, adj.

uncleaned ungebutzt, adj.

uncoil ab/wickle, v.; abgewickelt, pp.

uncombed schtruwwli(ch), adj.

uncomfortable 1.umleidich, adj.; 2.umleitlich, adj.; 3. unbequem, adj.; 4.uuleidich, adj.

uncommon 1.arich, adj.; 2.arig, adj.; 3.arrick, adj.; 4. ungewehnlich, adj.

unconcerned gleichgiltich, adj.

unconscionable 1.gwisselos, adj.; 2.unne Gwisse, adj.

unconscious um(m)echdich, adj.

uncontrollable 1.unbennich, adj.; 2.uubennich, adj.

unconverted 1.umbekehrt, adj.; 2.unbekehrt, adj.; 3. uubekehrt, adj.

uncouth fellow 1.Rauschebeidel (der)n.; 2.Schtoffelgluck (die)n.

uncover 1.ab/decke, v.; abgedeckt, pp.; 2.uff/decke, v.; uffgedeckt, pp.

uncovered blott, adj.

undecided 1.Schtutz (der)n. (uff der --); 2.uff der Schnepp, adj. 3.Waahl (die)n. (in -- schteh); 4.waahle, v.; gewaahlt, pp.

undependable person Windbeidel (der)n.

under 1.drunne, prep.; 2.drunner, prep.; 3.unner, prep.; 4.unnich, prep.; **a (but not "without" [fem])** unnichre = unnich re; **age** Elt (die)n. (unnich --); **under-handedly** verschtohle, adv.; **her** unnerre = unner re; **him** 1.unnerm = unner em; 2.unnern = unner en; 3.unnichem = unnich em; **it** 1.unners = unner es; 2.unnichs = unnich es; **one** unnerme = unner me; **one (but not "without a")** unnichme = unnich me; **that** dattdrunner, adv.; **this** dodrunner, adv.

underbid runner/biede, v.; runnergebodde, pp.

underbrush 1.Heck (die)n.; Hecke, pl.; 2.Unnerholz (es)n.

underclothes Unnergleeder (die)n., pl.

undercurrent Unnerzuck (der)n.

undergo erleide, v.; erlidde, pp.

underground 1.unner/aerdisch, adj.; 2.unnererdisch, adj.; **conduit for water** Dohl (es)n.; **container** Grub (die) n.; Gruwe, pl.

underhanded 1.geheem, adj.; 2.geheim, adj.

underjacket Unnerrock (der)n.; Unnerreck, pl.

underling Unnerdaahn (der)n.

undermine unnergraawe, v.; unnergegraawe, pp.; **(in business)** Abdrack duh (der)v.

underneath 1.drunne, adv.; 2.drunner, adv.; 3.unner, prep.

underpants Unnerhosse (die)n.

underrate 1.aa/schlagge, v.; aagschlagge, pp. (zu gering --); 2.unner/schetze, v.; unnergschetzt, pp.; 3.unnerschetze, v.; unnergschetzt, pp.

undershirt Unnerhemm (es)n.; Unnerhemmer, pl.

undershot unnerschlechdich, adj.

understand 1.begreife, v.; begriffe, pp.; 2.eisehne, v.; eigsehne, pp.; 3.nei/sehne, v.; neigsehne, pp.; 4.vernemme, v.; vernumme, pp.; 5.verschteh, v.; verschtanne, pp.

understandable verschtendlich, adj.

understanding Verschtendnis (es)n.

undertake 1.iwwernemme, v.; iwwernumme, pp.; 2.unner/ nemme, v.; unnergenumme, pp.; 3.unnernemme, v.; unnernumme, pp.

undertaker 1.Ausleger (der)n.; 2.Begrawwer (der)n.; 3. Dode-ausleger (der)n.; 4.Dodemann (der)n.; 5. Eibalsamierer (der)n.; 6.Laademacher (der)n.; Laademacher, pl.; 7.Laademecher (der)n.;

(Continued on page 403)

Uu

undertaker (continued) unpack

(Continued from page 402)

8.Laademesser (der)n.; 9.Leichde(n)berichder (der) n.; 10.Leichenbefaahrer (der)n.; 11.Leichtmann (der) n.; 12.Leichtversaryer (der)n.

undertaking 1.Unnernemmung (die)n.; 2.Vornemmes (es)n.

underwear 1.Unnergleeder (die)n., pl.; 2.Unnerrock (der) n.; Unnerreck, pl.

undeserved unverdient, adj.

undesigning absichtlos, adj.

undesirable person 1.Gschmees (es)n.; 2.Unrot (der)n.

undeterred unverdrosse, adj.

undisciplined youth 1.Umgraut (es)n.; 2.Ungraut (es)n.

undiscovered unendeckt, adj.

undismayed 1.unverschrocke, adj.; 2.unverzaacht, adj.; 3.unverzaakt, adj.

undisputed unbeschtritte, adj.

undisturbed unverschtaert, adj.

undivided unverdeelt, adj.

undo 1.los/mache, v.; losgemacht, pp.; 2.mache, v.; gemacht, pp. (zu nix --); 3.uff/mache, v.; uffgemacht, pp.; 4.vernichde, v.; vernicht, pp.

undress 1.aus/duh (sich --)v.; ausgeduh, pp.

uneasy 1.dusslich, adj.; 2.uffriehrisch, adj.; 3.unheemlich, adj.; 4.unruhich, adj.

unending endlos, adj.

uneven 1.bucklich, adj.; 2.rubbich, adj.; 3.ruppich, adj.; 4.unewe, adj.; 5.ungraad, adj.; **(field, road)** 1.huberich, adj.; 2.rub(b)lich, adj.

unexpected 1.sunderbaar, adj.; 2.sunnerbaar, adj.; 3.umbedenkt, adj.; 4.unaerwaart, adj.; 5.unbehofft, adj.; 6.unerwaard, adj.; 7.ungfaahr, adj.; 8.unverhofft, adj.; **success** Glickschuss (der)n.

unfailing unfehlbaar, adj.

unfamiliar 1.fremd, adj.; 2.fremm, adj.; 3.umbekannt, adj.; 4.unbekannt, adj.

unfasten 1.los/mache, v.; losgemacht, pp.; 2.uff/mache, v.; uffgemacht, pp.

unfinished stocking Schtrickschtrump (der)n.

unfit net fit, adj.

unfold ab/wickle, v.; abgewickelt, pp.

unforgettable unvergesslich, adj.

unfriendly unfreindlich, adj.

ungodly gottlos, adj.

ungrateful undankbaar, adj.

unhandy 1.umhendich, adj.; 2.unbeholfe, adj.; 3.unhendich, adj.; 4.uuhendich, adj.

unharness 1.ab/gscharre, v.; abgschatt, pp.; 2.ab/schaere, v.; abgschaerrt, pp.; 3.raus/schpanne, v.; rausgschpannt, pp.

unhealthy 1.umgsund, adj.; 2.ungsund, adj.; 3.unwohl, adj.; 4.uugsund, adj.

unheard-of 1.unaerheert, adj.; 2.unaerlebt, adv.

unhinge ab/henke, v.; abghonke, pp.

unhitch (horses from a wagon) 1.aus/schpanne, v.; ausgschpannt, pp.; 2.raus/schpanne, v.; rausgschpannt, pp.

unhook 1.ab/henke, v.; abghonke, pp.; 2.aus/henke, v.; ausghenkt, pp.; 3.los/hoke, v.; 4.uff/hoke, v.; uffghokt, pp.

unhurt unverletzt, adj.

unicorn root Deiwelsabbis (watzel) (die)n.

uniform gleichfermich, adj.

unify vereeniche, v.; vereenicht, pp.

unimportant (meaning little to anyone) niemand, pron. (net gross mit --)

union Gemeeschaft (die)n.

unique eenzich, adj.

unite 1.verbinne, v.; verbunne, pp.; 2.vereeniche, v.; vereenicht, pp.

United Brethern (church) Vereinichde Brieder (die)n., pl.

united gemeescheflich, adj.

uniting of new and old members of Grundsau lodge Verbinn rei (die)n.

unity 1.Eenichkeit (die)n.; 2.Friede (der)n.; 3.Ruh (die)n.

universal 1.allgebreichlich, adj.; 2.allgemee, adj.; 3.allgemei, adj.; 4.allgemein, adj.

unjust 1.ungerecht, adj.; 2.uugerecht, adj.

unjustly ungerechterweis, adv.

unkempt 1.schlabbich, adj.; 2.schtruwwli(ch), adj.; 3.zoppich, adj.

unkind unfreindlich, adj.

unknowingly unwissend, adj.

unknown 1.unbekannt, adj.; 2.uubekannt, adj.

unlace 1.aus/schniere, v.; ausgschniert, pp.; 2.uff/schniere, v.; uffgschniert, pp.

unlearn verlaerne, v.; verlaernt, pp.

unless mitaus, conj.

unlike 1.unaehnlich, adj.; 2.ungleich, adj.

unlikely unwaahrscheinlich, adv.

unload 1.ab/laade, v.; abgelaade, pp.; 2.ab/schtelle, v.; abgschtellt, pp.; 3.aus/laade, v.; ausgelaade, pp.; 4.aus packe, v.; ausgepackt, pp.; **grain or hay** (with a fork) ab/gawwle, v.; abgegawwelt, pp.

unlock uff/schliesse, v.; uffgschlosse, pp.

unloveable 1.umleidlich, adj.; 2.unleid(l)ich, adj.

unlucky unglicklich, adj.; **day** Unglicksdaag (der)n.

unmannerly 1.fleggelhaft, adj.; 2.fleggelhaft, adv.; 3.raubeenich, adj.; 4.raubelzich, adj.; 5.rilpsich, adj.; 6.ummanierlich, adj.; 7.unaardich, adj.; 8.ungebutzt, adj.; 9.unmanierlich, adj.; 10.unmanierlich, adv.; adj.; 11.uumanierlich, adj.; **fellow** 1.Fleggel (der)n.; Fleggel, pl.; 2.Raubelz (der)n.; 3.Raubiggel (der)n.

unmerciful 1.unbaremhartzich, adj.; 2.unbarmhaerzich, adj.; 3.uubarmhaerzich, adj.

unmercifulness Unbarmhaerzichkeet (die)n.

unnatural unnadierlich, adj.

unnecessary unneedich, adj.

unnerve schweche, v.; gschwecht, pp.

unnoticed unbeschraue, adj.

unoccupied space Lick (die)n.; **spaces** lickich, adj.

unpack (emotionally) aus/packe, v.; ausgepackt, pp.

Uu

unpleasant — upper

unpleasant 1.umblessierlich, adj.; 2.unblessierlich, adj.; 3.ungemietlich, adj.; 4.uublessierlich, adj.; **(of weather)** unfreindlich, adj.

unpleasantness Widderwaerdichkeet (die)n.

unproductive maager, adj.

unprotected unversichert, adj.

unravel 1.ab/wickle, v.; abgewickelt, pp.; 2.aus/zabbe, v.; ausgezappt, pp.; 3.aus/zobbe, v.; ausgezoppt, pp.; 4.los/ wickle, v.; losgewickelt, pp.

unreasonable 1.alwer(n), adj.; 2.umverschtennich, adj.; 3.unmanierlich, adj.; 4.unverninfdich, adj.; 5.unverschtennich, adj.

unreel (fishing line, yarn, etc.) ab/haschble, v.; abghaschbelt, pp.

unreliable 1.safdich, adj.; 2.unverlessich, adj.

unrest 1.Umruh (die)n.; 2.Unruh (die)n.

unrighteous 1.ungerecht, adj.; 2.uugerecht, adj.

unripe 1.grie(n), adj.; 2.unzeidich, adj.

unroll 1.ab/rolle, v.; abgerollt, pp.; 2.uff/rolle, v.; uffgerollt, pp.

unroof ab/decke, v.; abgedeckt, pp.

unruliness Wildheet (die)n.

unruly 1.ausgelosse, adj.; 2.umbennich, adj.; 3.ungezogge, adj.; 4.wiescht, adj.; 5.wild, adj.

unsaddle ab/saddle, v.; abgsaddelt, pp.

unsalted ungsalze, adj.

unsatisfactory mangelhaft, adj.

unscrew 1.ab/schrauwe, v.; abgschraubt, pp.; 2.aus/schrauwe, v.; ausgschraubt, pp.; 3.los/schrauwe, v.; losgschraubt, pp.

unseasoned lebbisch, adj.

unseem ab/drenne, v.; abgedrennt, pp.

unseemliness Uuzucht (die)n.

unskilled surgeon 1.Grottegelser (der)n.; 2.Gelser (der)n.

unsound (paper) money Geld (es)n. (lumbich --)

unstable wanke, v.; gewankt, pp.; **(of boards)** schneberich, adj.

unsteady 1.schwankich, adj.; 2.wanklich, adj.; **(as a table)** gnackere, v.; gegnackert, pp.; **(in gait)** schranklich adj.

unsuccessful attempt Fehlschlack (der)n.

untamable 1.unbennich, adj.; 2.uubennich, adj.

unthinkable undenklich, adj.

unthinking gedankelos, adj.

untidy 1.kaflich, adj.; 2.koslich, adj.; 3.kutzlich, adj.; 4. noochlessich, adj.; 5.schlabbich, adj.; 6.schlappich, adj.; **woman** 1.Kusel (die)n.; 2.Kutzel (die)n.; 3.Schlapp (die)n.

untie 1.los/binne, v.; losgebunne, pp.; 2.los/mache, v.; losgemacht, pp.

until bis, prep.

untried unbrowiert, adj.

untrue 1.falsch, adj.; 2.unwaahr, adj.; 3.unwohr, adj.

untruth 1.Falschheet (die)n.;2.Lieg (die)n.; Liege, pl.; 3. Unwaahret (die)n.;4.Unwaahrheet (die)n.; 5.Unwaahrheit (die)n.

untwine 1.uff/drehe,v.;ufgedreht,pp.; 2.uff/wickle, v.;uffgewickelt, pp.

untwist los/drehe, v.; losgedreht, pp.

unused ends of warp in carpet weaving Drassem (der)n.

unusual umgwehnlich, adj.

unusually small egg Unglicksoi (es)n.

unwell 1.umgsund, adj.; 2.ungsund, adj.; 3.unwohl, adj.; 4. uugsund, adj.

unwilling 1.ungern, adv.; 2.unwillens, adj.

unwillingly ungaern, adj.

unwind ab/wickle, v.; abgewickelt, pp.

unwise 1.ungscheit, adj.; 2.uugscheit, adj.

unwrap 1.aus/wickle, v.; ausgewickelt, pp.; 2.uff/wickle, v.; uffgewickelt, pp.

unyoke ab/yoche, v.; abgeyocht, pp.

up 1.howwe, adv.; 2.ruff, adv.; 3.uff, prep.; **(thither)** nuff, adv.; **above** 1.drowwe, adv.; 2.drowwedrauss, adv.; 3. owwedrowwe, adv.; **against in the rear** hinnewedder, adv.; **against it** hinnewedder, adv.; **along there** dattdraanuff, adv.; **by the back way** hinnenuff, adv.; **by the front** vannenuff, adv.; **country** 1.Land nufzus, adj.; 2.nuffzus, adj.; 3.owwedraus, adj.; 4.owwenaus, adj.; **from below** unneruff, adv.; **front here** dovaerrizus, adv.; **front there** dattvaerizus, adv.; **here** 1.do howwe, adv.; 2.do howwe, adv.; 3.dodrowwe, adv.; 4.dodrowwe, adv.; 5.donuff, adv.; 6.doruff, adv.; 7.howwe, adv. (do --); **hold** uff/hewe, v.; uffghowe, pp.; **in above** 1.owwedrin, adv.; 2.owwenei, adv.; **in front** vannenuff, adv.; **in that direction** dattnuffzus, adv.; **in the air (excited)** Heh (der) (in --); **in this direction** donuffzus, adv.; **land grazing are** Baschdert (der)n.; **se-daisy! (used in ri infant on knee)** hup-die-duden-du!; **set** um/schmeisse, v.; umgschmisse, pp.; **that way** dattdruffzus, adv.; **there** 1.dattdrowwe, adv.; 2.dattnuff, adv.; 3.dattruff, adv.; **this way** doruffzus, adv.; **through here** 1.dodarrichnuff, adv.; 2.dodarrichnuff, adv.; 3.dodarrichruff, adv.; 4.dodarrichruff, adv.; 5.dattdarichnuff, adv.; **to** 1.bis uff, prep.; 2.bis, prep. 3.vorhawwe, v.; vorghatt, pp.; **to a place** 1.nuff, adv.; 2.ruff, adv.; **to the knees** gniedief, adv.

upbraid 1.ab/zanke, v.; abgezankt, pp.; 2.vor/halde, v.; vorghalde, pp.; 3.vor/lege, v.; vorgelegt, pp.

uphill 1.Hiwwel (der)n. (-- nuff); 2.hiwwelnuff, adv.; **(to where the speaker or thinker is)** 1.baerrickruff, adj.; 2.barigruff, adv.

upholster 1.iwwerziege, v.; iwwerzogge, pp.; 2.iwwerziehe, v.; iwwerzogge, pp.

upkeep Uffhalding (die)n.

upon 1.auf, prep. (rare usage);2.druff, adv.; 3.iwwer, prep.; 4.uff, prep.

upper 1.ewwer, adv.; 2.ewwerscht, adj.; 3.owwer, adj.; **hand** 1.Iwwerhand (die)n.; 2.Owwerhand (die)n.; 3.Owwerhand (die)n.; 4.Wipphand (die)n.; **leather** 1.Rindledder (es)n.; 2.Rinsledder (es)n.; **part** Ewwerdeel (es)n.; **part of a shoe** Owweledder (es)n.

Uu

uppermost · uvula

uppermost ewwerscht, adj.

upright 1.Schtenner (der)n.; Schtenner, pl.; 2.uffrichdich, adj.

uproar 1.Uffrohr (der)n.; 2.Uffruhr (der, die)n.

upset 1.um/renne, v.; umgerennt, pp.; 2.um/schtaerze, v.; umgschtaertzt, pp.; 3.um/schtatze, v.; umgschtatzt, pp.; 4.verriessle, v.; verriesselt, pp.

upside down unnerscht's ewwersch, adv., adj.

upstairs 1.drowwe, adv.; 2.drowwedrauss, adv.; 3.owwedrowwe, adv.; 4.owwedrowwe, adv.; 5.owwenuff, adv.

upward nuffzus, adj.

upwards 1.ewwerschich, adv.; 2.ewwersich, adv.; 3.iwwerschich, adj.; 4.iwwerschich, adv.; 5.iwwersich, adv.; 6.ruff, adv.; 7.uffwaerts, adv.

urchin 1.Schpringer (der)n.; Schpringer, pl.; 2.Zickel (es)n.

urge 1.aa/befehle, v.; aabefohle, pp.; 2.aa/dreiwe, v.; aagedriwwe, pp.; 3.aa/dreiwe, v.; aagedriwwe, pp.; 4.aa/schpanne, v.; aagschpannt, pp.; 5.aab(e)fehle, v.; aab(e)fohle, pp.; 6.drenge, v.; gedrengt, pp.; 7.dringe, v.; gedrunge, pp.; 8.sch(i)ere, v.; gschiert, pp.; **(to accept)** neediche, v.; geneedicht, pp.; **against doing something** 1.ab/waere, v.; abgwore, pp.; 2.ab/wehre, v.; abgewehrt, pp.; **on** zu/schpreche, v.; zugschproche, pp.; **to come in** rei/neediche, v.; reigeneedicht, pp.; **to eat heartily** zu/schpreche, v.; zugschproche, pp.

urgent dringend, adj.

urging of the bowels 1.Nadurtrieb (der)n.; 2.Zwang (der)n.

urinate 1.aa/wende, v.; aagewendt, pp.; 2.brunse, v.; gebrunst, pp.; 3.pisse, v.; gepisst, pp.; 4.seeche, v.; gseecht, pp.; 5.Wasser (es)n. (-- ab/schlagge); (-- losse); **into** nei/brunse, v.; neigebrunst, pp.

urine 1.Bruns (der)n.; 2.Seech (der)n.

uropygial gland 1.Barzel (der)n.; 2.Eelkennli (es)n.; 3.Eelkessli (es)n.; 4.Eelkewwich (es)n.; 5.Eelzeppli (es)n.; 6.Fettheffli (es)n.; 7.Fettpann (die)n.; Fettpanne, pl.; 8.Fettschnebbel (der)n.; 9.Schmelzpann (die)n.; 10.Schmutzheffli (es)n.; 11.Schmutzkeidel (es)n.; 12.Schmutzkennli (es)n.; 13.Schnewwli (es)n.; 14.Schwanzgribs (es)n.; 15.Zibbel (der)n.

us uns, pron.

use 1.aa/wende, v.; aagewendt, pp.; 2.aa/wenne, v.; aagewennt, pp.; 3.benutze, v.; benutzt, pp.; 4.brauche, v.; gebraucht, pp.; 5.breiche, v.; gebreicht, pp.; 6.Gebrauch (der)n.; Gebreich, pl.; 7.Nutz (der)n.; 8.Nutze (der)n.; 9.nutze, v.; genutzt, pp.; 10.Verbrauch (der)n.; 11.yuuse, v.; gyuust, pp.; **a pick** picke, v.; gepickt, pp.; **a sledge** schleggle, v.; gschleggelt, pp.; **as a chaser** nunner/schwenke, v.; nunnergschwenkt, pp.; **in living** verlewe, v.; verlebt, pp.; **moderation** tempere (sich --)v.; getempert, pp.; **part of** aa/reisse, v.; aagerisse, pp.; **up** 1.uff/brauche, v.; uffgebraucht, pp.; 2.verbrauche, v.; verbraucht, pp.; **up as fodder** uff/fiedre, v.; uffgfiedert, pp.; **up in baking** 1.uff/backe, v.; uffgebackt, pp.; 2.verbacke, v.; verbacke, pp. ; **up in living** uff/lewe, v.; uffglebt,

pp.; **up in scribbling** uff/gritzle, v.; uffgegritzelt, pp.; **up in sewing** vernaehe, v.; vernaeht, pp.; **up in shooting** 1.verschiesse, v.; verschosse, pp.; 2.weck/schiesse, v.; weckgschosse, pp.; **up in spinning** 1.uff/schpinne, v.; uffgschpinnt, pp.; 2. verschpinne, verschpunne, pp.

used as a noun (geb mir eigei) eigei, interj.; **as ending of a compound noun adding the meaning of a collection of or variety** dings (Kuchedings); **contemptuously of a human face** Schnarefeggelgsicht (es)n.; **to** als, adv.

useful 1.behilf(l)ich, adj.; 2.brauchba(a)r, adv.; 3.brauchbaar, adj.; 4.nitzlich, adj.

useless 1.ausgedient, adj.; 2.nix waert, adj.

usher Eifiehrer (der)n.; **in** eifiehre, v.; eigfiehrt, pp.

usual gwehnt, adj.

usually 1.gemeenichlich, adj.; 2.gwehnlich, adj., adv.

utensils 1.Kochegscharr (es)n.; 2.Kochgscharr (es)n.

uterus Mudder (die)n.; **of animals** Draagsack (der)n.

utility Nitzlichkeet (die)n.

utilize benutze, v.; benutzt, pp.

utmost eissaerscht, adv.

utter raus/bringe, v.; rausgebrocht, pp.; **incautiously** raus/blatsche, v.; rausgeblatscht, pp.; **no sound** Laut (der)n. (kenn -- vun sich gewwe); **one's mind** aus/losse, v.; ausg(e)losst, pp.; **profanity** ab/flucke, v.; abgflucht, pp. (eens --); **unguardedly** raus/schnabbe, v.; rausgschnappt, pp.; **with a growl** raus/schnaare, v.; rausgschnarrt, pp.

uvula 1.Zebbche (es)n.; 2.Zeppelche (es)n.

Vv

vacant — vertical

vacant 1.leer, adj.; 2.leer/schteh, v.; leergschtanne, pp.; 3.lickich, adj.

vacation Ferien (die)n., pl.

vaccinate Parble (die)n. (-- blanze)

vaccine Parbleblanz (die)n.

vagabond Rumleefer (der)n.; Rumleefer, pl.

vagina Desch (die)n.

vague undeitlich, adj.

vain person (in dress) 1.Hochmutsnarr (der)n.; 2.Hochmutszibbel (der)n.

vale Daal (es)n.; Daale; Daaler, pl.; **of tears** Yammerdaal (es)n.

Valentine 1.Feldi (der)n.; 2.Wall(i) (der)n.

valerian Marien(s)watzel (die)n.

valley 1.Daal (es)n.; Daale; Daaler, pl.;2.Deich (es)n.; Deicher, pl.

valuable 1.hawweswaert, adj.; 2.schetzbaar, adj.; 3.waertvoll, adj.

valuation Schetzung (der)n.

value 1.schetze, v.; gschetzt, pp.; 2.Waert (der)n.; 3.Waertung (die)n.; 4.Wart (der)n.

vamp (of a shoe, boot) 1.aa/schuhe, v.; aagschu pp.; 2.Owwerledder (es)n.

vanish 1.schwinne, v.; gschwin gschwunne, pp.; 2.verfliege, v.; verflogge, pp.; 3.verschalle, v.; verschallt, pp.; 4. verscholle, v.; verschollt, pp.; 5.verschwinne, v.; verschwunne, pp.

vapor 1.Damp (der)n.; 2.Dunscht (der)n.; **forming on a polished surface** Duft (der)n.

vaporous dambich, adj.

vapory dunschdich, adj.

variable verennerlich, adj.

varied 1.verschiddlich, adj.; 2.verschiedlich, adj.

variegated 1.darichschlachdich, adj.; 2.darichschlachdich, adj.; 3.dupplich, adj.; 4.flechich, adj.; 5.scheckich, adj.

variety 1.Abwechslung (die)n.; 2.Abwexling (die)n.; 3.Manchfaltichkeet (die)n.; 4.Schlack (der)n.; **of apple** 1.Schofnaas (die)n.; 2.Wasserabbel (der)n.; **of large beet** Rummel (die)n.; **of ungrafted sweet red cherry** Rotsiesskasche (die)n.

various 1.allerhand, adj.; 2.annerschder, adj.; adv.; 3.ettlich, adj.; 4.mancherlee, adj.; 5.unnerschittlich, adj.; 6.verschiddlich, adj.; 7.verschieden, adj.; 8.verschiedlich, adj.; 9.vielerlee, adj.; **kinds** 1.allerlee, adv.; 2.allerlei, adv.

varnish 1.aa/wesche, v.; aagewesche, pp.; 2.Aaschtrich (der)n.

vary 1.ab/wexle, v.; abgewexelt, pp.; 2.verennere, v.; verennert, pp.

vascillating wankelmiedich, adj.

vast ungeheier, adj.

vat for holding flaxseed oil Olichschtenner (der)n. Olichschtenner, pl.

veal Kalbfleesch (es)n.

vegetable garden Gmiesgaarde (der)n.; **soup** Gekreidersupp (die)n.

vegetables Gaardesach (es)n.

vegetation 1.Graut (es)n.; Greider, pl.; 2.Kraut (es)n.

vehemence 1.Hefdichkeet (die)n.; 2.Hefdichkeet (die)n.

vehemently hefdich, adj.

vehicle 1.Fuhrwaerick (es)n.; 2.Fuhrwese (es)n. (usually applied to a carriage or buggy)

vein 1.Aader (die)n.; Aadere, pl.; 2.Blutaader (die) Blutaadere, pl.; 3.Blutoder (die)n.; Blutodere, pl.; 4.Bulsoder (die)n.; 5.Oder (die)n.; Odere, pl.; 6.Oder (die)n.; Odere, pl.

veined 1.darichfaahre, adj.; 2.oderich, adj.

velocity 1.Schnellichkeet (die)n.; 2.Schnellichkeit (die)n.

velvet Samt (der)n.; **leaf** 1.Buddermoddel (die)n.; 2.Buttermoddel (die)n.

veneer finiere, v.; finiert, pp.

venerable ehrwaerdich, adj.

venerate verehre, v.; verehrt, pp.

veneration Verehrung (die)n.

venereal disease Franzose (die)n., pl.

venison 1.Haschfleesch (es)n.; 2.Wildbret (es)n.

venom Gift (es)n.

venomous gifdich, adj.

venter (of insects) Hinnerleib (der)n.

ventilate 1.aus/lifde, v.; ausgelift, pp.; 2.lifde, v.; gelift, pp.; 3.lufde, v.; geluft, pp.

ventilation Auslifting (die)n.

ventricle Hatzkammer (die)n.

ventriloquism Bauchrede (es)n.

ventriloquist 1.Bauchredner (der)n.; 2.Bauchschwetzer (der)n.; Bauchschwetzer, pl.

venture 1.fendere (sich --)v.; 2.vendere (sich --)v.; gvendert, pp.; 3.vendere, v.; gvendert, pp.; 4.waage, v.; gewaagt, pp.; 5.woge, v.; gewogt, pp.; **away** weck/ vendere (sich --)v.; weckvendert, pp.; **out** 1.naus/vendere (sich --)v.; nausgvendert, pp.; 2.raus/woge (sich --)v.; rausgewoge, pp.; **up** nuff/woge (sich --)v.; nuffgewogt, pp.

veracious 1.verhaftich, adj.; 2.wohrhaftich, adj.

verb Zeitwaart (es)n.

verbal 1.waddlich, adj.; 2.waertlich, adj.

verdancy Unaerfaahring (die)n.

verdant 1.grie, adj.; 2.grien, adj.

verdigris Grieschpaa (der)n.

verify bschteediche, v.; bschteedicht, pp.; **the weight** no(och)wiege, v.; no(och)gwoge, pp.

verily 1.Waahretlich, adj.; 2.Waahrlich, adj.; 3.wohretlich, adj.; 4.wohrlich, adj.

vermifuge Waremmiddel (es)n.

vermin 1.Geziffer (es)n.; 2.Ungeziffer (es)n.

vernacular 1.Mudderschprooch (die)n.; 2.Umgangsschproch (die)n.

verse 1.Vaersch(t) (der)n.; 2.Varscht (der)n.

verses Dichte (die)n., pl.

vertical 1.kaerzegraad, adj.; 2.kerzegraad, adj.; 3.senkrecht, adj.

Vv

vertigo

vertigo 1.Dariyel (der)n.; 2.Schwindel (der)n.

vervain root Eisegrautwatzel (die)n.

very 1.aich, adv.; 2.allmechdich, adv.; 3.arich, adv.; 4.arig, adv.; 5.arrick, adj.; 6.gaar, adv.; 7.gewaltich, adj.; 8.gwaldich, adv.; 9.iwweraus, adv.; 10.leschderlich, adv.; 11. mechdich, adv.; 12.recht, adv.; 13.schtaerns, adv.; 14. verdarebt, adv.; 15. verdeihenkert, adv.; 16.verdeiwelt, adj.; 17.sehr, adv. (used rarely); **first** allererscht, adj.

vessel 1.Gfess (es)n.; 2.Schiff (es)n.; Schiffer, pl.; 3.Schissel (die)n.; Schissle, pl.; **(tin, smaller than a pail)** Blicki (es)n.

vest 1.Bruschtlappe (der)n.; 2.Wammes (der)n.; Wammes, pl.; 3.Wescht (die)n.

vestibule Vorgang (der)n.

vestments Messgewand (es)n.

vesture Begleedung (die)n.

veterinarian 1.Geilsdokder (der)n.; 2.Geilsdokter (der)n.; 3.Kiehdokder (der)n.; 4.Viehdokder (der)n Viehdok- der, pl.

vex 1.aeryere, v.; geaeryert, pp.; 2.grenke, v.; gegrenkt, pp.; 3.greppe, v.; gegreppt, pp.; 4.krenke, v.; gekrenkt, pp.; 5.petze, v.; gepetzt, pp.; 6.veraryere, v.; veraiyert, pp.; 7.verdriesse, v.; verdrosse, pp.; 8.verzanne, v.; ver- zannt, pp.

vexation 1.Aeryernis (die)n.; 2.Aeyer (der)n.; 3.Aiyer (der) n.; 4.Druwwel (der)n (en --); 5.Elend (es) (en --); 6. Veraeryernis (die)n.

vexatious 1.aeryerlich, adj.; 2.aiyerlich, adj.; 3.veraeryerlich, adj.; 4.veraiyerlich, adj.

vexed 1.aeryere (sich --)v.; gaeryert, pp.; 2.aeryerlich, adj.; 3.aiyerlich, adj.; 4.uffsetzich, adj. 5.veraeryere (sich --)v.

vial Boddelche (es)n.

vibrate 1.schiddle, v.; gschiddelt, pp.; 2.schwinge, v.; gschwunge, pp.

vice Laschder (es)n.

vicinity 1.Nochberschaft (die)n.; 2.Umgegend (die)n.

vicious laschderhaft, adj.

victim Opfer (es)n.

victorious siechreich, adj.

victory Siek (der)n.

victuals 1.Ess-sach(e) (die)n.; pl.; 2.Koscht (die)n.

view 1.aa/blicke, v.; aageblickt, pp.; 2.aa/schaue, v.; aagschaut, pp.; 3.Aablick (der)n.; 4.Aasicht (die)n.; 5. Aussicht (die)n.; 6.bedrachde, v.; bedracht, pp.; 7. begucke, v.; beguckt, pp.; 8.Sicht (die)n.

vigilant wach(t)sa(a)m, adj.

vigor 1.Graft (die)n.; Grefde, pl.; 2.Kraft (die)n.

vigorous 1.hatz(h)aftich, adj.; 2.hatzhafdich, adj.; 3.kreftich, adj.; 4.raschdich, adj.; 5.rischdich, adj.

vigorously drufflos, adv.

vile 1.nidderbeenich, adj.; 2.nidderdrechdich, adj.; 3.schlecht, adj.; **smelling animal** Schtinkert (der)n.

vilify verschimbiere, v.; verschimbiert, pp.

village 1.Schteddel (es)n.; 2.Schteddelche (es)n.;

visiting

3.Schtedt(el)che, (es)n.; 4.Schtedtche (es)n.; **(in nurs- ery rhyme only)** Dorf (es)n.

villager Schtedler (der)n.; Schtedler, pl.

villagers 1.Schtadtleit (die)n., pl.; 2.Schteddelleit (die)n.

villain Lump (der)n.

villainy Schelmerei (die)n.

vindicate 1.recht schtelle, v.; gschtellt, pp.; 2.rechtschtelle, v.; rechtgschtellt, pp.

vindictiveness Raachgier (die)n.

vine 1.Rank (die)n.; Ranke, pl.; 2.Reb(e) (die)n.; Rebe, pl.; 3.Weischtock (der)n.

vinegar Essich (der)n.; **barrel** Essichfass (es)n.; **jug** Essichgruck (der)n.; **punch** (vinegar, sugar, water mixed as a drink for field workers) 1.Essichbunsch (der)n.; 2.Essichschling (die)n.

vineyard 1.Weibarig (der)n.; 2.Weigaarde (der)n.

violable verletzlich, adj.

violate schende, v.; gschendt, pp.

violation Verletzung (die)n.

violence Gewalt (die)n.

violent 1.gewaltsam, adj.; 2.grob(b), adj.; adv.; 3.gwaltsam, adj.; 4.hefdichlich, adj.; **quarrel** 1.Grageel (der)n.; 2.Grakeel (der)n.; 3.Krageel (der) n.; **quarreling** 1.Gebaf(f)z (es)n.; 2.Gebef(f)z (es)n.

violently hefdich, adj.

violet 1.Maerzeblumm (die)n.; 2.Veilche (es)n.; 3.Veiolich (die)n.; 4.Violi (es)n.

violin Geig (die)n.; Geige, pl.; **bow** 1.Fiddelboge (der)n.; Fiddelboge, pl.; 2.Geigeboge (der)n.; **bridge** Geigesaddel (der)n.; **maker** Geigemacher (der)n.; Geigemacher, pl.; **string** Geigesaet (die)n.

violinist Geiger (der)n.

viper's bugloss 1.Ochsezung (die)n.; 2.Yoch (die)n.

virago 1.Mannweib (es)n.; 2.Zenkrin (die)n.

Virgin Mary 1.Mareia (die)n.; 2.Maria (die)n.; 3.Mariche (die)n.; **Mary's thistle** Marien(s)dischdel (die)n.

virgin Yungfraa (die)n.

Virginia creeper 1.Zaahreeb (die)n.; 2.Zaahrieb (die)n.; Zaahriewe, pl.; 3.Zohreeb (die)n.; 4.Zohrieb (die)n.; **snakeroot** 1.niddri Schlange (die)n.; 2.Schlang (die)n. (gleeni --); 3.Schlangwatzel (die)n. (gleeni, niddri --)

virginity Kasch (die)n.

Virgo (6th sign of the zodiac)1.Blummefraa(die)n.; 2.Yungfraa(die)n.

virtue 1.Reinheet (die)n.; 2.Sauwerkeet (die)n.; 3.Sauwerkeit (die)n.

virtuous 1.rechtschaffe, adj.; 2.rechtschaffich, adj.; 3.reschaffe, adj.

virulence Giftichkeet (die)n.

viscera 1.Eigeweid(e) (es)n.; 2.Ingeweid (es)n.

viscous 1.zaeh, adj.; 2.zeah, adj.

vise Schraubschtock (der)n.

visible sichtbaar, adj.; **part of a decayed tooth** Schtarre (der)n.

visit 1.Bsuch (der)n.; 2.bsuche, v.; bsucht, pp.

visiting (confounded) Bsucherei (die)n.

Vv

visitors   vulture

visitors Bsuch (der)n.

visor (of a cap) Schnawwel (der)n.; Schnawwel, pl.

vitality Lewe(n)skraft (die)n.

vitreous glessern, adj.

vituperative term 1.Dunnerwetter (es)n. (applied to a person;) 2.Oos (es)n.; 3.Rinsvieh (es)n.; 4.Schtinkluder (es)n.

vivacious 1.belebt, adj.; 2.lebhaft, adj.

vivacity 1.Lebhaftichkeet (die)n.; 2.Munterkeet (die)n.

vivify belewe, v.; belebt, pp.

vocabulary 1.Waddebuch (es)n.; Waddebicher, pl.; 2.Watterbuch (es)n.

voice 1.Mundschtick (es)n.; 2.Schprooch (die)n.; 3.Schtimm (die)n.; Schtimme, pl.

void leer, adj.; **an agreement** um/schmeisse, v.; umgschmisse, pp. **the bowels** 1.kacke, v.; gekackt, pp.; 2.pubbe, v.; gepuppt, pp.; 3.scheisse, v.; gschisse, pp.

voluntarily 1.freiwillich, adj.; 2.freiwillich, adv.; 3.gutwillich, adj.; 4.gutwillicherweis, adj.; 5.vun selwer(t) willichweis, adv.

volunteer aa/biede (sich --), v.; aagebodde, pp.

vomit 1.Kotz (der)n.; 2.kotze, v.; gekotzt, pp.; 3.uff/schmeisse, v.; uffschmisse, pp.; 4.um/schmeisse, v.; umgschmisse, pp.; 5.warixe, v.; gewarixt, pp.; **(it) out** raus/kotze, v.; rausgekotzt, pp.

vomiting Breche(s) (es)n.

voracious 1.g(e)fressich, adj.; 2.gfressich, adj.; 3.gierich, adj.; 4.wolfich, adj.; **appetite** Fresshunger (der)n.

vote 1.Schtimm (die)n.; Schtimme, pl.; 2.schtimme, v.; gschtimmt, pp.; **down** 1.ab/schtimme, v.; abgschtimmt, pp.; 2.nunner/schtimme, v.; nunnergschtimmt, pp.; **in** nei/schtimme, v.; neigschtimmt, pp.; **on the other side** niwwer/schtimme, v.; niwwergschtimmt, pp.

voter Schtimmgewwer (der)n.; Schtimmgewwer, pl.

vow 1.Schwur (der)n.; 2.verschweere (sich --)v.; verschwore, pp.; **to discontinue** ab/schweere, v.; abgschwore, pp.

voyage 1.Rees (die)n.; Reese, pl.; 2.Reis (die)n.; Reise, pl.; 3.Seereis (die)n.; 4.Seeschaal (die)n.

vulgar 1.frefelhaft, adj.; 2.nidder, adj.; 3.rau, adj.; adv.; **adornment** Kritzelfixel (es)n.

vulgarity Gemeinheet (die)n.

vulture Geier (der)n.

Ww

wabble — want

wabble 1.wabble, v.; gewabbelt, pp.; 2.wibble, v.; gewibbelt, pp.

wabbling or shaking Gewackel (es)n.

wack Buff (der)n.

wad Schtopper (der)n.

wad(ding) Watt (die)n.

wade 1.baade, v.; gebaade; gebaadt, pp.; 2.waade, v.; gewaade, pp.; 3.wadde, v.; gewaade, pp. ; **through** darich/baade, v; darichgebaadt, pp.; **through the water** Wasser (es)n. (darich's -- baade [weaade])

waffle Waffel (die)n.; **iron** Waffeleise (es)n.

wag 1.Schalk (der)n.; 2.Schallack (der)n.; 3.Schallicks (der) n.; 4.schiddle, v.; gschiddelt, pp.; 5.schwenzle, v.; gschwenzelt, pp.; **the tail** (of a dog) weddle, v.; geweddelt, pp. **the tongue** zingle, v.; gezingelt, pp.

wage(s) Verdi(e)nscht (der)n.

wager 1.uff/schtecke, v.; uffgschteckt; uffgschtocke, pp. 2. wedde, v.; g(e)wett, pp.

wages 1.Loh (der)n.; 2.Luh (der)n.

wagon 1.Waache (der)n.; 2.Waachen (der)n.; 3.Wagge (der)n.; Wegge, pl.; **builder** 1.Wangner (der)n.; 2.Wegner (der)n.; **cover** Waggedeck (die)n.; **rigged for hauling stones** Schteewagge (der)n.; **shed** Waggeschopp (der)n.; Waggeschepp, pl.; **tongue** 1.Deichsel (die)n.; 2.Deixel (die)n.; Deixle, pl.; 3.Waggedeixel (die)n.; **wheel** Waggeraad (es)n.; Waggeredder, pl.; **with side-ladders** (for hauling wood) Holswagge (der)n.; **without springs** Blotzwagge (der)n.

wail heil, v.; gheilt, pp.

wainscoating 1.Bruschtgsims (es)n.; 2.Wandbegleedung (die)n.

waistcoat Wammes (der)n.; Wammes, pl.

wait 1.harre, v.; gharrt, pp.; 2.verziege, v.; verzogge, pp.; 3.waared, v.; gwaard, pp.; 4.waarte, v.; gewaart, pp.; **at table** ab/waarde, v.; abgewaardt, pp.; **for** erwaarte, v.; erwaart, pp.; **on** uff/waarde, v.; uffgewaart, pp.

waiter 1.Abwaarder (der)n.; 2.Bedienter (der)n.

waiting on Uffwaarting (die)n.

waitress Abwaarden (die)n.

wake 1.uff/wecke, v.; uffgeweckt, pp.; 2.Wacht (die)n.; 3.wacker mache, v.; gemacht, pp.; 4.wecke, v.; geweckt, pp.; (funeral) Wach(t)nacht (die)n.; **up** 1.uff/wache, v.; uffgewacht, pp.; 2.wacker waare, v.; wacker waare, pp.

wakeful 1.wacker, adj.; 2.wackerich, adj.; 3.wackrich, adj.

waken erwache, v.; erwacht, pp.

walk 1.Laaf (der)n.; Leef, pl.; 2.laafe, v.; g(e)loffe, pp.; 3.schtiwwle, v.; gschtiwwelt, pp.; 4.Tour (die)n.; 5.Tour (die)n.; 6.wandle, v.; gewandelt, pp.; **ahead** vorlaafe, v.; vorgeloffe, pp.; **along with** mit/laafe, v.; geloffe, pp.; **alongside of each other** newenannerlaafe, adv.; **around** 1.rum/geh, v.; rumgange, pp.; 2.rum/laafe, v.; rumg(e)loffe, pp.; 3.rumhaer/laafe, v.; rumhaergeloffe, pp.; **around in**

the wet rum/schlappe, v.; rumgschlappt, pp.; **away** 1.fatt/laafe, v.; fattgeloffe, pp.; 2.weck/laafe, v.; weckgeloffe, pp.; **away from** devunlaafe, v.; **back** zerick/laafe, v.; zerickgeloffe, pp.; **clumsily** 1.dappe, v.; gedappt, pp.; 2.hie/dappe, v.; hiegedappt, pp.; **down** runner/laafe, v.; runnergeloffe, pp.; **heavily** 1.hie/zackere, v.; hiegezackert, pp.; 2.hie/zackere, v.; hiegezackert, pp.; **in** 1.nei/dabbe, v.; neigedappt, pp.; 2.nei/laafe, v.; neigeloffe, pp.; 3.rei/laafe, v.; reigloffe, pp.; **or go alongside of each other** newenannergeh, adv.; **out** 1.naus/laafe, v.; nausgeloffe, pp.; 2.raus/laafe, v.; rausgeloffe, pp.; **out heavily** raus/dappe, v.; rausgedappt, pp.; **over** 1.driwwerlaafe, v.; driwwergeloffe, pp.; 2.niwwer/laafe, v.; niwwergeloffe, pp.; **past** verbei/laafe, v.; verbeigeloffe, pp.; **rapidly** fiessle, v.; gfiesselt, pp.; **rapidly with a cane** schtocke, v.; gschtockt, pp.; **slowly** 1.loddele, v.; geloddelt, pp.; 2.schleiche, v.; gschliche, pp.; **stealthy** schleiche, v.; gschliche, pp.; **through** darich/laafe, v.; darichgeloffe, p.; **to a place** hie/laafe, v.; hiegeloffe, pp.; **to meet** engegelaafe, adj.; **to the head** vorlaafe, v.; vorgeloffe, pp.; **too fast** (of horses) huddle, v.; ghuddelt, pp.; **unsteadily** (from weakness) schrankle, v.; gschrankelt, pp.; **up** ruff/laafe, v.; ruffgelofe, pp.; **up against** 1.wedder/dappe, v.; weddergedappt, pp.; 2.wedder/laafe, v.; weddergeloffe pp.; **up to** uff/laafe, v.; uffgelofe, pp.; **with a mimicking gate** 1.rum/fiessle, v.; rumgfiesselt, pp.; 2.schwenzle, v.; gschwenzelt, pp.

walker Laafer (der)n.; Laafer, pl.

walking frame of a sawmill Gerischt (der)n.; **in a slovenly manner** schlappfiessich, adj.; **or gadding** Gelaaf (es) n.; **stick** Schtock (der)n.; Schteck, pl.; **with a stooping gait** grempisch, adv.; **with difficulty** 1.boddegraemisch, adj.; 2.boddegrempisch, adj.

wall Mauer (die)n.; **eye** Glessaag (es)n.; **paper** Wandbabier (es)n.; **surrounding a cemetery** Karichhofmauer (die)n.; **up** zumaure, v.; zugemauert, pp.

wallet Backebuch (es)n.; Backebicher, pl.

wallflower 1.Logeige (die)n.; 2.Wandbopp (die)n. (sarcastic)

wallow welse, v.; gewelst, pp.

walnut Walnus (die)n.; Walnis, pl.; **shell** Walnusschaal (die)n.; **tree** Walnusbaam (der)n.; Walnusbeem, pl.; **wood** Walnusholz (es)n.

Walter 1.Wall(i) (der)n.; 2.Welti (der)n.

waltz Walzer (der)n.

wander 1.rum/laafe, v.; rumg(e)loffe, pp.; 2.rum/wandre, v.; rumgewandert, pp.; 3.umher/laafe, v.; is umhergeloffe, pp.; 4.wandere, v.; gewandert, pp.; **around** rum/dappe, v.; rumgedappt, pp.

waning Abnemmes (es)n.

want 1.bedaerfe, v.; bedaerft, pp.; 2.Mangel (der)n.;

(Continued on page 410)

Ww

want (continued)   water

(Continued from page 409)

3.Not (die)n.; 4.verlange, v.; verlangt, pp.; 5.welle, v.;
gewellt, pp.; **to come (get) out** raus/wolle, v.;
rausgewollt, pp.; **to come in** rei/wolle, v.;
reigewollt, pp.; **to come to this place** haer/wolle,
v.; **to follow** no(och)wolle, v.; no(och)gewollt, pp.; **to
get across** niwwer/wolle, v.; niwwergewollt, pp.; **to
get or come up** ruff/wolle, v.; ruffgewollt, pp.; **to get
together** zamme/wolle, v.; zammegewollt, pp.; **to
get up** uff/wolle, v.; uffgewollt, pp.; **to go along**
mit/wolle, v.; mitgewollt, pp.; **to go away**
1.fatt/wolle, v.; fattgewollt, pp.; 2.weck/wolle, v.;
weckgewollt, pp.; **to go back** zerick/wolle, v.;
zerickgewollt, pp.; **to go in** nei/wolle, v.; neigewollt,
pp.; **to go through** darich/wolle, v.; darichgewollt,
pp.; **to go to a place** hie/wolle, v.; hiegewollt, pp.; **to
go up** nuff/wolle, v.; nuffgewollt, pp.

wanting to go home heemwolle, adj.
war 1.Grieg (der)n.; 2.Kriek (der)n.; **for independence**
Friedensgriek (der)n.; **vessel** Grieksschiff (es)n.
warble 1.singe, v.; gsunge, pp.; 2.zwillere, v.; gezwillert,
pp.
ward off 1.ab/wehre, v.; abgewehrt, pp.; 2.weck/halde,
v.; weckgehalde, pp.
wardrobe 1.Gleederkammer (die)n.; 2.Gleederschank
(der)n.; Gleederschenk, pl.
ware Waar (die)n.
warehouse Waarhaus (es)n.
wares Kramm (der)n.
wariness Vorsicht (die)n.
warm 1.baehe, v.; gebaeht, pp.; 2.waar(e)m, adj.;
3.waarem, adj.; 4.waerme, v.; gewaermt, pp.; **oneself**
waerme (sich --)v.; gewaermt, pp.; **up** 1.aa/hitze, v.;
aaghitzt, pp.; 2.uff/waerme, v.; uffgewaermt, pp.
warmth Waerming (die)n.
warn 1.ab/warne, v.; abgewarnt, pp.; 2.wanne, v.;
gewarnt; gwannt, pp.; 3.warne, v.; gewarnt, pp.
warning 1.Beischpiel (es)n.; 2.Priefing (die)n.; 3.Wanning
(die)n.; 4.Warning (die)n.
warp 1.verziege, v.; verzogge, pp.; 2.verziehe, v.; verzoge,
pp.; 3.Webzettel (der)n.; 4.Wewerzeddel (der)n.;
5.wickle, v.; gewickelt, pp.
warped winnisch, adj.
warrant versichere, v.; versichert, pp.
warranty Versichering (die)n.
warrior 1.Grieger (der)n.; 2.Griegsmann (der)n.
wart Waarz (die)n.; Waarze, pl.
wartime Griegzeit (die)n.
warty 1.waarzich, adj.; 2.zwackich, adj.
wash 1.Wesch (die)n.; 2.wesche, v.; gwesche, pp.;
(oneself) wesche (sich --)v.; gewescht, pp.; **away**
weck/wesche, v.; weckgewesche, pp.; **off**
ab/wesche, v.; abgewesche, pp.; **out** raus/wesche,
v.; rausgewesche, pp.; **up** 1.fege (sich --)v.; gfekt,
pp.; 2.uff/wesche, v.; uffgewesche, pp.
washbasin 1.Weschbool (die)n.; 2.Weschschissel (die)n.;

Weschschissle, pl.
washboiler Weschkessel (der)n.
washcloth Weschlumbe (der)n.
washday Weschdaag (der)n.
washerwoman 1.Weschern (die)n.; 2.Weschfraa (die)n.;
Weschweiwer, pl.
washhouse 1.Weschhaus (es)n.; 2.Weschkich (es)n.
washing 1.Gewesch (es)n.; 2.Wesches (es)n.; 3.Wesching
(die)n.; **(confounded laundry)** Wescherei (die)n. ;
machine Weschmachien (die)n.; **stool** 1.Weschblock
(der)n.; 2.Weschbock (der)n.
washline Weschlein (die)n.; Weschleine, pl.
washrag Weschlumbe (der)n.
washtub Weschzuwwer (der)n.; Weschziwwer, pl.
wasp 1.Weschb (die)n.; Weschbe, pl.; 2.Weschp (die)n.;
nest 1.Weschbenescht (es)n.; 2.Weschpenescht (es)
n.
waste 1.verschlenkere, v.; verschlenkert, pp.;
2.verschwende, v.; verschwendt, pp.;
3.verschwenne, v.; verschwendt, pp.;
4.weck/bemble, v.; weckgebembelt, pp.; **away**
uff/zehre, v.; uffgezehrt, pp.; **in drink** verleppere, v.;
verleppert, pp.; **in scribbling** vergritzle, v.; vergritzelt,
pp.; **material** Abfall (der)n.; **money or possessions
riotously** verdunnere, v.; verdunnert, pp.; **one's living with harlots** verhure, v.; verhurt, pp.; **time**
verbemble, v.; verbembelt, pp.
wasteful verdunisch, adj.
wasting away Abnemmes (es)n.
watch 1.lauere, v.; gelauert, pp.; 2.wache, v.; gwacht, pp.;
3. Wacht (die)n.; **(clock)** Sackuhr (die)n.; **(funeral)**
Wach(t)nacht (die)n.; **(look)** Lauer (die)n.; **dog**
1.Kettehund (der)n.; 2.Wachthund (der)n.; **for**
ab/lauere, v.; abgelauert, pp.; **out** uff/basse, v.;
uffgebasst, pp.; **something** Aag (es)n. (ebbes
im -- hawwe); **spring** Schpringfedder (die)n.
watchmaker Uhremacher (der)n.; Uhremacher, pl.
watchman Wechder (der)n.; Wechder, pl.
water 1.Genswei (der)n.; 2.Wasser (es)n.; 3.wessere, v.;
gewessert, pp.; **barrel** Wasserfass (es)n.; **bench**
Wasserbank (die)n.; Wasserbenk, pl.; **bird**
Wasservoggel (der)n.; **bottle** Wasserboddel (die)n.;
Wasserboddle, pl.; **brash** Sodbrenne(s) (es)n.; **channel of a spring house** Millichgraawe (der)n.; **engine**
Wasserschpritz (die)n.; **famine** Wassernot (die)n.;
gap Wasserkaft (die)n.; **hole** Wasserloch (es)n.;
Wasserlecher, pl.; **in the hollow of a stump**
Schtumbewasser (es)n.; **in which clothes have been
washed** Weschwasser (es)n.; **lily** Wasserlilye (die)n.;
mill Wassermiehl (die)n.; **right** Wasserrecht (es)n.;
snake Wasserschlang (die)n.; Wasserschlange, pl.;
space in a spring house Schpringegraawe (der)n.;
speedwell Bachbumbel (die)n.; **trough** Wassergrog
(der)n.; **used by a blacksmith for cooling his iron**
Kiehlwasser (es)n.; **wagon** Wasserwagge (der)n.;
well Brunne (der)n.

410

Ww

watercress — weigh

watercress 1.Brunnegress (es)n.; 2.Schpringegress (es)n.; 3.Wassersenf (der)n.

waterfall Wasserfall (der)n.

watering bucket Drenkeemer (der)n.; **place** 1.Drenk (die) n.; 2.Drenkloch (es)n.; **place for cattle** Ochsedrenk (die)n.

watermark Wassermaerrick (es)n.

watermelon 1.Wassermelon (die)n.; 2.Wassermelun (die) n.; Wassermelune, pp.

waterwheel Wasserraad (es)n.; Wasserredder, pl.

waterworks Wasserwaerrick (es)n.

watery 1.wass(e)rich, adj.; 2.wasserich, adj.; 3.wesserich, adj.

wattle Wangelabbe (der)n.

wave 1.schwenke, v.; gschwenkt, pp.; 2.weddle, v.; geweddelt, pp.; 3.wehe, v.; geweht, pp.; 4.Well (die) n.; Welle, pl.; 5.wewe, v.; gewewe, pp.

waver 1.wanke, v.; gewankt, pp.; 2.wankle, v.; gewankelt, pp.

wax 1.wachse, v.; gewachst, pp.; 2.Wax (der)n.; (threads) beche, v.; gebecht, pp.; **doll** Waxbopp (die)n.; **ends** Drohtschtumbe, (der)n.; **flower** Waxblumm (die)n.

waxen 1.wachsich, adj.; 2.waxich, adj.

way 1.Aart (die)n.; 2.Laaf (der)n.; Leef, pl.; 3.Ort (die)n.; 4.Weg (der)n.; Wege, pl.; **coming** 1.Haerweeg (der) n.; 2. Haerweeg (der)n.; **going** Hieweg (der)n.; **home** Heemweg (der)n.; **up back** hinnedrowwe, adv.

we (accented form) mir, pron.; **(unaccented form)** mer, pron.; **are at wit's end** ausbacke, v.; ausgebacke, pp. (do iss ausgebacke); **are in a dilemma** Rot (der)n. (do is guter -- deier); **do** dumer; **have overcome the main difficulty** Hund (der)n. (kummt mer iwwer der -- so kummt mer iwwer der schwans); **will await with interest** gaern, adv. (mer wolle -- sehne)

weak 1.langaarschich, adj.; 2.matt, adj.; 3.schwach, adj.; 4. zimberlich, adj.; **(of the eyes)** bleed, adj.; **coffee** (contemptuous usage) Madlenewasser (es)n.; **minded** schwachsinnich, adj.

weaken 1.schweche, v.; gschwecht, pp.; 2.verschweche, v.; verschwecht, pp.; **(by suckling)** ab/saufe, v.; abgsoffe, pp.

weakly 1.mattlich, adj.; 2.schwechlich, adv.

weakness 1.Schwachheet (die)n.; 2.Schwachheit (die)n.; 3.Schwechlichkeet (die)n.; 4.Schwechlichkeit (die)n.

wealth Reichdum (der)n.

wealthy reich, adj.

wean 1.ab/gewehne, v.; abgewehnt, pp.; 2.ab/gwehne, v.; abgwehnt, pp.

weapon Gewehr (es)n.

wear 1.draage, v.; gedraage, pp.; 2.naage, v.; genaagt, pp.; 3.uff/hawwe, v.; uffghat, pp.; 4.waere, v.; gewore, pp.; **(of clothes)** aa/hawwe, v.; aaghatt, pp.; **away by whetting** ab/wetze, v.; abgewetzt, pp.; **off** 1.ab/drede, v.; abgedrede, pp.; 2.ab/waere, v.; abgwore, pp.; 3.(by stubbing) ab/schtubbe, v.; abschtuppt, pp.; 4.(by dragging) abschleefe, v.;

abgschleeft, pp.; **out** 1.aus/bautsche, v.; ausgebautscht, pp.; 2.aus/schpiele (sich --)v.; ausgschpielt, pp.; 3.aus/weare, v.; ausgwore, pp.; **the nap off** ab/rutsche, v.; abgerutscht, pp.; **through by rubbing** darich/rutsche, v.; darichgerutscht, pp.; **through by treading** darich/drede, v.; darichgedrede, pp.; **to a fringe** aus/fransle, v.; ausgfranselt, pp.

weariness 1.Miedichkeet (die)n.; 2.Miedichkeit (die)n.; 3. Miehlseelichkeit (die)n.; 4.langweilich, adj.; 5.leschdich, adj.; 6.miehseelich, adj.; 7.verleedtsam, adj.

wearisome talker 1.Blaschder (es)n.; 2.Plaschder (die)n.

weary 1.iwwerdrissich, adj.; 2.matt, adj.; 3.mied, adj.

weasel 1.Wissel (der)n.; 2.Wisselche (es)n.; **skin** Wisselhaut (die)n.

weather 1.Wedder (es)n.; 2.weddere, v.; geweddert, pp.; 3.Wittrung (die)n.; **prophet** 1.Wedderbrofeet (der) n.; 2.Wedderbrophet (der)n.

weathercock Wedderhaahne (der)n.

weatherglass Wedderglaas (es)n.; Wedderglesser, pl.

weatherman Weddermann (der)n.

weave wewe, v.; gewewe, pp.

weaver Wewer (der)n.; Wewer, pl.

weaver's shuttle Schiffel (der)n.

web 1.Geweb(b) (es)n.; 2.Webb (es)n.; 3.Weeb (es)n.

wedding 1.Hochzich (die)n.; Hochziche, pl.; 2.Mohlzeit (die)n.; **clothes** Hochzichgleeder (die)n.,pl.; **day** Hochzichdaag (der)n.; **dinner** Hochzichschmaus (der) n.; **ring** Hochzichring (der)n.

wedge 1.Keidel (der)n.; 2.keidle, v.; gekeidelt, pp.

Wednesday Mittwoch (der)n.

wee 1.glee, adj.; 2.wuns(l)ich, adj.; 3.wunz(l)ich, adj.

weed 1.Graut (es)n.; Greider, pl.; 2.robbe, v.; geroppt, pp. (Ungraut --); 3.Schtengel (der)n.; 4.Schtengli (es)n.; 5.Umgraut (es)n.; 6.Ungraut (es)n.; **(a lawn)** graase, v.; gegraast, pp.

weedy graasich, adj.

week Woch (die)n.; Woche, pl.; **of October 16** Gallewoch (die)n.; **of the Elevation of the Holy Cross** (Sept. 14) Greizwoch (die)n.

weekday 1.Schaffdaag (der)n.; Schaffdaage, pl.; 2.Wardaag (der)n.

weekdays 1.waerdaags, adv.; 2.wardaags, adv.

weekend Wochend (es)n.

weekly 1.alli Woch, adv.; 2.wechentlich, adj.; 3.wechlich, adj.

weel Fischschlupp (der)n.

weep 1.brille, v.; gebrillt, pp.; 2.flenne, v.; gflennt, pp.; 3.greine, v.; gegreint, pp.; 4.schluchze, v.; gschluchzt, pp.; 5.schnippse, v.; gschnippst, pp.; 6.seifze, v.; gseifzt, pp.; 7.weine, v.; geweint, pp.

weeping Geheil (es)n.; **willow** 1.Drauerweide (der, die)n.; 2.Henkweide (der, die)n.

weevil Wiwwel (die)n.; Wiwwle, pl.

weigh 1.wiege (sich --)v.; gwoge, pp.; 2.wiege, v.; gewoge, pp.; **(for retail)** 1.ab/wiege, v.; abgewoge, pp.; 2.aus/wiege, v.; ausgewoge, pp.

Ww

weight ... which

weight 1.Gewicht (es)n.; 2.Gewichtschtee (der)n.; 3.Gwicht (es)n.; Gwichder, pl.

weighty 1.gewichtich, adj.; 2.schwer, adj.; 3.wichdich, adj.

weir Weiher (der)n.

weird 1.unheemlich, adj.; 2.uuheemlich, adj.

welcome 1.aagenehm, adj.; 2.Willkumm (der)n.; 3.Willkumm!, interj.

weld zamme/schweese, v.; zammegschweest, pp.; **(solder)**schwees(s)e, v.; gschwees(s)t, pp.

welfare Wohlfaahrt (die)n.

Well, I'm sure! Ich denk awwer aa!

well 1.aa, adv. (ich denk awwer --); 2.Aart (die)n. (das es en -- hot); 3.gut, adv.; 4.Gwell (die)n.; 5.munder, adj.; 6.munder, adv.; 7.well, interj.; 8.wohl, adj., adv.; 9.woll; adj.; 10.wull, adj.; **behaved** 1.aaschtennich, adj.; 2.braff, adj.; 3.verschtendich, adj.; 4.verschtennich, adj.; **built** 1.gepuschdurt, adj. (gut --); 2.gsetzt, adj. (gut --); **digger** Brunne(r)graawer (der)n.; **done** 1.gaar, adj.; 2.maer(r)b, adj.; **educated** gutgelannt, adj.; **fitting** (of clothes) schnack, adj.; **fixed** ab, adj. (gut --); **known** bekannt, adj. (gut --); **liked** gegliche, adj. (gut --); **off** 1.ab, adj. (gut --); 2.ab, prep. (net iw-wel --); **shaped** (of girls) schnack, adj.; **to-do** gut, adj. (-- ab sei); **water** Brunne(r)wasser (es)n.; **with bucket and rope or chain** Ziegbrunne (der)n.

Well! 1.Ai!, interj.; 2.ei!, interj.; 3.wohlaan!; 4.gottslebbdaag, interj.; 5.gottsdausich, interj.

Welsh Welsche (die)n.

welt 1.Raan (die)n.; 2.Ran (die)n.; 3.Roon (die)n.; Raane, pl.; 4.Schtraeme (der)n.; 5.Schtriehme (der)n.; 6.Schtrieme (der)n.; 7.Schuhraahme (der)n.

welts Rune (die)n., pl.

were waer, v. past tense of be

west Wescht (der)n.

western 1.wescht, adj.; adv.; 2.weschtlich, adv.

westward weschtlich, adv.

wet 1.nass adj. (-- mache); 2.nass, adj.; 3.netze, v.; genetzt, pp.; 4.schwammich, adj.; 5.suddlich, adj.; **fart** Fatzebrieh (die)n.; **through** darichnass, adj.; **wasteland used for pasture** Baschdert (der)n.

wether 1.Hammel (der)n.; 2.Schofhammel (der)n.

wettish 1.nasslich, adj.; 2.nesslich, adj.

whack Schlack (der)n.

whale 1.Waalfisch (der)n.; 2.Walfisch (der)n.

whalebone Fischbee (der)n.

wharf Warf (der)n.

what was, pron.; **has happened** gewwe, v.; gewwe, pp. (was hot's --); **kind of** 1.faerrich, adj. (was --); 2.far, prep. (was --); 3.fer, prep. (was --); 4.was fa(e)rich?; 5.was fer?; **number** 1.wievielt, adv.; 2.wiffelt, adv.; **sort** (of) ----? 1.was fer ----?; 2.faerrich, adj. (was --); 3.far, prep. (was --); 4.fer, prep. (was --); 5.was fa(e)rich?; **the deuce!** 1.Grammenot (die)n. (was dei --); 2.Grampet (die)n. (was dei --); 3.grenk (was dei --); **the dickens!** 1.Deixel! interj.; 2.Was der Dausich!;

under the sun himmelswelt (was in der --) **What's the matter here?** Wass iss do uff?; **your name?** Wie heescht?

what's the news gewwe, v.; gewwe, pp. (was gebt's neies); **your hurry?** Huddel (der)n. (was is dei --)

whatever? was ewwer?, pron.

wheat Weeze (der)n.; **(white) bread** 1.Weissbrot (es)n.; 2. Weezebrot (es)n.; **bin** Weezekaschde (der)n.; Weezekaschde, pl.; **chaff** Weezeschprau (die)n.; **field** Weezefeld (es)n.; **flour** 1.Weezemehl (es)n.; 2.Weissmehl (es)n.; **fork** Fruchtgawwel (die)n.; Fruchtgawwle, pl.; **harvest** Weeze-aern(t) (die)n.; **straw** Weezeschtroh (es)n.

wheather Wittring (die)n.

wheedle aa/schmeechle, v.; aagschmeechelt, pp.

wheel Raad (es)n.; Redder, pl.; **rut** Waggeglees (der)n.

wheelbarrow 1.Schuppkaich (der)n.; 2.Schuppkarich (der) n.; Schuppkariche, pl.

wheelchair Raadschtul (der)n.; Raadschtiel, pl.

wheelwright Wagner (der)n.

wheeze 1.haerchle, v.; ghaerchelt, pp.; 2.herchle, v.; geherschelt, pp.; 3.keich(l)e, v.; gekeiche(l)t, pp.; 4.keiche, v.; gekeicht, pp.

whelp Hundli (es)n.; Hindlin, pl.

when 1.nochdem, conj.; 2.nochdem, pron.; conj.; 3.wann, conj.; pron.; **everything in the dishes on the table at a meal is eaten** Wedder (es)n. (es gebt gut --) ; **he** wanndem = wann du em; **it** wanns = wann es; **one** wannderne = wann du me; **she** wanndre = wann du re; **the horns of the moon point up** iwwerschtende (im); **the horns of the moon are turned downward** Unnerschtehende (im); **you** 1.wannd = wann du; 2.wannde = wann du

whence 1.woher, adv.; 2.wuher, adv.

where 1.wo, pron.; 2.wu, pron.; **have you been keeping yourself** schtecke, v.; gschtocke, pp. (wu hoschde gschtocke); **to** 1.wu anne, adv.; 2.wu hie, adv.; 3.wuhie, adv.

whereabout wurum, adv.

whereabouts 1.Aufenthalt (der)n.; 2.Uffen(t)halt (der)n.

whereby 1.wodarich, adv.; 2.wudarich, adv.

wherewith wu mit, adv.

whet wetze, v.; gewetzt, pp.; **hot pressing iron** (with finger to see if it is hot) 1.putze, v.; geputzt, pp.; 2.puuze, v.; gepuuzt, pp.; 3.Wetzkump (der)n.; 4.Gump (der)n.; 5.Kump (der)n.; 6.Wetzkoom (der)n.

whether 1.eb, conj.; prep.; 2.ob, conj.; 3.oob, conj.; **he** owwer = ob er

whetstone 1.Wettschtee (der)n.; 2.Wetzschtee (der)n.

whetting Wetz (der)n.

whew! puh!, inter.

whey 1.Kaesmolke (die)n., pl.; 2.Keesmolke (die)n.; 3.Molke (die)n., pl.

which 1.well, adv., pron.; 2.weller, adv.; pron.; 3.welli, adv.; pron.; 4.wievielt, adv.; 5.wiffelt, adv.; 6.wo, rel. pron.; 7.wu, rel. pron.

Ww

whiffletree — wild

whiffletree 1.S(ch)illscheit (es)n.; S(ch)illscheider, pl.;
  2. Sillscheit (es)n.; Sillscheider, pl.

while 1.als, adv.; 2.dieweil, conj.; 3.diweil, conj.; 4.Lick
  (die)n.; 5.weil, conj.; 6.weile, v.; geweilt, pp.; **away**
  (time) verweile, v.; verweilt, pp.

whim Eifall (der)n.; Eifalle, pl.

whimper winsle, v.; gewinselt, pp.

whims Grille (die)n., pl.

whine 1.weine, v.; geweint, pp.; 2.winsle, v.; gewinselt, pp.

whining Gewinsel (es)n.

whinny 1.lache, v.; gelacht, pp.; 2.Kutschel (es)n.

whip 1.Beitsch (die)n.; 2.fitze, v.; gfitzt, pp.; 3.Fitzeel (es)n.
  (mit -- schmiere); 4.fitzle, v.; gfitzelt, pp.; 5.gadde, v.;
  gegaddt, pp.; 6.gaerde, v.; gegaerdt, pp.; 7.Gatt (die)n.;
  Gadde, pl.; 8.Geart (die)n.; 9.Geeschel (die)n.;
  Geeschle, pl.; 10.Schwing (die)n.; **(with a rod)** abfitze,
  v.; abgfitzt, pp.; **stock** Geeschelschtock (der)n.

whipping Schlaek (die)n., pl.

whippoorwill Wibberwill (der)n.

whirl 1.Waerwel (der)n.; 2.waerwle, v.; gewaerwelt, pp.;
  3.Zwaerl (der)n.; 4.Zwaerwel (der)n.; 5.zwaerwle, v.;
  gezwaerwelt, pp.; **around** rum/waerwle, v.; rumgewaerwelt, pp.

whirlwind Windwaerwel (der)n.

whisk Wedel (der)n.

whiskers Backebaart (der)n.

whiskey 1.Brandewei (der)n.; 2.Dramm (der)n.;
  3.Schnapps (der)n.; **barrel** Brandeweifass (es)n.

whisper 1.flischbere, v.; gflischbert, pp.; 2.pischbere, v.;
  gepischbert, pp.; **into one's ear** ei/blose, v.;
  eigeblose, pp.

whispering Gepischber (es)n.

whistle 1.Peif (die)n.; Peife, pl.; 2.peife, v.; gepiffe, pp.;
  after no(och)peife, v.; no(och)gepiffe, pp.; **made of
  chestnut bark** Keschdepeif (die)n.

whistler Peifer (der)n.; Peifer, pl.

whistling Gepeif (es)n.

white weiss, adj.; **as chalk** greideweiss, adj.; **ash**
  Weissesche (die)n.; **cedar** Weisszedre (der)n.; **clover**
  Glee (der)n. (weisser --); **face** (of a horse) Blessgsicht
  (es)n.; **headed** weisskebbich, adj.; **hellebore**
  (Veratrum virde) 1. Niesgraut (es)n.; 2.Mesgraut (es)
  n.; **horse with small black spots** Schimmel (der)
  n.;Schimmel,pl.; **lead** Bleiweiss (es)n.; **mark on the
  forehead of a cow or horse** 1.Bless (die)n.;
  2.Schtaern (die)n.; Schtaern, pl.; 3.Schtann (die)n.;
  Schtanne, pl.; **mulberry** Weissmaulbeer (die)n.; **oak**
  Weisseeche (der, die)n.; **of an egg** Oi (es)n. (es weiss
  vum --); **of the eye** Aag (es)n. (weiss vum --); **pine**
  Weissbeind (die)n.; **poplar** 1.Babble (der)n.; Babble,
  pl.; 2.Silwerbabble (die)n.; 3.Weissbabble (die)n.;
  willow Grieweide (der, die)n.

whiten weiss mache, v.; weiss gemacht, pp.

whitewash 1.weisse, v.; geweisst, pp.; 2.weissle, v.;
  geweisselt, pp.; **(the inside of)** aus/weisse, v.;
  ausgeweisst, pp.; **brush** Weisspensil (der)n.

whither 1.welke, v.; gewelkt, pp.; 2.wuhie, adv.

whithered welk, adj.

whitish weisslich, adj.

whitlow 1.Beesding (es)n.; 2.Middel (es)n.; 3.Naggelfluss
  (der)n.; 4.Umlaaf (der)n.

Whitmonday Pingschtmundaag (der)n.

Whitsunday Pingschtsunndaag (der)n.

Whitsuntide Pingschde (die)n., pl.

whittle 1.aus/schnitzle, v.; ausgschnitzelt, pp.;
  2.schnipsle, v.; gschnipselt, pp.; 3.schnitzle, v.;
  gschnitzelt, pp.; **away** verschnitzle, v.; verschnitzelt,
  pp.; **off** ab/schnitzle, v.; abgschnitzelt, pp.

whittling Gschnepper (es)n.

whiz! wuppsch, adv.

who 1.daer, rel pro.; 2.wer, pron.; 3.wo, rel. pron.; 4.wu,
  rel. pron.

whoever werewwer, pron.

whole ganz, adj.; **ago** vor(d)ich, adj.; **distance** alldeweeg,
  adv.; **kernel of half a walnut or hickory nut** Addler
  (der)n.; Addler, pl.; **lot** ewich, adj, adv. (gaar -- viel)

wholesale business Grosshandel (der)n.

wholesome heilsam, adj.

wholly genzlich, adv.

whom 1.wem, pron.; 2.wen, pron.

whooping cough Blohuschde (der)n.

whoremonger 1.Hurebull (der)n.; 2.Hurehengscht (der)n.

whoring Hurerei (die)n.

whose wem sei, pron.

why 1.ei!, interj.; 2.fer was, conj.; 3.ferwas, adv.;
  4.wa(a)rum, adv.;5.wei!, interj.; **yes** (pleasant assent)
  iya

wick 1.Docht (der)n.; 2.Wieche (der)n.; Wieche, pl.; **cord**
  Wiechgaarn (es)n.

wicked 1.bees, adj.; 2.gottlos, adj.; 3.heillos, adj.;
  4.schlecht, adj.; **shame** Sin(d) (die)n. (ee -- un ee
  schand)

wickedness 1.Frewel (der)n.; 2.Schlechdichkeit (die)n.;
  3.Schlechtichkeet (die)n.

wicker basket Weidekareb (der)n.

wide 1.breet, adj.; 2.weit, adj.; **(open)** schpaerreweit, adj.

widen erweitre, v.; erweitert, pp.

wider weider, adv.

widow Wittfraa (die)n.; Wittweiwer, pl.

widow's dower 1.Driddel (es)n.; 2.Drittel (es)n.

widower Wittmann (der)n.; Wittmenner, pl.

width 1.Breeding (die)n.; 2.Weiting (die)n.

wierdness Unheemlichkeit (die)n.

wife 1.Ehefraa (die)n.; 2.Fraa (die)n.; Weibsleit; Weiwer,
  pl.; 3.Weib (es)n.; Weiwer, pl.

wifey Weiwel (es)n.

wig Barick (die)n.; **wag** wewe, v.; gewewe, pp.

wiggle 1.schwenzle, v.; gschwenzelt, pp.; 2.zawwle, v.;
  gezawwelt, pp.

wiggling zawwlich, adj.

wild 1.ausgelosse, adj.; 2.rum/schpringe, v.;

(Continued on page 414)

413

Ww

wild (continued)   wish

(Continued from page 413)

rumgschprunge, pp.; 3.verzickt, adj.; 4.wild, adj.;
(ungrafted) apple Holsebbli (es)n.; **carrot** Gehlrieb
(die)n. (wildi --); **cherry** 1.Bitterkasch (die)n.;
2.Wildkasch (die)n.; Wildkasche, pl.; **ginger**
1.Budderwatzel (die)n.; 2.Butterwatzel (die)n.;
3.Wassersuchtgraut (es)n.; **goose** Schneegans (die)
n.; **honey suckle** Gicklifiess (die)n., pl.; **indigo**
Mickegraut (es)n.; **lettuce** 1.Millichgraut (es)n.;
2.Raahmgraut (es)n.; 3.Selaat (der)n. (wilder --);
4.Zelaat (der)n. (wilder --); **marjoram**
1.Marien(s)watzel (die)n.; 2.Wohlgemut (der)n.;
3.Wollgemut (der)n.; **parsnip** Giftbaschnaad (der)n.;
peppergrass 1.Dischligraut (es)n.; 2.Dischligraut (es)
n.; 3.Peffergraas (es)n.; 4.Peffergraut (es)n.; **radish**
Reddichmostert (der)n.; **rose** Ros (die)n. (wildi --);
sensitive plant Schaamgraut (es)n.; **yam**
1.Gehlwarzel (die)n.; 2.Rhummediswarzel (die)n.

wildcat Wildkatz (die)n.

wilderness Wildernis (die)n.

wildfire Wildfeier (es)n.

wildness Wildheet (die)n.

wilds 1.Gliftse (die)n., pl.; 2.Kliftse, (die)n., pl.

will 1.losse, v.; gelosst, pp. (ebber ebbes --); 2.vermache,
v.; vermacht, pp.; 3.verwille, v.; verwillt, pp.;
4.waerre, v.; warre; waerre, pp.; 5.welle, v.; gewellt,
pp.; 6.wolle, v.; gewollt, pp.; **(legal paper)** Wille (der)
n.; ; **he be sure to come** aa, adv. (kummt er --); **it be**
convenient tomorrow? mariye, adv. (dienders --); **o'**
the wisp 1.Drach (der)n.; Drache, pl.; 2.Erdlichdel
(es)n.

willful eegesinni(s)ch, adj.

willfulness Eegesinn (der)n.

willing 1.willens, adj.; 2.willich, adj.

willingly 1.garn, adv.; 2.gern, adv.

willow Weide (der, die)n.; **tree** Weidebaam (der)n.;
Weidebeem, pl.

willy-nilly iwwel, adj. (-- odder wohl)

wilt welke, v.; gewelkt, pp.; **(of plants)** 1.drau(e)re, v.;
gedrauert, pp.; 2.Trau(e)re, v.; getrauert, pp.

wilted welk, adj.

win gewinne, v.; gewunne, pp.; **or gain from** abgewinne,
v.; abgewinne, pp.

winch Drehhendel (der)n.

wind wickle, v.; gewickelt, pp.; **(air)** Wind (der)n.; **up**
1.uff/wickle, v.; uffgewickelt, pp.; 2.uff/ziehe, v.;
uffgezoge, pp.; **a warp on a cylinder preparatory to**
weaving rag carpet uff/bome, v.; **up with** letscht,
adj. (-- zu guter); **over** iwwerwickle, v.; iwwergewickelt, pp.

wind bringing snow Schneewind (der)n.; **colic** Windkolick
(der)n.; **gap** Windkaft (die)n.; **on spools** schpule, v.;
gschpult, pp.; ; **wheel** Windraad (es)n.

windfall Glicksfall (der)n.

winding frame Wickel (der)n.

winding stairs Schneckeschteek (die)n.

windlass 1.Walz (die)n.; 2.Winn (die)n.; Winne, pl.; **(for**
drawing water) Brunnewalz (die)n.

windmill Windmiehl (die)n.

window 1.Fenschder (es)n.; Fenschdere, pl.; 2.Finschder
(es)n.; Finschdere, pl.; **curtain** Umhenkel (es)n.;
frame Fenschdergschtell (es)n.; **sash** Fenschderraam
(der)n.; **seat** 1.Fenschdergschtell (es)n.;
2.Fenschdersitz (der)n.; **sill** 1.Fenschdergschtell (es)
n.; 2.Fenschdersitz (der)n.

windowpane Fenschderglaas (es)n.

windpipe 1.Luftrehe (die)n.; 2.Luftrohr (es)n.;
3.Sunndaagshals (der)n.

windrow Windroi (die)n.

windy windich, adj.

wine Wei (der)n.; **barrel** Weifass (es)n.; **grape** Weidraub
(die)n.

wineglass 1.Schtangeglaas (es)n.; 2.Schtengelglaas (es)n.;
3.Weiglaas (es)n.

winepress 1.Kelder (die)n.; 2.Weibress (die)n.

wing Fliggel (der)n.; Fliggel, pl.; **of turkey or goose used**
for dusting Fladderwisch (der)n.; **wall of a bridge**
Fliggelmauer (die)n.

wink 1.blinsle, v.; geblinselt, pp.; 2.Wink (der)n.; 3.winke,
v.; gewunke, pp.

winner Gewinner (der)n.

winnow sichte, v.; gsicht, pp.; **grain** 1.butze, v.; gebutzt,
pp. (frucht --); 2.uff/butze (sich --)v.; uffgebutzt, pp.

winnowing mill Windmiehl (die)n.

winter 1.Winder (der)n.; 2.windere, v.; gewindert, pp.;
apple Winderabbel (der)n.; **clothes** Windergleeder
(die)n., pl.; **cress** Leffelgraut (es)n.; **crookneck**
squash Holskaerbs (die)n.; **day** Winderdaag (der)n.;
fruit Winderobscht (es)n.; **month** Windermunet
(der)n.; **morning** Windermarye (der)n.; **pear**
Winderbeer (die)n.; **radish** Winderreddich (der)n.;
set in eiwintre, v.; eigewintert, pp.; **weather**
Winderwedder (es)n.; **wheat** Winderweeze (der)n.

wintergreen 1.Bruschttee (der)n.; 2.Buchs (der)n.;
3.Buchs (der)n. (nidderer --); 4.Windergrie (die)n.

wintery 1.winderisch, adj.; 2.windrich, adj.; 3.winterisch,
adj.; 4.wintrich, adj.

wipe 1.ab/butzt, v.; abgebutzt, pp.; 2.butze, v.; gebutzt,
pp.; 3.wische, v.; gewischt, pp.; **away** weck/wische,
v.; weckgewischt, pp.; **off** ab/wische, v.; abgewischt,
pp.

wiper 1.Abwischer (der)n.; Abwischer, pl.; 2.Wisch (der)
n.; 3.Wischer (der)n.

wire Droht (der)n.; **grass** 1.Blograas (es)n.; 2.Eisegraas
(es)n.; **nail** Drohtnaggel (der)n.; **staple** 1.Glowe (der)
n.; 2.Klowe (der)n.

wisdom 1.Gscheidheet (die)n.; 2.Weisheet (die)n.;
3.Weisheit (die)n.; 4.Weltlaerning (die)n.

wise klu(u)ch, adj.

wish 1.begehre, v.; begehrt, pp.; 2.Gwinsch (der)n.;
Gwinsche, pl.; 3.Winsch (der)n.; Winsche, pl.;

(Continued on page 415)

414

Ww

wish (continued)   woof

(Continued from page 414)

4.winsche, v.; gewinscht, pp.; 5.Winsches (es)n.;
6.wolle, v.; gewollt, pp.; 7.wott, v.; 8.Wunsch (der)n.;
(someone in a place) nei/winsche, v.; neigewinscht,
pp.; **back** zerick/winsche, v.; zerickgewinscht, pp.;
one ill gunne, v.; gegunnt, pp.; **oneself there**
hie/winsche (sich --)v.; hiegewinscht, pp.; **someone
would leave** naus/winsche, v.; nausgwinscht, pp.;
success Glick (es)n. (es -- winsche); **well** gunne, v.;
gegunnt, pp. (gaern --)

wishbone 1.Bruschtgnoche (der)n.; 2.Hinkelgnoche (der)n.
wishwish welle, v.; gewellt, pp.
wisp 1.Wisch (der)n.; 2.Wischel (es)n.; 3.Wischli (es)n.; **(of
hair)** Haarpusch (der)n.; **of hay** Hoiwisch (der)n.; **of
straw** Schtrohwisch (der)n.
wit 1.Verschtand (der)n.; 2.Witz (der)n.
witch doctor Hexedokder (der)n.; **grass** 1.Flaumgraas (es)
n.; 2.Kitzelgraas (es)n.
witchcraft Verblennerei (die)n.
witchery Verblennerei (die)n.
with 1.bei, prep.; 2.mit, prep.; 3.zamt(e), adv.; **a sigh**
1.seiferich, adv.; 2.seifzerich, adj.; **alacrity**
unverdrosse, adj.; **all might** Deiwelsgewalt (die)
(mit --); **all possible means** Gotteskrefte (die)n., pl.
(mit --); **that** 1.datt(de)mit, adv.; 2.dattmit, adj.; **the
exception of** ausgenumme, prep.; **this** 1.do(de)mit,
adv.; 2.do(de)mit, adv.; 3.domit, adv.; **young**
1.draagend, adj.; 2.draagich, adj.; 3.drechdich, adj.
withdraw zerick/ziehe, v.; zerickgezoge, pp.
withdrawal Abdritt (der)n.
withe Widd (die)n.
wither 1.verdarre, v.; verdatt, pp.; 2.verwelke, v.;
verwelkt, pp.; 3.verwenkle, v.; verwenkelt, pp.; **(and
fall off)** ab/welke, v.; abgewelkt, pp.
withered verdatt, adj.
withhold permission versaage, v.; versaagt, pp.
within 1.drin, adv.; 2.inne, adv.; 3.inner, prep.
without 1.unne, prep.; 2.unni, prep.; 3.unnich, prep.;
energy baamblich, adj.; **fail** unnefehl, adj.; **feeling**
gfiehllos, adj.; **it** 1.unnes = unne es; 2.unnichs =
unnich es; **kernels** (of nuts and grains) daab, adj.;
measure Maas (es)n. (iwwer --); **sure footing**
boddemlos, adj.; **thinking** 1.unbedacht, adj.;
2.unbedenkt, adj.
withstand 1.wedderschteh, v.; wedderschtanne, pp.;
2.widderschteh, v.; widderschtanne, pp.
witness Zeige (der)n.; **fee** Zeigegeld (es)n.
witticism Witz (der)n.
witty witzich, adj.
wobble wanke, v.; gewankt, pp.
wobbly 1.baamblich, adj.; 2.wacklich, adj.
woe 1.Beschwerde (die)n.; 2.Drauer (die)n.; 3.Elend (es)
n.; 4.Gwaal (die)n.; 5.Leed(e) (der)n.
woeful elendich, adj.
wolf Wolf (der)n.; Welf, pl.; **robe** Wolfhaut (die)n.
wolfisch wolfich, adj.

woman Weibsmensch (es)n.; Weibsleit, pl.; **(feminine
term corresponding to der Mannskall)** Weibsbild
(es)n.; **(rarely used singular in both meanings)** Weib
(es)n.; Weiwer, pl.; **(very pretty)** Fraa (die)n. (en
iwwerausi scheni --); **in child-bed** Kindbettern (die)
n.; **who changes residence frequently** Rutsch (die)n.;
who dispenses homemade remedies Dokterfraa (die)
n.; **who is very fond or sells flowers** Blummefraa
(die)n.
woman's sun bonnet Schtripphut (der)n.
womanly weiblich, adj.
womb Mudder (die)n.
womenfolk Weibsleit (die)n., pl.
wonder 1.erschtaune; 2.verwunnere (sich --)v.;
verwunnert, pp.; 3.Wunner (die, es)n.; 4.wunnere
(sich --)v.; gewunnert, pp.; 5.wunnere, v.;
gewunnert, pp.
wonderful 1.wunderbaar, adj.; 2.wunnerbaar, adj.;
3.wunnerlich, adj.; 4.wunnervoll, adj.
wonderfully wunners, adv.
woo freie, v.; gfreit, pp.
wood Holz (es)n.; **ashes** Holzesch (die)n.; **bit** Holzbohre
(der)n.; **carver** Holzschneider (der)n.; **fire** Holzfeier
(es)n.; **saw** Schpannsaeg (die)n.; **shaving** 1.Holschpaa
(der)n.; 2.Schpaa (der)n.; 3.Schpoo (der)n.; Schpee,
pl.; **sorrel** Sauerglee (der)n.
woodchest Holzkischt (die)n.; Holzkischde, pl.
woodchopper Holzhacker (der)n.
woodchuck 1.Grund(d)ax (der)n.; Grund(d)axe, pl.;
2.Grundsau (die)n.; Grundsei, pl.
wooden 1.helse, adj.; 2.hilsch, adj.; 3.hilze, adj.;
4.holzich, adj.; 5.unbeholfe, adj.; **baking bowl**
Backschissel (die)n.; Backschissle, pl.; **dish in which
butter is worked** 1.Budderschissel (die)n.;
2.Butterschissel (die)n.; **fork** Schiddelgawwel (die)n.;
Schiddelgawwle, pl.; **gun for shooting pins and other
light projectiles by blowing** Bolsrohr (es)n.; **part of
an old time gun or rifle** 1.Gscheft (es)n.; 2.Schaft
(der)n.; Schafde, pl.; **peg** Holzzabbe (der)n.; **screw**
Holzschraub (die)n.; **shaft of a mill wheel** Wellbaam
(der)n.; **shelf** (for storing canned goods in cellar)
Schaft (der)n.; Schafde, pl.; **spoon for working butter**
Butterleffel (der)n.; **spoon for working butter**
Budderleffel (der)n.
woodjack Saegbock (der)n.; Saegbeck, pl.
woodland 1.Buschland (es)n.; 2.Holzland (es)n.;
Holzlenner, pl.
woodpecker 1.Schpaech(t) (der)n.; 2.Schpechthaahne
(der)n.; 3.Schpeecht (der)n.; Schpeechde, pl.
woodpile Holzhaufe (der)n.; Holzheife, pl.
woods Busch (der)n.; Bisch, pl.
woodsaw Holzsaeg (die)n.
woodshed 1.Holzheisel (es)n.; 2.Holzheisli (es)n.;
3.Holzschopp (der)n.
woodstove Holzoffe (der)n.; Holzeffe, pl.
woof Eischlack (der)n.

Ww

wooing — wrapper

wooing Freierei (die)n.

wool Woll (die)n.; **from the rear quarters of a sheep where it is mixed with manure** Gnoddelwoll (die)n.; **gathering** Aaschlaek (die)n., pl. (-- fresse)

woolen 1.wolle, adj.; 2.wollich, adj.woolen fleece; **fleece** Wolleflies (der)n.

word 1.Wart (es)n.; 2.Watt (es)n.; Wadde, pl.; 3.Wattche (es)n.; **of honor** Ehrewatt (es)n.

worded laute, v.; gelaut, pp.

wordy wartreich, adj.

work 1.Arewet(t) (die)n.; 2.Arwet (die)n.; 3.schaffe, v.; gschafft, pp.; 4.Warick (es)n.; **(any long continued smeary or greasy)** 1.Gschleff (es)n.; 2.Schmiererei (die)n.; **along with** mit/schaffe, v.; mitgschafft, pp.; **at a small job** (especially in wood) beschdle, v.; gebeschdelt, pp.; **clothes** 1.Alldaagsgleeder (die)n.; 2..Schaffgleeder (die)n., pl.; 3.Wadaagsgleeder (die)n., pl.; 4.Waerdaagsgleeder (die)n., pl.; 5.Wardaagsgleeder (die)n.; **folk** Schaffleit (die)n.; **for a man** mannsaerwet (die)n.; **for someone on a day by day basis** daaglehnere, v.; gedaaglehnert, pp.; **in a hasty and unsatisfactory manner** huddle, v.; ghuddelt, pp.; **in a slow and poky manner** gnoddle, v.; gegnoddelt, pp.; **in different places** rumhaer/schaffe, v.; rumhaergschafft, pp.; **leisurely without accomplishing much** rum/gnoddle, v.; rumgegnoddelt, pp.; **like crazy** baerschdebinner, adj. (wie en -- schaffe [saufe, schpringe]); **of man** Menschewaerrick (es)n.; **one's way into a place** nei/schaffe (sich --)v. neigschaft, pp.; **one's way up** nuff/schaffe (sich --)v.; nuffgschafft, pp.; **out** aus/schaffe, v.; ausgschafft, pp.; **slovenly** weck/zackere, v.; weckgezackert, pp.; **slowly** leiere, v.; geleiert, pp.; **to excess** ab/schaffe (sich --)v.; abschafft, pp.; **together** zamme/schaffe, v.; zammegschaft, pp.; **up material** verschaffe, v.; verschafft, pp.

work(s) Waerrick (es)n.

workbench 1.Bank (die)n.; Benk, pl.; 2.Howwelbank (die)n.; Howwelbenk, pl.; 3.Schaffbank (die)n.; Schaffbenk, pl.

workday 1.Schaffdaag (der)n.; Schaffdaage, pl.; 2.Wadaag (der)n.; Wadaage, pl.

worker Schaffmann (der)n.; Schaffleit, pl.

workhouse Waerrickhaus (es)n.

working Gschaff (es)n.

workman 1.Schaffmann (der)n.; Schaffleit, pl.; 2.Scheffer (der)n.; Scheffer pl.

works of a clock Uhrewaerrick (es)n.

world 1.Erd (die)n.; 2.Welt (die)n.; 3.Weltkreis (der)n.; **war** Weltgrieg (der)n.

worldliness 1.Weltlichkeet (die)n.; 2.Weltlieb (die)n.; 3.Weltsinn (der)n.

worldling Weltmensch (der)n.

worldly weltlich, adj.

worm 1.Warem (der)n.; 2.Warm (der)n.; Waerm, pl.; **(in distilling apparatus)** Schlang (die)n.; Schlange, pl.; **eaten** 1.aagschtoche, adj.; 2.warmschtichich, adj.; **fence** Schtaagefens (die)n.; Schtaagefense, pl.

wormhole Warmschtich (der)n.

wormseed Warmgraut (es)n.

wormwood Warmet (der)n. (zaahmer --)

wormy 1.waermich, adj.; 2.waremich, adj.; 3.warmich, adj.

worn down verlumpt, adj.; **off** abgschtumpt, adj.; **out** 1.abgelbt, adv.; 2.abgewore, adj.; 3.ausgedient, adj.; 4.ausgewore, adj.; 5.verranst; **out roue** Glopphaahne (der)n.

worry 1.ab/maertre, v.; abgemaertert, pp.; 2.ab/quaele (sich --)v.; abgequaelt, pp.; 3.Badder (der, die)n.; 4.Blog (die)n.; 5.bloge (sich --)v.; geblogt, pp.; 6.Druwwel (der)n.; 7.druwwle (sich --)v.; gedruwwelt, pp.; **about something** uff/halde, v.; uffghalde, pp. (sich iwwer ebbes --)

worse aer(ri)yer, adj.; **worst** arrick; arrickscht, adj.

worsen verschlimmere, v.; verschlimmert, pp.

worship 1.aa/bede, v.; aagebet, pp.; 2.Goddesdi(e)nscht (der)n.; **service** Dinscht (der)n.

worst Schlimmscht (es)n.; **(in a fight)** leddere, v.; geleddert, pp.; **of all** 1.allerarrickscht, adj.; 2.allerwiescht, adj.

worsted 1.Gorn (es)n.; 2.Wollgaarn (es)n.

worth 1.Nutz (der)n.; 2.nutz, adv.; 3.Waert (der)n.; 4.waert, adv.; 5.Wart (der)n.; 6.wart, adv.; **listening to** heereswatt, adj.; **mentioning** nenneswaert, adj.; **seeing** sehneswaert, adj.; **thanking for** dankeswaert; **the trouble** Mieh (die)n. (-- wert dei)

worthless nixnutz(ich), adj.; **fellow** 1.Kannegiesser (der)n.; 2.Nixnutz (der)n.; **gun** (facetious usage) Gnalleise (es)n.

worthlessness Nixnutzichkeit (die)n.

worthwhile 1.waert, adj. (-- waert); 2.wunnerswaert, adj.

worthy waerdich, adj.; **of love** 1.liewenswaert, adj.; 2.lieweswaert, adj.

would 1.wett = wott; 2.wott, v.; **be** waer, v. pp. of be

wound 1.verwunde, v.; verwundt, pp.; 2.Wund (die)n.; 3.wunde, v.; gewundt, pp.

wraith Schpuck(s) (es)n.; Schpucke, pl.

wrangle 1.baffze, v.; gebaffzt, pp.; 2.beffze, v.; gebeffzt, pp.; 3.rechtle, v.; gerechtelt, pp.; 4.renkle, v.; gerenkelt, pp.; 5.schtreide, v.; gschtridde, pp.; 6.Schtreit (der)n.; 7.zaerife, v.; gezaerift, pp.; 8.zanke, v.; gezankt, pp.; 9.zareffe, v.; gezarefft, pp.

wrap 1.ei/wickle, v.; eigewickelt, pp.; 2.uff/wickle, v.; uffgewickelt, pp.; 3.wickle, v.; gewickelt, pp.; **into** 1.ei/wickle, v.; eigewickelt, pp.; 2.nei/wickle, v.; neigewickelt, pp.; **together** zamme/wickle, v.; zammegewickelt, pp.; **up** 1.ei/binne, v.; eigebunne, pp.; 2.eihille, v.; eighillt, pp.; 3.zu/wickle, v.; zugewickelt, pp.; **up thickly in clothes** ei/balsamiere, v.; eigebalsamiert, pp.; **up well** ei/mummle, v.; eigemummelt, pp.

wrapper Umschlack (der)n.

Ww

wraps   wry

wraps Sache (die)n.

wrath Wut (die)n.

wreak aus/iewe, v.; ausgeiebt, pp.; **upon** aus/losse, v.; ausg(e)losst, pp.

wreath 1.Blumme(r)krans (der)n.; 2.Krans (der)n.; **of flowers** Blummering (der)n.

wren 1.Mausekeenich (der)n.; Mausekeenich, pl.; 2.Mausevoggel (der)n.; Mauseveggel, pl.; 3.Zaahkeenich (der)n.; 4.Zaahschlibber (der)n.; 5.Zaaschlipper (der)n.; 6.Zaunkeenich (der)n.; 7.Zooschlipper (der)n.

wrench 1.schtauche, v.; gschtaucht, pp.; 2.schtrenge, v.; gschtrengt, pp.; 3.verdrehe, v.; verdreht, pp.; **(tool)** Wenneise (es)n.

wrest from ab/geege, v.; abgegeet, pp.

wrestle 1.packe, v.; gepackt, pp.; 2.raessle, v.; graesselt, pp.

wretch 1.Deiwel (der)n. (armer --); 2.Dropp (der)n. (aarmer --); 3.Schel(l)em (der)n.; 4.Schlucker (der)n. (aarmer --)

wretched 1.lumbich, adj.; 2.miehseelich, adj.; 3.unglicklich, adj.

wretchedness Miehlseelichkeit (die)n.

wring (out) 1.aus/drehe, v.; ausgedreht, pp.; 2.drehe, v.; gedreht, pp.

wrinkle 1.Falt (die)n.; Falde, pl.; 2.Runsel (die)n.; 3.runsle, v.; gerunselt, pp.; 4.verrunsle, v.; verrunselt, pp.

wrinkled 1.runslich, adj.; 2.verhutzelt, adj.; **old woman** Hutzel (die)n. (en aldi --)

wrinkles False (die)n., pl.

wristband 1.Breis (es)n.; 2.Hemmerbreis (es)n.

write schreiwe, v.; gschriwwe, pp.; **as a copy** vorschreiwe, v.; vorgschriwwe, pp.; **down** 1.hie/schreiwe, v.; hiegschriwwe, pp.; 2.nunner/duh, v.; nunnergeduh, pp.; 3.uff/schreiwe, v.; uffgschriwwe, pp.; **out** aus/schreiwe, v.; ausgschriwwe, pp.; **to someone at a distance** fatt/schreiwe, v.; fattgschriwwe, pp.

writer Schreiwer (der)n.; Schreiwer, pl.

writing 1.Gschreib (es)n.; 2.Gschriwwenes (es)n.; 3.Schreiwes (es)n.; 4.schriftlich, adj.; **in Gothic letters** frakture, v.; gfrakturt, pp.; **paper** Schreibbabier (es)n.; **table** Schreibdisch (der)n.

written agreement Schreiwes (es)n.

wrong 1.letz sei, v.; is letz gewest, pp.; 2.verkehrt, adj.; **road** Abweg (der)n.

wroth zannich, adj.

wry schepp, adj.; **mouth** 1.Scheppmaul (es)n.; 2.Schnaut (die)n.; 3.Schnut (die)n.; 4.scheppmeilich, adj.

Yy

yank up ... yule

yank up nuff/reisse, v.; nuffgerisse, pp.

Yankee Neienglenner (der)n.

yard Hof (der)n.; Hef, pl.; **(measure)** Yaard (es)n.

yardstick Yaardschtecke (der)n.

yarn 1.Gaarn (es)n.; 2.Netz (es)n.

yarrow Schofrippe (die)n., pl.

yawn 1.gaebbe, v.; gegaeppt, pp.; 2.uff/schpaerre, v.; uffgschpaerrt, pp. (es Maul --)

yawning Gruft (die)n.

year 1.Yaahr (es)n.; Yaahre, pl.; 2.Yohr (es)n.; 3.Yohrzaahl (die)n.; **in** yohrei, adv.; **of poor crops** Fehlyaa(h)r (es) n.; **old** 1.yae(h)rich, adj.; 2.yearich, adv.; **out** yohraus, adv.; **rich in fruit** Obschtyaahr (es)n.

yearbook Yaahrbuch (es)n.; Yaahrbiche pl.

yearling Yaehrling (der)n.

yearly 1.alli Yaahr, adv.; 2.yaahrlich, adv.

yearning 1.Aageleges (es)n.; 2.Aalanges (es)n.

years of indiscretion Delbelyaahre (die)n., pl.

yeast 1.Bierheef, (die)n.; 2.Satz (der)n.; **cake** Satzkuche (der)n.; **ladle** Satzbritsch (die)n.; **pot** Satzhaffe (der) n.

yeasty satzich, adj.

yell 1.gilbse, v.; gegilbst, pp.; 2.Greische, v.; gegrische, pp.; 3.Grisch (der)n.; 4.Mardgrisch (der)n.; **in** nei/greische, v.; neigegrische, pp.; **to split one's ears** maerderlich, adj. (-- greische)

yelling Gegr(e)isch (es)n.

yellow gehl, adj.; **adders tongue** Drechderblumm (die)n.; **foxtail** Kolwegraas (es)n.; **hop clover** Hoppeglee (der)n.; **jacket** 1.Gehliem (die)n.; Gehlieme, pl.; 2.Gehlweschp (die)n.; **pond lily** 1.Bachbledder (die) n., pl.; 2. Schillgrottebletter (die)n., pl.; 3.Wallebletter (die)n., pl.; 4. Wellebletter (die)n., pl.; **trefoil** Hoppeglee (der)n.; **week** Gehlwoch (die)n.

yellowish gehlich, adj.; **green** griegehl, adj.

yelp yaunse, v.; geyaunst, pp.

yes 1.hu hu; 2.iya; 3.ya, adv.; 4.Yawatt (es)n.; 5.yo, adv.; 6.Yowatt (es)n.; 7.aaha!, interj.

yesterday geschder, adv.

yet 1.doch, adv.; 2.noch, adv.; **a little while** glee, adj. (iwwer en gleenes)

yield (amount) 1.eibringe, v.; eigebrocht, pp.; 2.eidraage, v.; eigedraage, pp.; 3.fiege, v.; gfiekt, pp. (sich in ebbes --); 4.no(och)gewwe, v.; no(och)gewwe, pp.; **(to)** 1.aus/gewwe, v.; ausgewwe, pp.; 2.dreigewwe, adj.; 3.ei/gewwe, v.; eigewwe, pp. 4.weiche, v.; gewiche, pp.; **a point** dreisehne, v.; **fragrance** dufte, v.; geduft, pp.

yodel yodle, v.; geyodelt, pp.

yoeman Landeegner (der)n.; Landeegner, pl.

yoke 1.yoche, v.; geyocht, pp.; 2.Yochholz (es)n.; **in** nei/yoche, v.; neigeyicht, pp.; **of oxen** Ochsefuhr (die)n.; **put on geese to prevent them from creeping through fences** Gensyoch (es)n.; **put on hogs to prevent them from creeping through fences** Seiyoch (es)n.

yokel Delbel (der)n.

yolk of an egg 1.Dodder (der)n.; 2.Oidodder (der)n.

yonder datt, adv.

You old slowpoke! Die Faasnacht kummt hinneno!

you 1.dich, (acc.) pron.; 2.dir, (dative) pron.; 3.du, pron.; 4.eich, pron.; 5.Sie, pron. (occasionally used as a mark of respect in addressing a person especially a minister); **know** ewwe, adj.; **might know that** ab/zeehle, v. (des kannscht der Finger --); **must obey** heere, v.; gheert, pp. (du muscht mer --); **need not fear** Bang (die)n. (du brauscht kenn -- hawwe)

young yung, adj.; **cattle** Schpringer (der)n. (en gleener --); **girl** 1.Grott (die)n. (gleeni --); 2.Krott (die)n. (gleeni --); **people** Gezewwel (es)n. (yung --); **person** Yingling (der)n.; **rabbit** Haesche (es)n.; **shoot** (of a plant) Ausschlack (der)n.

youngster Schisser (der)n.; Schisser, pl.

your 1.dei, adj.(singular); 2.eier, adj. (plural); **equal** deinesgleiche, indecl. pronoun; **turn will come** Roi (die)n. (du kummscht aa in die --)

youth 1.Yingling (der)n.; 2.Yuchend (die)n.; 3.Yugend (die) n.; **and-old-age** (plant) Aldimeed (die)n.

yule Grischtdaag (der)n.; Grischtdaage, pl.

Zz

zany   zounds!

zany verrickt, adj.
zeal Eifer (der)n.
zealot Eiferer (der)n.
zealous 1.eiferich, adj.; 2.eifrich, adj.
zero 1.nix, adj.; 2.Null (die)n.; 3.null, adj.
zigzag 1.schtaagefensich, adj.; 2.zickzack, adv.
zinc Zink (es)n.
Zion Zion (es)n.
zither Zidder (die)n.
zoological garden Dieregaarde (der)n.
zounds! sapperlott!, interj.

NOTES

NOTES

NOTES

NOTES